The Nation's Health

EIGHTH EDITION

Edited by

Leiyu Shi, DrPH, MBA, MPA
Professor of Health Policy and Services Research
Department of Health Policy and Management
Johns Hopkins Bloomberg School of Public Health
Co-Director, Johns Hopkins Primary Care Policy Center
Baltimore, Maryland

Douglas A. Singh, PhD, MBA
Associate Professor of Management
School of Business and Economics
Indiana University-South Bend
South Bend, Indiana

JONES & BARTLETT
L E A R N I N G

World Headquarters
Jones & Bartlett Learning
40 Tall Pine Drive
Sudbury, MA 01776
978-443-5000
info@jblearning.com
www.jblearning.com

Jones & Bartlett Learning
Canada
6339 Ormindale Way
Mississauga, Ontario L5V 1J2
Canada

Jones & Bartlett Learning
International
Barb House, Barb Mews
London W6 7PA
United Kingdom

Jones & Bartlett Learning books and products are available through most bookstores and online booksellers. To contact Jones & Bartlett Learning directly, call 800-832-0034, fax 978-443-8000, or visit our website, www.jblearning.com.

Substantial discounts on bulk quantities of Jones & Bartlett Learning publications are available to corporations, professional associations, and other qualified organizations. For details and specific discount information, contact the special sales department at Jones & Bartlett Learning via the above contact information or send an email to specialsales@jblearning.com.

This publication is designed to provide accurate and authoritative information in regard to the Subject Matter covered. It is sold with the understanding that the publisher is not engaged in rendering legal, accounting, or other professional service. If legal advice or other expert assistance is required, the service of a competent professional person should be sought.

Production Credits
Publisher: Michael Brown
Associate Editor: Catie Heverling
Editorial Assistant: Teresa Reilly
Associate Production Editor: Kate Stein
Production Assistant: Rebekah Linga
Senior Marketing Manager: Sophie Fleck
Manufacturing and Inventory Control Supervisor: Amy Bacus
Composition: Auburn Associates, Inc.
Cover Design: Scott Moden
Photo Research and Permissions Manager: Kimberly Potvin
Assistant Photo Researcher: Emily Howard
Cover Image: © Olga Bogatyrenko/ShutterStock, Inc.
Printing and Binding: Malloy, Inc.
Cover Printing: Malloy, Inc.

Library of Congress Cataloging-in-Publication Data
The nation's health. — 8th ed. / [edited by] Leiyu Shi and Douglas A. Singh.
    p. ; cm.
Includes bibliographical references and index.
ISBN-13: 978-0-7637-8457-7 (pbk.)
ISBN-10: 0-7637-8457-5 (pbk.)
  1. Public health—United States. 2. Medical care—United States. 3. Medical policy—United States. 4. Health care reform—United States. 5. Health status indicators—United States. I. Shi, Leiyu. II. Singh, Douglas A., 1946-
  [DNLM: 1. Public Health—trends—United States. 2. Delivery of Health Care—United States. 3. Epidemiologic Factors—United States. 4. Health Policy—United States. 5. Health Status—United States. 6. Socioeconomic Factors—United States. WA 100 N2841 2011]
  RA445.N36 2011
  362.10973—dc22
                            2010017559

6048
Printed in the United States of America
14 13 12 11 10   10 9 8 7 6 5 4 3 2 1

Contents

Preface

Arguments over the health of Americans as a society have often focused on unequal access to medical care services by virtue of either having or not having insurance coverage. However, a nation's health is the outcome of multiple determinants that interact in complex ways at both the individual and population levels. This Eighth Edition of *The Nation's Health* evaluates health and well-being from this broad perspective.

On March 21, 2010, the House Democrats in the United States Congress passed, without bipartisan support, the final version of the Patient Protection and Affordable Health Care Act, commonly referred to as the "Health Care Reform Bill." On March 24, 2010, President Obama signed it into law. It is expected that the new law will extend health insurance coverage to an additional 32 million uninsured Americans, provide subsidies to help individuals purchase health insurance, mandate the coverage of pre-existing conditions, and provide billions of dollars of funding for public health and preventive activities. However, the law does not go into effect until 2014. Over half of the American people opposed this bill as too ambitious and too costly, and at the time of this writing, over one third of the states have threatened to mount a legal challenge over the constitutionality of this law. Hence, its final outcome remains somewhat uncertain. Even assuming its legal vindication, the effects of this legislation on the nation's health and economic sustainability are uncertain. As stated earlier, factors other than medical care have a significant effect on health and well-being. Secondly, even though access to timely medical services is an important factor, without a robust infrastructure of primary and preventive care, universal health insurance coverage can do little to improve the nation's health. From an eco-

nomic standpoint, no one in their right mind believes that expanding health insurance to several million people will save money unless the government nationalizes the entire health care system, enforces massive rationing of health care services, and imposes severe limits on payments to providers. Only the latter half of the next decade will begin to reveal whether the unusual political maneuvers employed by the Democrats in pushing the reform bill through Congress will turn out to be a good deal or a bad one for the nation as a whole.

In the meantime, the objectives of this new edition are to highlight the major accomplishments and limitations in health, identify and analyze the major determinants of health, and suggest interventions to positively impact the determinants of health. To accomplish these objectives and to organize the 18 chapters and 72 independent readings in this book, we have developed a framework, illustrated in Figure 1.

The book is organized into six parts that reflect a comprehensive framework of health determinants. The first two chapters contained in Part I, "Health of the Nation," provide a glimpse into the state of the nation's health and the dominant models of health determinants. Chapter 1, "Health Outcomes," explains the main health outcomes and includes readings on health outcome measurement, health status of the U.S. population, achievements and progress made over time, and international comparisons. Chapter 2, "Conceptual Framework of Health Determinants," covers the most dominant frameworks on health determinants as found in current literature.

In Part II, "The Determinants of Health," three chapters explain the non-medical determinants of health. Chapter 3, "Social Determinants of Health," looks at the non-medical social determinants of

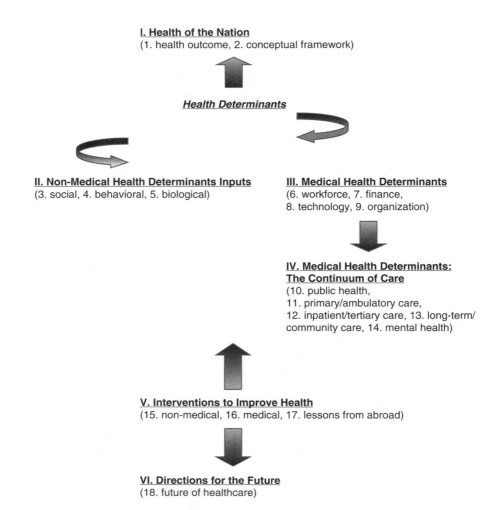

Figure 1 Framework of Health Determinants and Organization of the Book

health, including socioeconomic, political, economic, and environmental factors. Chapter 4, "Behavioral Determinants of Health," includes the non-medical behavioral determinants, such as cultural factors. In Chapter 5, "Biological Determinants of Health," the non-medical biological determinants, such as, genetics, aging, and certain internal factors are highlighted.

In Part III, "Medical Health Determinants: Inputs," three chapters are included that demonstrate the medical determinants of health from an input/ resources perspective. Chapter 6, "The Health Workforce," looks at the medical determinants of health, specifically the role of health workforce. Chapter 7, "Health Care Financing," is based on the close relationship between health insurance, access to and utilization of health care, reimbursement to providers for services delivered, and health care expenditures. Chapter 8, "Medical Technology," addresses the role

of medical technology that includes equipment, pharmaceuticals, and information systems.

Part IV, "Medical Health Determinants: The Continuum of Care," includes six chapters that demonstrate the medical determinants of health from a process/services continuum perspective. Chapter 9, "Organization of Health Care," points to the complexities of the U.S. health care delivery system, the role of managed care, care coordination, and patient activation and involvement in medical care. Chapter 10, "The Public Health System," looks at the medical determinants of health, specifically the public health continuum of care. Chapter 11, "Primary Care," covers the primary and ambulatory care continuum. Chapter 12, "Inpatient and Tertiary Care," incorporates inpatient hospital services, physician-owned specialty hospitals, and critical care. Chapter 13, "Long-Term and Community Care," covers senior housing and long-term care services. Chapter 14, "Mental Health Care," provides an overview of mental health care, including trends, issues related to race and ethnicity, and managed care carve-outs for mental health services.

The three chapters in Part V, "Interventions to Improve Health," illustrate targeted medical and non-medical interventions that can be developed to positively influence the determinants of health. Chapter 15, "Non-Medical Interventions," looks at the non-medical interventions to improve health including political, regulatory, socioeconomic, behavioral, cultural, community, and environmental factors. Chapter 16, "Medical Interventions," reports on the status of quality initiatives in the delivery of health care. Chapter 17, "Lessons from Abroad," considers interventions used in other countries including examples of representative health care systems around the world, and approaches to address health determinants and improving population health in selected countries.

Part VI, "Directions for the Future," provides a glimpse into the future. Chapter 18, "The Future of Health Care Delivery," sheds some light on why in the recent passage of health reform, solutions to health care problems are being imposed upon the public and the professionals by ambitious politicians and bureaucrats. How to deliver health care cost effectively will be a growing challenge for the United States and other developed countries.

Each chapter begins with a discussion of the major issues and challenges pertinent to the main theme of that chapter, followed by summaries of the four readings included in that chapter. This will help readers clearly grasp the essential elements related to that chapter and understand the main objectives of each of the selected readings.

In selecting the readings for the book, we struck a balance between classic readings and new readings published within the last five years. We included not only articles published in peer-reviewed journals, but also excerpts from government and organizational reports. Efforts were made to include international articles. It is to be understood that the selected readings in no way provide a comprehensive coverage of the chapter themes or capture all the important works in a given field. They are meant to illustrate the various themes within the scope of the book.

As an enhancement over the previous editions, this edition expands its scope by incorporating readings pertaining to health care delivery and interventions undertaken in other countries of the world. The United States can learn useful lessons from these countries. This book can be used either as a standalone text in courses dealing with health care policy or challenges and issues in health care, or it can be used to supplement materials covered in our two other related textbooks: *Delivering Healthcare in America: A Systems Approach* and *Essentials of the U.S. Health Care System.*

As a teaching aid for instructors, the book is accompanied by an Instructor's Manual that includes discussion/exam questions. The manual includes suggested answers in bulleted format.

We appreciate the work of our research assistants Angeli Bueno and Krista Beckwith who provided assistance with literature review and synthesis of materials on selected portions of the book. The views expressed are those of the authors only and do not necessarily reflect those of our institutions. As in the past, we invite comments from our readers. Communications can be directed to either or both authors:

Leiyu Shi
Department of Health Policy and Management
Bloomberg School of Public Health
Johns Hopkins University
624 North Broadway
Baltimore, MD 21205-1996
lshi@jhsph.edu

Douglas A. Singh
School of Business and Economics
Indiana University-South Bend
1700 Mishawaka Avenue
PO Box 7111
South Bend, IN 46634-7111
dsingh@iusb.edu

About the Editors

Leiyu Shi, DrPH, MBA, MPA is Professor of health policy and health services research in the Department of Health Policy and Management at the Johns Hopkins University Bloomberg School of Public Health. He is Co-Director of Johns Hopkins Primary Care Policy Center. He received his doctoral education from the University of California Berkeley, majoring in health policy and services research. He also has a master's in business administration focusing on finance. Dr. Shi's research focuses on primary care, health disparities, and vulnerable populations. He has conducted extensive studies about the association between primary care and health outcomes, particularly on the role of primary care in mediating the adverse impact of income inequality on health outcomes. Dr. Shi is also well known for his extensive research on the nation's vulnerable populations, in particular community health centers that serve vulnerable populations, including their sustainability, provider recruitment and retention experiences, financial performance, experience under managed care, and quality of care. Dr. Shi is the author of 8 textbooks and over 130 journal articles.

Douglas A. Singh, PhD, MBA teaches graduate and undergraduate courses in health care delivery, policy, finance, and management in the School of Business and Economics and in the Department of Political Science at Indiana University-South Bend. He has authored/coauthored four books and has published in several peer-reviewed journals.

I

HEALTH OF THE NATION

Part I of the book presents the broad outcomes achieved by the health care system and a conceptual framework for understanding health determinants. This part consists of two critical areas represented by two chapters: health outcomes (Chapter 1) and conceptual framework of health determinants (Chapter 2). Chapter 1 focuses on the nation's health outcomes. After a summary of the U.S. achievements in combating behavior risks, health problems and disparities are highlighted, with particular attention to vulnerable populations. Since the United States is often compared to other nations in terms of its achievements and deficiencies, the concept of global health is also introduced. Chapter 2 introduces some dominant health determinants conceptual framework both international and domestic. The chapter also includes articles that illustrate what a conceptual framework is and how a conceptual framework might be used to understand health and healthcare problems and identify solutions. Part I provides the outcome measurement for the other parts of the book that address input and process respectively. Part I is also a foundation for the rest of the book, providing a "big-picture" view on how much we have accomplished and how much we have yet to achieve. A clear grasp of the materials in Part I will assist in developing a more comprehensive and balanced critique of the U.S. health care system.

1

Health Outcomes

The World Health Organization (WHO) defines health as "a complete state of physical, mental, and social well-being, and not merely the absence of disease or infirmity" (WHO 1948). Over the past century, the United States has made great strides in improving the health of its populations. Since 1900, the average lifespan of persons in the U.S. has lengthened by greater than 30 years and 25 years of this gain are attributable to advances in public health (CDC 1999). The ten public health achievements include vaccination, motor-vehicle safety, safer workplaces, control of infectious diseases, decline in deaths from coronary heart disease and stroke, safer and healthier foods, healthier mothers and babies, family planning, fluoridation of drinking water, and recognition of tobacco use as a health hazard.

Despite these achievements, the U.S. still ranks low among the developed nations in health status. Out of 30 developed nations in the Organization for Economic Cooperation and Development (OECD), the U.S. is near the bottom in all standard measures of health status (Schroeder 2007). In 2004, the U.S. ranked 46th in life expectancy and 42nd in infant mortality out of 192 nations. While it is true that there are wide discrepancies in the health status of populations within the country, comparing only the health status of white Americans to other countries produced the same dismal results. White Americans are still doing worse than other developed nations for all standard measures of health status. The U.S. also has one of the highest amendable death rates, defined as mortality caused by bacterial infections, treatable cancers, diabetes, cardiovascular disease, cerebrovascular disease, and complications from common surgical procedures (Nolte and McKee 2008). Comparing 50-to-74-year-old Americans to Europeans while adjusting for wealth still placed Americans at worse health than the Europeans (Davies et al. 2007). While Americans were worse off for all levels of health, the discrepancy between Americans and Europeans were worst for poor Americans.

Yet, the U.S. has by far the most costly health system in the world, using up 17 percent of the country's gross domestic product, and has the highest rate of specialist physicians per capita (Davies et al. 2007; Simms 2009). Both physicians and patients consistently provide low ratings to the health care system, with reports of facing numerous barriers to care as well as inadequacies of insurance coverage. Compared to other counties, U.S. patients pay much more out of pocket for their medical expenses and are less likely to have a regular source of care, which then affects getting timely care (Avendano et al 2009).

In addition, the health status of individuals in the U.S. is mired with inequalities and disparities as a result of numerous factors, including but not limited to socioeconomic status (SES), race/ethnicity, and insurance coverage. SES most commonly incorporates measures of income, education, and occupation. An unfortunate truism in the U.S., and in nearly every other developed country, is that individuals with higher SES have better health. They also have greater ability to access health services and obtain better quality care. SES is related to health and health care in two ways that have been previously labeled material deprivation and lack of social participation (Marmot 2002). Material deprivation includes access to material goods that are required for good health, including clean water and good sanitation, adequate nutrition and housing, reliable transportation, and a safe and comfortable environment. Social participation includes having time for leisure activity and group participation, having friends or family around for entertainment and support, opportunities for professional achievement, and ultimately having sufficient control over one's life that leads to fulfillment and satisfaction. Without access to material goods and supportive social participation, health may falter, and greater barriers may be experienced in obtaining needed health care services.

One of the most prominent inequalities within the U.S. health care system is defined by race (Davies et al. 2007; Blendon et al. 2007). However, race/ethnicity frequently serves as a proxy measure for other factors that are more appropriate explanatory factors than skin color. Race/ethnicity can be a reflection of biological factors; socioeconomic status; cultural practices, beliefs, or acculturation; or political factors (King and Williams 1995). Race/ethnicity may also serve as a proxy measure of experiencing discrimination. In the case of health outcomes, race/ethnicity may serve as a proxy for biological factors (blacks are more prone to sickle cell anemia, for example), cultural behaviors or practices regarding health, or access to material goods and services that support health. In the case of health care experiences, race/ethnicity may serve as a proxy for socioeconomic factors (enabling the purchase of services), language factors (creating barriers to accessing services), or discrimination based on skin color.

Until recently, the U.S. was the only developed nation that does not guarantee its citizens access to health care through a system of universal health coverage. In 2000, WHO released a report ranking countries on the quality of their health systems. The report placed the U.S. in the 37th spot for health system performance and 72nd for health outcome performance (out of 191), primarily because of its failure to ensure access to primary care for the uninsured and because of the relatively low life expectancy and high infant mortality despite the fact that the U.S. spends more than all the other nations on health care (World Health Organization 2000). With the exception of individuals living in close proximity to free health care clinics or community health centers, the uninsured are particularly vulnerable to financial barriers in accessing health care (Kronick 2009; Levy and Meltzer 2008). Once a person is insured, there are three mechanisms by which insurance may be related to health and health care experiences: (1) health plan policies may affect care-seeking and cost-sharing behaviors of beneficiaries, (2) providers' incentives and reimbursement strategies may influence provider behavior, and (3) perceptions of health insurance plans may create feelings of stigma and affect the use of services and reports of quality.

This chapter focuses on the nation's health. After summarizing our achievements in combating behavior risks, we highlight our health problems and disparities, particularly for one of the most vulnerable populations, the American Indians. Since the United States is often compared to other nations in terms of its achievements and deficiencies, the concept of global health is also introduced. Below are synopses of the readings included for this chapter.

In **We Can Do Better—Improving the Health of the American People**, the author points out that the greatest opportunity to improve the health of Americans and reduce the number of premature deaths lies in personal behavior. History has shown this as a possible solution. There has been a marked increase in the use of seatbelts in the last couple of decades, and recently, Americans have decreased their high consumption of saturated fats. There was also the rapid fall of tobacco use from the mid-1960s to the present with the help of laws, regulations, and litigations, including smoke-free public areas and increased tax on cigarettes.

The next problem to be tackled will be obesity, which poses the same obstacles smoking once did on the population. The largest hurdle in dealing with the obesity epidemic is the use of BMI to classify obesity, since the method often misclassifies individuals with large amounts of muscle mass as obese. Litigation is also more difficult since the food industry is not as concentrated as the tobacco industry.

There are more stakeholders involved in the food industry.

Improving population health also requires using non-behavioral determinants of health, such as social and environmental factors. Class, as defined by income, total wealth, education, employment, and residential neighborhood, is often an ignored determinant of health, despite obvious gradients in health among members of different social classes. The United Kingdom is at the forefront of addressing effects of class on health. In 1998, they placed the Acheson Commission in charge of reducing health disparities, focusing particularly on social policies for health care, which is absent in the U.S. health care policy framework. Access and quality of care can also influence the health status of a population. The U.S. trails in access to care with 45 million people lacking insurance and several million more underinsured. Lack of insurance or insufficient insurance often leads to poor health because it limits an individual's access to the health care system.

It is difficult to improve population health in the U.S. for several reasons. The system focuses on the health of the middle and upper class, more so than it does on the affected poor with worse health outcomes. Most progress in health care only occurs when the middle class takes action and brings the problem to the forefront. One of the reasons for this is that the poor have no representation in politics. There is no active labor movement in the U.S., unlike other developed nations. In addition, it is difficult to increase the role of U.S. government in health care due to the American culture of individual responsibility that results in reluctance to intervene.

In **U.S. Disparities in Health: Descriptions, Causes, and Mechanisms**, the authors cite Healthy People 2010's definition of "health disparities" as differences that occur by gender, race or ethnicity, education or income, disability, geographic location, or sexual orientation. Disparities in race/ethnicity have been shown in certain diseases. Compared to whites, blacks have higher standard mortality rates (SMR) for homicides, hypertensive heart disease, esophageal cancer, and pulmonary circulation, and lower SMRs for suicide, leukemia, and COPD. Socioeconomic status (SES) has been found to contribute to a large portion of racial/ethnic disparities. A gradient within the SES correlates to a gradient in health outcomes with lower SES associated with poorer health.

Disparities have also been known to change over a life course. There are higher disparities among infants at birth depending on their mother's education, income, and lifestyle behaviors, but these disparities drop off during childhood, adolescence, and young adulthood. Disparities widen once again during middle age and finally decrease in older populations, most likely as a result of the "weaker" individuals in the population dying off at earlier ages to leave a healthier population at this late stage of life.

In **Changing Patterns of Mortality Among American Indians**, the authors note that the mortality rates of American Indians have shown an alarmingly increasing trend in recent years. For the Navajos, the largest tribe living on a reservation, the mortality rate began to increase at 46 per 100,000 individuals since the mid-1980s, while whites continued to decrease their rates within that same time period. The major source of mortality came from lung cancer, diabetes, and cardiovascular disease while there were decreases in deaths caused by infectious diseases. Morbidity among Navajos saw an increase in non-insulin-dependent diabetes as a result of the increasing rates of obesity made worse by changes in diet and activity patterns. Access to screening and prevention services is limited to the Navajo community. The best solutions to tackle the growing problem of mortality from chronic conditions within this population are primary prevention, i.e., the prevention or reduction of the underlying causes of risk factors. In addition, implementing a broad range of services, rather than only health services, may be better at solving chronic diseases.

In **Towards a Common Definition of Global Health**, the authors start by reviewing two related terms: public health and international health. Public health emerged in Europe and the United States from social reforms and an increased understanding of medicine, including a better understanding of the causes and treatments of infectious diseases. Public health has four important factors: (1) evidence-based decisions, (2) a focus on population care, rather than individual needs, (3) an emphasis on seeking social justice and equity, and (4) prevention rather than treatment. International health focuses on health care abroad, relating more to health practices, policies and systems, and stressing differences among countries. Public health is applied to international health as a means to fix the problems and challenges that affect mostly low-income or middle-income countries.

Global health is considered a mixture of both public health and international health. It focuses on problems with an international scope, rather than where the problem exists, embracing all health threats in addition to infectious diseases and maternal and child care that are problems in low-income and middle-income countries. Important topics in global health consist of under- and over-nutrition,

HIV/AIDS, tobacco use, malaria, and mental health. While global health emphasizes prevention, it also covers aspects of clinical medicine, including treatment and rehabilitation. The proposed definition of global health states that "global health is an area for study, research, practice that places a priority on improving health and achieving equity in health for all people worldwide . . . emphasizing transnational health issues, determinants, and solutions involving many disciplines within and beyond the health sciences and promotes interdisciplinary collaboration synthesis of population-based prevention with individual clinician care."

● ● ● **References**

Avendano et al. "Health Disadvenatges in US Adults Aged 50 to 74 Years: A Comparison of the Health of Rich and Poor Americans With That of Europeans." *American Journal of Public Health*. 99(2009):540-548.

Blendon et al. Disparities in Health: Perspectives of A Multi-Ethnic, Multi-Racial America. *Health Affairs*. 26(2007):1437-1447.

The Centers for Disease Control and Prevention (CDC). Ten Great Public Health Achievements—United States, 1900-1999. *MMWR* April 02, 1999/ 48(12);241-243.

Davies et al. "Mirror, Mirror on the Wall: An International Update on the Comparative Performance of American Health Care." *The Commonwealth Fund*, 2007.

King G; Williams D. Race and health: A multidimensional approach to African-American health. In B. Amick III, S. Levine, A.Talov, and D. Chapman Walsh (Eds.), *Society and Health*. Pp.93-130, New York, Oxford University Press, 1995.

Kronick, R. Health Insurance Coverage and Mortality Revisited. *Health Services Research* 44(2009): 1211-1231

Levy, H; Meltzer, D. The Impact of Health Insurance on Health. *Ann. Rev. Public Health* 29(2008):399-409.

Marmot, M. The influence of income on health: Views of an epidemiologist. Does money really matter? Or is it a marker for something else? *Health Affairs* 21(2):31-46, 2002.

Nolte E; McKee CM. Measuring the health of nations: Updating an earlier analysis. *Health Aff* 2008;27: 58-71.

Schroeder SA. Shattuck Lecture. We can do better—improving the health of the American people. *N Engl J Med* 2007;357:1221-8.

Simms, Chris. Inequalities in the Ameican health-care system. *The Lancet*. 373(2009):1252

World Health Organization (WHO). *Preamble to the Constitution*. Geneva, Switzerland, 1948.

World Health Organization (WHO). *World health report 2000: Health system performance*. Geneva, Switzerland, 2000.

1

We Can Do Better—Improving the Health of the American People

Source: Schroeder SA. Shattuck Lecture. We can do better—improving the health of the American people. *N Engl J Med* 2007;357:1221-8. Copyright © 2007 Massachusetts Medical Society. All rights reserved.

The United States spends more on health care than any other nation in the world, yet it ranks poorly on nearly every measure of health status. How can this be? What explains this apparent paradox?

The two-part answer is deceptively simple—first, the pathways to better health do not generally depend on better health care, and second, even in those instances in which health care is important, too many Americans do not receive it, receive it too late, or receive poor-quality care. In this lecture, I first summarize where the United States stands in international rankings of health status. Next, using the concept of determinants of premature death as a key measure of health status, I discuss pathways to improvement, emphasizing lessons learned from tobacco control and acknowledging the reality that better health (lower mortality and a higher level of functioning) cannot be achieved without paying greater attention to poor Americans. I conclude with speculations on why we have not focused on improving health in the United States and what it would take to make that happen.

HEALTH STATUS OF THE AMERICAN PUBLIC

Among the 30 developed nations that make up the Organization for Economic Cooperation and Development (OECD), the United States ranks near the bottom on most standard measures of health status (Table 1).[1-4] (One measure on which the United States does better is life expectancy from the age of 65 years, possibly reflecting the comprehensive health insurance provided for this segment of the population.) Among the 192 nations for which 2004 data are available, the United States ranks 46th in average life expectancy from birth and 42nd in infant mortality.[5,6] It is remarkable how complacent the public and the medical profession are in their acceptance of these unfavorable comparisons, especially in light of how carefully we track health-systems measures, such as the size of the budget for the National Institutes of Health, trends in national spending on health, and the number of Americans who lack health insurance. One reason for the complacency may be the rationalization that the United States is more ethnically heterogeneous than the nations at the top of the rankings, such as Japan, Switzerland, and Iceland. It is true that within the United States there are large disparities in health status—by geographic area, race and ethnic group, and class.[7-9] But even when comparisons are limited to white Americans, our performance is dismal (Table 1). And even if the health status of white Americans matched that in the leading nations, it would still be incumbent on us to improve the health of the entire nation.

Table 1	Health Status of the United States and Rank among the 29 Other OECD Member Countries		
Health-Status Measure	United States	U.S. Rank Country in OECD*	Top-Ranked in OECD
Infant mortality (first year of life), 2001			
All races	6.8 deaths/ 1000 live births	25	Iceland (2.7 deaths/ 1000 live births)
Whites only	5.7 deaths/ 1000 live births	22	
Maternal mortality, 2001†			
All races	9.9 deaths/ 100,000 births	22 --	Switzerland (1.4 deaths/ 100,000 births)
Whites only	7.2 deaths/ 100,000 births	19	
Life expectancy from birth, 2003			
All women	80.1 yr	23	Japan (85.3 yr)
White women	80.5 yr	22	
All men	74.8 yr	22	Iceland (79.7 yr)
White men	75.3 yr	19	
Life expectancy from age 65, 2003‡			
All women	19.8 yr	10	Japan (23.0 yr)
White women	19.8 yr	10	
All men	16.8 yr	9	
White men	16.9 yr	9	

*The number in parentheses is the value for the indicated health-status measure.

†OECD data for five countries are missing.

‡OECD data for six countries are missing.

PATHWAYS TO IMPROVING POPULATION HEALTH

Health is influenced by factors in five domains—genetics, social circumstances, environmental exposures, behavioral patterns, and health care (Fig. 1).[10,11] When it comes to reducing early deaths, medical care has a relatively minor role. Even if the entire U.S. population had access to excellent medical care—which it does not—only a small fraction of these deaths could be prevented. The single greatest opportunity to improve health and reduce premature deaths lies in personal behavior. In fact, behavioral causes account for nearly 40% of all deaths in the United States.[12] Although there has been disagreement over the actual number of deaths that can be attributed to obesity and physical inactivity combined, it is clear that this pair of factors and smoking are the top two behavioral causes of premature death (Fig. 2, not included).[12]

Addressing Unhealthy Behavior

Clinicians and policymakers may question whether behavior is susceptible to change or whether attempts to change behavior lie outside the province of traditional medical care.[13] They may expect future successes to follow the pattern whereby immunization and antibiotics improved health in the 20th century. If the public's health is to improve, however, that improvement is more likely to come from behavioral change than from technological innovation. Experience demonstrates that it is in fact possible to change behavior, as illustrated by increased seat-belt use and decreased consumption of products high in saturated fat. The case of tobacco best demonstrates how rapidly positive behavioral change can occur.

The Case of Tobacco

The prevalence of smoking in the United States declined among men from 57% in 1955 to 23% in 2005 and among women from 34% in 1965 to 18% in 2005.[14,15] Why did tobacco use fall so rapidly? The 1964 report of the surgeon general, which linked smoking and lung cancer, was followed by multiple reports connecting active and passive smoking to myriad other diseases. Early antismoking advocates, initially isolated, became emboldened by the cascade of scientific evidence, especially with respect to the risk of exposure to secondhand smoke. Counter-marketing—first in the 1960s and more recently by several states and the American Legacy Foundation's "truth®" campaign—linked the creativity of Madison Avenue with messages about the duplicity of the tobacco industry to produce compelling anti-smoking messages[16] (an antismoking advertisement is available with the full text of this article at www.nejm.org). Laws, regulations, and litigation, particularly at the state and community levels, led to smoke-free public places and increases in the tax on cigarettes—two of the strongest evidence-based tobacco-control measures.[14,17,18] In this regard, local governments have been far ahead of the federal government, and they have inspired European countries such as Ireland and the United Kingdom to make public places smoke-free.[14,19] In addition, new medications have augmented face-to-face and telephone counseling techniques to increase the odds that clinicians can help smokers quit.[15,20,21]

It is tempting to be lulled by this progress and shift attention to other problems, such as the obesity epidemic. But there are still 44.5 million smokers in the United States, and each year tobacco use kills 435,000 Americans, who die up to 15 years earlier than nonsmokers and who often spend their final years ravaged by dyspnea and pain.[14,20] In addition, smoking among pregnant women is a major contributor to premature births and infant mortality.[20] Smoking is increasingly concentrated in the lower socioeconomic classes and among those with mental illness or problems with substance abuse.[15,22,23] People with chronic mental illness die an average of 25 years earlier than others, and a large percentage of those years are lost because of smoking.[24] Estimates from the Smoking Cessation Leadership Center at the University of California at San Francisco, which are based on the high rates and intensity (number of cigarettes per day plus the degree to which each is finished) of tobacco use in these populations, indicate that as many as 200,000 of the 435,000 Americans who die prematurely each year from tobacco-related deaths are people with chronic mental illness, substance-abuse problems, or both.[22,25] Understanding why they smoke and how to help them quit should be a key national research priority. Given the effects of smoking on health, the relative inattention to tobacco by those federal and state agencies charged with protecting the public health is baffling and disappointing.

The United States is approaching a "tobacco tipping point"—a state of greatly reduced smoking prevalence. There are already low rates of smoking in some segments of the population, including physi-cians (about 2%), people with a postgraduate education (8%), and residents of the states of Utah (11%) and California (14%).[25] When Kaiser Permanente of northern California implemented a multisystem approach to help smokers quit, the smoking rate dropped from 12.2% to 9.2% in just 3 years.[25] Two basic strategies would enable the United States to meet its Healthy People 2010 tobacco-use objective of 12% population prevalence: keep young people from starting to smoke and help smokers quit. Of the two strategies, smoking cessation has by far the larger short-term impact. Of the current 44.5 million smokers, 70% claim they would like to quit.[20] Assuming that one half of those 31 million potential non-smokers will die because of smoking, that translates into 15.5 million potentially preventable premature deaths.[20,26] Merely increasing the baseline quit rate from the current 2.5% of smokers to 10%—a rate seen in placebo groups in most published trials of the new cessation drugs—would prevent 1,170,000 premature deaths. No other medical or public health intervention approaches this degree of impact. And we already have the tools to accomplish it.[14,27]

Is Obesity the Next Tobacco?

Although there is still much to do in tobacco control, it is nevertheless touted as a model for combating obesity, the other major, potentially preventable cause of death and disability in the United States. Smoking and obesity share many characteristics (Table 2). Both are highly prevalent, start in childhood or adolescence, were relatively uncommon until the first (smoking) or second (obesity) half of the 20th century, are major risk factors for chronic disease, involve intensively marketed products, are more common in low socioeconomic classes, exhibit major regional variations (with higher rates in southern and poorer states), carry a stigma, are difficult to treat, and are less enthusiastically embraced by clinicians than other risk factors for medical conditions.

Nonetheless, obesity differs from smoking in many ways (Table 2). The binary definition of smoking status (smoker or nonsmoker) does not apply to obesity. Body-mass index, the most widely used measure of obesity, misclassifies as overweight people who have large muscle mass, such as California governor Arnold Schwarzenegger. It is not biologically possible to stop eating, and unlike moderate smoking, eating a moderate amount of food is not hazardous. There is no addictive analogue to nicotine in food. Nonsmokers mobilize against tobacco because they fear injury from secondhand exposure, which is not a peril that attends obesity. The food industry is less concentrated than the tobacco

Table 2	Similarities and Differences between Tobacco Use and Obesity	
Characteristic	Tobacco	Obesity
High prevalence	Yes	Yes
Begins in youth	Yes	Yes
20th-century phenomenon	Yes	Yes
Major health implications	Yes	Yes
Heavy and influential industry promotion	Yes	Yes
Inverse relationship to socioeconomic class	Yes	Yes
Major regional variations	Yes	Yes
Stigma	Yes	Yes
Difficult to treat	Yes	Yes
Clinician antipathy	Yes	Yes
Relative and debatable definition	No	Yes
Cessation not an option	No	Yes
Chemical addictive component	Yes	No
Harmful at low doses	Yes	No
Harmful to others	Yes	No
Extensively documented industry duplicity	Yes	No
History of successful litigation	Yes	No
Large cash settlements by industry	Yes	No
Strong evidence base for treatment	Yes	No
Economic incentives available	Yes	Yes
Economic incentives in place	Yes	No
Successful counter-marketing campaigns	Yes	No

industry, and although its advertising for children has been criticized as predatory and its ingredient-labeling practices as deceptive, it has yet to fall into the ill repute of the tobacco industry. For these reasons, litigation is a more problematic strategy, and industry payouts—such as the Master Settlement Agreement between the tobacco industry and 46 state attorneys general to recapture the Medicaid costs of treating tobacco-related diseases—are less likely.[14] Finally, except for the invasive option of bariatric surgery, there are even fewer clinical tools available for treating obesity than there are for treating addiction to smoking.

Several changes in policy have been proposed to help combat obesity.[28-30] Selective taxes and subsidies could be used as incentives to change the foods that are grown, brought to market, and consumed, though the politics involved in designating favored and penalized foods would be fierce.[31] Restrictions could also apply to the use of food stamps. Given recent data indicating that children see from 27 to 48 food advertisements for each 1 promoting fitness or nutrition, regulations could be put in place to shift that balance or to mandate support for sustained social-marketing efforts such as the "truth®" campaign

against smoking.[16,32] Requiring more accurate labeling of caloric content and ingredients, especially in fast-food outlets, could make customers more aware of what they are eating and induce manufacturers to alter food composition. Better pharmaceutical products and counseling programs could motivate clinicians to view obesity treatment more enthusiastically. In contrast to these changes in policy, which will require national legislation, regulation, or research investment, change is already underway at the local level. Some schools have banned the sale of soft drinks and now offer more nutritionally balanced lunches. Opportunities for physical activity at work, in school, and in the community have been expanded in a small but growing number of locations.

Nonbehavioral Causes of Premature Death

Improving population health will also require addressing the nonbehavioral determinants of health that we can influence: social, health care, and environmental factors. (To date, we lack tools to change our genes, although behavioral and environmental factors can modify the expression of genetic risks such as obesity.) With respect to social factors, people with lower socioeconomic status die earlier and have more disability than those with higher socioeconomic status, and this pattern holds true in a stepwise fashion from the lowest to the highest classes.[33-38] In this context, class is a composite construct of income, total wealth, education, employment, and residential neighborhood. One reason for the class gradient in health is that people in lower classes are more likely to have unhealthy behaviors, in part because of inadequate local food choices and recreational opportunities. Yet even when behavior is held constant, people in lower classes are less healthy and die earlier than others.[33-38] It is likely that the deleterious influence of class on health reflects both absolute and relative material deprivation at the lower end of the spectrum and psychosocial stress along the entire continuum. Unlike the factors of health care and behavior, class has been an "ignored determinant of the nation's health."[33] Disparities in health care are of concern to some policymakers and researchers, but because the United States uses race and ethnic group rather than class as the filter through which social differences are analyzed, studies often highlight disparities in the receipt of health care that are based on race and ethnic group rather than on class.

But aren't class gradients a fixture of all societies? And if so, can they ever be diminished? The fact is that nations differ greatly in their degree of social inequality and that—even in the United States—earning potential and tax policies have fluctuated over time, resulting in a narrowing or widening of class differences. There are ways to address the effects of class on health.[33] More investment could be made in research efforts designed to improve our understanding of the connection between class and health. More fundamental, however, is the recognition that social policies involving basic aspects of life and well-being (e.g., education, taxation, transportation, and housing) have important health consequences. Just as the construction of new buildings now requires environmental-impact analyses, taxation policies could be subjected to health-impact analyses. When public policies widen the gap between rich and poor, they may also have a negative effect on population health. One reason the United States does poorly in international health comparisons may be that we value entrepreneurialism over egalitarianism. Our willingness to tolerate large gaps in income, total wealth, educational quality, and housing has unintended health consequences. Until we are willing to confront this reality, our performance on measures of health will suffer.

One nation attempting to address the effects of class on health is the United Kingdom. Its 1998 Acheson Commission, which was charged with reducing health disparities, produced 39 policy recommendations spanning areas such as poverty, income, taxes and benefits, education, employment, housing, environment, transportation, and nutrition. Only 3 of these 39 recommendations pertained directly to health care: all policies that influence health should be evaluated for their effect on the disparities in health resulting from differences in socioeconomic status; a high priority should be given to the health of families with children; and income inequalities should be reduced and living standards among the poor improved.[39] Although implementation of these recommendations has been incomplete, the mere fact of their existence means more attention is paid to the effects of social policies on health. This element is missing in U.S. policy discussions—as is evident from recent deliberations on income-tax policy.

Although inadequate health care accounts for only 10% of premature deaths, among the five determinants of health (Fig. 1, not included), health care receives by far the greatest share of resources and attention. In the case of heart disease, it is estimated that health care has accounted for half of the 40% decline in mortality over the past two decades.[40] (It may be that exclusive reliance on international mortality comparisons shortchanges the results of America's health care system. Perhaps the

high U.S. rates of medical technology use translate into comparatively better function. To date, there are no good international comparisons of functional status to test that theory, but if it could be substantiated, there would be an even more compelling claim for expanded health insurance coverage.) U.S. expenditures on health care in 2006 were an estimated $2.1 trillion, accounting for 16% of our gross domestic product.[41] Few other countries even reach double digits in health care spending.

There are two basic ways in which health care can affect health status: quality and access. Although qualitative deficiencies in U.S. health care have been widely documented,[42] there is no evidence that its performance in this dimension is worse than that of other OECD nations. In the area of access, however, we trail nearly all the countries: 45 million U.S. citizens (plus millions of immigrants) lack health insurance, and millions more are seriously underinsured. Lack of health insurance leads to poor health.[43] Not surprisingly, the uninsured are disproportionately represented among the lower socioeconomic classes.

Environmental factors, such as lead paint, polluted air and water, dangerous neighborhoods, and the lack of outlets for physical activity also contribute to premature death. People with lower socioeconomic status have greater exposure to these health-compromising conditions. As with social determinants of health and health insurance coverage, remedies for environmental risk factors lie predominantly in the political arena.[44]

THE CASE FOR CONCENTRATING ON THE LESS FORTUNATE

Since all the actionable determinants of health—personal behavior, social factors, health care, and the environment—disproportionately affect the poor, strategies to improve national health rankings must focus on this population. To the extent that the United States has a health strategy, its focus is on the development of new medical technologies and support for basic biomedical research. We already lead the world in the per capita use of most diagnostic and therapeutic medical technologies, and we have recently doubled the budget for the National Institutes of Health. But these popular achievements are unlikely to improve our relative performance on health. It is arguable that the status quo is an accurate expression of the national political will—a relentless search for better health among the middle and upper classes. This pursuit is also evident in how we consistently outspend all other countries in the use of alternative medicines and cosmetic surgeries and in how frequently health "cures" and "scares" are featured in the popular media.[45] The result is that only when the middle class feels threatened by external menaces (e.g., secondhand tobacco smoke, bioterrorism, and airplane exposure to multidrug-resistant tuberculosis) will it embrace public health measures. In contrast, our investment in improving population health—whether judged on the basis of support for research, insurance coverage, or government-sponsored public health activities—is anemic.[46-48] Although the Department of Health and Human Services periodically produces admirable population health goals—most recently, the Healthy People 2010 objectives[49]—no government department or agency has the responsibility and authority to meet these goals, and the importance of achieving them has yet to penetrate the political process.

WHY DON'T AMERICANS FOCUS ON FACTORS THAT CAN IMPROVE HEALTH?

The comparatively weak health status of the United States stems from two fundamental aspects of its political economy. The first is that the disadvantaged are less well represented in the political sphere here than in most other developed countries, which often have an active labor movement and robust labor parties. Without a strong voice from Americans of low socioeconomic status, citizen health advocacy in the United States coalesces around particular illnesses, such as breast cancer, human immunodeficiency virus infection and the acquired immunodeficiency syndrome (HIV–AIDS), and autism. These efforts are led by middle-class advocates whose lives have been touched by the disease. There have been a few successful public advocacy campaigns on issues of population health—efforts to ban exposure to secondhand smoke or to curtail drunk driving—but such efforts are relatively uncommon.[44] Because the biggest gains in population health will come from attention to the less well off, little is likely to change unless they have a political voice and use it to argue for more resources to improve health-related behaviors, reduce social disparities, increase access to health care, and reduce environmental threats. Social advocacy in the United States is also fragmented by our notions of race and class.[33] To the extent that poverty is viewed as an issue of racial injustice, it ignores the many whites who are poor, thereby reducing the ranks of potential advocates.

The relatively limited role of government in the U.S. health care system is the second explanation. Many are familiar with our outlier status as the only developed nation without universal health care coverage.[50] Less obvious is the dispersed and relatively weak status of the various agencies responsible for population health and the fact that they are so disconnected from the delivery of health services. In addition, the American emphasis on the value of individual responsibility creates a reluctance to intervene in what are seen as personal behavioral choices.

HOW CAN THE NATION'S HEALTH IMPROVE?

Given that the political dynamics of the United States are unlikely to change soon and that the less fortunate will continue to have weak representation, are we consigned to a low-tier status when it comes to population health? In my view, there is room for cautious optimism. One reason is that despite the epidemics of HIV–AIDS and obesity, our population has never been healthier, even though it lags behind so many other countries. The gain has come from improvements in personal behavior (e.g., tobacco control), social and environmental factors (e.g., reduced rates of homicide and motor-vehicle accidents and the introduction of fluoridated water), and medical care (e.g., vaccines and cardiovascular drugs). The largest potential for further improvement in population health lies in behavioral risk factors, especially smoking and obesity. We already have tools at hand to make progress in tobacco control, and some of these tools are applicable to obesity. Improvement in most of the other factors requires political action, starting with relentless measurement of and focus on actual health status and the actions that could improve it. Inaction means acceptance of America's poor health status.

Improving population health would be more than a statistical accomplishment. It could enhance the productivity of the workforce and boost the national economy, reduce health care expenditures, and most important, improve people's lives. But in the absence of a strong political voice from the less fortunate themselves, it is incumbent on health care professionals, especially physicians, to become champions for population health. This sense of purpose resonates with our deepest professional values and is the reason why many chose medicine as a profession. It is also one of the most productive expressions of patriotism. Americans take great pride in asserting that we are number one in terms of wealth, number of Nobel Prizes, and military strength. Why don't we try to become number one in health?

ACKNOWLEDGMENTS
Supported in part by grants from the Robert Wood Johnson and American Legacy Foundations. The sponsors had no role in the preparation of the Shattuck Lecture.

No potential conflict of interest relevant to this article was reported.

I thank Stephen Isaacs for editorial assistance; Michael McGinnis, Harold Sox, Stephen Shortell, and Nancy Adler for comments on an earlier draft; and Kristen Kekich and Katherine Kostrzewa for technical support.

● ● ● **References**

1. OECD health data 2006 (2001 figures). Paris: Organisation for Economic Cooperation and Development, October 2006.

2. Infant, neonatal, and postneonatal deaths, percent of total deaths, and mortality rates for the 15 leading causes of infant death by race and sex: United States, 2001. Hyattsville, MD: National Center for Health Statistics. (Accessed August 24, 2007, at http://www.cdc.gov/search.do? action=search &queryText=infant+mortality +rate+2001&x= 18&y=15.)

3. Hoyert DL. Maternal mortality and related concepts. *Vital Health Stat 3* 2007;33:4.

4. Chartbook on trends in the health of Americans. Table 27: life expectancy at birth, at age 65 years of age, and at age 75 years of age, by race and sex: United States, selected years 1900-2004:193. Hyattsville, MD: National Center for Health Statistics. (Accessed August 24, 2007, at http://www. cdc.gov/nchs/fastats/lifexpec.htm.)

5. WHO core health indicators. Geneva: World Health Organization. (Accessed August 24, 2007, at http://www3.who.int/whosis/core/core_select_ process.cfm.)

6. Minino AM, Heron M, Smith BL. Deaths: preliminary data for 2004. *Health E-Stats*. Released April 19, 2006. (Accessed August 24, 2007, at http://www.cdc.gov/nchs/products/pubs/pubd/hestats/ prelimdeaths04/preliminarydeaths04.htm.)

7. Harper S, Lynch J, Burris S, Davey Smith G. Trends in the black-white life expectancy gap in the United States, 19832003. *JAMA* 2007;297:1224-32.

8. Murray JL, Kulkarni SC, Michaud C, et al. Eight Americas: investigating mortality disparities across races, counties, and race-counties in the United States. *PLoS Med* 2006;3(9):e260.

9. Woolf SH, Johnson RE, Phillips RL, Philipsen M. Giving everyone the health of the educated: an examination of whether social change would save more lives than medical advances. *Am J Public Health* 2007;97:679-83.

10. McGinnis JM, Williams-Russo P, Knickman JR. The case for more active policy attention to health promotion. *Health Aff (Millwood)* 2002;21(2):78-93.

11. McGinnis JM, Foege WH. Actual causes of death in the United States. *JAMA* 1993;270:2207-12.

12. Mokdad AH, Marks JS, Stroup JS, Gerberding JL. Actual causes of death in the United States, 2000. *JAMA* 2004;291: 1238-45. [Errata, *JAMA* 2005;293:293-4, 298.]

13. Seldin DW. The boundaries of medicine. *Trans Assoc Am Phys* 1981;38:lxxv-lxxxvi.

14. Schroeder SA. Tobacco control in the wake of the 1998 Master Settlement Agreement. *N Engl J Med* 2004;350:293-301.

15. *Idem.* What to do with the patient who smokes? *JAMA* 2005;294:482-7.

16. Farrelly MC, Healton CH, Davis KC, et al. Getting to the truth: evaluating national tobacco countermarketing campaigns. *Am J Public Health* 2002; 92:901-7. [Erratum, *Am J Public Health* 2003;93:703.]

17. Warner KE. Tobacco policy research: insights and contributions to public health policy. In: Warner KE, ed. *Tobacco control policy*. San Francisco: Jossey-Bass, 2006:3-86.

18. Schroeder SA. An agenda to combat substance abuse. *Health Aff (Millwood)* 2005;24:1005-13.

19. Koh HK, Joossens LX, Connolly GN. Making smoking history worldwide. *N Engl J Med* 2007;356:1496-8.

20. Fiore MC, Bailey WC, Cohen SJ, et al. Treating tobacco use and dependence: clinical practice guideline. Rockville, MD: *Public Health Service*, 2000.

21. Schroeder SA, Sox HC. Trials that matter: varenicline—a new designer drug to help smokers quit. *Ann Intern Med* 2006;145:784-5.

22. Lasser K, Boyd JW, Woolhandler S, Himmelstein DU, McCormick D, Bor DH. Smoking and mental illness: a population-based prevalence study. *JAMA* 2000;284: 2606-10.

23. Zeidonis DM, Williams JM, Steinberg ML, et al. Addressing tobacco dependence among veterans with a psychiatric disorder: a neglected epidemic of major clinical and public health concern. In: Isaacs SL, Schroeder SA, Simon JA, eds. *VA in the vanguard: building on success in smoking cessation*. Washington, DC: Department of Veterans Affairs, 2005: 141-70. (Accessed, August 24, 2007, at http://smokingcessationleadership.ucsf. edu/AboutSCLC_vanguard.html.)

24. Colton CW, Manderscheid RW. Congruencies in increased mortality rates, years of potential life lost, and causes of death among public mental health clients in eight states. *Prev Chronic Dis* 2006;3:April (online only). (Accessed August 24,

2007, at http://www.cdc.gov/pcd/issues/2006/ apr/ 05_0180.htm.)

25. Smoking Cessation Leadership Center. Partner highlights. (Accessed August 24, 2007, at http:// smokingcessationleadership.ucsf.edu/Partner Featured.html.)

26. Doll R, Peto R, Boreham J, Sutherland I. Mortality in relation to smoking: 50 years' observations on male British doctors. *BMJ* 2004;328:1519-27.

27. Fiore MC, Croyle RT, Curry SJ, et al. Preventing 3 million premature deaths and helping 5 million smokers quit: a national action plan for tobacco cessation. *Am J Public Health* 2004;94:205-10.

28. Nestle M. Food marketing and childhood obesity—a matter of policy. *N Engl J Med* 2006;354:2527-9.

29. Mello MM, Studdert DM, Brennan TA. Obesity—the new frontier of public health law. *N Engl J Med* 2006;354:2601-10.

30. Gostin LO. Law as a tool to facilitate healthier lifestyles and prevent obesity. *JAMA* 2007;297: 87-90.

31. Pollan M. You are what you grow. *New York Times Sunday Magazine.* April 22, 2007:15-8.

32. *Food for thought: television food advertising to children in the United States.* Menlo Park, CA: Kaiser Family Foundation, March 2007:3.

33. Isaacs SL, Schroeder SA. Class—the ignored determinant of the nation's health. *N Engl J Med* 2004;351:1137-42.

34. Adler NE, Boyce WT, Chesney MA, Folkman S, Syme SL. Socioeconomic inequalities in health: no easy solution. *JAMA* 1993;269:3140-5.

35. McDonough P, Duncan GJ, Williams DR, House J. Income dynamics and adult mortality in the United States,1972 through 1989. *Am J Public Health* 1997;87:1476-83.

36. Marmot M. Inequalities in health. *N Engl J Med* 2001;345:134-6.

37. Williams DR, Collins C. US socioeconomic and racial differences in health: patterns and explanations. *Annu Rev Sociol* 1995;21:349-86.

38. Minkler M, Fuller-Thomson E, Guralnik JM. Gradient of disability across the socioeconomic spectrum in the United States. *N Engl J Med* 2006;355:695-703.

39. Independent inquiry into inequalities in health report. London: Stationery Office, 1998 (Accessed August 24, 2007, at http://www.archive.official-doc uments.co.uk/document/doh/ih/contents.htm.)

40. Ford ES, Ajani UA, Croft JB, et al. Explaining the decrease in U.S. deaths from coronary disease, 1980–2000. *N Engl J Med* 2007;356:2388-98.

41. Poisal JA, Truffer C, Smith S, et al. Health spending projections through 2016: modest changes obscure Part D's impact. *Health Aff (Millwood)* 2007;26:w242-w253 (Web only). (Accessed August 24, 2007, at http://content.healthaffairs.org/cgi/ content/full/26/2/w242.)

42. Institute of Medicine. *To err is human: building a safer health system.* Washington, DC: National Academy Press, 2000.

43. *Idem. Hidden costs, value lost: uninsurance in America.* Washington, DC: National Academy of Sciences, 2003.

44. Isaacs SL, Schroeder SA. Where the public good prevailed: lessons from success stories in health. *The American Prospect.* June 4, 2001:26-30.

45. Gawande A. Annals of medicine: the way we age now. *The New Yorker.* April 30, 2007:50-9.

46. McGinnis JM. Does proof matter? Why strong evidence sometimes yields weak action. *Am J Health Promot* 2001;15:391-6.

47. Kindig DA. A pay-for-population health performance system. *JAMA* 2006; 296:2611-3.

48. Woolf SH. Potential health and economic consequences of misplaced priorities. *JAMA* 2007;297:523-6.

49. Healthy People 2010: understanding and improving health. Washington, DC: Department of Health and Human Services, 2001.

50. Schroeder SA. The medically uninsured—will they always be with us? *N Engl J Med* 1996;334:1130-3.

2

U.S. Disparities in Health: Descriptions, Causes, and Mechanisms

Source: Adler NE, Rehkopf DH. U.S. disparities in health: descriptions, causes, and mechanisms. *Annu Rev Public Health* 2008;29:235-52.

ABSTRACT

Eliminating health disparities is a fundamental, though not always explicit, goal of public health research and practice. There is a burgeoning literature in this area, but a number of unresolved issues remain. These include the definition of what constitutes a disparity, the relationship of different bases of disadvantage, the ability to attribute cause from association, and the establishment of the mechanisms by which social disadvantage affects biological processes that get into the body, resulting in disease. We examine current definitions and empirical research on health disparities, particularly disparities associated with race/ethnicity and socioeconomic status, and discuss data structures and analytic strategies that allow causal inference about the health impacts of these and associated factors. We show that although health is consistently worse for individuals with few resources and for blacks as compared with whites, the extent of health disparities varies by outcome, time, and geographic location within the United States. Empirical work also demonstrates the importance of a joint consideration of race/ethnicity and social class. Finally, we discuss potential pathways, including exposure to chronic stress and resulting psychosocial and physiological responses to stress, that serve as mechanisms by which social disadvantage results in health disparities.

INTRODUCTION

Few terms have had such a meteoric rise into common usage in the health literature as has "health disparities." In the 1980s this was a key word in only one article, and in the 1990s there were fewer than 30 such articles. In contrast, during the five years from 2000 through 2004, more than 400 such articles appeared.[3] An equivalent increase occurred in the number of articles containing the key term of "health inequalities." Prior to this time, there was substantial work on the problem of health disparities, but it was usually framed in terms of specific factors such as race or poverty.[60]

One of the first uses of the term inequality with respect to health differences was in the title of the Working Group on Inequalities in Health, which issued the Black Report in Great Britain in 1980. In advance, it seemed likely that the working group would find reductions in social class differences in mortality following the provision of universal health care through the National Health Service. However, they found that the gap between the health of low and high social class individuals had actually widened. Around the same time, the Whitehall Study of British Civil Servants[68] revealed significant differences in cardiovascular disease and mortality[69] by occupational level within a population of office-based workers. Notably, differences were not just between those at the top and bottom. Rather, disease prevalence and mortality increased at each step down in occupational grade. Spurred by these and other data, another commission, the Independent Inquiry into Inequalities in Health, made recommendations for policies in Great Britain to reduce health inequalities.[2]

During this period, research on socioeconomic and racial/ethnic differences in health was also being conducted in the United States. Beginning in the 1970s, investigators linked death records to socioeconomic data from the Current Population Study, to the U.S. Census, and to Social Security Administration records. The findings documented at a nationwide level substantially higher age-adjusted mortality rates for nonwhites, individuals with less education, individuals with low incomes, and for some occupational categories.[16,58,59] These data and the British findings provided an impetus to determine the extent and nature of health disparities in the United States and identify ways to reduce them. Efforts have included a report from the National Center for Health Statistics on differences in mortality and morbidity by socioeconomic status,[80] *Healthy People 2010*,[100] which established the goal of eliminating health disparities in addition to the goal of improving health, and the passage of the Minority Health and Health Disparities Research and Education Act of 2000. This legislation established the National Center on Minority Health and Health Disparities to coordinate activities among the NIH institutes. The Institute of Medicine recently reviewed the NIH plan and made a number of recommendations to improve its effectiveness.[99]

As reflected in the dual goals of *Healthy People 2010*, public health research and practice aim both to improve health and to eliminate disparities. Previous papers in the *Annual Review of Public Health* have examined substantive and methodological aspects of specific types of disparities. Some reviews concerned measurement issues and health effects of poverty, class, and/or socioeconomic status(e.g.,[1,36,61]), of race and ethnicity (e.g.,[64,70,105]), and of rural residence.[88] None has considered disparities per se. Eliminating disparities requires a clear definition to allow measurement and monitoring of progress toward that goal and to understand their causes. Here we examine the definition of health dis-

parities and empirical findings on disparities associated with race/ethnicity and socioeconomic status. We then consider methodological challenges and solutions to understanding the causes of health disparities.

DEFINITION OF HEALTH DISPARITIES

The literature lacks a consensually agreed on definition of health disparities. *Healthy People 2010* referenced "differences that occur by gender, race or ethnicity, education or income, disability, geographic location, or sexual orientation."[100,p.14] Carter-Pokras & Baquet[17] identified 11 different definitions of health disparities. Some were inclusive, some limited disparities to those associated with race and ethnicity, and still others defined it only in terms of disparities in health care.

The various definitions imply and sometimes explicitly suggest the relevant comparison group for establishing a disparity. Definitions of racial/ethnic disparities suggest that a group's health status be compared with the majority, the population average, or the healthiest group. Thus, one might compare African American mortality rates to national rates, to European Americans who are the majority group in the United States, or to Asian Americans, who have in aggregate the lowest mortality rates. Depending on the relative size and the relative health of the majority group and the healthiest group, one could reach different conclusions about the extent of a disparity.

With the exception of Murray and colleagues,[78] who examined a range of socio-demographic characteristics of groups with markedly different life expectancies, most approaches to disparities start with bases of social disadvantage, which result in differences that are unjust and avoidable.[13,15] *Healthy People 2010* distinguishes between a health difference, which results from inherent biological differences (e.g., only women are subject to ovarian cancer and men to prostate cancer), and a disparity, which results from social factors. What constitutes a difference versus a disparity may sometimes be unclear, however. In the example of ovarian and prostate cancer, differential investment in research on treatment and prevention of one disease versus the other could reflect the relative advantage of males versus females. If men have more power to allocate resources for research and health care and differentially provide funding for prostate versus ovarian cancer, the resulting death rates from these diseases could constitute a disparity. This suggests that simple comparisons of mortality rates are not an adequate basis on which to evaluate health disparities. One also needs to know the biological potential of each group. Although women outlive men (a fact pointed to by some who advocate for more attention to men's health as a disparity issue), the gap between current life expectancy and life expectancy under optimal conditions could potentially be greater for women than for men.

Differences in biological potential have been raised in relation to racial/ethnic health disparities, suggesting these are differences rather than disparities. However, the contribution of unavoidable biological differences to overall disparities by race/ethnicity is relatively small. A few diseases (e.g., sickle cell anemia) have a clear primary genetic basis, but these are of a limited number and there is little evidence for a differential genetic basis for the many diseases for which disparities occur.[75] For example, African Americans have higher rates of hypertension than do European Americans, which some attribute to differential genetic vulnerability. However, prevalence of hypertension among blacks is lower in Caribbean countries than in the United States and lower still among blacks in Africa. Hypertension rates in Africa are, in fact, equivalent to or lower than rates among whites in the United States.[26] These findings suggest that higher rates of hypertension for blacks in the United States compared with other racial/ethnic groups are more likely to be due to social factors than to underlying biological vulnerability.

Health disparities result from both biological differences and social disparities. We focus on the latter not just because the effect is greater, but also because they are avoidable and inherently unjust.

EMPIRICAL WORK ON DISPARITIES

The bulk of research has focused either on disparities due to race/ethnicity or disparities due to social class and socioeconomic resources. Disparities by gender and geography have also been investigated, often in terms of how these factors modify racial/ethnic or social class disparities. Most research has not invoked an explicit model of disparities and studies are shaped and constrained by the availability of relevant data. For example, British studies emphasize social class as determined by occupational status using the Registrar General's measure of social class. This measure has been in use for many years and provides a fine-grained hierarchical ordering of occupations. Nothing comparable exists in the United States,

where national data are more likely to include race/ethnicity than measures of socioeconomic position. For example, it was not until 1989 that education was added to the U.S. standard certificate of death, and health records of large population groups such as those enrolled in Kaiser Permanente often include only race/ethnicity but not socioeconomic status (SES). Thus, it has been easier to characterize racial/ethnic disparities in the United States than those linked to social class. The data show that African Americans have higher mortality and poorer health status than does any other group, as do Native Americans. Overall mortality rates are surprisingly higher for non-Hispanic whites than for Hispanics or Asian Americans; relative mortality varies for specific causes of death.[3,94] For 1999-2001, male life expectancy for U.S.-born blacks and whites was 67.5 and 74.8 years, respectively. Life expectancy for U.S.-born Hispanic males (75.2 years) was greater than for non-Hispanic whites and was greater still for U.S.-born Asian/Pacific Islanders (78.9 years). The same pattern is shown for women. For both men and women, the health advantage of Hispanic and Asians compared to U.S.-born whites is even greater for recent immigrants in these groups (see Foreign-Born Populations box).

Intersection of SES and Race/Ethnicity

Some definitions limit disparities to those associated with race/ethnicity. This focus has been fostered both by relative availability of data as described above and by social equity concerns based on current and historical racism and discrimination. Such a limitation can be problematic, however, given marked differences in the distribution of racial/ethnic groups across levels of education, income, occupation, and wealth.[29,56] Examining race/ethnicity without simultaneously considering socioeconomic position can attribute too much influence to race/ethnicity per se, and may inadvertently foster an emphasis on biological differences. This point is forcefully made by Isaacs & Schroeder,[52] who argue that social class is the "ignored determinant" of health in the United States.

Researchers are increasingly looking at how SES and race/ethnicity function jointly and independently to affect health. Socioeconomic measures often account for a large part of racial/ethnic differences, although independent effects of race/ethnicity on health outcomes also exist, depending on what outcome is examined. Adequate control for SES across racial/ethnic groups may be difficult to achieve.[54]

FOREIGN-BORN POPULATIONS

Place of birth is a critical and frequently ignored component of socioeconomic and racial/ethnic disparities. To the extent that first-generation immigrants make up a substantial proportion of a given group's population in the United States, immigrants' health advantage may contribute to differences between groups. For most health outcomes (notable exceptions are stomach cancer and liver disease), foreign-born individuals in the United States have lower rates of disease than do their native-born peers. Controlling for demographic and socioeconomic factors, immigrant men and women 25 years of age and older had mortality rates 18% and 13% lower, respectively, than did nonimmigrants.[95] Immigrants as a group lived 3.4 years longer on average than did those born in the United States in 1999-2001, an increase over a gap of 2.3 years two decades earlier.[94] The gap was largest for native-born vs. immigrant blacks and Hispanics.

Most analyses of health disparities do not include birth place and do not account for the generally lower rates of disease among foreign-born individuals.[79] U.S. Hispanics as a group have lower all-cause mortality rates than do non-Hispanic blacks or non-Hispanic whites; a difference that becomes even greater after controlling for household income. The relatively lower rates of all-cause mortality among Hispanics as compared with non-Hispanics in the United States have been well documented, and a large literature investigating the substantive and potentially artifactual reasons for this has emerged (although no clear consensus has been reached yet).[79] Asian Americans, too, show favorable health profiles, with the lowest prevalence of a number of diseases and the lowest all-cause mortality rate of any major racial/ethnic group, and the role of migration processes in these disparities is also an area of active research.

SES indicators may have different meanings for different groups. For example, at the same income level, the amount of wealth and debt differ substantially by racial/ethnic group; Hispanics and African Americans have lower wealth than non-Hispanic whites and Asians at a given income level.[14,24] Similarly, at any given educational level, these groups have lower incomes than do whites.[14] Although some studies "control" for SES by adjusting for an indicator such as education or income, this adjustment is insufficient given evidence for independent effects of the different domains of SES. Controlling for a single measure is unlikely to capture the effects of social class per se, and residual confounding may be erroneously interpreted as racial/ethnic differences.[14,54]

Descriptive Findings

A descriptive understanding of socioeconomic and racial/ethnic disparities is important for (a) understanding both long- and short-term trends in health disparities, (b) informing causal investigations of health disparities, (c) targeting resources for prevention and treatments to reduce disparities in specific diseases, and (d) increasing public awareness of the existence and characteristics of health disparities. Below we briefly consider descriptive data regarding mortality disparities, cause-specific disparities, geographic variation in disparities, and time trends in these disparities.

All-cause mortality. The first U.S. study with a sample size sufficient to allow the examination of socioeconomic disparities within race/ethnicity based on individual-level data was done by Kitigawa & Hauser,[58] although data constraints limited comparisons to whites and nonwhites. Using data from the 1960 matched records of persons age 25 and over, they documented that compared with whites, age-adjusted all-cause mortality rates for nonwhites were 34% higher for females and 20% higher for males, correcting for net census undercount. They also examined mortality by education, occupation, income, and geographical location. For white men and women ages 25-64 mortality was respectively 64% and 105% higher for the least compared with the most educated. For nonwhite men and women the comparable difference in mortality by education was 31% and 70%, respectively. Pappas et al.[81] revisited this work, with data from 1986, showing a relatively sharper decrease in mortality over this time period for higher-income and more-educated individuals, thus creating greater relative disparities by income and education overall and within racial/ethnic groups over time. This and other work also highlights the importance of disparities based on social class for both women and men, despite some earlier work that suggested smaller social class disparities among women.[72]

In addition to dichotomizing race into white and nonwhite, earlier U.S. research generally dichotomized income into below versus above the poverty line. Publication of the Whitehall study inspired researchers to see if SES formed a graded association with health in the United States, as it did in England. Multiple studies have now demonstrated SES gradients by income and by education for a range of health outcomes including mortality, incidence of cardiovascular disease, arthritis, diabetes, asthma, cervical cancer, depression, and disability in children, adolescents, and both younger and older adults.[4,22,43,76] Although these associations occur across the distribution, they are generally stronger at the lowest levels of income and education.[8,33,91]

Cause-specific mortality. Studies uniformly find higher all-cause mortality for blacks than for whites under age 65, but within this overall trend there is heterogeneity by cause of death. For example, data from the National Longitudinal Mortality Study (NLMS) of 1.3 million persons[89] reveal a racial/ethnic difference for mortality from many but not all diseases. Black and white men under age 65 had approximately the same standardized mortality ratio (SMR) for ischemic heart disease, whereas (in order of magnitude of difference) black men had substantially higher SMRs than did whites for homicide, hypertensive heart disease, esophageal cancer, and pulmonary circulation but had relatively lower SMRs for aortic aneurysm, suicide, leukemia, and chronic obstructive pulmonary disease (COPD). Black women had substantially higher rates of homicide, hypertensive heart disease, diseases of pulmonary circulation, nephritis, and stomach cancer than did white women, with comparatively lower levels of suicide, COPD, and leukemia.

Howard et al.[51] also used data from the NLMS and found that SES accounted for different amounts of black-white mortality differences depending on the cause of death. For men, SES accounted for 30%-55% of the black-white mortality differences for accidents, lung cancer, stomach cancer, stroke, and homicide, but less than 17% of the differences for prostate cancer, pulmonary disease, and hypertension. For women, SES accounted for 37%-67% of differences for accidents, ischemic heart disease, diabetes, and homicide, but less than 17% for hypertension, infections, and stomach cancers. However, only income and education were used as SES controls, which could underestimate the contribution of SES to black-white mortality differences. Kington & Smith[57] found that with more complete demographic controls including wealth, racial/ethnic differences in functional limitation in health of older individuals were eliminated, although differences remain for other chronic diseases.

Wong et al.[106] also studied the contribution of education and race/ethnicity to different causes of death. Whereas many causes of death contributed in a similar way to both racial/ethnic and educational disparities in mortality (e.g., cardiovascular disease, liver disease), other causes were responsible for greater educational differentials (e.g., cancer, lung disease) or greater black-white differences (e.g., hypertension, lung disease, homicide). The data from these studies show that although the direction of disparities is fairly consistent, the extent of socioeconomic and racial/ethnic disparities and their interactions differ substantially by cause.

Geographic variation. Although marked differences in mortality rates across the United States have been noted, the extent to which socioeconomic factors and race/ethnicity explain these variations had not been adequately studied. However, data from within metropolitan areas reveal a geographic variation that can be substantially explained by considering these factors. These data also suggest that differences in local socioeconomic conditions have a greater impact on African American mortality than white mortality, resulting in an interaction between socioeconomic factors and race/ethnicity with respect to geography.[23,98] This is consistent with data from the NLMS[89] showing that the locations with the lowest mortality rates for whites and for blacks were at an equivalent level, even as overall rates were higher for blacks. These studies of geographic differences show the importance of area context for disparities and note that relationships among race/ethnicity, class, and health are not fixed, even within the United States during a given time period.

Changes in disparities over time. The magnitude of disparities in mortality by race/ethnicity and by SES have changed over time, providing further evidence that these disparities are changeable and preventable. Preston & Ilo[86] confirmed Pappas's finding of increasing education gradients for all-cause mortality for men since 1960 but also found that education differentials in mortality declined for women 25-64 and remained stationary for women 65-74. Ward et al.[104] examined disparities in cancer mortality by race/ethnicity 1975-2000. Prior to 1980 investigators saw no black/white disparities in breast cancer mortality among women and saw slightly higher rates of colorectal cancer mortality among white as compared with black men. But this changed, and by 2000, black women had higher breast cancer mortality than did white women and black men had higher colorectal cancer mortality than did white men. The black-white gap in overall life expectancy decreased from 1975 to1984, increased from 1984 to 1992-1994, then decreased again through 2004.[48] Most of these changes stemmed from relative improvements for blacks in specific causes of death (e.g., relatively greater decreases from 1994 to 2004 in homicide and unintentional injuries for both sexes and for HIV for men and heart disease for women).

Disparities in risk factors for disease have also changed over time. For example, Zhang & Wang[108] examined obesity rates among U.S. women 20-60 years old from 1971 to 2000 using data from the National Health and Nutrition Examination Survey

(NHANES). Owing to rapid increases in obesity prevalence among all educational groups, education disparities actually decreased, although all groups were worse off. These results highlight the importance of overall population trends for assessing progress in reducing health disparities.

Changes in disparities over the life course. The extent and nature of health disparities changes over the life course. Substantial disparities begin at birth; babies born to mothers who are poor, have lower education, and/or are African American are smaller at birth and are more likely to die within the first year of life. Disparities are smallest during childhood, adolescence, and early adulthood and greatest in middle age, becoming weaker again in older populations.[5] The primary explanation for diminished disparities in older populations is that the least healthy individuals are no longer in the population, and mortality will eventually be experienced by all regardless of socioeconomic status and race/ethnicity. Although selection over time can produce artifactual population patterns,[102] the proportion of the narrowing of disparities explained by selection is unclear. There may also be etiologic reasons, including the provision of safety net supports such as Social Security and Medicare, which are available to older adults and may reduce and/or buffer the effects of disadvantage.

Variation by measure of SES. Occupation, income, and education have different associations with health outcomes.[58,89] As currently operationalized, education and income are generally more strongly associated with health in U.S. data than are measures of occupation other than employed versus nonemployed. However, weaker associations with occupation may be due to the use of standard U.S. occupational measures.[14] Using a classification based on the new U.K. national statistics social class measure—which categorizes individuals as managers/professionals, intermediate, small employers and self employed, lower supervisory and technology, and semiroutine/routine or not in labor force—Barbeau et al.[9] found occupational associations with current smoking status as strong as those with education or income. Variations by SES measure used speak to the frequent recommendation of using discrete measures of SES such as education or income rather than a composite.[32] In addition to empirical reasons, use of specific SES measures clarifies intervention possibilities.

UNDERSTANDING THE NATURE AND CAUSES OF DISPARITIES

General patterns of disparities over the late twentieth century in the United States are similar: Those with fewer resources have worse health outcomes for a number of different causes. But variations by health outcome, place, time, and age point to the fact that these associations are not fixed or immutable, and that this heterogeneity should be used to better understand the causes of disparities. Kunitz[63] places links between distribution of resources and health within particular historical, socioeconomic, and cultural contexts. Given these variations, a deeper understanding of off-diagonals may be informative about the nature of disparities. This analysis would include diseases that do not show disparities or are more prevalent in more advantaged groups (e.g., black-white differences in kidney function and socioeconomic differences in breast cancer). It would also include those who do not show expected patterns such as immigrants, low-SES individuals in good health, and high-SES individuals in poor health. Finally, international comparisons of socioeconomic disparities highlight the importance of national contexts for understanding the nature of health disparities.

Establishing Causality

There are clearly documented associations of SES and health outcomes, but the causal link is still debated. Some questions are methodological, dealing with alternative explanations for the associations. Others are concerned with the nature of the mechanisms by which these upstream factors influence health. SES is unlikely to affect health directly (e.g., having more dollars in one's pocket is not health protective). Rather, it shapes life conditions that, in turn, influence health. In this section we first consider the methodological challenges to understanding causes of health disparities and then consider potential mechanisms by which SES may affect morbidity and mortality.

Methodological challenges—alternative explanations. When asserting that a measure of SES leads to sub-optimal health and premature mortality, researchers must address possible alternative explanations for the associations that are found.[42,45] The first possibility is that associations result from random chance; this possibility can be assessed by specifying confidence intervals around the effect estimate or p-values. Second, associations may be due to conditioning on an effect of the exposure and outcome occurring either through the selection of the sample (i.e., selection bias) or through use of inappropriate control variables.[42,50] Avoiding this possibility requires using a causal understanding of the process that created the data to inform sample selection and an appropriate choice of control covariates.

A third challenge is that the presumed health outcome may cause the exposure (reverse causation or health selection bias).[58,96] For example, illness may prompt individuals to decrease work hours, change to less demanding and lucrative jobs, or leave the labor force entirely. Using data from the Health and Retirement Study of individuals over the age of 50, Smith[96] found that wealth decreased by $17,000, and earnings by $2,600 per year with the onset of major disease. Collecting measures of income that predate the health assessment through longitudinal designs, data linkage or retrospective earnings recall can decrease reverse causation potential between income and health. Using a lagged approach with longitudinal data, McDonough et al.[71] found little difference in predicting all-cause mortality between a one-year lag and a five-year lag, thus questioning the importance of reverse causation for explaining the mortality associations. Using another approach to account for health selection, Benzeval & Judge[10] controlled for initial health status in addition to using measures of income prior to disease onset, and the associations between income and health outcomes remained.

There is less reason for concern about reverse causation between education and health. Generally the temporal lag between education exposure and adult health outcomes argues against adult health impacting education.[58] However, childhood illnesses and low birth weight may contribute to lower educational attainment.[18,25] These factors are themselves a function of SES. Haas[46] demonstrated that disadvantaged social background led to sub-optimal health in childhood, which made a subsequent impact on adult social class.

Overall, although health can affect SES, SES significantly affects health. The extent of reciprocal influence for specific outcomes is generally not understood. Longitudinal data with health, education, income, labor force participation, and wealth measures over time can more accurately model the process of social stratification and the extent to which causation and selection impact specific health outcomes at different points in the life course.

A fourth concern is whether associations result from the joint association of SES and health with a common underlying cause such as genetic factors, time preferences/delayed gratification,[39] or cognitive ability.[44] As with reverse causation, these confounders may themselves reflect SES. Early family environments affected by parents' education and income may shape all three of these potential confounders, including the extent to which genetic potential is realized through epigenetic processes. As evidence of the importance of SES and child environments for adult health increases, rather than viewing these factors as undermining evidence for the importance of socioeconomic factors on health, they should be viewed as part of the dynamic process between SES and health over the life course.

Data structure and methods. In addition to collecting appropriate data to control for potential alternative explanations in regression models, several types of data structures can also facilitate better determination of causal relationships and help rule out alternative explanations for observed correlations. True experiments are rare because individuals cannot easily be randomly assigned to levels of education, income, or occupation. However, experimental trials of interventions that modify some aspect of SES or factors associated with it are informative. Researchers have also taken advantage of natural experiments to assess the effects of economic or policy changes that affect an individual's SES but are not due to his or her own characteristics or behaviors. These reduce confounding and allow for a more easily conceptualized counterfactual.[45] Relevant examples include using German reunification to estimate the effects of income on health,[38] changes in the Earned Income Tax Credit to estimate the effects of household income on children's test scores,[28] enactment of schooling laws to estimate the effects of education on mortality,[66] and changes in legislation affecting Social Security benefits to estimate the effects of income on mortality in an older population.[97] With the exception of the Social Security payments, these studies confirm the effects from observational studies of socioeconomic factors to health.

Data with repeated measures on individuals over time also provide some strength for making causal claims.[87] Repeated measures allow observation of the temporal sequence of cause and effect. Birth cohorts provide particularly rich data for modeling early life confounders and exposures of interest. Three British studies of representative samples of children born in 1946, 1958, and 1970 have provided critical data about the causes of health disparities and have shown the impact on adult health and behaviors of early life exposures and socioeconomic position at different points in life.[84,103] Using data from the 1958 cohort, Power at al.[85] found a number of causes of health inequalities at age 33, including class at birth, socioemotional adjustment, educational level, and psychosocial job strain. In the absence of a birth cohort, follow-up of members of completed studies of children and adolescents can provide some of the same advantages.[41]

Analytic approaches. In addition to the design approaches described above, new analytic methods are facilitating a better understanding of the causes of health disparities. Five methods that may be particularly useful are propensity score matching, instrumental variables, time-series analysis, causal structural equation modeling, and marginal structural models.

Propensity scores provide an analytical method for balancing factors associated with being in either of the analytical comparison groups of interest in a particular study (e.g., high versus low education). If assumptions are met it allows for unbiased causal estimates of the exposure under study.[27,90] They have been used to identify the effects of gun violence exposure on subsequent violent activity,[11] neighborhood characteristics on dropping out of high school,[47] and neighborhood socioeconomic environment on cardiovascular mortality.[30] This approach is based on the same principle as adjusting for confounders in a regression model and similarly requires all confounders be measured. However, they facilitate assessment of whether overlap of confounding variables actually allows one to compare the analytic groups of interest appropriately, and they also provide power to control for a larger number of confounding covariates.

Instrumental variables (IV) offer advantages when analyzing data from natural experiments or similar designs. The crucial assumption is the availability of a variable (the instrument) that does not directly affect the outcome but is only associated with the predictor of interest, and where the exposure (instrument) is not itself influenced by known confounders.[7] This approach has been used to show causal effects of income on health outcomes[34] and to demonstrate the effect of years of schooling on all-cause mortality.[66]

Time-series analyses are particularly helpful for evaluating policy changes or other population exposures by analyzing the variation in health outcomes over time, while allowing investigators to identify and remove temporal autocorrelation and also account for lag effects between exposure and outcome. Particularly useful are data from multiple locations with different temporal ordering of the exposure to remove more general temporal trends. This approach has been used to demonstrate the effects of unemployment on alcohol abuse[19] and on very low birth weight[20] and to examine trends in black-white disparities over time.[65]

Structural equation models have been used extensively in the social sciences to understand complex relations between variables and to test relationships among hypothesized causes, mediators, and outcomes. Despite controversy, work over the past two decades by Pearl and others[82,83] has clarified the conditions under which the models may be used to represent cause. A significant innovation for gaining this understanding is the use of directed acyclic graphs (DAGs), a graphical language for describing causal relations. These form a framework for representing assumptions about elements of the causal pathways from social exposures to outcomes and information about possible confounders. Explicit delineation of the proposed causal structures through DAGs allows other researchers to evaluate the assumptions made and to build on the proposed structures. These models facilitate identification of valid empirical tests of proposed causal models.[31] This is helpful in testing proposed mediators between social class and health.[55] A causal structural modeling approach using DAGs is also mathematically equivalent to marginal structural models,[82] which allow (when assumptions are met) a determination of the overall causal effect of an exposure within a framework based on treating unobserved counterfactuals as missing data.[101]

Chandola et al.[21] used this approach with data from the 1958 British Birth Cohort to examine the relative contributions of six different pathways connecting education and health. The structural model included factors at age 7 (cognitive ability, father's social class), age 16 (adolescent health), age 23 (education), age 33 (adult social class, sense of control, healthy behaviors), and age 42 (adult health). It showed no direct effect of education on adult health but showed significant effects through adult social class, control, and behaviors, with differences by gender in the strength of pathways.[21] A similar approach was taken by Mulatu & Schooler[77] in examining the relative strength of behavioral and psychosocial pathways between SES and health.

Pathways and Mechanisms

Much recent research has attempted to explicate the pathways and the mechanisms by which SES influences health. Although few studies have explicitly tested these through structural equation models, the studies provide many candidates. Physical and social environments, including a person's home, school, work, neighborhood, and community, vary by SES and affect the likelihood of individuals' exposure to both health-damaging conditions and health-protecting resources. Health-damaging exposures within these pathways include early life conditions, inadequate nutrition, poor housing, exposure to lead and other toxins, inadequate healthcare, unsafe working conditions, uncontrollable stressors, social exclusion, and discrimination.[5,6,105]

Some of the exposures listed above have direct effects on health, whereas others may influence psychological dispositions and behaviors that have health consequences. A vast literature demonstrates the contribution of psychosocial and behavioral factors to morbidity and mortality. These factors include cognition and emotion (e.g., depression, hopelessness, hostility, and lack of control) and behavior (e.g., use of cigarettes, alcohol, and other substances). Gallo & Matthews[40] observed that substantial evidence links negative emotions with many health outcomes and links SES with negative emotions, but few studies have analyzed these pathways together. For example, hostility and hopelessness are strongly predicted by childhood socioeconomic position[49] and are linked, in turn, to poorer health.[12,37,40] However, the extent to which the links between childhood SES and adult health are accounted for by hostility and hopelessness has not been determined.

The few studies that have considered mediation by psychosocial factors provide supportive findings, but these have used regression rather than structural equation models. For example, Marmot et al.[67] examined the role of sense of control over one's work in explaining health disparities within the Whitehall sample. The higher the grade of the civil servants, the more control they experienced in relation to their work conditions. Consistent with hypothesized mediation, the association of occupational grade with health was substantially reduced when adjusted for sense of control.

A common element in many of the proposed mechanisms linking SES to health is differential exposure to stress. Disadvantaged environments expose individuals to greater uncertainty, conflict, and threats for which there are often inadequate resources to respond effectively. These experiences cumulate to create chronic stress. Until recently, stress research focused primarily on acute stress, which is more easily modeled in the lab, and was based on a model of homeostasis. The development of the model of "allostatic load" (AL)[73] provided a major conceptual advancement to understand health disparities. This model posits that the body does not simply reestablish homeostasis after experiencing a perturbation associated with a stressor. Rather, with repeated exposures, set points for various systems involved in the stress response, including the endocrine, metabolic, cardiovascular, and immune systems, may shift. Although the body may be in balance, the systems become burdened and dysregulated by the costs of the repeated adaptation cycles.[74] Precise ways to assess AL are still being developed,

but early findings suggest that it is a useful approach. Seeman et al.[92,93] assessed AL in terms of 10 dysregulation indicators in a sample of older adults who had no major diseases at baseline. AL scores were higher in those with less education and predicted subsequent decline in physical and cognitive functioning, new cardiovascular disease, and seven-year mortality. Using data from the Normative Aging Study, Kubzanksy et al.[62] also found higher AL among those with less education and further found evidence that the effect was partially mediated by hostility.

Although the effects of chronic stress cumulate over time, the biological manifestations may be seen relatively early in life. Evans[35] found that children from disadvantaged environments had higher AL than did children from more affluent backgrounds, and one indicator of AL was found in structural equation models to mediate the impact of poorer housing conditions on illness-related school absences.[53]

These examples are a few of thousands of studies on a variety of potential mechanisms and pathways. Most of these have not been linked specifically with health disparities but provide detailed information on different levels of cause that could result in disparities. Data sets with adequate measures of socioeconomic factors and race/ethnicity, potential psychosocial and biological mechanisms, and health outcomes are necessary to best understand pathways. These then can be analyzed using techniques such as causal structural models that allow modeling and testing of multiple direct and indirect pathways to health outcomes that are the bases of disparities.

CONCLUSION

Substantial health disparities exist in the United States by social class and race/ethnicity. It would, of course, be preferable to eliminate disparities by addressing the root causes, changing the inequitable resource distribution that now accompanies SES and race/ethnicity as well as other bases of disparity. For effective policy development and interventions, we need persuasive data on the causes of disparities. This entails moving beyond associations to establish causal relationships. In addition, understanding the pathways and mechanisms that mediate these effects provides more information about the multiple causes of health disparities and offers possible interventions to alleviate their occurrence.

SUMMARY POINTS

1. In the United States, health disparities associated with race/ethnicity and socioeconomic status (SES) are widespread.

2. Variation in disparities by cause of death, geographic region, and time suggest that disparities are modifiable and avoidable.

3. Differences in distribution across levels of SES for blacks and whites may account for many racial/ethnic health disparities; socioeconomic causes of racial/ethnic disparities cannot be ruled out without comprehensive measures of SES.

4. A variety of strategies can be used to provide stronger evidence of causal influences of SES on health, including use of data structures, such as natural experiments, and analytic methods, such as structural equation modeling.

5. Identifying pathways and mechanisms by which SES and race/ethnicity affect health provides better evidence of causation and more options for intervention to eliminate disparities.

6. Evidence shows multiple pathways from SES and race/ethnicity to health; one pathway is through differential exposure to chronic stress and its resulting biological toll.

Disclosure Statement

The authors are not aware of any biases that might be perceived as affecting the objectivity of this review.

ACKNOWLEDGMENTS

We appreciate helpful input on earlier drafts from S. Leonard Syme, Belinda Needham, Candyce Kroenke, James Scott, Lisa Bates, Maria Glymour, and Judith Stewart. We also thank Marilyn Vella for her skilled and cheerful help on the manuscript's preparation, and the Robert Wood Johnson Foundation Health and Society Scholars Program and the MacArthur Foundation for their financial support.

● ● ● **References**

1. Aber JL, Bennett NG, Conley DC, Li J. 1997. The effects of poverty on child health and development. *Annu. Rev. Public Health* 18:463-83.

2. Acheson D. 1998. *Independent Inquiry into Inequalities in Health*. London: Station. Off.

3. Adler NE. 2006. Overview of health disparities. In *Examining the Health Disparities Research Plan of the National Institutes of Health: Unfinished Business*, ed. GE Thompson, F Mitchell, M Williams, pp. 129-88. Washington: Natl. Acad. Press.

4. Adler NE, Boyce WT, Chesney M, Folkman S, Syme SL. 1993. Socioeconomic inequalities in health: no easy solution. *JAMA* 269(24):3140-45.

5. Adler NE, Marmot M, McEwen B, Stewart J. 1999. *Socioeconomics Status and Health in Industrialized Nations*. New York: Ann. N.Y. Acad. Sci.

6. Adler NE, Newman K. 2002. Socioeconomic disparities in health: pathways and policies. *Health Affairs* 21(2):60-76.

7. Angrist JD, Krueger AB. 2001. Instrumental variables and the search for identification: from supply and demand to natural experiments. *J. Econ. Perspect.* 15:69-85.

8. Backlund E, Sorlie PD, Johnson NJ. 1996. The shapes of the relationship between income and mortality in the United States: evidence from the National Longitudinal Mortality Study. *Ann. Epidemiol.* 6:12-20.

9. Barbeau EM, Krieger N, Soobader MJ. 2004. Working class matters: socioeconomic disadvantage, race/ethnicity, gender, and smoking in NHIS 2000. *Am. J. Public Health* 94:269-78.

10. Benezeval M, Judge K. 2001. Income and health: the time dimension. *Soc. Sci. Med.* 52:1371-90.

11. Bingenheimer JB, Brennan RT, Earls FJ. 2005. Firearm violence exposure and serious violent behavior. *Science* 308(5726):1323-26.

12. Boyle SH, Williams RB, Mark DB, Brummett BH, Siegler IC, Barefoot JC. 2005. Hostility, age, and mortality in a sample of cardiac patients. *Am. J. Cardiol.* 96(1):64-66.

13. Braveman P. 2006. Health disparities and health equity: concepts and measurement. *Annu. Rev. Public Health* 27:167-94.

14. Braveman P, Cubbin C, Egerter S, Chideya S, Marchi KS, et al. 2005. Socioeconomic status in health research-one size does not fit all. *JAMA* 294:2879-88.

15. Braveman P, Gruskin S. 2003. Defining equity in health. *J. Epidemiol. Community Health* 57:254-28.

16. Caldwell S, Diamond T. 1979. Income differential in mortality: preliminary results based on IRS-SSA linked data. In *Statistical Uses of Administrative Records with Emphasis on Mortality and Disability Research*, ed. L Delbene, F Scheuren, pp. 51-59. Washington, DC: Soc. Secur. Admin., Off. Res. Stat.

17. Carter-Pokras O, Baquet C. 2002. What is a "health disparity"? *Public Health Rep.* 117(5):426-34.

18. Case A, Lubotsky D, Paxson C. 2002. Economic status and health in childhood: the origins of the gradient. *Am. Econ. Rev.* 92(5):1308-34.

19. Catalano R, Dooley D, Wilson G, Hough R. 1993. Job loss and alcohol abuse: a test using data from the Epidemiologic Catchment Area project. *J. Health Soc. Behav.* 34(3):215-25.

20. Catalano R, Hansen H, Hartig T. 1999. The ecological effect of unemployment on the incidence of very low birthweight in Norway and Sweden. *J. Health Soc. Behav.* 40:422-28.

21. Chandola T, Clarke P, Morris JN, Blane D. 2006. Pathways between education and health: a causal modelling approach. *J. R. Stat. Soc.: Series A (Stat. Soc.)* 169(2):337-59.

22. Chen E, Matthews K, Boyce WT. 2002. Socioeconomic differences in children's health: How and why do these relationships change with age? *Psychol. Bull.* 128(2):295-329.

23. Chen JT, Rehkopf DH, Waterman PD, Subramanian SV, Coull BA, et al. 2006. Mapping and measuring social disparities in premature mortality: the impact of census tract poverty within and across Boston neighborhoods, 1999-2001. *J. Urban Health* 83:1063-84.

24. Conley D. 1999. *Being Black, Living in the Red: Race, Wealth, and Social Policy in America.* Berkeley: Univ. Calif. Press.

25. Conley D, Bennett NG. 2000. Is biology destiny? Birth weight and life chances. *Am. Sociol. Rev.* 65:458-67.

26. Cooper R, Rotimi C, Ataman S, McGee D, Osotimehin B, et al. 1997. The prevalence of hypertension in seven populations of West African origin. *Am. J. Public Health* 87(2):160-68.

27. D'Agostino RB. 1998. Propensity score methods for bias reduction in the comparison of a treatment to a nonrandomized control group. *Stat. Med.* 17(19):2265-81.

28. Dahl G, Lochner L. 2005. *The impact of family income on child achievement.* Work. Pap.11729, Natl. Bur. Econ. Res.

29. Davey Smith G. 2000. Learning to live with complexity: ethnicity, socioeconomic position,and health in Britain and the United States. *Am. J. Public Health* 90:1694-98.

30. Diez Roux AV, Borrell LN, Haan M, Jackson SA, Schultz R. 2004. Neighborhood environments and mortality in an elderly cohort: results from the cardiovascular health study. *J. Epidemiol. Community Health* 58:917-23.

31. Ditlevsen S, Christensen U, Lynch J, Damsgaard MT, Keiding N. 2005. The mediation proportion: a structural equation approach for estimating the proportion of exposure effect on outcome explained by an intermediate variable. *Epidemiology* 16:114-20.

32. Duncan GJ, Magnuson KA. 2003. Off with Hollingshead: socioeconomic resources, parenting, and child development. In *Socioeconomic Status, Parenting, and Child Development*, ed. MH Bornstein, RH Bradley, pp. 83-106. London: Erlbaum.

33. Ecob R, Davey Smith G. 1999. Income and health: What is the nature of the relationship? *Soc. Sci. Med.* 48:693-705.

34. Ettner SL. 1996. New evidence on the relationship between income and health. *J. Health Econ.* 15(1): 67-85.

35. Evans G. 2003. A multimethodological analysis of cumulative risk and allostatic load among rural children. *Dev. Psychol.* 39(5):924-33.

36. Evans GW, Kantrowitz E. 2002. Socioeconomic status and health: the potential role of environmental risk exposure. *Annu. Rev. Public Health* 23:303-31.

37. Everson-Rose SA, Lewis TT, Karavolos K, Matthews KA, Sutton-Tyrrell K, Powell LH. 2006. Cynical hostility and carotid atherosclerosis in African American and white women: the Study of Women's Health Across the Nation (SWAN) Heart Study. *Am.Heart J.* 152(5):982.e7-13.

38. Frijters P. 2005. The causal effect of income on health: evidence from German reunification. *J. Health Econ.* 24:997-1017.

39. Fuchs VR. 1992. Poverty and health: asking the right questions. *Am. Econ.* 36(2):12-18.

40. Gallo LC, Matthews KA. 2003. Understanding the association between socioeconomic status and physical health. *Psychol. Bull.* 129(1):10-51.

41. Gilman SE, Abrams DB, Buka SL. 2003. Socioeconomic status over the life course and stages of cigarette use: initiation, regular use, and cessation. *J. Epidemiol. Community Health* 57:802-8.

42. Glymour M. 2006. Using causal diagrams to understand common problems in social epidemiology. In *Methods in Social Epidemiology*, ed. J Kaufman, M Oakes, pp. 393-428. New York: Josey-Bass.

43. Goodman E, McEwen BS, Huang B, Dolan LM, Adler NE. 2005. Social inequalities in biomarkers of cardiovascular risk in adolescence. *Psychosom. Med.* 67:9-15.

44. Gottfredson LS, Deary IJ. 2004. Intelligence predicts health and longevity, but why? *Psychol. Sci.* 13(1):1-4.

45. Greenland S, Morgenstern H. 2001. Confounding in health research. *Annu. Rev. Public Health* 22:189-212.

46. Haas SA. 2006. Health selection and the process of social stratification: the effect of childhood health on socioeconomic attainment. *J. Health Soc. Behav.* 47:339-54.

47. Harding DJ. 2003. Counterfactual models of neighborhood effects: the effect of neighborhood poverty on dropping out and teenage pregnancy. *Am. J. Sociol.* 109:676-719.

48. Harper S, Lynch J, Burris S, Davey Smith G. 2007. Trends in the black-white life expectancy gap in the United States, 1983-2003. *JAMA* 297:1224-32.

49. Harper S, Lynch J, Hsu WL, Everson SA, Hillemeier MM, et al. 2002. Life course socioeconomic conditions and adult psychosocial functioning. *Int. J. Epidemiol.* 31:395-403.

50. Hernan MA, Hernandez-Diaz S, Robins JM. 2004. A structural approach to selection bias. *Epidemiology* 15:615-25.

51. Howard G, Anderson RT, Russell G, Howard VJ, Burke GL. 2000. Race, socioeconomic status, and cause-specific mortality. *Ann. Epidemiol.* 10:214-23.

52. Isaacs SL, Schroeder SA. 2004. Class—the ignored determinant of the nation's health. *N. Engl. J. Med.* 351(11):1137-42.

53. Johnston-Brooks CH, Lewis MA, Evans GW, Whalen CK. 1998. Chronic stress and illness in children: the role of allostatic load. *Psychosom. Med.* 60(5):597-603.

54. Kaufman JS, Cooper JS, McGee DL. 1997. The problem of residual confounding and the resiliency of race. *Epidemiology* 8:621-28.

55. Kaufman JS, MacLehose RF, Kaufman S. 2004. A further critique of the analytic strategy of adjusting for covariates to identify biologic mediation. *Epidemiol. Perspect. Innov.* 1:4.doi:10.1186/1742-5573-1-4.

56. Kawachi I, Daniels N, Robinson DE. 2005. Health disparities by race and class: why both matter. *Health Affairs* 24:343-52.

57. Kington RS, Smith JP. 1997. Socioeconomic status and racial and ethnic differences in functional status associated with chronic diseases. *Am. J. Public Health* 87:805-10.

58. Kitagawa E, Hauser P. 1973. *Differential Mortality in the United States*. Cambridge, MA: Harvard Univ. Press.

59. Kliss B, Scheuren FJ. 1978. The 1973 CPS-IRS-SSA exact match study. *Soc. Secur. Bull.* 41:14-22.

60. Krieger N, Fee E. 1996. Measuring social inequalities in health in the United States: a historical review, 1900-1950. *Int. J. Health Serv.* 26(3):391-418.

61. Krieger N, Williams DR, Moss NE. 1997. Measuring social class in US public health research: concepts, methodologies, and guidelines. *Annu. Rev. Public Health* 18:341-78.

62. Kubzansky LD, Kawachi I, Sparrow D. 1999. Socioeconomic status, hostility, and risk factor clustering in the Normative Aging Study: any help from the concept of allostatic load? *Ann. Behav. Med.* 21(4):330-38.

63. Kunitz SJ. 2007. Sex, race and social role-history and the social determinants of health. *Int. J. Epidemiol.* 36(1):3-10.

64. Lara M, Gamboa C, Kahramanian MI, Morales LS, Bautista DE. 2005. Acculturation and Latino health in the United States: a review of the literature and its sociopolitical context. *Annu. Rev. Public Health* 26:367-97.

65. Levine RS, Foster JE, Fullilove RE, Fullilove MT, Briggs N, et al. 2001. Black-white inequalities in mortality and life expectancy, 1933-1999: implications for Healthy People 2010. *Public Health Rep.* 116:474-83.

66. Lleras-Muney A. 2005. The relationship between education and adult mortality in the United States. *Rev. Econ. Stud.* 72(1):189-221.

67. Marmot MG, Bosma H, Hemingway H, Brunner E, Stansfeld S. 1997. Contribution of job control and other risk factors to social variations in coronary heart disease incidence. *Lancet* 350:235-39.

68. Marmot MG, Rose G, Shipley M, Hamilton PJS. 1978. Employment grade and coronary heart disease in British Civil Servants. *J. Epidemiol. Community Health* 32:244-49.

69. Marmot MG, Shipley MJ, Rose G. 1984. Inequalities in death—specific explanations of a general pattern? *Lancet* 323:1003-6.

70. Mays VM, Ponce NA, Washington DL, Cochran SD. 2003. Classification of race and ethnicity: implications for public health. *Annu. Rev. Public Health* 24:83-110.

71. McDonough P, Duncan G, Williams D, House JS. 1997. Income dynamics and adult mortality in the United States, 1972 through 1989. *Am. J. Public Health* 87:1476-83.

72. McDonough P, Williams DR, House JS, Duncan GJ. 1999. Gender and the socioeconomic gradient in mortality. *J. Health Soc. Behav.* 40:17-31.

73. McEwen B. 1998. Protective and damaging effects of stress mediators. *N. Engl. J. Med.* 338(3):171-79.

74. McEwen BS, Seeman T. 1999. Protective and damaging effects of mediators of stress: elaborating and testing the concepts of allostasis and allostatic load. *Ann. N. Y. Acad. Sci.* 896:30-47.

75. Merikangas KR, Risch N. Genomic priorities and public health. *Science* 302:599-601.

76. Minkler M, Fuller-Thomson E, Guralnik JM. 2006. Gradient of disability across the socioeconomic spectrum in the United States. *N. Engl. J. Med.* 355(7):695-703.

77. Mulatu MS, Schooler C. 2002. Causal connections between socio-economic status and health: reciprocal effects and mediating mechanisms. *J. Health Soc. Behav.* 43:22-41.

78. Murray CJL, Kulkarni SC, Michaud C, Tomijima N, Bulzacchelli MT, et al. 2006. Eight Americas: investigating mortality disparities across races, counties, and race-counties in the United States. *PLoS. Med.* 3(9):e260.

79. Palloni A. 2004. Paradox lost: explaining the Hispanic adult mortality advantage? *Demography* 41(3):385-415.

80. Pamuk E, Makuc D, Heck K, Reuben C, Lochner K. 1998. *Health, United States, 1998 with Socioeconomic Status and Health Chartbook*. Hyattsville, MD: Natl. Cent. Health Stat., Cent. Dis. Control Prev.

81. Pappas G, Queen S, Hadden W, Fisher G. 1993. The increasing disparity in mortality between socioeconomic groups in the United States, 1960 and 1986. *N. Engl. J. Med.* 392:103-9.

82. Pearl J. 2000. *Causality: Models, Reasoning, and Inference*. Cambridge, UK: Cambridge Univ. Press.

83. Pearl J. 2001. Causal inference in the health sciences: a conceptual introduction. *Health Serv. Outcomes Res. Methodol.* 2:189-220.

84. Power C, Matthews S. 1997. Origins of health inequalities in a national population sample. *Lancet* 350:1584-89.

85. Power C, Matthews S, Manor O. 1998. Inequalities in self-rated health: explanations from different stages of life. *Lancet* 351:1009-14.

86. Preston SH, Ilo IT. 1995. Are educational differentials in mortality increasing in the United States? *J. Aging Health* 7:476-96.

87. Raudenbush SW. 2001. Comparing personal trajectories and drawing causal inferences from longitudinal data. *Annu. Rev. Psychol.* 52:501-25.

88. Ricketts TC. 2000. The changing nature of rural health care. *Annu. Rev. Public Health* 21:639-57.

89. Rogot E, Sorlie PD, Johnson NJ, Schmitt C. 1992. *A Mortality Study of 1.3 Million Persons by Demographic, Social and Economic Factors: 1979-1985 Follow-Up. Second Data Book*. NIH Publ. No. 92-3297. Bethesda, MD: Natl. Inst. Health, Public Health Serv., Dep. Health Hum. Serv.

90. Rosenbaum PR, Rubin DB. 1983. The central role of the propensity score in observational studies for causal effects. *Biometrika* 70:41-55.

91. Schnittker J. 2004. Education and the changing shape of the income gradient in health. *J. Health Soc. Behav.* 45:286-305.

92. Seeman TE, McEwen BS, Rowe JW, Burton H, Singer BH. 2001. Allostatic load as a marker of cumulative biological risk: MacArthur studies of successful aging. *Proc. Natl. Acad. Sci. USA* 98: 4770-75.

93. Seeman TE, Singer BH, Rowe JW, Horwitz RI, McEwen BS. 1997. Price of adaptation—allostatic load and its health consequences. MacArthur studies of successful aging. *Arch. Intern. Med.* 157(19): 2259-68.

94. Singh GK, Hiatt RA. 2006. Trends and disparities in socioeconomic and behavioral characteristics, life expectancy, and cause-specific mortality of native-born and foreign-born populations in the United States, 1979-2003. *Int. J. Epidemiol.* 35(4):903-19.

95. Singh GK, Siahpush M. 2001. All-cause and cause-specific mortality of immigrants and native born in the United States. *Am. J. Public Health* 91(3):392-99.

96. Smith JP. 1999. Healthy bodies and thick wallets: the dual relation between health and economic status. *J. Econ. Perspect.* 13:145-66.

97. Snyder SE, Evans WN. 2006. The effect of income on mortality: evidence from the social security notch. *Rev. Econ. Stat.* 88:482-95.

98. Subramanian SV, Chen JT, Rehkopf DH, Waterman P, Krieger N. 2005. Racial disparities in context: a multilevel analysis of neighborhood variation in poverty and excess mortality among black populations in Massachusetts. *Am. J. Public Health* 95:260-65.

99. Thompson G, Mitchell F, Williams M, eds. 2006. *Health Disparities Research Plan of the National Institutes of Health*. Washington: Natl. Acad. Press.

100. U.S. Dep. Health Hum. Serv. 2000. *Healthy People 2010*.Washington, DC: U.S. GPO.

101. van der Laan MJ, Robins JM. 2003. *Unified Methods for Censored Longitudinal Data and Causality*. Cambridge, MA: Springer.

102. Vaupel JW, Yashin AI. 1985. Heterogeneity's ruses: some surprising effects of selection on population dynamics. *Am. Stat.* 39(3):176-85.

103. Wadsworth ME, Kuh DJ. 1997. Childhood influences on adult health: a review of recent work from the British 1946 national birth cohort study, the MRC National Survey of Health and Development. *Paediatr. Perinat. Epidemiol.* 11:2-20.

104. Ward E, Jemal A, Cokkinides V, Singh GK, Cardinez C, et al. 2004. Cancer disparities by race/ethnicity and socioeconomic status. *CA Cancer J. Clin.* 54:78-93.

105. Williams DR, Collins C. 1995. US socioeconomic and racial differences in health: patterns and explanations. *Annu. Rev. Sociol.* 21:349-86.

106. Wong MD, Shapiro MF, Boscardin J, Ettner SL. 2002. Contributions of major diseases to disparities in mortality. *N. Engl. J. Med.* 347:1585-92.

107. Wright EO. 1997. *Class Counts: Comparative Studies in Class Analysis*. Cambridge, UK: Cambridge Univ. Press.

108. Zhang Q, Wang Y. 2004. Trends in the association between obesity and socioeconomic status in U.S. adults: 1971 to 2000. *Obes. Res.* 12:1622-32.

3

Changing Patterns of Mortality Among American Indians

Source: Kunitz SJ. Ethics in public health research: changing patterns of mortality among American Indians. *Am J Public Health* 2008;98:404-11. Reprinted with permission of the American Public Health Association.

Mortality rates for American Indians (including Alaska Natives) declined for much of the 20th century, but data published by the Indian Health Service indicate that since the mid-1980s, age-adjusted deaths for this population have increased both in absolute terms and compared with rates for the White American population.

This increase appears to be primarily because of the direct and indirect effects of type 2 diabetes. Despite increasing appropriations for the Special Diabetes Program for Indians, per capita expenditures for Indian health, including third party reimbursements, remain substantially lower than those for other Americans and, when adjusted for inflation, have been essentially unchanged since the early 1990s. I argue that inadequate funding for health services has contributed significantly to the increased death rate. (*Am J Public Health.* 2008;98: 404-411. doi:10. 2105/AJPH.2007.114538)

Over the past century, mortality among American Indians (including Alaska Natives) declined roughly in parallel with that of the rest of the U.S. population, although rates continue to be higher than for white Americans. The decline, which persisted for most of the 20th century despite the vicissitudes of federal policies, practices, and appropriations, is an example of the epidemiological transition from a regime characterized by infectious diseases to one characterized by noninfectious, chronic diseases.[1] It is generally assumed that in advanced economies this progression is more or less inevitable; infectious diseases recede and are replaced in relative importance by noninfectious diseases, but total mortality continues to fall.

The collapse of the Soviet Union and the catastrophic reversal of declining mortality in its former republics and elsewhere in Eastern Europe show that such progress is not inevitable.[2] There are other cases of reversal or, at the very least, stagnation of declining mortality in advanced economies. For example, the life expectancy of Aboriginal Australians has been largely stagnant for several decades,[3] and recent changes in the mortality rates of American Indians indicate something similar.

I use published data to examine recent changes in age-adjusted mortality of American Indians in general and of Navajos in particular. Navajo data are included for several reasons: (1) the Navajos, as the largest tribe living on a reservation in the United States, have an important impact on overall rates; (2) during the period under consideration, Navajo health services were provided by the Indian Health Service (IHS) and not by tribally managed programs; and (3) historical data on Navajo health services and mortality are more readily available than for other, smaller American Indian populations.

Causes of death are classified as either amenable or not amenable to interventions by the health care system. This classification is usually traced to the work of David Rutstein et al. in the mid-1970s.[4] As Holland has said,

> Here medical care is defined in its broadest sense, that is prevention, cure and care, including the application of all relevant medical knowledge, the services of all medical and allied personnel, the resources of governmental, voluntary, and social agencies, and the cooperation of the individual himself. An excessive number of such unnecessary events serves as a warning signal of possible shortcomings in the health care system, and should be investigated further.[5(p1)]

Avoidable deaths, which are described in more detail in the following section, may thus arise for a variety of reasons, including unusual genetic and epidemiological characteristics of particular populations, inadequate funding, inaccessible services or populations, incompetent staff, uninformed populations, and noncompliant patients. Although all of these factors may be contributory, the fact that some populations have higher rates than others is an indication that adequate health services responsive to the unique needs of particular populations may not be available.[6]

I briefly consider two other issues. The first has to do with the impact of devolution of responsibility for services to American Indian tribal governments or other entities. Self determination in American Indian affairs has been federal policy since 1974, and some attempts have been made to examine the impact, if any, on health of changes in management.[7] The second has to do with a question debated in public health since the early years of the 20th century: the degree to which programs should be vertical or horizontal. The former refers to programs aimed at the eradication or control of a particular disease. The latter refers to programs covering a broad range of services.[8-11]

METHODS

Data for my analyses of time trends in American Indian mortality from the early 1970s through the 1990s came from IHS publications.[12,13] They included only deaths in the IHS service area, which comprises primarily states in the Midwest and West.

Data for the Navajo Area of the IHS came from two different sources. Historical data, taken from previously published material,[14] were for the population living on the Navajo Reservation. Data from the late 1990s and early 2000s, published by the Navajo Area IHS,[15] refer to the service area, which comprises both the reservation and adjacent nonreservation lands where many Navajos live.

Because death data were available only for New Mexico and Arizona, only the populations of the service areas in those two states were used as the denominator for calculating rates. The number of Navajos living in the Utah portion of the service area is very small, and their exclusion did not significantly influence the results. The classifications of cause of death on the Navajo Reservation in 1972 through 1978 and in the Navajo service area in 1998 through 2002 were from different revisions of the *International Classification of Diseases*[16,17] and thus may not be precisely comparable. Nonetheless, the codings of several of the most important causes of death, most notably diabetes, are similar enough to be useful for broad comparative purposes.

Causes of death amenable and not amenable to interventions by the health care system are the same as have been used elsewhere.[18] The IHS does not publish death rates for all causes, nor are age data published for most causes. (The causes that are available for the analysis of deaths caused by conditions amenable to health care interventions can be found as a supplement to the online version of this article at http://www.ajph.org.[13,19,20])

RESULTS

Mortality Trends among American Indians

Figure 1 displays all-cause, age-adjusted (to the 1940 U.S. population) death rates from 1973 through 1997 for American Indian and white Americans. Although rates for the former are higher than for the latter, they both declined during the first half of the period. Starting in the mid-1980s, however, they diverged as the rate for American Indians began to increase. At its nadir in 1986, the death rate for American Indians was 669.1 per 100,000. Over the next 10 years, it rose to 715.2 per 100,000, an increase of about 46 per 100,000. Over the same period, the rate for white Americans declined from 520.1 per 100,000 to 456.5 per 100,000 and has continued to decline in subsequent years.

Figures 2 and 3 display age-adjusted death rates from 1973 through 1997 for causes amenable and

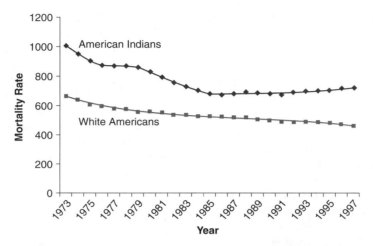

FIGURE 1 Mortality rates, per 100 000, by race, from all causes of mortality: American Indians[a] and white Americans, 1973–1997.

not amenable to intervention by the health care system. Among the former causes, deaths from diabetes among American Indians increased most significantly, whereas deaths from heart disease and cerebrovascular diseases declined, but at lower rates than among white Americans—so much so, indeed, that over the 24-year period the relative positions of the death rates of American Indians and of white Americans reversed.

The increased all-cause death rate of American Indians starting in the mid-1980s seems to have been partly the result of a stagnation in rates of decline of alcohol-related and cirrhosis deaths, and of deaths from pneumonia or influenza and tuberculosis, and an increase in rates of death from lung cancer and diabetes, the latter almost doubling from 29 per 100,000 to 53 per 100,000. Although there are insufficient data to explain the entire increase in all-cause mortality, it is clear that slightly more than half the increase (24 of 46 per 100000) was directly caused by diabetes. Over the same 10-year period, deaths from lung cancer increased from 24 per 100,000 to 34 per 100,000, accounting for about 20% of the increase.

The Navajo Area

Per capita allocations of the IHS budget among service areas vary greatly; in 1993 they ranged from $575 per enumerated American Indian in the Oklahoma area to $1906 in Alaska.[6] Among rural populations, the Navajo Area, which is located in Arizona, New Mexico, and a small strip of southern Utah, had one of the lowest allocations, whether

measured per user of services ($608) or per enumerated American Indian in the service area ($717). At the time to which the following data apply, all services were provided directly by the IHS and not by the Navajo Nation, although two of the eight service units have since come under the control of community boards.

Table 1 (not included) shows that the number of hospital beds per 1000 population has declined steadily over the past 70 years, as have occupancy rates, hospitalizations per 1000 population, and average length of stay.

Table 2 (not included) shows that since the 1970s, nursing staff has become more professionalized as registered nurses have replaced licensed practical nurses, but overall, the ratio of nursing staff to population has remained the same. Likewise, the ratio of public health nurses to population, considered separately, has remained almost unchanged. By contrast, the number of physicians per 10,000 population has almost doubled over the same period, from 8.3 to 15.5; this figure, although substantially less than the nationwide figure of 23.2 per 10,000,[15(p41)] is similar to those for Arizona (17.2 per 10,000) and New Mexico (16.8 per 10,000).[21,22] At the same time, median household income increased substantially (Table 3). Although the rate of increase in income was greater on the Navajo Reservation than in the surrounding states in the 1990s, absolute income was still substantially less.

From the early 1970s to the years 1996 through 1998, life expectancy increased from 58.8 years for men and 71.8 years for women to 68 and 76.5 years for men and women, respectively.[12,26]

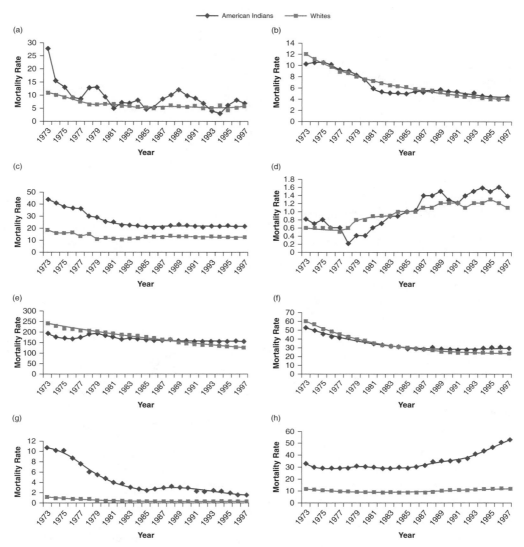

FIGURE 2 Mortality rates, per 100 000, by race, from maternal causes (a), neonatal causes (b), influenza and pneumonia (c), asthma (d), heart disease (e), cerebrovascular disease (f), tuberculosis (g), and diabetes (h): American Indians[a] and white Americans, 1973–1997.

This reflects the continuing epidemiological transition experienced by the Navajos over the past century. Infectious diseases have declined and noninfectious conditions have increased, some in relative importance and others in absolute importance. Table 4 displays crude average annual death rates for the periods 1972 to 1978 and 1998 to 2002 for several different broadly defined causes. Among conditions considered not amenable to health service interventions, accidents declined, suicide increased, and homicide and cirrhosis remained essentially unchanged. Among conditions amenable to intervention by the health care system, tuberculosis, neonatal mortality, pneumonia, and influenza all declined, whereas death rates from heart and cerebrovascular disease and from diabetes increased.

The epidemic of non-insulin-dependent diabetes among American Indians was relatively late in affecting the Navajos. Although prevalence seems to have begun to increase in the 1960s, it began to receive increasing attention only in the 1980s.[27,28] It is widely agreed to be the consequence of increasing obesity and changing dietary and activity

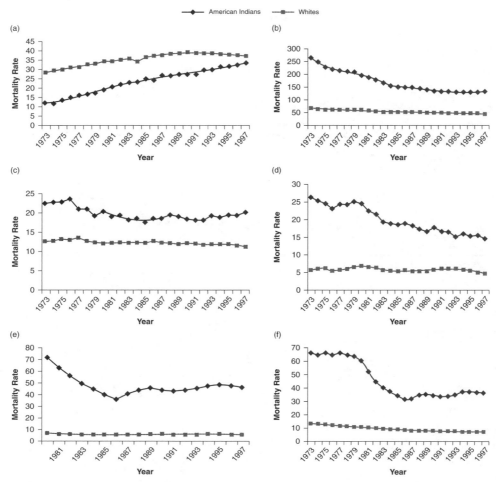

Note: Mortality are rates age-adjusted to the 1940 US population. These causes of mortality are not amenable to intervention by the health care system. Data for earlier years of alcohol-related causes were not available.
[a]Includes Alaska Natives.

FIGURE 3 Mortality rates, per 100,000, by race, from lung cancer (a), unintentional injuries (b), suicide (c), homicide (d), alcohol-related causes (e), and chronic liver disease and cirrhosis (f): American Indians[a] and white Americans, 1973–1997.

Table 1	Health Facilities and Utilization of Services in the Navajo Area of the Indian Health Service: 1933–2003					
Year	Hospital Beds, No.	Occupancy Rate,%	Average Beds/ 1000 Population	Hospitalizations/ Length of Stay,d	1000 Population	Outpatient Visits/Person
1933	352	111.0[a]	. . .	. . .	. . .	. . .
1940	564	50.0	11.3	20.5	182.8	1.1
1960	. . .	. . .	. . .	. . .	. . .	1.5–1.7
1966	547	83.6	5.2–5.9	8.9	158–181	. . .
1977/78	557	60.0	3.9	5.4	152.0	4.5
2003	351	43.3	1.5	3.3	72.5	5.1

[a]The 111% occupancy rate indicates overcrowding.

Note: Ellipses indicate that no data are available.

Source: Data are from Kunitz[14] and the Navajo Area Indian Health Service.[15]

Table 2	Medical Personnel at Health Facilities in the Navajo Area of the Indian Health Service: 1977 and 2003				
Year	Registered Nurses	Public Health Nurses	Licensed Practical Nurses	Total Nursing Staff	Physicians
1977	16.9	2.81	10.8	30.5	8.3
2003	26.9	2.4	2.2	31.5	15.5

Note: Personnel are per 100,000 population.

Source: Data are from Kunitz[14] and the Navajo Area Indian Health Service.[15]

Table 3	Median Family Income in Current and 1999 Dollars on the Navajo Reservations and in Neighboring States: 1969–1999					
	Navajo Reservation		New Mexico[a]		Arizona[a]	
Year	Current $	1999 $	Current$	1999 $	Current $	1999 $
1969	3,084[b]	12,083	7,096	27,803	8,199	32,125
1979	...	...	14,654	31,350	16,448	35,118
1989	10,958[c]	14,296	24,087	31,425	27,540	35,930
1999	20,005[d]	20,005	34,133	34,133	40,558	40,558

Note: Ellipses indicate that no data are available.

[a]Data are from the U.S. Census Bureau.[23]

[b]Figure is from the U.S. Census Bureau.[24]

[c]Figure is from Rodgers.[25]

[d]Figure is from Navajo Area Indian Health Service.[15]

Table 4	Crude Average Annual Death Rates in the Navajo Area of the Indian Health Service: 1972–1978 and 1998–2002	
	Death Rate per 100,000	
Cause	1972–1978	1998–2002
Accidents (motor vehicle accidents)	213.0 (106.0)	99.5 – 106.9 (63.6–68.4)
Homicide	15.6	13.0 – 13.9
Suicide	8.3	16.4 – 17.6
Neoplasms	38.0	63.6 – 68.4
Circulatory/ cardiovascular disease	72.8	108.0–116.1
Tuberculosis	6.8	1.7 – 1.8
Diabetes	10.1[a]	28.6 – 30.7
Infant mortality	17.6	6.2
Neonatal	8.7	4.1
Postneonatal	8.9	2.1
Cirrhosis/ chronic liver disease	18.1	18.4 – 19.8
Pneumonia/influenza	56.1[a]	24.6 – 26.4
Estimated population	132,156	200,000 – 215,000

[a]Figures are from an unpublished report by the Navajo Area Indian Health Service,Office of Program Planning and Evaluation, Window Rock, Ariz, June, 1998.

Source: Data are from Kunitz[14] and the Navajo Area Indian Health Service.[15]

patterns,[29-31] and it carries with it increased risk of morbidity and of mortality from cardiovascular diseases.[28,32-34] Moreover, hypertension is also strongly associated with diabetes, but only about 50% of hypertensive individuals found in a community survey had been told by a physician that they had hypertension.[35] About one third of diabetics in the same survey were unaware that they had diabetes, suggesting that both screening and prevention were not widely available.[36]

DISCUSSION

Although all the data I present have been published previously, most appeared in government publications, both federal and tribal, and are not widely known to the public health community. The data are important both in their own right, reflecting as they do a deterioration in the health of a small but significant population of Americans, and because they may foreshadow changes experienced more broadly in the United States, especially among the poor. Income has increased among American Indians in general[37] and Navajos in particular, but mortality caused by several chronic conditions amenable to intervention by the health care system has increased. This is similar to what has occurred in many poor countries, in which the emergence of ischemic heart disease and other chronic conditions is now recognized as a widespread phenomenon.[38] Such changes are usually attributed to changes in diet and exercise patterns attendant on the shift to relatively sedentary occupations and the increased availability of processed foods.

Avoidable Deaths

Important as changes in lifestyle are, however, health services have an important role to play in the prevention and treatment of these conditions. Health care systems in general, including the IHS, have been effective in reducing death rates from many conditions. Typically, these conditions have been primarily infectious diseases; however, the incidence and severity of stroke, hypertension,[39,40] and ischemic heart disease[41] in non–American Indian populations have also been affected by treatment. In addition, diabetics, who are at substantially increased risk of death from cardiovascular disease, also benefit from tight control of their diabetes, treatment of hypertension, and use of anticoagulants such as aspirin.[42,43]

Reduction of diabetes-related deaths is not simply a matter of primary prevention and changes in lifestyle. Compared with whites, American Indians have higher rates of self-reported obesity, smoking, diabetes, and heart disease; spend less time in leisure-time physical activity; and have worse self-assessed health, even after adjustment for sociodemographic variables.[44-46] Primordial prevention (the prevention of the underlying causes of risk factors) and primary prevention (the reduction of risk factors) are thus crucially important in this population. High death rates, however, cannot simply be accepted as the result of too many fast food restaurants and irresponsible or uninformed lifestyle choices and personal behavior. As the concept of amenable conditions suggests,

> an excessive number of such unnecessary events serves as a warning signal of shortcomings in the health care system, and should be investigated further.[5(p1)]

Indeed, this has been recognized by both the IHS and the U.S. Congress. A Special Diabetes Program for Indians was mandated in 1997 that has provided substantial and increasing funds for the prevention and treatment of diabetes: $30 million per year in 1997 through 2000, $100 million per year in 2001 through 2003, and $150 million per year since 2004.[13,47] The results have been encouraging: among treated diabetics, such measures as average diastolic blood pressure and cholesterol, hemoglobin A1c, and triglyceride levels all declined from 1995 through 2001, although mortality rates from diabetes have not declined.[48,49]

Although these declines are statistically significant, their clinical and epidemiological significance is uncertain because (1) these measures are still high, and cardiovascular disease risk factors are more important for diabetics than for nondiabetics, and (2) some of the results may be shifted downward by lead-time bias, whereby more-thorough screening leads to more cases being detected at an earlier and milder stage. Nonetheless, the recognition of the magnitude of the problem presented by diabetes, and the attempt to intervene, is of great significance.

Unfortunately, even taking these new funds and third-party payments into account, per capita expenditures for American Indian health remain well below those for other citizens, and in constant dollars they have remained essentially flat for well over a decade.[13] At the beginning and end of the 1990s, per capita expenditures for the IHS service population were about $1662; according to recent unpublished analyses by the IHS, they remain about the same (Cliff Wiggins, IHS, oral communication, February 27, 2007).

Horizontal and Vertical Programs

In this context, specially targeted funds such as the Special Diabetes Program for Indians are no doubt important and welcome, but they raise a question that has been debated in public health for much of the 20th century: the appropriateness of vertical as opposed to horizontal programs. The justification for vertically organized programs aimed at specific diseases has been that once diseases are eradicated or at least controlled, they no longer need to be a concern for the health care system.[8] Smallpox is the best example. By contrast, horizontal programs are justified because they provide the full range of services and indeed may be necessary if vertical programs are to have a lasting effect.[9]

One may also speculate that vertical programs are less likely to successfully stand alone when they are targeted at chronic diseases rather than, for instance, vaccine-preventable diseases. Chronic diseases may require a full range of services. Diabetes, for example, causes complications that may require dialysis and surgical intervention, which are best provided by a comprehensive health care system. With an essentially unchanging budget, however, provision of a broad range of services—that is, horizontal programs—becomes increasingly difficult to sustain, because expenditures fail to keep pace with population growth and inflation of health care costs.

The shift from inpatient to outpatient care on the Navajo Reservation over the past 70 years is largely the result of the change from infectious to noninfectious diseases, as well as changes in medical practice. The evidence cited here, however, also indicates that a high proportion of people with hypertension and diabetes are unaware of their diagnoses, suggesting that services are not reaching many who could benefit from them. This may be, at least in part, a consequence of having too few health care providers to meet the needs of the population, which in turn results from the very low per capita health expenditures for the Navajo population. Another possible cause, however, is that even in areas in which there are about the same number of providers as for nearby non–American Indian populations, the ability to provide needed services has been compromised by deficient budgets.

Self-Determination

Budgetary issues also confound attempts to assess the impact of self-determination on health. The years since the early 1970s have been a time of major change in American Indian health programs. It was in 1974 that President Nixon declared that, henceforth, tribal self-determination rather than termination (i.e., ending recognition of tribes as domestic sovereign nations) would be his administration's policy.[50] That has been government policy ever since, and an increasing number of tribal governments have assumed responsibility for providing services to their populations. One appraisal of the policy in 1998 claimed that IHS data showed a continuing improvement in the health status of American Indians over the previous 20 years,[7(p227)] which at the very least demonstrated that self-determination was not having deleterious consequences. More-recent data presented here, however, indicate that there have been changes for the worse in health status. Indeed, unpublished data from the IHS indicate that American Indian mortality has continued to stagnate since 1997 (Edna Paisano and Joanne Papallardo, IHS, written and oral communication, February 16, 2007).

The reversal of mortality decline cannot, however, be attributed to the management of health services by tribal entities. First, regional analyses published elsewhere show no clear association—either positive or negative—between rates of death from causes amenable to intervention and the proportion of services managed by tribes, beyond what could be better explained by median household income.[6,51] Second, over the years for which Navajo Area data were analyzed, during which deaths from diabetes and cardiovascular diseases increased, none of the health programs were managed by the Navajo Nation.

Although the temporal association between a stagnant budget and stagnant mortality rates do not prove causation, the relationship is not likely to be entirely fortuitous. The continuing low level of funding for American Indian health programs, regardless of whether services are provided directly by the IHS or by tribal entities, seems likely to have had an impact on health status. Health care for American Indians is not treated as an entitlement in the federal budget[49] but is a discretionary item subject to changing administration and congressional priorities.[52] This is why spending has been flat, and it is reasonable to suggest that it is also why American Indians have not benefited from health services as they should.

About the Author

The author is with the Department of Community & Preventive Medicine, University of Rochester School of Medicine, Rochester, NY, and the Department of Family & Community Medicine, University of New Mexico School of Medicine, Albuquerque, NM. Requests for reprints should be sent to Stephen J. Kunitz, MD, PhD, Department of Community & Preventive Medicine, University of Rochester Medical Center, PO Box 278969, Rochester, NY 14627-8969 (e-mail: stephen_kunitz@urmc.rochester.edu).

This essay was accepted August 11, 2007.

────────

ACKNOWLEDGMENTS

Edna Paisano, Joanne Papallardo, and Cliff Wiggins provided unpublished data from the Indian Health Service. Helpful comments and advice were provided by Michael Everett, Laurence Jacobs, and Matthew C. Riddle.

• • • References

1. Omran AR. The epidemiologic transition: a theory of the epidemiology of population change. *Milbank Mem Fund Q*. 1971;49:509-538.

2. *World Development Indicators* [CD-ROM]. Washington, DC: World Bank; 2002.

3. Kunitz SJ. *Disease and Social Diversity: The Impact of Europeans on the Health of Non-Europeans*. New York, NY: Oxford University Press; 1994.

4. Rutstein DD, Berenberg W, Chalmers TC, Child CG, Fishman AP, Perrin EB. Measuring the quality of medical care: a clinical method. *N Engl J Med*. 1976;294:582-588.

5. Holland WW, ed. *European Community Atlas of "Avoidable Death."* Vol 2. Oxford, England: Oxford University Press; 1993.

6. Kunitz SJ. The history and politics of health care for Native Americans. In: Healy J, McKee M, eds. *Accessing Health Care: Responding to Diversity*. Oxford, England: Oxford University Press; 2004: 303-324.

7. Dixon M, Shelton BL, Roubideaux Y, Mather D, Smith CM. Tribal perspectives on Indian self-determination and self-governance in health care management. In: *Amending the Indian Self Determination and Education Assistance Act to Provide for Further Self-Governance by Indian Tribes, and for Other Purposes*, Report 106-221, 106th Cong, 1st Sess (1999).

8. Soper FL. *Building the Health Bridge: Selections From the Work of Fred L. Soper*. Bloomington: Indiana University Press; 1970.

9. Djukanovic V, Mach EP. *Alternative Approaches to Meeting Basic Health Needs in Developing Countries*. Geneva, Switzerland: World Health Organization; 1978.

10. Berman P. Selective primary health care: is efficient sufficient? *Soc Sci Med*. 1982;16:1054-1059.

11. Gish O. Selective primary health care: old wine in new bottles. *Soc Sci Med*. 1982;16:1049-1053.

12. *Regional Differences in Indian Health 2000-2001*. Rockville, Md: Indian Health Service, Division of Program Statistics; 2003.

13. *Trends in Indian Health 2000-2001*. Rockville, Md: Indian Health Service, Division of Program Statistics; 2004.

14. Kunitz SJ. *Disease Change and the Role of Medicine: The Navajo Experience*. Berkeley: University of California Press; 1983.

15. *2005 Navajo Community Health Status Assessment*. Window Rock, Ariz: Navajo Area Indian Health Service, Office of Program Planning and Evaluation; 2005.

16. *International Classification of Diseases, Ninth Revision*. Geneva, Switzerland: World Health Organization; 1980.

17. *International Classification of Diseases, 10th Revision*. Geneva, Switzerland: World Health Organization; 1990.

18. Kunitz SJ, Pesis-Katz I. Mortality of white Americans, African Americans, and Canadians: the causes and consequences for health of welfare state institutions and policies. *Milbank Q*. 2005;83:5-39.

19. Manuel DG, Mao Y. Avoidable mortality in the United States and Canada, 1980-1996. *Am J Public Health*. 2002;92:1481-1484.

20. EC Working Group on Health Services and "Avoidable Deaths." *European Community Atlas of "Avoidable Death" 1985-89*. Oxford, England: Oxford University Press; 1997.

21. National Center for Health Workforce Analysis. The Arizona Health Workforce: Highlights from the Health Workforce Profile. Available at: http:// bhpr.hrsa.gov/healthworkforce/reports/statesummaries/ arizona.htm. Accessed December 1, 2007.

22. National Center for Health Workforce Analysis. The New Mexico Health Workforce: Highlights from the Health Workforce Profile. Available at: http:// bhpr.hrsa.gov/healthworkforce/reports/ statesummaries/newmexico.htm. Accessed December 1, 2007.

23. Table S1. Median household income by state: 1969, 1979, 1989, and 1999. Income Surveys Branch/ HHES Division, US Census Bureau. Available at: http://www.census.gov/hhes/www/ income/histinc/ state/state1.html. Accessed December 1, 2007.

24. *Final Report PC(2)-1F, American Indians*. Washington, DC: US Bureau of the Census; 1973:Table 14.

25. Rodgers L. *1990 Census: Population and Housing Characteristics of the Navajo Nation*. Window Rock, Ariz: Division of Community Development, Navajo Nation; 1993.

26. Thornton R. The Navajo-US population mortality crossover since the mid-20th century. *Popul Res Policy Rev*. 2004; 23:291-308.

27. Hoy W, Light A, Megill D. Cardiovascular disease in Navajo Indians with type 2 diabetes. *Public Health Rep*. 1995;110:87-94.

28. Sugarman JR, Hickey M, Hall T, Gohdes D. The changing epidemiology of diabetes mellitus among Navajo Indians. *West J Med*. 1990;153:140-145.

29. Sugarman JR, Gilbert TJ, Weiss NS. Prevalence of diabetes and impaired glucose tolerance among Navajo Indians. *Diabetes Care*. 1992;15:114-120.

30. Sugarman JR, White LL, Gilbert TJ. Evidence for a secular change in obesity, height, and weight among Navajo Indian schoolchildren. *Am J Clin Nutr*. 1990;52:960-966.

31. White LL, Ballew C, Gilbert TJ, Mendlein JM, Mokdad AH, Strauss KF. Weight, body image, and weight control practices of Navajo Indians: findings

from the Navajo Health and Nutrition Survey. *J Nutr.* 1990;127(suppl 10): 2094S-2098S.

32. Freedman DS, Serdula MK, Percy CA, Ballew C, White L. Obesity, levels of lipids and glucose, and smoking among Navajo adolescents. *J Nutr.* 1997;127(suppl 10):2120S-2127S.

33. O'Connor PJ, Crabtree BF, Nakamura RM, Kelley D. Hospitalization experience of Navajo subjects with type II diabetes and matched controls: an historical cohort study. *J Clin Epidemiol.* 1990;43: 881-890.

34. O'Connor PJ, Crabtree BF, Nakamura RM. Mortality experience of Navajos with type 2 diabetes mellitus. *Ethn Health.* 1997;2:155-162.

35. Will JC, Strauss KF, Mendlein JM, Ballew C, White LL, Peter DG. Diabetes mellitus among Navajo Indians: findings from the Navajo Health and Nutrition Survey. *J Nutr.* 1997;127(suppl 10): 2106S-2113S.

36. Percy C, Freedman DS, Gilbert TJ, White L, Ballew C, Mokdad A. Prevalence of hypertension among Navajo Indians: findings from the Navajo Health and Nutrition Survey. *J Nutr.* 1997;127(suppl 10): 2114S-2119S.

37. Taylor JB, Kalt JP. *American Indians on Reservations: A Databook of Socioeconomic Change Between the 1990 and 2000 Censuses.* Cambridge, Mass: Harvard Project on American Indian Economic Development, Harvard University; 2005.

38. World Health Organization. 2002. Global Burden of Disease Project. Available at: http://www.who.int/healthinfo/statistics/gbdwhoregionmortality2002.xls. Accessed February 15, 2007.

39. Barker WH, Mullooly JP. Stroke in a defined elderly population, 1967-1985: a less lethal and disabling but no less common disease. *Stroke.* 1997;28: 284-290.

40. Barker WH, Mullooly JP, Linton KLP. Trends in hypertension prevalence, treatment, and control in a well-defined older population. *Hypertension.* 1998; 31(pt 2):552-559.

41. Tunstall-Pedoe H, Vanuzzo D, Hobbs M, et al. Estimation of contribution of changes in coronary care to improving survival, event rates, and coronary heart disease mortality across the WHO MONICA Project populations. *Lancet.* 2000; 355:688-700.

42. Sunder M. Intense management of diabetes mellitus: role of glucose control and antiplatelet agents. *J Clin Pharmacol.* 2004;44:414-422.

43. Ostgren CJ, Lindblad U, Melander A, Rastam L. Survival in patients with type 2 diabetes in a Swedish community: Skaraborg Hypertension and Diabetes Project. *Diabetes Care.* 2002;25:1297-1302.

44. Centers for Disease Control and Prevention. Diabetes prevalence among American Indians and Alaska Natives and the overall population—United States, 1994-2002. *MMWR Morb Mortal Wkly Rep.* 2003;52:702-704.

45. Centers for Disease Control and Prevention. Prevalence of Heart Disease—United States, 2005. *MMWR Morb Mortal Wkly Rep.* 2007;56: 113-118.

46. Denny CH, Holtzman D, Goins RT, Croft JB. Disparities in chronic disease risk factors and health status between American Indian/Alaska Native and white elders: findings from a telephone survey, 2001 and 2002. *Am J Public Health.* 2005;95:825-827.

47. Vogt DU, Walke R. *Indian Health Service: Health Care Delivery, Status, Funding, and Legislative Issues.* Washington, DC: Congressional Research Service, Library of Congress; September 12, 2006.

48. Wilson C, Gilliland S, Cullen T, et al. Diabetes outcomes in the Indian health system during the era of the Special Diabetes Program for Indians and the Government Performance and Results Act. *Am J Public Health.* 2005; 95:1518-1522.

49. *Interim Report to Congress, Special Diabetes Program for Indians.* Albuquerque, NM: Indian Health Service National Diabetes Program; December 2004.

50. Kunitz SJ. The history and politics of health care policy for American Indians. *Am J Public Health.* 1996;86:1464-1473.

51. Adams A. The road not taken: how tribes choose between tribal and Indian Health Service management of health care resources. *Am Indian Cult Res J.* 2000;24:21-38.

52. Westmoreland TM, Watson KR. Redeeming hollow promises: the case for mandatory spending on health care for American Indians and Alaska Natives. *Am J Public Health.* 2006;96:600-605.

4

Towards a Common Definition of Global Health

Source: Reprinted from *The Lancet*; 373: 1993-95, Koplan et al. *Towards a Common Definition of Global Health*. Copyright 2009 with permission from Elsevier.

Global health is fashionable. It provokes a great deal of media, student, and faculty interest, has driven the establishment or restructuring of several academic programmes, is supported by governments as a crucial component of foreign policy,[1] and has become a major philanthropic target. Global health is derived from public health and international health, which, in turn, evolved from hygiene and tropical medicine. However, although frequently referenced, global health is rarely defined. When it is, the definition varies greatly and is often little more than a rephrasing of a common definition of public health or a politically correct updating of international health. Therefore, how should global health be defined?

Global health can be thought of as a notion (the current state of global health), an objective (a world of healthy people, a condition of global health), or a mix of scholarship, research, and practice (with many questions, issues, skills, and competencies). The need for a commonly used and accepted definition extends beyond semantics. Without an established definition, a shorthand term such as global health might obscure important differences in philosophy, strategies, and priorities for action between physicians, researchers, funders, the media, and the general public. Perhaps

most importantly, if we do not clearly define what we mean by global health, we cannot possibly reach agreement about what we are trying to achieve, the approaches we must take, the skills that are needed, and the ways that we should use resources. In this Viewpoint, we present the reasoning behind the definition of global health, as agreed by a panel of multidisciplinary and international colleagues.

Public health in the modern sense emerged in the mid-19th century in several countries (England, continental Europe, and the United States) as part of both social reform movements and the growth of biological and medical knowledge (especially causation and management of infectious disease).[2] Farr, Chadwick, Virchow, Koch, Pasteur, and Shattuck helped to establish the discipline on the basis of four factors: (1) decision making based on data and evidence (vital statistics, surveillance and outbreak investigations, laboratory science); (2) a focus on populations rather than individuals; (3) a goal of social justice and equity; and (4) an emphasis on prevention rather than curative care. All these elements are embedded in most definitions of public health.

The definition of public health that has perhaps best stood the test of time is that suggested by Winslow almost 90 years ago:[3]

"Public health is the science and art of preventing disease, prolonging life and promoting physical health and efficacy through organized community efforts for the sanitation of the environment, the control of communicable infections, the education of the individual in personal hygiene, the organization of medical and nursing services for the early diagnosis and preventive treatment of disease, and the development of social machinery which will ensure every individual in the community a standard of living adequate for the maintenance of health; so organizing these benefits in such a fashion as to enable every citizen to realize his birthright and longevity."

The U.S. Institute of Medicine (IOM), in its 1988 *Future of public health* report,[4] described public health in terms of its mission, substance, and organisational framework, which, in turn, address prevention, a community approach, health as a public good, and the contributions of various partners. The IOM report defined the mission of public health as "fulfilling society's interest in assuring conditions in which people can be healthy".[4] In the *Dictionary of Epidemiology* (2001), Last[5] defined public health as "one of the efforts to protect, promote and restore the people's health. It is the combination of sciences, skills and beliefs that is directed to the maintenance and improvement of the health of all the people through collective or social actions".

International health has a more straightforward history. For decades, it was the term used for health work abroad, with a geographic focus on developing countries and often with a content of infectious and tropical diseases, water and sanitation, malnutrition, and maternal and child health.[6] Many academic departments and organisations still use this term, but include a broader range of subjects such as chronic diseases, injuries, and health systems. The Global Health Education Consortium defines international health as a subspecialty that "relates more to health practices, policies and systems . . . and stresses more the differences between countries than their commonalities".[7] Other research groups define international health as limited exclusively to the diseases of the developing world.[8] But many find international health a perfectly usable term and have adapted it to coincide with the philosophy and content of today's globalised health practice.[7,8] International health is defined by Merson, Black, and Mills[9] as "the application of the principles of public health to problems and challenges that affect low and middle-income countries and to the complex array of global and local forces that influence them".

Global health has areas of overlap with the more established disciplines of public health and international health (Table). All three entities share the following characteristics: priority on a population-based and preventive focus; concentration on poorer, vulnerable, and underserved populations; multidisciplinary and interdisciplinary approaches; emphasis on health as a public good and the importance of systems and structures; and the participation of several stakeholders. In view of these commonalities, we are left with key questions that need to be resolved to arrive at a useful and distinctive definition for global health. We address some of these questions here.

What is global? Must a health crisis cross national borders to be deemed a global health issue? We should not restrict global health to health-related issues that literally cross international borders. Rather, in this context, global refers to any health issue that concerns many countries or is affected by transnational determinants, such as climate change or urbanisation, or solutions, such as polio eradication. Epidemic infectious diseases such as dengue, influenza A (H5N1), and HIV infection are clearly global. But global health should also address tobacco control, micronutrient deficiencies, obesity, injury prevention, migrant-worker health, and migration of health workers. The global in global health refers to the scope of problems, not their location. Thus—like public health but unlike international health—global health can focus on domestic health disparities as well as cross-border issues. Global health also incorporates the training and distribution of the healthcare workforce in a manner that goes beyond the capacity-building interest of public health.

Is global health mainly directed to infectious disease and maternal and child health issues or does it also address issues such as chronic diseases, injuries, mental health, and the environment? Infectious diseases and maternal and child health have dominated international health and continue to receive the most attention and interest in global health. However, global health has to embrace the full breadth of important health threats. This broad set of priorities might mean accepting that, for many countries, the epidemiological transition is a continuing process. Simultaneous effort needs to be expended on undernutrition and overnutrition, HIV/ AIDS and tobacco, malaria and mental health, tuberculosis and deaths due to motor vehicle accidents. Infectious agents are communicable and so are parts of the western lifestyle (i.e., dietary changes, lack of physical activity, reliance on automobile transport, smoking, stress, urbanisation). Burden of illness should be used as a criterion for global-health priority setting.

How does global health relate to globalisation? The spread of health risks and diseases across the world, often linked with trade or attempted conquest, is not new to public health or international

Table	Comparison of global, international, and public health		
	Global health	**International health**	**Public health**
Geographical reach	Focuses on issues that directly or indirectly affect health but that can transcend national boundaries	Focuses on health issues of countries other than one's own, especially those of low-income and middle-income	Focuses on issues that affect the health of the population of a particular community or country
Level of cooperation	Development and implementation of solutions often requires global cooperation	Development and implementation of solutions usually requires binational cooperation	Development and implementation of solutions does not usually require global cooperation
Individuals or populations	Embraces both prevention in populations and clinical care of individuals	Embraces both prevention in populations and clinical care of individuals	Mainly focused on prevention programmes for populations
Access to health	Health equity among nations and for all people is a major objective	Seeks to help people of other nations	Health equity within a nation or community is a major objective
Range of disciplines	Highly interdisciplinary and multidisciplinary within and beyond health sciences	Embraces a few disciplines but has not emphasised multidisciplinarity	Encourages multidisciplinary approaches, particularly within health sciences and with social sciences

health. Plague spread across Europe and Asia in the middle ages; quarantine was developed in 14th-century Venice; smallpox and measles were introduced to the New World by European invaders in the 16th century; the same explorers took tobacco from the Americas to Europe and beyond, leading to premature disease and death; and opium was sold to China in the 18th and 19th centuries as a product of trade and subjugation by imperial western powers. Nevertheless, the rapid increase in speed of travel and communication, as well as the economic interdependency of all nations, has led to a new level and speed of global interconnectedness or globalisation, which is a force in shaping the health of populations around the world.

Must global health operate only within a context of a goal of social/economic equity? The quest for equity is a fundamental philosophical value for public health. The promotion of social and economic equity, and reduction of health disparities, has been a key theme in domestic public health, international health, and global health. Up to now, most health initiatives in countries without sufficient resources to deal with their own health problems have come about through the assistance of wealthier countries, organisations, and foundations. Although this assistance is understandable, it does not help us to distinguish global health as a specialty of study and practice.

Global health has come to encompass more complex transactions between societies. Such societies recognise that the developed world does not have a monopoly on good ideas and search across cultures for better approaches to the prevention and treatment of common diseases, healthy environments, and

more efficient food production and distribution. The preference for use of the term global health where international health might previously have been used runs parallel to a shift in philosophy and attitude that emphasises the mutuality of real partnership, a pooling of experience and knowledge, and a two-way flow between developed and developing countries. Global health thus uses the resources, knowledge, and experience of diverse societies to address health challenges throughout the world.

What is the interdisciplinary scope of global health? Professionals from many diverse disciplines wish to contribute to improving global health. Although global health places greater priority on prevention, it also embraces curative, rehabilitative, and other aspects of clinical medicine and the study of basic sciences. But these latter areas are less central to the core elements of public health than are its population-based and preventive orientations. Clearly, many disciplines, such as the social and behavioural sciences, law, economics, history, engineering, biomedical and environmental sciences, and public policy can make great contributions to global health. Thus, global health encompasses prevention, treatment, and care; it is truly an interdisciplinary sphere.

A steady evolution of philosophy, attitude, and practice has led to the increased use of the term global health. Thus, on the basis of this analysis, we offer the following definition: global health is an area for study, research, and practice that places a priority on improving health and achieving equity in health for all people worldwide. Global health emphasises transnational health issues, determinants, and solutions; involves many disciplines within and beyond the health sciences and promotes interdisciplinary collaboration; and is a synthesis of population-based prevention with individual-level clinical care.

We call for the adoption of a common definition of global health. We will all be best served (and best serve the health of others around the world) if we share a common definition of the specialty in which we work and to which we encourage others to lend their efforts.

Contributors

All authors contributed to the writing and editing of the manuscript. The Consortium of Universities for Global Health (CUGH) Executive Board developed the definition and reviewed and edited the manuscript.

CUGH Executive Board

Haile Debas (University of California, San Francisco, CA, USA); King Holmes (University of Washington, Seattle, WA, USA); Gerald Keusch (Boston University, Boston, MA, USA); Jeffrey Koplan (Emory University, Atlanta, GA, USA); Michael Merson (Duke University, Durham, NC, USA); Thomas Quinn (Johns Hopkins University, Baltimore, MD, USA); Judith N Wasserheit (University of Washington, Seattle, WA, USA).

Conflicts of interest

We declare that we have no conflicts of interest.

ACKNOWLEDGMENTS

We thank George Alleyne, Lincoln Chen, William Foege, Andy Haines, Mohammed Hassar, Venkat Narayan, Sharifa Saif Al-Jabri, Barry Schoub, and Olive Shisana for their comments and suggestions.

Correspondence to

Prof Jeffrey P Koplan, Robert W Woodruff Health Sciences Center, Emory University, 1440 Clifton Road Suite 410, Atlanta, GA 30322, USA. jkoplan@emory.edu.

● ● ● References

1. Institute of Medicine. *The U.S. commitment to global health: recommendations for the new administration*. Washington, DC: Institute of Medicine, Dec 15, 2008. http://www.iom.edu/CMS/3783/51303/60714.aspx (accessed Feb 19, 2009).

2. Porter R. *The greatest benefit to mankind: a medical history of humanity*. New York: W W Norton & Company, 1997.

3. Winslow C. The untilled field of public health. *Mod Med* 1920; 2: 183-91.

4. Institute of Medicine. *The future of public health*. Washington, DC: National Academy Press, 1988.

5. Last J. *A dictionary of epidemiology*. New York: Oxford, 2001.

6. Brown TM, Cueto M, Fee E. The World Health Organization and the transition from "international" to "global" public health. *Am J Public Health* 2006; **96**: 62-72.

7. Global Health Education Consortium. *Global vs international*. http://globalhealthedu.org/Pages/GlobalvsInt.aspx (accessed Feb 19, 2009).

8. Brown University International Health Institute. *Welcome to the International Health Institute*. http://med.brown.edu/ihi/ (accessed Feb 19, 2009).

9. Merson MH, Black RE, Mills AJ. *International public health: diseases, programs, systems, and policies*, 2nd ed. Sudbury MA: Jones and Bartlett Publishers, 2006.

Conceptual Framework of Health Determinants

Conceptual frameworks are maps constructed to define the causal relationship between a problem and the factors contributing to it.[1-4] A key step in the understanding of a problem to be studied is the development of a conceptual framework. Wolfson described the importance of a conceptual framework when he asserted, "Data and facts are not like pebbles on a beach, waiting to be picked up and collected. They can only be perceived and measured through an underlying theoretical and conceptual framework, which defines relevant facts, and distinguishes them from background noise." (p.309)[5] As Wolfson's quote describes, the conceptual framework is a preliminary model of the problem under study, and is reflective of relationships among critical variables of interest. Conceptual frameworks on health have transgressed over time as our understanding and values of health change.[1] Dominant conceptual frameworks on health care systems, specifically those focusing on the United States, encompass a broad range of problems, including the social, environment, and structural factors impacting the quality and quantity of health across populations. Yet, within this diverse problem set lies the commonality of health equity as the proposed solution to addressing our health care system.[1-4]

To begin with, in order to successfully understand conceptual frameworks there must be a clear definition of how the various identified factors contributing to a problem relate to each other.[1] Many prominent conceptual frameworks categorize factors into distinct levels, with the factor at one level leading to the causation of a factor at the next level. For example, in a conceptual framework on the environment's impact on health, it is the absence of reserved open space that leads to the implementation of industrial factories, which in turn lead to the development of poor air quality and adverse health outcomes.[1,3] However, rarely do discrete levels exist in factors contributing to health care problems.[1] Rather, these elements continuously penetrate the health of a population through interconnected pathways, resulting in the fluid decrease or improvement of health over time.[1] So, while the industrial factories lead to poor air quality, they also lead to an increase in jobs and economic wealth for a community, thereby acting as part of an interconnected pathway of both positive and negative health outcomes.[1,3] Nancy Krieger's article **Proximal, Distal and** the Politics of Causation, proposes that, with a shift of language, conceptual frameworks can more accurately represent this degree relationship.[1] According to Krieger, spatial defining terminology should be replaced with terms like levels and pathways to more accurately represent the relationships of social determinants of health.[1] It is not the distinct presence or absence of an element causing poor health outcomes, but, rather, how the elements interconnect with each other to cause an adverse impact on a population's health.[1]

Globally, the most prominent conceptual frameworks is that proposed by the World Health Organization's (WHO) Commission on Social Determinants of Health.[2] This framework is distinguished due to its ability to identify the structural determinants of health inequities, and the impact of power and government influence on population health. Structural determinants encompass those that stratify individuals into social classes of hierarchical power, including income, education, gender and race.[2] The Commission connects these structural determinants to the resulting inequity in health through intermediary determinants, material circumstances, biological factors, behaviors and psychosocial factors. These intermediary benefits are supported by the social capital and social cohesion of society, including the norms, social trust and networks that facilitate coordination of mutual benefit.[2] The Commission concludes its framework by stressing the integration of structural determinants in policy formulation addressing social determinants to effectively address the inequities of health across populations.[2]

The WHO conceptual framework transcribes to national frameworks on environmental conditions impacting the quality of health across populations.[2,3] One example of a conceptual framework contextualizing the impact of the environment on health is Northridge et al.'s work, as described in **Sorting Out the Connections Between the Built Environment and Health.**[3] A built environment is characterized as the environment built by people for people, the product of urban planning efforts to provide livable settings for populations.[3] This framework contextualizes how modifications made to the natural environment by urban planning translate into built environmental stressors that ultimately influence individual health status.[3] This framework mirrors the outcomes established by the WHO commission, including the impact of power and government intervention on the health outcomes of communities.[2,3] Those most susceptible to poor built environments are those with the least power, alluding to government intervention as the

only measure to ensure adequate environmental standards within a given community.[2,3]

Additionally, in order to fully represent dominant frameworks in U.S. health care, a conceptual framework identifying the prominent structural challenges in delivering efficient health care services must be recognized.[4] Bentley et al. defines a framework surrounding waste in the U.S. health care system in the article **Waste in the U.S. Health Care System: A Conceptual Framework.**[4] This framework successfully defines the venues in which health care waste flows, including administrative, operational and clinical waste.[4] Administrative waste is characterized as any spending on administrative activities that exceeds what is necessary to achieve the organization's goals, such as insurance product design and excess claims processing.[4] Operational waste is characterized as any unnecessary use of resources in the production or delivery of health services, including increased patient waiting times and medical errors.[4] Clinical waste can be defined as any spending to produce services that provide little to no marginal health benefit over less costly alternatives, excessive diagnostic testing and lost medical records.[4] Again, as with environmental frameworks, conceptual frameworks on structural problems in U.S. health care mirror the proposed contexts set forth by the WHO commission. [2,3,4] The most vulnerable to being collateral damage to health care waste are those with the least power, suggesting to the need for government action to ensure population health. [2,4]

Conceptual frameworks are only as useful as their ability to induce action into finding solutions for the defined problems.[1-4] These frameworks are best utilized by those possessing the power to induce change in communities and among populations as well as those committed to implementing solutions.[1-4] As referenced by Bentley et al. in discussions of conceptual frameworks on waste in the U.S. health care system, while the problems are easily identified the potential fixes are much more complex.[4]

This chapter includes four readings that illustrate what a conceptual framework is and how conceptual frameworks might be used to understand health and health care problems and identify solutions. In **Proximal, Distal and the Politics of Causation: What's Level Got To Do With It?** Krieger proposes that a relative shift in terminology is needed in order to advance public health science. Historically, public health frameworks on social determinants utilized proximal and distal terminology to define, and categorize, distinctions among social and economic factors in relationship to an individual's health. Proximal and distal terminology has allowed biological and social sciences to define the spatial location and relative importance of factors describing disease origination. According to Krieger, spatial defining terminology should be replaced with terms like levels and pathways to more accurately represent the relationships of social determinants of health. Unlike proximal and distal events, which occur sequentially through time and space, social determinants are interconnected, existing simultaneously in causal relationships that impact an individual's health. For example, as Krieger examines within her paper, in order to fully analyze the health consequences embodied within tobacco products, one must study both the biological ecology and political economy as they simultaneously relate to each other. A cigarette is simultaneously: (1) a flammable mass of carcinogens providing toxic elements to human lungs upon inhalation; and (2) a product whose high profitability relies on the intentional production and marketing to lower socioeconomic classes. To not recognize the dual biological and social existence of cigarettes would provide an incomplete illustration of the impact of tobacco products on the public's health. Yet, can this simultaneous causal relationship be reflected through frameworks grounded in terms like proximal and distal? According to Krieger, in order to evolve public health knowledge and application, one must abandon the confusion that comes with theories founded on proximal and distal segments and, instead, clearly identify the interweaving pathways and levels of social determinants.

In an excerpt from **America's Health Rankings: A Call to Action for Individuals & Their Communities**, we present the longest running annual assessment of the nation's health on a state-by-state basis. The report uses data from the U.S. Departments of Health and Human Services, Commerce, Education and Labor; U.S. Environmental Protection Agency; the American Medical Association; the Dartmouth Atlas Project; and the Trust for America's Health. The rankings are published jointly by United Health Foundation, the American Public Health Association and Partnership for Prevention. It provides *state-specific rankings* from 1 to 50 across a variety of national health benchmarks such as smoking, obesity, children in poverty, access to care, and incidence of preventable disease. America's Health Rankings are based on the perspective that, in addition to our individual genetic predisposition to disease, health is the result of four essential and controllable components: our behaviors, the environment of the community in which we live and work, the public and health policies and practices made by government and community leaders, and the clinical care we receive. The four components are viewed as the primary health determinants that impact the health outcomes of a state, as well as the nation as a whole. The health determinants interact with each other in a complex web of cause and effect that impact the healthy outcomes we desire. Actions to improve these determinants will eventually improve health outcomes.

In **Sorting Out the Connections Between the Built Environment and Health**, Northridge et al. state a built environment is characterized as the environment built by people for people. More specifically, the built environment is the product of urban planning efforts to adapt natural surroundings into livable settings. The relationship between the built environment and health has been present continuously throughout history, thriving up until the post World War II era. Increased attention on disease manifestation gradually led to the deterioration of this relationship. Northridge et al.'s work analyzes the relative importance, and challenges, of reviving the relationship between urban planning and public health. A joint urban planning and public health conceptual framework is introduced, linking the natural, physical environment to the individual and population health levels. This framework contextualizes how modifications made to the natural environment by urban planning translate into built environmental stressors that ultimately influence individual health status. Northridge et al. use this framework as a foundation to then analyze previous research on the health effects of housing and housing interventions. This analysis acts as an example showing the difficulty in identifying the direct causal relationship between health outcome and the built environment. Physical health problems, including infections and respiratory troubles, have long been associated with residing in slums and ghettos. However, previous studies show that, while relative associations can be made, it is often difficult to isolate the direct impact of housing on physical health. Data from various studies give mixed reviews, with some showing improved physical health upon transitioning to improved housing conditions while others show no change in health outcomes. However, improvements in housing have shown to increase social outcomes, with individuals reporting less fear and isolation upon improvements to their living environment. Thus, when analyzing the relationship between the built environment and health, it is important to define the health outcome targeted by the planning. Northridge et al. conclude the article by recommending that concrete measurements and relevant empirical data be collected in order to fully utilize the partnership between urban planning and public health.

In 2007, the World Health Organization's Commission on Social Determinants of Health (CSDH) published its latest installment of recommendations to address the growing prominence of health inequities. In **A Conceptual Framework for Action on the Social Determinants of Health**, these recommendations are presented as a framework for action founded on principles of health equity across populations that are preserved by the power of governments. This framework is distinguished from other social determinant frameworks by beginning with the identification of the structural determinants of health inequities. Structural determinants encompass those that stratify individuals into social classes of hierarchical power, including income, education, gender and race. These social markers are borne from the socioeconomic political contexts of society, including the policies, culture, and societal values that determine the amount of social mobility from one classification to the next. CSDH connects these structural determinants to the resulting inequity in health through intermediary determinants, material circumstances, biological factors, behaviors and psychosocial factors. Material circumstances are defined as the determinants linked to the physical environment, including housing, neighborhoods and financial means to buy necessities. Biological factors and behaviors include diet, smoking, alcohol consumption and genetic predisposition to disease. Psychosocial factors are characterized by stress, social support and coping styles utilized when facing life challenges. These intermediary benefits are supported by the social capital and social cohesion of society, including the norms, social trust and networks that facilitate coordination of mutual benefit. Additionally, the health care system acts as a supporting element of the intermediary determinants in which access, or lack thereof, increases the inequity of health. By integrating these factors into the identified social determinants CSDH illustrates the frequently overlooked fact of inequalities within determinants themselves. Inequalities between social determinants are widely known, but amongst a classification of determinants inequities exist due to the varying nature of community culture and values. CSDH concludes its framework by stressing the integration of structural determinants in policy formulation addressing social determinants to effectively address the inequities of health across populations.

● ● ● References

1. Krieger N. Proximal, Distal and the Politics of Causation: What's Level Got To Do With It? *American Journal of Public Health*. February 2008; 98(2):221-30.

2. WHO Commission on Social Determinants of health. V. CSDH framework for Action. In: *A Conceptual Framework for Action on the Social Determinants of Health*. Geneva, Switzerland: World Health Organization, 2007: 15-49, 71-75. http://www.who.int/social_determinants/resources/csdh_framework_action_05_07.pdf. Accessed November 4, 2009.

3. Northridge, ME, Sclar ED, Biswas P. Sorting Out the Connections between the Built Environment and Health: A Conceptual Framework for Navigating Pathways and Planning Healthy Cities. *Journal of Urban Health*. December 2003;80(4):556-568.

4. Bentley TG, Effros RM, Palar K, Keeler EB. Waste in the U.S. Health Care System: A Conceptual Framework. *The Milbank Quarterly*. 2008; 86(4): 629-659.

5. Wolfson M. Social proprioception: Measurement, data and information from a population health perspective. In RC Evans, ML Barer, and T Marmor (Eds.) *Why Are Some People Healthy and Others Not?* New York: Aldine de Gruyter, 1994.

Proximal, Distal, and the Politics of Causation: What's Level Got to Do With It?

Source: Krieger N. Proximal, distal, and the politics of causation: what's level got to do with it? *Am J Public Health* 2008;98:221-30. Reprinted with permission of the American Public Health Association.

Causal thinking in public health, and especially in the growing literature on social determinants of health, routinely employs the terminology of *proximal* (or *downstream*) and *distal* (or *upstream*).

I argue that the use of these terms is problematic and adversely affects public health research, practice, and causal accountability. At issue are distortions created by conflating measures of space, time, level, and causal strength.

To make this case, I draw on an ecosocial perspective to show how public health got caught in the middle of the problematic proximal-distal divide—surprisingly embraced by both biomedical and social determinist frameworks—and propose replacing the terms *proximal* and *distal* with explicit language about levels, pathways, and power. (*Am J Public Health.* 2008;98:221-230. doi: 10.2105/AJPH.2007.111278)

PROXIMAL. DISTAL. UPSTREAM.

Downstream. Risk factor. Determinant. Level. Multilevel. These terms feature prominently in current discussions of causal pathways and public health, especially in work on the social determinants of health. A central focus is on how "upstream" so-cietal influences-typically referred to as *distal*—shape "downstream," or *proximal*, exposures, thereby affecting population health.[1-16]

Exemplifying this line of thought are recent reports issued by the World Health Organization Commission on Social Determinants on Health[2] and the World Health Organization Regional Office for Europe.[3] Common assumptions are that (1) diseases are attributable to many causes, located outside and within the body; (2) the social lies in the realm of the *distal*; (3) the biological belongs to the *proximal*; and (4) the distal and proximal are connected by *levels*, e.g., societal, institutional, household, individual, which can be conceptualized as *near to* or *far from* the causes under consideration. For example, as discussed in both reports, "distal" societal factors drive the risk of smoking; how smoking harms health involves "proximal" biology.[2,3] What could be more obvious?

Yet what seems clear-cut can be deceiving. I argue that although notions of *proximal, distal*, and *level* all matter for elucidating causal pathways, clear thinking—and, hence, public health research, practice, and causal accountability—is distorted by conflating measures of space, time, level, and causal strength. When it comes to causation, it is one thing to think about *near* and *far* in relation to space and time; it is another matter entirely to do so for levels. To make this intellectual argument, I draw on an ecosocial perspective[1,17-21] to show how public health got caught in the middle of the problematic proximal-distal divide- surprisingly embraced by both biomedical and social determinist frameworks—and propose replacing the terms *proximal* and *distal* with explicit language about levels, pathways, and power.

PROXIMAL AND DISTAL IN PUBLIC HEALTH THOUGHT

The idea that disease etiology and distribution are attributable to causes deemed "far" from and "near" (including within) the body is ancient[22-27]; Hippocratic tradition, in the 5th century BCE, famously invoked both atmosphere and individual constitution as explanations for epidemic disease.[22,25] By contrast, the idea that there is a causal etiological hierarchy, spanning from distal to proximal, is relatively new. It became a core part of the public health canon only in the mid-20th century CE. How this change happened and its public health implications have been little discussed.

Strand 1. 19th Century Emergence of Proximal and Distal as Scientific Terms for Spatiotemporal Scale

Only in the early 19th century CE did the terms *proximal* and *distal* enter the scientific discourse.[28] Invented to describe anatomical location and distance, as measured on a spatial scale, these words were coined by biologists at a time when comparative anatomy occupied a key place in debates over the classification and nature of species.[29,30] *Proximal*, derived from the Latin noun *proximus* ("nearest"), took on the meaning "situated toward the center of the body, or the point of origin or attachment of a limb, bone, or other structure."[28] Its antonym, *distal*, derived from *distant*, was intended to echo two other widely used biological concepts: *ventral* and *dorsal*.[28] Soon other natural sciences adopted the terms, albeit with some critical modifications. In geology, for example, the terms took on a temporal as well as a spatial dimension, reflecting how adjacent geological strata typically are "close" in time as well as in space.[28]

The moment time entered the picture, however, the terms *proximal* and *distal* were primed to develop new meanings. This is because of the ubiquitous metaphorical linkage of time, space, and causal reasoning.[31(pp133-138)] In all known languages, temporal events are described in spatial terms: Time moves through space.[31(p134)] This metaphorical relationship, as argued by the linguist Deutscher, is essential to causal reasoning, because it enables us to "talk freely about one thing coming 'from' another, 'out of' another, or happening 'through' another, to express abstract chains of cause and event."[31(p137)]

New European scientific discoveries of powerful physical laws for gravity, electricity, and magnetism[32-34] further affected scientific thinking about causation. These inverse square laws, expressed as pithy equations, clarified that force depends on distance: The more proximal the mass or the charge of the interacting objects, the greater the force—and the more powerful the effect. It was a short step from here to equate distance with causal strength, in not only the physical but also the life sciences.

Strand 2. From Spatiotemporal Scale to Causal Hierarchies and Levels

Not until the later 19th century, however, did the scientific meanings of *proximal* and *distal* leap from referring only to *spatiotemporal scale* to also describing *levels* and *causal hierarchies*. In their new usage, the "closeness"—or "distance"—of levels defined a new type of proximity, one that could be measured only conceptually, not in meters or minutes.

Initially, this conceptual change occurred within disciplines focused on a different type of body: that of body politic, i.e., the social sciences.[35-42] In books with such titles as *Social Pathology*[41] and *Organism and Society*,[42] influential late-19th century sociologists drew parallels between the biologically nested hierarchies of cell-organism-species and the socially nested hierarchies of individuals-families-societies.[35,36,37(pp4-8),38(pp231-323),40-42] In their view, just as organs, composed of their constituent cells, must collectively work together for an organism to survive, so too do social groups and their constituent individuals have complementary roles they must perform for society to thrive.[35,36,41,42] The intent was counter not only to the ruthless competition of Social Darwinism[30(pp87-90),39,40(pp196-199),42(p10)] but also to the contending Marxist view that class conflict determined societies' structure and development.[35,37(pp4-8),41,42(pp182-186),43,44(pp178-179)]

Borrowing biological terminology, these sociologists newly deployed the terms *proximal* and *distal* to describe societies' structural "levels."[41(xxiii)] Ranging from individual to institutional, these levels and the "distance" between them became defined by their nested relationships: Adjacent levels were "close," and nonadjacent levels were "far."

Meanwhile, biologists likewise expanded the use of the terms *proximal*, *distal*, and *level*, bringing these terms explicitly into their thinking about causal distance. As part of the early 20th century modern evolutionary synthesis, which integrated Darwinian evolutionary biology, paleontology, and Mendelian genetics,[29,45,46(pp503-591),47] these biologists newly contrasted what they termed "proximate" (physiological) versus "ultimate" or "distal" (evolutionary) causes.[29(pp313-321),35,46(pp1340-1343),47] This distinction recognized that asking *how* a biological event occurs (e.g., a muscle contraction) is not the same as asking *why* a biological phenomenon exists (e.g., muscles enable locomotion to find food and flee predators). Drawing on holistic thinking,[35,48] they argued that valid explanations could coexist across levels (e.g., species, organism, cell, molecule) and involve the distant past (evolution) *and* the immediate present (current stimulus). In the instant of a muscle contraction, both proximal and distal causes were at play.

The Mid-20th Century Public Health Embrace of Proximal and Distal

By mid-20th century, to be close or far could thus refer to space, to time, to lineage, or to location in hierarchical conceptual levels. The terms *proximal* and *distal* thus became widely encompassing terms to express—and contest—causal conceptions in both the social and the natural sciences. Amid these divergent uses, the terms *proximal* and *distal* finally entered the public health causal lexicon.

Prompting their adoption was growing recognition that the field of public health, still riding the crest of enormous success against infectious diseases in the 19th and 20th centuries CE, had to move beyond a monocausal to a multifactorial account of disease causation, which involved not only the agent but also the host and the environment.[1,17,24,49-51] As exemplified by the findings of the Framingham study of heart disease, rising rates of chronic disease and cardiovascular mortality seemed to be attributable not to any one single exposure but instead to a variety of factors,[51-53] leading the Framingham researchers to coin the term *risk factor* to describe these partial—i.e., not sufficient, not always necessary, but nonetheless contributing—component causes.[53]

It was through the multifactorial perspective that the terms *proximal* and *distal* emerged as terms for the discussion of causality in the public health literature.[17] Unfortunately, however, their new usage drew on shallow understandings of the terms *near* and *far* that impeded rather than deepened multilevel thinking. The essential features of the multifactorial framework remain well-sketched by the still highly influential spiderless[17] "web of causation," first articulated in the 1960s[54] and which, as I have previously argued,[17] (1) leveled all exposures to a single plane; (2) defined "proximal" factors to be those operating directly on or within the body, and relegated all other exposures to the murky realm of "distal"; (3) linked causal potency to distance—i.e., the "closer" the cause, the greater the effect (following the logic of the previously described physical inverse square laws); (4) held that distal causes necessarily exerted their influence through successively more proximal factors; (5) took a studied agnosticism as to what accounted for the array of exposures included in the web and eschewed any discussion of power or injustice; and, hence, (6) adopted a narrow stance of what may best be termed *causal pragmatism*[55,56] that prioritized focusing on what they considered to be "proximal" factors ostensibly amenable to control by either individuals or by public health or medical professionals (including by health education) rather than what they termed the more "distal" determinants requiring societal change.

The use of the terms *proximal* and *distal* persists to this day. It underlies the 21st century successor to the web of causation—that is, the "gene—environment interaction" framework,[57-60] which posits that the occurrence of common and complex diseases reflects the interplay of individual genetic variability with an array of exogenous exposures.[57-60] Work in this area is chiefly engaged[57-60] (albeit with some exceptions[61-65]) in the quest to discover genetic determinants of biological susceptibility and to develop pharmacological interventions that can block deleterious gene expression.

The proximal-distal discourse likewise pervades the social determinants of health perspective,[1-16] which holds that "distal" institutional priorities and practices of government and the private sector shape people's cumulative exposure, across the life course via intermediary pathways, to the proximal physical, behavioral, psychosocial, and biological exposures that trigger pathogenic processes (including gene expression), thereby causing disease. Secondarily, once illness occurs, the social determinants of health framework ask how prognosis is affected by socially produced inequities in access to needed medical care.[1-16]

In both cases, causal distance still matters for causal strength: In the gene-environment interaction model, "proximal" causes remain most potent, whereas for the social determinants of health perspective, "distal" causes are decisive. Despite their fundamentally different approaches, both frameworks cling to the proximal-distal divide. This little remarked convergence hints that some causal logic may be askew.

AN ALTERNATIVE ECOSOCIAL APPROACH TO LEVELS, EMBODIMENT, AND ACCOUNTABILITY

I suggest that one reason the proximal-distal terminology can be so readily used by such totally disparate frameworks is their now deeply entrenched conflation of relationships among space, time, distance, levels, and causal potency. Three examples, based on arguments offered from an ecosocial perspective (Figure 1, Table 1),[1,17-21] illustrate the problems that can arise when logics of scale are confused with analysis of levels and when distance is conflated with power.

The basic point is that societal patterns of disease represent the biological consequences of the ways of living and working differentially afforded to the social groups produced by each society's economy and political priorities.[1,17-21] Class and racial inequality, for example, differentially affect the living standards, working conditions, and environmental exposures of the dominant and subordinated classes and racial/ethnic groups, thereby creating class and racial/ethnic health disparities. Stated more generally, a society's economic, political, and social relationships affect both how people live and their ecologic context, and, in doing so, shape patterns of disease distribution. The understanding of the societal distributions of health thus cannot be divorced from considerations of political economy and political ecology.[1,17-21] Driving health inequities are how power—both *power over* and *power to do*,[66-68] including constraints on and possibilities for exercising each type—structures people's engagement with the world and their exposures to material and psychosocial health hazards. Notably, neither type of power readily maps onto a metric of proximal or distal. Nor do they neatly partition across levels. A critical corollary is that, contrary to the logic of the proximal-distal divide, within the very phenomena of disease occurrence and distribution—just as in a muscle contraction—the distal and the proximal are conjoined.

Example 1. Why Spatiotemporal Scale Is Not the Same as Level

The first example, drawn from ecology, the original multilevel science, clarifies why population sciences cannot afford to confuse metrics of spatiotemporal scale with the phenomena of levels. The example concerns, literally, the forest and the trees. Forests are levels within ecosystems, which involve not only trees but also the other plants and animals that inhabit them.[69-75] Notably, forests can be large or small (a spatial metric), as well as old or young (a temporal metric). Indeed, one key issue in conservation ecology today, spurred by intensified commercially driven logging and deforestation, forest fragmentation, habitat degradation, and spread of zoonoses (e.g., Lyme disease), is just what size, spatially, an expanse of woods needs to be—and how close it needs to be to other such expanses—to function as a particular type of forest.[69-75] Too small, with the ratio of edge-to-interior too high, or too spatially isolated, without connecting corridors, and its species composition will change, often losing diversity, including to the point of outright extinction.[69-75]

The phenomenon of a forest (a level), and interactions among both the entities that constitute it and also between the forest and its environs, is affected by, but not identical to, the forest's size (spatiotemporal scale). Similarly, for measles to become endemic with a community (a level), community size (a scale) must exceed 250,000 people.[76,77] Hence, argument 1: Confuse scale and level—or consider only one, not both—and understanding of population phenomena will be undermined.

Example 2. On Nonlinear Causal Pathways, with Immediate and Long-Term Effects

The second example illustrates that levels need not play by the proximal-distal schema that the path from what is considered "far" to "near" necessarily travels through what is termed "intermediate." This is because events at one level can directly and profoundly affect nonadjacent levels, instantly and persistently, without intermediaries.[29,46-48,66,78,79]

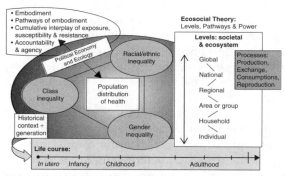

Note: To explain current and changing population distributions of disease, including health inequities, and who and what is accountable for the societal patterning of health, it is necessary to consider causal pathways operating at multiple levels and spatiotemporal scales, in historical context and as shaped by the societal power relations, material conditions, and social ans biological processes inherent in the political economy and ecology of the populations being analyzed. The embodied consequences of societal and ecologic context are what manifest as population distributions of and inequities in health, disease, and well-being.

Figure 1 A heuristic diagram for guiding ecosocial analyses of disease distribution, population health, and health inequities. See References 1, 17-21.

Table 1	Core Constructs of Ecosocial Theory—an Epidemiological Theory of Disease Distribution—and Some Predictions

Construct	Elaboration
Embodiment	A concept that refers to how we literally incorporate, biologically, the material and social world in which we live, from in utero to death; a corollary is that no aspect of our biology can be understood absent knowledge of history and individual and societal ways of living. Epidemiologically, "embodiment" is thus best understood: (1) As a construct, process, and reality, contingent upon bodily existence; (2) As a multilevel phenomenon, integrating soma, psyche, and society, within historical and ecological context, and, hence, an antonym to disembodied genes, minds, and behaviors; (3) As a clue to life histories, hidden and revealed; and (4) As a reminder of entangled consequences of diverse forms of social inequality.
Pathways of embodiment	Causal pathways that involve exposure, susceptibility, and resistance (as both social and biological phenomena), structured simultaneously by (1) societal arrangements of power, property, and contingent patterns of production, consumption, and reproduction, and (2) constraints and possibilities of our biology, as shaped by our species' evolutionary history, our ecologic context, and individual histories, that is, trajectories of biological and social development, and that involve gene expression, not just gene frequency.
Cumulative interplay among exposure, susceptibility, and resistance	Expressed in pathways of embodiment, with each factor and its distribution conceptualized at multiple levels (individual, neighborhood, regional or political jurisdiction, national, international, or supranational) and in multiple domains (e.g., home, work, school, other public settings), in relation to relevant ecologic niches, and manifested in processes at multiple scales of time and space.
Accountability and agency	Refers to who and what is responsible for social inequalities in health and for rectifying them, as well as for the overall current and changing contours of population health, as expressed in pathways of and knowledge about embodiment. At issue are the accountability and agency of not only institutions (government, business, and public sector), communities, households, and individuals, but also of epidemiologists and other scientists for theories used and ignored to explain social inequalities in health. A corollary is that, given likely complementary causal explanations at different scales and levels, epidemiological studies should explicitly name and consider the benefits and limitations of their particular scale and level of analysis.
Analytic implications and predictions	Determinants of disease distribution (a population-level phenomenon) presume but are not reducible to mechanisms of disease causation (which occur within individuals' bodies). Key contingent hypotheses are: (1) population patterns of health and disease constitute the embodied biological expression of ways of living and working differentially afforded by each society's political economy and political ecology, and (2) policies and practices that benefit and preserve the economic and social privileges of dominant groups simultaneously structure and constrain the living and working conditions they impose on everyone else, thereby shaping particular pathways of embodiment.

Source: See References 1, 17-21.

Consider, for example, the 1973 U.S. Supreme Court ruling that legalized abortion, on the grounds of individuals' rights to privacy.[80] Here, the levels at issue were defined jurisdictionally, with the federal judicial ruling on individual constitutional rights overturning federal and state laws that interfered with individual privacy by prohibiting abortion. In this case, the so-called distal determinant (1) directly affected individual girls' and women's reproductive rights and (2) reverberated up to other levels, by requiring changes in state laws and by expanding the permitted range of services that could be provided by health professionals and health facilities.

The positive health consequences were both immediate and long-term: U.S. girls and women alike no longer were forced, by law, to face the risk of having an unsafe illegal abortion and they were also less likely to bear unwanted children, thereby reducing risks of adverse maternal and birth outcomes.[81-84] More recent U.S. Supreme Court decisions restricting the right to abortion likewise illustrate this principle of skipping levels, with contrary effects.[85,86]

Analogous examples can readily be drawn from the health and human rights literature, whereby state obligations to respect, protect, and fulfill individuals' human rights affect policies and interventions at multiple levels.[87] The implication, argument 2, is that nonadjacent levels can have direct causal relationships, an insight obscured by the proximal-distal logic.

Example 3. On Levels and the Perils of Commodity Fetishism—the Simultaneity of Material Properties and Social Relations

The third example involves a key problem that permeates the proximal-distal divide: its incompatibility with truly multilevel thinking. This problem can be likened to the old-fashioned error of "commodity fetishism," albeit multiplied. In its original usage, this concept, introduced by Karl Marx (1818-1883), referred to how the value of commodities was mistakenly assumed to be an intrinsic property, rather than a consequence of the complex relationships of ownership,

Table 2   Proximal and Distal, Spatiotemporal Scale Versus Level—Meanings, Contrasts, and Causal Implications

Category	Spatiotemporal Scale		Level
	Space	Time	
Metric of distance	Units of spatial distance, measured in nested increments; examples include: kilometer-meter-millimeter-micron; or mile-foot-inch	Units of temporal distance, measured in nested increments; examples include: millennium-century-year-day-hour-minute-second-millisecond	Adjacency of levels, which can be organized–theoretically, conceptually, or structurally–as nested or nonnested hierarchies; examples include: (1) nested: nation-region-city-neighborhood-household; or ecosystem-species-organism-organ system-organ-cell; (2) nonnested: school I workplace I neighborhood-individual
"Near" "Far"	Proximal, near in space, close Distal, distant in space, far away	Proximal, near in time, recent Distal, distant in time, long ago	Conceptual or structural nonscalar relationship: adjacent levels Conceptual or structural nonscalar relationship: nonadjacent levels
Strength of effect	Usually inverse relationship of spatial distance and force: closer=stronger, hence proximal=powerful; farther=weaker, hence distal=dilute	Usually inverse relationship of temporal distance and force: closer=stronger, hence proximal=powerful; farther=weaker, hence distal=dilute	Cannot predict "strength" of "effect" based solely on level: a given phenomenon at any given level potentially can powerfully or weakly affect or be affected by phenomena at the same level, adjacent levels, and nonadjacent levels
Typical causal inference	Proximal=stronger cause Distal=weaker cause	Proximal=stronger cause Distal=weaker cause	Causal inference depends on level of question being asked: There may be different explanations for phenomena at different levels, and explanations for events observed within any given level may involve solely phenomena within that level or also interactions between levels; adjacency of levels may or may not predict causal strength of cause-effect relationship
Relationship to space and time	Physical distance is a spatial dimension distinct from time, but space and time can be related mathematically, e.g., distance=speed×time (and the length of a meter is now defined in relation to time and the speed of light[32][p537])	Chronological distance is a temporal dimension distinct from space, but time and space can be related mathematically, e.g., time=distance/speed (and initial time units were based on the earth's rotation, involving spatial distance[32][pp3–5])	Level is not a spatiotemporal phenomenon. It is, instead, a conceptual nonspatiotemporal relational construct that organizes and distinguishes (conceptually or structurally) different orders of hierarchically linked systems and processes (including both nested and nonnested hierarchies). "Distance" for levels does not involve spatiotemporal separation: For any phenomenon at any given point in space and time, all levels co-occur simultaneously, even though some levels may be more causally relevant than others to phenomena occurring at any given level. Space and time nevertheless do matter for levels in the case of nested hierarchies, whereby units within lower-order levels typically are smaller and involve faster processes than units in higher-order levels.

labor, and exchange inherently involved in their production, sale, and consumption.[43(pp35-41,71-83),88] Erring, however, in both directions, whether looking up or down levels, the proximal-distal divide simultaneously does the following:

(1) It promotes analysis of specific exposures and their biological embodiment stripped from the political economy, social relations, actual labor, and engagement with the material world that set the basis for their existence (the error of biomedical individualism and decontextualized "lifestyle" analyses[1-21,89-91]) *and*

(2) It encourages analysis of population health as if all that matters are social hierarchies, and not also the tangible properties of the commodities, i.e., goods and services, at issue (the error of public health nihilism[5,92-94]).

Thus, on the proximal side, official conventional reports[95,96] urge individuals to avoid specific risk factors without mention of the societal changes needed to curtail these factors' production, distribution, and consumption (precisely what the social determinant of health framework appropriately criticizes),[1-21] whereas on the distal side, some contend that public health initiatives that focus on specific risk factors or diseases are futile as long as "distal" or "fundamental" causes are at play.[13,14,97-99]

But insofar as health is concerned, the material substances *and* the social relations inherent in any given product or process *both* matter, precisely because of the physical and social exposures involved. To focus on only one or the other misses the fact we embody both.[1,17-21,94,100-103] To take but one example, consider the political economy and ecology of tobacco products and their embodied health consequences. A cigarette (or Freud's infamous cigar[104]) is *simultaneously*:

(1) A combustible mass of tobacco leaves and additives whose burning smoke transports psychoactive and addictive chemicals (e.g., nicotine) and carcinogens deep down the respiratory tract to the innermost parts of the lung and its alveolar capillaries, thereby increasing risk of cancer, cardiovascular and pulmonary disease, and other smoking-related ailments, *and*

(2) A highly profitable product whose production, distribution, advertisement, and consumption involves relentless corporate marketing (including manipulation of ideologies involving freedom, class, gender, sexuality, and race/ethnicity and targeting of marginalized groups), government regulation and taxation, tobacco farmers and workers, land ownership, trade agreements, and international treaties.[105-109]

Consequently, as recognized by several new sophisticated multilevel initiatives (e.g., Sweden's 2003 new public health policy,[110] the American Legacy Foundation's Truth Campaign,[111] and the Corporations and Health Watch project[112]), effective action to curb tobacco use and social disparities in tobacco-related diseases requires integrated, multifaceted, multilevel campaigns that are relentlessly honest about who gains and who loses from the status quo. The same could be said for any other public health concerns deemed "proximal" or "downstream," whether about environmental and occupational hazards,[6,8,9,113-116] access to safe water,[117,118] access to affordable nutritious food,[119,120] or violence,[121-123]—just as could be said for efforts focused on such ostensibly "distal" or "upstream" social determinants as economic poverty.[124-130]

Hence, argument 3: Unlike distal and proximal events separated by space or time, levels coexist simultaneously, not sequentially, and exert influence accordingly. The proximal-distal divide, however, inherently cleaves levels rather than connects them, thereby obscuring the intermingling of ecosystems, economics, politics, history, and specific exposures and processes at *every* level, macro to micro, from societal to inside the body. As William Blake (1757-1827) famously put it, the challenge instead is "to see a world in a grain of sand"[131]—because it is there.

SCALE, LEVEL, AND THE POLITICS OF CAUSATION

In summary, efforts to advance public health thinking and work about the causes of disease distribution, including health inequities, would do well to abandon the deeply confused language of the terms *proximal* and *distal*. The point is not simply semantic. Clear action requires clear thinking. By deleting the terms *proximal* and *distal* from the public health lexicon, we would have to expose our causal assumptions and also promote greater accountability for the public's health, both within our field and more broadly.

A final example suffices. In recent years, the Bill and Melinda Gates Foundation has become an enormous presence in work on global health,[132-135] funding technically oriented[136] research and medical interventions to address malaria, tuberculosis, HIV/AIDS, and other diseases that disproportionately burden poorer regions of the world. In January 2007, however, the *Los Angeles Times* published a two-part exposé,[137,138] "showing that the foundation reaps vast financial gains every year from investments that contravene its good works."[139] The foundation's response[140]:

"The stories you told of people who are suffering touched us all. But it is naive to suggest that an individual stockholder can stop that suffering. Changes in our investment practices would have little or no impact on these issues. While shareholder activism has worthwhile goals, we believe a much more *direct* [italics added] way to help people is by making grants and working with other donors to improve health, reduce poverty and strengthen education."[141]

The foundation's view that its real-world health portfolio somehow includes only its explicit biomedical research and health intervention projects and not also the health impacts of its financial investment strategies is the mind-set fostered by the proximal-distal divide. The distance and contradictions created by the proximal-distal discourse—in conceptual understanding and in professional and political accountability—are unacceptable. The extensive reach of this flawed logic is made only the more manifest by its equal use among those who profess a narrow biomedical vantage and those who articulate a more expansive social determinant of health framework. I accordingly propose that we banish the terms *proximal* and *distal* from the public health lexicon and refer instead explicitly to levels, pathways, and power, as one small but needed step toward developing better thinking and strategies for leveling health inequities.

About the Author

Nancy Krieger is with the Department of Society, Human Development, and Health at the Harvard School of Public Health, Boston, Mass.

Requests for reprints should be sent to Nancy Krieger, PhD, Professor, Department of Society, Human Development, and Health, Harvard School of Public Health, Kresge 717, 677 Huntington Ave, Boston, MA 02115 (e-mail: nkrieger@ hsph.harvard.edu).

This article was accepted June 7, 2007.

ACKNOWLEDGMENTS
The author thanks the following colleagues for useful discussions about the ideas in this article: George Davey Smith, Mary Bassett, Madeline Drexler, Sofia Gruskin, and Elizabeth Barbeau.

Human Participant Protection

No research on human subjects was performed.

• • • References

1. Krieger N. Theories for social epidemiology in the 21st century: an ecosocial perspective. *Int J Epidemiol.* 2001;30:668-677.

2. World Health Organization Commission on Social Determinants of Health. Towards a conceptual framework for analysis and action on the social determinants of health. Discussion paper for the Commission on the Social Determinants of Health [draft]. May 5, 2005. Available at: http://www.who.int/social_determinants/knowledge_networks/en. Accessed March 2, 2006.

3. Whitehead M, Dahlgren G. Leveling up (part 1): a discussion paper on concepts and principles for tackling social inequities in health. Studies on social and economic determinants of population health, No. 2, WHO Europe. Copenhagen, Denmark: World Health Organization Regional Office for Europe; 2006. Available at: http://www.euro.who.int. Accessed November 29, 2006.

4. Black D, Morris JN, Smith C, Townsend P. *The Black Report (Report of the Working Group on Inequalities in Health).* London, England: Penguin; 1982.

5. Kunitz S. *The Health of Populations: General Theories and Particular Realities.* Oxford, England: Oxford University Press; 2006.

6. Levy BS, Sidel VW, eds. *Social Injustice and Public Health.* New York, NY: Oxford University Press; 2006.

7. Wilkinson R, Marmot M, eds. *Social Determinants of Health: The Solid Facts.* 2nd ed. Oxford, England: Oxford University Press; 2006.

8. Navarro V, Muntaner C, eds. *Political and Economic Determinants of Population Health and Well-Being: Controversies and Developments.* Amityville, NY: Baywood Publishing Co; 2004.

9. Hofrichter R, ed. *Health and Social Justice: Politics, Ideology, and Inequity in the Distribution of Disease.* San Francisco, Calif: Jossey-Bass; 2003.

10. Evans T, Whitehead M, Diderichsen F, Bhuiya A, Wirth M, eds. *Challenging Inequities in Health: From Ethics to Action.* Oxford, England: Oxford University Press; 2001.

11. Berkman L, Kawachi I, eds. *Social Epidemiology.* Oxford, England: Oxford University Press; 2000.

12. Shaw M, Dorling D, Gordon D, Davey Smith G. *The Widening Gap: Health Inequalities and Policies in Britain.* Bristol, England: Policy Press; 1999.

13. McKinlay JB, Marceau LD. To boldly go . . . . *Am J Public Health.* 2000;90:25-33.

14. Link BG, Phelan J. Social conditions as fundamental causes of disease. *J Health Soc Behav.* 1995; 35(extra issue): 80-94.

15. Glass TA, McAtee MJ. Behavioral science at the crossroads in public health: extending horizons, envisioning the future. *Soc Sci Med.* 2006;62: 1650-1671.

16. Richard L, Potvin L, Kishchuk N, Prlic H, Green LW. Assessment of the integration of the ecological approach in health promotion programs. *Am J Health Promot.* 1996;318-328.

17. Krieger N. Epidemiology and the web of causation: has anyone seen the spider? *Soc Sci Med.* 1994;39: 887-903.

18. Krieger N. Ecosocial theory. In: Anderson N, ed. *Encyclopedia of Health and Behavior.* Thousand Oaks, Calif: Sage; 2004:292-294.

19. Krieger N. Embodiment: a conceptual glossary for epidemiology. *J Epidemiol Community Health.* 2005;59: 350-355.

20. Krieger N, ed. *Embodying Inequality: Epidemiologic Perspectives.* Amityville, NY: Baywood Publishers; 2004.

21. Krieger N. Stormy weather: *race*, gene expression, and the science of health disparities. *Am J Public Health.* 2005;95:2155-2160.

22. Sigerist HE. *History of Medicine. Vol. 1: Primitive and Archaic Medicine; Vol. 2: Early Greek, Hindu, and Persian Medicine.* New York, NY: Oxford University Press; 1955-1961.

23. Rosen G. *A History of Public Health* [1958]. [Introduction by Elizabeth Fee; bibliographical essay and new bibliography by Edward T. Morman.] Expanded ed. Baltimore, Md: Johns Hopkins University Press; 1993.

24. Porter D. *Health, Civilization and the State: A History of Public Health From Ancient to Modern Times.* London, England: Routledge; 1999.

25. Lloyd GER, ed. *Hippocratic Writings.* London, England: Penguin; 1983.

26. Temkin O. *Galenism: Rise and Decline of a Medical Philosophy.* Ithaca, NY: Cornell University Press; 1973.

27. Greenwood M. *Epidemiology: Historical and Experimental.* Baltimore, Md: Johns Hopkins; 1931;1-26.

28. *Oxford English Dictionary.* OED online. Available at: http://dictionary.oed.com.ezp2.harvard.edu (password required). Accessed January 8, 2006.

29. Grene M, Depew D. *The Philosophy of Biology.* Cambridge, England: Cambridge University Press; 2004.

30. Coleman W. *Biology in the Nineteenth Century: Problems of Form, Function, and Transformation.* New York, NY: John Wiley & Sons Inc; 1971.

31. Deutscher G. *The Unfolding of Language.* London, England: William Henemann; 2005.

32. Holton G, Brush SG. *Physics, the Human Adventure: From Copernicus to Einstein and Beyond.* 3rd ed. New Brunswick, NJ: Rutgers University Press; 2001.

33. Gleick J. *Isaac Newton.* New York, NY: Pantheon Books; 2003.

34. Gillmor CT. *Coulomb and the Evolution of Physics and Engineering in Eighteenth-Century France.* Princeton, NJ: Princeton University Press; 1971.

35. Cohen IB. An analysis of interactions between the natural sciences and the social sciences. In: Cohen IB, ed. *The Natural Sciences and the Social Sciences: Some Critical and Historical Perspectives.* Dordrecht, The Netherlands: Kluwer Academic Publishers; 1994:1-100.

36. Maasen S, Mendelsohn E, Weingart P, eds. *Biology as Society, Society as Biology: Metaphors.* Dordrecht, The Netherlands: Kluwer Academic Publishers; 1995.

37. Harris JG. *Foreign Bodies and the Body Politic: Discourses of Social Pathology in Early Modern England.* Cambridge, England: Cambridge University Press; 1998.

38. Maclay GR. *The Social Organism: A Short History of the Idea That a Human Society May Be Regarded as a Gigantic Living Creature.* Croton-on-Hudson, NY: North River Press; 1990.

39. Chase A. *The Legacy of Malthus: The Social Costs of the New Scientific Racism.* New York, NY: Knopf; 1977.

40. Durkheim E. *The Division of Labor in Society* [1893]. Halls WD, trans-ed. [Introduction by Lewis A. Coser.] New York, NY: Free Press; 1984.

41. Lilienfeld P. *La Pathologie Sociale.* [Avec une préface de René Worms.] Paris, France: V. Giard, and EBrière; 1896.

42. Worms R. *Organisme et Société.* Paris, France: V. Giard, and EBrière; 1896.

43. Marx K. *Capital: A Critique of Political Economy. Vol. 1. The Process of Capitalist Production* [1867]. Engels F, ed; Moore S, Aveling E, trans-ed. New York, NY: International Publishers; 1967.

44. Levitas R. *The Inclusive Society?: Social Exclusion and New Labour.* 2nd ed. Basingstoke, England: Macmillan; 2005.

45. Mayr E. Prologue: some thoughts on the history of the evolutionary synthesis. In: Mayr E, Provine WB. *The Evolutionary Synthesis: Perspectives on the Unification of Biology.* Cambridge, Mass: Harvard University Press; 1998: 1-48.

46. Gould SJ. *The Structure of Evolutionary Theory.* Cambridge, Mass: The Belknap Press of Harvard University Press; 2002.

47. Eldredge N. *The Pattern of Evolution.* New York, NY: W.H. Freeman & Co; 1999.

48. Lawrence C, Weisz G, eds. *Greater Than the Parts: Holism in Biomedicine, 1920-1950.* New York, NY: Oxford University Press; 1998.

49. Gordon JE. The world, the flesh and the devil as environment, host, and agent of disease. In: Galdston I, ed. *The Epidemiology of Health.* New York, NY: Health Education Council; 1953: 60-73.

50. Terris M. The epidemiologic tradition. The Wade Hampton Frost Lecture. *Public Health Rep.* 1979; 94:203-209.

51. Susser M. *Causal Thinking in the Health Sciences; Concepts and Strategies of Epidemiology.* New York, NY: Oxford University Press; 1973.

52. Marmot M, Elliott P, eds. *Coronary Heart Disease Epidemiology: From Aetiology to Public Health.* Oxford, England: Oxford University Press; 1992.

53. Rothstein WG. *Public Health and the Risk Factor: A History of an Uneven Medical Revolution.* Rochester, NY: University of Rochester Press; 2003.

54. MacMahon B, Pugh TF, Ipsen J. *Epidemiologic Methods.* Boston, Mass: Little, Brown and Company; 1960.

55. Gannett L. What's in a cause? The pragmatic dimensions of genetic explanations. *Biol Philos.* 1999;14:349-374.

56. Gillies D. An action-related theory of causality. *Br J Philos Sci.* 2005;85: 823-842.

57. National Human Genome Research Institute, National Institutes of Health. The Genes, Environment and Health Initiative (GEI). Available at: http://www.genome.gov/19518663. Accessed January 10, 2007.

58. *Genomics 2006 Program Review Book.* Atlanta, Ga: Centers for Disease Control and Prevention; 2006. Available at: http://www.cdc.gov/genomics/activities/ogdp/2006.htm. Accessed January 20, 2007.

59. Costa LG, Eaton DL, eds. *Gene-Environment Interactions: Fundamentals of Ecogenetics.* Hoboken, NJ: John Wiley & Sons; 2006.

60. Lewontin R. *The Triple Helix: Gene, Organism, and Environment.* Cambridge, Mass: Harvard University Press; 2000.

61. Smith GD, Gwinn M, Ebrahim S, Palmer LJ, Khoury MJ. Make it HuGE: human genome epidemiology reviews, population health, and the IJE. *Int J Epidemiol* 2006;35:507-510.

62. Keavney B, Danesh J, Parish S, et al. Fibrinogen and coronary heart disease: test of causality by "Mendelian randomization." *Int J Epidemiol.* 2006; 35:935-943.

63. Nitsch D, Molokhia M, Smeeth L, DeStavola BL, Whittaker JC, Leon DA. Limits to causal inference based on Mendelian randomization: a comparison with randomized controlled trials. *Am J Epidemiol.* 2006;163:397-403.

64. Davey Smith G, Lawlor DA, Harbord R, et al. Association of C-reactive protein with blood pressure and hypertension: life course confounding and mendelian randomization tests of causality [published correction appears in *Arterioscler Thromb Vasc Biol.* 2005; 25:e129]. *Aterioscler Thromb Vasc Biol.* 2005;25:1051-1056.

65. Davey Smith G, Ebrahim S. "Mendelian randomization": can genetic epidemiology contribute to understanding environmental determinants of disease? *Int J Epidemiol.* 2003;32:1-22.

66. McLennan G. Power. In: Bennett T, Grossberg L, Morris M, eds. *New Keywords: A Revised Vocabulary of Culture and Society.* Malden, Mass: Blackwell Publishing; 2005:274-278.

67. McFarland AS. Power: political. In: *International Encyclopedia of the Social & Behavioral Sciences* [online]. Elsevier; 2004:11936-11939. Available at: http://www.sciencedirect.com.ezp1. harvard. edu/science (password required). Accessed May 30, 2007.

68. Clegg SR. Power in society. In: *International Encyclopedia of the Social & Behavioral Sciences* [online]. Elsevier; 2004:11932-11936. Available at: http://www.sciencedirect.com.ezp1.harvard. edu/science (password required). Accessed May 30, 2007.

69. Peterson DL, Parker VT, eds. *Ecological Scale: Theory and Application.* New York, NY: Columbia University Press; 1998.

70. Patz JA, Daszak P, Tabor GM, et al; Working Group on Land Use Change and Disease Emergence. Unhealthy landscapes: policy recommendations on land use change and infectious disease emergence. *Environ Health Perspect.* 2004;112:1092-1098.

71. Rudel TK. Shrinking tropical forests, human agents of change, and conservation policy. *Conserv Biol.* 2006; 20:1604-1609.

72. Laurance WF, Nascimento HE, Laurance SG, et al. Rain forest fragmentation and the proliferation of successional trees. *Ecology.* 2006;87:469-482.

73. Ferraz G, Russell GJ, Stouffer PC, Bierregaard RO Jr, Pimm SL, Lovejoy TE. Rates of species loss from Amazonian forest fragments. *Proc Natl Acad Sci U S A.* 2003;100:14069-14073.

74. Damschen EI, Haddad NM, Orrock JL, Tewksbury JJ, Levey JJ. Corridors increase plant species richness at large scales. *Science.* 2006;313:1284-1286.

75. Brownstein JS, Skelly DK, Holford TR, Fish D. Forest fragmentation predicts local scale heterogeneity of Lyme disease risk. *Oecologia.* 2005; 146: 469-475.

76. Keeling MJ, Grenfell BT. Disease extinction and community size: modeling the persistence of measles. *Science*. 1997;275:65-67.

77. Bartlett MS. Measles periodicity and community size. *J R Stat Soc [Ser A]*. 1957;120:48-60.

78. Ahl V, Allen TFH. *Hierarchy Theory: A Vision, Vocabulary, and Epistemology*. New York, NY: Columbia University Press; 1996.

79. Gunderson L, Holling CS, eds. *Panarchy: Understanding Transformations in Human and Natural Systems*. Washington, DC: Island Press; 2002.

80. Goldstein LF, ed. *Contemporary Cases in Women's Rights*. Madison, Wis: University of Wisconsin Press; 1994:3-32.

81. Institute of Medicine. *Legalized Abortion and the Public Health: Report of a Study, by a Committee of the Institute of Medicine*. Washington, DC: National Academy of Sciences; 1975.

82. Lee KW, Paneth N, Gartner LM, Pearlman MA, Gruss L. Neonatal mortality: an analysis of the recent improvement in the United States. *Am J Public Health*. 1980;70:15-21.

83. Pakter J, Nelson F. Factors in the unprecedented decline in infant mortality in New York City. *Bull NY Acad Med*. 1974;50:839-868.

84. Lanham JT, Kohl SG, Bedell JH. Changes in pregnancy outcome after liberalization of the New York State abortion law. *Am J Obstet Gynecol*. 1974;118:485-492.

85. Wright AA, Katz IT. Roe versus reality—abortion and women's health. *New Engl J Med*. 2006; 355:1-9.

86. Stout D. Supreme court upholds ban on abortion procedure. *New York Times*, April 18, 2007. Available at: http://www.nytimes.com/2007/04/18/ us/18cnd-scotus.html?ex=1180756800&en=f3466a0d04fb44bb&ei=5070. Accessed May 31, 2007.

87. Gruskin S, Grodin MA, Annas GJ, Marks SP, eds. *Perspectives on Health and Human Rights*. New York, NY: Routledge; 2005.

88. Frow J. Commodity. In: Bennett T, Grossberg L, Morris M, eds. *New Keywords: A Revised Vocabulary of Culture and Society*. Malden, Mass: Blackwell Publishing; 2005:45-47.

89. Tesh S. *Hidden Arguments: Political Ideology and Disease Prevention Policy*. New Brunswick, NJ: Rutgers University Press; 1988.

90. Lock M, Gordon D, eds. *Biomedicine Examined*. Dordrecht, The Netherlands: Kluwer Academic Publishers; 1988.

91. Fee E, Krieger N. Understanding AIDS: historical interpretations and the limits of biomedical individualism. *Am J Public Health*. 1993;83: 1477-1486.

92. Fairchild AL, Oppenheimer GM. Public health nihilism vs pragmatism: history, politics, and the control of tuberculosis. *Am J Public Health*. 1998; 88: 1105-1117.

93. Szreter S. *Health and Wealth: Studies in History and Policy*. Rochester, NY: University of Rochester Press; 2005.

94. Krieger N. Sticky webs, hungry spiders, buzzing flies, and fractal metaphors: on the misleading juxtaposition of "risk factor" vs "social" epidemiology. *J Epidemiol Community Health*. 1999;53:678-680.

95. US Department of Health and Human Services. *A Healthier You*. Washington, DC: US Government Printing Office; 2005.

96. Bush GW. Healthier US: The President's Health and Fitness Initiative. Washington, DC: The White House; 2004. Available at: http://www.whitehouse. gov/infocus/fitness. Accessed January 22, 2007.

97. Wilkinson R. *The Impact of Inequality: How to Make Sick Societies Healthier*. New York, NY: The New Press; 2005.

98. Raphael D. Barriers to addressing the societal determinants of health: public health units and poverty in Ontario, Canada. *Health Promot Int*. 2003;18: 397-405.

99. Phelan JC, Link BG. Controlling disease and creating disparities: a fundamental cause perspective. *J Gerontol B Psychol Sci Soc Sci*. 2005;60(special issue):27-33.

100. Krieger N, Davey Smith G. "Bodies count," and body counts: social epidemiology and embodying inequality. *Epidemiol Review*. 2004;26:92-103.

101. Weiss G, Haber HF, eds. *Perspectives on Embodiment: The Intersections of Nature and Culture*. New York, NY: Routledge; 1999.

102. Scheper-Hughes N, Lock MM. The mindful body: a prolegomenon to future work in medical anthropology. *Med Anthro Q*. 1987;1:6-41.

103. Eldredge N, Grene M. *Interactions: The Biological Context of Social Systems*. New York, NY: Columbia University Press; 1992.

104. The Freud Museum. Frequently asked questions. Available at: http:// www.freud.org.uk/fmfaq.htm. Accessed January 12, 2007.

105. Kluger R. *Ashes to Ashes: America's Hundred-Year Cigarette War, the Public Health, and the Unabashed Triumph of Philip Morris*. New York, NY: Alfred A. Knopf; 1996.

106. Lock S, Reynolds A, Tansey EM, eds. *Ashes to Ashes: The History of Smoking and Health: Symposium and Witness Seminar Organized by the Wellcome Institute for the History of Medicine and the History of the Twentieth Century Medicine Group on 26-27 April 1995*. Amsterdam, The Netherlands: Rodopi; 1998.

107. Brandt AM. *The Cigarette Century: The Rise, Fall, and Deadly Persistence of the Product That Defined America.* New York, NY: Basic Books; 2007.

108. Mackay J, Eriksen E, Shafey O. *The Tobacco Atlas.* Atlanta, Ga: American Cancer Society; 2006.

109. Washington HA. Burning love: big tobacco takes aim at LGBT youths. *Am J Public Health.* 2002; 92:1086-1095.

110. Swedish National Institute of Public Health. *Sweden's New Public Health Policy: National Public Health Objectives for Sweden.* Rev ed. 2003. Available at: http://www.fhi.se. Accessed April 13, 2006.

111. American Legacy Foundation. Programs: overview. Available at: http://www.americanlegacy.org/18. htm. Accessed January 21, 2007.

112. Corporations and Health Watch [Web site]. Available at: http://www.corporationsandhealth. org. Accessed January 15, 2007.

113. Markowitz G, Rosner D. *Deceit and Denial: The Deadly Politics of Industrial Pollution.* Berkeley, Calif: University of California Press; 2002.

114. Richardson JW. *The Cost of Being Poor: Poverty, Lead Poisoning, and Policy Implementation.* Westport, Conn: Praeger; 2005.

115. McMichael AJ. *Human Frontiers, Environments, and Disease: Past Patterns, Uncertain Futures.* Cambridge, England: Cambridge University Press; 2001.

116. Mooney C. *The Republican War on Science.* New York, NY: Basic Books; 2005.

117. *Human Development Report 2006: Beyond Scarcity: Power, Poverty, and the Global Water Crisis.* New York, NY: United Nations Development Programme; 2006.

118. Whiteford L, Whiteford S, eds. *Globalization, Water, & Health: Resource Management in Times of Scarcity.* Santa Fe, NM: School of American Research Press; and Oxford, England: James Currey; 2005.

119. Nestle M. *Food Politics: How the Food Industry Influences Nutrition and Health.* Berkeley, Calif: University of California Press; 2002.

120. Schlosser E. *Fast Food Nation: The Dark Side of the All-American Meal.* Boston, Mass: Houghton Mifflin; 2001.

121. Krug EG, Dahlberg LL, Mercy JA, Zwi AB, Lozano R, eds. *World Report on Violence and Health.* Geneva, Switzerland: World Health Organization; 2002.

122. Hemenway D. *Private Guns Public Health.* Ann Arbor, Mich: University of Michigan Press; 2004.

123. Sokoloff NJ, Pratt C, eds. *Domestic Violence at the Margins: Readings on Race, Class, Gender, and Culture.* New Brunswick, NJ: Rutgers University Press; 2005.

124. Blank RM. Selecting among antipoverty policies: can an economist be both critical and caring? *Rev Social Economy.* 2003;61:447-469.

125. Townsend P, Gordon D, eds. *World Poverty: New Policies to Defeat an Old Enemy.* Bristol, England: The Policy Press; 2002.

126. *Human Development Report 2005: International Cooperation at the Crossroads—Aid, Trade and Security in an Unequal World.* New York, NY: United Nations Development Programme; 2005.

127. Katz MB. *In the Shadow of the Poorhouse: A Social History of Welfare in America.* Rev ed. New York, NY: Basic Books; 1996.

128. Sachs J. *The End of Poverty: Economic Possibilities for Our Time.* New York, NY: Penguin Press; 2005.

129. Stiglitz JE. *Making Globalization Work.* New York, NY: WW Norton & Co; 2006.

130. Monbiot G. *Manifesto for a New World Order.* New York, NY: WW Norton; 2004.

131. Blake W. *Auguries of Innocence.* Available at: http://rpo.library.utoronto.ca/poem/161.html. Accessed May 31, 2007.

132. Bill & Melinda Gates Foundation. Global health program. Available at: http://www.gates foundation.org/Global-Health. Accessed January 17, 2007.

133. Okie S. Global health—the Gates-Buffett effect. *New Engl J Med.* 2006; 355:1084-1088.

134. Garrett L. The challenge of global health. *Foreign Affairs.* Jan/Feb 2007. Available at: http://www. foreignaffairs.org/20070101faessay86103-p90/ laurie-garrett/the-challenge-of-globalhealth.html. Accessed January 22, 2007.

135. [No authors listed.] Governance questions at the Gates Foundation [editorial]. *Lancet.* 2007; 369:163.

136. Birn AE. Gates's grandest challenge: transcending technology as public health ideology. *Lancet.* 2005;366:514-519.

137. Piller C, Sanders E, Dixon R. Dark cloud over good works of Gates Foundation [Part I]. *Los Angeles Times,* January 7, 2007. Available at: http://www.latimes.com/news/nationworld/nation/ la-na-gatesx07jan07,0,6827615.story. Accessed January 17, 2007.

138. Piller C. Money clashes with mission: The Gates Foundation invests heavily in sub-prime lenders and other businesses that undercut its good works [Part II]. *Los Angeles Times,* January 8, 2007. Available at: http://www.latimes. com/news/ nationworld/nation/la-na-gates8jan08,1,6069951,

full.story?coll=la-headlines-nation. Accessed January 17, 2007.

139. Piller C. Gates Foundation to reassess investments. *Los Angeles Times*, January 11, 2007. Available at: http://www.latimes.com/business/la-fi-gates11 jan11,1,7943560.story. Accessed January 17, 2007.

140. Piller C. Gates Foundation to keep its investment approach. *Los Angeles Times*, January 14, 2007.

Available at: http://www.latimes.com/business/la-na-gates14jan14,1,1844117.story. Accessed January 17, 2007.

141. Stonesifer P. A foundation states its case [letter]. *Los Angeles Times*, January 14, 2007. Available at: http://www.latimes.com/news/printedition/opinion/la-le-sunday14.3jan14,1,1775487.story. Accessed: January 17, 2007.

2

A Call to Action for
Individuals & Their Communities

Source: United Health Foundation. Excerpts from America's Health Rankings: A Call to Action for Individuals & Their Communities. pp.4-37. www.americashealthrankings.org. 2009. Courtesy of America's Health Rankings™(c)2009 United Health Foundation. All rights reserved.

INTRODUCTION

Health is a result of our behaviors, our individual genetic predisposition to disease, the environment and the community in which we live, the clinical care we receive and the policies and practices of our health care and prevention systems. Each of us, individually, as a community, and as a society, strives to optimize these health determinants, so that all of us can have a long, disease-free and robust life regardless of race, gender or socio-economic status. This report looks at the four groups of health determinants that can be affected:

1. **Behaviors** the everyday activities we do that affect our personal health. It includes habits and practices we develop as individuals and families that have an effect on our personal health and on our utilization of health resources. These behaviors are modifiable with effort by the individual supported by community, policy and clinical interventions.

2. **Community and environment** the reality that the daily conditions in which we live our lives have a great effect on achieving optimal individual health.

3. **Public and health policies** indicative of the availability of resources to encourage and maintain health and the extent that public and health programs reach into the general population.

4. **Clinical care** the quality, appropriateness and cost of the care we receive at doctors' offices, clinics and hospitals.

All health determinants are and must work together to be effective. For example, an initiative that addresses tobacco cessation requires not only efforts on the part of the individual but also support from the community in the form of public and health policies that promote non-smoking and the availability of effective counseling and care at clinics. Similarly, sound prenatal care requires individual effort, access to and availability of prenatal care coupled with high quality of health care services. Obesity, a health epidemic now facing this country, requires coordination among almost all sectors of the economy including food producers, distributors, restaurants, grocery and convenience stores, exercise facilities, parks, urban and transportation design, building design, educational institutions, community organizations, social groups, healthcare delivery and insurance to complement and augment individual actions.

America's Health Rankings™ combines individual measures of each of these determinants with the resultant health outcomes into one comprehensive view of the health of a state. Additionally, it discusses health determinants separately from health outcomes and provides related health, economic and social information to present a comprehensive profile of the overall health of each state.

America's Health Rankings™ employs a unique methodology, developed and periodically reviewed by a panel of leading public health scholars, which balances the contributions of various factors, such as smoking, obesity, binge drinking, high school graduation rates, children in poverty, access to care and incidence of preventable disease, to a state's health. The report is based on data from the U.S. Departments of Health and Human Services, Commerce, Education and Labor; U.S. Environmental Protection Agency; the American Medical Association; the Dartmouth Atlas Project; and the Trust for America's Health.

PURPOSE

The ultimate purpose of *America's Health Rankings*™ is to stimulate action by individuals, elected officials, healthcare professionals, employers, and communities to improve the health of the population of the United States. We do this by promoting public conversation concerning health in our states, as well as providing information to facilitate citizen, community and group participation. We encourage participation in all elements: behaviors, community, environment, clinical care, and public and health policies. Each person individually, and in their capacity as an employee, employer, voter, community volunteer, health official or elected official, can contribute to the advancement of the healthiness of their

state. Proven, effective and innovative actions can improve the health of people in every state whether the state is first or 50th.

SCIENTIFIC ADVISORY COMMITTEE

In 2002, United Health Foundation, in concert with the American Public Health Association (APHA) and Partnership for Prevention, commissioned the School of Public Health at the University of North Carolina at Chapel Hill to undertake an ongoing review of *America's Health Rankings*™. The Scientific Advisory Committee, led by Thomas Ricketts, Ph.D., M.P.H., was charged with conducting a thorough review of the current index and recommending improvements that would maintain the value of the comparative, longitudinal information; reflect the evolving role and science of public health; utilize new or improved measures of health as they become available and acceptable; and incorporate new methods as feasible. Minor issues with data are always addressed immediately and incorporated into the contents of the next edition of the report. However, more significant issues, such as new measurements of health conditions, require more indepth study and analysis.

The Scientific Advisory Committee continues its review, and its input is reflected in this Edition. The Committee emphasizes the importance of this tool as a vehicle to promote and improve the general discussion of public health and, also, to encourage balance among public health efforts to benefit the entire community.

This Edition includes several suggestions discussed by the committee including:

- Changing the method of scoring metrics from a change relative to the national mean to a change measured in units of standard deviation

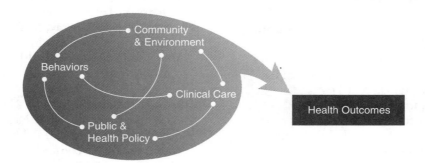

Figure 2-2 Components of Health

of the measure (Z-score). This method represents a major change to *America's Health Rankings*™ and required a recalculation of all prior years of rankings.

- Revising the Air Pollution measure to better accommodate nonreporting areas of states. Nonreporting counties were assigned a baseline value of exposure to fine particulate matter equal to the average of the lowest annual readings for fine particulate matter for the last three years in their Air Quality Control Region or, if not available, in their state.

- Geographic Disparity was reviewed and suggested that counties with a low number of deaths and deemed unreliable should be handled separately. The current calculation assigns the state's average total mortality rate to those counties that are unreliable.

In addition, the committee continues to work on issues concerning improved environmental health indicators, methods of expressing variability within the rankings, oral health indicators, mental health indicators, improved health disparities, improved cost measures, quality of care measures and international benchmarking. (Some of these measures are included in the expanded detail of each state's health profile at www.americashealth rankings.com/StateRank/details. aspx.) The committee also stresses the importance of focusing on health determinants as improving these measures can improve the healthiness of the states and the nation. This year, the overall ranks for combined determinants, as well as outcomes are presented in each state snapshot.

The methodology review group represents a variety of stakeholders, including representatives from state health departments and the Centers for Disease Control and Prevention, members of APHA, as well as experts from many academic disciplines.

Scientific Advisory Committee members include:

Thomas C. Ricketts, Ph.D., M.P.H.
Chair
Professor of Health Policy and Administration
and Social Medicine
School of Global Public Health
University of North Carolina at Chapel Hill
Dennis P. Andrulis, Ph.D., M.P.H.
Associate Dean for Research
Director, Center for Health Equality
Drexel University School of Public Health
Jamie Bartram, Ph.D.
Professor and Director of Global Water Institute
Gillings School of Global Public Health
University of North Carolina at Chapel Hill

John M. Booker, Ph.D.
Bureau Chief, Injury and Behavioral
Epidemiology
Epidemiology and Response Division
New Mexico Department of Health
William Dow, Ph.D.
Associate Professor of Health Economics
School of Public Health
University of California-Berkeley
Paul Erwin, M.D., M.P.H.
Director, Center for Public Health
Policy and Research
University of Tennessee
Jonathan Fielding, M.D., M.P.H., M.B.A., M.A.
Professor of Health Services and Pediatrics
UCLA School of Public Health
Director of Public Health and Health Officer,
Los Angeles County
Marthe Gold, M.D.
Logan Professor and Chair
Department of Community Health
CUNY Medical School
Dave Kindig, M.D., Ph.D.
Professor Emeritus
Senior Adviser, Population Health Institute
University of Wisconsin-Madison, School of
Medicine
Sheila Leatherman, M.S.W.
Research Professor and Gillings Visiting
Professor
School of Global Public Health
University of North Carolina at Chapel Hill
Glen P. Mays, Ph.D., M.P.H.
Associate Professor, Vice Chair, Director of
Research
Department of Health Policy and Management
Fay W. Boozman College of Public Health
University of Arkansas for Medical Sciences
Matthew McKenna, M.D., M.P.H.
Captain, U.S. Public Health Service
Director, Office on Smoking and Health
Centers for Disease Control and Prevention
Christopher J. L. Murray, M.D., D.Phil.
Professor of Global Health
Director, Institute for Health Metrics and
Evaluation
University of Washington
Patrick Remington, M.D., M.P.H.
Associate Dean for Public Health
School of Medicine and Public Health
University of Wisconsin-Madison
Barbara Rimer, DrPH
Dean, Gillings School of Global Public Health
University of North Carolina at Chapel Hill

William L. Roper, M.D., M.P.H.
  Chair Emeritus
  Dean, School of Medicine
  University of North Carolina at Chapel Hill
Leiyu Shi, Ph.D.
  Professor
  Department of Health Policy and Management
  Co-Director, Primary Care Policy Center for the
    Underserved
  Johns Hopkins University School of Public
    Health
Steven Teutsch, M.D., M.P.H.
  Chief Science Officer
  Los Angeles County Department of Public
    Health
Tom Eckstein, M.B.A.
  Principal
  Arundel Street Consulting, Inc.

FINDINGS

The 2009 Edition of *America's Health Rankings*™ is considered a benchmark of the relative health of states due to its longevity and its sound model. Numerous states incorporate this report into their annual review of programs, and several organizations use this study as a reference point when assigning goals for health improvement programs.

One of the major goals of this report is to continuously improve. Along this line, the underlying methodology used to calculate the final score and rank of each state has been substantially changed this year. Prior editions calculated the final score using a weighted average of the percent each state varied from the nation. This edition calculated the final score using a weighted average of number of standard deviations that a state is different than the nation.

The effect of this change is that the final score is much more representative of the real variation of the state from the nation. It reduces the effect of measures that are widely scattered among states and highlights where the state statistically differs from the nation as a whole. See the Methodology section for additional information.

The 2009 Edition of *America's Health Rankings*™ uses this improved methodology to calculate state ranks. Rankings presented in this edition are not comparable to rankings published in prior editions. However, all prior rankings have been recalculated using the improved method. The recalculated rankings are available at www.americashealthrankings.org, and can be compared to the rankings in this edition.

All historical comparisons discussed in this report are to rankings calculated using the improved method.

2009 Results

America's Health Rankings™—2009 Edition shows Vermont at the top of the list of healthiest states. The state has had a steady climb in the rankings for the last twelve years from a ranking of 17th in 1997 and 1998. Utah is ranked second this year, an improvement from ranking around 5th for the prior five years. Massachusetts is number three, followed by Hawaii and New Hampshire. Mississippi is 50th and the least healthy state, while Oklahoma is 49th. Alabama, Louisiana and South Carolina complete the bottom five states.

Vermont moved from 20th in 1990 and 1991 to the top position with sustained improvement in the last twelve years. Vermont's strengths include its number one position for all health determinants combined which includes ranking in the top ten states for a high rate of high school graduation, a low violent crime rate, a low percentage of children in poverty, high per capita public health funding, a low rate of uninsured population and ready availability of primary care physicians. Vermont's two challenges are low immunization coverage with 74.4 percent of children ages 19 to 35 months receiving complete immunizations and a high prevalence of binge drinking at 17.6 percent of the population. For further details, see Vermont's state snapshot at www.america shealth rankings.org/2009/vt.aspx.

Mississippi is 50th this year, the same as the last eight years. It has been in the bottom three states since the 1990 Edition. The state ranks well for a low prevalence of binge drinking and a low violent crime rate. It ranks in the bottom five states on 11 of the 22 measures including a high prevalence of obesity, a low high school graduation rate, a high percentage of children in poverty, limited availability of primary care physicians, and many preventable hospitalizations. It ranks 50th for all health determinants combined, so its overall ranking is unlikely to change significantly in the near future. For further details, see Mississippi's state snapshot at www. americashealthrankings.org/2009/ms.aspx.

Table 1 lists the score and ranking for each of the 50 states.

Scores presented in the tables indicate the weighted number of standard deviation units a state is above or below the national norm. For example, Vermont with a score of 1.064 is slightly more than one standard deviation unit above the national norm.

Table 1	2009 Overall Rankings				
ALPHABETICAL BY STATE			**RANK ORDER**		
RANK	**STATE**	**SCORE***	**RANK**	**STATE**	**SCORE***
48	Alabama	−0.546	1	Vermont	1.064
34	Alaska	−0.091	2	Utah	1.006
27	Arizona	0.082	3	Massachusetts	0.905
40	Arkansas	−0.416	4	Hawaii	0.892
23	California	0.278	5	New Hampshire	0.886
8	Colorado	0.606	6	Minnesota	0.828
7	Connecticut	0.779	7	Connecticut	0.779
32	Delaware	−0.082	8	Colorado	0.606
36	Florida	−0.200	9	Maine	0.569
43	Georgia	−0.469	10	Rhode Island	0.557
4	Hawaii	0.892	11	Washington	0.538
14	Idaho	0.524	12	Wisconsin	0.534
29	Illinois	−0.056	13	Oregon	0.530
35	Indiana	−0.188	14	Idaho	0.524
15	Iowa	0.503	15	Iowa	0.503
24	Kansas	0.245	16	Nebraska	0.475
41	Kentucky	−0.434	17	North Dakota	0.421
47	Louisiana	−0.530	18	New Jersey	0.414
9	Maine	0.569	19	Wyoming	0.343
21	Maryland	0.281	20	South Dakota	0.286
3	Massachusetts	0.905	21	Maryland	0.281
30	Michigan	−0.063	22	Virginia	0.281
6	Minnesota	0.828	23	California	0.278
50	Mississippi	−0.789	24	Kansas	0.245
38	Missouri	−0.238	25	New York	0.203
26	Montana	0.192	26	Montana	0.192
16	Nebraska	0.475	27	Arizona	0.082
45	Nevada	−0.482	28	Pennsylvania	−0.031
5	New Hampshire	0.886	29	Illinois	−0.056
18	New Jersey	0.414	30	Michigan	−0.063
31	New Mexico	−0.067	31	New Mexico	−0.067
25	New York	0.203	32	Delaware	−0.082
37	North Carolina	−0.206	33	Ohio	−0.084
17	North Dakota	0.421	34	Alaska	−0.091
33	Ohio	−0.084	35	Indiana	−0.188
49	Oklahoma	−0.566	36	Florida	−0.200
13	Oregon	0.530	37	North Carolina	−0.206
28	Pennsylvania	−0.031	38	Missouri	−0.238
10	Rhode Island	0.557	39	Texas	−0.320
46	South Carolina	−0.492	40	Arkansas	−0.416
20	South Dakota	0.286	41	Kentucky	−0.434
44	Tennessee	−0.480	42	West Virginia	−0.446
39	Texas	−0.320	43	Georgia	−0.469
2	Utah	1.006	44	Tennessee	−0.480
1	Vermont	1.064	45	Nevada	−0.482
21	Virginia	0.281	46	South Carolina	−0.492
11	Washington	0.538	47	Louisiana	−0.530
42	West Virginia	−0.446	48	Alabama	−0.546
12	Wisconsin	0.534	49	Oklahoma	−0.566
19	Wyoming	0.343	50	Mississippi	−0.789

*Scores presented in this table indicate the weighted number of standard deviations a state is above or below the national norm.

When comparing states from year to year, differences in score are more important than changes in ranking.

Determinants and Outcomes

The 22 measures that comprise *America's Health Rankings*™ are of two types—health determinants and health outcomes. Health determinants represent those actions that can affect the future health of the population, whereas health outcomes represent the result of what has already occurred, either through death or missed days due to illness.

For a state to improve the health of its population, efforts must focus on changing the determinants of health. If a state is significantly better in its ranking for health determinants than its ranking for health outcomes, it will be more likely to improve its overall health ranking in the future. Conversely, if a state is worse in its ranking for health determinants than its ranking for health outcomes, its overall health ranking will be more likely to decline over time.

Table 2 presents the overall rankings for the health determinants, health outcomes and implications for the future. If the current trend is positive, the future overall ranking is more likely to increase; if it is neutral, the future overall ranking will probably stay the same; or if it is negative, the future overall ranking is more likely to decline.

The top ten states for strong determinants are, in order from the top ranked state: Vermont, Utah, Massachusetts, New Hampshire, Hawaii, Connecticut, Minnesota, Maine, Colorado and Rhode Island.

The states with the weakest determinants, beginning with the lowest listed first, are: Mississippi, Nevada, Oklahoma, Georgia, Texas, South Carolina, Louisiana, Alabama, Tennessee and Arkansas.

The top ten states for strong health outcomes are, in order from the top ranked state: Minnesota, Hawaii, Nebraska, Massachusetts, Iowa, Utah, Connecticut, New Hampshire, Vermont and Washington. The states with the weakest determinants, beginning with the lowest listed first, are: Mississippi, Alabama, West Virginia, Kentucky, Louisiana, Tennessee, Oklahoma, Arkansas, South Carolina and Georgia.

When compared to other states, South Dakota, Maryland and Maine have a much higher ranking for health determinants than for health outcomes, showing a stronger indication they will improve over time. Texas, Nebraska and New York show a stronger indication that they will decline over time compared to other states.

There are many other measures that states can use to compare themselves, especially as action plans are created and implemented. The measures are posted on the Web site. These supplemental measures can be accessed by viewing the state's snapshot at http://www.americashealthrankings.org/StateRank/details.aspx.

Health Diparities within States

One of the primary goals of *Healthy People 2010* to eliminate health disparities among segments of the population, including differences that occur by gender, race or ethnicity, education or income, disability, geographic location, or sexual orientation.[1]

The statewide measures used in *America's Health Rankings*™ reflect the condition of the "average" resident. However, when those measures are examined more closely, startling differences can exist within a state when race, gender, geographic location and/or economic status are considered.

The National Healthcare Disparities Report (http://www.ahrq.gov/qual/nhdr08/nhdr08.pdf), released each year by the Agency for Healthcare Research and Quality, highlights disparities at a national level. The report analyzes numerous measures and indicates that disparities exist for many groups, including women, children, the elderly, rural residents, and among racial and socioeconomic groups. The report also indicates that such disparities affect all aspects of health and health care delivery, including preventive care, acute care and chronic disease management, and affect many delivery locations including primary care, home health care, hospice, emergency care, hospitals and nursing homes.

The report highlights three themes:

- Disparities persist in health care quality and access.
- The magnitude and pattern of disparities are different within subpopulations.
- Some disparities exist across multiple priority populations.

While each state has unique issues that contribute to disparities, states that have been successful in reducing disparities in health indicators while retaining high overall health can serve as models for other states.

The 2009 Edition of *America's Health Rankings*™ contains an explicit metric for disparities—Geographic

---

[1.]Office of Disease Prevention and Health Promotion, U.S. Department of Health and Human Services, Rockville, Md., http://www.healthypeople.gov/About/goals.htm.

Table 2	Health Determinants and Health Outcomes, 2009		
STATE	RANK FOR ALL DETERMINANTS	RANK FOR ALL OUTCOMES	INFLUENCE ON FUTURE OVERALL RANK
Alabama	43	49	Positive
Alaska	34	28	Negative
Arizona	27	23	Neutral
Arkansas	41	43	Neutral
California	24	19	Negative
Colorado	9	13	Neutral
Connecticut	6	7	Neutral
Delaware	32	32	Neutral
Florida	34	40	Positive
Georgia	47	41	Negative
Hawaii	5	2	Neutral
Idaho	12	15	Neutral
Illinois	33	24	Negative
Indiana	38	33	Negative
Iowa	18	5	Negative
Kansas	25	22	Neutral
Kentucky	40	47	Positive
Louisiana	44	46	Neutral
Maine	8	21	Positive
Maryland	16	34	Positive
Massachusetts	3	4	Neutral
Michigan	30	31	Neutral
Minnesota	7	1	Negative
Mississippi	50	50	Neutral
Missouri	37	39	Neutral
Montana	23	27	Neutral
Nebraska	21	3	Negative
Nevada	49	37	Negative
NewHampshire	4	8	Neutral
NewJersey	17	16	Neutral
NewMexico	31	29	Neutral
NewYork	26	12	Negative
North Carolina	36	38	Neutral
NorthDakota	19	14	Negative
Ohio	28	36	Positive
Oklahoma	48	44	Neutral
Oregon	14	11	Neutral
Pennsylvania	29	29	Neutral
RhodeIsland	10	18	Positive
South Carolina	45	42	Neutral
SouthDakota	15	35	Positive
Tennessee	42	45	Neutral
Texas	46	26	Negative
Utah	2	5	Neutral
Vermont	1	9	Positive
Virginia	20	25	Positive
Washington	13	10	Neutral
WestVirginia	39	48	Positive
Wisconsin	11	16	Positive
Wyoming	22	20	Neutral

Disparity. This indicator reflects the range of age adjusted mortality rates that exist within a state at the county level. Graph 1 shows geographic disparity increasing in the United States over the last five years. Disparity in mortality rates occur for many reasons, including differences in behaviors, genetics, community and environmental situations, health care policies and clinical interventions. State data is at www.america shealthrankings.org/2009/disparity.aspx.

While this overall disparity metric provides a broad view of the challenges facing a state, specific measures shed more light on the sources of the disparity and how disparity exists in behaviors, disease and mortality for subgroups in the United States.

While it is helpful to understand disparity across all factors, data for disparity differences by race/ethnicity is the most readily available in the United States. Tables 3 and 4 show how the prevalence of smoking and the prevalence of obesity vary by race/ethnicity within the states. These tables show how disparities are a local issue; in some states, there is a wide difference among race/ethnicity groups whereas in other groups, the difference is much less pronounced. This type of analysis, especially when expanded to encompass a broad range of social, economic and health indicators, allows communities, their organizations and public health officials to target programs to address the biggest areas of concern.

Disparities also exist in the prevalence of diseases, especially chronic disease. Table 5 shows how diabetes affects the various race/ethnic groups in each state. It is notable that diabetes among non-Hispanic blacks is consistently higher than diabetes among either non-Hispanic whites or Hispanics.

The effect of disparities continues throughout life, resulting in higher mortality rates among certain race/ethnic groups, as shown in Table 6.

Comparison to Other Nations

When health in the United States is compared to health in other countries, the picture is disappointing. The World Health Organization, in its annual World Health Statistics 2009, compares the United States to the nations of the world on a large variety of measures. While the U.S. does exceed many countries, it is far from the best in many of the common measures used to gauge our healthiness and lags behind its peers in other developed countries.

Healthy life expectancy (HALE) is a measure that indicates the number of years that a newborn can expect to live a healthy and productive life. Japan is the perennial leader in this measure with a HALE of 76

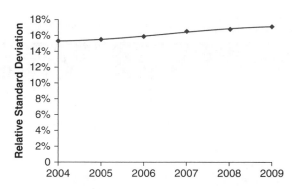

Graph 1 Geographic Disparity for United States Since 2004

years on average for both genders. At 70 years, the United States has the same HALE as Czech Republic and Chile. There are 30 other countries that exceed the United States in healthy life expectancy, including Australia, Italy, Spain, France, Germany, Greece and United Kingdom. The difference between Japan and the United States for females is 7 years; the difference for males is 5 years (Table 7).

One of the underlying causes for these differences is the gap in infant mortality rates between the United States and many other countries (Table 7). The infant mortality rate for the U.S. in 2007 was six deaths per 1,000 live births; the infant mortality rates for Sweden, Japan, France, Norway, Portugal and the Czech Republic were three deaths or fewer per 1,000 live births—one-half of the rate in the United States. Of the 193 countries rated, 36 countries had lower infant mortality rates than the United States.

Differences in healthy life expectancy are also affected by the effectiveness of treating diseases, especially those that are amenable to care, including bacterial infections, treatable cancers, diabetes, cardiovascular and cerebrovascular disease, some ischemic heart disease and complications from common surgical procedures. The age-adjusted amenable mortality rate before age 75 for the United States was 109.7 deaths per 100,000 population in 2002, which meant it ranked last among the 19 countries of the Organization for Economic Cooperation and Development (OECD) nations studied. The rate in the U.S. is 50 percent higher than the rate in France, Japan, Spain, Italy, Canada and Australia.

Additionally, the study indicated that despite spending more than any other country on health care, the United States continues to slip further behind other countries. In 1997, the U.S. ranked 15th in this mortality rate. Since then, Finland, Portugal, United Kingdom and Ireland have reduced their

Table 3	Prevalence of Smoking by Race/Ethnicity and State (percent of adult population)						
STATE	NON-HISPANIC WHITE	NON-HISPANIC BLACK	HISPANIC	NON-HISPANIC ASIAN	NON-HISPANIC HAWAIIAN/ PACIFIC ISLANDER	NON-HISPANIC AMERICAN INDIAN OR ALASKAN NATIVE	NON-HISPANIC MULTIRACIAL
Alabama	23.6%	20.0%	23.1%	—	—	28.5%	24.6%
Alaska	19.0%	—	21.9%	9.3%	—	39.9%	40.2%
Arizona	18.0%	23.0%	16.2%	20.5%	—	19.1%	20.2%
Arkansas	22.3%	24.0%	21.5%	—	—	31.2%	35.9%
California	14.7%	21.0%	13.5%	8.2%	22.2%	29.3%	23.9%
Colorado	16.5%	25.2%	21.5%	13.0%	—	38.3%	31.7%
Connecticut	15.5%	19.4%	21.2%	9.0%	—	—	38.8%
Delaware	19.8%	17.0%	22.4%	4.2%	—	—	26.0%
Florida	21.2%	15.5%	15.5%	8.4%	—	32.0%	27.2%
Georgia	20.1%	17.5%	17.3%	16.2%	—	31.1%	32.4%
Hawaii	13.9%	11.0%	24.1%	12.7%	21.9%	—	22.2%
Idaho	17.4%	—	18.8%	—	—	33.9%	23.7%
Illinois	20.2%	24.1%	20.6%	10.9%	—	—	21.1%
Indiana	24.1%	27.8%	28.6%	—	—	—	32.4%
Iowa	19.5%	34.8%	21.9%	—	—	—	—
Kansas	18.1%	22.9%	19.4%	6.7%	—	31.7%	32.4%
Kentucky	27.1%	27.5%	25.7%	—	—	49.5%	41.2%
Louisiana	22.1%	21.8%	25.9%	18.4%	—	33.7%	26.6%
Maine	19.4%	—	24.4%	—	—	41.6%	28.1%
Maryland	17.0%	18.3%	11.1%	6.8%	—	29.6%	17.1%
Massachusetts	16.8%	17.6%	17.7%	6.6%	—	28.2%	28.4%
Michigan	20.4%	24.9%	25.6%	7.9%	—	35.9%	29.2%
Minnesota	16.9%	21.8%	25.2%	14.8%	—	—	—
Mississippi	24.2%	22.6%	24.7%	—	—	—	37.4%
Missouri	23.6%	26.6%	27.8%	—	—	37.2%	37.8%
Montana	17.3%	—	26.4%	—	—	43.5%	31.8%
Nebraska	18.5%	24.8%	17.4%	10.5%	—	47.2%	39.4%
Nevada	21.4%	24.3%	20.0%	13.2%	—	29.0%	34.9%
New Hampshire	18.3%	—	22.7%	3.8%	—	35.9%	38.2%
New Jersey	17.2%	19.6%	15.6%	7.2%	—	23.0%	22.7%
New Mexico	19.2%	26.4%	21.1%	20.2%	—	17.3%	34.4%
New York	18.8%	17.6%	17.4%	8.4%	—	29.7%	22.0%
North Carolina	22.2%	22.4%	16.3%	10.4%	—	36.4%	36.0%
North Dakota	18.1%	—	17.0%	—	—	47.7%	—
Ohio	20.8%	26.5%	32.2%	6.3%	—	59.4%	39.4%
Oklahoma	24.1%	29.1%	20.6%	12.8%	—	33.6%	31.4%
Oregon	16.9%	—	13.3%	6.0%	—	33.1%	32.1%
Pennsylvania	20.4%	26.7%	23.4%	15.1%	—	47.1%	32.8%
Rhode Island	18.1%	17.7%	14.8%	13.5%	—	—	—
South Carolina	22.2%	18.7%	19.6%	12.5%	—	44.0%	31.4%
South Dakota	17.0%	—	23.2%	—	—	48.8%	45.7%
Tennessee	23.9%	21.5%	19.1%	—	—	—	22.7%
Texas	18.9%	22.6%	16.9%	7.3%	—	37.1%	28.0%
Utah	9.4%	—	15.2%	7.0%	—	19.0%	15.8%
Vermont	17.0%	—	25.4%	—	—	40.8%	29.6%
Virginia	17.8%	20.7%	14.4%	7.6%	—	31.0%	31.1%
Washington	16.3%	21.8%	13.4%	7.8%	16.3%	35.0%	26.8%
West Virginia	26.4%	28.3%	21.3%	—	—	—	32.9%
Wisconsin	19.3%	30.5%	21.2%	—	—	46.9%	36.3%
Wyoming	19.8%	—	28.0%	—	—	47.8%	28.8%
United States	19.5%	21.1%	16.1%	9.2%	23.3%	34.4%	28.2%
District of Columbia	9.9%	23.0%	13.4%	9.7%	—	—	25.0%

Source: Centers for Disease Control and Prevention (CDC). Behavioral Risk Factor Surveillance System Survey Data. Atlanta, Georgia: U.S. Department of Health and Human Services, Centers for Disease Control and Prevention, 2006-2008.

Table 4	Prevalence of Obesity by Race/Ethinicity and State (percent of adult population)						
STATE	NON-HISPANIC WHITE	NON-HISPANIC BLACK	HISPANIC	NON-HISPANIC ASIAN	NON-HISPANIC HAWAIIAN/ PACIFIC ISLANDER	NON-HISPANIC AMERICAN INDIAN OR ALASKAN NATIVE	NON-HISPANIC MULTIRACIAL
Alabama	28.2%	41.1%	32.5%	—	—	28.8%	24.9%
Alaska	26.2%	—	25.6%	14.0%	—	35.0%	26.6%
Arizona	22.4%	32.9%	32.0%	11.0%	—	34.8%	31.3%
Arkansas	27.7%	38.2%	25.8%	—	—	28.0%	37.5%
California	21.1%	36.7%	29.3%	6.6%	13.4%	28.6%	26.2%
Colorado	17.1%	26.7%	26.0%	7.5%	—	28.8%	23.9%
Connecticut	20.7%	31.7%	24.1%	7.3%	—	—	40.9%
Delaware	25.5%	40.2%	28.2%	9.5%	—	—	28.4%
Florida	21.8%	35.9%	26.9%	9.7%	—	29.7%	30.0%
Georgia	24.7%	37.4%	24.6%	8.1%	—	25.6%	34.1%
Hawaii	18.3%	24.0%	28.3%	12.6%	56.1%	—	32.7%
Idaho	24.6%	—	25.8%	—	—	38.1%	34.4%
Illinois	24.5%	34.0%	30.1%	7.2%	—	—	19.8%
Indiana	27.2%	36.7%	22.7%	—	—	—	30.8%
Iowa	26.6%	36.1%	26.6%	—	—	—	—
Kansas	26.6%	42.6%	31.2%	6.9%	—	36.7%	30.7%
Kentucky	28.4%	40.5%	25.4%	—	—	22.3%	35.4%
Louisiana	26.1%	36.8%	25.1%	—	—	31.3%	30.9%
Maine	24.6%	—	24.8%	—	—	33.6%	30.9%
Maryland	23.8%	35.2%	20.0%	11.3%	—	29.6%	27.6%
Massachusetts	20.8%	30.1%	26.4%	4.0%	—	32.3%	23.9%
Michigan	27.4%	38.0%	29.4%	9.0%	—	44.3%	35.7%
Minnesota	25.4%	28.4%	28.0%	11.5%	—	—	—
Mississippi	28.2%	41.0%	26.3%	—	—	—	46.5%
Missouri	27.3%	37.2%	29.2%	—	—	39.8%	32.3%
Montana	21.9%	—	21.4%	—	—	37.4%	29.4%
Nebraska	26.6%	37.0%	25.5%	7.9%	—	35.8%	35.7%
Nevada	24.2%	27.4%	28.3%	9.0%	—	37.1%	27.9%
New Hampshire	24.1%	—	32.2%	5.9%	—	33.6%	32.5%
New Jersey	23.0%	34.1%	24.3%	8.3%	—	20.5%	21.9%
New Mexico	20.2%	39.2%	28.8%	7.9%	—	34.7%	25.9%
New York	24.0%	31.4%	27.0%	5.3%	—	24.6%	25.3%
North Carolina	25.9%	40.0%	25.3%	4.3%	—	36.0%	35.5%
North Dakota	25.8%	—	35.5%	—	—	45.4%	—
Ohio	27.7%	43.1%	24.4%	5.4%	—	34.3%	24.8%
Oklahoma	28.2%	33.4%	31.8%	9.6%	—	36.6%	33.6%
Oregon	25.5%	—	23.2%	10.8%	—	29.4%	29.5%
Pennsylvania	25.9%	37.0%	31.0%	6.4%	—	31.1%	31.7%
Rhode Island	21.1%	27.7%	25.6%	12.2%	—	—	—
South Carolina	26.1%	40.1%	28.4%	6.5%	—	43.4%	27.5%
South Dakota	26.2%	—	27.7%	—	—	39.8%	26.2%
Tennessee	28.2%	40.3%	40.9%	—	—	—	31.4%
Texas	24.7%	39.2%	31.8%	8.7%	—	31.6%	30.9%
Utah	22.5%	—	20.5%	8.2%	—	27.2%	32.9%
Vermont	22.1%	—	22.6%	—	—	24.6%	29.1%
Virginia	24.8%	35.9%	24.2%	5.8%	—	30.6%	28.7%
Washington	25.2%	29.1%	29.5%	7.8%	30.4%	39.3%	30.2%
West Virginia	31.1%	35.9%	28.7%	—	—	—	35.4%
Wisconsin	25.4%	37.9%	26.4%	—	—	36.7%	32.0%
Wyoming	23.6%	—	28.9%	—	—	37.4 %	32.8%
United States	24.7%	36.8%	28.4%	7.6%	19.5%	32.8%	29.3%
District of Columbia	9.4%	34.0%	19.7%	5.6%	—	—	20.7%

Source: Centers for Disease Control and Prevention (CDC). Behavioral Risk Factor Surveillance System Survey Data. Atlanta, Georgia: U.S. Department of Health and Human Services, Centers for Disease Control and Prevention, 2006-2008. Note: Differences between groups may be more or less than shown because of variations in the correctioness of self-report data varies by ethinic and racial groups[2].

[2.]S.Yun et. al, A comparison of national estimates of obestiy prevalence from the behavioral risk factor surveillance systems and the national health and nutrition examination survey. *International Journal of Obesity*, 2006, pg 164-170.

Table 5	Prevalence of Diabetes by Race/Ethnicity and State (percent of adult population)						
STATE	NON-HISPANIC WHITE	NON-HISPANIC BLACK	HISPANIC	NON-HISPANIC ASIAN	NON-HISPANIC HAWAIIAN/ PACIFIC ISLANDER	NON-HISPANIC AMERICAN INDIAN OR ALASKAN NATIVE	NON-HISPANIC MULTIRACIAL
Alabama	9.6%	12.9%	12.0%	—	—	—	12.2%
Alaska	5.9%	—	8.6%	5.8%	—	7.2%	3.5%
Arizona	7.6%	13.1%	9.7%	2.8%	—	15.0%	—
Arkansas	8.8%	10.9%	5.5%	—	—	12.6%	12.5%
California	6.9%	14.2%	8.8%	7.4%	—	15.6%	8.1%
Colorado	4.8%	11.1%	7.4%	—	—	9.9%	6.3%
Connecticut	6.4%	13.9%	7.1%	5.2%	—	—	9.6%
Delaware	8.2%	10.7%	4.6%	6.0%	—	—	—
Florida	8.6%	12.5%	7.9%	6.7%	—	15.8%	13.8%
Georgia	8.5%	12.4%	10.1%	8.9%	—	10.2%	9.0%
Hawaii	4.6%	—	8.0%	9.5%	11.1%	—	8.8%
Idaho	7.2%	—	5.8%	—	—	—	16.9%
Illinois	7.3%	14.6%	7.8%	7.1%	—	—	9.2%
Indiana	8.4%	12.9%	7.7%	—	—	—	11.9%
Iowa	7.1%	9.5%	4.6%	—	—	—	—
Kansas	7.4%	10.9%	7.2%	5.8%	—	16.7%	6.7%
Kentucky	9.6%	13.1%	—	—	—	14.1%	14.2%
Louisiana	8.9%	12.9%	8.0%	—	—	—	11.3%
Maine	7.7%	—	6.1%	—	—	10.8%	9.9%
Maryland	7.5%	11.4%	5.3%	7.1%	—	6.6%	6.2%
Massachusetts	6.5%	10.9%	9.1%	5.3%	—	14.5%	6.5%
Michigan	8.1%	13.4%	8.8%	—	—	—	12.1%
Minnesota	5.8%	5.0%	5.6%	—	—	—	—
Mississippi	10.0%	13.5%	5.8%	—	—	—	8.0%
Missouri	7.9%	9.3%	—	—	—	12.3%	13.3%
Montana	6.1%	—	6.8%	—	—	12.2%	10.2%
Nebraska	7.4%	10.4%	6.9%	4.1%	—	8.1%	8.1%
Nevada	8.6%	11.5%	5.1%	8.6%	—	—	10.3%
New Hampshire	7.2%	—	11.5%	5.8%	—	9.5%	10.3%
New Jersey	7.4%	13.6%	8.9%	6.0%	—	15.7%	—
New Mexico	6.1%	—	9.2%	8.2%	—	11.3%	8.3%
New York	7.6%	11.5%	7.0%	5.7%	—	12.5%	—
North Carolina	8.5%	14.3%	4.5%	4.4%	—	12.2%	10.5%
North Dakota	6.5%	—	8.9%	—	—	12.8%	—
Ohio	8.1%	14.4%	8.8%	—	—	12.6%	11.2%
Oklahoma	9.0%	13.5%	8.0%	—	—	17.1%	13.3%
Oregon	6.8%	14.6%	4.4%	5.1%	—	—	9.3%
Pennsylvania	8.0%	14.4%	8.0%	2.4%	—	—	13.1%
Rhode Island	7.0%	13.2%	9.0%	—	—	—	—
South Carolina	8.4%	13.1%	7.8%	4.7%	—	13.3%	11.0%
South Dakota	6.3%	—	3.7%	—	—	12.6%	4.9%
Tennessee	11.0%	12.7%	2.6%	—	—	—	—
Texas	8.1%	12.2%	10.6%	5.7%	—	—	13.2%
Utah	5.8%	—	5.6%	2.8%	—	13.0%	10.4%
Vermont	6.2%	—	13.8%	—	—	11.8%	8.4%
Virginia	7.0%	14.9%	4.7%	5.3%	—	10.3%	—
Washington	7.0%	8.0%	6.0%	5.8%	6.2%	10.8%	8.5%
West Virginia	11.6%	11.1%	10.0%	—	—	—	16.5%
Wisconsin	6.2%	12.6%	5.4%	—	—	11.7%	6.5%
Wyoming	6.6%	—	9.2%	—	—	—	12.1%
United States	7.7%	12.8%	8.8%	6.6%	7.2%	13.1%	10.1%
District of Columbia	2.4%	13.3%	4.8%	3.1%	—	—	—

Source: Centers for Disease Control and Prevention (CDC). Behavioral Risk Factor Surveillance System Survey Data. Atlanta, Georgia: U.S. Department of Health and Human Services, Centers for Disease Control and Prevention, 2006-2008.

Table 6	Mortality by Race/Ethnicity and State (deaths per 100,000 population, age adjusted)				
STATE	WHITE*	BLACK*	ASIAN*	AMERICAN INDIAN OR ALASKAN NATIVE*	HISPANIC**
Alabama	950.9	1147.2	349.5	323.2	313.7
Alaska	735.2	710.2	458.6	1054.4	468.5
Arizona	750.1	861.9	373.8	844.9	690.1
Arkansas	897.4	1141.9	394.7	349.7	326.9
California	753.1	1014.9	466.7	421.3	588.0
Colorado	748.5	835.3	431.8	497.1	715.4
Connecticut	739.8	835.9	337.7	413.7	563.3
Delaware	811.0	995.1	313.9	617.6	582.1
Florida	728.9	945.4	325.4	303.8	586.1
Georgia	863.7	1028.2	380.2	681.9	308.2
Hawaii	692.3	431.2	639.3	362.4	1104.8
Idaho	776.0	493.3	419.3	819.3	581.5
Illinois	788.7	1083.1	379.3	247.0	467.2
Indiana	862.0	1069.4	341.5	190.5	455.9
Iowa	755.0	1000.9	370.3	615.9	404.5
Kansas	803.9	1125.9	379.9	1125.7	542.0
Kentucky	941.6	1075.2	388.0	197.8	570.0
Louisiana	931.1	1199.6	456.8	332.3	378.5
Maine	822.1	554.0	376.9	1218.4	306.5
Maryland	786.7	994.0	391.5	409.5	345.1
Massachusetts	760.2	818.4	369.3	362.0	484.3
Michigan	810.7	1084.2	383.8	977.5	714.6
Minnesota	697.3	864.7	522.3	1045.4	405.5
Mississippi	937.8	1145.4	489.4	749.5	253.3
Missouri	855.3	1116.9	423.8	435.3	556.6
Montana	784.3	605.6	405.9	1196.9	574.1
Nebraska	752.1	1016.2	431.5	1173.9	508.5
Nevada	905.4	946.7	481.7	674.5	474.7
New Hampshire	769.1	520.5	304.4	—	328.1
New Jersey	765.5	979.2	357.6	403.9	480.9
New Mexico	795.4	741.5	322.3	802.6	769.2
New York	744.0	802.0	386.1	263.8	576.3
North Carolina	839.7	1056.9	369.8	880.3	266.3
North Dakota	711.3	603.1	—	1343.8	216.7
Ohio	856.7	1093.4	320.1	202.3	469.7
Oklahoma	943.9	1135.1	447.9	929.2	516.8
Oregon	804.7	880.2	464.8	797.0	436.7
Pennsylvania	823.8	1083.9	358.8	279.0	526.9
Rhode Island	786.3	875.0	421.7	647.1	416.7
South Carolina	848.4	1071.2	403.0	443.0	413.6
South Dakota	719.0	832.6	487.2	1417.4	413.4
Tennessee	918.9	1139.6	409.3	302.0	294.2
Texas	807.0	1053.0	402.0	188.5	674.7
Utah	742.5	778.8	528.3	705.4	552.1
Vermont	757.6	587.0	—	—	191.6
Virginia	791.6	1012.4	421.6	292.6	387.2
Washington	764.2	882.9	480.0	902.6	473.3
West Virginia	976.9	1057.4	149.2	—	218.2
Wisconsin	759.3	1075.9	476.3	1085.9	384.8
Wyoming	816.3	830.6	350.9	982.4	711.0
United States	797.0	1022.2	446.9	656.0	590.2
District of Columbia	592.4	1162.7	439.9	315.7	248.7

* Includes both Hispanic and non-Hispanic ethnicities
** Includes all races

Source: Centers for Disease Control and Prevention, National Center for Health Statistics. Compressed Mortality File, CDC WONDER, 2004-2006

Table 7	International Comparisons	
LOCATION	HEALTHY LIFE EXPECTANCY* (HALE) AT BIRTH (YEARS)	INFANT MORTALITY RATE* (DEATHS BETWEEN BIRTH AND AGE 1 PER 1,000 LIVE BIRTHS)
Japan	76	3
San Marino	75	2
Switzerland	75	4
Iceland	74	2
Sweden	74	2
Andorra	74	3
Italy	74	3
Spain	74	4
Australia	74	5
Singapore	73	2
France	73	3
Luxembourg	73	3
Ireland	73	3
Norway	73	3
Monaco	73	4
Germany	73	4
Israel	73	4
Netherlands	73	4
Canada	73	5
New Zealand	73	5
Finland	72	3
Austria	72	4
Belgium	72	4
Greece	72	4
Denmark	72	4
Malta	72	5
United Kingdom	72	5
Slovenia	71	3
Portugal	71	3
Republic of Korea	71	4
Czech Republic	70	3
Cyprus	70	3
United States of America	70	6
Chile	70	8
Cuba	69	5
Kuwait	69	9
Costa Rica	69	10

Source: World Health Statistics, 2009, World Health Organization, Geneva, Switzerland

mortality rate from disease amenable to care more rapidly than the United States. All now have better rates than the U.S.[3]

Equally discouraging are results from a UNICEF study of child well-being, in which the U.S. ranked second to last when compared to 21 comparably "rich" countries based on 40 different measures. When UNICEF looked specifically at child health aspects of well-being, the United States fared very poorly due to a high infant mortality rate, a high percentage of low birth weight infants and only an average rate of immunization coverage.[4]

The Commonwealth Fund rates the U.S. last in health care system performance when compared to a group of six countries that include Australia, Canada, Germany, New Zealand and the United Kingdom. The U.S. spends twice as much as these six countries on a per-capita basis, yet it is last on dimensions of access, patient safety, efficiency and equity[5], while the U.S. is spending more on total health care when compared to other countries, the country is getting less access, patient safety, efficiency and equity.

The results of these studies should be a wake-up call to everyone in the United States to strive to improve all aspects of our health system however possible, including education, prevention and clinical care. Other countries have improved their overall health by improving their health care system, indicating that we too can do the same.

CHANGES FROM 1990

National

The 20-year perspective provided by this report allows us to view health over time. During the past 20 years, this report has tracked our nation's 20.1 percent improvement in overall health (Graph 2). This national success stems from improvements in the reduction of infant mortality, infectious disease, prevalence of smoking, cardiovascular deaths, violent crime and children in poverty, and an increase in immunization coverage (Table 8). However, success has

eluded us in two very significant measures—the rapid increases in both the prevalence of obesity and the rate of uninsured population. In addition, the high school graduation rate remains relatively stagnant with fewer than three of four incoming freshmen graduating within four years.

Graph 2 shows that the rate of improvement experienced in the health of the United States' population occurred in two phases. During the 1990s, annual improvement in health was 1.5 percent per year on average. During this decade, the annual improvement in health has been 0.4 percent per year. Special concern surrounds the decline in health determinants, as those measures point to the future health of the population.

The United States has the potential to return to the rates of improvement typical in the 1990s. However, to do so, it must address the drivers of declining health more directly while focusing on reducing important risk factors. For example, the prevalence of smoking has been stagnant for many years and only just recently started to show improvement, declining from 19.8 percent in 2008 to 18.3 percent in 2009, the lowest level in 20 years.

Unprecedented and unchecked growth in the prevalence of obesity has also dramatically affected the overall health of the United States. The prevalence of obesity has increased 129 percent from 11.6 percent of the in 1990 to 26.6 percent of the population in 2009. Now, more than one in four people in the U.S. is considered obese—a category that the Centers for Disease Control and Prevention reserves for those who are significantly over the suggested body weight given their height. This alarming rate of increase shows little evidence of slowing or abating (Graph 4). These very high obesity rates are gathered from the Behavioral Risk Factor Surveillance System, the nation's largest phone survey about health, and rely on selfreported height and weight. Actual obesity rates, as measured by health professionals, may be almost 10 percent higher, meaning that over one-third of the population is now obese.[6]

Lack of health insurance coverage increased from 13.9 percent in 2001 to 15.3 percent of the population in 2009 (Graph 5). Lack of health insurance not only inhibits people from getting the proper care when needed but also reduces access to necessary preventive care to curtail or minimize future illnesses.

3. Nolte, Ellen and McKee, C. Martin, Measuring the Health of Nations: Updating an Earlier Analysis, Health Affairs, 27, No 1 (2006): 58-71 http://content.healthaffairs.org/cgi/content/abstract/27/1/58.

4. "UNICEF, Child poverty in perspective: An overview of child well-being in rich countries, Innocents Report Card 7" 2007, UNICEF Innocenti Research Centre, Florence, http://www.unicef-irc.org.

5. Davis, K. et. al. Mirror, Mirror on the Wall: An International Update on the Comparative Performance of American Health Care, The Commonwealth Fund, May 2007. www.common wealthfund.org http://content.healthaffairs.org/cgi/content/abstract/hlthaff.25.w457.

6. Yun, S. et. al. A comparison of national estimates of obesity prevalence from the behavioral risk factor surveillance system and the national health and nutrition examination survey, *International Journal of Obesity* (2006) 30, 164–170.

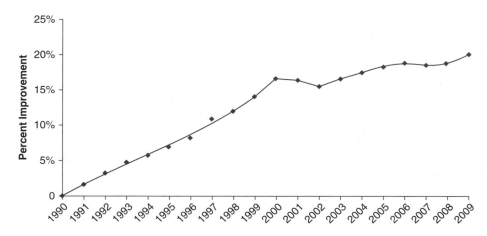

Graph 2 Improvements since 1990

Table 8	National Measures of Successes and Challenges: Long Term

MEASURE	EDITION TO EDITION CHANGES
Successes	
Infectious Disease	53 percent decrease in the incidence of infectious disease from 40.7 cases in 1990 to 19.1 cases per 100,000 population in 2009.
Infant Mortality	33 percent decrease in the infant mortality rate from 10.2 deaths in 1990 to 6.8 deaths per 1,000 live births in 2009.
Prevalence of Smoking	38 percent decline in the prevalence of smoking from 29.5 percent in 1990 to 18.3 percent of the population in 2009.
Violent Crime	25 percent decline in the violent crime rate from 609 offenses in1990 to 455 offenses per 100,000 population in 2009.
Cardiovascular Deaths	29 percent decline in the rate of deaths from cardiovascular disease from 405.1 deaths in 1990 to 287.9 deaths per 100,000 population in 2009.
Children in Poverty	8 percent decline in the percentage of children in poverty from 20.6 percent in 1990 to 19.0 percent of persons under age 18 in 2009.
Immunization Coverage	42 percent increase in immunization coverage from 55.1 percent in 1999 to 78.2 percent of children ages 19 to 35 months receiving complete immunizations in 2009.
Premature Death	14 percent decline from 8,716 years of potential life lost before age 75 per 100,000 population in 1990 to 7,511 years of potential life lost before age 75 per 100,000 population in 2009.
Air Pollution	The average amount of fine particulate in the air continues to decline from 13.2 micrograms in 2003 to 11.7 micrograms per cubic meter in 2009.
Challenges	
Prevalence of Obesity	129 percent increase in the prevalence of obesity from 11.6 percent in 1990 to 26.6 percent of the population in 2009.
Lack of Health Insurance	14 percent increase in the rate of uninsured population from 13.4 percent in 1990 to15.3 percent in 2009.
High School Graduation Rate	The high school graduation rate continues to remain around 73 percent of incoming freshman that graduate within four years.
Poor Mental Health Days	In the last eight years, the number of poor mental health days per month has stagnated at 3.4 days in the previous 30 days.
Poor Physical Health Days	In the last six years, the number of poor physical health days per month has stagnated at 3.6 days in the previous 30 days.
Prenatal Care	Adequate prenatal care is available to only about 70 percent of pregnant women.

Source: World Health Statistics, 2009, World Health Organization, Geneva, Switzerland.

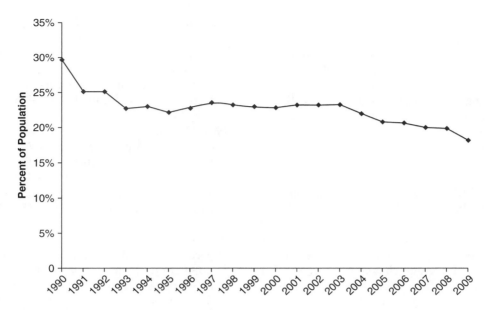

Graph 3 Prevalence of Smoking since 1990

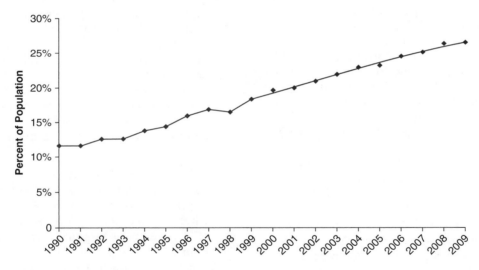

Graph 4 Prevalence of Obesity since 1990

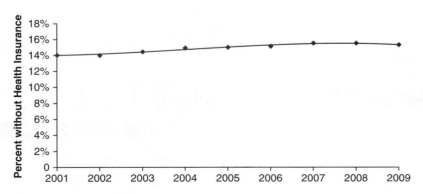

Graph 5 Lack of Health Insurance since 2001

High school graduation, poor mental health days and poor physical health days have had minimal improvement in the last decade and restrict more significant improvements in health.

While there have been improvements since 1990, these worsening influences have caused and will continue to cause slower rates of improvement than experienced in the 1990s.

States

All states except Oklahoma show a positive change in overall score between 1990 and 2009. New York, Vermont, Hawaii, New Hampshire, New Jersey and Minnesota have improved 32.5 percent or more overall since the 1990 Edition, or 12 percent more than the national average change in score of 20.1 percent (Table 9). Twenty-three states in total have exceeded the national rate of improvement.

The principal reasons for the changes in these states from 1990 to 2009 are:

New York: The violent crime rate dropped by 60 percent from 1,007 to 398 offenses per 100,000 population, the infant mortality rate declined from 10.7 to 5.7 deaths per 1,000 live births and the prevalence of smoking declined from 28.7 percent to 16.7 percent of the population. In the last ten years, immunization coverage increased from 62.6 percent to 76.2 percent of children ages 19 to 35 months receiving complete immunizations.

Vermont: The prevalence of smoking decreased by 46 percent from 30.7 percent to 16.7 percent of the population and the percentage of children in poverty declined by 39 percent from 15.9 percent to 9.8 percent of persons under age 18. In the last ten years, immunization coverage increased from 55.8 percent to 74.4 percent of children ages 19 to 35 months receiving complete immunizations.

Hawaii: The prevalence of smoking decreased by 44 percent from 27.6 percent to 15.4 percent of the population and the infant mortality rate declined from 9.1 to 6.0 deaths per 1,000 live births. In the last ten years, the incidence of infectious disease declined from 47.5 to 17.6 cases per 100,000 population.

New Hampshire: The prevalence of smoking decreased by 45 percent from 30.7 percent to 17.0 percent of the population, the infant mortality rate from 8.4 to 5.7 deaths per 1,000 live births and the rate of deaths from cardiovascular disease decreased from 392.3 to 255.4 deaths per 100,000 population.

New Jersey: The violent crime rate declined by 40 percent from 541 to 327 offenses per 100,000 population, the prevalence of smoking decreased by 47 percent from 27.9 percent to 14.7 percent of the population and the infant mortality rate declined by 44 percent from 9.6 to 5.4 deaths per 1,000 live births.

Minnesota: The prevalence of smoking decreased by 39 percent from 28.7 percent to 17.5 percent of the population, the infant mortality rate declined from 8.9 to 5.1 deaths per 1,000 live births and the percentage of children in poverty decreased from 21.2 percent to 15.6 percent of persons under age 18. In the last ten years, immunization coverage increased from 41.2 percent to 77.4 percent of children ages 19 to 35 months receiving complete immunizations.

Twenty-seven states are below the national rate of improvement and are slipping further behind in healthiness when compared to the nation as a whole. Oklahoma has declined 2.7 percent since 1990 while West Virginia, Mississippi and Kentucky have improved by less than 7 percent compared to the 20.1 percent improvement in the U.S. on average (Table 10).

The principal reasons for changes in these states from 1990 to 2009 are:

Oklahoma: The prevalence of obesity surged from 11.6 percent in 1990 to 30.9 percent of the pop-

Table 9	States with the Greatest Overall Health Score Improvement 1990 to 2009

STATE	CHANGE IN SCORE
New York	+37.5
Vermont	+36.5
Hawaii	+35.0
New Hampshire	+34.8
New Jersey	+32.5
Minnesota	+32.5

Table 10	States with the Least Overall Health Score Improvement 1990 to 2009

STATE	CHANGE IN SCORE
Oklahoma	−2.7
West Virginia	+3.9
Mississippi	+6.2
Kentucky	+6.7

ulation in 2009. The percentage of children in poverty increased from 17.7 percent to 21.8 percent of persons under age 18 and the violent crime rate increased from 419 to 527 offenses per 100,000 population.

West Virginia: The prevalence of smoking declined less rapidly in West Virginia than other states, declining from 34.0 percent to 26.5 percent of the population, and is now ranked 50th in the country. The violent crime rate increased by 98 percent from 138 to 274 offenses per 100,000 population.

Mississippi: Infant mortality rates continue to stay high in Mississippi at 11.0 deaths per 1,000 live births, the highest in the nation. Improvements in the prevalence of smoking are slower than in other states and the prevalence of obesity continues to rise rapidly with one-third of the population now considered obese.

Kentucky: The percentage of children in poverty increased slightly from 23.7 percent in 1990 to 24.4 percent of persons under age 18 in 2009. The prevalence of smoking and the violent crime rate both improved since 1990, but at a much slower rate than in other states.

The changes in scores and rankings for all 50 states since the 1990 Edition of *America's Health Rankings*™ are at www.americashealthrankings. org/2009/1990state.aspx. States that have changed less than 20.1 percent are not improving as quickly as the nation as a whole.

CHANGES FROM 2008

National

Since the 2008 Edition, overall health in the United States has increased slightly from 18.9 percent to 20.1 percent above the 1990 baseline. This increase is primarily due to a decline in the prevalence of smoking, a significant decline from 19.8 percent to 18.3 percent of the population.

Table 11 shows the national changes in the last year. In addition to a decrease in the prevalence of smoking, other improvements included decreases in the occupational fatalities rate, the rate of deaths from cardiovascular disease and the incidence of infectious disease, and an increase in per capita public health funding. These improvements were offset by a deterioration in several measures, including an increase in the prevalence of obesity from 26.3 percent to 26.6 percent of the population, an increase in the percentage of children in poverty from 18.0 percent to 19.0 percent of persons under age 18 and a decrease in the high school graduation rate from 74.7 percent to 73.4 percent of incoming ninth graders who graduate within four years.

States

Comparisons of state scores for these two years indicate that 34 states had positive changes in their overall scores on health, 14 states experienced declines and two did not change. The largest positive increases were in Mississippi, Louisiana, Utah and Oregon, all of which increased by 3.0 points or more (Table 12).

The principal reasons for the changes in these states are:

Mississippi: The percentage of children in poverty declined from 32.8 percent to 23.5 percent of persons under age 18 and the rate of preventable hospitalizations also declined from 109.8 to 101.3 discharges per 1,000 Medicare enrollees.

Louisiana: The violent crime rate decreased by 10 percent from 730 to 656 offenses per 100,000

Table 11	National Measures of Successes and Challenges: 2008 to 2009
MEASURE	**EDITION TO EDITION CHANGES**
Successes	
Prevalence of Smoking	Decreased from 19.8 percent to 18.3 percent of the population.
Occupational Fatalities	Decreased from 5.2 to 4.8 deaths per 100,000 workers.
Infectious Disease	Decreased from 20.1 to 19.1 cases per 100,000 population.
Cardiovascular Deaths	Decreased from 298.2 to 287.9 deaths per 100,000 population.
Public Health Funding	Increased from $88 to $94 per person.
Challenges	
Prevalence of Obesity	Increased from 26.3 percent to 26.6 percent of the population who are obese.
Children in Poverty	Increased from 18.0 percent to 19.0 percent of persons under age 18.
High School Graduation	Decreased from 74.7 percent to 73.4 percent of incoming ninth graders who graduate within four years.

Table 12	States with the Greatest Overall Health Score Improvement: 2008 to 2009
STATE	**CHANGE IN SCORE**
Mississippi	+4.7
Louisiana	+4.0
Utah	+3.6
Oregon	+3.0

population and the levels of air pollution declined by 8 percent from 12.3 to 11.3 micrograms of fine particulate per cubic meter of air. Immunization coverage increased by 7 percent from 77.7 percent to 83.0 percent of children ages 19 to 35 months receiving complete immunizations.

Utah: The percentage of children in poverty declined from 12.6 percent to 8.8 percent of persons under age 18, the rate of preventable hospitalizations also declined from 46.8 to 43.5 discharges per 1,000 Medicare enrollees, and the rate of deaths from cardiovascular disease decreased from 243.2 to 230.8 deaths per 100,000 population.

Oregon: Air pollution declined by 5 percent from 8.5 to 8.1 micrograms of fine particulate per cubic meter of air, the rate of preventable hospitalizations also declined from 51.2 to 46.6 discharges per 1,000 Medicare enrollees, and the rate of deaths from cardiovascular disease decreased from 265.1 to 254.6 deaths per 100,000 population.

No state declined by 3 points or more in the last year.

The comparisons of scores and rankings between 2008 and 2009 are shown at www.americashealthrankings.org/2009/2008state.aspx.

METHODOLOGY

The methodology underlying *America's Health Rankings*™ reflects the evolving expectations and role of health in our society and our ability to measure various aspects of health. This year, the methodology was revised to better capture and reflect the variation in health metrics among the states. All prior editions have been recalculated to reflect the new methodology such that the 20-year history can be maintained to provide a resource for tracking and evaluating progress. All years of data are available at www.americashealthrankings.org.

For each measure, the raw data as obtained from the stated sources and adjusted for age as appropriate is presented and referred to as "value." All age-adjusted data utilizes the population profile for the middle year of data. For example, if the data is from 2006 to 2008, the standard population is set at 2007.

The score for each state is based on the following formula. The score is stated as a decimal.

$$\text{SCORE} = \frac{\text{STATE VALUE} - \text{NATIONAL MEAN}}{(\text{STANDARD DEVIATION OF ALL STATE VALUES})}$$

Often referred to as a "Z-score," this score indicates the number of standard deviations a state is above or below the national mean. This results in a score of 0.00 for a state with the same value as the national mean. States that have a higher value than the national average will have a positive score while those with lower values will have a negative score. Scores are calculated to three decimal places and, to prevent an extreme value from excessively influencing a final score, the maximum score any state could receive for a measure is plus or minus 2.

Confidence intervals, where available, are presented in the online version of the tables and calculated according to the description for each metric. Confidence intervals are presented at a 95 percent confidence level unless indicated otherwise.

For several measures, such as Infant Mortality and Infectious Disease, the data from multiple years are combined to provide sufficient sample size to be meaningful.

Where a value for the United States overall is not available, the national average is set at the average value of the states and the District of Columbia.

The overall score was calculated by adding the scores of each measure multiplied by its weight or the percent of total overall ranking. (Note: Scores reported for individual measures may not add up to the overall scores due to the rounding of numbers.)

The ranking is the ordering of each state according to value. Ties in scores are assigned equal rankings.

Overall comparisons to prior years, such as Changes from 1990, are based upon the relative change in the values of a measure compared to the national average for each measure. The overall result is the weighted sum of these variations. The change between years is the summation of all changes between those years for the components included in the models used for the years of interest.

All earlier results have been revised to correct any errors discovered since the release of prior editions. Because of the new methodology, scores in this edition are not comparable to scores presented in prior editions and overall ranks presented in this edition are not comparable to overall ranks in prior printed editions. However, all prior editions have been recalculated and are presented online at www.americashealthrankings.org.

MEASURES

Selection of Measures

Four primary considerations drove the design of *America's Health Rankings*™ and the selection of the individual measures:

1. The overall rankings had to represent a broad range of issues that affect a population's health,
2. Individual measures needed to use common health measurement criteria,
3. Data had to be available at a state level, and
4. Data had to be current and updated periodically.

While not perfect, the measures selected are believed to be the best available indicators of the various aspects of healthiness at this time and are consistent with past reports.

The Scientific Advisory Committee suggested that the measures be divided into two categories—Determinants and Outcomes. For further clarity, determinants are divided into four groups: Behaviors, Community and Environment, Public and Health Policies, and Clinical Care. These four groups of measures influence the health outcomes of the population in a state, and improving these inputs will improve outcomes over time. Most measures are actually a combination of activities in all four groups. For example, the prevalence of smoking is a behavior that is strongly influenced by the community and environment in which we live, by public policy, including taxation and restrictions on smoking in public places and by the care received to treat the chemical and behavioral addictions associated with tobacco. However, for simplicity, we placed each measure in a single category.

For *America's Health Rankings*™ to continue to meet its objectives, it must evolve and incorporate new information as it becomes available. The Scientific Advisory Committee provides guidance for the evolution of the rankings, balancing the need to change with the desire for longitudinal comparability. Over the last few years, change is being driven by:

(1) the acknowledgment that health is more than years lived but also includes the quality of those years; (2) data about the quality and cost of health care delivery are becoming available on a comparative basis; and (3) measurement of the additional determinants of health are being initiated and/or improved. The committee also emphasizes that the real impact on health will be made by addressing the health determinants, and making improvements on these items will affect the long-term health of the population. The determinants are the predictors of our future health.

Health outcomes are traditionally measured using mortality measures including premature death, infant mortality, cancer and cardiovascular mortality. While these measures overlap significantly, they do present different views of mortality outcomes of the population. Two measures of the quality of life—poor mental health days and poor physical health days—are also included and defined as the number of days in the previous 30 days when a person indicates their activities are limited due to mental or physical health difficulties. Disparity in health outcomes is now explicitly captured in the Geographic Disparity measure.

As with all indices, the positive and negative aspects of each measure must be weighed when choosing and developing them. These aspects for consideration include: (1) the interdependence of the different measures; (2) the possibility of the overall ranking disguising the effects of individual measures; (3) an inability to adjust all data by age and race; (4) an overreliance on mortality data; and (5) the use of indirect measures to estimate some effects on health. These concerns cannot be addressed directly by adjusting the methodology; however, assigning weights to the individual measures can mitigate their impact (Table 17).

Each measure is assigned a weight that determines its percentage of the overall score. Determinants account for 75 percent of the overall ranking and outcomes account for 25 percent, a shift from the 50/50 balance in the original 1990 index. This reflects the importance and growing availability of determinant measures.

Description of Measures

Table 13 is a summary of each of the measures in *America's Health Rankings*™. The table includes the core measures included in the current model, plus supplemental measures that can be used to further understand the situation. The supplemental measures are more fully described at www.americas healthrankings.org/measure.aspx.

Table 13 Summary Description of Measures CORE MEASURES

Core Measures

DETERMINANTS	DESCRIPTION
Behaviors	
Prevalence of Smoking	Percentage of population over age 18 that smokes on a regular basis. This is an indication of known, addictive, health-adverse behaviors within the population. (www.americashealthrankings.org/measure/2009/smoking.aspx)
Prevalence of Binge Drinking	Percentage of population over age 18 that has drunk excessively in the last 30 days. Binge drinking is defined as 5 drinks for a male and 4 for a female in one setting. It is a proxy indicator for excessive drug and alcohol use within a population. (www.americashealthrankings.org/measure/2009/binge.aspx)
Prevalence of Obesity	Percentage of the population estimated to be obese, with a body mass index (BMI) of 30.0 or higher. Obesity is known to contribute to a variety of diseases, including heart disease, diabetes and general poor health. (www.americashealthrankings.org/measure/2009/obesity.aspx)
High School Graduation	Percentage of incoming ninth graders who graduate in four years from a high school with a regular degree, as reported by NCES in compliance with the No Child Left Behind initiative. It is an indication of the individual's ability to learn about, create and maintain a healthy lifestyle and to understand and access health care when required. (www.americashealthrankings.org/measure/2009/graduation.aspx)
Community & Environment	
Violent Crime	The number of murders, rapes, robberies and aggravated assaults per 100,000 population. It reflects an aspect of overall lifestyle within a state and its associated health risks. (www.americashealthrankings.org/measure/2009/crime.aspx)
Occupational Fatalities	Number of fatalities from occupational injuries per 100,000 workers. This measure reflects job safety as a part of public health. (www.americashealthrankings.org/measure/2009/WorkFatalities.aspx)
Infectious Disease	Number of AIDS, tuberculosis and hepatitis (A and B) cases reported to the Centers for Disease Control and Prevention per 100,000 population. This is an indication of the toll that infectious disease is placing on the population. (www.americashealthrankings.org/measure/2009/disease.aspx)
Children in Poverty	The percentage of persons under age 18 who live in households at or below the poverty threshold. Poverty is an indication of the lack of access to health care by this vulnerable population. (www.americashealthrankings.org/measure/2009/ChildPoverty.aspx)
Air Pollution	The average exposure of the general public to particulate matter of 2.5 microns or less in size (PM2.5). Health studies have shown a significant association between exposure to fine particles and premature death from heart or lung disease. Fine particles can aggravate heart and lung diseases and have been linked to effects such as: cardiovascular symptoms; cardiac arrhythmias; heart attacks; respiratory symptoms; asthma attacks; and bronchitis. (www.americashealthrankings.org/measure/2009/air.aspx)

(continues)

Table 13   Summary Description of Measures CORE MEASURES (continued)

Core Measures

DETERMINANTS	DESCRIPTION
Public & Health Policies	
Lack of Health Insurance	Percentage of the population that does not have health insurance privately, through their employer or the government. This is an indicator of the ability to access care as needed, especially preventive care. (www.americashealthrankings.org/measure/2009/insurance.aspx)
Public Health Funding	State funding dedicated to public health as well as federal funding directed to states by the Centers for Disease Control and Prevention and the Health Resources and Services Administration, expressed on a per capita basis. This represents the annual investment being made in public health programs to monitor and improve population health. (www.americashealthrankings.org/measure/2009/PH_Spending.aspx)
Immunization Coverage	Percentage of children ages 19 to 35 months who have received four or more doses of DTP, three or more doses of poliovirus vaccine, one or more doses of any measles-containing vaccine, three or more doses of HiB, and three or more doses of HepB vaccine. (www.americashealthrankings.org/measure/2009/immunize.aspx)
Clinical Care	
Prenatal Care	Percentage of pregnant women receiving adequate prenatal care, as defined by Kotelchuck's Adequacy of Prenatal Care Utilization (APNCU) Index. This measures how well women are receiving the care they require for a healthy pregnancy and development of the fetus. (www.americashealthrankings.org/measure/2009/prenatal.aspx)
Primary Care Physicians	Number of primary care physicians (including general practice, family practice, OB-GYN, pediatrics and internal medicine) per 100,000 population. This measure reflects the availability of physicians to assist the population with preventive and regular care. (www.americashealthrankings.org/measure/2009/PCP.aspx)
Preventable Hospitalizations	Discharge rate among the Medicare population for diagnoses that are amenable to non-hospital based care. This reflects how well a population uses the various delivery sites for necessary care. (www.americashealthrankings.org/measure/2009/preventable.aspx)

(continues)

Table 13 Summary Description of Measures CORE MEASURES (continued)

Core Measures

OUTCOMES	DESCRIPTION
Poor Mental Health Days	Number of days in the previous 30 days when a person indicates their activities are limited due to mental health difficulties. This is a general indication of the population's ability to function on a day-to-day basis. (www.americashealthrankings.org/measure/2009/MentalDays.aspx)
Poor Physical Health Days	Number of days in the previous 30 days when a person indicates their activities are limited due to physical health difficulties. This is a general indication of the population's ability to function on a day-to-day basis. (www.americashealthrankings.org/measure/2009/PhysicalDays.aspx)
Geographic Disparity	The variation among the overall mortality rates among the counties within a state. Equality among counties would be expressed by low variation. This measure indicates how equal the outcomes are across a state. (www.americashealthrankings.org/measure/2009/disparity.aspx)
Infant Mortality	Number of infant deaths (before age 1) per 1,000 live births. This is an indication of the prenatal care, access and birth process for both child and mother. (www.americashealthrankings.org/measure/2009/IMR.aspx)
Cardiovascular Deaths	Number of deaths due to all cardiovascular diseases, including heart disease and strokes, per 100,000 population. This is an indication of the toll that these types of diseases place on the population. (www.americashealthrankings.org/measure/2009/CVD.aspx)
Cancer Deaths	Number of deaths due to all causes of cancer per 100,000 population. This is an indication of the toll cancer places on the population. (www.americashealthrankings.org/measure/2009/cancer.aspx)
Premature Death	Number of years of potential life lost prior to age 75 per 100,000 population. This is an indication of the number of useful years of life that are not available to a population due to early death. (www.americashealthrankings.org/measure/2009/PrematureDeath.aspx)

(continues)

Table 13   Summary Description of Measures CORE MEASURES (continued)

Supplemental Measures

DETERMINANTS	DESCRIPTION
Behaviors	
Cholesterol Check	Percentage of adults who have had their blood cholesterol checked within the last five years. (www.americashealthrankings.org/measure/2009/CholesterolTest.aspx)
Dental Visit	Percentage of adults who have visited the dentist or dental clinic within the past year for any reason. (www.americashealthrankings.org/measure/2009/dental.aspx)
Physical Activity	Percentage of adults who, during the past month, participated in any physical activities. (www.americashealthrankings.org/measure/2009/activity.aspx)
Teen Birth Rate	The number of births per 1,000 mothers age 15 to 19. (www.americashealthrankings.org/measure/2009/teenbirth.aspx)
Chronic Disease	
Cardiac Heart Disease	Percentage of adults who have been told by a health professional that they had angina or coronary heart disease. (www.americashealthrankings.org/measure/2009/Cardiac.aspx)
Diabetes	Percentage of adults who have been told by a health professional that they had diabetes(does not include pre-diabetes or diabetes during pregnancy). (www.americashealthrankings.org/measure/2009/diabetes.aspx)
High Cholesterol	Percentage of adults who have had their cholesterol checked and been told that it was high. (www.americashealthrankings.org/measure/2009/HighCholesterol.aspx)
Heart Attack	Percentage of adults who have been told by a health professional that they had a heart attack(myocardial infarction). (www.americashealthrankings.org/measure/2009/HeartAttack.aspx)
Stroke	Percentage of adults who have been told by a health professional that they had a stroke. (www.americashealthrankings.org/measure/2009/stroke.aspx)
Hypertension	Percentage of adults who have been told by a health professional that they had high blood pressure. (www.americashealthrankings.org/measure/2009/hypertension.aspx)
Economic	
Personal Income	Per capita personal income in current dollars.(www.americashealthrankings.org/measure/2009/income.aspx)
Unemployment Rate	Total unemployed as a percent of the civilian labor force (U-3 definition). This is the usual number cited by officials and in the media. The annual unemployment rate is at www.americashealthrankings.org/measure/2009/annual unemployment.aspx; the August 2009 unemployment rate, seasonally adjusted,is at www.americashealthrankings.org/measure/2009/augustunemployment.aspx.
Underemployment Rate	Total unemployed, plus all marginally attached workers, plus total employed part time for economic reasons, as a percent of the civilian labor force plus all marginally attached workers (U-6 Definition).This more comprehensive definition accounts for individuals that are not fully employed, are involuntarily working part time or have stopped looking for employment. (www.americashealthrankings.org/measure/2009/underemployment.aspx)
IncomeDisparity (Ginicoefficient)	A common measure of income in equality that varies between 0, which reflects complete equality of income and 1, which indicates complete inequality (one person has all the income or consumption, all others have none). (www.americashealthrankings.org/measure/2009/gini.aspx)

A short discussion of each measure immediately follows. The data for each year is the most current data available at the time the report was compiled.

The data tables are available at www.americas healthrankings.org/measure.aspx.

Determinants

Behaviors

Four measures reflect behaviors that are potentially modifiable through a combination of personal, community and clinical interventions: the prevalence of smoking, the prevalence of obesity, the percentage of the population that binge drinks and high school graduation. These items are determinants that measure behaviors and activities having an immediate or delayed effect on health and are prominently included in these rankings. However, the selection of these four does not imply that they are the only underlying behaviors that need to be addressed in a comprehensive public health effort. For example, the American Academy of Family Physicians suggests that to improve health, individuals should:

- Avoid any form of tobacco,
- Eat a healthy diet,
- Exercise regularly,
- Drink alcohol in moderation, if at all,
- Avoid use of illegal drugs,
- Practice safe sex,
- Use seat belts (and car seats for children) when riding in a car or truck,
- Avoid sunbathing and tanning booths,
- Keep immunizations up-to-date, and
- See a doctor regularly for preventive care.

Additional suggestions for individual initiatives are in *Healthy People in Healthy Communities, A Community Planning Guide Using Healthy People 2010*, published by the U.S. Department of Health and Human Services, Washington, D.C., available at http://www.healthypeople.gov/Publications/HealthyCommunities2001/ default.htm.

The impact of changing behaviors is huge. CDC estimates that if tobacco use, poor diet and physical inactivity were eliminated, 80 percent of heart disease and stroke, 80 percent of Type 2 diabetes and 40 percent of cancer would be prevented.[7]

Prevalence of Smoking measures the percent of the population over age 18 that smokes tobacco products regularly. The information is obtained from the Behavioral Risk Factor Surveillance System (BRFSS) and measures the percentage of the population that has smoked at least 100 cigarettes and currently smokes regularly.

The prevalence of smoking in the population has an adverse impact on overall health by causing increased cases of respiratory diseases, heart disease, stroke, cancer and other illnesses (http://www.cdc.gov/tobacco/). It is a lifestyle behavior that an individual can directly influence with support from the community and, as required, clinical intervention.

The 2009 ranks, based on 2008 data (Behavioral Risk Factor Surveillance System, Centers for Disease Control and Prevention), can be found at www.americashealthrankings.org/measure/2009/smoking.aspx. The national average is 18.3 percent of the population, a significant decrease of 1.5 percent from the rate last year. This means that over 40 million American adults smoke on a regular basis. Cigarette smoking is estimated to be responsible for about one in five deaths annually, or about 443,000 deaths per year.[8] The proportion of the population that smokes varies from a low of 9.3 percent in Utah to more than 25 percent in Kentucky, Indiana and West Virginia. The prevalence of smoking decreased significantly in Wyoming, from 22.1 percent to 19.3 percent of the population, and in Ohio, from 23.1 percent to 20.1 percent of the population. If all states were to accomplish a smoking rate equal to the best state (Utah), the number of smokers in the United States would be halved.

Since the 1990 Edition, the prevalence of smoking decreased in the United States by 11.2 percent. Rhode Island, Virginia, Maryland, Florida, Delaware and Vermont each lowered the prevalence of smoking since 1990 by 14 percent or more. Every state experienced a decrease since the 1990 Edition. Missouri had the smallest decrease in percentage of the population and continues to hover around one-quarter of the population smoking on a regular basis. Due to the limits of the BRFSS, caution must be used in comparing changes in prevalence of smoking in states with small populations.

Prevalence of Binge Drinking measures the percentage of the population who binge drink. Binge

---

[7.]Mensah, George A., Associate Director for Medical Affairs, CDC "Global and Domestic Health Priorities: Spotlight on Chronic Disease," National Business Group on Health Webinar, May 23, 2006.

[8.]Centers for Disease Control and Prevention. Smoking-Attributable Mortality, Years of Potential Life Lost, and Productivity Losses-United States, 2000-2004. *Morbidity and Mortality Weekly Report* [serial online]. 2008;57(45):1226-1228.

drinking is defined as males having five or more drinks and females having four or more drinks on one occasion. Binge drinking has an adverse effect on health due to increased injuries and deaths, increased aggression, damage to the fetus and liver diseases along with other health concerns (http://www.cdc.gov/alcohol/).

Prevalence of Binge Drinking is measured over a two-year span to increase the reliability of the estimates and to allow better state-to-state comparisons. The measure reflects the impact of excessive alcohol on increased motor vehicle deaths, liver damage and unintentional injuries.

The 2009 ranks, based on 2007 and 2008 data (Behavioral Risk Factor Surveillance System, Centers for Disease Control and Prevention) are at www.americashealthrankings.org/mea sure/2009/binge.aspx. The prevalence of binge drinking varies from less than 10 percent in Tennessee, West Virginia and Utah to more than 20 percent in Iowa, North Dakota and Wisconsin. The national average is 15.7 percent of the adult population who binge drinks and has varied from 14.3 percent to 16.8 percent of the population over the last seven years. The largest decrease in the last year was in West Virginia where the prevalence of binge drinking decreased from 10.5 percent to 9.3 percent of the population, however this decline may not be statistically significant. New Mexico also declined in overall ranking in the last year, but its notable gain is the decline in binge drinking from 15.4 percent in 2002 to 11.9 percent of the population in 2009. Even though the definition of binge drinking has changed during this time span, the state has shown consistent declines in the last seven years. The largest increase in the last year was in Kentucky, but it also may not be statistically significant in that it increased from 8.4 percent to 10.1 percent of the population and just returned to historical levels.

Prevalence of Obesity is the percentage of the population estimated to be obese, defined as having a body mass index (BMI) of 30.0 or higher. BMI is equal to your weight in pounds divided by your height in inches squared and then multiplied by 703. CDC has a calculator for BMI at http://www.cdc.gov/nccdphp/dnpa/bmi/ calc-bmi.htm. Weight status is determined per Table 14. Obesity is known to contribute to a variety of diseases, including heart disease, diabetes and general poor health (http://www.cdc.gov/nccdphp/dnpa/ obesity/). The data are collected by each state as part of the Behavioral Risk Factor Surveillance System of the Centers for Disease Control and Prevention.

The 2009 ranks, based on 2008 data (Behavioral Risk Factor Surveillance System, Centers for Disease Control and Prevention), are at www.americas healthrankings.org/measure/2009/obesity.aspx. The average for the United States is 26.6 percent of the adult population, up from 26.3 percent of the population in 2008 and substantially more than double the rate of 11.6 percent of the population in 1990. In the United States, this means that more than one-in-four are obese—that is 56 million adults with a body mass index of 30.0 or higher. If the population of the United States could return to the weight status of 1990, there would be 25 million fewer obese individuals—more than the entire population of the second most populous U.S. state, Texas.

The prevalence of obesity ranges from 19.1 percent of the population in Colorado to over 30 percent of the population in Kentucky, South Carolina, Oklahoma, Tennessee, West Virginia, Alabama and Mississippi. In the last year, no state experienced a significant change in obesity, however over the last five years, obesity has significantly increased in 80 percent of all states. There has been no significant decline in obesity in the last five years. Since 1990, the prevalence of obesity increased in all states. The largest increases have been in Alabama, Tennessee and Oklahoma.

High School Graduation estimates the percentage of incoming ninth graders who graduate within four years and are considered regular graduates. The National Center for Education Statistics collects the enrollment and completion data and, now, as part

Table 14	**Body Mass Index (BMI)**			
BMI	**WEIGHT STATUS**	**EXAMPLES (ADULTS)** 5'6"	5'10"	6'2"
Below 18.5	Underweight	Under 115 lbs	Under 129 lbs	Under 144 lbs
18.5 to 24.9	Normal	115 to 154 lbs	129 to 174 lbs	144 to 194 lbs
25.0 to 29.9	Overweight	155 to 185 lbs	175 to 208 lbs	195 to 233 bls
30.0 and above	Obese	Over 186 lbs	Over 208 lbs	Over 233 lbs

of the No Child Left Behind initiative, estimates the graduation rate for each state. The rate is the number of graduates divided by the estimated count of freshmen four years earlier. This average freshman enrollment count is the sum of the number of 8th graders five years earlier, the number of 9th graders four years earlier (because this is when current year seniors were freshmen) and the number of 10th graders three years earlier divided by three. Enrollment counts include a proportional distribution of students not enrolled in a specific grade.

Data are not adjusted for the presence or quality of basic health and consumer health education in the curriculum, for continuing education programs nor for other non-traditional learning programs. Also, individual states are increasingly altering graduation requirements, which may affect their reported number of regular graduates, their graduation rate and the comparability of these rates across time.

Education is a vital contributor to health as consumers must be able to learn about, create and maintain a healthy lifestyle and understand and participate in their options for care.

The 2009 ranks, based on 2005 to 2006 data (National Center for Education Statistics, Washington, D.C., U.S. Department of Education), are at www.americashealthrankings.org/measure/2009/graduation.aspx. The rate varies from 87.5 percent of incoming ninth graders who graduate within four years in Wisconsin to 55.8 percent in Nevada. The national average is 73.4 percent, down 1.3 percent from 74.7 percent in the 2008 Edition. Graduation rates have stagnated in the last five years with around 73 percent of incoming ninth graders graduating within four years. Arizona's rate returned back to more historical levels dropping from 84.7 percent to 70.5 percent of incoming ninth graders who graduate within four years. Utah, California and Virginia indicated a drop of 5 percent or more in the last year.

Community & Environment

Five measures are used to represent the community and the environment: the violent crime rate, the occupational fatalities rate, the percentage of children in poverty, the incidence of air pollution. Measures of community and environment reflect the reality that the daily conditions in which we live our lives have a great effect on achieving optimal individual health. The presence of pollution, violence, illegal drugs, infectious disease and unsafe workplaces are detrimental. In addition, studies indicate that the general socio-economic conditions and the level of education have a significant relationship to the healthiness of a community's residents.

These determinants measure both positive and negative aspects of the community and environment of each state and their effects on the population's health. Again, there are many additional efforts of communities that improve the overall health of a population but are not directly reflected in these five measures. Each community has its strengths, challenges and resources and should undertake a careful planning process to determine what action plans are best for them.

Violent Crime measures the effect of criminal behavior on a population's health. It represents factors such as illegal drug use and various social ills. Violent crime measures the annual number of murders, rapes, robberies and aggravated assaults per 100,000 population. Violent crime reflects an aspect of current U.S. lifestyle and is an indicator of health risk and death.

The 2009 ranks, based on 2008 data (Crime in the United States: 2008. Washington, D.C., Federal Bureau of Investigation), are at www.americas healthrankings.org/measure/2009/crime.aspx. The violent crime rate is dependent upon many factors, not just population; thus when taking action to combat crime, each state must consider its specific circumstances.

The violent crime rate varies from less than 175 offenses per 100,000 population in Maine, Vermont, New Hampshire and North Dakota to more than 700 offenses per 100,000 population in South Carolina, Nevada, Tennessee and Delaware. The national average is 455 offenses per 100,000 population, down 12 offenses per 100,000 population from the prior year and down 154 offenses per 100,000 population from the 1990 Edition. Crime peaked in 1993 and 1994 at 758 offenses per 100,000 population and has since dropped by 40 percent.

The largest reported decreases in violent crime from the 2008 Edition occurred in Louisiana where reported offenses decreased by 74 offenses per 100,000 population and in South Carolina where reported offenses decreased by 58 offenses per 100,000 population. The largest reported increases occurred in Connecticut, from 256 to 298 offenses per 100,000 population, and in South Dakota, from 169 to 201 offenses per 100,000 population.

This is the tenth year that the national violent crime rate is lower than the 1990 Edition. However, several states experienced significant increases since 1990, led by Delaware, Alaska and Tennessee with increases of 271 offenses, 197 offenses and 188 offenses per 100,000 population, respectively. New York, California and Florida reduced violent crime the most since the 1990 Edition, decreasing from

1,007 to 398 offenses per 100,000 population, from 918 to 504 offenses per 100,000 population, and from 1,024 to 689 offenses per 100,000 population, respectively.

Occupational Fatalities represents the impact of hazardous jobs on the population. Occupational injuries would be a preferred measure; however, there is not a uniform reporting system used by all 50 states. Due to the different industry mixes in each state, occupational fatalities are adjusted to more accurately reflect the actual safety differences between the states.

Occupational fatalities are measured over a three-year span because of their low incidence rate. The industry adjustment is based on the ratio of workers in the following industries: construction, manufacturing, trade, transportation, utilities, professional and business services as defined by the North American Industry Classification System (NAICS).

The 2009 ranks, based on 2006 to preliminary 2008 data (Census of Fatal Occupational Injuries, Bureau of Labor Statistics, U.S. Department of Labor, Washington, D.C.), are at www.americashealth rankings.org/measure/2009/WorkFatalities.aspx. Scores vary from 3.1 deaths per 100,000 workers in Massachusetts and Minnesota to over 10 deaths per 100,000 workers in Wyoming and Alaska. The national norm is 4.8 deaths per 100,000 workers, down from 5.2 deaths per 100,000 workers in the 2008 Edition. The occupational fatalities rate decreased the most in the last year in Florida, by 1.3 deaths per 100,000 workers. The rate did not significantly increase in any state.

Children in Poverty measures the percentage of related persons under age 18 living in a household that is below the poverty threshold. The poverty threshold established by the U.S. Census Bureau for a household of four people which includes two children living in the lower 48 states is approximately $22,050 in household income.

The 2009 ranks, based on 2008 data (March 2009 Current Population Survey, Washington, D.C., U.S. Census Bureau), are at www.americashealth rankings.org/measure/2009/ChildPoverty.aspx. The percentage of children in poverty ranged from less than 10 percent of persons under age 18 in New Hampshire, Utah, Alaska and Vermont to a high of more than 25 percent in New Mexico and Arizona. The national average is 19.0 percent, up 1.0 percent from the 2008 Edition and up 3.2 percent from the low of 15.8 percent of persons under age 18 reported in the 2002 Edition. It is only 1.6 percent below the 1990 Edition. In the past year, the percentage of chil-

dren in poverty increased in 35 of 50 states, though no individual changes are statistically significant. Since 1990, the percentage of children in poverty has increased in 17 of 50 states. Children in poverty increased by 5 percent or more in Rhode Island, Arizona and Delaware, while during the same time period, it decreased by 10 percent or more in Louisiana and Mississippi.

Infectious Disease includes the occurrence of Acquired Immune Deficiency Syndrome (AIDS), tuberculosis and hepatitis (A and B) as representative of all major infectious diseases in a state. It is a running three-year average.

It should be noted that this measure is neither age nor race adjusted, and, as reporting comes from each individual state health department, the level of accuracy may differ from state to state. Despite these drawbacks, the data remains the best available.

The 2009 ranks, based on 2006 to 2008 data (*Mortality and Morbidity Weekly Reports*, Centers for Disease Control and Prevention), are at www.americashealthrankings.org/2008/disease.aspx. AIDS cases in 2008 were not available as the data collection system for this measure is being revised. The incidence of infectious disease per 100,000 population varies from a reported low of less than five cases in North Dakota, Wyoming, Montana, Idaho and Vermont to a reported high of more than 30 cases in New York, Maryland and Florida. The national average is 19.1 cases per 100,000 population, down from 20.1 cases per 100,000 population in the 2008 Edition and down considerably from 40.7 cases per 100,000 population in the 1990 Edition.

In Georgia, reported infectious disease decreased by 4.8 cases per 100,000 population and continues a five-year decline in the state. No state had a considerable increase. Since the 1990 Edition, Oregon, Alaska, Arizona and Washington have seen the greatest decreases in reported cases with more than 70 fewer cases per 100,000 population and all show a gradual, continued decline in infectious disease rates. None of the states have experienced increases in the incidence of infectious disease since the 1990 Edition.

Air Pollution measures the fine particulates in the air we breathe. The fine particulates, too small to see individually but appearing as haze in the air, can enter the deepest portions of the lungs. Air pollution has been shown to have an adverse effect on health, including decreased lung function, aggravated asthma, development of chronic bronchitis, irregular heartbeat, nonfatal heart attacks, and premature death in people with heart or lung disease. See www.epa.gov/air/particlepollution/health.html for more information.

Air Pollution was a new measure in the 2008 Edition. It is the population weighted average exposure to particulates 2.5 micron and smaller for each county reporting within a state. Air pollution is monitored in many counties where population density is significant and/or where there have been pollution concerns in prior years. Population weighting of the county data adjusts the information to reflect the actual number of people potentially exposed to the particulate. In counties where pollution data is not available, the population was assumed to be exposed to the background level of particulate in the air quality control region and/or state. Background levels are estimated to be the average of the lowest measures in each region or state for each of the last three years. The data is collected by the EPA and available at http://www.epa.gov/air/data/. (Due to modification in the method used to estimate particulate exposure in background areas, the data for the 2008 Edition is restated in this report.)

The 2009 ranks, based on 2006 to 2008 data (U.S. Environmental Protection Agency, Washington, D.C. and the U.S. Census Bureau, Washington, D.C.), are at www.americashealthrankings.org/ measure/2009/air.aspx. Air pollution varies from a low of 4.8 micrograms of fine particulate per cubic meter in Hawaii to 13.9 micrograms of fine particulate per cubic meter in California, Delaware, Georgia and Pennsylvania. The average for reporting counties in the United States is 11.7 micrograms of fine particulate per cubic meter, down slightly from 12.2 micrograms in 2008 and 12.8 micrograms five years ago in the 2004 Edition.

Public & Health Policies

Three measures are used to represent public and health policies and programs: public health funding, immunization coverage and lack of health insurance. These measures are indicative of the availability of resources and the extent of the program's reach to the public.

Every state has many excellent and effective public health programs, too numerous and individualized to list, that contribute to the overall health of the population but are not explicitly included in these rankings. Contact your state public health officials to obtain additional information about programs in your state that are enacted to optimize individual and community health. Each state summary lists the Web site for that state's health department. Individuals can also see the spectrum of options available to states and communities by visiting www.thecommunityguide.org, a Web site that pro-

vides a systemic review of programs and evidence-based recommendations for health and community officials.

Lack of Health Insurance measures the percentage of the population not covered by private or public health insurance. Individuals without health insurance have greater difficulty accessing the health care system, frequently are not able to participate in preventive care programs and can add substantially to the cost of health care due to delayed care and emergency department treatment.

The 2009 ranks, based on 2008 data (March 2009 Current Population Survey, Washington, D.C., U.S. Census Bureau), are at www.americashealth rankings.org/measure/2009/insurance.aspx.

The rate of uninsured population ranged from 5.4 percent in Massachusetts to over 20 percent in Texas, New Mexico and Florida. The national average is 15.3 percent (46.3 million people) uninsured.[9] If the United States as a whole could emulate the best state, the number of uninsured would decrease by over 25 million people or more than the population of Texas, the second most populous state in the United States.

In the last year, the two-year average rate of uninsured population decreased in 16 states, led by Massachusetts with a significant decline of 2.5 percent. The rate of uninsured population increased in 32 states, including an increase of 1.0 percent or more in Rhode Island and Alaska. Over a five-year period, Washington and Massachusetts have experienced a significant decrease in the uninsured rate and Tennessee and South Carolina (as well as the United States as a whole) have experienced a significant increase.

Public Health Funding measures the dollars per person that are spent on public or population health through funding from Centers for Disease Control and Prevention, Health Resources Services Administration and the state. This does not include spending from other sources such as county or city governments. High spending on these health programs are indicative of states that are proactively implementing preventive and education programs targeted at improving the health of at-risk populations within a state. Recent research has shown that an investment of $10 per person per year in proven community-based programs to increase physical activity, improve nutrition, and prevent smoking and other tobacco use could save the country more than $16 billion annually within five years. This is a return of $5.60 for every $1 invested (http://healthyamericans.org/reports/prevention 08/Prevention08.pdf).

The 2009 ranks, based on 2006 and 2007 data (Trust for America's Health, Washington, D.C.) are at www.americashealthrankings.org/measure/2009/PH_Spending.aspx. It ranges from more than $150 per person in Vermont, Alaska and Hawaii to less than $40 per person in Wisconsin, Indiana, Nevada and Ohio. The average funding in the United States is $94 per person, up from $88 per person last year and $76 per person two years ago.[9]

Immunization Coverage is the percentage of children ages 19 to 35 months who have received the suggested early childhood immunizations listed in Table 15. Early childhood immunization has been shown to be a safe and cost-effective manner of controlling diseases within the population.

The 2009 ranks, based on 2008 data (National Immunization Program, Centers for Disease Control and Prevention), are at www.americas healthrank ings.org/measure/2009/immunize.aspx. It ranges from immunization coverage of 85.0 percent in New Hampshire to less than 70 percent in Montana, Idaho and Wyoming. Compared to coverage in the prior year, coverage for the complete series of immunizations in the United States decreased from 80.1 percent to 78.2 percent of children ages 19 to 35 months. In the last year, immunization coverage dropped significantly in Connecticut from 89.3 percent to 72.5 percent of children ages 19 to 35 months and in Maryland from 92.4 percent to 82.6 percent of children ages 19 to 35 months. (The latter is less troubling since 2008 data was reported to be unusually high compared to prior years.) In the last 14 years, coverage in the United States increased from 55.1 percent to 78.2 percent of children ages 19 to 35 months who received the complete set of immunizations. The rate peaked in 2005 and 2006 at almost 81 percent of children receiving a full set of immunizations. The recent decline is not significant

at the 95 percent confidence level, yet is still troubling in its direction.

The Guide to Community Preventive Services has numerous proven methods to increase the rate of vaccinations in a community that include ways to increase the demand in the community, improving access and system-based or provider-based innovations. See their suggestions at http://www.thecommunityguide.org/vaccine/default.htm.

Clinical Care

Preventive and curative care must be delivered in an effective, appropriate and timely manner. In the 2009 Edition, three measures are included in this section: Prenatal Care, Primary Care Physicians and Preventable Hospitalizations. Prenatal Care has been included since the 1990 Edition and Primary Care Physicians and Preventable Hospitalizations were added in the 2007 Edition.

Prenatal Care is a measure of both access to and frequency of prenatal care based on the Adequacy of Prenatal Care Utilization (APNCU) Index developed by Kotelchuck. This index considers two aspects of prenatal care: the month it was initiated and the number of visits occurring after initiation. The 1990 through 2004 Editions of the report defined Prenatal Care using the Kessner Index, a measure highly correlated to Kotelchuck; however, it does not consider both initiation and frequency of visits. The introduction of a new birth certificate, the information of record from which the APNCU is derived, is an additional complication to the data. The adoption of the new birth certificate is gradual across the system and directly comparing the APNCU from the different certificates is not valid. Therefore, starting with this Edition, the APNCU index only compares a state to another state using the same birth certificate. While this does allow a score to be calculated among peer states, it doesn't allow for ranking the states for this measure.

Prenatal care is not adjusted for age or race.

The 2009 Edition is based on 2006 data (National Center for Health Statistics. Adequacy of Care by State, United States, Hyattsville, Md.) and can be found at www.americashealthrankings.org/measure/2009/prenatal.aspx.

Primary Care Physicians is a measure of access to primary care for the general population as measured by number of primary care physicians per 100,000 population. Primary care physicians provide a combination of direct care to the patient and, as necessary, counsel the patient in the appropriate use of specialists and advance treatment locations.

---

[9]·U.S. Bureau of the Census; Income, Poverty and Health Insurance Coverage in the United States: 2008, September 2009.

Table 15	Immunization Coverage
IMMUNIZATION	**DOSES**
DTP	4 or more
Poliovirus	3 or more
MCV	1 or more
HiB	3 or more
HepB	3 or more

The 2009 ranks, based on 2007 data (American Medical Association, Physician Characteristics and Distribution in the United States, 2009 Edition, Chicago, Ill. Data used with permission), are at www.americashealthrankings.org/measure/2009/PCP .aspx. Primary care physicians include all those who identify themselves as Family Practice physicians, General Practitioners, Internists, Pediatricians, Obstetricians or Gynecologists.

The number of Primary Care Physicians per 100,000 population will change because of changing state population, physician retirements, new physicians, and physicians moving between states and specialties. Primary Care Physicians range from 190.0 physicians per 100,000 population in Massachusetts to 78.1 physicians in Idaho. The national average is 120.6 physicians per 100,000 population, essentially unchanged in the last few years.

Preventable Hospitalizations is a measure of the discharge rate from hospitals for ambulatory care-sensitive conditions. Ambulatory care-sensitive conditions are those "for which good outpatient care can potentially prevent the need for hospitalization, or for which early intervention can prevent complications or more severe disease."[10] These hospitalizations can often be reduced by strong outpatient care systems and include conditions such as adult asthma, bacterial pneumonia, congestive heart failure, chronic obstructive pulmonary disease, diabetes, low birth weight, urinary tract infection and other conditions. It is not adjusted by characteristics of the population served, such as age or health status.

These discharges are also highly correlated with general admissions and reflect the tendency for a population to overuse the hospital setting as a site for care.

The 2009 ranks, based on 2006 data (The Dartmouth Atlas of Health Care, The Dartmouth Institute for Health Policy and Clinic Practice, Lebanon, N.H.), are at www.americashealthrank ings.org/measure/2009/preventable.aspx. The rate of preventable hospitalizations ranges from a low of under 50 discharges per 1,000 Medicare enrollees in Washington, Oregon, Hawaii and Utah to over 100 discharges per 1,000 Medicare enrollees in West Virginia, Kentucky and Mississippi. The national average is 74.2 discharges per 1,000 Medicare enrollees, down from 78.4 discharges last year. Four of five states had a significant improvement in this measure in the last year. In the last eight years, the national discharge rate declined

from 82.5 to 74.2 discharges per 1,000 Medicare enrollees, a notable improvement in this metric that reflects improving clinical care and follow-up for preventable hospitalizations.

Health Outcomes

Health outcomes include the length of life, the disparity among outcomes in a state and the quality of life. These seven measures represent the burden placed on the overall health of a population by death, disparity and depressed quality of life. Measures range from counting days in which people feel their normal activities are limited due to poor health to disease-specific mortality and years of potential life lost.

Poor Mental Health Days is the average number of days in the previous 30 days that a person could not perform work or household tasks due to mental illness. The data is collected by the Behavioral Risk Factor Surveillance System of the Centers for Disease Control and Prevention and rely on the accuracy of each respondent's estimate of the number of limited activity days lost in the previous 30 days.

Poor mental health days highlight the fact that good health outcomes preclude days in which mental health prohibits an individual from accomplishing everyday activities.

The 2009 ranks, based on 2008 data (Behavioral Risk Factor Surveillance System, Centers for Disease Control and Prevention), are at www.americas healthrankings.org/measure/2009/MentalDays.aspx. The number of poor mental health days in the previous 30 days ranges from an average of 2.2 days in North Dakota to 4.0 or more days in Oklahoma, Alabama, Mississippi, West Virginia and Kentucky. The average number of poor mental health days in the previous 30 days for the United States is 3.4 days, essentially unchanged from the prior eight editions. Kentucky had a significant increase of 0.9 days in the previous 30 days, returning it to more historical values. Florida had a significant increase of 0.5 days, rising to 3.7 days in the previous 30 days, and continues to trend upward over the last ten years.

Poor Physical Health Days is the average number of days in the 30 days that a person could not perform work or household tasks due to physical illness. The data are collected by the Behavioral Risk Factor Surveillance System of the Centers for Disease Control and Prevention and rely on the accuracy of each respondent's estimate of the number of limited activity days lost in the previous 30 days.

Poor physical health days highlight that good health outcomes preclude days in which physical

---

10. http://www.qualityindicators.ahrq.gov/.

health prohibits an individual from accomplishing everyday activities.

The 2009 ranks, based on 2008 data (Behavioral Risk Factor Surveillance System, Centers for Disease Control and Prevention), are at www.americas healthrankings.org/measure/2009/PhysicalDays. aspx. The number of poor physical health days in the previous 30 days ranges from an average of 2.7 days in Nebraska, 2.8 days in North Dakota, 2.9 days in Connecticut and Minnesota and 5.5 days in West Virginia. The average number of poor physical health days in the previous 30 days for the United States is 3.6 days, and it has remained the same for the last six years.

Geographic Disparity measures the variation in the age-adjusted mortality rate among counties within a state. Ideally, health and mortality should be equal among the populations of every county within a state and not vary based upon the physical location where a person lives. Many things may differ among counties, including natural features such as altitude, latitude, moisture and temperature and man-made features such as land use, population density, roads and communications. But even with all these variations, health should still be equal.

Geographic Disparity was a new measure in the 2008 Edition. It indicates the amount of variation among the counties of a state. It is the standard deviation of the three-year average, age-adjusted all-cause mortality rate for all counties within a state divided by the three-year age-adjusted all-cause mortality rate for the state. The lower the percent, the closer each county is to the state average and the more uniform the mortality rate is across the state. For counties with fewer than 20 deaths in the three year period (about 20 to 30 counties in the United States each year), the county was assumed to have an age-adjusted death rate equal to the state's age-adjusted death rate and thus has no effect on the geographic disparity of the state.

The 2009 ranks, based on 2004 to 2006 data (Centers for Disease Control and Prevention), are at www.americashealthrankings.org/measure/ 2009/disparity.aspx. It varies from a low geographic disparity of less than 6 percent in Connecticut, New Hampshire and Delaware to a high geographic disparity of more than 20 percent in Florida and South Dakota. For the United States as a whole, the geographic disparity among all counties is 17.1 percent, up slightly from 16.8 percent in the 2008 Edition and on a consistently upward trend since the 2004 Edition, the first year it was calculated.

Infant Mortality represents many factors surrounding birth, including but not limited to: the health of the mother, prenatal care, quality of the health services delivered to the mother and child and infant care. In addition, high infant mortality rates are often considered preventable and, thus, can be influenced by various educational and care programs.

The 2009 ranks, based on a two-year average using 2005 and 2006 data (National Center for Health Statistics, Washington, D.C. Some data is provisional), are at www.americashealthrankings. org/measure/2009/IMR.aspx. Infant mortality varies greatly among states, from less than 5.0 deaths per 1,000 live births in Washington and Utah to more than 10.0 deaths per 1,000 live births in Mississippi. The national average is 6.8 deaths per 1,000 live births. The data has not been updated since the 2008 Edition.

States with a low number of births will experience more fluctuations in the two-year average infant mortality rate than states with a higher number of births.

Cardiovascular Deaths is measured using a three-year average, age-adjusted death rate due to heart disease, strokes and other cardiovascular disease. The effect of cardiovascular disease on health was measured using mortality data due to the improved accuracy of the data and the ability to adjust for age and race.

The use of mortality data does not reflect the full impact of cardiovascular disease as data indicates that even though mortality rates are declining, more individuals are living with cardiac disease as new procedures prolong the lives of these individuals.

The 2009 ranks, based on 2004 to 2006 data (Centers for Disease Control and Prevention), are at www.americashealthrankings.org/measure/2009/ CVD.aspx. This measure varies from a low of 212.6 deaths from cardiovascular disease per 100,000 population in Minnesota to over 350 deaths per 100,000 population in Alabama, Oklahoma and Mississippi. The national average is 287.9 deaths per 100,000 population, down from 298.2 deaths per 100,000 population last year and 405.1 deaths per 100,000 population in 1990.

In the last year, 38 of 50 states had a significant decline in cardiovascular deaths led by declines in Oklahoma from 371.0 deaths to 354.4 deaths per 100,000 population and in Tennessee from 353.8 deaths to 338.1 deaths per 100,000 population. No state experienced an increase. All states have had a significant decline in cardiovascular deaths since the 2007 Edition and the nation overall has experienced a steady decline since the 1990 Edition.

Cancer Deaths is measured using a three-year average, age-adjusted death rate due to cancer. The effect of cancer on health was measured using mortality data due to the improved accuracy of the data and the ability to adjust for age.

The 2009 ranks, based on 2004 to 2006 data (Centers for Disease Control and Prevention), are at www.americashealthrankings.org/measure/2009/cancer.aspx. The rate varies from less than 150 cancer deaths per 100,000 population in Utah to over 220 deaths per 100,000 population in West Virginia, Louisiana and Kentucky. The national average is 192.6 deaths per 100,000 population, a decrease of 0.8 deaths per 100,000 population from the 2008 Edition and a decrease of only 4.9 deaths per 100,000 population from the 1990 Edition. Cancer deaths peaked in 1996 when the national rate was 205.5 deaths per 100,000 population, but unlike cardiovascular deaths, there has not been a significant decline in cancer deaths over the last 20 years.

In the last five years, cancer deaths have declined significantly in about half of the states led by declines in Virginia, Alaska, New Jersey, Nevada and New York.

Premature Death measures the loss of years of productive life due to death before age 75 as defined by Centers for Disease Control and Prevention's Years of Potential Life Lost (YPLL-75). Thus, the death of a 25-year-old would account for 50 years of lost life, while the death of a 60-year-old would account for 15 years.

The 2009 ranks, based on 2006 data (Centers for Disease Control and Prevention), are at www.americashealthrankings.org/measure/2009/premature Death.aspx. The age-adjusted data vary from less

than 6,000 years lost per 100,000 population in Minnesota, New Hampshire and Vermont to more than 10,000 years lost per 100,000 population in Mississippi, Louisiana and Alabama. The national average is 7,511 years lost before age 75 per 100,000 population, which is 21 years more than the 2008 Edition. Premature death has essentially plateaued in the last decade and hovers around 7,500 years lost before age 75 per 100,000 population.

Supplemental Measures

The core measures used in the Rankings are a small fraction of those measures available to the public and public health officials. *The America's Health Rankings™* Web site contains additional measures that are useful in understanding the health of your state and provide information for more in-depth analysis.

Table 13 contains a brief definition of the supplemental measures and a link to the data.

Cholesterol Check: The National Cholesterol Education Program (NCEP) recommends that adults aged 20 years or older have their cholesterol checked every 5 years. A simple blood test can measure total cholesterol levels, including LDL (low-density lipoprotein, or "bad" cholesterol), HDL (high-density lipoprotein, or "good" cholesterol), and triglycerides. More than 107 million people are considered to have high cholesterol, of which 38 million are over 240 mg/dL, a level which puts them are a higher risk for heart disease.[11]

[11.]Division of Heart Disease and Stroke Prevention, Centers for Disease Control and Prevention, http://www.cdc.gov/dhdsp/library/fs_cholesterol.htm, accessed Sept 3, 2009.

Table 16	Supplemental Chronic Disease Measures	
MEASURE	**QUESTION**	**TABLE**
Cardiac Heart Disease	Has a doctor, nurse, or other health professional EVER told you that you had any of the following? (Ever told) you had angina or coronary heart disease?	www.americashealthrankings.org/measure/2009/cardiac.aspx
Diabetes	Have you EVER been told by a doctor that you have diabetes?	www.americashealthrankings.org/measure/2009/diabetes.aspx
High Cholesterol	Have you EVER been told by a doctor, nurse or other health professional that your blood cholesterol is high?	www.americashealthrankings.org/measure/2009/HighCholesterol.aspx
Heart Attack	Has a doctor, nurse, or other health professional EVER told you that you had any of the following? (Ever told) you had a heart attack, also called a myocardial infarction?	www.americashealthrankings.org/measure/2009/HeartAttack.aspx
Stroke	Has a doctor, nurse, or other health professional EVER told you that you had any of the following? (Ever told) you had a stroke?	www.americashealthrankings.org/measure/2009/stroke.aspx
Hypertension	Have you EVER been told by a doctor, nurse, or other health professional that you have high blood pressure?	www.americashealthrankings.org/measure/2009/hypertension.aspx

These data are collected through the Behavioral Risk Factor Surveillance System by Centers for Disease Control and Prevention. A table of the percentage of adults receiving a blood cholesterol check within the last five years is at www.americas healthrankings.org/measure/2009/Cholesterol Test.aspx. Factors that influence individuals receiving a blood cholesterol check include access, cost, education and motivation.

The National Heart, Lung and Blood Institute at the National Institute of Health provides additional background information on cholesterol and actions you can take to manage high cholesterol at http://www.nhlbi.nih.gov/health/public/heart/index. htm#chol.

Dental Visit: Oral health is a vital part of a comprehensive preventive health program. The Division of Oral Health at the CDC notes, "There are threats to oral health across the lifespan. Nearly one-third of all adults in the United States have untreated tooth decay. One in seven adults aged 35 to 44 years has gum disease; this increases to one in every four adults aged 65 years and older. In addition, nearly a quarter of all adults have experienced some facial pain in the past six months. Oral cancers are most common in older adults, particularly those over 55 years who smoke and are heavy drinkers."[12]

These data are collected through the Behavioral Risk Factor Surveillance System by Centers for Disease Control and Prevention. A table of the percentage of adults visiting a dental office within the last year is at www.americashealthrankings.org/measure/2009/dental.aspx. Factors that influence individuals receiving dental include access, cost, education and motivation.

Additional information on oral health can be obtained from the Division of Oral Health, Centers for Disease Control and Prevention (http://www.cdc. gov/OralHealth) and from the American Dental Association (http://www.ada.org/public/index.asp). Both Websites address questions about personal oral health and community programs to improve overall oral health, such as water fluoridation.

Physical Activity: Regular physical activity is one of the most important things you can do for your health. It can help:[13]

- Control your weight
- Reduce your risk of cardiovascular disease
- Reduce your risk for type 2 diabetes and metabolic syndrome
- Reduce your risk of some cancers
- Strengthen your bones and muscles
- Improve your mental health and mood
- Improve your ability to do daily activities and prevent falls, if you're an older adult
- Increase your chances of living longer

These data are collected through the Behavioral Risk Factor Surveillance System by Centers for Disease Control and Prevention. A table of the percentage of adults who have participated in any physical activities in the last 30 days is at www.americas healthrankings.org/measure/2009/activity.aspx. These physical activities range from walking through exercise programs, so the range includes activities that are available to almost every individual.

Centers for Disease Control and Prevention presents guidelines for physical activities for adults, children and older adults at http://www.cdc.gov/physical activity/everyone/guidelines/index.html.

Diet: According to the Dietary Guidelines for Americans published by the CDC, a healthy eating plan:[14]

- Emphasizes fruits, vegetables, whole grains, and fat-free or low-fat milk and milk products
- Includes lean meats, poultry, fish, beans, eggs, and nuts
- Is low in saturated fats, trans fats, cholesterol, salt (sodium), and added sugars
- Stays within your daily calorie needs

Data collected for this measure focus on the consumption of vegetables and fruits at the recommended five portions per day. These data are collected through the Behavioral Risk Factor Surveillance System by Centers for Disease Control and Prevention. A table of the percentage of adults who consume five or more servings of vegetables and fruit a day is at www. americashealthrankings.org/measure/2009/diet.aspx.

Nutritional information is abundant and overwhelming, but two sound starting points for information are the Centers for Disease Control and

---

[12.]Division of Oral Health, Centers for Disease Control and Prevention, http://www.cdc.gov/OralHealth/topics/adult.htm, accessed Sept 3, 2009.

[13.]Centers for Disease Control and Prevention, http://www. cdc.gov/physicalactivity/everyone/health/index.html accessed Sept 3, 2009.

[14.]Centers for Disease Control and Prevention, http://www. cdc.gov/healthyweight/healthy_eating/index.html, accessed Sept 3, 2009.

Prevention (http://www.cdc.gov/healthyweight/index.html) resources about healthy weight and the National Heart, Lung and Blood Institute DASH nutrition plan (http://www.nhlbi.nih.gov/health/public/heart/hbp/dash/introduction.html). The DASH eating plan was originally developed as an eating plan to reduce high blood pressure, i.e., hypertension. (DASH stands for Dietary Approaches to Stop Hypertension.) However, the plan also represents a healthy approach to eating for those who do not have a problem with hypertension.

Teen Birth Rate: Prevention of teen and unplanned pregnancy is an important part of a healthy community. The CDC notes, "In 2006, there were 435,436 births to mothers aged 15-19 years in the United States, a birth rate of 41.9 per 1,000 women in this age group. The majority, nearly two thirds among mothers under age 18 and more than half among mothers aged 18-19 years, of teen births are unintended—they occurred sooner than desired or were not wanted at any time. U.S. teen pregnancy, birth, and abortion rates are considerably higher than most other developed countries."[15]

Data collected for this measure focus on the rate of birth to mothers age 15 through 19. These data are collected by the Centers for Disease Control and Prevention. The birth rate for teens is at www.americashealthrankings.org/measure/2009/teenbirth.aspx.

A valuable resource for further information about teen and unplanned pregnancy is available from The National Campaign to Prevent Teen and Unplanned Pregnancy (http://www.thenationalcampaign.org/default.aspx).

Chronic Disease: Six diseases are included in this category: cardiac heart disease, diabetes, high cholesterol, heart attack, stroke and hypertension (high blood pressure). These diseases are long term illnesses that many individuals can manage through lifestyle changes and healthcare interventions. However, they do place a burden on many of the affected individuals by constraining options and activities available to them and can mean expensive and on-going expenditures for health care.

All measures are self-reported by respondents to the Behavioral Risk Factor Surveillance System to the following questions.

Resources for heart and vascular diseases are at National Heart, Lung and Blood Institute (http://www.nhlbi.nih.gov/health/public/heart/index.htm) as well as at the Division for Heart Disease and Stroke Prevention, Centers for Disease Control and Prevention (http://www.cdc.gov/DHDSP/index.htm).

Diabetes information is available at National Center for Chronic Disease Prevention and Health Promotion, Centers for Disease Control and Prevention (http://www.cdc.gov/diabetes/ and http://www.cdc.gov/nccdphp/publications/aag/ddt.htm) and the American Diabetes Association (http://www.diabetes.org/).

Median Household Income: Median household income is the amount that divides the income distribution into two equal groups, half with income above that amount, and half with income below that amount. The household's income reflects the ability for that household to afford aspects of a healthy lifestyle, preventive medicine and curative care not provided to the individual through government, business, trade groups or other sources.

Data for household income is from the U.S. Census Bureau, Current Population Survey, Annual Social and Economic Supplements and presented at www.americashealthrankings.org/measure/2009/MedianIncome.aspx.

Personal Income: An individual's income reflects the ability for that individual to afford aspects of a healthy lifestyle, preventive medicine and curative care not provided to the individual through government, business, trade groups or other sources. Personal income has also been shown to be negatively correlated to morbidity and mortality, that is higher income relates to lower illness and death.[16]

Data for personal income is from the Regional Economic Information System, Bureau of Economic Analysis, U.S. Department of Commerce and presented at www.americashealthrankings.org/measure/2009/income.aspx. Per capita personal income is total personal income divided by total midyear population.

Unemployment Rate: For many individuals, their employer is the source for their healthcare insurance. For most, employment is the source of income for sustaining a healthy life and for accessing healthcare.

The Bureau of Labor Statistics, U.S. Department of Labor releases unemployment figures monthly and annually. The official definition of the unemployment rate is "total unemployed, as a percent of the

[15]·Centers for Disease Control and Prevention, http://www.cdc.gov/reproductivehealth/AdolescentReproHealth/AboutTP.htm, accessed Sept 3, 2009.

[16]."Poverty or income inequality as predictor of mortality: longitudinal cohort study" by Fiscella, Frank and Franks, Peter; *BMJ*1997;314:1724 (14 June), http://www.bmj.com/cgi/content/ full/314/7096/1724.

civilian labor force" and is the figure most widely published by the media.

Data for the most recent annual unemployment rate is at www.americashealthrankings.org/measure/2009/annualunemployment.aspx.

Data for the August 2009 unemployment rate is at www.americashealthrankings.org/measure/2009/augustunemployment.aspx.

Underemployment Rate: Many suggest that the official unemployment rate does not reflect the full impact of employment on the market. The Bureau of Labor Statistics uses an expanded definition to allow for individuals that are no longer seeking employment, those employed only part time when they desire full time work and workers that are only marginally attached, that is persons who currently are "neither working nor looking for work but indicate that they want and are available for a job and have looked for work sometime in the recent past."

Data for the most recent annual underemployment rate is at www.americashealthrankings.org/measure/2009/underemployment.aspx.

Income Disparity (Gini): The Gini coefficient is a common measure of income inequality. It varies between 0, which reflects complete equality of income and 1, which indicates complete inequality (one person has all the income or consumption, all others have none). Historically, the U.S. index has varied from .386 in 1968 to .470 in 2006.

There is debate among the public health and economic communities as to the effect of income disparity on health of a population. However, that need not be resolved to acknowledge that income disparity does play a factor in how a community will develop plans and take actions to change health. As such, income disparity provides a valuable description of the environment in which health improvement programs must be implemented.

The source for the data is U.S. Census Bureau, Current Population Survey, 1978 to 2008 Annual Social and Economic Supplements and it is presented at www.americashealthrankings.org/measure/2009/gini.aspx.

Historically, the U.S. index has varied from .386 in 1968 to .470 in 2006 (http://www.census.gov/hhes/www/income/histinc/h04.html). Most developed European nations and Canada have Gini indices between .24 and .36. (The Gini Index, which is the Gini coefficient times 100, is reported for other countries by the Central Intelligence Agency at https://www.cia.gov/library/publications/the worldfactbook/fields/2172.html and in Human Development Reports, United Nations Development Program at http://hdrstats.undp.org/en/indicators/147.html.)

Weighting of Measures

Three criteria were considered when assigning weights to measures.

1. What effect does a measure have on overall health?

2. Is the effect measured solely by this measure or is it included in other measures?

3. How reliable is the data supporting a measure?

The final weights, presented in Table 17, are based on input from the experts in 1990 and 1991 and from input from the Scientific Advisory Committee and its continuing methodological review. The weights of the measures total 100 percent. The column labeled "% of Total" indicates the weight of each measure in determining the overall ranking. For example, prevalence of smoking is 7.5 percent of the *America's Health Rankings*™. The column labeled "Effect on Score" presents how each measure positively or negatively relates to the overall ranking. For example, a high prevalence of smoking has a negative effect on score and will lower the ranking of a state. An increase in the percent of high school graduates has a positive effect on score and will increase the overall ranking of a state.

Table 17 | **Weight of Individual Measures**

NAME OF MEASURE	% OF TOTAL	EFFECT ON SCORE
Determinants		
Behaviors		
Prevalence of Smoking	7.5	Negative
Prevalence of Binge Drinking	5.0	Negative
Prevalence of Obesity	7.5	Negative
Community & Environment		
High School Graduation	5.0	Positive
Violent Crime	5.0	Negative
Occupational Fatalities	2.5	Negative
Infectious Disease	5.0	Negative
Children in Poverty	5.0	Negative
Air Pollution	5.0	Negative
Public & Health Policies		
Lack of Health Insurance	5.0	Negative
Public Health Funding	2.5	Positive
Immunization Coverage	5.0	Positive
Clinical Care		
Prenatal Care	5.0	Positive
Primary Care Physicians	5.0	Positive
Preventable Hospitalizations	5.0	Negative
Health Outcomes		
Poor Mental Health Days	2.5	Negative
Poor Physical Health Days	2.5	Negative
Geographic Disparity	5.0	Negative
Infant Mortality	5.0	Negative
Cardiovascular Deaths	2.5	Negative
Cancer Deaths	2.5	Negative
Premature Death	5.0	Negative
Overall Health Ranking	100.0	—

Sorting Out the Connections Between the Built Environment and Health: A Conceptual Framework for Navigating Pathways and Planning Healthy Cities

Source: With kind permission from Spring Science + Business Media: Northridge ME, Sclar ED, Biswas P. Sorting out the connections between the built environment and health: a conceptual framework for navigating pathways and planning healthy cities. *J Urban Health* 2003;80:556-68.

ABSTRACT

The overarching goal of this article is to make explicit the multiple pathways through which the built environment may potentially affect health and well-being. The loss of close collaboration between urban planning and public health professionals that characterized the post–World War II era has limited the design and implementation of effective interventions and policies that might translate into improved health for urban populations. First, we present a conceptual model that developed out of previous research called Social Determinants of Health and Environmental Health Promotion. Second, we review empirical research from both the urban planning and public health literature regarding the health effects of housing and housing interventions. And third, we wrestle with key challenges in conducting sound scientific research on connections between the built environment and health, namely: (1) the necessity of dealing with the possible health consequences of myriad public and private sector activities; (2) the lack of valid and reliable indicators of the built environment to monitor the health effects of urban planning and policy decisions, especially with regard to land use mix; and (3) the growth of the "megalopolis" or "super urban region" that requires analysis of health effects across state lines and in circumscribed areas within multiple states. We contend that to plan for healthy cities, we need to reinvigorate the historic link between urban planning and public health, and thereby conduct informed science to better guide effective public policy.

While it has been stated before, it nonetheless bears repeating that the connections between urban planning and public health are not new.[1] What has changed is the magnitude of the population health crisis that we presently face in both the developed and less developed areas of the world. The United Nations Human Settlements Programme (UN-HABITAT) estimates that approximately 1 billion people out of a global population of close to 6 billion people are presently living in slumlike conditions.[2] By 2030, the global population is expected to increase by about 2 billion people; the slum-dwelling population is expected to account for half of this increase.[2] The squalid living conditions of industrialized cities in the middle of the 19th century that gave rise to both the urban planning and public health professions are again fully manifest at the beginning of the 21st century,[3] as large segments of the world's population lack basic shelter and sanitation, especially in developing countries.[2]

Unfortunately, the loss of close collaboration between urban planning and public health professionals that characterized the post–World War II era has limited the design and implementation of effective interventions and policies that might translate into improved health for urban populations. While the theory that connects the built environment to health and well-being is intuitively plausible, we still have a long way to go in collecting sufficient empirical data to make convincing appeals for planning and policy changes by the weight of the evidence.

In the interest of reviving strategic collaborations between urban planning and public health professionals, next we outline three major aims for this article. First, we present a conceptual model that developed out of previous research conducted separately by colleagues at the University of Michigan[4] and our group at Columbia University,[3] which we then connected and built upon to construct a framework for "Social Determinants of Health and Environmental Health Promotion."[5] Unlike other approaches in which the built environment is considered as background or context, our conceptual model specifically focuses on urban morphology and responds to Hebbert's conjectures about where the streets and buildings belong in the "new public health."[6(p446)]

Second, we review empirical research from both the urban planning and public health literature regarding the health effects of housing and housing interventions, both to illustrate how connections between the built environment and health and well-being have been investigated to date, and to recommend strategies that may be useful in future scientific inquiry. An earlier article by Greenberg et al. found only minor overlap in a review of all articles and book reviews published between 1978 and 1990 in the *Journal of the American Planning Association* and the *American Journal of Public Health*.[7] Since

that time, the "new urbanism" has devoted rather more attention to the new public health than vice versa,[6] but recent campaigns spearheaded by the National Center for Environmental Health of the Centers for Disease Control and Prevention[8] and the National Institute of Environmental Health Sciences of the National Institutes of Health[9] are helping to redirect the attention of public health researchers toward investigating the health outcomes of urban design choices and community revitalization projects. In September 2003, the *American Journal of Public Health*[10] and the *American Journal of Health Promotion*[11] both published theme issues devoted to the built environment and health. The current issue of the *Journal of Urban Health* provides additional scientific and policy focus on these connections, with particular emphasis on the urban context.

Finally, we wrestle with key challenges in conducting sound scientific research on connections between the built environment and health, namely: (1) the necessity of dealing with the possible health consequences of myriad public and private sector activities, including those primarily concerned with commerce, housing, transportation, labor, energy, and education;[12] (2) the lack of valid and reliable indicators of the built environment to monitor the health effects of urban planning and policy decisions, especially with regard to land use mix;[13] and (3) the growth of the "megalopolis" or "super urban region" that requires analysis of health effects across state lines and in circumscribed areas within multiple states.[14] While they are by no means panaceas, we suggest strategies for addressing each of these challenges, in order to advance the science of connections between the built environment and health, and better plan for healthy cities.

FOCUS ON URBAN ENVIRONMENTS AND POPULATIONS

More of us are urban dwellers than ever before. According to the 2000 census, nearly 80% of the approximately 280 million people counted in the United States live in metropolitan areas or, more correctly, *metropolitan statistical areas*, defined as urban agglomerations of 50,000 people or more.[15] The largest of these is the New York consolidated metropolitan statistical area, which spreads out over four states (New York, New Jersey, Connecticut, and Pennsylvania) and contains over 21 million people. The U.S. Bureau of the Census defines a *consolidated metropolitan statistical area* as an agglomeration of over 1 million people living in adjacent primary metropolitan statistical areas or metropolitan statistical areas that by local common agreement are effectively aggregated into one region.[15]

The importance of this observation rests upon its implications for the relevant spatial unit for analyzing data, as well as the "level" for intervention to improve population health. For instance, most of the environmental interventions conducted to date, such as ameliorating lead paint, have occurred at the neighborhood, site, and building levels. Increasingly, however, the most important environmental and population health interventions, such as decreasing emissions of greenhouse gases, will require collaboration at the national, regional, and even global levels.

A CONCEPTUAL FRAMEWORK FOR UNDERSTANDING THE CONNECTIONS BETWEEN THE BUILT ENVIRONMENT AND HEALTH

Our joint urban planning and public health framework is centrally concerned with the social, political, economic, and historical processes that generate the urban built environment.[3] By the built environment, we mean that part of the physical environment made by people for people, including buildings, transportation systems, and open spaces. The remainder of the physical environment is the natural environment. None of the natural environment per se remains in cities, since even the parks and waterways have been created—or at least significantly modified—by people, and are therefore part of the built environment.[16] Nonetheless, the natural environment is essential to all life, including urban dwellers. Thus, while we consider the natural environment to be a fundamental determinant of health and well-being, in the context of our joint urban planning and public health framework it is background, while the built environment is foreground.

Mary Northridge recently collaborated with Amy Schulz, a University of Michigan sociologist, to delineate the various mechanisms and pathways through which social, political, and economic processes interface with the physical configurations of cities to affect the health and well-being of urban populations.[5] The conceptual model we jointly devised is presented in Figure 1 (not included).

Figure 1 (not included) was adapted from a conceptual model for understanding racial disparities in health that was developed by Dr. Schulz and her colleagues at the University of Michigan,[4] and draws upon a joint urban planning and public health frame-

work for use in health impact assessment that our group at Columbia University previously introduced.[3] The model posits that three domains—the natural environment (including topography, climate, and water supply), macrosocial factors (including historical conditions, political and economic orders, and human rights doctrines), and inequalities (including those related to the distribution of wealth, employment and educational opportunities, and political influence)—contain the fundamental factors that underlie and influence health and well-being via multiple pathways through differential access to power, information, and resources.[17]

Fundamental factors, in turn, influence two domains of intermediate factors: the built environment (including land use, transportation systems, and buildings) and the social context (including community investment, public and fiscal policies, and civic participation). Structurally, our model posits a set of simultaneous and dynamic relationships among four of the five domains that comprise the first two levels of our model. For analytic purposes, the natural environment is treated as an exogenous domain. It is important to note, however, that this last assumption does not hold over extended time frames. In the longer term, anthropomorphic choices about transportation systems and energy sources do, in fact, change the natural environment. Nonetheless, for our purposes, holding the natural environment relatively constant does little damage to more sophisticated models in which it, too, becomes an endogenous domain.

In terms of the synthesis we seek between the urban built environment and population health and well-being, it is the intermediate factors that we choose to emphasize, in particular. Whether purposefully or inadvertently, it is here that the impact of the built environment is especially subject to policy manipulation. A corollary is that these types of interventions may have the greatest potential benefit for improved population health and well-being. Intermediate factor interventions include the development of land use strategies based upon densification, land use mixing, and microscale design considerations. Because urban planners work at the interface between the built environment and social context applying the knowledge of social science and urban design to generate the physical configurations of cities, we believe that stronger collaborations between urban planners and public health practitioners may prove effective in designing and planning for healthy cities.

Moving from the intermediate factors to the proximate factors in Figure 1 (not included), we shift from the familiar territory of the urban planner to the familiar territory of the public health practitioner. The proximate factors influencing health and well-being are dominated by two domains: stressors (including violent crime, financial insecurity, and environmental toxins) and social integration and social support (including the shape of social networks and the resources available within networks). A somewhat transitional domain is depicted for health behaviors, as they are conceptually separate and distinct from the other two proximate domains, and yet are impossible to practically disentangle from them. Interactive and dynamic relationships among the various domains, between the fundamental and intermediate factors as well as between the intermediate and proximate factors, are depicted by the arrows in Figure 1.

In the past several decades, public health research and practice has focused on understanding and influencing health behaviors, such as smoking cessation, mammography screening, and consumption of more fruits and vegetables. As early as the 1970s and 1980s, however, economic insecurity—unemployment in particular—was implicated in the creation of both physical and mental illness.[18,19] More recently, a broader set of proximate factors, including the effects of racism on health[20] and social support on longevity,[21] have been given greater scientific attention.

Finally, the last column in Figure 1, Health and Well-Being, contains two domains: health outcomes include obesity, injury and violence, respiratory health, and others; well-being effects include hope/despair, life satisfaction, and happiness, to name but a few. As these in turn clearly influence civic life, Figure 1 illustrates the interactive and dynamic nature of the proximate factors and health and well-being domains through the use of arrows between these levels.

Increased interest in the life course approach to chronic disease epidemiology has helped inform population health theory and practice over the past several years, even as this approach is not new to public health or unique to epidemiology.[22] As defined by Ben-Shlomo and Kuh, the life course approach to chronic disease epidemiology is "the study of long-term effects on chronic disease risk of physical and social exposures during gestation, childhood, adolescence, young adulthood, and later adult life."[22(p285)] This perspective includes studies of the biological, behavioral, and psychosocial pathways that operate across an individual's life course as well as across generations to influence the development of chronic diseases and is clearly consonant with the conceptual model presented in Figure 1.

EVIDENCE BASE FOR CONNECTIONS BETWEEN HOUSING AND HOUSING INTERVENTIONS AND HEALTH AND WELL-BEING

On October 25, 1967, at the engineering and sanitation section program at the 95th annual meeting of the American Public Health Association in Miami Beach, Florida, M. Allen Pond, Assistant Surgeon General for Special Projects of the Public Health Service, presented a paper on the role of the public health service in housing and urban life:

> Health problems associated with housing—and the neighborhood that the housing services—are too important to be dealt with on a strictly categorical basis. The problems of the slums and the ghettos in America demand the broadest possible attention, and health officials at all levels must give the highest priority to their solution. The job to be done is simply too big to be handled in a unified, sharply delineated way. Indeed, much of what the Public Health Service does in support of research and development, preparation of standards, training of manpower, provision of technical assistance, and sharing in the costs of program development and operation bears significantly on our national efforts to improve the quality of housing and urban living.[23(p101)]

Our interest in housing interventions is both long-standing[24] and contemporary,[25] renewed in part from ongoing efforts to address the childhood asthma epidemic in Harlem, New York City.[26] Presently, the shortage of affordable housing is so severe in New York City that the homeless population is larger than it has ever been at 38,200 people, including 17,000 children. Fully 85% of the homeless population in New York City is composed of families; 40% of these homeless children have asthma, and lack a regular physician or health care worker to oversee their medical care.[27]

In searching the public health literature for research linking housing and health, we came across a comprehensive review of evidence related to the health and social effects of housing improvements.[28] Upon turning to the urban planning literature, we found an equally thoughtful review on both links between housing and health, and the effects of urban regeneration on health.[29] The following discussion draws heavily on these two current reviews.

Thomson et al. reviewed studies from the observational public health literature on hazards in domestic buildings and identified hygrothermal conditions, radon, falls, house dust mites, environmental tobacco smoke, and fires as the major health risks.[28] Meanwhile, Curtis et al. reviewed studies from the urban planning literature and concluded that poor housing may affect physical health through greater risks of injury and violence, increased levels of respiratory disease and gastrointestinal problems associated with cold, damp conditions and mold growth, and increased rates of infection because of crowded living conditions, especially in temporary accommodations.[29]

Nonetheless, Thomson et al.'s comprehensive review of the health effects of housing improvements concluded that there was insufficient evidence to support improved housing as a means to improved health.[28] In terms of general physical health and illness episodes, 10 of the studies reviewed found some health improvements, 5 studies found no differences on certain measures, and some studies found mixed effects. A more consistent pattern was found for mental health, suggesting that improved housing generates mental health gains. The findings on respiratory health were more equivocal, although one study found children's respiratory symptoms improved and fewer days were missed from school due to asthma 3 months after installation of central heating.[30]

In terms of well-being, the intervention results were more positive. On the basis of four studies that assessed social outcomes, the overall findings were that, after relocation, residents reported a reduced sense of isolation, a reduced fear of crime, an increased sense of belonging and feelings of safety, increased involvement in community affairs, greater recognition of neighbors, and improved outlook on the area as a good place to live.[28] Conversely, two of the reviewed studies on rehousing and area regeneration highlighted the potential for unintended adverse effects because of increased rents. One older study reported increases in standardized mortality rates in the rehoused residents, which was attributed to a doubling of rents, and the household members' consequent inability to afford adequate food.[31]

Curtis et al.[29] concluded that it is difficult to disentangle the health effects of housing renewal from other factors. Housing improvements to windows and bathrooms, fencing of semiprivate spaces, closing alleyways, calming traffic, and improving children's play spaces in an English town estate resulted in reduced anxiety and depression, improved self-esteem, reduced fear of crime, and greater perceived "friendliness" of the area.[32] In an area of Sweden that had undergone improvements to local services and facilities, the population showed reduced levels of mental illness and increased levels of social support.[33] Finally, Collard recorded the experiences of Bangladeshi families in temporary accommodations, who reported that financial assistance in moving, and redecorating and furnishing the home would have been helpful.[34] Not surprisingly, high levels of mobility had detrimental effects on the families' access to primary health care and education.

Saegert et al.[35] have reviewed and evaluated the key characteristics, methods, and results of housing interventions designed to improve health. Of the 64 interventions reviewed from 12 electronic databases, 90% addressed a single condition (most often lead, injury, or asthma), 59% were targeted to children, and 13% were designed for older adults. The message is that current interventions linking housing and health are woefully limited in both scope and scale. The lack of an evidence base relating improved housing to improved health may be due in part to the failure of public health researchers and practitioners to engage in meaningful housing development projects from the initial planning stages and to evaluate them longitudinally and across the life course using valid and reliable measures of health and well-being.

Calls for broad-based studies of the health impacts of the built environment and needed planning and policy interventions at the intermediate level in our conceptual model have historic precedent. On November 16, 1967, Richard A. Prindle, Assistant Surgeon General and director of the Bureau of Disease Prevention and Environmental Control, Public Health Service, gave a speech titled, "The City as Environment: Biological and Social Implications," at a centennial symposium at Wayne State University in Detroit, Michigan. He concluded:

We public health workers must begin to concern ourselves with land use policy in the broadest sense. We must develop criteria of effective use of resources, and in order to develop these criteria we must relate them to standards concerning the health and well-being of people.

We in the health professions also have a specific job of collecting the kind of information on which public planning and policy can be based and of translating these data for the decision makers—which ultimately is the general public. Finally, we in public health, in concert with others, must move from the ivory tower into the community to observe and work with situations as they exist. Epidemiology may not be the full answer, but it certainly is the beginning. We need measurements and plans based on those measurements. We need actions to correct the problems as those affected see them if our solutions are to be accepted, put in practice, and have lasting benefits.[36]

This is not to say it will be easy. We turn our attention next to two key hurdles we have identified in conducting sound scientific research on connections between the built environment and health, and our proposed strategies for surmounting them.

CHALLENGES IN CONDUCTING SOUND SCIENTIFIC RESEARCH ON THE BUILT ENVIRONMENT AND HEALTH

Rather than compiling an exhaustive list of the challenges likely to be encountered in conducting research on connections between the built environment and health, we have elected instead to discuss two key areas and how we have sought to address each of the difficulties we faced. The first is the lack of valid and reliable indicators of the built environment to monitor effects of urban planning and policy decisions, especially with regard to land use mix. For instance, current land use policies not only facilitate automobile use and dependence but also actually hinder the ability to safely access even nearby urban destinations on foot or bike, or by mass transit. Prior to the establishment of a precedent for exclusionary zoning in 1926 (*Euclid, Ohio v Ambler Realty),* land uses were most often intermixed. Afterward, *euclidean* emerged as a euphemism to convey homogeneous zoning, which predominates in the United States today.[13]

Mixed use or heterogeneous zoning allows compatible but different land uses to locate in close proximity to one another and thereby decreases the travel distances between activities.[37] The effects of land use mix on travel choices vary as distances between complementary land uses increase. Thus, one strategy for mitigating air quality and traffic problems and encouraging walking, biking, and transit is to improve accessibility to work sites, services, and transit stations within existing urban settings.[38]

Empirical research regarding the relationship between land use mix and travel behavior has been limited by the relative complexity of measurement, thereby hampering investigations of proposed theoretical ideas involving population health effects.[13] For instance, if a zone is more than half a mile across, then the benefit of mixing uses at a scale in which residents may choose to walk for shopping or a meal may not be captured. For this reason, measuring land use mix at the census block group level rather than at the census tract level may be more meaningful. In addition, when measured at a zonal level, land use mix also needs to take into account the effects of complementary land uses located in adjacent zones, since people do not recognize census borders when selecting destinations. If services are located within a convenient and pleasurable walk, that is, a safe and comfortable one, more people will access these services on foot rather than in automobiles.

Other methodological complications arise in examining the effects of land use mix on transportation modes. For instance, to reduce automobile use, there needs to be pedestrian connectivity between nearby, complementary land uses. Handy notes that access is a function of both travel times and the number and quality of nearby destinations, which need to be accounted for in empirical investigations.[39]

As important as land use mix is to urban planning, there is a dearth of empirical evidence in the public health literature regarding the effects of zoning and land use policies that may potentially affect population health and well-being. An exception is Maantay's longitudinal case study of New York City over the period 1961 to 1998, in which she found that noxious industrial uses are increasingly concentrated within poor communities of color.[40] Employing geographical information systems along with block-by-block canvassing for walkability and verification of service locations, it may be possible to generate improved measures of land use mix across a range of urban and suburban communities that may be usefully employed in future investigations of connections between land use mix and population health.

A second major challenge in conducting sound research on the built environment and health relates to the growth of the megalopolis or super urban region, which requires the analysis of health effects across state lines and in circumscribed areas within multiple states.[14] Not only is the United States a metropolitan nation, it is highly skewed in its distribution of residents. The 10 largest consolidated metropolitan statistical areas account for one third of the entire population. Hence, to effectively plan for urban design and health services, regional analyses are required.

The methodologies for conducting the necessary empirical investigations far surpass the cooperative arrangements that would be needed to implement meaningful policy interventions such as interstate compacts in state and local taxing and land use policy. For example, Rodwin and Gusmano, as part of their World Cities Project, first defined an urban core for New York City, London, Paris, and Tokyo, and then examined the similarities and differences among them.[41] Their current studies illuminate inequalities in health care use and health status, the importance of neighborhoods in protecting population health, and the quality of life in diverse urban communities. Nelson et al., using data from the Behavioral Risk Factor Surveillance System, found significant intrastate differences for binge drinking among metropolitan areas in New York, Tennessee, and Utah.[42] They concluded that metropolitan area estimates might be useful in guiding local efforts to reduce binge drinking. Such methods could be extended to investigate, for example, injury, diabetes, and obesity estimates by metropolitan area, and might then be related to transportation systems, land use policies, and other features of the built environment that have been calculated for these metropolitan statistical areas.[14]

Given sufficient resources, it may even be possible to conduct public health surveillance by city and "megacity," in addition to the current monitoring conducted by states. Certainly the methodological capabilities exist, including using census blocks, census block groups, and census tracts, to construct meaningful agglomerations of the areas of interest.[43]

EFFECTING MEANINGFUL CHANGE

When asked if he ever gets discouraged in his efforts to address urban poverty, Robert M. Coard, the president of Action for Boston Community Development, replied: "[Y]ou know that there's a need. But the need changes. And the face of poverty changes. And what we do changes."[44(p4)]

The needs of the world's poor are profound. The 21st century began with almost 2 billion people living in urbanized regions of the developing world, three quarters of whom live in wretched poverty. Over the next 30 years, the number of city dwellers will double to 4 billion, in a global population that by then will total 8 billion.[3]

According to de la Barra, "Cities are the physical expression of the societies that build them, and the political, social, and economic interactions of their inhabitants.[45(p7)] If we are to collectively revive a passion for "urbanism as a way of life"[46] in the 21st century, it is essential to pay careful attention to the physical definitions of streets and buildings, and ensure that public spaces are places of shared use.

One method of translating research into action on the built environment and health may be through some form of health impact assessment, which is ex-pressly designed to deal with the population health effects of myriad public and private activities, including those primarily concerned with commerce, housing, transportation, labor, energy, and education.[12] In August 2002, Mary Northridge and Elliott Sclar attended a small working meeting of 25 scholars and practitioners from over eight disciplines and 10 countries at the Harvard School of Public Health in Boston, Massachusetts. The aim was to foster a critical exchange about the promises, process, and pitfalls of health impact assessment. In recognition of the fact that public health is strongly influenced by nonmedical health determinants, recent government policies in the United Kingdom and Canada, especially, have provided the impetus for conducting health impact assessments on policies that have not been traditionally viewed as the responsibility of the health sector.[47]

While considerable caution was voiced at the meeting about institutionalizing health impact assessment in the United States, much was learned from the informed and engaged dialogue and debate. A greater appreciation on the part of urban planners and public health professionals of the political processes (from local to federal) that ultimately determine what policies are enacted and what projects are constructed is a first step toward ensuring that research on the built environment and health is more usefully directed toward planning for healthy cities. Yet scientific and professional input is not sufficient to promote healthy living conditions at increasingly high levels of density—the essence of urban life.[3] Only by including the views of the people who bear the brunt of enacted policies and programs will any devised strategies prove acceptable and thus capable of improving population health and well-being. Methodologically, health impact assessment has the potential to improve diverse approaches to developing, testing, validating, implementing, and disseminating research on policies that affect population health, including but not limited to community-based participatory action research.[12,48]

Ultimately, rather than institutionalize health impact assessment in the United States, it may eventually be possible to revamp the environmental impact statement process,[49] which has not been amended in 30 years. Concerns on the part of both environmentalists and developers regarding either erosions of current requirements or further impediments to building projects have hampered efforts to restore it as a meaningful tool of land use decision making.[1] Such improvements might include stronger consideration of environmental health impacts on human populations, consequential public input from the start rather than only at the end of the process via litigation, and follow-up assessments of the predictions of environmental impact statements which rarely, if ever, are conducted.[12]

CONCLUSION

The conceptual model presented here, Social Determinants of Health and Environmental Health Promotion, includes both the built environment and the social context as intermediate determinants of health and well-being. We seek to integrate this model with other multilevel frameworks, notably the ecosocial perspective,[50] in addition to various complementary and reinforcing frameworks, including the life course approach,[22] health and human rights,[51] the precautionary principle,[52] and sustainable production.[53] In order to meaningfully sort out the connections between the built environment and health, however, we need to do more than be explicit about the hypothesized pathways. We also need to test our theories empirically and use these data to refine our models.

The current public health literature lacks concrete measures of the physical dimensions of the neighborhoods and communities it purports to study. The current urban planning literature fails to take into account the distribution of health determinants within and across social groups defined by age, gender, race/ethnicity, class, and sexuality. We contend that in order to plan effectively for healthy cities, we need to reinvigorate the historic collaborative link between urban planning and public health professionals, and together conduct informed science. Perhaps then we can amass sufficient empirical data to make convincing "weight of the evidence" appeals for essential planning and policy changes to improve the health and lives of urban populations.

ACKNOWLEDGMENT

The authors thank Amy Schulz for her joyful collaboration on the model of Social Determinants of Health and Environmental Health Promotion used in this article, and Nancy Krieger for her valued conversations and related references on the history of public health and the life course perspective. We also thank two anonymous reviewers for their critical comments on an earlier draft of this paper, as well as the members of our Urbanism and Public Health university seminar and the students in our Urban Environmental Planning classes at Columbia University for informing our approach and allowing us to talk out loud about our ideas. Partial support for Dr. Northridge is provided by the Centers for Disease Control and Prevention through core funding for the Harlem Health Promotion Center, and the Robin Hood Foundation through major funding for the Harlem Children's Zone Asthma Initiative.

● ● ● REFERENCES

1. Sclar E, Northridge ME. Property, politics, and public health. *Am J Public Health*. 2001; 91:1013-1015.

2. United Nations Human Settlements Programme (UN-HABITAT). Available at: http:// www.unhabitat. org/about/challenge.asp. Accessed June 1, 2003.

3. Northridge ME, Sclar E. A joint urban planning and public health framework: contributions to health impact assessment. *Am J Public Health*. 2003;93: 118-121.

4. Schulz AJ, Williams DR, Israel BA, Lembert LB. Racial and spatial relations as fundamental determinants of health in Detroit. *Milbank Q*. 2002;20(4): 677-707.

5. Schulz A, Northridge ME. Social determinants of health and environmental health promotion. *Health Educ Behav*. In press.

6. Hebbert M. A city in good shape: town planning and public health. *Town Planning Rev*. 1999:70; 433-453.

7. Greenberg M, Popper F, West B, Krueckeberg D. Linking city planning and public health in the United States. *J Plann Lit*. 1994;8:235-239.

8. Dannenberg AL, Jackson RJ, Frumkin H, et al. The impact of community design on public health: a scientific research agenda. *Am J Public Health*. 2003; 93:1500-1508.

9. Srinivasan S, O'Fallon LR, Dearry A. Creating healthy communities, healthy homes, healthy people: initiating a research agenda on the built environment and public health. *Am J Public Health*. 2003;93:1446-1450.

10. Jackson RJ. The impact of the built environment on health: An emerging field. *Am J Public Health*. 2003;93:1382-1384.

11. Killingsworth R, Earp J, Moore R. Supporting health through design: Challenges and opportunities. *Am J Health Promotion*. 2003;18:1-2.

12. Krieger N, Northridge ME, Gruskin S, et al. Assessing health impact assessment: multidisciplinary and international perspectives. *J Epidemiol Community Health*. 2003;57:659-662.

13. Frank LD. Land use and transportation interaction: implications on public health and quality of life. *J Plann Educ Res*. 2000;20:6-22.

14. Sclar E. A metropolitan nation. *Am J Public Health*. In press.

15. US Bureau of the Census. Available at: http://fact finder.census.gov/servlet/GCT Table?ds_name= DEC_2000_SF1_U&geo_id=01000US&_box_ head_nbr=GCT-PH1- R&format=US-10S. Accessed December 21, 2002.

16. Health and Environment: Partners for Life. Ottawa, Ontario: Health Canada; 1997. Report available at http://www.atl.ec.gc/community/resources.html.

17. Link BG, Phelan J. Social conditions as fundamental causes of disease. *J Health Soc Behav.* 1995;spec no:80-94.

18. Brenner MH. Fetal, infant, and maternal mortality during periods of economic instability. *Int J Health Serv.* 1973;3:145-159.

19. Sclar ED. Community economic structure and individual well-being: a look behind the statistics. *Int J Health Serv.* 1980;10:563-579.

20. Krieger N. Does racism harm health? Did child abuse exist before 1962? On explicit questions, critical science, and current controversies: an ecosocial perspective. *Am J Public Health.* 2003; 93:194-199.

21. Glass TA, Dym B, Greenberg S, Rintell D, Roesch C, Berkman LK. Psychosocial intervention in stroke: Families in Recovery from Stroke Trial (FIRST). *Am J Orthopsychiatry.* 2000;70:169-181.

22. Ben-Shlomo Y, Kuh D. A life course approach to chronic disease epidemiology: conceptual models, empirical challenges, and interdisciplinary perspectives. *Int J Epidemiol.* 2002;31:285-293.

23. Pond MA. Role of the public health service in housing and urban life. *Public Health Reports.* 1968;83:101-107.

24. Sclar ED. Homelessness and housing policy: a game of musical chairs. *Am J Public Health.* 1990;80:1039-1040.

25. Northridge ME, Sclar ED. Housing and health. *Am J Public Health.* 2002;92:701.

26. Northridge ME, Jean-Louis B, Shoemaker K, Nicholas S. Advancing population health in the Harlem Children Zone Project. *Soz Praventiv Med.* 2002;47:201-204.

27. Newfield J. How the other half still lives: in the shadow of wealth, New York's poor increase. *The Nation.* March 17, 2003:11-17.

28. Thomson H, Pettricrew M, Douglas M. Health impact assessment of housing improvements: incorporating research evidence. *J Epidemiol Community Health.* 2003;57:11-16.

29. Curtis C, Cave B, Coutts A. Is urban regeneration good for health? Perceptions and theories of the health impacts of urban change. *Environ Plann C: Gov Policy.* 2002;20:517-534.

30. Somerville M, Mackenzie I, Owen P, et al. Housing and health: does installing heating in the home improve the health of children with asthma? *Public Health.* 2000;114: 434-440.

31. McGonigle G, Kirby J. *Poverty and Public Health.* London, England: Gillencz, 1936.

32. Halpern D. *Mental Health and the Built Environment: More Than Bricks and Mortar.* London, England: Taylor and Francis, 1995.

33. Dalgard O, Tambs K. Urban environment and mental health: a longitudinal study. *J Psychiatry.* 1997;171:530-536.

34. Collard A. *Settling Up: Towards a Strategy for Resettling Homeless Families.* London, England: Homeless Forum, 1997.

35. Saegert SC, Klitzman S, Freudenberg N, Cooperman J, Nassar S. Healthy housing: a structured review of published evaluations of U.S. interventions to improve health by modifying housing in the United States, 1990-2001. *Am J Public Health.* 2003;93: 1471-1477.

36. Prindle RA. Health aspects of the urban environment. *Public Health Rep.* 1968;83: 617-621.

37. Parker T. *The Land Use Air Quality Linkage: How Land Use and Transportation Affect Air Quality.* Sacramento: California Air Resources Board, 1994.

38. Handy S. Understanding the link between urban form and network travel behavior. *J Plann Educ Res.* 1996;15:183-198.

39. Handy S. Regional versus local accessibility: neo-traditional development and its implications for non-work travel. *Built Environ.* 1992;18:253-267.

40. Maantay, J. Zoning, equity and public health. *Am J Public Health.* 2001; 91:1033-1041.

41. Rodwin VG, Gusmano MK. The World Cities Project: rationale, organization, and design for comparison of megacity health systems. *J Urban Health.* 2002;79:445-463.

42. Nelson DE, Naimi TS, Brewer RD, Bolen J, Wells HE. Metropolitan area estimates of binge drinking in the United States. *Am J Public Health.* In press.

43. Krieger N, Chen JT, Waterman PD, Soobader MJ, Subramanian SV, Carson R. Geocoding and monitoring of US socioeconomic inequalities in mortality and cancer incidence: does the choice of area-based measure and geographic level matter? The Public Health Disparities Geocoding Project. *Am J Epidemiol.* 2002;156:471-482.

44. Weiss J. *Boston Globe Magazine.* October 27, 2002:4.

45. de la Barra X. Fear of epidemics: the engine of urban planning. *Plann Pract Res.* 2000; 15:7-16.

46. Wirth L. Urbanism as a way of life. In: LeGates RT, Stout F, eds. *The City Reader.* 2nd ed. London, England: Routledge; 2000:97-105.

47. Department of Health. *Independent Inquiry Into Inequalities in Health: Report.* Chairman Sir Richard Acheson. London, England: Stationery Office; 1998.

48. Israel BA, Schulz AJ, Parker A, Becker AB. Review of community-based research: assessing partnership approaches to improve public health. *Annu Rev Public Health.* 1998; 19:173-202.

49. Gilpin A. *Environmental Impact Assessment (EIA): Cutting Edge for the Twenty-First Century.* Cambridge, England: Cambridge University Press; 1995.

50. Krieger N. Theories for social epidemiology in the 21st century: an ecosocial perspective. *Int J Epidemiol.* 2001;30:668-677.

51. Gruskin S, Tarantola D. Health and human rights. In: Detels R, McEwen J, Beaglehole R, Tanaka K, eds. *The Oxford Textbook of Public Health.* 4th ed. New Yok, NY: Oxford University Press; 2001:311-335.

52. Kriebel D, Tickner J, Epstein P, et al. The precautionary principle in environmental health. *Environ Health Perspect.* 2001;109:871-876.

53. Quinn MM, Kriebel D, Geiser K, Moure-Eraso R. Sustainable production: a proposed strategy for the work environment. *Am J Ind Med.* 1998;34:297-304.

4

A Conceptual Framework for Action on the Social Determinants of Health

Source: WHO Commission on Social Determinants of Health. V. CSDH framework for action. In: *A Conceptual Framework for Action on the Social Determinants of Health* (http://www.who.int/social_determinants/resources/csdh_framework_action_05_07.pdf, accessed November 4, 2009). Geneva, Switzerland: World Health Organization, 2007: 15-49, 71-75.

Key messages from this section:

- In contemporary social epidemiology, the three main theoretical frameworks for explaining disease distribution are: (1) psychosocial approaches; (2) social production of disease/political economy of health; and (3) ecosocial and other emerging multi-level frameworks. All represent theories of disease distribution, which presume but cannot be reduced to mechanism-oriented theories of disease causation.

- The main social pathways and mechanisms through which social determinants affect people's health can usefully be seen through three perspectives: (1) 'social selection', or social mobility; (2) 'social causation'; and (3) lifecourse perspectives.

- These frameworks/directions and models are not mutually exclusive. On the contrary, they are complementary, and all contribute elements to the CSDH framework.

- Some previous frameworks for understanding SDH and disease distribution have paid insufficient attention to political variables. The CSDH framework will systematically incorporate these factors.

V. CSDH FRAMEWORK FOR ACTION

V.1.—Purpose of constructing a model for the CSDH

We now proceed to present in detail the specific conceptual framework developed for the CSDH. This is an action-oriented framework, whose primary purpose is to support the CSDH in identifying the level(s) at which it will seek to promote change in tackling SDH through policy. The framework helps to situate these levels of intervention, clarify their relationships and suggest the scope and limits of policy action in each area. A comprehensive SDH model should achieve the following:

(a) Identify the social determinants of health and the social determinants of inequities in health;

(b) Show how major determinants relate to each other;

(c) Clarify the mechanisms by which social determinants generate health inequities;

(d) Provide a framework for evaluating which SDH are the most important to address; and

(e) Map specific levels of intervention and policy entry points for action on SDH.

To include all these aspects in one model is difficult and may complicate understanding. In an earlier version of the CSDH conceptual framework, drafted in 2005, we attempted to include all of these elements in a single synthetic diagram. However, this approach was not necessarily the most helpful. In the current presentation, we separate out the various major components of the framework, and we present and discuss each element separately, in detail.

We begin the presentation by sketching some additional important background elements: first, insights from the theorization of social power, which can help to clarify the dynamics of social stratification; second, an existing model of the social production of disease developed by Diderichsen and colleagues, from which the CSDH framework draws significantly. With these background elements in place, we proceed to examine the key components of the CSDH framework in turn, including: (1) the socio-political context; (2) structural determinants and socioeconomic position; (3) intermediary determinants. We conclude the presentation with a synthetic review of the framework as a whole. The issue of entry points for policy action will be taken up explicitly in the next chapter.

V.2.—Theories of power to guide action on social determinants

Health inequities flow from patterns of social stratification—that is, from the systematically unequal distribution of power, prestige and resources among groups in society. As a critical factor shaping social hierarchies and thus conditioning health differences among groups, 'power' demands careful analysis from researchers concerned with health equity and SDH. Understanding the causal processes that underlie health inequities, and assessing realistically what may be done to alter them, requires understanding how power operates in multiple dimensions of economic, social and political relationships.

The theory of power is an active domain of inquiry in philosophy and the social sciences, and developing a full-fledged theory of power lies beyond the mandate of the CSDH. What the Commission can do is draw elements from philosophical and political analyses of power to guide its framing of the relationships among health determinants and its recommendations for interventions to alter the social distribution of health and sickness.

Power is 'arguably the single most important organizing concept in social and political theory',[67] yet this central concept remains contested and subject to diverse and often contradictory interpretations. Classic treatments of the concept of power have emphasized two fundamental aspects: (1) 'power to', i.e., what Giddens has termed 'the transformative capacity of human agency', in the broadest sense 'the capability of the actor to intervene in a series of events so as to alter their course";[68] and (2) 'power

over', which characterizes a relationship in which an actor or group achieves its strategic ends by determining the behavior of another actor or group. Power in this second, more limited but politically crucial sense may be understood as 'the capability to secure outcomes where the realization of these outcomes depends upon the agency of others'.[69] 'Power over' is closely linked to notions of coercion, domination and oppression; it is this aspect of power which has been at the heart of most influential modern theories of power.[70] It is important to observe, meanwhile, that 'domination' and 'oppression' in the relevant senses need not involve the exercise of brute physical violence, nor even its overt threat. In a classic study, Steven Lukes showed that coercive power can take covert forms. For example, power expresses itself in the ability of advantaged groups to shape the agenda of public debate and decision making in such a way that disadvantaged constituencies are denied a voice. At a still deeper level, dominant groups can mold people's perceptions and preferences, for example through control of the mass media, in such a way that the oppressed are convinced they do not have any serious grievances. 'The power to shape people's thoughts and desires is the most effective kind of power, since it pre-empts conflict and even pre-empts an awareness of possible conflicts'.[71] Iris Marion Young develops related insights on the presence of coercive power even where overt force is absent. She notes that 'oppression' can designate, not only 'brutal tyranny over a whole people by a few rulers', but also 'the disadvantage and injustice some people suffer . . . because of the everyday practices of a well-intentioned liberal society'. Young terms this 'structural oppression', whose forms are 'systematically reproduced in major economic, political and cultural institutions'.[72]

For all their explanatory value, power theories which tend to equate power with domination leave key dimensions of power insufficiently clarified. As Angus Stewart argues, such theories must be complemented by alternative readings that emphasize more positive, creative aspects of power. A crucial source for such alternative models is the work of philosopher Hannah Arendt. Arendt challenged fundamental aspects of conventional western political theory by stressing the inter-subjective character of power in collective action. In Arendt's philosophy, 'power is conceptually and *above all politically* distinguished, not by its implication in agency, but above all by its character as *collective action*'[73]. For Arendt, 'Power corresponds to the human ability not just to act, but to act in concert. Power is never the property of an individual; it belongs to a group and remains in existence only so long as the group keeps together'[74]. From this vantage point, power can be understood as 'a relation in which people are not dominated but empowered' through critical reflection leading to shared action[75].

Recent feminist theory has further enriched these perspectives. Luttrell, Quiroz and Scrutton (2007) follow Rowland (1997) in distinguishing four fundamental types of power:

- Power over (ability to influence or coerce)
- Power to (organize and change existing hierarchies)
- Power with (power from collective action)
- Power within (power from individual consciousness)

They note that these different interpretations of power have important operational consequences for development actors' efforts to facilitate the empowerment of women and other traditionally dominated groups. An approach based on 'power over' emphasizes greater participation of previously excluded groups within existing economic and political structures. In contrast, models based on 'power to' and 'power with', emphasizing new forms of collective action, push towards a transformation of existing structures and the creation of alternative modes of power-sharing: 'not a bigger piece of the cake, but a different cake'.[76]

This emphasis on power as collective action connects suggestively with a model of social ethics based on human rights. As one analyst has argued: 'Throughout its history, the struggle for human rights has a constant: in very different forms and with very different contents, this struggle has consisted of one basic reality: a demand by oppressed and marginalized social groups and classes *for the exercise of their social power*'.[77] Understood in this way, a human rights agenda means supporting the collective action of historically dominated communities to analyze, resist and overcome oppression, asserting their shared power and altering social hierarchies in the direction of greater equity.

The theories of power we have reviewed are relevant to analysis and action on the social determinants of health in a number of ways. First and most fundamentally, they remind us that any serious effort to reduce health inequities will involve changing the distribution of power within society to the benefit of disadvantaged groups. Changes in power relationships can take place at various levels, from the 'micro' level of individual households or workplaces to the 'macro' sphere of structural relations among social constituencies, mediated through economic, social and political institutions. Power analysis makes clear, however, that micro-level modifications will be insufficient to reduce health inequities unless micro-level action is supported and reinforced through structural changes.

By definition, then, action on the social determinants of health inequities is a political process that engages both the agency of disadvantaged communities and the responsibility of the state. This political process is likely to be contentious in most contexts, since it will be seen as pitting the interests of social groups against each other in a struggle for power and control of resources. Theories of power rooted in collective action, such as Arendt's, open the perspective of a less agonistic model of equity-focused politics, emphasizing the creative self-empowerment of previously oppressed groups. 'Here the paradigm case is not one of command, but one of enablement in which a disorganized and unfocused group acquires an identity and a resolve to act'.[78] However, there can be little doubt that the political expression of vulnerable groups' 'enablement' will generate tensions among those constituencies that perceive their interests as threatened. On the other hand, theories that highlight both the overt and covert forms through which coercive power operates provide a sobering reminder of the obstacles confronting collective action among oppressed groups.

Theorizing the impact of social power on health suggests that the empowerment of vulnerable and disadvantaged social groups will be vital to reducing health inequities. However, the theories reviewed here also encourage us to problematize the concept of 'empowerment' itself. They point to the different (in some cases incompatible) meanings this term can carry. What different groups mean by empowerment depends on their underlying views about power. The theories we have discussed acknowledge different forms of power and thus, potentially, different kinds and levels of empowerment. However, these theories urge skepticism towards depoliticized models of empowerment and approaches that claim to empower disadvantaged individuals and groups while leaving the distribution of key social and material goods largely unchanged. Those concerned to reduce health inequities cannot accept a model of empowerment that stresses process and psychological aspects at the expense of political outcomes and downplays verifiable change in disadvantaged groups' ability to exercise control over processes that affect their well-being. This again raises the issue of state responsibility in creating spaces and conditions under which the empowerment of disadvantaged communities can become a reality. A model of community or civil society empowerment appropriate for action on health inequities cannot be separated from the responsibility of the state to guarantee a comprehensive set of rights and ensure the fair distribution of essential material and social goods among population groups. This theme is explored more fully in section VI.4.3, below.

> **Key messages from this section:**
>
> - An explicit theorization of power is useful for guiding action to tackle health inequities.
> - Classic conceptualizations of power have emphasized two basic aspects: (1) 'power to', i.e., the ability to bring about change through willed action; and (2) 'power over', the ability to determine other people's behavior, associated with domination and coercion.
> - Theories that equate power with domination can be complemented by alternative readings that emphasize more positive, creative aspects of power, based on collective action. In this perspective, human rights can be understood as embodying a demand on the part of oppressed and marginalized communities for the expression of their collective social power.
> - Any serious effort to reduce health inequities will involve changing the distribution of power within society to the benefit of disadvantaged groups.
> - Changes in power relationships can range from the 'micro' level of individual households or workplaces to the 'macro' sphere of structural relations among social constituencies, mediated through economic, social and political institutions. Micro level modifications will be insufficient to reduce health inequities unless supported by structural changes.
> - This means that action on the social determinants of health inequities is a political process that engages both the agency of disadvantaged communities and the responsibility of the state.

V.3.—Relevance of the Diderichsen model for the CSDH framework

The CSDH framework for action draws substantially on the contributions of many previous researchers, prominently including Finn Diderichsen. Diderichsen's and Hallqvist's 1998 model of the social production of disease was subsequently adapted by Diderichsen, Evans and Whitehead (2001)[79]. The concept of social position is at the center of Diderichsen's interpretation of "the mechanisms of health inequality"[80]. In its initial formulation, the model emphasized the pathway from society through social position and specific exposures to health. The framework was subsequently elaborated to give greater emphasis to "mechanisms that play a role in stratifying health outcomes,"[81] including "those central engines of society that generate and distribute power, wealth and risks" and thereby determine the pattern of social stratification. The model emphasizes how social contexts create social stratification and assign individuals to different social positions. Social stratification in turn engenders differential exposure to health damaging conditions and differential vulnerability, in terms of health conditions and material resource availability. Social stratification likewise determines differential consequences of ill health for more and less advantaged groups (including economic and social consequences, as well as differential health outcomes per se).

At the individual level, the figure depicts the pathway from social position, through exposure to specific contributing causal factors, and on to health outcomes. As many different interacting causes in the same pathway might be related to social position, the effect of a single cause might differ across social positions as it interacts with some other cause related to social position[82]. Diderichsen's most recent version of the model provides some additional insights.[83] Both *differential exposure* (Roman numeral 'I' in the diagram below[not included]) and *differential vulnerability* (II) may contribute to the relation between social position and health outcomes, as can be tested empirically[84]. Ill health has serious social and economic consequences due to inability to work and the cost of health care. These consequences depend not only on the extent of disability but also on the individual's social position (III—*differential consequences)* and on the society's environment and social policies. The social and economical consequences of illness may feed back into the etiological pathways and contribute to the further development of disease in the individual (IV). This effect might even, on an aggregate level, feed into the context of society, as well, and influence aggregate social and economic development[85].

Many of the insights from Diderichsen's model will be taken up into the CSDH framework, which we will now begin to explain, presenting its key components one by one.

> **Key messages from this section:**
>
> - Social position is at the center of Diderichsen's model of 'the mechanisms of health inequality'.

- The mechanisms that play a role in stratifying health outcomes operate in the following manner:
  - **Social contexts** create social stratification and assign individuals to different social positions.
  - **Social stratification** in turn engenders **differential exposure** to health-damaging conditions and **differential vulnerability,** in terms of health conditions and material resource availability.
  - Social stratification likewise determines **differential consequences** of ill health for more and less advantaged groups (including economic and social consequences, as well differential health outcomes per se).

V.4 .—First element of the CSDH framework: socio-economic and political context

The social determinants framework developed by the CSDH differs from some others in the importance attributed to the *socioeconomic-political context*. This is a deliberately broad term that refers to the spectrum of factors in society that cannot be directly measured at the individual level. 'Context' therefore encompasses a broad set of structural, cultural and functional aspects of a social system whose impact on individuals tends to elude quantification but which exert a powerful formative influence on patterns of social stratification and thus on people's health opportunities. Within the context in this sense will be found those social and political mechanisms that generate, configure and maintain social hierarchies, such as for example the labor market, the educational system, and political institutions including the welfare state.

One point noted by some analysts, and which we also wish to emphasize, is the relative inattention to issues of political context in a substantial portion of the literature on health determinants. It has become commonplace among population health researchers to acknowledge that the health of individuals and populations is strongly influenced by SDH. It is much less common to aver that the quality of SDH is in turn shaped by the policies that guide how societies (re)distribute material resources among their members[86]. In the growing area of SDH research, a subject rarely studied is the impact on social inequalities and health of political movements and parties and the policies they adopt when in government[87].

Meanwhile, Navarro and other researchers have compiled over the years an increasingly solid body of evidence that the quality of many social determinants of health is conditioned by approaches to public pol-

icy. To name just one example, the state of Kerala in India has been widely studied, showing the relationship between its impressive reduction of inequalities in the last 40 years and improvements in the health status of its population. With very few exceptions, however, these reductions in social inequalities and improvements in health have rarely been traced to the public policies carried out by the state's governing communist party, which has governed in Kerala for the longest period during those 40 years[88]. Hung and Muntaner find similarly that few studies have explored the relationship between political variables and population health at the national level, and none has included a comprehensive number of political variables to understand their effect on population health, while simultaneously adjusting for economic determinants.[89] As an illustration of the powerful impact of political variables on health outcomes, these researchers concluded in a recent study of 18 wealthy countries in Europe, North America and the Asia-Pacific region that 20% of the differences in infant mortality rate among countries could be explained by the type of welfare state. Similarly, different welfare state models among the countries accounted for about 10% of differences in the rate of low birth weight babies.[90]

Raphael similarly emphasizes how policy decisions impact a broad range of factors that influence the distribution and effects of SDH across population groups. Policy choices are reflected for example in: family-friendly labor policies; active employment policies involving training and support; the provision of social safety nets; and the degree to which health and social services and other resources are available to citizens[91]. The organization of health care is also a direct result of policy decisions made by governments. Public policy decisions made by governments are of course themselves driven by a variety of political, economic, and social forces, constituting a complex space in which the relationship between politics, policy and health works itself out.

It is safe to say that these specifically political aspects of context are important for the social distribution of health and sickness in virtually all settings, and have been seriously understudied. On the other hand, it is also the case that the most relevant contextual factors, i.e., those that play the greatest role in generating social inequalities, may differ considerably from one country to another.[92] For example, in some countries religion will be a decisive factor, in others less so. In general, the construction/mapping of context should include at least six points: (1) **governance** in the broadest sense and its processes, including definition of needs, patterns of discrimination, civil society participation, and accountability/transparence in public administration; (2) **macroeconomic policy,** including fiscal, monetary, balance of payments and trade policies, and underlying labour market structures; (3) **social policies** affecting factors such as labor, social welfare, land and housing distribution; (4) **public policy** in other relevant areas such as education, medical care, water and sanitation;[93] (5) **culture and societal values;** (6) **epidemiological conditions,** particularly in the case of major epidemics such as HIV/AIDS, which exert a powerful influence on social structures and must be factored into global and national policy-setting. In what follows, we highlight some of these contextual elements, focusing particularly on those with major importance for health equity.

We have adopted the UNDP definition of governance, which is as follows: "[the] system of values, policies and institutions by which society manages economic, political and social affairs through interactions within and among the state, civil society and private sector. It is the way a society organizes itself to make and implement decisions. It comprises the mechanisms and processes for citizens and groups to articulate their interests, mediate their differences and exercise their legal rights and obligations. It is the rules, institutions and practices that set limits and provide incentives for individuals, organizations and firms. Governance, including its social, political and economic dimensions, operates at every level of human enterprise, be it the household, village, municipality, nation, region or globe".[94] It is important to acknowledge, meanwhile, that there is no general agreement on the definition of governance, or of good governance. Development agencies, international organizations and academic institutions define governance in different ways, this being generally related to the nature of their interests and mandates.[95]

Regarding labour market policies, we adopt aspects included in the glossary elaborated for the CSDH's Employment Conditions Knowledge Network[96]: "Labour market policies mediate between supply (jobseekers) and demand (jobs offered) in the labour market and their intervention can take several forms. There are policies that contribute directly to matching workers to jobs and jobs to workers or enhancing workers' skills and capacities, reducing labour supply, creating jobs or changing the structure of employment in favour of disadvantaged groups (e.g. employment subsidies for target groups). Typical passive programmes are unemployment insurance and assistance and early retirement; typical active measures are labour market training, job cre-

ation in form of public and community work programmes, programmes to promote enterprise creation and hiring subsidies. Active policies are usually targeted at specific groups facing particular labour market integration difficulties: younger and older people, women and those particularly hard to place such as the disabled".

The concept of the 'welfare state' is one in which the state plays a key role in the protection and promotion of the economic and social well-being of its citizens. It is based on the principles of equality of opportunity, equitable distribution of wealth, and public responsibility for those unable to avail themselves of the minimal provisions for a good life. The general term may cover a variety of forms of economic and social organization. A fundamental feature of the welfare state is social insurance. The welfare state also usually includes public provision of basic education, health services, and housing (in some cases at low cost or without charge). Anti-poverty programs and the system of personal taxation may also be regarded as aspects of the welfare state. Personal taxation falls into this category insofar as it is progressively used to achieve greater justice in income distribution (rather than merely to raise revenue) and also insofar as it used to finance social insurance payments and other benefits not completely financed by compulsory contributions. In socialist countries the welfare state also covers employment and administration of consumer prices.[97]

One of the main functions of the welfare state is 'income redistribution'; therefore, the welfare state framework has been applied to the fields of social epidemiology and health policy as an amendment to the 'relative income hypothesis'. Welfare state variables have been added to measures of income inequality to determine the structural mechanism through which economic inequality affects population health status.[98]

Chung and Muntaner provide a classification of welfare state types and explore the health effects of their respective policy approaches. Their study concludes that countries exhibit distinctive levels of population health by welfare regime types, even when adjusted by the level of economic development (GDP per capita) and intra-country correlations. They find, specifically, that Social Democratic countries exhibit significantly better population health status, i.e., lower infant mortality rate and low birth weight rate, compared to other countries.[99]

Institutions and processes connected with globalization constitute an important dimension of context as we understand it. 'Globalization' is defined by the CSDH Globalization Knowledge Network, following Jenkins, as: '"a process of greater integration within the world economy through movements of goods and services, capital, technology and (to a lesser extent) labour, which lead increasingly to economic decisions being influenced by global conditions"—in other words, to the emergence of a global marketplace'[100]. Non-economic aspects of globalization, including social and cultural aspects, are acknowledged and relevant. However, economic globalization is understood as the force that has driven other aspects of globalization over recent decades. The importance of globalization signifies that contextual analysis on health inequities will often need to examine the strategies pursued by actors such as transnational corporations and supranational political institutions, including the World Bank and International Monetary Fund.

'Context' also includes social and cultural values. The value placed on health and the degree to which health is seen as a collective social concern differs greatly across regional and national contexts. We have argued elsewhere, following Roemer and Kleczkowski, that the social value attributed to health in a country constitutes an important and often neglected aspect of the context in which health policies must be designed and implemented.[101] In constructing a typology of health systems, Roemer and Kleczkowski have proposed three domains of analysis to indicate how health is valued in a given society:

- The extent to which health is a priority in the governmental/societal agenda, as reflected in the level of national resources allocated to health.

- The extent to which the society assumes collective responsibility for financing and organizing the provision of health services. In maximum collectivism (also referred to as a state-based model), the system is almost entirely concerned with providing collective benefits, leaving little or no choice to the individual. In maximum individualism, ill health and its care are viewed as private concerns.

- The extent of societal distributional responsibility. This is a measure of the degree to which society assumes responsibility for the distribution of its health resources. Distributional responsibility is at its maximum when the society guarantees equal access to services for all.[102]

These criteria are important for health systems policy and evaluating systems performance. They are also relevant to assessing opportunities for action on SDH.

To fully characterize all major components of the socioeconomic and political context is beyond the scope of the present paper. Here, we have considered only a small number of those components likely to have particular importance for health equity in many settings.

V.5.—Second element of the framework: structural determinants and socioeconomic position

Graham observes that the concept of 'social determinants of health' has acquired a dual meaning, referring both to the social factors promoting and undermining the health of individuals and populations and to the social processes underlying the unequal distribution of these factors between groups occupying unequal positions in society. The central concept of 'social determinants' thus remains ambiguous, referring simultaneously to the determinants of health and to the determinants of inequalities in health. Graham notes that: "using a single term to refer to both the social factors influencing health and the social processes shaping their social distribution would not be problematic if the main determinants of health—like living standards, environmental influences, and health behaviors—were equally distributed between socioeconomic groups". But the evidence points to marked socioeconomic differences in access to material resources, health-promoting resources, and in exposure to risk factors. Furthermore, policies associated with positive trends in health determinants (e.g., a rise in living standards and a decline in smoking) have also been associated with persistent socioeconomic disparities in the distribution of these determinants (marked socioeconomic differences in living standards and smoking rates).[103] We have attempted to resolve this linguistic ambiguity by introducing additional differentiations within the field of concepts conventionally included under the heading 'social determinants'. We adopt the term *'structural determinants'* to refer specifically to the components of people's socioeconomic position. Structural determinants, combined with the main features of the socioeconomic and political context described above, together constitute what we call the *social determinants of health inequities*. This concept corresponds to Graham's notion of the 'social processes shaping the distribution' of downstream social determinants. When referring to the more downstream factors, we will use the term *'intermediary determinants of health'*. We attach to this term specific nuances that will be spelt out in a later section (see section V.6.,).

Within each society, material and other resources are unequally distributed. This inequality can be portrayed as a system of social stratification or social hierarchy[104]. People attain different positions in the social hierarchy according mainly to their social class, occupational status, educational achievement and income level. Their position in the social stratification system can be summarized as their socioeconomic position. (A variety of other terms, such as social class, social stratum, and social or socioeconomic status, are often used more or less interchangeably in the literature, despite their different theoretical bases.)

The two major variables used to operationalize socioeconomic position in studies of social inequities in health are *social stratification* and *social class*. The term stratification is used in sociology to refer to social hierarchies in which individuals or groups can be arranged along a ranked order of some attribute. Income or years of education provide familiar examples.

Measures of social stratification are important predictors of patterns of mortality and morbidity. However, despite their usefulness in predicting health outcomes, these measures do not reveal the social mechanisms that explain how individuals arrive at different levels of economic, political and cultural resources. 'Social class', meanwhile, is defined by relations of ownership or control over productive resources (i.e. physical, financial, organizational)[105]. This concept adds significant value, in our view, and for that reason we have chosen to include it as an additional, distinct component in our discussion of socioeconomic position. The particularities of the concept of social class will be described in greater detail when we analyze this concept under point V.5.4.

Two central figures in the study of socioeconomic position were Karl Marx and Max Weber. For Marx, socioeconomic position was entirely determined by "social class", whereby an individual is defined by their relation to the "means of production" (for example, factories, land). Social class, and class relations, is characterized by the inherent conflict between exploited workers and the exploiting capitalists or those who control the means of production. Class, as such, is not an a priori property of individual human beings, but is a social relationship created by societies. One explicit adaptation of Marx's theory of social class that takes into account contemporary employment and social circumstances is Wright's social class classification. In this scheme, people are classified according to the interplay of three forms of exploitation: (a) ownership of capital

assets, (b) control of organizational assets, and (c) possession of skills or credential assets[106].

Weber developed a different view of social class. According to Weber, differential societal position is based on three dimensions: class, status and party (or power). Class is assumed to have an economic base. It implies ownership and control of resources and is indicated by measures of income. Status is considered to be prestige or honor in the community. Weber considers status to imply "access to life chances" based on social and cultural factors such as family background, lifestyle and social networks. Finally, power is related to a political context.[107] In this paper, we use the term "socioeconomic position", acknowledging the three separate but linked dimensions of social class reflected in the Weberian conceptualization.

Krieger, Williams and Moss refer to *socioeconomic position* as an aggregate concept that includes both resource-based and prestige-based measures, as linked to both childhood and adult social class position. Resource-based measures refer to material and social resources and assets, including income, wealth, and educational credentials; terms used to describe inadequate resources include "poverty" and "deprivation". Prestige-based measures refer to individuals' rank or status in a social hierarchy, typically evaluated with reference to people's access to and consumption of goods, services, and knowledge, as linked to their occupational prestige, income, and educational level. Given distinctions between resource-based and prestige-based aspects of socioeconomic position and the diverse pathways by which they affect health, epidemiological studies should state clearly how measures of socioeconomic position are conceptualized.[108] Educational level creates differences between people in terms of access to information and the level of proficiency in benefiting from new knowledge, whereas income creates differences in access to scarce material goods. Occupational status includes both these aspects and adds to them benefits accruing from the exercise of specific jobs, such as prestige, privileges, power and social and technical skills.

Kunst and Mackenbach have argued that there are several indicators for socioeconomic position, and that the most important are occupational status, level of education and income level. Each indicator covers a different aspect of social stratification, and it is therefore preferable to use all three instead of only one. They add that the measurement of these three indicators is far from straightforward, and due attention should be paid to the application of appropriate classifications, for example, children, women and economically inactive people, for whom one or more of these indicators may not be directly available. Information on education, occupation and income may be unavailable, and it may then necessary to use proxy measures of socioeconomic status such as indicators of living standards (for example, car ownership or housing tenure).

Singh-Manoux and colleagues have argued that the social gradient is sensitive to the proximal/distal nature of the indicator of socioeconomic position employed. The idea is that there is valid basis for causal and temporal ordering in the various measures of socioeconomic position. An analysis of the socioeconomic status of individuals at several stages of their lives showed that socioeconomic origins have enduring effects on adult mortality through their effect on later socioeconomic circumstances such as education, occupation and financial resources. This approach is derived from the life course perspective, where education is seen to structure occupation and income. In this model, education influences health outcomes both directly and indirectly through its effect on occupation and income.[109] The disadvantage with education is that it does not capture changes in adult socioeconomic circumstances or accumulated socioeconomic position.

Reporting that educational attainment, occupational category, social class, and income are probably the most often used indicators of current socioeconomic status in studies on health inequalities, Lahelman and colleagues find that each indicator is likely to reflect both common impacts of a general hierarchical ranking in society, and particular impacts specific to the indicator. (1) Educational attainment is usually acquired by early adulthood. The specific nature of education is knowledge and other non-material resources that are likely to promote healthy lifestyles. Additionally, education provides formal qualifications that contribute to the socioeconomic status of destination through occupation and income. (2) Occupation-based social class relates people to social structure. Occupational social class positions indicate status and power, and reflect material conditions related to paid work. (3) Individual and household income derive primarily from paid employment. Income provides individuals and families necessary material resources and determines their purchasing power. Thus income contributes to resources needed in maintaining good health. Following these considerations, education is typically acquired first over the life course. Education contributes to occupational class position and through this to income. The effect of education on income is assumed to be mediated mainly through occupation[110].

Socioeconomic position can be measured meaningfully at three complementary levels: individual, household, and neighborhood. Each level may independently contribute to distributions of exposure and outcomes. Also, socioeconomic position can be measured meaningfully at different points of the lifespan: e.g., infancy, childhood, adolescent, adult (current, past 5 years, etc.). Relevant time periods depend on presumed exposures, causal pathways, and associated etiologic periods. Today it is also vital to recognize gender, ethnicity and sexuality as social stratifiers linked to systematic forms of discrimination.[111]

The CSDH framework posits that *structural determinants* are those that generate or reinforce social stratification in the society and that define individual socioeconomic position. These mechanisms configure the health opportunities of social groups based on their placement within hierarchies of **power, prestige** and **access to resources** (economic status). We prefer to speak of *structural determinants*, rather than 'distal' factors, in order to capture and underscore the causal hierarchy of social determinants involved in producing health inequities. Structural social stratification mechanisms, joined to and influenced by institutions and processes embedded in the socioeconomic and political context (e.g., redistributive welfare state policies), can together be conceptualized as *the social determinants of health inequities*.

We now examine briefly each of the major variables used to operationalize socioeconomic position. First we analyse the proxies use to measure social stratification, including income, education and occupation. Income and education can be understood as social outcomes of stratification processes, while occupation serves as a proxy for social stratification. Having reviewed the use of these variables, we then turn to analyse social class, gender and ethnicity, which operate as important structural determinants.

V.5.1.—Income

Income is the indicator of socioeconomic position that most directly measures the material resources component. As with other indicators such as education, income has a "dose-response" association with health, and can influence a wide range of material circumstances with direct implications for health[112,113]. Income also has a cumulative effect over the life course and is the socioeconomic position indicator that can change most on a short term basis. It is implausible that money in itself directly affects health, thus it is the conversion of money and assets into health-enhancing commodities and services via expenditure that may be the more relevant concept for interpreting how income affects health. Consumption measures are, however, rarely used in epidemiological studies,[114] and are in fact seriously flawed when used in health equity research because high medical costs (an element of consumption) may make a household appear non-poor[115].

Income is not a simple variable. Components include wage earning, dividends, interest, child support, alimony, transfer payments and pensions. Kunst and Mackenbach argued that this is more proximate indicator of access to scarce material resources or of standard of living. It can be expressed most adequately when the income level is measured by: adding all income components (this yield total gross income); subtracting deductions of tax and social contribution (net income); adding the net income of all household members (household income); or adjusting for the size of the household (household equivalent income)[116].

While individual income will capture individual material characteristics, household income may be a useful indicator, since the benefits of many elements of consumption and asset accumulation are shared among household members. This cannot be presumed, especially in the context of gender divisions of labour and power within the household, in particular for women, who may not be the main earners in the household. Using household income information to apply to all the people in the household assumes an even distribution of income according to needs within the household, which may or may not be true. However income is nevertheless the best single indicator of material living standards. Ideally, data are collected on disposable income (what individuals/households can actually spend), but often data are collected instead on gross incomes, or incomes that do not take account in-kind transfers that function as hypothecated income. The meaning of current income for different age groups may vary and be most sensitive during the prime earning years. Income for young and older adults may be a less reliable indicator of their true socioeconomic position because income typically follows a curvilinear trajectory with age. Measures at one point in time may thus fail to capture important information about income fluctuations.[117,118] Macinko, Shi, Starfield and Wulu propose the following summary table of explanations for the relationship between income inequality and health[119]. Galobardes, Shaw, Lawler, Lynch and Davey Smith, conversely, have argued that income primarily influences health through a direct effect on material resources that are in turn mediated by more proximal factors in the causal chain,

Explanation	Synopsis of the Argument
Psychosocial (micro): Social status	Income inequality results in "invidious processes of social comparison" that enforce social hierarchies causing chronic stress leading to poorer health outcomes for those at the bottom.
Psychosocial (macro): Social cohesion	Income inequality erodes social bonds that allow people to work together, decreases social resources, and results in less trust and civic participation, greater crime, and other unhealthy conditions.
Neo-material (micro): Individual income	Income inequality means fewer economic resources among the poorest, resulting in lessened ability to avoid risks, cure injury or disease, and/or prevent illness.
Neo-material (macro): Social disinvestment	Income inequality results in less investment in social and environmental conditions (safe housing, good schools, etc.) necessary for promoting health among the poorest.
Statistical artifact	The poorest in any society are usually the sickest. A society with high levels of income inequality has high numbers of poor and consequently will have more people who are sick.
Health selection	People are not sick because they are poor. Rather, poor health lowers one's income and limits one's earning potential.

such as behaviors. The mechanisms through which income could affect health are:

- Buying access to better quality material resources such as food and shelter.

- Allowing access to services, which may improve health directly (such as health services, leisure activities) or indirectly (such as education).

- Fostering self esteem and social standing by providing the outward material characteristics relevant to participation in society.

- Health selection (also referred to as 'reverse causality') may also be considered as income level can be affected by health status.

V.5.2.—Education

Education is a frequently used indicator in epidemiology. As formal education is frequently completed in young adulthood and is strongly determined by parental characteristics[120,121], it can be conceptualized within a life course framework as an indicator that in part measures early life socioeconomic position. Education can be measured as a continuous variable (years of completed education), or as a categorical variable by assessing educational milestones such as completion of primary or high school, higher education diplomas, or degrees. Although education is often used as a generic measure of socioeconomic position, specific interpretations explain its association with health outcomes:

- Education captures the transition from parents' (received) socioeconomic position to adulthood (own) socioeconomic position and it is also a strong determinant of future employment and income. It reflects material, intellectual, and other resources of the family of origin, begins at early ages, is influenced by access to and performance in primary and secondary school and reaches final attainment in young adulthood for most people. Therefore it captures the long term influences of both early life circumstances on adult health, as well as the influence of adult resources (for example, through employment status) on health.

- The knowledge and skills attained through education may affect a person's cognitive functioning, make them more receptive to health education messages, or more able to communicate with and access appropriate health services.

- Ill health in childhood could limit educational attendance and/or attainment and predispose

to adult disease, generating a health selection influence on health inequalities.

Finally, measuring the number of years of education or levels of attainment may contain no information about the quality of the educational experience, which is likely to be important if conceptualizing the role of education in health outcomes specifically related to knowledge, cognitive skills, and analytical abilities but may be less important if education is simply used as a broad indicator of socioeconomic position.

V.5.3.—Occupation

Occupation-based indicators of socioeconomic position are widely used. Kunst and Mackenbach emphasize that this measure is relevant because it determines people's place in the societal hierarchy and not just because it indicates exposure to specific occupational risk, such as toxic compounds. Galobardes, Shaw, Lawler, Lynch & Davey Smith suggest that occupation can be seen as a proxy for represent Weber's notion of socioeconomic position, as a reflection of a person's place in society related to their social standing, income and intellect. Occupation can also identify working relations of domination and subordination between employers and employees or, less frequently, characterize people as exploiters or exploited in class relations.

The main issue, then, is how to classify people with a specific job according to their place in the social hierarchy. The most usual approach consists of classifying people based on their position in the labour market into a number of discrete groups or social classes. People can be assigned to social classes by means of a set of detail rules that use information on such items as occupational title, skills required, income pay-off and leadership functions. For example Wright's typology distinguishes among four basic class categories: wage laborers, petty bourgeois (self-employed with no more than one employee; small employers (2-9 employees) and capitalist (10 or more employees). Also other classifications-called "social class" but more accurately termed "occupational class"—have been used in European public health surveillance and research. Among the best known and longest lived of these occupational class measures is the British Registrar General's social class schema, developed in 1913. This schema has proven to be powerfully predictive of inequalities in morbidity or mortality, especially among employed men[122,123]. The model has five categories based on a graded hierarchy of occupations ranked according to skill. Importantly, these occupational categories are not necessarily reflective of class relations.

Most studies use the current or longest held occupation of a person to characterize their adult socioeconomic position. However, with increasing interest in the role of socioeconomic position across the life course, some studies include parental occupation as an indicator of childhood socioeconomic position in conjunction with individuals' occupations at different stages in adult life. Some of the more general mechanisms that may explain the association between occupation and health related outcomes are presented by:

- Occupation (parental or own adult) is strongly related to income and therefore the association with health may be one of a direct relation between material resources—the monetary and other tangible rewards for work that determines material living standards—and health.

- Occupations reflect social standing and may be related to health outcomes because of certain privileges—such as easier access to better health care, access to education, and more salubrious residential facilities—that are afforded to those of higher standing.

- Occupation may reflect social networks, work based stress, control, and autonomy and thereby affect health outcomes through psychosocial processes.

- Occupation may also reflect specific toxic environmental or work task exposures such as physical demands (for example, transport driver, labourer).

One of the most important limitations of occupational indicators is that they cannot be readily assigned to people who are not currently employed. As a result, if used as the only source of information on socioeconomic position, socioeconomic differentials may be underestimated through the exclusion of retired people, people whose work is inside the home (mainly affecting women), disabled people (including those disabled by work-related illness and injury), the unemployed, students, and people working in unpaid, informal, or illegal jobs.[124] Given the growing prevalence of insecure and precarious employment, knowing a person's occupation is of limited value without further information about the individual's employment history and the nature of the current employment relationship. Further, socioeconomic indicators based on occupational classification may not adequately capture disparities in working and living conditions across divisions of race/ethnicity and gender.[125]

V.5.4.—Social Class

Social class is defined by relations of ownership or control over productive resources (i.e. physical, financial, and organizational). Social class provides an explicit relational mechanism (property, management) that explains how economic inequalities are generated and how they may affect health. Social class has important consequences for the lives of individuals. The extent of an individual's legal right and power to control productive assets determines an individual's strategies and practices devoted to acquire income and, as a result, determines the individual's standard of living. Thus the class position of 'business owner' compels its members to hire 'workers' and extract labour from them, while the 'worker' class position compels its members to find employment and perform labour. Most importantly, class is an inherently relational concept. It is not defined according to an order or hierarchy, but according to relations of power and control. Although there have been few empirical studies of social class and health, the need to study social class has been noted by social epidemiologists.[126]

Class, in contrast to stratification, indicates the employment relations and conditions of each occupation. The criteria used to allocate occupations into classes vary somewhat between the two major systems presently in widespread use: the Goldthorpe schema and the Wright schema. According to Wright, power and authority are 'organisational assets' that allow some workers to benefit from the abilities and energies of other workers. The hypothetical pathway linking class (as opposed to prestige) to health is that some members of a work organization are expending less energy and effort and getting more (pay, promotions, job security, etc.) in return, while others are getting less for more effort. So the less powerful are at greater risk of running down their stocks of energy and ending up in some kind of physical or psychological 'health deficit'. French industrial sociologists called this 'l'usure de travail'—the usury of work. At the most obvious level, the manager sits in an office while the routine workers are exposed to all the dangers of heavy loads, dusts, chemical hazards and the like[127].

The task of class analysis is precisely to understand not only how macro structures (e.g., class relations at the national level) constrain micro processes (e.g., interpersonal behavior) but also how micro processes (e.g., interpersonal behavior) can affect macro structures (e.g. via collective action)[128].

Social class is among the strongest known predictors of illness and health and yet is, paradoxically, a variable about which very little research has been conducted.[129] Muntaner and colleagues have observed that, while there is substantial scholarship on the psychology of racism and gender, little research has been done on the effects of class ideology (i.e., classism). This asymmetry could reflect that in most wealthy democratic capitalist countries, income inequalities are perceived as legitimate while gender and race inequalities are not[130].

V.5.5.—Gender

'Gender' refers to those characteristics of women and men which are socially constructed, whereas 'sex' designates those characteristics that are biologically determined[131]. Gender involves 'culture-bound conventions, roles, and behaviours' that shape relations between and among women and men and boys and girls[132]. In many societies, gender constitutes a fundamental basis for discrimination, which can be defined as the process by which 'members of a socially defined group . . . are treated differently (especially unfairly)' because of their inclusion in that group[133]. Socially constructed models of masculinity can have deleterious health consequences for men and boys (e.g., when these models encourage violence or alcohol abuse). However, women and girls bear the major burden of negative health effects from gender-based social hierarchies.

In many societies, girls and women suffer systematic discrimination in access to power, prestige and resources. Health effects of discrimination can be immediate and brutal: e.g., in cases of female infanticide, or when women suffer genital mutilation, rape or gender-based domestic violence. Gender divisions within society also affect health through less visible biosocial processes, whereby girls' and women's lower social status and lack of control over resources exposes them to health risks. Disproportionately high levels of HIV infection among young women in some sub-Saharan African countries are fueled by patterns of sexual coercion, forced early marriage, and economic dependency among women and girls[134]. Widespread patterns of underfeeding girl children, relative to their male siblings, provide another example of how gender-based discrimination undermines health. As Doyal argues, 'A large part of the burden of preventable morbidity and mortality experienced by women is related directly or indirectly to the patterning of gender divisions. If this harm is to be avoided, there will need to be significant changes in related aspects of social and economic or-

ganization. In particular, strategies will be required to deal with the damage done to women's health by men, masculinities and male institutions'[135].

Gender-based discrimination often includes limitations on girls' and women's ability to obtain education and to gain access to respected and well remunerated forms of employment. These patterns reinforce women's social disadvantage and, in consequence, their health risks. Gender norms and assumptions define differential employment conditions for women and men and fuel differential exposures and health risks linked to work. Women generally work in different sectors than men and occupy lower professional ranks. 'Women are more likely to work in the informal sector, for example in domestic work and street vending'[136]. Broadly, gender disadvantage is manifested in women's often fragmented and economically uncertain work trajectories: domestic responsibilities disrupt career paths, reducing lifetime earning capacity and increasing the risks of poverty in adulthood and old age[137]. For these reasons, Doyal argues that 'the removal of gender inequalities in access to resources' would be one of the most important policy steps towards gender equity in health. 'Since it is now accepted that gender identities are essentially negotiated, policies are needed which will enable people to shape their own identities and actions in healthier ways. These could include a range of educational strategies, as well as . . . employment policies and changes in the structure of state benefits'[138].

V.5.6.—Race/ethnicity

Constructions of racial or ethnic differences are the basis of social divisions and discriminatory practices in many contexts. As Krieger observes, it is important to be clear that 'race/ethnicity is a social, not biological, category'. The term refers to social groups, often sharing cultural heritage and ancestry, whose contours are forged by systems in which 'one group benefits from dominating other groups, and defines itself and others through this domination and the possession of selective and arbitrary physical characteristics (for example, skin colour)'[139].

In societies marked by racial discrimination and exclusion, people's belonging to a marginalized racial/ethnic group affects every aspect of their status, opportunities and trajectory throughout the lifecourse. Health status and outcomes among oppressed racial/ethnic groups are often significantly worse than those registered in more privileged groups or than population averages. Thus, in the United States, life expectancy for African-Americans is significantly lower than for whites, while an

African-American woman is twice as likely as a white woman to give birth to an underweight baby[140]. Indigenous groups endure racial discrimination in many countries and often have health indicators inferior to those of non-indigenous populations. In Australia, the average life expectancy of Aboriginal and Torres Strait Islanders lags 20 years behind that of non-Aboriginal Australians. Perhaps as a result of the compounded forms of discrimination suffered by members of minority and oppressed races/ethnicities, the 'biological expressions of racism' are closely intertwined with the impact of other determinants associated with disadvantaged social positions (low income, poor education, poor housing, etc.).

V.5.7.—Links and mutual influence between social-political context and structural determinants

A close relationship exists between the social-political context and what we term the structural determinants of health inequities. The CSDH framework posits that *structural determinants* are those that generate or reinforce stratification in the society and that define individual socioeconomic position. In all cases, structural determinants present themselves in a specific political and historical context. It is not possible to analyze the impact of structural determinants on health inequities, nor to assess policy and intervention options, if contextual aspects are not included. As we have noted, key elements of the context include: governance patterns; macroeconomic policies; social policies; and public policies in other relevant sectors, among other factors. Contextual aspects, including education, employment and social protection policies, act as modifiers or buffers influencing the effects of socioeconomic

position on health outcomes and well-being among social groups. At the same time, the context forms part of the 'origin' and sustenance of a given distribution of power, prestige and access to material resources in a society and thus, in the end, of the pattern of social stratification and social class relations existing in that society. The positive significance of this linkage is that it is possible to address the effects of the structural determinants of health inequities through purposive action on contextual features, particularly the policy dimension.

V.5.8.—Diagram synthesizing the major aspects of the framework presented thus far

In this diagram we have summarized the main elements of the social and political context that model and directly influence the pattern of social stratification and social class existing in a country. We have included in the diagram, in the far left column, the main contextual aspects that affect inequities in health, e.g., governance, macroeconomic policies, social policies, public policies in other relevant areas, culture and societal values, and epidemiological conditions. The context exerts an influence on health through socioeconomic position.

Moving to the right, in the next column of the diagram, we have situated the main aspects of social hierarchy, which define social structure and social class relationships within the society. These features are given according to the distribution of power, prestige and resources. The principal domain is social class/position within the social structure, which is connected with the economic base and access to resources. This factor is also linked with people's degree of power, which is in turn again influenced by

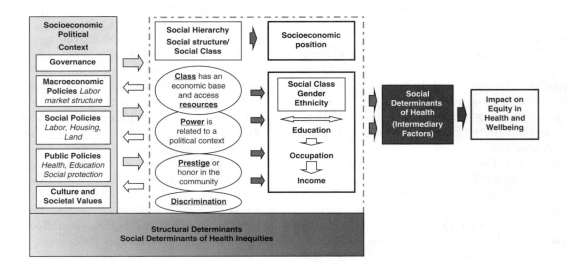

the political context (functioning democratic institutions or their absence, corruption, etc.). The other key domain in this area encompasses systems of prestige and discrimination that exist in the society.

Again moving to the right, in the next column, we have described the main aspects of socioeconomic position. Studies and evaluations of equity frequently use income, education and occupation as proxies for these domains (power, prestige and economic status). When we refer to the domains of prestige and discrimination, we find them strongly related to gender, ethnicity and education. Social class also has a close connection to these different domains, as previously indicated. As an inherently relational variable, class is able to provide greater understanding of the mechanisms associated with the social production of health inequities.

Meanwhile, the patterns according to which people are assigned to socioeconomic positions can turn back to influence the broader context, for example by generating momentum for or against particular social welfare policies, or affecting the level of participation in trade unions.

Proceeding again to the next column to the right (blue rectangle), we see that it is socioeconomic position as assigned within the existing social hierarchy which determines differences in exposure and vulnerability to intermediary health-affecting factors, (what we call the 'social determinants of health' in the limited and specific sense), depending on people's positions in the hierarchy.

Together, context and socioeconomic position constitute the social determinants of health inequities, whose effect is to give rise to an inequitable distribution of health, wellbeing and disease across social groups.

Key messages from this section:

- The CSDH framework is distinguished from some others by its emphasis on the socio-economic and political context and the structural determinants of health inequity
- 'Context' is broadly defined to include all social and political mechanisms that generate, configure and maintain social hierarchies, including: the labor market; the educational system political institutions and other cultural and societal values.
- Among the contextual factors that most powerfully affect health are the welfare state and its redistributive policies (or the absence of such policies)
- In the CSDH framework, *structural determinants* are those that generate stratification and social

class divisions in the society and that define individual socioeconomic position within hierarchies of power, prestige and access to resources. Structural determinants are rooted in the key institutions and mechanisms of the socioeconomic and political context. The most important structural stratifiers and their proxy makers include:
  - o Income
  - o Education
  - o Occupation
  - o Social Class
  - o Gender
  - o Race/ethnicity
- Together, context and structural determinants constitute the *social determinants of health inequities*. We began this study by asking the question of where health inequities come from. The answer to that question lies here. The structural mechanisms that shape social hierarchies according to these key stratifiers are the root cause of inequities in health.

V.6.—Third element of the framework: intermediary determinants

The structural determinants operate through a series of what we will term *intermediary social factors or social determinants of health*. The social determinants of health inequities are causally antecedent to these intermediary determinants, which are linked, on the other side, to a set of individual-level influences, including health-related behaviors and physiological factors. The intermediary factors flow from the configuration of underlying social stratification and, in turn, determine differences in exposure and vulnerability to health-compromising conditions. At the most proximal point in the models, genetic and biological processes are emphasized, mediating the health effects of social determinants.[141] The main categories of intermediary determinants of health are: material circumstances; psychosocial circumstances; behavioral and/or biological factors; and the health system itself as a social determinant. We once again review these elements in turn.

V.6.1.—Material circumstances include determinants linked to the physical environment, such as housing (relating to both the dwelling itself and its location), consumption potential, i.e., the financial means to buy healthy food, warm clothing, etc., and the physical working and neighbourhood environments. Depending on their quality, these circumstances both provide resources for health and contain health risks.

Differences in material living standards are probably the most important intermediary factor. The material standards of living are probably directly significant for the health status of marginalized groups, and also for the lower socioeconomic position, especially if we include environmental factors. Housing characteristics measure material aspects of socioeconomic circumstances[142]. A number of aspects of housing have direct impact on health: the structure of dwellings; internal conditions such as damp, cold and indoor contamination. Indirect housing effects related to housing tenure, including wealth impacts, and neighborhood effects are seen as increasingly important. Housing as a neglected site for public health action, include indoor and outdoor housing condition, as well as, material and social aspect of housing, and local neighborhood have an impact on health of occupants. Galobardes, Shaw, Lawler, Lynch and Davey Smith propose a number of household amenities include access to hot and cold water in the house, having central heating and carpets, sole use of bathrooms and toilets, whether the toilet is inside or outside the home, having a refrigerator, washing machine, or telephone. These household amenities are markers of material circumstances and may also be associated with specific mechanisms of disease. For example, lack of running water and a household toilet may be associated with increased risk of infection[143]. In addition to household amenities, household conditions such as the presence of damp and condensation, building materials, rooms in the dwelling, and overcrowding are housing-related indicators of material resources. These are used in both industrialized and non-industrialized countries.[144] Crowding is calculated as the number of persons living in the household per number of rooms available in the house. Overcrowding can plausibly affect health outcomes through a number of different mechanisms: overcrowded households are often households with few economic resources and there may also be a direct effect on health through facilitation of the spread of infectious diseases. Galobardes et al. add that recent efforts to better understand the mechanisms underlying socioeconomic inequalities in health have lead to the development of some innovative area level indicators that use aspects of housing. For example, a "broken windows" index measured housing quality, abandoned cars, graffiti, trash, and public school deterioration at the census block level in the USA[145].

An explicit definition incorporating the causal relationship between work and health is given by the Spanish National Institute of Work, Health and Safety: "The variables that define the making of any given task as well as the environment in which it is carried out, determining the health of the workers in threefold sense: physical, psychological and social".[146] There are clear social differences in physical, mental, chemical and ergonomic strains in the workplace. The accumulation of negative environmental factors throughout working life probably has a significant effect on variations in the general health of the population, especially when people are exposed to such factors over a long period of time. Main types of hazards at the workplace include physical, chemical, ergonomic, biological, and psychosocial risk factors. General conditions of work define, in many ways, peoples' experience of work. Minimum standards for working conditions are defined in each country but the large majority of workers, including many of those whose conditions are most in need of improvement, are excluded from the scope of existing labour protection measures. In many countries, workers in cottage industries, the urban informal economy, agricultural workers (except for plantations), small shops and local vendors, domestic workers and home workers are outside the scope of protective legislation. Other workers are deprived of effective protection because of weaknesses in labour law enforcement. This is particularly true for workers in small enterprises, which account for over 90% of enterprises in many countries, with a high proportion of women workers.

V.6.2.—Social-environmental or psychosocial circumstances include psychosocial stressors (for example, negative life events, job strain), stressful living circumstances (e.g., high debt) and (lack of) social support, coping styles, etc. Different social groups are exposed to different degrees to experiences and life situations that are perceived as threatening, frightening and difficult to deal with. This partly explains the long-term pattern of social inequalities in health.

Stress may be a causal factor and trigger direct many forms of illness, and detrimental, long-term stress may also be part of the causal complex behind many somatic illnesses. A person's socioeconomic position may itself be a source of long-term stress, and will also affect the opportunities to deal with stressful and difficult situations. However, there are also other, more indirect explanations of the pathway from stress to social inequalities in health. Firstly, there is an on-going international debate on what is often called Wilkinson's "income inequality and social cohesion" model. The model states that, in rich societies, the size of differences in income is more important from a health point of view than the size of the average income. Wilkinson's hypothesis is that the greater the income disparities are in a society, the greater becomes the distance between the social strata. Social interaction is thus characterized by less solidarity and community spirit.[147] The people who lose most are those at the bottom of the income hierarchy, who are particularly affected by psychosocial stress linked to social exclusion, lack of self-respect and more or less concealed contempt from the people around them. Secondly, there are significant social differences in the prevalence of episodes of stress occurrence of short-term and long-term episodes of mental stress, linked to uncertainty about the financial situation, the labor market and social relations. The same applies to the probability of experiencing violence or threats of violence. Disadvantaged people have experienced far more insecurity, uncertainty and stressful events in their life course, and this affects social inequalities in health. This is illustrated in the following table published in the Norwegian Action Plan to Reduce Social Inequalities in Health 2005-06.[148]

Some studies refer to the association between socio-economical status and health locus control. This concept refers to the way people perceive the events related to their healthy: as controllable (internal control), or as controlled by others (external control). People with education below university level more frequently identified an external locus of control.[149] Other important challenges arise from increased incidence and prevalence of precarious and informal employments consequent on changes in the labor market raise many issues and challenges for health care providers, organizational psychologists, personnel and senior managers, employers and trade union representatives, and workers and their families. Job insecurity and non-employment are also matters of concern to the wider community.[150]

V.6.3.—Behavioural and biological factors include smoking, diet, alcohol consumption, and lack of physical exercise, which again can be either health protecting and enhancing (like exercise) or health damaging (cigarette smoking and obesity), between biological factor we are including genetics factor and from perspective of social determinants of health age and sex distribution could be including.

Social inequalities in health have also been associated with social differences in lifestyle or behaviors. Such differences are found in nutrition, physical activity, tobacco and alcohol consumption. This indicates that differences in lifestyle could partially explain social inequalities in health, but researchers do not agree on their importance: some regard differences in lifestyle as a sufficient explanation without further elaboration; others regard them as contributory factors that in turn result from more fundamental causes. For example, Margolis et al. found that the prevalence of both acute and persistent respiratory symptoms in infants showed dose response relationships with SEP. When risk factors such as crowding and exposure to smoking in the household were adjusted for, relative risk associated with SEP was reduced but still remained significant. The data further suggest that risk factors operated differently for different SEP levels; being in day care was associated with somewhat reduced incidence in lower SEP families but with increased incidence among infants from high SEP families.[151] Health risk behaviors such as cigarette smoking, physical inactivity, poor diet, and substance abuse are closely tied to

	Social status:[1]	
PERCENTAGES WHO HAVE EXPERIENCED IN THEIR ADULT LIFE:	**LOW:**	**HIGH:**
– several episodes of 3+ months of unemployment	11%	1%
– lost their job serveral times (involuntarily)	7%	2%
– received social security benefits	11%	2%
– had a serious accident	21%	6%
– been unemployed at the age of 55	29%	7%
– been unmarried/had no cohabitant at the age of 55	26%	14%
– had a low income at the age of 53	20%	2%

[1]Low status = the third with the lowest occupational prestige, high status = the third with the highest occupational prestige

both SEP and health outcomes. Despite the close ties, the association of SEP and health is reduced but not eliminated when these behaviors are statistically controlled.[152]

Cigarette smoking is strongly linked to SEP, including education, income, and employment status, and it is significantly associated with morbidity and mortality, particularly from cardiovascular disease and cancer[153]. A linear gradient between education and smoking prevalence was also shown in a community sample of middle-aged women: Additionally, among current smokers the number of cigarettes smoked was related to SEP.[154] Significant employment grade differences in smoking were found in the Whitehall II study, which examined a new cohort of 10,314 subjects from the British Civil Service beginning in 1985.[155] Moving from the lowest to the highest employment grades, the prevalence of current smoking among men was 33.6%, 21.9%, 18.4%, 13.0%, 10.2%, and 8.3%, respectively. For women, the comparable figures were 27.5%, 22.7%, 20.3%, 15.2%, 11.6%, and 18.3%, respectively. Social class differences in smoking are likely to continue because rates of smoking initiation are inversely related to SEP and because rates of cessation are positively related to SEP[156].

Lifestyle factors are relatively accessible for research, so this is one of the causal areas we know a good deal about. Although descriptions of the correlation of lifestyle factors with social status are relatively detailed and well-founded, this should not be taken to indicate that these factors are the most important causes of social inequalities in health. Other, more fundamental factors may cause variations in both lifestyle and health. Some surveys indicate that differences in lifestyle can only explain a small proportion of social inequalities in health.[157] For instance, material factors may act as a source of psychosocial stress, and psychosocial stress may influence health related behaviors. Each of them can influence health through specific biological factors. For example a diet rich in saturated fat will lead to atherosclerosis, which will increase the risk of a myocardial infarction. Stress will activate hormonal systems that may increase blood pressure and reduce the immune response. Adoption of health-threatening behaviors is a response to material deprivation and stress. Environments determine whether individuals take up tobacco, use alcohol, have poor diets, and engage in physical activity. Tobacco and excessive alcohol use, and carbohydrate-dense diets, are means of coping with difficult circumstances.[158]

V.6.4.—The health system as a social determinant of health.

As previously discussed, various models that have tried to explain the functioning and impact of SDH have not made sufficiently explicit the role of the health system as a social determinant. The role of the health system becomes particularly relevant through the issue of access, which incorporates differences in exposure and vulnerability. On the other hand, differences in access to health care certainly do not fully account for the social patterning of health outcomes. Adler, Boyce, Chesney, Folkman and Syme, for instance, have considered the role of access to care in explaining the SEP-health gradient and concluded that access alone could not explain the gradient[159].

In a comprehensive model, the health system itself should be viewed as an intermediary determinant. This is closely related to models for the organization of personal and non-personal health service delivery. The health system can directly address differences in exposure and vulnerability not only by improving equitable access to care, but also in the promotion of intersectoral action to improve health status. Examples would include food supplementation through the health system and transport policies and intervention for tackling geographic barrier to access health care. A further aspect of great importance is the role the health system plays in mediating the differential consequences of illness in people's lives. The health system is capable of ensuring that health problems do not lead to a further deterioration of people's social status and of facilitating sick people's social reintegration. Examples include programmes for the chronically ill to support their reinsertion in the workforce, as well as appropriate models of health financing that can prevent people from being forced into (deeper) poverty by the costs of medical care. Another important component to analyze relates to the way in which the health system contributes to social participation and the empowerment of the people, if in fact this is defined as one of the main axes for the development of pro-equity health policy. In this context, we can reflect on the hierarchical and authoritarian structure that predominates in the organization of most health systems. Within health systems, people enjoy little participatory space through which to take part in monitoring, evaluation and decision-making about system priorities and the investment of resources.

Diderichsen suggests that services through which the health sector deals with inequalities in health can be of five different types: (1) reducing the inequality level among the poor with respect to the causal factors that mediate the effects of poverty on health in such areas as nutrition, sanitation, housing, and working conditions; (2) reinforcing factors that might reduce susceptibility to health effects from inequitable exposures, using various means including vaccination, empowerment, and social support; (3) treating and rehabilitating the health problems that constitute the socioeconomic gap of burden of disease (the rehabilitation of disabilities, in particular, is often overlooked as a potential contributor to the reduction of health inequalities); (4) strengthening policies that reproduce contextual factors such as social capital that might modify the health effects of poverty; (5) protecting against social and economic consequences of ill health though health insurance sickness benefits and labor market policies.[160] Even if there were some dispute as to whether the health system can itself be considered an indirect determinant of health inequities, it is clear that the system influences how people move among the social strata. Benzeval, Judge and Whitehead argue that the health system has three obligations in confronting inequity: (1) to ensure that resources are distributed between areas in proportion to their relative needs; (2) to respond appropriately to the health care needs of different social groups; and (3) to take the lead in encouraging a wider and more strategic approach to developing healthy public policies at both the national and local level, to promote equity in health and social justice.[161] On this point the UK Depart-

ment of Health has argued that the health system should play a more active role in reducing health inequalities, not only by providing equitable access to health care services but also by putting in place public health programmes and by involving other policy bodies to improve the health of disadvantaged communities[162].

V.6.5.—Diagram summarizing the content of the preceding section on intermediary determinants

Socioeconomic context directly affects intermediary factors, e.g. through kind, magnitude and availability (large yellow arrow). But for the population, the more important path of influence is through socioeconomic position. Socioeconomic position influences health through more specific, intermediary determinants. Those intermediary factors include: material circumstances, such as neighborhood, working and housing conditions; psychosocial circumstances, and also behavioral and biological factors. The model assumes that members of lower socioeconomic groups live in less favorable material circumstances than higher socioeconomic groups, and that people closer to the bottom of the social scale more frequently engage in health-damaging behaviors and less frequently in heath-promoting behaviors than do the more privileged. The unequal distribution of these intermediary factors (associated with differences in exposure and vulnerability to health-compromising conditions, as well as with differential consequences of ill-health) constitutes the primary mechanism

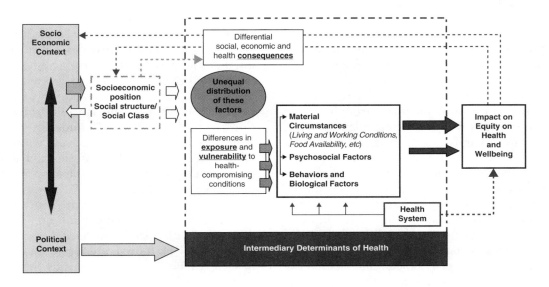

Figure Mechanisms and intermediary factors of social determinants of health elaborated for EQH/EIP (OPSH) 2006

through which socioeconomic position generates health inequities. The model includes the health system as a social determinant of health and illustrates the capacity of the heath sector to influence the process in three ways, by acting upon: differences in exposures, differences in vulnerability and differences in the consequences of illness for people's health and their social and economic circumstances.

V.6.6.—A crosscutting determinant: social cohesion/ social capital[163].

The concepts of social cohesion and 'social capital' occupy an unusual (and contested) place in understandings of SDH. Over the past decade, these concepts have been among the most widely discussed in the social sciences and social epidemiology. Influential researchers have proclaimed social capital a key factor in shaping population health.[164,165,166,167] However, controversies surround the definition and importance of social capital.

In the most influential recent discussions, three broad approaches to the characterization and analysis of social capital can be distinguished: communitarian approaches, network approaches and resource distribution approaches. The *communitarian approach* defines social capital as a psychosocial mechanism, corresponding to a neo-Durkheimian perspective on the relation between individual health and society[168]. This school includes influential authors such as Robert Putnam and Richard Wilkinson. Putnam defines social capital as "features of social organization, such as networks, norms, and social trust, that facilitate coordination and cooperation for mutual benefit"[169]. Social capital is looked upon as an extension of social relationships and the norms of reciprocity[170], influencing health by way of the social support mechanisms that these relationships provide to those who participate on them. The *network approach* considers social capital in terms of resources that flow and emerge through social networks. It begins with a systemic relational perspective; in other words, an ecological vision is taken that sees beyond individual resources and additive characteristics. This involves an analysis of the influence of social structure, power hierarchies and access to resources on population health[171]. This approach implies that decisions that groups or individuals make, in relation to their lifestyle and behavioural habits, cannot be considered outside the social context where such choices take place. Two of the most outstanding conceptualisations in this regard have been elaborated by James Coleman and Pierre Bourdieu, whose work has focused primarily on notions of social cohesion. Finally, the *resource distribution approach*, adopting a materialistic perspective, suggests that there is a danger in promoting social capital as a substitute for structural change when facing health inequity. Some representatives of this group openly criticize psychosocial approaches that have suggested social capital and cohesion as the most important mediators of the association between income and health inequality[172]. The resource distribution approach insists that psychosocial aspects affecting population health are a consequence of material life conditions[173].

Recent work by Szreter and Woolcock (2004)[174] has enriched the debates around social capital and its health impacts. These authors distinguish between bonding, bridging and linking social capital. *Bonding social* capital refers to the trust and cooperative relationships between members of a network that are similar in terms of their social identity. *Bridging social capital*, on the other hand, refers to respectful relationships and mutuality between individuals and groups that are aware that they do not possess the same characteristics in socio-demographic terms. Finally, *linking social capital* corresponds with the norms of respect and trust relationships between individuals, groups, networks and institutions that interact from different positions along explicit gradients of institutionalised power[175].

Some scholars have critiqued what they see as the faddish, ideologically driven adoption of the term 'social capital'. Muntaner, for example, has suggested that the term serves primarily as a 'comforting metaphor' for those in public health who wish to maintain that 'capitalism . . . and social cohesion/ social integration are compatible'. Beyond such ideological reassurance, Muntaner argues, the vocabulary of social capital provides few if any fresh insights, and may in fact provoke confusion. Those innovations that have been achieved by researchers investigating social capital could just as well 'have been carried out under the label of "social integration" or "social cohesion"'. Indeed, 'it would be more adequate to use terms such as "cohesion" and "integration" to avoid the confusion and implicit endorsement of [a specific] economic system that the term [social capital] conveys'[176].

We share with Muntaner the concern that the current interest in 'social capital' may further encourage depoliticized approaches to population health and SDH. Indeed, it is clear that the concept of social capital has not infrequently been deployed as part of a broader discourse promoting reduced state responsibility for health, linked to an emphasis on individual and community characteristics, values and lifestyles as primary shapers of health outcomes.

Logically, if communities can take care of their own health problems by generating 'social capital', then government can be increasingly discharged of responsibility for addressing health and health care issues, much less taking steps to tackle underlying social inequities. Navarro suggests that foundational work on social capital, including Putnam's, 'reproduced the classical . . . dichotomy between civil and political society, in which the growth of one (civil society) requires the contraction of the other (political society—the state)'. From this perspective, the adoption of social capital as a key for understanding and promoting population health is part of a broader, radically depoliticizing trend.[177]

On the other hand, however, it can be argued that the recognition of linking social capital through Szreter's and Woolcock's work has contributed to a higher consideration of the dimension of power and of structural aspects in tackling social capital as a social determinant of health. This may help move discussions of social capital resolutely beyond the level of informal relationships and social support. The idea of linking social capital has also been fundamental as a new element when discussing the role that the state occupies or should occupy in the development of strategies that favour equity. Linking social capital offers the opportunity to analyse how relationships that are established with institutions in general, and with the state in particular, affect people's quality of life. Such discussions highlight the role of political institutions and public policy in shaping opportunities for civic involvement and democratic behaviour[178,179]. The CSDH adopts the position that the state possesses a fundamental role in social protection, ensuring that public services are provided with equity and effectiveness. The welfare state is characterized as systematic defense against social insecurity, this being understood as individuals', groups' or communities' vulnerability to diverse environmental threats[180]. In this context, while remaining alert to ways in which notions of 'social capital' or community may be deployed to excuse the state from responsibility for the well-being of the population[181,182,183], we can also look for aspects of these concepts that shed fresh light on key state functions.

The notion of linking social capital speaks to the idea that one of the central points of health politics should be the configuration of cooperative relationships between citizens and institutions. In this sense, the state should assume the responsibility of developing more flexible systems that facilitate access and develop real participation by citizens. Here, a fundamental aspect is the strengthening of local or regional governments so that they can constitute concrete spaces of participation[184,185]. The development of social capital, understood in these terms, is based on citizen participation. True participation implies a (re)distribution of empowerment, that is to say, a redistribution of the power that allows the community to possess a high level of influence in decision-making and the development of policies affecting its well being and quality of life.

The competing definitions and approaches suggest that 'social capital' cannot be regarded as a uniform concept. Debate surrounds whether it should be as seen a property of individuals, groups, networks, or communities, and thus where it should be located with respect to other features of the social order. It is unquestionably difficult to situate social capital definitively as either a structural or an intermediary determinant of health, under the categories we have developed here. It may be most appropriate to think of this component as 'cross-cutting' the structural and intermediary dimensions, with features that link it to both.

V.7.—Impact on equity in health and well-being

This section summarizes some of the outcomes that emerge at the end of the social 'production chain' of health inequities depicted in the framework. At this stage (far right side of the framework diagrams), we find the measurable impacts of social factors upon comparative health status and outcomes among different population groups, i.e., health equity. According to the analysis we have developed, the structural factors associated with the key components of socioeconomic position (SEP) are at the root of health inequities measured at the population level. This relationship is confirmed by a substantial body of evidence.

Socioeconomic health differences are captured in general measures of health, like life expectancy, all-cause mortality and self-rated health.[186] Differences correlated with people's socioeconomic position are found for rates of mortality and morbidity from almost every disease and condition[187]. SEP is also linked to prevalence and course of disease and self-rated health[188]. Socioeconomic health inequalities are evident in specific causes of disease, disability and premature death, including lung cancer, coronary heart disease, accidents and suicide. Low birth weight provides an additional important example. This is a sensitive measure of child health and a major risk factor for impaired development through childhood, including intellectual development[189]. There are marked differences in national rates of low birth weight, with higher rates in the U.S. and UK and lower rates in Nordic countries like Sweden, Norway and the Netherlands. These rates vary in line with the proportion of the child population living in poverty (in households with incomes below 50% of average income): at their lowest in lowpoverty countries like Sweden and Norway, and at their highest in high-poverty countries like the UK and U.S.[190].

a) *Impact along the gradient:* There is evidence that the association of SEP and health occurs at every level of the social hierarchy, not simply below the threshold of poverty. Not only do those in poverty have poorer health than those in more favored circumstances, but those at the highest level enjoy better health than do those just below[191]. The effects of severe poverty on health may seem obvious through the impact of poor nutrition, crowded and unsanitary living conditions, and inadequate medical care. Identifying factors that can account for the link to health all across the SEP hierarchy may shed light on new mechanisms that have heretofore been ignored because of a focus on the more readily apparent correlates of poverty. The most notable of the studies demonstrating the SEP-health gradient is the Whitehall study of mortality (Marmot et al., 1984), which covered British civil servants over a period of 10 years. Similar findings emerge from census data in the United Kingdom (Susser, Watson and Hopper 1985)[192]. Surprisingly, we know rather little about how SEP operates to influence biological functions that determine health status. Part of the problem may be the way in which SEP is conceptualized and analyzed. SEP has been almost universally relegated to the status of a control variable and has not been systematically studied as an important etiologic factor in its own right. It is usually treated as a main effect, operating independently of other variables to predict health.

b) *Life course perspective on the impact:* Children born into poorer circumstances are at greater risk of the forms of developmental delay associated with intellectual disability, including speech impairments, cognitive difficulties and behavioral problems[193,194]. Some other conditions, like stroke and stomach cancer, appear to depend considerably on childhood circumstances, while for others, including deaths from lung cancer and accidents/violence, adult circumstances play the more important role. In another group are health outcomes where it is cumulative exposure that appears to be important. A number of studies suggest that this is the case for coronary heart disease and respiratory disease, for example[195].

c) *Selection processes and health-related mobility:* As discussed above, people with weaker health resources, allegedly, have a tendency to end up or remain low on the ladder of socioeconomic position. According to some analysts, the status of research on selection processes and health-related mobility within the socioeconomic structure can be summarized in three points: (1) Variations in health in youth have some significance for educational paths and for the kind of job a person has at the beginning of his or her working career; (2) For those who are already established in working life, variations in health have little significance for the overall progress of a person's career; (3) People who develop serious health problems in adult life are often excluded from working life, and often long before the ordinary retirement age[196].

Graham argues that people with intellectual disabilities are more exposed to the social conditions associated with poor health and have poorer health than the wider population[197]. She adds that, for example, those with mild disabilities are more likely than non-disabled people to have employment histories punctured by repeated periods of unemployment. Women with mild intellectual disabilities are further disadvantaged by high rates of teenage motherhood[198]. In both childhood and adulthood, co-morbidity—the experience of multiple illnesses and functional limitations—disproportionately affects people with intellectual disabilities[199]. For example, in the British 1958 birth cohort study, children with mild mental retardation were at higher risk of sensory impairments and emotional difficulties; they were also more likely to be in contact with psychiatric services. In adulthood, mild mental retardation was associated with limiting long-term illness and disability, and, particularly for women, with depressed mood.

One might assume such effects to be inevitable. But they are in part due to discriminatory practices, in part also to failures to adapt educational institutions and working life to special needs. To the extent that this is the case, social selection is neither necessary, nor inevitable, nor fair. This phenomenon particularly affects persons with disabilities, persons from immigrant backgrounds and, to a certain extent, women[200].

d) *Impact on the socioeconomic and political context:* From a population standpoint, we observe that the magnitude of certain diseases can translate into direct effects on features of the socioeconomic and political context, through high prevalence rates and levels of mortality and morbidity. The HIV/AIDS pandemic in sub-Saharan Africa can be seen in this light, with its associated plunge in life expectancy and stresses on agricultural productivity, economic growth, and sectoral capacities in areas such as health and education. The magnitude of the impact of epidemics and emergencies will depend on the historical, political and social contexts in which they occur, as well as on the demographic composition of the societies affected. These are aspects that must be considered when analyzing welfare state structures, in particular models of health system organization that may be considered to respond to such challenges[201].

Key messages from this section:

- The underlying social determinants of health inequities operate through a set of intermediary determinants of health to shape health outcomes. The vocabulary of 'structural determinants' and 'intermediary determinants' underscores the causal priority of the structural factors.
- The main categories of intermediary determinants of health are: material circumstances; psychosocial circumstances; behavioral and/or biological factors; and the health system itself as a social determinant
- Material circumstances include factors such as housing and neighborhood quality; consumption potential (i.e., the financial means to buy healthy food, warm clothing, etc.), and the physical work environment.
- Psychosocial circumstances include psychosocial stressors, stressful living circumstances and relationships, and social support and coping styles (or the lack thereof).
- Behavioral and biological factors include nutrition, physical activity, tobacco consumption and alcohol consumption, which are distributed differently among different social groups. Biological factors also include genetic factors.
- The CSDH framework departs from many previous models by conceptualizing the health system itself as a social determinant of health. The role of the health system becomes particularly relevant through the issue of access, which incorporates differences in exposure and vulnerability, and through intersectoral action led from within the health sector. The health system plays an important role in mediating the differential consequences of illness in people's lives.
- The concepts of social cohesion and social capital occupy a conspicuous (and contested) place in discussions of SDH. Social capital cuts across the structural and intermediary dimensions, with features that link it to both.
- Focus on social capital risks reinforcing depoliticized approaches to public health and SDH; however, certain interpretations, including Szreter's and Woolcock's notion of 'linking social capital', have spurred new thinking on the role of the state in promoting equity.
- A key task for health politics is nurturing cooperative relationships between citizens and institutions. The state should take responsibility for developing flexible systems that facilitate access and participation on the part of the citizens.
- The social, economic and other consequences of specific forms of illness and injury vary significantly, depending on the social position of the person who falls sick.
- Illness and injury have an indirect impact in the socioeconomic position of individuals. From the population perspective, the magnitude of certain illnesses can directly impact key contextual factors (e.g., the performance of institutions).
- Looking at the ultimate impact of social processes on health equity, we find that the structural factors associated with the key components of socioeconomic position (SEP) are at the root of health inequities at the population level. This relationship is confirmed by a substantial body of evidence.
- Differences correlated with people's socioeconomic position are found for rates of mortality and morbidity from almost every disease and condition. SEP is also linked to prevalence and course of disease and self-rated health.
- The magnitude of certain diseases can directly affect features of the socioeconomic and political context, through high prevalence rates and levels of mortality and morbidity. The HIV/AIDS pandemic in sub-Saharan Africa provides one example, with its impact on agriculture, economic growth and sectoral capacities in areas such as health and education.

V.8.—Summary of the mechanisms and pathways represented in the framework

In this section, we summarize key features of the CSDH model and begin to sketch some of the considerations for policymaking to which the model gives rise. The next chapter will explore policy implications and entry points in greater depth.

The figure below illustrates the main processes captured in the CSDH framework, as we have explored them, step by step, in the present chapter. The diagram also highlights the reverse or feedback effects through which illness may affect individual social position, and widely prevalent diseases may affect key social, economic and political institutions. Reading the diagram from left to right, we see the social and political context (in yellow), which gives rise to a set of unequal socioeconomic positions or social classes (red column). (Phenomena related to socioeconomic position can also influence aspects of the context, as suggested by the pale red arrows pointing back to the left.) Groups are stratified according to the economic status, power and prestige they enjoy, for which we use income levels, education, occupation status, gender, race/ethnicity and other factors as proxy indicators. This column of the diagram ("socioeconomic position") locates the underlying mechanisms of social stratification and the creation of social inequities.

Moving to the right, we observe how these socioeconomic positions then translate into specific determinants of individual health status reflecting the individual's social location within the stratified system. The model shows that a person's socioeconomic position affects his/her health, but that this effect is not direct. Socioeconomic position influences health through more specific, intermediary determinants.

Based on their respective social status, individuals experience differences in exposure and vulnerability to health-compromising conditions. Socioeconomic position directly affects the level or frequencies of exposure and the level of vulnerability, in connection with intermediary factors. Also, differences in exposure can generate more or less vulnerability in the population after exposure.

Once again, a distinctive element of this model is its explicit incorporation of the health system. Socioeconomic inequalities in health can in fact be partly explained by the "feedback" effect of health on socioeconomic position, e.g., when someone experiences a drop in income because of a work-induced disability or the medical costs associated with major illness. Persons who are in poor health less frequently move up and more frequently move down the social ladder than healthy persons. This implies that the health system itself can be viewed as a social determinant of health. This is in addition to the health sector's key role in promoting and coordinating SDH policy, as regards interventions to alter differential exposures and differential vulnerability through action on intermediary factors (material circumstances, psychosocial factors and behavioral/biological factors). It may be noted, in addition, that

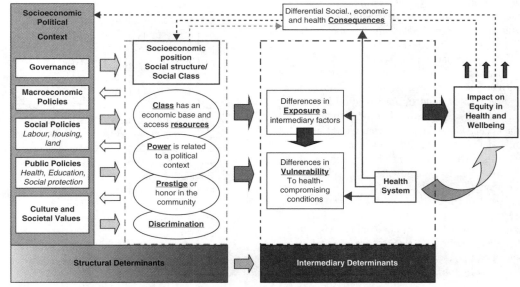

Figure summary pathway and mechanism of social determinants of health inequities elaborated EQH/EI

some specific diseases can impact people's socioeconomic position not only by undermining their physical capacities, but also through associated stigma and discrimination, e.g., in the case of HIV/AIDS. Because of their magnitude, certain diseases, such as HIV/AIDS and malaria, can also impact key contextual components directly, e.g., the labour market and governance institutions. This effect is illustrated by the blue arrow in the diagram. The whole set of 'feedback' mechanisms just described is brought together under the heading of 'differential social, economic and health consequences'. We have included the impact of social position on these mechanisms, indicating that path with a red arrow.

We have repeatedly referred to Hilary Graham's warning about the tendency to conflate the social determinants of health and the social processes that shape these determinants' unequal distribution, by lumping the two phenomena together under a single label. Maintaining the distinction is more than a matter of precision in language. As Graham argues, blurring these concepts may lead to seriously misguided policy choices. "There are drawbacks to applying health-determinant models to health inequalities." To do so may "blur the distinction between the social factors that influence health and the social processes that determine their unequal distribution. The blurring of this distinction can feed the policy assumption that health inequalities can be diminished by policies that focus only on the social determinants of health. Trends in older industrial societies over the last 30 years caution against assuming that tackling "the layers of influence" on individual and population health will reduce health inequalities. This period has seen significant improvements in health determinants (e.g., rising living standards and declining smoking rates) and parallel improvements in people's health (e.g., higher life expectancy). But these improvements have broken neither the link between social disadvantage and premature death nor the wider link between socioeconomic position and health. As this suggests, those social and economic policies that have been associated with positive trends in health-determining social factors have also been associated with persistent inequalities in the distribution of these social influences.'[202]

Many existing models of the social determinants of health may need to be modified in order to help the policy community understand the social causes of health inequalities. Because inequalities in determinants are not factored into the models, their central role in driving inequalities in health may not be recognized. They are designed to capture schematically the distinction between health determinants and

health inequality determinants, which can be obscured in the translation of research into policy. Evidence points to the importance of representing the concept of social determinants to policymakers in ways that clarify the distinction between the social causes of health and the factors determining their distribution between more and less advantaged groups. Our CSDH framework attempts to fulfill this objective. Indeed, this is one of its most important intended functions.

Graham argues that what is obscured in many previous treatments of these topics '*is that tackling the determinants of health inequalities is about tackling the **unequal distribution of health determinants**'. Focusing on the unequal distribution of determinants is important for thinking about policy. This is because policies that have achieved overall improvements in key determinants such as living standards and smoking have not reduced inequalities in these major influences on health. When health equity is the goal, the priority of a determinants-oriented strategy is to reduce inequalities in the major influences on people's health. Tackling inequalities in social position is likely to be at the heart of such a strategy. For, according to Graham, social position is the pivotal point in the causal chain linking broad ('wider') determinants to the risk factors that directly damage people's health.

Graham emphasizes that policy objectives will be defined quite differently, depending on whether our aim is to address determinants of health or determinants of health inequities:

- *Objectives for health determinants* are likely to focus on reducing overall exposure to health-damaging factors along the causal pathway. These objectives are being taken forward by a range of current national and local targets: for example, to raise educational standards and living standards (important constituents of socioeconomic position) and to reduce rates of smoking (a major intermediary risk factor).

- *Objectives for health inequity determinants* are likely to focus on leveling up the distribution of major health determinants. How these objectives are framed will depend on the health inequities goals that are being pursued. For example, if the goal is to narrow the health gap, the key policies will be those which bring standards of living and diet, housing and local services in the poorest groups closer to those enjoyed by the majority of the population. If the health inequities

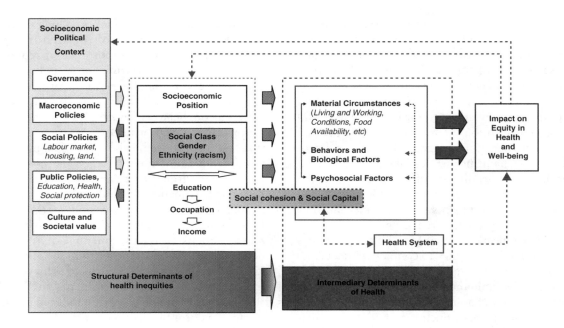

goal is to reduce the wider socioeconomic gradient in health, then the policy objective will be to lift the level of health determinants across society towards the levels in the highest socioeconomic group.[203]

V.9.—Final form of the CSDH framework

The diagram above brings together the key elements of the account developed in successive stages throughout this chapter. This image seeks to summarize visually the main lessons of the preceding analysis and to organize in a single comprehensive framework the major categories of determinants and the processes and pathways that generate health inequities.

The framework makes visible the concepts and categories discussed in this paper. It can also serve to situate the specific social determinants on which the Commission has chosen to focus its efforts, and can provide a basis for understanding how these choices were made (balance of structural and intermediary determinants, etc.).

• • • REFERENCES

67. Ball T, New faces of power. In Wartenberg T (ed). 1992. *Rethinking power*. Albany: SUNY Press: 14.

68. Cited in Stewart A 2001. *Theories of power and domination: the politics of empowerment in late modernity*. London /Thousand Oaks, Calif.: SAGE: 15.

69. Giddens 1976 cited in Stewart 2001: 14.

70. Stewart A 2001. *Theories of power and domination: the politics of empowerment in late modernity*. London/Thousand Oaks, Calif.: SAGE.

71. Quiroz S (2006). *Empowerment: a selected annotated bibliography*, p 6-7.

72. Young IM. Five Faces of Oppression. In Wartenberg T (ed). 1992. *Rethinking power*. Albany: SUNY Press: 175-76.

73. Stewart A 2001. *Theories of power and domination: the politics of empowerment in late modernity*. London/Thousand Oaks, Calif.: SAGE: p 36, emphasis in original.

74. Arendt, cited in Wartenberg 22.

75. Fay B, cited in Ball T, New faces of power. In Wartenberg, 23.

76. In Luttrell C, with Quiroz S and Scrutton C (2007). *Empowerment: an overview* (poverty-wellbeing.net).

77. Instituto de Estudios Politicos para America Latina y Africa. http://www.iepala.es/curso_ddhh/ddhh27.htm. Emphasis ours.

78. Fay, cited in Ball, in Wartenberg 23.

79. In Evans T, Whitehead M, Diderichsen F, Bhuiya A, Wirth M (eds). 2001. *Challenging inequities in health*. New York: Oxford UP.

80. (Diderichsen 1998, 102).

81. (Diderichsen, Evans, and Whitehead 2001, 15).

82. (Hallqvist, et al. 1998).

83. Resource allocation for *Health Equity : Issues and Methods*. Finn Diderichsen, September 2004.

Health, Nutrition and Population (HNP) The World Bank.

84. (Whitehead, Diderichsen, and Burström 2000).

85. (Sen 1999).

86. Esping-Andersen G. *Why we need a new Welfare State*. Oxford University 2002.

87. Navarro V. and Shi L. The Political context of Social Inequalities and Health. *International Journal of Health Services*, Vol 31, Pages 1-21, 2001.

88. Navarro V. and Shi L. The Political context of Social Inequalities and Health. *International Journal of Health Services*, Vol 31, Pages 1-21, 2001.

89. Chung H, Muntaner C. 2006. Political and welfare state determinants of infant and child health indicators: an analysis of wealthy countries. *Soc Sci Med*. 2006 Aug;63(3):829-42.

90. Chung H, Muntaner C. 2006. Political and welfare state determinants of infant and child health indicators: an analysis of wealthy countries. *Soc Sci Med*. 2006 Aug;63(3):829-42.

91. Raphael D. 2006. Social determinants of health: present status, unanswered questions, and future directions. *Int J Health Serv*. 2006;36(4):651-77. Raphael D, Bryant T. 2006. Maintaining population health in a period of welfare state decline: political economy as the missing dimension in health promotion theory and practice. *Promot Educ*. 2006;13(4):236-42.

92. Socieconomic inequalities in health, Part 1, Mackenbach , Bakker, Kunst and Diderichsen. reducing Inequalities in health: *European Perspective*. 2002.

93. Rockefeller Health Equity programme, from Concept and trends in research on Social determinants of Health in Latin America and the Caribbean J.A. Casas WHO.

94. As cited in Gender-sensitive and Pro-poor Indicators of Good Governance.

95. A first approach to Labour Market, Governance and Educational Indicators, Update 7th December 2006, Antía Castedo García.

96. CSDH Employment Conditions Knowledge Network (EMCONET). A Glossary of key concepts 2006.

97. 'Welfare state'. Encyclopædia Britannica. 2006. Encyclopædia Britannica Online. 14 Dec. 2006 <http://www.search.eb.com/eb/article-9076482>.

98. Coburn D. Income inequality, social cohesion and the health status of populations: the role of neo-liberalism. *Social Science & Medicine* 2000; 51(1):135-46.

99. Chung H, Muntaner C. 2007. Welfare state matters: a typological multilevel analysis of wealthy countries. *Health Policy*. 2007 Feb;80(2):328-39.

100. Labonte R, Schrecker T. 2005. Globalization and social determinants of health: strategic and analytic review paper. http://www.who.int/social_determinants/resources/globalization.pdf.

101. Orielle HSR and repro health paper.

102. Solar O, Irwin A, Vega J. 2004. Equity in Health Sector Reform and Reproductive Health: Measurement Issues and the Health Systems Context. WHO Health Equity Team working paper. [i] Kleczkowki BM, Roemer M, Van Der Werff A. 1984. *National health systems and their reorientation toward health for all: guidance for policymaking*. Geneva: WHO.

103 (Hills 1998; Howden-Chapman and Tobias 2000; Kubzansky et al. 2001; Perrson et al. 2001).

104. Giddens E. 1993 cited in A. Kunst and Johan P Mackenbach. Measuring socioeconomic inequalities in Health WHO Regional Office Europe 2000.

105. Muntaner C, Borell C, Benach J Pasarin MI Fernadez E. The associations of social class and social stratification with patterns of general and mental health in a Spanish population. *International journal of epidemiology* 2003;32:950-958.

106. Wright EO The class analysis of poverty *Int J Health Serv* 1995.25:85-100.

107. Liberatos P Link BG Kelsey JL. The measurement of social class in epidemiology. *Epidemiology Review* 1988;10:87-121.

108. Krieger, Willimas and Moss. Measuring Social Class. *Annu. Review Public Health* 1997,18:341-378.

109. Singh-Manoux, Clarke P, Marmot M Multiple measure of socioeconomic position and psychosocial health: proximal and distal measures. *International Journal of Epidemiology* 2002; 31:1192 -1199.

110. Pathways between socioeconomic determinants of health. E Lahelma, P Martikainen, M Laaksonen and A Aittomäki. *Journal Epidemiol. Community Health* 2004;58;327-332.

111. Krieger N, Rowley DL, Herman AA, Avery B, Phillips MT.1993. Racism, sexism and social class, implications for studies of health, diseases and well being *Ann J Prev. Med* 9:82-122.

112. Ecob R. Davey Smith G. Income and health: what is the nature of the relationship? *Soc Sci Med 1999*, 48 693-705.

113. Liberatos P Link BG Kelsey JL. The measurement of social class in epidemiology. *Epidemiology Review* 1988;10:87-121.

114. Galobardes B. Shaw M Lawler D Lynch J Davey Smith G. *J. Epidemiol Community Health* 2006; 60:7-12.

115. See E. van Doorslaer et al. (2006), Effect of payments for health care on poverty estimates in 11 countries in Asia: an analysis of household survey data, *Lancet* 368:1357-1364.

116. Kunst and Johan P Mackenbach. Measuring socioeconomic inequalities in Health WHO Regional Office Europe 2000.

117. Galobardes B. Shaw M Lawler D Lynch J Davey Smith G. *J. Epidemiol Community Health* 2006; 60:7-12.

118. Krieger, Williams and Moss. Measuring Social Class. *Annu. Review Public Health* 1997,18: 341-378.

119. Macinko J., Shi L. Starfield B. AND Wulu J. Income Inequality and Health: A critical Review of the Literature. *Medical Care Research and review*, Vol 60 n 4 (December 2003) 407-452.

120. Matthijs Kalmijn Mother's Occupational Status and Children's Schooling *American Sociological Review*, Vol. 59, No. 2. (Apr., 1994), pp. 257-275.

121. Duane F. Alwin Family of Origin and Cohort Differences in Verbal Ability. *American Sociological Review*, Vol. 56, No. 5. (Oct., 1991), pp. 625-638.

122. Marmot M Bobak M Smith DG 1995 Explanations for social inequalities on Health, In Society and Health. Oxford Univ. Express.

123. Towsend P, Davinson N Whitehead M 1990, *Inequalities in Health: The Black Report and the Health Divide*. London: Peguin Books.

124. Galobardes B. Shaw M Lawler D Lynch J Davey Smith G. *J. Epidemiol Community Health* 2006; 60:7-12.

125. Krieger, Williams and Moss. Measuring Social Class. Annu. *Review Public Health* 1997,18: 341-378

126. Oakes JM, Rossi PH. The measurement of SES in health research: current practice and steps toward a new approach. *Soc Sci Med* 2003;56:769-84.

127. M Bartley Commentary: Relating social structure and health *International Journal of Epidemiology* 2003;32:958-960.

128. Muntaner, Lynch and Oates The Social class determinants of income inequality and social cohesion International *Journal of Health service* 1999, Vol 20, Number 4 : 699-732.

129. Socioeconomic Status and Health The challenge of the gradient Adler N, Boyce T, and colleagues *American Psychologist* January 1994: 15-24

130. Muntaner, Lynch and Oates The Social class determinants of income inequality and social cohesion *International Journal of Health service* 1999, Vol 20, Number 4 : 699-732.

131. WHO (2002). Gender glossary. Appendix to Integrating gender perspectives in the work of WHO: WHO gender policy. Geneva: WHO, 2002.

132. Krieger N. 2001. Theories for social epidemiology in the 21st century: an ecosocial perspective. *Int J Epidemiol.* 2001 Aug;30(4):668-77.

133. Krieger N. 2001. Theories for social epidemiology in the 21st century: an ecosocial perspective. *Int J Epidemiol.* 2001 Aug;30(4):668-77.

134. Centre for AIDS Development, Research and Evaluation. 2003. Gender-based violence and HIV/AIDS in South Africa : organisational responses / developed by Centre for AIDS Development, Research and Evaluation (CADRE), for the Department of Health, South Africa. Braamfontein: Centre for AIDS Development, Research and Evaluation.

135. Doyal 2000.

136. WHO, http://www.who.int/gender/other_health/ Gender,HealthandWorklast.pdf.

137. (Walby 1999).

138. Doyal 2000.

139. Krieger N. 2001. Theories for social epidemiology in the 21st century: an ecosocial perspective. *Int J Epidemiol.* 2001 Aug;30(4):668-77.

140. UNDP. Human Development Report 2005. New York: UNDP.

141. Hilary Graham Social Determinants and their unequal distribution: clarifying policy understandings. *The Milkbank* Vol 82, n 1, 2004. pp 101-124.

142. P Howden-Chapman Housing Standards: a glossary of housing and Health *J Epidemiol Community Helath* 2004;58:162-168.

143. Dedman DJ, Gunnell D, Davey Smith G, et al. Childhood housing conditions and later mortality in the Boyd Orr cohort. *J Epidemiol Community Health* 2001;55:10-15.

144. Lenz R. Jakarta kampung morbidity variations: some policy implications. *Soc Sci Med* 1988;26: 641-9.

145. Cohen D, Spear S, Scribner R, et al. ''Broken windows'' and the risk of gonorrhea. *Am J Public Health* 2000;90:230-6.

146. Employment Conditions Knowledge Network (EMCONET) A Glossary of key concepts for EMCONET 2006.

147. R. G. Wilkinson: Unhealthy societies. The Affliction of inequality. London: Routlegde, 1996.

148. Reference Published : Jon Ivar Elstad/Statistisk sentralbyrå: Livsløpsundersøkelse blant 55-årige menn i 2001 (previously unpublished).

149. Willems Sara.*The socioeconomic gradient in health: a never-ending history? A descriptive and explorative study in Belgium*. October 2005 Department of General Practice and Primary Health Care.

150. Labour market changes and job insecurity: a challenge for social welfare and health promotion *Edited by* Jane E. Ferrie, Michael G. Marmot, John Griffiths *and* Erio Ziglio WHO 1999

151. Margolis, P. A., Greenberg, R. A., Keyes, L. L., Lavange, L. M., Chapman, R. S., Denny, F. W, Bauman, K. E., & Boat, B. W. (1992). Lower respiratory illness in infants and low socioeconomic status. *American Journal of Public Health, 82,* 1119-1126.

152. (Marmot et al., 1984).

153. Adelstein, 1980; Centers for Disease Control, 1987; Devesa & Diamond, 1983; Escobedo, Anda, Smith, Remington, & Mast, 1990; Kraus et al., 1980; Marmot et al., 1991; Pugh, Power, Goldblatt, & Arber, 1991; Remington et al., 1985; Seccareccia, Menotti,& Prati, 1991; U.S. Department of Health, Education, and Welfare [DHEW], 1979; Winkleby, Fortmann,& Barrett, 1990.

154. (Matthews, Kelsey, Meilahn, Kuller, & Wing, 1989).

155. (Marmot et al., 1991).

156. (Escobedo et al., 1990; Kaprio & Koskenvuo, 1988; Pugh etal., 1991).

157. M. G. Marmot, G. Rose, M. Shipley and P. J. S. Hamilton: "Employment grade and coronary heart disease in British civil servants". *Journal of Epidemiology and Community Health* 32 (1978), pp. 244-249.

158. ref Mackenbach book.

159. (Adler, Boyce, Chesney, Folkman, & Syme, 1993).

160. Diderichsen.

161. Benzeval, Judge and Whitehead.

162. J, Mackenbach, L.J. Gunning-Schepers How should interventions to reduce inequalities in helath be evaluated? *Journal of Epidemiology and Communities Health* 1997;51:359-364.

163. This part of the paper was taken of the background paper elaborated for Pamela Bernales May 2006 Internship of the Department Equity, Poverty and Social Determinants, EIP,WHO.

164. Ferguson, K. (2006). Social capital and children's wellbeing: a critical synthesis of the international social capital literature. *International Journal of Social Welfare,* 15: 2-18.

165. Kawachi, I., Kennedy, B. P., Lochner, K. and Prothrow-Stith, D. (1997). Social capital, income inequality, and mortality. *American Journal of Public Health,* 87: 1491-1498.

166. Putnam, R. (2000). *Bowling alone: The collapse and revival of American community.* New York: Simon & Schuster.

167. Putnam, R. (2001). Foreword. In S. Saegert, J. P. Thompson and M. R. Warren (Eds.), *Social capital and poor communities* (pp. xv-xvi). New York: Russell Sage Foundation.

168. Popay, J. (2000). Social capital: the role of narrative and historical research. *Epidemiology and Community Health,* 54: 401.

169. Putnam, R. (1995). Bowling alone: America's declining social capital. *Journal of Democracy,* 6: 65-78. (p. 67).

170. Szreter, S. and Woolcock, M. (2004). Health by association?. Social capital, social theory, and the political economy of public health. *International Journal of Epidemilogy,* 33: 650-667.

171. Moore, S., Haines, V., Hawe, P. and Shiell, A. (2006). Lost in translation: a genealogy of the "social capital" concept in public health. *Journal of Epidemiology and Community Health,* 60: 729-734.

172. Lynch, J., Due, P., Muntaner, C. and Davey Smith, G. (2000). Social capital—Is it a good investment strategy for public health?. *Journal of Epidemiology and Community Health,* 54: 404-408.

173. Lynch, J. (2000). Income inequality and health: expanding the debate. *Social Science and Medicine,* 51: 1001-1005.

174. Szreter, S. and Woolcock, M. (2004). Health by association?. Social capital, social theory, and the political economy of public health. *International Journal of Epidemilogy,* 33: 650-667.

175. Szreter, S. and Woolcock, M. (2004). Health by association?. Social capital, social theory, and the political economy of public health. *International Journal of Epidemilogy,* 33: 650-667.

176. Muntaner C 2004 Social capital, social class and the slow progress of psychosocial epidemiology. *Int J Epidemiol* 2004;33: 1-7.

177. Navarro V (2004). Is capital the solution or the problem? *Int J of Epidemiology* 2004;33: 672-74.

178. Cropper, S. (2002). What contributions might ideas of social capital make to policy implementation for reducing health inequalities?. *Paper to HAD Seminar Series 'Tackling Health Inequalities: turning policy into practice'. Seminar 3: Organisational Change and Systems Management.* 17th September 2002, Royal Aeronautical Society, London.

179. Lowndes, V. and Wilson, D. (2001). Social capital and local governance: exploring the institutional design variable. *Political Studies,* 49: 629-647.

180. Castel, R. (2005). Estado e inseguridad social. Conferencia Subsecretaría de la Gestión Pública, República de Argentina, 03 Agosto de 2005.

181. Crawshaw, P., Bunton, R. and Gillen, K. (2002). Health action zones and the problem of community. *Health and Social Care in the Community,* 11 (1): 36-44.

182. Labra, M. (2002). Capital social y consejos en salud en Brasil. ¿Un círculoo virtuoso?. *Cuadernos de Saúde Pública vol. 18 suppl.* Río de Janeiro. Download 13-07-2006 de http://www.scielo.br/scielo.php?script=sci_arttext&pid=S0102-311X 2002000700006&.

183. Rose, N. (1999). Inventiveness in politics. *Economy and Society,* 28 (3): 467-493.

184. Castel, R. (2005). Estado e inseguridad social. Conferencia Subsecretaría de la Gestión Pública, República de Argentina, 03 Agosto de 2005.

185. Szreter, S. and Woolcock, M. (2004). Health by association?. Social capital, social theory, and the political economy of public health. *International Journal of Epidemilogy,* 33: 650-667.

186. (Drever & Whitehead 1997; Kubzansky et al. 2001; Mackenbach et al. 2002; Singh & Yu 1996).

187. (Antonovsky, 1967; Ulsley& Baker, 1991).

188. Quality of life fundation.

189. Graham H. 2005. Intellectual disabilities and Socieconomic inequalities in Health : An overview of research Journal of Applied Research in Intellectualities 2005,18,101-111.

190. (Emerson 2004) .

191. Adelstein, 1980; Kraus, Borhani, & Franti, 1980; Marmot et al., 1991; Marmot, Shipley, & Rose, 1984).

192. Marmot, Kogevinas, and Elston (1987).

193. (Power & Hertzman 2004).

194. (Maughan et al. 1999).

195. Davey Smith at al 2001.

196. Ref

197. (Cf. Leonard & Wen 2002; US Department of Health and Human Services (USDHSS) 2002; Elliott et al. 2003). Graham 2004.

198. (Maughan et al. 1999).

199. (Elliott et al. 2003).

200. Graham H. Social Determinants and their unequal distribution: clarifying policy understandings. *The Milbank Quarterly* Vol 82, n 1, 2004.

201. Buscar referencia.

202. Graham H. 2004. Social Determinants and their unequal distribution: clarifying policy understandings. *The Milbank Quarterly* Vol 82, n 1, 2004 pp. 101-124.

203. Graham H. 2004. Social Determinants and their unequal distribution: clarifying policy understandings. *The Milbank Quarterly* Vol 82, n 1, 2004 pp. 101-124.

II

THE DETERMINANTS OF HEALTH

In our conceptual framework for this book, Part II, the Determinants of Health, represents a general overview of the non-medical factors (i.e., determinants) that affect both the average and distribution of health within populations. These determinants include the distal political, legal, institutional, and cultural factors, and the more proximate elements of socioeconomic status, physical environment, living and working conditions, family and social network, lifestyle or behavior, and demographics. In addition, inequalities in health have become increasingly more prominent over the past ten years both within and among populations across the world. This part highlights three of the most critical determinants: social determinants of health (Chapter 3), behavioral determinants of health (Chapter 4), and biological determinants of health (Chapter 5).

Chapter 3 includes selected papers related to social determinants reflecting both US and international contexts. The readings in Chapter 4 include conceptual, evaluative, as well as intervention pieces related to health promotion and behavioral change. Chapter 5 illustrates the biological determinants of health. The biological makeup of a person is where ultimately the social and behavioral elements, discussed in the previous two chapters, coalesce with the human biology to determine the individual's health and well-being. Readings in this chapter focus on both overall biological aspects and specific biological measures such as race/ethnicity and age.

Part II provides an overview of the non-medical inputs toward health outcomes. It is also a foundation for understanding the limitations of medical care, providing a "big-picture" view on how to achieve meaningful progress in health improvement. A clear grasp of the materials in Part II will assist students in developing a more comprehensive and balanced strategy to improving the health for the U.S. population

Social Determinants of Health

Social determinants of health represent non-medical factors that affect both the average and distribution of health within populations. These determinants include the distal political, legal, institutional, and cultural factors, and the more proximal elements of socioeconomic status, physical environment, living and working conditions, family and social network, lifestyle or behavior, and demographics. In addition, inequalities in health have become increasingly more prominent over the past ten years both within and among populations across the world.

As evidenced from the literature, social determinants of health are defined as those factors contributing to the social welfare of an individual that make him or her more or less vulnerable to disease or poor health status.[1-7] The major categories of social determinants include race/ethnicity, socioeconomic status, surrounding environment and social status.[1-7] These major determinants act as vertical hierarchies, in which the farther up the hierarchy an individual is placed the more or less likely he or she is susceptible to a given disease.[4] Social determinants of health can largely vary within and across populations, with defined social values and health care system structures acting as in-

fluencing factors in the degree of variation.[2] These determinants exist as connecting factors, with the hierarchal placement on one vertical axis influencing the placement on another.

To begin with, race is identified as one of the dominant social determinants of health due to its influence in determining the position an individual resides at within the other determinants.[5] This is particularly true in a multi-racial society such as the United States. Race is correlated with the given level obtained by a population in other social determinants, including education, socioeconomic status and social class.[5] As a social category, race is a concept that varies across societies and has changed over time.[5] Health researchers have historically experienced numerous problems with solidifying race as a measurement, as a majority of the categorization is based on physical appearance and culture, both of which are fluid characteristics with subjective definitions.[5] Yet, substantial contrasts in morbidity and mortality exist among groups of varying racial differences.[5] And these health indicators are further illustrated by differences in health behaviors, health-care access, and utilization of health services across varying racial groups.[5]

Socioeconomic status is also one of the most defined social determinants of health, with direct correlation being measured between the economic stability of a population and their health status.[1,4] Socioeconomic status encompasses a broad range of population characteristics, including income level, economic prosperity, definitions of wealth and ability to transgress across economic levels.[1,4] Within the U.S. healthcare system socioeconomic status acts as the gatekeeper to healthcare access because the ability to purchase health insurance allows for increased access to healthcare services. Education level is closely intertwined with socioeconomic status because higher levels of education enable people to have better paying jobs. Education level and income as direct determinants of health status have received contrasting evaluations when correlated to health status.[2] Numerous studies have measured education level as a positive correlating factor to health status within populations, with increasing education level leading to increased access to medical care and more efficient usage of health services.[2] However, contrasting studies indicate that, with increasing education level and increased income, comes increased stress.[2] This increased stress, in turn, decreases the health status of populations, illustrating a negative correlation between education and health.[2]

Additionally, an individual's built environment influences health.[6] A built environment is characterized as the environment built by people for people, the product of urban planning efforts to adapt natural surroundings into livable settings.[6] Common examples of the built environment include cities, roadways, parks and neighborhoods, but can also include the urban planning efforts addressing pollution in cities and clean water filtration in community dwellings.[6] When analyzing the relationship between the built environment and health, it is important to define the health outcome targeted by the planning.[6] Physical health problems, including infections and respiratory troubles, have long been associated with residing in slums and ghettos.[6] However, previous studies show that, while relative associations can be made, it is often difficult to isolate the direct impact of housing on physical health.[6] Data from various studies give mixed reviews, with some showing improved physical health upon transitioning to improved housing conditions while others show no change in health outcomes.[6] However, improvements in housing have shown to increase social outcomes, with individuals reporting less fear and isolation upon improvements to their living environment.[6]

Social status, or social class, as a health determinant is often underrepresented.[7] Identification within a given social class is characterized by an individual's socioeconomic status, education level, income, race, and residing neighborhood.[7] Social class acts as the foundation that connects other social determinants, including an individual's built environment and socioeconomic status.[7] What social status represents through the combination of these characteristics, allowing it to be classified as a separate social determinant, is power.[7] The status of individuals in relation to their peers, including the power they hold over their desired situation, weighs heavily on their health outcomes.[7] A consistent inverse relationship exists between class and premature death, with individuals in lower social classes dying earlier than those of a higher status.[7] While the underlying factors of socioeconomic status, education, race and other determinants can help explain the age of death, the lack of power individuals of a lower social class have over their own outcomes must also be considered.[7] The lower the social status, the less voice individuals have in advocating for their own health and prosperity.[7] Instead, their future is left to the responsibility of those with the power.

As a field of research, social determinants of health have dramatically increased as a priority in addressing poor health outcomes. Public health officials and policy makers must now look beyond the genetic causes of both communicable and noncommunicable disease to better understand the social causes of disease vulnerability among populations. As public health professionals and policy makers alike better understand the influence of public policy in defining social determinants, they can better conceptualize how to construct policies that better influence the social determinants, and thus health, of societies.

This chapter includes four prominent readings related to social determinants reflecting both U.S. and international context. In **Social Epidemiology: Social Determinants of Health in the United States: Are We Losing Ground?** Berkman provides a U.S. perspective on social determinants. The United States consistently ranks low in life expectancy, with socioeconomic inequalities widening in parallel to this decreased ranking. While rigorous studies have sought to identify social, behavioral and environmental factors that may reduce these inequalities, few studies have produced effective interventions and policy changes. Observational and experimental data illicit varying conclusions of behavioral and social risks, resulting in the delayed implementation of health interventions that then seek to address a proposed risk no longer present in a population. Berkman's article proposes that in order to rectify the differences in data conclusions and delayed implementation of interventions we must incorporate life course models into intervention planning and better understand the relationship between interventions and the context in which they are delivered. To begin with, Berkman illustrates how life course models can effectively identify the potential health risks that occur over an individual's lifetime with respect to how they age. Interventions to curb negative health outcomes must then align with the life course of the targeted disease in order to be effective. By recognizing these changes, public health policy and programming seek to intentionally integrate health interventions that parallel the health risks incurred over an individual's lifetime. For example, when analyzing effective interventions for the risk of cardiovascular disease from tobacco usage, we must look at the life course of tobacco smoking and where, in an individual's lifetime, a person will be most receptive to intervention. While cardiovascular disease impacts older populations, tobacco usage originates in early adulthood, indicating that a tobacco intervention early in a person's life will be most effective in curbing a negative health outcome later on. Additionally, Berkman argues that both epidemiologists and public health professionals alike must better understand the social, behavioral and environmental contexts in which an intervention thrives. For example, occupational risks associated with certain jobs stems into both behaviors engaged in while on the job as well as the education level of the employee. An occupation encompassing health risks is more likely to be pursued by individuals of lesser education and economic status, indicating that the most effective intervention for this risk must include measures that improve education and economic status. Berkman concludes the article by emphasizing the need to improve average life expectancy and reduce inequalities in order to effectively impact population health.

In **Income Inequality and Socioeconomic Gradients in Mortality,** Wilkinson and Pickett touch upon inequality and health. The association between population health and income distribution is vital to public health practice. Income distribution has widely been considered an indicator of population health, with lower income communities experiencing higher mortality rates. The unequal distribution of wealth on health outcomes has historically been equated to the relationship between health disparities and health outcomes. Yet, while both research and practice have indicated an interaction between in-

come distribution and health outcomes that is similar to that of other health disparities, disagreement still exists as to whether the processes responsible for health disparities are the same as those between income inequality and health. Wilkinson and Pickett's paper seeks to increase the understanding of the relationship between income distribution and population health by analyzing whether the same mortality rates that are susceptible to the causes of health disparities are also susceptible to income inequality. Through multi-level regression analysis models, Wilkinson and Pickett compared 10 age- and county-specific mortality rates to county median incomes and state income inequalities across the United States. Overall, findings indicate that states with more income equality were more likely to experience lower mortality rates of diseases negatively associated with county income level, such as ischemic heart disease and homicide. However, when comparing states with similar county-level median incomes, findings showed that mortality rates were lower among states with more income equality regardless of a varying range of county-level median income. Additionally, results indicate that contextual differences exist between varying mortalities, with interaction gradients of mortality rates for ischemic heart disease differing from those of respiratory disease. These contradicting findings indicate that, while lower income differences may result in fewer health disparities, the contextual benefits of lower mortality rates extend to the larger population. Thus, while a more income equal state may experience improved health standards, the overall health inequalities may not differ from those of other states. Wilkinson and Pickett conclude their article with the introduction of social status mobility, and lack thereof, as a potential reason for why income alone does not necessarily determine health. Poor health outcomes within a state, including mortality, may be strongly linked to varying social status amongst populations rather than income.

In **Social Determinants of Health Inequalities,** Marmot provides a global perspective. Currently, there are major health inequalities both between and within countries resulting from both communicable and non-communicable disease. While the treatment of existing disease will remain imperative and at the forefront of public health practice we now must begin to look at the root causes of health problems, the underlying social determinants that result in health disparities. In order to better understand the nature and operation of social determinants of health, The World Health Organization has structured an independent commission to link knowledge on social determinants with action. By increasing understanding of the structure of social determinants, policy makers can be better equipped to create policies that promote the health of populations. Marmot's article reads as a persuasive report, arguing that all policy should be focused on improving the health of populations regardless of whether it is health policy or not. Marmot highlights mortality rates both across continents and within countries, bringing to light the social inequalities that these mortality differences stem from. Mortality rates for children under 5 years of age increase hundred-fold from Iceland to Sierra Leone. Within countries there exists a 20-year gap in life expectancy among Australian Aboriginal and Torres Strait Islander peoples. These health disparities are used as the platform in which Marmot argues that an increased understanding of social determinants of health inequalities will improve the ability of social and economic policies to address the root causes of disparities. All policies should be focused on improving the health of populations since the overall success of a policy is based on its ability to meet human needs. Marmot concludes his paper by emphasizing that action on social determinants of health is necessary in order for society to thrive.

Finally, in **Socioeconomic Inequalities in Health in 22 European Countries**, Mackenbach et al. present a European perspective. One of the primary challenges of public health is the inequalities in health status among groups that arise due to varying levels of socioeconomic status. These inequalities are increasingly apparent when comparing countries. Mortality data segmented by occupational class and education level was obtained for 22 diverse European countries that encompass the northern, western, southern, eastern and Baltic regions. Two separate analyses on death were conducted to focus on both common causes of death, such as cancer and cardiovascular disease, and more specific causes of death, such as smoking- and alcohol-related causes. Self-reported health status was also obtained and compared to mortality rates across education and occupation levels. As Mackenbach et al. report education is inversely related to health status across all European countries, with lower educated populations experiencing higher rates of mortality and poor health status. Additionally, poor self-reported health status was greater among lower socioeconomic groups, indicating that self-assessment of health is associated with the social determinants of

education level and socioeconomic status. Both obesity and smoking were more common among lower education levels, with men experiencing larger education-related inequalities in smoking and women experiencing larger education-related inequalities in obesity. However, prominent differences were identified among countries. Education-related smoking inequalities were greatest among northern, western and continental regions and smallest in the southern regions, indicating that lower educated female groups in southern regions experience a difference in obesity and smoking than females of higher education levels. Mackenbach et al. conclude that socioeconomic health inequalities exist across varying countries and may not be the direct indicator of mortality. As illustrated by their analyses, variations in health could be a result of socioeconomic differences in smoking behavior, alcohol usage and access to health care. Policies targeting these immediate determinants may be the most effective interventions of health inequalities.

● ● ● **References**

1. Berkman LF. Social epidemiology: Social Determinants of Health in the United States: Are We Losing Ground? *Annu. Rev. Public Health.* 2009; 30:27-41.

2. Mackenbach JP, Stirbu I, Roskam AJ, et al. Socioeconomic Inequalities in Health in 22 European Countries. *The New England Journal of Medicine.* June 2008;358(23):2468-81.

3. Marmot M. Social Determinants of Health Inequalities. *The Lancet.* March 2005; 365: 1099-104.

4. Wilkinson RG, Pickett KE. Income Inequality and Socioeconomic Gradients in Mortality. *American Journal of Public Health.* April 2008; 98(4): 699-704.

5. Laveist TA. Beyond Dummy Variables and Sample Selection: What Health Services Researchers Ought to Know About Race as a Variable. *Health Services Research.* April 1994;29(1):1-16.

6. Northridge ME, Sclar ED, Biswas P. Sorting Out the Connections between the Built Environment and Health: A Conceptual Framework for Navigating Pathways and Planning Healthy Cities. *Journal of Urban Health.* December 2003;80(4):556-568.

7. Isaacs SL, Schroeder SA. Class—The Ignored Determinant of the Nation's Health. *The New England Journal of Medicine.* 9 September 2004; 351(11):1137-1142.

Social Epidemiology: Social Determinants of Health in the United States: Are We Losing Ground?

Source: Berkman LF. Social epidemiology: social determinants of health in the United States: are we losing ground? *Annu Rev Public Health* 2009;30:27-41.

ABSTRACT

The United States ranks in the lower tiers of OECD countries in life expectancy, and recent studies indicate that socioeconomic inequalities in health have been widening in the past decades. Over this period, many rigorous longitudinal studies have identified important social, behavioral, and environmental conditions that might reduce health disparities if we could design effective interventions and make specific policy changes to modify them. Often, however, neither our policy changes nor our interventions are as effective as we hoped they would be on the basis of findings from observational studies. Reviewed here are issues related to causal inference and potential explanations for the discrepancy between observational and experimental studies. We conclude that more attention needs to be devoted to (*a*) identifying the correct etiologic period within a lifecourse perspective and (*b*) understanding the dynamic interplay between interventions and the social, economic, and environmental contexts in which interventions are delivered.

THE STATE OF THE STATE: SETTING THE STAGE FOR UNDERSTANDING SOCIAL DETERMINANTS OF HEALTH IN THE UNITED STATES

The United States has consistently ranked in the bottom half or bottom third of OECD (Organisation for Economic Cooperation and Development) countries in life expectancy in the past several decades. In 2005, the United States ranked 24th among 30 OECD countries, with a life expectancy of 77.8 years.[58] Recently, the United States has been confronted with a new possibility that some segments of our population may either be losing ground as compared with others or may even be experiencing absolute declines in critical indicators of health and well being.[17] At a time in U.S. history (and, in fact, in a number of industrialized nations) when relative disparities in a wide range of health outcomes may be increasing, it is important to turn our attention to understanding why this is occurring and what we can do to reduce social and economic health disparities. Although social inequalities in health are persistent over time and in all countries, the magnitudes of the differences are highly variable across time and place,[46,47,62,72] which suggests that we can reduce health disparities if we can better understand the forces that determine the magnitude of the differences among different social, economic, and racial/ethnic groups.

A host of recent papers have documented this rise in disparities in the past several decades. Some have focused on geographic disparities without regard to social or economic conditions.[17] Ezzati and colleagues, for instance, have recently shown, in an examination of U.S. county mortality data between 1961 and 1999, that after 1983, 180 counties for women and 11 counties for men experienced declines in life expectancy. In the period between 1961 and 1983, no counties experienced such declines. Although the percentage of the total population impacted by these county-level changes is small, it nonetheless may signal an important trend. Because many other counties experienced substantial improvements in life expectancy during this period while others stagnated, county-level health disparities widened during this same time. Epidemiologists and economists have explicitly noted the rising health inequalities in the United States related to socioeconomic conditions and among racial/ethnic groups.[19,30,36,53,62,73] Meara[53] reports that life expectancy hardly changed for people with low levels of education over the 20-year period from 1981 to 2000, and among women with low levels of education, it actually declined during that period. For men and women with higher levels of education, life expectancy at age 25 improved 1.8 years for white men, 1.0 years for white women, 3.3 years for black men, and 1.6 years for black women. Harper and colleagues[30] likewise report that black/white gaps in life expectancy have been growing since the mid-1980s. Augmenting this picture, Krieger and colleagues[37] show that the widening socioeconomic and racial/ethnic relative and absolute disparities in premature mortality and infant mortality in recent decades were preceded by a narrowing of these inequities that started in the mid-1960s and extended up to 1980. Almond et al.[1] also reported shrinking black/white disparities in infant mortality in the U.S. rural south in the mid-1960s, followed by an increase. Such short-term temporal changes, including shrinking as well as widening of the magnitude of disparities, suggest strong environmental forces are at play.

Increasing inequalities in health occurring over the last several decades have been documented for a large number of European countries and for the UK as well during this period[45,69,76] with some variation in the extent of change and some reports of stable risks especially in Nordic countries.[38] Substantial improvements among the best off in many countries serve to widen differences, leaving the poor and disadvantaged farther behind even as population means improve. An important note to understanding this pattern is to recognize the differences between relative risks and absolute risks. In some cases, as population health improves, relative risks may grow even as absolute risks decline. Krieger[37] has noted that this association is not consistently linked and that it will be important in future studies to show both absolute and relative risks. Studies by Mackenbach[45] in European Union countries show widening relative socioeconomic inequalities occurring in a number of industrialized countries. Others have documented the difficult circumstances in former Soviet states and in many Eastern European countries that have experienced declines in life expectancy.[70] In fact, some demographic forecasts indicate that improvements in life expectancy may not continue into the future as they have occurred in the past. These demographic forecasts are based on changes in behaviors related to tobacco consumption[66] and obesity[18,39,59,60] as well as to rising socioeconomic inequality and patterns of immigration and social exclusion and isolation.[51]

On the basis of national averages for an outcome such as life expectancy, it is well known that for many years the United States has not performed nearly as well as one would expect, given both our gross domestic product (GDP) and our spending on health care. The United States may be doing particularly poorly vis à vis countries we consider as quite comparable to us in GDP such as the United Kingdom. For instance, a particularly interesting paper by Banks and colleagues[2] showed that among people in similar socioeconomic positions, men and women in the United Kingdom have a considerable health advantage compared with their U.S. counterparts for a number of health outcomes ranging from biomarkers of cardiovascular and metabolic risk to self reports of chronic conditions. The prevalence of diabetes in the United States was 9.5 and 8.2 for those with the highest levels of education and income, respectively, compared with rates of 5.7 and 4.4 in U.K. counterparts.[2] Even though these uppersocioeconomic status men and women have access to the best possible medical care in the United States, they still assume some risk just by living in the United States.

Although social epidemiology as a field has perhaps made its greatest advances over the past three decades, it has occurred at a time when health inequalities have widened across many countries. This situation implores us to examine both the methodological approaches to document social determinants of health, and it challenges us to understand the drivers of social disparities in health so that we can better inform policy, both improving population health and reducing disparities. On a more positive note, even though social inequalities in health are pervasive and present in virtually all societies examined, the magnitude, both absolute and relative, varies widely across time as well as among countries or states or provinces within countries. This latter finding, along with the several policy initiatives within countries and across countries,[33] implies that by identifying the forces that serve to reduce inequalities, those in public and private sectors can better implement those actions and policies in all places.

Because the trends reviewed above clearly identify that some environmental conditions increase or decrease health disparities even as many countries have experienced overall improvements in population health, the aim of this article is to explore two major paradigms that are fundamental to social epidemiology to see if they can help us understand these current trends in health. The first is related to integrating a life course perspective into planning interventions and interpreting the reasons for changing patterns of health. The second is related to Rose's paradigm[67] about the determinants of population health and understanding contextual-level influences on population health. Both these perspectives can help investigators interpret the trends in mortality in the United States and in many other countries. The two perspectives also help us to understand why observational and experimental data have so often come to different conclusions about social and behavioral risks to health and can lead us to more effective interventions. It is critical to reconcile these divergent results from observational and intervention studies to improve population health and reduce health inequalities. Thus, the aim of this review is not to compile the literature on each of the major social determinants of health (e.g., socioeconomic conditions, social networks, discrimination, work conditions) but quite the contrary: to identify provocative and important paradigms that can help us interpret research findings so that public health as a field can move forward substantively, methodologically, and theoretically.

Life course issues have recently come to permeate thinking about a broad number of exposures in public health. It is now commonplace to think of critical or sensitive periods in exposure to risk as well as to understand dynamics related to cumulative exposure. And yet, there is little consensus about which specific exposures are related to which life course dynamics for which health outcomes. Life course perspectives have been the focus of much recent attention and have im-

plications for study design and causal inference as well as for points of intervention. First, life course models pose interesting challenges to classical approaches to randomized experiments as well as to observational studies. Second, a review and critique of Rose's paradigm of population health indicate ways in which this paradigm is useful in interpreting patterns of health and well-being and in shaping interventions. The paradigm may have limitations in helping determine for whom new interventions should be planned. This paradigm while of interest in many areas of public health has been centrally important to social epidemiologists because of the way in which Rose originally challenged us to think about the macro forces that might shape population patterns of disease prevalence and distribution of risk. Recently, this work has been scrutinized more critically by epidemiologists.

INTERPRETING THE RESULTS OF SOCIAL AND BEHAVIORAL INTERVENTIONS FROM A LIFE COURSE PERSPECTIVE

Over the past two decades, a series of randomized controlled experiments hoping to change social, behavioral, and psychological conditions have produced null or modest results in terms of improving health outcomes. To be sure, some have had greater impacts than others, but on the whole, most of the investigators leading these interventions hoped the results would show much stronger effects, considering the magnitude of risks reported in observational studies. The adoption of a life course approach provides insight into why trials may have not yielded the effects anticipated on the basis of observational studies. Because life course approaches attempt to identify the etiologic period of risk, they are critical to the design of interventions. Life course issues have permeated much of epidemiology.[41,42,49,56,57,61,64,74] Although life course approaches were once commonplace only for developmental outcomes, epidemiologists have come to recognize that concepts related to etiologic period, latency, and sensitive periods are all relevant to epidemiology.[29,31,65]

Although there has been some debate among epidemiologists about the value of randomized controlled trials (RCTs) as an effective study design in which to test large-scale social and behavioral interventions, experimental designs have critical advantages related to randomization. They limit the kinds of confounding and selection issues that are inherent in many observational studies. Furthermore, ultimately public health sciences are aimed at improving population health not just furthering basic sciences related to understanding the world around us. To accomplish this goal, we need interventions and/or policies that have public health impact. Using experimental approaches, whether they are full-scaled randomized trials or more quasiexperimental approaches building on natural experiments, is important in public health. Experimental approaches help to identify interventions that work and identify the critical periods in which interventions will maximize public health benefits.

To discuss issues related to life course dynamics and subsequently to understand the need to embed interventions more deeply into the social conditions in which people live, I draw on two recent RCTs related to social support and social network interventions: The two studies are Enhancing Recovery for Coronary Heart Disease Patients (ENRICHD) and Families in Recovery from Stroke (FIRST). The results of these interventions, and in fact, their designs, serve to illustrate the issues related to life course and social context.

ENRICHD was an RCT aimed at improving social support and reducing depression in post-myocardial-infarction (MI) patients.[7] The primary outcome was the reduction of reinfarction and all-cause mortality. ENRICHD enrolled post-MI patients from more than 80 hospitals and 8 clinical centers across the United States ($n = 2481$). ENRICHD was based on evidence from a large number of longitudinal observational studies indicating that both depression and social support were related to survival post MI.[13] Most of the studies indicated that both men and women who were depressed or were socially isolated had elevated mortality or reinfarction risks ranging from ~2 to 4.[9,11,14,35,77] Results from related clinical trials were inconsistent.[23,24,26] The results from M-HEART, a study[22] published just before the launch of ENRICHD, showed null results but suggested a trend that women in the intervention group fared worse than women in the usual care group ($p = 0.064$).

With a follow-up of 3.4 years using an intent-to-treat analysis, there were no differences between the intervention and control groups in ENRICHD ($p = 0.89$).[7] In fact, the survival curves completely overlap when looking at the primary endpoint of reinfarction or all-cause mortality. The ENRICHD study did find reductions in the mediating conditions related to depression and low social support, suggesting the intervention was changing the conditions upon which it was designed to intervene.[7] The magnitude and long-term differences were smaller than expected, however, causing concerns about the in-

tervention's effectiveness. At six months, at the conclusion of the main intervention, however, investigators noted significant differences between the intervention and usual care (UC) groups in social support and depressive symptoms.

Subgroup Differences in Outcome: Does Social Context Influence Treatment Outcomes?

The most intriguing and controversial analysis from ENRICHD is the subgroup analysis of outcomes looking at gender and racial/ethnic differences. In prespecified analyses, statistically significant interactions between gender and the intervention revealed that men in the intervention had better outcomes than did men in the UC group. Women in the intervention group had worse outcomes than did women in the UC group. In post hoc analysis with stratification by both gender and race/ethnicity, one trend demonstrated that white men benefitted from the intervention (HR = 0.80, $p = 0.10$), whereas other groups showed no benefit from participating in the intervention.[68] Furthermore, using outcomes related specifically to cardiovascular disease, white men had a risk of 0.63 ($p = 0.004$) of reinfarction or cardiovascular mortality, and white women and black men and women experienced no benefit from being in the intervention group. See Figure 1. White men were more likely to be married and better educated; have the fewest chronic conditions, better ejection fractions, and less severe myocardial infarctions; and were more likely to receive thrombolytic therapy and cardiac catheterization and coronary revascularization. None of these conditions accounted for the difference in outcomes by treatment group seen in ENRICHD. However, such differences might suggest that unmeasured covariates may account for these gender and racial/ethnic differences.

A second much smaller RCT designed to improve functioning in stroke patients was based on social network intervention models.[27] This trial was conducted with 291 patients from 8 Boston-area hospitals and rehabilitation centers. The intervention was based on family systems and cognitive behavioral therapy. It aimed to enlarge social networks, improve social support, and increase recovery efficacy and effective problem solving. The primary outcome was functional independence at six months poststroke. The results of this trial showed no difference between intervention and UC in the primary endpoint at either three or six months, using an intention-to-treat approach.[28] An examination of prespecified subgroups revealed that those who were not depressed and had little cognitive impairment,

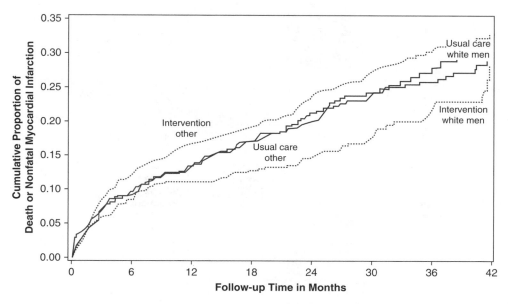

Figure 1 ENRICHD cumulative all-cause mortality and nonfatal MI by gender, race/ethnicity, and treatment group (69).

more minor strokes, and fewer preexisting chronic conditions tended to benefit from the intervention. Those who were frailer tended to do better in the UC group compared with the intervention group. Post hoc subgroup differences were very revealing in this study as well. A frailty summary score based on the above conditions[16] showed that among nonfrail participants, those in the intervention group did better than did those in the control in functional outcomes ($p = 0.001$) and they had lower mortality rates ($p = 0.03$). Among those who were frail, those in the UC group tended to do better in terms of functional outcomes and mortality risk. See Figure 2.

The results of these two trials, also coupled with the results from M-HEART, consistently demonstrated overall null results from the trials when using an intent-to-treat analysis. The intervention may have had more positive results in some subgroups, whereas in other subgroups, those in the UC group did better. Some investigators suggest that frailer, less healthy participants actually fared worse in the intervention group when compared with the UC group. We are left with a stark contrast between the observational studies, which indicate that those with low levels of social support and weak networks and high levels of depression were at substantial risk, and the results of the trials, which showed null results in intention-to-treat analysis. In post hoc analyses, there is some indication that the interventions may have been harmful in some subgroups. Only a few types of hypotheses can explain the discrepancy between the findings from the observational studies, which almost uniformly show strong ties between these exposures and

health outcomes, and the results of the RCTs, which show much weaker results. The first explanation is that the interventions failed to change the exposure or, to be more specific, did not change the exposure sufficiently or during the correct etiologic period. The second explanation posits that the exposure is causally related to the outcomes and that the intervention changed the exposure but treatment effects were heterogeneous. The third explanation proposes that the exposures are not causally related to the outcomes and the observational findings are the result of confounding by some unmeasured variable or reverse causation. The contrasts between findings from observational studies and randomized clinical trials are growing, and discrepancies in findings have been observed for a number of recent interventions. Of particular interest is the possibility that observational studies rarely help us identify the etiologic period clearly enough to know when to intervene. Thus, many interventions may be targeted at a population when their period of etiologic risk has largely passed.

Most observational studies identify a risk factor at one period in time. In such studies, it is impossible to identify the etiologic period of risk. For some exposures, especially those related to tobacco consumption and selected cardiovascular risk factors, longitudinal information on exposures over long time periods does exist, and epidemiologists can start to identify etiologic periods of risk with some accuracy. In social epidemiology, we are just starting this research endeavor. Life course models identify where exposures may have the most important impacts. Three distinct trajectories have been linked with each

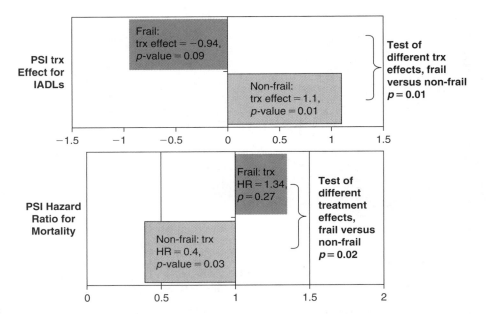

Figure 2 FIRST: differential treatment effects by frailty (16).

of the most common life course models.[6,31,40,65] The first life course model that has been dominant in developmental studies is related to critical or sensitive periods in which early childhood or even prenatal exposures shape subsequent outcomes that may or may not be evident for years. In this model, early exposures shape subsequent outcomes independently of later experiences or changes in exposure. The exposure may not lead to obvious outcomes until later life owing to some latency period. In the second life course model, exposures throughout life have a cumulative effect. In such cases, there do not appear to be sensitive periods, but rather, it is the exposures over many years that have the largest impacts. In the final life course model, early exposures may shape opportunities or barriers to critical exposures in later life, which are themselves the critical exposure linked to disease outcomes. This latter model is often called a social trajectory. In the next section, each of these three models is discussed in greater depth (all three models are shown in Figure 3).

Sensitive Periods and Latency: Childhood Origins of Adult Health

Developmentalists interested in early development and childhood have focused for decades on the importance of early life exposures in shaping cognition and brain function.[71] Over the past two decades, epidemiologists have come to understand the early origins of diseases, often focusing on fetal origins, which evidence suggests shape patterns of metabolic func-

tion related to diabetes and other health outcomes.[3,4] The causal pathway invoked in this trajectory can be seen in the top diagram of Figure 3. According to this causal diagram, early life conditions (in this case social conditions of interest) become embodied immediately and may go on to influence either adult social conditions or adult health outcomes. In this model, there is only a causal link between early exposure and subsequent adult disease, with no pathway leading from adult social conditions to adult health. In this case of early embodiment, intervention in adulthood cannot offset the harm incurred in childhood.

Which types of exposures and outcomes are linked to this trajectory? Many examples relate to cognitive and brain development in both animals and humans. Of interest to us, though, are exposures related to both social experiences and health outcomes. Examples here are harder to find, but some interesting studies do exist. For instance, with regard to cognitive function in old age, Meaney has produced a host of studies related to nurturing experiences in early postnatal life in rats.[10,12,15,52,55,63,75,78] In these experiments, rats were randomized to handling and not handling postnatally. Rats randomized to both groups were very similar to each other at earlier ages, but by midlife and at older ages, the nonhandled rats developed significant cognitive impairment and simultaneously had higher levels of corticosterone. More recent studies by Meaney and colleagues show differences in epigenetic processes, leading to behavioral outcomes.[20,21]

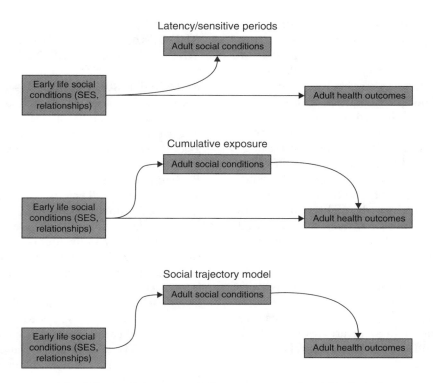

Latency/sensitive periods

Cumulative exposure

Social trajectory model

Figure 3 Three life course models of disease: latency, cumulative exposures, and social trajectories.

Cumulative Exposure Over the Life Course

Many epidemiologists interested in life course issues hypothesize that most adult disease is not likely the result of early childhood or prenatal exposure but rather the result of a lifetime of accumulated exposures.[43,44] Such a model can relate to early exposures and simultaneously to adult exposures because it is the impact of cumulative exposures across the life course that takes a toll at older ages. Early experiences may produce some independent impact on outcomes but that is not the central issue in this model. In this model, the etiologic period is long and covers decades of an individual's life, starting either in early childhood or in adulthood. In this model, we see that even if early experiences set people up for adult experiences, it is the cumulative impact that is critical. Of central importance to the development of effective interventions is the understanding that intervention in adulthood can offset some of the harm caused by the exposures. This process is illustrated in the middle diagram of Figure 3, in which causal arrows go from the adult experience/exposure to the health outcome, even though a causal arrow extends directly from the early exposure to adult health outcomes. Ben-Shlomo & Kuh[6] as well as Lynch & Davey Smith[43] offer fuller reviews of life course models in epidemiology. They point out that in risk models of accumulative exposure there can be both independent and uncorrelated insults as well as correlated insults with risk clustering or chains of risk.

One of the risk factors we know the most about is tobacco consumption. We put tobacco consumption into this life course model to understand effective points of intervention. For instance, almost all smokers start to smoke as adolescents. If we had a goal of preventing tobacco consumption, our goal would most likely be to stop adolescents from starting to smoke because quitting is very difficult. Once people start smoking, the effects on specific disease outcomes are varied. Quitting after the diagnosis of lung cancer does not change the prognosis related to lung cancer because the cumulative impact has already taken its toll to produce disease. However, quitting after a diagnosis of heart disease can alter prognosis because quitting produces an immediate effect that soon alters cardiovascular function. In these two cases, there are different etiologic periods, and because epidemiologists have studied tobacco exposure so well for so long, we have a good understanding of the differential impacts that exposures have on specific disease outcomes. Unfortunately, data on social exposures is much more limited.

With regard to the relation between, for instance, socioeconomic disadvantage and cardiovascular disease, data from a number of studies suggest that both early life and cumulative exposures over the life course play a role in disease etiology. Evidence suggests that early exposures, even fetal exposures, play a role in shaping risk of cardiovascular disease. Differences in blood pressure, cardiovascular reactivity, and metabolic function are evident in childhood and early adulthood.[5,25,50] Early life anthropometry is associated with adult cardiovascular disease.[41] Although early events may shape risks and perhaps trajectories of risks, it is also becoming increasingly clear that accumulated exposures over the life course impact cardiovascular risk in old age. For instance, studies from Alameda county in the United States[44] and from the GAZEL study of French Gas and Electricity workers show that socioeconomic disadvantage experienced multiple times over adulthood increases the mortality risks net of early childhood experiences.[54] In fact, the preponderance of evidence would suggest that sustained economic disadvantage is strongly associated with many health outcomes.[42] This model of cumulative risk argues that changes in adulthood to modify risk or prevent the onset of risk will partially offset the risks set by trajectories in early childhood.

Social Trajectories of Risk

In a social trajectory model of health and disease, early life exposures impact adult exposures, which in turn directly influence disease risk. In the bottom diagram of Figure 3, the causal pathways indicate that early life exposures do not directly affect adult health. They influence adult social conditions, which, in turn, affect adult health. In this case, intervention in adulthood can completely offset harm incurred in childhood.

A clear example of such causal patterns relates to occupational exposures. One can imagine that early life experiences, education, and training in young adulthood place people on a trajectory to obtain certain jobs. Certain occupations, however, carry with them risks related to the physical environment (toxic exposures to chemicals or ergonomic risks) as well as to challenging and stressful conditions. These job exposures have risks related to a multitude of poor health outcomes involving cardiovascular, musculoskeletal, and cancer disease. In this model, altering the job exposure will completely offset the individual's risk. Even though specific social or other experiences in childhood may place people at risk for entering certain occupations, risks can be substantially reduced by interventions aimed at adult exposures, especially at the work site level. Parallel findings may be related to other adult exposures related to neighborhood or other adult contexts.

ROSE REVISITED: THE DYNAMICS OF POPULATION HEALTH AND THE ROLE OF SOCIAL CONTEXT

In the mid 1980s, Geoffrey Rose, a British cardiovascular epidemiologist, started to write about population health, making a clear distinction between understanding what might produce sick individuals as opposed to what produces sick populations. By 1992, he had written a book, *The Strategy of Preventive Medicine*,[67] which framed his ideas into a coherent story. "The critical insight of Rose's was that an individual's risk of illness cannot be considered in isolation from the disease risk of the population to which the individual belongs."[8] Rose makes two points, which follow from this paradigm. The first indicates that the mean of the risk distribution influences the tail of the distribution, implying that it makes little sense to change the tail without understanding that it belongs to the population. He uses a host of cardiovascular risk factors to illustrate this point. The second point demonstrates that the distribution of risk produces a "prevention paradox" in which a large number of people with a relatively modest risk may produce more cases of disease than would a small number of people at high risk. These two phenomena give rise to the need to shape prevention strategies that acknowledge the entire risk distribution and rarely target high-risk individuals or segments of the population. Most investigators have interpreted his findings to support strategies that shift the risk distribution entirely to a lower-risk position. Figure 4a illustrates the shift from a high-risk distribution (curve 1) to a lower-risk distribution (curve 2) without changing the shape of the curve. The paradigm is compelling and serves public health well to suggest that rather than focusing on a rather small number of individuals who are embedded in some larger population, those in public health identify the forces that shape why specific populations have particular risk distributions.

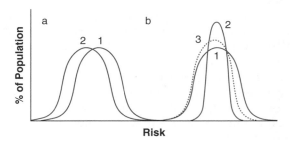

Figure 4 Variations on risk distributions based on Rose's paradigm.

Over time, however, several epidemiologists have questioned some of the assumptions Rose made, particularly concerning risk distribution.[34,48] Although the paradigm serves as a helpful heuristic for understanding population dynamics, the paradigm might not apply in some cases exactly as it did in Rose's examples of coronary heart disease in the 1970s and 1980s. Most of Rose's examples show (a) the distribution of risk to be relatively normal with few people in the tails of risk and (b) relative risks increasing continuously. This specific distribution and relative risk give rise to the prevention paradox. Rose said the "distribution of health-related characteristics move up and down as a whole: the frequency of cases can be understood only in the context of the population's characteristics."[8,67] For instance, in the United States, obesity has been on the rise over the past few decades, and a careful examination supports Rose's proposition that the entire risk distribution has shifted during this time. In fact, the mean has driven the tail.

However, if increasingly more people are in the tails of the distribution or if the distribution itself is not normally distributed, then Rose's strategies may not be effective, and specific high-risk strategies may become more effective. In fact, this rather straightforward empirical question has rarely been examined. Similarly if relative risks do not increase linearly or show clear threshold effects, different actions may be appropriate. In some instances, reducing population risk brings people to the formerly low-risk side of the distribution into higher risk. For example, reducing overweight at the population level may produce more people with eating disorders at the very low end of the weight distribution. So, for instance, the curves in Figure 4b show the normal distribution again with an illustration of the optimal shift in the curve if the goal is to reduce the high-risk end of the curve but to maintain the distribution of the curve below the mean so as not to increase risk (see Figure 4b, curve 3). Some evidence also indicates that if the risk distribution is not normally distributed or if many are in the extreme tails of risk, a population strategy of risk reduction may not always produce the same results. Rose himself acknowledged that under certain circumstances, high-risk strategies may be more effective on a population level than population-wide strategies would be. Certainly, from a purely hypothetical perspective, if the risk distribution is very skewed, Rose's paradigm may be more problematic. This issue at hand is whether this is actually the case with regard to some risks or if it is a purely hypothetical situation.[32,34]

Another issue also relates to the shape of the curve. For instance, considering the issue of economic inequality and health, one can imagine two curves:

both normally distributed but with very different standard deviations (Figure 4b, curves 1 and 2). If there is something harmful about inequality itself, its relative nature, not just the absolute prevalence of poverty, then shifting the curve to the left or giving everyone the same amount of money will do little to improve population health. Reducing the standard deviation or the percentage of people in the tails of the distribution is critical to improving health. In this case, the mean may stay exactly the same, but the tails move toward the center. One could imagine population strategies that might produce a tighter risk distribution around the mean or one could employ specific high-risk strategies to pull in the tails, especially the tail with highest risk. In any case, it is time for a second critical look at the population paradigm developed by Rose and to subject the theories to empirical tests so that optimal strategies to improve population health will be developed.

CONCLUSIONS

In this article, we argue that epidemiologists and especially social epidemiologists will have to integrate a deeper understanding of (a) the etiologic period, (b) the social and environmental context in which interventions are rolled out, and (c) the potential for heterogeneous treatment effects to develop successful interventions and policies. In addition, population approaches to disease prevention, which draw heavily on Rose's strategy of preventive medicine, where entire distributions of risk move toward lower risk levels, may be applicable much but not all of the time. A more critical look into population approaches that evaluate high-risk strategies that may reduce inequalities more effectively is necessary. Population health depends on both improving the average health expectancy of the population as well as reducing the risk inequalities within the population.

DISCLOSURE STATEMENT

The author is not aware of any biases that might be perceived as affecting the objectivity of this review.

● ● ● LITERATURE CITED

1. Almond DV, Cay KY, Greenstone M. 2006. *Civil rights, the war in poverty and black-white convergence in infant mortality in the rural south and Mississippi.*Work. Pap., Dep. Econ., Mass. Inst. Technol.

2. Banks J, Marmot M, Oldfield Z, Smith JP. 2006. Disease and disadvantage in the United States and in England. *JAMA* 295:2037-45.

3. Barker DJ, Forsen T, Uutela A, Osmond C, Eriksson JG. 2001. Size at birth and resilience to effects of poor living conditions in adult life: longitudinal study. *BMJ* 323:1273-76.

4. Barker DJ, Martyn CN. 1992. Maternal and fetal origins of cardiovascular disease. *J. Epidemiol. Community Health* 46:8.

5. Barker DJ, Winter PD, Osmond C, Margetts B, Simmonds SJ. 1989. Weight in infancy and death from ischaemic heart disease. *Lancet* 2:577-80.

6. Ben-Shlomo Y, Kuh D. 2002. A life course approach to chronic disease epidemiology: conceptual models, empirical challenges and interdisciplinary perspectives. *Int. J. Epidemiol.* 31:285-93.

7. Berkman LF, Blumenthal J, Burg M, Carney RM, Catellier D, et al. 2003. Effects of treating depression and low perceived social support on clinical events after myocardial infarction: the Enhancing Recovery in Coronary Heart Disease Patients (ENRICHD) Randomized Trial. *JAMA* 289:3106-16.

8. Berkman LF, Kawachi I. 2000. *Social Epidemiology.* New York: Oxford Univ. Press.

9. Berkman LF, Leo-Summers L, Horwitz RI. 1992. Emotional support and survival after myocardial infarction. A prospective, population-based study of the elderly. *Ann. Intern. Med.* 117:1003-9.

10. Bredy TW, Grant RJ, Champagne DL, Meaney MJ. 2003. Maternal care influences neuronal survival in the hippocampus of the rat. *Eur. J. Neurosci.* 18:2903-9.

11. Bush DE, Ziegelstein RC, Tayback M, Richter D, Stevens S, et al. 2001. Even minimal symptoms of depression increase mortality risk after acute myocardial infarction. *Am. J. Cardiol.* 88:337-41.

12. Cameron N, Del Corpo A, Diorio J, McAllister K, Sharma S, Meaney MJ. 2008. Maternal programming of sexual behavior and hypothalamic-pituitary-gonadal function in the female rat. *PLoS ONE* 3:e2210.

13. Carney RM, Rich MW, Tevelde A, Saini J, Clark K, Jaffe AS. 1987. Major depressive disorder in coronary artery disease. *Am. J. Cardiol.* 60:1273-75.

14. Case RB, Moss AJ, Case N, McDermott M, Eberly S. 1992. Living alone after myocardial infarction. *JAMA* 267:515-19.

15. Champagne FA, Meaney MJ. 2006. Stress during gestation alters postpartum maternal care and the development of the offspring in a rodent model. *Biol. Psychiatry* 59:1227-35.

16. Ertel KA, Glymour MM, Glass TA, Berkman LF. 2007. Frailty modifies effectiveness of psychosocial intervention in recovery from stroke. *Clin. Rehabil.* 21:511-22.

17. Ezzati M, Friedman AB, Kulkarni SC, Murray CJ. 2008. The reversal of fortunes: trends in county mortality and cross-county mortality disparities in the United States. *PLoS Med.* 5:e66.

18. Flegal KM, Graubard BI, Williamson DF, Gail MH. 2005. Excess deaths associated with underweight, overweight, and obesity. *JAMA* 293:1861-67.

19. Ford ES, Ajani UA, Croft JB, Critchley JA, Labarthe DR, et al. 2007. Explaining the decrease in U.S. deaths from coronary disease, 1980-2000. *N. Engl. J. Med.* 356:2388-98.

20. Francis DD, Caldji C, Champagne F, Plotsky PM, Meaney MJ. 1999. The role of corticotropin-releasing factor-norepinephrine systems in mediating the effects of early experience on the development of behavioral and endocrine responses to stress. *Biol. Psychiatry* 46:1153-66.

21. Francis DD, Szegda K, Campbell G, Martin WD, Insel TR. 2003. Epigenetic sources of behavioral differences in mice. *Nat. Neurosci.* 6:445-46.

22. Frasure-Smith N, Lesperance F, Prince RH, Verrier P, Garber RA, et al. 1997. Randomised trial of home-based psychosocial nursing intervention for patients recovering from myocardial infarction. *Lancet* 350:473-79.

23. Frasure-Smith N, Lesperance F, Talajic M. 1993. Depression following myocardial infarction. Impact on 6-month survival. *JAMA* 270:1819-25.

24. Frasure-Smith N, Prince R. 1985. The ischemic heart disease life stress monitoring program: impact on mortality. *Psychosom. Med.* 47:431-45.

25. Freedman DS, Dietz WH, Srinivasan SR, Berenson GS. 1999. The relation of overweight to cardiovascular risk factors among children and adolescents: the Bogalusa Heart Study. *Pediatrics* 103:1175-82.

26. Friedman M, Thoresen CE, Gill JJ, Ulmer D, Powell LH, et al. 1986. Alteration of type A behavior and its effect on cardiac recurrences in post myocardial infarction patients: summary results of the recurrent coronary prevention project. *Am. Heart J.* 112: 653-65.

27. Glass TA. 2000. Psychosocial intervention. See Ref. 8, pp. 267-305.

28. Glass TA, Dym B, Greenberg S, Rintell D, Roesch C, Berkman LF. 2000. Psychosocial intervention in stroke: Families in Recovery from Stroke Trial (FIRST). *Am. J. Orthopsychiatry* 70:169-81.

29. Hallqvist J, Lynch J, Bartley M, Lang T, Blane D. 2004. Can we disentangle life course processes of accumulation, critical period and social mobility? An analysis of disadvantaged socio-economic positions and myocardial infarction in the Stockholm Heart Epidemiology Program. *Soc. Sci. Med.* 58:1555-62.

30. Harper S, Lynch J, Burris S, Davey Smith G. 2007. Trends in the black-white life expectancy gap in the United States, 1983-2003. *JAMA* 297:1224-32.

31. Hertzman C, Power C. 2003. Health and human development: understandings from life-course research. *Dev. Neuropsychol.* 24:719-44.

32. Hunink MG, Goldman L, Tosteson AN, Mittleman MA, Goldman PA, et al. 1997. The recent decline in mortality from coronary heart disease, 1980-1990. The effect of secular trends in risk factors and treatment. *JAMA* 277:535-42.

33. Irwin A, Valentine N, Brown C, Loewenson R, Solar O, et al. 2006. The commission on social determinants of health: tackling the social roots of health inequities. *PLoS Med.* 3:e106.

34. Jackson R, Lynch J, Harper S. 2006. Preventing coronary heart disease. *BMJ* 332:617-18.

35. Kawachi I, Colditz GA, Ascherio A, Rimm EB, Giovannucci E, et al. 1996. A prospective study of social networks in relation to total mortality and cardiovascular disease in men in the USA. *J. Epidemiol. Community Health* 50:245-51.

36. Krieger N. 2008. Proximal, distal, and the politics of causation: What's level got to do with it? *Am. J. Public Health* 98:221-30.

37. Krieger N, Rehkopf DH, Chen JT, Waterman PD, Marcelli E, Kennedy M. 2008. The fall and rise of US inequities in premature mortality: 1960-2002. *PLoS Med.* 5:e46.

38. Kunst AE, Bos V, Lahelma E, Bartley M, Lissau I, et al. 2005. Trends in socioeconomic inequalities in self-assessed health in 10 European countries. *Int. J. Epidemiol.* 34:295-305.

39. Lakdawalla DN, Goldman DP, Shang B. 2005. The health and cost consequences of obesity among the future elderly. *Health Aff (Millwood)* 24(Suppl. 2):W5R30-41.

40. Lawlor D, Ben-Shlomo Y, Leon D. 2004. *Pre-Adult Influences on Cardiovascular Disease.* New York: Oxford Univ. Press.

41. Lu MC, Halfon N. 2003. Racial and ethnic disparities in birth outcomes: a life-course perspective. *Matern. Child Health J.* 7:13-30.

42. Lynch J, Kaplan GA. 2000. Socioeconomic position. See Ref. 8, pp. 15-35.

43. Lynch J, Smith GD. 2005. A life course approach to chronic disease epidemiology. *Annu. Rev. Public Health* 26:1-35.

44. Lynch JW, Kaplan GA, Shema SJ. 1997. Cumulative impact of sustained economic hardship on physical, cognitive, psychological, and social functioning. *N. Engl. J. Med.* 337:1889-95.

45. Mackenbach JP, Bos V, Andersen O, Cardano M, Costa G, et al. 2003. Widening socioeconomic inequalities in mortality in six Western European countries. *Int. J. Epidemiol.* 32:830-37.

46. Mackenbach JP, Kunst AE, Cavelaars AE, Groenhof F, Geurts JJ. 1997. Socioeconomic inequalities in morbidity and mortality in western Europe. The EU Working Group on Socioeconomic Inequalities in Health. *Lancet* 349:1655-59.

47. Mackenbach JP, Roskam AJR, Schaap MM, Menvielle G, Leinsalu M, Kunst AE. 2008. Socioeconomic status and health inequalities in European countries. *N. Engl. J. Med.* 358:1-14.

48. Manuel DG, Lim J, Tanuseputro P, Anderson GM, Alter DA, et al. 2006. Revisiting Rose: strategies for reducing coronary heart disease. *BMJ* 332:659-62.

49. Marmot MG, Wadsworth MEJ. 1997. Fetal and early childhood environment: long-term health implications. *Br. Med. Bull.* 53:210-21.

50. Matthews KA, Salomon K, Brady SS, Allen MT. 2003. Cardiovascular reactivity to stress predicts future blood pressure in adolescence. *Psychosom. Med.* 65:410-15.

51. McPherson M, Smith-Lovin L, Brashears M. 2006. Social isolation grows in America. Changes in core discussion networks over two decades. *Am. Soc. Rev.* 71:353-75.

52. Meaney MJ, Aitken DH, Bodnoff SR, Iny LJ, Sapolsky RM. 1985. The effects of postnatal handling on the development of the glucocorticoid receptor systems and stress recovery in the rat. *Prog. Neuropsychopharmacol. Biol. Psychiatry* 9:731-34.

53. Meara ER, Richards S, Cutler DM. 2008. The gap gets bigger: changes in mortality and life expectancy, by education, 1981-2000. *Health Aff. (Millwood)* 27:350-60.

54. Melchior M, Berkman LF, Kawachi I, Krieger N, Zins M, et al. 2006. Lifelong socioeconomic trajectory and premature mortality (35-65 years) in France: findings from the GAZEL Cohort Study. *J. Epidemiol. Community Health* 60:937-44.

55. Menard JL, Champagne DL, Meaney MJ. 2004. Variations of maternal care differentially influence 'fear' reactivity and regional patterns of cFos immunoreactivity in response to the shock-probe burying test. *Neuroscience* 129:297-308.

56. Naess O, Claussen B, Smith GD, Leyland AH. 2008. Life course influence of residential area on cause specific mortality. *J. Epidemiol. Community Health* 62:29-34.

57. Nguyen CT, Couture MC, Alvarado BE, Zunzunegui MV. 2008. Life course socioeconomic disadvantage and cognitive function among the elderly population of seven capitals in Latin America and the Caribbean. *J. Aging Health* 20:347-62.

58. OECD. 2008. *Health data 2008.* http://oecd.org/documents/16/0,3343.

59. Olshansky SJ. 2005. Projecting the future of U.S. health and longevity. *Health Aff. (Millwood)* 24(Suppl. 2):W5R86-89.

60. Olshansky SJ, Passaro DJ, Hershow RC, Layden J, Carnes BA, et al. 2005. A potential decline in life expectancy in the United States in the 21st century. *N. Engl. J. Med.* 352:1138-45.

61. Owen CG, Martin RM, Whincup PH, Smith GD, Cook DG. 2005. Effect of infant feeding on the risk of obesity across the life course: a quantitative review of published evidence. *Pediatrics* 115:1367-77.

62. Pappas G, Queen S, Hadden W, Fisher G. 1993. The increasing disparity in mortality between socioeconomic groups in the United States, 1960 and 1986. *N. Engl. J. Med.* 329:103-9.

63. Plotsky PM, Thrivikraman KV, Nemeroff CB, Caldji C, Sharma S, Meaney MJ. 2005. Long-term consequences of neonatal rearing on central corticotropin-releasing factor systems in adult male rat offspring. *Neuropsychopharmacology* 30:2192-204.

64. Pollitt RA, Rose KM, Kaufman JS. 2005. Evaluating the evidence for models of life course socioeconomic factors and cardiovascular outcomes: a systematic review. *BMC Public Health* 5:7.

65. Power C, Hertzman C. 1997. Social and biological pathways linking early life and adult disease. *Br. Med. Bull.* 53:210-21.

66. Preston SH, Wang H. 2006. Sex mortality differences in the United States: the role of cohort smoking patterns. *Demography* 43:631-46.

67. Rose G. 1992. *The Strategy of Preventive Medicine.* New York: Oxford Univ. Press.

68. Schneiderman N, Saab PG, Catellier DJ, Powell LH, DeBusk RF, et al. 2004. Psychosocial treatment within sex by ethnicity subgroups in the Enhancing Recovery in Coronary Heart Disease clinical trial. *Psychosom. Med.* 66:475-83.

69. Shaw M, Dorling D, Gordon D, Davey Smith G. 1999. *The Widening Gap: Health Inequalities and Policy in Britain.* Bristol: Policy.

70. Shkolnikov VM, Andreev EM, Jasilionis D, Leinsalu M, Antonova OI, McKee M. 2006. The changing relation between education and life expectancy in central and eastern Europe in the 1990s. *J. Epidemiol. Community Health* 60:875-81.

71. Shonkoff JP. 2003. From neurons to neighborhoods: old and new challenges for developmental and behavioral pediatrics. *J. Dev. Behav. Pediatr.* 24:70-76.

72. Singh GK. 2003. Area deprivation and widening inequalities in US mortality, 1969-1998. *Am. J. Public Health* 93:1137-43.

73. Singh GK, Siahpush M. 2006. Widening socioeconomic inequalities in US life expectancy, 1980-2000. *Int. J. Epidemiol.* 35:969-79.

74. Wainwright NW, Surtees PG. 2002. Childhood adversity, gender and depression over the life-course. *J. Affect. Disord.* 72:33-44.

75. Weaver IC, Cervoni N, Champagne FA, D'Alessio AC, Sharma S, et al. 2004. Epigenetic programming by maternal behavior. *Nat. Neurosci.* 7:847-54.

76. White C, Galen FV, Huang Chow Y. 2003. Trends in social class differences by cause, 1986-2000. *Health Stat. Q.* 20:25-37.

77. Williams RB, Barefoot JC, Califf RM, Haney TL, Saunders WB, et al. 1992. Prognostic importance of social and economic resources among medically treated patients with angiographically documented coronary artery disease. *JAMA* 267:520-24.

78. Zhang TY, Bagot R, Parent C, Nesbitt C, Bredy TW, et al. 2006. Maternal programming of defensive responses through sustained effects on gene expression. *Biol. Psychol.* 73:72-89.

2

Income Inequality and Socioeconomic Gradients in Mortality

Source: Wilkinson RG, Pickett KE. Income inequality and socioeconomic gradients in mortality. *Am J Public Health* 2008;98: 699-704. Reprinted with permission of the American Public Health Association.

Objectives. We investigated whether the processes underlying the association between income inequality and population health are related to those responsible for the socioeconomic gradient in health and whether health disparities are smaller when income differences are narrower.

Methods. We used multilevel models in a regression analysis of 10 age- and cause-specific U.S. county mortality rates on county median household incomes and on state income inequality. We assessed whether mortality rates more closely related to county income were also more closely related to state income inequality. We also compared mortality gradients in more- and less-equal states.

Results. Mortality rates more strongly associated with county income were more strongly associated with state income inequality: across all mortality rates, $r=-0.81$; $P=.004$. The effect of state income inequality on the socioeconomic gradient in health varied by cause of death, but greater equality usually benefited both wealthier and poorer counties.

Conclusions. Although mortality rates with steep socioeconomic gradients were more sensitive to income distribution than were rates with flatter gradients, narrower income differences benefit people in both wealthy and poor areas and may, paradoxically, do little to reduce health disparities. (*Am J Public Health.* 2008;98:699-704. doi:10.2105/AJPH.2007.109637)

The nature of the association between income distribution and population health is of crucial importance to public health. The United States has wider income differences and a lower life expectancy than other developed countries, which appears to fit the international correlation between the two.[1] Likewise, life expectancy among the 50 states also appears to be correlated with state income distribution.[2] However, despite a growing body of research and supportive findings from a large majority of published papers, disagreement remains about whether income inequality is a determinant of population health,[3,4] the nature of the processes through which it might influence population health, and how those processes might be related to the causes of health inequalities. A deeper understanding of these issues may pave the way for policymakers to improve population health and reduce health inequalities.

An initially plausible hypothesis is that both the socioeconomic gradient in health and the association between health and income distribution reflect the effects of socioeconomic disadvantage on health; if narrower income differences reduce disadvantage, they might improve average health by reducing health disparities. However, it is also possible that any effects of income distribution could reflect quite separate causal processes from those responsible for the socioeconomic gradient in health. Although health disparities are sometimes attributed primarily to material and behavioral factors such as smoking, diet, bad housing, and lack of health care,[5-7] we and others have suggested that income inequality is more likely to influence health through processes of social comparison.[8-10] It is even possible that there are two completely separate domains: health inequalities may reflect the direct effects of material living standards, and income inequality may reflect the psychosocially mediated effects of social comparisons.

Determining whether income inequalities work through the same or different processes from those responsible for health disparities is complicated by our lack of precise knowledge of the causal processes for either. Therefore, it would be informative to examine whether mortality rates that have steep socioeconomic gradients are also those most strongly related to income inequality and whether mortality rates that have little or no socioeconomic gradient have little or no relation to income inequality. Are mortality rates that are sensitive to the causes of health disparities also sensitive to income inequality?

METHODS

We measured the strength of the relation between median county income and 10 different mortality rates across all 3,139 counties in the United States. We used county-level data instead of individual-level data to measure socioeconomic gradients in health because individual-level data on mortality by income were not available by age and cause of death for each state. In multilevel models, we also measured the strength of the relationship between county mortality rates and state income inequality, conditional on county median incomes. We then compared how strongly each mortality rate was related to county median income with how strongly related it was to state income inequality. Finally, we investigated how health inequalities, as measured by the gradients between the mortality rates and county median income, were affected by differences in state income inequality.

County- and State-Level Data

We took data on median household income for all 3,139 U.S. counties, in 1999 dollars, from the U.S. Census 2000 Summary File 3.[11] Mortality was drawn from the Compressed Mortality File, a county-level national mortality and population database. For each county we extracted 10 mortality rates: infant mortality, all-cause working-age mortality (mortality among those of working age, 25-64 years), all-cause elderly mortality (among those aged ≥65 years), ischemic heart disease mortality, mortality from diseases of the respiratory system, and mortality from diabetes mellitus, breast cancer, prostate cancer, alcoholic liver disease (liver disease caused by alcohol consumption), and homicide. Except for breast and prostate cancer, all mortality rates were for both genders combined. All rates except that for infant mortality were age-adjusted rates per 100,000 population and were averaged over the 4-year period of 1999 to 2002.

We used published information[12,13] to select age- and cause-specific mortality rates that would include cause-specific mortality rates with contrasting strong and weak socioeconomic gradients as well as all-cause mortality rates for contrasting age groups covering a large majority of all deaths.

For each mortality rate, we excluded from analysis any county for which the mortality was zero and the population was not sufficiently large to expect at least 1 death during the 4-year period. We also excluded a few counties (usually fewer than 8) for which an implausibly high mortality, usually attributable to small numbers, made them extreme outliers. After these exclusions, county mortality rates were approximately normally distributed. Means and standard deviations are shown in Table 1.

Data on income inequality for the 50 U.S. states were taken from the U.S. Census Bureau.[14] Income inequality was measured as the Gini coefficient of family income for 1999. Gini coefficients vary between 0 (complete equality) and 1 (maximum inequality—all income to a single recipient).[15]

Statistical Analysis

Our statistical analyses were designed to answer two questions: Are causes of death with steeper socioeconomic gradients more closely associated with income inequality than those with flatter gradients? How does the socioeconomic gradient in mortality differ in more and less-equal states?

Association of income inequality and causes of death. We first performed a single-level ecological analysis at the county level to assess the steepness of the socioeconomic gradient by estimating the Pearson correlation coefficient for each mortality rate in relation to county median household income. We then examined the contextual effect of state-level income inequality on county-level mortality, independent of county-level median income, in multilevel mixed-effects linear regression models, with a random effect

| | Table 1 | Associations of Mortality Rates With County-Level Median Household Income and State-Level Income Inequality: United States, 1999–2002 |

Mortality Rate	Single-Level Analyses of County-Level Income		Multilevel Analyses of State-Level Income Inequality (Adjusted for County-Level Income)	
	Rate per 100,000, Mean (SD)	Correlation (*r*) with County-Level Income	Standardized Parameter Estimate for State-Level Income Inequality	Significant Interaction between Income and Income Inequality (*P* < .1)
Infant	730 (443)	0.204***	0.118**	No
All causes, working age[a]	390 (113)	0.533***	0.328***	Yes
All causes, elderly[b]	5,298 (711)	0.198***	0.211*	No
Ischemic heart disease	180 (50)	0.263***	0.213**	Yes
Respiratory disease	90 (23)	0.203***	0.161**	Yes
Diabetes	27 (12)	0.231***	0.078	No
Breast cancer	25 (9.5)	0.006	0.059	No
Prostate cancer	12 (6)	0.116***	−0.014	No
Alcoholic liver disease	4 (4)	0.167***	0.024	Yes
Homicide	4 (5)	0.309***	0.255***	Yes

[a]Aged 25–64 years.
[b]Aged 65 years or older.
*P < .05; **P < .01; ***P < .001.

of state. We used z scores of mortality rates (mean=0; SD=1) to compare the multilevel model coefficients for different causes of death. We also used z scores of state-level income inequality so that the standardized parameter estimates (B) for income inequality from these models could be interpreted as correlation coefficients.

Across all mortality, we compared the strength of the association between state-level income inequality with the strength of the mortality gradient with median county income. To do this we estimated the Pearson correlation coefficient between the correlations with county-level income from the single-level models and the correlation coefficients for state-level income inequality the B's from the multilevel models. The association between mortality and state income inequality was therefore a contextual effect of income inequality conditional on county median incomes.

Socioeconomic gradients in more- and less-equal states. We categorized states into two equal groups of high- and low-inequality states and tested for a crosslevel interaction between these categories of state-level income inequality and county-level income in relation to county mortality in multilevel models. In these models, we interpreted $P \le .10$ as indicating statistically significant interaction effects. For causes of death with statistically significant in-

teractions, we graphed the socioeconomic gradients in mortality for more- and less-equal states. All analyses were conducted with Stata version 9 (StataCorp LP, College Station, TX).

RESULTS

Nine of the 10 mortality rates had statistically significant negative gradients by countylevel median income (Table 1). There was no socioeconomic gradient in breast cancer mortality.

Multilevel regression analysis, accounting for the clustering of counties within states, showed that state-level income inequality was related to 6 of the 10 mortality rates independently of differences in county incomes in each state. These included infant mortality and all-cause mortality for the working-age population and the elderly, as well as cause specific mortality for heart disease, respiratory disease, and homicides. Deaths caused by diabetes, breast and prostate cancers, and alcoholic liver disease—all with weak or nonexistent socioeconomic gradients—were unrelated to state income inequality in these models. We then held county-level median household income constant to obtain the contextual effect of income inequality only. We found that a 1-standard-deviation increase in state-level income inequality was associated with increased mortality per 100,000 of 38 deaths among the working-age population, 150 for deaths among the elderly, 52 for deaths among infants, 11 for deaths from ischemic heart disease, 4 for deaths from respiratory disease, and 1 for deaths from homicide.

Figure 1 shows that there was a clear tendency for the strength of the 10 mortality rates correlations with county-level median income to be related to the strength of their correlations with the contextual effect of state-level income inequality. The stronger the relation with county median income, the stronger the relation with state inequality ($r=-.0814$; $P=.004$).

Statistically significant interactions between county-level median income and state-level income inequality (showing that greater equality does not have the same effect on mortality in wealthier and poorer counties) were found for 5 of the 10 causes of death. For all-cause mortality among the working age population, mortality from respiratory disease, and mortality from homicide, the socioeconomic gradient was flatter in more-equal states compared with less-equal states, and more-equal states had lower mortality at any given level of county median income, as illustrated in Figure 2. For mortality from ischemic heart disease, the socioeconomic gradient was marginally steeper in more-equal states; people living in wealthier counties appeared to benefit slightly from greater state equality than did people living in poorer counties. For mortality from alcoholic liver disease, the socioeconomic gradients crossed over; compared with the socioeconomic gradients in more-equal states, greater inequality was associated with higher mortality from alcoholic liver disease in wealthier counties and lower mortality in poorer counties. There were no significant interaction effects for all-cause mortality among the elderly or for infant mortality, suggesting that greater state equality benefited wealthy and poor counties alike.

DISCUSSION

Causal Processes

Our findings show that mortality that was more strongly related to county median income was also more strongly associated with state-level income inequality. This suggests that the factors responsible for the tendency for more-egalitarian societies to have better health may be closely related to those factors that account for the socioeconomic gradient in health. We believe this is the first demonstration of

links between health inequalities and effects of income distribution.

Rather than suggesting compositional reasons for worse health in more-unequal states—resulting from lower incomes in less-equal compared to more-equal states—our results reveal strong contextual effects of inequality. A contextual effect of state income inequality means that even counties (or people) at the same level of income will have lower mortality if they are in more—rather than in less—equal states. After adjusting for differences in county median incomes, we found more-equal states had lower rates of infant mortality and both of the age-specific all cause mortalities as well as of three cause-specific mortalities (homicide, heart disease, and respiratory disease) than did less-equal states.

For each mortality rate, the strength of its relation to these contextual effects of state inequality was related to the strength of its relationship to county median income (Figure 1). Only death from diabetes and the three mortalities most weakly related to county income (breast cancer, prostate cancer, and alcoholic liver disease) showed no contextual effect of state income inequality. The data in Figure 1 suggest that the contextual effects of inequality were proportional to the compositional effects of income differences.

Income Inequality and Health Disparities

If the processes responsible for health disparities are closely related to those that explain the association between income inequality and health, we might expect health disparities to be smaller when income differences are smaller. However, when we explored how the gradient in mortality by county income differed between more- and less-equal states, we found that mortality was reduced across a wide range of county median incomes in more-equal states.

Although compositional effects of greater equality would almost inevitably reduce the socioeconomic gradient in health, we found that the contextual effects of inequality on the slope of gradients varied from one mortality rate to another. For infant mortality and for all causes of death among the elderly, there were no interaction effects; reduced income inequality lowered mortality across all levels of county income without changing the slope of the socioeconomic gradients.

The gradients for all-cause working-age mortality showed that decreased inequality benefited the least well off the most, making the socioeconomic gradient less steep (Figure 2). The same was true of mortality from respiratory disease and homicide. For

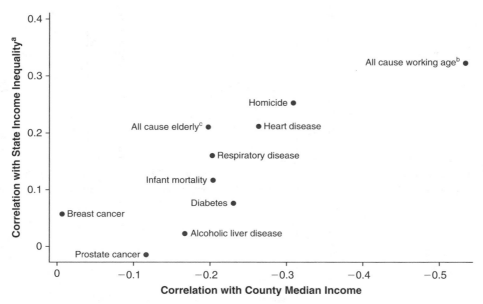

Note: r = −0.814; P = 0.004

[a]Standardized parameter estimates (B) from multilevel model after county-level income was controlled.
[b]Aged 25–64 years.
[c]Aged ≥ 65 years.

Figure 1 The effect of county-level median household income in relation to contextual effect of state-level income inequality.

mortality from alcoholic liver disease, there was no overall effect of state inequality (Table 1), but a significant interaction effect suggested that a decrease in equality shifts the social distribution of the disease from wealthy to poor counties. Although statistically significant, the interaction effect for ischemic heart disease was small. The benefits of greater equality were spread to all county income levels, but were, if anything, slightly greater in the more-wealthy counties (Figure 2). The remaining 5 mortality rates showed no significant interactions, indicating that there was no significant difference in the benefits of greater inequality in wealthy compared with poor counties.

The effect of inequality on the socioeconomic gradient in infant mortality and both all-cause mortality rates (among people of working age and the elderly) may be regarded as summarizing the effects of all their component cause-specific mortality rates. Our findings suggest that greater equality had contextual benefits that were widely shared across income groups: only among people of working age was there a contextual effect of smaller income inequalities that reduced the socioeconomic gradient in health. For all 6 of the mortality rates that showed a main effect of state income inequality (including infant mortality and the 2 all-cause mortality rates),

the benefits of greater equality extended to income groups covering the vast majority of the population. It is important to note that almost 98% of counties had a median household income between $20,000 and $65,500 (Figure 2).

Findings from Other Studies

Results of other studies that have tried to identify who benefits from greater equality are equivocal. In a review of multilevel studies of income inequality and health, Subramanian and Kawachi point out that "the question of who is most harmed by greater inequality has not been systematically addressed."[15] Four multilevel studies have examined crosslevel interactions in relation to self-rated health, rather than to mortality.[2,16-18] All showed main effects of state-level income inequality, suggesting that the health of the population at large benefited from greater equality.

Two studies provided evidence suggesting that some income groups may not share in the benefits. Kahn et al. analyzed data from the National Maternal and Infant Health Survey. Their results suggest that although the effects of inequality on maternal depressive symptoms were widespread (considering effect estimates rather than P values), the association between greater equality and better

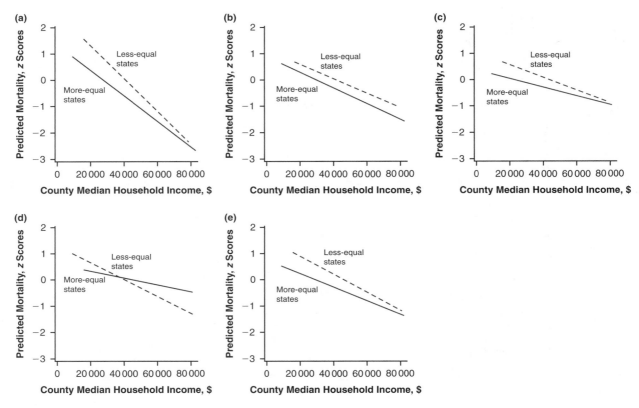

Figure 2 Mortality gradients, by mean county household income in 1999 dollars, in more- and less-equal states for all-cause mortality among those of working age (25–64 years) (a), ischemic heart disease (b), respiratory disease (c), alcoholic liver disease (d), and homicide (e).

self-rated health was confined to poor women.[16] Kennedy et al. used data from the Behavioral Risk Factor Surveillance System to examine the effect of individual income on self-rated health in analyses stratified by state income inequality. They found that odds ratios for worse self-rated health associated with greater state inequality were above 1 for all income groups—consistent with widespread health costs of greater inequality—but they were larger and only reached statistical significance among the poor.[2]

Subramanian et al., who studied data from the same sample in a multilevel interaction model that included state-level social capital, not only found benefits among the poor, but also discovered significant adverse effects of greater equality on self-rated health among high-income individuals.[18] In a later, more powerful analysis of self-reported health combining data from the 1970, 1980, and 1990 Current Population Surveys, Subramanian and Kawachi found no clear support for differential effects of state inequality across different population groups.[17] They concluded that their results suggested "an overall contextual effect of state income inequality."

The only study before ours to examine the effects of these crosslevel interactions on mortality did not use multilevel models. Lochner et al. used the National Health Interview Survey linked to the National Death Index.[19] They found that beneficial health effects of greater state equality were strongest among the "near poor" and disappeared among both the wealthier and the poorer income groups.

Lochner et al.'s study is the only one we know of suggesting that the poor do not share the benefits of greater state-level equality. Otherwise, the picture from our own and other studies is consistent with widespread benefits, tending to be larger among the poor and becoming smaller or nonexistent (or possibly leading to adverse consequences) among the wealthy.

Relative versus Absolute Gradients

If ill health is reduced in all income groups but is more reduced in poor than in wealthy groups, absolute health disparities will be smaller. However, relative differences—which express rates of ill health (or mortality) among the poor as a multiple of rates of ill health (or mortality) among the wealthy—may be undiminished.

Although more-egalitarian countries, similar to more-egalitarian U.S. states, tend to have better health,[4] several attempts to compare the size of health inequalities internationally have reported that, despite lower overall mortality, some more-egalitarian countries, such as Sweden, may not have smaller relative mortality differentials between higher and lower social status groups.[20,21] Similar findings came from a recent comparison of health in the United States and in England.[22] Average health standards were better in England than in the United States (where income inequalities are larger). Although absolute health differences by income and education were smaller in England, they were not smaller when expressed in relative terms. These findings are consistent with our own and other results.

Discussing the contextual health effects of income inequality, which they found spread widely across income groups, Subramanian and Kawachi suggested that they implied a "pollution" model of the effects of inequality spreading throughout society.[17] Inequality has often been regarded as socially corrosive, and recent evidence on the relationship between inequality and levels of violence, trust, and social capital seems to corroborate this.[23,24]

If the effects of greater inequality are not confined to the poor, but extend—like a pollutant—far up the income distribution, that may go some way to explaining why disparities in health may be smaller when expressed in absolute, but not in relative, terms in more-egalitarian countries.

Status, Status Competition, and Social Mobility

We have shown elsewhere that ill health may be just one of many social problems related to relative deprivation that are more common in more-unequal societies.[24] Others include adolescent births, violence, poor educational performance, mental illness, and imprisonment rates. This suggests that causal thinking should not be confined to factors likely to influence health alone.

If causes of death with strong socioeconomic gradients are most sensitive to the contextual effects of income inequality, this lends weight to suggestions that social relativities—such as social position, relative income, or relative deprivation—may be determinants of health. Recent interpretations of research findings on health inequalities suggest that social status differentiation may be close to the center of the problem.[23,25] If greater income inequality increases

social status differences, it may also heighten status competition and status insecurities across low- and high-income groups. If the socioeconomic gradient in health—which runs right across society—is related to social status differences, then bigger income differences may worsen health across society by increasing status insecurities and competition.

However, an alternative, or perhaps additional, explanation of why income inequality appears to have rather little impact on relative health disparities might involve the role of social mobility. In an international comparison, we found that social mobility seemed to be greater in more-equal societies.[24] If social mobility is selective for health potential established in early life, then perhaps any tendency for greater income equality to reduce health disparities would be masked by contributions to the gradient resulting from increased social mobility.

Limitations

Our study had two main weaknesses. Because it was cross-sectional, we had no direct evidence of causal ordering. However, in the relationship between income inequality and health, it seems unlikely that health determined income inequality rather than the other way around. A weakness of the ecological nature of our data was that county mortality was influenced by the fact that most counties contained both wealthy and poor households. That we used median county income rather than average county income reduced, but did not overcome, this problem. In addition, there may have been systematic differences, related to state inequality, in the material living standard that could be bought by any given level of median county income. However, using ecological rather than individual data allowed us to analyze data for the entire geographic population of the United States, rather than a sample, to include all deaths over a 4-year period, and to use age- and cause-specific mortality rates.

We are aware of no data sets large enough to have allowed us to analyze the relationship between individual income and deaths categorized by age and cause of death and how that relation was affected by state income inequality. As well as making our findings robust, using county data enabled us to look at age and cause-specific mortality rates. Another advantage was that our data included a wider spread of income than did previous studies. County median household income in our study ranged from $9333 to $82,929. The highest income categories in previous studies that used samples of individuals in cross-level interactions were $50,000 and greater in one study[19] and $35,000 and greater in others.[2,16,18]

Conclusions

Although the compositional effects of narrower income differences may reduce health inequalities, the contextual benefits extend to a large majority of the population and therefore do little to reduce relative differences in mortality between income groups. This may explain the otherwise perplexing finding that, despite their higher overall health standards, health inequalities are sometimes no smaller in more equal societies. Although the compositional effect of a narrower dispersion of income reduces health inequalities, this effect appears to be offset by contextual effects that spread far up the income range. If the strength of the contextual effects tends to be proportional to the strength of the compositional effects (Figure 1), relative measures of health inequalities may vary little between more- and less-equal societies.

However, our finding that mortality rates with stronger income gradients were also more sensitive to the contextual effects of income inequality implies the two were nevertheless linked. Such a picture could arise if health inequalities resulted, among other influences, from social status differentiation. The effects of status differences might then be amplified or reduced right across society by bigger or smaller income differences. Observable symptoms of such a process might include increased status competition and status insecurity.

About the Authors

Richard G. Wilkinson is with the Division of Epidemiology and Public Health, University of Nottingham Medical School, Nottingham, England. Kate E. Pickett is with the Department of Health Sciences, University of York, York, England.

Requests for reprints should be sent to Professor Richard Wilkinson, Division of Epidemiology and Public Health, University of Nottingham Medical School, Nottingham NG7 2UH, UK (e-mail: richard.wilkinson@nottingham.ac.uk).

This article was accepted February 6, 2007.

Contributors

R.G. Wilkinson originated and designed the study and helped write the article. K.E. Pickett conducted the statistical analysis and helped write the article.

ACKNOWLEDGMENTS

Thanks to Jeremy Miles, RAND Corporation, for statistical advice.

Human Participant Protection

No protocol approval was required for this ecological study.

● ● ● References

1. De Vogli R, Mistry R, Gnesotto R, Cornia GA. Has the relation between income inequality and life expectancy disappeared? Evidence from Italy and top industrialised countries. *J Epidemiol Community Health.* 2005;59:158-162.
2. Kennedy BP, Kawachi I, Glass R, Prothrow-Stith D. Income distribution, socioeconomic status, and self rated health in the United States: multilevel analysis. *BMJ.* 1998;317:917-921.
3. Lynch J, Davey Smith G, Harper S, et al. Is income inequality a determinant of population health? Part 1. A systematic review. *Milbank Q.* 2004;82:5-99.
4. Wilkinson RG, Pickett KE. Income inequality and population health: a review and explanation of the evidence. *Soc Sci Med.* 2006;62:1768-1784.
5. Lynch JW, Kaplan GA, Salonen JT. Why do poor people behave poorly? Variation in adult health behaviours and psychosocial characteristics by stages of the socioeconomic lifecourse. *Soc Sci Med.* 1997;44: 809-819.
6. Blane D, Bartley M, Davey Smith G. Disease aetiology and materialist explanations of socioeconomic mortality differentials. *Eur J Public Health.* 1998;7:385-391.
7. Lynch JW, Davey Smith G, Kaplan GA, House JS. Income inequality and mortality: importance to health of individual income, psychosocial environment, or material conditions. *BMJ.* 2000;320:1200-1204.
8. Marmot M, Wilkinson RG. Psychosocial and material pathways in the relation between income and health: a response to Lynch et al. *BMJ.* 2001;322: 1233-1236.
9. Kawachi I, Kennedy BP. Income inequality and health: pathways and mechanisms. *Health Serv Res.* 1999;34(1 Pt 2):215-227.
10. Wilkinson RG. Comment: income, inequality, and social cohesion. *Am J Public Health.* 1997;87: 1504-1506.
11. *Census 2000 Summary File 3.* Washington, DC: US Census Bureau; 2003.
12. Steenland K, Henley J, Thun M. All-cause and cause-specific death rates by educational status for two million people in two American Cancer Society cohorts, 1959-1996. *Am J Epidemiol.* 2002;156:11-21.
13. Steenland K, Hu S, Walker J. All-cause and causespecific mortality by socioeconomic status among employed persons in 27 US states, 1984-1997. *Am J Public Health.* 2004;94:1037-1042.
14. Table S4: Gini ratios by state: 1969, 1979, 1989, 1999. Washington, DC: Income Statistics Branch/

Housing and Household Economics Statistics Division, US Census Bureau; 2004. Available at: http://www. census.gov/hhes/www/income/ histinc/state/state4. html. Accessed August 16, 2007.

15. Subramanian SV, Kawachi I. Income inequality and health: what have we learned so far? *Epidemiol Rev.* 2004;26:78-91.

16. Kahn RS, Wise PH, Kennedy BP, Kawachi I. State income inequality, household income, and maternal mental and physical health: cross sectional national survey. *BMJ.* 2000;321:1311-1315.

17. Subramanian SV, Kawachi I. Whose health is affected by income inequality? A multilevel interaction analysis of contemporaneous and lagged effects of state income inequality on individual self-rated health in the United States. *Health Place.* 2006;12:141-156.

18. Subramanian SV, Kawachi I, Kennedy BP. Does the state you live in make a difference? Multilevel analysis of self-rated health in the US. *Soc Sci Med.* 2001;53:9-19.

19. Lochner K, Pamuk E, Makuc D, Kennedy BP, Kawachi I. State-level income inequality and individual mortality risk: a prospective, multilevel study. *Am J Public Health.* 2001;91:385-391.

20. Cavelaars AE, Kunst AE, Geurts JJ, et al. Differences in self reported morbidity by educational level: a comparison of 11 western European countries. *J Epidemiol Community Health.* 1998;52:219-227.

21. Mackenbach JP, Kunst AE, Cavelaars AE, Groenhof F, Geurts JJ. Socioeconomic inequalities in morbidity and mortality in western Europe. The EU Working Group on Socioeconomic Inequalities in Health. *Lancet.* 1997;349:1655-1659.

22. Banks J, Marmot M, Oldfield Z, Smith JP. Disease and disadvantage in the United States and in England. *JAMA.* 2006;295:2037-2045.

23. Wilkinson RG. *The Impact of Inequality.* New York, NY: New Press; 2005.

24. Wilkinson RG, Pickett KE. The problems of relative deprivation: why some societies do better than others. *Soc Sci Med.* 2007. In press. doi: 10.1016/j. socscimed.2007.05.041.

25. Marmot M. *Status Syndrome: How Your Social Standing Directly Affects Your Health and Life Expectancy.* London, England: Bloomsbury; 2004.

3

Social Determinants
of Health Inequalities

Source: Reprinted from *The Lancet;* 365: 1099-104. Marmot M. Social determinants of health inequalities, Copyright 2005, with permission from Elsevier.

The gross inequalities in health that we see within and between countries present a challenge to the world. That there should be a spread of life expectancy of 48 years among countries and 20 years or more within countries is not inevitable. A burgeoning volume of research identifies social factors at the root of much of these inequalities in health. Social determinants are relevant to communicable and non-communicable disease alike. Health status, therefore, should be of concern to policy makers in every sector, not solely those involved in health policy. As a response to this global challenge, WHO is launching a Commission on Social Determinants of Health, which will review the evidence, raise societal debate, and recommend policies with the goal of improving health of the world's most vulnerable people. A major thrust of the Commission is turning public-health knowledge into political action.

There are gross inequalities in health between countries. Life expectancy at birth, to take one measure, ranges from 34 years in Sierra Leone to 81.9 years in Japan.[1] Within countries, too, there are large inequalities—a 20-year gap in life expectancy between the most and least advantaged populations in the USA, for example.[2] One welcome response to these health inequalities is to put more effort into the control of major diseases that kill and to improve health systems.[3,4]

> **Panel 1: The Commission on Social Determinants of Health**
>
> The Commission will not only review existing knowledge but also raise societal debate and promote uptake of policies that will reduce inequalities in health within and between countries.
>
> The Commission's aim is, within 3 years, to set solid foundations for its vision: the societal relations and factors that influence health and health systems will be visible, understood, and recognised as important. On this basis, the opportunities for policy and action and the costs of not acting on these social dimensions will be widely known and debated. Success will be achieved if institutions working in health at local, national, and global level will be using this knowledge to set and implement relevant public policy affecting health. The Commission will contribute to a long-term process of incorporating social determinants of health into planning, policy and technical work at WHO.

A second belated response is to deal with poverty. This issue is the thrust of the Millennium Development Goals.[5,6] These goals challenge the world community to tackle poverty in the world's poorest countries. Included in these goals is reduction of child mortality, the health outcome most sensitive to the effects of absolute material deprivation.

To reduce inequalities in health across the world there is need for a third major thrust that is complementary to development of health systems and relief of poverty: to take action on the social determinants of health. Such action will include relief of poverty but it will have the broader aim of improving the circumstances in which people live and work. It will, therefore, address not only the major infectious diseases linked with poverty of material conditions but also non-communicable diseases—both physical and mental—and violent deaths that form the major burden of disease and death in every region of the world outside Africa and add substantially to the burden of communicable disease in sub-Saharan Africa.

To understand the social determinants of health, how they operate, and how they can be changed to improve health and reduce health inequalities, WHO is setting up an independent Commission on Social Determinants of Health, with the mission to link knowledge with action (panel 1). Public policy—both national and global—should change to take into account the evidence on social determinants of health and interventions and policies that will address them.

This introduction to the Commission's task lays out the problems of inequalities in health that the Commission will address and the approach that it will take. This report will argue that health status should be of concern to all policy makers, not merely those within the health sector. If health of a population suffers it is an indicator that the set of social arrangements needs to change. Simply, the Commission will seek to have public policy based on a vision of the world where people matter and social justice is paramount.

INEQUALITIES IN HEALTH BETWEEN AND WITHIN COUNTRIES: POVERTY AND INEQUALITY

A catastrophe on the scale of the Indian Ocean tsunami rightly focuses attention on the susceptibility of poor and vulnerable populations to natural disasters. It is no less important to keep on the agenda the more enduring problem of inequalities in health among countries.

Children

Under-5 mortality varies from 316 per 1000 livebirths in Sierra Leone to 3 per 1000 livebirths in Iceland, 4 per 1000 livebirths in Finland, and 5 per 1000 livebirths in Japan.[1] In 16 countries (12 in Africa), child mortality rose in the 1990s,[7] by 43% in Zimbabwe, 52% in Botswana, and 75% in Iraq.[8]

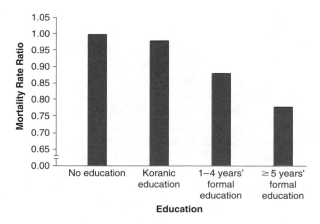

Figure 3 Mortality and education in men aged 45–90 years in Matlab, Bangladesh, 1982–98[11]

Figure 1 shows under-5 mortality rates for four countries with households classified according to socioeconomic quintile. Child mortality varies among countries.[9] Within countries, not only is child mortality highest among the poorest households but also there is a social gradient: the higher the socioeconomic level of the household the lower the mortality rate.

Adults

Differences in adult mortality among countries are large and growing. Figure 2 shows probability of death between age 15 and 60 years by region of the world between 1970 and 2002.[7] Mortality rose in Africa and in the countries of central and eastern Europe whereas it declined in the world as a whole. By 2002, for example, men in the high mortality countries of Europe had more than 40% probability of death between age 15 and 60 years compared to a 25% probability in southeast Asia. These data are

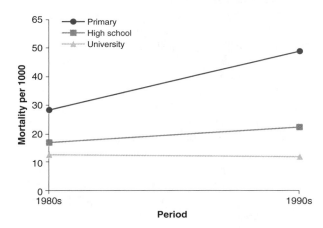

Figure 4 Increase in educational differentials in mortality between the 1980s and 1990s in St Petersburg men[16]

for regions. Among countries, the differences are even more dramatic. The probability of a man dying between age 15 and 60 years is 8.3% in Sweden, 82.1% in Zimbabwe, and 90.2% in Lesotho.[7]

A particularly telling example of health inequalities within countries is the 20-year gap in life expectancy between Australian Aboriginal and Torres Strait Islander peoples—life expectancy is 56.3 years for men and 62.8 years for women—and the Australian average.[10] The men in this population would look unhealthy in India (male life expectancy 60.1 years) whereas Australian life expectancy is among the highest in the world, marginally behind Iceland, Sweden, and Japan. The poor health of Aboriginal and Torres Strait Islander peoples is not the result of a high rate of child deaths. Infant mortality is 12.7 per 1000 livebirths. This figure is high by Australian standards, but on a scale from Iceland to Sierra Leone, it is much closer to Iceland than to Sierra Leone. The shortened life expectancy of Aboriginal and Torres Strait Islander peoples results from mortality in adults from non-communicable disease and injury. In this sense, the population is typical of the world health picture. Of the 45 million deaths among adults age 15 years and older in 2002, 32 million were due to noncommunicable disease and a further 4.5 million to violent causes.[7]

Aboriginal and Torres Strait Islander peoples are a socially excluded minority within their country. But poor health is not confined to poor populations or those who are socially excluded. As with child mortality, there is a socioeconomic gradient in adult mortality rates within countries. Figure 3 shows that in Bangladesh, adult mortality rates vary inversely with level of education.[11] This gradient in mortality is quite remarkable. Within rich countries, with strikingly different material conditions from Bangladesh, there is a social gradient in mortality prompting consideration of the causal links between status and health.[12] Whether the social gradient in poor countries can be attributed to the same causal pathways is an urgent task for review. It is especially important because, in many countries, inequalities in health have been increasing.[13-15] In Russia for example, where life expectancy is low, social inequalities have grown (Figure 4).[16]

Mortality statistics are readily available. They should not, however, lead to ignorance of the burden of nonfatal disease. In particular, mental illness causes much suffering but its effect is not clear by inspection of mortality data. Worldwide, the second highest cause of disease burden among adults age 15-59 years is unipolar depressive disorder.[7]

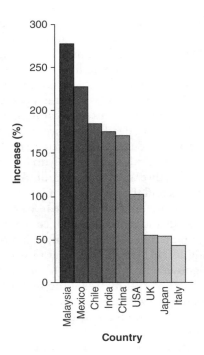

Figure 5 Projected percentage increase in the elderly population (older than 65 years) from 2000 to 2030 in selected countries Adapted from reference 17 with permission of the US Census Bureau.

The Ageing of the World's Population

It is convenient, but quite wrong, to think that the greying of the world's population is an issue only for the rich countries. Figure 5 shows the projected increase between 2000 and 2030 in the population older than 65 years in selected countries.[17] The fastest rates of increase are in countries at an intermediate level of human development, starting from a low base. The social determinants of the health of older people claim attention alongside those of health at younger ages.

SOCIAL DETERMINANTS: POVERTY, INEQUALITY, AND THE CAUSES OF THE CAUSES

In consulting widely in developing the plan for the Commission on Social Determinants of Health, a common question was: "What's new? We know that poverty is bad for health. Does that need a Commission?"

It is not difficult to understand how poverty in the form of material deprivation—dirty water, poor nutrition—allied to lack of quality medical care can account for the tragically foreshortened lives of people in Sierra Leone. Such understanding is insufficient in two important ways. First, it fails properly to take into account that relief of such material deprivation is not simply a technical matter of providing clean water or better medical care. Who gets these resources is socially determined.[18] Second, and related, international policies have not been pursued as if they had people's basic needs in mind. The critics of the policies pursued by the International Monetary Fund in the global South have argued eloquently that the economic policies pursued under structural adjustment have not benefited disadvantaged people in poor countries.[19] Recognising the health effects of poverty is one thing. Taking action to relieve its effects entails a richer understanding of the health effects of social and economic policies.

Dirty water, lack of calories, and poor antenatal care cannot account for the 20-year deficit in life expectancy of Australian Aboriginal and Torres Strait Islander peoples. On a world scale, their infant mortality rate, at 12.7 per 1000 live births, is low. Their high rate of adult mortality is from cardiovascular diseases, cancers, endocrine nutritional and metabolic diseases (including diabetes), external causes (violence), respiratory disorders, and digestive diseases.[10] This fact is not to deny that poverty is important. But the form that poverty takes and its health consequences are quite different when considering chronic disease and violent deaths in adults, compared to deaths from infectious disease in children. It entails a richer understanding of the social determinants of health.

The health experience of Aboriginal and Torres Strait Islander peoples has relevance for the health of disadvantaged people worldwide. While in Africa the major contributor to premature mortality is communicable disease, in every other region of the world it is non-communicable disease.[1] Careful analysis of the global burden of disease has pointed to the importance of risk factors, such as being overweight, smoking, alcohol, and poor diet.[20] These are indeed potent causes. But would it be helpful to go into a deprived Australian Aboriginal population and point out that they should really take better care of themselves—that their smoking and obesity were killing them; and if they must drink, please do so in moderation? Unlikely. To borrow Geoffrey Rose's term, we need to examine the causes of the causes:[21] the social conditions that give rise to high risk of non-communicable disease whether acting through unhealthy behaviours or through the effects of impossibly stressful lives[12] (panel 2).

A further answer to the what's new question: although it might be obvious that poverty is at the root of much of the problem of infectious disease, and needs to be solved, it is less obvious how to break the link between poverty and disease. Income poverty provides, at best, an incomplete explanation of differences in mortality among countries or among subgroups within countries. It is well known that among rich countries, there is little correlation between gross national product (GNP) per person and life expectancy. Greece for example, with a GNP at purchasing power parities of just more than U.S. $17,000, has a life expectancy of 78.1 years; the USA, with a GNP of more than $34,000, has a life expectancy of 76.9 years. Costa Rica and Cuba stand out as countries with GNPs less than $10,000 and yet life expectancies of 77.9 years and 76.5 years.[23]

There are many examples of relatively poor populations with similar incomes but strikingly different health records.[8] Kerala and China, famously, have good health, despite low incomes.[24] The social processes that lead to this beneficial state of health need not wait for the world order to be changed to relieve poverty in the worst-off countries. A social determinants perspective is crucial. It is also important to enquire whether the action that is taking place

---

Panel 2: The Solid Facts

Because the causes of the causes are not obvious, the WHO Regional Office for Europe asked a group at University College London to summarise the evidence on the social determinants of health, published as *The Solid Facts*.[22] It had ten messages on the social determinants of health based on:

- the social gradient
- stress
- early life
- social exclusion
- work
- unemployment
- social support
- addiction
- food
- transport

As an indication that there was a ready audience for these messages, in the first 12 months after publication of the second edition it was downloaded from the Internet 218,000 times.

The Solid Facts reviewed evidence from Europe, aimed mainly at reducing inequalities in health within countries. The task of the Commission will be to review evidence on the social determinants of health that are relevant to global health: inequalities among countries and within.

to relieve poverty is having the desired effect not only on average incomes but also on income distribution and hence on the poorest people.

The social gradient in health is a particular challenge. Where material deprivation is severe, a social gradient in mortality could arise from degrees of absolute deprivation. In rich countries with low levels of material deprivation the gradient changes the focus from absolute to relative deprivation.[25] Relative deprivation relates to a broader approach to social functioning and meeting of human needs[12]—capabilities in the words of Amartya Sen,[26] spiritual resources to use Robert Fogel's term.[27] It is likely that both material or physical needs and capability, spiritual, or psychosocial needs are important to the gradient in health, which will, therefore, be an important focus.

A focus on material conditions and control of infectious disease must not be to the exclusion of social determinants. The circumstances in which people live and work are as important for communicable as they are for non-communicable disease. Social conditions powerfully influence both the onset and response to treatment of the major infectious diseases that kill.[28,29]

The Commission on Social Determinants of Health will need to have in its sights poverty of the sub-Saharan African sort and the social determinants that account for Bolivia having 14 fewer years of life expectancy than Costa Rica or Aboriginal and Torres Strait Islander peoples having 20 years fewer than other Australians. As these examples illustrate, it will examine inequalities in health between countries and inequalities within.

ACTION IS POSSIBLE AND NECESSARY

A review of policies in European countries identified several that took action on the social determinants of health.[30] Although the reason for the policies was not necessarily to improve health they were nevertheless relevant to health: taxation and tax credits, old-age pensions, sickness or rehabilitation benefits, maternity or child benefits, unemployment benefits, housing policies, labour markets, communities, and care facilities.

In Sweden, the new strategy for public health is "to create social conditions that will ensure good health for the entire population".[31] Of 11 policy domains, five relate to social determinants: participation in society, economic and social security, conditions in childhood and adolescence, healthier working life, and environment and products. These

are in addition to health-promoting medical care and the usual health behaviours. The UK set reduction of health inequalities as a key aim of health policy. It assembled evidence and expert judgments on areas suitable for policy development.[32] These then formed the basis of a plan of action to reduce health inequalities.[33]

These are examples from rich countries. There are further encouraging examples. Familias en Accion in Colombia transfers cash to poor families. To qualify, families must ensure their children receive preventive health care, enroll in school, and attend classes. The results are encouraging: favourable growth of children and fewer episodes of diarrhoea.[34] The Oportunidades programme in Mexico had somewhat similar aims with similarly encouraging results.[35]

MEETING HUMAN NEEDS

Two linked themes provide the rationale for the Commission on Social Determinants of Health. First, there is no choice. If the major determinants of health are social, so must be the remedies. Treating existing disease is urgent and will always receive high priority but should not be to the exclusion of taking action on the underlying social determinants of health. Disease control, properly planned and directed, has a good history, but so too does social and economic development in combating major disease and improving population health. Wider social policy will be crucial to reduction of inequalities in health.

There is a second theme that relates to the question of how one can tell if a population is thriving. One standard answer is to measure economic well-being with measures such as GNP, average income, or consumption patterns. A better answer is to measure health status.[36] There is no difficulty in convincing medical and health personnel that health is important—that is what we do. It is more challenging, but necessary, to convince policy makers and others that the health of the population is important precisely because it is a measure of whether, in the end, a population is benefiting as a result of a set of social arrangements.

In other words, action on the social determinants of health is necessary not only to improve health but also because such improvement will indicate that society has moved in a direction of meeting human needs.[37] There is a great deal of dogmatic dispute about the rights and wrongs of economic and social policies. People use labels—globalisation, neoliberal economic policies—as badges of allegiance and terms of abuse. The Commission will have one basic dogma: policies that harm human health need to be identified and, where possible, changed. From this perspective, globalisation and markets are good or bad in so far as the way they are operated affects health. Inequalities in health between and within countries are avoidable.[38] There is no necessary biological reason why life expectancy should be 48 years longer in Japan than in Sierra Leone or 20 years shorter in Australian Aboriginal and Torres Strait Islander peoples than in other Australians. Reducing these social inequalities in health, and thus meeting human needs, is an issue of social justice.

Conflict of interest statement

Michael Marmot is chairman of the Commission on Social Determinants of Health.

ACKNOWLEDGMENTS

Grateful thanks to Ruth Bell, Hilary Brown, Tim Evans, Alec Irwin, Rene Loewenson, Nicole Valentine, Jeanette Vega, and members of the WHO Equity team who have worked to develop the Commission and the ideas in this report.

About the Author

International Centre for Health and Society, University College London, 1–19 Torrington Place, London WC1E 6BT, UK. (Prof Sir M Marmot) m.marmot@ucl.ac.uk.

● ● ● **References**

1. WHO. The World Health Report 2004: changing history. Geneva: World Health Organization, 2004.

2. Murray CJL, Michaud CM, McKenna MT, Marks JS. US patterns of mortality by county and race: 1965-94. Cambridge: Harvard Center for Population and Development Studies, 1998.

3. WHO. Treating 3 million by 2005: making it happen: the WHO strategy—the WHO and UNAIDS global initiative to provide retroviral therapy to 3 million people with HIV/AIDS in developing countries by the end of 2005. Geneva: World Health Organization, 2003.

4. The Global Fund to fight AIDS, tuberculosis, and malaria. http://www.theglobalfund.org.

5. United Nations Development Group. Millennium Development Goals, http://www.developmentgoals. org.

6. Sachs JD, McArthur JW. The Millennium Project: a plan for meeting the Millennium Development Goals. *Lancet* 2005; **365**: 347-53.

7. WHO. World Health Report 2003: shaping the future. Geneva: World Health Organization, 2003.

8. United Nations. Human Development Report 2004. New York: United Nations Development Programme, 2004.

9. Victora CG, Wagstaff A, Schellenberg JA, Gwatkin D, Claeson M, Habicht JP. Applying an equity lens to child health and mortality: more of the same is not enough. *Lancet* 2003; **362**: 233-41.

10. Aboriginal and Torres Strait Commissioner, Statistics Human Rights and Equal Opportunity Commission. A statistical overview of Aboriginal and Torres Strait Islander peoples in Australia. http://www.humanrights.gov.au/social_justice/ statistics/index.html (accessed Oct 28, 2004).

11. Hurt LS, Ronsmans C, Saha S. Effects of education and other socioeconomic factors on middle age mortality in rural Bangladesh. *J Epidemiol Community Health* 2004; **58**: 315-20.

12. Marmot M. Status syndrome. London: Bloomsbury, 2004.

13. Donkin A, Goldblatt P, Lynch K. Inequalities in life expectancy by social class 1972-1999. *Health Stat Q* 2002; **15**: 5-15.

14. Mackenbach JP, Bos V, Andersen O, et al. Widening socioeconomic inequalities in mortality in six Western European countries. *Int J Epidemiol* 2003; **32**: 830-37.

15. Crimmins EM, Saito Y. Trends in healthy life expectancy in the United States, 1970-1990: gender, racial, and educational differences. *Soc Sci Med* 2001; **52**: 1629-41.

16. Plavinski SL, Plavinskaya SI, Klimov AN. Social factors and increase in mortality in Russia in the 1990s: prospective cohort study. *BMJ* 2003; **326**: 1240-42.

17. Kinsella K, Velkoff VA, US Census Bureau. An aging world: 2001-series P95/01-1. Washington: US Government Printing Office, 2001.

18. Kim JY, Millen JV, Irwin A, Gershman J. Dying for growth: global inequality and the health of the poor. Monroe: Common Courage Press, 2000.

19. Stiglitz JE. Globalization and its discontents. London: Allen Lane, 2002.

20. WHO. Reducing risks, promoting healthy life: World Health Report 2002. Geneva: World Health Organization, 2002.

21. Rose G. Strategy of preventive medicine. Oxford: Oxford University Press, 1992.

22. Wilkinson R, Marmot M. The Solid Facts. Copenhagen: World Health Organization, 2003.

23. United Nations Development Programme. Human development report. New York: Oxford University Press, 2003.

24. Sen A. Development as freedom. New York: Alfred A Knopf, 1999.

25. Wilkinson RG. The impact of inequality: how to make sick societies healthier. London: Routledge, 2005.

26. Sen A. Inequality reexamined. Oxford: Oxford University Press, 1992.

27. Fogel RW. The fourth great awakening and the future of egalitarianism. Chicago: University of Chicago Press, 2000.

28. Farmer P. Infections and inequalities. Berkeley: University of California Press, 1999.

29. Farmer P. Pathologies of power: health, human rights, and the new war on the poor. Berkeley: University of California Press, 2003.

30. Crombie IK, Irvine L, Elliott L, Wallace H. Closing the health inequalities gap: an international perspective. Dundee: NHS Health Scotland and University of Dundee, 2004.

31. Hogstedt H, Lundgren B, Moberg H, Pettersson B, Agren G. Swedish public health policy and the National Institute of Public Health. *Scan J Public Health* 2004; **32** (suppl 64): 1-64.

32. Acheson D. Inequalities in health: report of an independent inquiry. London; HMSO, 1998.

33. Department of Health. Tackling health inequalities: a programme for action. London, Department of Health, 2003.

34. Attanasio O, Vera-Hernandez M. Medium and long run effects of nutrition and child care: evaluation of a community nursery programme in rural Colombia-IFS working papers EWP04/06. London: Institute for Fiscal Studies, 2004.

35. World Bank. Mexico's Oportunidades program. http://www.worldbank.org/wbi/reducingpoverty/case-Mexico-OPORTUNIDADES.html (accessed Feb 9, 2005).

36. Sen A. Mortality as an indicator of success and failure: Innocenti Inaugural Lecture 1995. Instituto degli Innocenti, Florence, Italy; March 3, 1995.

37. Doyal L, Gough I. A theory of human need. London: Macmillan, 1991.

38. Whitehead M. The concepts and principles of equity and health. Copenhagen: World Health Organization, 1990

Socioeconomic Inequalities in Health in 22 European Countries

Source: Mackenbach JP, Stirbu I, Roskam AJ, et al. Socioeconomic inequalities in health in 22 European countries. *N Engl J Med* 2008;358:2468-81. Copyright [(c)] 2008 Massachusetts Medical Society. All rights reserved.

ABSTRACT

Background

Comparisons among countries can help to identify opportunities for the reduction of inequalities in health. We compared the magnitude of inequalities in mortality and self-assessed health among 22 countries in all parts of Europe.

Methods

We obtained data on mortality according to education level and occupational class from census-based mortality studies. Deaths were classified according to cause, including common causes, such as cardiovascular disease and cancer; causes related to smoking; causes related to alcohol use; and causes amenable to medical intervention, such as tuberculosis and hypertension. Data on self-assessed health, smoking, and obesity according to education and income were obtained from health or multipurpose surveys. For each country, the association between socioeconomic status and health outcomes was measured with the use of regression-based inequality indexes.

Results

In almost all countries, the rates of death and poorer self-assessments of health were substantially higher in groups of lower socioeconomic status, but the magnitude of the inequalities between groups of higher and lower socioeconomic status was much larger in some countries than in others. Inequalities in mortality were small in some southern European countries and very large in most countries in the eastern and Baltic regions. These variations among countries appeared to be attributable in part to causes of death related to smoking or alcohol use or amenable to medical intervention. The magnitude of inequalities in self-assessed health also varied substantially among countries, but in a different pattern.

Conclusions

We observed variation across Europe in the magnitude of inequalities in health associated with socioeconomic status. These inequalities might be reduced by improving educational opportunities, income distribution, health-related behavior, or access to health care.

Inequalities in health among groups of various socioeconomic status (as measured by education, occupation, and income) constitute one of the main challenges for public health,[1] but it is unknown to what extent such inequalities are modifiable. Because international comparative studies can help identify opportunities for reducing inequalities in health, we conducted a study aimed at measuring variations in the magnitude of inequalities in health among 22 European countries and at identifying some of the immediate determinants of these variations.

Europe offers excellent opportunities for this type of research because of the intercountry variety of political, cultural, economic, and epidemiologic histories and because good data on inequalities in health are often available.[2] In a previous study, we compared socioeconomically based inequalities in mortality and morbidity among 10 countries in western Europe during the 1980s.[3-7] We now report a study of the magnitude of inequalities in health in a much larger number of countries in both western and eastern Europe during the 1990s and early 2000s. The inclusion of eastern Europe allows us to determine whether countries that have gone through a turbulent period of political, economic, and health care reform[8-12] have larger inequalities in health than countries elsewhere in Europe.

METHODS

We obtained data on mortality according to age, sex, cause of death, and indicators of socioeconomic status from mortality registries (Table 1). The data were based on 3.5 million deaths in 16 countries among more than 54 million persons ranging in age from 30 to 74 years at the beginning of the study. The data were drawn from national populations, except for the United Kingdom, with data from England and Wales only; Italy, with data from Turin only; and Spain, with data from Madrid, Barcelona, and the Basque country only. With regard to the mortality data from England and Wales, this article has received clearance from the Office for National Statistics Longitudinal Study (reference number 20037C). We performed two analyses of the data on death according to cause; one analysis focused on common causes of death (cancer, cardiovascular disease, and injuries), and the other focused on more specific causes of death (smoking-related causes, alcohol-related causes, and causes amenable to medical intervention, such as tuberculosis and hypertension[13,14]). Code numbers of the causes of death according to the ninth and tenth revisions of the *International Classification of Diseases, Clinical Modification* (ICD-9-CM and ICD-10-CM) are given in Table 1 in the Supplementary Appendix, available with the full text of this article at www.nejm.org.

Data on self-assessed health and risk factors for disease (e.g., smoking and obesity) according to age, sex, and indicators of socioeconomic status were obtained from national health or multi-purpose surveys that also included self-reported socioeconomic data (Table 1). The data came from 19 countries and almost 350,000 respondents who ranged in age from 30 to 64 years in some surveys and from 30 to 69 years in others. All data are nationally representative. For self-reported illness, our study focused on the single-item question on self-assessed health ("How is your health in general?"), which has five possible answers, ranging from "very good" to "bad." In order to make use of the full range of levels of self-assessed health, we gave quantitative weights to each level (i.e., a multiplicative factor of 1.85 for each level worse than "very good") that were derived from the average number of chronic conditions in each level[15] (details of the calculation are given in the legend to Fig. 2). The only risk factors for disease for which data were available in a form that enabled them to be compared across countries were current tobacco smoking and obesity, defined as a body-mass index (the weight in kilograms divided by the square of the height in meters) greater than 30.

Socioeconomic status was measured by education, occupation, and income. Education levels were categorized as no education or primary education (up to approximately 6 years of education), lower secondary education (up to approximately 9 years), higher secondary education (up to approximately 11 years), and tertiary education (bachelor's degree or higher). Data on education level were available in a comparable form for most countries from both mortality registries and health interviews or multipurpose surveys. Occupations were classified as "manual" (considered the lower level) or "nonmanual." Data on occupation were available from mortality registries for middle-aged men in a limited number of countries only. Income was categorized in approximate quintiles of equivalent net household income. The self-reported after-tax incomes of all household members, including benefits, were added, and the total was corrected for household size by dividing it by the total number of persons in the household to the power of 0.36. Income data were available from surveys in a limited number of countries only. Tables 2 and 3 (not included) show the distribution of study populations according to education level, occupational classification, and income level. The proportion of the population with less education tended to be large in the southern and eastern regions, whereas inequalities in income were large in England and Wales and in Portugal.

Table 1 Countries Included in the Analysis and Sources of Data

European Region	Country	Mortality Data				Morbidity Data		
		Type of Study*	Years	Person-years of Follow-up	No. of Deaths	Survey	Years	No. of Respondents
North	Finland	National, longitudinal, census-linked mortality study	1990–2000	25,874,201	269,781	Finbalt Health Monitor — National Public Health Institute, Helsinki	1994, 1998, 2000, 2002, 2004	16,963
	Sweden	National, longitudinal, census-linked mortality study	1991–2000	43,537,681	404,151	Swedish Survey of Living Conditions — Statistics Sweden, Stockholm	2000–2001	9,918
	Norway	National, longitudinal, census-linked mortality study	1990–2000	19,956,767	213,022	Norwegian Survey of Living Conditions — Statistics Norway, Oslo	2002	5,918
	Denmark	National, longitudinal, census-linked mortality study	1996–2000	13,926,291	136,065	Danish Health and Morbidity Survey — Danish National Institute of Public Health, Copenhagen	2000	14,503
West	United Kingdom	National, longitudinal, census-linked mortality study for a representative sample of 1% of the population of England and Wales	1991–1999	2,295,029	21,234	Health Survey for England — Department of Health, London	2001	13,960
	Ireland	Not available				Living in Ireland Panel Survey — Economic and Social Research Institute, Dublin	1995–2002	5,294
Continental	The Netherlands	Not available				General Social Survey — Statistics Netherlands, Voorburg	2003–2004	13,782
	Belgium	National, longitudinal, census-linked mortality study	1991–1995	24,861,015	283,349	Health Interview Survey — Institute of Public Health, Brussels	1997–2001	16,268
	Germany	Not available				German National Health Examination and Interview Survey — Robert Koch Institut, Berlin	1998	6,403
	Switzerland†	National, longitudinal, census-linked mortality study	1990–2000	27,910,587	255,251	Not available		
	France‡	National, longitudinal, census-linked mortality study for a representative sample of 1% of population	1990–1999	2,404,246	20,465	French Health, Health Care and Insurance Survey — Institut de Recherche et Documentation en Economie de la Santé, Paris	2004	14,727
South	Italy	Urban, longitudinal, census-linked mortality study for the city of Turin	1991–2001	4,873,109	50,621	Health Conditions and Use of Health Services — National Institute of Statistics, Rome	1999–2000	102,832
						Multipurpose Family Survey, Aspects of Daily Living — National Institute of Statistics, Rome	2000	43,011

(continued)

Table 1 Countries Included in the Analysis and Sources of Data (continued)

Region	Country	Study	Period	Population	Deaths	Source	Survey year(s)	Survey N
	Spain	Urban, longitudinal, census-linked mortality study for the city of Barcelona	1992–2001	8,151,810	77,101	National Health Survey — Ministry of Health and Consumption, Madrid	2001	17,517
		Regional, longitudinal, census-linked mortality study for the region of Madrid	1996–1997	3,663,333	22,585			
		Regional, longitudinal, census-linked mortality study for the Basque country	1996–2001	6,098,485	41,704			
	Portugal	Not available				National Health Survey — Instituto Nacional de Saude Dr. Ricardo Jorge, Lisbon	1998–1999	34,840
East	Slovenia	National, longitudinal, census-linked mortality study	1991–2000	9,647,452	101,557			
	Hungary	National, unlinked, cross-sectional mortality study	1999–2002	21,031,348	363,508	National Health Interview Survey Hungary — National Public Health and Medical Officer Service, Budapest	2000–2003	9,179
	Czech Republic	National, unlinked, cross-sectional mortality study	1999–2003	25,759,210	344,973	Health Interview Survey — Institute of Health Information and Statistics of the Czech Republic, Prague	2002	2,028
	Slovakia	Not available				Health Monitor Survey — Public Health Institute of the Slovak Republic, Bratislava	2002	1,200
	Poland	National, unlinked, cross-sectional mortality study	2001–2003	54,883,245	717,743	Not available		
Baltic	Lithuania	National, unlinked, cross-sectional mortality study	2000–2002	5,156,703	78,399	Finbalt Health Monitor — National Public Health Institute, Helsinki	1994, 1998, 2000, 2002, 2004	10,336
	Latvia	Not available				Finbalt Health Monitor — National Public Health Institute, Helsinki	1998, 2000, 2002, 2004	6,779
	Estonia	National, unlinked, cross-sectional mortality study	1998–2002	3,435,255	60,794	Health Behavior among Estonian Adult Population — National Institute for Health Development, Tallinn	2002, 2004	3,525
Total	Europe			303,540,302	3,462,053			348,983

* In longitudinal, census-linked, follow-up studies of mortality, socioeconomic status as determined during a census is linked to mortality data during a follow-up period after the census. In unlinked, cross-sectional studies of mortality, socioeconomic data mentioned on death certificates and elicited during the census have been used to classify the numerator and denominator of mortality, respectively.

† Non-Swiss nationals are excluded.

‡ Residents of overseas territories, members of the military, and students were excluded.

All measures were adjusted for age. Because both relative and absolute measures of inequalities in health are important, we have presented both the relative index of inequality and the slope index of inequality[16,17] for each country separately. Both indexes are regression-based measures that take into account the whole socioeconomic distribution and that remove variability in the size of socioeconomic groups as a source of variation in the magnitude of inequalities in health.[17] In the regression analysis, mortality, morbidity, or risk-factor prevalence was related to a measure of the rank of education, occupation, or income, in which the rank was calculated as the mean proportion of the population having a higher level of education, occupation, or income.

The relative index of inequality is the ratio between the estimated mortality, morbidity, or risk-factor prevalence among persons at rank 1 (the lowest education, occupation, or income level) and rank 0 (the highest level). The relative index of inequality was calculated with the use of Poisson regression analysis, which also generated 95% confidence intervals. The slope index of inequality measures absolute differences in rates (e.g., in deaths per 100,000 person-years) between the lowest and the highest ends of the socioeconomic scale. The slope index of inequality is derived from the relative index of inequality and the age-adjusted overall mortality rate according to the following formula: slope index of inequality = 2 × mortality rate × (relative index of inequality − 1) ÷ (relative index of inequality + 1).[16] Because the slope index of inequality depends on the overall mortality rate in the population, we have presented these overall mortality rates together with the slope indexes of inequality.

RESULTS

Figures 1A and 1B show relative inequalities in the rate of death from any cause according to education level. The relative index of inequality is greater than 1 for both men and women in all countries, indicating that, throughout Europe, mortality is higher among those with less education. The magnitude of these inequalities varies substantially among countries. For example, in Sweden, the relative index of inequality for men is less than 2, indicating that mortality among those with the least education is less than twice that among those with the most education; on the other hand, in Hungary, the Czech Republic, and Poland, the relative index of inequality for men is 4 or higher, indicating that mortality

differs by a factor of more than 4 between the lower and upper ends of the education scale. The smallest inequalities for both men and women are found in the Basque country of Spain, whereas the largest inequalities are found in the Czech Republic and Lithuania. Education-related inequalities in mortality are smaller than the average for Europe in all southern European populations included in this analysis and larger than average in most countries in the eastern and Baltic regions. Data on occupation-related inequalities in mortality among middle-aged men (Fig. 1C) confirm that relative inequalities in mortality tend to be smaller in southern European populations.

Table 2 shows that the international pattern observed for relative education-related inequalities in mortality also generally applies to absolute education-related inequalities in mortality, as indicated by the slope index of inequality. In Europe as a whole, persons with less education have higher rates of death from all causes except breast cancer, as indicated by a negative slope index of inequality for this cause of death. Inequalities in the rate of death from cardiovascular disease account for 34% of education-related inequalities in the rate of death from any cause among men (451 of 1333 deaths per 100,000 person-years) and 51% of those among women (251 of 492 deaths per 100,000 person-years). Although death from almost any cause is more frequent among those with less education than among those with more education, the range of variation for a single cause of death sometimes includes both "reverse" inequalities (higher mortality in groups with higher education) and "regular" inequalities (higher mortality in groups with lower education).

These data help to explain how smaller education-related inequalities in the rate of death from any cause in southern European populations and larger inequalities in the eastern and Baltic regions arise. Among men and women, smaller inequalities in the rate of death from any cause in the southern region are due mainly to smaller inequalities in the rate of death from cardiovascular disease. For example, among men in the Basque country, where the education-related inequality in the rate of death from any cause is below the European average, death from cardiovascular disease accounts for 46% of this difference (i.e., [451 − 16 deaths per 100,000 person-years] ÷ [1333 − 384 deaths per 100,000 person-years]). Larger inequalities in the rate of death from cardiovascular disease make an important contribution to larger inequalities in the rate of death from any cause in the eastern and Baltic regions as well; however, important contributions are also made

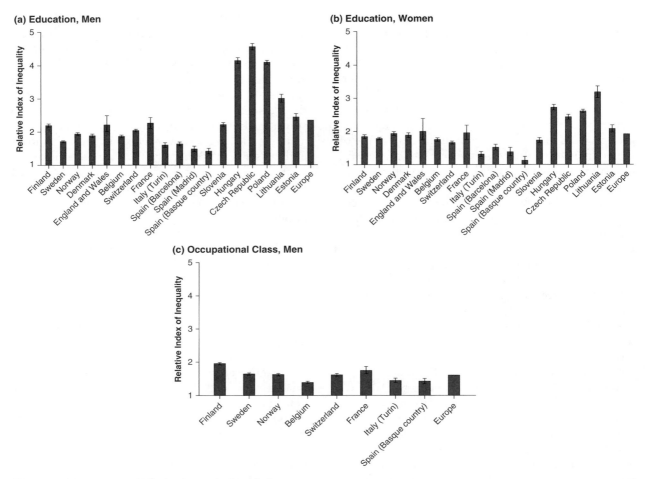

Figure 1 Relative Inequalities in the Rate of Death from Any Cause.

by cancer in the eastern region and injuries in the Baltic region.

In Europe as a whole, inequalities in mortality from smoking-related conditions account for 22% of the inequalities in the rate of death from any cause among men and 6% of those among women (Table 2). Inequalities in smoking-related mortality tend to be larger in the eastern and Baltic regions (among men only) and smaller (or even "reverse") in the southern region. In Europe as a whole, inequalities in alcohol-related mortality account for 11% of inequalities in the rate of death from any cause among men and 6% of those among women. Larger inequalities in alcohol related mortality contribute to larger inequalities in the rate of death from any cause in Hungary (among men and women) and the Baltic region (among men only). In Europe as a whole, deaths from conditions amenable to medical intervention account for 5% of inequalities in the rate of death from any cause. However, these inequalities are larger than the European average in Lithuania and Estonia, where

they contribute to the larger inequalities in the rate of death from any cause (among men only).

Figure 2 shows the relative inequalities in the prevalence of poorer self-assessed health (weighted on the basis of the burden of chronic disease) according to education and income level. The relative index of inequality is greater than 1 in all countries, indicating worse health in groups of lower socio-economic status throughout Europe. The variation of this measure among countries is considerably less than that of inequalities in the rate of death from any cause, and the international pattern also tends to be different from that of death from any cause. In Italy and Spain, education-related inequalities in self-assessed health are smaller than average, a finding that mirrors the smaller education-related inequalities in the rate of death from any cause observed in Turin, Barcelona, Madrid, and the Basque country. In the Baltic region, on the other hand, education-related inequalities in self-assessed health are smaller than average, whereas education-

Table 2 Absolute Inequalities in Overall and Cause-Specific Mortality Rates between Persons with the Lowest and Those with the Highest Level of Education.*

Country	Average Rate of Death from Any Cause†	Slope Index of Inequality According to Cause of Death											
		All Causes	All Cancer-Related Causes	Breast Cancer‡	Lung Cancer	All Cardiovascular Disease	Ischemic Heart Disease	Cerebrovascular Disease	Injuries	All Other Diseases	Alcohol-Related Causes§	Smoking-Related Causes¶	Causes Amenable to Medical Intervention‖
						deaths/100,000 person-years							
Men													
Finland	1673	1255	213		135	533	393	94	143	347	101	215	88
Sweden	1188	625	90		37	309	229	50	52	175	50	71	26
Norway	1529	980	169		95	434	307	78	70	305	62	166	49
Denmark	1344	828	126		75	235	157	39	89	363	23	60	44
United Kingdom (England and Wales)	1124	862	225		141	401	284	67	19	157	28	241	NA
Belgium	1510	915	274		179	233	99	55	64	340	36	302	28
Switzerland	1475	1012	283		136	401	132	61	91	348	117	260	61
France	1241	1044	333		71	232	67	68	109	357	196	204	114
Italy (Turin)	1377	639	232		107	140	57	52	23	243	63	177	24
Spain (Barcelona)	1370	662	230		90	88	26	40	38	304	77	218	36
Spain (Madrid)	1355	530	181		56	38	−16	11	26	278	75	170	34
Spain (Basque country)	1108	384	107		39	16	−6	3	63	177	46	107	24
Slovenia	1902	1439	303		124	405	67	219	203	482	224	327	83
Hungary	2110	2580	666		260	1003	482	385	222	671	420	508	66
Czech Republic	1664	2130	676		247	825	472	259	138	489	146	364	73
Poland	1804	2192	589		260	750	295	223	187	637	145	408	75
Lithuania	2531	2536	383		197	807	505	159	643	677	304	424	195
Estonia	2799	2349	355		191	929	610	263	436	618	286	323	162
Europe total	1635	1333	328		153	451	233	131	147	425	141	288	72

(continued)

Table 2   Absolute Inequalities in Overall and Cause-Specific Mortality Rates between Persons with the Lowest and Those with the Highest Level of Education.* (continued)

Women

Finland	811	483	49	−8	14	262	168	72	25	161	31	28	42
Sweden	673	381	73	−6	20	172	104	44	8	128	15	39	18
Norway	811	518	103	−14	44	239	141	62	5	169	16	79	30
Denmark	830	511	103	−12	63	160	90	42	22	230	9	70	27
United Kingdom (England and Wales)	672	462	111	−22	59	236	154	31	1	96	7	103	NA
Belgium	761	417	47	−11	11	198	77	55	11	163	6	29	10
Switzerland	676	337	53	−3	10	158	74	46	5	120	10	21	22
France	536	375	50	35	6	130	33	44	36	163	30	17	82
Italy (Turin)	721	197	15	−17	−9	94	34	34	−3	94	8	−4	11
Spain (Barcelona)	569	236	7	−12	−14	103	36	34	5	126	7	−14	12
Spain (Madrid)	543	175	−12	−29	−17	96	30	29	−1	94	−3	−17	9
Spain (Basque country)	422	51	−76	−19	−20	56	23	17	7	74	3	−24	2
Slovenia	853	459	−13	−21	−18	263	62	127	28	180	44	−3	33
Hungary	1023	948	120	−17	20	511	237	216	51	258	82	61	26
Czech Republic	868	726	144	10	17	356	182	134	26	203	23	33	32
Poland	840	750	139	6	10	356	117	142	29	222	23	28	27
Lithuania	1053	1099	130	7	7	535	297	162	178	251	87	39	51
Estonia	1213	851	7	−5	4	493	273	187	109	252	101	16	48
Europe total	778	492	55	−9	10	251	120	85	30	172	30	28	27

* Code numbers of the causes of death according to the 9th and 10th revisions of the *International Classification of Diseases, Clinical Modification* (ICD-9-CM and ICD-10-CM) are given in Table 1 of the Supplementary Appendix. The slope index of inequality is a regression-based measure of absolute differences in mortality rates between the lowest and the highest ends of the socioeconomic scale. NA denotes not available.

† Age-standardized rates of death for all educational groups are given.

‡ Rates of death from breast cancer among men are not given.

§ Alcohol-related causes are accidental poisoning by alcohol and alcoholic psychosis, dependence, abuse, cardiomyopathy, and cirrhosis of the liver and pancreas.

▮ Smoking-related causes are chronic obstructive pulmonary disease and cancer of the buccal cavity, pharynx, esophagus, larynx, trachea, bronchus, and lung.

‖ Causes amenable to medical intervention are tuberculosis and other infectious and parasitic diseases, cervical cancer, breast cancer, Hodgkin's disease, leukemia, hypertension, cerebrovascular disease, pneumonia or influenza, appendicitis, hernia, peptic ulcer, cholelithiasis and cholecystitis, and complications of childbirth.

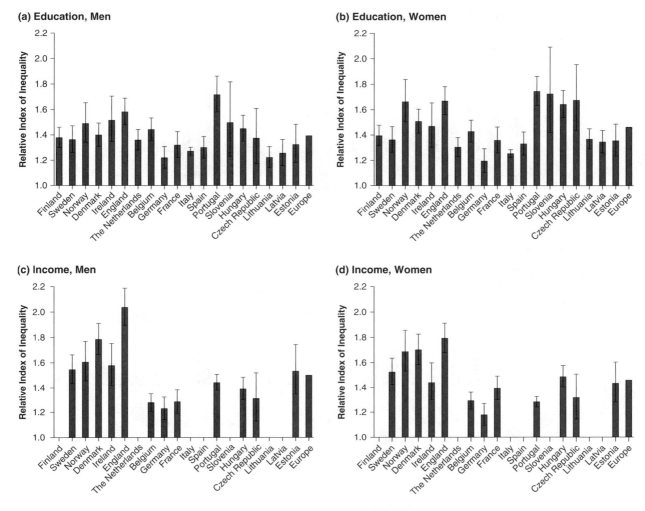

Figure 2 Relative Inequalities in the Prevalence of Poorer Self-Assessed Health.

related inequalities in death from any cause are larger. Income-related inequalities in self-assessed health are not larger in the eastern and Baltic regions than in other parts of Europe and are remarkably large in the northern and western regions, particularly England and Wales, where income inequalities are also large.

In Europe as a whole, both smoking and obesity are more common among people of lower education level; education-related inequalities in smoking are larger among men, and education-related inequalities in obesity are larger among women (Fig. 3). There are striking differences among countries in the magnitude and even the direction of these inequalities, however. Large education-related inequalities in smoking are seen in the northern, western, and continental regions; small inequalities (and, among women, even reverse inequalities, in which smoking rates are higher in groups with more

education) are seen in the southern region. In the eastern and Baltic regions, the pattern is unclear. Large education-related inequalities in obesity are seen in the southern region, particularly among women, for whom the relative indexes of inequality are above 4, indicating that the prevalence of obesity among those with the least education is more than four times higher than that among those with the most education. By contrast, education-related inequalities in obesity tend to be smaller than average in the eastern and Baltic regions.

DISCUSSION

As compared with our study of inequalities in mortality and morbidity related to socioeconomic status in 10 western European countries during the 1980s,[3] the present, more extensive study of the situation

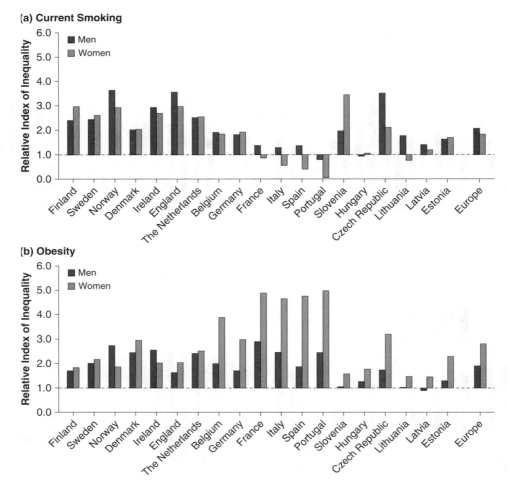

Figure 3 Relative Inequalities in the Prevalence of Current Smoking (Panel A) and Obesity (Panel B) between Persons with the Lowest and Those with the Highest Level of Education, According to Sex.

during the 1990s and early 2000s found much larger among-country variability in the magnitude of inequalities in health. Inequalities in mortality from selected causes suggest that some variations may be attributable to socioeconomic differences in smoking, excessive alcohol consumption, and access to health care. We also found among-country variations in the magnitude of inequalities in self-assessed health, but in a different pattern, precluding a generalization from inequalities in mortality to inequalities in overall health.

Our study had several limitations. International comparability of data on socioeconomic inequalities in health is still imperfect, and the degree of comparability is likely to decline with increasing geographical coverage. There are differences among countries in various aspects of data collection, and some of these might affect the size of inequalities in health, as we have shown previously.[18] We found

smaller inequalities in mortality in some urban, relatively prosperous southern European populations that are not necessarily representative of the whole of Italy or Spain. Some studies have shown, however, that inequalities in health tend to be larger in urban than in rural areas.[19] Our previous study in the 1980s, which used national data for Italy and Spain from methodologically less-refined sources, also showed smaller inequalities in mortality in these countries.[4,5] We found larger inequalities in mortality in the eastern and Baltic regions. All these countries except Slovenia, which has smaller inequalities in mortality, provided data from cross-sectional, noncensus-linked studies. Although this may suggest bias,[20] it is also possible that Slovenia, which is close to Italy, shares some of the favorable characteristics of the southern region.

Internationally comparable data on inequalities in specific determinants of mortality and morbidity are scarce, and we could study only smoking and obesity. The contribution to inequality of other factors, such as alcohol consumption, use of health care, working and housing conditions, and psychosocial stressors, could not be studied directly.

Both smoking and obesity have been shown to contribute to inequalities in health related to socioeconomic status in studies of individual persons in some countries.[21-23] Obesity, however, is unlikely to be a major contributor to international variations in inequalities in health, because inequalities in obesity related to socioeconomic status are large where inequalities in mortality related to socioeconomic status, particularly mortality from cardiovascular disease, are small (i.e., in the southern region). Smoking, on the other hand, does appear to be a major explanatory factor. It has been well documented that countries in the southern region are in an earlier stage of the smoking epidemic than countries in the northern, western, and continental regions.[24,25] We still found reverse inequalities in smoking among women and small inequalities among men, findings that are consistent with the smaller inequalities in mortality in the southern region, particularly from conditions related to smoking. The history of the smoking epidemic is much less well documented for the eastern and Baltic regions,[26,27] and it is therefore difficult to determine why inequalities in mortality from smoking-related conditions are large, whereas inequalities in smoking are often small.

The role of hazardous drinking (daily consumption of large amounts of alcohol-containing beverages, binge drinking, or consumption of surrogate alcohols) in generating high mortality rates in eastern Europe, particularly among men, has been well documented.[28-30] We have not been able to find comparable survey data on inequalities in alcohol consumption related to socioeconomic status in eastern Europe, but our analysis of cause-specific mortality suggests that rates of hazardous drinking are substantially higher in the lower than in the higher socioeconomic groups, particularly among men. Low levels of social support, lack of control over one's life, and material hardship, combined with a culture that approves of excessive alcohol consumption, are likely to be involved.[8,9]

Although the role of deficiencies in health care in the high mortality rates of eastern Europe has been pointed out before,[31,32] our study demonstrates the magnitude of inequalities in mortality related to socioeconomic status from conditions amenable to medical intervention in this part of Europe. Our results suggest that inequalities in access to good-quality health care have a role in generating inequalities in mortality. Inequalities in access to health care leading to inequalities in survival from chronic conditions may also partly explain the discrepancy between our results for mortality and those for self-assessed health. Inequalities in the prevalence of poorer self-assessed health are the result of inequalities in both the incidence and the duration of health problems, which may be shortened by lower survival rates among less-educated persons in eastern Europe.

Smoking, obesity, excessive alcohol consumption, and deficiencies in health care represent only some of the immediate determinants of inequalities in health, and both lifestyle choices and patterns of use of health care are likely to be constrained by inequalities in general living conditions, as structured by political, economic, social, and cultural forces. Within western Europe, there is little evidence that among-country variations in the magnitude of inequalities in health are related to variations in political factors. For example, Italy and Spain have welfare policies that are less generous and less universal than those of northern Europe,[33,34] but they appear to have substantially smaller inequalities in mortality, perhaps partly because of cultural factors, such as the Mediterranean diet and the reluctance of women to take up smoking.[35,36] Cultural factors seem to have prevented differences in access to material and other resources in these populations from translating into inequalities in lifestyle-related risk factors for mortality.

We also found no evidence for systematically smaller inequalities in health in countries in northern Europe. This is surprising, because these countries have long histories of egalitarian policies, reflected by, among other things, welfare policies. These policies provide a high level of social-security protection to all residents of the country, resulting in smaller income inequalities and lower poverty rates.[33,34,37] Our results suggest that although a reasonable level of social security and public services may be a necessary condition for smaller inequalities in health, it is not sufficient. Lifestyle-related risk factors have an important role in premature death in high-income countries[38] and also appear to contribute to the persistence of inequalities in mortality in the northern region.[39]

Our study shows that although inequalities in health associated with socioeconomic status are present everywhere, their magnitude is highly variable, particularly for inequalities in mortality. This result implies that there is opportunity to reduce inequalities in mortality. Developing policies and interventions that effectively target the structural and immediate determinants of inequalities in health is an urgent priority for public health research.[40]

Disclosure

Supported by a grant (2003125) from the Health and Consumer Protection Directorate-General of the European Union as a part of the Eurothine Project.

No potential conflict of interest relevant to this article was reported.

We thank the members of the Eurothine consortium for their comments and suggestions on a previous version of this manuscript.

● ● ● Appendix

In addition to the authors, the following members of the European Union Working Group on Socioeconomic Inequalities in Health participated in this study: Scientific Institute of Public Health, Brussels—H. van Oyen, S. Demarest; Department of Demography and Geography, Faculty of Science, Charles University in Prague, Prague, Czech Republic—J. Rychtarikova; Department of Social Geography and Regional Development, Faculty of Science, Charles University in Prague, Prague, Czech Republic—D. Dzurova; National Institute of Public Health, Copenhagen—O. Andersen; National Institute of Public Health, University of Southern Denmark, Copenhagen—O. Ekholm; School for Health, University of Bath, Bath, England—K. Judge; National Institute for Health Development, Department of Epidemiology and Biostatistics, Tallinn, Estonia—M. Tekkel; Department of Health Promotion and Chronic Disease Prevention, National Public Health Institute, Helsinki—R. Prättälä; Department of Sociology, University of Helsinki, Helsinki—P. Martikainen; Institut National de la Statistique et des Études Économiques, Paris—G. Desplanques; Research and Information Institute for Health Economics, Paris—F. Jusot; Center for Social Policy Research, University of Bremen, Bremen, Germany—U. Helmert; Demographic Research Institute, Hungarian Central Statistical Office, Budapest, Hungary—K. Kovacs; Hungarian National Center of Epidemiology, Budapest, Hungary—F. Marton; Economic and Social Research Institute, Dublin—R. Layte; Department of Public Health, University of Turin, Turin, Italy—G. Costa; Servizio di Epidemiologia, Grugliasco, Italy—F. Vannoni; Faculty of Public Health, Riga Stradins University, Riga, Latvia—A. Villerusa; Kaunas University of Medicine, Kaunas, Lithuania—R. Kalediene, J. Klumbiene; Centraal Bureau voor de Statistiek, Voorburg, the Netherlands—J.J.M. Geurts; Research Program Care, Health and Welfare,

Oslo University College, Oslo—E. Dahl; Division of Epidemiology, Norwegian Institute of Public Health, Oslo—B.H. Strand; Department of Medical Statistics, National Institute of Hygiene, Warsaw, Poland—B. Wojtyniak; Centro de Estudos Geográficos, Universidade de Coimbra, Coimbra, Portugal—P. Santana; Košice Institute for Society and Health, Pavol Josef Safarik University, Košice, Slovakia—A. Madarasova Geckova; Department of Public Health, Faculty of Medicine, Ljubljana, Slovenia—B. Artnik; Agencia de Salut Pública de Barcelona, Barcelona—C. Borrell; Research Unit, Department of Health, Basque Government, Vitoria-Gasteiz, Spain—S. Esnaola; Department of Preventive Medicine and Public Health, Universidad Complutense de Madrid, Madrid—E. Regidor; Department of Public Health Sciences, Karolinska Institute, Stockholm—B. Burström; Center for Health Equity Studies Stockholm, Stockholm University, Stockholm—J. Fritzell, O. Lundberg; Institute of Social and Preventive Medicine, University of Zurich, Zurich, Switzerland—M. Bopp; Office of National Statistics, Newport, United Kingdom—M. Glickman.

About the Author

From the Department of Public Health, Erasmus University Medical Center, Rotterdam, the Netherlands (J.P.M., I.S., A.-J.R.R., M.M.S., G.M., A.E.K.); INSERM Unité 687, Saint-Maurice, France (G.M.); the Stockholm Center on Health of Societies in Transition, Södertorn University College, Södertorn, Sweden (M.L.); and the Department of Epidemiology and Biostatistics, National Institute for Health Development, Tallinn, Estonia (M.L.).

Address reprint requests to Dr. Mackenbach at the Department of Public Health, Erasmus University Medical Center, P.O. Box 2040, 3000 CA Rotterdam, the Netherlands, or at j.macken bach@erasmusmc.nl.

Other investigators who participated in the study are listed in the Appendix.

● ● ● References

1. Marmot M. Social determinants of health inequalities. *Lancet* 2005;365:1099-104.

2. Kunst AE, Bos V, Mackenbach JP. *Guidelines for monitoring health inequalities in the European Union.* Rotterdam: the Netherlands: Department of Public Health, 2001.

3. Mackenbach JP, Kunst AE, Cavelaars AEJM, Groenhof F, Geurts JJ. Socioeconomic inequalities in morbidity and mortality in Western Europe. *Lancet* 1997;349:1655-9.

4. Kunst AE, Groenhof F, Mackenbach JP, Heath EW. Occupational class and cause specific mortality in middle aged men in 11 European countries: compar-

ison of population based studies. *BMJ* 1998;316:
1636-42.

5. Kunst AE, Groenhof F, Mackenbach JP. Mortality
by occupational class among men 30-64 years in 11
European countries. *Soc Sci Med* 1998;46:1459-76.

6. Cavelaars AEJM, Kunst AE, Geurts JJM, et al.
Differences in self-reported morbidity by educational level: a comparison of 11 Western European
countries. *J Epidemiol Community Health* 1998;52:
219-27.

7. Cavelaars AEJM, Kunst AE, Geurts JJM, et al.
Morbidity differences by occupational class among
men in seven European countries: an application of
the Erikson-Goldthorpe social class scheme. *Int J
Epidemiol* 1998;27:222-30.

8. Bobak M, Marmot M. East-West mortality divide
and its potential explanations: proposed research
agenda. *BMJ* 1996;312:421-5.

9. McKee M, Shkolnikov V. Understanding the toll of
premature death among men in eastern Europe.
BMJ 2001;323:1051-5.

10. Leinsalu M, Vågerö D, Kunst AE. Estonia 1989-
2000: enormous increase in mortality differences by
education. *Int J Epidemiol* 2003;32:1081-7.

11. Shkolnikov VM, Andreev EM, Jasilionis D, Leinsalu
M, Antonova OI, McKee M. The changing relation
between education and life expectancy in central
and eastern Europe in the 1990s. *J Epidemiol
Community Health* 2006;60:875-81.

12. Murphy M, Bobak M, Nicholson A, Rose R,
Marmot M. The widening gap in mortality by edu-
cational level in the Russian Federation, 1980-2001.
Am J Public Health 2006;96:1293-9.

13. Charlton JR, Hartley RM, Silver R, Holland WW.
Geographical variation in mortality from conditions
amenable to medical intervention in England and
Wales. *Lancet* 1983;1:691-6.

14. Nolte E, McKee M. Measuring the health of
nations: analysis of mortality amenable to health
care. *BMJ* 2003;327:1129. [Erratum, *BMJ*
2004;328:494.]

15. Kunst AE, Roskam AJ. *Comparison of educational
inequalities in general health in 12 European countries: application of an integral measure of self-
assessed health.* Rotterdam, the Netherlands:
Department of Public Health, 2007. (Accessed May
12, 2008, at http://www.eurothine.org.)

16. Pamuk ER. Social class inequality in mortality from
1921 to 1972 in England and Wales. *Popul Stud*
(Camb) 1985;39:17-31.

17. Mackenbach JP, Kunst AE. Measuring the magnitude
of socio-economic inequalities in health: an overview
of available measures illustrated with two examples
from Europe. *Soc Sci Med* 1997;44:757-71.

18. Kunst AE. *Cross-national comparisons of socioeconomic differences in mortality.* (Ph.D. thesis.
Rotterdam, the Netherlands: Erasmus University,
1997.)

19. Bos V, Kunst AE, Mackenbach JP. Socio-economic
inequalities in mortality in the Netherlands: analyses
on the basis of information at the neighborhood
level. *TSG Tijdschrift voor Gezondheidsweten-
schappen* 2002;80:158-65. (In Dutch.)

20. Shkolnikov VM, Jasilionis D, Andreev EM, Jdanov
DA, Stankuniene V, Ambrozaitiene D. Linked versus
unlinked estimates of mortality and length of life by
education and marital status: evidence from the first
record linkage study in Lithuania. *Soc Sci Med*
2007;64:1392-406.

21. Davey Smith G, Blane D, Bartley M. Explanations
for socio-economic differentials in mortality evidence from Britain and elsewhere. *Eur J Public
Health* 1994;4:131-44.

22. Pekkanen J, Tuomilehto J, Uutela A, Vartiainen E,
Nissinen A. Social class, health behaviour, and mor-
tality among men and women in eastern Finland.
BMJ 1995;311:589-93.

23. van Oort FVA, van Lenthe FJ, Mackenbach JP.
Material, psychosocial, and behavioural factors in
the explanation of educational inequalities in mortality in the Netherlands. *J Epidemiol Community
Health* 2005;59:214-20.

24. Lopez AD, Collishaw NE, Piha T. A descriptive
model of the cigarette epidemic in developed countries. *Tobacco Control* 1994;3:242-7.

25. Huisman M, Kunst AE, Mackenbach JP.
Educational inequalities in smoking among men and
women aged 16 years and older in eleven European
countries. *Tobacco Control* 2005;14:106-13.

26. Kubik AK, Parkin DM, Plesko I, et al. Patterns of
cigarette sales and lung cancer mortality in some
central and eastern European countries, 1960-1989.
Cancer 1995;75:2452-60.

27. Pudule I, Grinberga D, Kadziauskiene K, et al.
Patterns of smoking in the Baltic Republics. *J
Epidemiol Community Health* 1999;53:277-82.

28. Leon DA, Chenet L, Shkolnikov VM, et al. Huge
variation in Russian mortality rate 1984-94: arte-
fact, alcohol, or what? *Lancet* 1997;350:383-8.

29. Britton A, McKee M. The relation between alcohol
and cardiovascular disease in Eastern Europe: explaining the paradox. *J Epidemiol Community
Health* 2000; 54:328-32.

30. Powles JW, Zatonski W, Vander Hoorn S, Ezzati M.
The contribution of leading diseases and risk factors
to excess losses of healthy life in Eastern Europe:
Burden of Disease study. *BMC Public Health*
2005;5:116.

31. Velkova A, Wolleswinkel-van den Bosch JH, Mackenbach JP. The East-West life expectancy gap: differences in mortality from conditions amenable to medical intervention. *Int J Epidemiol* 1997;26:75-84.

32. Nolte E, McKee M. Population health in Europe: how much is attributable to health care? *World Hosp Health Serv* 2004;40:12-4,40,42.

33. Esping-Andersen G. *The three worlds of welfare capitalism*. Oxford: Polity Press, 1999.

34. Ferrera M. The "Southern model" of welfare in social Europe. *J Eur Soc Policy* 1996;6:17-37.

35. Mackenbach JP, Cavelaars AEJM, Kunst AE, Groenhof F. Socioeconomic inequalities in cardiovascular disease mortality: an international study. *Eur Heart J* 2000;21:1141-51.

36. Knoops KTB, de Groot LCPGM, Kromhout D, et al. Mediterranean diet, lifestyle factors, and 10-year mortality in elderly European men and women: the HALE project. *JAMA* 2004;292:1433-9.

37. Fritzell J. Still different? Income distribution in the Nordic countries in a European comparison. In: Kautto M, Fritzell J, Hvinden B, Kvist J, Uusitalo H, eds. *Nordic welfare states in the European context*. London: Routledge, 2001:18-41.

38. Ezzati M, Hoorn SV, Rodgers A, Lopez AD, Mathers CD, Murray CJ. Estimates of global and regional potential health gains from reducing multiple major risk factors. *Lancet* 2003;362:271-80. [Erratum, Lancet 2005;365:28.]

39. Dahl E, Fritzell J, Lahelma E, Martikainen P, Kunst A, Mackenbach J. Welfare state regimes and health inequalities. In: Siegrist J, Marmot M, eds. *Health inequalities in Europe*. Oxford: Oxford University Press, 2006:193-222.

40. Mackenbach JP, Bakker MJ. Tackling socioeconomic inequalities in health: an analysis of recent European experiences. *Lancet* 2003;362:1409-14.

4

Behavioral Determinants of Health

Certain individual behaviors and personal lifestyle choices represent important risk factors for illness and disease. As the rates of communicable and non-communicable diseases continue to rise, public health practitioners have turned attention to the behavioral determinants of health. Many of the diseases sweeping through populations no longer occur by random chance, instead they flourish as a result of the behaviors individuals choose to engage, or not engage, in. Behavioral determinants can be defined as behaviors that can alter the health of an individual, and include such factors as smoking, substance abuse, a high-fat diet, inadequate physical exercise, alcohol consumption, irresponsible use of motor vehicles, unsafe sex, and various other lifestyle choices. Poor health outcomes attributable to behavioral determinants of health include hypertension, diabetes, cancer, and coronary heart disease.[5]

Smoking has been identified as a leading cause of preventable disease and death in the United States because it significantly increases the risk of heart disease, stroke, lung cancer, and chronic lung disease.[6] As another example, studies have shown that diet and foods play a major role in most of the significant health problems of today. Heart disease, diabetes, stroke, and cancer are but some of the diseases with direct links to dietary choices. Throughout the world, incidence and mortality rates for many forms of cancer are rising. Yet research has clearly indicated that a significant portion of cancer is preventable. The role of diet and nutrition in cancer prevention has been one of the most exciting and promising research areas. Researchers now estimate that 40% to 60% of all cancers, and as many as 35% of cancer deaths, are linked to diet.[7] Research also shows that a diet rich in fruits, vegetables, and low-fat dairy foods, and with reduced saturated and total fat can substantially lower blood pressure. Thus a nutritional approach can be effective in both preventing and treating hypertension.[7] As nutrition is fast becoming a major modifiable determinant of chronic disease, public health professionals are working on strategies that reduce nutrition-related risk factors (e.g., high total blood cholesterol, high systolic blood pressure, high body mass index, and inadequate vegetable and fruit intake) and make dietary recommendations that may reduce such diseases as cancer, cardiovascular disease, and diabetes.

The role of exercise and physical activity as a potentially useful, effective, and acceptable method for reducing the risk of colon cancer is also significant.[8] Research findings have also confirmed the association between recreational and/or occupational physical activity and a reduced risk of colon cancer.[9]

The resulting health impact of behavioral determinants of health may not be noticeable for years, making the strength of the relationship between the determinant and the health outcome hard to solidify. In order to address these behavioral determinants, thus changing a community's health outcome, promotion of good behaviors must coincide with the prevention of bad behaviors. This complex strategy is most often administered at the population and community levels through health promotion programs and worksite wellness programs.

Obesity is now often included in research and discussions related to behavioral determinants of health.[5] Obesity has become a forefront issue in public health due to the devastating impact extra weight can have on organ and tissue systems in the body, including diabetes and coronary heart disease. Research for determining the underlying causes of obesity as the culprit of many chronic illnesses has predominantly focused on one weight category, overweight, and the effects of various factors on the likelihood of someone becoming overweight.[5] Exercise, diet choices, tobacco use, and alcohol consumption are all common behavioral determinants correlated with increased weight gain and risk for obesity complications. Yet, these determinants interact with each other, further illustrating the complex nature of behavioral health determinants. For example, the amount of tobacco use interacts with the amount, and intensity, of exercise an individual engages in.[5] Additionally, the diet and alcohol choices an individual makes may decrease the positive impact of exercise on their health.

The health promotion and risk reduction campaign launched with the Healthy People initiative was in response to the growing importance of chronic diseases as leading causes of death and the prevalence of such behavioral risks as tobacco use, alcohol abuse, high-fat diet, and sedentary lifestyles. Specific public health interventions include lifestyle and related behavioral change such as smoking cessation, alcohol consumption reduction, drug abuse control, and use of screening and preventive services. These ongoing interventions have been attributed to delaying the onset of disease, early detection and treatment of disease, and prolonging life for the general public.

Work site health promotion programs are employer-sponsored programs targeting the well-being and health of their workers. These programs encompass primary, secondary and tertiary prevention, including initiatives such as access to exercise facilities, nutrition programs, smoking cessation programs and reduced-cost medication for high cholesterol. Work site health promotion programs provide the means for employers to reduce the amount of sick time employees must take. Health promotion campaigns and programs are social awareness strategies employed to promote the engagement of healthy behaviors as opposed to unhealthy behaviors.

The readings in this chapter cover conceptual, evaluative, as well as interventional aspects of health promotion and behavior. In **Evaluating the Public Health Impact of Health Promotion Interventions: The RE-AIM Framework**, Glasgow and colleagues introduce the RE-AIM model to solve a practical problem and emphasize the reach and representativeness of both settings and participants. Interventions have long since been a primary tool utilized in public health to address population health outcomes. Yet little research has shown the significance of these interventions. While research often utilizes subjects experiencing only the health problem addressed by an intervention, the reality of treating population health means dealing with multiple health problems simultaneously. This problem leads many health intervention models to be effective in a controlled setting yet ineffective when implemented in real-life situations. As described by Glasgow et al., this challenge indicates a need for research and formulation of models that better reflect the complex environments in which public health interventions are implemented. The RE-AIM model summarizes public health interventions as a function of five factors: reach, efficacy, adoption, implementation and maintenance. Failure to address all five factors can lead to adverse outcomes, wasted resources, and ineffectiveness of the intended intervention. Glasgow et al. conclude that the RE-AIM model provides a sufficient representation of the quality of a public health intervention. As the paradigms of healthcare services and delivery shift over time, the resulting evaluation of program intervention must also shift. As Glasgow et al. reiterate, the RE-AIM effectively accounts for the evolving state of healthcare when providing evaluation and should be utilized within public health interventions.

In **A Framework for Assessing the Effectiveness, Efficiency, and Equity of Behavioral Healthcare**, Aday and colleagues note that the terms "behavioral health" and "behavioral healthcare" have increasingly gained prominence in public health programming. With the absence of a general definition the most closely aligned health-related term remains to be mental health, which includes the mental and psychological aspects of health. And, with the absence of a solidified definition for behavioral healthcare, comes the lack of dominant frameworks for policy related to behavioral health. Aday et al. address this gap by introducing a framework, which is a compilation of previous conceptual work conducted by the authors, maintaining the underlying assumptions that the denominator for behavioral healthcare services must encompass the entire population's needs and the delivery system must address both primary prevention and aftercare services. The defined framework both uncovers a new surge of motivation in addressing the mental health of populations while defining the current gaps in behavioral healthcare. The framework encompasses key elements of behavioral health, including the structure, process, intermediate outcomes, and ultimate outcomes of programming, all of which reside under the power of health policy at the federal, state, and local levels. Structure defines the delivery system, population at risk, and environment while process includes both the realized access and health risks of the targeted population. Additionally, intermediate outcomes link the effectiveness of a mental health service to the equity and efficiency in the delivery of the service, culminating in the ultimate outcome of individual and community health. This framework further allows for the recognition of current policy and practice gaps, including the absence of a comprehensive continuum of care for behavioral health and the effect of limited research on the inadequate knowledge base for policy formulation. Aday et al. conclude the article reflecting on the transgression of behavioral health programming from its initial era of cost saving prioritization to the current era emphasizing equity and access to services.

In **The Health and Cost Benefits of Work Site Health-Promotion Programs**, Goetzel and Ozminkowski think that most employers still hesitate to implement work site health promotion programs because of the barriers to implementing such programs. Such barriers include costs of implementing such programs, the intrusion some employers feel they are making on employees' personal choices and resistance by employees' to having employer intervention into their personal lives. Yet, as indicated by Goetzel and Ozminkowski, work sites offer the prime venue for health promotion activities, as they

provide the setting for a group of individuals with diverse backgrounds to gather together on a consistent basis. Goetzel and Ozminkowski further explore effective best practices for implementing health promotion activities by reviewing the prominent research in the field. Relevant findings include conducting needs assessments at work sites to both ensure a high participation rate as well as effective tailoring of messages to bring about behavioral change. Additionally, successful health promotion programs include providing the means for individuals to easily access a variety of engagement modalities and follow-up tools while supporting self-management and self-care throughout the process. Goetzel and Ozminkowski conclude the article with the recognition that, while literature and research pertaining to work site health promotion programs is available, many employers lack the knowledge to successfully implement such programs independently. In order to further the health of employees, employers must look to collaborate with experts in the field of health promotion to work together in implementing such innovative health improvement measures.

In **Healthy Communities Preventing Chronic Disease by Activating Grassroots Change**, the Centers for Disease Control and Prevention (CDC) states that chronic disease has become a primary health concern among public health officials in developed countries. Chronic diseases are defined as non-infectious diseases that individuals may live with for years and can include heart disease, arthritis, cancer, stroke and diabetes. According to the CDC, almost 50% of Americans have at least one chronic illness, and 7 out of 10 of the top causes of death are the result of a chronic disease. More concerning to public health officials than the prevalence of chronic disease is the number of preventable chronic illnesses flourishing due to poor health behaviors, including tobacco use and obesity. Additionally, chronic disease epidemiology is susceptible to the threat of health disparities, with minority populations and those with a lower socioeconomic status experiencing a higher rate of chronic disease complications than their counterparts. The CDC, along with state and local community partners, have initiated the Healthy Communities Program to create thriving, health communities amongst those most severely affected by chronic illnesses. The CDC provides technical assistance and training over a five-year period to communities committed to reducing the health problems of their populations. The program operates by mobilizing communities from within, supporting the utilization of their own resources and strategies to induce change in their surrounding environments. To date, over 240 successful community programs have been funded by the CDC, including work site wellness programs in Austin, Texas, and increased fruit and vegetable intake among school-age children in Broome County, New York. Community partnerships and local leadership cultivation remains a prioritized goal of the CDC in future endeavors.

● ● ● References

1. Aday LA, Begley CE, Lairson DR, Slater CH, Richard AJ, Montoya ID. A Framework for Assessing the Effectiveness, Efficiency, and Equity of Behavioral Healthcare. *The American Journal of Managed Care*. 1999; 5 Spec No:SP25-44.

2. Glasgow RE, Vogt TM, Boles SM. Evaluating the Public Health Impact of Health Promotion Interventions: The RE-AIM Framework. *American Journal of Public Health*. 1999;89:1322-27.

3. Goetzel RZ, Ozminkowski RJ. The Health and Cost Benefits of Work Site Health-Promotion Programs. *Annu. Rev. Public Health*. 2008;29:303-23.

4. Healthy Communities Preventing Chronic Disease by Activating Grassroots Change. National Center for Chronic Disease Prevention and Health Promotion. 2009. Accessible at http://www.cdc.gov/chronicdisease/resources/publications/AAG/pdf/healthy_communities.pdf. Accessed on January 21, 2010.

5. Yen ST, Chen Z, Eastwood DB. Lifestyles, Demographics, Dietary Behavior, and Obesity: A Switching Regression Analysis. *Health Research and Educational Trust*. 2009;44:1345-69.

6. Centers for Disease Control and Prevention. Tobacco use—United States, 1900-1999. *Morbidity and Mortality Weekly Report* 48(43):986-993, 1999.

7. Appel L. A clinical trial of the effects of dietary patterns on blood pressure. *New England Journal of Medicine* 336(16):1117-1124, 1997.

8. Macfarlane GI, Lowenfels AB. Physical activity and colon cancer. *European Journal of Cancer Prevention* 3(5):393-398, 1994.

9. White E. Physical activity in relation to colon cancer in middle-aged men and women. *American Journal of Epidemiology* 144(1):42-50, 1996.

Evaluating the Public Health Impact of Health Promotion Interventions: The RE-AIM Framework

Source: Glasgow RE, Vogt TM, Boles SM. Evaluating the public health impact of health promotion interventions: the RE-AIM framework. *Am J Public Health* 1999;89:1322-7. Reprinted with permission of the American Public Health Association.

Although the field of health promotion has made substantial progress,[1-13] our advances are limited by the evaluation methods used. We have the potential to assess the population-based impact of our programs. However, with few exceptions, evaluations have restricted their focus to 1 or 2 of 5 "dimensions of quality" we believe to be important.

There is a great need for research methods that are designed to evaluate the public health significance of interventions.[14] The efficacy-based research paradigm that dominates our current notions of science is limiting and not always the most appropriate standard to apply.[14,15] A reductionistic scientific paradigm oversimplifies reality[16-18] in the quest to isolate efficacious treatments. Most clinical trials focus on eliminating potential confounding variables and involve homogeneous, highly motivated individuals without any health conditions other than the one being studied. This approach provides important information and strong internal validity; from an external validity perspective, however, it results in samples of nonrepresentative participants and settings.[15,19,20]

Similarly, the emphasis on developing clinically significant outcomes often produces interventions that are intensive, expensive, and demanding of both patients and providers.[21] These interventions tend to be studied in the rarified, "controlled" atmosphere of specialty treatment centers using highly standardized protocols. This "efficacy" paradigm[22] does not address how well a program works in the world of busy, understaffed public health clinics, large health systems, or community settings.[15]

Our medical culture emphasizes pharmacosurgical interventions that produce immediate results and whose dosage can be easily defined and controlled. There is little research on interventions that address whole populations, are long lasting, or become "institutionalized."[23-26] Indeed, many interventions that prove efficacious in randomized trials are much less effective in the general population.[14,15,19,27]

In this commentary we describe the RE-AIM evaluation model, which emphasizes the reach and representativeness of both participants and settings, and discuss the model's implications for public health research. The representativeness of participants[19,28] is an important issue for outcome research.[20,29] The representativeness of settings-clinics, worksites, or communities for public health interventions is equally important. Many evaluations, such as the otherwise well-designed Community Intervention Trial for Smoking Cessation,[30] explicitly restrict selection of participating communities (and research centers) to those most motivated, organized, and prepared for change.[30] This results in expert, highly motivated research teams and settings, which are, by definition, unrepresentative of the settings to which their results are to be applied.

Recognizing some of the foregoing issues, both the National Cancer Institute and the National Heart, Lung, and Blood Institute have proposed sequential "stages" of research.[14,22,31] These steps move from hypothesis generation to testing under controlled conditions, evaluations in "defined populations," and, finally, dissemination research. Interventions found to be efficacious then undergo "effectiveness" evaluations, and programs that prove to be effective—especially cost-effective[22,32]—are selected for dissemination research.

There is often difficulty, however, in making the transition across phases. We think this may be due to a flaw in the basic model, in that many characteristics that make an intervention efficacious (e.g., level of intensity of the intervention and whether it is designed for motivated, homogeneous populations) work against its being effective in more complex, less advantageous settings with less motivated patients and overworked staff.[8,33,34] Low-intensity interventions that are less efficacious but that can be delivered to large numbers of people may have a more pervasive impact.[35-37]

Abrams and colleagues[38] defined the impact of an intervention as the product of a program's reach, or the percentage of population receiving the intervention, and its efficacy ($I = R \times E$). We expand on this "RE" (Reach × Efficacy) concept by adding 3 dimensions that apply to the settings in which research is conducted (Adoption, Implementation, and Maintenance: "AIM") to more completely characterize the public health impact of an intervention.

RE-AIM MODEL

We conceptualize the public health impact of an intervention as a function of 5 factors: reach, efficacy, adoption, implementation, and maintenance. Each of the 5 RE-AIM dimensions is represented on a 0 to 1 (or 0% to 100%) scale.

This framework is compatible with systems-based and social-ecological thinking[16,39,40] as well as community-based and public health interventions.[41,42] A central tenet is that the ultimate impact of an intervention is due to its combined effects on 5 evaluative dimensions. The RE-AIM model expands on earlier work[12,38,43] and is summarized in Table 1.

Reach

Reach is an individual-level measure (e.g., patient or employee) of participation. Reach refers to the percentage and risk characteristics of persons who receive or are affected by a policy or program. It is measured by comparing records of program participants and complete sample or "census" information for a defined population, such as all members in a given clinic, health maintenance organization, or worksite. If accurate records are kept of both the numerator (participants) and the denominator (population), calculation of participation rates is straightforward.

Reach (as well as adoption) also concerns the characteristics of participants. Assessing representativeness is challenging.[20,43,44] It requires demographic information—and preferably psychosocial, medical history, or case mix information—on nonparticipants as well as participants. Detailed infor-

Table 1	RE-AIM Evaluation Dimensions

Dimension[a]	Level
Reach (proportion of the target population that participated in the intervention)	Individual
Efficacy (success rate if implemented as in guidelines; defined as positive outcomes minus negative outcomes)	Individual
Adoption (proportion of settings, practices, and plans that will adopt this intervention)	Organization
Implementation (extent to which the intervention is implemented as intended in the real world)	Organization
Maintenance (extent to which a program is sustained over time)	Individual and organization

[a]The product of the 5 dimensions is the public health impact score (population-based effect).

mation on non-participants is often challenging to collect and raises ethical issues in that non-participants have typically not consented to be studied.[28,45] Cooperative arrangements that permit investigation of the extent to which participants are representative of the larger "denominator" population should be a priority for future research.

Unfortunately, participants in health promotion activities sometimes are those who need them least (e.g., the "worried well,"[46,47] those in the more affluent segments of the population, and nonsmokers).[20] With the increasing gap between the "haves" and "have-nots" in our country,[48] and the dramatic impact of socioeconomic status on health status,[49] understanding the degree to which a program reaches those in need is vital. Because public health interventions are addressed to large numbers of people, even small differences in risk levels between participants and nonparticipants can have a significant impact on cost-effectiveness.[35]

Efficacy

Entire textbooks have been devoted to evaluating the efficacy of interventions.[44,50,51]

We discuss two specific issues: the importance of assessing both positive and negative consequences of programs and the need to include behavioral, quality of life, and participant satisfaction outcomes as well as physiologic endpoints.

Positive and negative outcomes. Most population-based evaluations focus on improvement in some targeted health or risk indicator. Interventions delivered to large populations can also have unanticipated negative effects. Labeling someone with a potential illness may have profound social and psychological consequences.[52,53] Many effective services remain underdelivered, while others are delivered that are not necessary or effective in the groups receiving them. Even services that cost only a few dollars can have substantial negative (as well as positive) societal effects, including misplaced resources and large opportunity costs, when delivered to millions of people. It is critical not only to determine benefits but also to be certain that harm does not outweigh benefits.

Outcomes to be measured. Clinical research emphasizes biologic outcomes—in particular, disease risk factors[44,54]—and concerns about limited resources have led to an increasing emphasis on health care use.[8,55,56] Such outcomes are important, but a public health evaluation should include more than simply biologic and use measures. Two other types of outcomes merit inclusion. First, behavioral outcomes should be assessed for participants (e.g., smoking cessation, eating patterns, physical activity), for staff who deliver an intervention (approaching patients, delivering prompts and counseling, making follow-up calls), and for the payers and purchasers who support the intervention (adopting an intervention, changing policies). Second, participant-centered quality-of-life perspective[8,57] should be included to allow evaluation of patient functioning, mental health, and consumer satisfaction, since these factors provide a critical check on the impact of delivery practices.

Adoption

Adoption refers to the proportion and representativeness of settings (such as worksites, health departments, or communities) that adopt a given policy or program.[58] There are common temporal patterns in the type and percentage of settings that will adopt an innovative change.[43,59] Adoption is usually assessed by direct observation or structured interviews or surveys. Barriers to adoption should also be examined when nonparticipating settings are assessed.

Implementation

The term *effectiveness* is used to describe evaluations conducted in real-world settings by individuals who are not part of a research staff.[22,31] Implementation refers to the extent to which a program is delivered as intended. It can be thought of as interacting with efficacy to determine effectiveness (Efficacy $\times$ Implementation = Effectiveness). There are both individual-level and program-level measures of implementation.

At the individual level, measures of participant follow-through or "adherence" to regimens are necessary for interpreting study outcomes.[60,61] At the setting level, the extent to which staff members deliver the intervention as intended is important. Stevens et al.[62] demonstrated that differential levels of protocol implementation were, in large part, the reason that a brief hospital-based smoking-cessation program was more successful when implemented by research staff than by hospital respiratory therapy staff. Implementation research is crucial in determining which of a set of interventions may be practical enough to be effective in representative settings.

Maintenance

A major challenge at both individual and organization-community levels is long term maintenance of behavior change.[24,63,64] At the individual level, relapse following initial behavior change is ubiquitous.[65,66] Equally essential is the collection of program-level measures of institutionalization,[25] that is, the extent to which a health promotion practice or policy becomes routine and part of the everyday culture and norms of an organization. Recently, there have been advances in identifying factors related to the extent to which a change is institutionalized.[23,25] At the community level, maintenance research is needed to document the extent to which policies are enforced over time (e.g., laws concerning alcohol sales, no-smoking policies). Maintenance measures the extent to which innovations become a relatively stable, enduring part of the behavioral repertoire of an individual (or organization or community).

Combining Dimensions

The public health impact score, represented as a multiplicative combination of the component dimensions (Table 1), is probably the best overall representation of quality. The RE-AIM model is silent on the choice of efficacy measure; any outcome that is quantifiable, reliable, valid, and important to scientific, citizen, and practitioner communities is admissible. Examples include hypertension, mammography screening, and smoking status.

Implicit in the constructs of implementation and maintenance is the length of the period during which data are collected: a minimum of 6 months to 1 year for implementation and 2 years or longer for maintenance. Frequency of assessment should be based on the particular issue, goals, and setting. If RE-AIM dimensions are assessed multiple times, then a RE-AIM profile can be plotted. Repeated measurements and visual displays[67,68] can enhance understanding of intervention effects and be used to compare different interventions (Figure 1). (Additional tables and fig-

ures related to application of the RE-AIM framework are available at www.ori.org/~shawn/public/reaim/reaim.long.pdf.)

DISCUSSION

The last several years have seen a variety of provocative articles on changing paradigms of health care.[8,12,34, 69-73] Unfortunately, there have been few discussions of evaluation models for these new population based paradigms. Even economic analyses and outcomes research[32] do not address several of the core evaluation issues and key dimensions of these evolving approaches. Evaluation methods must match the conceptual issues and interventions being studied. With the shift to a multiple causation and holistic or systems approach to medical science,[12,17,35,73,74] recognition of the complexity and various levels of disease determinants is required.[38,75-77]

While classic randomized controlled trials have significantly advanced our knowledge of pharmacotherapy and medi-cosurgical interventions,[44,78] they have limitations when applied to behavioral issues and, especially, community interventions.[51,79-83] Randomized controlled trials emphasize efficacy to the de facto exclusion of factors such as adoption, reach, and institutionalization.[51,79,80] RE-AIM provides a framework for determining what programs are worth sustained investment and for identifying those that work in real-world environments. RE-AIM can be used to evaluate randomized controlled studies as well as studies with other designs, and it is compatible with evidence-based medicine; RE-AIM asserts, however, that evidence should be broadened to include dimensions in addition to efficacy. The model can also be used to guide qualitative research

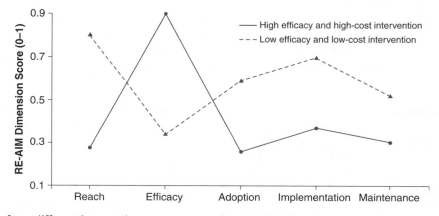

Figure 1 Display of two different intervention programs on various RE-AIM dimensions.

efforts by focusing inquiry on each of these issues. To the extent that REAIM dimensions are incorporated into evaluations, decision makers will have more complete information on which to base adoption or discontinuance of programs.

Data collected via the RE-AIM model can serve several evaluative purposes: (1) assessing an intervention's overall public health impact, (2) comparing the public health impact of an intervention across organizational units or over time, (3) comparing two or more interventions across RE-AIM dimensions (Figure 1), and (4) making decisions about redistributing resources toward more effective programs.

Future Research and Policy Issues

There are several implications of the RE-AIM model. Empirical evaluations involving these implications would greatly help in assessing the utility of the model and informing policy and funding decisions.

1. From the RE-AIM perspective, we expect that programs that are very efficacious (under highly controlled, optimal conditions) may have poor implementation results. Such an inverse relationship between program efficacy and implementation, or between reach and efficacy,[43] has significant implications for the types of interventions that should receive high priority.

2. The RE-AIM model does not explicitly include economic factors.[32] However, cost issues are addressed in three ways. First, we think that cost is often a major factor determining whether a program will be adopted, implemented consistently, or maintained.[84-86] This hypothesis should be tested and substantiated or refuted. Second, cost-effectiveness and cost-benefit are certainly appropriate outcomes. They determine how well resources are being used and whether or not more good could be accomplished through alternative uses (opportunity costs). Finally, a population-based cost-effectiveness index could be calculated by dividing the resulting public health impact by the total societal costs[32] of a program. Dividing each RE-AIM component score by the costs relevant to that dimension could help identify areas of efficiency and waste. There is a need for further work on similar formulas and evaluation of the extent to which providing decision makers with information on REAIM dimensions influences decisions.

3. Systematic reviews that determine the extent to which different research fields have studied—or neglected—each of the RE-AIM dimensions are needed. We hypothesize that adoption and maintenance-institutionalization will be the most understudied dimensions, but this needs to be documented for different research topics.

Limitations of RE-AIM

The precise nature of the relationships among the 5 RE-AIM dimensions, and how they combine to determine overall public health impact, is unknown. We have represented these factors as interacting multiplicatively because we believe that this is closer to reality than an additive model. A highly efficacious program that is adopted by few clinics or that reaches only a small proportion of eligible citizens will have little population-based impact. In future research, it will be necessary to determine the precise mathematical functions that best characterize the interplay of these dimensions.

In this initial model, we have implicitly assumed, in the absence of data to the contrary, that all 5 RE-AIM dimensions are equally important and therefore equally weighted. This may not always be the case. In situations in which one or more of the RE-AIM dimensions are considered most important, differential weights could be assigned. Similarly, it may not be necessary to assess all RE-AIM components in every study.

Finally, the time intervals we have suggested for assessing implementation (6 months-1 year) and maintenance (2+ years) are arbitrary. Future research is needed to determine whether there are necessary or optimal intervals for evaluating these dimensions.

CONCLUSION

Public health interventions should be evaluated more comprehensively than has traditionally been done.[42,55,71] Dimensions such as reach, adoption, and implementation are crucial in evaluating programs intended for wide-scale dissemination. We hope that the RE-AIM framework, or similar models that focus on overall population-based impact, will be used to more fully evaluate public health innovations. Such an evaluation framework helps remind us of the key purposes of public health, organizational change, and community interventions.[71,83,87,88] It is time to re-aim our evaluation efforts.

Contributors

R. E. Glasgow originated the idea for the RE-AIM framework and served as editor. T. M. Vogt drafted sections on implications and coined the acronym RE-AIM. S. M. Boles drafted content on the various uses of the model and contributed the figure and ideas about displays. All authors contributed substantially to the writing of the paper.

ACKNOWLEDGMENTS

Preparation of this manuscript was supported by grants ROI DK51581, ROI DK35524, and ROI HL52538 from the National Institutes of Health.

Appreciation is expressed to Drs Gary Cutter, Mark Dignan, Ed Lichtenstein, and Deborah Toobert for their helpful comments on an earlier version of this article.

About the Author

Russell E. Glasgow is with the AMC Cancer Research Center, Denver, Colo. Thomas M. Vogt is with the Kaiser Permanente Center for Health Research, Honolulu, Hawaii. Shawn M. Boles is with the Oregon Research Institute, Eugene, OR. Requests for reprints should be sent to Russell E. Glasgow, PhD, AMC Cancer Research Center, 1600 Pierce St, Denver, CO 80214 (e-mail: glasgowr@amc.org). This paper was accepted April 17, 1999.

● ● ● References

1. Bandura A. *Social Foundations of Thought and Action: A Social Cognitive Theory.* Englewood Cliffs, NJ: Prentice Hall; 1986.

2. Green LW, Kreuter MW. *Health Promotion Planning: An Education and Environmental Approach.* Mountain View, Calif: Mayfield Publishing Co; 1991.

3. Green LW, Richard L, Potvin L. Ecological foundations of health promotion. *Am J Health Promotion.* 1996;10:270-281.

4. Glanz K, Rimer BK. *Theory at a Glance. A Guide for Health Promotion Practice.* Bethesda, Md: National Cancer Institute; 1995.

5. Glasgow RE, La Chance P, Toobert DJ, et al. Long term effects and costs of brief behavioral dietary intervention for patients with diabetes delivered from the medical office. *Patient Educ Counseling.* 1997;32:175-184.

6. Meenan RT, Stevens VJ, Hornbrook MC, et al. Cost-effectiveness of a hospital-based smoking cessation intervention. *Med Care.* 1998;36: 670-678.

7. Wasson J, Gaudette C, Whaley F, et al. Telephone care as a substitute for routine clinic follow-up. *JAMA.* 1992;267:1788-1793.

8. Kaplan RM. *The Hippocratic Predicament: Affordability, Access, and Accountability in American Health Care.* San Diego, Calif: Academic Press Inc; 1993.

9. *Health Plan Employer Data and Information Set 3.0.* Washington, DC: National Committee for Quality Assurance; 1996.

10. Ferguson T. *Health Online.* Reading, Mass: Addison-Wesley Publishing Co; 1996.

11. Street RL Jr, Rimal RN. *Health promotion and interactive technology: a conceptual foundation.* In: Street RL Jr, Gold WR, Manning T, eds. *Health Promotion and Interactive Technology: Theoretical Applications and Future Directions.* Mahwah, NJ: Lawrence Erlbaum Associates; 1997:1-18.

12. Glasgow RE, Wagner E, Kaplan RM, et al. If diabetes is a public health problem, why not treat it as one? A population-based approach to chronic illness. *Ann Behav Med.* 1999;21:1-13.

13. Shaw KM, Bulpitt CJ, Bloom A. Side effects of therapy in diabetes evaluated by a self-administered questionnaire. *J Chronic Dis.* 1977;30: 39-48.

14. Sorensen G, Emmons KM, Dobson AJ. The implications of the results of community intervention trials. *Annu Rev Public Health.* 1998; 19:379-416.

15. Starfield B. Quality-of-care research: internal elegance and external relevance [commentary]. *JAMA.* 1998;280: 1006-1008.

16. Stokols D. Establishing and maintaining healthy environments: toward a social ecology of health promotion. *Am Psychol.* 1992;47:6-22.

17. Capra F. *The Web of Life: A New Understanding of Living Systems.* New York, NY: Doubleday;1997.

18. Gould SJ. *Full House: The Spread of Excellence From Plato to Darwin.* Pittsburgh, Pa: Three Rivers Press; 1997.

19. Glasgow RE, Eakin EG, Toobert DJ. How generalizable are the results of diabetes self-management research? The impact of participation and attrition. *Diabetes Educ.* 1996;22:573-585.

20. Conrad P. Who comes to worksite wellness programs? A preliminary review. *J Occup Med.* 1987;29:317-320.

21. DCCT Research Group. Lifetime benefits and costs of intensive therapy as practiced in the Diabetes Control and Complications Trial. *JAMA.* 1996;276:1409-1415.

22. Flay BR. Efficacy and effectiveness trials (and other phases of research) in the development of health promotion programs. *Prev Med.* 1986; 15:451-474.

23. Hofstede G. *Cultures and Organization. Software of the Mind.* New York, NY: McGraw-Hill International Book Co; 1997.

24. Goodman RM, Steckler A. The life and death of a health promotion program: an institutionalization perspective. *Int Q Community Health Educ.* 1988;89:5-19.

25. Goodman RM, McLeroy KR, Steckler A, et al. Development of level of institutionalization scales for health promotion programs. *Health Educ Q.* 1993;20:161-178.

26. Clarke GN. Improving the transition from basic efficacy research to effectiveness studies: methodologi-

cal issues and procedures. *J Consult Clin Psychol.* 1995;63:718-725.

27. Paul GL, Lentz RJ. *Psychosocial Treatment of Chronic Mental Patients.* Cambridge, Mass: Harvard University Press; 1977.

28. Dertouzos ML. *What Will Be: How the New World of Information Will Change Our Lives.* New York, NY: HarperEdge Publishers Inc; 1997.

29. Glasgow RE, Fisher E, Anderson BJ, et al. Behavioral science in diabetes: contributions and opportunities. *Diabetes Care.* 1999;22:832-843.

30. COMMIT Research Group. Community Intervention Trial for Smoking Cessation (COMMIT): summary of design and intervention. *J Natl Cancer Inst.* 1991;83:1620-1628.

31. Cullen JW. Design of cancer prevention studies. *Cancer Detect Prev.* 1986;9: 125-138.

32. Gold MR, Siegel JE, Russell LB, et al. *Cost-Effectiveness in Health and Medicine.* New York, NY: Oxford University Press Inc; 1996.

33. Bodenheimer TS, Grumbach KE. *Understanding Health Policy: A Clinical Approach.* Stamford, Conn: Appleton & Lange; 1995.

34. Califano JA Jr. *Radical Surgery: What's Next for America s Health Care.* New York, NY: Random House; 1994.

35. Vogt TM, Hollis JF, Lichtenstein E, et al. The medical care system and prevention: the need for a new paradigm. *HMO Pract.* 1998; 12:6-14.

36. Kristein MM, Arnold CB, Wynder EL. Health economics and preventive care. *Science.* 1977; 195: 457-462.

37. Hatziandrew EJ, Sacks JJ, Brown R, et al. The cost-effectiveness of three programs to increase use of bicycle helmets among children. *Public Health Rep.* 1995;110:251-259.

38. Abrams DB, Orleans CT, Niaura RS, et al. Integrating individual and public health perspectives for treatment of tobacco dependence under managed health care: a combined stepped care and matching model. *Ann Intern Med.* 1996;18:290-304.

39. Green LW, Kreuter MW Behavioral and environmental diagnosis. In: Green LW, Kreuter MW, eds. *Health Promotion and Planning: An Educational and Environmental Approach.* Mountain View, Calif: Mayfield Publishing Co; 1991:125-149.

40. Stokols D. Translating social ecological theory into guidelines for community health promotion. *Am J Health Promotion.* 1996;10:282-298.

41. Bracht N. *Community Organization Strategies for Health Promotion.* Newbury Park, Calif: Sage Publications; 1990.

42. Green LW, Johnson JL. Dissemination and utilization of health promotion and disease prevention knowledge: theory, research and experience. *Can J Public Health.* 1996;87(suppl 2):S11-S17.

43. Glasgow RE, McCaul KD, Fisher KJ. Participation in worksite health promotion: a critique of the literature and recommendations for future practice. *Health Educ Q.* 1993;20:391-408.

44. Meinert CL. *Clinical Trials: Design, Conduct and Analysis.* New York, NY: Oxford University Press Inc; 1986.

45. Rind DM, Kohane IS, Szolovits P, et al. Maintaining the confidentiality of medical records shared over the Internet and the World Wide Web. *Ann Intern Med.* 1997;127:138-141.

46. Vogt TM, LaChance PA, Glass A. Screening interval and stage at diagnosis for cervical and breast cancer. Paper presented at: Annual Meeting of the American Society of Preventive Oncology; March 1998; Bethesda, Md.

47. Emmons KM. Maximizing cancer risk reduction efforts: addressing risk factors simultaneously. *Cancer Causes Control.* 1997;8(suppl 1):S31-S34.

48. Athanasiou T. *Divided Planet: The Ecology of Rich and Poor.* Boston, Mass: Little Brown & Co Inc; 1996.

49. Marmot MG, Bobak M, Smith GD. Explanations for social inequities in health. In: Amick BC, Levine S, Tarlov AR, Walsh DC, eds. *Society and Health.* New York, NY: Oxford University Press Inc; 1995: 172-210.

50. Cook TD, Campbell DT. *Quasi-Experimental Design and Analysis Issues for Field Settings.* Chicago, Ill: Rand McNally; 1979.

51. Bradley C. Designing medical and educational intervention studies. *Diabetes Care.* 1993; 16: 509-518.

52. Bloom JR, Monterossa S. Hypertension labeling and sense of well-being. *Am J Public Health.* 1981;71: 1228-1232.

53. Downs WR, Robertson JF, Harrison LR. Control theory, labeling theory, and the delivery of services for drug abuse to adolescents. *Adolescence.* 1997; 32:1-24.

54. Glasgow RE, Osteen VL. Evaluating diabetes education: are we measuring the most important outcomes? *Diabetes Care.* 1992;15:1423-1432.

55. Nutbeam D. Evaluating health promotion progress, problems and solutions. *Health Promotion Int.* 1998;13:27-44.

56. Vinicor F. Is diabetes a public-health disorder? *Diabetes Care.* 1994;17:22-27.

57. Spilker B. *Quality of Life in Clinical Trials.* New York, NY: Raven Press; 1990.

58. Emont SL, Choi WS, Novotny TE, et al. Clean indoor air legislation, taxation, and smoking behaviour in the United States: an ecological analysis. *Tob Control.* 1992;2:13-17.

59. Rogers EM. *Diffusion of Innovations.* New York, NY: Free Press; 1983.

60. Glasgow RE. Compliance to diabetes regimens: conceptualization, complexity, and determinants. In:

Cramer JA, Spilker B, eds. *Patient Compliance in Medical Practice and Clinical Trials.* New York, NY: Raven Press; 1991:209-221.

61. Mahoney MJ, Thoresen CE. *Self-Control: Power to the Person.* Monterey, Calif: Brooks/Cole; 1974.

62. Stevens VJ, Glasgow RE, Hollis JF, et al. Implementation and effectiveness of a brief smoking cessation intervention for hospital patients. *Med Care.* In press.

63. Marlatt GA, Gordon JR. Determinants of relapse: implications for the maintenance of behavior change. In: Davidson P, Davidson S, eds. *Behavioral Medicine: Changing Health Lifestyles.* New York, NY: Brunner/Mazel;1980:410-452.

64. Steckler A, Goodman RM. How to institutionalize health promotion programs. *Am J Health Promotion.* 1989;3:34 44.

65. Marlatt GA, Gordon JR. *Relapse Prevention: Maintenance Strategies in the Treatment of Addictive Behaviors.* New York, NY: Guilford Press; 1985.

66. Stunkard AJ, Stellar E. *Eating and Its Disorders.* New York, NY: Raven Press; 1984.

67. Cleveland WS. *The Elements of Graphing Data.* Monterey, Calif: Wadsworth Advanced Books and Software; 1985.

68. Tufte ER. *Visual Explanations: Images and Quantities, Evidence and Narrative.* Cheshire, Conn: Graphics Press; 1997.

69. Greenlick MR. Educating physicians for population-based clinical practice. *JAMA.* 1992;267:1645-1648.

70. Von Korff M, Gruman J, Schaefer J, et al. Collaborative management of chronic illness. *Ann Behav Med.* 1997;127:1097-1102.

71. Abrams DB, Emmons K, Niaura RD, et al. Tobacco dependence: an integration of individual and public health perspectives. In: Nathan PE, Langenbucher JW, McCrady BS, Frankenstein W, eds. *The Annual Review of Addictions Treatment and Research.* New York, NY: Pergamon Press; 1991:391-436.

72. Sobel D. Rethinking medicine: improving health outcomes with cost-effective psychosocial interventions. *Psychosom Med.* 1995;57:234-244.

73. McKinlay JB. A tale of 3 tails. *Am J Public Health.* 1999;89:295-298.

74. Stokols D, Pelletier KR, Fielding JE. The ecology of work and health: research and policy directions for the promotion of employee health. *Health Educ Q.* 1996;23:137-158.

75. Glasgow RE, Eakin EG. Issues in diabetes self-management. In: Shumaker SA, Schron EB, Ockene JK, McBee WL, eds. *The Handbook of Health Behavior Change.* New York, NY: Springer Publishing Co; 1998:435-461.

76. Amick BC III, Levine S, Tarlov AR, et al. *Society and Health.* New York, NY: Oxford University Press Inc; 1995.

77. Gochman DS. *Handbook of Health Behavior Research* II. New York, NY: Plenum Press; 1997.

78. Kazdin AE. *Research Design in Clinical Psychology.* Boston, Mass: Allyn & Bacon; 1992.

79. Bradley C. Clinical trials-time for a paradigm shift? *Diabet Med.* 1988;5:107-109.

80. Pincus T. Randomized controlled clinical trials versus consecutive patient questionnaire databases. Paper presented at: Annual Conference of the Society of Behavioral Medicine; March 1998; Rockville, Md.

81. Biglan A. *Changing Cultural Practices: A Contextualist Framework for Intervention Research.* Reno, Nev: Context Press; 1995.

82. Weiss SM. Community health demonstration programs. In: Matarazzo JD, Weiss SM, Herd JA, Miller NE, eds. *Behavioral Health: A Handbook of Health Enhancement and Disease Prevention.* New York, NY: John Wiley & Sons Inc; 1984.

83. Fisher EB Jr. The results of the COMMIT Trial [editorial]. *Am J Public Health.* 1995;85:159-160.

84. Smith TJ, Hillner BE, Desh CE. Efficacy and cost-effectiveness of cancer treatment: rational allocation of resources based on decision analysis. *J Natl Cancer Inst.* 1993; 85:1460-1473.

85. Russel LB. Some of the tough decisions required by a national health plan. *Science.*1989;246:8923-8926.

86. Aaron H, Schwartz WB. Rationing health care: the choice before us. *Science.* 1990;247:418-422.

87. Lichtenstein E, Glasgow RE. Smoking cessation: what have we learned over the past decade? *J Consult Clin Psychol.* 1992;60:518-527.

88. Susser M. The tribulations of trials- intervention in communities [editorial]. *Am J Public Health.* 1995;85:156-158.

A Framework for Assessing the Effectiveness, Efficiency, and Equity of Behavioral Healthcare

Source: Aday LA, Begley CE, Lairson DR, Slater CH, Richard AJ, Montoya ID. A framework for assessing the effectiveness, efficiency, and equity of behavioral healthcare. *Am J Manag Care.* 1999;5 Spec No:SP25-44.

ABSTRACT

Objective: To evaluate the effectiveness, efficiency, and equity of behavioral healthcare and to guide an assessment of the current state of the art of behavioral health-oriented health services research.

Study Design: The framework is grounded in previous conceptual work by the authors in defining a prevention- and outcomes-oriented continuum of healthcare and in identifying and integrating the concepts and methods of health services research and policy analysis for assessing healthcare system performance.

Patients and Methods: The defining assumptions are that (1) the denominator for behavioral healthcare services must encompass a look at the population, not just the patients, who manifest behavioral health risks; and (2) the delivery system to address these needs must extend beyond acute, treatment-oriented services to include both primary prevention and aftercare services for chronic relapsing conditions.

Results: Current policy and practice in behavioral healthcare reveal the absence of a comprehensive, coordinated continuum of care; substantial variation in policy and financial incentives to encourage such development; and poorly defined or articulated outcome goals and objectives. The current state of the art of research in this area reflects considerable imprecision in conceptualizing and measuring the effectiveness, efficiency, and equity criteria. Further, these three criteria have not been examined together in evaluating system performance.

Conclusions: The first era of behavioral healthcare focused on cost savings in managed care alternatives; the second is focusing on quality and outcomes; a third must consider the issues of equity and access to behavioral healthcare, especially for the most seriously ill and vulnerable, in an increasingly managed care–dominated public and private policy environment.

Although the terms "behavioral health" and "behavioral healthcare" sound precise and measurable, there are in fact no generally accepted definitions of these concepts. Their wide use in the managed care market owes more to a rhetorical history that implies precision rather than to any actual precision. Attempts to define these terms sometimes have merely served to underline their ambiguity. For instance, the Joint Commission on Accreditation of Healthcare Organizations (JCAHO) defined behavioral healthcare as "a broad array of mental health, chemical dependency, forensic, mental retardation or developmental disabilities, and cognitive rehabilitation services provided in settings providing services such as acute, long term, and ambulatory care."[1(p1)] Here, the "array" of "disorders" or "disabilities" that might fall under the rubric of behavioral health is broad and apparently open ended. Consequently, it is not clear what sorts of services this definition would exclude.

Because behavioral healthcare appears to be a reimbursement category that will be in use for some time, it is important that practitioners of behavioral healthcare come to an agreement regarding a working definition. Based on a brief review of the history of behavioral healthcare and an overview of health services research on the measurement of effectiveness, efficiency, and equity, this article introduces a framework for defining behavioral healthcare and for guiding research on its performance and impact.

BEHAVIORAL HEALTHCARE

"Behavioral"

The use of the adverb "behavioral" to modify "health" in "behavioral healthcare" has a precedent in the behavioral medicine movement of the 1970s, itself heavily dependent on behaviorism as it was interpreted by American psychologists in the 1950s and 1960s. Behavioral medicine was an attempt to integrate the goals of psychiatry and allied mental health disciplines with those of physical medicine. Interior emotional or cognitive states, and even mental illnesses as traditionally defined, concerned behavioral medicine "only insofar as they contribute to physical disorders as an end point."[2(p7)]

The most important legacy of behavioral medicine for today's behavioral healthcare industry may lie in a subtle but nevertheless real shift of emphasis toward the treatment of behavior with undesirable consequences and away from the treatment of disordered cognition or affect. Behavioral medicine's use of a strict, medically driven criterion for therapy and its insistence on observable behavioral change grow out of its sharp focus on behavioral symptoms. McKegney and Schwartz note that "one of the cardinal principles of behavioral medicine as a field is that well-defined treatment techniques are used for specific target symptoms or signs of illness."[3(p330)] This behavioral symptomatology at the heart of behavioral medicine also represents a movement away from neurobiologic symptomatology. This raises suspicions among some practitioners that the "behavioral" emphasis in behavioral healthcare will result in an emphasis on treating the emotional and personal problems of neurobiologically healthy individuals at the expense of persons with severe, chronic mental disorders.[4]

"Health"

What behavioral healthcare is also depends on what we mean by "health." Caplan and colleagues observed that "the concept of health may have as many nuances as there are diseases, and it may be a derivative from these particular disease concepts."[5(p32)] Traditional negative physical concepts of health may place practitioners of behavioral healthcare in some very awkward positions if physicians, nurses, and payers expect these practitioners to intervene to influence behavior change whenever a patient's behavior poses a potential "health" risk. Skydiving, rock climbing, and even automobile driving are behaviors that significantly increase the chances of physical mortality or morbidity, but does that mean that they are behavioral disorders? Because people can derive considerable joy and fulfillment from activities that pose significant health risks, practitioners of behavioral medicine risk becoming pleasure police, maximizing the maintenance of functioning bodies without regard for the flourishing of persons. More holistic definitions of health have been endorsed by the World Health Organization (WHO). In its 1946 constitution, WHO defined health as "a complete state of physical, mental and social well-being and not merely the absence of illness."[6(p29)] More recently, it defined health as the ability "to identify and to realize aspirations, to satisfy needs, and to change or cope with the environment. Health is therefore a resource for everyday life, not the objective of living. Health is a positive concept emphasizing social and personal resources, as well as physical capacities."[7(p1)]

"Care"

The meaning of the term "care" in the phrase "behavioral healthcare" depends to a large extent on the meaning given to the other words in the phrase. If we adapt the notion of behavioral health to the WHO's conception of health, the scope of behavioral health shifts substantially. Syndromes such as clinical depression, bipolar disorder, schizophrenia, and the like can be consistently treated as direct threats to health, not simply as potential generators of unhealthy behaviors. In the process, however, much of the apparent clarity of purpose and outcome that distinguished behavioral medicine from mental health practice and psychiatry is lost.

Practitioners who provide behavioral healthcare do not face this problem alone. With the aging of the population, the entire healthcare community has shifted its focus away from acute care and toward the prevention, delay, and management of chronic conditions. During the period when the American mental health system was being developed, clinical medicine was primarily occupied with the treatment of infectious diseases. The outcomes of such treatments are more easily measured than the outcomes of therapies for chronic physical illness or behavioral health problems such as depression or substance abuse. If these outcomes are measured at the time of discharge, the result is different from what it would be if they were measured a year later.

Like chronic diseases and conditions, chronic behavioral health conditions are often preceded by biological anomalies, environments, traits, states, and events that statistically or theoretically predispose individuals toward disease.[8] For instance, exposure to shift work,[9] avoidant problem solving, stressful, fateful, or disruptive life events such as marital breakup or job separation,[10-13] and neuroticism[14] all have been shown to predict the occurrence of major depressive disorders. Adult alcoholism has been shown to be preceded and predicted by a variety of factors, including a family history of alcoholism,[15] poor early school performance,[16] and low level of response to alcohol.[17] Behavioral interventions can sometimes reduce the amount of suffering individuals and communities experience as a result of chronic, symptomatic, debilitating mental health or substance abuse conditions. Thus, once a positive definition of health is adopted, the scope of care expands to encompass a continuum extending from prevention to long-term maintenance and harm reduction.

CONCEPT AND CONTINUUM OF BEHAVIORAL HEALTHCARE

Based on the review of the defining elements of behavioral healthcare, we propose the following definition: *Behavioral healthcare represents a continuum of services aimed at promoting physical, mental, and social well-being through thoughtful and respectful intervention in human behavior, behavioral antecedents, and behavioral consequences.*

The array of programs and services that would be encompassed in a comprehensive continuum of behavioral healthcare is displayed in Figure 1. The continuum implies continuity, integration over time,

and integration among components in the context of promoting and protecting the health of individuals and populations through primary prevention to inhibit the onset of mental health and substance abuse problems, secondary prevention to restore a person who is already affected to maximum functioning in the least restrictive environment, and tertiary prevention to minimize the deterioration of mental and physical functioning for those experiencing chronic, relapsing conditions.

The provision of ambulatory and acute institutional care within the conventional clinical care system encompasses the treatment-oriented (secondary prevention) center of the continuum. Community social and economic resources, as well as mental health and substance abuse prevention programs, define the primary prevention-oriented beginning of the continuum. Long-term institutional, home, and community-based care extend the continuum toward enhancing quality of life and maximizing functioning of those with chronic mental illness or addictions. The prevention-oriented and long-term-care poles encompass an array of clinical, as well as nonclinical, programs and services directed toward promoting or protecting the physical, mental, and social health of populations and individuals.[18(p117)]

POLICY ISSUES

The magnitude of unmet need for mental health and substance abuse services is estimated to be high in many communities. Based on the Epidemiological Catchment Area survey, around 30% of individuals with a diagnosable mental disorder go untreated, whereas 56% to 59% receive care in the general medical sector and only 8% to 12% in the specialty mental health sector.[19] The National Household Survey of Drug Abuse estimated even higher rates of unmet need among serious drug users. In 1996 around 63% of those in need of treatment did not receive it.[20] The rates of untreated disorders have been estimated to be even higher for children, the elderly, blacks, and Hispanics. Primary prevention and aftercare services also are poorly developed in many communities.

Much mental health and substance abuse policy in this country is shaped by state and local governments because of their historical role in caring for people with serious mental and behavioral disorders. State mental health authorities have extensive experience with providing services directly for citizens (primarily through state mental hospitals)

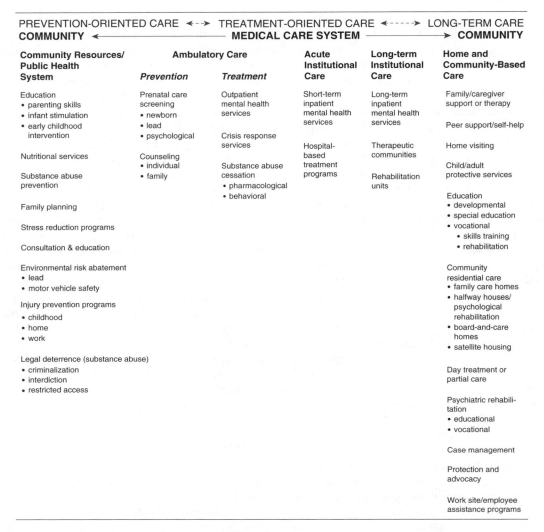

Figure 1 Continuum of Behavioral Healthcare. Adapted from Aday LA. At Risk in America: The Health and Health Care Needs of Vulnerable Populations in the United States. San Francisco, CA: Jossey-Bass; 1993:Figure 5.1 (p 117), Table 5.4 (p 134), and Table 5.5 (p 139).[18] Used with permission.

under conditions of limited budgets and excess demand. In recent years, with deinstitutionalization, states have become engaged in developing community mental health systems that provide an array of home, clinical, and social support services, including case management, for their priority populations. The federal government has played a major role with the passage of the Community Mental Health Centers Construction Act of 1963, providing federal funding to establish community mental health centers so that clients could be served in community settings instead of mental hospitals. In addition, over the past 30 years, federal eligibility, coverage, and payment policies in the Medicare, Medicaid, Social and Security Disability Insurance and Supplemental Security Income, and other welfare programs have had a major impact on behavioral healthcare practice.[21]

Governments at all levels are increasingly purchasing behavioral healthcare services from the private sector, typically from local private community mental health centers, psychiatric hospitals, and social service agencies. In response to rising costs, federal, state, and local governments also are learning to compete in the managed care market both as providers of behavioral healthcare services and as payers through state Medicaid managed care programs. They are implementing managed care practices such as risk-based contracting, utilization management, and protocols for contract development and credentialing that will impact mental health services.[22]

Governments also are involved in extending behavioral healthcare insurance coverage through their role as regulators of insurance plans. Mental health benefit parity requirements, recently addressed by national legislation, have been a major focus of this regulation. A major effort is being made to determine how much and what type of government regulation is needed to ensure quality behavioral healthcare in the managed care environment and the appropriate integration with general healthcare. Governments are working on developing consistent financial reporting, cost-accounting methods, and outcomes reporting as they assume the role of "watchguards of the privatized public safety net."[21(p96)] Other areas of attention include standards for participation, monitoring access and quality, establishing patient rights, fair marketing, supporting professional responsibility and ethical behavior, and restricting perverse financial incentives.[23]

The use of health services research in policy development can be illustrated by the number of studies focusing on the effects of managed care on the mentally ill. Policy makers need to know whether the care provided in managed care plans is equal to or more effective than that in traditional plans (and whether it is more or less costly). An example of a study addressing these questions is a randomized, controlled trial with Medicaid clients in the Medicaid managed care demonstration project in Hennepin County, Minnesota, done by Lurie et al.[24] This study indicated that neither general health status nor psychiatric symptoms were significantly different between the managed care and the fee-for-service groups. The Medical Outcomes Study, a 4-year longitudinal study started in 1986, involved more than 20,000 patients in different practice settings in competing financing systems in three cities. It found that overall for nonpsychiatric patients there were no differences in mental health outcomes. Among patients with major depression or dysthymia who were seen by psychiatrists, however, the outcomes were poorer for those in health maintenance organizations.[25]

This article provides a framework for guiding the conduct of policy-oriented health services research to assess the performance and impact of privately and publicly supported managed care arrangements. The defining assumptions of the perspective offered here are that (1) the denominator for behavioral healthcare services must encompass a look at the population, not just the patients, that manifest behavioral health risks; and (2) the delivery system to address these needs must extend beyond acute, treatment-oriented services to include both primary prevention and aftercare services for chronic relapsing conditions.

FRAMEWORK FOR ASSESSING BEHAVIORAL HEALTHCARE

The framework for assessing behavioral healthcare, provided in Figure 2,[26] acknowledges the importance of including both clinical and nonclinical factors, as well as the associated continuum of behavioral healthcare programs and services (Figure 1), when evaluating the effectiveness, efficiency, and equity of mental healthcare and substance abuse programs and policies. It also recognizes the large role played by physical, social, and economic environments and the associated health risks in influencing health outcomes.

The design and conduct of evaluations of healthcare system performance often are motivated by questions related to the formulation or evaluation of health policy. The access, cost, and quality dilemmas faced by governmental and private policy makers and institutions at the national, state, and local level in providing and paying for mental health and substance abuse services serve as invitations to investigators to contribute to the knowledge and expertise needed to address them.

The concepts and methods of behavioral healthcare research provide guidance by describing, analyzing, and evaluating the structure, process, and outcomes of the healthcare system. *Structure* refers to the availability, organization, and financing of behavioral healthcare programs; the characteristics of the populations to be served by them; and the physical, social, and economic environment to which they are exposed. Process encompasses the transactions between patients and providers in the course of actual care delivery, as well as the environmental and behavioral transactions exacerbating behavioral health risks.

The delivery of healthcare services is ultimately concerned with enhancing the health of individuals and communities. Improving the health of individuals and communities is, however, best viewed as a dynamic and ongoing process. Effectiveness, efficiency, and equity research provide evaluative indicators of this process.

Clinical effectiveness, production efficiency, and procedural equity focus on behavioral healthcare services. Clinical effectiveness addresses the impact of care on improvements for individual patients; production efficiency is concerned with the combination of inputs required to produce these and related

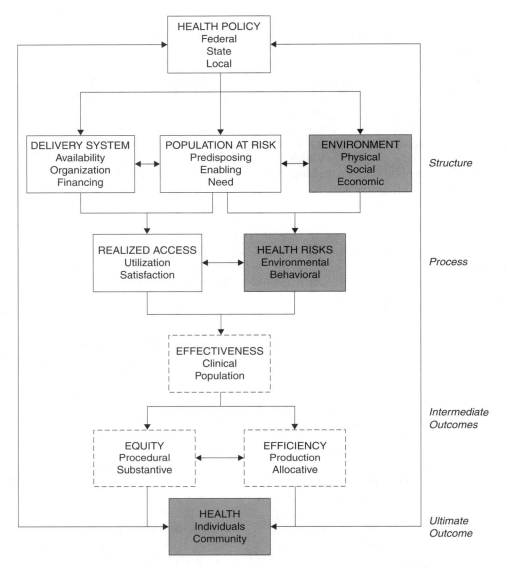

Figure 2 Framework for Assessing Behavioral Healthcare. Adapted from Aday LA, Begley CE, Lairson DR, et al. Evaluating the Healthcare System: Effectiveness, Efficiency, and Equity. 2nd ed. Chicago, IL: Health Administration Press; 1998:Figure 1.4.[26(p10)] Used with permission.

services at the lowest costs; and procedural equity assesses the fairness of care delivery.

Population effectiveness, allocative efficiency, and substantive equity focus on the ultimate outcome of interest: community-wide behavioral health improvements. Population effectiveness addresses the role of clinical and nonclinical factors in influencing the health of populations as a whole; allocative efficiency analysis attempts to address what combination of inputs produce the greatest health improvements given the available resources; and substantive equity is judged ultimately by the extent to which those health benefits are shared equally across groups in the community.

Effectiveness—or the production of behavioral health benefits—is arrayed before efficiency and equity in the framework to indicate the central role it plays in assessing the cost effectiveness of producing behavioral health benefits (efficiency), as well as the distribution of these benefits and costs across groups (equity). Effectiveness, efficiency, and equity research can assist policy makers in deciding, given constrained resources, how most fairly *and* effectively to distribute these benefits.

Behavioral healthcare research provides basic descriptive data on the organization and operation of the behavioral healthcare system (number and distribution of providers, percentage of the population uninsured, rates of service utilization).[27-29] It also analyzes likely relationships between and among components (reflected in the arrows in Figure 2), examining the impact of a health policy on the delivery system and the individuals and populations affected by this initiative; on the effectiveness, efficiency, and equity of the delivery system; and ultimately—and most importantly—on the health of the population the policy was intended to serve.[23]

The structure, process, and outcomes of behavioral healthcare can be studied at the macro or micro level of analysis. The macro level refers to a population perspective on the determinants of the behavioral health of communities as a whole, and the micro level represents a clinical perspective on the factors that contribute to the health of individuals at the system, institution, or patient level. The community encompasses the population in a defined area and the physical, social, and economic environment in which they reside. This perspective acknowledges the intimate linkage between mental health and substance abuse and related sociomedical health risks (e.g., homicide, suicide, family abuse, homelessness). The system level refers to the healthcare system, including the resources (money, people, physical infrastructure, and technology) and the organizational configurations used to transform these resources into healthcare services.[30(p2)] The institution level references a specific organizational entity such as a mental hospital, substance abuse clinic, or health maintenance organization. The patient level refers to the microcosm of clinical decision making and treatment.

Information from each of these levels is required to understand and interpret fully the effects of behavioral healthcare policies and programs. Commitments to developing high-cost technologies or procedures to optimize individual patient outcomes may fail to consider whether, in the light of limited resources, these are the best investments to enhance the health and well-being of the population as a whole. Treatments that have been demonstrated to be efficacious at the individual patient level may not be applied similarly across institutions, or even within the same institution. System-level outcomes may be influenced by organizational and financial incentives that influence the patterns of healthcare provision. The expanded role of managed care in behavioral healthcare provision calls, in particular, for research on the impact of alternative forms of managed care on the access, quality, and cost of behavioral healthcare services. Community-level outcome studies allow exploration of the variations in health outcomes that may be due to differential exposures

to health risks and access to healthcare or to different styles of practice not detectable by outcomes research at the institutional or system level alone.

CONCEPTS AND CRITERIA FOR ASSESSING PERFORMANCE: EFFECTIVENESS, EFFICIENCY, AND EQUITY

Effectiveness

Effectiveness research—more popularly known as outcomes research—attempts to link structure, process, or both to the outcomes of healthcare at the community, system, institution, or patient level.[31] Effectiveness research reflects two seemingly competing, but complementary, definitions of effectiveness. One definition represents a population perspective, or macro-level view, which considers the role of the physical, social, and economic environments on the health of the population. It includes in its purview both patients who have received care and individuals in the population as a whole who have not.[26] The second is a clinical perspective, or micro-level view, focused on the interactions of patients and providers in the clinical care system and institutions and the resulting improvement or health benefits achieved by patients. Research conducted from this point of view examines the impact of the structures and processes associated with delivering care on the achievement of improvements in the health of patients.

Dimensions of Effectiveness. Structure, process, and outcome are linked conceptually in a research paradigm. This paradigm assumes that structural elements of healthcare influence what is and is not done in the process, in addition to how well it is done. This process in turn influences the outcome (health) that people experience as a result of their encounters with the process.

Efficacy and effectiveness are key concerns in assessing the performance of behavioral healthcare.[32-36] Efficacy is concerned with the benefits achievable from a therapy or an intervention under ideal conditions, such as are found in randomized clinical trials.[32] The efficacy of psychotherapeutic interventions has been confirmed in a comprehensive meta-analysis of studies.[37] According to Lyons et al, the effectiveness of mental health services is now of concern: specifically, the questions of "what services work for whom, under what conditions, when should they be offered, and by which providers?"[38(p1)]

Framework for Effectiveness Research. To empirically address these questions, Table 1 shows a

| Table 1 | Framework for Effectiveness Research* |

	Level of Analysis			
		Clinical Perspective		
Dimension	Population Perspective Community	System	Institution	Patient
Outcome measures	Population relapse rates Population functioning rates Mental health status Population reduction rates Mental health incidence and prevalence rates Perceived mental health	Relapse rates Functioning rates Mental health status Reduction rates Diagnosis rates Averaged self-report	Relapse rates Functioning rates Mental health status Reduction rates Diagnosis rates Averaged self-report	Relapse/recidivism Functioning Mental health status Symptom reduction Diagnosis Self-reported mental health
Risk adjustment	Demographic characteristics	Demographic characteristics Comorbidity rates Risk adjustment sytems	Demographic characteristics Comorbidity rates Risk adjustment systems	Patient profiles Comorbidity Diagnoses
Study design	Observational- epidemiological	Observational- interorganizational	Observational- intraorganizational	Observational Case reports/series Experimental— randomized clinical trials Synthetic Meta-analysis Decision analysis
Data source	Records Population health information system Surveillance Surveys	Records Medical records Discharge data Claims data Surveys	Records Medical records Discharge data Claims data Surveys	Records Medical records Discharge data Claims data Surveys

*The following are typical effectiveness research questions by level of analysis:
Community: What is the contribution of behavioral healthcare to the mental health of the population?
System: What is the impact of system-level variables (e.g., provider specialty mix, organizational form, payment mechanism) on the processes and outcomes of behavioral healthcare?
Institution: What is the impact of the quality of care on the outcomes of behavioral healthcare?
Patient: What patient treatment options result in the best mental health outcomes for patients with a specific condition?

Adapted from Aday LA, Begley CE, Lairson DR, et al. Evaluating the Healthcare System: Effectiveness, Efficiency, and Equity. 2nd ed. Chicago, IL: Health Administration Press; 1998:Table 2.2.[26(p53)] Used with permission.

framework for effectiveness research that attempts to integrate the two perspectives (i.e., population and clinical) and the four levels (i.e., community, system, institution, and patient). The population perspective focuses on addressing these questions in the context of a community-level analysis, whereas the clinical perspective could seek to address them at the system, institution, or patient level of analysis. Outcome measures, risk adjustment procedures, study designs, and data sources represent the defining dimensions of this framework.

The outcome measures, risk adjustment procedures, study designs, and data sources that might be drawn upon at each level, as well as examples that il-

lustrate the application of these methods at each of the levels, are highlighted in Table 1 and in the discussion that follows. Specific illustrations of tools and methods applicable to behavioral healthcare also are provided.

OUTCOME MEASURES

Outcome measures in behavioral healthcare include indicators such as improved functioning, reduction in symptoms, employment, and school behavior as well as performance on various rating scales and self-report questionnaires. Mental health performance measures have been identified and examined for their feasibility in a 5-state study.[39] An annotated bibliography of these rating scales and questionnaires is provided by Lyons et al.[38] Specific indicators of each of these broad outcome measures may be used at the different levels. Community-level outcome measures include overall population rates. For examining outcomes across institution and system levels, outcomes are aggregated from patient data within each of these levels.

RISK ADJUSTMENT

Ultimately the value of all effectiveness research depends on the ability to validly adjust for differences in risks associated with final outcomes. Risk adjustment of patient outcomes is undertaken and necessary in effectiveness research to account for the differing risks patients bring to the clinical setting. Clearly, patients who differ in their risks at entry to care or admission to a hospital—and who receive similarly effective treatments—will experience different outcomes. When randomized clinical trials are possible, these differences can be minimized by the random allocation of subjects to experimental and control groups. However, under nonexperimental conditions (the conditions under which most effectiveness research is conducted), these differences and their potential confounding should be adjusted for in the analysis. Differing risks in behavioral healthcare that require adjustments include differences in patient demographic characteristics (e.g., age, gender, race); functioning; motivation; personality; severity of illness; social, marital, or family support; and symptom severity.[38]

At the patient level, two general approaches may be taken to this risk adjustment. A subjective approach, relying on the informed judgments of experienced clinicians in rating the severity of the patient's illness at entry, may provide a valid assessment of a patient's status. This type of assessment, however, rarely is feasible because of the considerable therapist time required to provide a sufficiently sensitive and specific diagnosis.[40] In its place, an objective approach, based on clearly identified data related to the patient's risk, clinical state, and probable outcome, is used in an algorithm or formula to generate a score characterizing the patient's risk. These data may include characteristics of patients, their comorbid conditions, and their diagnoses, which at the institution and system levels may be incorporated into risk adjustment systems such as the Computerized Psychiatric Severity Index developed by Horn et al.[41] Also at the institution and system levels, where some of the detailed patient data may be lacking (as in discharge and claims data), demographic characteristics or comorbidity rates may be used as proxies for actual severity measures. At the community level, demographic characteristics (e.g., age, gender) are used to adjust for differing risk of illness.

STUDY DESIGNS

Study designs for effectiveness research cover a range of possibilities. The design principles are the same as those for any study: namely, maximize experimental variance, control extraneous variance, and minimize error variance. Applying these principles results, on the one hand, in outcomes research designs that follow true experimental design principles of random allocation, control groups, blinding, and homogeneity and that lead to efficacy studies. On the other hand are nonexperimental observational designs, in which investigators do not directly intervene but instead develop methods for describing events that occur naturally and their effect on study subjects. An alternative is what has been called synthetic design[42]: meta-analysis and decision analysis. Meta-analysis involves statistically combining the results of several randomized clinical trials to estimate the results of therapy. A decision analysis requires information on the actual treatment of patients with a disease, the outcomes, and the value of those outcomes to patients.

A comprehensive meta-analysis of psychotherapeutic interventions has been done by Lipsey and Wilson.[37] They reviewed more than 300 prior meta-analyses and concluded that the efficacy of these interventions has been well established. Given this conclusion, the effectiveness of these services and particularly their effectiveness under managed care arrangements still need investigation. The few studies related to their effectiveness under managed care are inconclusive, and the tools for a comprehensive assessment need further development. Agreed-on outcome measures and risk adjustment procedures are sorely needed and are under development. Data sources, particularly of the performance-monitoring type reflected in the Health Employer Data and Information Set (HEDIS) system, need development and implementation to make good effectiveness research possible.

DATA SOURCES

When clinical trials and true experiments are not possible, effectiveness research relies on a variety of data sources for cross-sectional type studies (as shown in Table 1). Surveys of institutions, providers, and patients as well as records of clinical care, discharges, and claims provide information for effectiveness research at the patient, institution, and system levels, depending on the level of aggregation of the data. At the community level, the following types of sources provide the data for effectiveness studies: state and county governments charged with the responsibility for administering mental health services, police records reflecting arrests related to mental health or drug abuse problems, the Drug Abuse Warning Network medical examiner and emergency room databases,[43] and prevalence surveys such as the National Comorbidity Survey[44] and the National Household Survey on Drug Abuse.[45]

EXAMPLES

Studies of the effectiveness of behavioral healthcare under managed care are limited and at this point inconclusive, which in itself argues the need for further research in this arena. A good overview of these studies is provided by Christianson and Osher,[46] who document studies done in four settings: the Northwest region (Kaiser Permanente); the RAND Medical Outcomes Study (Boston, MA: Chicago, IL; Los Angeles, CA); Hennepin County, Minnesota (the Medicaid demonstration); and Monroe and Livingston counties in New York. These studies taken together fail to provide a conclusive or coherent picture of the impact of managed care on patients with mental health problems,[46] a conclusion confirmed by Wells and Sturm.[25]

One other example study, not focused on managed care and specific to drug abuse treatment only, is the National Drug Abuse Treatment Outcome Study. This study, funded by the National Institute on Drug Abuse, "is a multisite prospective study of drug treatment effectiveness based on a sample of 120,010 treatment admissions from approximately 100 treatment programs in 11 cities."[47(p497)] This is an example of outcomes research at the patient level.

CRITERIA

The effectiveness framework also can be used to develop a set of criteria for assessing the adequacy of behavioral healthcare services. The conceptualization of the Community Healthcare Management System by Shortell and colleagues provides the theoretical basis for these criteria.[48] Such a system, they suggest, begins with the assessment of needs on a population level and proceeds to the development of (1) resources and services across the continuum of care to meet those needs, (2) guidelines and protocols to guide the care, and (3) a potential monitoring system to ensure that the needs are met. This conceptualization implies a set of criteria related to improving the effectiveness of behavioral healthcare; namely, behavioral healthcare options should be based on population mental health information, should address the continuum of behavioral healthcare services, should specify guidelines for clinical performance, and should seek to improve the performance of behavioral healthcare through monitoring of process and outcomes indicators. The first two criteria reflect the population perspective; the latter two, the clinical perspective. The impact of the behavioral health continuum has been investigated for children and adolescents in a military setting through the Civilian Health and Medical Program of the Uniformed Services (CHAMPUS) program.[49] In a quasi-experimental evaluation design, comparing Fort Bragg as the demonstration site with two other military bases, this study showed that with a continuum-of-care philosophy, children in this setting were less likely to leave treatment inappropriately; thus, time in treatment was extended.

Guideline development in the field of mental health has been as active as in medical fields. The Clinical Practice Guidelines for Depression in Primary Care developed by the Agency for Health Care Policy and Research,[50] the Practice Guideline for Major Depressive Disorder in Adults developed by the American Psychiatric Association,[51] and the Treatment Improvement Protocols developed by the Center for Substance Abuse Treatment[52] are prominent examples of these guidelines.

There are also significant efforts to develop monitoring systems for mental healthcare. One is the Performance Measures for Managed Behavioral Healthcare Programs developed by the American Managed Behavioral Health Care Association in a desire to supplement the HEDIS set. It consists of 16 measures covering the domains of access, consumer satisfaction, and quality of care. The effectiveness measures included are ambulatory follow-up after hospitalization for major depressive disorder and treatment failure for substance abuse.[53] Another monitoring approach is in the form of a report card. This activity represents a collaboration among consumers, the Mental Health Statistics Improvement Program, and the Center for Mental Health Services of the Substance and Mental Health Services Administration.[54,55]

In summary, the efficacy of behavioral healthcare services has been established.[37] It is the effectiveness of these services and particularly their effectiveness under managed care arrangements that need investigation now. The few studies related to their effectiveness under managed care are inconclusive, and the tools for a comprehensive assessment need further development. Agreed-on outcome measures and risk adjustment procedures are sorely needed and are under development. Data sources, particularly of the performance-monitoring type reflected in the HEDIS system, need development and implementation to make good effectiveness research possible. Given the current need, the will, the concepts developed here, and the previous work with physical health effectiveness research, it should be possible to chart a course for assessing the effectiveness of behavioral healthcare in general and under managed care specifically.

Efficiency

For society as a whole, efficiency requires that the combination of goods and services with the highest attainable total value be produced, given limited resources and technology.[56] This requires attainment of both allocative and production efficiency. Allocative efficiency depends on attainment of the "right" (most valued) mix of outputs.[57] Production efficiency refers to producing a given level of output at minimum cost. As implied in the conceptual framework (Figure 2), improving the health of communities and individuals is the desired and valued endpoint (or output) of societal investments in behavioral health programs and policies. There is a need for a better understanding of these problems and how the healthcare system operates, as well as for policies that will improve the access, cost, and quality of behavioral healthcare. The tools of efficiency analysis can assist in formulating and assessing these policies.

Allocative Efficiency. Where behavioral healthcare is viewed as an input in the production of health improvements, the focus is on allocative efficiency (maximizing health with constrained resources). Allocative-efficiency problems arise in healthcare delivery, for example, when substantial resources are allocated to treatments of questionable effectiveness while proven preventive services are neglected. Primary health policy areas that reflect concerns with allocative efficiency in relationship to behavioral health improvements are (1) behavioral medicine versus nonmedical policy alternatives, (2) coverage of preventive services, and (3) mix or types of treatment.

BEHAVIORAL MEDICINE VERSUS NONMEDICAL ALTERNATIVES

In a broader context of health-oriented social policy, a society may achieve much greater health benefits by diverting resources from healthcare to investment in social capital (e.g., education, job training, safe communities, community development).[58,59] For example, a British study links increased job insecurity to worse health measures and health risks. From a position of no advantage at baseline, self-reported morbidity and physiologic risk factors tended to

increase among respondents from the threatened department compared with those from other departments.[60] Grossman[61] has proposed that schooling improves the efficiency by which one produces one's own health; that is, better-educated people have more know-how regarding what is needed to stay healthy and know better how to use medical and other inputs, as well as their time, to produce better health.[62-64] These findings present interesting challenges to state policy makers in particular, who face significant trade-offs in deciding the relative allocation of state tax dollars to Medicaid versus public education and the effects of fiscal policy on employment.

PREVENTIVE SERVICES

Within the behavioral healthcare sector, there is concern that too much is spent on the treatment of persons with existing illness for whom health improvements are limited and too little is spent on preventive services. To date, however, behavioral healthcare lacks a workable paradigm for developing, implementing, and evaluating such services. School-based substance abuse prevention is the most heavily supported and researched preventive behavioral healthcare strategy in the United States. Studies indicate that participation in these programs does not delay drug use significantly once the former participants enter adolescence.[65,66] Although researchers are improving their ability to predict the onset of mental disorders, including schizophrenia,[67] and research has indicated that interventions conducted in preadolescence can affect the severity of anxiety symptoms,[68] little has been written regarding the implications of these advances for the prevention of mental illness. To date, the United States lacks any effort to match Italy's Sonda Project,[69] an ambitious preventive undertaking designed to lower the risk of the development of debilitating mental illness in children.

As in medical care, it is difficult to document the effectiveness and cost effectiveness of behavioral healthcare preventive programs.[70,71] Mechanic[23] described the potential, but unproven, advantage of managed care organizations to improve the allocation of resources and production efficiency by taking a population view of behavioral health problems, that is, by assessing the behavioral health needs in the population and having the flexibility to organize the most efficient preventive and therapeutic services to address those needs. In contrast, studies have documented poor performance of health maintenance organizations in covering and providing a broad range of behavioral healthcare services, especially services targeted to the most severely impaired patients.[72] Although research has documented no overall variation in mental health outcomes in general by practice setting or payment plan, there is evidence that psychiatrically treated managed care patients with the most severe mental illnesses fare less well under managed care than under more traditional practices.[25,73,74]

Economic controls imposed at the governmental level constitute another level of intervention in terms of primary prevention. For example, increasing the cost of substances such as drugs, alcohol, and cigarettes can reduce the incidence and quantity of use by youths.[75-77] In fact, a series of studies published over the past decade indicating that price significantly affects the consumption of so-called "addictive" substances poses one of the most interesting challenges to conventional notions of addiction-and one of the most promising avenues for prevention.[78-86]

MIX OR TYPES OF TREATMENT

There is a corresponding concern regarding the appropriate and efficient mix or types of services delivered in treating patients. This is reflected, for example, in the overuse of institutionalization for alcohol problems.[87,88] When appropriately supported, less intensive outpatient care may be just as effective and less costly.[89] However, under managed care arrangements, there are questions about whether the reduction in inpatient care is truly more efficient, given the lack of studies on patient outcomes over the long term.[23] This may simply represent a reduction in services and shifting of costs without appropriate augmentation of community services such as outpatient and home treatment to achieve the same or improved outcomes for patients.

Production Efficiency. Health is viewed as the final output and behavioral health services as an intermediate output of the healthcare system. Production efficiency (producing output at the least cost) is of concern for both intermediate and final outputs. Production efficiency addresses whether resources are organized and managed in a manner that minimizes the cost of production (for a given level of quality), as well as whether personnel, supplies, and equipment are paid for at rates that represent their cost in their next-best alternative use. Inefficiency occurs when physicians provide services that could be provided just as well by nurses or other less expensive health personnel and when practice does not take advantage of economies of scale, as in the production of laboratory services.

The key methods for assessing allocative and production efficiency involve both micro- and macrolevel analysis. These methods are described below.

Key Methods of Assessing Efficiency Economic analysis typically is divided into micro and macro levels. The micro level encompasses the three health services research levels defined earlier as part of the clinical perspective on effectiveness: patient, institution, and system. Macroeconomics focuses on the population as a whole. This parallels the population perspective on health outcomes at the community level (as shown in Table 1).

MICRO LEVEL

The principal methods used in micro-level analyses of efficiency include (1) estimating production functions and (2) cost-effectiveness, cost-benefit, and related cost-utility analyses.

Production Functions. Economists have developed a comprehensive theoretical model of production efficiency, expressing how the total, average, and marginal costs of a given product or commodity change under a given set of assumptions regarding the relationship between inputs and outputs (the production function), the cost of inputs, and technology. For example, inputs for behavioral healthcare may include physician and therapist time and prescription drugs, and outputs may be defined in terms of services rendered or their effect on the mental health of patients. Input costs include therapist and physician earnings, rents, and the cost of drugs. Technology is defined broadly as the information and techniques for transforming inputs into outputs. The cost functions represent the minimum total and unit costs attainable for alternative combinations of inputs and the size of the production units (e.g., the number of beds in an inpatient facility).

Cost-Effectiveness Analysis, Cost-Benefit Analysis, and Cost-Utility Analysis. Other efficiency analysis methods frequently applied in healthcare are cost-effectiveness analysis, cost-benefit analysis, and cost-utility analysis.[90] (See Table 2 for a comparison of these methods.) These methods have not been extensively applied in the field of behavioral healthcare, except to the extent they are used to evaluate new drug therapies. Difficulty in measuring outcome is a major impediment to these studies in this field.[23]

Cost-effectiveness analysis is a systematic analysis of the effects and costs of alternative methods or programs for achieving the same objective (e.g., saving lives, preventing disease, providing services). Cost-effectiveness analysis is used when the concern is with determining production efficiency, and effects are measured in nonmonetary units.[91] Cost-benefit analysis is a systematic analysis of one or more meth-

Table 2	Comparisons of Cost-Effectiveness, Cost-Benefit, and Cost-Utility Analyses		
Type of Study	Measurement/ Valuation of Costs in Both Alternatives	Identification of Consequences	Measurement/ Valuation of Consequences
Cost-effectiveness analysis	Dollars	Single effect of interest, common to both alternatives, but achieved to different degrees (e.g., the ratio of incremental costs to incremental effectiveness [life-years saved] with usual care vs an enhanced program to screen and treat patients with substance abuse problems in primary care settings)	Natural units (e.g., life-years gained, disability)
Cost-benefit analysis	Dollars	Single or multiple effects not necessarily common to both alternatives, and common effects may be achieved to different degrees by the alternatives (e.g., dollars saved from investment in substance abuse prevention compared with treatment programs)	Dollars
Cost-utility analysis	Dollars	Single or multiple effects, not necessarily common to both alternatives, and common effects may be achieved to different degrees by the alternatives (e.g., the ratio of incremental costs to incremental effectiveness [quality-adjusted life-years] added from investment in substance abuse prevention compared with treatment programs)	Healthy days or (more often) quality-adjusted life-years

Adapted from Drummond MF, O'Brien B, Stoddart GL, et al. Methods for the Economic Evaluation of Health Care Programmes. Oxford, UK: Oxford University Press; 1997: Table 1.1.[90(p2)] Used with permission.

ods or programs for achieving a given objective and measures both benefits and costs in monetary units. In cost-utility analysis, effects are weighted by utility measures denoting the patient's or member of the general public's preference for or desirability of a particular outcome.[92]

Cost-benefit analysis can determine whether a program is worth doing in the sense that its benefits are greater than its costs (allocative efficiency), whereas cost-effectiveness analysis compares the costs of alternatives for achieving a common objective (production efficiency) without determining whether the objective itself is worth achieving. For example, what are the costs and associated savings of screening and treatment for alcohol problems in primary care settings? A broader view might compare this program with other medical alternatives (e.g., a self-management program for chronic disease) or public health alternatives (e.g., population-based health risk reduction programs).

Determination of net economic benefits in monetary terms, especially in programs for the elderly and poor, is difficult and controversial. Regardless, society generally supports such investments if they yield net health benefits. All programs with net health benefits cannot be funded and therefore should be compared in terms of cost per life-year gained or cost per quality-adjusted life-year gained. Instead of monetary values, life-years are valued (quality adjusted) according to utility values or how people feel about time spent in alternative health states ranging from states they think would be worse than death to being completely healthy.[25,27] For example, while being completely healthy may be assigned a utility value of 1, the condition of severe depression may be assigned a value of 0.6. If an otherwise-healthy person could avert depression for 1 year, the gain would be 0.4 quality-adjusted life-years. This information provides a guide to resource allocation among programs to achieve the greatest health improvement with the available funds.[93,94]

There is a paucity of cost-effectiveness studies in the field of behavioral healthcare primarily because the precise nature of the interventions and outcomes to be measured is difficult to specify. The economic evaluation of pharmaceutical remedies for mental and related behavioral disorders is probably the area in which the most work has been done in this regard.[95-97]

LEVEL

The principal macro-level approaches to efficiency analysis are based on international comparisons of the performances of healthcare systems in different countries.[98] Although there are major problems with comparisons at the system level (e.g., measurement of health outcomes, cultural and demographic differences, data comparability), such comparisons do serve to raise questions about the efficiency and equity of health systems and to stimulate inquiry into reasons for major observed differences.[99] International surveys also can identify alternative approaches to treatment and prevention of behavioral health problems.

Analysts have emphasized the need to broaden the policy framework beyond healthcare to include the social and physical environment and to focus more on primary prevention and health promotion services that are usually underfunded because of the large expenditure for medical care treatment. Healthcare purchasers in a few countries (e.g., Canada, United Kingdom, Ireland, Iceland, New Zealand) have established health goals for the population and are searching for alternative ways of achieving those health goals, including preventive healthcare and more effective integration of health and other policy issues such as education, housing, and social policy. Methods of allocative-efficiency analysis are applied in making these decisions.[98]

In summary, with population health as the goal, allocative efficiency concerns attainment of maximum population health using the limited resources that society has available for that objective during any given period of time. Attainment of this goal requires that societies choose the "right," most-valued mix of medical and nonmedical services and that these services be produced at minimum cost (maximal production efficiency).

Equity

Three primary philosophic traditions have focused primarily on individuals, institutions, or the community in judging justice. These may be used to illuminate the correlates and indicators of equity in behavioral health and healthcare.[26]

The distinctions between the individual and community perspectives are most deeply lodged in the debate between liberal and communitarian values.[100] The liberal political tradition focuses on the norms of personal well-being and individual freedom. Policies grounded in this tradition have been concerned with protecting or ensuring individual rights and the tradition's underlying distributive justice paradigm. Rights are those benefits to which one has a claim, based on assessment of what a fair distribution of benefits and burdens might be. This assessment includes consideration of both negative rights (i.e., noninterference and freedom of choice)

and positive rights (i.e., the conferring of specific material or nonmaterial benefits). Posed from this point of view, the essential question regarding equity is, What can I justly claim? This perspective has focused most notably on the availability, organization, and financing of behavioral healthcare services.

Communitarian sentiments are based on norms of the common good, social solidarity, and protecting the public welfare. The concept of justice on which this perspective is based is concerned with the underlying social, economic, and environmental underpinnings of inequity. Rather than focusing on conferring or ensuring positive or negative rights (or benefits) to individuals, this paradigm encompasses a broader consideration of public health and social and economic interventions required to enhance the well-being of groups or communities as a whole. Posed from this perspective, the essential question regarding equity is, What's good for us? Health policy ultimately directed toward improving the health of individuals and populations demands investments in more comprehensive, integrated, and effective clinical and nonclinical interventions (see Figure 1).

Contemporary social theorists, most notably German philosopher Jürgen Habermas, have argued for a new synthesis of these competing foundations for fairness, based on a theory of deliberative democracy.[26] Policies attuned to this perspective address the extent to which norms of participation appear to guide decision making. Posed from this point of view, the question regarding equity is, Who decides and how? This deliberative justice paradigm recognizes and attempts to resolve conflicts rooted in the other dominant paradigms of fairness through posing the need for rational discourse on the part of affected groups and individuals. Habermas argues that strategic or technical-rational aims of decision makers at either the macro or micro level (e.g., negotiating contract provisions for a state Medicaid behavioral healthcare managed care program, achieving patient adherence to therapeutic regimens) are unlikely to be orchestrated and achieved unless affected stakeholders (e.g., providers, payers, patient advocates) have the opportunity to present and have their points of view heard and respected in the process.

Table 3 summarizes empiric indicators of equity as they relate to the primary dimensions of the framework for assessing behavioral healthcare (Figure 2) and the underlying criteria of justice. The ultimate test of the equity of health policy from the social justice perspective is the extent to which disparities or inequalities in health among subgroups of the population are minimized. Substantive equity refers to the minimization of disparities in health

Table 3	Criteria for and Indicators of Equity

Dimension	Criteria	Indicators
Procedural Equity		
Deliberative justice		
Health policy	Participation	Type and extent of affected groups' participation in formulating and implementing policies and programs
Distributive justice		
Delivery system	Freedom of choice	
Availability		Distribution of providers
Organization		Types of facilities
Financing		Sources of payment
Realized access	Cost effectiveness	
Utilization		Type and volume of services used
Satisfaction		Public opinion, patient opinion
Distributive and social justice		
Population at risk	Similar treatment	
Predisposing		Age, sex, race, education, etc.
Enabling		Regular source, insurance coverage, income, etc.
Need		Perceived, evaluated
Social justice		
Environment	Common good	
Physical		Toxic, environmental hazards
Social		Social capital (family structure, voluntary organizations, social networks)
Economic		Human and material capital (schools, jobs, income, housing)
Health risks	Need	
Environmental		Toxic, environmental exposures
Behavioral		Lifestyle, health promotion practices
Substantive Equity		
Health	Need	
Individuals		Clinical indicators
Community		Population rates

From Aday LA, Begley CE, Lairson DR, et al: Evaluating the Healthcare System: Effectiveness, Efficiency, and Equity. 2nd ed. Chicago, IL: Health Administration Press; 1998:Table 6.2.[26(p186)] Used with permission.

among subgroups. Procedural equity refers to the extent to which the structure and process (or procedures) for achieving these outcomes may be judged to be fair, grounded in norms of deliberative, distributive, and social justice. The normative import of these procedural factors for substantive equity can be judged empirically, based on the extent to which they predict inequalities in health across groups and communities. Data may be gathered to assess dimensions of procedural and substantive equity descriptively, as well as to conduct analytic or evaluative research, exploring those factors that are most predictive of persistent substantive inequities (mirrored in subgroup variations in health). The challenge to analytic and evaluative research is how best to design studies and gather data to assess what factors are most likely to influence this endpoint and what health policy interventions are suggested as a consequence.

Participation. Empiric indicators of deliberative justice attempt to express the type and extent of affected groups' participation in formulating and implementing policies and programs. Such participation is manifest, for example, in the extent to which patients or patient advocacy groups are involved in influencing the provisions of behavioral healthcare managed care contracts, the mix of clinical and nonclinical services provided, and the criteria for assessing plan performance. An issue of central importance in working out programs of treatment for individuals who may be seriously compromised in terms of their decision-making capacity because of mental or related behavioral disorders is how to ethically and legally specify the protocol of informed consent for such treatment.

Freedom of Choice. Empiric indicators of access, based on the freedom-of-choice norm, are the distribution and availability of healthcare resources to consumers. For example, the ratios of personnel (e.g., primary care physicians, mental healthcare specialists) and facilities (e.g., inpatient and outpatient services) to population and the related inventories of behavioral healthcare personnel or providers (e.g., managed care providers and contractors) in a given target or market area are indicators of the basic supply of providers and delivery sites available to consumers.

Cost Effectiveness. The costs and benefits of care are reflected in the type and comprehensiveness of services received and how satisfied patients and their families are with them relative to some standard. Studies comparing the costs and outcomes of behavioral healthcare services delivered in alternative managed care models (health maintenance organizations versus preferred provider organizations) would, for example, provide useful guidance in terms of how best to invest limited healthcare dollars.

Similar Treatment. The similar-treatment criterion emphasizes that age, sex, race, income, or whether a person is covered by Medicaid, has private insurance, or has no insurance should not dictate that people with similar needs enter different doors (e.g., private versus public providers) or be treated differently (in terms of the type or intensity of services provided). This criterion is a defining tenet of the egalitarian concept of justice. A primary concern about care delivery in the mental health and substance abuse fields is that the existing system of financing such services lacks both parity and equity; that is, coverage comparable to that for medical care

services and comparable coverage across groups, respectively.[18(p183)]

Common Good. Empiric indicators related to the common good involve the array of social status, social capital, and human and material capital resources available to the population at risk in a given area, as well as the significant physical environmental exposures likely to exist. The role of interventions is not to alter individual actions and motivations, but to affect the more distal, foundational roots of health problems, such as the social-structural correlates of health and healthcare inequalities rooted in the physical, social, and economic environments in which individuals live and work. Health risks in the physical environment include toxic and environmental contaminants or stressors (e.g., lead paint, violent crime) in a given neighborhood or community. The social environment includes social resources (or social capital) associated with the family structure, voluntary organizations, and social networks that both bind and support individuals in a community. The economic environment encompasses both human and material capital resources, such as the schools, jobs, income, and housing that characterize the community.[18]

Need. Indicators of equity from the perspective of need attempt to measure health risks and health disparities in a population. The ultimate test of the equity of a health policy is the extent to which disparities or inequalities in health persist among subgroups of the population. The normative relevance of variations in the structure and process of care, however, can ultimately be judged empirically by the ability of these variations to predict inequalities in behavioral health risks and outcomes across groups and communities.

CRITIQUE AND NEW DIRECTIONS

Behavioral healthcare is not reducible to mental health therapy, substance abuse treatment, health psychology, or the sum of these. It is a product of a larger trend toward service integration, driven by managed care's concern with cost savings. As such, it still lacks a coherent sense of itself as a systemic whole. Achieving more clarity and integration requires a serious effort on the part of behavioral healthcare practitioners and researchers to arrive at a definition that is broad enough to encompass the various specialties subsumed under it, but precise enough to possess a clear mission and a coherent set of goals.

In designing programs and policies to enhance the effectiveness, efficiency, and equity of behavioral healthcare (as well as in designing and conducting research to assess the extent to which these goals have been achieved), the following issues are particularly important to consider:

- Current policy and practice in behavioral healthcare reveal the absence of a comprehensive, coordinated continuum of care and substantial variation in policy and financial incentives to encourage its development through behavioral healthcare contracting.

- The current state of the art of research in this area reflects considerable imprecision in conceptualizing and measuring the effectiveness, efficiency, and equity criteria. The goals of behavioral healthcare are not well articulated. Therefore, it is difficult to design research to evaluate "outcomes." Further, these three criteria have not been examined together when evaluating system performance.

- The limitations of the research in this area have resulted in a less-than-adequate knowledge base for the formulation of behavioral healthcare policy and program design.

The first era of behavioral healthcare focused on the cost savings to be realized in service integration and managed care alternatives. We are now entering a second era, which is focusing on quality and outcomes. To face the challenges of this era, we must put more effort into resolving questions related to definition,[5] goal setting, and measurement. In a third era, we must consider the issues of equity and access to behavioral healthcare, especially for the most seriously ill and vulnerable, in a public and private environment increasingly dominated by managed care.

ACKNOWLEDGMENTS
The authors gratefully acknowledge permission to reprint originals or adaptations of the following materials: selected excerpts from Chapters 1, 2, 4, and 6; Figure 1.4; and Tables 2.2, 4.1, and 6.2 from Aday LA, Begley CE, Lairson DR, et al. *Evaluating the Healthcare System: Effectiveness, Efficiency, and Equity.* 2nd ed. Chicago, IL: Health Administration Press, 1998; Figure 5.1 and Tables 5.4 and 5.5 from Aday LA. *At Risk in America: The Health and Health Care Needs of Vulnerable Populations in the United States.* San Francisco, CA: Jossey-Bass, 1993; and Table 1.1 from Drummond MF, O'Brien B, Stoddart GL, et al. *Methods for the Economic Evaluation of Health Care Programmes.* Oxford, UK: Oxford University Press, 1997.

About the Author
From The University of Texas School of Public Health, Houston, TX (L.A.A., C.E.B, D.R.L., C.H.S), and Affiliated Systems Corporation, Houston, TX (A.J.R., I.D.M). Opinions expressed herein are solely those of the authors. Address correspondence to: Lu Ann Aday, PhD, The University of Texas School of Public Health, PO Box 20186, Houston TX 77225. E-mail: laday@utsph.sph.uth.tmc.edu.

● ● ● **REFERENCES**

1. Joint Commission on Accreditation of Healthcare Organizations. Glossary of terms for performance measurement systems. Available at: http://www.jcaho.org/nssearch/perfmeas/oryx/10table3.htm. Accessed May 22, 1998.

2. Schwartz GE, Weiss SM. Yale Conference on Behavioral Medicine: A proposed definition and statement of goals. *J Behav Med* 1978;1:3-12.

3. McKegney FP, Schwartz CE. Behavioral medicine: Treatment and organizational issues. *Gen Hosp Psychiatry* 1986;8:330-339.

4. Backlar P. What's in a name? Mental health? Behavioral health? *Community Ment Health J* 1996;32:5-8.

5. Caplan A, Engelhardt HT, McCartney J. *Concepts of Health and Disease.* Reading, MA: Addison-Wesley; 1981.

6. World Health Organization Interim Commission. Constitution of the World Health Organization. *Chronicle of the World Health Organization* 1997;1:29-40.

7. World Health Organization. *Ottawa Charter for Health Promotion.* First International Conference on Health Promotion; November 17-21, 1986; Ottawa, Ontario, Canada.

8. Shah C. *Public Health and Preventive Medicine in Canada.* 3rd ed. Toronto, Ontario, Canada: University of Toronto Press; 1994.

9. Scott AJ, Monk TH, Brink LL. Shiftwork as a risk factor for depression: A pilot study. *Int J Occup Environ Health* 1997;3(suppl 2):S2-S9.

10. Kendler KS, Karkowski LM, Prescott CA. Stressful life events and major depression: Risk period, long-term contextual threat, and diagnostic specificity. *J Nerv Ment Dis* 1998;186:661-669.

11. Roy A. A case-control study of social risk factors for depression in American patients. *Can J Psychiatry* 1997;42:307-309.

12. Salokangas RK, Poutanen O. Risk factors for depression in primary care. Findings of the TADEP Project. *J Affect Disord* 1998;48:171-180.

13. Shrout PE, Link BG, Dohrenwend BP, et al. Characterizing life events as risk factors for depression: The role of fateful loss events. *J Abnorm Psychol* 1989;98:460-467.

14. Maier W, Lichtermann D, Minges J, et al. Personality traits in subjects at risk for unipolar major depression: A family study perspective. *J Affect Disord* 1992;24:153-163.

15. Peterson JB, Pihl RO, Gianoulakis C, et al. Ethanolinduced change in cardiac and endogenous opiate function and risk for alcoholism. *Alcohol Clin Exp Res* 1996;20:1542-1552.

16. Crum RM, Ensminger ME, Ro MJ, et al. The association of educational achievement and school dropout with risk of alcoholism: A twenty-five-year prospective study of inner-city children. *J Stud Alcohol* 1998;59:318-326.

17. Schuckit MA, Smith TL. Assessing the risk for alcoholism among sons of alcoholics. *J Stud Alcohol* 1997;58:141-145.

18. Aday LA. *At Risk in America: The Health and Health Care Needs of Vulnerable Populations in the United States*. San Francisco, CA: Jossey-Bass; 1993.

19. Hough, RL, Landsverk JA, Karno M, et al. Utilization of health and mental health services by Los Angeles Mexican Americans and non-Hispanic whites. *Arch Gen Psychiatry* 1987;44:702-709.

20. Epstein J, Gfroerer J. Changes affecting NHSDA estimates of treatment need for 1994-1996. In: *Analyses of Substance Abuse and Treatment Need Issues*. Rockville, MD: US Dept of Health and Human Services, Substance Abuse and Mental Health Services Administration, Office of Applied Studies; 1998:127-145. DHHS publication (SMA) 98-3227.

21. Mechanic DS. Emerging trends in mental health policy and practice. *Health Aff* 1998;17(6):82-98.

22. Essock SM, Goldman HH. States' embrace of managed mental health care. *Health Aff* 1995;14(3):34-44.

23. Mechanic DS. Key policy considerations for mental health in the managed care era. In: Manderscheid RW, Sonnenschein MA, eds. *Mental Health, United States, 1996*. Washington, DC: US Dept of Health and Human Services; 1996:1-16. DHHS publication (SMA) 96-3098.

24. Lurie N, Moscovice IS, Finch M, et al. Does capitation affect the health of the chronically mentally ill? Results from a randomized trial. *JAMA* 1992;276:3300-3304.

25. Wells KB, Sturm R. Care for depression in a changing environment. *Health Aff* 1995;14(3):78-89.

26. Aday LA, Begley CE, Lairson DR, et al. *Evaluating the Healthcare System: Effectiveness, Efficiency, and Equity*. 2nd ed. Chicago, IL: Health Administration Press; 1998.

27. Dial TH, Kantor A, Buck JA, et al. Behavioral health care in HMOs. In: Manderscheid RW, Sonnenschein MA, eds. *Mental Health, United States, 1996*. Washington, DC: US Dept of Health and Human Services; 1996:45-58. DHHS publication (SMA) 96-3098.

28. Frank RG, McGuire TG, Norman EH, et al. Developments in Medicaid managed behavioral health care. In: Manderscheid RW, Sonnenschein MA, eds. *Mental Health, United States, 1996*. Washington, DC: US Dept of Health and Human Services; 1996:138-153. DHHS publication (SMA) 96-3098.

29. Redick RW, Witkin MJ, Atay JE, et al. Highlights of organized mental health services in 1992 and major national and state trends. In: Manderscheid RW, Sonnenschein MA, eds. *Mental Health, United States, 1996*. Washington, DC: US Dept of Health and Human Services; 1996:90-137. DHHS publication (SMA) 96-3098.

30. Longest BB Jr. *Health Policymaking in the United States*. Chicago, IL: The Association of University Programs in Health Administration; 1994.

31. Slater C. What is outcomes research and what can it tell us? *Eval Health Prof* 1997;20:243-264.

32. Brook R, Lohr K. Efficacy, effectiveness, variations, and quality: Boundary-crossing research. *Med Care* 1985;23(suppl):710-722.

33. Donabedian A. *Explorations in Quality Assessment and Monitoring*, vol I. *The Definition of Quality and Approaches to Its Assessment*. Ann Arbor, MI: Health Administration Press; 1980.

34. Cochrane A. *Effectiveness and Efficiency*. London, UK: The Nuffield Provincial Hospitals Trust; 1971.

35. Sackett DL. Evaluation of health services. In: Last J, ed. *Maxcy-Rosenau Public Health and Preventive Medicine*. Norwalk, CT:Appleton-Century-Crofts; 1980:1800-1823.

36. Williamson J. The estimation of achievable health care benefit. In: Williamson J, ed. *Assessing and Improving Health Care Outcomes*. Cambridge, MA: Ballinger Publishers; 1978:51-69.

37. Lipsey M, Wilson D. The efficacy of psychological, educational, and behavioral treatment. *Am Psychol* 1993;12:1181-1209.

38. Lyons J, Howard K, O'Mahoney M, et al. *The Measurement and Management of Clinical Outcomes in Mental Health*. New York, NY: John Wiley & Sons; 1997.

39. National Association of State Mental Health Program Directors Research Institute, Inc. Five state feasibility study on state mental health agency performance measures. Available at: http://www.mentalhealth.org/mhstats/FeaFinal.htm. Accessed November 24,1998.

40. Charlson M, Sax F, MacKenzie C, et al. Assessing illness severity: Does clinical judgment work? *J Chronic Dis* 1986;39:439-452.

41. Horn S, Chambers A, Sharkey P, et al. Psychiatric severity of illness: A case mix study. *Med Care* 1989;27:69-84.

42. Fineberg H. The quest for causality in health services research. In: *Research Methodology: Strengthening Causal Interpretations of Nonexperimental Data*. Rockville, MD: Agency for Health Care Policy and Research; 1990:215-220. DHHS Publication No. (PMS) 90-3454.

43. Substance Abuse and Mental Health Services Administration. *Year-End Preliminary Estimates from the 1996 Drug Abuse Warning Network*. Rockville, MD: US Dept of Health and Human Services; 1997. DHHS Publication (SMA) 98-3175.

44. Kessler RC. The National Comorbidity Survey: Preliminary results and future directions. *International Journal of Methods in Psychiatric Research* 1995;5:139-151.

45. Substance Abuse and Mental Health Services Administration. *National Household Survey on Drug Abuse: Population Estimates, 1995*. Rockville, MD: US Dept of Health and Human Services; 1996. DHHS Publication (SMA) 96-3095.

46. Christianson J, Osher F. Health maintenance organizations, health care reform, and persons with serious illness. *Hosp Community Psychiatry* 1994;45:898-905.

47. Hser Y, Grella C, Chou C, et al. Relationships between drug treatment careers and outcomes: Findings from the National Drug Abuse Treatment Outcome Study. *Evaluation Review* 1998;22:496-519.

48. Shortell S, Gillies R, Devers K. Reinventing the American hospital. *Milbank Q* 1995;73:131-160.

49. Foster E. Does the continuum of care influence time in treatment? Evidence from the Fort Bragg Evaluation. *Evaluation Research* 1998;22:447-469.

50. Agency for Health Care Policy and Research. *Clinical Practice Guidelines for Depression in Primary Care*. Rockville, MD: Agency for Health Care Policy and Research; 1993. AHCPR Publication No. 93-0550.

51. American Psychiatric Association. Practice guideline for major depressive disorder in adults. *Am J Psychiatry* 1993;150(suppl):1-26.

52. McLellan T, Dembo T. *Screening and Assessment of Alcohol- and Other Drug-Abusing Adolescents*. Rockville, MD: Substance Abuse and Mental Health Services Administration; 1993. DHHS Publication (SMA) 93-2009.

53. Ross E. Managed behavioral health care premises, accountable systems of care, and AMBHA's PERMS. *Evaluation Review* 1997;21:318-321.

54. Substance Abuse and Mental Health Services Administration. Consumer-oriented mental health report card. Available at: http://www.mentalhealth.org/resource/rptcrd.htm. 1996. Accessed December 3, 1998.

55. Teague G, Ganju V, Hornik J, et al. The MHSIP mental health report card: A consumer-oriented approach to monitoring the quality of mental health plans. *Evaluation Review* 1997;21:330-341.

56. Byrns RT, Stone GW. *Microeconomics*, 6th ed. New York, NY: Harper Collins College Publishers; 1995.

57. Davis K, Anderson G, Rowland D, et al. *Health Care Cost Containment*. Baltimore, MD: The Johns Hopkins University Press; 1990.

58. Kennedy BP, Kawachi I, Glass R, et al. Income distribution, socioeconomic status, and self-rated health in the United States: Multilevel analysis. *Br Med J (Clinical Research Ed)* 1998;317:917-921.

59. Kennedy BP, Kawachi I, Prothrow-Stith D, et al. Social capital, income inequality, and firearm violent crime. *Soc Sci Med* 1998;47:7-17.

60. Ferrie JE, Shipley MJ, Marmot M, et al. An uncertain future: The health effects of threats to employment security in white-collar men and women. *Am J Public Health* 1998;88:1030-1036.

61. Grossman M. On the concept of health capital and the demand for health. *J Political Economy* 1972;80:223-255.

62. Behrman M, Wolfe BL. Does more schooling make women better nourished and healthier? Adult sibling and fixed effects estimates for Nicaragua. *J Hum Resour* 1989;24:644-663.

63. Berger MC, Lee JP. Schooling, self-selection, and health. *J Hum Resour* 1989;24:433-455.

64. Wolfe BL, Behrman JR. Women's schooling and children's health: Are the effects robust with adult sibling control for the women's childhood background? *J Health Econ* 1987;6:239-254.

65. Clayton RR, Cattarello AM, Johnstone BM. The effectiveness of Drug Abuse Resistance Education (project DARE): 5-year follow-up results. *Prev Med* 1996;25:307-318.

66. Shope JT, Copeland LA, Kamp ME, et al. Twelfth grade follow-up of the effectiveness of a middle school-based substance abuse prevention program. *J Drug Educ* 1998;28:185-197.

67. Yung AR, Phillips LJ, McGorry PD, et al. Prediction of psychosis. A step towards indicated prevention of schizophrenia. *Br J Psychiatry* 1998;172(suppl):14-20.

68. Dadds MR, Spence SH, Holland DE, et al. Prevention and early intervention for anxiety disorders: A controlled trial. *J Consult Clin Psychol* 1997;65:627-635.

69. Buscema M. The Sonda Project: Prevention, prediction, and psychological disorder. *Subst Use Misuse* 1997;32:1053-1153.

70. Ennett ST, Tobler NS, Ringwalt CL, et al. How effective is drug abuse resistance education? A meta-

analysis of project DARE outcome evaluations. *Am J Public Health* 1994;84:1394-1401.

71. Gorman D. The effectiveness of DARE and other drug use prevention programs. *Am J Public Health* 1995;85:873.

72. Schlesinger M, Mechanic DS. Challenges for managed competition from chronic illness. *Health Aff* 1993;12(suppl):123-137.

73. Wells KB, Astrachan BM, Tischler GL, et al. Issues and approaches in evaluating managed mental health care. *Milbank Q* 1995;73:57-75.

74. Rogers WH, Wells KB, Meredith LS, et al. Outcomes for adult outpatients with depression under prepaid or fee for service financing. *Arch Gen Psychiatry* 1993;50:517-525.

75. Grossman M. Health benefits of increases in alcohol and cigarette taxes. *Br J Addict* 1989;84:1193-1204.

76. Grossman M, Chaloupka FJ. The demand for cocaine by young adults: A rational addiction approach. *J Health Econ* 1998;17:427-474.

77. Chaloupka FJ, Wechsler H. Price, tobacco control policies and smoking among young adults. *J Health Econ* 1997;16:359-373.

78. Becker GS, Grossman M, Murphy K. An empirical analysis of cigarette addiction. *Am Econ Rev* 1994;84(3):396-418.

79. Keeler TE, Hu T-W, Barnett PG, et al. Taxation, regulation, and addiction: A demand function for cigarettes based on time-series evidence. *J Health Econ* 1993;12:1-18.

80. Chaloupka F. Rational addictive behavior and cigarette smoking. *J Political Economy* 1991;99(4):722-742.

81. Ornstein SI. Control of alcohol consumption through price increase. *J Stud Alcohol* 1980;41:807-818.

82. Chaloupka FJ, Grossman M, Saffer H. The effects of price on the consequences of alcohol use and abuse. *Recent Dev Alcohol* 1998;14:331-346.

83. Ponicki W, Holder HD, Gruenewald PJ, et al. Altering alcohol price by ethanol content: Results from a Swedish tax policy in 1992. *Addiction* 1997;92:859-870.

84. Treno AJ, Nephew TM, Ponicki WR, et al. Alcohol beverage price spectra: Opportunities for substitution. *Alcohol Clin Exp Res* 1993;17:675-680.

85. Levy D, Sheflin N. New evidence on controlling alcohol use through price. *J Stud Alcohol* 1983;44:929-937.

86. Rabow J, Schwartz C, Stevens S, et al. Social psychological dimensions of alcohol availability: The relationship of perceived social obligations, price considerations, and energy expended to the fre-

quency, amount, and type of alcoholic beverage consumed. *Int J Addict* 1982;17:1259-1271.

87. Miller W, Hester R. Inpatient alcoholism treatment: Who benefits? *Am Psychol* 1986;41:794-805.

88. Firshein J. Alcohol-treatment programmes are comparable. *Lancet* 1997;349:40.

89. McCrady B, Longabaugh R, Fink E, et al. Cost-effectiveness of alcoholism treatment in partial hospital versus inpatient settings after brief inpatient treatment: 12 month outcomes. *J Consult Clin Psychol.* 1986;54:708-713.

90. Drummond MF, O'Brien B, Stoddart GL, et al. *Methods for the Economic Evaluation of Health Care Programmes*. Oxford, UK: Oxford University Press; 1997.

91. Clark RE, Teague GB, Ricketts SK, et al. Cost-effectiveness of assertive community treatment versus standard case management for persons with co-occurring severe mental illness and substance use disorders. *Health Serv Res* 1998;33:1285-1308.

92. Gold M, Siegel J, Russell L, et al. *Cost-Effectiveness in Health and Medicine*. New York, NY: Oxford University Press; 1996.

93. Torrance G, Feeny D. Utilities and quality adjusted lifeyears. *Int J Technol Assess Health Care* 1989;5:559-575.

94. Torrance G, Feeny DK, Furlong WJ, et al. Multiattribute utility function for a comprehensive health status classification system—Health Utilities Index Mark 2. *Med Care* 1996;34(7):702-722.

95. Agency for Health Care Policy and Research. *Report to Congress: Progress of Research on Outcomes of Health Care Services and Procedures*. Rockville, MD: Agency for Health Care Policy and Research; 1991. AHCPR publication 91-0004.

96. Power EJ. Current efforts in standards development: United States. *Med Care* 1996;34(suppl):DS204-DS207.

97. Hillman AL. Summary of economic analysis of health care technology: A report on principles. *Med Care* 1996;34 (suppl):DS193-DS196.

98. Organization for Economic Cooperation and Development. *New Directions in Health Care Policy*. Paris, France: Organization for Economic Cooperation and Development; 1995. Health Policy Studies; No. 7.

99. Schieber G, Poullier J. Overview of international comparisons of health care expenditures. In: *Health Care Systems in Transition: The Search for Efficiency*. Paris, France: Organization for Economic Cooperation and Development;1990. Social Policy Series; No. 7.

100. Mulhall S, Swift A. *Liberals and Communitarians*. Oxford, UK: Blackwell; 1992.

The Health and Cost Benefits of Work Site Health-Promotion Programs

Source: Goetzel RZ, Ozminkowski RJ. The health and cost benefits of work site health-promotion programs. *Annu Rev Public Health* 2008;29:303-23.

ABSTRACT

We review the state of the art in work site health promotion (WHP), focusing on factors that influence the health and productivity of workers. We begin by defining WHP, then review the literature that addresses the business rationale for it, as well as the objections and barriers that may prevent sufficient investment in WHP. Despite methodological limitations in many available studies, the results in the literature suggest that, when properly designed, WHP can increase employees' health and productivity. We describe the characteristics of effective programs including their ability to assess the need for services, attract participants, use behavioral theory as a foundation, incorporate multiple ways to reach people, and make efforts to measure program impact. Promising practices are noted including senior management support for and participation in these programs. A very important challenge is widespread dissemination of information regarding success factors because only ~7% of employers use all the program components required for successful interventions. The

need for more and better science when evaluating program outcomes is highlighted. Federal initiatives that support cost-benefit or cost-effectiveness analyses are stressed, as is the need to invest in healthy work environments, to complement individual based interventions.

INTRODUCTION

In a 1993 report prepared by the Office of Disease Prevention and Health Promotion, McGinnis, former Deputy Assistant Secretary of Health, wrote, "Worksite health promotion has taken on increasing importance as a contributor to improved health for many Americans." He continued, "With the expanded activity comes an interest and obligation to assess the results of such programs to ensure that we have a clearer notion of what works best in various settings."[83]

The report, written a decade and a half ago, spotlighted the experience of 61 employers, large and small, public and private, that were providing work site health-promotion (WHP) programs aimed at improving the health and well-being of their employees and reducing health care, workers' compensation, and disability costs. Since that report was released, researchers and program evaluators, largely university based, have increased the knowledge base related to health-promotion efforts in the workplace. However, that experience and the insights garnered from the research have not been well communicated and applied to the audience that would benefit the most: employers.

Here, we critically examine WHP and discuss how knowledge from this field has advanced since the early 1990s. We review the literature supporting the hypotheses that WHP programs positively influence workers' health, medical service use, and productivity, and we evaluate the quality of the evidence. We discuss ways in which evidence-based WHP practices can and should be disseminated more broadly so that the positive health and economic outcomes from such initiatives can be realized.

DEFINING WORK SITE HEALTH PROMOTION

WHP programs are employer initiatives directed at improving the health and well-being of workers and, in some cases, their dependents. They include programs designed to avert the occurrence of disease or the progression of disease from its early unrecognized stage to one that's more severe.[27] At their core, WHP programs support primary, secondary, and tertiary prevention efforts. Primary prevention efforts in the workplace are directed at employed populations that are generally healthy. They also offer opportunities for workers who do not maintain good health and who may fall prey to diseases and disorders that can be prevented or delayed if certain actions are taken. Examples of primary prevention include programs that encourage exercise and fitness, healthy eating, weight management, stress management, use of safety belts in cars, moderate alcohol consumption, recommended adult immunizations, and safe sex.[53]

Health promotion also incorporates secondary prevention directed at individuals already at high risk because of certain lifestyle practices (e.g., smoking, being sedentary, having poor nutrition, practicing unsafe sex, consuming excessive amounts of alcohol, and experiencing high stress) or abnormal biometric values (e.g., high blood pressure, high cholesterol, high blood glucose, overweight). Examples of secondary prevention include hypertension screenings and management programs, smoking cessation telephone quit lines, weight loss classes, and reduction or elimination of financial barriers to obtaining prescribed lipid-lowering medications.

Health promotion sometimes also includes elements of tertiary prevention, often referred to as disease management, directed at individuals with existing ailments such as asthma, diabetes, cardiovascular disease, cancers, musculoskeletal disorders,

and depression, with the aim of ameliorating the disease or retarding its progression. Such programs promote better compliance with medications and adherence to evidence-based clinical practice guidelines for outpatient treatment. Because patient self-management is stressed, health-promotion practices related to behavior change and risk reduction are often part of disease management protocols. Full-service disease management programs also encourage collaboration among patients, their families, physicians, other health care providers, and the staff of the disease management program, and routine feedback loops are established among these groups.[33]

ESTABLISHING A BUSINESS CASE FOR WORK SITE HEALTH PROMOTION

The Centers for Disease Control and Prevention (CDC), in conjunction with its *Healthy People in Healthy Places* initiative, has observed that workplaces are to adults what schools are to children, because most working-age adults spend a substantial portion of their waking hours in their workplaces.[113] Historically, WHP programs have been referred to as wellness, health management, health promotion, health enhancement, and health and productivity management (HPM) programs. For the sake of simplicity, we use the term WHP and define it as a set of workforce-based initiatives that focus primarily on providing traditional health-promotion services (e.g., health management or wellness programs) and may also include disease management (e.g., screening, care management, or case management programs), demand management (e.g., self-care, nurse call line programs), and related efforts to optimize employee productivity by improving employee health.[54]

Today, many employers associate poor health with reduced employee performance, safety, and morale. The organizational costs of workers in poor health, and those with behavioral risk factors, include high medical, disability, and workers' compensation expenses; elevated absenteeism and employee turnover; and decreased productivity at work (often referred to as presenteeism).[44,48,51] In addition, one worker's poor health may negatively affect the performance of others who work with him or her.[44,48,80]

The question for employers is whether well-conceived WHP programs can improve employees' health, reduce their risks for disease, control unnecessary health care utilization, limit illness-related absenteeism, and decrease health-related productivity losses.[1,26,43,92,93] If effective, WHP programs could reach large segments of the population that would not normally be exposed to and engaged in organized health improvement initiatives. Still, many employers are reluctant to offer sufficiently intensive and comprehensive work site programs because they are not convinced that these programs deliver on the promise that they can reduce risk factors for their employees and achieve a positive financial return on investment (ROI).[8,42,73,90]

BARRIERS TO IMPLEMENTING WORK SITE PROGRAMS

A 1999 survey of WHP fielded by the U.S. Office of Disease Prevention and Health Promotion reported that 90% of work sites offered workers at least one type of health-promotion activity.[68] The key word in that report was "activity." Almost all employers reported having one or a string of activities loosely connected to WHP, but most had no organizing framework for these programs. The most recent National Worksite Health Promotion Survey[68] reports that only 6.9% of employers provide all five elements considered key components of a comprehensive program: (*a*) health education, (*b*) links to related employee services, (*c*) supportive physical and social environments for health improvement, (*d*) integration of health promotion into the organization's culture, and (*e*) employee screenings with adequate treatment and follow up. Some employers do not opt to invest in WHP, and some even cut funding to existing programs, sometimes in spite of compelling data showing that these programs achieve good results. Their reasons for not supporting new or existing work site initiatives are multifaceted.

A subset of employers are philosophically opposed to interfering with their workers' private lives, health habits, and medical decision-making, considering such actions as akin to playing the role of big brother. Some employers consider WHP programs as luxuries and not central to the organization's main business purpose. Still others may be concerned that programs promoted during work hours may distract workers from their day-to-day duties and consequently negatively impact worker productivity. Some employers argue that there is no grassroots support for WHP, as evidenced by poor attendance in health education sessions, or that labor unions may object, claiming that company cash outlays for such programs reduce workers' take-home pay.[16,97]

Other employers' objections to health promotion may be less defined, and in fact, they may believe that these programs exert a positive effect. However, they may find it difficult and expensive to prove positive outcomes to senior managers seeking hard evidence of program impacts. Furthermore, it may also be difficult to isolate specific program elements that are more effective than others—those that deliver the "biggest bang for the buck."

Furthermore, some employers may be reluctant to institute programs that achieve a positive ROI only after many years of investment, and the promises of quick returns never match reality. Also, they contend, even if they wished to start such programs, there are too few best practices to emulate. Finally, small businesses complain they lack the resources necessary to implement initiatives similar to those of large companies because they lack the advantages of scalability and infrastructure possessed by larger employers.[112]

RATIONALE FOR INVESTING IN WORK SITE HEALTH PROMOTION

Despite these objections to WHP, our recent informal discussions with health-promotion vendors report a heightened interest in and demand for their services. Vendors report that they are besieged with requests for proposals (RFPs) from employers wishing to provide to their employees health risk appraisals (HRAs), health education programs, health decision support tools, health improvement coaching, and other preventive care services, within the context of a more holistic way to manage employee health and costs (R. Goetzel, personal communication, October 2, 2007). Benefit consultant surveys that usually target large employers report that almost two thirds of those responding to their surveys now offer wellness programs, and 15% more plan to do so.[73]

There are several reasons offered by employers for investing in WHP.

Workplaces Offer a Practical Setting for Health Promotion

The workplace presents a useful setting for introducing and maintaining health-promotion programs for working-age adults. It contains a concentrated group of people, usually situated in a small number of geographic sites, who share a common purpose and common culture. Communication and information exchange with workers are relatively straightforward. Individual goals and organizational goals, including those related to increasing profitability, generally are aligned with one another.

Because good worker health has the potential to enhance company profitability and help achieve other organizational goals, the objectives of health promotion can be aligned with the organization's mission. Social and organizational support is likely to be available when behavior change efforts are attempted. Organizational policies and social norms can help guide certain behaviors and discourage others, and financial or other incentives can be introduced to encourage participation in programs. Finally, measurement of program impact is often practical, using available administrative data collection and analysis systems.

Health Care and Health-Promotion Expenditures

The main driving force behind employers' growing interest in providing WHP services to their workers is undoubtedly rapidly rising health care costs.[74,78]

Employers' health care costs, primarily focused on sickness care, are increasing exponentially with no immediate attenuation in sight. In 2006, U.S. health care spending totaled $2.1 trillion—about 16.0% of the gross domestic product.[95] Employers pay more than one third of the total annual medical bill, and the balance is funded by Medicare, Medicaid, other government programs, individual insurance coverage, and patient out-of-pocket expenditures.[65] In 2006, employer premiums for medical care averaged $3615 a year for single coverage and $8508 for family coverage.[61]

At the same time, the prevalence of illnesses that are at least partly caused by modifiable health risk factors and poor lifestyle habits also continues to rise. For example, the United States has been witnessing alarming increases in obesity, contributing to heightened rates of diabetes and related disorders.[84] These strain the health care system's resources because individuals who are burdened by them generate significantly higher health care costs.[36]

A large body of medical and epidemiological research confirms the links between chronic illnesses and common modifiable risk factors, such as smoking, obesity, physical inactivity, excessive alcohol consumption, poor diet, high stress, and social isolation.[3,18,72,75] Preventable or postponable illnesses make up ~70% of the total burden of disease (as measured in terms of premature deaths and potential years of life lost and their associated costs).[113] The World Health Organization[77] has observed that smoking, alcohol misuse, physical inactivity, and poor diet are among the top five contributors to disease and injury worldwide. McGinnis & Foege and Mokdad et al. showed that about half of all deaths in the United States may be premature because they are caused by behavioral risk factors and behavior patterns that are modifiable.[71,72,75]

MODIFIABLE HEALTH RISKS AND EMPLOYER COSTS

Studies by Goetzel et al.[45] and Anderson et al.[7] examined the relationships between ten modifiable health risk factors and medical claims for more than 46,000 employees from private and public sector employers over a 6-year period. The risk factors studied included obesity, high serum cholesterol, high blood pressure, stress, depression, smoking, diet, excessive alcohol consumption, physical fitness and exercise, and high blood glucose. The authors found that these risk factors accounted for ~25% of total employer health care expenditures for the employees included in the study. Moreover, employees with seven of the risk factors (tobacco use, hypertension, hypercholesterolemia, overweight/obesity, high blood glucose, high stress, and lack of physical activity) cost employers 228% more in health care costs compared with those lacking any of these risk factors.[45] Other reports have shown that workers with these modifiable risk factors are also more likely to be absent, have higher rates of disability, and be less productive.[2,9,11,13,17,24,29,30,58-60,62,63,66,103,105,110,111,118]

Synthesizing the health-promotion literature spanning 15 years, Aldana[1] concluded that there is consistent evidence of a relationship between obesity, stress, multiple risk factors, and subsequent health care expenditures as well as subsequent worker absenteeism. Thus, the health risk profile of an employer's workforce is likely to have a significant impact on total labor costs.

Work Site Health-Promotion Programs' Effects on Behaviors and Health Risks

Work site programs have been associated with changes in the health habits of workers. A systematic review of the literature pertaining to workplace-based health-promotion and disease-prevention programs was commissioned by the CDC in 1995,[117] and a more recent review was concluded by the Community Preventive Services Task Force in 2007.[109]

One specific focus of the earlier review was multicomponent WHP programs and their impact on employee health and productivity. In that review,

Heaney & Goetzel examined 47 peer-reviewed studies over a 20-year period[57] and found that WHP programs varied widely in terms of their comprehensiveness, intensity, and duration. Consequently, the measurable impact of these programs was shown to be uneven because different intervention and evaluation methods were employed.

Despite the variability in programs and study designs, the authors concluded that there was "indicative to acceptable" evidence supporting the effectiveness of multicomponent WHP in achieving long-term behavior change and risk reduction among workers. The most effective programs offered individualized risk-reduction counseling to the highest risk employees, but they did so within the context of broader health awareness programs and a "healthy company" culture. On the basis of the evidence, the reviewers noted that changing the behavior patterns of employees and reducing their health risks were achievable objectives in a work site setting, assuming favorable conditions exist, including proper program design and execution.[26,57,117] Unfortunately, this review did not report on the average effect sizes of the interventions, but instead only on whether the program achieved "significant" reductions in the health and productivity outcomes examined.

Findings from the Community Guide Review of Work Site Health Promotion

In February 2007, the Community Guide Task Force released the findings of a comprehensive and systematic literature review focused on the health and economic impacts of WHP.[109] Using established and rigorous guidelines for their review,[119] the Task Force examined the literature for work site programs that include an assessment of health risks with feedback, delivered verbally or in writing, followed by health education or other health-improvement interventions. Additional health-promotion interventions included counseling and coaching of at-risk employees, invitations to group health education classes, and support sessions aimed at encouraging or assisting employees in their efforts to adopt healthy behaviors. Interventions with an environmental or ecological focus included enhancing access to physical activity programs (exercise facilities or time off for exercise), providing healthy food choices in cafeterias, and enacting policies that support a healthier work site environment (such as a smoke-free workplace). In most cases, WHP interventions provided at the work site were offered free of charge to encourage participation.

Health and productivity outcomes from these interventions were reported from 50 studies qualifying for inclusion in the review. The outcomes included a range of health behaviors, physiologic measurements, and productivity indicators linked to changes in health status. Although many of the changes in these outcomes were small when measured at an individual level, such changes at the population level were considered substantial.[109]

Specifically, the Task Force found strong evidence of WHP program effectiveness in reducing tobacco use among participants (with a median reduction in prevalence rates of 1.5 percentage points), dietary fat consumption as measured by self-report (median reduction in risk prevalence of 5.4 percentage points), high blood pressure (median prevalence risk reduction of 4.5 percentage points), total serum cholesterol levels (median prevalence reduction of 6.6 percentage points), the number of days absent from work because of illness or disability (median reduction of 1.2 days per year), and improvements in other general measures of worker productivity.

However, insufficient evidence of effectiveness was found for some desired program outcomes, such as increasing dietary intake of fruits and vegetables, reducing overweight and obesity, and improving physical fitness. Also, in a parallel review, the Task Force concluded that evidence was insufficient to determine the effectiveness of HRAs with feedback when implemented alone, without follow-up programs.[109] Thus, employers that administered an HRA but provided no meaningful follow-up interventions would likely not realize changes in employees' health and related outcomes. These findings confirmed an earlier review that reached similar conclusions.[6]

Aside from changes in health risks, the Task Force noted that there may be additional benefits associated with work site programs, including increasing worker awareness of health issues; increasing detection of certain diseases, or risk for disease at an earlier or presymptomatic stage; referral to medical professionals for employees at high risk for disease; and creation of need-specific health promotion programs based on the analysis of aggregate results. The Task Force also identified some possible negative consequences associated with these programs, including workers' fear of breaches in confidentiality and the possibility that those who think or know they have significant health risks may be unwilling to participate in programs that expose those risks.

Several threats to internal and external validity inherent in work site studies were also highlighted in the Task Force review. These included using biased samples comprised of volunteers willing or even anxious to participate in health improvement-initiatives (the so-called worried well, who actively seek out medical information on their own); high attrition rates; the possibility that the social desirability of responses to HRA questions will yield invalid answers to survey questions; maturation effects; unaccounted for secular changes (e.g., introduction of new laws or company policies); and publication bias (whereby studies that report positive results are more likely to be reported, leading to an overly optimistic view of health-promotion impacts).

Return on Investment from Work Site Health-Promotion Programs

If WHP programs can influence employees' health habits and behaviors, can they also reduce health care costs? Over the past 20 years, several studies have addressed that question, and there is growing evidence that work site programs can yield acceptable financial returns to employers that invest in them. Several literature reviews that weigh the evidence from experimental and quasi-experimental studies suggest that programs grounded in behavior change theory and that utilize tailored communications and individualized counseling for high-risk individuals are likely to produce a positive return on the dollars invested in those programs.[1,26,50,93,114]

The ROI research is largely based on evaluations of employer-sponsored health programs. One important caveat in assessing those evaluations is that they are most often funded by employers implementing the programs, and these employers may desire a positive assessment to justify their investment decisions. Studies often cited with the strongest research designs and large numbers of subjects include those performed at Johnson and Johnson,[15,19] Citibank,[86] Dupont,[12] Bank of America,[38,67] Tenneco,[10] Duke University,[63] the California Public Retirees System,[39] Procter and Gamble,[49] and Chevron Corporation.[46] Even accounting for inconsistencies in design and results, most of these work site studies produced positive financial results.

A 1998 review of early WHP studies, mostly conducted in the 1980s and early 1990s,[50] estimated ROI savings ranging from $1.40 to $3.14 per dollar spent, with a median ROI of ~$3.00 saved per dollar spent on the program. The review acknowledged that negative results were not likely to be reported in the literature and that the quality of many of the studies was less than optimal.

In 2001, Aldana[1] performed a comprehensive literature review of the financial impact of health-promotion programming on health care costs in which he rated the rigor of the evaluations. In his analysis, only 4 of 32 studies reviewed reported no effects of health promotion on health care costs. However, these four studies did not employ a randomized design, whereas several of the other studies that reported positive results applied experimental or rigorous quasi-experimental methods. The average ROI for seven studies reporting costs and benefits was $3.48 for every dollar expended.

In the same review, Aldana[1] also reported the impact of work site programs on absenteeism. All 14 absenteeism studies reviewed by Aldana found reductions in employee absenteeism, regardless of the research design used, but only three reported ROI ratios, from $2.50 to $10.10 saved for every dollar invested.

In a more recent review of economic outcomes, summarizing results from 56 qualifying financial impact studies conducted over the past two decades, Chapman in 2005 concluded that participants in work site programs have 25%-30% lower medical and absenteeism costs compared with nonparticipants, over an average study period of 3.6 years.[26] However, Chapman's review included a mix of cross-sectional and prospective research studies and did not adjust for study design as rigorously as did Aldana, so his higher estimates of cost savings may be inflated.

Some researchers point to selection bias as the likely reason for finding cost savings and high ROI estimates in work site studies. In many studies, it is unclear whether program participants are healthier or more highly motivated than nonparticipants to begin with. Such a priori differences in health or motivation may explain why participants use fewer medical care or other services and may continue to do so even if a program was not available. Under this scenario, changes in medical expenditures or absenteeism may be due to underlying health and motivational factors that are independent of the program being evaluated, and these should not be counted in the program's favor. This type of selection bias can be minimized, however, if researchers are able to obtain data explaining why the decision to participate was made. Recent financial impact studies of work site programs have attempted to control for such inherent differences between participants and nonparticipants at baseline, referred to as selection bias, using methods suggested by Heckman, such as propensity matching and weighting, to yield more accurate estimates of program savings and ROI.[87]

ELEMENTS OF PROMISING PRACTICES

As illustrated above, when WHP programs are grounded in behavior theory, implemented effectively using evidence-based principles, and measured accurately, they are more likely to improve workers' health and performance. These results can contribute to the organization's competitiveness and potentially enhance the organization's standing in the community. However, we need to learn more about the mechanisms and processes that facilitate behavior change among workers, as well as those that are ineffective.

Research is also needed to investigate the relationships between program design and implementation and the amount of time needed to develop new participant health habits initiated by such programs. An oft-cited example pertains to weight-reduction programs that help participants lose weight within a relatively short period, only to have them regain much of that weight after the program ends. Investigators must seek to understand more fully whether such behavior is due to poor program design, poor follow-up, or overriding influences of the environment that cannot easily be corrected.

Recent benchmarking and best-practice studies suggest that the effectiveness of work site programs is influenced greatly by such factors as having senior management support, a champion at the work site promoting the program, alignment between the program and broader organizational objectives, data documenting program achievements, and the ability to create a healthy company culture[31,40-42,47,81,82,116] (D. Anderson, unpublished information).

In addition, several other key components frequently found in successful WHP programs are described below.

Needs Assessment

As highlighted in the *Community Guide* review, using an HRA to assess employees' health risks is a necessary but insufficient component of successful WHP programs.[109] Nonetheless, most effective programs begin with the administration of an HRA in which employees answer questions about their health behaviors, biometric measures may be collected, and a series of estimates of health risks are provided to the individual. These HRAs also include questions designed to shape interventions most likely to improve employees' health risk profiles. For example, HRAs often assess participants' readiness to change, perceived level of self-efficacy, or other psychosocial factors affecting their willingness or ability to change

behaviors. Without an HRA, it is difficult to tailor interventions that fit well with individuals' states of readiness to change behavior and learning style.

The HRA is usually a fairly low-cost tool, ranging in price from a few pennies to ~$50 per respondent depending on whether it is administered electronically or through the mail, and whether biometric measures are also taken.[102] Thus, the HRA can be an efficient method of providing a gateway to follow-up interventions that are more costly and that should be recommended for those who are most in need.

One illustration of the value HRAs was provided in a study of retirees conducted by Ozminkowski et al.[88] In their financial analysis of Medicare claims data, the investigators found that the HRA was the cornerstone of successful programs for the elderly and that its administration, along with other health-promotion programs, was associated with significant cost savings. They used growth-curve analyses to account for preexisting trends in utilization for program participants and nonparticipants, along with propensity score weighting and other multiple regression analyses to control for differences in baseline health status, prior to estimating the impact of program participation.

The researchers found that cost trends were lowest (and savings were therefore highest) for HRA participants who also engaged in one or more follow-up interventions. These interventions included on-site biometric screenings, telephone lifestyle management counseling for high-risk individuals, nurse-support telephone lines, and wellness classes. In general, the more programs in which seniors participated, the lower were their subsequent health care costs. Cost savings were not observed for beneficiaries who engaged in follow-up programs without also completing an HRA; in some analyses, these beneficiaries even cost more. The authors therefore surmised that the HRA was an effective tool to triage and direct beneficiaries to other programs in an appropriate manner. Indeed, combining HRA results with other data, such as medical and pharmacy claims, may offer additional triage and targeting opportunities.

Achieving High Participation Rates

A high participation rate is a key element of any successful risk-reduction program. As Anderson opines, "Nothing happens until [people] participate"[101] (D. Anderson, unpublished information). As described below, many methods can be used to achieve high participation rates, including the shrewd use of incentives. Participation is defined in many ways including taking HRAs, enrolling in programs, completing programs, and participating in self-care and self-management activities that are difficult to monitor. In a survey of Koop Award winners, Goetzel et al.[52] found that the majority of former winners considered high participation rates "very important," especially among employees who are hard to reach, and that the average participation rate among exemplary WHP programs was 60%.

Providing Tailored Behavior Change Messages

A number of studies have demonstrated the increased efficacy of tailored messages relative to generic ones. For example, Kreuter and Strecher[65] compared the effects of tailored HRA feedback with generic feedback and found that individuals receiving the tailored feedback were 18% more likely to change at least one risk factor (usually cholesterol screening, dietary fat consumption, or physical activity).

This finding was confirmed in studies addressing single risk behaviors as well. For example, Rimer et al.,[96] in a smoking cessation study, found that participants who received tailored print material were significantly more likely to reread the material and believe that the ideas were new, that the material was helpful, and that it was easy to use. In a randomized study of exercise behavior, Peterson & Aldana[94] found that individuals who received written messages tailored to their stage of change (as defined by Prochaska) demonstrated a 13% increase in physical activity, compared with 1% for those who received generic messages, and an 8% decrease for the control group over a six-week period.

Supporting Self-Care and Self-Management

Self-care or self-management refers to the notion that the individual is an active participant in his or her medical treatment or in ensuring health maintenance.[69] For the chronically ill, effective self-management increases patients' ability to manage their prescribed medical treatment, by teaching or otherwise helping them adhere to medication or diet regimens, teaching them to use medical care services appropriately, and helping to address the emotional sequelae of health conditions.

Thus, self-management education is designed to teach skills and increase the participant's confidence in his or her ability to define and solve problems, make decisions, find resources, and form partnerships with health care providers. Such an approach can reduce symptoms and distress caused by many chronic diseases and improve psychological well-being as measured by standardized instruments.[69] For example, in a review of self-management programs, Lorig & Holman[69] found that goal setting and action planning were critical to perceived health improvements.

As shown above, a key component of self-care and self-management is goal setting, which enhances treatment compliance and motivates behavior change. Lovato & Green[70] found that goal setting was the most effective method to maintain employee participation in WHP programs. They further noted that goal setting was most effective when goals are realistic, short-term, flexible, and set by the participant rather than imposed by program staff.[70]

Guided self-help strategies are also key elements of self-management. These come in the form of printed materials or conversations with trained counselors that help participants define their goals (e.g., manage their symptoms or reduce their morbidity or mortality risks) and develop action plans (e.g., find better ways to adhere to pharmacotherapy or other treatments).[69] Orleans et al.[85] presented evidence that self-help smoking cessation guides are a promising addition to clinical treatments such as nicotine patches and that complementing pharmacotherapy with self-help guides and frequent interactions with trained counselors can help achieve high smoking-cessation rates.

In short, individualized and tailored behavioral interventions that use goal-setting techniques, reflective counseling, and motivational interviewing, provided in a personalized and consistent manner, are more effective than general awareness building and information and education sharing programs.[35,55,57,91,104]

Addressing Multiple Risk Factors

Addressing multiple risk factors simultaneously can increase the impact of the intervention because it facilitates individuals' involvement in the program through many entry channels. However, a strategic approach to addressing a participant's multiple risks is important. Several studies cited by Strecher et al.[108] suggest a need to break bad habits one at a time. People with multiple risk factors may be overwhelmed with the sheer number of health risks they have and may find it difficult to sort out the major from the minor. Thus a program should avoid recommending too much too quickly.

Risks can be prioritized on the basis of their near-term likelihood of morbidity or mortality and the participant's readiness to change any given risk factor. This approach is based on the presumption that an individual's high intrinsic motivation to change one even relatively benign behavior is more likely to achieve success, thus generating a sense of self-efficacy and continued motivation to change more behaviors. Thus, once one behavior or risk is successfully mitigated, the individual may feel greater confidence in his or her ability to address other health issues. Offering a comprehensive program that allows participants to move from one risk category to another is therefore desirable.

Offering a Variety of Engagement Modalities

With the understanding that some individuals prefer to work on behavior change on their own while others prefer to utilize social support, most work site programs offer a menu of interventions, including printed health education materials, individualized counseling, group classes, and work site–wide health promotion activities. Although classes appeal to some, Erfurt et al.[34] found that offering a menu, including guided self-help, one-to-one, mini group, and full-group interventions, is more successful than offering only didactic sessions. Fries analyzed two programs for retirees delivered entirely through the mail and found that tailored print materials had a significant behavioral impact.[38,39] However, he did not test whether impacts would have been greater with additional engagement modalities. Several studies support the idea that with tailored interventions, on-site, face-to-face encounters between health educators and participants may not be necessary.[35] However, this area requires further research because it is not clear what might be the relative effects of different engagement modalities.[109]

Providing Easy Access to Programs and Effective Follow-Up

In WHP programs, easy access to programs is key to recruiting and maintaining participation. Erfurt et al.[34] found that, although half of employees indicated interest in smoking and weight-loss classes, fewer than 1% enrolled in the classes when offered off-site, compared with 8%-12% when offered on-site. Lovato & Green[70] cite several studies based on surveys of employees who dropped out of health-promotion programs; that the surveys identified logistical barriers (time and location) as the most often cited reasons for dropping out of the program.

For employees who participated in blood pressure treatment, work site weight-loss, or smoking-cessation programs, gains made are best maintained when the program includes ongoing routine and persistent follow-up counseling.[34] Several studies reviewed by Pelletier[91] in these three areas found that one-time screening and counseling can have short-term impacts (up to three months), but without additional follow-up, the effect disappears within a year.

Social Support

Lovato & Green[70] cited social support and reinforcement as important factors in influencing participation in exercise programs, especially the support of a spouse, family, or significant others. Feedback from program staff can also be a source of social support. In a review of smoking-cessation studies, Orleans[85] noted that successful quitters reported more positive support from significant others than did relapsers or continued smokers.

Use of Incentives

In WHP programs, incentives have been offered for participation, compliance with behavior change recommendations, or achievement of certain health goals. Researchers have observed that an incentive valued at ~$100 (in 2006 dollars) is necessary to encourage the majority of employees to complete an HRA.[101] However, others have argued that incentives should be used sparingly or intermittently to avoid situations in which positive health improvements are tied directly to incentives and then healthy actions stop when incentives are removed.[25] Anderson[5] presented preliminary data at a recent conference showing that increasing incentives (typically through reductions in medical premiums) at $100 intervals (from a base of $100 in 2007 dollars) will result in incremental 10% improvements in HRA and program participation.

Culture of Health

Workplace programs embedded within a healthy company culture are more likely to succeed. A healthy company culture allows for the use of company equipment, facilities, and other forms of infrastructure to support health behaviors. In larger companies, physical plants are used to house fitness centers, on-site health education classes, and cafeterias featuring healthy food choices. Employers embodying a healthy culture can establish policies to reinforce desired behaviors and brand health improvement programs in ways that mirror other organizational initiatives.[54]

Assuring Sufficient Duration of Programs

Evaluation studies have followed WHP participants from as short a period as six months to as long as 10 years.[91] Heaney & Goetzel[57] suggest that a program must be in operation for at least one year to bring about risk reductions among employees, and Gome[55] and Moore[76] state that it may be misleading to evaluate the program in less than a year because changes that occur in the first few months of a program may not be maintained over time. Aldana[1] calculated an average study duration of 3.25 years. Consensus opinion is that WHP programs need to be in place for at least three years to measure health and financial outcomes but that annual assessments of those outcomes are necessary to track progress and fine-tune the interventions.[1,26,50,93]

SUMMARY FINDINGS FROM BENCHMARK STUDIES

This review has touched on several individual components of WHP. Large-scale benchmarking and promising practice studies, conducted over the past decade, have looked at broad and general themes emanating from successful WHP programs. A review of benchmarking and best-practice studies was recently published by Goetzel et al.,[54] and their observations mirror many of the individual success factors already noted. On the basis of findings from previous studies, coupled with discussions with subject matter experts and observations from site visits to several exemplary programs, the authors identified the following as effective WHP practices: (*a*) integrating WHP programs into the organization's central operations; (*b*) addressing individual, environmental, policy, and cultural factors affecting health and productivity; (*c*) targeting several health issues simultaneously; (*d*) tailoring programs to address specific needs of the population; (*e*) attaining high participation rates; (*f*) rigorously evaluating outcomes; and (*g*) effectively communicating these outcomes to key stakeholders.

REPRODUCIBILITY OF PROMISING PRACTICE PROGRAMS

Although insights about effective WHP programs are available in the scientific literature, many employers, especially small businesses, lack the knowledge and experience to design, implement, and evaluate effective programs likely to achieve desired outcomes.[42] No large-scale education, communication,

and dissemination efforts have been launched in this area, and consequently, we need better marketing and real-world application of current and emerging knowledge related to WHP—knowledge about what works, what does not work, and where significant gaps in knowledge exist.

More consistent evaluation of these interventions, their impact, and their potential for translation into public health practice is needed. Careful evaluation can improve the information relevant to translation issues (e.g., critical success factors, impediments) and thus provide needed data to public health practitioners, employers, local communities, organizations, and individual consumers to make informed health-promotion practice decisions.

Moreover, well-structured and large-scale experiments examining the application of commercially developed health-promotion programs are still in their infancy. Although several key process components leading to successful program outcomes have been documented and applied by leading employers, there is insufficient evaluation of program outcomes, especially financial outcomes, using rigorous study methods. Thus more research is needed before early successful WHP applications can be generalized to the broader employer community.

CONCLUSIONS

Recently, interest in WHP has increased dramatically. Examples of increased activity in this area include the work of Partnership for Prevention in promoting the Leading by Example Initiative,[89] the Score Card Project from the Health Enhancement Research Organization (HERO),[56] the National Committee for Quality Assurance (NCQA) interest in accrediting and certifying health-promotion vendors,[79] the CDC Foundation Worksite Initiative,[22] the Conference Board Health Promotion Consortium,[28] the NIOSH/CDC Work-Life Symposium,[23] and several research studies funded by the CDC[21] and National Institutes of Health[115] focused on work site health promotion and disease prevention programs.

To maintain their momentum and achieve the status of a must-have company benefit, WHP programs will need to document enduring health improvements for their targeted population and related cost impacts. This involves periodically measuring the health risks of their workers and evaluating changes in health behaviors, biometric measures, and utilization of health care services. Furthermore, for WHP programs to be deemed successful, they will need to engage large segments of the population, especially those with the greatest need for such programs.

In addition, to remain viable and sustainable as a business investment, WHP programs will need to produce data supporting their cost-effectiveness and cost-benefit. To achieve a positive ROI, programs will need to be funded at an optimal investment level so that program savings can be deemed acceptable or, ideally, equal to or greater than program expenses. Knowing the tipping point—how much to spend to improve health and save money—is currently an unanswered question for most employers. Hence, more research is needed on the optimal design and cost of interventions, and this research must reach employers for these programs to be applied more broadly.

The notion of delivering health improvement at a reasonable cost through WHP is the key to achieving greater support from private and public employers. Very few newly approved medical interventions actually save money, but they can improve health at a reasonable expense. However, this notion has rarely been used when considering the value of health-improvement programs. Instead, the more difficult-to-achieve objective of realizing net savings has been required in WHP program evaluations.[16] As employers and other payers acknowledge that investments in WHP are long-term in nature, and that there may be a significant lag between improvements in health and savings in medical expenditures or improvements in productivity, the importance of documenting cost-effectiveness may become a higher priority.

Today, many employers (especially large ones) provide WHP programs because they believe that good health care programs increase worker productivity and organizational effectiveness. Their view is that paying for quality health care and WHP programs is not just the cost of doing business, but rather is an investment in their human capital. As evaluations of WHP programs become more sophisticated, program impact estimates are likely to expand to include productivity measures and their effects on ROI. This will require the ability to link multiple sources of data to fully investigate the impact of WHP programs.

Sophisticated employers are also becoming increasingly aware that to improve the health and well-being of workers, they also need to address the organizational, environmental, and ecological elements of the workplace. Preliminary evidence suggests that the physical environment affects workers' physical activity levels and dietary habits.[4,14,20,37,98,99]

An organization is supportive of individual health-improvement efforts when it provides environmental and ecological supports for health improvement such as offering healthy food choices in cafeterias, stocking vending machines with nutritious snacks, requiring company-sponsored meals to be healthy, providing opportunities for physical activity, having a campus-wide no-smoking policy, making staircases attractive, and providing benefit coverage for recommended preventive screenings. Although many of these environmental and policy innovations have already been introduced at work sites, there is still sparse research on their individual and combined effects on such outcomes as improving the health of workers, reducing utilization of health care services, and improving worker productivity.

Consistent with this notion is a small but growing movement to integrate occupational safety initiatives with work site health promotion.[32,44,100,106,107] Evidence shows that poor health increases the likelihood of industrial accidents or injuries.[32,100,106] If that is the case, successfully integrated WHP and safety initiatives can also help ensure the safety of work environments, leading to healthier and more productive employees.

Finally, as noted above, several large federally funded studies are currently underway to test alternative WHP models. Armed with better and more practical data on program effects, federal, state, and local governments can play a larger role in disseminating information about evidence-based programs, with the expectation that such dissemination will prompt more employers to adopt these programs. Through legislative or other initiatives, government agencies may also support financial incentives (e.g., tax credits) to encourage employers to implement effective programs.

DISCLOSURE STATEMENT

The authors have been engaged in work site health promotion evaluation research for over a decade. Support for such research has been provided by organizations implementing programs, federal, state and local governments. They have also functioned as paid consultants to businesses wishing to design, implement, and evaluate their work site programs.

ACKNOWLEDGMENTS
No external funding was provided for the preparation of this paper. The authors would like to thank Jennie Bowen for her help in providing background research and editing the final manuscript. The opinions expressed in this paper are the authors' and do not necessarily represent the opinions of Thomson Healthcare or Cornell University. This article was written while R.G. was Director of the Institute for Health and Productivity Studies at Cornell University. R.G. is now a Professor in the Department of

Health Policy and Management, Rollins School of Public Health, at Emory University.

• • • References

1. Aldana SG. 2001. Financial impact of health promotion programs: a comprehensive review of the literature. *Am. J. Health Promot.* 15:296-320.

2. Aldana SG, Pronk NP. 2001. Health promotion programs, modifiable health risks, and employee absenteeism. *J. Occup. Environ. Med.* 43:36-46.

3. Amler RW, Dull HB, eds. 1987. *Closing the Gap: The Burden of Unnecessary Illness.* New York: Oxford Univ. Press.

4. Andersen RE, Franckowiak SC, Snyder J, Bartlett SJ, Fontaine KR. 1998. Can inexpensive signs encourage the use of stairs? Results from a community intervention. *Ann. Intern. Med.* 129:363-69.

5. Anderson D. 2007. *EHM: What really works?* Presented at HERO Forum for Empl. Health Manag. Solut. New Orleans, LA.

6. Anderson DR, Staufacker MJ. 1996. The impact of worksite-based health risk appraisal on health-related outcomes: a review of the literature. *Am. J. Health Promot.* 10:499-508.

7. Anderson DR, Whitmer RW, Goetzel RZ, Ozminkowski RJ, Dunn RL, et al. 2000. The relationship between modifiable health risks and group-level health care expenditures: a group-level analysis of the HERO database. *Am. J. Health Promot.* 15:45-52.

8. Assoc. Worksite Health Promot. 1999. *1999 National Worksite Health Promotion Survey.* Northbrook, IL: AWHP.

9. Baun WB. 1995. The impact of worksite health promotion programs on absenteeism. In *Health Promotion Economics: Consensus and Analysis,* pp. 131-45. Champaign, IL: Hum. Kinet. Publ.

10. Baun WB, Bernacki EJ, Tsai SP. 1986. A preliminary investigation: effect of a corporate fitness program on absenteeism and health care cost. *J. Occup. Med.* 28:18-22.

11. Bell B, Blanke D. 1989. The effects of a worksite fitness program on employee absenteeism. *Health Values* 13:3-11.

12. Bertera RL. 1990. The effects of workplace health promotion on absenteeism and employment costs in a large industrial population. *Am. J. Public Health* 80:1101-5.

13. Bertera RL. 1991. The effects of behavioral risks on absenteeism and health-care costs in the workplace. *J. Occup. Med.* 33:1119-24.

14. Blamey A, Mutrie N, Aitchison T. 1995. Health promotion by encouraged use of stairs. *BMJ* 311:289-90.

15. Bly JL, Jones RC, Richardson JE. 1986. Impact of worksite health promotion on health care costs and utilization. Evaluation of Johnson & Johnson's Live for Life program. *JAMA* 256:3235-40.

16. Bondi MA, Harris JR, Atkins D, French ME, Umland B. 2006. Employer coverage of clinical preventive services in the United States. *Am. J. Health Promot.* 20(3):214-22. Abstract: http://www.rwjf.org/pr/product.jsp?id=15085.

17. Bowne DW, Russell ML, Morgan JL, Optenberg SA, Clarke AE. 1984. Reduced disability and health care costs in an industrial fitness program. *J. Occup. Med.* 26:809-16.

18. Breslow L, Breslow N. 1993. Health practices and disability: some evidence from Alameda County. *Prev. Med.* 22:86-95.

19. Breslow L, Fielding J, Herrman AA, Wilbur CS. 1990. Worksite health promotion: its evolution and the Johnson & Johnson experience. *Prev. Med.* 19:13-21.

20. Brownell KD, Stunkard AJ, Albaum JM. 1980. Evaluation and modification of exercise patterns in the natural environment. *Am. J. Psychiatry* 137:1540-45.

21. Cent. Dis. Control Prev. 2007. *CDC home page.* http://www.cdc.gov/.

22. Cent. Dis. Control Prev. 2007. *Healthier worksite initiative.* http://www.cdc.gov/nccdphp/dnpa/hwi/program design/funding.htm.

23. Cent. Dis. Control Prev. Natl. Inst. Occup. Safety Health. 2007. *NIOSH WorkLife Initiative.* http://www.cdc.gov/niosh/worklife/.

24. Chaney C. 1988. *Effects of an Employee Fitness and Lifestyle Modification Program upon Health Care Costs, Absenteeism, and Job Satisfaction.* Ann Arbor, MI: Univ. Microfilms.

25. Chapman LS. 2003. Meta-evaluation of worksite health promotion economic return studies. *Art Health Promot. (Am. J. Health Promot. Suppl.)* 6:1-16.

26. Chapman LS. 2005. Meta-evaluation of worksite health promotion economic return studies: 2005 update. *Am. J. Health Promot.* 19:1-11.

27. Comm. Chronic Illness. 1957. *Chronic Illness in the United States.* Cambridge, MA: Harvard Univ. Press.

28. Conf. Board. 2007. *The Conference Board home page.* http://www.conference-board.org/.

29. Conrad KM, Blue CL. 1995. Physical fitness and employee absenteeism: measurement considerations for programs. *AAOHN J.* 43:577-87; quiz 88-89.

30. Conrad KM, Riedel JE, Gibbs JO. 1990. Effect of worksite health promotion programs on employee

absenteeism. A comparative analysis. *AAOHN J.* 38:573-80.

31. Dalton BA, Harris JS. 1991. A comprehensive approach to corporate health management. *J. Occup. Med.* 33:338-48.

32. DeJoy DM, Southern DJ. 1993. An integrative perspective on worksite health promotion. *J. Occup. Med.* 35:1221-30.

33. DMAA Care Contin. Alliance. 2007. *Welcome to DMAA: The Care Continuum Alliance.* http://www.dmaa.org/.

34. Erfurt JC, Foote A. 1990. Maintenance of blood pressure treatment and control after discontinuation of work site follow-up. *J. Occup. Med.* 32:513-20.

35. Erfurt JC, Foote A, Heirich MA. 1991. Worksite wellness programs: incremental comparison of screening and referral alone, health education, follow-up counseling, and plant organization. *Am. J. Health Promot.* 5:438-48.

36. Finkelstein E, Fiebelkorn C, Wang G. 2005. The costs of obesity among full-time employees. *Am. J. Health Promot.* 20:45-51.

37. French SA, Story M, Jeffery RW. 2001. Environmental influences on eating and physical activity. *Annu. Rev. Public Health* 22:309-35.

38. Fries JF, Bloch DA, Harrington H, Richardson N, Beck R. 1993. Two-year results of a randomized controlled trial of a health promotion program in a retiree population: the Bank of America Study. *Am. J. Med.* 94:455-62.

39. Fries JF, Harrington H, Edwards R, Kent LA, Richardson N. 1994. Randomized controlled trial of cost reductions from a health education program: the California Public Employees' Retirement System (PERS) study. *Am. J. Health Promot.* 8:216-23.

40. Fronstin P, Helman R. 2000. Small employers and health benefits; findings from the 2000 Small Employer Health Benefits Survey. *EBRI Issue Brief.* 226:1-22.

41. Goetzel RZ. 1997. Essential building blocks for successful worksite health promotion programs. *Manag. Employ Health Bene.* 6:1-6.

42. Goetzel RZ. 2001. A corporate perspective: reflections from the economic buyer of health promotion programs. *Am. J. Health Promot.* 15:357.

43. Goetzel RZ. 2001. The role of business in improving the health of workers and the community. *Report prepared under contract for the Inst. Med. (IOM) of the Natl. Acad. Sci. (NAS).*

44. Goetzel RZ. 2005. *Examining the Value of Integrating Occupational Health and Safety and Health Promotion Programs in the Workplace.* Rockville, MD: US Dep. Health Hum. Serv., Public Health Serv., Cent. Dis. Control, Natl. Inst. Occup. Saf. Health.

45. Goetzel RZ, Anderson DR, Whitmer W, Ozminkowski RJ, Dunn RL, et al. 1998. The relationship between modifiable health risks and health care expenditures: an analysis of the multi-employer HERO health risk and cost database. *J. Occup. Environ. Med.* 4:843-57.

46. Goetzel RZ, Dunn RL, Ozminkowski RJ, Satin K, Whitehead D, Cahill K. 1998. Differences between descriptive and multivariate estimates of the impact of Chevron Corporation's Health Quest Program on medical expenditures. *J. Occup. Environ. Med.* 40:538-45.

47. Goetzel RZ, Guindon A, Humphries L, Newton P, Turshen J, Webb R. 1998. *Health and Productivity Management: Consortium Benchmarking Study Best Practice Report.* Houston, TX: Am. Prod. Qual. Cent. Int. Benchmarking Clear.

48. Goetzel RZ, Hawkins K, Ozminkowski RJ, Wang S. 2003. The health and productivity cost burden of the "top 10" physical and mental health conditions affecting six large U.S. employers in 1999. *J. Occup. Environ. Med.* 45:5-14.

49. Goetzel RZ, Jacobson BH, Aldana SG, Vardell K, Yee L. 1998. Health care costs of worksite health promotion participants and nonparticipants. *J. Occup. Environ. Med.* 40:341-46.

50. Goetzel RZ, Juday TR, Ozminkowski RJ. 1999. What's the ROI? A systematic review of return on investment (ROI) studies of corporate health and productivity management inititatives. *AWHP's Worksite Health.* 6:12-21.

51. Goetzel RZ, Long SR, Ozminkowski RJ, Hawkins K, Wang S, Lynch W. 2004. Health, absence, disability, and presenteeism cost estimates of certain physical and mental health conditions affecting U.S. employers. *J. Occup. Environ. Med.* 46:398-412.

52. Goetzel RZ, Ozminkowski RJ, Asciutto AJ, Chouinard P, Barrett M. 2001. Survey of Koop Award winners: life-cycle insights. *Art Health Promot. (Am. J. Health Promot. Suppl.)* 5:2-8.

53. Goetzel RZ, Reynolds K, Breslow L, Roper WL, Shechter D, et al. 2007. Health promotion in later life: It's never too late. *Am. J. Health Promot.* 21:1-5, iii.

54. Goetzel RZ, Shechter D, Ozminkowski RJ, Marmet PF, Tabrizi MJ. 2007. Promising practices in employer health and productivity management efforts: findings from a benchmarking study. *J. Occup. Environ. Med.* 49:111-30.

55. Gomel M, Oldenburg B, Simpson JM, Owen N. 1993. Work-site cardiovascular risk reduction: a

randomized trial of health risk assessment, education, counseling, and incentives. *Am. J. Public Health* 83:1231-38.

56. Health Enhanc. Res. Organ. *HERO Health management best practice scorecard*. http://www.the-hero.org/scorecard.htm.

57. Heaney C, Goetzel RZ. 1998. A review of health-related outcomes of multi-component worksite health promotion programs. *Am. J. Health Promot.* 11:290-307.

58. Horowitz SM. 1987. Effects of aWorksite Wellness Program on absenteeism and health care costs in a small federal agency. *Fit. Bus.* April:167-72.

59. Jacobson BH, Aldana SG. 2001. Relationship between frequency of aerobic activity and illness-related absenteeism in a large employee sample. *J. Occup. Environ. Med.* 43:1019-25.

60. Jeffery RW, Forster JL, Dunn BV, French SA, McGovern PG, Lando HA. 1993. Effects of work-site health promotion on illness-related absenteeism. *J. Occup. Med.* 35:1142-46.

61. Kaiser Family Found., Health Res. Educ. Trust, Cent. Stud. Health Syst. Change. 2006. *Employer Health Benefits: 2006 Annual Survey*. Menlo Park, CA: Kaiser Family Found.

62. Kerr JH. 1996. Employee fitness programmes and reduced absenteeism: a case study. In *Workplace Health-Employee Fitness and Exercise*, ed. JH Kerr, T Cox, A Griffiths, pp. 159-67. London: Taylor & Francis.

63. Knight KK, Goetzel RZ, Fielding JE, Eisen M, Jackson GW, et al. 1994. An evaluation of Duke University's LIVE FOR LIFE health promotion program on changes in worker absenteeism. *J. Occup. Med.* 36:533-36.

64. Koretz G. 2002. Employers tame medical costs: but workers pick up a bigger share. *Bus. Week:* 26:26.

65. Kreuter MW, Strecher VJ. 1996. Do tailored behavior change messages enhance the effectiveness of health risk appraisal? Results from a randomized trial. *Health Educ. Res.* 11:97-105.

66. Lechner L, de Vries H, Adriaansen S, Drabbels L. 1997. Effects of an employee fitness program on reduced absenteeism. *J. Occup. Environ. Med.* 39:827-31.

67. Leigh JP, Richardson N, Beck R, Kerr C, Harrington H, et al. 1992. Randomized controlled study of a retiree health promotion program. The Bank of American Study. *Arch. Intern. Med.* 152:1201-6.

68. Linnan L, Bowling M, Lindsay G, Childress J, Blakey C, et al. 2008. Results of the 2004 NationalWorksite Health Promotion Survey. *Am. J. Public Health.* 98:In press.

69. Lorig KR, Holman H. 2003. Self-management education: history, definition, outcomes, and mechanisms. *Ann. Behav. Med.* 26:1-7.

70. Lovato CY, Green LW. 1990. Maintaining employee participation in workplace health promotion programs. *Health Educ. Q.* 17:73-88.

71. McGinnis JM. 2001. Does proof matter? Why strong evidence sometimes yields weak action. *Am. J. Health Promot.* 15:391-96.

72. McGinnis JM, Foege WH. 1993. Actual causes of death in the United States. *JAMA* 270:2207-12.

73. Mercer Health Benefits. 2006. *National Survey of Employer-Sponsored Health Plans, 2005*. http://mercerhr.com/ushealthplansurvey.

74. Mercer Healthc. Consult. 2007. *After a three-year lull, health benefit cost growth picks up a little speed in 2008*. http://www.mercer.com/pressrelease/details.jhtml?idContent=1279545.

75. Mokdad AH, Marks JS, Stroup DF, Gerberding JL. 2004. Actual causes of death in the United States, 2000. *JAMA* 291:1238-45.

76. Moore JE, Von Korff M, Cherkin D, Saunders K, Lorig KR. 2000. A randomized trial of a cognitive-behavioral program for enhancing back pain self care in a primary care setting. *Pain* 88:145-53.

77. Murray CJ, Lopez AD. 1997. Global mortality, disability, and the contribution of risk factors: Global Burden of Disease Study. *Lancet* 349:1436-42.

78. Natl. Bus. Group Health. 2007. *Summary of cost analyses of employment-based health care*. http://www.businessgrouphealth.org/members/secureDocument.cfm?docid=715.

79. Natl. Comm. Qual. Assurance. 2007. *NCQA home page*. http://web.ncqa.org/.

80. Nicholson S, Pauly MV, Polsky D, Baase CM, Billotti GM, et al. 2005. How to present the business case for healthcare quality to employers. *Appl. Health Econ. Health Policy* 4:209-18.

81. O'Donnell M. 1996. *Corporate Health Promotion and Demand Management Consortium Benchmarking Study, Final Report*. Houston, TX: Am. Prod. Qual. Cent.

82. O'Donnell M, Bishop C, Kaplan K. 1997. Benchmarking best practices in workplace health promotion. *Art Health Promot. (Am. J. Health Promot. Suppl.)* 1:1-8.

83. Off. Dis. Prev. Health Promot. 1993. Health Promotion Goes to Work: Programs with an Impact.Washington, DC: Public Health Serv., U.S. Dep. Health Hum. Serv.

84. Ogden CL, Fryar CD, Carroll MD, Flegal KM. 2004. Mean Body Weight, Height, and Body Mass Index, United States 1960-2002. Atlanta, GA:

Cent. Dis. Control Prev. http://www.cdc.gov/nchs/data/ad/ad347.pdf.

85. Orleans CT, Schoenbach VJ, Wagner EH, Quade D, Salmon MA, et al. 1991. Self-help quit smoking interventions: effects of self-help materials, social support instructions, and telephone counseling. *J. Consult. Clin. Psychol.* 59:439-48.

86. Ozminkowski RJ, Dunn RL, Goetzel RZ, Cantor RI, Murnane J, Harrison M. 1999. A return on investment evaluation of the Citibank, N.A. health management program. *Am. J. Health Promot.* 14:31-43.

87. Ozminkowski RJ, Goetzel RZ. 2001. Getting closer to the truth: overcoming research challenges when estimating the financial impact of worksite health promotion programs. *Am. J. Health Promot.* 15:289-95.

88. Ozminkowski RJ, Goetzel RZ, Wang F, Gibson TB, Shechter D, et al. 2006. The savings gained from participation in health promotion programs for Medicare beneficiaries. *J. Occup. Environ. Med.* 48:1125-32.

89. Partnersh. Prev. 2005. *Leading by Example: Improving the Bottom Line through a High Performance, Less Costly Workforce.* Washington, DC: Partnership. Prev.

90. Partnersh. Prev. 2007. *Partnership for Prevention home page.* http://www.prevent.org.

91. Pelletier KR. 1999. A review and analysis of the clinical and cost-effectiveness studies of comprehensive health promotion and disease management programs at the worksite: 1995-1998 update (IV). *Am. J. Health Promot.* 13:333-45, iii.

92. Pelletier KR. 2001. A review and analysis of the clinical- and cost-effectiveness studies of comprehensive health promotion and disease management programs at the worksite: 1998-2000 update. *Am. J. Health Promot.* 16:107-16.

93. Pelletier KR. 2005. A review and analysis of the clinical and cost-effectiveness studies of comprehensive health promotion and disease management programs at the worksite: update VI 2000-2004. *J. Occup. Environ. Med.* 47:1051-58.

94. Peterson TR, Aldana SG. 1999. Improving exercise behavior: an application of the stages of change model in a worksite setting. *Am. J. Health Promot.* 13:229-32, iii.

95. Poisal JA, Truffer C, Smith S, Sisko A, Cowan C, et al. 2007. Health spending projections through 2016: modest changes obscure part D's impact. *Health Affairs (Project Hope)* 26:w242-53.

96. Rimer BK, Orleans CT, Fleisher L, Cristinzio S, Resch N, et al. 1994. Does tailoring matter? The impact of a tailored guide on ratings and short-

term smoking-related outcomes for older smokers. *Health Educ. Res.* 9:69-84.

97. Robert Wood Johnson Found. 2007. *Grant results: Partnership for Prevention survey of employers reveals their barriers to supporting tobacco-control.* http://www.rwjf.org/ reports/grr/043596.htm.

98. Russell WD, Dzewaltowski DA, Ryan GJ. 1999. The effectiveness of a point-of-decision prompt in deterring sedentary behavior. *Am. J. Health Promot.* 13:257-59, ii.

99. Sallis JF. 2005. The built environment can encourage or obstruct healthful behavior. In *Ecology of Obesity Conference*, pp. 3-4. Ithaca, NY: Cornell Univ. Coll. Hum. Ecol.

100. Schulte PA, Wagner GR, Ostry A, Blanciforti LA, Cutlip RG, et al. 2007. Work, obesity, and occupational safety and health. *Am. J. Public Health* 97:428-36.

101. Serxner S, Anderson DR, Gold D. 2004. Building program participation: strategies for recruitment and retention in worksite health promotion programs. *Am. J. Health Promot.* 18:1-6, iii.

102. Shechter D, Goetzel RZ, Ozminkowski RJ, Stapleton D, Lapin P. 2004. *An Inventory of Senior Risk Reduction Programs and Services Offered by Health Promotion Vendors.* Omaha, NE: Wellness Counc. Am.

103. Shephard RJ. 1995. Worksite health promotion and productivity. In *Health Promotion Economics: Consensus and Analysis*, ed. RL Kaman, pp. 147-74. Champaign, IL: Hum. Kinet. Publ.

104. Shi L. 1992. The impact of increasing intensity of health promotion intervention on risk reduction. *Eval. Health Prof.* 15:3-25.

105. Song T, Shephard RJ, Cox M. 1981. Absenteeism, employee turnover and sustained exercise participation. *J. Sports Med. Phys. Fit.* 22:392-99.

106. Sorensen G, Barbeau E. 2004. *Steps to a Healthier U.S. Workforce: Integrating Occupational Health and Safety and Worksite Health Promotion: State of the Science.* Rockville, MD: US Dep. Health Hum. Serv., Public Health Serv., Cent. Dis. Control and Prev., Natl. Inst. Occup. Saf. Health. http://www.cdc.gov/niosh/worklife/steps/pdfs/ NIOSH%20integration%20ms post-symp%20 revision trckd%20done.pdf.

107. Stokols D. 1992. Establishing and maintaining health environments: toward a social ecology of health promotion. *Am. Psychol.* 47:6-22.

108. Strecher V, Wang C, Derry H, Wildenhaus K, Johnson C. 2002. Tailored interventions for multiple risk behaviors. *Health Educ. Res.* 17:619-26.

109. Task Force Comm. Prev. Serv. 2007. *Proceedings of the Task Force Meeting: Worksite Reviews.* Atlanta, GA: Cent. Dis. Control Prev.

110. Tucker LA, Aldana SG, Friedman GM. 1990. Cardiovascular fitness and absenteeism in 8,301 employed adults. *Am. J. Health Promot.* 5:140-45.

111. Univ. Mich. Health Manag. Res. Cent. 2000. *The Ultimate 20th Century Cost Benefit Analysis and Report.* Ann Arbor: Univ. Mich.

112. U.S. Dep. Health Hum. Serv. 2000. Use of the 2010 objectives by the business community. *Proc. Meet. Secr. Counc. Natl. Health Promot. Dis. Prev. Object. 2010,* Sept. 12 http://www.healthypeople. gov/Implementation/Council/council9-12-00/panel Use Business Comm.htm.

113. U.S. Dep. Health Hum. Serv. 2000. Healthy People 2010: national health promotion and disease prevention objectives. *Publ. No. (PHS) 91-50213,* Washington, DC.

114. U.S. Dep. Health Hum. Serv. 2003. *Prevention makes common "cents."* http://aspe.hhs.gov/ health/prevention/.

115. U.S. Dep. Health Hum. Serv., Natl. Inst. Health. 2007. *NIH home page.* http://www.nih.gov/.

116. Wellness Counc. Am. 2007. *Seven benchmarks of success.* http://www.welcoa.org/wellworkplace/ index.php?category=2.

117. Wilson M, Holman P, Hammock A. 1996. A comprehensive review of the effects of worksite health promotion on health related outcomes. *Am. J. Health Promot.* 10:429-35.

118. Wood EA, Olmstead GW, Craig JL. 1989. An evaluation of lifestyle risk factors and absenteeism after two years in a worksite health promotion program. *Am. J. Health Promot.* 4:128-33.

119. Zaza S, Wright-De Aguero LK, Briss PA, Truman BI, Hopkins DP, et al. 2000. Data collection instrument and procedure for systematic reviews in the Guide to Community Preventive Services. Task Force on Community Preventive Services. *Am. J. Prev. Med.* 18:44-74.

4

Healthy Communities Preventing Chronic Disease by Activating Grassroots Change: At a Glance 2009

Source: Center for Disease Control and Prevention. Healthy Communities Preventing Chronic Disease by Activating Grassroots Change: At a Glance 2009. Accessible at http://www.cdc.gov/chronicdisease/resources/publications/AAG/pdf/healthy_communities.pdf

NATIONAL CHRONIC DISEASE CRISIS: THE TIME TO ACT IS NOW

Our nation faces a crisis in the burden of chronic disease. Today, 7 of the 10 leading causes of death in the United States are chronic diseases, and almost 50% of Americans live with at least one chronic illness. People who suffer from chronic diseases, such as heart disease, stroke, diabetes, cancer, obesity, and arthritis, experience limitations to function, health, activity, and work, affecting the quality of their lives as well as the lives of their families.

Treatment for people with chronic conditions accounts for more than 75% of the $2 trillion spent on annual U.S. medical care costs. Effectively addressing the national chronic disease crisis is central to the future of health care in our nation and a priority for policy makers and those who pay for public and private health insurance plans.

Preventable health risk factors such as lack of physical activity, poor diet, and tobacco and excessive alcohol use contribute to the development and severity of many chronic diseases. For example,

- In the last 15 years, the number of people in the United States with diagnosed diabetes has more than doubled, reaching 17.9 million in 2007. If current trends continue, one-third of all children born in 2000 will develop type 2 diabetes during their lifetime.

- More than one-third of all adults do not meet recommendations for aerobic physical activity based on the 2008 *Physical Activity Guidelines for Americans*.

- Tobacco use is the single-most avoidable cause of disease, disability, and death in the United States. Each year, an estimated 443,000 people die prematurely from smoking or exposure to secondhand smoke. Despite these risks, more than 43 million (approximately 1 in 5) American adults still smoke.

- During 2001-2005, there were approximately 79,000 deaths annually caused by excessive alcohol use. Excessive alcohol use is the third leading lifestyle-related cause of death for Americans each year.

Health disparities continue to be a serious threat to the health and well-being of specific population groups. For example,

- Death rates for heart disease are 23.4% higher among African Americans than whites; death rates for stroke are 31.4% higher.

- Native American adults are twice as likely as white adults to have diabetes.

Chronic Diseases: The Facts

- **Heart disease** and **stroke** remain the first and third leading causes of death, accounting for more than 30% of all mortality. One million Americans are disabled from strokes; many can no longer perform daily tasks, such as walking or bathing, without help.
- Nearly 24 million Americans have **diabetes,** and an estimated 57 million American adults have prediabetes and are at increased risk for developing type 2 diabetes. Diabetes is the leading cause of kidney failure, non-traumatic lower-extremity amputations, and blindness among adults aged 20-74 years.
- **Cancer** claims more than half a million lives each year and remains the nation's second leading cause of death. The total number of Americans living with a previous diagnosis of cancer is currently estimated at 11 million.
- 1 in every 3 adults and almost 1 in 5 children between the ages of 6 and 19 are obese. **Obesity** has been linked to increased risk for heart disease, high blood pressure, type 2 diabetes, arthritis-related disability, and some cancers.
- An estimated 46 million adults in the United States reported being told by a doctor that they have some form of **arthritis,** rheumatoid arthritis, gout, lupus, or fibromyalgia. Arthritis results in activity limitations for nearly 19 million Americans

PRODUCING RESULTS

Strong action at the community level is critical to reversing chronic disease trends. Communities have responded with a groundswell of energy, ideas, and the will to make needed changes by targeting chronic diseases and their major risk factors including tobacco and excessive alcohol use, insufficient physical activity, and poor nutrition. CDC's investments in local communities are producing results. For example, CDC invested in 40 Steps communities during Fiscal Years 2003-2008, with the following impressive outcomes:

- **Broome County, New York,** increased fruit and vegetable consumption by 14% in all 46 elementary and middle schools by using a consolidated bid to purchase healthy foods at lower costs. More than 50,000 people enrolled in an innovative walking program and the percentage of adults who walked for more than 30 minutes on 5 or more days each week increased from 47% to 54% in 1 year.
- **Austin, Texas,** established a work site wellness program at Capital Metro, the Austin

transit authority. Employee absences dropped more than 44% and the annual increases in health care costs were reduced from 27% to 9%.

- The **River Region of Alabama** worked with communities to control diabetes. Emergency room visits among participants decreased by more than 50%.
- Across the **40 funded communities,** the percentage of adult smokers who were advised to quit by a health care provider increased from 63% to 71% during 2004-2006, and the percentage of adults with diabetes who reported having a foot exam in the past year increased from 71% to 77%.

Building upon the lessons learned from these communities, CDC is expanding its efforts to assist hundreds of communities across the nation.

CDC EXPANDS EFFORTS

CDC and its partners—local and state health departments and national organizations—are working through CDC's Healthy Communities Program to create healthier, thriving communities and help those communities most severely effected by chronic disease. The program mobilizes community resources to bring change to the places and organizations that touch people's lives every day-at work sites, schools, community centers, and health care settings-to stem the growth of chronic disease.

Local Investments

CDC funds and supports local communities for 5-year periods. Participating communities create online action guides, which give step-by-step instructions for replicating effective strategies from their communities. CDC currently provides guidance, technical assistance, and training to 12 Strategic Alliance for Health (SAH) communities selected to represent a mix of urban, rural, and tribal communities. During 2003-2008, CDC supported 40 SAH communities.

CDC will train and support over 200 **ACHIEVE** (Action Communities for Health, Innovation, and Environmental Change) communities over the next several years. ACHIEVE selects communities to participate in an Action Institute, in which community leaders receive technical assistance and support to start a local action plan. Technical assistance is provided by national and state experts for a minimum of 3 years, and communities also receive modest financial support. CDC collaborates with five key national organizations to provide this technical and financial support, including

- The National Association of Chronic Disease Directors
- The National Association of County and City Health Officials
- The National Recreation and Park Association
- The Society for Public Health Education
- The YMCA of the USA

CDC also supports the **YMCA of the USA's Pioneering Healthier Communities** initiative. Since 2004, CDC has provided funding and technical support to the YMCA and used its vast network to bring together key local leaders to improve health and confront the national crises of obesity and chronic disease. Through its Pioneering Healthier Communities Program, the YMCA of the USA has developed innovative models for community change and has convened, trained, and supported teams of key leaders in 81 communities. By 2010, approximately 100 communities will have made changes to their communities to support healthy lifestyles and reduce risk factors for chronic disease.

Action Institutes

CDC provides **Action Institutes**, which convene community action teams and train community leaders making policy, systems, and environmental changes to prevent and control chronic diseases and their risk factors. Community action teams receive training from innovative national experts and develop a plan of action during the 3-day institute. They also hear from peer communities about how to undertake an effective community-change process and gain access to a range of tools and resources for putting programs into action.

Mobilizing National Networks for Community Change

Through its Healthy Communities Program, CDC is engaging in innovative new partnerships that reach across communities and engage local planners, decision makers, and community organizations whose primary mission is not necessarily health, but whose efforts can have a profound impact on health and chronic disease.

Tools for Community Action

CDC provides national leadership in health promotion at the community level by making the following tools for local action universally available to individuals and organizations:

Community Health Resources Web Site. This CDC Web site (http://www.cdc.gov/community healthresources) gives communities a searchable portal through which they can access a wide range of tools and data for local health promotion.

Action Guides. CDC and Partnership for Prevention® have developed *The Community Health Promotion Handbook,* available at http://www. prevent.org/actionguides, which provides communities with step-by-step guidance for implementing five effective community-level health promotion strategies identified in *The Guide to Community Preventive Services.*

Additional Action Guides are planned.

CHANGE (Community Health Assessment and Group Evaluation). This tool provides community leaders with a snapshot of local policy, systems, and environmental change strategies currently in place in their community; identifies areas where such health strategies are lacking; and assists communities in defining and prioritizing areas for improvement.

Promoting Health Equity—A Resource to Help Communities Address Social Determinants of Health. This workbook, available at http://www. cdc.gov/nccdphp/dach/chaps, shows communities how to address social determinants of health as part of health and social service efforts through real examples from communities that are using this approach.

Future Directions: Spreading Change Across the Nation. Turning the tide on chronic disease requires changes in our communities that support health where we live, learn, work, and play. To date, more than 240 communities have received funding and technical support through CDC's Healthy Communities Program, which has resulted in measurable changes at the local level. An additional 260 communities will receive funding to improve the health of their communities during the next 5 years. The Healthy Communities Program will continue to disseminate effective strategies and provide communities with funding; tools; and training for creating policy, systems, and environmental changes. Working with key partners, CDC will activate these changes in a widening network of communities that are ready to take action.

For More Information

For more information about CDC's Healthy Communities Program, please contact the Centers for Disease Control and Prevention National Center for Chronic Disease Prevention and Health Promotion: 4770 Buford Highway NE, Mail Stop K–93, Atlanta, GA 30341-3717. Telephone: 770-488-6452. E-mail: cdcinfo@cdc.gov. Web: http://www.cdc.gov/HealthyCommunitiesProgram.

5

Biological Determinants of Health

The biological makeup of a person is where ultimately the social and behavioral elements, discussed in the previous two chapters, coalesce with the human biology to determine the individual's health and well-being. In fact, there is significant interaction between the social, behavioral, and biological factors in determining an individual's health.

A person's genetic makeup has been well recognized as an important determinant of health, well-being, and premature death (Blum 1981; CDC 1979). Hence, a person's ancestry, race, and ethnicity play a role in determining susceptibility to disease, disability, and longevity apart from social and behavioral factors and access to medical care. Family health history and risk assessment have, therefore, become important tools in the delivery of medical care. Although race is a dominant social determinant of health, its biological implications cannot be ignored. For example, sickle cell anemia is a blood disorder that affects primarily the African American population in the United States. Certain genetic diseases affect individuals of Eastern European Jewish descent.

Genomic medicine—the use of information from genomes and their derivatives (RNA, proteins, and metabolites) to guide medical decision-making—is now a key component of personalized medicine. A rapidly advancing field of health care, *personalized medicine* is informed by each person's unique clinical, genetic, genomic, and environmental information (Ginsburg & Willard, 2009).

There is now clear evidence that the pace and pathway of early growth is a major risk factor for the development of a group of chronic diseases that include coronary heart disease, stroke, type-2 diabetes and hypertension (Barker et al. 2009). This understanding has led to a new biological model called the *fetal origins hypothesis* which states that low-birthweight babies born because of malnutrition are predisposed to adult diseases. Henriksen and Clausen (2002) propose that fetal malnutrition may be caused by placental insufficiency apart from inadequate maternal nutrition. Placental insufficiency is the failure of the placenta to supply nutrients to the unborn child and remove toxic wastes, and is clearly a biological factor. Among women with placental insufficiency syndromes, there is an increased prevalence of risk factors for cardiovascular disease (CVD). Maternal cardiovascular risk factors may therefore increase the risk of adult diseases in the offspring. In fact, malnutrition not only during fetal life but also during infancy and early childhood can permanently change the structure and function of the body, a phenomenon known as *programming*. These children can later develop coronary heart disease and type-2 diabetes (Barker et al. 2009).

Numerous studies support the notion that cumulative exposure to chronic stress is a risk factor for CVD. Various stress-related hormones have been proposed as potential mediators of the relationship between psychological stress and CVD (Kubzansky & Adler 2010). Childhood stress—which may emanate from psychological, social, and/or economic adversity—can result in negative health outcomes in later life.

Aging is another well-known biological phenomenon that is often accompanied by irreversible chronic problems, comorbidities, and disability. Certain biological functions seem to change as a person ages. For example, blood glycemic levels tend to rise with normal aging (Pani et al. 2008). The *homeostatic theory of aging* focuses on the fact that as the human body ages it becomes less able to regulate the internal environment of the body, such as regulation of body temperature and fluid balance. Aging also reduces the immune system capacity (Watson 2008). The extreme forms of memory loss which accompany dementia are associated with profound damage to areas of the brain. This may represent an acceleration of the aging process in the brain and, while many risk factors have been identified, increasing age is the strongest (Woods 2005). Atrophy is another feature of aging. The implications of muscle atrophy lead to less strength in the limbs, lowered mobility and, in extreme cases, a tendency to falls (Watson 2008). Current research suggests that many of the adverse biological processes can be slowed through appropriate lifestyle interventions.

In the first reading for this chapter, **Biological Basis of Determinants of Health**, Bortz proposes a conceptual framework according to which genes, external agency, internal agency, and aging are the determinants that effectively describe the biological experience of the organism. Although genes may determine 15% to 20% of the differences in human longevity, their real significance lies not in their essence, but in their interrelations with the other three components of health. The second component in this framework, external agency, refers to health threats that the external world presents. Apart from the treatments available through medical science, the issue of disease prevention is important when considering external agency as a health determinant.

Bortz asserts that a disordered internal function (internal agency) is the principal cause of chronic disease patterns prevalent today. Both stress (too much energy) and disuse (too little energy as manifested through a sedentary lifestyle) result in disease. Bortz refers to aging as wear and tear minus repair in a biological sense. A summation of the four agencies determines a person's health. However, only the determinants caused by faulty external and internal agency are susceptible to clinical intervention.

In **The Health of U.S. Racial and Ethnic Populations**, Williams examines several conceptual and methodological issues that can affect our knowledge of the underlying pattern of racial differences in health. The main issues are: (1) Age-adjusted rates (such as mortality rates) are not actual measures of risk; they should be used for comparison purposes only. (2) Racial comparisons that are limited to the entire population can mask subgroups that have elevated risk. (3) Magnitude of the disparity varies depending on whether we use absolute differences between rates or the relative difference, i.e., ratio between two rates. (4) Quality of the data can lead to errors. For example, there are reporting errors on death certificates, and many Hispanics report their national identity when requested to indicate their race on surveys. (5) Census data are not based on a count of all residents and the undercount varies by age, gender, and race. (6) The health status of various racial groups varies according to whether they are recent immigrants, long-term immigrants, or U.S. born. Immigration, acculturation, and socioeconomic status of foreign-born racial groups add complexity to racial health profiles. (7) Racial differences in health persist despite socio-economic status. Factors such as perceptions of discrimination, occupational contexts, housing conditions and other stressors likely play a role. Williams notes that in spite of various methodological limitations, the overall pattern of persisting racial differences in health remains. The article includes recommendations for further research.

The Effects of Childhood Stress on Health Across the Lifespan focuses on the negative aspects of childhood stress that overwhelms a child's ability to cope effectively. The authors of this report, Middlebrooks and Audage, point out that stress can disrupt early brain development and compromise functioning of the nervous and immune systems. Manifestations of early-life stress include alcoholism, depression, eating disorders, heart disease, cancer, and other chronic conditions in adults. Research differentiates between positive stress, tolerable stress, and toxic stress. Examples of the latter include violence, various types of abuse, neglect, and custodial interference. Results from the Adverse Childhood Experiences (ACE) Study of toxic stress in childhood suggest that as the number of ACE increases, the number of comorbid health conditions also increases. There is also a link between ACE and suicide attempts. The authors propose a social-ecological model to prevent child mistreatment.

In the final reading for this chapter, **Behavioral Determinants of Health Aging Revisited: An Update on the Good News for the Baby Boomer Generation,** Potkanowicz and colleagues present the latest recommendations that our growing number of older adults can use to maximize their quality of life. With the growing elderly population there is also a growing need to clarify how to approach fitness because a lack of specific information can lead to inactivity. Being the least active of all age groups, the older adult population needs this information. The authors include both physical and mental health. Physical fitness includes health-related and skill-related fitness. However, benefits of health-related fitness outweigh those of skill-related fitness in averting premature onset of hypokinetic conditions such as obesity, diabetes, and hypertension. A tool called EASY (Exercise Assessment and Screening for You) is now available that older adults can use to begin a self-directed physical activity program. The program should incorporate at least the recommended minimum levels of aerobic activity, muscle strengthening, and flexibility/balance. Recommendations for improving cognitive capacity are based on the cognitive reserve theory and the theory of neurogenesis. In practical terms, the concept of "enriched environments"—opportunities for physical activity, learning, and social interaction—seems to be the key to improving cognitive capacity. When both cognitive training and physical training are employed, they appear to have a multiplier effect in which each enhances the impact of the other.

● ● ● **References**

Barker, D.J.P., et al. 2009. Growth and chronic disease: Findings in the Helsinki Birth Cohort. *Annals of Human Biology* 36(5):445-458.

Blum, H.L. 1981. *Planning for health.* 2nd ed. New York: Human Sciences Press.

Centers for Disease Control and Prevention (CDC). 1979. *Healthy people: The Surgeon General's report on health promotion and disease prevention.* Washington, DC: US Department of Health and Human Services.

Ginsburg, G.S. and H.F. Willard. 2009. Genomic and personalized medicine: Foundations and applications. *The Journal of Laboratory and Clinical Medicine* 154(6):277-287.

Henriksen, T. and T. Clausen. 2002. The fetal origins hypothesis: placental insufficiency and inheritance versus maternal malnutrition in well-nourished populations. *Acta Obstetricia & Gynecologica Scandinavica* 81(2):112-114.

Kubzansky, L.D. and G.K. Adler. 2010. Aldosterone: A forgotten mediator of the relationship between psychological stress and heart disease. *Neuroscience & Biobehavioral Reviews* 34(1):80-86.

Pani, L.N., et al. 2008. Effect of aging on A1C levels in individuals without diabetes. *Diabetes Care* 31(10): 1991-1996.

Watson, R. 2008. Research into ageing and older people. *Journal of Nursing Management* 16(2):99–104.

Woods, B. 2005. Dementia. In *The Cambridge Handbook of Age and Ageing* (M.L. Johnson ed.), pp. 252–260. Cambridge University Press, Cambridge.

1

Biological Basis of Determinants of Health

Source: Bortz, W.M. 2005. Biological basis of determinants of health. *American Journal of Public Health* 95 (3): 389-392. Reprinted with permission of the American Public Health Association.

Zimmerman's Law states "No one notices when things go right." This simple homily underlies the fact that 95% of the U.S. healthcare economy is allocated for direct medical care, and only 5% is allocated to health improvement.[1]

Aligned with this economic reality is the fact that medical science has devoted almost the entirety of its intellectual and financial capital to the elucidation of disease mechanisms and their relief. The pathogenesis of most illness is now known in great detail, yet the causative features that underlie health remain largely unexplored.

It is commonly acknowledged that the root causes of both disease and health involve multiple agencies. The hierarchical nature of multiple causes, "causes of causes," recognizes that some causes are more proximate or immediate than others.[2] The death certificate form in California requests the following information: (1) immediate cause of death, (2) secondary cause of death, and (3) other contributing conditions. McGinnis and Foege examined this "cause of cause" idea in their article "Actual Causes of Death in the United States."[3] McGinnis and Foege contrasted the traditional list of causes of death with actual causes, most of which were behavioral and lifestyle in origin.

The summary of the determinants of health provided in *Healthy People 2010* displays multiple contributing agencies within an interactive matrix formulation (Figure 1).[4(p18, Figure 7)] However, within the formulation, it is evident that the biological factors are more proximate determinants than the socioeconomic contributors, which are upstream and ultimate in their role. Nearly the entirety of the March-April 2002 issue of *Health Affairs* was devoted to the determinants of health and emphasized the social ecology in which health is enmeshed. Deaton lamented the ignorance of the biological determinants that are not revealed by clinical measurements and that are obscured by the long time interval between cause and outcome.[2] However, it is from biological factors that the functional well-being of the organism basically derives as the final common pathway to health. I explore these biological determinants of health and provide a new simple conceptual framework for their consideration. I hope that such a proposition assists in strategic planning that differentiates those determinants that are tractable and those that currently lie outside clinical approach.[4]

DETERMINANTS OF HEALTH

To establish a conceptual framework for the biological determinants of health, I propose 4 discrete agencies. The metaphor of car health may help establish this scheme. The life of a car depends on 4 elements:

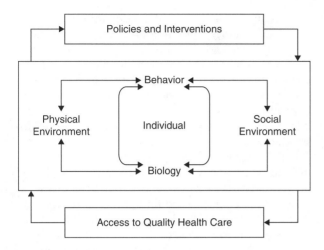

Figure 1 Determinants of health. *Source:* Adapted from Healthy People 2010: Understanding and Improving Health.[4]

design, accidents, maintenance, and aging. If the car is a "lemon," is involved in many accidents, or is poorly maintained, it will not have the chance to grow old. These same 4 categories apply to the human organism but are more appropriately designated as (1) genes, (2) external agency, (3) internal agency, and (4) aging.

I propose that these 4 factors account, occurring in innumerable combinations and chronologies, for the totality of the human health experience, both individual and collective. Hypothetically, if the first 3 of these 4 factors could be eliminated through a perfect design or gene set, no accidents or external disruptions, and ideal maintenance or balanced internal dynamics, then the car or body would have the opportunity to die of "natural causes"-aging, which rarely if ever occurs with either.

Genes

The 30,000-gene human genome was widely touted as the ultimate determinant of well-being and illness. This conjecture has now largely been displaced by the recognition that genes actually represent only restricted arbiters of health whose repertoire depends on differential cueing.[5]

Quantitatively, Strohman estimated that less than 2% of human illness is attributable to a faulty single gene locus.[6] Virtually all diseases exhibit mosaic patterns with genetic complexity. An approach widely used to quantify genetic contribution is to investigate the health history of identical twins. If genes were ultimately determinative, and the other 3 agencies were only negligible factors, identical twins would die simultaneously of the same disease. This

situation is far from the case. Common neurological diseases of older persons have been shown to have low concordance among twins.[7,8] Further, studies of monozygotic and dizygotic twins indicate that heredity accounts for 15% to 20% of the differences in human longevity.[9] Genes matter; however, their real significance lies not in their essence, but in their interrelations with the other components of health.[10]

External Agency as a Health Determinant

Throughout recent history, the major threat to human health has been the byproduct of an adverse encounter with a hostile threat. Pasteur demonstrated that the previously held attribution of sickness to metaphysical punishment motifs was wrong and that a microbe was more properly labeled as the devil.[11] The appropriate recourse to this new reality was to construct a therapeutic armor to shield the unsuspecting host from his or her dangerous environment. The varieties of health threat that the external world presents are immense in scope and timing. Injury, infection, and malignancy each are huge demerits. These threats may diminish the health reserve catastrophically or may conspire through the accumulation of trivial or sequential insults. For the most part, they are acute in their representation and are usually confined to a defect in one of the body's component parts.

In my opinion, the conditions involved in external agency are responsible for the development of the majority of the current medical enterprise of hospitals, surgery, technology, and pharmacy. Medical science has gaudy credentials gained by confronting the conditions secondary to faulty external agency. Technical advance has allowed address and redress of countless illness states that were unapproachable just a few decades ago. In addition, the issue of prevention is presented when considering external agency as a health determinant. Most infection, injury, and malignancy is preventable—and preventing them is a strategy far preferable to curing them (cheaper, too). To paraphrase Oliver Wendell Holmes, "The shield is nobler than the spear."[12]

Internal Agency as a Health Determinant

The era of the dominance of external agents as prime determinants of health has been replaced by the reality of disordered internal function as the principal causes of the chronic illness patterns prevalent today. Conditions caused by faulty internal agency do not feature a dominant external perturbation. These conditions tend to involve the entire system rather than components as in external agency problems. Instead of the environment being a threat to well-being, internal agency connotes an appropriate and constant interplay of the host and environment. The environment becomes the source of organic order, stability, and, therefore, health. This new conceptualization is captured by the term homeodynamics, as specified by Yates.[13]

Homeodynamics is a substantially more effective term than homeostasis, helpfully supplied by Cannon more than 80 years ago.[14] Homeostasis addresses the reality of our internally stabilizing processes, but the connotation of stasis is alien to living processes. Yates's proposition defines how environmental energetic stimuli are inscribed onto the organism through myriad transduction processes. The extraordinary plasticity of all parts of our body is a vivid demonstration of how form follows function and how the body is constantly remodeling in response to the energetic field in which it is immersed. We become what we do through homeodynamic reshaping at every level.

Environmental interfacing with a healthy body has two primary expressions: fuel and energy. The role of adequate nutrition in health maintenance has been voluminously documented. Excesses and deficiencies exact certain tolls. Less well displayed is the health risk posed by inappropriate energetic stimulation. This maladaptation becomes increasingly important as age proceeds. This misapplied energy comes in two forms: too much and too little. Too much energetic interfacing is known by the term stress; too little is known as disuse. Both have vast negative consequences on the afflicted organism, and both are inadequately recognized as basic health threats. Part of the reason for their lack of proximal recognition, diagnosis, and treatment is the long timeline from cause to effect.

Selye first elaborated the diverse spectrum of stressors with which organisms are assaulted. He labeled the host response to these challenges the "general adaptation syndrome."[15] McEwen coined the term "allostatic load" to quantitate the cumulative physiological toll exerted on a body over time by efforts to adapt to life experience.[16] A 1997 report by Seeman et al. indicated that allostatic load was a better predictor of cognitive decline and cardiovascular performance in older persons than more standard parameters.[17]

The converse of stress is disuse; disuse means too little energetic interchange, usually manifested through a sedentary lifestyle. I codified the common clinical parameters within the rubric of the "disuse syndrome"[18]: cardiovascular vulnerability, musculoskeletal fragility, immunologic susceptibility, metabolic instability, depression, and precocious aging. Each of these diverse components has discrete, deterministic mechanisms that relate insufficient energetic throughput to the frequently observed disease byproduct. They are not genetic or externally produced, nor are they secondary to aging per se; instead, they are the byproducts of protracted disuse.

The most vivid demonstration of disuse occurs in muscle. With continued use, muscle strength and power deteriorates at a slow rate, but with disuse, as in space travel or a casted limb, muscle strength can decay at 1% per day.[19] Every organ, tissue, and function is beholden to this appropriate homeodynamic linkage. The energy transduction and gene expression details inherent in this remodeling are now known in great detail.

"VO$_2$ max" is a congregate, physiological parameter that collectively reflects how an organism extracts oxygen from the atmosphere and conducts it through the respiratory and circulatory systems to every cell, where it is used to provide the spark that fuels metabolism and runs life. A physically fit person exhibits a decline in VO$_2$ max at the rate of 0.5% per year. An unfit person, conversely, loses this basic competence at the rate of 2% per year—4 times as fast. This is not the result of bad genes or extrinsic agency or aging; it is the result of faulty internal agency.[20] Both muscle strength and VO$_2$ max have been shown to be powerful, predictive biomarkers for subsequent disability and death.[21,22]

In my opinion, this category—defective internal agency—is the predominant determinant of failing health in older people, particularly because chronic, time-sensitive illnesses are our most common demons. Unfortunately, the competence of the medical enterprise and its curing mission finds only limited success with the conditions attributable to defective internal agency. Heart disease, arthritis, type II diabetes, and strokes are palliated at great cost, but they are not cured. However, they are preventable through redress of energetic imbalance and nutritional excess.

Aging

The participation of the process of aging in the human condition has long been the province of playwrights, theologians, and charlatans. Only recently has aging been held to rigorous analysis. No longer is it considered a disease susceptible to a curing potion, gland, or surgery. Instead, it is seen as a lifelong development and undevelopment process that lends itself to a thermodynamic analysis within Yates' formulation of homeodynamics.[13] Aging is the result of entropic decay inherent in metabolic process, which is partially but incompletely offset by countering mechanisms. Aging is wear and tear minus repair.

In the past 10 years, 2 reports provided a vital, quantitative measure of the basic rate of aging.[23,24] The decline in function in 12 organ systems has an underlying rate of 0.5% per year in all systems, from ages 30 through 70, where most data are available. This figure is thought, therefore, to represent the underlying rate at which health reserves are debited, specifically, because of chronological, entropic age process. The 0.5% per year rate of decline also describes the age rate of decline in several athletic performances.[23] Previously noted were observed rates ranging from 2% per year to 1% per week. Such declines are commonly ascribed to aging. However, these declines are caused not by aging but by more tractable agencies.

DISCUSSION

Consideration of the healthy state leads directly to an estimate of the functional capacity of the organism. A wide range of function assessment tools exist, ranging from daily activity rating scales to technical physiological measurements. The recognition that there is a maximum, total capacity is intrinsic to an effort to assess the amount of health an organism possesses. Health not only exists at the basal resting state but also exhibits substantial reserve. Such reserve relates clearly to the evolutionary need for organisms to withstand environmental perturbation of substantial variety and extent. Food and fluid availability, temperature extremes, elevation, and energetic loads are the major challenges. For example, a Tour de France cyclist may expend 8,000 calories per day for a month, which is several times basal energetic turnover. Physical conditioning implies a full expansion of reserve capacities in which linked, but separate, bodily functions scale together. This systemic, morphological, and physiological reaction to an increased load lies, in my view, at the heart of why physical exercise displays such a wide scope of anabolic benefit.

Diamond surveyed a series of "biological safety factors" in a variety of species from squid to primates and found a range of 1.3 to 10 total functional to basal capacity.[25] In humans, the reserve margin of health is most easily observed in the case of the paired organs in which a total loss of 1 organ leads to little apparent loss in function. Many other capacities—cardiac reserve, oxygen transport, neurotransmitter levels, muscle power, arterial cross-section, creatinine clearance, liver mass, sensory and cognitive capacities—exhibit similar safety margins. A common, but not universal, implication is that not until 70% of maximal capacity is lost does symptomatic impairment of health appear.[26] Verdery termed the zone of 20% to 40% of maximal function "the disability to survival span."[27] The World Health Organization proposed that health represents that state before impaired health becomes apparent.[28] Clearly the lack of awareness of symptomatic loss involves a substantial physiological reserve (Figure 2, not included). This concept suggests that health exists above the symptomatic threshold value of 30% of optimal/maximal function. Below 30% of maximum, there is only a small margin of safety before profound threat to function and survival occurs. I propose that it is in this 20% to 30% range where most medical encounters occur, and most expenses are generated.

A 2001 article about the ecology of medical care confirmed a 1961 report that in 1 month, 80% of adults encounter some life event perceived as ill health.[29,30] Fortunately, most of these people do not eventuate in entry to the medical system and the precipitating conditions are reversible. Only 25% call a physician in that month. Fewer than 1% require hospitalization. The clustering of serious medical encounters and expenses in a small minority of persons is repeatedly noted.[31] Most people spend most of their lives above the symptomatic threshold level of 30% of maximum capacity in the health zone.

The range of 20% to 30% of maximum capacity represents the frailty zone of precariously limited vital reserve. A person can lose 70% of his or her full function catastrophically as a result of external events, or the loss may occur more slowly from accumulated minor decrements caused by internal agency or to aging. In the real world, health is determined by a summation of the effects of 4 listed agencies. What is crucial to observe, however, is that only those determinants caused by faulty external and internal agency are susceptible to clinical intervention. Genetic aberration and the process of aging, which, although theoretically approachable, are still remote in their practicability.

Redress of disordered external and internal agencies, which quantitatively are the major biological determinants of health, is eminently practicable, and attention to the behavioral causes of these causes appears acutely necessary. Such active pursuit is the most likely strategy to succeed in fulfilling the goals of *Healthy People 2010.*[4]

About the Authors

Walter M. Bortz, MD, is with the Stanford University School of Medicine, Portola Valley, Calif.

Requests for reprints should be sent to Walter M. Bortz, MD, Stanford University School of Medicine, 167 Bolivar Lane, Portola Valley, CA, 94028 (e-mail: drwbortz@aol.com).

This article was accepted March 12, 2004.

● ● ● References

1. Iglehart JK. Influences on the health of population. *Health Aff.* 2002; 21:7-8.

2. Deaton A. Policy implications of the gradient of health and wealth. *Health Aff.* 2002;21:13-30.

3. McGinnis JM, Foege WH. Actual causes of death in the United States. *JAMA.* 1993;270:2207-2212.

4. US Department of Health and Human Services. *Healthy People 2010: Understanding and Improving Health.* Washington, DC: US Department of Health and Human Services; 2001.

5. Keller EF. *The Century of the Gene.* Cambridge, Mass: Harvard University Press; 2000.

6. Strohman R. Ancient genomes, wise bodies, and unhealthy people: limits of a genetic paradigm in biology and medicine. *Perspect Biol Med.* 1993;37: 112-145.

7. Tanner CM, Ottman R, Goldman SM, et al. Parkinson's disease in twins. *JAMA.* 1999;281: 341-346.

8. Breitner JC. Alzheimer's disease, National Academy of Sciences National Research Council Registry of Aging Twin Veterans III. Detection of cases, longitudinal results, and observations on twin concordance. *Arch Neurol.* 1995;52:763-771.

9. McGue M, Vaupel JW, Holm N, Harvald B. Longevity is moderately heritable in a sample of Danish twins born 1870-1880. *J Geront Biol Sci.* 1993; 48:3237-3244.

10. Finch CE, Tanzi RE. Genetics of aging. *Science.* 1997;278:407-411.

11. Schwartz, N. The life and work of Louis Pasteur. *J Appl Microbiol.* 1991:91:597-601.

12. Holmes OW. "Songs in Many Keys." Project Gutenberg EBook The Poetical Works of O.W. Holmes, Volume 4. Songs in Many Keys #18 in our series by Oliver Wendell Holmes, Sr. 1893. Available at: http://www2.cddc. vt.edu/gutenberg/etext05/ohp0410.txt. Accessed December 6, 2004.

13. Yates FE. Order and complexity in dynamic systems: homeodynamics as a generalized mechanism for biology. *Mathematics and Computer Modeling.* 1994;14:49-74.

14. Cannon W. Organization for load and its health consequences. *Physiol Rev* 1922;9:399-431.

15. Selye H. *The Story of the Adaptation Syndrome.* Montreal, Ontatio, Canada, ACTA; 1952.

16. McEwen BS. Allostasis, allostatic load, and the aging nervous system: role of excitatory amino acids and excitotoxicity. *Neurochem Res.* 2001;25: 1219-1231.

17. Seeman TE, Singer BH, Rowe JW, Horwitz I, McEwen BS. Price of adaptation—Price of allostatic load and its health consequences. *Arch Intern Med.* 1997;157:2259-2268.

18. Bortz W. The disuse syndrome. *West J Med.* 1984;141:691-699.

19. Muller LA. Influences of training and inactivity on muscle strength. *Arch Phys Med Rehab.* 1970;51:449-462.

20. Kasch FW, Boyer JL, VanCamp S. Cardiovascular changes with age and exercise. *Scand J Med Sci Sports.* 1995;5:147-151.

21. Laukkanen P, Heikkinem EJ, Kauppinen M. Muscle strength and mobility are predictors of survival in 75-year-old people. *Age Ageing.* 1995;24:465-473.

22. Blair SN, Kuhn KW, Barlow CE, Paffenbarger R, Gibbons LW, Macera CA. Changes in physical fitness and all cause mortality. Prospective study of healthy and non-healthy men. *JAMA.* 1995; 273:1094-1100.

23. Bortz W IV, Bortz W II. How fast do we age? Exercise performance over time as a biomarker. *J Geront.* 1996;51a:223-225.

24. SehI M, Yates FE. Rates of senescence between ages 30 and 70 years in healthy people. *J Geront.* 2000; 13:198-208.

25. Diamond J. Evaluation of biological safety factors: a cost/benefit analysis. In: Weibel ER, Taylor CR, Bolis L, eds. *Principles of Animal Design.* Cambridge, Mass: Cambridge University Press;1998:21-29.

26. Bortz W. A conceptual framework of frailty. *J Gerontol A Biol Sci Med Sci.* 2002;57:M283-M288.

27. Verdery R. Failure to thrive. In: Hazzard RR, Bierman E, Blass J, Ettinger WH, Halter JB, eds. *Principles of Geriatric Medicine and Gerontology.* 3rd ed. New York, NY: McGraw Hill;1994: 1205-1211.

28. *International Classification of Impairments, Disabilities, and Handicaps.* Geneva, Switzerland: World Health Organization: 1980.

29. White. KL, Williams TF. Greenburg BC. The ecology of medical care. *N Engl J Med.* 1961:265: 885-892.

30. Green. LA, Fryer GE, Yawn BP, Lanier D, Dovey SM. The ecology of medical care revisited. *N Engl J Med.* 2001:344:2021-2025.

31. Hogan C. Lunney J, Gabel J, Lynn J. Medicare beneficiaries costs of care in the last year of life. *Health Aff.* 2001;20:188-195

The Health of U.S. Racial and Ethnic Populations

Source: Williams, D.R. 2005. The health of U.S. racial and ethnic populations. *Journals of Gerontology: Series B* 60B (Special Issue II): 53-62.

This article provides an overview of racial and ethnic disparities in health in the United States. It describes limitations linked to the quality and method of presentation of the available data. It also considers the complex ways in which immigrant status, race, and SES combine to affect health and outlines important directions for research that would enhance our understanding of the ways in which social factors can lead to changes in health status.

The United States has a long history of collecting and reporting health statistics by race. This article provides an overview of racial disparities in health and examines multiple conceptual and methodological issues linked to the quality of racial statistics and how they are reported that can affect our knowledge of the underlying pattern of health differentials by race. It considers the ways in which migration and socioeconomic status (SES), singly and in combination, can affect patterns of the distribution of disease. It outlines research that is needed to enhance our understanding of how conditions linked to the lives of socially disadvantaged groups can positively and negatively affect health and emphasizes the importance of understanding how these unfold over the life course.

This article views "race" as capturing ethnicity: common geographic origins, ancestry, family patterns, language, cultural norms, and traditions. Historically, racial categories have also reflected oppression, exploitation, and inequality. Accordingly, race has been an important marker of differential access to societal resources and rewards, and health status is no exception. Given the arbitrary nature of racial categorization and the preference of the majority of Hispanics to have this category treated as a racial category (Tucker et al., 1996), in the interest of economy of presentation, the term "race" is used to refer to all of the official Office of Management and Budget (OMB) racial and ethnic categories. Moreover, in recognition of individual dignity, I use the most preferred terms for each group (such as Black and African American or Hispanic and Latino) interchangeably.

RACIAL DIFFERENCES IN HEALTH

Mortality statistics are among the most readily available indicators of health status for multiple racial groups. However, the magnitude of racial disparities in mortality is related to how they are reported. Table 1 illustrates this by comparing age-adjusted mortality rates with age-specific ones. It presents mortality rates for Whites and the minority/White ratios for the major racial groups in the United States. Ratios greater than 1.0 indicate a higher rate and those less than 1.0 indicate a lower mortality rate than the White population. The first row of Table 1 presents overall age-adjusted data. Blacks have an overall

Table 1	Overall Age-Adjusted Mortality Rates for 1998–2000* and Age-Specific Death Rates for 2000† for Whites and Minority/White Rates				

Age (y)	Non-Hispanic White Rate	Black/ White Ratio	AmInd/ White Ratio	API/ White Ratio	Hispanic/ White Ratio
All ages	85.5	1.3	0.9	0.6	0.8
1–4	2.79	2.0	2.0	0.7	1.0
5–14	1.72	1.5	1.0	0.5	1.0
15–24	7.21	1.9	1.7	0.6	1.3
25–34	9.26	2.2	1.8	0.6	1.1
35–44	17.97	2.1	1.7	0.5	0.9
45–54	39.31	2.1	1.3	0.5	0.8
55–64	96.00	1.8	1.2	0.6	0.8
65–74	240.94	1.4	1.0	0.6	0.7
75–84	572.87	1.2	0.7	0.6	0.6
85+	1582.64	0.9	0.4	0.6	0.6

Note: Rates per 10,000 population.
*National Center for Health Statistics (2003).
†National Center for Health Statistics (2004).
AmInd = American Indian; API = Asian and Pacific Islander.

death rate that is 30% higher than that of Whites. All other racial groups have death rates that are lower than that of Whites, with the Asian and Pacific Islander (API) population manifesting the lowest overall death rate. However, limiting racial comparisons only to the age-adjusted rate for the entire population can mask subgroups that have an elevated risk.

Limits of Age Adjustment

Age adjustment is a routine and widely used statistical procedure to make rates of health events comparable across various population groups that may differ in their age structures. An age-adjusted rate is a weighted average of age-specific rates, with the weights being determined by the age structure of the age standard. There is considerable variation in the age structure of the various racial populations in the United States. Table 4 indicates, for example, that the median age for Whites (37.7 years) is 10 years more than that of American Indians (28.0), Native Hawaiians and other Pacific Islanders (27.5), and Hispanics (25.8). It is also considerably greater than that of Blacks (30.2) and Asians (32.7). The other rows of Table 1 make comparisons across racial groups without using an artificially created age-adjusted mortality rate. The National Center for Health Statistics (NCHS, 2003) indicates that age-adjusted rates are relative indexes for comparison but not actual measures of risk. However, they are often misinterpreted by researchers and policy makers.

Strikingly different patterns emerge when age-specific mortality rates are compared across racial groups. In contrast to an overall age-adjusted rate that is 30% higher than that of Whites, age-specific rates reveal that African Americans have mortality rates that are markedly higher than those of Whites across the age span with age-specific ratios being higher than the overall ratio from birth through age 75 years. The death rates for Blacks are at least twice as high as those of Whites between ages 1-4 and ages 25-54 years. They decline in the later years, eventually falling to be 20% higher than those of Whites between ages 75 and 84 years and lower than that of Whites over age 85 years. Similarly, in contrast to an overall age-adjusted rate that is slightly lower than that of the White population, American Indians have death rates that are higher than those of the White population for ages 1-4 and ages 15-64 years. The rates are equivalent between ages 5-14 and 65-74 years and fall below those of the White population at ages greater than 75 years.

The overall age-adjusted mortality data for Hispanics indicated that this population had lower rates than that of Whites but a more complex pattern emerges with age-specific data. Hispanics have mortality rates that are comparable with those of Whites up through age 14 years and that are slightly higher than those of Whites in young adulthood (ages 15-34 years). Beyond age 35 years, rates for Hispanics are lower than those of Whites and decline with increasing age. It is only for the API population that the pattern with the overall age-adjusted data and the age-specific data is consistent with that of markedly lower death rates for this group than Whites throughout the life course. However, the combination of Asians and Pacific Islanders into a single subgroup skews the elevated rates of mortality for Pacific Islanders compared with that of the U.S. population (Frisbie, Cho, & Hummer, 2001; Zane, Takeuchi, & Young, 1994). The OMB's recent revision of the racial categories that requires a new separate category for Native Hawaiians and other Pacific Islanders will allow for better tracking of the health of this group in the future.

The magnitude of racial disparities over time also varies with the age adjustment standard utilized. For over 50 years, the NCHS has employed an age standard for creating age-adjusted rates for the U.S. population, called the 1940 Standard Million, which was based on the age distribution of the U.S. population in 1940. In 1998, the age standard was changed to the 2000 Standard Million—the projected age distribution of the U.S. population in the year 2000. The new age standard attempts to more accurately reflect the aging population of the United States and gives more weight to the older population where racial disparities in mortality are smaller. Importantly, this technical change in the age standard attenuates racial and some SES inequalities in health (Krieger & Williams, 2001). Moreover, it has occurred at the same time of Healthy People 2010— the first national commitment on the part of the federal government to eliminate these disparities.

Table 2 shows trends in all-cause mortality rates for Blacks and Whites from 1950 to 1998, adjusted for the 1940 Standard Million, and the same rates adjusted for the year 2000 Standard Million. It also presents both the absolute and the relative racial differences in rates. Patterns of disparity also vary by whether an absolute or a relative measure of inequality is used (Carter-Pokras & Baquet, 2002). Both rate differences and ratio measures are used to provide a complete picture of disparities over time. For both racial groups, mortality rates adjusted for the year 2000 Standard Million are larger than those adjusted for the 1940 Standard Million. However, regardless of the age adjustment standard or the measure of disparity used, racial disparities in mortality existed in 1950 and persist through 1998. At the same time, different patterns are evident for the two age adjustment standards. With use of the 1940 Standard Million, the Black/White differences have declined from 4.4 deaths per 1,000 population in 1950 to 2.4 in 1998, while the Black/White ratio at 1.5 in 1998 is identical to what it was in 1950. In contrast, when the 2000 Standard Million is used as the adjustment standard, there is only a slight decline (from 3.1 to 2.9) in the difference in rates from 1950 to 1998, and an increase in the Black/White ratio from 1.2 in 1950 to 1.3 in 1998.

Infant mortality rates provide another striking example of the persistence of racial disparities in health in over time and of how the magnitude of the disparity varies depending on the indicator utilized. Table 3 presents infant mortality rates for Blacks and Whites from 1950 to 2000. Infant mortality rates have declined over time for both racial groups, but a large disparity persists in the year 2000. The measure of the absolute difference between the rates indicates that they have declined by more than 50%, from 17.1 in 1950 to 8.4 in the year 2000. In contrast, the measure of the relative difference between

| Table 2 | Mortality Rates From All Causes, 1950–1998 |

| | Adjusted for 1940 Standard Million* | | | | Adjusted for 2000 Standard Million† | | | |
Year	White	Black	Diff. (B − W)	Ratio (B/W)	White	Black	Diff. (B − W)	Ratio (B/W)
1950	8.0	12.4	4.4	1.5	14.1	17.2	3.1	1.2
1960	7.3	10.8	3.5	1.5	13.1	15.8	2.7	1.2
1970	6.8	10.4	3.6	1.5	11.9	15.2	3.3	1.3
1980	5.6	8.4	2.8	1.5	10.1	13.1	3.0	1.3
1990	4.9	7.9	3.0	1.6	9.1	12.5	3.4	1.4
1998	4.5	6.9	2.4	1.5	8.5	11.4	2.9	1.3

Note: Deaths per 10,000 population.
*National Center for Health Statistics (2000).
†National Center for Health Statistics (2001).
B = Black; W = White.

Table 3	Infant Mortality Rates, 1950–2000			
		Infant Mortality		
Year	White (W)	Black (B)	Difference (B – W)	Ratio (B/W)
1950	26.8	43.9	17.1	1.6
1960	22.9	44.3	21.4	1.9
1970	17.8	32.6	14.8	1.8
1980	10.9	22.2	11.3	2.0
1990	7.6	18.0	10.4	2.4
2000	5.7	14.1	8.4	2.5

Notes: Deaths per 1,000 live births. From National Center for Health Statistics (2003).

the two rates (the Black/White ratio) has markedly increased from 1.6 in 1950 to 2.5 in the year 2000.

Numerator Problems

Errors linked to data quality can also affect the validity of the mortality statistics. There are problems with the accuracy of the numerator that vary across the major racial populations. The numerator for mortality statistics comes from death certificates. Race is typically recorded on the death certificate by the funeral home director. A comparison of racial status as reported in the Current Population Survey while respondents were alive to that indicated on their death certificate revealed that the racial designation on the death certificate was highly consistent with self-reported race for Blacks and Whites (Sorlie, Rogot, & Johnson, 1992). However, 26% of American Indians and 18% of APIs were misclassified on the death certificate, with most of these persons being misclassified as White. Similarly, some 10% of Hispanics were misclassified as non-Hispanic on the death certificate.

A recent analysis of a cohort of elderly Mexican Americans indicated that the mortality rates for this group are seriously underestimated when compared with the National Death Index (NDI) (Patel, Eschbach, Ray, & Markides, 2004). This study compared the mortality of elderly Mexican Americans in a community-based cohort from five southwestern states using the NDI with that obtained from proxy data that collected the date, location, and cause of death from family members of the deceased and other informants. The NDI is more likely to miss Hispanics than non-Hispanic Whites for multiple reasons (Patel et al., 2004). Compared with Whites, the use and accuracy of Social Security numbers may be lower for Hispanics, the matching of names may be more unreliable because Hispanic naming customs are different from those used by non-Hispanics,

and Hispanics may also be more likely to die outside of the United States and such deaths are not reflected in the NDI.

This study found that proxy-reported death rates were higher than those obtained from matches with the NDI (Patel et al., 2004). Specifically, 20% of deaths reported by proxy reports were missed by the NDI. NDI underreporting of Hispanic deaths was especially likely among older Mexican Americans, women, and the foreign-born. For example, proxy-reported rates were 9% higher for men and 28% higher for women compared with the NDI. Importantly, the study found that adjusting nationally reported mortality rates for Mexican Americans by the underascertainment documented in this study completely eliminated the pattern of lower mortality rates for Mexican Americans compared with Whites for women and narrowed the gap for men (Patel et al., 2004). Strikingly, once mortality patterns for elderly Mexican-American women were adjusted for underreporting, Mexican-American women over age 65 had higher age-adjusted mortality rates than White women. Similarly, in contrast to national vital statistics data that show lower heart disease mortality rates for Hispanics, community-based cohort studies find equivalent (Pandey, Labarthe, Goff, Chan, & Nichaman, 2001) or higher (Swenson, Trepka, Rewers, Scarbo, Hiatt, & Hamman, 2002) rates for Mexican Americans compared with Whites.

Denominator Problems

The quality and accuracy of the denominator data used to calculate the rates of various health events could also importantly affect the accuracy of the reported rates. Census counts for population subgroups are routinely used to calculate mortality and other health rates. The use of a denominator that has an undercount inflates the obtained rate in exact proportion to the magnitude of the undercount in the denominator. Throughout the history of the U.S. Census, the census has failed to count all residents and this undercount varies by age, sex, and race. For over 50 years, the U.S. Census Bureau has evaluated the extent of undercount for Blacks and Whites by using demographic analysis. This approach estimates the population based on administrative data and demographic trends (Robinson, Bashir, Prithwis, & Woodrow, 1993). The unavailability of consistent birth, death, and immigration data by detailed race has made demographic analysis difficult for the other major racial populations in the United States.

Demographic analyses reveal that census undercount is higher for Blacks than for Whites and has been declining over time. Within the African American population, census undercount is markedly higher for Black males than for Black females and varies considerably by age such that the census undercount in 1990 was between 11% and 13% for all of the 10-year age groups for Black males between the ages of 25 and 64 (NCHS, 1994). The net undercount in the 2000 Census was 10% for Black males aged 30-49 years (Robinson, 2001). Thus, all of the officially reported mortality rates (and rates for multiple other health events that use census data as denominators) for middle-aged Black males are likely to be at least 10% higher than they are in reality. In recent decades, the census has also done postenumeration surveys as a second means of estimating the net undercount. Data from these analyses suggests that the net census undercount is even higher for American Indians and Hispanics than for Blacks, with Asians having rates intermediate between Whites and African Americans (Anderson & Feinberg, 1999). However, there has been little systematic analysis of how the misclassification of race in the numerator combines with undercounts in the denominator to affect the officially reported rates of health events for multiple racial groups.

UNDERSTANDING RACIAL DISPARITIES IN HEALTH

In spite of various methodological limitations, the overall pattern of persisting racial differences in health remains. How do we make sense of these differences? Historically in the United States, research has focused on racial differences in underlying biological characteristics as crucial for creating racial differences in rates of disease and death (Krieger, 1987). The health field currently gives greater attention to differences in the social circumstances of racial groups in the United States (Cooper & David, 1986; Krieger, Rowley, Herman, Avery, & Phillips, 1993; Williams, 1997).

Race and Sociodemographic Variation

Table 4 illustrates how race is a crude proxy for location in varying social contexts by presenting a broad range of demographic and socioeconomic characteristics for the major racial categories in the United States. These data indicate that America's racial groups are characterized by considerable demographic and socioeconomic diversity. The first row shows that there is marked variation across race in the percentage who identify as Hispanic (U.S. Census, 2000). Reporting Hispanic ancestry varies from 1.2% among Asians and 2% among Blacks to 8% of Whites, 16% of American Indians, and 11% of Native Hawaiians and other Pacific Islanders. At the same time, an overwhelming 97% of people who mentioned that they belonged to a racial category

| Table 4 | Demographic and Socioeconomic Characteristics by Race and Ethnicity: United States, 2000 |

Indicator	White	Black	Am. Indian/ Alaska Native	Asian	Native Hawaiian and Pacific Islander	Other	Hispanic Race
Hispanic, %	8.0	2.0	16.4	1.2	11.4	97.0	—
Foreign born, %	3.5	6.1	5.4	68.9	19.9	43.4	40.2
Median age, %	37.7	30.2	28.0	32.7	27.5	24.6	25.8
Female-headed, %	9.2	30.8	20.9	9.1	16.1	19.3	17.8
White collar, %	36.6	25.2	24.3	44.6	23.3	14.2	18.1
High school+, %	85.5	72.3	70.9	80.4	78.3	46.8	52.4
College grad+, %	27.0	14.3	11.5	44.1	13.8	7.3	10.4
Poor, %	8.1	24.9	25.7	12.6	17.7	24.4	22.6
Own home, %	71.3	46.3	55.5	53.4	45.0	40.5	48.0

Source: U.S. Census (2000).

other than the standard OMB ones offered in the census indicated that they were Hispanic. That is, many Hispanics report their national identity when requested to indicate their race. Table 4 also indicates that a relatively high proportion of Asians (69%) and Hispanics (40%) are immigrants (Malone, Baluja, Costanzo, & Davis, 2003). As noted, the median ages for American Indians, Native Hawaiians and other Pacific Islanders, and Hispanics are considerably lower than those for Whites, Asians, and Blacks (U.S. Census, 2000). Whites and Asians also have the lowest levels of female-headed households, Blacks have the highest, and the rates are intermediate for Hispanics and American Indians (U.S. Census, 2000).

Table 4 also shows that there is variation across race on multiple markers of SES: occupational status, educational attainment, poverty rates, and home ownership rates. The probability of being employed in upper-white collar jobs (professionals, executives, and managers) is much higher for Whites and Asians than for the other racial populations (Fronczek & Johnson, 2003). There are relatively high rates of high school completion for people aged 25 years or older of all races, but this ranges from only 52% for Hispanics to 86% for Whites (Bauman & Graf, 2003). Much lower proportions of Americans from all racial groups have completed a college degree, with 44% of Asians and 27% of Whites, but only about 10% of Hispanics and American Indians, and 14% of Blacks and Native Hawaiians having a college degree or more education. Similarly, Blacks, American Indians, and Hispanics have poverty rates that are considerably higher than those of Whites and Asians (Bishaw & Iceland, 2003). Racial differences in wealth are much larger than those for income. Table 4 provides data for rates of home ownership, one of the most common economic assets in American households (U.S. Census, 2000). Seventy-one percent of White households own homes, compared with slightly more than half of all American Indians and Asians, and less than half of Blacks, Native Hawaiians, and Hispanics. These demographic and SES variations point to two major influences on the health patterns of the United States: immigration and socioeconomic disadvantage.

Immigration and Health

Because processes linked to migration make an important contribution to health, the large number of immigrants within both the Asian and Hispanic population importantly affects the health status of these groups. National data reveal that immigrants of all of the major racial groups in the United States have lower rates of adult and infant mortality than their native-born counterparts (Hummer, Rogers, Nam, & LeClere, 1999; Singh & Miller, 2004; Singh & Yu, 1996). However, with length of stay in the United States and acculturation to American society, the health advantage of immigrants tends to decline over time. For example, research on Latinos reveals that adult mortality, infant mortality, psychiatric disorders, psychological distress, substance use, low birth weight, poor health practices, and other indicators of morbidity all increase with increasing acculturation (Finch, Hummer, Reindl, & Vega, 2002; Vega & Amaro, 1994). Similarly, an analysis of the prevalence of chronic disease in the National Health Interview Survey from 1992 to 1995 showed a consistent trend across multiple populations in which recent immigrants reported better health than long-term immigrants and the U.S. born (Singh & Miller, 2004). This pattern existed for non-Hispanic Whites and Blacks, Chinese, Japanese, Filipinos, Asian Indians, Koreans, Vietnamese, other APIs, Mexicans, Cubans, and Central and South Americans.

At the same time, a more complex pattern emerges for the relationship between immigrant status and health for some subgroups of the Asian and Hispanic population. For example, although White, Black, and Hispanic immigrants had markedly lower overall death rates than their native-born counterparts, the death rates for API immigrants were only slightly lower than those of their native-born peers (Singh & Miller, 2004). Moreover, Chinese, Japanese, and Filipino immigrants had all-cause mortality rates that were higher than those of their native-born peers. For the Chinese and Japanese, death rates for multiple causes of death (respiratory diseases, liver cirrhosis, unintentional injuries, suicide, homicide, and liver cancer) were higher for immigrants than their native-born counterparts. The health profile of Puerto Ricans is also distinctive. The infant mortality rate for mainland Puerto Ricans was identical to that of island-born Puerto Ricans, and recent Puerto Rican immigrants report higher levels of chronic disease than the U.S. (mainland)-born and long-term immigrants (Singh & Miller, 2004). The relationship between immigrant status and health also varies by the health status indicator under consideration, such that our knowledge of the health of immigrants may be importantly shaped by the availability of data for certain health outcomes. A study of pregnancy-related mortality between 1991 and 1997 revealed that Hispanic and Asian immigrant women had higher pregnancy-related mortality rates than their U.S.-born counterparts (Centers for

Disease Control and Prevention, 2001). Moreover, the pregnancy related mortality risk of both U.S.-born and foreign-born Black women was four times as high as that of White women. Other data reveal that women of all Hispanic immigrant groups have a higher risk of low birth weight and prematurity than do Whites (Frisbie, Forbes, & Hummer, 1998). These data point to complex associations between immigration, acculturation, ethnicity, and health.

Immigrant SES, Social Mobility, and Health Trajectories

The health literature has also given inadequate attention to the SES characteristics of immigrant populations. The differences between these groups in SES

levels upon arrival in the United States and their trajectories for socioeconomic mobility in the United States are likely to lead to diverging patterns of health over time. Table 5 presents the rate of college graduation, employment in white collar (managerial and professional) and blue-collar occupations, and poverty rates for the major immigrant and native-born racial groups (Rumbaut, 1996a,b). Within each subcategory, groups are ranked by the percentage graduating from college. Several Asian immigrant groups have higher occupational status and markedly higher levels of education than native-born Asians and other native-born Americans of all racial backgrounds. However, Cambodian, Laotian, and, to a lesser extent, Vietnamese immigrants diverge from this pattern with strikingly lower levels of education

| Table 5 | Socioeconomic Status of Immigrants and Native-Born Persons, 1990 |

Group	Education College Grads %	Occupation White %	Occupation Blue %	Income Poor %
Native born				
Asian (U.S. born)	35.9	34	8	9.8
White (non-Hisp.)	22.0	29	13	9.2
Black (non-Hisp.)	11.4	18	21	29.5
Puerto Rican	9.5	17	21	31.7
Mexican (U.S. born)	8.6	16	19	24.5
Immigrants				
Asian				
India	64.9	48	8	8.1
Taiwan	62.2	47	4	9.8
Philippines	43.0	28	11	5.9
Japan	35.0	39	7	12.8
Korea	34.4	25	13	15.6
China	30.9	29	16	15.7
Vietnam	15.9	17	21	25.5
Cambodia	5.5	9	23	38.4
Laos	5.1	7	41	40.3
Hispanic/Latin American				
Venezuela	37.2	34	11	21.1
Brazil	34.2	20	12	10.8
Argentina	27.7	33	11	11.0
Cuba	15.6	23	18	14.9
Nicaragua	14.6	11	24	24.4
Dominican Republic	7.5	11	31	30.0
El Salvador	4.6	6	27	24.9
Mexico	3.5	6	32	29.7
Blacks				
Africa (Sub-Saharan)	47.1	37	12	15.7
Guyana	15.8	19	12	11.9
Trinidad and Tobago	15.6	20	10	14.9
Jamaica	14.9	22	11	12.1
Haiti	11.8	14	21	21.7
Barbados	8.6	11	8	9.4

Notes: College grad=college graduate or more for persons aged 25 years or older; White=white collar=professionals, executives, and managers; Blue=blue collar=operators, fabricators, laborers. [From Rumbaut (1996a,b).]

and managerial employment than U.S.-born persons. Many of these latter immigrants entered the United States with refugee status. With regard to poverty rates, with the exception of Japanese, Filipino, and Indian immigrants, all of the Asian immigrants have higher rates of poverty than native-born Asians. Instructively, the Cambodian and Laotian immigrants have higher rates of poverty than native-born Blacks and Hispanics.

The socioeconomic profile of Latin American immigrants differs markedly from that of Asians. The rates of college graduation and managerial employment are low for migrants from Mexico, the Dominican Republic, and El Salvador, considerably higher for immigrants from Venezuela, Brazil, and Argentina, and intermediate for those from Cuba and Nicaragua. Rates of poverty are high for some Hispanic immigrants (e.g., Mexicans, Dominicans, and Nicaraguans) but low for others (e.g., Brazilians and Argentineans). The final grouping in Table 5 provides the profile of Black immigrants. Not all immigrants from Africa are Black, and persons of African descent are currently outnumbered by persons of Indian (Asian) ancestry for two of the countries listed here (Guyana and Trinidad and Tobago). Nonetheless, Africa and the Caribbean countries included are the major sources of Black immigrants to the United States. Black immigrants from Africa have rates of college graduation that are more than twice that of the U.S.-born population and four times the college graduation rate of native-born Blacks. Most Black immigrants in the United States come from the Caribbean. The data from the five largest sending countries suggests that Black immigrants from the English-speaking Caribbean (with the exception of Barbados) have slightly higher levels of college completion than the native-born Black population but lower than that of the native-born U.S. population in general. In contrast, immigrants from French-speaking Haiti have levels of SES very similar to those of African Americans. Their poverty rates are also higher than those of other Black immigrants.

What are the implications of these patterns for health and trajectories of immigrant health status? The socioeconomic data indicate that both native-born Asians and most Asian immigrants have higher levels of education and occupational status than U.S. Whites. Thus, although the health advantage of Asian immigrants declines somewhat over time (Cho & Hummer, 2000; Frisbie et al., 2001), the maintenance of a relatively high SES profile suggests that Asians are likely to continue to lead the United States on multiple health indictors. In contrast, the low SES profile of Hispanic immigrants, combined with the low SES levels of native-born Latinos and the ongoing challenges that Hispanics face with educational and occupational mobility (Camarillo & Bonilla, 2001), suggest that the health status of Latinos is likely to decline more rapidly than that of Asians and to be worse than the U.S. average in the future.

The SES trajectory of Black immigrants is likely to importantly affect their future patterns of health. Some evidence suggests that the SES trajectory of second-generation Caribbean immigrants is importantly related to the SES of their parents, with those from low SES backgrounds faring considerably worse than their middle-class counterparts (Waters, 1999). Inadequate research attention has been given to the health of Black immigrants in general and immigrants from Africa in particular. These groups provide a unique opportunity to identify how SES, acculturation, and exposure to racism relate to each other and combine to affect health and health trajectories.

The data in Table 5 also highlight the heterogeneity within immigrant populations. Although some 60% of Hispanics in the United States are of Mexican ancestry, there is considerable variation within the Hispanic category, and health researchers should attempt to assess this whenever feasible. There is similar variation within the Black and Asian categories. For example, combining all Asians into one category or focusing only on the subgroups that have a long history of settlement in the United States will mask those Asian subgroups that have higher levels of risks. Research reveals that the Laotians, Hmong, Cambodians, Vietnamese, and Pacific Islanders have levels of health status markedly worse than the overall Asian category and generally inferior to that of Whites (Cho & Hummer, 2000; Frisbie et al., 2001). Similarly, the health profile of black immigrants varies by the specific group and health outcome under consideration (Fruchter et al., 1990). Inadequate research attention has also been given to health status variations within the White population.

Race, SES, and Health

Table 4 noted that there were large racial differences in SES. SES is one of the strongest known determinants of variations in health (Williams & Collins, 1995). Across a broad range of societies, persons of higher social status enjoy better health than their lower SES counterparts. Data on self-assessed health by income level for Blacks, Whites, and Hispanics illustrate the complex role that SES plays in racial differences in health in the United States. Self-assessed health is a global indicator of health status that is a strong predictor of mortality and changes in physical functioning (Idler & Benyamini, 1997; Idler & Kasl, 1995). Racial differences exist on this overall indicator of health. In 1995, 9.1% of non-Hispanic Whites indicated that they were in fair or poor health compared with 15.1% of Hispanics and 17.3% of non-Hispanic Blacks (NCHS, 2003).

Several points are noteworthy regarding the data in Table 6 (not included). First, the differences by SES are large within each group for both men and women. Second, the SES differences are much larger than the racial ones. Within each racial and gender group, the differences between the poor and high income categories are more than three times larger than the overall Black/White difference in health and more than four times larger than the overall Hispanic/White difference in health. Third, there is the persistence of racial differences in health at comparable levels of income. At every level of income, African American men and women report poorer health than their White counterparts. This independent effect of race is especially marked among poor Black men and among Black women. A similar pattern exists for Hispanic men at the two highest income categories and for Hispanic women for the three nonpoor categories. It is instructive that among the poor, Hispanic women do not differ from White women in self-rated ill-health and Hispanic men report lower levels of self-rated ill health than White males. The interplay of migration with SES may underlie this pattern. A large number of Hispanic immigrants are low in SES, but are in relatively good health. However, as noted earlier, with increasing acculturation and length of stay in the United States, the health of many Hispanics worsens even as SES increases (Vega & Amaro, 1994).

Table 7 (not included) presents infant mortality rate by mother's education among women aged 20 years and older in the United States and further illustrates the complexity of the association between race, SES, and health. Infant mortality rates are inversely related to mother's education for each racial group. At the same time, the size of the association varies by group, with the relationship being stronger for non-Hispanic Whites and American Indians than for Blacks, Hispanics, and APIs. Compared with college graduates, women who have not completed high school have infant mortality rates that are 1.5 times higher for Blacks, 1.4 times higher for Hispanics, and 1.4 times higher for APIs compared with 2.4 times higher for Whites and 2.2 times higher for the highest available education group (women with some college education) for American Indians.

The racial differences in infant mortality at comparable levels of education are also striking. Infant mortality rates for the API population are equivalent to or lower than those of Whites at every level of education. Hispanics have lower rates than Whites at the two lower education levels but higher rates than Whites at the two highest levels. In contrast, both American Indians and African Americans have infant mortality rates that are higher than those of Whites at every level of education. The differences are especially striking for African American women. The Black/White difference in mortality rates does not decline with increasing years of education, and the Black/White ratio becomes larger as education levels increase. Most strikingly, the most advantaged group of African American women (college graduates) have higher rates of infant mortality than the most disadvantaged group of White, Hispanic, and API women (those who have not completed high school).

These data highlight that race and SES are two related but not interchangeable systems of inequality. The striking pattern of excess risk for African American women at all levels of SES, but especially among the college educated, is not unique to infant mortality data. In national data, the highest SES group of African-American women also has equivalent or higher rates of low birth weight, hypertension, and overweight than the lowest SES group of White women (Pamuk, Makuk, Heck, & Reuben, 1998). Other evidence suggests that middle-class African-American males also have elevated health risks for a number of stress-related outcomes such as suicide, hypertension, and reported levels of stress (Williams, 2003). Understanding these unique effects linked to race and the conditions under which they occur requires increased research attention to the nonequivalence of all SES indicators across racial groups (Kaufman, Cooper, & McGee, 1997; Williams & Collins, 1995), the multiple ways in which racism can affect the health of socially disadvantaged populations (Williams, 2004), and the ways in which risk factors and resources for health combine over the life course to affect the social distribution of disease.

Research on the stressful consequences for health of perceptions of racial discrimination may provide one of the missing links to understanding the elevated health risks that are sometimes linked to middle-class status among members of minority groups. Levels of reported racial discrimination are positively related to SES among African Americans (Forman, Williams, & Jackson, 1997). Some evidence suggests that perceptions of discrimination make an incremental contribution to explaining the residual effect of race after SES is controlled (Williams, Neighbors, & Jackson, 2003). However, future research must seek to comprehensively characterize other risk factors that may either uniquely or disproportionately affect middle-class members of minority populations. Some of the unique stressors of middle-class minorities may arise from their occupational contexts. For example, exposure to tokenism at work and persistent glass ceilings can lead to frustration that could adversely affect health (Jackson & Stewart, 2003). Other health risks may arise from residential conditions. Compared with Whites with similar incomes, Blacks and Puerto Ricans live in neighborhoods that are poorer in quality (Alba & Logan, 1993). An analysis of 1990 Census data revealed that Blacks who reside in the suburbs lived in housing conditions that were equivalent or inferior to those of Blacks living within central cities (Harris, 1999). Not surprisingly, one recent study found that whereas suburban residence was associated with lower mortality for Whites, it predicted elevated mortality rates for Blacks, especially for Black men (House et al., 2000).

Another understudied risk factor for middle-class members of historically disadvantaged populations is the "costs of caring" (Kessler, McLeod, & Wethington, 1985) involved in the provision of material and other support to lower SES family members. Many of these middle-class persons have large family networks that exist in high stress, low SES contexts. The extent to which some middle-class minority members also experience health costs linked to caring for relatives has not been systematically explored. Still another understudied pathogenic factor may be the disidentification, distancing, and alienation from one's community of origin that may be true of some portion of middle-class minority group members (Cole & Omari, 2003).

Identifying Health Risks Over the Life Course

There is growing recognition that psychological, social, and economic adversity in childhood can have long-term consequences for health. Several recent studies highlight the importance of attending to these issues. For example, in the CARDIA Study, low childhood SES, as measured by parental education, was associated with poorer baseline pulmonary function among young adults, as well as declines in pulmonary function over time (Jackson, Kubzansky, Cohen, Weiss, & Wright, 2004). This graded association remained significant after adjustment for current SES, asthma history, smoking history, and other risk factors. Importantly, this pattern was evident for

Blacks and Whites, males and females, in this large cohort. Hispanics and Blacks are more likely than Whites to reside in areas with poor air quality, and one recent study of 226 African American and Dominican women in New York documented that prenatal exposure to air pollution adversely affected the neurodevelopment of children beyond the neonatal period (Rauh et al., 2004). Infants born to mothers who had been exposed to indoor and ambient air pollutants were twice as likely to be classified as significantly delayed cognitively at 24 months compared with nonexposed children. Moreover, the study found an interaction between exposure to air pollution and material hardship, with children having both exposures manifesting the greatest cognitive deficits. This study also illustrates the importance of attending to complex interactions that may exist between factors in the physical environment with those in the social and psychological context. A study of childhood SES and adult psychological functioning from Kuopio, Finland, also highlights the importance of understanding how childhood and adult risk factors relate to each other and combine to affect health (Harper et al., 2002). The study found that childhood SES measured by parental education and occupation at age 10 years predicted higher levels of cynical hostility, hopelessness, and depressive symptoms in a cohort of men some 30-50 years later. However, childhood SES and adult SES were independently related to cynical hostility and hopelessness, but only adult SES was independently related to depressive symptoms.

Taking the life course seriously also requires greater attention to identifying critical time points and transitions that may be important in the development of health risk. For example, the period of transition from late adolescence to early adulthood appears to be pregnant with health risks for African Americans. During this time, elevated rates of blood pressure emerge or become pronounced, cigarette use, problem drinking, and illicit drug use show a larger increase for African Americans than for Whites, and if heavy use is initiated for Blacks, it continues for a longer period of time (Williams, 2003). Similarly, elevated rates of mood disorders are evident for African Americans compared with Whites only for the 18- to 29-year age group (Robins & Regier, 1991). These patterns may reflect the reality that the transition to adulthood is associated with heightened awareness of restricted opportunities that lead to elevated levels of stress and maladaptive patterns of coping (Williams, 2003). A recent study found that an increasingly disadvantaged post-high school educational pathway that led to the underrepresentation of Blacks and Hispanics in 4-year colleges largely accounted for their elevated rate of depressed mood compared with Whites and Asians (Gore & Aseltine, 2003).

Alternatively, the transition to adulthood may be associated with the declining influence of religious institutions and their potential health-enhancing effects. Black adolescents are much less likely than White adolescents to use a broad range of substances, including alcohol, tobacco, and marijuana (Wallace, Bachman, O'Malley, Johnston, Schulenberg, & Cooper, 2002). Among high school seniors in the United States, religious involvement is a powerful predictor of adolescent risk behavior. National data reveal that religious high school seniors are less likely than their nonreligious peers to carry a weapon to school, get into fights or hurt someone, drive after drinking, ride with a driver who had been drinking, smoke cigarettes, engage in binge drinking, or use marijuana (Wallace & Forman, 1998). In addition, religious seniors were more likely than nonreligious seniors to wear seatbelts; eat breakfast, green vegetables and fruit; get regular exercise; and sleep at least 7 hours per night. A recent analysis of these same data indicated that religious involvement among African-American adolescents is a key determinant of their lower levels of substance use (Wallace, Brown, Bachman, & Laveist, 2003). These findings for the role of religion in health risk behavior highlight the importance of understanding resilience factors and processes and identifying how they combine with other individual and social factors to affect health risks.

The high level of childhood poverty in the United States emphasizes the importance of attending to life course factors in understanding adult health. In 1996, 11% of White non-Hispanic children under the age of 18 years lived in poor households (Pamuk et al., 1998). However, the poverty rate was twice as high for API children and four times as high for Black and Hispanic children. A large number of children are also at high risk of becoming poor. Households that are near poor (incomes above poverty but less than twice the poverty level) are at high risk of falling into poverty at some time while these children are being raised (Duncan, 1988). When the poor and near poor are combined into an economically vulnerable category, it becomes evident that 43% of all children in the United States are at risk of being exposed to economic adversities in childhood that may have long-term health consequences (Pamuk et al., 1998). This includes 31% of White, 36% of API, 68% of Black, and 72% of Hispanic children.

A recent review documented the broad range of risk factors that are associated with being raised in a family living in poverty (Evans, 2004). Compared with high SES children, poor children are more exposed to family turmoil, violence, separation, instability, and chaotic households. In addition, they experience less support and have parents that are less responsive and more authoritarian. They also are read to less frequently, watch more TV, and have less access to books and computers. Poor children are also less likely to have parents involved in their school activities and to be exposed to negative risk factors in their housing and residential environments. Poor children are more likely to consume air and water that is polluted and live in homes that are crowded, noisy, and of low quality (Evans, 2004). In addition, they live in neighborhoods that are more dangerous, have access to poorer city services, and have greater physical deterioration. Poor children are also more likely to attend schools and daycare institutions that are of inferior quality. Social adversities and stressors tend to co-occur and cumulate over the life course, with individuals and groups disadvantaged with exposure to a given pathogenic factor also being exposed to multiple risk factors. An important priority for future research on the health of racial populations is to better understand how adult health is affected by events earlier in life as well as by the accumulation of health risks over the life course.

Identifying the Biological Pathways

There is also a pressing need to identify the biological pathways by which psychosocial adversities affect health. Chronic exposure to stressors can also lead to dysregulation across multiple physiological systems of the body. The concept of allostatic load captures the cumulative burden of this physiological wear and tear on the human organism that can increase the risk of disease (McEwen & Seeman, 1999). A recent study of elderly adults suggests that a measure of allostatic load can shed light on understanding social inequalities in health (Seeman et al., 2004). In this study of high functioning elders, a summary measure of allostatic load that consisted of 16 biological indicators of cardiovascular risk (6), hormones (4), inflammation (4), and renal function and lung function was inversely related to SES. This composite measure of biological dysregulation explained one third of educational differences in morbidity. Importantly, allostatic load explained more variance when operationalized as a composite measure of biological risk than as multiple individual risk factors.

Conclusion

Clarity remains an elusive goal with regard to the patterns of racial disparities in health for each of America's racial groups. Future research on racial differences in health should be attentive to the ethnic heterogeneity of each racial category, the distinctiveness of each racial group, and the data limitations attendant to the assessment and presentation of racial data. There is also an urgent need to identify the determinants of racial disparities in health so that the effectiveness of efforts to eliminate elevated health risks for socially disadvantaged populations can be enhanced. More research is needed that is attentive to individual and group histories and to the particular social and geographic locations of America's racial populations. Efforts that catalogue and quantify the patterned ways in which risk and protective factors emerge in specific contexts and cumulate over the life course can deepen our understanding of how the larger social environment can shape the distribution of disease.

ACKNOWLEDGMENTS

An earlier version of this article was presented at the Pennsylvania State University Conference on Health Inequalities Across the Life Course, June 6-7, 2004.

Preparation of this article was supported in part by the John D. and Catherine T. McArthur Foundation Research Network on Socioeconomic Status and Health.

I thank Trisha Matelksi for assistance with research and the preparation of the manuscript.

Address correspondence to David R. Williams, PhD, MPH, Departments of Sociology and Epidemiology and Survey Research Center, Institute for Social Research, University of Michigan, Post Office Box 1248, 426 Thompson St., Ann Arbor, MI 48106-1248. E-mail: wildavid@umich.edu.

• • • REFERENCES

Alba, R. D., & Logan, J. R. (1993). Minority proximity to whites in suburbs: An individual-level analysis of segregation. *American Journal of Sociology*, 98, 1388-1427.

Anderson, M. J., & Feinberg, S. E. (1999). *Who counts? The politics of census-taking in contemporary America.* New York: Russel Sage Foundation.

Bauman, K. J., & Graf, N. L. (2003). Educational attainment: 2000 (Census 2000 Brief C2KBR-24). Washington, D.C.: U.S. Government Printing Office.

Bishaw, A., & Iceland, J. (2003). *Poverty: 1999* (Census 2000 Brief C2KBR-19). Washington, D.C.: U.S. Government Printing Office.

Camarillo, A. M., & Bonilla, F. (2001). Hispanic in a multicultural society: A new American dilemma? In N. J. Smelser, W. J. Wilson, & F. Mitchell (Eds.), America becoming: *Racial trends and their consequences, vol. I* (pp. 103-134). Washington, D.C.: National Academy Press.

Carter-Pokras, O., & Baquet, C. (2002). What is a "health disparity"? *Public Health Reports 117*, 426-434.

Centers for Disease Control and Prevention. (2001). Pregnancy-related deaths among Hispanic, Asian/Pacific Islander and American Indian/Alaska Native women-United States, 1991-1997. *MMWR Morbidity and Mortality Weekly Report, 50*, 361-364.

Cho, Y., & Hummer, R. A. (2000). Disability status differentials across fifteen Asian and Pacific Islander groups and the effect of nativity and duration of residence in the U.S. *Social Biology, 48*, 171-195.

Cole, E. R., & Omari, S. R. (2003). Race, class, and the dilemmas of upward mobility for African Americans. *Journal of Social Issues, 59*, 785-802.

Cooper, R. S., & David, R. (1986). The biological concept of race and its application to public health and epidemiology. *Journal of Health and Politics, Policy and Law*, 11, 97-116.

Duncan, G. J. (1988). The volatility of family income over the life course. In P. Bates, D. Featherman, & R. M. Lerner (Eds.), *Life span development and behavior* (pp. 317-358). Hillsdale, NJ: Lawrence Erlbaum.

Evans, G. W. (2004). The environment of childhood poverty. *American Psychologist*, 59, 77-92.

Finch, B. K., Hummer, R. A., Reindl, M., & Vega, W. A. (2002). Validity of self-rated health among Latino(a)s. *American Journal of Epidemiology*, 155, 755-759.

Forman, T. A., Williams, D. R., & Jackson, J. S. (1997). Race, place, and discrimination. In C. Gardner (Ed.), *Perspectives on social problems* (pp. 9, 231-261). New York: JAI Press.

Frisbie, W. P., Cho, Y., & Hummer, R. A. (2001). Immigration and the health of Asian and Pacific Islander adults in the United States. *American Journal of Epidemiology*, 153, 372-380.

Frisbie, W. P., Forbes, D., & Hummer, R. A. (1998). Hispanic pregnancy outcomes: Additional evidence. *Social Science Quarterly, 79*, 149-169.

Fronczek, P., & Johnson, P. (2003). Census 2000 Brief. *Occupations: 2000.* Washington, D.C.: U.S. Government Printing Office.

Fruchter, R. G., Nayeri, K., Remy, J. C., Wright, C., Feldman, J. D., Boyce, J. G., & Burnett, W. S. (1990). Cervix and breast cancer incidence in immigrant Caribbean women. *American Journal of Public Health*, 80, 722-724.

Gore, S., & Aseltine, R. H. (2003). Race and ethnic differences in depressed mood following the transition from high school. *Journal of Health & Social Behavior, 44*, 370-389.

Harper, S., Lynch, J., Hsu, W. L., Everson, S. A., Hillemeier, M. M., Rhaghunatian, T. E., et al. (2002). Life course socioeconomic conditions and adult psychosocial functioning. *International Journal of Epidemiology, 31*, 395-403.

Harris, D. R. (1999). *All suburbs are not created equal: A new look at racial differences in suburban locations* (research report no. 99-440). Ann Arbor: University of Michigan, Population Studies Center.

House, J. S., Lepkowski, J. M., Williams, D. R., Mero, R. P., Lanz, P. M., Robert, S. A., et al. (2000). Excess mortality among urban residents: How much, for whom, and why. *American Journal of Public Health, 90*, 1898-1904.

Hummer, R. A., Rogers, R. G., Nam, C. B., & LeClere, F. B. (1999). Race/ethnicity, nativity, and U.S. adult mortality. *Social Science Quarterly, 80*, 136-153.

Idler, E. L., & Benyamini, Y. (1997). Self-rated health and mortality: A review of twenty-seven community studies. *Journal of Health and Social Behavior, 38*, 21-37.

Idler, E. L., & Kasl, S. V. (1995). Self-ratings of health: Do they also predict change in functional ability? *Journals of Gerontology Series B: Psychological Sciences & Social Sciences, 50*, S344-S353.

Jackson, B., Kubzansky, L. D., Cohen, S., Weiss, S., & Wright, R. J. (2004). A matter of life and breath: Childhood socioeconomic status is related to young adult pulmonary function in the CARDIA study. *International Journal of Epidemiology, 33*, 271-278.

Jackson, P. B., & Stewart, Q. T. (2003). A research agenda for the black middle class: Work stress, survival strategies, and mental health. *Journal of Health and Social Behavior, 44*, 442-455.

Kaufman, J. S., Cooper, R. S., & McGee, D. L. (1997). Socioeconomic status and health in blacks and whites: The problem of residual confounding and the resiliency of race. *Epidemiology, 8*, 621-628.

Kessler, R. C., McLeod, J. D., & Wethington, E. (1985). The costs of caring: A perspective on the relationship between sex and psychological distress. In I. Sarason & B. Sarason (Eds.), *Social support: Theory, research, and applications* (pp. 491-506). Dordrecht, Netherlands: Martinus Nijhoff.

Krieger, N. (1987). Shades of difference: Theoretical underpinnings of the medical controversy on black/white differences in the United States, 1830-1870. *International Journal of Health Services, 17*, 259-278.

Krieger, N., Rowley, D. L., Herman, A. A., Avery, B., & Phillips, M. T. (1993). Racism, sexism, and social class: Implications for studies of health, disease, and well-being. *American Journal of Preventive Medicine, 9*(suppl 6), 82-122.

Krieger, N., & Williams, D. R. (2001). Changing to the 2000 standard million: Are declining racial/ethnic and socioeconomic inequalities in health real progress or statistical illusion? *American Journal of Public Health, 91*, 1209-1213.

Malone, N., Baluja, K. F., Costanzo, J. M., & Davis, C. J. (2003). *The foreign-born population: 2000* (Census 2000 Brief C2KBR-34). Washington, D.C.: U.S. Government Printing Office.

McEwen, B. S., & Seeman, T. (1999). Protective and damaging effects of mediators of stress: Elaborating and testing the concepts of allostasis and allostatic load. *Annals of the New York Academy of Sciences, 896*, 30-47.

National Center for Health Statistics. (1994). *Vital statistics of the United States, 1990, vol. ii, mortality, part a. Public Health Services.* Washington, D.C.: U.S. Government Printing Office.

National Center for Health Statistics. (2000). *Health, United States, 2000 with adolescent health chartbook.* Hyattsville, MD: U.S. Government Printing Office.

National Center for Health Statistics. (2001). *Health, United States, 2001 with urban and rural health chartbook.* Washington, D.C.: U.S. Government Printing Office.

National Center for Health Statistics. (2003). *Health, United States, 2003, with chartbook on trends in the health of Americans.* Hyattsville, MD: U.S. Government Printing Office.

National Center for Health Statistics Center for Disease Control and Prevention. (2004). *U.S. Department of Health and Human Services, mortality tables.* Washington, DC: U.S. Department of Health and Human Services. Retrieved on January 25, 2005, from http://www. cdc.gov/nchs/datawh/statab/ unpubd/mortabs.htm.

Pamuk, E., Makuk, D., Heck, K., & Reuben, C. (1998). *Health, United States, 1998 with socioeconomic status and health chartbook.* Hyattsville, MD: National Center for Health Statistics.

Pandey, D. K., Labarthe, D. R., Goff, D. C., Chan, W., & Nichaman, M. Z. (2001). Community-wide coronary heart disease mortality in Mexican Americans equals or exceeds that in non-Hispanic whites: The Corpus Christi Heart Project. *American Journal of Medicine, 110*, 81-87.

Patel, K. V., Eschbach, K., Ray, L. A., & Markides, K. S. (2004). Evaluation of mortality data for older Mexican Americans: Implications for the Hispanic paradox. *American Journal of Epidemiology, 159*, 707-715.

Rauh, V. A., Whyatt, R. M., Garfinkel, R., Andrews, H., Hoepner, L., Reyes, A., et al. (2004). Developmental effects of exposure to environmental tobacco smoke and material hardship among inner-city children. *Neurotoxicology and Teratology, 26,* 373-385.

Robins, L. N., & Regier, D. A. (1991). *Psychiatric disorders in America: The epidemiologic catchment area study.* New York: Free Press. Robinson, J. G. (2001). ESCAP II: Demographic analysis results (U.S. Census Bureau Report No. 1). Washington, D.C.: U.S. Government Printing Office.

Robinson, J. G. (2001) *ESCAP II: Demographic analysis results* (U.S. Census Bureau Report No. 1). Washington, D.C.: U.S. Government Printing Office.

Robinson, J. G., Bashir, A., Prithwis, D. G., & Woodrow, K. A. (1993). Estimation of population coverage in the 1990 United States Census based on demographic analysis. *Journal of the American Statistical Association, 88,* 1061-1071.

Rumbaut, R. G. (1996a). Immigrants from Latin America and the Caribbean: A socioeconomic profile. In Rochin, R. I. (Ed.), *Immigration and ethnic communities: A focus on Latinos.* East Lansing, MI: Julian Samora Research Institute.

Rumbaut, R. G. (1996b). Origins and destinies: Immigration, race, and ethnicity in contemporary America. In S. Pedraza & R. G. Rumbaut (Eds.), *Origins and destinies: Immigration, race, and ethnicity in America* (pp. 21-42). Belmont, CA: Wadsworth.

Seeman, T. E., Crimmins, E., Huang, M. H., Singer, B., Bucur, A., Gruenewald, T., Berkman, L. F., et al. (2004). Cumulative biological risk and socioeconomic differences in mortality: MacArthur Studies of Successful Aging. *Social Science & Medicine, 58,* 1985-1997.

Singh, G. K., & Miller, B. A. (2004). Health, life expectancy, and mortality patterns among immigrant populations in the United States. *Canadian Journal of Public Health, 95,* I14-I21.

Singh, G. K., & Yu, S. M. (1996). Adverse pregnancy outcomes: Differences between US- and foreign-born women in major US racial and ethnic groups. *American Journal of Public Health, 86,* 837-843.

Sorlie, P. D., Rogot, E., & Johnson, N. J. (1992). Validity of demographic characteristics on the death certificate. *Epidemiology, 3,* 181-184.

Swenson, C. J., Trepka, M. J., Rewers, M. J., Scarbo, S., Hiatt, W. R., & Hamman, R. F. (2002). Cardiovascular disease mortality in Hispanics and non-Hispanic whites. *American Journal of Epidemiology, 156,* 919-928.

Tucker, C., McKay, R., Kojetin, B., Harrison, R., de la Puente, M., Stinson, L., & Robison, E. (1996). Testing methods of collecting racial and ethnic information: Results of the current population survey supplement on race and ethnicity. *Bureau of Labor Statistical Notes, 40,* 1-149.

U.S. Census 2000. (2000). *General demographic characteristics by race for the United States: 2000.* (PHC-T-15). Washington, D.C.: U.S. Government Printing Office.

Vega, W. A., & Amaro, H. (1994). Latino outlook: Good health, uncertain prognosis. *Annual Review of Public Health, 15,* 39-67.

Wallace, J. M., Bachman, J. G., O'Malley, P. M., Johnston, L. D., Schulenberg, J. E., & Cooper, S. M. (2002). Tobacco, alcohol, and illicit drug use: Racial and ethnic differences among U.S. high school seniors, 1976-2000. *Public Health Reports, 117,* S67-S75.

Wallace, J. M., Brown, T. N., Bachman, J. G., & Laveist, T. A. (2003). The influence of race and religion on abstinence from alcohol, cigarettes and marijuana among adolescents. *Journal of Studies on Alcohol, 64,* 843-848.

Wallace, J. M., & Forman, T. A. (1998). Religion's role in promoting health and reducing risk among American youth. *Health Education and Behavior, 25,* 725-741.

Waters, M. C. (1999). Black identities: *West Indian Immigrant dreams and American realities.* New York: Russell Sage Foundation.

Williams, D. R. (1997). Race and health: Basic questions, emerging directions. *Annals of Epidemiology, 7,* 322-333.

Williams, D. R. (2003). The health of men: Structured inequalities and opportunities. *American Journal of Public Health, 93,* 724-731.

Williams, D. R. (2004). *Racism and health.* In K. E. Whitfield (Ed.), *Closing the gap: Improving the health of minority elders in the new millennium* (pp. 69-80). Washington, D.C.: Gerontological Society of America.

Williams, D. R., & Collins, C. (1995). U.S. socioeconomic and racial differences in health: Patterns and explanations. *Annual Review of Sociology, 21,* 349-386.

Williams, D. R., Neighbors, H. W., & Jackson, J. S. (2003). Racial/ethnic discrimination and health: Findings from community studies. *American Journal of Public Health, 93,* 200-208.

Zane, N. W. S., Takeuchi, D. T., & Young, K. N. S. (1994). *Confronting critical health issues of Asian and Pacific Islander Americans.* Thousand Oaks, CA: Sage.

3

The Effects of Childhood Stress on Health Across the Lifespan

Source: Middlebrooks, J.S. and N.C. Audage. 2008. *The Effects of Childhood Stress on Health Across the Lifespan.* Atlanta, GA: Centers for Disease Control and Prevention, National Center for Injury Prevention and Control.

Stress is an inevitable part of life. Human beings experience stress early, even before they are born. A certain amount of stress is normal and necessary for survival. Stress helps children develop the skills they need to cope with and adapt to new and potentially threatening situations throughout life. Support from parents and/or other concerned caregivers is necessary for children to learn how to respond to stress in a physically and emotionally healthy manner.

The beneficial aspects of stress diminish when it is severe enough to overwhelm a child's ability to cope effectively. Intensive and prolonged stress can lead to a variety of short- and long-term negative health effects. It can disrupt early brain development and compromise functioning of the nervous and immune systems. In addition, childhood stress can lead to health problems later in life including alcoholism, depression, eating disorders, heart disease, cancer, and other chronic diseases.

The purpose of this publication is to summarize the research on childhood stress and its implications for adult health and well-being. Of particular interest is the stress caused by child abuse, neglect, and repeated exposure to intimate partner violence (IPV).

We hope this publication provides practitioners, especially those working in violence prevention, with ideas about how to incorporate this information into their work.

TYPES OF STRESS

Following are descriptions of the three types of stress that The National Scientific Council on the Developing Child has identified based on available research:[1]

Positive stress results from adverse experiences that are short-lived. Children may encounter positive stress when they attend a new daycare, get a shot, meet new people, or have a toy taken away from them. This type of stress causes minor physiological changes including an increase in heart rate and changes in hormone levels. With the support of caring adults, children can learn how to manage and overcome positive stress. This type of stress is considered normal and coping with it is an important part of the development process.

Tolerable stress refers to adverse experiences that are more intense but still relatively short-lived. Examples include the death of a loved one, a natural disaster, a frightening accident, and family disruptions such as separation or divorce. If a child has the support of a caring adult, tolerable stress can usually be overcome. In many cases, tolerable stress can become positive stress and benefit the child developmentally. However, if the child lacks adequate support, tolerable stress can become toxic and lead to long-term negative health effects.

Toxic stress results from intense adverse experiences that may be sustained over a long period of time—weeks, months or even years. An example of toxic stress is child maltreatment, which includes abuse and neglect. Children are unable to effectively manage this type of stress by themselves. As a result, the stress response system gets activated for a prolonged amount of time. This can lead to permanent changes in the development of the brain. The negative effects of toxic stress can be lessened with the support of caring adults. Appropriate support and intervention can help in returning the stress response system back to its normal baseline.

THE EFFECTS OF TOXIC STRESS ON BRAIN DEVELOPMENT IN EARLY CHILDHOOD

The ability to manage stress is controlled by brain circuits and hormone systems that are activated early in life. When a child feels threatened, hormones are released and they circulate throughout the body. Prolonged exposure to stress hormones can impact the brain and impair functioning in a variety of ways.

- Toxic stress can impair the connection of brain circuits and, in the extreme, result in the development of a smaller brain.[1]

- Brain circuits are especially vulnerable as they are developing during early childhood. Toxic stress can disrupt the development of these circuits. This can cause an individual to develop a low threshold for stress, thereby becoming overly reactive to adverse experiences throughout life.[1]

- High levels of stress hormones, including cortisol, can suppress the body's immune response. This can leave an individual vulnerable to a variety of infections and chronic health problems.[1]

- Sustained high levels of cortisol can damage the hippocampus, an area of the brain responsible for learning and memory. These cognitive deficits can continue into adulthood.[1]

The National Scientific Council on the Developing Child has been studying the effects of toxic stress on brain development. Papers summarizing the scientific literature can be found on-line at www.developingchild.net.

THE EFFECTS OF TOXIC STRESS ON ADULT HEALTH AND WELL-BEING

Research findings demonstrate that childhood stress can impact adult health. The Adverse Childhood Experiences (ACE) Study is particularly noteworthy because it demonstrates a link between specific (1) violence-related stressors, including child abuse, neglect, and repeated exposure to intimate partner violence, and (2) risky behaviors and health problems in adulthood.

The ACE Study

The ACE Study, a collaboration between the Centers for Disease Control and Prevention (CDC) and Kaiser Permanente's Health Appraisal Clinic in San Diego, uses a retrospective approach to examine the link between childhood stressors and adult health. Over 17,000 adults participated in the research, making it one of the largest studies of its kind. Each participant completed a questionnaire that asked for detailed information on their past history of abuse, neglect, and family dysfunction as well as their current behaviors and health status. Researchers were particularly interested in participants' exposure to the following ten ACE:[3]

Abuse
- Emotional
- Physical
- Sexual

Neglect
- Emotional
- Physical

Household Dysfunction
- Mother treated violently
- Household substance abuse
- Household mental illness
- Parental separation or divorce
- Incarcerated household member

General ACE Study Findings

The ACE Study findings have been published in more than 30 scientific articles. The following are some of the general findings of the study:

Childhood abuse, neglect, and exposure to other adverse experiences are common. (See Table 1.) Almost two-thirds of study participants reported at least one ACE, and more than one in five reported three or more.[3] (See Table 2.)

Table 1	Prevalence of Individual Adverse Childhood Experiences[3]

ACE Category		Women (N = 9,367)	Men (N = 7,970)	Total (N = 17,337)
Abuse				
	Emotional Abuse	13.1%	7.6%	10.6%
	Physical Abuse	27.0%	29.9%	28.3%
	Sexual Abuse	24.7%	16.0%	20.7%
Neglect				
	Emotional Neglect*	16.7%	12.4%	14.8%
	Physical Neglect*	9.2%	10.7%	9.9%
Household Dysfunction				
	Mother Treated Violently	13.7%	11.5%	12.7%
	Household Substance Abuse	29.5%	23.8%	26.9%
	Household Mental Illness	23.3%	14.8%	19.4%
	Parental Separation or Divorce	24.5%	21.8%	23.3%
	Incarcerated Household Member	5.2%	4.1%	4.7%

* Collected during the second survey wave only (N = 8,667).

Table 2	ACE Score[3]

Number of Adverse Childhood Experiences (ACE Score)	Women	Men	Total
0	34.5%	38.0%	36.1%
1	24.5%	27.9%	26.0%
2	15.5%	16.4%	15.9%
3	10.3%	8.6%	9.5%
4 or more	15.2%	9.2%	12.5%

The short- and long-term outcomes of ACE include a multitude of health and behavioral problems. As the number of ACE a person experiences increases, the risk for the following health outcomes also increases:[3]

- alcoholism and alcohol abuse
- chronic obstructive pulmonary disease
- depression
- fetal death
- illicit drug use
- ischemic heart disease
- liver disease
- risk for intimate partner violence

- multiple sexual partners
- sexually transmitted diseases
- smoking
- suicide attempts
- unintended pregnancies

ACE are also related to risky health behaviors in childhood and adolescence, including pregnancies, suicide attempts, early initiation of smoking, sexual activity, and illicit drug use.[3]

As the number of ACE increases, the number of co-occurring health conditions increases.[3]

Violence-Related ACE Study Findings

Findings from the ACE Study confirm what we already know—that too many people in the United States are exposed early on to violence and other childhood stressors. The study also provides strong evidence that being exposed to certain childhood experiences, including being subjected to abuse or neglect or witnessing intimate partner violence (IPV), can lead to a wide array of negative behaviors and poor health outcomes. In addition, the ACE Study has found associations between experiencing ACE and two violent outcomes: suicide attempts and the risk of perpetrating or experiencing IPV.[3]

The following section will summarize some of the ACE Study findings relevant to violence. Some findings relate to participants' past history of abuse, neglect, and IPV exposure, while others involve the link between ACE and adult behaviors and health status.

Child Maltreatment and its Impact on Health and Behavior

- 25% of women and 16% of men reported experiencing child sexual abuse.[4]
- Participants who were sexually abused as children were more likely to experience multiple other ACE.[4]
- The ACE score increased as the child sexual abuse severity, duration, and frequency increased and the age at first occurrence decreased.[4]
- Women and men who experienced child sexual abuse were more than twice as likely to report suicide attempts.[5]
- A strong relationship was found between frequent physical abuse, sexual abuse, and wit-

nessing of IPV as a child and a male's risk of involvement with a teenage pregnancy.[6]
- Women who reported experiencing four or more types of abuse during their childhood were 1.5 times more likely to have an unintended pregnancy at or before the age of twenty.[7]
- Men and women who reported being sexually abused were more at risk of marrying an alcoholic and having current marital problems.[5]

Witnessing Intimate Partner Violence (IPV) as a Child and its Impact on Health and Behavior

- Study participants who witnessed IPV were two to six times more likely to experience another ACE.[8]
- As the frequency of witnessing IPV increased, the chance of reported alcoholism, illicit drug use, IV drug use, and depression also increased.[8]
- Exposure to physical abuse, sexual abuse, and IPV in childhood resulted in women being 3.5 times more likely to report IPV victimization.[9]
- Exposure to physical abuse, sexual abuse, and IPV in childhood resulted in men being 3.8 times more likely to report IPV perpetration.[9]

The Link Between ACE and Suicide Attempts

- 3.8% of study participants reported having attempted suicide at least once.[10]
- Experiencing one ACE increased the risk of attempted suicide two to five times.[10]
- As the ACE score increased so did the likelihood of attempting suicide.[10] (See Figure 1, not included.)
- The relationship between ACE and the risk of attempted suicide appears to be influenced by alcoholism, depression, and illicit drug use.[10]

ACE and Associated Health Behaviors

Associations were found between ACE and many negative health behaviors. A partial list of behaviors is included below. For a complete list, see the ACE Study web site at www.cdc.gov/nccdphp/ace/index.htm.

- Participants with higher ACE scores were at greater risk of alcoholism.[11]
- Those with higher ACE scores were more likely to marry an alcoholic.[12]

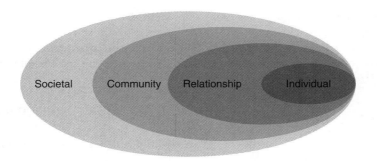

Figure 2 The Social-Ecological Model

- Study participants with higher ACE scores were more likely to initiate drug use and experience addiction.[13]

- Those with higher ACE scores were more likely to have 30 or more sexual partners, engage in sexual intercourse earlier, and feel more at risk of contracting AIDS.[14,15]

- Higher ACE scores in participants were linked to a higher probability of both lifetime and recent depressive disorders.[16]

IMPLICATIONS FOR CHILD MALTREATMENT PREVENTION

Child maltreatment is one example of toxic stress. CDC works to stop maltreatment, including abuse and neglect, before it initially occurs. Prevention of child maltreatment requires understanding the circumstances and factors that cause it. CDC uses a four-level social ecological model to better understand potential strategies for prevention. This model considers the complex interplay between individual, relationship, community and societal factors. (See Figure 2.)

INDIVIDUAL LEVEL STRATEGIES

Parent Education

Educational programs that occur in group settings are used to reduce the risk factors and enhance the protective factors that are associated with the perpetration of child maltreatment. Often, these programs contain multiple components that include training on parenting topics (e.g., discipline), moderated discussions with the children, and facilitated parent-child interactions. This model provides parents with new skills and gives them an opportunity to apply the skills in a safe environment. There is

some scientific research showing that programs of this type are effective. The evidence base continues to grow.[18]

Some of these parent education programs occur in clinical settings. For example, a hospital-based program has been developed to teach new parents about the dangers of violently shaking an infant. This program was found to reduce the rates of abusive head trauma to infants.[19]

Child Education

Most schools in the United States provide curricula to help children avoid or report abuse. Research has shown that this method is effective in teaching children about safety and providing them with skills that may reduce their risk of abuse.[18] However, the research has also shown that children are less likely to believe they are at risk from parents or caregivers, the same people who are most likely to abuse them.[18] Additional information is needed about how these skills transfer in abusive situations where the perpetrator is someone the child knows well and trusts.

Screening and Treatment

The early identification and treatment of toxic stress, including child maltreatment, can lessen the associated long-term negative health and behavioral outcomes. Daycare providers, teachers, and other adults who interact frequently with children should have sufficient knowledge and skills to identify and care for children who have been exposed to traumatic childhood experiences. They should be familiar with support services to meet the needs of children whose problems cannot be adequately addressed by frontline staff.[20] Social service agencies that are responsible for investigating suspected cases of abuse and neglect should include a thorough assessment of a child's developmental status.[20] This assessment should include the measurement of cognitive, linguistic, emotional, and social competence.[1] Individuals who have experienced ACE should receive help. This may involve psychotherapy, theater workshops, movement therapy, hypnotherapy, expressive writing, diary programs or some combination.[21]

RELATIONSHIP LEVEL STRATEGIES

Parent-Child Centers

Parent training and education is often delivered within comprehensive parent-child centers. These centers provide a stable learning environment in which parents and their children can interact. Studies have found that families participating in these centers have lower levels of child maltreatment.[22]

Home Visitation

This type of program involves trained personnel visiting families in their homes to deliver training, education, and support. The trained personnel can be nurses, social workers, paraprofessionals, or peers. Home visits often begin before birth and continue past a child's second birthday. These programs include training on prenatal and infant care as well as child development. They also enhance problem solving skills, assist with educational and work opportunities, and provide referrals to community services. A systematic review conducted by the non-federal Task Force on Community Preventive Services found that early childhood home visitation results in a 40% reduction in episodes of abuse and neglect.[23] Not all home visitation programs were found to be equally effective. Those deemed to be successful in preventing child maltreatment were specifically aimed at high-risk families, lasted two years or longer, and were conducted by professionals (as opposed to trained paraprofessionals).[23]

COMMUNITY, ORGANIZATIONAL, AND SOCIAL LEVEL STRATEGIES

Public Awareness Campaigns

Public awareness campaigns have long been used as a prevention strategy for a variety of health issues, including child maltreatment. These campaigns include a variety of public service announcements involving television, radio, the Internet, print media, and billboards. Research has shown that these campaigns are effective in raising awareness about the existence of child maltreatment and its devastating impact on

victims.[18] However, there is not yet conclusive evidence to show that public awareness campaigns change the attitudes and behaviors of parents.[18] Research in this area is ongoing.

USING THIS INFORMATION

Many violence prevention practitioners are unaware of the research on toxic stress and Adverse Childhood Experiences. The following suggestions are meant to help CDC's partners make the case that stopping violence before it occurs can reduce risky behaviors, prevent chronic disease, and foster adult health.

1. Share Knowledge

There are many ways you can share the research with your partners and constituents:

- Incorporate the research into presentations for professional and lay audiences.
- Invite a Subject Matter Expert to give a conference keynote address, participate in Grand Rounds, or provide staff training.
- Work with reporters to highlight the issue on the Internet, television, radio or in print media, including newspapers and magazines.
- Reference the research in scholarly journal articles.
- Use the data in a mayoral or gubernatorial proclamation to prevent child maltreatment or intimate partner violence.
- Work with local colleges and universities to incorporate the research into the curricula of psychology, nursing, medicine, social work, and public health programs.

2. Collect Data

Survey instruments are available on-line (www.cdc.gov/NCCDPHP/ACE/questionnaires.htm). These can be used to assess the prevalence of ACE in populations that are of interest to you. The data can be incorporated into any of the strategies mentioned in "Share Knowledge."

3. Secure Additional Resources

The data can be incorporated into grant applications or used when other opportunities to secure additional resources become available. Several CDC partners have used the data to demonstrate that violence prevention leads to overall health and well-being.

ADDITIONAL INFORMATION

- The National Center for Injury Prevention and Control www.cdc.gov/ncipc
- The National Scientific Council on the Developing Child www.developingchild.net
- The Adverse Childhood Experiences (ACE) Study www.cdc.gov/nccdphp/ace/index.htm

References

1. National Scientific Council on the Developing Child. Cambridge: The Council: 2005 [cited 2007 April 9]. Excessive stress disrupts the architecture of the developing brain. Working Paper No. 3. Available from: http://www.developingchild.net/pubs/wp/Stress_Disrupts_Architecture_Developing_Brain.pdf.

2. Finkelhor D, Ormrod, R,Turner H, Hamby S. The victimization of children and youth: a comprehensive, national survey. *Child Maltreatment.* 2005;10(1):5-25.

3. Centers for Disease Control and Prevention. Atlanta: CDC; 2006 [cited 2007 April 9]. Adverse Childhood Experiences Study Available from: http://www.cdc.gov/nccdphp/ace/index.htm.

4. Dong M,Anda RF, Dube SR, Giles WH,Felitti VJ. The relationship of exposure to childhood sexual abuse to other forms of abuse, neglect and household dysfunction during childhood. *Child Abuse Negl.* 2003;27(6):625-39.

5. Dube SR, Anda RF, Whitfield CL, Brown DW,Felitti VJ, Dong M,et al. Long-term consequences of childhood sexual abuse by gender of victim. *Am J Prev Med.* 2005;27(5):430-8.

6. Anda RF, Felitti VJ, Chapman DP, Croft JB, Williamson DF, Santelli JS, et al. Abused boys, battered mothers, and male involvement in teen pregnancy. *Pediatrics.* 2001;107(2):E19.

7. Dietz PM, Spitz AM,Anda RF, Williamson DF, McMahon PM, Santelli JS, et al. Unintended pregnancy among adult women exposed to abuse or household dysfunction during their childhood. *JAMA.* 1999;282(14):1359-64.

8. Dube SR, Anda RF, Felitti VJ, Edwards VJ, Williamson DF. Exposure to abuse, neglect and household dysfunction among adults who witnessed intimate partner violence as children: Implications for health and social services. *Violence Vict.* 2002;17(1):3-17.

9. Whitfield CL, Anda RF, Dube SR, Felitti VJ. Violent childhood experiences and the risk of intimate partner violence in adults: assessment in a large health maintenance organization. *J Interpers Violence.* 2003;18(2):166-85.

10. Dube SR, Anda RF, Felitti VJ, Chapman D, Williamson DF, Giles WH.Childhood abuse, household dysfunction and the risk of attempted suicide throughout the life span: findings from the Adverse Childhood Experiences Study. *JAMA.* 2001;286(24):3089-96.

11. Anda RF, Whitfield CL, Felitti VJ, Chapman D, Ewards VJ, Dube SR, et al. Adverse childhood experiences, alcoholic parents, and later risk of alcoholism and depression. *Psychiatr Serv.* 2002; 53(8):1001-9.

12. Dube SR, Anda RF, Felitti VJ, Edwards VJ, Croft JB. Adverse childhood experiences and personal alcohol abuse as an adult. *Addict Behav.* 2002;27(5):713-25.

13. Dube SR, Felitti VJ, Dong M,Chapman DP, Giles WH,Anda RF. Childhood abuse, neglect and household dysfunction and the risk of illicit drug use: the Adverse Childhood Experience Study. *Pediatrics.* 2003;111(3):564-72.

14. Dube SR, Felitti VJ, Dong M,Giles WH,Anda RF. The impact of adverse childhood experiences on health problems: evidence from four birth cohorts dating back to 1900. *Prev Med.* 2003;37(3):268-77.

15. Hillis SD, Anda RF, Felitti VJ, Marchbanks PA. Adverse childhood experiences and sexual risk behaviors in women: a retrospective cohort study. *Fam Plann Perspect.* 2001;33:206-211.

16. Chapman DP, Whitfield CL, Felitti VJ, Dube SR, Edwards VJ, Anda RF. Adverse childhood experiences and the risk of depressive disorders in adulthood. *J Affect Disord.* 2004;82(2):217-25.

17. National Scientific Council on the Developing Child. Cambridge: The Council: 2004 [cited 2007 april 9]. Young children develop in an environment of relationships. Working Paper No. 1. Available from: http://www.developingchild.net/pubs/wp/Young_Children_Environment_ Relationships.pdf.

18. Daro D, McCurdy K. Interventions to prevent child maltreatment. In: Doll L, Bonzo S, Sleet D, Mercy J, Hass E, editors. *Handbook of Injury and Violence Prevention.* New York: Springer; 2007. p.137-56.

19. Dias MS, Smith K, deGuehery K, Mazur P, Li V, Shaffer ML. Preventing abusive head trauma among infants and young children: a hospital-based, parent education program. *Pediatrics.* 2005;115(4):470-7.

20. National Scientific Council on the Developing Child. Cambridge: The Council: 2006 [cited 2007 April 9]. Children's emotional development is built into the architecture of their brains. Working Paper No. 2. Available from: http://www.developingchild.net/pubs/wp/Childrens_Emotional_Development_Architecture_Brains.pdf.

21. Edwards VJ, Anda RF, Felitti VJ, Dube SR. Adverse childhood experiences and health-related quality of life as an adult. In: K. Kendall-Tackett, editor. *Victimization and Health*. Washington, D.C.: American Psychological Association;2003.

22. Reynolds AJ, Temple JA, Ou SR. School-based early intervention and child well-being in the Chicago longitudinal study. *Child Welfare*. 2003;82:633-56.

23. Centers for Disease Control and Prevention. First reports evaluating the effectiveness of strategies for preventing violence: early childhood home visitation and firearms laws. Findings from the Task Force on Community Preventive Services. *MMWR* 2003; 52(No. RR-14):1-9.

4

Behavioral Determinants of Health Aging Revisited: An Update on the Good News for the Baby Boomer Generation

---

Source: Potkanowicz, E., P. Hartman-Stein, and J. Biermann. 2009. Behavioral Determinants of Health Aging Revisited: An Update on the Good News for the Baby Boomer Generation" *OJIN: The Online Journal of Issues in Nursing* 14 (3).

ABSTRACT

On October 15th, 2007, Kathleen Casey-Kirschling became the first Baby Boomer to ride the "silver tsunami" by applying for her social security benefits. Riding a wave is an appropriate analogy for Baby Boomers given the expectations they have for their later years. Now, just as it was in the original 2003 Behavioral Determinants article, the answer to the question, "Can this generation of Americans expect to achieve a satisfying, high-quality life as older adults?" is still a resounding yes. But now, there is greater clarity and more specific detail as to exactly what the Baby Boomer generation should, and can, be doing to insure that they have the quality of life as older adults that they have become accustomed to in their younger years. To that end, this article will examine the updated recommendations for physical activity and psychological elements associated with healthy aging.

On October 15th, 2007, Kathleen Casey-Kirschling became the first of the Baby Boomer generation to ride the "silver tsunami" (a term coined by Mary Finn Maples in 2002 to represent the rising swell of Baby Boomers moving towards older adulthood) by applying for her social security benefits. Having been born at one second past midnight on January 1, 1946, Ms. Casey-Kirschling has the unique distinction of being regarded as Baby Boomer #1. The "wave" is not only a figurative symbol for the Baby Boomers. The wave is also this group's literal expectation for continuing an active and fulfilling lifestyle into their later years. In other words, Baby Boomers want to hike, bike, and surf their way into retirement.

In the original Behavioral Determinants article (Hartman-Stein & Potkanowicz, 2003), we spoke of the leading edge of the Baby Boomer generation moving steadily towards their older adult years. Those born between 1946 and 1964 will start to reach the age of 65 by 2011; and estimates now suggest that by 2030 the number of adults 65 years of age and over will be 71 million, or, 20% of the United States (U.S.) population (Centers for Disease Control and Prevention [CDC], 2007). The wave is a big one.

Like the steady march of this Baby Boomer generation, the recommendations for healthy aging have continued to move forward and change as well. As such, an update to the original (2003) article is warranted. The foundation for this update is the recent position stand released jointly by the American College of Sports Medicine and the American Heart

Association (AHA) (Nelson et al., 2007). This position stand incorporates the recommendations of numerous health and fitness organizations, findings from the research community, and literature reviews. This position stand suggests that now, just as it was in 2003, the answer to the question, "Can this generation of Americans expect to achieve a satisfying, high-quality life as older adults?" is still a resounding yes. But now, there is greater clarity and more specific detail as to exactly what the Baby Boomer generation should be doing to insure that they have the quality of life as older adults that they have become accustomed to in their younger years. To that end, this article will examine both the updated recommendations for physical activity and psychological elements associated with healthy aging.

THE KEY TO REMAINING PHYSICALLY FIT

Physical fitness includes both health-related fitness and skill-related fitness. In this section the authors will define physical fitness, discuss the role of physical activity in fitness, offer guidance for pre-exercise screening, and review the updated recommendations for aerobic activity, muscle strengthening, and flexibility and balance. They will conclude by considering how much physical activity is enough.

What Physical Fitness Really Is

For the sake of clarity, physical fitness is defined by the American College of Sports Medicine (ACSM) as:

> . . . a set of attributes or characteristics that people have or achieve that relates to the ability to perform physical activity. These characteristics are usually separated into either health-related or skill-related components (2009, p. 2).

Although many people aspire to possess the skill-related components associated with physical fitness, e.g., agility, balance, coordination, speed, power, and reaction time, we benefit more on a day-to-day basis, and certainly in the long term, from the health-related components of physical fitness. That is not to say that skill-related attributes cannot be attained or achieved by the older adult; but rather that the general population of older adults benefits more significantly from possessing the health-related attributes. As defined by the ACSM (2006, p. 3), health-related physical fitness:

> . . . is associated with the ability to perform daily activities with vigor, and the possession of traits and capacities that are associated with a low risk of premature development of hypokinetic diseases (e.g. those associated with physical inactivity, like obesity, diabetes, and hypertension).

The combination of high levels of both health-related fitness, and its associated traits and capacities, such as cardiovascular endurance, muscular fitness, flexibility, body composition, and physiologic fitness (fitness that relates to the status of metabolic systems, body compositional factors, and bone mineral density) can increase a Baby Boomer's chances of enjoying a life filled with satisfying personal experiences, a life of good quality, and a life of pursuits not hindered by physiological setbacks . . .

The Role of Physical Activity in Fitness

Fitness and healthcare professionals have made great strides in improving the public's recognition of the importance of regular physical activity. Through the work of organizations, such as the American College of Sports Medicine (ACSM), The American Heart Association (AHA), and The National Institutes of Health (NIH), as well as through initiatives like Healthy People 2010, the public's recognition of the importance of regular physical activity has improved appreciably. However, there are those who suggest that the biggest challenge that the fitness and healthcare professions face is clearing up the confusion that the public has with regard to exactly what they should be doing in terms of physical activity. In other words, the public is unsure as to what types of actual activities are needed, how often these activities should be performed, and with what intensity they should be performed (Howley, Bassett, & Thompson, 2005; U.S. Department of Agriculture & the U.S. Department of Health and Human Services, 2005).

What makes the topic of exercise recommendations particularly problematic and troublesome is that this lack of specific information can potentially lead to inactivity and/or indifference. According to the CDC (2007), physical inactivity is one of the three behaviors (along with smoking and poor diet) that contributed to almost 35% of all deaths in the U.S. in the year 2000, as these behaviors often contributed to the development of diseases. Sadly, the older adult population is the least active of all age groups (CDC, 2003). In 2002, 32% of adults age 65 and older died from heart disease, 22% died from cancer, and 8% died from a stroke. In total, these three conditions represented 61% of all deaths among this age group (CDC, 2007). Perhaps the most disturbing recognition is that the eventual deaths associated with these conditions were largely preventable. Baby Boomers today stand a very good chance of dramatically reducing their risk for developing a chronic disease as long as they include regular physical activities in their daily lives and receive appropriate direction regarding these activities.

Pre-Exercise Screening

In the original 2003 article, the recommendations offered for physical activity were prefaced by the recommendations that (a) before beginning any exercise program, the individual should consult with a physician to insure that he or she is healthy enough to begin an exercise program, and (b) the individual should seek the advice and guidance of an exercise professional certified through a recognized certifying body, such as the ACSM or National Strength and Conditioning Association. Both of these recommendations still stand and are strongly encouraged.

However, the screening process is changing today. While not a substitute for direct contact with an exercise or medical professional, older adults can now begin the screening process and initiate a self-directed physical activity program through the use of a new screening tool called the EASY tool, which is an acronym for Exercise Assessment and Screening for You. The EASY tool, according to the authors (Resnick et al., 2008, p. 215):

> . . . is a tool developed to help older individuals, their health care providers, and exercise professionals identify different types of exercise and physical activity regimens that can be tailored to meet the existing health conditions, illnesses, or disabilities of older adults.

The authors go on to say that the EASY tool can be completed either independently by the older adult or with the assistance of a healthcare or exercise professional. The authors contend that pre-exercise screening should not keep people from being physically active (and many screening tools do so), but rather should set people on their way to being physically active, given that physical activity in all age groups is good. The EASY tool is available online at the EASY website www.easyforyou.info.

Updated Recommendations for Aerobic Activity

When one considers the number of activities in any given day that require aerobic activity, commonly called endurance, and the important role of endurance in independent living, the importance of sufficient aerobic capacity becomes apparent. Older adults need sufficient aerobic capacity to get through their day and to retain their independent lifestyle. Spirdusso, Francis, and MacRae (2005) noted that estimates of minimal levels of aerobic capacity for independent living are approximately 13 milliliters of oxygen per kilogram of mass for each minute of activity (or 3.7 METS, where 1 MET $= 3.5$ ml $\times$ kg^{-1} $\times$ min^{-1}).

Research has demonstrated that aerobic capacity changes as one ages. Estimates place the age-related decline in aerobic capacity at approximately 1% per year, for each year after the age of 25 (Spirdusso et al., 2005). Furthermore, the rate of decline is thought to increase between the ages of 65 and 75 and then again between the ages of 75 and 85. Sufficient aerobic capacity not only helps to maintain an independent lifestyle, it also contributes to the prevention of multiple chronic disease processes. Being physically active is an important tool in promoting healthy aging.

Before examining the updated recommendations for aerobic activity, it is important to operationally define some aerobic-related terms. With respect to aerobic activity, and relative to one's fitness level, moderate-intensity aerobic activity is defined as a rating of 5-6 on a 10-point scale, where 0 is sitting, 10 is an all out effort, and 5-6 involves a noticeable increases in heart rate and breathing (Nelson et al., 2007). Similarly, and using the same 10-point scale, vigorous-intensity aerobic activity is defined as a rating of 7 or 8, at which point large increases in heart rate and breathing are noted (Nelson et al.).

The new recommendations from the ACSM and the AHA (Nelson et al., 2007) suggest that in order to maintain and promote health, the older adult needs to participate in moderate-intensity aerobic activity for a minimum of 30 minutes on five (5) days each week. Or, if capable, the older adult can engage in vigorous-intensity aerobic activity for 20 minutes on three (3) days each week. It should be noted that the recommendations also indicate that a combination of both moderate- and vigorous-intensity aerobic activity can be performed to meet these aerobic activity recommendations. An important point to remember is that these recommendations for aerobic activity are in addition to the normal, light-intensity activities of daily living (ADLs) which include self care or cooking, or moderate-intensity activities (e.g., walking around the office or walking from the parking lot) lasting less than 10 minutes respectively. For a comparison of the full 2003 and 2008 recommendations please refer to Table 1.

Updated Recommendations for Muscle Strengthening

Within the context of activities of daily living, there are a number of activities that require moderate levels of strength and power (e.g., carrying groceries, lifting grandchildren, and getting into and out of a car) (Spirdusso, Francis, & MacRae, 2005). More complex activities, too, require more than minimal levels of muscular strength. A muscular strength training regimen is necessary to have the lifestyle outcomes desired by the Baby Boomers. The importance of muscular strength training cannot be understated.

Before examining the recommendations for muscular strength, it is again appropriate to operationally define some terms with respect to level of effort. With respect to muscle-strengthening activities, a moderate-intensity effort is defined as a rating of 5-6 on a 10-point scale, where 0 is no movement and 10 is a

Table 1	Comparison Table—Physical Activity: Recommendations for Older Adults, 2003 vs. 2007	
Category	**2003 Physical Activity Recommendations** (Hartman-Stein & Potkanowicz, 2003)	**2007 Physical Activity Recommendations** (Nelson et al., 2007)
Aerobic Activity (i.e., cardiorespiratory fitness)	3–5 days/week 30–60 minutes accumulated time 55–90% of Maximum Heart Rate	Minimum 30 minutes, on 5 days each week at moderate intensity (5–6 on a 10-point [pt]. scale) Or If capable, 20 minutes, on 3 days each week at vigorous intensity (7–8 on a 10 pt. scale)
Muscle Strengthening	Progressive in nature and individualized, 8–10 exercises, consisting of one set of 8–12 repetitions on 2–3 days per week	Minimum 2 non-consecutive days per week, 8–10 exercises, 10–15 repetitions at moderate (5–6 on a 10 pt. scale) to high (7–8 on a 10 pt. scale) intensity
Flexibility	Participate in flexibility training that addresses the major muscle groups and their respective ranges of motion 2–3 days per week	Participate in flexibility training that addresses the major muscle groups and their respective ranges of motion on at least two days of the week for at least 10 minutes each time
Balance	No formal recommendation Passively addressed as a part of the overall recommendation	Older adults should intentionally pursue and participate in exercise to improve/maintain balance rather than passive inclusion as part of an overall program

maximal effort for the muscle group (Nelson et al., 2007). Using the same 10-point scale, a high-intensity effort is defined as a rating of 7 or 8.

According to the new recommendations (Nelson et al., 2007), older adults should strive to engage in activities that maintain or increase muscular strength on a minimum of two days each week. To that end, older adults should choose 8-10 exercises that use major muscle groups and perform them on two or more non-consecutive days each week. Each exercise, and its associated resistance (weight) should allow for 10-15 repetitions, with the level of effort being moderate to high (relative to one's ability).

Updated Recommendations for Flexibility and Balance

The recommendations for flexibility have remained relatively unchanged, except for recommendations regarding frequency and duration. Older adults are still encouraged to participate in some form of flexibility training; however, they are now encouraged to do so on at least two days of each week for at least 10 minutes each time. As we stated in the original article (Hartman-Stein & Potkanowicz, 2003), "When we take the time to consider just how important freedom of movement and flexibility are in everyday living, it becomes easier to see the significant role that flexibility training can play in maintaining one's quality of life."

An element not directly addressed in the 2003 article is the current recommendation that older adults should intentionally pursue and participate in exercises and training that improve balance and reduce the risk of falls. In the past, balance training was considered a passive component of some other training mechanism or regimen. The current recommendations suggest that as a way to prevent falls in those individuals with a known risk for falls; for example, older adults with mobility problems or those who fall frequently, the older adult should perform exercises that will contribute to the maintenance and improvement of balance (Nelson et al., 2007). To add to that, the older adult should pursue these activities even if he or she does not present with known risks, given that prevention is the key to reducing the risk of falls.

Some Is Good, More Is Better

The preceding recommendations represent the minimum levels of involvement with respect to aerobic activity and muscle strengthening. Being minimum recommendations, the older adult can expect to experience the minimum in the way of outcomes. While this amount of improvement is not necessarily a bad thing, Nelson et al. (2007) point out that if older adults wish to: (a) improve their personal fitness, (b) improve their management of an existing condition or disease where higher levels of physical activity may have greater therapeutic value, and/or (c) reduce their risk of premature health conditions or mortality from chronic conditions related to physical inactivity, they should strive to engage in activities that exceed the minimum levels. This recommendation assumes that the older adult does not have a condition that would preclude higher levels of physical activity. Further, the older adult should also pursue additional muscle-strengthening, higher-impact, and weight-bearing activities in an effort to further maintain and enhance skeletal health. Examples of these muscle-strengthening and weight-bearing activities include increasing the number of muscles or muscle groups trained, working at progressively higher intensities, and jogging rather than walking.

Perhaps most encouraging for the older adult are studies showing that the older adult possesses a capacity for change, both aerobically and muscularly, that is similar to the young adult (Frontera, Meredith, O'Reilly & Evans, 1988; Kohrt et al., 1991; Meredith et al., 1989). While the exact mechanism of change in the older adult has yet to be fully elucidated, the message is quite clear: physical activity contributes to successful and healthy aging. Although it cannot be definitively stated that physical activity extends life, it can be said that physical activity improves life, given its influence on the incidence and onset of chronic disease.

THE KEY TO A SHARP MIND

In the original 2003 article, we noted, "cognitive decline, especially memory deficit associated with aging, is a concern of many Baby Boomers in regard to their parents as well as themselves." We also reviewed the topics of maintaining cognitive abilities, emotional health, and the relationship between religion and physical and mental health. While the latter two areas remain important elements of healthy aging, maintaining cognitive ability and slowing age-related cognitive decline have become hot topics for researchers and the general public. Many new resources related to cognitive abilities are available for the general public. In the last few years, however, the media has been abuzz with hopeful news that we may be able to keep our brain fit just as we keep our body fit, and thereby age successfully. In this section we will examine recent findings addressing the preservation of the older adult's cognitive capacity as we discuss theoretical perspectives related to cognitive functioning, such as cognitive reserve and neurogenesis; interventions to enhance cognitive functioning, for example, enriched environments and cognitive activities; the relationships between and among physical activities, cognition, and social functioning; and commercial brain fitness products.

Cognitive Reserve

Until relatively recently, the dominant view of cognitive aging has been that of pervasive, progressive, and irreversible decline. However, current theoretical underpinnings of enhancing cognitive fitness later in life, i.e., at age 65 and older, are based on the concepts of cognitive reserve and neural plasticity. Both constructs are exciting and hopeful because they imply that the older adult can actively help to preserve his/her intellectual capacity. Cognitive reserve theory explains why some individuals are more resilient or adaptive to brain pathology and can function well in everyday life despite neuronal damage. It implies that people have more cognitive capacity than needed for survival, and that we can draw from an extra "reserve" when needed (Stern, 2006; Vance & Crowe, 2006).

According to cognitive reserve theory, a higher reserve arises from a combination of greater overall cognitive efficiency, greater proliferations of brain neurons, more connections between neurons, and an enhanced ability to compensate by recruiting generalized neurons for specific tasks at hand and using alternative strategies to solve problems (Grady, 2006). The investigations into the hypotheses of cognitive reserve suggest that childhood cognition, educational and IQ levels, professional attainment, occupational complexity, and lifestyle characteristics, such as level of activity and nutrition, all lead to greater cognitive reserve (Richards & Sacker, 2003; Scarmeas & Stern, 2003). Although older, retired adults are not able to build cognitive reserve via childhood educational and occupational attainment, they can make changes in their current lifestyle through engagement in educational and other cognitive-enhancing activities. Vance and Crowe (2006) suggest that the steps to prevent loss or to increase cognitive reserve include engaging in cognitively stimulating activities and using cognitive training techniques. The reserve model is a dynamic

process that applies across the life course, suggesting that cognitive ability is modifiable at all life stages (Richards, Sacker, & Deary, 2006). These notions clearly have significant positive implications for the aging Baby Boomer.

Neurogenesis

Similarly encouraging is the theory of neurogenesis. For most of the twentieth century, scientists believed that brain cells, unlike hair cells, skin cells and other cells in the body, could not reproduce; i.e., a human would have no more neurons at death than he or she had at birth—and would probably have significantly fewer. Then, near the end of the last century, researchers discovered that two brain structures, the hippocampus (a structure involved in memory and learning) and the olfactory bulb (the brain structure involved in the perception of odor) could generate new cells. Even adults beyond the age of 65 had the capacity for neurogenesis in these two structures (Gould, Beylin, Tanapat, Reeves, & Shors, 1999). This phenomenon, originally discovered in bird models, has also been found in other animal models, most often rats or mice, and sometimes dogs. Such research must use animal models because it entails sacrificing animals to examine their brain for signs of new cells. However, among neuroscientists, there is no doubt that what has been observed in other mammals is also true of humans, and that this potential exists throughout the lifespan (Bruel-Jungerman, Rampon, & Laroche, 2007).

Along the lines of neurogenesis, there is evidence to suggest that there can also be growth in the connections between neurons. Vigorous physical activity appears to enhance neuronal growth, while learning, which involves using the cells, appears to promote new connections (Olson, Eadie, Ernst, & Christie, 2006). Taken together, the factors that can produce structural and functional changes in the brain are referred to collectively as an "enriched environment." Although all of the research to date has used animal models, usually rats or mice, the potential is encouraging for humans.

Improving Cognitive Capacity through Enriched Environments

In 2006 the community of scientists on the cutting edge of research regarding the role of physical and cognitive exercise in promoting cognitive vitality made the following recommendation: The concept of the "enriched environment" currently employed in animal studies to promote physical activity, socialization, and problem solving, needs to be explored in human studies (Studenski et al., 2006).

Having an "enriched environment" seems to be the key to improving cognitive capacity. Such an environment comprises increased opportunities for physical activity, learning, and social interaction. In their experiments using animal models, Kempermann, Kuhn, and Gage (1997) found that even a short-term exposure to such an environment led to a striking, five-fold increase in new neurons, along with a substantial improvement in behavioral performance. They observed more learning, more exploratory behavior, and more locomotor activity in enriched environments. These results are strong evidence that signs of neuronal aging in humans can be diminished by sustaining an active and challenging life, even if these stimulating activities start later in life. There are both cognitive and physical pursuits which, if performed to an appropriate level of intensity and frequency, will promote various benefits for older adults. For example, an eight-year, longitudinal study of over 1,000 older adults in Finland found that higher levels of physical and leisure activity were associated with, and predictive of, mental well-being in later life, thus suggesting these activities are appropriate target areas for prevention of cognitive decline (Lampinen, Heikkinen, Kauppinen, & Heikkinen, 2006).

Cognitive Activities

Cognitive scientists study cognition in terms of specific functions, such as attention, recall, expressive and receptive language, motor coordination, and executive functions that include planning and problem solving as well as stress management and emotional modulation. Many researchers, as well as the general public, believe that these skills inevitably decline with age. Hence, there have been quite a few attempts over the past decades to train people in these specific functions as a defense against time. In general, results of empirically supported studies using healthy older adults suggest that specific skills can be improved when targeted by an intervention (Studenski et al., 2006; Willis et al., 2006).

A few studies have found evidence of generalized benefit from cognitive training programs. For example, the Advanced Cognitive Training for Independent and Vital Elderly (ACTIVE) study (Willis et al., 2006) showed that cognitive training in the areas of reasoning, memory, or speed of processing improved cognitive function in adults 65 years and older who are living independently, and the improvement lasted at least five years, if there was some booster training. The benefits of all types of cognitive training were detectable on the specific trained skill after five years, but only training in reasoning ability had a self-reported impact on preserving ability to function well in everyday life.

One emerging and promising area of research is the design and evaluation of interventions that offer ecologically valid activities in "real life" environments, because of their increased likelihood for acceptance and adherence by older adults. One example is the Experience Corps (EC) project that has forged a partnership between older adults and the public schools (Glass et al., 2004). In this project, teams of older adults worked in elementary school classrooms where they participated in teaching literacy and math skills as well as conflict resolution. Older adults deemed at the greatest risk for cognitive impairment who participated in this project showed improvement in executive functioning and memory skills (Carlson et al., 2004).

Another innovative program is the first intergenerational Charter School in Cleveland, Ohio. In this program, children aged six to twelve learn in the company of older adults, some of whom have been diagnosed as having Alzheimer's Disease (Whitehouse & George, 2008). The program, initiated in 2003, creates opportunities for older adults to contribute to their community by sharing their knowledge and experience, while exercising multiple cognitive skills. Specific activities are described on the school website <www.tisonline.org/>. The long-term cognitive benefits of participating in such a program are not yet known, but anecdotal evidence suggests that volunteering in this award-winning program enhances quality of life for the older adult while providing service in the community.

Physical Activities and Cognition

Physical fitness training, specifically aerobic training, has been found to have robust benefits for cognition. In the original 2003 article, the work of Colcombe and Kramer (2003) was cited as evidence of the relationship between physical activity and cognition. In our 2003 article we noted these researchers had concluded that when it came to the question of whether or not aerobic fitness training is beneficial to the older adult, the researchers had provided an unequivocal yes. While Colcombe and Kramer were successful in validating the beneficial effects of physical activity on cognition, they noted that numerous moderating effects, such as type of fitness training, program duration, session duration, and their respective influences on the effectiveness of the training, need to be considered in future research.

Spirdusso, Poon, and Chodzko-Zajko (2008) observed that there are moderators, e.g., age, gender, or education, and mediators, e.g., physical activity, physical resources, disease state, or mental resources that influence the effectiveness of physical activity on cognition. While it is often stated in the literature that physical activity has an effect on one's cognitive ability, including one's ability to learn, retrieve, and problem solve, Spirdusso et al. have suggested that there are mediating factors, such as our physical resources, our disease state, and our mental resources that influence just how well physical activity will work in effecting a positive change in cognition. Further, they have observed that moderating factors, such as age, gender, education, estrogen levels, and genotype, must be considered. The reader is directed to the book, *Exercise and Its Mediating Effects on Cognition,* by Spirduso et al. for a more complete discussion of this particular topic.

More recently, new evidence has surfaced that has further validated the role of aerobic conditioning in the preservation of cognition. Colcombe et al. (2006), in an effort to determine whether aerobic fitness training of older adults increased brain volume in regions associated with age-related decline, subjected two groups of volunteers to either six months of aerobic training or six months of toning and stretch training (20 young adults served as controls and underwent no training). It was determined that the training promoted significant increases in both grey (the neurons of the cortex) and white (the connecting pathways) matter regions. Their evidence suggests that cardiovascular fitness and training is associated with the sparing of brain tissue in aging humans, and with maintaining and enhancing cognitive functioning in older adults.

Cognitive, Physical, and Social Functioning

Cognitive training alone and physical training alone each have benefits for cognitive function. However, when an individual engages in both types of training, there appears to be a multiplier effect in which each enhances the impact of the other. Olson et al. (2006) noted that the two work together to enhance cognitive function, especially in the hippocampus where learning occurs. Oswald et al. (2006) provided cognitive, physical, and also psycho-education training together. They reported that over a five-year period, they observed significant training effects, including fewer depressive symptoms in the participants compared to a control group, which did not receive the training.

Newson and Kemps (2006), too, found that the combination of physically and cognitively stimulating activities was related to better cognitive performance. In their study, participants recorded their engagement (time and effort) in such physical activities as running, swimming, and jogging; and cognitive activities, such as reading a book and completing crossword puzzles. They were then tested on a visual imagery task which made demands on cognitive function. By choosing this task for their test, Newson and Kemps claimed that the results of their study are indicative of a broad range of cognitive demands people face. The data analysis suggested that cognitive activities promoted performance on complex cognitive tasks better than the physical activity, but both physical and cognitive activity promoted general cognitive function. The authors concluded that both physical and cognitive stimulation offer protection against cognitive decline with age, but likely take different paths in doing so.

Meaningful activities are those that require skill, concentration, feedback, deep involvement, and also a sense of flow, i.e, loss of awareness of the passage of time due to focused concentration (Hartman-Stein & Potkanowicz, 2003). Professionally conducted, community-based cultural programs are examples of such activities. In a study of 166 healthy older adults, participants were assigned to a singing chorale intervention or comparison group of usual activities and were followed for 12 months (Cohen et al., 2006). The intervention group reported better morale and less loneliness, as well as a higher overall rating of physical health, including less medication use, fewer doctor visits, and fewer instances of falls. This positive effect suggests that organized group activities have potentially important health promotion and disease prevention benefits.

Additionally, Cohen et al. (2006) identified health-promoting activities for older adults, to be those that provide either a sense of mastery, and/or require the involvement of simultaneous bilateral brain involvement, and/or include meaningful social engagement. Fave and Massimini (2005) surveyed people from several cultures on the psychological features of optimal activity in daily life. They consistently found that optimal experience was most closely associated with activities that were complex, highly structured, and enjoyable, and that provided opportunities for self-expression, required a high level of concentration to do the task, and would lead to skill development. Stern (2006) stated that what seems to matter is that there be a variety of activities both intellectual and social in nature that are challenging to the individual.

Table 2	Brain Activities Websites

Brain games available on the web without charge
- www.fitbrains.com/games
- www.gamesforthebrain.com
- www.freerice.com/index.php

Commercial brain fitness programs
- www.mybraintrainer.com
- www.cogmed.com
- www.positscience.com
- www.calibex.com/nintendo-brain-game
- www.luminosity.com

Brain Fitness Blog
- www.sharpbrains.com/

Commercial Brain Fitness Products

Several commercial brain exercise products are currently available such as Posit Science's "Brain Fitness," "My Brain Trainer," and Nintendo's "Brain Age" programs. Some of these are listed in Table 2. Currently, though, there are more commercial products designed as brain exercises than there are empirically supported research studies of the effectiveness of these products. Based on her review of the current literature, LaRue (2008) concluded that there is no one cognitive activity or combination of activities that can currently be identified for reducing the risk of dementia. She made the following cognitive-activity recommendations for older adults:

- Carve out time for cognitively stimulating activities that have been enjoyable throughout your life.
- Add some new challenging pursuits, as time and energy allow.
- Aim to engage in cognitively challenging pursuits several times a week.
- Participate in social interactions.

Table 3 provides a listing of self-help books and consumer education related to brain fitness. The sources cited throughout this paper speak with one voice: the characteristics of activities that people most want to engage in are challenging, require skill, allow the person to get involved at a deep level, and at least some of the time, have an element of social involvement.

SUMMARY

In summary, as was the case in the original article from 2003, "the news for the baby boomer generation is indeed positive regarding their upcoming late

Table 3	Resources for Brain Fitness: Self-help Books and Consumer Education

Alvaro, F., & Elkhonon, G. (2009). *The sharp brain's guide to brain fitness: 18 interviews with scientists, practical advice, and product reviews, to keep your brain sharp*. North Charleston, SC: BookSurge, LLC.

Amen, D.G. (2008). *Magnificent mind at any age*. New York, NY: Harmony Books.

Cohen, G.D. (2005). *The mature mind: The positive power of the aging brain*. New York, NY: Basic Books.

Engleman, M., Ragsdale, E., & Kinney, T. (2006). *Whole brain workouts*. Verona, WI: Attainment Company, Inc.

Golberg, E. (2005). *The wisdom paradox. How your mind can grow stronger as your brain grows older*. New York, NY: Gotham Books.

Green, C.R. (1999). *Total memory workout: 8 Easy steps to maximum memory fitness*. New York, NY: Bantam Books.

Maples, M.F. (2002). Holistic adult development: A spirituality perspective. Paper presented at the Connection of the Association for Counselor Education and Supervision. San Antonio, TX.

McKhann, G., & Albert, M. (2002). *Keep your brain young: The complete guide to physical and emotional health and longevity*. New York, NY: John Wiley & Sons, Inc.

Nussbaum, P. (2003). *Brain health and wellness*. Tarentum, PA: Word Association Publishers.

Perlmutter, D., & Colman, C. (2004). *The better brain book: The best tools for improving memory and sharpness and for preventing aging of the brain*. New York, NY: Riverhead Books.

Small, G. (2002). *The memory bible: An innovative strategy for keeping your brain young*. New York, NY: Hyperion.

Small, G., & Vorgan, G. (2004). *The memory prescription: Dr. Gary Small's 14-day plan to keep your brain and body young*. New York, NY: Hyperion.

Weil, A., & Small, G. (2007). *The healthy brain kit*. Louisville, CO: Sounds True.

life years" (Hartman-Stein & Potkanowicz, 2003). The research community has provided evidence that just as physical exercise benefits the body, so also exercising the brain can have protective and enhancing effects. We are beginning to gather the evidence that just as physical exercise is not only good but also necessary for the body, so also cognitive challenge is necessary to keep the brain working well. These new understandings make it an exciting time to contemplate the future of aging, a time when older adults can be fully functioning without the prevalence of some of the declines and deficits that we have here-to-fore accepted as an unavoidable side effect of getting older.

The Next Wave

As was stated at the beginning of this article, on October 15th, 2007, Kathleen Casey-Kirschling became the first of the Baby Boomer generation to ride the silver tsunami by applying for her social security benefits. The actual definition of a tsunami is a series of waves. With the expectations of the first wave of Baby Boomers being as high as they are, the assumption can safely be made that the next wave of Baby Boomers and the waves of Baby Boomers to follow will have higher and greater expectations for themselves compared to those in the first wave. Simply put, they will want more out of life in their later years compared to their predecessors. In order to accommodate them we, as fitness and healthcare professionals, must champion the cause of making regular physical activity and cognitive training a part of every Baby Boomer's daily life.

Authors

Edward S. Potkanowicz, PhD, ACSM HFS
E-mail: potkanow@ohio.edu
Dr. Edward S. Potkanowicz received his PhD degree from Kent State University in 2003. He received his Bachelor of Science degree in Exercise Science from Youngstown State University and his Master's in Physical Education, with an Exercise Physiology concentration, from Kent State University. Dr. Potkanowicz is currently an Assistant Professor at Ohio University and has spent a number of years working closely with the older adult population conducting research related to the effects of aging on thermoregulation, as well as research into methods for improving and maintaining functional fitness within the older adult population. Dr. Potkanowicz is a certified Health Fitness Specialist (HFS) member of the American College of Sports Medicine, as well a member of The American Physiological Society, The European Group for Research in Physical Activity and Aging, and The International Society for Aging and Physical Activity.

Paula Hartman-Stein, PhD
E-mail: cha@en.com
Dr. Paula E. Hartman Stein is a clinical psychologist specializing in issues related to aging. She provides clinical and consulting services in her private practice, the Center for Healthy Aging, located in Kent, Ohio, In addition, Dr. Hartman-Stein is the Director of Geriatric Psychology at Summa Health System in Akron, Ohio, where she chairs a geriatric mental health alliance. She is currently directing a multi-year grant that provides cognitive fitness programs for older adults at Laurel Lake Retirement Community in Hudson, Ohio. Academic affiliations include Assistant Professor of Psychology in Psychiatry at the Northeastern Ohio Universities College of Medicine; Senior Fellow at the University of Akron Institute for Life Span Development and Gerontology; and Adjunct Associate Professor of Psychology in the Department of Psychology at Kent State University, Kent, Ohio.

Jeanette S. Biermann, PhD, MBA, MA
E-mail: jsb37@uakron.edu
Dr. Biermann received her BA in Mathematics from Valparaiso University, her MBA from Cleveland State University, and her PhD in Operations Research from Case Western Reserve University in Cleveland, Ohio. After 25 years she left her career in the business/corporate world to prepare for a new career in geropsychology. She expects to soon complete requirements for the PhD in Counseling Psychology degree at the University of Akron. An important part of her preparation has included working under the supervision of Dr. Paula Hartman-Stein at the Center for Healthy Aging in Kent, Ohio, and also working at the Summa Health System Hospital in Akron, Ohio. She is currently completing a geropsychology internship at the Veterans Administration Medical Center in Miami, Florida. Her dissertation, which is in progress, is focused on aspects of older adults' cognition, attention, and decision making.

● ● ● References

American College of Sports Medicine (2009). *ACSM's guidelines for exercise testing and prescription (8th ed.)*. Baltimore, MD: Lippincott Williams and Wilkins.

Bruel-Jungerman, E., Rampon, C., & Laroche, S. (2007). Adult hippocampal neurogenesis, synaptic plasticity and memory: facts and hypotheses. *Review of Neuroscience, 18*, 93-114.

Carlson, M.C., Saczynski, J.D., Rebok, G. W., Glass, T. A., McGill, S., Tielsch, J., et al. (2004). *Experience Corps: Results of a pilot randomized controlled trial of a senior service program on cognitive function*. Paper presented at the 57th Annual Scientific Meeting of the Gerontological Society of America, Washington, D.C.

Centers for Disease Control and Prevention. (2003). Prevalence of physical activity, including lifestyle activities among adults-United States, 2000-2001. *Morbidity and Mortality Weekly Report, 52*: 764-769.

Centers for Disease Control and Prevention and The Merck Company Foundation (2007). *The state of aging in America*. Whitehouse Station, NJ: The Merck Company Foundation.

Cohen, G.D., Perlstein, S., Chapline, J., Kelly, J., Firth, K.M., & Simmens, S. (2006). The impact of professionally conducted cultural programs on the physical health, mental health, and social functioning of older adults. *The Gerontologist, 46,* 726-734.

Colcombe, S. J., Erickson, K. I., Scalf, P. E., Kim, J. S., Prakash, R., McAuley, E., et al. (2006). Aerobic exercise training increases brain volume in aging humans. *Journals of Gerontology, 61,* 1166-1170.

Colcombe, S.J., & Kramer, A.F. (2003). Neurocognitive aging and cardiovascular fitness. *Journal of Molecular Neuroscience, 24,* 9-14.

Fave, D., & Massimini, F. (2005). The relevance of subjective well-being to social policies: Optimal experience and tailored intervention. In F. A. Huppert, N. Baylis, & B. Keverne (Eds.). *The Science of well-being.* (pp. 379-404). New York: Oxford University Press.

Frontera, W.R., Meredith, C.N., O'Reilly, K.P., & Evans, W.J. (1988). Strength conditioning in older men: Skeletal muscle hypertrophy and improved function. *Journal of Applied Physiology, 64,* 1038-1044.

Glass, T.A., Freedman, M., Carlson, M.C., Hill, J., Frick, K.D., Ialongo, N., et al. (2004). Experience Corps: design of an intergenerational program to boost social capital and promote the health of an aging society. *Journal of Urban Health. 81,* 94-105.

Gould, E., Beylin, A., Tanapat, P., Reeves, A., & Shors, T. J. (1999). Learning enhances adult neurogenesis in the hippocampal formation. *Nature Neuroscience. 2,* 260-265.

Grady, C. L. (2006). In Y. Stern, (Ed.). *Cognitive reserve: Theory and application* (pp. 265-283). New York, NY: Taylor and Francis, Inc.

Hartman-Stein, P., & Potkanowicz, E.S. (2003). Behavioral determinants of healthy aging: Good news for the baby boomer generation. *Online Journal of Issues in Nursing 8(2).* Available: www.nursingworld.org/MainMenuCategories/ ANAMarketplace/ANAPeriodicals/OJIN/Tableof Contents/Volume82003/No2May2003/Behavior andHealthyAging.aspx.

Howley, E.T., Bassett Jr., D.R., & Thompson, D.L. (2005). Get them moving: Balancing weight with physical activity, part II. *ACSM's Health and Fitness Journal, 9,* 19-23.

Kempermann, G., Kuhn, H.G., & Gage, F.H. (1997). More hippocampal neurons in adult mice living in an enriched environment, *Nature, 386,* 493-495.

Kohrt, W.M., Malley, M.T., Coggan, A.R., Spina, R.J., Ogawa, T., Ehsani, A.A., et al. (1991). Effects of gender, age and fitness level on response of VO_2max to training in 60-71 yr olds. *Journal of Applied Physiology, 71,* 2004-2011.

Lampinen, P., Heikkinen, R.L., Kauppinen, M. & Heikkinen, E. (2006). Activity as a predictor of mental well-being among older adults. *Aging and Mental Health, 10,* 454-466.

LaRue, A. (2008, October). *Brain fitness: Public policy, entrepreneurs and a little science.* Paper presented at the Geriatric Behavioral Healthcare Conference on evidence-based community interventions for geriatric depression and cognitive decline, Summa Health System, Akron, Ohio.

Meredith, C.N., Frontera, W.R., Fisher, E., Hughes, V., Herland, J., Edwards, J., et al. (1989). Peripheral effects of endurance training in young and old subjects. *Journal of Applied Physiology, 66,* 2844-2849.

Nelson, M., Rejeski, W., Blair, S., Duncan, P., Judge, J., King, A., et al. (2007). Physical activity and public health in older adults: Recommendation from the American College of Sports Medicine and the American Heart Association. *Medicine and Science in Sport and Exercise, 39,* 1435-1445.

Newson, R. S., & Kemps, E. B. (2006). The influence of physical and cognitive activities on simple and complex cognitive tasks in older adults. *Experimental Aging Research, 32,* 341-362.

Olson, A.K., Eadie, B.D., Ernst C., & Christie, B.R. (2006). Environmental enrichment and voluntary exercise massively increase neurogenesis in the adult hippocampus via dissociable pathways. *Hippocampus, 16,* 250-60.

Oswald, W. D., Gunzelmann, T., Rupprecht, R., & Hagen, B. (2006). Differential effects of single versus combined cognitive and physical training with older adults: The SimA study in a 5-year perspective. *European Journal of Ageing, 3,* 179-192.

Resnick, B., Ory, M.G., Hora, K., Rogers, M.E., Page, P., Bolin, J.N., et al. (2008). A Proposal for a new screening paradigm and tool called Exercise Assessment and Screening for You (EASY). *Journal of Aging and Physical Activity, 16,* 215-233.

Richards, M., & Sacker, A. (2003). *Lifetime antecedents of cognitive reserve. Journal of Clinical and Experimental Neuropsychology, 25,* 614-624.

Richards M., Sacker A., & Deary I. J. (2006). Lifetime antecedents of cognitive reserve. In Y. Stern (Ed.), *Cognitive Reserve.* (pp. 37-52). New York, NY: Psychology Press.

Scarmeas, N., & Stern, Y. (2003). Cognitive reserve and lifestyle. *Journal of Clinical and Experimental Neuropsychology, 25,* 625-633.

Spirduso, W., Francis, K.L., & MacRae, P.G. (2005). *Physical dimensions of aging.* Champaign, IL: Human Kinetics.

Spirduso, W., Poon, L.W., & Chodzko-Zajko, W. (2008). *Exercise and its mediating effects on cognition.* Champaign, IL: Human Kinetics.

Stern, Y. (2006). *Cognitive reserve: Theory and application.* New York, NY: Taylor and Francis, Inc.

Studenski, S., Carlson, M.S., Fillit, H., Greenough, W.T., Kramer, A., & Rebok, G.W. (2006). From bedside to bench: Does mental and physical activity promote cognitive vitality in late life? *Science of Aging Knowledge Environment, 2006(10)*, 21.

U.S. Department of Agriculture and U.S. Department of Health and Human Services. (2005). *Dietary guidelines for Americans 2005*. Washington, DC: U.S. Government Printing Office.

Vance, D.E., & Crowe, M. (2006). A proposed model of neuroplasticity and cognitive reserve in older adults. *Activities, Adaptation & Aging, 30*, 61-79.

Whitehouse, P.J., & George, D. (2008). *The Myth of Alzheimer's: What you aren't being told about today's most dreaded diagnosis*. New York, NY: St. Martin's Press.

Willis, S.L., Tennstedt, S. L., Marsiske, M., Ball, K., Elias, J., Koepke, K. M., et al. (2006). Long-term effects of cognitive training on everyday functional outcomes in older adults. *The Journal of the American Medical Association, 296*, 2805-2814.

III

Medical Health Determinants: Inputs

Inputs and infrastructure are both essential for ensuring the supply of health care services in quantities sufficient to address the levels of demand. This part of the book covers three main health system inputs: workforce, financing, and technology. Actually, all three play a dual role. They are important inputs in determining the nature and quantity of services available, and they are also important determinants of the demand for medical services. Health system infrastructure is covered in Part IV.

The health care workforce constitutes a critical input in supporting the health delivery infrastructure. Supply of medical services, such as the availability of primary care, is largely dependent on the supply of a generalist medical workforce. On the other hand, the high demand for specialist care in the United States is partly driven by the abundance of specialists in the U.S. health care system. In the global health workforce, critical shortages of physicians and nurses exist in both developing and underdeveloped countries. Various factors affecting the workforce supply and the main workforce-related issues are addressed in Chapter 6.

Demand for medical services is created primarily through the financing of health insurance which plays a significant role in determining access to medical services. In the United States, both private and tax-financed public insurance sources are prevalent. The supply of medical services is determined mainly in two ways. (1) Reimbursement levels, that is, the amount that providers of services get paid in exchange for the services delivered, affect supply indirectly. Providers often base their decisions to expand or contract services on the amount of reimbursement, favorable or unfavorable changes in reimbursement methodologies, and the opportunity to make a profit. For example, physicians' decisions to accept Medicaid patients are based largely on the level of reimbursement from Medicaid. Technological innovation and utilization are also driven by the level of reimbursement from both private and public insurance sources. (2) The government's direct investment in public health and safety net infrastructure determines supply of certain basic health care services for the uninsured and underprivileged. Through its influence on both demand and supply of health care, financing eventually determines total health care expenditures. The cost-effectiveness of medical care in the United States remains a hot topic for now and the future. Chapter 7 sheds additional light on these topics.

Some of the main controversies surrounding medical technology are discussed in Chapter 8. While other nations have used various mechanisms to ration the use of technology and, in turn, restrain innovation, the United States has not employed any supply-side measures to slow down the growth of technological innovation and utilization. As a result, Americans outdo other nations in technological innovations, and new technologies find their own demand when they are covered by insurance. Unrestricted use of technology is one reason why the United States surpasses all other countries in health care spending. Whether commonly used medical technologies add value by promoting health and longevity in relation to their cost is open to debate because relatively little research has been done to evaluate the cost-effectiveness of these technologies. At least one thing is clear: Not all technology adds value.

6

The Health Workforce

With over 3 percent of the total labor force, the U.S. health care industry is the largest employer in the nation. The U.S. Bureau of Labor Statistics (2005) projects seven of the ten fastest growing occupations for 2004-2014 are health related. The health care sector of the U.S. economy will continue to grow for two main reasons: (1) growth in population mainly due to immigration, and (2) aging of the population, especially as the baby boom generation starts to hit retirement age in 2011 and beyond.

The health workforce includes physicians, nurses, dentists, pharmacists, optometrists, psychologists, podiatrists, chiropractors, nonphysician practitioners (NPPs), health services administrators, and allied health professionals. The latter category incorporates therapists, laboratory and radiology technicians, social workers, and health educators. These professionals work in a variety of healthcare settings including hospitals, managed care organizations, nursing care facilities, mental health institutions, insurance firms, pharmaceutical companies, outpatient facilities, community health centers, migrant health centers, mental health centers, school clinics, physicians' offices, laboratories, voluntary health agencies, professional health associations, colleges of medicine and allied health professions, and research institutions.

Growth of the number and type of health workforce is closely associated with factors associated with both the need and demand for healthcare services. These include population trends, disease and illness trends, advances in research and technology, and changes in healthcare financing and delivery. Population growth and the aging of the population enhance the demand for health services. The changing patterns of disease from acute to chronic have led to an increasing emphasis on behavioral risk factors, and the need for health services professionals who are prepared to address these health risks, their consequences, and their prevention. Advances in scientific research and new and complex medical techniques and machines contribute to new methods of preventing, diagnosing, and treating illness. Scientific research and technological advancement have also contributed to specialization in medicine and the proliferation of different types of medical technicians. With the passage of the healthcare reform act, the widespread availability of insurance from both the public and private sectors would further contribute to the increase in medical care utilization, which would then create a greater demand for health care providers. Changes in reimbursement from retrospective to prospective payment methods and increased enrollment in managed care have contributed to a slowdown in cost escalation, a shift from inpatient to outpatient care, and an emphasis on the role of primary care providers.

However, the U.S. health workforce is still characterized by an imbalance between primary and specialty care services, which has contributed to an imbalance in the ratio of generalists to specialists. There is a growing disparity between primary care physicians and specialists as more graduates choose more specialized branches of medicine such as anesthesiology, dermatology, and radiology over primary care specialties, such as general pediatrics, general internal medicine, and general and family practice. Another growing trend among physicians is the decline of small, self-owned practices. Now there are large group practices as well as independent practices that contract their services to hospitals or clinics. Multispecialty practices fare better in the US healthcare system because they have greater leverage in negotiating payments from private insurance companies due to a larger patient pool and the ability to offer a variety of services (Pham and Ginsburg 2007). The current health workforce also sees a large disparity in regional distribution as well as racial and ethnic composition of the workforce, which does not represent the population of the country.

The chasm between the supply of specialists and primary care physicians only continues to widen as no significant reform is done to control the situation. Evidence has shown that a healthcare system that emphasizes primary care has better overall health than one that focuses on specialization (Goodman and Grumbach 2008). Yet, the US healthcare system continues to graduate more specialists than primary care physicians (Shortell and Swartzberg 2008). This is the result of poor job satisfaction among primary care providers (PCP) and the gap in income between specialists and PCPs. PCPs are not pleased with reimbursements from Medicaid and Medicare, which pay less than private insurance (Freed and Stockman 2009). The current market response to the shortage of primary care physicians has been to use NPPs such as physician assistants and nurse practitioners. In addition, multispecialty practices have begun to employ more PCPs because they can provide profit to the medical group through referrals (Pham and Ginsburg 2007).

One of the proposals to fix the growing shortage of PCPs is to increase the physician workforce by expanding the number of medical school graduates. Unfortunately, fixing the system through expansion has severe limitations. Increasing the number of students enrolled in medical school would not increase the workforce, it will only displace the number of international applicants who currently take up the first year resident slots that are not filled by American graduates. Also, increasing the number of physicians will most likely cause similar problems seen in areas with high physician supply: lack of coordination in the delivery of care and increased costs due to higher utilization of hospital-based specialty services (Goodman and Grumbach 2008).

More viable solutions to solving the problem in primary care shortage are restructuring physician payment schemes, developing integrated and coordinated care, and use of a "medical home" (Pham and Ginsburg 2007). Restructuring the physician payment scheme would involve moving away from the fee for service (FFS) system that pays physicians for volume of services administered to the patient, and moving towards positive-sum capitation that will reward or penalize physicians based on rates of spending on patients during a typical care episode or a chronic disease management period (Pham and Ginsburg 2007). This reformed payment system would push physicians to compete to improve their results, which could then improve the overall quality of care for the patients—an outcome that is not produced by the current method of cost-shifting and cost-reduction to "fix" the payment system (Porter and Teisberg 2007).

It is important to fix the problem with primary care physician supply in the United States in the face of growing prevalence for chronic diseases. Multidisciplinary teams are best suited to delivering higher-quality and lower-cost chronic care and prevention—teams that include an even balance of specialists and primary care physicians. At the moment, the proportions are skewed toward specialists, making it difficult to control preventable chronic diseases, such as diabetes, obesity, hypertension, and asthma (Bodenheimer 2009).

The other significant problem for the US health workforce is its lack of diversity. The nation's ethnic diversity is not mirrored in the population of health professions with African Americans, Latinos, and Native American Indians/Alaskan Natives underrepresented. Almost all health professions have an underrepresentation of these ethnic groups, with the exception of public health whose proportions of racial and ethnic groups are up to population parity. The lack of diversity can be linked to the failure of primary education (grades K-12) in meeting the needs of minority and low-income students and the rigorous admission policies of medical schools, which focus on quantitative measures (standardized exams and GPA). A focus on quantitative measures adversely affects minority students as they have been shown to perform worse than their non-minority peers despite having the same likelihood of graduating medical school, passing their boards, and practicing medicine as a physician (Grumbach and Mendoza 2009).

The proportion of underrepresented minorities must be increased to help produce better outcomes. Racial, ethnic, and linguistic diversity has been associated with better access to and the quality of care for racial and ethnic groups and socioeconomically disadvantage populations. Racial and ethnic minorities from disadvantaged backgrounds are more likely to serve this population during their careers than others from a dissimilar background. Racial and ethnic concordance between providers and patients has also been associated with improved quality of interpersonal care. When patients are treated by someone of the same culture and background, they are often left more satisfied with the care they have received. Increasing the number of underrepresented Latino and Asian health professionals might also broaden access to care by patients who have limited English proficiency from these backgrounds. Another result of diversity and racial and ethnic concordance is an increase of trust in the health care system among minority and socioeconomically disadvantaged populations. Most important, health professionals from disadvantaged backgrounds are more likely to provide leadership and advocate for policies and programs aimed at improving the health care of vulnerable populations. Increasing diversity should be an important focus for the health workforce and underrepresented minorities should not be limited to the public service of caring for the underserved (USDHHS 2006; Grumbach and Mendoza 2009).

Outside the United States, the shortage of healthcare workers is much more significant, especially in poorer countries, as reported by the World Health Report, *Working Together for Health*. In 2006, the global shortage of healthcare workers was estimated at 4.3 million. To address this problem, WHO established the Task Force for Scaling up Education and Training for Health Workers to draw up proposals for massive increases in education and training of health workers to build up the health systems of developing countries (Crisp 2008). The readings included in this chapter provide a glimpse of the issues identified above. Following are synopses of these readings.

In **The Physician Workforce: Projections and Research into Current Issues Affecting Supply and Demand**, USDHHS used both active supply and full-time equivalent (FTE) supply methods to produce national projections on physician supply. In 2005, there were 817,500 physicians in the workforce, a third of which were generalists (general and family practitioners, general pediatricians, and general internal medicine) while the remaining two-thirds were in specialties. Women are more likely to choose primary care specialties over surgical and other subspecialties. Women make up 52 percent of general pediatrics and 41 percent of OB/GYN, while only 2 percent of orthopedic surgeons and 5 percent of urologists. At the same time, women are also less likely to work in non-metropolitan areas, or rural areas due to spousal employment opportunities, flexible hours, availability of childcare, and opportunities for part-time employment. In terms of minority make-up of the physician workforce, only 9 percent was black or Hispanic while 25 percent of the population was black or Hispanic in the United States. Factors that have impacted current need in the physician workforce supply included the growth in managed care in the 1990s, which moved the system toward salary and capitation rather than self-employment and fee-for-service; increase in malpractice premiums, which has pushed some physicians to pursue early retirement along with physician burnout; and the aging of the physician workforce as a large physician population is nearing retirement while demand continuous to grow. If these trends continue, the supply is predicted to grow to 951,700 or 866,000 FTE, by 2020.

In **Forecasting the Global Shortage**, the authors noted that 57 countries had a shortage of physicians, nurses, and midwives totaling 2.3 million. While the number did not take into account recruitment and retention of the workforce, it still demonstrated a growing problem in the global health workforce. In 2004, the United States spent over 50 percent of the global health expenditure with 20 percent of the world's physicians and 10 percent of the global burden of disease. The European region had 35 percent of the physicians with 32 percent health expenditure. On the other hand, the global burden of disease in South-East Asia is 29 percent, but only had 11 percent of the world's physicians and 1 percent of the world's health expenditure. Similarly, the African region had 24 percent of the global disease burden, 2 percent of the world's physicians, and less than 1 percent of health expenditure.

Using both need-based and demand-based approaches to determine shortages (a shortage was defined as falling below 80 percent of the projected need and demand), 45 countries were found to have physician shortages based on need and 37 countries based on demand. Demand-based shortages correlated with countries that experienced strong economic growth, but did not have the means to grow their health workforce to keep pace with economic growth. Need-based shortage was linked to the lack of physicians to meet the determined benchmark of 80 percent live births covered by a skilled attendant. Countries facing only a need-based shortage could expand medical training programs. Countries with only a demand-based shortage could strengthen retention of medical professionals. Countries with both need- and demand-based shortages would have to adopt a mixture of both solutions. African countries showed shortages on both the need- and demand-based models.

In **The Rationale for Diversity in the Health Professions: A Review of the Evidence**, USDHHS reported that the racial/ethnic and sociodemographic compositions of the US population were not captured by the US health professionals. In particular, racial and ethnic minority groups (i.e., African-Americans, Mexican Americans, Native Americans, and mainland Puerto Ricans) and people from socioeconomically disadvantaged backgrounds were significantly underrepresented. While programs aiming to increase diversity have recently been under attack, evidence has shown that a more diverse workforce would benefit public health.

Minority physicians provide a disproportionately large portion of health care for patients in their own racial and ethnic groups despite making up a much smaller portion of the health workforce. In addition, they are also more likely to provide care to patients in lower income brackets, those insured by Medicaid, those with no insurance, and those in health professional shortage areas. Diversity in the workforce then lends to broader access to care since physicians from racial and ethnic minorities tend to care for the underserved.

A review of the literature also showed a positive effect on both racial/ethnic concordance and language concordance on access, utilization, and outcomes. Increasing diversity and providing patients with access to providers who are from similar backgrounds and speak the same language improves the quality of communication between provider and patient. Patients with limited proficiency of the English language benefit most from language concordance as they are better able to comprehend the situation. Diversity also increases the trust among minority and socioeconomically disadvantaged patients on the health care system. Patients were more likely to trust a provider from a similar background than one who was not.

The reading '*Physician Workforce Crisis: Wrong Diagnosis, Wrong Prescription,*' addresses the issues surrounding future physician shortages. In 2020, there will be a 10% shortage of physicians which brings up a concern for access to care. To resolve the problem, the Association of American Medical Colleges has called for a 30% expansion of U.S. medical schools and to lift the current cap on Medicare funding for graduate medical education to expand the workforce. Unfortunately, increasing the physician supply does not necessarily translate to better care.

Increasing physician supply may actually make the problem worse. It could continue to widen regional inequities, and undermine primary care while fostering specialization because the U.S. health care system rewards procedure-oriented specialties. In addition, expanding the supply of physicians would be expensive due to the high cost of training involved in obtaining a medical degree.

A better method of correcting the problems in the health care system may be reforming the delivery system to reduce fragmentation of care and lack of coordination. There have recently been pilot programs in both the private and public sector to address the growing problems in health care, including primary-care-based medical homes, enhanced care coordination, programs for chronic-disease management, and payment reforms. In addition, medical education funding could be reallocated towards programs that lead to improved care coordination and chronic-disease management or efforts to reform the payment process that fosters integration and more efficient care.

There is a lack of scientific support for current workforce policies. Academic medicine should take the initiative and research better methods of delivering high-quality, affordable care.

● ● ● **References**

Bodenheimer, Thomas; Chen, Ellen; Bennett, Heather. "Confronting the Growing Burden of Chronic Disease: Can the U.S. Health Care Workforce Do the Job?" *Health Affairs*. 28(2009):64-74.

Crisp, Nigel; Gawanas, Bience; Sharp, Imogen. "Training the health workforce: scaling up, saving lives." *Lancet*. 371(2008):689-691

Freed, Gary L; Stockman, James A. "Oversimplifying Primary Care Supply and Shortages." *JAMA*. 301(2009):1920-1922.

Goodman, David C.; Grumbach, Kevin. "Does Having More Physicians Lead to Better Health System Performance?" *JAMA*. 299(2008):335-337.

Grumbach, Kevin; Mendoza, Rosalia. "Disparities in Human Resources: Addressing the Lack of Diversity in The Health Professions." *Health Affairs*. 27 (2009):413-422.

Pham, Hoangmai; Ginsburg, Paul B. "Unhealthy Trends: The Future of Physician Services." *Health Affairs*. 26(2007):1586-1598.

Porter, Michael E.; Teisberg, Elizabeth Olmstead. "How Physicians Can Change the Future of Health Care." *JAMA*. 297(2007):1103-1111.

Shortell, Stephen; Swartzberg, John. "The Physician as Public Health Professional in the 21st Century." *JAMA*. 300(2008):2916-2918.

The US Bureau of Labor Statistics. Charting the US labor market in 2005. Available at: www.bls.gov/cps/labor2005/chart1-19.pdf. Accessed 2007.

United States Department of Health and Human Services (USDHHS). *The Rationale for Diversity in the Health Professions: A Review of the Evidence*. October 2006.

The Physician Workforce: Projections and Research into Current Issues Affecting Supply and Demand

Source: US Department of Health and Human Services, Health Resources and Services Administration, Bureau of Health Professions. *The Physician Workforce: Projections and Research into Current Issues Affecting Supply and Demand* (ftp://ftp.hrsa.gov/bhpr/workforce/physicianworkforce.pdf, accessed November 4, 2009). Washington, DC: US Department of Health and Human Services, 2008, pp. iv-v, 36-61, 99-106.

PHYSICIAN REQUIREMENTS

Physician "requirements" refers to an assessment of the total number of physicians needed to provide a specified level of services to a given population. Estimating physician requirements and projecting future requirements is often the most difficult and controversial component of assessing the adequacy of the physician supply. There exists no consensus on

- what constitutes an adequate level of services (given the needs of a population and its ability to pay for services),

- the relationship between requirements and certain key determinants, and

- how the characteristics of the health care system and other key determinants of physician requirements will change over time.

In the remainder of this Chapter we discuss approaches to modeling physician requirements, pro-

vide an overview of the PRM, describe the major determinants of physician requirements, and present projections from the PRM.

A. Approaches to Model Physician Requirements

Approaches to estimate physician requirements range from estimating some socially optimal number (a needs-based analysis), to estimating the number that society will likely employ (a demand-based analysis), to some variation of these approaches. In addition to simply extrapolating current physician-to-population ratios, four major approaches have been used to estimate physician requirements:

1. **Needs-based approach.** The Committee on the Costs of Medical Care (CCMC) might be considered the first attempt to apply scientific principles to determine the adequacy of physician supply in the United States. In 1933, the CCMC published its finding that the Nation needed 140.5 physicians per 100,000 population (an estimate that exceeded existing supply by 10 percent), and that 82 percent of the physician workforce should be generalists. CCMC reached its conclusion by estimating (1) the incidence of disease and other health problems, (2) the expected number of patient-physician encounters per incidence of disease, (3) the average amount of physician time per encounter with a patient, and (4) the average amount of physician time per year spent in patient

care activities. A major criticism of this approach is that it ignores the economic realities of the health care system.[16] Schroeder (1994) and others have criticized this approach as being open to bias because it relies heavily on the subjective assessments of expert panels. A further complication of using this needs-based approach is that it fails to account for the technological changes in the practice of medicine which increase the ability to treat complex clinical conditions; these technological advances are also heavily concentrated in specialty care, thereby having a larger impact on the need or demand for specialists than for primary care. GMENAC (1981) estimated physician requirements using an "adjusted" needs-based approach, similar to the CCMC study, but adjusted downward their initial requirements estimates to reflect "realistic" physician and patient behavior.

2. **Demand/utilization-based approach.** The demand-based approach extrapolates current patterns of utilization of physician services taking into account changing demographics and trends in key determinants of the demand for physician services. This approach relies primarily on empirical analysis to estimate the relationship between utilization of health care services and its determinants, and relies less on subjective assessments from a panel of experts. This approach forms the basis for HRSA's requirements models, as well as for numerous studies on individual clinical specialties. A major criticism of the demand-based approach is that because it extrapolates current health care utilization and service delivery patterns, inequities in the current system are carried into future requirements projections.

3. **Benchmarking approach.** Benchmarking involves the identification of a certain standard of care, and then extrapolating that standard to a different population. Examples of benchmarks include: (1) physician staffing patterns in HMOs (e.g., Weiner, 1994; Weiner 2004), and (2) physician-to-population ratios in other countries. Some utilization-based projections of physician requirements could be considered benchmarking, where the physi-

cian staffing patterns in future years are compared to physician staffing patterns in the reference year. The implicit assumption of benchmarking is that the benchmark (e.g., HMO, country, time period, etc.) reflects an efficient (or at least adequate) mix and number of physicians for the population served. A challenge with using this approach is that health care delivery systems might be very different between the benchmark entity and the population of interest such that a comparison of physician-to-population ratios requires substantial adjustments. For example, the role of primary care physicians in the United States might be quite different than the role of primary care physicians in other countries, which complicates the comparison of simple statistics such as physician-to-population ratios. Weiner (2004) studied three prepaid group plans and found that compared to the U.S. population as a whole, physician-to-population ratios at the three prepaid group plans were about 25 percent lower for primary care physicians and 32 percent lower for specialists.

4. **Trend analysis approach.** Cooper (2000) and colleagues (2002) use a "Trend Model" that estimates the correlation between a proxy for the demand for physician services (they use physician-to-population ratios under the assumption that historically, supply has equaled demand) and factors hypothesized to be major determinants of demand. Cooper uses aggregate-level, time-series data to estimate the relationship between physicians-per-population and its hypothesized determinants: per capita GDP and demographics to control for population growth and aging. Cooper concludes that there is a trend to desiring a higher level of care (specialist care, in particular) that is limited primarily by our ability and willingness to pay.

B. Physician Requirements Model Overview

The PRM uses a utilization-based approach to project future physician requirements. The PRM projects requirements for 18 medical specialties through 2020. Projections are based on current use patterns of physician services and expected trends in U.S. demographics, insurance coverage, and patterns of care delivery. These use patterns are expressed as physician-to-population ratios for each specialty and population segment defined by age, sex, metropolitan/

---

[16] A survey of 835 physicians by Hojat et al. (2000) found that 59 percent agreed with the statement that "cost should be considered an important factor by physicians in their decisions concerning the care of their patients."

| Population projections by age, sex, and metro/non-metro | × | Insurance distribution by age, sex, and metro/non-metro | × | Physician-per-population ratios by age, sex, metro/non-metro, insurance, and physician specialty | = | Physician requirements by population characteristics and physician specialty |

Exhibit 27 Overview of the Physician Requirements Model

non-metropolitan location, and insurance type. The baseline ratios are established using 2000 data. Thus, the major components of the model are:

1. Population projections by age,[17] sex, and metropolitan/non-metropolitan location;

2. Projected insurance distribution by insurance type, age, sex, metropolitan/non-metropolitan location; and

3. Detailed physician-to-population ratios (Exhibit 27).

The model's base year is 2000, which means that the model's baseline scenario projects growth in demand for physician services based on the level of care provided to the U.S. population in 2000. Population growth and aging, as projected by the U.S. Census Bureau, are the main drivers of growth in demand for physician services in the baseline projections. Alternative scenarios are projected using different assumptions regarding changes in insurance coverage and type, economic growth, and the increased use of NPCs. We explore trends in major determinants of physician requirements and their implications for future physician requirements.

C. Determinants of Physician Demand

Physician requirements derive from the demand for physician-related services. The demand for such services is the outcome of countless decisions made by consumers, physicians providing services, and other entities involved in the health care system such as insurers. The PRM is a simplified model of a complex health care system and tries to capture the major trends that affect the demand for physician services, and thus the number of physicians needed to provide that level of service. The major determinants of physician requirements are population growth and aging, changes in medical insurance coverage and type, economic growth, the growing role of NPCs, advances in science and technology, changing public expectations,

the price of physician services, and government policy. We discuss each of these determinants in turn.

1. Population Growth and Aging

The United States Census Bureau projects a rapid increase in the elderly population beginning in 2010 when the leading edge of the baby boom generation approaches age 65 (Exhibit 28). Between 2005 and 2020, the population younger than age 65 is expected to grow by about 9 percent, while the population age 65 to 74 is projected to grow by about 71 percent and the age 74 and older population is projected to grow by about 26%.

The elderly, especially those over age 85, use much greater levels of physician services relative to the non-elderly, so the rapid growth of the elderly population portends a significant increase in demand for physician services. To estimate differences in use of physician services by different demographic groups, for each physician specialty we estimated per capita encounters for segments of the United States population categorized by age, sex, and insurance status. We analyzed health care use data from the National Ambulatory Medical Care Survey (NAMCS), National Hospital Ambulatory Medical Care Survey (NHAMCS), National Inpatient Sample (NIS), National Nursing Home Survey (NNHS), and National Home and Health Survey (NHHS) (BHPr, 2003). After determining what portion of physicians' time is spent with each segment of the population, we calculated physician-per-population ratios that reflect current use patterns and current patterns of care.

For presentation purposes, these ratios are summarized in estimates of physician requirements per 100,000 population for four categories of physicians and six age groups (Exhibit 29). In 2000, for the United States population as a whole, approximately 253 active physicians (MDs and DOs) were engaged primarily in patient care per 100,000 population.[18] The aggregate estimates ranged from a low of 149

---

[17] The eight categories are ages 0-4, 5-17, 18-24, 25-44, 45-64, 65-74, 75-84, and 85 and older.

[18] As with the physician supply estimate, this count uses AMA and AOA Masterfile data on physicians' activity status for physicians younger than age 75.

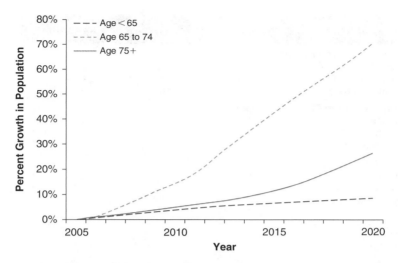

Exhibit 28 Projected Percent Growth in Population, by Age: 2005 to 2020. *Source:* United States Census Bureau population projections (April 2005 release).

for the population ages 0 to 17, to a high of 781 for the population ages 75 and older. The ratios vary substantially by medical specialty. These data suggest that the aging of the population will contribute to faster growth, in percentage terms, for specialist services relative to the growth in demand for primary care services.

The PRM segments the U.S. population into 176 mutually exclusive categories based on age, gender, metropolitan/non-metropolitan location, medical insurance status, and insurer type. The PRM considers differences in per capita health care utilization in each of these 176 categories and uses this information to estimate physician-to-population ratios in the base year for each population category. Combining these physician-to-population ratios with population

projections creates the baseline demand projections in the PRM.

2. Medical Insurance Coverage and Type

Whether a person has medical insurance and type of insurance plan are important determinants of the amount and type of physician services utilized. Insured persons have greater access to physician services, relative to the uninsured, because insurers typically negotiate discounts with providers and cover much of the cost of services. Modeling insurance coverage and type is especially important for projecting how demand for physician services will likely change under alternative insurance scenarios (e.g., implementing Federal policies or programs that expand medical coverage), and in response to trends in the

Age Group	Specialty				
	Primary[1] Care	Medical[2] Specialties	Surgery[3]	Other[4] Care	Total
0–17 years	95	10	16	29	149
18–24 years	43	15	54	48	159
25–44 years	59	23	52	62	196
45–64 years	89	41	59	81	270
65–74 years	175	97	125	145	543
75+ years	270	130	161	220	781
Total	95	33	55	70	253

Exhibit 29 Estimated Requirements for Patient Care Physicians per 100,000 Population, by Patient Age and Physician Specialty, 2000. *Source:* PRM. [1]Includes general and family practice, general internal medicine, and pediatrics. [2]Includes cardiology and other internal medicine subspecialties. [3]Includes general surgery, obstetrics/gynecology, ophthalmology, orthopedic surgery, otolaryngology, urology and other surgical specialties. 4Includes anesthesiology, emergency medicine, pathology, psychiatry, radiology, and other specialties.

Insurance Category	Population (in millions)	% of U.S. Population
Government Sponsored Programs (Population ≥ 65)		
Fee-for-service	29.2	10
Exclusive network HMO	4.6	2
All other managed care	1.2	0
Government Sponsored Programs (Population < 65)		
Fee-for-service	9.8	3
Exclusive network HMO	11.8	4
All other managed care	0.7	<1
Private		
Fee-for-service	32.1	11
Exclusive network HMO	71.1	25
All other managed care	71.8	25
Uninsured	49.2	17
Total Insured		
Fee-for-service	71.1	25
HMO	87.5	31
All other managed care	73.6	26

Exhibit 30 Estimated U.S. Population, by Insurance Status: 2000 Analysis of the 1999, 2000 and 2001 NHIS. *Source:* Analysis of the 1999, 2000 and 2001 NHIS.

health care system (e.g., such as changes in managed care enrollment rates).

Managed care plans attempt to control health care costs through the use of gatekeepers, preferred providers, utilization review and other managed care practices. The lower physician-to-population ratios among managed care plans form the basis for Weiner's (2004) analysis that suggests that the Nation could get by with substantially fewer physicians—especially specialists.

The PRM models 10 insurance categories. These include four payer categories: private insurance; Medicare (defined for modeling purposes as all government-sponsored insurance for the age 65 and older[19]); government-sponsored insurance for the age < 65 (which is primarily Medicaid); and uninsured. The three insured categories are each divided into three subcategories: traditional fee-for-service; exclusive network HMO (i.e., group-, staff-, network- or mixed-model HMO); and all other managed care plans (to include preferred provider organizations [PPOs], point-of-service [POS] plans organized as open-ended HMO, non-HMO POS, and other HMO/managed care plans).

The PRM starts with the insurance distribution in 2000 (Exhibit 30), with the probability of being in a particular insurance category differing by age and sex. The baseline projections in the PRM assume that, controlling for age and sex, the probability of being in a particular insurance category remains constant over time.

The PRM uses an index to scale the physician-to-population ratios used for each demographic group in different insurance categories (Exhibit 31).[20] In this index, the fee-for-service (FFS) setting is used as the comparison group and has an index value of 1. Consider the index values for anesthesiology. The value of 0.86 for the exclusive network HMO indicates that a person enrolled in an HMO will tend to utilize only 86 percent of anesthesiologist time, on average, compared to a similar person insured under a fee-for-service plan. Enrollees in other types of managed care plans will use approximately 98 percent and the uninsured will use only 29 percent of anesthesiologist time, on average, relative to a comparable population insured under a fee-for-service plan.

3. Economic Growth

Economic theory and empirical research suggest a positive correlation between ability to pay for physician services and demand for such services.[21] At the

---

[19] The entire population age 65 and older is assumed insured under Medicare.

[20] These index values are based on an analysis of health care utilization patterns using 1999 to 2001 data from the NAMCS, NHAMCS, NIS, NNHS and NHHS (see BHPr, 2003).

[21] Macro-level measures of ability to pay include gross domestic product (GDP) per capita and personal income per capita. An example of a micro-level measure of ability to pay is average household income.

Specialty	Fee-for-service	Exclusive Network HMO	All Other Managed Care	Uninsured
Anesthesiology	1.00	0.86	0.98	0.29
Cardiovascular Diseases	1.00	0.92	1.00[1]	0.18
Emergency Medicine	1.00	0.41	0.47	0.78
General/Family Practice	1.00	0.87	0.99	0.60
General Surgery	1.00	0.86	0.98	0.33
General Surgery Subspecialties	1.00	0.86	0.98	0.33
Internal Medicine	1.00	1.03	1.18	0.25
Internal Medicine Subspecialties	1.00	0.90	1.00[1]	0.24
Obstetrics/Gynecology	1.00	0.83	0.95	0.30
Ophthalmology	1.00	1.00[1]	1.00[1]	0.67
Orthopedic Surgery	1.00	0.78	0.90	0.22
Other Specialties	1.00	0.59	0.68	0.32
Otolaryngology	1.00	0.66	0.76	0.45
General Pediatrics	1.00	1.00[1]	1.00[1]	0.62
Pathology	1.00	0.86	0.98	0.27
Psychiatry	1.00	0.65	0.75	1.00[1]
Radiology	1.00	0.86	0.98	0.22
Urology	1.00	0.94	1.00[1]	0.21

Exhibit 31 Per Capita Index for Use of Physician Services (relative to a fee-for-service). *Source:* BHPr (2003). [1]Estimates capped.

micro level, the ability of an individual or a household to afford medical insurance and out-of-pocket expenses influences whether a person seeks needed medical services. At the macro level, the Nation's ability to pay determines the number of persons who receive medical insurance and the generosity of such insurance in terms of services covered and out-of-pocket costs to beneficiaries.[22] For example, during an economic expansion, employers might provide more generous medical benefits to attract and retain employees (Christianson and Trude, 2003). Economic growth also affects tax revenues, which in turn affect the ability of the Federal and State governments to fund programs such as Medicaid, Medicare, and the State Children's Health Insurance Program (SCHIP).

Income elasticity, the economic term for a measure that quantifies the relationship between ability to pay and demand, is defined as the percent increase in demand for physician services for each 1 percent increase in ability to pay. While the direction of the relationship between ability to pay and overall demand for physician services is clear, there exists no consensus regarding the size of this relationship. Obtaining precise estimates of this relationship is complicated by several factors:

1. The relationship likely varies by medical specialty (e.g., elective and cosmetic procedures being among the most sensitive to ability to pay). Cooper et al. (2002) find a positive correlation across States between the number of active physicians per capita (which they use as a proxy for demand) and personal income per capita, with the relationship being stronger for specialists compared to generalists.

2. The relationship reflects decisions made at the household level (e.g., whether or not to visit the doctor), at the employer level (e.g., whether to offer medical insurance), and at the societal level (e.g., whether or not to expand a government-sponsored medical insurance program).

---

[22] Holahan and Pohl (2002) find, however, that changes in per capita GDP in the United States during the period 1994 to 2000 results in little change in the overall number of insured persons. While downturns in economic activity result in a decline in number of persons insured under private plans, economic downturns result in an increased number of households eligible for Medicaid. The analysis does not, however, indicate whether the quality of the insurance products changes with changes in per capita GDP.

3. The relationship is distorted by the nature of a three-party health care system-patients, physicians and insurers. Once insured, most patients are relatively shielded from the costs of physician services and physicians are less constrained by patients' ability to pay. This tends to be true regardless of whether the insurance is public or private.

4. The relationship is confounded by variables that are correlated with both ability to pay and utilization of physician services (e.g., health status, adequacy of physician supply, and implementation of new technology).

The following is a brief summary of key and recent studies of the relationship between ability to pay and demand for health care or physician services, as well as our own empirical analysis.

Cooper et al. (2002, p. 143) state that "the major trend affecting the [per capita] demand for physician services is the economy." Assuming that historical, national rates of physicians per capita reflect demand for physician services, the authors estimate the relationship between physicians per capita and per capita GDP using annual data from 1929 to 2000. The authors conclude that each 10 percent increase in per capita GDP results in a 7.5 percent increase in demand for physician services (i.e., income elasticity [ε]=0.75). They view changes in economic growth over time as both an indicator of increased ability to pay and a proxy for technological advances, and argue that because of increased ability to pay for health care services consumers will demand a higher level of services in the future than is provided under the current health care system. Cooper et al. project the future supply of and demand for physicians and conclude that we face a looming shortage of specialists.

Other researchers have expressed concerns with Cooper et al.'s assumptions and conclusions (e.g., Barer, 2002; Grumbach, 2002; Reinhardt, 2002; Weiner, 2002). One critique is that the authors do not establish a causal relationship between economic well-being and demand for physicians despite the finding of a statistical correlation. Another critique is the assumption that physician supply and demand were in equilibrium during the 70 year period included in the analysis, which assumption is necessary when using physicians per capita (a supply measure) as a proxy for demand. Cooper et al. assume that in the past market (and other) forces helped keep a balance of supply and demand, but in the future supply and demand will diverge.

Exhibit 32 illustrates one of the problems with using a simple correlation between physicians per capita and measures of economic well-being to estimate the relationship between demand and ability to pay. This exhibit shows a positive correlation across States between personal income per capita (controlling for cross-State differences in cost of living) and physicians per 100,000 population. Two series are plotted: (1) a series that <u>adjusts</u> for out-of-State consumption of health care services, and (2) a series that <u>does not adjust</u> for out-of-State consumption of health care services. The adjusted series is computed based on work by MEDPAC (2002),

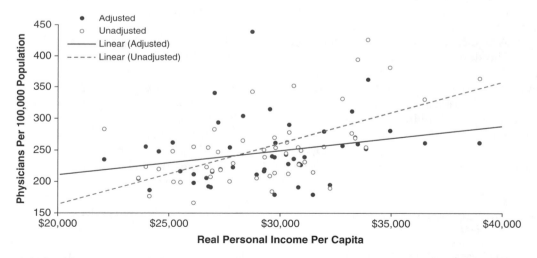

Exhibit 32 Relationship across States between Real Per Capita Personal Income and Physicians per 100,000 Population: 2001
Source: Income estimates from the U.S. Bureau of Economic Analysis. Population estimates from the U.S. Census Bureau. State-level estimates of physician supply from AMA's Physician Characteristics and Distribution in the U.S. (AMA, 2003). Note: The District of Columbia, which is omitted from this graph, has a physician-to-100,000 population ratio of 698.

which estimates Medicare payments per beneficiary with and without adjusting for out-of-State service use and health status. The unadjusted series suggests that each $1,000 increase in personal income per capita increases the number of physicians per 100,000 population by approximately 9.7. Evaluated at the mean personal income per capita, this translates to an elasticity of 1.12, meaning a 10 percent increase in personal income per capita is correlated with an 11.2 percent increase in physicians per capita. The series that adjusts for out-of-State consumption of health care services suggests that each $1,000 increase in personal income per capita results in an increase of 3.8 physicians per 100,000 population. Evaluated at the mean personal income per capita, a 10 percent increase in personal income per capita is correlated with a 4.7 percent increase in the supply of physicians. The 95 percent confidence interval for this estimate is quite large, though, ranging from 0.06 to 0.87.

This comparison of the adjusted and unadjusted series suggests that States with higher per capita income are net exporters of physician services. Controlling for where patients receive services explains away approximately 60 percent of the observed cross-State relationship between physicians per capita and personal income per capita. While the adjusted series still shows a positive correlation between personal income per capita and physicians per capita, the estimated relationship is substantially smaller than Cooper et al.'s estimate, which in turn is substantially smaller than the estimate from the unadjusted series.

Anderson et al. (2003) report statistics that show a positive correlation between a country's per capita GDP and the percentage of GDP spent on health care for the Organization for Economic Cooperation and Development (OECD) countries (Exhibit 33, not included).[23] Although the United States spends a disproportionate amount of GDP on health care relative to other countries, Anderson et al. attribute this phenomenon largely to higher prices for health care goods and services in the United States rather than higher utilization of such goods and services.

A visual inspection of Exhibit 33 (not included) suggests that the relationship between per capita

GDP and percent of GDP spent on health care is strongest among countries with per capita GDP less than $25,000. Close to 60 percent of the OECD countries have per capita GDP in the $25,000 to $35,000 range, and among this subset of countries there is little relationship between per capita GDP and the percent of GDP spent on health care.

Using data on physicians per capita from Anderson et al., we estimated the relationship between physicians per capita and per capita GDP by estimating a log-log model using a bivariate regression analysis. The estimated income elasticity is 0.4, which suggests that each 10 percent increase in per capita GDP is associated with a 4 percent increase in physicians per capita. The estimated 0.4 elasticity is roughly half the 0.75 estimate found by Cooper et al., but the 95 percent confidence interval is large, ranging from 0.10 to 0.70.

Exhibit 34 (not included) plots the relationship between per capita GDP and supply of physicians per 100,000 population for OECD countries.[24] The number of physicians per capita in the United States falls below the trend line, suggesting that demand for physicians exceeds supply if economic well-being is the major determinant of demand for physicians. A caution against drawing causal conclusions from observed statistical correlations, such as presented here, is the failure to control for differences across countries in the health care system, demographics, and indicators of health care needs. For example, the United States has a much greater supply of other trained health workers (e.g., NPCs, nurses, technicians, etc.) compared to other countries, which distorts the observed simple relationship between physicians per capita and measures of economic well-being. Demographics, lifestyle, the public health infrastructure, and other important determinants of physician demand vary substantially by country.

Koenig et al. (2003) estimate the relationship between income and expenditures for physician services both using aggregate-level data and using beneficiary-level data. The authors simultaneously control for nine categories of factors hypothesized to affect expenditures for physician services: demographics, health status, insurance product and benefit design, provider supply and organization, provider payment, practice operating costs, health care regulation, medical technology, and economic activity. One analysis uses State-level data from 1990 to 1998 to estimate the relationship between per capita expenditures for

---

[23] Note that this graph excludes Luxembourg, a small OECD country with the highest per capita GDP ($46,960 in U.S. dollars) and one of the lowest percentages of GDP spent on health care (6 percent). The simple correlation of per capita GDP and the percent of GDP spent on health care produces a correlation coefficient of 0.75 when Luxembourg is omitted, and a coefficient of 0.52 when Luxembourg is included.

[24] Again, Luxembourg is omitted as an extreme outlier. Slovakia is omitted because data on physicians per capita is unavailable.

Source	Elasticity (95% CI)	Economic Variable	Physician/Healthcare Services Demand Variable	Description of Regression Analysis
Cookson and Reilly (1994)	0.88	Lagged per capita GDP	National health care expenditures	Time series analysis (1961–1993) relating national health care expenditures to lagged per capita GDP.
Koenig et al. (2003)	0.76 $(0.57 \leq \varepsilon \leq 0.95)$	Disposable income per capita	Expenditures for physician services	Time-series, cross-sectional analysis using State-level data from multiple years. This analysis controls for demographics, health status, medical insurance products, physician practice characteristics, health care regulations, medical technology, and physician supply.
Cooper et al. (2002)	0.75	Per capita GDP	Physicians per capita	Time series analysis (1929–2000) relating physicians per capita to per capita GDP.
Authors' analysis of State-level data	0.47 $(0.06 \leq \varepsilon \leq 0.87)$	Income per capita	Physicians per capita	Cross-sectional analysis of State-level physicians per capita and personal income per capita, adjusted for out-of-State health care utilization, in 2000.
Authors' analysis of data from Anderson et al. (2003)	0.40 $(0.10 \leq \varepsilon \leq 0.70)$	Per capita GDP	Physicians per capita	Cross-sectional analysis using OECD country data on physicians per capita and per capita GDP in 2000.
Koenig et al. (2003)	0.31 $(0.10 \leq \varepsilon \leq 0.53)$	Income per capita	Expenditures for physician services	Analysis using data on 3+ million beneficiaries enrolled in a large national group health insurer. This analysis controls for demographics, health status, medical insurance products, physician practice characteristics, health care regulations, medical technology, and physician supply.

Exhibit 35 Income Elasticity Estimates

Year	Patient Care			Non-patient Care	Total
	Primary Care	Non-primary Care	Total Patient Care		
2000*	267,100	446,800	713,800	42,200	756,100
2005	281,800	475,500	757,300	44,800	802,100
2010	297,500	507,900	805,400	47,700	853,100
2015	316,300	544,300	860,600	50,900	911,500
2020	337,400	584,100	921,500	54,500	976,000
Change: 2005–2020	20%	23%	22%	22%	22%

* Base year assumes that physician supply and demand are balanced.

Exhibit 36 Baseline Projections of Physician Requirements

physician services and various explanatory variables. This analysis produces an income elasticity estimate of 0.76 with a 95 percent confidence interval of 0.57 to 0.95. The second analysis uses data on beneficiaries enrolled in a national preferred provider organization from May 1998 to May 2000. This second analysis produced an income elasticity estimate of 0.31 with a 95 percent confidence interval of 0.10 to 0.53. This lower estimate, however, is based on a subset of the population that is insured and thus excludes the income impact on ability to purchase medical insurance.

Cookson and Reilly (1994) model health care consumption using a trend analysis, where national health care expenditures are modeled as a function of numerous factors including measures of real personal income. These authors find a significant lagged "wealth effect," with change in real income being a statistically significant predictor of change in health care expenditures 3, 4 and 5 years into the future. The estimated income elasticities for 3, 4 and 5 years are, respectively, 0.17, 0.39 and 0.33. The cumulative effect is approximately 0.88, which implies that a 10 percent increase in real per capita personal income eventually translates into an 8.8 percent increase in health care expenditures.

The findings and methods used in these studies are summarized in Exhibit 35. The estimated elasticities range from 0.31 to 0.88, with relatively large standard errors on these estimates.

The extant research sheds little light on how to incorporate national economic growth into the PRM projections. Empirical questions raised include:

- **How does the relationship between national economic growth and demand for physician services differ by medical specialty?** Theory would suggest that elective services (e.g., some plastic surgery services) are more responsive to ability to pay than are less elective services (e.g., cardiologist services). Indeed, when Cooper et al. look at the relationship between States' physician-per-population ratio and income per capita they find a stronger relationship for specialists compared to generalists. Therefore, separate estimates of income elasticity are needed for each specialty.
- **To what extent is the relationship between national economic growth and demand for physician services already built into the PRM via the insurance distribution assumptions?** If the main effect of national economic growth is to move people into more generous insurance status (e.g., from uninsured to insured, from managed care into fee-for-service), then the research needed to incorporate economic growth into the PRM is very different from the research needed to estimate health care utilization changes within insurance status.
- **Does the size of the relationship between ability to pay and demand for physician services diminish at higher income levels?** As discussed earlier, when using country-level data the relationship between per capita GDP and health care measures such as percent of GDP spent on health care and physicians per capita seems to diminish as a country's per capita wealth increases.

The argument that economic growth should be considered in the PRM projections raises a philosophical question regarding how the PRM projections should be used. Incorporating economic growth into the model will result in higher demand projections because the hypothesized impact is that consumers will demand higher-quality care as the Nation's wealth increases. Historically, projections of an impending physician shortage have had large policy implications and have been instrumental in securing additional Federal funding for training new doctors. Should the government role be to help ensure sufficient supply to meet demand (even if society wants the "sport-utility vehicle [SUV] version of health care" as discussed by Grumbach [2002])?

For this study we project the future demand for physicians under alternative scenarios. The baseline scenario omits economic growth, and in essence projects future demand for physicians assuming the

Year	Patient Care			Non-patient Care	Total
	Primary Care	Non-primary Care	Total Patient Care		
2000*	95	158	253	15	268
2005	95	161	256	15	271
2010	96	164	261	15	276
2015	98	169	267	16	283
2020	100	174	274	16	291
Change: 2005–2020	5%	8%	7%	7%	7%

* Base year assumes that physician supply and demand are balanced.

Exhibit 37 Baseline Physician Requirements per 100,000

same level of care that is currently supplied is provided in the future. An alternative scenario incorporates economic growth. Projections under this alternative scenario are presented in a later section, but these alternative projections assume the following:

- **Economic growth of 2 percent annually between 2000 and 2020.** The CBO projects a 3 percent annual growth rate in real GDP between 2003 to 2013, which is approximately equal to about a 2 percent average annual growth in real per capita GDP.

- **Income elasticity of 0.25, 0.5, and 0.75 varies by specialty.** There is no consensus on what the income elasticity of demand is for physician services. Physician requirements are projected under the assumption that demand for some specialties is relatively insensitive (elasticity=0.25)[25], modestly sensitive (elasticity=0.50)[26], or more sensitive (elasticity =0.75)[27] to economic growth.

Real, per capita economic growth occurs through increased productivity. The CBO's economic growth projections, therefore, imply that productivity will increase by approximately 2 percent annually, on average, throughout the economy. Productivity growth will differ by industry and occupation, and because physician services are labor intensive it is reasonable to assume that growth in physician productivity (however measured) will lag behind overall productivity growth in the economy. An increase in physician productivity of 1 percent annually would offset the increased demand for physician services under the scenario and accompanying assumptions described above. Trends in physician productivity are discussed in more detail in a later section, but the limited available data suggest physician productivity appears to be growing at about 1 percent annually.

4. Role of Nonphysician Clinicians

Three trends during the past decade have increased the proportion of health care services being provided by NPCs (Cooper, Laud and Dietrich, 1998; Druss et

al., 2003). First, the number of NCPs has grown substantially. Second, State legislatures have expanded the legal scope of practice for NCPs (Cooper, Henderson and Dietrich, 1998). Third, pressure to contain rising health care costs has fueled demand for NPCs.

The size of the NPC workforce has grown significantly in recent years and is projected to continue growing rapidly. Assessments of the adequacy of the future physician supply should take into consideration changes in the growth and use of NPCs. The BLS projects that between 2000 and 2010 employment of PAs will increase 53 percent, employment of chiropractors will increase 24 percent, employment of optometrists will increase 19 percent, and employment of podiatrists will increase 11 percent. Cooper et al. (2002) report that by 2015 there could be as many as 525,000 NPCs—including 275,000 nurse practitioners, physician assistants and nurse-midwives; 150,000 acupuncturists and chiropractors; and 100,000 other NPCs engaged in various medical specialties. These authors calculate that by 2015 these NPCs could be providing services that are the equivalent of 40 physicians per 100,000 population (with most of the services displacing services that historically have been provided by primary care physicians).

Physicians view NPCs in their role as both a complement and a competitor in the provision of care (Grumbach, 1998).

1. **NPCs as complements to physicians.** The view of NPCs as complements to physicians is one in which NPCs allow physicians to leverage their expertise. In this model of care, there is a division of labor such that NPCs provide those services within the scope of their training, with physicians handling the more complex cases. Druss et al. (2003) find evidence of increased collaboration between NPCs and physicians over the period 1987 to 1997, and Trude (2003) reports that between 1997 and 2001 the proportion of physicians in non-institutional practice settings who worked with NPCs increased from 40 percent to 48 percent. The increase in working with NPCs was most noticeable for group practices of three or more physicians where the percentage of physicians working with NPCs increased from 53 percent to 66 percent between 1997 and 2001. Part of the increased collaboration between physicians and NPCs might be considered voluntary on the part of physicians (e.g., physicians hiring

---

[25] Specialties hypothesized to be in this low-sensitivity category include general and family practice, general internal medicine, pediatrics, obstetrics/gynecology, and emergency medicine.

[26] Specialties hypothesized to be in this medium-sensitivity category include cardiology, internal medicine subspecialties, general surgery, otolaryngology, urology, anesthesiology, radiology, pathology, and "other" specialties.

[27] Specialties hypothesized to be in this high-sensitivity category include orthopedic surgery, ophthalmology, "other" surgery, and psychiatry.

NPCs), while part of the increased collaboration might be considered imposed (e.g., in the case of a managed care company that hires both physicians and NPCs). A recent survey by Farber and Murray (2001) found that 19 percent of responding physicians indicated that to counter lagging income they are considering hiring nurse practitioners or physician assistants.

2. **NPCs as competitors to physicians.** As noted by the American Academy of Physician Assistants (AAPA, 1999) and others, the increasing financial uncertainties in the health care system has increased concerns by physicians about encroachment into their practice territory by physicians in other specialties and by NPCs. Cooper, Henderson and Dietrich (1998) document legislation passed by States giving NPCs greater business and clinical autonomy. Because NPCs can provide some services currently offered by physicians but at a lower cost, there exists an economic incentive to use NPCs to provide services within their legal scope of practice.

Whether viewed as competitors or complements in delivering care, the increasing size of the NPC workforce will likely reduce demand for physicians. The growing role of NPCs raises several questions pertinent to modeling future demand for physicians in specific specialties:

1. How large is the overlap in services provided by NPCs and physicians. That is, what proportion of physician workload can legally and safely be transferred to NPCs?

2. Although the supply of NPCs is growing rapidly, is there a saturation point at which there will be a NPC surplus? Will all NPCs trained displace physicians, or will the United States reach a point at which there is no longer the ability to partially substitute NPCs for physicians?

3. To what extent are NPCs practicing in markets that are left unfilled by physicians? Physician assistants and nurse practitioners are disproportionately employed in rural areas that have difficulty attracting physicians.

Cooper, Laud, and Dietrich (1998) analyzed State distributions of physicians and NPCs per 100,000 population and found that for most NPC specialties, there were higher NPC-to-population ratios in States that also had high physician-to-population ratios. This finding suggests that economic growth is associated with higher demand for health care services, with little economic-related preference for physicians over NPCs. This analysis, though, does not control for cross-State variation in factors that would be correlated with demand for both NPC and physician services (e.g., health care needs of the population).

The baseline projections in the PRM assume that current patterns of health care delivery will continue over the projection horizon. Physicians and NPCs will continue to have overlapping scopes of practice, and each will maintain their share of total services provided. An alternative scenario assumes that the increased supply of NPCs will retard growth in demand for physicians by capturing a growing percentage of total patient volume. Projections for this scenario are produced for physicians in the aggregate, not by specialty. Specific assumptions are that (1) the number of active NPCs will double between 2000 and 2020, (2) all NPCs that are trained will become employed[28] and will provide services that otherwise would have been provided by physicians, and (3) on average each NPC will provide 40 percent of the work currently provided by a physician. The projections under this scenario are presented later.

5. Science and Technology

Advances in science and technology have great potential to affect the demand for physician services and thus physician requirements. Most health workforce projection models, however, do not include trends in science and technology in the set of determinants because there is too much uncertainty regarding how new innovations will impact the supply of or demand for certain health care services. Furthermore, technological advances will likely have differing impacts on individual physician specialties. Advances in science and technology have the capability to affect the demand for physicians by:

1. Creating additional demand for physician services so that consumers seek treatments that previously did not exist (e.g., fertility treatment) or that can now be provided at lower cost (e.g., minimally invasive surgery);

---

[28] The assumption that all NPCs that are trained will become employed thus reducing demand for physicians is a strong assumption. The National Health Service Corps (NHSC), which helps to place primary care physicians and NPCs in underserved areas, has reduced the number of new NPCs participating in the program because of recent difficulties in placing NPCs at NHSC-qualified sites despite strong demand for additional physicians at these sites.

2. Increasing physicians' productivity (which increases the amount of services that physicians can provide and thus <u>reduces the number of physicians needed</u> to adequately serve a given population); and

3. Eliminating certain illnesses or otherwise reducing the amount of time needed to treat certain health problems, thus <u>reducing demand for physician services</u>.

4. Increasing longevity that may eventually <u>increase the demand for physician services</u> as patients age and seek care for other health problems.

The following are areas of scientific and technological advancement with the potential to affect physician supply and demand.

- **Information technology:** Physician reliance on electronic medical records is increasing rapidly and will only continue to do so in the next decade. The goals of these systems are to "enhance patient safety and reduce the amount of paperwork for clinicians, giving them more time to devote to patient care" (Morrissey, 2004). Efforts to expand electronic data collection and allow for interoperability (exchange of data within a facility) and portability (exchange of data across facilities) are underway. Significant hurdles, such as privacy concerns and system compatibility, remain. *Improvements in physician productivity likely would reduce the demand for physicians because fewer physicians would be needed to provide the same level of services.*

- **Emerging forms of communication:** The Internet, telemedicine, video conferencing, and telesurgery are emerging innovations with the potential to transform the way some physician services are delivered. Currently, most physician services are provided through face-to-face encounters with patients. *The potential for technology to reduce the importance of geography in providing physician services has mixed implications for the amount of physician services utilized. There is the potential to increase utilization by improving access to care by rural and other underserved populations. There is also the potential for outsourcing some services (e.g., interpreting scans and test results) to physicians in foreign countries.* Telemedicine could potentially affect all medical specialties, but the greatest current applications are found in providing diagnostic-related services in radiology, pathology, and cardiology. Advances are also being made in systems that use robotics, minimally invasive surgical gear, and video equipment to provide surgical services remotely.

Miller and Derse (2002, p. 168) opine that "the emergence of the Internet portends a dramatic shift for health care and the relationships of patients and physicians," potentially improving the quality, timeliness, and efficacy with which physician services are provided. Miller and Derse document that physician services currently provided over the Internet include: (1) proscribing medications, (2) responding to consumers' medical questions, (3) providing psychotherapy, (4) reviewing biopsies and medical records, and (5) providing second opinions to a patient's physician. The overall impact of patient Internet access to physicians is uncertain. Such access will likely increase the level of correspondence between patients and physicians, but this increased demand for physician services might be offset by increased efficiency in the delivery of services.

While face-to-face encounters between physician and patient will continue in importance, these other forms of communication have great potential to alleviate the geographic misdistribution of physicians. For example, email may facilitate more productive interactions between patients and physicians without necessitating an office visit. Email, while not having the urgency of a phone call, allows both the patient and the physician to communicate efficiently. Physicians might find email useful for sending additional medical or condition-related information, thereby potentially reducing the need for an office visit.

Although the technology exists to provide a larger proportion of physician services remotely, third-party payers for medical services have been slow to change their reimbursement structure to compensate physicians for services provided remotely. Currently, only capitation allows physicians to fully realize the benefits of communicating with patients via nontraditional means such as email. Thus, reimbursement system and regulatory changes are needed before these new forms of communication with patients can be fully implemented (Terry, 2000).

- **Minimally invasive surgery:** Most surgical specialties increasingly use minimally invasive surgery (MIS) in place of open surgery. The benefits of MIS over open surgery include reducing patient recovery time, risk of infection, pain, and scaring. MIS requires greater surgical skill, and sometimes longer operating times are required compared to open surgery.

Because MIS greatly reduces the direct medical costs, patient indirect costs (e.g., lost time from work), and patient suffering, advances in MIS have increased demand for such procedures. For example, between 1990 and 1994 the number of patients that elected to have a cholecystectomy increased 84 percent (AHA TrendWatch, 2002). *Advances in MIS, therefore, will likely increase demand for surgeons because of increased time to perform surgeries and increased demand for such surgeries. These advances might decrease demand for hospitalists and primary care physicians because MIS reduces patient recovery time and risk of complications.*

- **Diagnostic equipment:** Advances in diagnostic equipment such as X-rays, ultrasound, CT and MRI scans allow physicians to identify health problems earlier and with greater accuracy. *Technological advances that increase the ability to diagnose health problems and reduce the cost of such equipment will likely lead to increased demand for physicians (e.g., radiologists, neurologists) and technicians who provide these diagnostic services. The ability to more quickly identify health problems has a mixed effect on demand for physician services.* There will likely be increased demand for services to correct health problems, while the ability to identify health problems at an earlier stage could reduce the need for more extensive physician services that would occur if a health problem becomes more advanced.

- **Pharmaceutical and vaccination advancement:** Rational Drug Design, the development of new chemical and molecular entities by looking at the physical structure and chemical composition, continues to shorten the drug discovery process. The discovery of new and more potent pharmaceuticals with fewer side effects will enable physicians to treat patients quickly and effectively, reducing the need for time consuming treatments and surgeries. In addition, pharmaceutical advancement will bring with it an increase in prophylactic drugs and vaccines. These in turn will reduce the overall burden of illness and help alleviate certain chronic conditions. Prophylactic and therapeutic pharmaceuticals and vaccines will reduce the demand for physicians by both reducing the number of face-to-face visits and surgical procedures required to treat a patients. (RWJF, Health and Health Care 2010).

  Pharmaceutical and vaccination advancement, therefore, is likely to reduce overall demand for physician services.

- **Genetic mapping, genetic testing, gene therapy, and transplantation:** Genetic mapping, genetic testing, gene therapy, and transplantation are technologies which will come to play an increasingly important role in medicine in the future. New innovations can increase demand for specific tests and therapies, but the ability to cure diseases and other ailments creates the potential to reduce overall, long-term demand for physician services. *Therefore, the likely long-term impact on demand for physician services is unknown and will likely differ substantially by medical specialty.*

6. Public Expectations

Public expectations of medicine are different today than they were 100 years ago, or even 20 years ago. New medicines have improved the ability to care for chronic conditions and have improved the quality of life for many individuals. The Institute of Medicine (2000) has highlighted the prevalence of medical errors which has led to increased scrutiny of quality of care by the public and by policymakers. The elderly baby boom population will not have experienced the same hardships as their grandparents which may also affect their expectations of the health care system. Rising public expectations will increase physician requirements.

7. Price of Physician Services

In most economic models, the price of goods and services is a major determinant of the quantity of such goods and services demanded. Likewise, theory would suggest that as the price of physician services rises (falls), utilization of such services would fall (rise). The scenarios modeled in the PRM assume no changes in the relative price of physician services over the projection horizon.

The responsiveness of physician requirements projections to changes in the cost of services is an area for future research. There are many challenges to quantifying the price of physician services, projecting how these prices will change over time, and determining the likely impact of price changes on utilization of physician services. The following are a few such challenges:

1. The quality of services changes over time due to technological advances and increased skill and sophistication of the services provided, thus increasing the difficulty of obtaining

historical price data on a give set of physician services.

2. It is difficult to predict how the price of physician services will change over time relative to the price of other goods and services. Because physician services are labor intensive and thus less likely to benefit from technological advances that increase productivity, it is reasonable to assume that physician services will become relatively more expensive over time. That is, the cost per unit of physician services is likely to become more expensive relative to the cost per unit of food, transportation, etc.

3. Additional research is needed to determine the *price elasticity* of various goods and services—that is, how responsive health care utilization is to changes in price. Price elasticities are particularly difficult to estimate for health care services because our third-party payment system reduces the cost-consciousness of patients and physicians making health care utilization decisions. Unlike the purchase of most goods and services, the majority of patients are shielded from the true cost of health care services. Employers and insurers, however, are relatively sensitive to the cost of health care services and have a strong financial incentive to keep physician payments to a minimum. Employers demonstrate their sensitivity to health care costs through the selection of insurers. Many insurers demonstrate their sensitivity to the cost of physician services through the use of selective contracting with physicians and the implementation of other managed care techniques.

4. Additional research is needed to quantify trends in the total price of medical services—including physician charges for services and indirect costs (e.g., wait times) associated with seeking services.

A final note regarding the price of physician services is that market pressures (e.g., competition among physicians, bargaining clout of employers and insurers) will help to correct imbalances in physician supply. A shortage (surplus) of physicians will tend to drive prices up (down), thus reducing (increasing) per capita utilization of services.

8. Government Policy

The changing role of government, which is closely linked to public expectations, may also have a significant impact on the demand for physician services. This includes the impact of regulation as well as payment policies. Policies that might increase demand for physician services include more generous Medicare and Medicaid benefits, while policies that might reduce physician requirements include giving NPCs greater clinical and business autonomy, and efforts to ration or otherwise limit access to certain services.

Government Medicare projections take into account expected changes in physician behavior resulting from changes in program policies and practices. For example, Nguyen (1994) finds that legislation that reduced physician fees for providing Medicare services in 1989 and 1990 had the unintended consequences of increasing the volume of services provided. Nguyen found that that each planned dollar decrease in physician payments due to fee reductions was offset by a $0.40 increase in payments attributed to higher volume. Nguyen attributes this volume offset to physician behavior motivated by a desire to maintain earnings. The size of the volume offset differs by medical specialty, with surgical specialties showing a larger volume offset, on average, compared to non-surgical specialties. Nguyen cites other studies with similar findings, as well as studies that find no evidence of a volume offset.

Although the PRM can be used to model the demand implications of policy changes, this report contains no projections modeling changes in government programs or policies.

D. Physician Requirements Projections

The baseline projections take into account the growth and aging of the population, but are calculated on the assumption that the United States will provide the same level of care in the future that is currently provided. Essentially, the baseline projections assume that the future will use today's health care system. Alternative projections are based on different assumptions of how the health care system will evolve over time.

The baseline projections suggest that between 2005 and 2020 overall requirements for physicians engaged primarily in patient care increase 22 percent, from approximately 757,300 to 921,500 (Exhibits 36, 38, and 39). In percentage terms, growth is lower for primary care (20 percent) than for non-primary care (23 percent). If it is assumed that requirements for physicians engaged primarily in non-patient care activities (e.g., administration, teaching, and research) remain relatively constant at

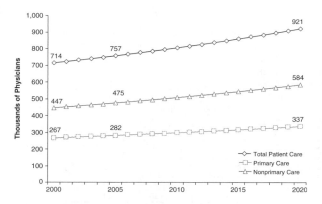

Exhibit 38 Physician Requirements

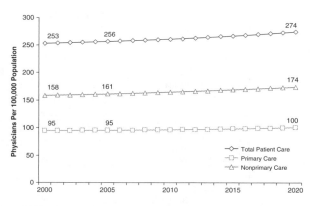

Exhibit 40 Requirements per 100,000 Population

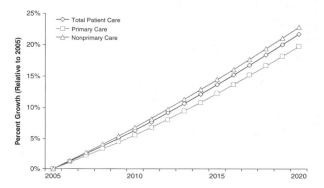

Exhibit 39 % Growth in Physician Requirements

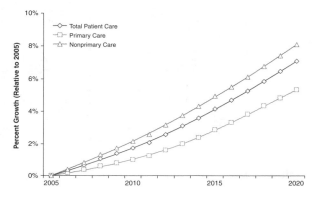

Exhibit 41 % Growth in Requirements per Capita

approximately 6 percent of total physicians, then total requirements for physicians will increase from about 802,100 to 976,000 during this period.[29]

On a per capita basis, demand for physicians is increasing as a result of an aging population (Exhibits 37, 40, and 41). For example, under the baseline scenario, requirements for physicians engaged in patient care increases from approximately 256 to 274 (7 percent) per 100,000 population between 2005 and 2020. In percentage terms, the increase is greater for non-primary care (8 percent) than for primary care (5 percent).

Projected growth in requirements between 2005 and 2020 varies substantially by specialty (Exhibit 42). Between 2005 and 2020, specialties with the highest percentage growth are cardiology (33 percent) and urology (30 percent). Specialties with the lowest percentage growth are pediatrics (9 percent) and obstetrics/gynecology (10 percent).

The baseline projections assume that patterns of health care use and delivery of care remain unchanged over the projection horizon and that changing demographics are the primary driver of changes in physician requirements. To better understand the implications of possible changes in utilization and delivery patterns, physician requirements are projected from 2005 to 2020 under alternative scenarios (Exhibits 43 and 44).

- **Growing role of NPCs.** This scenario assumes that (1) the number of active NPCs will increase 60 percent between 2005 and 2020, (2) all NPCs that are trained will become employed and will provide services that otherwise would have been provided by physicians, and (3) on average each NPC will provide 40 percent of the work currently provided by a physician. Under this scenario, by 2020 physician requirements would be approximately 90,000 physicians less than the baseline projections. NPCs will have a disproportionate impact by specialty, with NPCs having a greater impact on reducing demand for generalists.

---

[29] Over the past 20 years, the percentage of total Federal and non-Federal physicians engaged primarily in non-patient care activities has steadily declined from around 9 percent to its current level of about percent.

Specialty	Base Year	Projected				
	2000	2005	2010	2015	2020	% Change 2005 to 2020
Total	756,100	802,100	853,100	911,500	976,000	22%
Total Non-Patient Care	42,200	44,800	47,700	50,900	54,500	22%
Total Patient Care	713,800	757,300	805,400	860,600	921,500	22%
Primary Care	267,100	281,800	297,500	316,300	337,400	20%
General Family Practice	107,700	113,900	120,600	127,900	135,900	19%
General Internal Medicine	107,500	115,000	123,400	132,900	143,500	25%
Pediatrics	51,900	52,900	53,500	55,500	57,900	9%
Nonprimary Care	446,800	475,500	507,900	544,300	584,100	23%
Medical Specialties	86,400	93,000	100,700	109,800	119,800	29%
Cardiology	20,600	22,200	24,200	26,700	29,600	33%
Other Internal Medicine	65,900	70,800	76,500	83,100	90,200	27%
Surgical Specialties	159,400	169,000	179,900	192,000	205,100	21%
General Surgery	39,100	41,700	44,800	48,400	52,200	25%
OB/GYN	41,500	43,100	44,800	46,000	47,200	10%
Ophthalmology	18,400	19,700	21,200	23,100	25,200	28%
Orthopedic Surgery	24,100	25,600	27,300	29,300	31,600	23%
Other Surgery	16,200	17,400	18,800	20,300	22,000	26%
Otolaryngology	9,800	10,300	11,000	11,600	12,400	20%
Urology	10,400	11,100	12,000	13,200	14,400	30%
Other Specialties	200,900	213,500	227,300	242,500	259,200	21%
Anesthesiology	37,800	40,200	43,000	46,500	50,400	25%
Emergency Medicine	26,300	27,600	28,900	30,300	31,800	15%
Pathology	17,200	18,400	19,800	21,200	22,600	23%
Psychiatry	38,300	40,700	43,000	45,200	47,400	16%
Radiology	30,900	32,900	35,200	37,900	41,100	25%
Other Specialties	50,400	53,700	57,400	61,400	65,800	23%

Note: Totals might not equal sum of subtotals due to rounding.

Exhibit 43 Baseline Physician Requirements Projections

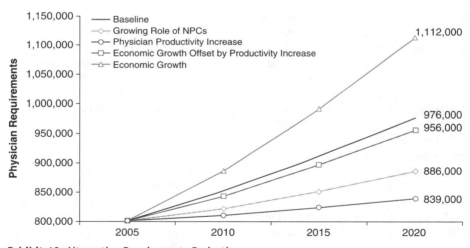

Exhibit 43 Alternative Requirements Projections

• **Economic growth.** This scenario assumes that economic growth will allow the Nation to afford a higher-quality health care system. This new health care system will require more physician and, in particular, more specialists.

Physician requirements are projected under the assumption that per capita income will grow by 2 percent annually, and that demand for some specialties is relatively insensitive (elasticity=0.25), modestly sensitive (elasticity

=0.50), or more sensitive (elasticity=0.75) to economic growth (Exhibit 34, not included). This scenario produces the highest projections, with requirements growing to 1.1 million physicians in 2020 (136,000 higher than the baseline projection).

- **Physician productivity increase.** Requirements are projected under the assumption that physician productivity increases 1 percent annually (i.e., each physician can see one percent more patients per year through improved use of staff and technology). Projected physician requirements remain relatively constant through 2020 under this scenario, with the 2020 projection suggesting 137,000 fewer physicians than projected under the baseline scenario.

- **Economic growth offset by physician productivity increase.** Combining the previous two scenarios, the growth in demand for physician services due to economic growth is offset by the increased productivity of physicians resulting in projected requirements of 956,000 in 2020 (20,000 fewer than under the baseline scenario).

The scenarios described here produce a large range in projected future demand for physicians. The sensitivity of the projections to key assumptions regarding the impact of economic growth and increases in physician productivity illustrate why researchers arrive at such different conclusions regarding the future requirements for physicians. These national projections use current patterns in the utilization and delivery of physician services as a starting point. Throughout the Nation there remain pockets of under service, especially in poor, rural and urban areas. These geographic disparities are discussed in **Chapter IV.**

Specialty	2005	2010	2015	2020	Percent Change 2005 to 2020	Elasticity Assumption
Total	**802,000**	**887,000**	**992,000**	**1,112,000**	**38%**	**NA**
Total Non-Patient Care	**45,000**	**48,000**	**51,000**	**55,000**	**22%**	**NA**
Total Patient Care	**757,000**	**839,000**	**941,000**	**1,057,000**	**39%**	**NA**
Primary Care	**282,000**	**306,000**	**334,000**	**367,000**	**30%**	**NA**
General Family Practice	114,000	124,000	135,000	148,000	30%	0.25
General Internal Medicine	115,000	127,000	140,000	156,000	36%	0.25
Pediatrics	53,000	55,000	59,000	63,000	19%	0.25
Nonprimary Care	**476,000**	**533,000**	**607,000**	**690,000**	**45%**	**NA**
Medical Specialties	**93,000**	**105,000**	**122,000**	**141,000**	**52%**	**NA**
Cardiology	22,000	25,000	30,000	35,000	59%	0.50
Other Internal Medicine	71,000	80,000	92,000	106,000	49%	0.50
Surgical Specialties	**169,000**	**189,000**	**215,000**	**243,000**	**44%**	**NA**
General Surgery	42,000	47,000	54,000	61,000	45%	0.50
OB/GYN	43,000	46,000	49,000	51,000	19%	0.25
Ophthalmology	20,000	23,000	27,000	32,000	60%	0.75
Orthopedic Surgery	26,000	29,000	34,000	40,000	54%	0.75
Other Surgery	17,000	20,000	24,000	28,000	65%	0.75
Otolaryngology	10,000	12,000	13,000	15,000	50%	0.50
Urology	11,000	12,000	14,000	16,000	45%	0.25
Other Specialties	**214,000**	**239,000**	**270,000**	**306,000**	**43%**	**NA**
Anesthesiology	40,000	45,000	52,000	59,000	48%	0.50
Emergency Medicine	28,000	30,000	32,000	35,000	25%	0.25
Pathology	18,000	21,000	23,000	27,000	50%	0.50
Psychiatry	41,000	46,000	53,000	60,000	46%	0.75
Radiology	33,000	37,000	42,000	48,000	45%	0.50
Other Specialties	54,000	60,000	68,000	77,000	43%	0.50

Note: Totals might not equal sum of subtotals due to rounding.

Exhibit 44 Physician Requirements by Medical Specialty: High Economic Growth Series

CONCLUSIONS

A. Summary

An adequate supply of physicians is needed to help ensure access to affordable, quality care. Over the past 70 years since the Committee on the Costs of Medical Care (CCMC, 1933) conducted the first major scientific study of the adequacy of physician supply in the United States, the approach to modeling physician supply and demand has evolved to reflect improvements in our understanding of the determinants of physician supply and demand, improved data collection, and improved analytical techniques. Still, workforce modeling remains as much art as it is science. As stated by Uwe Reinhardt (2002): it is a "daunting enterprise . . . to estimate the physician surplus or shortage one or two decades into the future. Any of the variables in the equation can change over time, sometimes in unforeseen ways" (p. 196). This is especially true when projecting demand for physician services, where there is much uncertainty regarding the characteristics of the future health care system.

While there is generally consensus with physician supply projections, physician requirements projections are often controversial. The lack of consensus on requirements projections reflects differences in assumptions about the major determinants of demand for physician services, incomplete information on future trends in health care utilization and delivery of services, different but valid approaches to modeling future requirements, and philosophical differences on the definition and purpose of requirements projections.

HRSA's Physician Supply Model and Physician Requirements Model, like all models, are simplified versions of a complex health care system that generalizes the millions of decisions made by physicians, patients, insurers, and other entities into probabilities that certain events will occur based on historical patterns of behavior. As stated by Ehrenberg and Smith (1991, p. 5), "models are not intended to capture every complexity of behavior; instead, they are created to strip away random and idiosyncratic factors so that we can focus on general principles." The PSM and PRM attempt to capture these major factors as identified based on theory, a review of the literature, and original analysis. The major trends with implications for the physician workforce include:

- **Changing demographics.** The U.S. population is growing, aging and becoming more racially and ethnically diverse. The physician workforce is also aging, and women constitute a growing proportion of physicians.

- **Rising cost of government programs for the elderly.** The aging population will place increasing cost pressure on State and Federal government retirement plans and social programs that serve the elderly (e.g., Medicare, Medicaid, and Social Security).

- **Increased cost consciousness.** Rising health care costs are spurring efforts by insurers to find new ways to contain costs.

- **Economic growth.** Increased prosperity has the potential to increase public expectations and demand for physician services.

- **Proliferation of health care specialties—including nonphysician clinicians.** The past few decades have seen a proliferation of health care specialties—both within the physician community and among NPCs—which both increases competition among health care providers but also provides patients with a broader range of health care services.

- **Scientific and technological advances.** Technological breakthroughs continue to change both demand for health care services and the way in which services are delivered.

For this study we computed a range of supply and requirements projections for scenarios reflecting different assumptions about the future health care system, the evolving role of physicians, and trends in other supply and demand determinants. The baseline projections assume that over the next 1 to 2 decades things will continue largely as they are. The Nation will continue to graduate a slightly growing number of new physicians, health care utilization and practice patterns will reflect current patterns, and the main driver of changing demand for physician services is the growth and aging of the population. Alternative supply and demand scenarios model the sensitivity of projections to these assumptions, as well as reflect differences in the literature on the main determinants of physician supply and demand.

The baseline projections suggest that overall demand for physician services is growing faster than supply. Without a modest increase in number of new graduates from U.S. medical schools, the Nation cannot continue to provide the same level of health care unless the health care system becomes more efficient at delivering care traditionally provided by physicians; reduces demand for physician services through improved science, technology, or use of other inputs to care; or becomes more dependent on foreign-trained physicians.

B. Policy Implications

The Federal Government, as a major player in the health care system via its role as health care insurer, subsidizer of physician training, and role to improve access to care to underserved populations has often exerted its influence in an attempt to create a coherent national workforce policy and to improve access to affordable, quality health care.

The modest but growing projected shortfall of physicians could impede national health care goals, if left unchecked, by contributing to greater geographic disparities in physician supply. For several decades the United States has been a net importer of medical school graduates. A growing demand for physicians that exceeds production from U.S. medical schools could make the Nation even more reliant on international medical schools, and this at a time when other nations face greater health workforce inadequacies.

As the population ages and places greater pressures on the health care system, economic realities will require some form of cost containment. Because physicians directly account for an estimated 20 percent of health care expenditures and indirectly account for the majority of health care spending, any attempt to control health care costs will directly affect physicians.

C. Areas for Future Research

Although the physician workforce literature continues to grow, there is still a need for additional research on the relationship between physician supply and its determinants, and between physician requirements and its determinants. Lack of data continues to be a major hindrance to conducting research on physician behavior and how practice patterns change over time and in response to changes in the health care operating environment. The high cost to collect such data in a timely and consistent manner requires collaboration on the part of payers, provider associations, researchers, and Federal and State stakeholders.

The health care system continues to evolve as does the role of physicians. Because of the long length of time needed to train physicians and to change the education infrastructure, policymakers, educators, physicians, and other stakeholders need to know at least a decade in advance how changes in the health care system and other trends will affect the adequacy of physician supply. Physician supply and demand projections should be updated every few years to reflect the latest trends and to provide this advance warning of changes in the adequacy of physician supply.

Finally, it should be remembered that the physician workforce is only one part of an increasingly complex health care system in which the final goal is a healthier society. The link between number and type of physicians, as well as the content of their education, and the health status of the populations they serve has yet to be completely understood. Further investigation regarding the impact of the physician workforce on health will better inform workforce planning.

• • • References

Abt Associates, Inc. 1991. *Reexamination of the Adequacy of Physician Supply Made in 1980 by the Graduate Medical Advisory Committee for Selected Specialties.* Final report prepared for Health Services and Resources Administration.

American Academy of Physician Assistants. 1999. *Into the Future: Physician Assistants Look to the 21st Century: A Strategic Plan for the Physician Assistant Profession.* Report prepared for the Bureau of Health Professions, Health Research and Services Administration.

American Association of Medical Colleges. 2001. *Data Book.*

American Association of Medical Colleges. 2005. National Resident Matching Program: U.S. Medical School Seniors Apply to Residency Programs in Record Numbers. http://www.aamc.org/newsroom/pressrel/2005/050317.htm (Accessible February 28, 2006).

American Hospital Association. 2002. *TrendWatch: Cutting Edge Costs: Hospitals and New Technology.* 4(4).

American Medical Association. *Physician Characteristics and Distribution in the U.S.* Various years.

American Medical Association, *Physician Socioeconomic Statistics.* Various years.

Anderson, GF; Reinhardt, UE; Hussey, PS; and Petrosyan, V. 2003. It's the Prices, Stupid: Why the United States is so Different from Other Countries. *Health Affairs.* 22(3):89-93.

Barer, M. 2002. New Opportunities for Old Mistakes. *Health Affairs.* 21(1):169-171.

Bickel, J and Ruffin, A. 1995. Gender-associated Differences in Matriculating and Graduating Medical Students. *Academic Medicine.* 70(6): 552-559.

Blumenthal, D. 2004. New Steam from an Old Cauldron—The Physician-Supply Debate. *New England Journal of Medicine.* 350(17): 1780-1787.

Bureau of Health Professions 2003. *Changing Demographics and the Implications for Physicians, Nurses, and Other Health Workers.* http://bhpr. hrsa.gov/healthworkforce/reports/changedemo/ (Accessible February 28, 2006).

Burnstein, PL and Cromwell, J. 1985. Relative Incomes and Rates of Return for U.S. Physicians. *Journal of Health Economics.* 4:63-78.

Christianson, J and Trude, S. 2003. Managing Costs, Managing Benefits: Employer Decisions in Local Health Care Markets. *Health Services Research.* 38(1): 355-371.

Congressional Budget Office. 2003. *The Budget and Economic Outlook: Fiscal Years 2004-2013.* A Report to the Senate and House Committees on the budget.

Cookson, JP and Reilly, P. 1994. Modeling and Forecasting Healthcare Consumption. http://www.op.net/~pkreilly/researchreports/mfnhe. html (Accessible February 28, 2006).

Cooper, RA. 2000. Adjusted Needs? Modeling the Specialty Physician Workforce. http://www.aans.org/library/Article.aspx?ArticleId= 10136 (Accessible February 28, 2006).

Cooper, RA; Getzen, TE; McKee, HJ; and Prakash, L. 2002. Economic and Demographic Trends Signal an Impending Physician Shortage. *Health Affairs.* 21(1):140-153.

Cooper, RA; Henderson, T; and Dietrich, CL. 1998. Roles of nonphysician clinicians as autonomous providers of patient care. *JAMA.* 280(9):795-802.

Cooper, RA; Laud, P; and Dietrich, CL. 1998. Current and projected workforce of nonphysician clinicians. *JAMA.* 280:788-794.

Cooper, RA; Prakash, L; and Dietrich, CL. 1998. Current and Projected Workforce of Nonphysician Clinicians. *JAMA.* 280:788-794.

Council on Graduate Medical Education. 1996. Eight Report. *Patient Care Physician Supply and Requirements: Testing COGME Recommendations.* Washington, DC, US Depart of Health and Human Services.

Council on Graduate Medical Education. 2003. Physician Workforce Policy Guidelines for the U.S. for 2000-2020. Washington, DC, US Depart of Health and Human Services.

Druss, BG; Marcus, SC; Olfson, M; Tanielian, T; and Pincus, HA. 2003. Trends in Care by Nonphysician Clinicians in the United States. *New England Journal of Medicine.* 348(2):130-7.

Ehrenberg R. and Smith R. 1991. *Modern Labor Economics, 4th edition.* HarperCollins Publishers, Inc., New York, NY.

Ellsbury, KE; Baldwin, L; Johnson, KE; Runyan, SJ; and Hart, GL. 2002. Gender-related factors in the re-cruitment of physicians to the rural northwest. *Journal American Board of Family Practice.* 15(5):392-400.

Farber, L and Murray D. 2001. A Slip in Net Worth. *Medical Economics.* 5(21).

Gamliel, S; Politzer, RM; Rivo, ML; and Mullan, F. 1995. Managed Care on the March: Will Physicians meet the Challenge? *Health Affairs,* 14(2):131-142.

GMENAC. April 1981. *Geographic Distribution Technical Panel, 3.* DHHS Publication No. HRA-81-651. Washington D.C.: U.S. Government Printing Office.

Grumbach, K. 2002.The Ramifications of Specialty-dominated Medicine. *Health Affairs.* 21(1):155-157.

Hart, LG; Wagner, E; Pirzada, S; Nelson, AF; and Rosenblatt, RA. 1997. Physician Staffing Ratios in Staff-Model HMOs: A Cautionary Tale. *Health Affairs.* Jan/Feb, pp. 55-89.

Hicks, JR. 1966. *The Theory of Wages,* 2nd ed. New York: St. Martin's Press.

Hogan, PF; Dobson, A; Haynie, B; DeLisa, JA; Gans, B; Grabois, M; LaBan, MM; Melvin, JL; and Walsh, NE. 1996. Physical Medicine and Rehabilitation Workforce Study: The Supply of and Demand for Physiatrists. *Arch Phys Med Rehabil.* 77: 95-99.

Hogan, PF; Hirchkorn, C; Hughes, J; Simonson, B; and Cardwell, MH. 2001. *Workforce Study of Endocrinologists.* Final report prepared for The Endocrine Society; The American Association of Clinical Endocrinologists; The American Diabetes Association; The Association of Program Directors of Endocrinology, Diabetes, and Metabolism; American Thyroid Association, and Lawson Wilkens Pediatric Endocrine Society. http://209.63.37.22/publicpolicy/legislative/ upload/workforce-study-report.pdf (Accessible February 28, 2006).

Hojat, M; Gonnella, JS; Erdman, JB; Veloski, JJ; Louis, DZ; Nasca, TJ; Rattner, SL. 2000. Physicians' Perceptions of the Changing Healthcare System: Comparisons by Gender and Specialties. *Journal of Community Health.* 25:455-471.

Holahan, J and Pohl, MB. 2002. Changes in Insurance Coverage: 1994-2000 and Beyond. *Health Affairs, Web Exclusives.* W162-W171.

Holliman, CJ; Wuerz, RC; and Hirshberg, AJ. 1997. Analysis of Factors Affecting U.S. Emergency Physician Workforce Projections. *Academic Emergency Medicine.* 4(7): 731-735.

Institute of Medicine. 1978. *A Manpower Policy for Primary Healthcare.* A National Academy of Sciences report, Washington D.C.

Institute of Medicine. 1996. *The Nation's Physician Workforce: Options for Balancing Supply and Requirements.* KN Lohr, NA Vanselow, and DE

Detmer, eds. Washington, DC: National Academy Press.

Institute of Medicine. 2000. To Error is Human: Building a Safer Health System. LT Kohn, JM Corrigan, and MS Donaldson, eds. Committee on Quality of Health Care in America, Washington, DC: National Academy Press.

Jacoby, I and Meyer, GS. 1998. Creating an Effective Physician Workforce Marketplace. *JAMA*. 280(9): 822-824.

Jonasson, O; Kwakwa F; and Sheldon, GF. 1995. Calculating the Workforce in General Surgery. *JAMA* 274:731-34.

Keith, SN; Bell, RM; Swanson, AG; and Williams, AP. 1985. Effects of Affirmative Action in Medical Schools: A Study of the Class of 1975. *New England Journal of Medicine*. 313:1519-1525.

Koenig, L; Siegel, JM; Donson, A; Hearle, K; Ho, S; and Rudowitz, R. 2003. Drivers of Healthcare Expenditures Associated With Physician Services. *The American Journal of Managed Care*. 9 (Special Issue 1): SP34-42.

Komaromy, M; Grumbach, K; Drake, M; Vranizan, K; Lurie, N; Keane, D; and Bindman, AB. 1996. The Role of Black and Hispanic Physicians in Providing Healthcare for Underserved Populations. *New England Journal of Medicine*. 334:1305-1310.

Lee PP; Jackson CA; and Relles DA. 1995. Estimating Eye Care Workforce Supply and Requirements. *Ophthalmology*. 102(12):1964-1971.

Lee PP; Jackson CA; and Relles DA. 1998. Demand-Based Assessment of Workforce Requirements for Orthopaedic Services. *The Journal of Bone and Joint Surgery*. 80:313-26.

McMurray, JE; Linzer, M; Konrad, TR; Douglas, J; Shugerman, R; and Nelson, K. 2000. The work lives of women physicians: results from the Physician Work Life Study. *J Gen Intern Med*. 15:372-380.

Medical Group Management Association. *Cost Survey of the Medical Group Management Association*. Englewood, CO. Various years.

Medical Group Management Association. 2002. *Physician Compensation and Production Survey*. Englewood, CO.

Meyer, GS; Jacoby, I; Krakauer, H; Powell, DW; Aurand, J; and McCardle, P. 1996. Gastroenterology Workforce Modeling. *JAMA*. 276(9):689-694.

Miller, RS; Dunn, MR; Richter, TH; and Whitcomb, ME. 1998. Employment-Seeking Experiences of Resident Physicians Completing Training During 1996. *JAMA*. 280(9):777-783.

Miller, TE. and Derse, AR. 2002. Between Strangers: The Practice of Medicine Online. *Health Affairs*. 21(4):168-179.

Mitka, M. June 2001. What Lures Women Physicians to Practice Medicine in Rural Areas? *JAMA*. 285(24): 3078-3079.

Moorhead, JC; Gallery, ME; Mannle, T; Chaney, WC; Conrad, LC; Dalsey, WC; Herman, S; Hockberger, RS; McDonald, SC; Packard, DC; Rapp, MT; Rorrie, CC; Schafermeyer, RW; Schulman, R; Whitehead, DC; Hirschkorn, C; and Hogan, PF. 1998. A study of the workforce in emergency medicine. *Ann Emerg Med*. 31(5):595-607.

Morrissey, J. 2004. CHW Plans IT Initiative. *Modern Healthcare*. 34(8):16.

Moy, E and Bartman, BA. 1995. Physician Race and Care of Minority and Medically Indigent Patients. *JAMA*. 273(16):1515-1520.

Neilson, EG; Hull, AR; Wish, JB; Neylan, JF; Sherman, D; and Suki, WN. 1997. The Ad Hoc Committee Report on Estimating the Future Workforce and Training Requirements for Nephrology. *Journal of the American Society of Nephrology*. 8(5 suppl 9):S1-S4.

Ness, RB; Ukoli, F; Hunt, S; Kiely, SC; NcNeil, MA; Richardson, V; Weissbach, N; and Belle, SH. 2000. Salary Equity among Male and Female Internists in Pennsylvania. *Annals of Internal Medicine*. 133(2): 104-110.

Nguyen, XN. (1994) Physician Behavioral Response to Price Control. *Human Capital Development and Operations Policy Working Papers*. World Bank.

Nonnemaker, L. 2000. Women physicians in academic medicine: New insights from cohort studies. *New England Journal of Medicine*. 342:399-405.

Novielli, K; Hojat, M; Park, PK; Gonnella, JS; and Veloski, JJ. 2001. Career Choice: Glass Ceiling or Glass Slipper? Change of Interest in Surgery during Medical School: A Comparison of Men and Women. *Academic Medicine*. 76:s58-s61.

Palepu, A; Carr, PK; Friedman, RH; Ash, AS; and Moskowitz, MA. 2000. Specialty Choices, Compensation, and Career Satisfaction of Under-represented Minority Faculty in Academic Medicine. *Academic Medicine*. 75:157-60.

Palepu, A; Carr, PL; Friedman, RH; Amos, H; Ash, AS; and Moskowitz, MA. 1998. Minority Faculty and Academic Rank in Medicine. *JAMA*. 280(9):767-771.

Randolph, GD. and Pathman, DE. 2001. Trends in the Rural-Urban Distribution of General Pediatricians. *Pediatrics*. 107(2): e18.

Reinhardt, UE. 2002. Analyzing Cause and Effect in the U.S. Physician Workforce. *Health Affairs*. 21(1): 165-166.

Robert Wood Johnson Foundation. 2000. *Health and Health Care 2010: The Forecast, The Challenge*. San Francisco: Jossey-Bass.

Ross, GS. 2001. Salary Equity among Male and Female Internists: Letter to the Editor. *Annals of Internal Medicine*. 134(9):798-799.

Schmitz, R.; Lantin, M. and White, A. 1998. *Future Needs in Pulmonary and Critical Care Medicine.* Report prepared by Abt Associates, Inc., for the American College of Chest Physicians, American Thoracic Society, and Society for Critical Care Medicine.

Schroeder, SA. 1994. Managing the U.S. Healthcare Workforce: Creating Policy Amidst Uncertainty. *Inquiry*. 31:266-275.

Showalter, MH and Thurston, NK. 1997. Taxes and Labor Supply of High-Income Physicians. *Journal of Public Economics*. 66(1):73-97.

Sloan, FA and Feldman, R. 1978. Competition Among Physicians. W. Greenberg, ed., *Competition in the Healthcare Sector: Past, Present and Future.* Conference proceedings sponsored by the Bureau of Economics, Federal Trade Commission. pp. 57-131.

Snyderman, R; Sheldon, GF; and Bischoff, TA. 2002. Gauging Supply and Demand: The Challenging Quest to Predict the Future Physician Workforce. *Health Affairs*. 21(1):167-168.

Spickard, A; Gabbe, SG; and Christensen, JF. 2002. Mid-Career Burnout in Generalist and Specialist Physicians. *JAMA*. 288(12):1447-1450.

Tarlov, AR. Estimating physician workforce requirements. *JAMA*. 294(1995):1558-1560.

Terry, K. 1999. What practices are Worth in Today's Market: The PPM Meltdown. *Medical Economics*. 76(2):169-70, 173-6.

Terry, NP. 2000. Structural and Legal Implications of E-Health. *Journal of Health Law*. 33(4):606-614.

Trude, S. So Much to Do, So Little Time: Physician Capacity Constraints, 1997-2001. *Center for Studying Health System Change Tracking Report*. May 2003.

Weiner, DM; McDaniel, R. and Lowe, F.C. 1997. Urologic Manpower Issues for the 21st Century: Assessing the Impact of Changing Population Demographics. *Urology*. 49:335-342.

Weiner, JP. 1994. Forecasting the Effects of Health Reform on the U.S. Physician Workforce Requirements: Evidence from HMO Staffing Patterns. *JAMA*. 272:222-230.

Weiner, JP. 2002. A Shortage of Physicians or a Surplus of Assumptions? *Health Affairs*. 21(1):160-162.

Weiner, JP. Prepaid Group Practice Staffing And U.S. Physician Supply: Lessons For Workforce Policy, *Health Affairs Web Exclusive*, February 4, 2004.

Wennberg, JE; Goodman, DC; Nease, RF; and Keller, RB. 1993. Finding Equilibrium in U.S. Physician Supply. *Health Affairs*. 12:89-103.

2

Forecasting the Global Shortage of Physicians: An Economic- and Needs-Based Approach

Source: Scheffler RM, Liu JX, Kinfu Y, Dal Poz MR. Forecasting the global shortage of physicians: an economic- and needs-based approach. *Bull World Health Organ* 2008;86:516-523B. Courtesy of the World Health Organization.

INTRODUCTION

The World Health Report 2006: working together for health has brought renewed attention to the global human resources required to produce health.[1]

It estimated that 57 countries have an absolute shortage of 2.3 million physicians, nurses and midwives. These shortages suggest that many countries have insufficient numbers of health professionals to deliver essential health interventions, such as skilled attendance at birth and immunization programmes. However, these estimates do not take into account the ability of countries to recruit and retain these workers, nor are they specific enough to inform policy-makers about how, and to what extent, health workforce investment should be channelled into training of different professions.

This paper focuses on physicians, who serve a key role in health-care provision. Using the most up-dated information on the supply of physicians over a 20-year period, we project the size of the future global need for, demand for and supply of physicians to year 2015, the target date for the Millennium Development Goals (MDGs).[2]

Objective Global achievements in health may be limited by critical shortages of health-care workers. To help guide workforce policy, we estimate the future demand for, need for and supply of physicians, by WHO region, to determine where likely shortages will occur by 2015, the target date of the Millennium Development Goals.

Methods Using World Bank and WHO data on physicians per capita from 1980 to 2001 for 158 countries, we employ two modelling approaches for estimating the future global requirement for physicians. A needs-based model determines the number of physicians per capita required to achieve 80% coverage of live births by a skilled health-care attendant. In contrast, our economic model identifies the number of physicians per capita that are likely to be demanded, given each country's economic growth. These estimates are compared to the future supply of physicians projected by extrapolating the historical rate of increase in physicians per capita for each country.

Findings By 2015, the global supply of physicians appears to be in balance with projected economic demand. Because our measure of need reflects the minimum level of workforce density required to provide a basic health service that is met in all but the least developed countries, the needs-based estimates predict a global surplus of physicians. However, on a regional basis, both models predict shortages for many countries in the WHO African Region in 2015, with some countries experiencing a needs-based shortage, a demand-based shortage, or both.

Conclusion The type of policy intervention needed to alleviate projected shortages, such as increasing health-care training or adopting measures to discourage migration, depends on the type of shortage projected.

Bulletin of the World Health Organization 2008; 86:516-523.

Needs-based estimates use an exogenous health benchmark to judge the adequacy of the number of physicians required to meet MDG targets. Demand estimates are based on a country's economic growth and the increase in health-care spending that results from it, which primarily goes towards worker salaries. We then compare the needs-based and demand-based estimates to the projected supply of physicians, extrapolated based on historical trends. Our results point to dramatic shortages of physicians in the WHO African Region by 2015. We provide estimates of shortages by country in Africa and discuss their implications for different workforce policy choices.

METHODS

For illustrative purposes, we provide a stylized version of the conceptual framework we employed for forecasting physician numbers in Fig. 1. First, we project the supply in the per capita number of physicians *(S)* based on historical data on physician numbers for each country; this serves as a baseline against which different forecasts can be evaluated. We employ two forecasting methods. The forecast for the needs-based estimate *(N)* is determined by calculating the number of physicians that would be required to reach *The world health report 2006* goal of having 80% of live births attended by a skilled health worker.[3] The second forecasting method reflects the demand for physicians in each country as determined by economic growth $(D_1$ and $D_2)$. With these different estimates, shortages or surpluses can be calculated. For example, by year 8, about 3.5 physicians

per 1000 population will be needed compared to the projected supply of 3.0 per 1000, producing a 0.5 per 1000 shortage. In comparison, 4.0 per 1000 will be demanded according to the scenario represented by D_1, resulting in a demand-based shortage of about 1.0 physicians per 1000. A different scenario can arise if supply exceeds demand, as represented by D_2, resulting in a surplus. We can then multiply this estimated shortage by projected population numbers to calculate the absolute deficit of the numbers of physicians. In this illustrative case, the needs-based shortage exceeds the demand-based shortage. This framework can be applied at the country, regional and global levels of analyses, depending on the level of aggregation of physician numbers.

We now describe our estimation procedures more formally. First, baseline supply projections to the year 2015 were estimated using the historical growth rate of physician densities in each country. The following regression equation was run for each country for time $t = \{1980, \ldots, 2001\}$:

$$\ln (\text{physicians per 1000 population}_t) = \alpha_0 + \alpha_1 \times \text{year}_t + \varepsilon_t$$

where ε_t is the random disturbance term, and α_0 and α_1 are unknown parameters to be estimated from the model. This exponential growth model assumes that current trends in the growth of physician numbers will continue as they have historically for each country.

The needs-based approach is based on an $\sin^{-1}$-log model that relates physician density with coverage of skilled birth attendants, weighted by population size. This model is used to identify a level

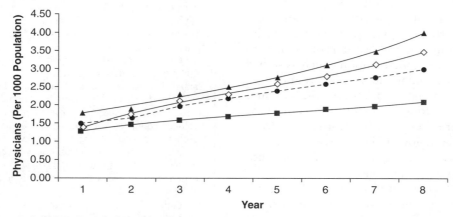

Figure 1 Conceptual Forecasting Framework

of physician density below which virtually no country has achieved 80% coverage. While physicians may not necessarily be the same workers who attend live births, we can determine the overall required number of health-care workers to achieve the goal and thus gauge the subset number of physicians needed to maintain the desired level of service coverage. This approach assumes that skills mix in health service delivery remains constant. The needs-based model estimates the following equation for all countries i at time t:

$$\sin^{-1}(\% \text{ coverage}_{it}) = \beta_0 + \beta_1 \times \ln(\text{physicians per 1000 population}_{it}) + \mu_i + \eta_t + \delta_{it}$$

where μ_i and η_t reflect country and time fixed effects, respectively, δ_{it} is a random error term, and β_0 and β_1 are unknown parameters to be estimated from the model. This threshold density figure, along with population estimates for future years, was subsequently used to calculate the number of physicians that would be needed in each country to attain the MDG of 80% coverage of live births. We opted for the $\sin^{-1}$ transformation because it is more consistent with statistical theory; the transformation of the dependent variable, which is a proportion, results in normally distributed responses (asymptotically). The $\sin^{-1}$-log model also achieved the highest R^2 and best goodness-of-fit to the data as measured by the deviance.[4] This approach is similar to that followed in *The world health report 2006*.

The demand-based approach utilizes gross national income (GNI) per capita as the predictor of demand for physicians per 1000 population, along with country fixed effects to account for unobservable heterogeneity across countries, weighted by population size. Previous research has shown that indicators of gross domestic product or national income are the best predictors of health expenditures, of which, labour is the principle component.[5-9]

This method has also been employed in other forecasts of physician demand.[10] This approach estimates the following relationship for country i at time t:

$$\ln(\text{physicians per 1000 population}_{it}) = \gamma_0 + \gamma_1 \times \ln(\text{GNI per capita}_{it-5}) + \gamma_2 \times \text{income level}_i + \mu_i + \zeta_{it}$$

where μ_i reflects a vector of country fixed effects, ζ_{it} is the disturbance term, and γ_0 and γ_1 are unknown parameters to be estimated from the model. GNI per capita is lagged 5 years to account for time required for economic growth to affect health-care spending and, in turn, influence changes in the health-care system and the workforce. Because GNI data were only available until 2002 at the time of data assembly, values for 2003-2010 were predicted using the historical growth rate. For each country at time t, the growth rate in GNI per capita was calculated as:

$$\exp(\lambda_1) - 1$$

from the equation:

$$\ln(\text{GNI per capita}_t) = \lambda_0 + \lambda_1 \times \text{year}_t + \upsilon_t$$

where υ_t is the disturbance term, and λ_0 and λ_1 are unknown parameters to be estimated from the model. Classification of countries by income level (low, medium and high) from the World Bank was included in the demand equation as countries at different levels of development may exhibit stronger or weaker relationships between economic growth and healthcare spending, depending on the complexities of the health-care system and structure of local markets.

Data

Data were compiled from several sources. The World Bank *Health, nutrition and population database* contains physician numbers from 1980 to 2001.[11] GNI per capita (adjusted for purchasing power parity using the atlas method) for 1975-2002 was obtained from the *World development indicators database*.[12] Physician numbers were updated with the most recent figures from the *World health statistics 2006* database and from the *OECD health data 2005* database for OECD countries.[13,14] Historic and projected population numbers were obtained from the United Nations Population Division.[15] We employ physician density (per 1000 population) in our analyses to account for differences in health-system size and weight all regressions by population size. Our benchmark indicator for need is the number of live births attended by a skilled health worker, also available from *World health statistics 2006*. We constructed a panel of 158 countries from 1980 to 2001, grouped according to WHOregional classifications (available at: http://www.who.int/about/regions). Data were missing for some countries, either due to unavailability or differences in reporting practices. Missing data points occurring between two data points were linearly interpolated; those that were not bounded by two real data points were not interpolated. For figures on physicians per capita, missing data for up to 6 consecutive years were interpolated as some countries only reported periodically in the 22-year span of our data compilation; interpolated values comprise 35.6% of the 2819 data points for physician supply numbers used in this analysis.

Because GNI per capita data are more readily available, only 4.7% of the 4238 GNI per capita data points used were interpolated. This method of treating missing data points raises concern over the robustness of our estimation results. To address this, we systematically drop countries from our sample for which the number of data points for physicians per capita are fewer than six (24 countries), fewer than seven (41 countries), and fewer than eight (63 countries). Estimated coefficients from these subsamples may differ from the main sample due to the fact that data reporting issues are more frequently encountered for lower-income countries. We carry out formal *F* tests of our economic demand model on these different subsamples in our robustness checks.

RESULTS

Current Distribution

We first describe the current distribution of physicians by level of health expenditures and burden of disease, displayed in Fig. 2. The size of the circle represents the proportion of world health expenditures comprised of the countries in a given region. In 2004, the WHO Americas Region registered the highest proportion of the world's health expenditures (over 50%), but had just over 20% of the world's supply of physicians, and only 10% of the global burden of disease. With a similar level of burden of disease, the WHO European Region has over 35% of the world's supply of physicians along with about 32% of the world's health expenditures. In contrast, countries in the WHO South-East Asia Region suffer the highest pro-

portion of the global burden of disease (29%) with only 11% of the world's supply of physicians and just about 1% of world health expenditures. Similarly, the WHO African Region experiences 24% of the global burden of disease, while having only 2% of the global physician supply and spending that is less than 1% of global expenditures. Clearly, there is a dramatic imbalance in the global distribution of physicians, with countries in the WHO African and South-East Asia Regions currently facing the largest disparities.

Forecasting Results

The results of our analysis of the future global distribution of physicians are shown in Table 1. If current trends continue, we will have 12.7 million physicians supplied by 2015 globally. Given the standard error of our estimated growth rates of physicians for each country, this supply number can range from 11.4 million to 14.3 million (95% confidence interval). Our needs-based model projects the ratio of physicians required to achieve 80% coverage of live births by a skilled attendant to be 0.55 per 1000 population, ranging from 0.41 to 0.61 based on a 95% confidence interval (regression results in Table 2 and Fig. 3, available at: http://www.who.int/bulletin/volumes/86/7/07-046474/en/index.html). Note that this criterion of need reflects a relatively low level of health-service provision that is already met in many middle- and high-income countries. Consequently, this needs-based approach estimates that the global required number of physicians to achieve 80% coverage is about 3.8 million, ranging from 3.4 million to 4.2 million. This implies that there will be many more physicians in 2015 than are needed to reach

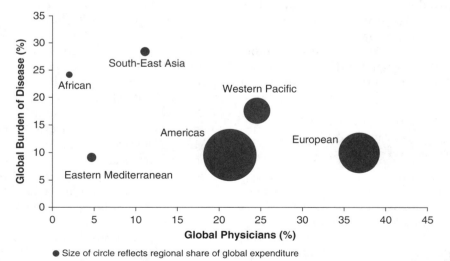

Figure 2 Physician distribution by burden of disease and health expenditure, by WHO region, 2004. *Source:* World health statistics 2006.[13]

Table 1	Projected supply of, need for and demand for physicians, by WHO region, 2015				
WHO region	Supply[a]	Need[b]		Demand[c]	
	(1000s)[d]	(1000s)[d]	Surplus (+) or shortage (−)[d,e]	(1000s)	Surplus (+) or shortage (−)[d,f]
African	255 (208–329)	422 (377–469)	−167 (−213 − −122)	144 (131–159)	111 (96–124)
Americas	2773 (2,509–3,120)	538 (481–599)	2235 (2,174–2,293)	1885 (1,620–2,196)	888 (578–1,153)
Eastern Mediterranean	1077 (914–1,297)	308 (275–343)	769 (734–802)	520 (442–612)	557 (465–635)
European	3222 (3,015–3,449)	480 (429–534)	2742 (2,687–2,793)	2913 (2,615–3,259)	309 (−38–607)
South-East Asia	1067 (931–1,225)	987 (882–1,097)	80 (−30–186)	910 (718–1,155)	157 (−87–350)
Western Pacific	4256 (3,853–4,883)	1016 (907–1,130)	3240 (3 126–3 348)	4432 (3,107–6,347)	−176 (−2,092–1,148)
World	12,650 (11,430–14,303)	3,752 (3,351–4,171)	8,898 (8,478–9,299)	10,804 (8,633–13,728)	1,846 (−1,078–4,017)

[a] Supply is projected based on the historical growth of physicians per capita in each country.
[b] Need is assessed based on reaching the goal of 80% of live births attended by a skilled health-care worker.
[c] Demand is projected based on economic growth (both historical and projected) of each country.
[d] Values in parentheses are 95% confidence intervals.
[e] Surplus (shortage) is calculated as mean projected supply minus estimated need. High and low estimates reflect the 95% confidence interval of the needs-based estimated 80% coverage attainment level.
[f] Surplus (shortage) is calculated as mean projected supply minus estimated demand. High and low estimates reflect the 95% confidence interval of the demand-based estimated coefficients.

Table 3	Number of countries with physician shortages[a] in 2015	
WHO region	Needs-based model	Demand-based model
African	32	15
Americas	1	3
Eastern Mediterranean	3	2
European	0	10
South-East Asia	3	0
Western Pacific	6	7
World	45	37

[a] Shortage is defined as having a projected supply of physicians that meets less than 80% of the forecasted demand or need, calculated at estimated means.

the benchmark outcome. However, the issue of equitable workforce distribution remains. Even though the global supply of physicians exceeds that of the "need", the WHO African Region is likely to experience a shortage of physicians (about 167,000 in 2015) according to the needs-based approach.

In contrast, based on projected GNI growth, there will be a global demand for about 10.8 million physicians by 2015 (regression results in Table 2). However, when we account for the 95% confidence interval, our demand-based global estimates of the number of physicians suggest a balance with the projected supply of physicians in 2015. Furthermore, countries in the WHO African, Americas and the Eastern Mediterranean Regions will likely experience surpluses of physicians of 111,000, 888,000 and 557,000 respectively in 2015. Such a projected surplus in excess of projected demand indicates that future economic growth based on the historical growth rate since 1975 may not sufficiently increase health expenditures in these areas to retain newly trained physicians. This has important implications for out-migration from shortage areas, as physicians may be attracted to areas with higher demand and higher salaries.

We further investigate whether the inclusion of countries with more missing data, and thus relatively more interpolated observations, affects the regression coefficients. We systematically drop countries with fewer than six, seven and eight actual data points from our full sample and re-ran our demand regression equation. In all cases, the coefficient for the elasticity of physicians per capita with respect to lagged GNI for the omitted category (high-income countries) is significant, does not appreciably vary across different subsamples and is precisely estimated.

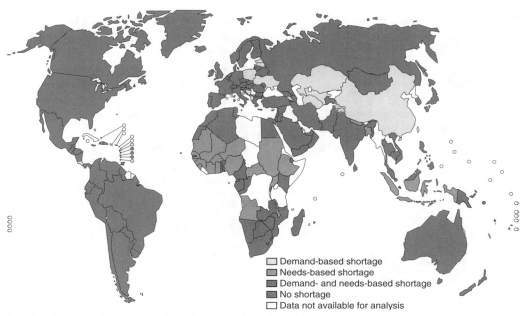

Figure 4 Physician shortages in 2015 based on demand and need models

However, coefficients on dummy variables for middle- and low-income countries do differ across subsamples, reflecting the fact that missing data are more likely to occur for these countries. Nevertheless, all coefficients on these dummy variables are negative and significant, consistently indicating that the elasticity of physicians per capita is less sensitive to GNI per capita in middle- and low-income countries than it is in higher-income countries. Results of F tests

comparing the full-sample specification to each of the restricted subsamples fail to reject the null hypothesis of no difference.

Table 3 compares the number of countries that are projected to experience shortages in 2015 from the needs- and demand-based models. We define a country as having a shortage if the projected supply of physicians meets less than 80% of the projected demand or need. Overall, we find that 45 countries

Table 2	Ordinary least squares regression results of needs-based and demand-based models			
	Needs-based model: % live births attended by a skilled physician[b]		Demand-based model: logged physicians per 1000	
	Estimated coefficient	Robust standard error	Estimated coefficient	Robust standard error
Logged physicians per 1000	0.204[c]	0.010		
Logged GNP per capita ($t-5$)			0.237[c]	0.074
Middle-income country			−0.568[c]	0.128
Low-income country			−1.565[c]	0.182
Country fixed effects	Yes		Yes	
N	409		2513	
R^2			0.974	
Wald-stat ($P > \chi^2$)	446.52	0.000		
F-stat (P-value)			74.15	0.000

GNP, gross national product.
[a] Full sample $n = 158$ countries. Standard errors are clustered at the country level. Regressions are weighted by population size.
[b] Sin^{-1} transformation applied.
[c] Significant at 1% level.

Data *Source:* World development indicators database,[12] World health statistics 2006,[13] Health nutrition population statistics, OECD health data 2005,[14] 2004 revision population database.[15]

will have a shortage in 2015 according to the needs-based approach, the overwhelming majority of which are located in the WHO African Region. According to the demand-based model, 37 countries are likely to experience a shortage in 2015; 15 of these countries are located in the WHO African Region, 10 in the WHO Eastern Mediterranean Region, and 7 in the WHO Western Pacific Region. These results for the world are graphically displayed in Fig. 4. Countries that are projected to experience demand-based shortages are also countries that will likely experience strong economic growth in the near future. For example, the demand for physicians will increase dramatically in China if the rapid economic growth experienced in recent history continues into the near future. Other countries, such as Indonesia, are projected to experience a needs-based shortage only, suggesting that even though their economies may grow strongly enough to support the supply of physicians, the overall workforce number will not be adequate to meet the needs-based benchmark of 80% of live births covered by a skilled attendant.

Results for Africa

In the WHO African Region, some countries will have both a needs-based and demand-based shortage. This indicates that, even though there is a critical need for more physicians, and projected economic growth will demand a larger physician workforce, the projected supply of physicians will not increase sufficiently by 2015 to achieve balance. These coun-

tries do not have the required capacity to train the numbers that will be demanded by 2015, and will likely need to depend on newly recruited workers from abroad, possibly from neighbouring countries with poor economic performance. Table 4 (available at: http://www.who.int/bulletin/ volumes/86/7/07-046474/en/index. html) displays the projected need for, demand for and supply of physicians in the year 2015 for all African countries included in our analysis. For example, Kenya will need 24,000 physicians on average in 2015 (a shortage of about 18,000 physicians) and the economy will be strong enough to demand 7600 physicians on average, but the supply in Kenya is only projected to reach an average of 6100 physicians. Algeria, on the other hand, will have an ample supply of 97,000 physicians, a surplus of almost 77,000 physicians beyond what is needed and a surplus of 67,000 physicians beyond what will be demanded. In Ethiopia, we see another scenario where 53,000 physicians will be needed by 2015, but the economy will only demand about 3000 physicians, even though the supply of physicians is projected to reach about 5000. These scenarios suggest that future migration of physicians could take an increasingly regional dimension.

DISCUSSION

Our projections suggest that, by the year 2015, the global supply of physicians will be roughly in balance with demand, while a significant surplus will

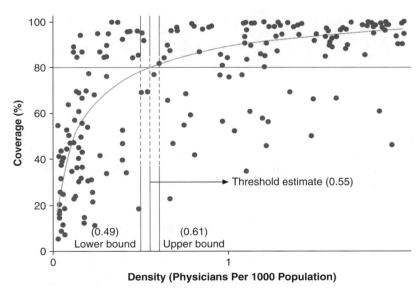

Figure 3 Needs-based estimate of the number of physicians per capita required to achieve 80% coverage of live births by a skilled attendant

| Table 4 | Projected supply of, need for and demand for physicians in 2015 for countries in the WHO African Region |

Country	Supply	Needs-based model		Demand-based model	
	(count)	(count)	Surplus (+) or shortage (−)[a]	(count)	Surplus (+) or shortage (−)[b]
Algeria	97 739	−0 896	76 843	30 682	67 057
Angola	2 593	11 493	−8 900	1 309	1 284
Benin	490	−6 154	−5 665	905	−415
Botswana	975	927	48	521	454
Burkina Faso	1 197	9 699	−8 503	679	517
Burundi	449	5 825	−5 376	628	−179
Cameroon	822	10 447	−9 625	1 539	−717
Cape Verde	105	345	−240	242	−137
Central African Republic	201	2 550	−2 349	210	−10
Comoros	322	559	−237	142	180
Congo	3 115	2 985	130	1 511	1 605
Côte d'Ivoire	2 975	11 825	−8 850	1 988	987
Equatorial Guinea	86	344	−258	296	−209
Ethiopia	4 916	53 306	−48 390	2 967	1 949
Gabon	188	881	−692	647	−459
Gambia	23	1 036	−1 014	76	−54
Ghana	3 414	14 574	−11 159	2 097	1 317
Guinea	1 552	6 524	−4 972	1 703	−151
Guinea-Bissau	504	1 170	−666	393	111
Kenya	6 105	24 248	−18 143	7 602	−1 497
Lesotho	51	957	−906	118	−67
Madagascar	2 376	13 065	−10 690	2 916	−540
Malawi	644	8 778	−8 134	413	231
Mali	890	9 927	−9 037	1 038	−148
Mauritania	599	2 188	−1 589	392	207
Mauritius	2 612	737	1 875	1 572	1 040
Mozambique	277	12 901	−12 624	683	−407
Namibia	2 623	1 233	1 389	756	1 867
Niger	802	10 580	−9 778	507	295
Nigeria	72 123	88 298	−16 176	36 580	35 543
Rwanda	395	6 179	−5 784	656	−261
Senegal	1 819	7 977	−6 158	1 396	423
Sierra Leone	759	3 784	−3 025	424	335
South Africa	35 882	26 282	9 599	33 543	2 338
Swaziland	537	544	−8	168	369
Togo	433	4 305	−3 873	720	−288
Uganda	2 282	22 999	−20 717	2 315	−33
Zambia	433	7 594	−7 162	1 518	−1 086
Zimbabwe	1 659	7 574	−5 915	2 363	−705

[a] Surplus (shortage) is calculated as supply minus need at means of predicted values.
[b] Surplus (shortage) is calculated as supply minus demand at means of predicted values.

arise according to the needs-based model. However, regional trends show that distributional problems will likely persist. More than any other region of the world, Africa will likely experience most of the physician shortages in 2015. Given the disproportionate burden of disease in this region, policies for increasing the supply of physicians are urgently needed to stem projected shortages. According to our needsbased target of 80% coverage of live births by a skilled attendant, a 65% increase in the physician supply in the WHO African Region will be required compared to an increase of 44% of

physicians to equilibrate demand with supply. These enormous increases will require significant increases in health-care spending and active policy intervention.

Policy Implications

The type of policy intervention pursued will depend on the type of shortage likely to be experienced. Given the difficulty of redistributing physicians across country borders, countries that may face only a needs-based shortage may want to consider expanding medical training programmes. For countries that face a demand-based shortage only, out-migration may be a particular concern, suggesting policies geared towards retention. Countries that face both demand-based and needs-based shortages may prefer a mixture of training and recruitment policies. Government and donor organizations should consider increasing financial support of health-care workers as a means of improving recruitment and retention.

The exact nature and extent of any policy intervention adopted will depend crucially on the characteristics of each country's health-care system and institutions. While this analysis provides a direction for where policies should be targeted, such cross-country comparisons cannot fully account for these complexities as well as other aspects of distribution (e.g., physician specialty, race/ethnicity), practice styles (e.g., work hours) and trends in the demographic characteristics of the workforce supply (e.g., ageing, gender mix), which have also been found to have important effects on health-care service delivery and access.[16-18] Moreover, health-worker mix is another critical factor in health-services production; further work is required in the area of predicting the future numbers of nurses, midwives and other ancillary health-care workers who will be needed and demanded. As the WHO report shows, nurses and other health workers can help to make the clinical work more productive, particularly in certain patient-care services where there are skill overlaps.[19] The use of telemedicine may also have merit as a cost-effective workforce model.[20,21] Limited resources clearly point to merits of these approaches.

Limitations and Future Directions

While we have sought to provide some indication of the numbers of physicians that will likely be required in the future, some caution is warranted in interpreting these figures. First, our criterion of need only reflects one aspect of health-care delivery; thus different numbers of physicians will be required to meet alternative normative criteria for health services. Second, our projections of demand and supply both rely on trends in either economic growth or physicians per capita, each of which are continually being affected by policy intervention. Comparable cross-country data along these dimensions are currently unavailable and consequently cannot be fully accounted for in this type of forecasting. Moreover, projections of demand will also likely be affected by other factors other than economic growth, suggesting directions for further work in refining such de-

mand models. Given these limitations, we nevertheless believe that this exercise has been useful and informative for providing an overall sense of where physician workforce policies should be undertaken.

ACKNOWLEDGMENTS

We thank Teh-wei Hu, Ray Catalano and Timothy Brown for their technical expertise and advice. Steeve Ebener and his team, including Yaniss Guigoz, at WHO also provided assistance with mapping tools. We also thank the numerous seminar participants at the London School of Economics, the London School of Hygiene and Tropical Medicine, the International Health Workforce Conference, the Advanced Health Leadership Forum and the International Health Economics Association for their comments and feedback. Members of the Department for Human Resources for Health at WHO provided logistical, administrative and technical support for this study.

● ● ● **References**

1. *The world health report 2006: working together for health*. Geneva: WHO; 2006.

2. *The millennium development goals report 2005*. New York, NY: United Nations; 2005.

3. Chen L, Evans T, Anand S, Boufford JI, Brown H, Chowdhury M, et al. Human resources for health: overcoming the crisis. *Lancet* 2004;364:1984-90. PMID:15567015 doi:10.1016/S0140-6736(04)17482-5.

4. Zar JH. *Biostatistical analysis*. Upper Saddle River, NJ: Prentice-Hall; 1996.

5. Cooper RA, Getzen TE, Laud P. Economic expansion is a major determinant of physician supply and utilization. *Health Serv Res* 2003;38:675-96. PMID:12785567 doi:10.1111/1475-6773.00139.

6. Scheffler RM. *Health expenditures and economic growth: an international perspective* [Occasional Papers on Globalization]. University of South Florida Globalization Research Center. Nov 2004:1.10.

7. Getzen TE. Macro forecasting of national health expenditures. In: Rossiter L, Scheffler RM, eds. *Advances in health economics* 11:27-48. Greenwood, CN: JAI Press;1990.

8. Newhouse JP. Medical care expenditure: a cross-national survey. *J Hum Resour* 1977;12:115-25 10.2307/145602. PMID:404354 doi:10.2307/145602.

9. Pfaff M. Differences in health care spending across countries: statistical evidence. [Medline]. *J Health Polit Policy Law* 1990;15:1-67. PMID:2108198 doi:10.1215/03616878-15-1-1.

10. Scheffler RM. *Is there a doctor in the house? market signals and tomorrow's supply of doctors*. Stanford, CA: Stanford University Press; 2008.

11. Stats HNP [online database]. Washington, DC: World Bank; 2006. Available from:

http://devdata.worldbank.org/hnpstats [accessed on 3 April 2008].

12. *World Development Indicators (WDI) database* [online database]. Washington, DC: World Bank; 2006. Available from: http://web.worldbank.org/ WBSITE/EXTERNAL/DATASTATISTICS [accessed on 3 April 2008].

13. *World health statistics 2006.* Geneva: WHO; 2006.

14. *Health data OECD, 2005.* Paris: OECD, 2005.

15. *World population prospects: the 2004 revision population database* [online database]. New York, NY: United Nations Population Division; 2005. Available from: http://esa.un.org/unpp/ [accessed on 3 April 2008].

16. Brown TT, Coffman JM, Quinn BC, Scheffler RM, Schwalm DD. Do physicians always flee from HMOs? New results using dynamic panel estimation methods. *Health Serv Res* 2006;41:357-73. PMID:16584453 doi:10.1111/j.1475-6773.2005.00485.x.

17. Brown TT, Scheffler RM, Tom SE, Schulman KA. Does the market value racial/ethnic concordance in physician-patient relationships? *Health Serv Res* 2007;42:706-26. PMID:17362214 doi:10.1111/j.1475-6773.2006.00634.x.

18. Liu JX, Brown TT, Scheffler RM. *Are there enough minority physicians in California to go around?* CPAC policy briefing, "Health research innovation: CPAC reports". Sacramento, CA; 2006.

19. Scheffler RM, Waitzman NJ, Hillman JM. The productivity of physician assistants and nurse practitioners and health work force policy in the era of managed health care. *J Allied Health* 1996;25:207-17. PMID:8884433.

20. *TeleHealth national program in support of the primary health care, Brazil.* 2007. Available from: http:/www.telessaudebrasil.org.br [accessed on 3 April 2008].

21. Vassallo DJ, Swinfen P, Swinfen R, Wootton R. Experience with a low-cost telemedicine system in three developing countries. *J Telemed Telecare* 2001;7:56-8. PMID:11576493 doi:10.1258/1357633011936732.

3

The Rationale for Diversity in the Health Professions: A Review of the Evidence

Source: HRSA. The Rationale for Diversity in the Health Professions: A Review of the Evidence. U.S. Department of Health and Human Services.

EXECUTIVE SUMMARY

Several racial and ethnic minority groups and people from socioeconomically disadvantaged backgrounds are significantly underrepresented among health professionals in the United States. Underrepresented minority (URM) groups have traditionally included African-Americans, Mexican Americans, Native Americans, and mainland Puerto Ricans. Numerous public and private programs aim to remedy this underrepresentation by promoting the preparedness and resources available to minority and socioeconomically disadvantaged health professions candidates, and the admissions and retention of these candidates in the health professions pipeline and workforce. In recent years, however, competing demands for resources, along with shifting public opinion about policies aimed to assist members of specific racial and ethnic groups, have threatened the base of support for "diversity programs." Continued support for these programs will increasingly rely on evidence that they provide a measurable public benefit.

The most compelling argument for a more diverse health professions workforce is that it will lead to improvements in public health. We therefore examined the evidence addressing the contention that health professions diversity will lead to improved population health outcomes. Specifically, we searched for, reviewed, and synthesized publicly available studies addressing four separate hypotheses:

1. The service patterns hypothesis: that health professionals from racial and ethnic minority and socioeconomically disadvantaged backgrounds are more likely than others to serve racial and ethnic minority and socioeconomically disadvantaged populations, thereby improving access to care for vulnerable populations and in turn, improving health outcomes;

2. The concordance hypothesis: that increasing the number of racial and ethnic minority health professionals—by providing greater opportunity for minority patients to see a practitioner from their own racial or ethnic group or, for patients with limited English proficiency, to see a practitioner who speaks their primary language—will improve the quality of communication, comfort level, trust, partnership, and decision making in patient-practitioner relationships, thereby increasing use of appropriate health care and adherence to effective programs, ultimately resulting in improved health outcomes;

319

3. The trust in health care hypothesis: that greater diversity in the health care workforce will increase trust in the health care delivery system among minority and socioeconomically disadvantaged populations, and will thereby increase their propensity to use health services that lead to improved health outcomes; and

4. The professional advocacy hypothesis: that health professionals from racial and ethnic minority and socioeconomically disadvantaged backgrounds will be more likely than others to provide leadership and advocacy for policies and programs aimed at improving health care for vulnerable populations, thereby increasing health care access and quality, and ultimately health outcomes for those populations.

We reviewed a total of 55 studies: 17 for service patterns, 36 for concordance, and 2 for trust in health care. We were not able to identify any empirical studies addressing the hypothesis that greater health professions diversity results in greater advocacy or implementation of programs and policies targeting health care for minority and other disadvantaged populations. Our review generated the following findings:

- URM health professionals, particularly physicians, disproportionately serve minority and other medically underserved populations;

- minority patients tend to receive better interpersonal care from practitioners of their own race or ethnicity, particularly in primary care and mental health settings;

- non-English speaking patients experience better interpersonal care, greater medical comprehension, and greater likelihood of keeping follow-up appointments when they see a language-concordant practitioner, particularly in mental health care; and

- insufficient evidence exists as to whether greater health professions diversity leads to greater trust in health care or greater advocacy for disadvantaged populations.

These findings indicate that greater health professions diversity will likely lead to improved public health by increasing access to care for underserved populations, and by increasing opportunities for minority patients to see practitioners with whom they share a common race, ethnicity or language. Race, ethnicity, and language concordance, which is associated with better patient-practitioner relationships and communication, may increase patients' likelihood of receiving and accepting appropriate medical care.

Several areas warrant further research. Most studies of health professional service patterns are limited to physicians. Studies are needed to determine whether the service patterns of non-physician professionals who serve as many patients' usual source of health care (e.g., nurse practitioners, physician assistants) vary according to race, ethnicity, or socioeconomic background. Studies of racial and ethnic concordance are primarily limited to physicians and mental health practitioners. Future studies should examine the impact of concordance between patients and other health professionals, particularly nurses, who interact closely with patients. Studies have not adequately examined the relative contributions of language concordance vs. combined language and ethnic concordance, an issue that has significant implications for which policy solutions will most enhance quality of care for patients with limited English proficiency. Researchers should thus compare the quality of care in encounters and relationships in at least three categories: concordant language/ethnicity, concordant language/discordant ethnicity, and discordant language/ethnicity.

Studies of the effect of institutional diversity on patients' trust in health care and propensity to use health care services are lacking. Research in this area could start by measuring trust, perceived access, satisfaction, and likelihood of using services among patients receiving care at institutions with differing levels of staff diversity. Finally, research is needed to test the proposed hypothesis that a greater presence of health professionals from minority and socioeconomically disadvantaged backgrounds will lead to greater advocacy, and ultimately better access and quality of care, for disadvantaged populations.

In summary, we found that current evidence supports the notion that greater workforce diversity may lead to improved public health, primarily through greater access to care for underserved populations and better interactions between patients and health professionals. We also identified several gaps in the evidence and proposed an agenda for future research that would help to fill those gaps.

Conducting this research will be essential to solidifying the evidence base underlying programs and policies to increase diversity among health professionals in the United States.

INTRODUCTION

Achieving a health care workforce that reflects the diversity of the U.S. population is an explicit goal supported by, among others, the Association of American Medical Colleges (AAMC),[1] the American Medical Association (AMA),[2] and the Institute of Medicine.[3,4] Expanding the workforce of underrepresented minority (URM) physicians has warranted significant attention. URMs have traditionally included African-Americans, Mexican Americans, Native Americans, and mainland Puerto Ricans. Since 2003, the AAMC has defined "underrepresented" as those racial and ethnic populations that are underrepresented in the medical profession relative to their numbers in the general population.[5] Several racial and ethnic groups, most notably African-Americans, Latinos, and American Indians continue to be significantly underrepresented in the health professions workforce when compared to their representation in the general U.S. population (Table 1).[6]

Several national programs have sought to expand the URM health care workforce. The AAMC sponsored "Project 3000 by 2000" in the 1990s, which aimed to expand the number of URM medical students to a total of 3000 by Year 2000. While the program did not achieve this goal, it did spawn two other programs still administered by the AAMC that aim to expand diversity. The first, the Health Professions Partnership Initiative (supported by the Kellogg Foundation and the Robert Wood Johnson Foundation), involves collaborative relationships between academic medical centers and schools with large minority student populations at the kindergarten through college level. The aim of this program is to provide academic support and to expose these students to the range of professional opportunities in health care. The second program is the Minority Medical Education Program (also sponsored by the Robert Wood Johnson Foundation). This is an intensive 6-week program targeted at minorities who are interested in becoming physicians to be better prepared academically for the rigors of medical school.

The Federal Government also sponsors programs to enhance health care workforce diversity, including the Health Careers Opportunity Program (HCOP), Centers of Excellence (COE), and Minority Faculty Fellowship Programs (MFFP), each administered through the Health Resources and Services Administration's Bureau of Health Professions (BHPr). The HCOP provides grants to programs with the goal of enhancing diversity across a wide range of health care fields. Programs recruit individuals from disadvantaged backgrounds (including, but not restricted to, racial/ethnic minority groups) and provide them with preparatory training, counseling, mentoring, and exposure to community-based primary health care. COE grants to health professional schools support a range of efforts related to recruiting

| Table 1 | Race/Ethnicity of U.S. Health Professionals Compared to U.S. Population, 2000 |

	Non-Hispanic White	Non-Hispanic Black	Hispanic	Asian/Pacific Islander	American Indian/ Alaska Native
U.S. Population (over age 18)	75.1%	12.3%	12.5%	3.7%	0.9%
Chiropractors	91.9%	1.2%	2.9%	2.7%	0.6%
Dentists	82.8%	3.4%	3.6%	9.1%	0.3%
Medical & Health Services Managers	78.5%	10.8%	5.9%	3.1%	1.0%
Optometrists	86.5%	1.7%	2.7%	8.1%	0.4%
Pharmacists	78.9%	5.1%	3.2%	11.5%	0.3%
Physician Assistants	76.2%	8.6%	8.1%	4.8%	0.6%
Physicians & Surgeons	73.6%	4.5%	5.1%	15.3%	0.3%
Podiatrists	90.0%	4.6%	1.7%	2.8%	0.3%
Registered Nurses	80.4%	9.0%	3.3%	6.0%	0.8%

Adapted from: Minorities in Medical Education: Facts & Figures 2005. Washington, DC: Association of American Medical Colleges, 2005.
Data sources: U.S. Census 2000 Special Equal Employment Opportunity (EEO) Tabulation Data; and U.S. Census Bureau, Census 2000 Summary File 1 (SF 1) 100-Percent Data.

and training minorities, including faculty development, a focus on minority health issues, improvements in academic and clinical training opportunities, and stipends to minority students served by these programs. In addition to COEs for minorities in general, there are also Hispanic COEs and Native American COEs. Finally, MFFP grants are awarded to institutions in an effort to increase the number of minority faculty. Salary support and training to foster skills that maximize the chances of academic success are provided to faculty fellows. In turn, the fellows provide clinical services in underserved communities, and engage in academic pursuits. In addition to these programs with national scope, there are many ongoing local efforts with similar aims.

Despite a paucity of high quality research on the effectiveness of these diversity-related programs, available data suggest that they are successful in enhancing diversity in health professions schools.[7] Nonetheless, there are significant challenges to achieving this goal, and trend data reveal that progress towards greater diversity in most of the health professions is slow (Figure 1). Furthermore, the current political climate has placed diversity programs at risk. The increasing number of lawsuits and ballot initiatives in recent years challenging or rescinding affirmative action policies, sometimes successfully, provides evidence that the general public may no longer be willing to accept at face value policies and programs intended to increase diversity in higher education or in the professional workforce. As such, diversity programs are under increasing pressure to demonstrate their value.

The purpose of this report is to review the evidence base related to the rationale for diversity in the health professions.* The strongest such rationale is that a more diverse health care workforce will lead to improvements in public health. We therefore examined the evidence addressing the contention that health professions diversity will lead to improved population health outcomes. Due to widespread disparities in measures of health and health care for racial and ethnic minority and low socioeconomic status populations,[8,9] it is critical to understand the state of the science supporting the notion that the health of the population is enhanced, either directly or indirectly, when the health professions more accurately reflect the racial, ethnic, and socioeconomic diversity of the population.

Conceptual Framework

There are no studies that definitively address the association between health professions diversity and health outcomes. Specifically, we know of no randomized controlled trials in which patients or communities have been assigned to receive care from a diverse vs. non-diverse group of health professionals

---

* Our review was commissioned by BHPr, whose diversity programs target individuals from URM groups and socioeconomically disadvantaged backgrounds. As such, we conceptualize diversity from this perspective. It should be noted that other underserved populations are also underrepresented in the health care workforce (e.g., rural populations), and investigation into the role of enhanced diversity in these areas is also warranted.

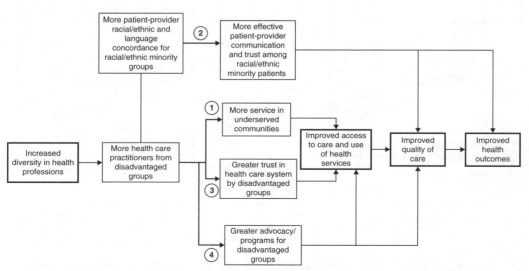

Figure 2 Conceptual Framework Linking Health Professions Diversity to Health Outcomes

and are then followed for clinical outcomes. In the absence of such direct evidence, examining the association between health professions diversity and health outcomes requires analyzing the links in a "chain of logic" connecting workforce diversity to improved health outcomes.

Before searching for evidence, therefore, we developed a conceptual model of how diversity might lead to improved health outcomes (Figure 2, not included). We derived this model from existing frameworks outlining the rationale for health professions diversity,[3,4,10-14] and through discussion with experts in the field. It is important to note that some arguments around diversity focus on the effects of a diverse student body on the quality of health professions education. Our framework does not include this potential effect of student body diversity on education but rather focuses on the effects of workforce diversity on public health. We posit four separate pathways through which diversity in the health care workforce might affect health outcomes:

- Service patterns. Greater diversity among health professionals may lead to greater diversity in the geographic locations where health professionals practice and in the populations they serve. Specifically, health professionals from racial and ethnic minority and socioeconomically disadvantaged backgrounds may be more likely than others to serve racial and ethnic minority and socioeconomically disadvantaged populations, who represent a disproportionately large segment of the Nation's medically underserved. If this were the case, greater health professions diversity would increase access to health care services for underserved populations, which would in turn lead to improved health outcomes.[15-17]

- Racial, ethnic, and language concordance. Increasing the number of racial and ethnic minority health professionals would provide greater opportunity for minority patients to see a practitioner from their own racial or ethnic group, or for patients with limited English proficiency, to see a practitioner who speaks their primary language. Racial, ethnic, and language concordance may improve the quality of communication, comfort level, or trust in patient-practitioner relationships and thereby improve partnership and decision making. This may in turn increase adherence to effective programs or regimens, ultimately resulting in improved health outcomes.

- Trust in the health care delivery system. Greater diversity in the health care workforce might increase trust in the health care delivery system. Racial and ethnic minority patients, in particular, may distrust health systems and institutions that are managed and staffed by predominantly White health professionals, due to historical segregation and discrimination. If this were the case, increasing diversity might increase minority populations' trust, and in turn, their propensity to use services at those systems and institutions. This hypothesis is similar to the concordance hypothesis articulated above, though at a system or institutional rather than interpersonal level.

- Professional advocacy. Greater diversity among health professionals may broaden the priorities of the health care delivery system. Specifically, health professionals from racial and ethnic minority and socioeconomically disadvantaged backgrounds may be more likely than others to advocate for and implement policies and programs to improve health care for disadvantaged populations. These programs and policies might expand access to health services or improve quality in the delivery of those services. They may also result in greater emphasis and resources devoted to research, advocacy, or service in areas relevant to minority and other disadvantaged populations. Increased access, quality, and attention to issues relevant to minority and other disadvantaged populations would be expected to improve health outcomes for those populations.

METHODS

Evidence Search We developed strategies to search the existing literature addressing each of the four lines of evidence discussed above: service patterns, concordance, trust in health care, and professional advocacy. We searched the MEDLINE, HealthSTAR, and CINAHL databases using search terms available in each database. For the concordance hypothesis, we also searched the PsycINFO database, because we knew that many of the studies related to patient-practitioner concordance were conducted in the context of mental health counseling and published in journals not included in the other three databases. We supplemented these database searches in four ways. First, we conducted a "gray" literature search, for studies that may not have been published as journal articles but rather as monographs or book chapters. Second, we manually searched the reference lists of included studies and relevant review articles. Third, we searched selected Web sites for relevant references. Finally, we presented our initial results to several audiences including experts in health professions diversity and solicited their input on relevant evidence not yet included in our review. We retrieved articles or documents identified by these supplementary approaches and reviewed them for relevance.

We reviewed titles and abstracts from our database searches and retrieved full articles for those that met inclusion criteria specific to each of our four lines of evidence. When it was not possible to determine from the title or abstract whether an article should be included, we reviewed the full article. We limited our review to articles that included original, empirical data generated within the United States. We believe that, due to the highly variable social significance and meaning of race, ethnicity, and social class, data from other countries would not be sufficiently generalizable to the U.S. In the same vein, we limited our review to studies published in or after 1985, since the social significance and meaning of race in particular has changed, and continues to change, over time. Studies published before 1985 often included data from a period when minority representation in the health professions was substantially lower and when racial attitudes were closer to those of the pre–Civil Rights era than they are today.

Evidence Abstraction and Synthesis We reviewed all retrieved articles and included those that met our inclusion criteria. We critically reviewed the included articles and abstracted relevant information about the health professional groups and patient populations examined, the principal results of the study, and important study features or limitations. For lines of evidence with more than a small number of studies available (service patterns and concordance), we tabulated the abstracted information in evidence tables, to facilitate comparison, discussion, and qualitative synthesis of the evidence. For minority professional service patterns and racial, ethnic, and language concordance, we also created tables in which we compared the number of studies that supported each hypothesis with the number that either did not support or refuted the hypothesis. We stratified these tables by race/ethnicity. For example, we counted the number of studies that supported the hypothesis that patient-practitioner race concordance improves quality of care for African-Americans, as well as the number that did not support this hy-

pothesis or refuted it. The purpose of these tables was to provide perspective on the balance of the evidence for each hypothesis. In creating these tables, we found that some studies assessed multiple outcomes related to a single hypothesis (e.g., self-reported delay in seeking care and emergency department visits as measures of access or utilization). When studies like this found evidence supporting the hypothesis in question for one outcome measure, we counted the study as supporting the hypothesis if, for the second outcome measure, the hypothesis was not refuted. If for the second outcome measure the hypothesis was refuted, we counted the study as one in which the overall hypothesis was not supported.

In this paper we present the overall results of our review and highlight findings from representative studies. The highlighted studies illustrate our qualitative synthesis of the evidence and make points that we considered important to understanding the state of the current evidence base—including its implications and limitations—on the rationale for health professions diversity.

RESULTS

Our initial search produced 586 titles and abstracts, of which 66 appeared potentially relevant. Of these, 35 met our inclusion criteria. Our supplemental search strategies added 20 studies meeting our inclusion criteria, resulting in a total of 55 included studies: 17 for service patterns, 36 for concordance, and two for trust in health care. We were not able to identify any empirical studies addressing the hypothesis that greater health professions diversity results in greater advocacy or implementation of programs and policies targeting health care for minority or other disadvantaged populations.

Service Patterns

Racial and Ethnic Minority Health Professionals We identified 17 studies addressing the service patterns of racial and ethnic minority health professionals. Of these, 16 examined physicians' and one reported dentists' service patterns. These studies were overwhelmingly consistent in supporting the hypotheses that minority health professionals are more likely than non-minorities to serve both minority and other underserved populations, including the poor and uninsured (Table 2).

Thirteen separate studies have documented that minority physicians tend to provide a disproportionately large share of health care for patients from their own racial and ethnic backgrounds.[18-30] In one recent study, Bach and colleagues found that in a national sample of Medicare beneficiaries, 22 percent of African-American patients' visits in 2001 were to African-American physicians, who make up roughly 4.5 percent of the Nation's physicians.[18] Notably, this disproportionate pairing appears to be a result of both African-American physicians locating their practices in African-American communities, and of African-American patients' preferentially seeking out African-American physicians. Bach at al. found that African-Americans physicians comprised 12.5 percent of physicians in the service areas where African-American patients sought care, well above the representation of African-Americans in the physician workforce, but well below the proportion of race concordant visits between African-American patients and physicians.[18] In another study, Saha and colleagues found that African-American patients tended to choose African-American physicians, independent of the convenience of the physicians' office location.[29] This disproportionate pairing of patients and physicians of the same race is true not only for African-Americans but also for other racial and ethnic minorities. In a national survey from 2001, 24.5 percent of African-Americans, 27.6 percent of Latinos, and 45.3 percent of Asians reported having a regular physician from their own racial group, figures that are all well above the proportion of each of these racial groups in the U.S. physician workforce.[28] Finally, it should be noted that minority physicians not only disproportionately serve patients from their own racial and ethnic groups, but they also disproportionately serve other minority patients as well.[20,24,31]

In addition to serving minority populations, minority health professionals tend to serve other disadvantaged populations to a greater extent than nonminority professionals do.[19,21-24,26,27,30-34] Studies have provided compelling evidence that minority physicians are more likely than nonminority physicians to care for poor patients,[19,21,23,24,30,33] those insured by Medicaid,[19,22-24,30-33] those without health insurance,[19,23,24,31,33] and those living in areas with health professional shortages.[22,23,33] In the one study we identified that examined service patterns for minority health professionals other than physicians, Mofidi et al. found that among dentists who had served in the National Health Service Corps (NHSC)—a program providing loan repayment to health professionals in exchange for a period of service in an underserved community—African-American race was the strongest predictor of continuing to work in the underserved community beyond the NHSC obligation period.[34]

Some of the studies cited above have addressed key issues relevant to minority providers' service of the underserved. First, some may argue that minority professionals serve in minority and underserved communities not by choice but because they are less able, possibly due to lower academic performance, to compete for positions in more affluent communities. Two studies, however, examined service patterns at the University of California, San Francisco, and the University of California, San Diego, both ranked among the most prestigious medical schools in the Nation.[35] These studies revealed that even among students from these elite institutions, whose graduates likely have substantial choice regarding practice type and location, minority physicians were substantially more likely than their non-minority classmates to serve minority and underserved communities.[23,27]

Second, several studies have demonstrated that race is a stronger predictor than socioeconomic

Table 2	Results of Studies of Health Professional Service Patterns									
	Number of Studies									
Practitioner Race:	**Black**		**Latino**		**Asian**		**AI/AN**		**URM**	
Hypothesis	+	0/−	+	0/−	+	0/−	+	0/−	+	0/−
Serve minority/same-race populations	12	−	8	−	4	−	1	−	2	−
Serve underserved/poor populations	6	−	4(1)	−	1	1	−	−	5	−

+ = supports hypothesis
0/− = does not support/refutes hypothesis
(#) = non-significant trend
URM = underrepresented minority, not broken down by specific race/ethnicity

background of serving the underserved.[19,31,33] For instance, Brotherton et al. demonstrated in a national sample of pediatricians that URM physicians cared for more Medicaid and uninsured patients than non-URM physicians, regardless of socioeconomic background. In fact, URM pediatricians from relatively privileged backgrounds, as measured by having parents who were professionals or had at least a college degree, cared for more uninsured and Medicaid patients than non-URM physicians from underprivileged backgrounds.[31] Findings such as this indicate that, with regard to increasing the number of health professionals caring for underserved populations, diversity programs targeting only individuals from socioeconomically disadvantaged backgrounds will likely be less effective than programs that explicitly consider race and ethnicity.

Finally, findings from several studies have countered the notion that providing health professionals with financial incentives to serve underserved populations may substitute for diversity programs as a way to ensure adequate access to care for the underserved.[30,31,33] These studies have examined the primary financial incentive program used for this purpose, the National Health Service Corps (NHSC). In each of these studies, while NHSC participation was associated with a higher likelihood of going on to care for underserved populations, URM race was always a stronger predictor than NHSC participation.[30,31,33] In fact, URM physicians *without* NHSC obligations were more likely to serve the underserved than non-URM physicians *with* NHSC obligations.[30,31] This suggests that diversity programs might be a more effective long-term investment than the NHSC, in terms of providing access to health professionals for the medically underserved.

Health Professionals from Socioeconomically Disadvantaged Backgrounds As noted above, several studies have examined physician service patterns as a function of socioeconomic background.[19,31,33] Rabinowitz et al. surveyed a national sample of physicians and asked about their family income during childhood. The authors found that this measure of socioeconomic background, stratified into quintiles, was not associated with care for underserved populations, designated as: working in a federally designated Health Professional Shortage Area or Medically Underserved Area; or having a practice in which over 40 percent of patients were either uninsured, or on Medicaid or poor.[33] Similarly, Brotherton et al. did not find an association between socioeconomic background, as measured by parental education and occupation, and the proportion of pediatricians' patients who were from racial or ethnic

minorities or were uninsured or on Medicaid.[31] Cantor et al. did find an association between disadvantaged socioeconomic background and care of underserved groups, though the association was relatively weak, and as noted above, was small in comparison to the effect of URM race.[19]

Concordance

We identified 36 studies addressing the effects of patient-practitioner racial, ethnic, and/or language concordance on health care access/utilization, quality, and outcomes. We defined a study as addressing *race* concordance when individuals were categorized according to the major racial/ethnic categories used by the U.S. Census Bureau: White/Caucasian, Black/African-American, Hispanic/Latino, Asian, Pacific Islander, and American Indian/Alaska Native. We labeled studies as addressing *ethnic* concordance if they considered concordance as being present between people who were from more specific subgroups, based on nationality or other affiliations. For instance, if a patient and practitioner who were both Latino were categorized as concordant, we considered this to represent race concordance. If concordance was considered present when patient and practitioner were both of Mexican origin, we considered this to represent ethnic concordance.

Most of the studies we identified examined concordance between patients and physicians, or between mental health clients and their therapists (Table 3). These studies addressed three different categories of outcome measures: access to care or utilization of health services, quality of care, and health care outcomes.

Racial/Ethnic Concordance

Studies addressing the effects of patient-practitioner racial or ethnic concordance on access to care and use of health services, quality of care, and health outcomes provided mixed results (Table 4).

Access/Utilization Four studies assessed the effect of patient-physician race concordance on access to care and use of health services.[28,36-38] In a national survey conducted in 1994, Saha and colleagues found that race concordance was associated with a lower likelihood of having unmet health needs and a greater likelihood of self-reported receipt of preventive care for African-Americans, but not for Latinos.[36] In two other studies, race concordance was not associated with receipt of appropriate preventive care or disease management services among African-Americans, Latinos, or Asians,[28] or with care seeking delays, emergency department use, or med-

Table 3	Numbers of Studies of Patient-Provider Concordance, by Provider Category and Concordant Characteristic

Health Professional Category:	Physicians	Mental health providers	Substance abuse counselors	Medical students
Race Concordance	13	4	4	1
Ethnic Concordance	0	7	0	0
Language Concordance	7	5	0	0

Table 4	Results of Studies of Patient-Provider Race and Ethnic Concordance

	Number of Studies							
Practitioner Race:	Black		Latino		Asian		Minority	
Hypothesis	+	0/−	+	0/−	+	0/−	+	0/−
Improves access/utilization	7	6	3	5	6	2	2	0
Improves quality	9	5	4	3	1	3	0	0
Improves outcomes	3	6	2	2	3	3	0	0

+ = supports hypothesis
0/− = does not support/refutes hypothesis

ication adherence among African-Americans with hypertension.[37] In the fourth study, Chen et al. tested the association between race concordance and use of coronary angiography among Medicare beneficiaries hospitalized for acute myocardial infarction (AMI).[38] This was an important study, in that it examined the role of patient-physician race discordance in explaining one of the most well-documented racial disparities in health care (i.e., disparities in the use of coronary angiography).[39] The authors found that race concordance was not associated with use of coronary angiography, in both unadjusted analyses and analyses accounting for patient, physician, and hospital characteristics. It should be noted, however, that the physician whose race was determined to be concordant or discordant with the patient's in this study was the attending physician for the hospital stay. This may or may not have been a physician with whom the patient had a relationship pre-dating the hospitalization or the physician who served as the patient's principal agent in guiding decision making.

Eleven studies examined the effect of client-therapist racial or ethnic matching on utilization of mental health services.[40-50] All but one of the studies were conducted in the context of county mental health agencies in California, many of them taking advantage of administrative databases maintained by those counties.[40-49] Therapists included a broad array of health professionals, including social workers, psychiatrists, psychologists, clinical nurse specialists, and unlicensed mental health workers. The studies examined the effect of client-therapist racial or ethnic concordance on measures intended to capture adherence to outpatient mental health therapy, including the total number of visits attended and dropout from therapy. In general, the studies demonstrated that racial and ethnic concordance was associated with greater use of mental health services and lower dropout rates,[40,42,43,45-50] as well as lower use of emergency services.[47] Two studies found mixed or null results.[41,44]

Four studies assessed whether race concordance between substance abuse clients and counselors was associated with greater attendance or participation in therapy.[51-54] With the exception of one isolated finding from two separate studies by the same authors, these studies found no effect of concordance on utilization patterns among substance abuse clients. In the two studies with significant findings, African-American clients with African-American counselors were less likely to use substance abuse treatment after therapy ended.[53,54]

Quality Thirteen studies evaluated the association between patient-physician race concordance and quality of care.[28,36,37,55-63] Most of the studies used patients' ratings of interpersonal care (e.g., patient satisfaction) as the principal measure of quality. The majority of these studies found that race concordance was associated with better interpersonal care.[36,55-58,60,61,63] Another study found a similar association between patient-counselor race concordance and empathy for substance abuse clients.[51]

Three of the studies went beyond interpersonal care to evaluate the impact of concordance on other measures of quality.[28,59,62] One study found no association between patient-physician race concordance and parents' evaluations of both interpersonal and technical aspects of their children's primary care.[62] In another study, race concordance was not associated with patients' self-reported receipt of appropriate primary care services, such as cholesterol screening or diabetes management for eligible patients.[28] In the third study, King and colleagues examined the quality of care for patients with human immunodeficiency virus (HIV) infection in a large national cohort. They found that patient-provider race concordance among African-Americans was associated with shorter time to receipt of protease inhibitors—medications known to reduce progression to the acquired immunodeficiency syndrome (AIDS) and to prolong life[64,65]—even after accounting for other patient and provider characteristics.[59] Moreover, the authors found that in the cohort overall, White patients received protease inhibitors earlier than African-Americans, but that among patients with race concordant providers, this disparity was eliminated.

This study is important for two reasons. First, it is one of only two studies that examined the effects of race concordance on the use of health care services proven to reduce morbidity and mortality.[28,59] Second, the study demonstrated that race concordance was associated with elimination of disparities in an important aspect of treating HIV/AIDS, a disease known to disproportionately affect African-Americans. These two facets of the study suggest that patient-physician race concordance has the capacity to reduce racial disparities not only in health care, but in health and mortality.

Another noteworthy study examined the impact of race concordance on the quality of patients' communication with their primary care providers.[56] In this study, Cooper and colleagues audiotaped doctor-patient encounters and analyzed the content of the encounters. They found that doctor-patient race concordance was associated with longer visits and measurably better communication.[56] They also found that patients were more satisfied with the visit and rated the doctor as fostering more doctor-patient partnership in race concordant encounters. Notably, however, the authors found that the differences in communication and the differences in patients' ratings of the visit were independent of each other; i.e., accounting for the differences in communication did not explain any of the differences in patients' ratings of their doctors. This finding is important in that it illustrates that race concordance is associated not only with better communication but also with other unmeasured aspects of the doctor-patient encounter that give rise to higher patient ratings of health care quality. This suggests that while communication training for health professionals may improve the quality of care for minority patients, it is unlikely to serve as a substitute for increasing the number of minority health professionals, which would increase minority patients' ability to see race concordant providers if they choose to.

Outcomes Twelve studies tested for associations between patient-practitioner racial or ethnic concordance and health outcomes.[38,41-44,48-51,53,54,63] In most of these studies, the outcome of interest was improvement in global mental health status after a course of mental health counseling or therapy.[41-44,48-50] These studies produced mixed results, with no clear pattern for patients from any specific racial or ethnic group or with any specific mental health condition. Four of the seven studies did find some evidence of a positive effect of racial or ethnic concordance on mental health outcomes.[43,44,48,50]

In a study comparing adjustment to disability among African-American patients with vitiligo, a disfiguring skin condition, Porter and Beuf found that patients treated at a clinic with predominantly African-American physicians and staff expressed better adjustment than those treated at a clinic with predominantly White physicians and staff.[63] This study was unique in examining race concordance with not only a single health care provider but with the majority of the clinic staff. The study was limited, however, in that it only examined two different health care settings.

Three studies examined the association between patient-counselor race concordance and substance abuse treatment outcomes.[51,53,54] One study assessed abstinence from substance use and found that race concordance was not associated with abstinence for any individual racial group, but that women with race concordant counselors were more likely to remain abstinent.[51] In the other two studies, which were conducted by the same group of authors, results were conflicting.[53,54] Both studies examined co-horts of African-American patients in cocaine treatment programs. In one study, patient-counselor race concordance was associated with more medical and legal problems nine months after treatment.[53] In the other study, race concordance was associated with a lower likelihood of having been jailed within nine months of treatment.[54] Notably, in both studies, the authors tested for multiple treatment outcomes, such that the statistically significant findings mentioned above may have occurred by chance.

Language Concordance

Studies of patient-practitioner language concordance were generally more consistent than those of racial/ethnic concordance in demonstrating a positive effect of concordance on access, utilization, and quality of care (Table 5). Findings of these studies did not reveal a consistent effect of language concordance on health outcomes.

Access/Utilization Seven studies assessed the impact of patient-practitioner language concordance on access to care and use of health services.[40-42,47-49,66] Most of these studies sought to determine whether client-therapist language concordance was associated with measures intended to capture adherence to outpatient mental health therapy, including the total number of visits attended and dropout from therapy.[40-42,48,49] The studies generally found beneficial effects for language concordance on these outcomes among both Latino and Asian mental health clients, though the findings were more consistent for Latinos. Another study found that client-therapist language concordance was associated with less use of emergency services for both Latinos and Asians.[47] Finally, in a study of Spanish-speaking patients with asthma, Manson found that patients in continuous

relationships with language concordant primary care physicians were less likely than those in language discordant relationships to miss appointments.[66] He also found non-significant trends suggesting that language concordance was associated with greater medication adherence and fewer emergency department visits.[66]

Quality Four studies of Latino populations tested the association between patient-physician language concordance and the quality of interpersonal care, particularly communication.[67-70] In three of the studies, language concordance was positively associated with interpersonal quality of care.[67,68,70] A fifth study examined the influence of patient-physician language concordance on patients' comprehension of medical information.[71] In this survey of Californians speaking one of eleven different non-English primary languages, respondents with limited English proficiency were more likely than English-proficient respondents to have problems understanding a medical situation and understanding medication labels.

When limited English-proficient patients with language discordant vs. concordant physicians were examined separately, the former group was much more likely to have problems in both of these areas. The latter group was only modestly more likely than English-proficient patients to have difficulty understanding a medical situation and were no more likely to have difficulty with medication labels. These findings, which took into account differences in demographic factors and access to care, indicate that language concordance was associated with significantly greater medical comprehension among individuals with limited English proficiency.[71]

Outcomes Seven studies assessed the association between language concordance and health outcomes.[41,42,48,49,69,71,72] Four of the studies examined

Table 5	Results of Studies of Patient-Provider Language Concordance					
	Number of Studies					
Practitioner Race:	**Latino**		**Asian**		**Minority**	
Hypothesis	+	0/−	+	0/−	+	0/−
Improves access/utilization	3	0	4	1	2	0
Improves quality	3	1	0	0	1	0
Improves outcomes	1 (1)	2	1	3	1	0

+ = supports hypothesis
0/− = does not support/refutes hypothesis
(#) = non-significant trend

improvements in global mental health status after a course of mental health counseling or therapy.[41,42,48,49] One study found a positive association between language concordance and improved mental health for Latinos but not for Asians;[48] the other studies found no significant associations. Another study examined a group of Latino patients with diabetes and found a non-significant trend suggesting better glycemic control among those with a language concordant primary care physician, though fewer than half of the language concordant providers were themselves Latino.[72]

Perez-Stable and colleagues found an association between patient-physician language concordance and several dimensions of patients' self-reported health status, though this was a cross-sectional study; the authors were therefore unable to determine whether language concordance was associated with improvements in health status.[69] Finally, in the study of Californians speaking non-English languages discussed in the previous section, limited English-proficient patients with a language discordant physician were significantly more likely than English-proficient patients to report having had a bad reaction due to problems understanding medication instruction. Limited English-proficient patients with a language concordant physician were no more likely than their English-proficient counterparts to have experienced a bad medication reaction.[71]

Trust in Health Care

We found limited evidence addressing the hypothesis that institutional diversity enhances trust among minority or socioeconomically disadvantaged patient populations. Our search generated only two studies that indirectly addressed this hypothesis.[73,74] In the first, Mouton and colleagues surveyed women who did not respond to an invitation to participate in a large clinical trial.[73] The authors found that 37 percent of the African-American women in the sample expressed a preference to be treated by an African-American scientist. This finding suggests that increasing the number of minority health scientists might enhance minority participation in clinical trials, which might reduce racial disparities in the benefits of medical research. This study, however, was limited in that only 29 African-American women were surveyed, and it was not clear that lack of diversity among researchers was a principal reason for lack of participation among the women who reported a preference.

In the second study, Reese et al. interviewed African-American pastors to elucidate barriers to hospice participation among terminally ill African-American patients.[74] Pastors identified lack of diversity among health professionals as a significant barrier to hospice enrollment. The authors developed and administered a survey of barriers to hospice participation that incorporated lack of diversity among health professionals as a potential barrier. While the authors found that African-Americans were more likely to endorse barriers to participation, they did not report findings for each specific barrier. It was thus not possible to determine whether lack of diversity among health care workers represented a significant barrier in their quantitative analysis.

Professional Advocacy

Insufficient evidence exists as to whether greater health professions diversity leads to greater advocacy for disadvantaged populations. While health professionals from racial and ethnic minority and socioeconomically disadvantaged backgrounds would seem more likely than others to advocate for and implement policies and programs to improve health care for disadvantaged populations, we could find no studies testing this hypothesis.

DISCUSSION

We conducted a review of publicly available studies addressing four separate hypotheses linking increased racial, ethnic, and socioeconomic diversity among health professionals to improved public health. We found a large and consistent body of evidence suggesting that minority health professionals, particularly physicians, disproportionately serve minority and other medically underserved populations. Data generally supported the notion that minority patients receive better interpersonal care from practitioners of their own race or ethnicity, particularly in primary care and mental health settings. Patient-practitioner language concordance similarly was associated with better interpersonal care, greater medical comprehension, and greater likelihood of keeping follow-up appointments, particularly in mental health care. For two of our hypotheses—that greater health professions diversity leads to greater trust in health care and greater advocacy for disadvantaged populations—empirical evidence was scant or lacking.

Collectively, the studies in our review suggest several mechanisms by which increasing numbers of minority and socioeconomically disadvantaged health professionals in the United States might lead to improved health outcomes. First, minority physicians, and to a lesser degree those from socioeconomically disadvantaged backgrounds, serve as a usual source of care for many of the nation's underserved populations, including those who are uninsured or underinsured. Studies have established that having access to a usual source of care improves health outcomes.[15-17] To the extent that future minority health professionals follow this pattern of disproportionately caring for the underserved, increasing minority representation among health professionals should increase access to health care for underserved groups and thereby improve population health.

Second, increasing health professions diversity would afford minority patients, particularly those from groups underrepresented in the health professions, greater opportunity to see practitioners of their own racial or ethnic background. Increased diversity would thereby improve the quality of interpersonal care that minority patients receive, and potentially increase their likelihood of receiving and accepting appropriate medical care, which would in turn lead to improved health. One study in our review supported this contention by demonstrating that African-American patients received lifeprolonging medications for HIV/AIDS in a more timely manner from African-American as opposed to White physicians.

Finally, increasing the presence of underrepresented Latino and Asian health professionals in particular might afford more limited English-proficient patients the opportunity to see practitioners that speak their native language. The observation of higher-quality care in language concordant relationships—most likely a result of effective communication and possibly of cultural congruence—suggests that greater linguistic diversity among health professionals will lead to improved health outcomes and greater patient safety.[75-77] This is particularly relevant in the current context of limited funding for and use of medical interpreter services.[78]

Some caveats to these arguments for health professions diversity warrant mention. First, considering minority practitioner service patterns as the primary rationale for diversity programs may lead to the problematic expectation that minority health professionals should all serve underserved patient populations. It is important to remember that our review supports the notion that increasing workforce diversity will lead to greater access to care through the choices of minority practitioners (to serve underserved populations) and minority patients (to seek care from minority practitioners). We would consider it unethical to require practitioners to serve specific populations based on their race, ethnicity, or socioeconomic background.

Second, we caution against the conclusion that, because race concordance is associated with higher quality care, patients should always be paired with practitioners of their own race. Although studies in our review suggested that interpersonal care was *on balance* better in race concordant patientpractitioner relationships, and that patients tended to prefer practitioners of their own race, these findings did not apply to all patients and practitioners. In most studies, the majority of patients had no preference regarding practitioner race and were very satisfied with the care they received from race discordant providers. The association between race concordance and interpersonal quality indicates that greater diversity might improve overall quality of care by affording those who do have a preference, and who do experience better care in race concordant relationship, greater opportunity to have such relationships.

Finally, it is important to note that we were not able to determine the separate effects of language concordance alone vs. language plus ethnic concordance. One path to greater patient-practitioner language concordance for limited English-proficient patients is to increase racial and ethnic diversity in the health professions. Another path is to train nonminority health professionals to speak non-English languages. This latter strategy could enhance language concordance but would lack the potential benefit of combined language and ethnic concordance. We were not able to determine whether this combined concordance was more beneficial than language concordance alone. Thus, while our review suggested a potential benefit from increasing language concordance in patient-practitioner encounters, it did not establish whether achieving this benefit is best accomplished by training more minority health professionals or by training existing and future health professionals to speak non-English languages.

Study Limitations

There were several limitations to our review. Our search strategies may not have captured all relevant studies. We took several measures to ensure a comprehensive search, including reviewing reference lists and Web sites and consulting with experts. It is possible, though, that important studies were missed. We only searched for publicly available studies. Some studies relevant to our review may have been conducted by private institutions that did not disseminate their findings to the general public. It is also possible that our review was affected by publication bias, as some authors may have selectively chosen not to publish results either supporting or refuting the hypotheses we addressed.

Recommendations for Future Research

Our review revealed several gaps in the evidence base related to health professions diversity that we believe are important areas for future research. Notably, nearly all the studies we found related to service patterns examined physician practices. More studies are needed to determine whether the service patterns of other professionals who serve as many patients' usual source of health care (e.g., nurse practitioners, physician assistants) vary according to race, ethnicity, or socioeconomic background. Likewise, studies of patient-practitioner racial and ethnic concordance were limited primarily to physicians and mental health practitioners. It would be useful to know about the impact of concordance between patients and other health professionals, particularly nurses, who interact closely with patients—in hospitals, long-term care facilities, doctors' offices, and even in patients' homes—and whose interpersonal interactions are therefore likely to substantially influence patients' experiences.

Future studies of racial and ethnic concordance should look beyond the quality of interpersonal care (e.g., patient satisfaction) and begin to study the impact of concordance on more objective measures of quality, including process measures (e.g., receipt of influenza vaccination among elderly and chronically ill patients) and health outcomes (e.g., glycohemoglobin level among patients with diabetes). In designing and conducting such studies, researchers should choose measures that are likely to be strongly influenced by interpersonal interactions between health care providers and patients, i.e., those for which a link with patient-practitioner concordance makes sense. Researchers should also be mindful in conducting these studies that, relative to measures of interpersonal quality, process and outcome measures are influenced by numerous factors other than the patient-practitioner interaction. Studies examining process and outcome measures must therefore take these potentially confounding factors into account and be adequately powered to detect the influence of concordance amidst the influence of many other variables. Using data from large clinical and administrative databases is one way to harvest the kind of power that may be needed for such studies, but it will require that the databases contain, or at least can be linked to, data on patient and practitioner race. Organizations such as Aetna, who are now collecting these data routinely,[79] may serve as a resource and a model for other health care organizations interested in health professions diversity.

Studies of language concordance to date have not adequately examined the relative contributions of language concordance alone vs. combined language and ethnic concordance. It is not clear, therefore, whether the observed effects in these studies are attributable solely to language concordance or are in part explained by the ethnic (and perhaps cultural) concordance that are often present in language concordant encounters. The policy implications of language concordance studies depend, at least in part, on the relative contributions of these separate effects. If common language accounts for all of the benefits of language concordance, then interventions to enhance practitioners' non-English skills (e.g., Spanish language courses) might suffice to improve care for patients with limited English proficiency. If ethnic concordance were influential, policies to increase ethnic diversity among health professionals would likely be needed. Therefore researchers should compare the quality of care in encounters and relationships in at least three categories: concordant language/ethnicity, concordant language/discordant ethnicity, and discordant language/ethnicity. In conducting such studies, researchers should pay attention to and measure non-English fluency among practitioners and English fluency among patients, since language concordance is best conceived as a continuous (or ordinal), rather than dichotomous variable.

Studies of the effect of institutional diversity on patients' trust in health care and propensity to use health care services are lacking. Research in this area could start by measuring trust, perceived access, satisfaction, and likelihood of using services among patients receiving care at (or with the option to receive care at) health care facilities with differing levels of staff diversity. It is important that such studies account for other differences across institutions that might affect patients' attitudes and choices. Because minority professionals are more likely to practice in underserved communities, the facilities they work in may be less well reimbursed than facilities staffed predominantly by nonminority professionals. Patients' attitudes toward certain health care facilities may appear negative, despite their diversity, if those institutions have long waiting times, inadequate resources, or even an unattractive physical appearance.

It is also important in studies of the effects of institutional diversity to measure both structural diversity—the proportion of a facility's staff from different racial/ethnic groups—and interactional diversity-the degree to which patients interact with staff from different racial or ethnic groups. Structural diversity alone may be important, in that patients may trust an institution more, simply because it has a diverse workforce. But it is more likely that the influence of diversity on patients' trust and use of services, if such an influence exists, will be mediated by their experiences and interactions with individuals within that institution.

Finally, research is needed to test the proposed hypothesis that a greater presence of professionals from minority and socioeconomically disadvantaged backgrounds in the health care workforce will lead to greater leadership and advocacy, and ultimately better access and quality of care for disadvantaged populations. This research could begin with a simple survey assessing the priorities of health care leaders from different racial, ethnic, and socioeconomic backgrounds. Another study might examine the research portfolios of researchers from different backgrounds. Do minority researchers spend relatively more effort on issues important to minority and other disadvantaged patient populations? This could be done, for instance, by examining the portfolios of NIH-funded researchers. The National Academy of Sciences (NAS) conducts periodic evaluations of NIH programs aimed at recruiting minority scientists and fostering their careers.[80] The NAS could incorporate into these evaluations an investigation of the research focus and populations studied among beneficiaries of these programs, as compared to other researchers.

CONCLUSION

Programs and policies to promote racial, ethnic, and socioeconomic diversity in the health professions are based, at least in part, on the principle that a more diverse health care workforce will improve public health. We developed a framework and reviewed publicly available evidence addressing that principle. We found that current evidence supports the notion that greater workforce diversity may lead to improved public health, primarily through greater access to care for underserved populations and better interpersonal interactions between patients and health professionals. We identified, however, several gaps in the evidence and proposed an agenda for future research that would help to fill those gaps. Conducting this research will be essential to solidifying the evidence base underlying programs and policies to increase diversity among health professionals in the United States.

ACKNOWLEDGMENTS

This publication was prepared under Contract No. 03-0285P for the U.S. Department of Health and Human Services, Health Resources and Services Administration by Somnath Saha, MD, MPH and of the Portland VA Medical Center and Oregon Health & Science University, and Scott A. Shipman, MD, MPH, of Dartmouth Medical School.

● ● ● **REFERENCES**

1. Cohen JJ. A word from the president: reaffirming our commitment to diversity. *AAMC Reporter*. 2000;9. Available at http://www.aamc.org/newsroom/reporter/august03/word.htm (accessed September 1, 2005).

2. Nelson JC. Testimony to the Sullivan Commission on Diversity in the Health care Workforce, from the American Medical Association. Chicago, IL; 2003. Available at http://www.amaassn.org/ama1/pub/upload/mm/20/testimonyoctober.pdf (accessed September 1, 2005).

3. Institute of Medicine. The Right Thing to Do, the Smart Thing to Do: Enhancing Diversity in the Health Professions. Washington, DC: *National Academies Press*; 2001.

4. Institute of Medicine. In the Nation's Compelling Interest: Ensuring Diversity in the Health Care Workforce. Washington, DC: *National Academies Press*; 2004.

5. Association of American Medical Colleges. Underrepresented in medicine definition. Available at http://www.aamc.org/meded/urm/start.htm (accessed September 1, 2005).

6. Association of American Medical Colleges. Minorities in Medical Education: Facts & Figures 2005. Washington, DC: *Association of American Medical Colleges*, 2005.

7. Grumbach K, Coffman J, Munoz C, Rosenoff E, Gandara P, Sepulveda E. Strategies for Improving the Diversity of the Health Professions. Woodland Hills, CA: The California Endowment, 2003.

8. Agency for Health care Research and Quality. National Health care Disparities Report. Rockville, MD: Agency for Health care Research and Quality, 2004.

9. Institute of Medicine. Unequal Treatment: Confronting Racial and Ethnic Disparities in Health Care. Washington, DC: *National Academies Press*; 2003.

10. Cohen JJ, Gabriel BA, Terrell C. The case for diversity in the health care workforce. *Health Aff. (Millwood)*. 2002;21(5):90-102.

11. Cohen JJ. The consequences of premature abandonment of affirmative action in medical school admissions. *JAMA*. 2003;289(9):1143-9.

12. Drake MV, Lowenstein DH. The role of diversity in the health care needs of California. *West J Med*. 1998;168(5):348-54.

13. Reede JY. A recurring theme: the need for minority physicians. *Health Aff (Millwood)*. 2003;22(4):91-3.

14. Smith LS. Are we reaching the health care consumer? *J Cult Divers*. 1998;5(2):48-52.

15. Bindman AB, Grumbach K, Osmond D, et al. Preventable hospitalizations and access to health care. *JAMA*. 1995;274(4):305-11.

16. Starfield B, Shi L. The medical home, access to care, and insurance: a review of evidence. *Pediatrics*. 2004;113(5 Suppl):1493-8.

17. Weissman JS, Stern R, Fielding SL, Epstein AM. Delayed access to health care: risk factors, reasons, and consequences. *Ann Intern Med*. 1991;114(4):325-31.

18. Bach PB, Pham HH, Schrag D, Tate RC, Hargraves JL. Primary care physicians who treat Blacks and Whites. *N Engl J Med*. 2004;351(6):575-84.

19. Cantor JC, Miles EL, Baker LC, Barker DC. Physician service to the underserved: implications for affirmative action in medical education. *Inquiry*. 1996;33(2):167-80.

20. Gray B, Stoddard JJ. Patient-physician pairing: does racial and ethnic congruity influence selection of a regular physician? *J Community Health*. 1997;22(4):247-59.

21. Johnson DG, Lloyd SM, Jr., Miller RL. A second survey of graduates of a traditionally Black college of medicine. *Acad Med*. 1989;64(2):87-94.

22. Keith SN, Bell RM, Swanson AG, Williams AP. Effects of affirmative action in medical schools. A study of the class of 1975. *N Engl J Med*. 1985;313(24):1519-25.

23. Komaromy M, Grumbach K, Drake M, et al. The role of Black and Hispanic physicians in providing health care for underserved populations. *N Engl J Med*. 1996;334(20):1305-10.

24. Moy E, Bartman BA. Physician race and care of minority and medically indigent patients. *JAMA*. 1995;273(19):1515-20.

25. Murray-Garcia JL, Garcia JA, Schembri ME, Guerra LM. The service patterns of a racially, ethnically, and linguistically diverse housestaff. *Acad Med*. 2001;76(12):1232-40.

26. Pathman DE, Konrad TR. Minority physicians serving in rural National Health Service Corps sites. *Med Care*. 1996;34(5):439-54.

27. Penn NE, Russell PJ, Simon HJ, et al. Affirmative action at work: a survey of graduates of the University of California, San Diego, Medical School. *Am J Public Health*. 1986;76(9):1144-6.

28. Saha S, Arbelaez JJ, Cooper LA. Patient-physician relationships and racial disparities in the quality of health care. *Am J Public Health*. 2003;93(10):1713-9.

29. Saha S, Taggart SH, Komaromy M, Bindman AB. Do patients choose physicians of their own race? *Health Aff (Millwood)*. 2000;19(4):76-83.

30. Xu G, Fields SK, Laine C, Veloski JJ, Barzansky B, Martini CJ. The relationship between the race/ethnicity of generalist physicians and their care for underserved populations. *Am J Public Health*. 1997;87(5):817-22.

31. Brotherton SE, Stoddard JJ, Tang SS. Minority and nonminority pediatricians' care of minority and poor children. *Arch Ped Adol Med*. 2000;154(9):912-7.

32. Perloff JD, Kletke PR, Fossett JW, Banks S. Medicaid participation among urban primary care physicians. *Med Care*. 1997;35(2):142-57.

33. Rabinowitz HK, Diamond JJ, Veloski JJ, Gayle JA. The impact of multiple predictors on generalist physicians' care of underserved populations. *Am J Public Health*. 2000;90(8):1225-8.

34. Mofidi M, Konrad TR, Porterfield DS, Niska R, Wells B. Provision of care to the underserved populations by National Health Service Corps alumni dentists. *J Public Health Dent*. 2002;62(2):102-8.

35. USNews.com. American's best graduate schools 2006. Top medical schools—research. Available at http://www.usnews.com/usnews/edu/grad/rankings/med/brief/mdrrank_brief.php (accessed September 1, 2005).

36. Saha S, Komaromy M, Koepsell TD, Bindman AB. Patient-physician racial concordance and the perceived quality and use of health care. *Arch Intern Med*. 1999;159(9):997-1004.

37. Howard DL, Konrad TR, Stevens C, Porter CQ. Physician-patient racial matching, effectiveness of care, use of services and patient satisfaction. *Res Aging*. 2001;23(1):83-108.

38. Chen J, Rathore SS, Radford MJ, Wang Y, Krumholz HM. Racial differences in the use of cardiac catheterization after acute myocardial infarction. *N Engl J Med*. 2001;344(19):1443-9.

39. Kressin NR, Petersen LA. Racial differences in the use of invasive cardiovascular procedures: review of the literature and prescription for future research. *Ann Intern Med*. 2001;135(5):352-66.

40. Flaskerud JH. The effects of culture-compatible intervention on the utilization of mental health services by minority clients. *Comm Ment Health J*. 1986;22(2):127-41.

41. Flaskerud JH, Liu PY. Influence of therapist ethnicity and language on therapy outcomes of Southeast Asian clients. *Int J Soc Psych*. 1990;36(1):18-29.

42. Flaskerud JH, Liu PY. Effects of an Asian client-therapist language, ethnicity and gender match on utilization and outcome of therapy. *Comm Ment Health J*. 1991;27(1):31-42.

43. Fujino DC, Okazaki S, Young K. Asian-American women in the mental health system: An examination of ethnic and gender match between therapist and client. *J Comm Psychol*. 1994;22(2):164-176.

44. Gamst G, Dana RH, Der-Karaberian A, Kramer T. Ethnic match and client ethnicity effects on global assessment and visitation. *J Comm Psychol*. 2000;28(5):547-564.

45. Jerrell JM. Effect of ethnic matching of young clients and mental health staff. *Cult Divers Ment Health*. 1998;4(4):297-302.

46. McCabe KM. Factors that predict premature termination among Mexican-American children in outpatient psychotherapy. *J Child Fam Stud*. 2002;11(3):347-359.

47. Snowden LR, Hu TW, Jerrell JM. Emergency care avoidance: ethnic matching and participation in minority-serving programs. *Comm Ment Health J*. 1995;31(5):463-73.

48. Sue S, Fujino DC, Hu L-t, Takeuchi DT, et al. Community mental health services for ethnic minority groups: A test of the cultural responsiveness hypothesis. *J Consult Clin Psychol*. 1991;59(4):533-540.

49. Yeh M, Eastman K, Cheung MK. Children and adolescents in community health centers: Does the ethnicity or the language of the therapist matter? *J Comm Psychol*. 1994;22(2):153-163.

50. Rosenheck R, Fontana A, Cottrol C. Effect of clinician-veteran racial pairing in the treatment of posttraumatic stress disorder. *Am J Psych*. 1995;152(4): 555-563.

51. Fiorentine R, Hillhouse MP. Drug treatment effectiveness and client-counselor empathy. *J Drug Iss*. 1999;29(1):59-74.

52. Gottheil E, Sterling RC, Weinstein SP, Kurtz JW. Therapist/patient matching and early treatment dropout. *J Addict Dis*. 1994;13(4):169-76.

53. Sterling RC, Gottheil E, Weinstein SP, Serota R. Therapist/patient race and sex matching: Treatment retention and 9-month follow-up outcome. *Addiction*. 1998;93(7):1043-1050.

54. Sterling RC, Gottheil E, Weinstein SP, Serota R. The effect of therapist/patient race- and sex-matching in individual treatment. *Addiction*. 2001;96(7):1015-22.

55. Chen FM, Fryer GE, Jr., Phillips RL, Jr., Wilson E, Pathman DE. Patients' beliefs about racism, preferences for physician race, and satisfaction with care. *Ann Fam Med*. 2005;3(2):138-43.

56. Cooper LA, Roter DL, Johnson RL, Ford DE, Steinwachs DM, Powe NR. Patient-centered communication, ratings of care, and concordance of patient and physician race. *Ann Intern Med*. 2003;139(11):907-15.

57. Cooper-Patrick L, Gallo JJ, Gonzales JJ, et al. Race, gender, and partnership in the patientphysician relationship. *JAMA*. 1999;282(6):583-9.

58. Garcia JA, Paterniti DA, Romano PS, Kravitz RL. Patient preferences for physician characteristics in university-based primary care clinics. *Ethn Dis*. 2003;13(2):259-67.

59. King WD, Wong MD, Shapiro MF, Landon BE, Cunningham WE. Does racial concordance between HIV-positive patients and their physicians affect the time to receipt of protease inhibitors? *J Gen Intern Med*. 2004;19(11):1146-53.

60. Lin X, Guan J. Patient satisfaction and referral intention: effect of patient-physician match on ethnic origin and cultural similarity. *Health Mark Q*. 2002;20(2):49-68.

61. Malat J. Social distance and patients' rating of health care providers. *J Health Soc Behav*. 2001;42(4):360-72.

62. Stevens GD, Shi L, Cooper LA. Patient-provider racial and ethnic concordance and parent reports of the primary care experiences of children. *Ann Fam Med*. 2003;1(2):105-12.

63. Porter JR, Beuf AH. The effect of a racially consonant medical context on adjustment of African-American patients to physical disability. *Med Anthropol*. 1994;16(1):1-16.

64. Hammer SM, Squires KE, Hughes MD, et al. A controlled trial of two nucleoside analogues plus indinavir in persons with human immunodeficiency virus infection and CD4 cell counts of 200 per cubic millimeter or less. AIDS Clinical Trials Group 320 Study Team. *N Engl J Med*. 1997;337(11):725-33.

65. Cameron DW, Heath-Chiozzi M, Danner S, et al. Randomised placebo-controlled trial of ritonavir in advanced HIV-1 disease. The Advanced HIV Disease Ritonavir Study Group. *Lancet*. 1998;351(9102):543-9.

66. Manson A. Language concordance as a determinant of patient compliance and emergency room use in patients with asthma. *Medical Care*. 1988;26(12):1119-28.

67. Fernandez A, Schillinger D, Grumbach K, et al. Physician language ability and cultural competence. An exploratory study of communication with Spanish-speaking patients. *J Gen Intern Med*. 2004;19(2):167-74.

68. Lee LJ, Batal HA, Maselli JH, Kutner JS. Effect of Spanish interpretation method on patient satisfaction in an urban walk-in clinic. *J Gen Intern Med*. 2002;17(8):641-5.

69. Perez-Stable EJ, Napoles-Springer A, Miramontes JM. The effects of ethnicity and language on medical outcomes of patients with hypertension or diabetes. *Med Care.* 1997;35(12):1212-9.

70. Seijo R, Gomez H, Freidenberg J. Language as a communication barrier in medical care for Latino patients. *Hisp J Behav Sci.* 1991;13(4):363-75.

71. Wilson E, Chen AH, Grumbach K, Wang F, Fernandez A. Effects of limited English proficiency and physician language on health care comprehension. *J Gen Intern Med.* 2005;20(9):800-6.

72. Lasater LM, Davidson AJ, Steiner JF, Mehler PS. Glycemic control in English- vs Spanish-speaking Hispanic patients with type 2 diabetes mellitus. *Arch Intern Med.* 2001;161(1):77-82.

73. Mouton CP, Harris S, Rovi S, Solorzano P, Johnson MS. Barriers to Black women's participation in cancer clinical trials. *J Nat Med Assoc.* 1997;89(11): 721-7.

74. Reese DJ, Ahern RE, Nair S, O'Faire JD, Warren C. Hospice access and use by African-Americans: addressing cultural and institutional barriers through participatory action research. *Soc Work.* 1999; 44(6):549-59.

75. Woloshin S, Bickell NA, Schwartz LM, Gany F, Welch HG. Language barriers in medicine in the United States. *JAMA.* 1995;273(9):724-8.

76. Flores G. The impact of medical interpreter services on the quality of health care: a systematic review. *Med Care Res Rev.* 2005;62(3):255-99.

77. Cohen AL, Rivara F, Marcuse EK, McPhillips H, Davis R. Are Language Barriers Associated With Serious Medical Events in Hospitalized Pediatric Patients? *Pediatrics.* 2005;116(3):575-579.

78. Ku L, Flores G. Pay Now Or Pay Later: Providing Interpreter Services In Health Care. *Health Aff (Millwood).* 2005;24(2):435-444.

79. Disparities in Health Care. Vol. 2005: Aetna; 2003.

80. Assessment for NIH Minority Research/Training Programs: Phase 3. Available at http://www4.nas. edu/webcr.nsf/ProjectScopeDisplay/BBXX-K-00-08-A?OpenDocument (accessed September 1, 2005).

4

Physician Workforce Crisis? Wrong Diagnosis, Wrong Prescription

Source: Goodman DC, Fisher ES. Physician workforce crisis? Wrong diagnosis, wrong prescription. N Engl J Med 2008;358:1658-61. Copyright (c) 2008 Massachusetts Medical Society. All rights reserved.

Despite the fact that there are now more physicians per capita in the United States than there have been for at least 50 years, the Council on Graduate Medical Education (COGME) recently predicted a 10% shortfall of physicians by 2020. Public concern about access to care, reports of difficulties in recruiting physicians in many specialties, and discussion of the looming collapse of primary care all contribute to the sense of crisis. The Association of American Medical Colleges has responded with calls for a 30% expansion of U.S. medical schools and a lifting of the current cap on Medicare funding for graduate medical education so that federal dollars can support the expansion of the workforce.

Before acting on these recommendations, we should carefully consider the accuracy of the diagnosis and the likely consequences of the prescription. Three observations should give policymakers pause (see Table 1).

Physician supply varies dramatically by region of the country. COGME is concerned about a 10% shortfall at a time when the regional supply of physicians varies by more than 50% (see Table 1). An analysis of the country's hospital-referral regions (re-

gional markets for tertiary care) in which regions are categorized into quintiles on the basis of their per-capita supply of physicians reveals that the ratio of the supply in the highest-quintile regions to that in the lowest-quintile regions is 1.56 for primary care, 1.89 for medical specialists, and 1.43 for surgical specialists.

But the presence of more physicians doesn't translate into better care. Medicare beneficiaries' satisfaction with their care and perceptions of access are no better in high-supply regions than in low-supply regions. Nor does more physicians generally mean better care for hospitalized patients (see Table 1). Physicians in high-supply regions are more likely to report concerns about inadequate continuity of care, inadequate communication among physicians, and greater difficulty providing high-quality care.[1] And certainly most important, patient outcomes are not better in regions with a very large supply of physicians.[2,3]

Having more physicians does, however, mean more spending on health care—a strong correlation that should not be surprising.[3] Physicians' incomes are an important component of medical spending, and physicians order most clinical services.

Taken together, these analyses contradict the notion that health care systems have inflexible physician requirements and call into question the significance of a 10% national "shortfall." They should also lead us to question the diagnosis of a crisis in the physician workforce.

Table 1	Supply of Physicians in U.S. Hospital-Referral Regions and Associated Quality of and Access to Care, 2005*			
Variable	Regions in Lowest Quintile of Supply	Regions in Middle Quintile of Supply	Regions in Highest Quintile of Supply	Ratio of Lowest to Highest
Total number of physicians per capita (per 100,000 population, adjusted for age and sex)	169.4	204.8	271.8	1.60
Primary care	61.5	72.7	95.7	1.56
Medical specialists	34.1	44.3	64.3	1.89
Surgical specialists	37.4	43.2	53.4	1.43
Hospital-based specialists	23.8	26.1	28.7	1.21
Medicare composite quality scores				
Acute myocardial infarction	91.0	91.7	93.1	1.02
Congestive heart failure	84.1	85.9	88.6	1.05
Pneumonia	79.5	78.8	79.2	1.00
Medicare access and satisfaction				
Ever had a problem and didn't see a doctor? (% responding no)	91.7	92.8	93.2	1.02
Do you have a particular place for medical care? (% responding yes)	95.0	94.8	95.5	1.01
Satisfied with ease of getting to the doctor? (% responding yes)	94.9	93.5	94.7	1.00
Satisfied with doctor's concern for overall health? (% responding yes)	95.5	94.2	95.7	1.00
Satisfied with quality of medical care? (% responding yes)	96.7	96.3	97.0	1.00

*Data are for hospital-referral regions according to quintile of beneficiary-weighted total number of physicians per capita for 2005. Total numbers of physicians include the number of full-time clinical postgraduate physicians and 0.35 times the number of residents and fellows. For acute myocardial infarction, the Medicare composite quality scores are the averages of scores for the use of aspirin within 24 hours before or after admission and at discharge, the use of a beta-blocker within 24 hours before or after admission, and the use of an angiotensin-converting–enzyme (ACE) inhibitor for left ventricular systolic dysfunction; for congestive heart failure, composite scores are the averages of scores for assessment of left ventricular function and the use of an ACE inhibitor for left ventricular dysfunction; for pneumonia, composite scores are the averages of scores for the timing of initial antibiotic therapy, the presence or absence of pneumococcal vaccination, and assessment of oxygenation. The percentages for Medicare access and satisfaction are calculated from responses to the Medicare Current Beneficiary Survey. Data are from the Dartmouth Atlas of Health Care Project.

What about the prescription? As we see it, increasing the number of physicians will make our health care system worse, not better.

First, unfettered growth is likely to exacerbate regional inequities in supply and spending. Research at our center has shown that physicians do not preferentially practice where the need is greatest. On the contrary, between 1979 and 1999, the physician supply per capita grew by 45% in primary care, 118% among medical specialists, and 21% among surgical specialists, yet four of every five new physicians settled in regions where the supply was already high.[4] Any plan to increase the supply should be crafted to reduce, not exacerbate, regional disparities.

Second, unrestricted expansion of graduate medical education (as would occur if the funding cap on residency positions were removed) would probably further undermine primary care and reinforce trends toward a fragmented, specialist-oriented health care system. Current reimbursement systems strongly favor procedure-oriented specialties, and training programs would almost certainly respond to these incentives, which would lead to a relative increase in subspecialty care that inefficiently disperses patients' care among multiple specialists. The flexibility of the workforce will diminish as more physicians learn narrower skill sets. In the absence of reform, expansion of specialist training risks further marginalizing primary care in medical education and limits our capacity for building patient-centered delivery systems.

Third, workforce expansion will be expensive. Although no formal estimates of the marginal costs have been offered by proponents of expanding training, we estimate that the additional costs of training the physicians who would expand the workforce by 30% would be $5 billion to $10 billion per year, depending on the proportion of subspecialists trained. Once these physicians are in practice, the costs will be many times greater. If outcomes and patients' perception of access improved as supply increased, then we could debate whether an expansion of training offers better value than investments in preventive care, disease management, or broader insurance coverage, which have known benefits. Instead, the costs of expansion will limit the resources available for necessary reform efforts without any evidence-based promise of a benefit.

The situation in Massachusetts reflects the problem with focusing narrowly on the physician workforce. Massachusetts has seen its supply of physicians per capita more than double since 1976, and it now has the highest physician-to-population ratio of any state, in primary care as well as overall. Yet the Massachusetts Medical Society has issued several annual reports asserting that there is a severe physician shortage, and patients report that the availability of primary care continues to decline.[5]

We believe that the perception of a physician shortage, both nationally and in Massachusetts, is just one symptom of the underlying problems in our health care system. The current delivery and payment systems often make it more "efficient" for primary care physicians to see patients they already know (diminishing others' access to primary care) and for all physicians to narrow their scope of practice (increasing referrals to specialists) and to admit patients to the hospital (where hospitalists manage their care). Data showing that physicians in high-supply regions are more likely to report difficulty gaining both hospital admissions and specialist referrals are consistent with this hypothesis.[1] In the absence of reform of the delivery system, additional growth will lead to further fragmentation of care that will exacerbate the problem of access and worsen the apparent scarcity it is intended to remedy.

Rather than treat the symptoms, we should focus on the underlying disease—a largely disorganized and fragmented delivery system characterized by lack of coordination, incomplete patient information, poor communication, uneven quality, and rising costs. Pilot projects intended to address these problems are under way in both the private and public sectors, with growing interest in primary care-based medical homes, enhanced care coordination, programs for chronic-disease management, and payment reform.

Policymakers therefore face a choice: respond to pressure to increase funding for medical education—and risk making things worse—or accept the evidence that the apparent shortage is but one symptom of the underlying problems with our health care system. We would offer three recommendations: do not remove the Medicare cap on funding for graduate medical education; find the best way of reallocating current medical education funding toward programs (such as primary care residencies and geriatric and palliative care fellowships) that could lead to improved care coordination and chronic-disease management; and accelerate efforts to reform payment systems so that they foster integration, coordination, and efficient care.

Physicians have a financial stake in this debate. Pressure to constrain costs is increasing. Growth of the physician workforce will make it harder to preserve individual physicians' incomes. And given the income disparities between procedural and cognitive specialties and the high costs of procedures, disproportionate growth in the specialist workforce will exacerbate the pressure on incomes.

Academic medicine, for its part, faces a challenge and an opportunity. The dramatic differences in practice—and spending—observed among major

Table 2	Average Number of Physicians (Full-Time Equivalents) Caring for Chronically Ill Medicare Beneficiaries in the Last 6 Months of Life at Five Top U.S. Hospitals, 1999–2003*				
Variable	Johns Hopkins	Mayo Clinic	UCLA Medical Center	Cleveland Clinic	Massachusetts General Hospital
Rank according to *U.S. News and World Report*	1	2	3	4	5
No. of clinical physicians (full-time equivalents) per 1000 patients					
Total	12.2	8.9	16.9	12.7	15.3
Primary care	5.0	3.0	3.5	4.3	6.3
Medical specialists	3.9	3.9	10.1	5.5	5.5
Surgical specialists	1.1	0.8	1.4	1.5	1.1
Hospital-based specialists	1.4	1.0	1.5	1.2	1.7
No. of days in the hospital	17.1	12.9	19.2	14.6	17.7
No. of days in intensive care	4.3	3.9	11.4	3.5	2.8

* Hospitals were ranked "top honor roll hospitals" by *U.S. News and World Report*.

academic medical centers challenge the assumption that their care is somehow uniformly scientific or evidence-based (see Table 2). Seriously ill Medicare beneficiaries cared for at the UCLA Medical Center, for example, spend many more days in the hospital and receive many more physician services than those cared for at the Mayo Clinic; as a consequence, UCLA patients require almost twice as many physicians (16.9 vs. 8.9 full-time-equivalent physicians per 1000 patients), a difference largely explained by greater use of specialists. But these differences also highlight an opportunity for academic medicine—to acknowledge the lack of an adequate scientific basis for current workforce policy and take the lead in organizing research to determine how best to deliver high-quality, affordable care. After all, why should the best medical care in the world require twice as many physicians as the best medical care in the world?

● ● ● **References**

1. Sirovich BE, Gottlieb DJ, Welch HG, Fisher ES. Regional variations in health care intensity and physician perceptions of quality of care. *Ann Intern Med* 2006;144:641-9.

2. Goodman DC, Fisher ES, Little GA, Stukel TA, Chang CH, Schoendorf KS. The relation between the availability of neonatal intensive care and neonatal mortality. *N Engl J Med* 2002;346:1538-44.

3. Fisher ES, Wennberg DE, Stukel TA, Gottlieb DJ, Lucas FL, Pinder EL. The implications of regional variations in Medicare spending. *Ann Intern Med* 2003;138:273-98.

4. Goodman DC. Twenty-year trends in regional variations in the U.S. physician workforce. Health Aff (Millwood) 2004;Suppl Web Exclusives:VAR90-VAR97.

5. 2007 MMS Physician Workforce Study. Waltham, MA: Massachusetts Medical Society, 2007. (Accessed March 28, 2008, at http://www.massmed.org/Content/NavigationMenu/NewsandPublications/ResearchReportsStudies/PhysicianWorkforceStudy/workforce07.htm.)

7

Health Care Financing

inancing is a broad area. At a very basic level, it refers to the financing of health insurance, private or public. People who are not covered by either private or government-sponsored health insurance programs are the uninsured. There is a close relationship—including cause and effect—between health insurance, access to and utilization of health care, reimbursement to providers for services delivered, and health care expenditures. For example, without rationing care, expansion of insurance increases both access and utilization, which in turn increase health care expenditures. There is a common misconception that Americans receive health care through private insurance. In fact, a variety of public insurance programs has been growing ever since the creation of Medicare and Medicaid in 1965. Other key public programs include the State Children's Health Insurance Program (SCHIP), TriCare (which provides health insurance to the armed forces personnel and their dependents), Veterans Health Administration, and Indian Health Service. In addition, federal and state governments fund public health services and community health centers. Of the total national health care expenditures in 2006, 54% were traced to private sources; the other 46% to public sources (National Center for Health Statistics 2009). Hence, public financing plays a substantial role in U.S. health care delivery.

To access health care services, the uninsured must predominantly depend on *safety net* providers. Such providers include traditional safety net providers—those who are legally obligated to provide care to persons who cannot afford it, such as public hospitals, federally funded health centers, hospital emergency rooms, and local health departments—and mainstream providers—those who provide uncompensated care voluntarily or as part of their community-service obligation (Gresenz et al. 2007). Other components of the safety net include free clinics and federally funded Health Care for the Homeless (HCH) Program which operates almost 200 HCH clinics across the country for homeless populations (Zlotnick & Zerger 2009). There is, however, wide variation in access to medical care among uninsured individuals living in different communities, one main reason being the safety net capacity and where the safety net providers are located (Hadley & Cunningham 2004). Also, crossing the border to obtain health care in Mexico is not uncommon for U.S. residents living in counties near the border. The reasons may include affordability, different prescription requirements, and cultural preferences. However, not having insurance is an important correlate of cross-border care utilization (Escobedo & Cardenas 2006).

Whether or not the uninsured suffer negative health consequences has been a subject of debate for quite some time. One recent research report (Kronick 2009) concluded that when adjusted for demographic, health status, and health behavior characteristics, the risk of subsequent mortality is no different for the uninsured than for those covered by employer-sponsored group insurance. Only when health status is excluded as a covariate, the uninsured have a 10% higher mortality rate. The author of this study concluded that there would not be much change in the number of deaths in the United States as a result of universal insurance coverage, although the difficulties in inferring causality from observational analyses temper the strength of this conclusion. Robust evidence can only come from a randomized experiment, in which the only difference between the insured and the uninsured is that some people are randomly assigned to insurance while others to being uninsured. However, no such experiment exists (Kronick 2009). On the other hand, the uninsured often do not have access to adequate primary care. Hence, intuition would suggest that uninsurance should cause poor health. After reviewing the evidence on this question, Levy and Meltzer (2008) reached three conclusions. First, many of the studies claiming to show a causal effect of health insurance on health do not do so convincingly because the observed correlation between insurance and good health may be driven by other, unobservable factors. Second, convincing evidence demonstrates that health insurance can improve health measures of some population subgroups, some of which, although not all, are the same subgroups that would be the likely targets of coverage expansion policies. Third, for policy purposes we need to know whether the results of these studies generalize. Solid answers to the multitude of important questions about how specific health insurance policy options may affect health seem likely to be forthcoming only with investment of substantial resources in social experiments. These conclusions appear valid in light of the fact that health insurance provides access to medical care, but does little to address social, cultural, lifestyle, and genetic factors that together have a much greater influence on health and well-being than medical care alone. On the other hand, there appears to be clear evidence that the aging population derives significant health benefits from Medicare cov-

erage. McWilliams and colleagues (2007) used a quasi-experimental design and nationally representative longitudinal data to demonstrate that eligibility for Medicare coverage at age 65 years was associated with significant improvements in self-reported health trends for previously uninsured adults relative to previously insured adults.

Rising health care expenditures continue to be a vital issue that the nation must grapple with. Rising costs of health care render it more and more unaffordable, and is one factor that is associated with uninsurance.

In the first reading for this chapter, **The Uninsured, A Primer: Key Facts About Americans Without Health Insurance**, Hoffman and colleagues explain that only 19% of the uninsured are in families that have no connection to the workforce; 81% are in working families. Many of them are either not offered health insurance by their employers or they cannot afford it. People with various characteristics but in low-wage jobs are likely to be uninsured. Hoffman and colleagues have concluded that health insurance makes a difference in whether and when people get necessary medical care, where they get the care, and how healthy people are. For example, the uninsured have to forgo regular preventive care. The authors also cite studies supporting the claim that the uninsured are more likely to be hospitalized, receive fewer services in the hospital, and incur higher mortality rates. Most of the care for the uninsured is funded by the government, and most of these dollars are paid to hospitals. Uncompensated care provided by physicians has continued to decline.

Medicare—the nation's public health insurance program for the elderly, disabled individuals receiving Social Security benefits, and people who have end-stage renal disease—gives beneficiaries an option to either enroll in the traditional fee-for-service (FFS) program or enroll in Medicare Advantage, also called Part C of Medicare, which is a risk contracting program. In the reading, **Trends in the Health Status of Medicare Risk Contract Enrollees**, Riley and Zarabozo first give an overview of the risk contracting program. Of particular note are the types of beneficiaries who enrolled in risk programs. The enrollees have been relatively healthy populations. Hence, a risk-adjusted payment system based on diagnoses was implemented to match payments to enrollee health status. One objective of risk-adjusted payments is to make the program more appealing to vulnerable populations which have complex health care needs and can benefit from savings in their out-of-pocket costs. The study finds that the health and functional status of risk contract enrollees has now become more similar to that of FFS beneficiaries, and may reflect the impact of risk-adjusted payment policies. The authors also point out other factors that may be responsible for the trend.

In **The Value of Medical Spending in the United States, 1960-2000**, Cutler and colleagues have attempted to evaluate the worth of medical care by comparing the increased expenditures to gains in life expectancy. This type of analysis is important in determining whether the United States spends too much on health care delivery. The researchers evaluate the present value of medical spending over the estimated life expectancy for newborns, and for those at age 15 years, 45 years, and 65 years, respectively. On the whole, between 1990 and 2000, the cost of $145,000 per year of life gained is considered reasonable. In arriving at this conclusion, it is assumed that 50% of the total gains in life expectancy are attributable to medical care. On the other hand, as a person ages, costs rise more rapidly than life expectancy. For the elderly, the cost-effectiveness of medical care has continued to decrease. However, is the increase in quality of life for the elderly worth the cost even though longevity may not improve? Such questions are not easily addressed.

In **High and Rising Health Care Costs: Demystifying U.S. Health Care Spending**, Ginsburg thinks that health care professionals may have more influence on health care spending than other entities such as consumers who are shielded from most of the cost implications of decisions regarding health care consumption. There are conflicting views about the value of medical technology, a major driver of costs. A more practical concern is the affordability of health insurance. Rising costs also put pressures on public insurance programs and the nation's safety net. The net result is a fragmentation of the delivery system according to ability to pay. Rising health care spending may also be a negative factor for the over-all U.S. economy. The notion that the United States spends too much on health care comes from spending comparisons with OECD countries. The reading concludes with the major drivers of health care costs in the United States, the most significant of which is medical technology.

● ● ● **References**

Escobedo, L.G. and V.M. Cardenas. 2006. Utilization and purchase of medical care services in Mexico by residents in the United States of America, 1989–1999. *Revista Panamericana de Salud Pública* 19(5):300-305.

Gresenz, C.R. et al. 2007. Health care markets, the safety net, and utilization of care among the uninsured. *Health Services Research* 42(1 Pt 1): 239-264.

Hadley, J. and P. Cunningham. 2004. Availability of Safety Net Providers Access to Care of Uninsured Persons. *Health Services Research* 39(5):1527-1546.

Kronick, R. 2009. Health insurance coverage and mortality revisited. *Health Services Research* 44(4): 1211-1231.

Levy, H. and D. Meltzer. 2009. The impact of health insurance on health. *Annual Review of Public Health* 29(1):399-409.

McWilliams, J.M. et al. 2007. Health of previously uninsured adults after acquiring Medicare coverage. *JAMA* 298(24):2886-2894.

National Center for Health Statistics. 2009. *Health, United States, 2008*. Hyattsville, MD: National Center for Health Statistics.

Zlotnick, C. and S. Zerger. 2009. Survey findings on characteristics and health status of clients treated by the federally funded (US) Health Care for the Homeless Programs. *Health and Social Care in the Community* 17(1):18-26.

1

The Uninsured: A Primer

Source: Excerpted from "The Uninsured: A Primer" (#7451-05), The Henry J. Kaiser Family Foundation, October 2009. This information was reprinted with permission from the Henry J. Kaiser Family Foundation. The Kaiser Family Foundation is a non-profit private operating foundation, based in Menlo Park, California, dedicated to producing and communicating the best possible analysis and information on health issues.

WHO ARE THE UNINSURED?

In 2008, 46 million people in the U.S. under age 65 lacked health insurance. Most of these individuals come from working families and have low incomes. Adults make up more than their share of the uninsured because they are less likely than children to be eligible for Medicaid—especially young adults whose low incomes make it more it difficult to afford coverage.

More than eight in ten of the uninsured are in working families—about two thirds are from families with one or more full-time workers and 14% are from families with part-time workers. Only 19% of the uninsured are from families that have no connection to the workforce (Figure 4). Even at lower income levels, the majority of the uninsured are in working families. Among the uninsured with incomes below the poverty level ($22,025 for a family of four in 2008), 55% have at least one worker in the family.

About two-thirds of the uninsured are poor or near poor (Figure 4). These individuals are less likely to be offered employer-sponsored coverage or to be able to afford to purchase their own coverage. Those who are poor (below 100% of the poverty level) are about twice as likely to be uninsured as the entire nonelderly population (35% vs.17%). Were it not for the Medicaid program, many more of the poor would be uninsured. The near-poor (those with incomes between 100% and 199% of the poverty level) also run a high risk of being uninsured (29%), in part, because they are less likely to be eligible for Medicaid. Only 10% of the uninsured are from families at or above 400% of poverty.

Adults are more likely to be uninsured than children. Adults make up 70% of the nonelderly population, but more than 80% of the uninsured (Figure 4). Most low-income children qualify for Medicaid or the Children's Health Insurance Program (CHIP), but low-income adults under age 65 typically qualify for Medicaid only if they are disabled, pregnant, or have dependent children. Income eligibility levels are generally much lower for parents than for children, and adults without children are generally ineligible.

Young adults, ages 19 to 29, comprise a disproportionately large share of the uninsured, largely due to their low incomes. Young adults have the highest uninsured rate (30%) of any age group. More than half of uninsured young adults are families with at least one full-time worker, but their low incomes make it more difficult for them to afford coverage.[1] The median income of uninsured young

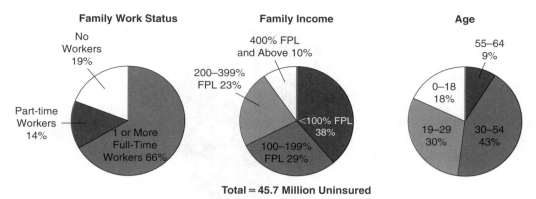

Figure 4 Characteristics of the Uninsured, 2008

adults in 2008 was $15,000. While young adults are the most likely to be uninsured, they do not comprise the majority of the uninsured. More than half (52%) of the uninsured are age 30 and older, and these older adults are at increased risk of serious health problems.

More than half (62%) of nonelderly uninsured adults have no education beyond high school, making them less able to get higher-skilled jobs that are more likely to provide health coverage. Those with less education are also more likely to be uninsured for longer periods of time.[2]

Minorities are much more likely to be uninsured than whites. About one third of Hispanics are uninsured compared to 13% of whites. The uninsured rate among African-Americans (21%) is also much higher than that of whites (Figure 5). Because racial and ethnic minority groups are more likely to come from low-income families, Medicaid is an important source of health insurance for them. However, its limited reach leaves large numbers of minorities uninsured.

The majority of the uninsured (80%) are native or naturalized U.S. citizens. Although non-citizens (legal and undocumented) are about three times more likely to be uninsured than citizens, they are not the primary cause of the uninsured problem. Non-citizens have less access to employer coverage because they are more likely to have low-wage jobs and work for firms that do not offer coverage. Further, until recently, states were precluded from using federal dollars to provide Medicaid or CHIP coverage to most recent legal immigrants who have been in the U.S. less than five years. However, in 2009, states were given the option of extending Medicaid coverage to children and pregnant women who previously would have been subject to the five year ban. Federal law bars undocumented immigrants from enrolling in Medicaid and CHIP coverage.

The uninsured tend to be in worse health than the privately insured. About 11% of the uninsured are in fair or poor health, compared to 5% of those with private coverage. Almost half of all uninsured nonelderly adults have a chronic condition.[3] Those with such conditions and others who are not in good health and who do not have access to employer-sponsored coverage may find non-group coverage to be unavailable or unaffordable.

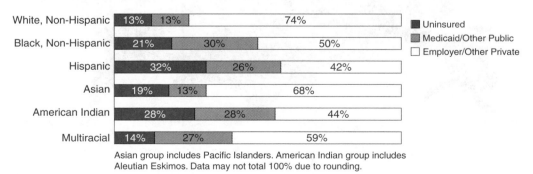

Figure 5 Insurance Coverage of Nonelderly, by Race/Ethnicity, 2008 *Source:* Summary Health Statistics for the U.S. Population: National Health Interview Survey, 2007. 2008.

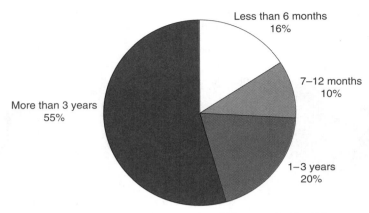

More than three years includes those who said they never had health insurance.
Percentages are age adjusted. Data may not total 100% due to rounding.

Figure 6 Duration of Time Without Coverage Among the Uninsured, 2007. *Source:* Summary Health Statistics for the U.S. Population: National Health Interview Survey, 2007. 2008.

About three-quarters of the uninsured (75%) have gone without coverage for more than one year (Figure 6). Because health insurance is primarily obtained as an employment benefit, health coverage is disrupted when people change or lose their jobs. When people are unable to obtain employer-sponsored coverage and are ineligible for Medicaid, they may be left uninsured for long periods of time if individual coverage is either unaffordable or unavailable due to their health status.

Insurance coverage varies by state depending on the share of families with low incomes, the nature of the state's employment, and the reach of state Medicaid programs.[4] Insurance market regulations and the availability of jobs with employer-sponsored coverage also influence the distribution of health coverage in each state. Uninsured rates tend to be higher in the southern and western regions of the United States. State uninsured rates range from less than 10% in Hawaii, Massachusetts, and Minnesota to over 25% in New Mexico and Texas (Figure 7).

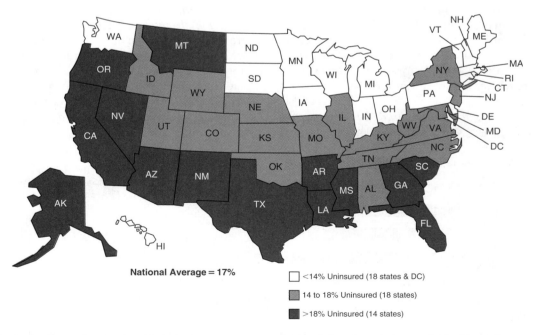

National Average = 17%

☐ <14% Uninsured (18 states & DC)

▨ 14 to 18% Uninsured (18 states)

■ >18% Uninsured (14 states)

Figure 7 Uninsured Rates Among Nonelderly by State, 2007-2008. *Source:* Kaiser Commission on Medicaid and the Uninsured/Urban Institute analysis of 2008 and 2009 ASEC Supplements to the CPS., two-year pooled data.

HOW DOES LACK OF INSURANCE AFFECT ACCESS TO HEALTH CARE?

Health insurance makes a difference in whether and when people get necessary medical care, where they get their care, and ultimately, how healthy people are. Uninsured adults are far more likely than the insured to postpone or forgo health care altogether. The consequences of this can be severe, particularly when preventable conditions go undetected.

The uninsured are far more likely than those with insurance to report problems getting needed medical care. Nearly one-quarter of uninsured adults say that they have forgone care in the past year because of its cost—compared to 4% of adults with private coverage. Part of the reason for this is that slightly more than half of uninsured adults do not have a regular place to go when they are sick or need medical advice (Figure 8).

Anticipating high medical bills, many of the uninsured are not able to follow recommended treatments. Just over a quarter of uninsured adults say they did not fill a drug prescription in the past year because they could not afford it. Regardless of a person's insurance coverage, those injured or newly diagnosed with a chronic condition receive similar follow-up care plans; however, the uninsured are less likely than the insured to actually obtain all the services that are recommended.[5]

Problems getting needed care also exist among uninsured children. Uninsured children are much more likely to lack a usual source of care, to delay care, or to have unmet medical needs than children with insurance (Figure 9). Uninsured children with common childhood illnesses and injuries do not receive the same level of care as others. As a result, they are at higher risk for preventable hospitalizations and for missed diagnoses of serious health conditions.[6] Disparities exist even among children with special needs, including access to specialists.[7]

Lack of health coverage, even for short periods of time, results in decreased access to care. Those who have been uninsured for less than six months are already more likely than those with continuous health coverage to report having an unmet need for medical care or a prescription drug in the past year.[8]

The uninsured are less likely to receive timely preventive care. Silent health problems, such as hypertension and diabetes, often go undetected without routine check-ups. Uninsured nonelderly adults, compared to those with coverage, are far less likely to have had regular preventive care, including cancer screenings.[9] Consequently, uninsured patients are diagnosed in later stages of diseases, including cancer, and die earlier than those with insurance.[10,11]

Because the uninsured are less likely than the insured to have regular outpatient care, they are more likely to be hospitalized for avoidable health problems and experience declines in their overall health. When they are hospitalized, the uninsured receive fewer diagnostic and therapeutic services and also are more likely to die in the hospital than insured patients.[12,13] Even among those injured in severe automobile accidents who are unable to participate in the initial treatment decisions, the

Percent of adults (age 18–64) reporting:

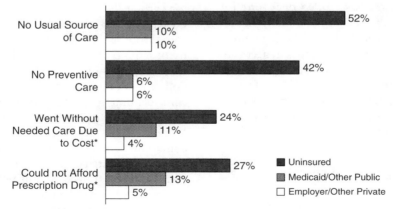

* In past 12 months.
Respondents who said usual source of care was the emergency room were included among those not having a usual source of care.

Figure 8 Barriers to Health Care Among Nonelderly Adults, by Insurance Status, 2008. *Source:* KCMU analysis of 2008 NHIS data.

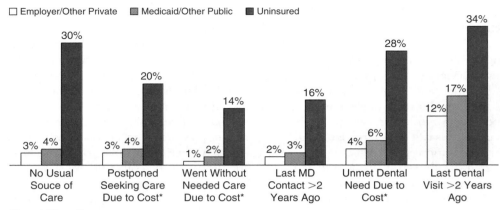

* In past 12 months
Questions about dental care were analyzed for children age 2–17. All other questions were analyzed for all children under age 18. MD contact includes other health professionals. Respondents who said usual source of care was the emergency room were included among those not having a usual source of care.

Figure 9 Children's Access to Care, by Health Insurance Status, 2008 *Source:* KCMU analysis of 2008 NHIS data.

uninsured receive less hospital services and have a substantially higher mortality rate.[14]

Research demonstrates that gaining health insurance restores access to health care considerably and diminishes the adverse effects of having been uninsured. Middle-aged adults who are continuously uninsured are much more likely to experience a decline in their health than those who are continuously insured.[15] However among previously uninsured adults who acquire Medicare coverage at age 65, use of preventive care increases, their access to physician and hospital care improves, and they experience improved health and functional status. When uninsured children gain health coverage, they receive more timely diagnosis, fewer preventable hospitalizations, and miss fewer days of school.[16]

Access to health care has eroded over time for many. Rising health care costs have made health care less affordable, particularly for the uninsured. Between 1997 and 2006, the differences in access to care between the uninsured and insured widened, even among those with chronic conditions. The insurance disparities in access to a usual source of care, annual check-ups, and preventive health care are the greatest and grew the most over the decade.[17,18]

HOW IS UNCOMPENSATED CARE FINANCED?

When the uninsured are unable to pay for the health care they receive, that uncompensated care is paid for through a patchwork of federal, state, and private funds. The bulk of such care is funded by the gov-

ernment and is crucial to the strength of the nation's safety-net hospitals and clinics.

The uninsured spend less than half of what the insured spend on health care. In 2008, the average person who was uninsured for a full-year incurred $1,686 in total health care costs compared to $4,463 for the nonelderly with coverage.[19] The uninsured pay for about a third of their care out of pocket, totaling $30 billion in 2008. This includes the health care costs for those uninsured all year and the costs incurred during the months the part-year uninsured have no health coverage.[20]

The remaining costs of their care, the uncompensated costs, amounted to about $57 billion in 2008. About 75% of this total ($42.9 billion) will be paid by federal, state, and local funds appropriated for care of the uninsured (Figure 11, not included). Nearly half of all funds for uncompensated care come from the federal government, with the majority of federal dollars flowing through Medicare and Medicaid. Although substantial, these government dollars amounted to a small slice (2%) of total health care spending in the U.S. in 2008.

Hospitals, community clinics, and physicians provide care to the uninsured. While physicians and community clinics see more uninsured patients, 60% of uncompensated care costs are incurred in hospitals because medical needs requiring hospitalization are the most expensive (Figure 12, not included).[21] Most government dollars for uncompensated care are paid to hospitals based indirectly on the share of uncompensated care they may provide.

The cost of uncompensated care provided by physicians is not directly or indirectly reimbursed by public dollars.[22] Financial pressures and time constraints, coupled with changing physician practice patterns, have contributed to a decline in charity care provided by physicians. The percent of all doctors who provide charity care fell to 68% in 2004-2005 from 76% in 1996-1997.[23]

Uncompensated care costs for direct service programs, such as the Veterans Affairs health system and community health centers, are funded largely by public dollars. Community health centers and public hospitals also rely heavily on the Medicaid program as their largest source of third-party insurance payments. About one-third of all revenues in Federally Qualified Health Centers and public hospitals are paid by Medicaid, evidence of the large share of low-income patients they serve.[24]

In recent years, federal funding for community health centers (CHCs) has been increasing; however it has not kept pace with the growing numbers of uninsured and the costs of caring for them.[25] Federal dollars cover a good share of the costs of caring for uninsured patients in health centers, but that share has declined between 2000 and 2007 from 56% to 48% (Figure 13, not included). Less than $1 billion out of $26 billion of federal spending for uncompensated care went to community health centers in 2008.[26]

Recognizing the growing need for CHC services, the American Recovery and Reinvestment Act passed in 2009, provided over $2 billion to expand the number of sites, increase services at existing CHCs, and provide supplemental payments for spikes in the number of uninsured CHCs serve as a result of the recession.

Table 1	Characteristics of the Nonelderly Uninsured, 2008				
	Nonelderly (millions)	Percent of Nonelderly	Uninsured Nonelderly (millions)	Percent of Uninsured Nonelderly	Uninsured Rate for Nonelderly
Total - Nonelderly[a]	**262.8**	**100.0%**	**45.7**	**100.0%**	**17.4%**
Age					
Children-Total	**78.7**	**29.9%**	**8.1**	**17.7%**	**10.3%**
Adults-Total	**184.1**	**70.1%**	**37.6**	**82.3%**	**20.4%**
Adults 19–24	24.3	9.2%	7.5	16.4%	30.8%
Adults 25–34	40.1	15.3%	10.8	23.5%	26.8%
Adults 35–44	41.1	15.6%	8.0	17.6%	19.6%
Adults 45–54	44.3	16.9%	7.1	15.4%	15.9%
Adults 55–64	34.3	13.0%	4.3	9.4%	12.5%
Annual Family Income					
<$20,000	60.6	23.1%	21.9	47.8%	36.1%
$20,000–$39,999	52.2	19.9%	13.3	29.1%	25.5%
$40,000+	150.0	57.1%	10.6	23.1%	7.0%
Family Poverty Level[b]					
<100%	**50.2**	**19.1%**	**17.5**	**38.2%**	**34.8%**
100–199%	**46.0**	**17.5%**	**13.3**	**29.2%**	**29.0%**
...100–149%	23.7	9.0%	7.4	16.2%	31.2%
...150–199%	22.3	8.5%	5.9	13.0%	26.6%
200–399%	**74.3**	**28.3%**	**10.5**	**22.9%**	**14.1%**
...200–299%	41.5	15.8%	7.3	15.9%	17.5%
...300–399%	32.8	12.5%	3.2	7.0%	9.8%
400%+	**92.3**	**35.1%**	**4.4**	**9.6%**	**4.8%**
Household Type					
Single Adults Living Alone	19.6	7.5%	3.9	8.5%	19.7%
Single Adults Living Together	31.3	11.9%	10.9	23.7%	34.7%
Married Adults	55.5	21.1%	8.1	17.6%	14.5%
1 Parent with children[c]	32.6	12.4%	5.9	13.0%	18.2%
2 Parents with children[c]	109.4	41.6%	12.8	28.1%	11.7%
Multigenerational/Other with children[d]	14.4	5.5%	4.2	9.1%	29.0%
Family Work Status					
2 Full-time	72.0	27.4%	5.4	11.7%	7.4%
1 Full-time	137.4	52.3%	25.0	54.7%	18.2%
Only Part-time[e]	21.1	8.0%	6.4	14.1%	30.4%
Non-Workers	32.2	12.3%	8.9	19.5%	27.6%

(continued)

Table 1	Characteristics of the Nonelderly Uninsured, 2008 (continued)

Race/Ethnicity

White only (non-Hispanic)	166.4	63.3%	21.1	46.1%	12.7%
Black only (non-Hispanic)	33.3	12.7%	6.9	15.0%	20.6%
Hispanic	44.7	17.0%	14.4	31.5%	32.2%
Asian/S. Pacific Islander	12.4	4.7%	2.3	5.1%	18.7%
Am. Indian/Alaska Native	1.7	0.7%	0.5	1.1%	27.9%
Two or More Races	4.3	1.6%	0.6	1.3%	14.1%

Citizenship

U.S. citizen - native	230.5	87.7%	33.7	73.8%	14.6%
U.S. citizen - naturalized	12.3	4.7%	2.7	5.9%	22.0%
Non-U.S. citizen, resident for < 6 years	5.4	2.0%	2.5	5.5%	46.3%
Non-U.S. citizen, resident for 6+ years	14.6	5.6%	6.8	14.9%	46.4%

Health Status

Excellent/Very Good	179.1	68.2%	26.2	57.4%	14.6%
Good	60.4	23.0%	14.3	31.3%	23.7%
Fair/Poor	23.2	8.8%	5.2	11.3%	22.2%

Confidence intervals and standard errors were calculated only for uninsured rates. ( )=Estimate has a large 95% confidence interval of +/−5.0 −7.9 percentage points. Estimates with relative standard errors greater than 30% are not provided.

Table 2	Characteristics of Uninsured Children, 2008

	Children (millions)	Percent of Children	Uninsured Children (millions)	Percent of Uninsured Children	Uninsured Rate for Children
Total - Children[f]	**78.7**	**100.0%**	**8.1**	**100.0%**	**10.3%**
Age					
<1	4.3	5.5%	0.5	5.8%	11.0%
1−5	21.0	26.7%	1.7	21.5%	8.3%
6−18	53.4	67.9%	5.9	72.6%	11.0%
Family Income					
<$20,000	18.5	23.5%	3.4	42.7%	18.6%
$20,000−$39,999	14.3	18.2%	2.1	26.4%	14.9%
$40,000+	45.9	58.3%	2.5	30.9%	5.4%
Family Poverty Level[b]					
, 100%	**19.3**	**24.5%**	**3.5**	**43.3%**	**18.1%**
100−199%	**15.6**	**19.8%**	**2.3**	**28.5%**	**14.8%**
...100−149%	8.3	10.6%	1.4	16.8%	16.2%
...150−199%	7.3	9.2%	0.9	11.8%	13.1%
200−399%	**22.4**	**28.5%**	**1.7**	**20.5%**	**7.4%**
...200−299%	12.8	16.2%	1.2	14.7%	9.3%
...300−399%	9.6	12.2%	0.5	5.8%	4.9%
400%+	**21.4**	**27.2%**	**0.6**	**7.7%**	**2.9%**
Household Type[g]					
1 Parent[c]	19.4	24.7%	2.2	27.5%	11.4%
2 Parents[c]	52.4	66.6%	4.2	52.2%	8.0%
Multigenerational/Other[d]	6.1	7.7%	1.4	17.4%	23.1%
Family Work Status					
2 Full-time	22.5	28.6%	1.4	17.0%	6.1%
1 Full-time	41.1	52.3%	4.1	51.3%	10.1%
Only Part-time[e]	5.4	6.9%	0.7	9.3%	13.8%
Non-Workers	9.6	12.3%	1.8	22.3%	18.7%

(continued)

| Table 2 | Characteristics of Uninsured Children, 2008 (continued) |

Race/Ethnicity

White only (non-Hispanic)	44.1	56.0%	3.1	38.5%	7.1%
Black only (non-Hispanic)	11.3	14.4%	1.3	15.7%	11.2%
Hispanic	17.2	21.9%	3.1	38.1%	17.9%
Asian/S. Pacific Islander	3.3	4.2%	0.4	4.7%	11.5%
Am. Indian/Alaska Native	0.6	0.7%	0.1	1.1%	(16.3%)
Two or More Races	2.2	2.8%	0.2	1.9%	6.8%

Citizenship

U.S. Citizen	76.3	97.0%	7.2	88.8%	9.4%
Non-U.S. citizen, resident for <6 years	1.1	1.4%	0.3	4.2%	(31.3%)
Non-U.S. citizen, resident for 6+ years	1.3	1.6%	0.6	7.0%	(44.8%)

Health Status

Excellent/Very Good	63.9	81.3%	6.0	73.9%	9.3%
Good	13.0	16.6%	1.9	23.8%	14.7%
Fair/Poor	1.7	2.2%	0.2	2.3%	10.7%

Confidence intervals and standard errors were calculated only for uninsured rates. ( ) = Estimate has a large 95% confidence interval of +/−5.0 − 7.9 percentage points. Estimates with relative standard errors greater than 30% are not provided.

| Table 3 | Health Insurance Coverage of the Nonelderly, 2008 |

		Percent Distribution by Coverage Type				
	Nonelderly (millions)	**Private**		**Public**		**Uninsured**
		Employer	Individual	Medicaid	Other[h]	
Total - Nonelderly[a]	**262.8**	**59.7%**	**5.3%**	**14.9%**	**2.7%**	**17.4%**
Age						
Children-Total	**78.7**	**54.4%**	**4.1%**	**29.7%**	**1.5%**	**10.3%**
Adults-Total	**184.1**	**62.0%**	**5.8%**	**8.6%**	**3.2%**	**20.4%**
Adults 19–24	24.3	43.8%	11.7%	12.3%	1.5%	30.8%
Adults 25–34	40.1	58.4%	4.1%	9.3%	1.4%	26.8%
Adults 35–44	41.1	66.6%	4.3%	7.7%	1.9%	19.6%
Adults 45–54	44.3	68.3%	4.9%	7.5%	3.4%	15.9%
Adults 55–64	34.3	65.3%	6.5%	7.7%	7.9%	12.5%
Annual Family Income						
<$20,000	60.6	16.9%	6.3%	36.4%	4.3%	36.1%
$20,000–$39,999	52.2	46.6%	5.5%	19.0%	3.5%	25.5%
$40,000+	150.0	81.5%	4.8%	4.9%	1.8%	7.0%
Family Poverty Level[b]						
, 100%	**50.2**	**14.2%**	**5.6%**	**42.1%**	**3.3%**	**34.8%**
100–199%	**46.0**	**36.4%**	**6.0%**	**24.1%**	**4.4%**	**29.0%**
...100–149%	23.7	28.3%	5.9%	29.5%	5.0%	31.2%
...150–199%	22.3	45.0%	6.1%	18.4%	3.8%	26.6%
200–399%	**74.3**	**71.2%**	**5.3%**	**6.9%**	**2.6%**	**14.1%**
...200–299%	41.5	65.5%	5.5%	8.6%	2.9%	17.5%
...300–399%	32.8	78.3%	5.0%	4.7%	2.2%	9.8%
400%+	**92.3**	**86.8%**	**4.7%**	**2.1%**	**1.6%**	**4.8%**
Household Type						
Single Adults Living Alone	19.6	57.3%	7.8%	10.1%	5.0%	19.7%
Single Adults Living Together	31.3	43.8%	8.5%	9.5%	3.5%	34.7%
Married Adults	55.5	70.5%	5.6%	5.1%	4.3%	14.5%
1 Parent with children[c]	32.6	36.5%	4.4%	39.5%	1.4%	18.2%
2 Parents with children[c]	109.4	69.2%	4.2%	13.1%	1.7%	11.7%
Multigenerational/Other with children[d]	14.4	36.1%	2.9%	29.4%	2.7%	29.0%
Family Work Status						
2 Full-time	72.0	83.5%	3.1%	4.8%	1.2%	7.4%
1 Full-time	137.4	62.4%	5.2%	12.4%	1.7%	18.2%
Only Part-time[e]	21.1	27.7%	11.6%	26.9%	3.4%	30.4%
Non-Workers	32.2	15.8%	6.1%	40.5%	10.0%	27.6%

(continued)

Table 3

Health Insurance Coverage of the Nonelderly, 2008 (continued)

Race/Ethnicity

White only (non-Hispanic)	166.4	68.0%	6.4%	10.1%	2.9%	12.7%
Black only (non-Hispanic)	33.3	47.0%	2.7%	26.1%	3.6%	20.6%
Hispanic	44.7	38.9%	2.8%	24.5%	1.6%	32.2%
Asian/S. Pacific Islander	12.4	62.1%	6.3%	11.3%	1.7%	18.7%
Am. Indian/Alaska Native	1.7	41.0%	2.9%	23.2%	4.9%	27.9%
Two or More Races	4.3	55.4%	3.6%	23.3%	3.6%	14.1%

Citizenship

U.S. citizen - native	230.5	61.6%	5.3%	15.5%	2.9%	14.6%
U.S. citizen - naturalized	12.3	61.0%	5.7%	9.0%	2.3%	22.0%
Non-U.S. citizen, resident for <6 years	5.4	35.6%	5.0%	12.1%	1.1%	46.3%
Non-U.S. citizen, resident for 6+ years	14.6	36.9%	3.7%	11.7%	1.3%	46.4%

Health Status

Excellent/Very Good	179.1	65.5%	5.9%	12.5%	1.5%	14.6%
Good	60.4	52.4%	4.3%	16.8%	2.9%	23.7%
Fair/Poor	23.2	34.3%	3.1%	29.1%	11.3%	22.2%

( ) = Estimate has a large 95% confidence interval of +/−5.0 − 7.9 percentage points. Estimates with larger margins of error or with standard errors greater than 30% are not provided.

Table 4

Health Insurance Coverage of Children, 2008

	Children (millions)	Percent Distribution by Coverage Type				
		Private		**Public**		**Uninsured**
		Employer	Individual	Medicaid	Other[h]	
Total - Children[f]	**78.7**	**54.4%**	**4.1%**	**29.7%**	**1.5%**	**10.3%**
Age						
<1	4.3	44.6%	2.7%	39.9%	1.9%	11.0%
1−5	21.0	51.6%	2.8%	35.6%	1.8%	8.3%
6−18	53.4	56.3%	4.7%	26.6%	1.4%	11.0%
Annual Family Income						
<$20,000	18.5	12.9%	3.0%	64.0%	1.4%	18.6%
$20,000−$39,999	14.3	32.5%	3.8%	46.9%	1.8%	14.9%
$40,000+	45.9	77.9%	4.6%	10.6%	1.5%	5.4%
Family Poverty Level[b]						
, 100%	19.3	13.2%	3.0%	64.3%	1.4%	18.1%
100−199%	15.6	34.7%	3.8%	44.9%	1.8%	14.8%
...100−149%	8.3	26.4%	3.3%	52.3%	1.8%	16.2%
...150−199%	7.3	44.2%	4.4%	36.4%	1.9%	13.1%
200−399%	22.4	72.3%	4.7%	13.8%	1.8%	7.4%
...200−299%	12.8	66.9%	4.6%	17.5%	1.7%	9.3%
...300−399%	9.6	79.5%	4.9%	8.8%	1.9%	4.9%
400%+	21.4	87.2%	4.6%	4.2%	1.2%	2.9%
Household Type[g]						
1 Parent with children[c]	19.4	33.2%	3.8%	50.5%	1.0%	11.4%
2 Parents with children[c]	52.4	66.0%	4.1%	20.1%	1.7%	8.0%
Multigenerational/Other with children[d]	6.1	25.2%	3.0%	47.5%	1.2%	23.1%
Family Work Status						
2 Full-time	22.5	78.5%	2.9%	11.3%	1.3%	6.1%
1 Full-time	41.1	55.3%	4.6%	28.5%	1.5%	10.1%
Only Part-time[e]	5.4	19.2%	5.8%	59.2%	2.0%	13.8%
Non-Workers	9.6	13.9%	4.0%	61.5%	1.9%	18.7%

(continued)

Table 4	Health Insurance Coverage of Children, 2008 (continued)					
Race/Ethnicity						
White only (non-Hispanic)	44.1	66.4%	5.4%	19.7%	1.5%	7.1%
Black only (non-Hispanic)	11.3	38.4%	2.2%	46.1%	2.0%	11.2%
Hispanic	17.2	33.7%	1.9%	45.4%	1.1%	17.9%
Asian/S. Pacific Islander	3.3	61.4%	4.7%	21.2%	---	11.5%
Am. Indian/Alaska Native	0.6	(36.0%)	---	---	---	(16.3%)
Two or More Races	2.2	52.3%	3.2%	34.6%	3.1%	6.8%
Citizenship						
U.S. citizen	76.3	55.1%	4.1%	29.8%	1.5%	9.4%
Non-U.S. citizen, resident for <6 years	1.1	(34.8%)	4.0%	28.6%	---	(31.3%)
Non-U.S. citizen, resident for 6+ years	1.3	24.9%	3.2%	26.7%	---	(44.8%)
Health Status						
Excellent/Very Good	63.9	58.7%	4.4%	26.1%	1.5%	9.3%
Good	13.0	36.9%	2.8%	44.0%	1.5%	14.7%
Fair/Poor	1.7	26.9%	2.2%	58.9%	---	10.7%

( ) = Estimate has a large 95% confidence interval of +/−5.0 − 7.9 percentage points. Estimates with larger margins of error or with standard errors greater than 30% are not provided.

• • • References

1. KCMU/Urban Institute analysis of 2009 ASEC Supplement to the CPS. More information on uninsured young adults is in the following report: Schwartz K and T Schwartz. 2008 "Uninsured Young Adults: A Profile and Overview of Coverage Options," Kaiser Commission on Medicaid and the Uninsured (#7785 June). Available at: http://www.kff.org/uninsured/7785.cfm.

2. National Center for Health Statistics. 2008. *Summary Health Statistics for the U.S. Population: National Health Interview Survey, 2007.*

3. Davidoff AJ and G Kenney. 2005. *Uninsured Americans with Chronic Health Conditions: Key Findings from the National Health Interview Survey.* Available at: http://www.urban.org/publications/411161.html.

4. Marks C, T Schwartz, and L Donaldson. 2009. "State Variation and Health Reform: A Chartbook". Kaiser Commission on Medicaid and the Uninsured. (#7942: July).

5. Hadley J. 2007. "Insurance Coverage, Medical Care Use, and Short-term Health Changes Following an Unintentional Injury or the Onset of a Chronic Condition." *JAMA* 297(10):1073-84.

6. Institute of Medicine. 2002. *Health Insurance is a Family Matter.* Washington, DC.

7. Institute of Medicine. 2009. *America's Uninsured Crisis, Consequences for Health and Health Care.* Washington, DC: National Academies Press. p. 60-63.

8. Haley J and S Zuckerman. 2003. *Is Lack of Coverage a Short-Term or Chronic Condition?* Kaiser Commission on Medicaid and the Uninsured (#4122; June).

9. NewsHour with Jim Lehrer/Kaiser Family Foundation National Survey on the Uninsured. March 2003.

10. Ayanian J et al. 2000. "Unmet Health Needs of Uninsured Adults in the United States." *JAMA* 284(16):2061-9.

11. Roetzheim R et al. 2000. "Effects of Health Insurance and Race on Colorectal Cancer Treatments and Outcomes." *American Journal of Public Health* 90(11):1746-54.

12. Hadley J. 2003. "Sicker and Poorer—The Consequences of Being Uninsured." *MCRR* 60(2): 3-76.

13. Canto J et al. 2000. "Payer Status and the Utilization of Hospital Resources in Acute Myocardial Infarction." *Arch Intern Med* 160(6):817-23.

14. Doyle JJ. 2005. "Health Insurance, Treatment, and Outcomes: Using Auto Accidents as Health Shocks." *Review of Economics and Statistics* 87:256-270.

15. Baker D et al. 2001. "Lack of Health Insurance and Decline in Overall Health in Late Middle Age." *New England Journal of Medicine* 345(15): 1106-12.

16. IOM, 2009. p. 82.

17. Hoffman C and K Schwartz. 2008. "Trends in Access to Care Among Working-Age Adults, 1997-2006." Kaiser Commission on Medicaid and the Uninsured (#7824; October).

18. Hoffman C and K Schwartz. 2008. "Eroding Access Among Nonelderly U.S. Adults with Chronic Conditions: Ten Years of Change." *Health Affairs* 27(5):w340-8 (published online July 22, 2008).

19. Hadley J, et al. 2008.

20. Hadley J, et al. 2008.

21. Hadley J, et al. 2008.

22. Hadley J, et al. 2008.

23. Cunningham P and JH May. 2006. *A Growing Hole in the Safety Net: Physician Charity Care Declines Again.* Center for Studying Health Systems Change Tracking Report.

24. National Association of Public Hospitals and Health Systems. 2009. *2007 Annual Survey Results Highlight the Importance of the Nation's Safety Net Hospitals and Health Systems.* Research Brief, May/June 2009.

25. Hadley J, M Cravens, T Coughlin, J Holahan. 2005. *Federal Spending on the Health Care Safety Net from 2001-2004: Has Spending Kept Pace with the Growth in the Uninsured?* Kaiser Commission on Medicaid and the Uninsured (#7425; November).

26. Hadley J, et al. 2008.

2

Trends in the Health Status of Medicare Risk Contract Enrollees

Source: Riley, G. and C. Zarabozo. 2006-2007. Trends in the Health Status of Medicare Risk Contract Enrollees. *Health Care Financing Review* 28 (2): 81–95.

Previous research has found Medicare risk contract enrollees to be healthier than beneficiaries in fee-for-service (FFS). Medicare Current Beneficiary Survey (MCBS) data were used to examine trends in health and functional status measures among risk contract and FFS enrollees from 1991 to 2004. Risk contract enrollees reported better health and functioning, but the differences tended to narrow over time. Most of the differences in trends were observed for functional status measures and institutionalization; differences in trends for perceived health status and prevalence rates of chronic conditions tended to be small or non-existent. The narrowing of functional and health status differences between the risk contract and FFS populations may have implications for payment policy, as well as implications for the role of private health plans in Medicare.

INTRODUCTION

Medicare's risk contracting program has been operational since 1985, following passage of the Tax Equity and Fiscal Responsibility Act of 1982 (TEFRA). Under TEFRA, risk contracts were entered into by health maintenance organizations (HMOs), which received capitation payments in return for providing covered services to their enrollees. The program was designed to produce cost savings for Medicare, as well as to expand the range of health plan choices available to Medicare beneficiaries (Brown et al., 1993). Risk-based plans were not available in all parts of the U.S., but tended to be concentrated in particular urban areas, where Medicare FFS expenditures (the basis of payment under risk contracts) were relatively high. The ability of risk-based plans to provide the Medicare benefit package for less than the level of expenditures in FFS enabled the plans to offer extra benefits and lower out-of-pocket costs, resulting in their ability to attract enrollees. Other factors also played a part in the extent to which Medicare plans attracted enrollment (Brown and Gold, 1999).

Legislative History

Congress has attempted to improve and expand Medicare's risk contracting program on several occasions, notably through the 1997 Balanced Budget Act (BBA) and the 2003 Medicare Modernization Act (MMA). One goal of each of these laws was to expand the availability of plans to rural areas and

Gerald Riley is with the Centers for Medicare & Medicaid Services (CMS). Carlos Zarabozo is an independent consultant. The statements expressed in this article are those of the authors and do not necessarily reflect the views or policies of CMS.

to other areas that did not have risk plans available to Medicare beneficiaries. The BBA created the Medicare+Choice program, which expanded the types of health plans permitted to enter into risk contracts to include preferred provider organizations (PPOs), provider-sponsored organizations, and private FFS plans. It also significantly changed the payment formula, including the phased introduction of a new risk adjustor. The BBA also introduced a payment floor for risk-based plans which resulted in health plan payment rates doubling in some counties. Further payment changes and expansions in plan types were made in subsequent legislation, including the 2000 Benefits Improvement and Protection Act (BIPA), which introduced a payment floor applicable to metropolitan statistical areas.

The MMA created the Medicare Advantage (MA) program and introduced two new types of plans—regional and special needs plans (SNPs). Regional plans were intended to be the means by which every part of the country would have a Medicare private health plan available; such plans have to be offered on a region-wide basis, among the 26 designated regions. By contrast, local plans can operate in an area as small as a single county. SNPs are unique in that they may limit their enrollment to certain categories of Medicare beneficiaries—those with special needs. Special needs beneficiaries include Medicare/Medicaid dual eligibles, the institutionalized, and those with chronic or disabling conditions. However, the SNP restricted enrollment provision sunsets at the end of 2008. That is, unless Congress extends the provision, after 2008 SNPs may not limit their enrollment to only individuals with special needs.

Because the MMA added outpatient prescription drug coverage as a voluntary choice available to all Medicare beneficiaries, risk-based plans lost a feature that many Medicare beneficiaries found attractive in contrast to the traditional FFS program. However, MA plans are able to use savings they generate in covering Medicare Parts A and B benefits to reduce their premiums for the Part D (drug) benefit and/or increase the generosity of the Part D benefit. Presumably, health plans should generally be able to provide the drug benefit at a lower cost than stand-alone prescription drug plans because of their ability to coordinate drug coverage with other health care coverage through the same network of providers.

The MMA also authorized the comparative cost adjustment program. Beginning in 2010 and authorized for 6 years, the program calls for the Medicare FFS program to compete against private plans in certain areas. The premium for traditional FFS Medicare will be adjusted to reflect its costs in relation to private health plans available in the area (as opposed to the current situation in which the Medicare FFS premium is uniform throughout the country).

Enrollment History

Medicare managed care enrollment grew rapidly throughout the 1990s, increasing from 1.8 million beneficiaries in 1990 to 6.7 million in 1999 (Centers for Medicare & Medicaid Services, 2005). Almost all of this increase was in risk-based plans. Enrollment decreased thereafter to 5.0 million beneficiaries in 2003, following widespread plan withdrawals and service area reductions in 1998-2002. Total managed care enrollment recovered to 6.1 million by December 2005 (Centers for Medicare & Medicaid Services, 2006), corresponding to increases in plan payments and other changes brought about by MMA as previously described.

Health Status in the Risk Program

Since its inception, Medicare's risk contracting program has contained an atypical mix of beneficiaries. Studies of enrollment patterns have found disproportionately few enrollees from vulnerable subgroups, such as disabled beneficiaries under age 65, beneficiaries age 85 or over, dual eligibles, and institutionalized individuals (Zarabozo et al., 1996; Riley et al., 1996; Murgolo, 2002). In addition, Medicare risk-based plans have been found to have relatively healthy populations according to a variety of health-related measures, including pre-enrollment costs, self-reported health and functional status measures, demographic factors, and mortality (Hellinger, 1995; Riley et al., 1996; Physician Payment Review Commission, 1996; Morgan et al., 1997; Call et al., 1999; Greenwald, Levy, and Ingber, 2000; Hellinger and Wong, 2000; Maciejewski et al., 2001; Mello et al., 2003). The health status of risk contract enrollees is of special policy concern because favorable selection may have led to overpayments under Medicare's capitation system (Brown et al., 1993; Riley et al., 1996). Such overpayments can arise if capitation payments do not account for the health status of plan members. In response to such payment concerns, a risk-adjustment system based on diagnoses has been developed to more appropriately match payments to enrollee health status (Pope et al., 2004). Risk adjustment is also meant to increase the viability of plans that serve vulnerable populations, thus safeguarding beneficiary access to appropriate care.

The health and functional status of Medicare's risk contract enrollees are also of interest as a measure of the risk program's appeal to vulnerable subpopulations. Individuals in poor health have complex health care needs and frequently have high out-of-pocket costs (Crystal et al., 2000). The Medicare managed care program may benefit many of these individuals through savings in out-of-pocket costs, improvements in coverage, and coordination of care.

The purpose of this study was to examine trends in the health and functional status of risk contract enrollees, in comparison to FFS. Several factors may have significantly influenced the mix of beneficiaries enrolled in risk-based plans. Such factors include the growth and subsequent decline in number of participating plans and in level of enrollment; legislative and regulatory developments in both the managed care and FFS sectors of Medicare; and changes in the managed care market, including the non-Medicare market. The implementation of risk-adjusted payments may have removed some of the disincentives for risk-based plans to enroll chronically ill people, which could result in a trend toward worse health status within the risk contract sector. The growth of SNPs may also have increased the number of chronically ill beneficiaries enrolled under risk contracts in recent years. It is notable that most studies of enrollee health status were based on data from the mid-1990s or earlier, before major legislative changes and plan withdrawals took place. This analysis used data from the MCBS and covers the years 1991-2004. The MCBS contains a variety of health and functional status measures that are not available in Medicare administrative records.

DATA AND METHODS

Data

The MCBS is a longitudinal, multipurpose survey of a nationally representative sample of the Medicare population (Adler, 1994). It has been conducted by CMS (formerly the Health Care Financing Administration) continuously since 1991. The survey employs a rotating panel design, with each panel consisting of about 4,000 respondents who participate in 12 interviews that produce data for three complete calendar years. The sample includes individuals residing in longterm care facilities, defined as nursing homes, retirement homes, domiciliary or personal care facilities, distinct long-term units in a hospital complex, mental health facilities and centers, assisted and foster care homes, and institutions for the mentally retarded and developmentally disabled (Centers for Medicare & Medicaid Services, 2006). A supplemental sample of HMO enrollees was added to the survey in 1996-1998.

Respondents are asked about perceived health status, difficulties with six activities of daily living (ADLs) and six instrumental activities of daily living (IADLs), and whether a doctor has ever told them they have 20 specific conditions. Information on demographics, income (reported in $5,000 intervals on the Access to Care Files), and supplemental health insurance is also collected. Medicare administrative records are routinely linked to survey information. This study used MCBSAccess to Care Files, which contain survey information collected in the fall round (September-December) of each year.

Methods

For each study year, Medicare administrative records were used to identify respondents in risk-based plans (including demonstration projects) and in FFS at the time of the fall round interview. Beneficiaries enrolled in plans with cost-based contracts were excluded from the study, as were any respondents who were not entitled to Medicare Parts A and B. Descriptive statistics on demographic, health, and functional status measures were computed separately for the risk contract and FFS samples for each year, using MCBS cross-sectional weights. These weights reflect the design of MCBS and represent the total Medicare population. Some measures are limited to the non-institutionalized population because of data limitations on institutionalized respondents.

Findings on health and functional status measures are presented graphically to highlight trends for the risk contract and FFS populations. In order to test whether trends were significantly different for the two populations, observations were pooled across the study years and regression models were estimated with individual health and functional status measures as the dependent variables. Because all measures were dichotomous, logistic regression models were used. Independent variables were year (entered as a continuous variable with values from 1 to 14); enrollment status (1 = risk contract enrollee, 0 = FFS); and an interaction term (YEAR X ENROLLMENT). If the coefficient for the interaction term was significantly different from 0 there was a difference in trends between the risk contract and FFS populations. Standard errors of the regression coefficients were adjusted using a method developed by Bye et al. (1994), which accounts for the MCBS complex sampling design, as well as the panel nature of the survey (i.e., individuals could contribute multiple observations). Regression models were estimated using MCBS cross-sectional weights.

Trends in health and functional status could be strongly influenced by demographic changes, e.g., the aging of the risk contract population. In order to detect differences in health status trends that were not attributable to demographic shifts, we estimated an additional set of regression models that incorporated age-sex covariates. In these models, a statistically significant interaction term between year and enrollment indicated a difference in trends between the risk contract and FFS populations that was independent of changes in age and sex. In general, age and sex adjustment did not have a strong effect on the findings related to differences in trends.

RESULTS

The demographic mix of the risk contract population has changed over time (Table 1). Females age 85 or over represented only 4.7 percent of risk contract enrollees in 1991, but accounted for 8.3 percent by 2004. The percent of risk contract enrollees who were female under age 65 remained relatively stable, but there was a large increase in this group in FFS. Medicaid enrollment increased substantially in the risk contract sector from 4.3 percent of risk contract enrollees in 1991 to 11.3 percent in 2004. Medicaid enrollment was measured from both self reports and from Medicare administrative records, which identify buy-in beneficiaries, i.e., those for whom a State pays the Medicare Part B premium.

Table 1	Trends in Demographic Characteristics of the Medicare Risk Contract and Fee-for-Service (FFS) Populations: 1991–2004							
	1991		**1995**		**2000**		**2004**	
Characteristic	Risk Contract	FFS	Risk Contract	FFS	Risk Contract	FFS	Risk Contract	FFS
N	380	11,786	1,140	13,618	2,717	13,050	1,895	12,912
				Percent				
Age and Sex	100.0	100.0	100.0	100.0	100.0	100.0	100.0	100.0
Male								
<65 Years	2.3	5.7*	2.4	6.6*	4.0	7.7*	4.3	8.0*
65–74 Years	25.0	21.2	24.9	19.8*	23.1	18.2*	17.2	18.7
75–84 Years	13.0	11.8	13.0	12.7	13.3	13.3	15.1	13.3
85 Years or Over	2.2	2.8	3.0	3.1	2.6	3.5*	3.3	3.7
Female								
<65 Years	2.4	3.5*	2.4	4.6*	2.8	6.3*	3.3	7.5*
65–74 Years	30.5	27.5	29.2	25.2*	27.4	22.9*	26.8	21.6*
75–84 Years	20.0	19.7	19.4	19.6	20.1	19.8	21.7	18.8*
85 Years or Over	4.7	7.7*	5.7	8.3*	6.6	8.4*	8.3	8.4
Race	100.0	100.0	100.0	100.0	100.0	100.0	100.0	100.0
White	82.9	88.5*	87.0	88.1	84.8	86.6	83.4	84.5
Black	12.3	8.8	7.4	9.1	9.6	9.2	9.7	9.8
Other[1]	4.8	2.7	5.6	2.9*	5.6	4.2*	6.9	5.8
Medicaid[2]	100.0	100.0	100.0	100.0	100.0	100.0	100.0	100.0
Yes	4.3	14.8*	4.5	17.3*	5.9	18.4*	11.3	20.1*
No	95.7	85.2*	95.5	82.7*	94.1	81.6*	88.7	79.9*
Census Region[3]	100.0	100.0	100.0	100.0	100.0	100.0	100.0	100.0
Northeast	6.0	22.8*	11.9	22.1*	21.7	20.0	24.2	19.1
Midwest	14.1	24.8*	7.8	26.3*	15.3	25.8*	9.6	25.4*
South	20.7	36.0*	22.2	37.3*	23.3	39.8*	22.3	39.5*
West	59.2	16.4*	58.1	14.3*	39.7	14.4*	44.0	15.9*

*p < 0.05 for difference between risk contract and FFS.
[1] Includes individuals reporting more than one race.
[2] Medicaid enrollment was defined from self reports and from administrative data on State buy-ins.
[3] Excludes Puerto Rico.
Notes: Includes beneficiaries entitled to Parts A and B. Enrollees in cost contract plans are excluded.
All percents are weighted.

Source: Centers for Medicare & Medicaid Services: Data from the Medicare Current Beneficiary Survey Access to Care Files. 2004.

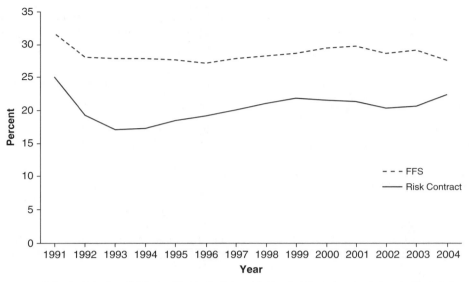

Notes: Includes beneficiaries entitled to Parts A and B. Enrollees in cost contract plans are excluded.

Figure 1 Percent of Non-Institutionalized Medicare Beneficiaries Who Reported Fair or Poor Heath, by Risk Contract and Fee-for-Service (FFS) Sector: 1991-2004. *Source:* Centers for Medicare & Medicaid Services: Data from the Medicare Current Beneficiary Survey Access to Care Files.

There was a strong regional shift in risk contract enrollment to the Northeast, from 6.0 percent in 1991 to 24.2 percent in 2004 (Table 1). The percent of risk contract enrollees residing in the West decreased during this period from 59.2 to 44.0 percent. During this extensive geographic shift, risk-based plans remained primarily an urban program. The percent of risk contract enrollees residing in non-metropolitan areas remained under 4.5 percent for all years (data not shown in tables).

Health and Functional Status

Non-institutionalized risk contract enrollees were significantly less likely to report fair or poor health than non-institutionalized beneficiaries in FFS (Figure 1 and Table 2). Risk contract enrollees reported lower rates of fair or poor health in each study year, with the difference between the two groups varying between 5.3 and 10.8 percent. The difference narrowed slightly over time; in the regression model the interaction between year and risk contract enrollment was positive and approached statistical significance ($p = 0.052$).

Prevalence rates for five relatively common and costly conditions are summarized in Figures 2-5 and Table 2. Risk contract enrollees reported significantly lower rates of heart disease than beneficiaries in FFS, with no significant difference in trends between the two groups. Cancer was less frequently reported by risk contract enrollees early in the study period, but was more frequently reported than in FFS after 1998;

the difference in trends was highly significant. Levels of diabetes were somewhat lower among risk contract enrollees early on, but rates were similar in risk-based plans and FFS after 1996, with both increasing over time. The increase in diabetes prevalence was marginally greater in risk-based plans than in FFS ($p = 0.051$). Reported rates of emphysema/asthma/chronic obstructive pulmonary disease, and stroke were non-significantly lower among risk contract enrollees and there were no differences in trends between the risk contract and FFS sectors.

Risk contract enrollees were significantly less likely to report any difficulties with IADLs and ADLs than beneficiaries in FFS (Figures 6-7 and Table 2). They were also less likely to report more than two IADL or ADL difficulties, which is a measure of greater frailty. The percents of risk contract enrollees reporting functional difficulties moved closer to FFS levels over the study period and approached some FFS levels in 2004. In the regression models the interactions between year and risk contract enrollment were positive and significant, indicating a significant narrowing of differences between the risk contract and FFS sectors (Table 2).

Rates of institutionalization among risk contract enrollees were one-half or less than those in FFS throughout the study period (Figure 8). In the FFS sector the rate of institutionalization decreased throughout much of the study period, whereas the rate generally increased among risk contract enrollees. The difference in trends was highly significant (Table 2). Adjusting for age and sex attenuated

| Table 2 | Results of Weighted Logistic Regressions for Trends in Health and Functional Status Differences Between Risk Contract and Fee-for-Service Enrollees: 1992–2004 |

	Independent Variables					
	Year		Risk Contract Enrollee		Year×Risk Contract Enrollee	
Dependent Variable	Coefficient	Standard Error	Coefficient	Standard Error	Coefficient	Standard Error
Fair/Poor Health	−0.0005	0.0021	−0.5568	0.0711***	0.0145	0.0075
Heart Disease[1]	−0.0062	0.0027*	−0.1934	0.0853*	0.0038	0.0090
Cancer[2]	−0.0023	0.0029	−0.2821	0.0929**	0.0320	0.0096***
Diabetes	0.0284	0.0030***	−0.2004	0.0990*	0.0195	0.0100
Emphysema/Asthma/COPD	0.0132	0.0031***	−0.0829	0.1064	−0.0102	0.0110
Stroke	0.0168	0.0035***	−0.1852	0.1134	0.0019	0.0117
Any IADL Difficulty	−0.0068	0.0020***	−0.4638	0.0646***	0.0145	0.0068*
GT 2 IADL Difficulties	−0.0054	0.0025*	−0.6708	0.0935***	0.0340	0.0098***
Any ADL Difficulty[3]	−0.0015	0.0022	−0.4499	0.0695***	0.0220	0.0073**
GT 2 ADL Difficulties[3]	−0.0079	0.0031*	−0.6233	0.1048***	0.0296	0.0109**
Institutionalized	−0.0135	0.0036***	−1.9512	0.2309***	0.0802	0.0226***

*$p < 0.05$

**$p < 0.01$

***$p < 0.001$

[1] Measure does not include other heart conditions such as congestive heart failure, problems with valves of the heart, or problems with rhythm of heartbeat.

[2] Measure does not include skin cancer.

[3] Data on ADL difficulties were not available for 1991.

Notes: Includes beneficiaries entitled to Parts A and B. Enrollees in cost contract plans are excluded. GT is greater than. COPD is chronic obstructive pulmonary disease. IADL is instrumental activities of daily living. ADL is activities of daily living.

Source: Centers for Medicare & Medicaid Services: Data from the Medicare Current Beneficiary Survey Access to Care Files.

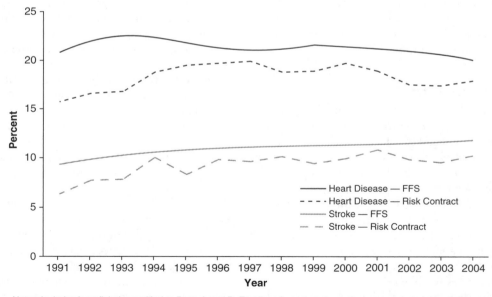

Notes: Includes beneficiaries entitled to Parts A and B. Enrollees in cost contract plans are excluded. Heart disease measure does not include other heart conditions such as congestive heart failure, problems with valves of the heart, or problems with rhythm of heartbeat.

Figure 2 Percent of Non-Institutionalized Medicare Beneficiaries Who Reported a History of Heart Attack/Angina/Coronary Heart Disease, or Stroke, by Risk Contract and Fee-for-Service (FFS) Sector: 1991-2004. *Source:* Centers for Medicare & Medicaid Services: Data from the Medicare Current Beneficiary Survey Access to Care Files.

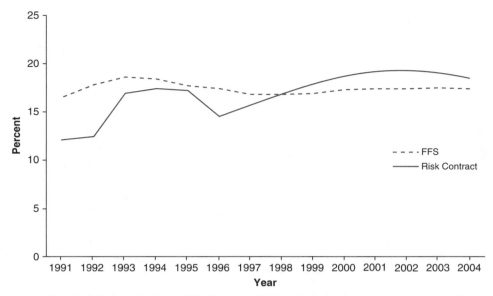

Notes: Includes beneficiaries entitled to Parts A and B. Enrollees in cost contract plans are excluded. Measure does not include skin cancer.

Figure 3 Percent of Non-Institutionalized Medicare Beneficiaries Who Reported a History of Cancer, by Risk Contract and Fee-for-Service (FFS) Sector: 1991-2004. *Source:* Centers for Medicare & Medicaid Services: Data from the Medicare Current Beneficiary Survey Access to Care Files.

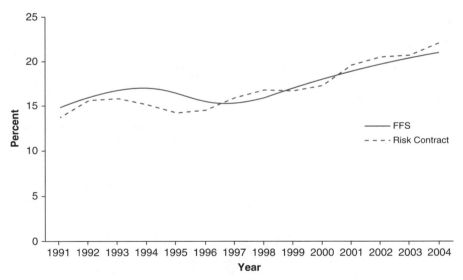

Notes: Includes beneficiaries entitled to Parts A and B. Enrollees in cost contract plans are excluded.

Figure 4 Percent of Non-Institutionalized Medicare Beneficiaries Who Reported a History of Diabetes, by Risk Contract and Fee-for-Service (FFS) Sector: 1991-2004. *Source:* Centers for Medicare & Medicaid Services: Data from the Medicare Current Beneficiary Survey Access to Care Files.

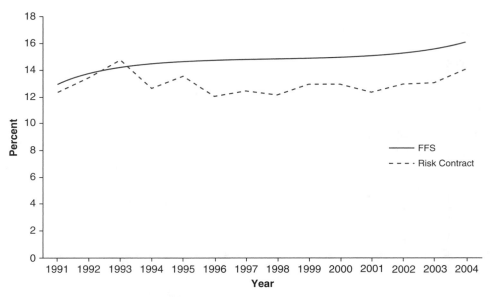

Notes: Includes beneficiaries entitled to Parts A and B. Enrollees in cost contract plans are excluded. COPD is chronic obstructive pulmonary disease.

Figure 5 Percent of Non-Institutionalized Medicare Beneficiaries Who Reported a History of Emphysema/Asthma/COPD, by Risk Contract and Fee-for-Service (FFS) Sector: 1991-2004. *Source:* Centers for Medicare & Medicaid Services: Data from the Medicare Current Beneficiary Survey Access to Care Files.

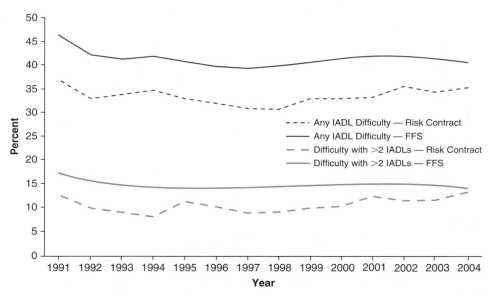

Notes: Includes beneficiaries entitled to Parts A and B. Enrollees in cost contract plans are excluded.

Figure 6 Percent of Non-Institutionalized Medicare Beneficiaries Who Reported Difficulties with Instrumental Activities of Daily Living (IADL), by Risk Contract and Fee-for-Service (FFS) Sector: 1991-2004. *Source:* Centers for Medicare & Medicaid Services: Data from the Medicare Current Beneficiary Survey Access to Care Files.

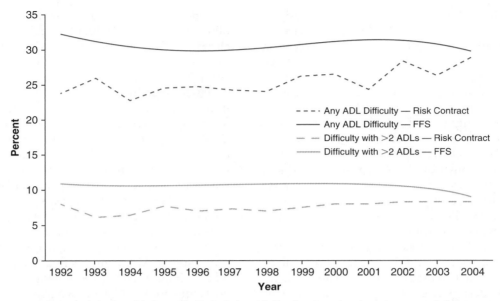

Notes: Includes beneficiaries entitled to Parts A and B. Enrollees in cost contract plans are excluded.

Figure 7 Percent of Non-Institutionalized Medicare Beneficiaries Who Reported Difficulties with Activities of Daily Living (ADL), by Risk Contract and Fee-for-Service (FFS) Sector: 1992-2004. *Source:* Centers for Medicare & Medicaid Services: Data from the Medicare Current Beneficiary Survey Access to Care Files.

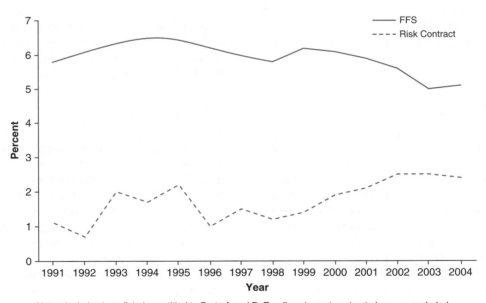

Notes: Includes beneficiaries entitled to Parts A and B. Enrollees in cost contract plans are excluded.

Figure 8 Percent of Medicare Beneficiaries Who Are Institutionalized, by Risk Contract and Fee-for-Service (FFS) Sector: 1991-2004. *Source:* Centers for Medicare & Medicaid Services: Data from the Medicare Current Beneficiary Survey Access to Care Files.

somewhat the differences in trends for IADLs, ADLs, and institutionalization, but the differences in trends remained statistically significant (with the exception of any IADL difficulty) after incorporation of age and sex covariates in the regression models.

Trends in enrollee health status may be strongly influenced by the growth in risk-based plans that target chronically ill and frail beneficiaries. Such plans include Programs of All-Inclusive Care for the Elderly (PACE), Evercare plans that target the institutionalized population, SNPs, social HMOs, and various demonstration projects focusing on disease management, dual eligibles, etc. Although enrollment in such plans comprises only a small portion of total risk contract enrollment, there has been significant growth in this area over the last several years. In order to evaluate the impact of this subset of plans on our findings, we re-estimated the regression models after excluding enrollees in plans that target chronically ill and frail beneficiaries. These exclusions varied from 1 percent of enrollees in 1992-1996 to 5 percent of enrollees in 2004. The exclusion of enrollees from selected plans resulted in some attenuation of the trend differences between risk contract and FFS enrollees in the area of functional status. However, most of these trends continued to show some significant narrowing of the difference between the risk contract and FFS sectors over time.

DISCUSSION

As Medicare's risk contracting program has matured, the characteristics of the enrolled population have evolved. The health and functional status of risk contract enrollees has become more similar to that of beneficiaries in FFS, although risk contract enrollees continue to report more favorable health over several domains. Most of the differences in trends were observed for functional status measures and institutionalization; differences in trends for perceived health status and prevalence rates of chronic conditions tended to be small or non-existent, with the exception of cancer. Part of the difference in trends for functional status and institutionalization was attributable to the aging of the risk contract population, but we found a narrowing of differences between the risk contract and FFS sectors even after controlling for age and sex.

The narrowing of functional and health status differences between the two populations may have implications for payment policy. The principal in-patient diagnostic cost group model (implemented in 2000), and the CMS hierarchical condition categories (HCC) model (implemented in 2004) adjusted capitation payments to reflect the health status of enrollees in risk-based plans. The adjustments were designed to reduce payment distortions resulting from biased selection, remove disincentives for plans to enroll and retain beneficiaries with chronic illnesses, and improve the viability of plans that enrolled significant numbers of such beneficiaries. Recent trends in enrollee health status may in part reflect the impact of risk-adjustment policies. The current CMS-HCC model incorporates diagnoses established through physician and hospital encounters, as well as demographic factors (Pope et al., 2004). It does not contain explicit measures of functional status. Although this model represents a significant improvement over previous risk adjusters, it does not capture all expected costs associated with risk contract enrollees. Any narrowing of differences between the risk contract and FFS sectors, particularly in the area of functional status, may result in more appropriate payments to risk-based plans to the extent that risk adjustment becomes less important. It should be noted, however, that risk adjustment is implemented on a plan-specific basis and is designed to account for health status differences among plans, and not only overall differences between the risk contract and FFS sectors. We were unable to address plan-by-plan patterns of health status or their corresponding trends, due to sample size limitations.

Several factors may be responsible for the growing similarity of the risk contract and FFS populations. As previously noted, the emergence of PACE, Evercare, SNPs, and various demonstration projects has expanded the target population for managed care to specifically include frail and chronically ill beneficiaries. Although enrollment in such plans is small, it is growing and appears to be affecting the composition of the Medicare risk contract population.

The expansions and contractions of the Medicare managed care market may have influenced the composition of the enrolled population. During expansion in the 1990s, a large percentage of risk contract enrollees tended to be recent joiners, who may be healthier than long-term enrollees because of regression toward the mean (Welch, 1985; Riley, Rabey, and Kasper, 1989). During market contraction (1998-2002), there were fewer new enrollees and the health status of the remaining long-term enrollees may have been more similar to that of beneficiaries in FFS.

Geographic factors may also have affected the composition of the risk contract population. The percent of beneficiaries with access to a Medicare managed care plan has changed considerably over time (Centers for Medicare & Medicaid Services, 2006), and our findings show there has been a marked interregional shift in enrollment. Health status has also been shown to vary significantly among geographic areas within the U.S. (Blumberg, 1987). Changes in the geographic distribution of the risk contract enrollees over time may have resulted in higher enrollments from areas tending to exhibit worse health.

Lastly, trends in the health and functional status of risk contract enrollees could be attributable in part to the effects of managed care on access to and quality of care.

Many studies have examined quality of care in managed care plans, and findings have been mixed (Miller and Luft, 1997; 2002). It was beyond the scope of this study to address whether observed health status differences between the risk contract and FFS populations were due to beneficiary selection or to sector effects.

Several vulnerable subpopulations, such as the very old, the dually eligible, and the institutionalized have grown as a proportion of risk contract population over time. The recent increase in Medicaid enrollment within the risk contract population could be related to outreach efforts begun in 1999 to enroll eligible individuals into Medicare savings programs, which provide various levels of Medicaid benefits (Haber et al., 2003). Managed care may be attractive to dual eligibles with less than full Medicaid benefits because it tends to reduce their out-of-pocket costs.

Disabled beneficiaries under age 65 continue to be underrepresented in risk-based plans. This may reflect reluctance on the part of these beneficiaries to sever ties with their own network of providers that they rely on for their care. The high percentage of disabled beneficiaries with dual eligibility also may continue to depress their levels of risk contract enrollment.

Some limitations should be noted: First, risk contract sample sizes tended to be small in the early years of the analysis, producing some instability in the estimates. Second, the health and functional status measures analyzed herein are relatively crude and do not distinguish levels of severity for chronic conditions. Survey-based measures of this type are not well suited to identifying the sickest individuals, who account for a very high percentage of total Medicare expenditures (Mello et al., 2003). It was therefore not possible to determine whether there has been a change in the proportion of very sick and high cost individuals within the risk contract population. Lastly, as previously noted the study did not have sufficient sample size to address plan-by-plan differences in enrollee characteristics.

Enrollment in risk-based plans has increased in recent months (Centers for Medicare & Medicaid Services, 2006) following recent improvements in benefits, cost sharing, and premiums (Achman and Harris, 2005). If enrollment continues to increase as expected under the MMA, it is unclear how the composition of the risk contract population will evolve. The recent growth in SNPs, focusing on individuals who are institutionalized, dually eligible, and/or have severe or disabling chronic conditions, may produce a more chronically ill risk contract population. On the other hand, a large influx of new enrollees, particularly in areas that previously did not have access to risk contracts, may produce a relatively healthy case mix, as happened early in the risk contracting program. The creation of regional PPOs may also affect the case mix of the risk contract population. Moreover, the introduction of the Part D drug benefit has radically altered the nature of choices Medicare beneficiaries face with regard to their health insurance options and may significantly affect selection into risk contracts. If the traditional FFS Medicare Program will one day be competing with private plans, each Medicare beneficiary should have a private plan option that is suitable for their needs. The narrowing of differences in health and functional status between the two sectors would indicate that private health plans are becoming an accepted choice for vulnerable populations. Continued monitoring of enrollee health status will be essential to understanding the long-term impacts of the MA program.

ACKNOWLEDGMENT

The authors wish to thank Brigid Goody and Al Esposito for their helpful comments on earlier versions of this manuscript.

Reprint Requests

Gerald Riley, Centers for Medicare & Medicaid Services, 7500 Security Boulevard, C3-20-17, Baltimore, MD 21244-1850. E-mail: gerald.riley@cms.hhs.gov.

● ● ● **References**

Achman, L. and Harris, L.: *Early Effects of the Medicare Modernization Act: Benefits, Cost Sharing, and Premiums of Medicare Advantage Plans, 2005.* AARP, Washington, DC. April 2005.

Adler, G.: A Profile of the Medicare Current Beneficiary Survey. *Health Care Financing Review* 15(4):153-163, Summer 1994.

Blumberg, M.S.: Inter-Area Variations in Age-Adjusted Health Status. *Medical Care* 25(4):340-353, April 1987.

Brown, R.S., Clement D.G., Hill, J.W., et al.: Do Health Maintenance Organizations Work for Medicare? *Health Care Financing Review* 15(1):7-23, Fall 1993.

Brown, R.S. and Gold, M.R.: What Drives Medicare Managed Care Growth? *Health Affairs* 18(6):140-149, November/December 1999.

Bye, B.V., Dykacz, J.M., and Gallicchio, S.J.: *Covariance Estimates for Regression Parameters from Complex Sample Designs.* Office of Research and Statistics, Working Paper Series Number 62. Social Security Administration, Baltimore, MD. September 1994.

Call, K.T., Dowd, B., Feldman, R., et al.: Selection Experiences in Medicare HMOs: Pre-Enrollment Expenditures. *Health Care Financing Review* 20(4):197-209, Summer 1999.

Centers for Medicare & Medicaid Services: Internet address: www.cms.hhs.gov. (Accessed 2006.)

Centers for Medicare & Medicaid Services: Medicare & Medicaid Statistical Supplement, 2003. *Health Care Financing Review,* February 2005.

Crystal, S., Johnson, R.W., Harman, J., et al.: Out-of-Pocket Health Care Costs Among Older Americans. *Journal of Gerontology: Social Sciences* 55B(1): S51S62, January 2000.

Greenwald, L.M., Levy, J.M., and Ingber, M.J.: Favorable Selection in the Medicare+Choice Program: New Evidence. *Health Care Financing Review* 21(3):127-134, Spring 2000.

Haber, S.G., Adamache, W., Walsh, E.G., et al.: *Evaluation of Qualified Medicare Beneficiary (QMB) and Specified Low-Income Medicare Beneficiary Programs.* Final Report prepared for CMS under Contract Number 500-95-0058. RTI International, Waltham, MA. October 2003.

Hellinger, F.J.: Selection Bias in HMOs and PPOs: A Review of the Evidence. *Inquiry* 32(2):135-142. Summer 1995.

Hellinger, F.J. and Wong, H.S.: Selection Bias in HMOs: A Review of the Evidence. *Medicare Care Research and Review* 57(4):405-439, December 2000.

Maciejewski, M.L., Dowd, B., Call, K.T., et al.: Comparing Mortality and Time Until Death for Medicare HMO and FFS Beneficiaries. *Health Services Research* 35(6):1245-1265, February 2001.

Mello, M.M., Stearns, S.C., Norton, E.C., et al.: Understanding Biased Selection in Medicare HMOs. *Health Services Research* 38(3):961-992, June 2003.

Miller, R.H. and Luft, H.S.: Does Managed Care Lead to Better or Worse Quality of Care? *Health Affairs* 16(5):7-25, September/October 1997.

Miller, R.H. and Luft, H.S.: HMO Plan Performance Update: An Analysis of the Literature, 1997-2001. *Health Affairs* 21(4):63-86, July/August 2002.

Morgan, R.O., Virnig, B.A., DeVito, C.A., et al.: The Medicare-HMO Revolving Door—The Healthy Go In and the Sick Go Out. *New England Journal of Medicine* 337(3):169-175, July 1997.

Murgolo, M.S.: Comparison of Medicare Risk HMO and FFS Enrollees. *Health Care Financing Review* 24(1):177-185, Fall 2002.

Physician Payment Review Commission: *Annual Report to Congress.* Washington, DC. 1996.

Pope, G.C., Kautter, J., Ellis, R.P., et al.: Risk Adjustment of Medicare Capitation Payments Using the CMS-HHC Model. *Health Care Financing Review* 25(4):119-141, Summer 2004.

Riley, G., Rabey, E., and Kasper, J.: Biased Selection and Regression Toward the MeaninThree Medicare HMO Demonstrations: A Survival Analysis of Enrollees and Disenrollees. *Medical Care* 27(4): 337351, April 1989.

Riley, G., Tudor, C., Chiang, Y., et al.: Health Status of Medicare Enrollees in HMOs and Fee-for-Service in 1994. *Health Care Financing Review* 17(4):65-76, Summer 1996.

Welch, W.P.: Medicare Capitation Payments to HMOs in Light of Regression Toward the Mean in Health Care Costs. In Scheffler, R., Rossiter, L. (eds): *Advances in Health Economics and Health Services Research: Biased Election in Health Care Markets* Volume 6:75-96. JAI Press, Inc. Greenwich. CT. 1985.

Zarabozo, C., Taylor, C., and Hicks, J.: Medicare Managed Care: Numbers and Trends. *Health Care Financing Review* 17(3):243-261, Spring 1996.

3

The Value of Medical Spending in the United States, 1960-2000

Source: Cutler, D.M., A.B. Rosen, and S. Vijan. 2006. The Value of Medical Spending in the United States, 1960-2000. *The New England Journal of Medicine,* 355(9): 920-927.

ABSTRACT

Background

The increased use of medical therapies has led to increased medical costs. To provide insight into the value of this increased spending, we compared gains in life expectancy with the increased costs of care from 1960 through 2000.

Methods

We estimated life expectancy in 1960, 1970, 1980, 1990, and 2000 for four age groups. To control for the influence of nonmedical factors on survival, we assumed in our base-case analysis that 50 percent of the gains were due to medical care. We compared the adjusted increases in life expectancy with the lifetime cost of medical care in the same years.

Results

From 1960 through 2000, the life expectancy for newborns increased by 6.97 years, lifetime medical spending adjusted for inflation increased by approximately $69,000, and the cost per year of life gained was $19,900. The cost increased from $7,400 per year of life gained in the 1970s to $36,300 in the 1990s. The average cost per year of life gained in 1960-2000 was approximately $31,600 at 15 years of age, $53,700 at 45 years of age, and $84,700 at 65 years of age. At 65 years of age, costs rose more rapidly than did life expectancy: the cost per year of life gained was $121,000 between 1980 and 1990 and $145,000 between 1990 and 2000.

Conclusions

On average, the increases in medical spending since 1960 have provided reasonable value. However, the spending increases in medical care for the elderly since 1980 are associated with a high cost per year of life gained. The national focus on the rise in medical spending should be balanced by attention to the health benefits of this increased spending.

Advances in medical care have led to sustained increases in medical spending over time. Adjusted for inflation, annual medical spending per person has increased from approximately $700 in 1960 to more than $6,000 today, tripling as a share of the gross domestic product (GDP).[1] At least half this increase is a result of more care, not higher prices for existing care.[2]

An evaluation of whether increased medical spending is useful requires the valuation of the increase in care. The enormous growth in spending has led many to argue that the increasing costs are excessive.[3] Others, however, suggest that spending more may provide good value, whether measured in costs per year of life gained or in overall measures of economic benefit.[4-7] The vast literature on the cost-effectiveness of specific medical treatments and other interventions suggests that many (though certainly not all) medical treatments provide reasonable value.[8] However, there has been comparatively little effort to understand the value of the medical system as a whole: Is the increase in spending by more than a factor of eight worth it?

We addressed this question by examining how medical spending has translated into gains in survival. We measured the increase in medical spending from 1960 through 2000 and compared it with the number of additional years of life lived, focusing on the gains in life expectancy that were likely to be due to medical care. We assumed in our base case that 50 percent of improvements in longevity resulted from medical care. We also conducted sensitivity analyses using various assumptions about the proportion of life-expectancy gains that was attributable to health care.

METHODS

We estimated life expectancies and the projected medical spending for four age groups in 1960, 1970, 1980, 1990, and 2000, according to the mortality rates and costs that prevailed in each year. For example, when calculating the lifetime costs (i.e., costs from birth) of health care for a newborn in 1960, we used the 1960 values for spending in all ages. In this way, we obtained an accurate picture of the medical system as it existed at each time, and we were able to explore how that picture changed over time.

Life Expectancy

Our data on life expectancy were based on U.S. life tables for 1959-1961, 1969-1971, 1979-1981, 1989-1991, and 2000.[9] For simplicity, we refer to the three-year periods by the middle year (1960, 1970, 1980, 1990). To estimate changes in life expectancy according to cause, we used cause-deletion methods.[10] Specifically, we obtained the rates of death from each cause in 1960 according to age. We then added the age-specific change in the mortality rate between 1960 and 2000 for a particular cause to the age-specific overall mortality rate in 1960 and calculated the life expectancy according to the new mortality rate. The difference between the life expectancy calculated with the new mortality rate and the life expectancy in 1960 was considered to reflect the effect of that cause on life expectancy.

We assumed that a portion of the gains in life expectancy were related to medical care. Analyses aggregated from treatments clearly shown to be medically effective suggest that at least half the life-expectancy gains since 1950 are due to medical advances.[11-13] About 90 percent of the gains in life expectancy are attributable to improvements in the rates of death in infancy and the rates of death from cardiovascular disease. Prevailing estimates suggest that at least half the reduction in these rates are due to medical care.[4,14-23] We therefore assumed in our base case that 50 percent of the total gains in life expectancy were due to medical care.

We examined this assumption by considering the importance of two causes of death that are unlikely to be due to changing medical treatment. The first was death attributable to smoking. Rates of smoking among adults fell from 42 percent in 1960 to 22 percent in 2000. To estimate the changes in life expectancy that were attributable to reduced rates of smoking, we constructed an alternative time series for mortality in 1970, 1980, 1990, and 2000, assuming that smoking rates were fixed at 1960 levels—in essence, assuming that none of the decline in the rate of smoking was due to medical treatment. Data on the prevalence of smoking were from the National Health Interview surveys for 1965-2000[24] and from a survey of adolescents in California.[25] Because the surveys did not collect information on smoking until 1965, the ratio of per capita cigarette use in 1960 was compared with that for 1965 to extrapolate the prevalence data before 1965.[26] By combining the prevalence of smoking with the relative risk of death for smokers,[27] we could estimate the contribution of reduced rates of smoking to increased longevity.

The second cause we investigated was the rate of death from external factors: accidents (most commonly involving motor vehicles), suicide, and homicide. The rates of death from external causes have declined by 44 percent since 1960. Although this decline is partly related to medical care (better emergency room care, for example), trends in survival are likely to reflect other factors to a far larger degree.[20] To estimate the effect of changes in the rate of death from external causes, we assumed that the rate was the same in 1970, 1980, 1990, and 2000 as it was in 1960.

The effect of medical care on improvements in health is uncertain. We therefore performed sensitivity analyses on the percentage of gains in life expectancy that was assumed to be due to medical care.

Medical Spending

We obtained data on medical spending according to age from Meara et al.[28] These researchers estimated spending for five years for which health expenditure surveys were available: 1963, 1970, 1977, 1987, and 2000. Spending was defined as total medical costs; we did not consider the indirect costs of medicine, such as improvements in productivity. We interpolated and extrapolated the data by using national spending trends to estimate age-specific spending in 1960, 1970, 1980, 1990, and 2000. Lifetime costs were calculated with the use of the probability of survival to each age. All spending was adjusted to 2002 dollars with the use of the GDP deflator and was discounted at a rate of 3 percent. The discounting, combined with the fact that not all people live to an advanced age, meant that the current value of lifetime spending at a younger age need not have exceeded the current value of spending at an older age.

Value of Medical Care

To measure the value of care, we divided the change in spending from one decade to the next (incremental costs) by the change in life expectancy from one decade to the next (incremental health benefits). We calculated the number of dollars spent per year of life gained during the entire life span (i.e., from birth to death) for 1960, 1970, 1980, 1990, and 2000 individually and for the four-decade period as a whole. We also estimated the costs per year of life gained between 15 years of age and death, 45 years of age and death, and 65 years of age and death by including the medical costs incurred and the increase in life expectancy after each age. A lower ratio of dollars spent to years of life gained indicated a better value (i.e., less money paid for each one-year increase in life expectancy).

RESULTS

The remaining life expectancy for four age groups (newborn and 15, 45, and 65 years of age) is listed in Table 1. The life expectancy for newborns increased by 6.97 years between 1960 and 2000. At 3.12 years, the increase in life expectancy between 1970 and 1980 was the largest increase during any decade. The increase was 0.86 year between 1960 and 1970, 1.5 years between 1980 and 1990, and 1.49 years between 1990 and 2000. The mortality rate fell between 1960 and 2000 for each age group.

The causes of the increases in life expectancy for newborns between 1960 and 2000 are shown in Table 2. Of the 6.97-year increase in life expectancy, 4.88 years (70 percent) resulted from a reduced rate of death from cardiovascular disease. An additional 1.35 years (19 percent) resulted from a reduced rate of death in infancy. A reduced rate of death from external causes led to an additional increase of 0.36 year (5 percent). The reduction in the rate of death from smoking (included in the rate of death from cardiovascular disease and other causes) led to an increase in life expectancy of 1.1 years (16 percent) (data not shown). The combined effect of reduced rates of death from external causes and smoking, 21 percent, is less than the increase in longevity of 50 percent that we attributed to nonmedical factors.

Estimates of the present value of medical spending for each of the four age groups, calculated with the use of age-specific spending rates that prevailed in each year, are listed in Table 3. In 1960, lifetime spending from birth was about $14,000 per person. That amount had increased to more than $83,000 by 2000, an increase by a factor of nearly six. At older ages, medical spending increased even more between 1960 and 2000—by a factor of more than 13 for people 65 years of age or older, for example.

Table 1	Life Expectancy According to Age Group and Year, 1960–2000.					
Age			**Life Expectancy**			**Cumulative Change (1960–2000)**
	1960	1970	1980	1990	2000	
			years			
Newborn	69.90	70.76	73.88	75.37	76.87	6.97
15 Yr	57.33	57.69	60.19	61.38	62.62	5.29
45 Yr	29.50	30.12	32.27	33.44	34.38	4.88
65 Yr	14.39	15.00	16.51	17.28	17.86	3.47

Table 2	Causes of Increases in Life Expectancy among Newborns, 1960–2000.*

Cause	Increase in Life Expectancy	Relative Contribution
	yr	%
Reduction in rate of death from cardio-vascular disease	4.88	70
Reduction in rate of death in infancy	1.35	19
Reduction in rate of death from external causes	0.36	5
Reduction in rate of death from pneumonia or influenza	0.28	4
Reduction in rate of death from cancer	0.19	3
Total	6.97	100

* The data do not sum to the total because of slight increases in the rates of death from other causes (not listed) and because of rounding.

Table 3	Present Value of Average Medical Spending per Person According to Age Group and Year.*

Age	Average per Capita Spending					Cumulative Change (1960–2000)
	1960	1970	1980	1990	2000	
				$		
Newborn	13,943	25,528	37,085	56,120	83,307	69,364
15 Yr	18,700	32,704	47,155	69,457	102,490	83,790
45 Yr	17,141	35,266	63,275	100,983	148,014	130,873
65 Yr	11,495	34,526	69,819	116,097	158,549	147,054

* Values are expressed in 2002 U.S. dollars. Costs were discounted with the use of an interest rate of 3 percent. Because of this discounting and the fact that not everyone lives to an advanced age, the present value of lifetime spending at younger ages need not exceed the present value of spending at older ages.

The lifetime incremental costs per year of life gained, based on the assumption that 50 percent of such increases were due to medical care, are shown in Figure 1. From birth, during the entire period from 1960 through 2000, an average of $19,900 was spent per year of life gained. Costs per year of life gained were lower in the first two decades than in the third and fourth decades but costs per year of life for newborns never exceeded $40,000 per year. At older ages, there were substantial increases in the cost of each additional year of life gained. For example, the average cost per year of life gained at 65 years of age was about $84,700 during the entire 1960-2000 period but rose from $75,100 between 1960 and 1970 to $145,000 between 1990 and 2000.

We used sensitivity analyses to examine how varying the proportion of increases in life expectancy gains assumed to be due to medical care would affect the estimates of cost-effectiveness (Fig. 2). If 25 percent of the gains in life expectancy were due to health care, then the average cost per year of life gained between 1960 and 2000 would have ranged from $39,800 at birth to $169,400 at 65 years of age. According to this scenario, each one-year increase in life expectancy cost more than $70,000 between 1990 and 2000 for each age group. Conversely, if 75 percent of the increase in life expectancy were due to health care, then the average cost per year of life gained between 1960 and 2000 would have ranged from $13,300 for newborns to $56,500 for people 65 years of age or older.

DISCUSSION

Medical spending has increased at more than 10 percent per year for most of the past four decades,

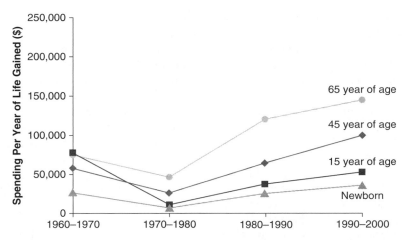

Figure 1 Longitudinal Trends in the Costs per Year of Life Gained in Four Age Groups. Spending per year of life gained was defined by the change in spending over the decade divided by the change in expected years of life over the decade.

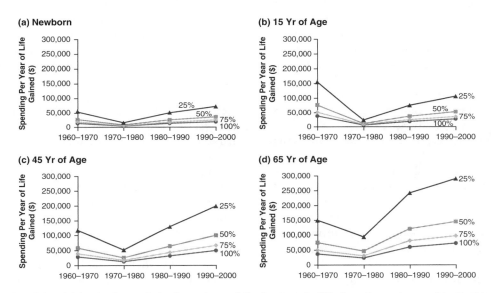

Figure 2 Results of Sensitivity Analyses of the Percentage of the Increase in Life Expectancy Assumed to Be Due to Medical Care from Birth (Panel A), from 15 Years of Age (Panel B), from 45 Years of Age (Panel C), and from 65 Years of Age (Panel D). Spending per year of life gained was defined by the change in spending over the decade divided by the change in expected years of life over the decade.

largely as a result of the development and widespread use of new medical techniques.[2] This dramatic increase in spending has contributed to political pressure to restrain costs.[3] Yet one of the most important questions remains unanswered: What is the value of this medical spending? We attempted to answer that question by comparing the trends in spending with the trends in life expectancy. During the period from 1960 through 2000, we estimated that increased spending on health care at birth resulted in an average cost of $19,900 per year of life gained. In analyses including spending and the increase in life expectancy for people 65 years of age, the average cost per additional year of life was about $84,700.

The value of a year of life as used in medical decision-making (known as the value of a statistical life) is the subject of some debate. Viscusi and Aldy[29] estimated the value of a statistical life for people of working age at approximately $7 million. For a person who is roughly 45 years old and thus has a remaining life expectancy of 30 years, the value is more than $200,000 per year of life remaining.[7] Some studies recommend a value of $100,000 per year of life,[4,30] whereas the National Institute for Health and Clinical Excellence, whose analysis is used to inform decisions about health coverage by the British National Health Service, seems to use a value of £25,000 to £35,000 per year of life (roughly

$50,000) as a general upper limit, though this is not specifically stated as policy.[31]

According to virtually any commonly cited value of a year of life, we found that if medical care accounts for about half the gains in life expectancy, then the increased spending has, on average, been worth it. However, the current trends are a cause for concern. There has been a sharp increase in the cost per additional year of life gained during the past two decades, primarily among the elderly. Analyses focused on spending and on the increase in life expectancy beginning at 65 years of age showed that the incremental cost of an additional year of life rose from $46,800 in the 1970s to $145,000 in the 1990s. The former amount certainly reflects a good value, but the latter fails to meet many cost-benefit criteria. Furthermore, it appears that although the rate of increase in spending had stabilized, if not declined, by 2000 for the newborn and 15-year-old groups, this rate is substantially outpacing the rate of increase in life expectancy in older age groups. If this trend continues in the elderly, the cost-effectiveness of medical care will continue to decrease at older ages.

The reasons for the substantially increased cost per year of life gained in older age groups cannot be ascertained from our analyses, although other investigators have examined possible reasons.[3] One is that the "low-hanging fruit" (less expensive therapies such as antihypertensive medications) were picked first, and incremental advances thereafter have necessarily been more costly. Another is that relatively more care for elderly patients than for younger patients is palliative or residential, which results in increased spending for the elderly and does improve quality of life but may not improve longevity.

Clearly, not all improvements in the mortality rate resulted from medical spending, but we used a conservative method to estimate the percentage that did. Consistently with past analyses,[11-13] we assumed that only 50 percent of the reduction in the mortality rate was due to medical care. This assumption is likely to be reasonable, given our finding that 90 percent of the increases in life expectancy during the past four decades have resulted from reductions in the rate of death from cardiovascular disease and death in infancy. Although reductions in the rate of death from cardiovascular causes are multifactorial, prior research has suggested that at least half the reductions in the rate have resulted from medical advances.[14-17] Among infants, more than half the reduction in the mortality rate between 1960 and 2000 resulted from a reduced rate of neonatal death among low-birth-weight infants (weighing <2500 g),

which is due almost entirely to medical advances.[18,19,21-23]

To validate our assumption, we considered other factors that were unlikely to be the result of medical care. Reduced rates of death from external causes and death related to smoking together accounted for 21 percent of the increase in longevity, well below the 50 percent that we attributed to nonmedical factors. Even if only 25 percent of the gains in longevity were due to medical care, the value of medical care is reasonable, on average.

Our primary conclusion is that although medical spending has increased over time, the return on spending has been high. In considering health policy, the concern about high medical costs needs to be balanced by the benefits of the care received.

Our results contrast with the conclusions that are often drawn from international data. The United States spends more on health care than other countries do, with similar or poorer overall outcomes. Of course, differences in culture, lifestyle, and social systems may confound these international comparisons. Still, it is clear that the U.S. health care system is not as efficient as it could be,[32] and improving its efficiency is an important goal. However, our results suggest that the increase in spending is not solely attributable to an increase in inefficiency. Indeed, medical spending has increased at roughly the same rate in all countries.[2,33] Taken as a whole, the average return on the increased spending has been high.

One possible scenario for the future of health care is that the costs per year of life gained will continually increase, resulting in wasted resources. However, extrapolation of any kind is inherently uncertain, and particularly so for medical advances. The genetic revolution is opening new avenues for medical inquiry, and some very cost-effective therapies could emerge. In addition, quality-improvement initiatives could increase the value of every dollar spent.

A number of limitations of our study should be mentioned. First, our estimate that 50 percent of the increase in longevity results from medical care is uncertain. Although reduced rates of death from tobacco use and from external causes accounted for only 21 percent of the increase in life expectancy, we did not consider all causes of changes in life expectancy that were due to nonmedical interventions. The most obvious omissions were the increased rate of obesity and the spread of acquired immunodeficiency syndrome, each of which results in worsened health. Second, our analysis was based on mortality alone, not on changes in the quality of life. Consistent data on the quality of life were not available for the period from 1960 through 2000. However, studies suggest that there were substantial improvements in the quality of life during this period, especially among the elderly.[13,34] Thus, our estimates are likely to have understated the value of medical spending. Finally, although we excluded gains in life expectancy that were due to nonmedical interventions, we did not exclude their associated costs, owing to the difficulty of disaggregating them from the overall costs of health care. This resulted in the overstatement of cost increases and thus the understatement of the value of medical advances.

In conclusion, although medical spending has increased substantially during the past 40 years, the money spent has provided good value. However, temporal trends suggest that the value of health care spending is decreasing over time, particularly for older age groups. We need to continue tracking trends in health care spending and its benefits to ensure that resources are allocated wisely. Such efforts should focus on specific diseases in order to provide a more detailed picture of the value of health care both within disease categories and across a spectrum of common diseases over time. Also, the United States should modify its system of tracking the health sector to include a measure of population health in addition to spending, so that policymakers and the public have an informed picture of the benefits obtained for the money spent.

About the Author

From the Department of Economics, Harvard University, and the National Bureau of Economic Research—both in Cambridge, Mass. (D.M.C.); and the Center for Practice Management and Outcomes Research, Ann Arbor Veterans Affairs Medical Center, and the Division of General Medicine, University of Michigan Health System—both in Ann Arbor (A.B.R., S.V.). Address reprint requests to Dr. Cutler at the Department of Economics, Harvard University, 1875 Cambridge St., Cambridge, MA 02138, or at dcutler@harvard.edu.

• • • References

1. National health expenditure accounts. Baltimore: Centers for Medicare and Medicaid Services, 2005. (Accessed August 4, 2006, at http://www.cms.hhs.gov/statistics/nhe/default.asp.)

2. Newhouse JP. Medical care costs: how much welfare loss? *J Econ Perspect* 1992; 6:3-29.

3. Bodenheimer T. High and rising health care costs. Part 1: seeking an explanation. *Ann Intern Med* 2005;142:847-54.

4. Cutler DM. *Your money or your life: strong medicine for America's health care system.* Oxford, England: Oxford University Press, 2004.

5. Lichtenberg FR. Are the benefits of newer drugs worth their cost? Evidence from the 1996 MEPS. *Health Aff (Millwood)* 2001;20(5):241-51.

6. Nordhaus W. The health of nations: the contribution of improved health to living standards. In: Murphy KM, Topel RH, eds. *Measuring the gains from medical research: an economic approach.* Chicago: University of Chicago Press, 2003:9-40.

7. Murphy KM, Topel RH. The economic value of medical research. In: Murphy KM, Topel RH, eds. *Measuring the gains from medical research: an economic approach.* Chicago: University of Chicago Press, 2003:41-73.

8. Comprehensive table of cost-utility ratios, 1976-2000. Boston: Harvard School of Public Health, 2003. (Accessed August 4, 2006, at http://www.hsph.harvard.edu/cearegistry/data/1976-2001_CEratios_comprehensive_4-7-2004.pdf.)

9. National Vital Statistics Reports. United States life tables. Atlanta: Centers for Disease Control and Prevention, 2005. (Accessed August 4, 2006, at http://www.cdc.gov/nchs/products/pubs/pubd/lftbls/lftbls.htm.)

10. Tsai SP, Lee ES, Hardy RJ. The effect of a reduction in leading causes of death: potential gains in life expectancy. *Am J Public Health* 1978;68:966-71.

11. Bunker JP. The role of medical care in contributing to health improvements within societies. *Int J Epidemiol* 2001;30:1260-3.

12. Bunker JP, Frazier HS, Mosteller F. Improving health: measuring effects of medical care. *Milbank Q* 1994;72:225-58.

13. Bunker JP. Medicine matters after all. *J R Coll Physicians Lond* 1995;29:105-12.

14. Goldman L, Cook EF. The decline in ischemic heart disease mortality rates: an analysis of the comparative effects of medical interventions and changes in lifestyle. *Ann Intern Med* 1984;101:825-36.

15. Capewell S, Morrison CE, McMurray JJ. Contribution of modern cardiovascular treatment and risk factor changes to the decline in coronary heart disease mortality in Scotland between 1975 and 1994. *Heart* 1999;81:380-6.

16. Hunink MG, Goldman L, Tosteson AN, et al. The recent decline in mortality from coronary heart disease, 1980-1990: the effect of secular trends in risk factors and treatment. *JAMA* 1997;277:535-42.

17. Unal B, Critchley JA, Capewell S. Modelling the decline in coronary heart disease deaths in England and Wales, 1981-2000: comparing contributions from primary prevention and secondary prevention. *BMJ* 2005;331:614.

18. Williams RL, Chen PM. Identifying the sources of the recent decline in perinatal mortality rates in California. *N Engl J Med* 1982;306:207-14.

19. Richardson DK, Gray JE, Gortmaker SL, Goldmann DA, Pursley DM, McCormick MC. Declining severity adjusted mortality: evidence of improving neonatal intensive care. *Pediatrics* 1998;102:893-9.

20. Li G, Shahpar C, Grabowski JG, Baker SP. Secular trends of motor vehicle mortality in the United States, 1910-1994. *Accid Anal Prev* 2001;33: 423-32.

21. Kliegman RM. Neonatal technology, perinatal survival, social consequences, and the perinatal paradox. *Am J Public Health* 1995;85:909-13.

22 Cutler DM, Meara ER. The technology of birth: is it worth it? In: Garber AM, ed. *Frontiers in health policy research*. Cambridge, Mass.: MIT Press, 2000:33-67.

23. Lee KS, Paneth N, Gartner LM, Pearlman MA, Gruss L. Neonatal mortality: an analysis of the recent improvement in the United States. *Am J Public Health* 1980; 70:15-21.

24. Tobacco Information and Prevention Source (TIPS). National Health Interview surveys, selected years— United States, 1965-2000. Atlanta: Centers for Disease Control and Prevention, 2005. (Accessed August 4, 2006, at http://www.cdc.gov/tobacco/ research_data/adults_prev/adstat1print.htm.)

25. Anderson CM, Burns DM. Patterns of adolescent initiation rates over time: national and California data. In: *Smoking and tobacco control*. Monograph no. 14: changing adolescent smoking prevalence. Washington, D.C.: National Cancer Institute, 2001.

26. Giovino GA, Schooley MW, Zhu BP, et al. Surveillance for selected tobacco-use behaviors— United States, 1900–1994. *MMWR CDC Surveill Summ* 1994;43:1-43.

27. Thun MJ, Myers DG, Day-Lally C, et al. Age and the exposure-response relationships between cigarette smoking and premature death in Cancer Prevention Study II. In: *Smoking and tobacco control. Monograph no. 8: changes in cigarette-related disease risks and their implications for prevention and control*. Washington, D.C.: National Cancer Institute, 1997.

28. Meara E, White C, Cutler DM. Trends in medical spending by age, 1963-2000. *Health Aff (Millwood)* 2004;23(4):176-83.

29. Viscusi WK, Aldy J. The value of a statistical life: a critical review of market estimates throughout the world. *J Risk Uncertainty* 2003;27:5-76.

30. Tolley GS, Kenkel DS, Fabian RG. *Valuing health for policy: an economic approach*. Chicago: University of Chicago Press,1994.

31. Rawlins MD, Culyer AJ. National Institute for Clinical Excellence and its value judgments. *BMJ* 2004;329:224-27.

32. Fisher ES, Wennberg DE, Stukel TA, Gottlieb DJ, Lucas FL, Pinder EL. The implications of regional variations in Medicare spending. Part 2: health outcomes and satisfaction with care. *Ann Intern Med* 2003;138:288-98.

33. Anderson GF, Frogner BK, Johns RA, Reinhardt UE. Health care spending and use of information technology in OECD countries. *Health Aff (Millwood)* 2006; 25:819-31.

34. Freedman VA, Martin LG, Schoeni RF. Recent trends in disability and functioning among older adults in the United States: a systematic review. *JAMA* 2002; 288:3137-46. [Erratum, *JAMA* 2003;289: 3242.]

High and Rising Health Care Costs: Demystifying U.S. Health Care Spending

Source: Ginsburg, P.B. 2008. *High and rising health care costs: Demystifying U.S. health care spending.* Research Synthesis Report No. 16. Princeton, NJ: The Synthesis Project. Reprinted with permission of the Robert Wood Johnson Foundation.

INTRODUCTION

Health care spending per capita has increased each year, at least since 1960, when the federal government began tracking U.S. health care spending through the National Health Expenditure Accounts (NHEA), a measure of all spending on health services. In addition to spending by private insurance and out-of-pocket spending, the NHEA include spending by public programs, such as Medicare and Medicaid, spending by the uninsured, and spending for services not covered by insurance, such as over-the-counter medications. Since it is the most comprehensive measure of spending, it will be the principal focus in this synthesis. Of greatest concern to policy-makers is spending on services typically covered by insurance, since those services are likely to be the most important to people (as evidenced by their coverage by insurance) and because so much public funding subsidizes them, whether directly (Medicare and Medicaid) or indirectly through tax subsidies to private health insurance.[a]

Another key conceptual distinction is between the level of spending during a period of time and trends in spending over time. U.S. health spending per person is very high in relation to that of other developed countries and also is increasing rapidly over time. The distinction is important to understanding what is driving spending and what can be done to address it. For example, many believe that the fragmentation of health care financing and delivery in the United States is a factor behind high spending per person, but it may not be an important factor behind the growth in spending over time. If fragmentation leads spending to be X percent higher than it could be, that X percent could be relatively constant over time. Other factors, such as medical technology, lead both to high spending per person—technology that has already been incorporated into care delivery—and spending increasing over time as new technologies are developed and diffuse.

This synthesis addresses the following questions:

1. What are the historical data on health care spending?

2. Are health care costs too high?

3. How does U.S. spending on health care compare with other developed nations?

4. What is driving the growth in health care spending?

5. What are the short-term spending trends?

---

[a] Employer contributions to employee health benefits are not taxable to the employee. Employee contributions made through a Section 125 cafeteria plan are made from pre-tax income.

FINDINGS

Are Health Care Costs Too High?

Nobody asks whether spending on computers or automobiles is too high because only private purchasing decisions are involved. Consumers decide what they want to buy, based on their preferences and their budgets. If spending on computers increased sharply, most would label this a success story, meaning that improvements in the products were so meaningful to consumers that they have decided to sacrifice other goods and services to spend more on computers.

Health care does have some critical differences, however. For one thing, much of it is paid for by private or public health insurance. This means that patients are shielded from most of the cost implications of their decisions—or their doctor's decisions—at the point of service. Health insurance products have long had features, such as administrative controls, to restrain somewhat the effects of these incentives. In addition, consumers do not perceive themselves to have as much control over spending on health care because of their dependence on physicians and standards of care to determine diagnosis and treatment. Although service providers outside of health care also have incentives to convince consumers to spend more, health care professionals are likely to have more influence because of consumers' limited technical knowledge and the urgency, fear and pain involved in many medical episodes.

Given these circumstances, some economists are unwilling to accept the current proportion of GDP spent on health care as optimal. It has motivated many to focus on the value of additional units of health spending in relation to costs as well as the burdens of increases in spending (meaning what must be sacrificed) on those individuals, businesses and governments that pay for health services.

Issue of Value

In recent years, some economists have estimated large values—in terms of increased longevity—for some new technologies and cautioned that cost-containment policies could diminish the rate of development of valuable technologies.[b] They have measured additional longevity from specific new technologies and assigned a value to them, using the concept of quality-adjusted life years (QALY). Two significant issues

arise with analyses of value of new technology. One is that while a technology may be valuable in the aggregate, it is often applied to some patients obtaining very large value and others gaining little value or even being made worse off. Many valuable technologies have been applied too broadly, for example the use of the drug Vioxx by many not expected to benefit from its unique characteristic of causing fewer gastrointestinal problems than existing drugs. Similarly, some have questioned the use of angioplasty for some patients for whom medical treatment (drugs and lifestyle changes) would be at least as effective. So evidence of the aggregate value of a technology does not justify all of its applications. According to Garber, Goldman and Jena.[35] "The variability in benefits that different patients achieve from similar interventions is at the heart of the conflicting views of the value of medical technology." Championing technology does not have to be inconsistent with advocating vigorous attempts to limit use to patients most likely to benefit.

Researchers may have a tendency to study only the most successful technologies, if only because they are better known. We do not know how much is spent for technologies that are less well known and whether they are less valuable. Indeed, Skinner, Staiger and Fisher,[75] using data from later years, estimated a far lower value for innovations to treat heart attacks than did Cutler and McClellan.[20]

Analysis of the extensive variation in rates of use of services across geographic areas within the United States is increasingly contributing to discussions of the value of additional spending on health care. Much of the research has focused on the Medicare program, which has uniform coverage throughout the country (except for private supplemental coverage and dual eligibility for Medicaid). A synthesis by Marsha Gold[42] describes the extensive variation in Medicare spending by hospital referral region, with half the variation not explained by population characteristics or prices. Those residing in high-cost regions did not receive better care or have superior outcomes. Fisher et al.,[33] included in the Gold synthesis, showed that the 60 percent higher utilization in higher spending regions was explained by more frequent physician visits, especially in the inpatient setting, more frequent tests and minor procedures, and increased use of specialists and hospitals. Quality of care was no better.

One striking consideration about the literature on the value of new technology is the lack of discussion about the implications of the results. For example, studies of the value of new technologies for heart attacks or of new drugs presumably are not addressing a policy option of banning those tech-

---

[b]See, for example, Cutler[19] and Lichtenberg[52].

nologies. The subtext is whether steps that would make new technologies less profitable for their developers—for example, through guidelines leading to their being applied to fewer patients—would reduce the development of the valuable new technologies. Although it goes without saying that less profitable research and development will reduce resources going into these activities, it is far less certain that it would reduce the flow of high-value new technologies. The law of diminishing marginal returns certainly applies to research and development, so whether this would occur would depend on the skill of those who allocate capital to different research and development projects in identifying those projects with potential for the highest value.

Issue of Affordability

Research on the value of new technologies strikes some as quite academic. When health care spending rises substantially more rapidly than GDP, insurance premiums rise more rapidly than earnings. In recent years, the gap between premium trends and earning trends has been particularly large, so that the inability to afford health insurance now affects many in the middle class (Figure 4, not included). For many, whether advances in medical technology are valuable or not has little relevance if their inability to afford insurance puts those technologies beyond their reach.

Many societies have values that lead to efforts to ensure universal access to some standard of care, even if those with the highest incomes can access additional care. In the United States, public policy reflects this by use of taxes to fund public insurance for the elderly and some poor, particularly children, and through support of the safety net hospitals and community health centers that serve predominantly low-income people. When costs rise more rapidly than incomes, financing of these activities becomes more challenging. Maintaining this policy will require subsidizing coverage for those no longer able to afford it and higher outlays in relation to revenues for existing commitments. The result is either crowding out of other public priorities, higher taxes or, at the federal level, larger deficits. When health spending increases more rapidly than growth in incomes, it has important fiscal ramifications for government, for those who depend on government programs and for those who pay taxes.

Another complicating perspective is that in most advanced countries most people use the same medical care delivery system, implying generally the same standard of care for those who access the system. This leads, theoretically at least, to conflict over the level of spending incurred between those with different means. A market resolution to this issue would involve a splintering of the delivery system into subsystems that deliver different standards of care. This is probably happening in the United States to a much larger degree than in other advanced countries, where health insurance tends to be comprehensive for all people. Unconstrained growth in health spending in the United States will inevitably lead to fragmentation in the delivery system according to the ability to pay, something that at least some leaders would see as a negative.

A distinct issue in affordability of health care is tied to the financing of coverage by employers. Many leaders of industry maintain that rising health insurance premiums hurt the competitiveness of American companies. They claim that it drives total compensation costs higher and reduces profitability in industries facing international competition, where prices cannot be raised.[51] Most economists have been skeptical of this argument, since economic theory predicts that employers would shift rising costs of employee health benefits to employees through lowering other components of compensation, such as cash wages.[68]

Some economists perceive that the opinion of business leaders has some merit due to institutional constraints. Nichols and Axeen[61] demonstrate how, during periods when the gap between premium trends and earning trends is very large, it would take a decline in nominal wage rates to fully shift increasing costs of health insurance to workers. Although wage cuts are theoretically possible, experience shows great resistance to them.

Source of Job Creation?

Those who attend meetings of local business leaders are very likely to have heard the argument that health care is an economic engine for the community, creating well-paying jobs for local residents. In certain areas, such as those that attract patients from all over the nation or the world for tertiary care or are centers of biomedical research and development, this is likely to be the case. The argument may also apply to a chronically depressed locality, where the benefit of additional Medicare and Medicaid spending is likely to offset the negative effect on the local economy of higher insurance premiums.

At the level of the entire nation, in times other than recessions, however, the story is different. If people spend more money on health care, they have less to spend on other goods and services. So jobs gained in health care are likely to come at the expense of jobs elsewhere in the economy. Pauly[65] argues that the impact of shifting resources from health care to other goods and services depends on the value of health care, which could be lower at the margin as a result of the extensive use of health insurance. Monaco and Phelps[57] model changes in health care spending and its effect on the role of government in the economy. If higher spending for Medicare and Medicaid leads to higher taxes, the loss of efficiency from higher tax rates will mean that higher spending detracts from the economy. Indeed, to the degree that rising health care spending hurts the competitiveness of American companies that compete internationally, rising spending on health care could be an even larger negative factor for the U.S. economy.

How Does U.S. Health Care Spending Compare with That of Other Developed Nations?

The question of whether U.S. health care costs are too high is the motivation for most analyses of international differences in spending. Many analyses have shown that per capita costs in the United States are much higher than those in other developed countries. These differences remain after adjustment for national incomes—and this is without taking into account that most other developed countries have universal coverage. The implication is that other systems are more efficient in providing health care to their populations and that U.S. spending is higher than it should be.

Drawing on data on spending created by the Organization for Economic Co-operation and Development (OECD),[63] numerous analyses have shown that health care spending in the United States is much higher than in the rest of OECD countries. For example, in 2006, U.S. spending was 15.3 percent of GDP, compared to an average of 8.9 percent of GDP for all OECD countries.[c] Many researchers have concluded that despite the difference in spending, growth trends have been similar.[40] A recent study suggests, however, that the U.S. trend has been higher than the OECD trend since the mid-1980s.[89] Decomposing the spending trend for 1970-2002 into population aging, economic growth and a residual called "excess growth," and using data on aggregate OECD spending rather than the median OECD country, the study finds that excess growth was similar for 1970-1985 (U.S. 2.0 percent, OECD 1.7 percent), but fell to 0.6 percent for OECD for 1985-2002 while the U.S. continued at 2.0 percent.

An extensive literature has examined a number of possible explanations for the differences; a recent comprehensive study by McKinsey Global Institute (MGI)[5] extended the number of explanations. The literature suggests that prices, efficiency and insurance administration are the most important differences. MGI estimates that drug prices are 70 percent higher in the United States compared with OECD countries. Physician compensation in the United States is 6.6 times per capita GDP for specialists and 4.2 times for primary care physicians, compared to ratios of 4 and 3.2 in the comparison OECD countries. Salaries of nurses are in line with OECD countries. The United States spends 54 percent more than OECD countries for the top-five inpatient medical devices (e.g., implants, stents). Anderson and others[4,2,3] explain that single-payer systems effectively exercise monopsony power in setting payment rates for providers, which fragmented U.S. payers cannot muster.

The MGI study also compares efficiency across OECD countries. U.S. costs in outpatient settings are higher because of subscale operation of facilities. With prices very high, outpatient facilities in the United States can earn a profit despite underutilizing capacity. In contrast to hospital CT equipment being used for 20-30 scans per day, freestanding outpatient facilities, which have lower overhead, can earn a profit at 4-8 scans per day. This leads to extensive investments in inefficiently used capacity—and a likelihood of higher service use in response to physician self-referral incentives.

Advocates of single-payer systems have long pointed to higher insurance administrative costs (marketing and sales, underwriting, claims processing, utilization review and profits) in the United States, often comparing them to Canada.[90] This and earlier work by Woolhandler and Himmelstein[91] attracted a great deal of criticism, dwelling on the likelihood the differences are overstated and pointing out that U.S. political history and institutions would require even a feasibly reformed U.S. health care system to spend more on administration than Canada's system.[1,24,74] MGI estimated that the United States spends six times more for administration than OECD countries, not including the costs borne by providers in interacting with payers.

What Is Driving the Growth in Health Care Spending?

An extensive literature examines which factors play the largest roles in explaining increases in health spending over time. Conclusions about which drivers are most important have been very consistent from study to study. For example, authors agree that

---

[c]Calculations by the author. Note that while the OECD data for the United States is based on NHEA data, adjustments are made to be comparable to data on other nations.

technological change is the most important driver of spending increases over time and that population aging plays only a minor role (Table 1, not included).

Technology. Measuring the contribution of changing medical technology is particularly challenging because of the inability to measure aggregate technological change directly. Nevertheless, all of the studies reviewed obtain broadly similar results. Most studies measure technology as a residual; that is, after estimating the contributions of all of the directly measurable drivers of spending, attributing the proportion of spending increases not otherwise explained as the contribution of technology. These approaches are vulnerable to confounding technological change with other factors for which the contribution is not fully captured (or measurement errors). For example, the role of increasing rates of obesity has not been studied until recently, so some of its impact on spending may have inadvertently been attributed to technology. In addition, separating the effects of technology from health insurance coverage is problematic because the contribution of technology would not be as great had the technologies not been covered by insurance.

A frequently cited study by Newhouse[59] attributes the bulk of the more than half of spending increases that could not be explained by other factors to technological change. Peden and Freeland[67] attribute about two-thirds of spending increases from 1960 to 1993 to technological change. Smith, Heffler and Freeland[79] and Cutler[19] also attribute substantial portions of spending increases to technological change. A technical review panel convened to advise CMS on future health care cost trends concluded that about half of real health expenditure growth is attributable to technology.[82]

A few studies, instead of estimating a residual, use proxies for technological change. Okunade and Murthy[62] use health care research and development spending as a proxy for technological change. Analyzing time series data from 1960 to 1997, they do not suggest a particular percentage but support Newhouse's conclusion that "technological change is a major escalator of health care expenditure." Di Matteo[27] uses a time trend to proxy technological change and estimates that it accounts for 62 percent of the increase in spending. With such similar research results across studies, little is to be gained at this point by debating the contrasting methodologies.

Cutler and McClellan[20] outline lucidly how technology advances affect aggregate spending trends through either treatment *substitution* or *expansion*. Treatment substitution can, in different cases, either increase or decrease spending. Examples of advances that increased spending per patient through treatment substitution are new treatments for heart attacks and breast cancer.

Examples where lower-cost treatments were substituted include cataract surgery, where advances in technology made the surgery a simple outpatient procedure, and treatment for depression with selective serotonin reuptake inhibitors (SSRI), where psychotherapy was reduced or eliminated. Treatment *expansion* occurs when treatment becomes more attractive to patients because of either better outcomes or reduced pain or disability connected with treatment. Treatment expansion almost always increases spending (some preventive services would be exceptions, although most effective preventive services increase spending.[70] Treatment substitutions that decrease costs often stimulate large treatment expansions, since lower unit costs often go along with reductions in pain and disability, as with cataract surgery and minimally invasive gall bladder surgery.

The contribution of technological change to spending probably varies by time period. For example, drug spending trends, which are highly influenced by technological change, have been low in recent years—after being particularly high during the 1990s—due to a combination of relatively few approvals of "blockbuster" drugs and older drugs coming off patent. The genomic revolution could lead to sharply higher drug spending down the road, with recent rapid growth of spending on biologics an early indication of that trend.

Demographics. The literature on the role population aging plays in spending trends is extensive and highly consistent. Most of the studies use survey data on spending per capita at different ages and combine that with data on demographic trends. All of the studies reviewed project contributions of aging to spending trends of less than 0.7 percentage point per year, with the more sophisticated studies tending to get the lower numbers.

Differences in results across studies often reflect differences in the period studied. Studies examining the period before baby boomers began reaching their mid-50s obtain smaller impacts than those focusing on the very recent past or making projections. Strunk and Ginsburg[80] focused on commercial insurance premiums and estimated the contribution of population aging to spending growth at an average 0.1 percentage point per year in the early 1990s, rising to 0.7 percentage point in 2001 and continuing at that rate throughout the current decade. Martini et al.,[54] using a health plan's administrative data, estimated that population aging will contribute 0.3 percentage point per year from 2000–2050.

Studies that incorporate high spending in the last year of life and project a continuation of increasing life expectancy get even lower estimates of the impact of aging. For example, Seshamani and Gray[72] find that their estimate of increasing spending due to aging in England was halved to about 0.4 percentage point per year for 2002-2026 by incorporating the end-of-life dimension. Cutler and Sheiner,[22] who focus on Medicare spending, find that between 1990 and 2030, the percentage of Medicare beneficiaries in their last year of life will decline from 5 percent to 4.2 percent. The impact of increasing longevity swamps the 0.14 percentage point per year estimate for the role of aging in Medicare spending trends for 1992-2050 that they estimate assuming constant life expectancy.[d]

Some studies have focused on differences in trends in health care spending by age group, raising concerns that spending per capita is increasing more rapidly for older people.[73] More recent research casts doubt on those findings, however.[55]

With the literature generally consistent in showing the effect of aging on spending is small, it is important to examine the enormous gulf between the beliefs of health care providers and the research. Commonly, hospital leaders justify expansions based on "aging baby boomers." This prompted research focused on the role of aging in the demand for inpatient hospital services,[81] which obtained results similar to earlier studies of only a small effect.

Health Status. Using data from the 1987 National Medical Expenditure Survey and the 2001 Medical Expenditure Panel Survey, a well-known analysis by Thorpe et al.[83] attributes 27 percent of increased inflation-adjusted spending from 1987 to 2001 to increasing rates of obesity and changing patterns of obesity treatment and associated conditions. Increasing incidence of obesity contributes only 12 percentage points of the 27 percent; the remaining increase results from changing treatment patterns, which would more appropriately be classified as a contribution of technology.[17,e]

Analyses that do not factor in life expectancy changes from trends in health status will tend to overstate the contribution of health status to spending trends. Van Baal et al.[87] highlighted how effective steps to reduce obesity would reduce spending in the short run but increase spending in the long run because of increased longevity and the resulting exposure to other illnesses. Simulating a cohort of 20-year-olds, those who are obese had the highest costs up to age 56. At older ages, smokers had the highest costs. But over a lifetime, neither obese people nor smokers were the most expensive. Possible implications of these results are that reductions in spending from declines in rates of smoking are mostly behind us, while the higher spending from increased longevity will predominate in the future, and reversing the trend toward obesity would lead to reduced spending for a long period until the effects of greater longevity eventually dominate.

Health Insurance. Most actuaries and budget analysts draw on the RAND Health Insurance Experiment to develop assumptions about the impact of changes in insurance benefit structure on medical care spending by a small group of enrollees.[60] CBO[17] asserts that under such a standard model, increased insurance coverage explains 10 percent to 13 percent of the long-term spending trend. However, the proportion of the population with health insurance has been slowly declining over time, so this factor will affect future spending only if policies are enacted to increase the proportion of the population covered by health insurance. Indeed, it is likely that changes in insurance coverage during this decade have slowed the rate of health spending growth rather than been a driver.

The question of the role that insurance plays in cost trends at the market level—rather than individual level—is much more complex. Newhouse outlined different possible mechanisms through which the amount of insurance could affect health care spending.[58] The traditional mechanism—the level of insurance coverage (or proportion of spending paid by insurance) influences the level of spending—does not address market dynamics in which the extent of insurance coverage influences the degree of development and introduction of new technology and affects prices charged by providers and the expensiveness of their approaches to treatment. Peden and Freeland[67] followed the Newhouse framework in explaining increases in spending by including both the average coinsurance rate and its percentage change in their model for changes in spending. The percentage change in coinsurance turns out to be the more important insurance variable, explaining 44.4 percent of spending increases.

---

[d]These analyses of the role of aging to Medicare costs do not include the large portion of long-term care not covered by Medicare.

[e]If the relative spending for obese and normal-weight people from 1987 had been used, the impact of increasing obesity would explain 4 percent of increased spending. Using the 2001 relative spending rates would explain 12 percent. Standard index number procedures would calculate a geometric mean between the results based on 1987 weights and 2001 weights, which is 8 percent. But the 2001 weights are most relevant for forecasting the role of obesity in the future-and obesity prevalence continues to increase.[10]

To investigate the implications of large changes in health insurance on spending, Finkelstein[31] analyzed the impact of the implementation of the Medicare program on national health spending and estimated that the creation of Medicare led to a 37 percent increase in inflation—adjusted hospital spending (by all patients)—six times the increase that would be expected on the basis of the results of the RAND Health Insurance Experiment. This was an example of changes in insurance coverage for a large segment of the population—the elderly—fundamentally affecting the character of medical care for all. She estimated that changes in insurance coverage may be responsible for half of the increase in spending from 1950-1990, an estimate that is consistent with that of Peden and Freeland.

Finkelstein suggests two models for how insurance coverage affects spending. A "fixed-costs" model has aggregate changes in health insurance sufficiently changing market demand to get hospitals to incur the fixed costs of entering a market or adopting new practice styles. A "spillovers" model has changes in insurance for one group of patients influencing treatment of other patients.

A summary of the evidence on the role of health insurance coverage in health spending shows two strands of thought. Standard assumptions about how a change in health insurance affects an individual's spending on health care lead to a conclusion that health insurance is not a dominant driver of spending trends. But the literature also suggests that a change in health insurance affecting large numbers of people is likely to influence the care delivered to all people and influence technological change and even provider productivity.

In the future, a decline in the comprehensiveness of insurance coverage may lead to a reversal of the phenomenon Finkelstein described following the introduction of Medicare. The combination of benefit "buy downs" (increased deductibles, coinsurance and copayments), changes in benefit structures to encourage patients to choose low-cost providers, and increased information on provider prices and quality could change the market dynamic to one in which consumers become more judicious in incurring health costs. This is more likely to affect outpatient services than inpatient services because current benefit structures, including high-deductible plans, have not changed incentives for inpatient care substantially. If the trend toward greater financial incentives for patients is large enough, it may affect spending to a greater degree than standard assumptions would predict.

Income. Newhouse[59] synthesized the literature on the role of income in health spending. Estimates based on cross-sectional analysis of data on individuals tend to underestimate the magnitude of the relationship because poor health, which leads to high spending on health care, depresses income. Elasticities (the relationship between changes in income and changes in spending) from these studies tend to be in the 0.2-0.4 range. Studies using aggregate data, such as cross sections of countries, tend to obtain elasticity estimates of 1.0 or higher, suggesting that as income rises, the proportion of income spent on health care is likely to stay the same or increase. However, CBO[17] argues that the difficulties in undertaking cross-national comparisons may bias these estimates upward. It concludes that the literature discussed above implies contributions of income trends to health spending trends anywhere between 5 percent and 20 percent of long-term spending growth. The most recent econometric literature, using more sophisticated methods, consistently obtains elasticities below 1.0, implying that health care is a necessity rather than a luxury.[84,26,34] An implication is that gains in income tend to ease the burdens of financing health care.

Physician Specialty Mix and Supplier-Induced Demand. A number of cross-sectional studies show that regions in which a higher proportion of physicians are specialists have higher spending, presumably because specialists practice a more expensive style of medicine—at least where they are in ample supply. Since the proportion of specialists in the overall physician workforce is increasing, this could be a driver of spending trends. Baicker and Chandra[7] use the Dartmouth Atlas to examine state-level Medicare claims data. They find that states with a higher proportion of specialists had higher spending and lower quality. Shifting one physician per 10,000 population from generalist to specialist increases spending per beneficiary per year by $526.

Greenfield et al.[43] analyzed 20,000 patients who visited physician offices during a nine-day period in 1986 (Medical Outcomes Study) using self-administered questionnaires completed by both patients and physicians. A multivariate analysis with detailed patient information showed that patients seeing internal medicine subspecialists had higher rates of hospitalization, higher rates of prescriptions and higher rates of tests than those seeing general internists or family physicians.

Since the 1970s, economists have battled over whether variations in the supply of health care resources, such as hospital facilities and physicians, impact the use health services. The challenge is to separate out variation in supply from factors other than variation in patient demand—in other words, getting the causation right.[50,64] Dranove[29] criticized the econometric techniques used to attempt to establish causation by using them to analyze the impact of physician supply on childbirth and finding a significant but unlikely impact. The most recent published work is from Australia. Using newer theoretical models and econometric techniques, Peacock and Richardson[66] found a substantial impact of the supply of health care resources on the use of health services. Although supplier-induced demand tends not to appear on lists of drivers of spending trends because of the controversy about its existence or magnitude, even without inducement, increases in supply will likely lead to higher spending; policies to constrain supply, if effective, are likely to lead to constrained spending. However, in health systems in which prices are not controlled centrally, such as the United States, constraining supply is also likely to lead to higher prices for services.

Productivity Trends. The health care industry has many characteristics that would lead one to expect relatively small increases in productivity over time. For example, there tends to be little competition among providers on the basis of price. Extensive third-party coverage dilutes consumer incentives to be price conscious, and benefit structures tend to offer little reward for choosing a low-priced provider. On the other hand, Medicare administered pricing likely increases incentives to be efficient in producing individual services or, in the case of hospitals, admissions.

In a study for the Medicare Payment Advisory Commission, Lichtenberg[52] outlines a number of additional factors leading one to expect relatively low productivity growth in hospitals. These include high labor intensity, low investment in computers and software, and low investment in research and development, although one should raise the question of whether the latter two factors result from lack of incentives to increase productivity. He notes that government statistics on constant dollar output and American Hospital Association data on full-time equivalent staff suggest productivity growth at less than half the rate of the general economy.

Cutler and McClellan[20] note that from 1960 to 1999, the medical component of the Consumer Price Index exceeded the overall index by about 1.8 percentage points a year, suggesting either increasing market power on the part of medical providers or much lower rates of productivity increases. They sug-

gest that the gap is due to lack of adjustment for quality increases, arguing that a quality-adjusted index for treatments for the conditions examined in the study would show productivity gains exceeding those for the economy as a whole.

Reflecting on these perspectives, one can conclude that most of the delivery mechanisms within health care are set up to have lower productivity increases than the general economy, but the health system also has a vibrant research and development component that over time creates more valuable treatments, many of which have higher quality or lower unit costs. The health care system, in turn, likely delivers these new technologies relatively inefficiently, both by using high levels of inputs per service and by using the technologies not only for patients who derive large benefits from them but also for those where the benefits are small or even negative.

Managed Care. Contributions of managed care to overall spending trends are covered in this synthesis mostly for historical reasons. The managed care of the 1980s and early 1990s, which was studied extensively, has long ago passed from the scene in response to an extensive backlash. In addition, because of data limitations, most of the literature defined managed care as health maintenance organizations (HMOs), entities that play a much smaller role in health care financing today. Instead of focusing on research on whether managed care reduced the level of spending, it is more useful to focus on whether managed care reduced the rate of spending growth. To put it differently, if a large stable part of the population had been served by HMOs, which clearly did have lower costs, would the rate of increase in spending be different?

Two excellent syntheses help to efficiently summarize this literature.[41,14] Glied raises a methodological concern with selection in the enrollment process. If managed care plans experience favorable selection, their growth will lead to higher cost trends for other plans and too high a measured difference in trends. More recent studies show a larger cost growth difference—about one percentage point per year—than studies using data from the early 1980s.

Glied notes that Cutler and Sheiner[23] is the only study to address the impact of managed care on technology diffusion. That study showed that states with high managed care penetration went from being first adopters to average adopters of new technology, suggesting potential—for better or for worse—of managed care slowing development or diffusion of new technology.

A synthesis by Chernew et al.[14] contrasted studies of health plans with studies of markets. The former did not show differences in cost growth but the latter did. He raised the prospect that other health plans benefited from spillovers from managed care, resulting in market comparisons looking more favorable to managed care's ability to slow cost growth than plan comparisons. Spillovers can occur from doctors treating all of their patients the same way, higher penetration by HMOs benefiting preferred provider organizations (PPOs) in provider negotiations, and the possibility that managed care plans cause a change in the health care infrastructure.

Studies covering the late 1980s and first half of the 1990s may have been picking up a growing impact of managed care through that period as increasing plan market share increased negotiating clout with providers and, as Chernew et al. noted, affecting the whole infrastructure of delivery. This is not the same as managed care having the potential to affect the rate of growth of spending long term, however.

Changing Market Structure and Entrepreneurship. Markets for hospital care and for health insurance are becoming more concentrated over time. During the 1990s, many hospitals merged into systems, increasing their clout in local markets. A synthesis of the research on this question concluded that hospital concentration leads to higher prices.[88] But considering the magnitude of the price increases measured, it is unlikely that the contribution of increasing concentration of hospitals is a major contributor to growth in health spending over time.

Health insurance also has become more consolidated over time. Mergers in the 1990s often increased concentration in markets. More recent mergers have not had that effect, perhaps due to antitrust restrictions. In recent years, however, mergers have involved national health plans acquiring regional plans in areas where they had only limited penetration. Because large employers increasingly want to contract with a single carrier, this has increased the advantage of being a large national plan.[f] This has led to a difficult business environment for local or regional health plans, increasing the shares of the dominant plans in local markets and increasing entry barriers.

Whether insurer concentration contributes to trends in overall spending is a difficult question.

Increasing power in the provider market could lead to lower payment rates, but increasing power in the insurance market could preclude passing the savings on to purchasers, or even lead to higher premiums. Like hospital concentration, however, it is unlikely that insurer concentration is a major driver of cost trends.

Medical Malpractice Liability. Sloan and Chepke[76] estimate that over a 30-year period (1970-2000), medical malpractice premiums increased from 5.5 percent to 7.5 percent of total physician practice expenses, so premiums cannot be an important cost driver. Research on whether defensive medicine affects spending is challenging because liability risk pushes physicians in the same direction as fee-for-service payment incentives—providing more services. The best research has focused on comparisons of states with tort reforms with other states. As a result, its potential contribution is more to the question of why health spending is high than on why it is rising.

Kessler and McClellan[48] analyzed Medicare data for beneficiaries with serious heart disease and found that reforms that directly reduce liability pressure (such as limits on noneconomic damages) lead to reductions of 5 percent to 9 percent in medical expenditures. They conclude that liability reform can reduce defensive medicine.

Studies of obstetrics find smaller impacts.[78,30] Only the latter study, which focused on cesarean delivery rates, found evidence of defensive medicine, concluding that a total cap on damages would reduce cesarean deliveries by 3 percent and total obstetrical charges by 0.27 percent. A 2006 synthesis of this literature concluded that caps on noneconomic damages do reduce award size substantially, but the reductions in medical malpractice premiums are modest.[56] Other tort reforms did not have significant impacts. A 2006 report by the Congressional Budget Office finds the evidence of impact of tort reforms to be inconsistent and dependent on particular relationships and specifications tested.[16]

These results confirm that the shortcomings of the liability system are not an important driver of cost trends or even a large factor behind costs being high. Indeed, the literature emphasizes that the larger potential for true reform is in the area of better quality of care and more equitable compensation of those suffering large losses.[77]

---

[f]Blue Cross and Blue Shield plans, which are regional, have achieved this advantage through their coordination, giving employers access to Blue networks all over the country.

ACKNOWLEDGMENTS
The author would like to acknowledge the superb research assistance of Johanna Lauer and editorial support of Alwyn Cassil, as

well as comments by the Synthesis Project advisory group and project staff.

For More Information

For more information about the Synthesis Project, visit the Synthesis Project Web site at www.policysynthesis.org. For additional copies of Synthesis products, please go to the Project's Web site or send an e-mail message to pubsrequest@rwjf.org.

• • • References

1. Aaron HJ. "The Costs of Health Care Administration in the United States and Canada—Questionable Answers to a Questionable Question." *New England Journal of Medicine*, vol. 349, no. 8, 2003.

2. Anderson GF, Frogner BK, Reinhardt UE. "Health Spending in OECD Countries in 2004: An Update." *Health Affairs*, vol. 26, no. 5, September/October 2007.

3. Anderson GF, Hussey PS, Frogner BK, Waters HR. "Health Spending in the United States and the Rest of the Industrialized World." *Health Affairs*, vol. 24, no. 4, July/August 2005.

4. Anderson GF, Reinhardt UE, Hussey PS, Petrosyan V. "It's the Prices, Stupid: Why the United States is so Different From Other Countries." *Health Affairs*, vol. 22, no. 3, May/June 2003.

5. Angrisano C, Farrell D, Laboissiere M, Parker S. "Accounting for the Cost of Health Care in the United States." McKinsey Global Institute, 2007. [http://www.mckinsey.com/mgi/reports/pdfs/healthcare/MGI_US_HC_fullreport.pdf.]

6. Antel JJ, Ohfeld RL, Becker ER. "State Regulations and Hospital Costs." *The Review of Economics and Statistics*, vol. 77, no. 3, August 1995.

7. Baicker K, Chandra A. "Medicare Spending, the Physician Workforce, and Beneficiaries Quality of Care." *Health Affairs*, Web Exclusive, April 7, 2004.

8. Boards of Trustees, Federal Hospital Insurance and Federal Supplementary Medical Insurance Trust Funds. "The 2002 Annual Report of the Boards of Trustees, Federal Hospital Insurance and Federal Supplementary Medical Insurance Trust Funds." 2002 [Available at: http://www.cms.hhs.gov/ReportsTrustFunds/downloads/tr2002.pdf].

9. Catlin A, Cowan C, Hartman M, Heffler S. "National Health Spending in 2006: A Year of Change for Prescription Drugs." *Health Affairs*, vol. 27, no. 1, January/February 2008.

10. Centers for Disease Control and Prevention. "Behavioral Risk Factor Surveillance System, Obesity Trends Among U.S. Adults, 2006," PowerPoint(c) presentation, 2007 [Available at: http://www.cdc.gov/nccdphp/dnpa/obesity/trend/maps/].

11. Centers for Medicare and Medicaid Services. "National Health Expenditures by Type of Service and Source of Funds, CY 1960-2006." 2008 [Available at: http://www.cms.hhs.gov/NationalHealthExpendData/02_NationalHealthAccountsHistorical.asp].

12. Centers for Medicare and Medicaid Services. "NHE Summary Including Share of GDP, CY 1960-2006." 2008 [Available at: http://www.cms.hhs.gov/NationalHealthExpendData/02_NationalHealthAccountsHistorical.asp].

13. Centers for Medicare and Medicaid Services. "Projections of National Health Expenditures: Methodology and Model Specification." February 2008 [Available at: http://www.cms.hhs.gov/NationalHealthExpendData/downloads/projections-methodology.pdf].

14. Chernew ME, Hirth RA, Sonnad SS, Ermann R, Fendrick AM. "Managed Care, Medical Technology, and Health Care Cost Growth: A Review of the Evidence." *Medical Care Research and Review*, vol. 55, no. 3, 1998.

15. Congressional Budget Office. *The Long-Term Outlook for Health Care Spending* (No. 3085). Washington, DC: Congressional Budget Office, November 2007.

16. Congressional Budget Office. *Medical Malpractice Tort Limits and Health Care Spending* (No. 2668). Washington, DC: Congressional Budget Office, April 2006.

17. Congressional Budget Office. *Technological Change and the Growth of Health Care Spending* (No. 2764). Washington, DC: Congressional Budget Office, January 2008.

18. Conover CJ, Sloan FA. "Does Removing Certificate-of-Need Regulations Lead to a Surge in Health Care Spending?" *Journal of Health Politics, Policy and Law*, vol. 23, no. 3, June 1998.

19. Cutler DM. "Technology, Health Costs, and the NIH." Paper prepared for the National Institute of Health Economics Roundtable on Biomedical Research, September 1995.

20. Cutler DM, McClellan M. "Is Technological Change in Medicine Worth It?" *Health Affairs*, vol. 20, no. 5, September/October 2001.

21. Cutler DM, McClellan M, Newhouse JP, Remler D. "Are Medical Prices Declining? Evidence From Heart Attack Treatments." *Quarterly Journal of Economics*, vol. 113, no. 4, November 1998.

22. Cutler DM, Sheiner L. "Demographics and Medical Care Spending: Standard and Nonstandard Effects." *National Bureau of Economic Research Working Paper No. 6886*, 1998.

23. Cutler DM, Sheiner L. "Managed Care and the Growth of Medical Expenditure." *Frontiers in Health Policy Research*, vol. 1, 1998.

24. Danzon PM. "Hidden Overhead Costs: Is Canada's System Really Less Expensive?" *Health Affairs*, vol. 11, no. 1, 1992.

25. DeNavas-Walt C, Proctor BD, Smith J, U.S. Census Bureau. *Income, Poverty, and Health Insurance Coverage in the United States: 2006.* Current Population Reports, P60-233. Washington, DC: U.S. Government Printing Offi ce, 2007.

26. Di Matteo L. "The Income Elasticity of Health Care Spending: A Comparison of Parametric and Nonparametric Approaches." *European Journal of Health Economics*, vol. 4, no. 1, 2003.

27. Di Matteo L. "The Macro Determinants of Health Expenditure in the United States and Canada: Assessing the Impact of Income, Age Distribution and Time." *Health Policy*, vol. 71, January 2005.

28. Dranove D, Lindrooth R, White WD, Zwanziger J. "Is the Impact of Managed Care on Hospital Prices Decreasing?" *Journal of Health Economics*, vol. 27, 2008.

29. Dranove D, Wehner P. "Physician-Induced Demand for Childbirths." *Journal of Health Economics*, vol. 13, no. 1, March 1994.

30. Dubay L, Kaestner R, Waidmann T. "The Impact of Malpractice Fears on Cesarean Section Rates." *Journal of Health Economics*, vol. 18, no. 4, 1999.

31. Finkelstein A. "The Aggregate Effects of Health Insurance: Evidence From the Introduction of Medicare." *Quarterly Journal of Economics*, vol. CXXII, no. 1, February 2007.

32. Finkelstein S, Temin P. *Reasonable Rx: Solving the Drug Price Crisis.* Upper Saddle River, NJ: FT Press, 2008.

33. Fisher ES, Wennberg DE, Stukel TA, Gottlieb DJ, Lucas FL, Pinder EL. "The Implications of Regional Variations in Medicare Spending. Part 1: The Content, Quality, and Accessibility of Care." *Annals of Internal Medicine*, vol. 138, 2003.

34. Freeman DG. "Is Health Care a Necessity Or a Luxury? Pooled Estimates of Income Elasticity From US State-Level Data." *Applied Economics*, vol. 35, no. 5, 2003.

35. Garber A, Goldman DP, Jena AB. "The Promise of Health Care Cost Containment." *Health Affairs*, vol. 26, no. 6, November/December 2007.

36. Getzen TE. "Forecasting Health Expenditures: Short, Medium, and Long (Long) Term." *Journal of Health Care Finance*, vol. 26, no. 3, Spring 2000.

37. Ginsburg, PB. "Competition in Health Care: Its Evolution Over the Past Decade." *Health Affairs*, vol. 24, no. 6, November/December 2005.

38. Ginsburg, PB. "Provider Payment Incentives and Delivery System Reform." Forthcoming in volume to be published by the Center for American Progress.

39. Ginsburg PB, Berenson RA. "Revising Medicare's Physician Fee Schedule—Much Activity, Little Change." *New England Journal of Medicine*, vol. 356, no. 12, March 22, 2007.

40. Glied S. *Chronic Condition: Why Health Reform Fails.* Cambridge, MA: Harvard University Press, 1997.

41. Glied S. "Managed Care." In *Handbook of Health Economics*, vol. 1A, Culyer AJ, Newhouse JP (eds.). San Diego, CA: Elsevier, Inc., 2000.

42. Gold M. "Geographic Variation in Medicare Per Capita Spending: Should Policy-Makers Be Concerned?" The Robert Wood Johnson Foundation Research Synthesis Report No. 6, 2004.

43. Greenfield S, Nelson EC, Zubkoff M, Manning W, Rogers W, Kravitz, Keller A, Tarlov AR, Ware JE. "Variations in Resource Utilization Among Medical Specialties and Systems of Care: Results From the Medical Outcomes Study." *Journal of the American Medical Association*, vol. 267, no. 12, 1992.

44. Grossman JM, Ginsburg PB. "As the Health Insurance Underwriting Cycle Turns: What Next?" *Health Affairs*, vol. 23, no. 6, November/December 2004.

45. Kaiser Family Foundation. "Kaiser Health Tracking Poll: Election 2008." April 2008 [Available at: http://www.kff.org/kaiserpolls/upload/7772.pdf].

46. Kaiser Family Foundation and Health Research and Educational Trust. "Employer Health Benefits: 2007 Annual Survey." 2007 [Available at: http://www.kff.org/insurance/7672/upload/76723.pdf].

47. Keehan S, Sisko A, Truffer C, Smith S, Cowan C, Poisal J, Clemens MK. "Health Spending Projections Through 2017: The Baby-Boom Generation is Coming to Medicare." *Health Affairs*, Web Exclusive, February 26, 2008.

48. Kessler D, McClellan M. "Do Doctors Practice Defensive Medicine?" *Quarterly Journal of Economics*, vol. 111, no. 2, May 1996.

49. Kronick R, Gilmer T. "Explaining the Decline in Health Insurance Coverage: 1979-1995." *Health Affairs*, vol. 18, no. 2, March/April 1999.

50. Labelle R, Stoddart G, Rice T. "A Re-Examination of the Meaning and Importance of Supplier-Induced Demand." *Journal of Health Economics*, vol. 13, no. 3, October 1994.

51. Leonard JA. *The Escalating Cost Crisis: An Update on Structural Cost Pressures Facing U.S. Manufacturers.* Washington, DC: National Association of Manufacturers, September 2006.

52. Lichtenberg FR. "Does Hospital Productivity Grow at the Same Rate as Productivity in the Rest of the Economy?" *American Hospital Association*, December 2003.

53. Lichtenberg FR. "The Impact of New Drugs on U.S. Longevity and Medical Expenditure, 1990-2003." *American Economic Review*, vol. 97, no. 2, May 2007.

54. Martini EM, Garrett N, Lindquist T, Isham GJ. "The Boomers Are Coming: A Total Cost of Care Model of the Impact of Population Aging on Health Care Costs in the United States by Major Practice Category." *Health Services Research*, vol. 42, no. 1, February 2007.

55. Meara E, White C, Cutler DM. "Trends in Medical Spending by Age: 1963-2000." *Health Affairs*, vol. 23, no. 4, July/August 2004.

56. Mello MM. "Medical Malpractice: Impact of the Crisis and Effect of State Tort Reform." *The Robert Wood Johnson Foundation Research Synthesis Report No. 10*, May 2006.

57. Monaco RM, Phelps JH. "Health Care Prices, the Federal Budget and Economic Growth." *Health Affairs*, vol. 14, no. 2, Summer 1995.

58. Newhouse JP. *Erosion of the Medical Marketplace*. Santa Monica, CA: RAND, 1978.

59. Newhouse JP. "Medical Care Costs: How Much Welfare Loss?" *Journal of Economic Perspectives*, vol. 6, no. 3, Summer 1992.

60. Newhouse JP, Insurance Experiment Group. *Free for All? Lessons From the RAND Health Insurance Experiment*. Cambridge, MA: Harvard University Press, 1993.

61. Nichols LM, Axeen S. *Employer Health Costs in a Global Economy: A Competitive Disadvantage for U.S. Firms*. Washington, DC: New America Foundation, May 2008.

62. Okunade AA, Murthy VNR. "Technology as a Major Driver of Health Care Costs: A Cointegration Analysis of the Newhouse Conjecture." *Journal of Health Economics*, vol. 21, no. 1, January 2002.

63. Organisation for Economic Co-Operation and Development. "OECD Health Data 2008: Statistics and Indicators for 30 Countries." June 2008.

64. Pauly MV. "Editorial: A Re-Examination of the Meaning and Importance of Supplier-Induced Demand." *Journal of Health Economics*, vol. 13, no. 3, October 1994.

65. Pauly MV. "When Does Curbing Health Care Costs Really Help the Economy?" *Health Affairs*, vol. 14, no. 2, Summer 1995.

66. Peacock SJ, Richardson JR. "Supplier-Induced Demand: Re-Examining Identification and Misspecification in Cross-Sectional Analysis." *European Journal of Health Economics*, vol. 8, no. 3, September 2007.

67. Peden EA, Freeland MS. "A Historical Analysis of Medical Spending Growth, 1960-1993." *Health Affairs*, vol. 14, no. 2, Summer 1995.

68. Reinhardt UE. "Health Care Spending and American Competitiveness." *Health Affairs*, vol. 8, no. 4, Winter 1989.

69. Rosenblatt A. "The Underwriting Cycle: The Rule of Six." *Health Affairs*, vol. 23, no. 6, November/December 2004.

70. Russell LB. *Prevention's Potential for Slowing the Growth of Medical Spending*. Washington, DC: National Coalition on Health Care, October 2007.

71. Salkever DS, Bice TW. "The Impact of Certificate of Need Controls on Hospital Investment." *The Milbank Memorial Fund Quarterly*, vol. 54, no. 2, 1976.

72. Seshamani M, Gray A. "Time to Death and Health Expenditure: An Improved Model for the Impact of Demographic Change on Health Care Costs." *Age and Ageing*, vol. 33, no. 6, November 2004.

73. Shactman D, Altman SH, Eilat E, Thorpe KF, Doonan M. "The Outlook for Hospital Spending." *Health Affairs*, vol. 22, no. 6, November/December 2003.

74. Sheils JF, Young GJ, Rubin RJ. "O Canada: Do We Expect Too Much From Its Health System?" *Health Affairs*, vol. 11, no. 1, 1992.

75. Skinner JS, Staiger DO, Fisher ES. "Is Technological Change in Medicine Always Worth It? The Case of Acute Myocardial Infarction." *Health Affairs*, Web Exclusive, February 7, 2006.

76. Sloan F, Chepke L. "From Medical Malpractice to Quality Assurance." *Issues in Science and Technology*, Spring 2008.

77. Sloan FA, Chepke LM. *Medical Malpractice*. Cambridge, MA: Massachusetts Institute of Technology, 2008.

78. Sloan F, Entman S, Reilly B, Glass C, Hickson G, Zhang H. "Tort Liability and Obstetrician's Care Levels." *International Review of Law and Economics*, vol. 17, no. 2, June 1997.

79. Smith SD, Heffler SK, Freeland MS. "The Impact of Technological Change on Health Care Cost Increases: An Evaluation of the Literature." Working Paper, 2000.

80. Strunk BC, Ginsburg PB. "Aging Plays Limited Role in Health Care Cost Trends." *Center for Studying Health System Change Data Bulletin No. 23*, 2002.

81. Strunk BC, Ginsburg PB, Banker MI. "The Effect of Population Aging on Future Hospital Demand." *Health Affairs*, Web Exclusive, March 28, 2006.

82. Technical Review Panel on the Medicare Trustees Report. "Review of Assumptions and Methods of the Medicare Trustees' Financial Projections." December 2000 [Available at: http://www .cms.hhs.gov/ReportsTrustFunds/downloads/ TechnicalPanelReport2000.pdf]

83. Thorpe KE, Florence CS, Howard DH, Joski P. "Trends: The Impact of Obesity on Rising Medical Spending." *Health Affairs*, Web Exclusive, October 20, 2004.

84. Tosetti E, Moscone F. "Health Expenditure and Income in the United States." University of Leicester, Department of Economics Working Paper No. 07/14, October 2007.

85. Tynan A, Berenson RA, Christianson JB. "Health Plans Target Advanced Imaging Services." *Center for Studying Health System Change Issue Brief No. 118*, 2008.

86. U.S. Department of Labor, Bureau of Labor Statistics. Current Employment Statistics. Average Hourly Earnings, Not Seasonally Adjusted, 1999-2007 [Available at: http://www.bls.gov/ces/#tables].

87. Van Baal PHM, Polder JJ, de Wit GA, Hoogenveen RT, Feenstra TL, Boshuizen HC, Engelfriet PM, Brouwer WBF. "Lifetime Medical Costs of Obesity: Prevention No Cure for Increasing Health Expenditure." *PLoS Medicine*, vol. 5, no. 2, February 2008.

88. Vogt WB, Town R. "How Has Hospital Consolidation Affected the Price and Quality of Hospital Care." *The Robert Wood Johnson Foundation Research Synthesis Report No. 9*, February 2006.

89. White C. "Health Care Spending Growth: How Different is the United States From The Rest of the OECD?" *Health Affairs*, vol. 26, no. 1, January/ February 2007.

90. Woolhandler S, Campbell T, Himmelstein DU. "Costs of Health Care Administration in the United States and Canada." *New England Journal of Medicine*, vol. 349, no. 8, 2003.

91. Woolhandler S, Himmelstein DU. "The Deteriorating Administrative Efficiency of the U.S. Health Care System." *New England Journal of Medicine*, vol. 324, no. 18, 1991.

8

Medical Technology

There is no standard definition of medical technology. In broad terms, it refers to "drugs, devices, medical and surgical procedures used in medical care, and the organizational and supportive systems within which such care is provided" (Office of Technology Assessment 1982). Medical technology continues to be influenced by new developments in areas other than biomedical research.

Technological innovation and the use of new drugs, devices, and procedures have made significant strides in the treatment of a variety of diseases, both old and new. Studies have suggested that pharmaceutical drugs are responsible for much of the marked gains in life expectancy observed over the last 50 years. However, a critical appraisal of these studies suggests that the biomedical determinants of life expectancy using aggregate data have been overstated (Grootendorst et al. 2009). The aggregate benefits of new drug launches are even less impressive. Using conservative estimates, Lichtenberg (2005) found that the average annual increase in life expectancy of the entire population resulting from new drug launches is about one week. When interpreting these results, some caution is advised. Even though at the population level pharmaceutical drugs may not have pro-

duced the level of health benefits that were earlier presumed, the benefits of both old and new drugs for individual patients or certain categories of patients remain unrefuted. For example, use of antiretroviral drug "cocktails" has produced tremendous gains in life expectancy for HIV-positive individuals. Lima and colleagues (2007) observed that life expectancy for a 20-year old HIV-positive patient increased by 9.1 years in 1993-1995 and to 23.6 years in 2002-2004. The increase in life expectancy and decrease in mortality were directly associated with the use of modern forms of highly active antiretroviral therapy (HAART). Similarly, medical technology has benefited other categories of patients such as those with heart disease, diabetes, and a host of other medical conditions.

This brings us to the question of the appropriate use of technology. Increasingly, the emphasis is being placed on evidence of health outcomes and risk-benefit. Outcomes or *efficacy* can be both positive and negative. Positive outcomes include better diagnosis and cure, better management of chronic conditions, decrease in morbidity and mortality, and increased life expectancy and quality of life. Negative outcomes result from the inappropriate application of medical technology or when the safety and efficacy of technology have not been adequately assessed. For example, hospitals have been plagued recently by numerous incidents of radiation overexposure during brain scans or CT scans. One hospital reported that some patients may have received up to eight times the normal dose because of computer error (McLaughlin 2009). In other instances, risk-benefit must be assessed. For example, medical science has found a variety of ways to examine the heart from the outside. Cardiologists can open clogged arteries without opening the chest and will someday be able to repair faulty valves that way. Radiation is the key to these advances. Yet exposure to radiation can also damage DNA, the operating manual of a cell. This damage can lead to uncontrolled cell division, the hallmark of cancer. The larger the dose, the greater the risk of developing cancer. This delicate balance between benefit and risk demands the judicious and appropriate use of radiation for diagnosing and treating disease (Harvard Heart Letter 2009).

As pointed out in Chapter 7, technology has been one of the most significant factors responsible for health care cost inflation. Without a doubt, ever-rising health care costs will be unsustainable in the future, which means that unrestricted diffusion and utilization of technology will be increasingly unaffordable. However, both unrestricted use and non-judicious rationing of technology are bad for society. To address this dilemma, experts have been pointing to an increased role of *health technology assessment* (HTA) to decide which technology is best suited for a given clinical situation. Cost-effectiveness of a given technology before it is recommended for widespread use is one approach. Assessment of cost-effectiveness is important because a given technology may offer improved outcomes, but the costs of development and production are often very high. However, even cost-effectiveness is not free from controversy because its assessment is at the aggregate level. At some point, we will have to confront the problem of cost-effectiveness at the level of the patient. For example, reallocating resources from cost-ineffective treatments for late-stage pancreatic cancer to cost-effective treatments for diabetes may improve health outcomes in the aggregate but not for patients with late-stage pancreatic cancer (Weinstein & Skinner 2010).

Organizational and supportive systems are particularly relevant to an understanding of medical technology because they include the increasing use of information technology in health care delivery. *Health information technology* (HIT) is the term used to describe the application of computers and technology in health care settings. Sometimes the term *information*

and communications technology (ICT) is used when the use of HIT has a strong networking or communications component (Hersh 2009). Integrated electronic patient records can reduce the likelihood of incorrect medical decisions (Dick et al. 1997); however, human errors are still possible.

We begin the readings in this chapter with a primer on medical technology and its cost implications. The article, **How Changes in Medical Technology Affect Health Care Costs**, cites two examples, heart attacks and low-birthweight babies, in which new drugs, diagnostic procedures, and treatments have remarkably reduced mortality and increased life expectancy. Medical technologies affect health care costs in several different ways based on their prescribed application and their effects on the use of other health care services such as hospital stays. Another factor is how widespread a new technology becomes available and the extent of utilization. Some technologies save money, such as a new vaccine that prevents expensive treatments down the road, can result in cost savings over time. In other situations, such as innovations in anesthesia that may reduce the cost of surgery per patient, technology may end up increasing costs if more surgeries are performed as a result of the innovation. Although a direct measure of the impact of new technology on total health care spending has not been possible, indirect estimates suggest that as much as half of the growth in real health care spending may be attributable to technology. Innovation is influenced by factors such as consumer demand, reimbursement, investments in basic science and research, and competition among providers to offer the "latest and best" to attract patients. Of the expenditures on health research in the United States, 55% is spent by private industry and 36% is spent by the government. As we move forward, the ongoing question facing Americans will be how much health care we can afford. Coverage and reimbursement decisions guided by cost-effectiveness analyses may be the way to address this issue.

The report by Beever, **The Cost of Medical Technologies: Maximizing the Value of Innovation**, goes beyond the first article by focusing on the use of medical technology on those patient segments where it truly adds value. Dissemination and, therefore, the use of technology varies by geographic region, but without producing corresponding differences in health benefits. Duplication of procedures incurs costs but add little or no value. Technologies that deliver significant medical benefits in some cases are sometimes used for low value-added situations. Four factors may account for such variations. (1) To obtain regulatory approval for a new medical technology, innovators focus their studies mainly on clinical situations where maximum value is added; situations where value is not added are not addressed. (2) Physicians and patients who select treatment options have little or no stake in the cost implications of their decisions. (3) Medical technology is reimbursed on the basis of its cost. (4) The practice of defensive medicine adds to costs, but its value is questionable. Beever suggests that a variety of solutions may be possible to address these issues. As a starting point, establish a commonly accepted definition of value, cover a variety of clinical situations in cost-effectiveness studies, and establish a credible agency to conduct value assessment studies in which both experts and stakeholders are involved.

The report by the U.S. Department of Commerce, **Pharmaceutical Price Controls in OECD Countries: Implications for U.S. Consumers, Pricing, Research and Development, and Innovation**, highlights the effects of government price controls in OECD countries that are designed to limit spending on pharmaceuticals. By contrast, in the United States, the government mainly provides incentives through direct and indirect funding, intellectual property laws, and other policies intended toward creating an environment that encourages innovation and competition. In the OECD countries, the government sets the sales price and makes it illegal to sell the drugs at higher prices. Also, being the dominant buyer of drugs, the government is able to leverage its monopsonistic power. In addition to price controls, OECD countries use approval delays and other procedural barriers, restrictions on dispensing and prescribing, and payment restrictions. The net effect is that drug companies charge less than a market-based price. As a result, they generate less revenue which curtails research and development (R&D). Other regulatory practices limit the competition that would otherwise accrue from generic pharmaceuticals. OECD countries can save money by promoting the use of generic drugs. If these countries would invest those savings in R&D, the benefit to U.S. consumers from new drugs developed by OECD countries would be in the range of $5 billion to $7 billion per year.

The final reading for this chapter, **Some Unintended Consequences of Information Technology in Health Care: The Nature of Patient Care Information System-Related Errors**, demonstrates from separate studies in the United States, The Netherlands, and Australia that information systems can generate errors rather than reduce their likelihood. In this article, Ash and colleagues point out that the care delivery system in which people, technologies, organizational routines, and regulations interact may actually be weakened rather than strengthened by patient care information systems or PCIS (the term used by the authors for HIT). The re-

sulting errors can be traced to HIT design and/or its implementation. Certain "silent errors" cannot be found by a technical analysis of the system design. One main category of errors is associated with entering and retrieving information. These errors are caused by either human-computer interface in a highly interruptive environment or by requirements to encode data entry in structured formats that are more time consuming to complete and read than paper medical records. The second main category of errors arises when computers undermine communication and coordination of events and activities involved in patient care delivery. The contingency-driven nature of health care work poses special challenges for system designers. The result can be faulty reporting and actions by those using the system. Patient safety may be compromised because users may tend to work around the system that is deemed to be unrealistic. The article discusses other issues and provides recommendations to overcome some of the IT-related problems.

References

Dick, R.S., E.B. Steen, and D.E. Detmer. 1997. *The Computer-Based Patient Record: An Essential Technology for Health Care.* Washington, DC: National Academy Press.

Grootendorst, P., E. Piérard, and M. Shim. 2009. Life-expectancy gains from pharmaceutical drugs: a critical appraisal of the literature. *Expert Review of Pharmacoeconomics & Outcomes Research* 9(4): 353-364.

Harvard Heart Letter. 2009. Radiation in medicine: a double-edged sword. *Harvard Heart Letter* 19(8):1-2.

Hersh, W. 2009. A stimulus to define informatics and health information technology. *BMC Medical Informatics & Decision Making* 9 (Special Section): 1-6.

Lichtenberg, F.R. 2005. The impact of new drug launches on longevity: evidence from longitudinal, disease-level data from 52 countries, 1982-2001. *International Journal of Health Care Finance and Economics* 5(1):47-73.

Lima, V.D., et al. 2007. Continued improvement in survival among HIV-infected individuals with newer forms of highly active antiretroviral therapy. *AIDS* 21(6):685-692.

McLaughlin, N. 2009. Do attempt to adjust the picture. *Modern Healthcare* 39(50):24.

Office of Technology Assessment. 1982. *Medical Technology Under Proposals to Increase Competition in Health Care.* Report OTA-H-190, Washington, DC: US Government Printing Office.

Weinstein, M.C. and J.A. Skinner. 2010. Comparative effectiveness and health care spending—implications for reform. *New England Journal of Medicine* 2010 Jan 6. [Epub ahead of print]

1

How Changes in Medical Technology Affect Health Care Costs

Source: "How Changes in Medical Technology Affect Health Care Costs", *Snapshots: Health Care Costs.* The Henry J. Kaiser Family Foundation, March 2007. This information was reprinted with permission from the Henry J. Kaiser Family Foundation. The Kaiser Family Foundation is a non-profit private operating foundation, based in Menlo Park, California, dedicated to producing and communicating the best possible analysis and information on health issues.

Health expenditures continue to grow very rapidly in the U.S. Since 1970, health care spending has grown at an average annual rate of 9.8%, or about 2.5 percentage points faster than the economy as measured by the nominal gross domestic product (GDP). Annual spending on health care increased from $75 billion in 1970 to $2.0 trillion in 2005, and is estimated to reach $4 trillion in 2015. As a share of the economy, health care has more than doubled over the past 35 years, rising from 7.2% of GDP in 1970 to 16.0% of GDP in 2005, and is projected to be 20% of GDP in 2015. Health care spending per capita increased from $356 in 1970 to $6,697 in 2005, and is projected to rise to $12,320 in 2015.[1]

The particularly rapid increases in health insurance premiums over the last few years have focused the health policy community on the issues of cost containment and health insurance affordability. A key question from policymakers is why spending on health care consistently rises more rapidly than spending on other goods and services. Health care experts point to the development and diffusion of medical technology as primary factors in explaining the persistent difference between health spending and overall economic growth, with some arguing that new medical technology may account for about one-half or more of real long-term spending growth. This paper briefly describes what health policy analysts mean by medical technology and the mechanisms by which it affects the growth in health care costs.

WHAT IS MEDICAL TECHNOLOGY?

Broadly speaking, the term "medical technology" can be used to refer to the procedures, equipment, and processes by which medical care is delivered. Examples of changes in technology would include new medical and surgical procedures (e.g., angioplasty, joint replacements), drugs (e.g., biologic agents), medical devices (e.g., CT scanners, implantable defibrillators), and new support systems (e.g., electronic medical records and transmission of information, telemedicine).[2] There is very little in the field of medicine that does not use some type of medical technology and that has not been affected by new technology.

Heart disease and its consequence, heart attack, is the leading cause of death in the U.S. and a good example of how new technology has changed the treatment and prevention of a disease over time. In the 1970s, cardiac care units were introduced, lidocaine was used to manage irregular heartbeat, beta-blockers were used to lower blood pressure in the first 3 hours after a heart attack, "clot buster" drugs began to be widely used, and coronary artery bypass surgery became more prevalent. In the 1980s, blood-thinning agents were used after a heart attack to prevent reoccurrences, beta-blocker therapy evolved from short-term therapy immediately after a heart attack to maintenance therapy, and angioplasty (minimally invasive surgery) was used after heart attack patients were stable. In the 1990s, more effective drugs were introduced to inhibit clot formation, angioplasty was used for treatment and revascularization along with stents to keep blood vessels open, cardiac rehabilitation programs were implemented sooner, and implantable cardiac defibrillators were used in certain patients with irregular heartbeats. In the 2000s, better tests became available to diagnose heart attack, drug-eluting stents were used, and new drug strategies were developed (aspirin, ACE inhibitors, beta-blockers, statins) for long-term management of heart attack and potential heart attack patients. From 1980-2000, the overall mortality rate from heart attack fell by almost half, from 345.2 to 186.0 per 100,000 persons.[3]

Another example of how advances in technology have changed health outcomes over time is in the treatment of preterm babies, for which very little could be done in 1950. But by 1990, changes in technology, including special ventilators, artificial pulmonary surfactant to help infant lungs develop, neonatal intensive care, and steroids for mother and/or baby, helped decrease mortality to one-third its 1950 level, with an overall increase in life expectancy of about 12 years per low-birthweight baby.[4]

HOW DOES NEW MEDICAL TECHNOLOGY AFFECT HEALTH CARE SPENDING AND COSTS?

While a particular new technology may either increase or decrease health care spending, researchers generally agree that, taken together, advances in medical technology have contributed to rising overall U.S. health care spending. Rettig describes how new medical technology affects the costs of health care through the following "mechanisms of action":[5]

- Development of new treatments for previously untreatable terminal conditions, including long-term maintenance therapy for treatment of such diseases as diabetes, end-stage renal disease, and AIDS;

- Major advances in clinical ability to treat previously untreatable acute conditions, such as coronary artery bypass graft;

- Development of new procedures for discovering and treating secondary diseases within a disease, such as erythropoietin to treat anemia in dialysis patients;

- Expansion of the indications for a treatment over time, increasing the patient population to which the treatment is applied;

- On-going, incremental improvements in existing capabilities, which may improve quality;

- Clinical progress, through major advances or by the cumulative effect of incremental improvements, that extends the scope of medicine to conditions once regarded as beyond its boundaries, such as mental illness and substance abuse.

Whether a particular new technology will increase or reduce total health expenditures depends on several factors. One is its impact on the cost of treating an individual patient. Does the new technology supplement existing treatment, or is it a full or partial substitute for current approaches? Do these changes result in higher or lower health spending for each patient treated? In looking at the impact on cost per patient, consideration needs to be given to whether the direct costs of the new technology include any effect on the use or cost of other health care services such as hospital days or physician office visits.

A second factor is the level of use that a new technology achieves (i.e., how many times is the new technology used?). Does the new technology extend treatment to a broader population?—examples would be innovations that address previously untreatable illness, diagnose new populations for existing treatments, or extend existing treatments to new conditions. New technologies can also reduce utilization—for example, new screening or diagnosis capacity that allows more targeted treatment. There also are temporal aspects to evaluating the impact of new technologies on costs. Some innovations, such as a new vaccine, may cost more immediately but may lead to savings down the road if the vaccine results in fewer people seeking more expensive treatment. New technologies also can extend life expectancy, which affects both the type and amount of health care that people use in their lifetime.

Evaluating the impact of new innovation can be complicated. For example, a case study that focuses on a single technology or disease may show cost savings based on the costs and benefits of the new technology if it replaces a more expensive technology and provides health improvements, while an analysis of health care system-wide costs may show cost increases if the new technology results in greater utilization than the old. A specific example is anesthesia, where substantial innovations have occurred in recent years. Better anesthetic agents and practices have reduced the burden of surgery on patients, producing faster patient recoveries, shorter hospital stays, and fewer medical errors. These changes reduce the cost per patient compared to surgery in the absence of these changes. At the same time, these innovations also make it possible to perform surgeries on patients who previously would have been considered too frail to undergo the surgery; this adds to the amount of health care that is delivered systemwide, thus perhaps increasing total health care spending.

It is not possible to directly measure the impact of new medical technology on total health care spending; innovation in the health care sector occurs continuously, and the impacts of different changes interrelate. The size of the health sector (16% of gross domestic product in 2005) and its diversity (thousands of procedures, products, and interventions) also render direct measurement impractical. Economists have used indirect approaches to try to estimate the impact of new technology on the cost of health care.[6] In an often-cited article, Newhouse estimates the impact of medical technology on health care spending by first estimating the impact of factors that can reasonably be accounted for (e.g., spread of insurance, increasing per capita income, aging of the population, supplier-induced demand, low medical sector productivity gains). He concludes that the factors listed above account for well under half of the growth in real medical spending, and that the bulk of the unexplained residual increase should be attributed to technological change—what he calls "the enhanced capabilities of medicine."[7]

WHAT FACTORS AFFECT THE GROWTH OF NEW MEDICAL TECHNOLOGY?

Many factors influence innovation in medical care. Consumer demand for better health is a prime factor. Research shows that the use of medical care rises with income: as people and the nation become wealthier, they provide a fertile market for new medical innovations. Consumers want medical care that will help them achieve and maintain good health, and advances in medical technology are perceived as

ways to promote those goals. Consumer demand is affected by the increased public awareness of medical technology through the media, the Internet, and direct-to-consumer advertising.

Health insurance systems that provide payment for new innovations also encourage medical advances. Medical treatments can be very expensive, and their cost would be beyond the reach of many people unless their risk of needing health care could be pooled though insurance (either public or private). The presence of health insurance provides some assurance to researchers and medical suppliers that patients will have the resources to pay for new medical products, thus encouraging research and development. At the same time, the promise of better health through improvements in medicine may increase the demand for health insurance by consumers looking for ways to assure access to the type of medical care that they want.

The continuing flow of new medical technology results from other factors including the desire by professionals to find better ways to treat their patients and the level of investment in basic science and research. Direct providers of care may incorporate new technology because they want to improve the care they offer their patients, but they also may feel the need to offer the "latest and best" as they compete with other providers for patients. Health care professionals, like people in other occupations, also may be motivated by professional goals (e.g., peer recognition, tenure, prestige) to find ways to improve practice. Commercial interests (such as pharmaceutical companies and medical device makers) are willing to invest large amounts in research and development because they have found strong consumer interest in, and financial reimbursement for, many of the new products they produce. In addition, public and private investments in basic science research lead directly and indirectly to advancements in medical practice; these investments in basic science are not necessarily motivated by an interest in creating new products but by the desire to increase human understanding.

An estimated $111 billion was spent on U.S. health research in 2005. The largest share was spent by Industry ($61 billion, or 55%), including the pharmaceutical industry ($35 billion, or 31%), the biotechnology industry ($16 billion, or 15%), and the medical technology industry ($10 billion, or 9%). Government spent $40 billion (36%), most of which was spent by the National Institutes of Health ($29 billion, or 26%), followed by other federal government agencies ($9 billion, or 8%), and state and local government ($3 billion, or 2%). Other Organizations (including universities, independent research institutes, voluntary health organizations, and philanthropic foundations) spent $10 billion (9%). About 5.5 cents of every health dollar was spent on health research in 2005, a decrease from 5.8 cents in 2004.[8] It is not known how much of health research was spent specifically on medical technology, though by definition most of the Industry spending ($61 billion) was spent on medical technology. Medical technology industries spent greater shares of research and development as a percent of sales in 2002 than did other U.S. industries: 11.4% for the Medical Devices industry and 12.9% for Drugs and Medicine, compared to 5.6% for Telecommunications, 4.1% for Auto, 3.9% for Electrical/Electronics, 3.5% for All Companies, and 3.1% for Aerospace/Defense.[9]

POLICY ISSUES

Rising health care expenditures lead to the question of whether we are getting value for the money we spend. Compared to other high-income countries, the U.S. spends more,[10] but this spending is not reflected in greater health care resources (such as hospital beds, physicians, nurses, MRIs, and CT scanners per capita)[11] or better measures of health.[12] However, studies have found that, on average, increases in medical spending as a result of advances in medical care have provided reasonable value. For example, Cutler et al. found that from 1960 to 2000, average life expectancy increased by 7 years, 3.5 years of which they attribute to improvements in health care. Comparing the value of a year of life (anywhere from $50,000 to $200,000) to the study's finding that each year of increased life expectancy cost about $19,900 in health spending (after adjusting for inflation), the authors concluded that the increased spending, on average, has been worth it.[13]

No matter the value of advances in medical care, as the rapid growth in health care costs increasingly strains personal, corporate, and government budgets, policymakers and the public must consider the question of how much health care we can afford. Can the U.S. continue to spend an expanding share of GDP on health (from 7.2% in 1970 to a projected 20% by 2015)? If the answer is no, then society must consider ways to reduce future health spending growth. And since, as described earlier, the development and diffusion of new medical technology is a significant contributor to the rapid growth in health care spending, it is new technology that we would look to for cost savings.

Currently, most suggestions to slow the growth in new medical technology in the U.S. focus on cost-effectiveness analysis. Other approaches have problems: some used by other countries are not popular in the U.S. (rationing, regulation, budget-driven constraints), some have been tried and found not to have a significant impact on technology-driven costs (managed care, certificate-of-need approval), while others are expected to have only limited impact on health care spending (consumer-driven health care, pay-for-performance, information technology). Cost-effectiveness analysis involves non-biased, well-controlled studies of a technology's benefits and costs, followed by dissemination of the findings so they can be applied in clinical practice. The method to control the use of inappropriate technology could be through coverage and reimbursement decisions, by using financial incentives for physician and patients to use cost-effective treatments. Use of the cost-effectiveness findings could be implemented at the health plan level[14] or through a centralized, institutional process, such as Britain's National Institute for Health and Clinical Excellence (NICE). If implemented at the national level, questions about the structure, placement, financing, and function of a centralized agency would have to be resolved.[15] Other issues include whether money would be saved by reducing costly technology where marginal value is low and how to monitor the cost impact, and whether a cost containment approach would discourage technological innovation.

● ● ● **References**

1. Centers for Medicare and Medicaid Services, Office of the Actuary, National Health Statistics Group, http://www.cms.hhs.gov/NationalHealthExpend Data/ (see Historical, NHE summary including share of GDP, CY 1960-2005, file nhegdp05.zip; and Historical, Projected, NHE Historical and projections, 1965-2015, file nhe65-15.zip).

2. George B. Moseley III, *Changing Conditions for Medical Technology in the Health Care Industry* (presented before the OGI School of Science and Engineering, Oregon Health and Science University, October 18, 2005), http://cpd.ogi.edu/Seminars05 /MoseleySeminarIndex.htm.

3. AdvaMed, *The Value of Investment in Health Care: Better Care, Better Lives* (January 2004): 14-21, at http://www.advamed.org /newsroom/medtap/ medtapreport.pdf.

4. David M. Cutler and Mark McClellan, "Is Technological Change in Medicine Worth It?" *Health Affairs* 20(5) (September/October 2001): 11-29.

5. Richard A. Rettig, "Medical Innovation Duels Cost Containment," *Health Affairs* (Summer 1994): 15.

6. Several approaches have been used to study and quantify the impact of technology on health care costs, including:

- The *residual approach*, where the impact of changes in other factors (such as prices, income, population growth and demographic changes, and utilization) is quantified, and the residual not accounted for is attributed to changes in technology. The most widely-used approach, it circumvents the need to specify a direct measure of technology and captures the impact of general technologies applied in the health sector, such as information technology. However, it is only a rough, indirect estimate (and perhaps an overestimate) of the impact of technology on health spending because other factors that cannot be quantified (such as lifestyle, environment, education) will also be included along with technology. Examples of residual studies include (1) Newhouse (1992), described in the text of this report; and (2) Edgar A. Peden and Mark S. Freeland, "Insurance Effects on US Medical Spending (1960-1993)," *Health Economics* 7 (1998):671-687, which found that nearly half (47%) of the 1960-1993 growth in real per capita U.S. medical spending and almost two-thirds (64%) of its 1983-1993 growth were due to increasing levels of insurance coverage (i.e., a decline in coinsurance levels paid by consumers). Because lower coinsurance levels and higher research spending are considered inducers of technology, the authors concluded that these results imply that about two-thirds (70%) of the 1960-1993 medical spending growth and about three-fourths (76%) of the 1983-1993 medical spending growth came from cost-increasing advances in medical technology.

- The *proxy approach*, where a proxy (such as research and development spending, or time) is used to measure the impact of technology. The usefulness of these studies depends on how good a substitute the proxy is for technology and how measurable it is. Examples include: (1) Albert A. Okunade and Vasudeva N.R. Murthy, "Technology as a "Major Driver" of Health Care Costs: a Cointegration Analysis of the Newhouse Conjecture," *Journal of Health Economics* 21 (2002):147-159, which found that technological change, proxied by total research and development (R&D) spending and health R&D spending, is a statistically significant long-run driver of 1960-1997 rising real health care expenditures per capita; and (2) Livio Di Matteo, "The Macro Determinants of Health Expenditure in the United State and Canada: Assessing the Impact of Income, Age Distribution and Time," *Health Policy* 71(1) (January 2005):23-42, which found that time, used as a proxy for technological change, accounted for about two-thirds of the 1975-2000 increases in real per capita health expenditures in the U.S. and Canada.

- *Case studies of specific technologies*, to determine their effects on the cost of treating a particular condition. While case studies can explain the impact of certain medical advances on health care costs, it is difficult to generalize from them to an aggregate or national level: (1) In an analysis of technological change at the disease level for 5 medical conditions, David M. Cutler and Mark McClellan, "Is Technological Change In Medicine Worth It?" *Health Affairs* 20(5) (September/October 2001):11-29, found that the benefits of 4 of the 5 conditions studied (heart attacks, low-birthweight infants, depression, and cataracts) were greater than the costs; costs and benefits were about equal for the fifth condition (breast cancer). For example, in 1984 nearly 90% of heart attack patients were managed medically; by 1998, more than half of patients received surgical treatment. Spending by Medicare on heart attack patients increased from $3 billion to $4.8 billion (a 3.4% annual change), despite a 0.8% annual decline in the number of heart attacks. From 1984-1998, the use of new technology helped to increase the average heart attack patient's life expectancy by one year (valued at $70,000 per case), while treatment costs increased $10,000 per case (4.2% per year), for a net benefit of $60,000 per case; and (2) Laurence Baker et al., "The Relationship Between Technology Availability And Health Care Spending," *Health Affairs*, Web Exclusive (November 5, 2003): W3-537-W3-551, studied the relationship between the supply of new technologies and health care utilization and spending at 3 levels (a particular technology, "category" spending on substitutable or complimentary technologies, and total health spending), using 10 diagnostic imaging, cardiac, cancer, and newborn care technologies. They found that more availability of the technologies was frequently associated with higher use and spending on the services. For example, a one unit increase in the number of freestanding MRI units per million people was associated with an increase of about $32,900 per million beneficiaries (commercial and Medicare) per month, or approximately $395,000 per year. Looking at "category" spending, they found an individual technology can increase or decrease spending on other technologies in the same category depending on whether they complement those technologies (e.g., an increase of one unit per million in availability of MRI equipment was associated with an increase of 0.33% in total diagnostic imaging spending) or substitute for those technologies (e.g., increases in the availability of cardiac services were typically associated with reductions in total spending on patients with cardiac diagnoses). For total health care spending, they found that greater availability of technologies was associated with higher total spending in the commercial population in all but 2 technologies studied, and these effects were larger than the technology-specific relationships.

This endnote borrows heavily from (1) Mark S. Freeland, Stephen K. Heffler, and Sheila D. Smith, *The Impact of Technological Change on Health Care Cost Increases: A Brief Synthesis of the Literature*, June 1998, Office of the Actuary, Health Care Financing Administration; (2) Fabio Pammolli et al., *Medical Devices: Competitiveness and Impact on Public Health Expenditure* (July 2005), Center for the Economic Analysis of Competitiveness, Markets and Regulation (CERM), Rome, Italy; prepared for the Directorate Enterprise of the European Commission, http://ec.europa.eu/enterprise/medical_devices/c_f_f/md_final_report.pdf; and (3) Productivity Commission, Australian Government, *Impacts of Advances in Medical Technology in Australia*, August 31, 2005, Melbourne, Australia, http://www.pc.gov.au/study/medicaltechnology/finalreport/index.html.

7. Joseph P. Newhouse, "Medical Care Costs: How Much Welfare Loss?" *Journal of Economic Perspectives* 6(3) (Summer 1992):3-21. For a thorough discussion of the components of health care spending growth and medical technology's significant role, see the report of the Technical Review Panel on the Medicare Trustees Reports, *Review of Assumptions and Methods of the Medicare Trustees' Financial Projections* (December 2000), http://www.cms.hhs.gov/ReportsTrustFunds/02_TechnicalPanelReports.asp#TopOfPage. The Panel concluded that estimates from the literature suggest that about half of real health care expenditure growth has been attributable to medical technology (p. 35).

8. Research!America, *2005 Investment in U.S. Health Research*, September 2006, http://www.researchamerica.org/publications/appropriations/healthdollar2005.pdf. Data for the medical technology industry, universities, state and local government, and philanthropic foundations is for 2004.

9. AdvaMed, *The Medical Technology Industry at a Glance* (Sept. 7, 2004):14, Chart 3.2, http://www.advamed.org/newsroom/chartbook.pdf.

10. Kaiser Family Foundation, *Health Care Spending in the United States and OECD Countries*, January 2007, http://www.kff.org/insurance/snapshot/chcm010307oth.cfm.

11. Gerard F. Anderson, Bianca K. Frogner, Roger A. Johns, and Uwe E. Reinhardt, "Health Care Spending And Use Of Information Technology In OECD Countries," *Health Affairs* 25(3) (May/June 2006):819-831.

12. Cathy Schoen, Karen Davis, Sabrina K.H. How, and Stephen C. Schoenbaum, "U.S. Health System Performance: A National Scorecard," *Health Affairs*, Web Exclusive (September 20, 2006):w459.

13. David M. Cutler, Allison B. Rosen, and Sandeep Vijan, "The Value of Medical Spending in the United States, 1960-2000," *The New England Journal of Medicine*, 355(9) (August 31, 2006): 920-927. See also Jonathan S. Skinner, Douglas O. Staiger, and Elliott S. Fisher, "Is Technological Change In Medicine Always Worth It? The Case Of Acute Myocardial Infarction," *Health Affairs*, Web Exclusive (February 7, 2006):W34-W47, and Cutler and McClellan (2001).

14. Mark. V. Pauly, "Competition And New Technology," *Health Affairs* 24(6) (November/December 2005):1523-1535.

15. Gail R. Wilensky, "Developing A Center For Comparative Effectiveness Information," *Health Affairs*, Web Exclusive (November 7, 2006):w572-w585; Molly Joel Coye and Jason Kell, "How Hospitals Confront New Technology," *Health Affairs* 25(1) (Januaryl/February 2006):163-173; and the NICE website: http://www.nice.org.uk/page.aspx?o=home.

2

The Cost of Medical Technologies: Maximizing the Value of Innovation

Source: Beever, C. 2007. *The Cost of Medical Technologies: Maximizing the Value of Innovation.* New York, NY: Booz Allen Hamilton, Inc. (Booz & Company). http://www.booz.com/media/uploads/ TheCostOfMedicalTechnologies.pdf.

BENEFITS OF INNOVATION

Innovation is a fundamental driver of progress that improves the quality of lives. This is true across a broad range of fields, none more so than medical technology. Advances in medical technology have turned diseases like cancer and HIV/AIDS into chronic conditions with dramatically increased survival rates. Thanks to improved diagnostics, diseases can be uncovered sooner, leading to earlier treatment and reduced mortality rates. One outstanding example of this is cardiovascular disease, one of the United State's biggest killers. Earlier diagnosis, combined with innovative advances in medical technology, including pacemakers, stents, and minimally invasive surgical devices, has led to a reduction in deaths over the last 20 years from roughly 400 per 100,000 of population to fewer than 300 per 100,000.

BY-PRODUCTS OF INNOVATION

Innovation does not come without a price. At the same time that they enhance and extend human life, medical technology advances also contributed to rising health care costs. Health care costs have been rising more quickly than the GNP for more than a decade, and that trend is expected to continue. Over the last five years, health care cost growth has on average exceeded GNP growth by over four percentage points. Today, health care costs this country $1.5 trillion a year. Medical technology has become one of the most significant drivers, representing about 20 percent of total cost growth (see Exhibit 1). For nonpharmaceutical medical technology, more than $100 billion in additional spend is expected in the next five years. The magnitude of these cost increases poses a serious challenge to the U.S. economy and society. It isn't surprising that medical technology costs have come under scrutiny—with the objective of identifying the drivers of cost in order to influence them. If manufacturers and health care providers want to play a pivotal role in how that influence will affect health care delivery, it is time for them to act together to develop an effective process for assessing the value of medical technologies and balancing costs against outcomes (see Exhibits 2 and 3).

Nobody questions the overall value of medical technology. To date, most of the studies on medical technology have focused on safety and efficacy. Cost effectiveness and value have played a subordinate role. What health care providers and equipment manufacturers must now determine is whether that value can be even further enhanced by focusing the use of medical technology on those patient segments where it truly adds value.

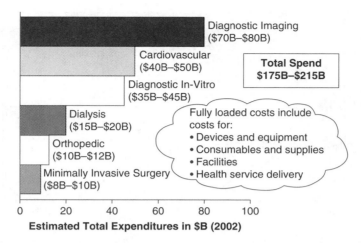

Exhibit 2 Estimated Spending by Category (Excluding Drugs) (2002). *Source:* Medical and Healthcare Marketplace Guide (2003); SG-2 reports; GE Medical; Booz Allen Hamilton interviews; Booz Allen Hamilton analysis

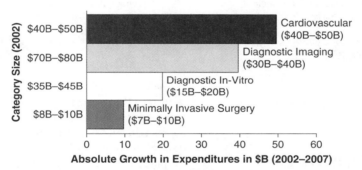

Note: Costs are fully loaded, i.e., include cost of devices, equipment, procedures, supplies, consumables, and facility

Exhibit 3 Projected Cost Growth by Technology Category (Excluding Drugs) (2002-2007). *Source:* Medical and Healthcare Marketplace Guide (2003); SG-2 reports; GE Medical; Booz Allen Hamilton interviews; Booz Allen Hamilton analysis

Payers have started to look at medical technology more closely, searching for ways to manage cost increases without sacrificing the benefits of innovation. For example, in March 2003, The Centers for Medicare and Medicaid Services (CMS) announced the creation of the Medical Technology Council to find ways to streamline the process for making reimbursement decisions. The Council will formalize the process for making CMS coverage decisions for medical technology dependent on safety, efficacy and cost-effectiveness, or value. Given the lead role that CMS often has in influencing coverage decisions made by private health insurance, this is likely to bring major changes for the future.

Booz Allen Hamilton's analysis has shown that there is indeed room to create more value from the money spent on medical technology. As with most discussions about health care value, this one is complicated by the third party payment system for health care in the U.S. (and elsewhere in the world), where those receiving the benefits of care are not in most cases paying directly for the care. Traditional market mechanisms for determining value don't work, and incentives to put money in places where it maximizes value are often misaligned. In the absence of market mechanisms and incentives that create a value screen for the use of medical technology, we have undertaken analysis to provide a fact base for a discussion about how to enhance the value delivered by medical technology. The fact base addresses three questions: What is contributing to the growth of medical technology spending; under what circumstances does medical technology spending exceed the value created; and how can value be

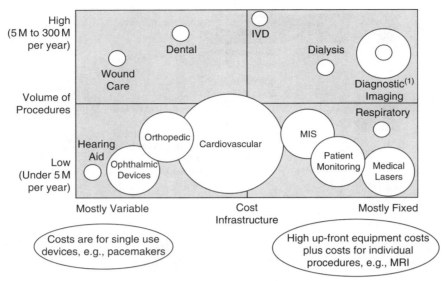

(1) Diagnostic imaging has low cost (e.g., X-ray) and medium cost (e.g., MRI) segments
Note: Costs are fully loaded, i.e., include cost of devices, equipment, procedures, supplies, consumables, and facility

Exhibit 4 Medical Technologies—Contributors to Growth. *Source:* Medical & Healthcare Marketplace guide; multiple secondary sources; Booz Allen Hamilton analysis

enhanced for all stakeholders (payers, providers, manufacturers, and patients)?

CONTRIBUTORS TO THE GROWTH OF MEDICAL TECHNOLOGY SPENDING

The largest components of the U.S. non-pharmaceutical medical technology market are diagnostic imaging, cardiovascular procedures, and in-vitro diagnostics. These three categories alone are expected to add $100 billion in spending by 2005.

There are three main contributors to growth within these categories: the number of procedures, the cost of an individual procedure, and what we call the cost infrastructure, i.e., whether there is a large upfront fixed cost for instance (for setting up a cath lab) or whether the costs are largely variable (for instance for a hearing device) (see Exhibit 4). For example, much of the growth in the diagnostic imaging field reflects the fact that the number of machines (MRI, PET, CT) has increased significantly over the last few years. From the larger installed base, a much larger number of scans have been made. As a result, the growth in expenditures is driven by the large upfront payments for machines (cost infrastructure) multiplied by the larger number of scans (number of procedures). In the cardiovascular area, several effects impact the huge cost growth: the growth in the number of cath labs, a similar cost infrastructure sit-

uation to the one just described for medical imaging, as well as the high costs of individual devices (cost of a procedure). As better and higher-cost alternative devices become available, they are increasingly used, "replacing" lower-cost alternatives.

CALCULATING THE COST-VALUE EQUATION

While not conclusive, there is evidence that spending on medical technology for some patients exceeds its value. Some examples are:

- **Variations in the amount of equipment per patient:** There are wide variations among regions in the U.S. in the number of diagnostic imaging machines per million of population, without corresponding differences in mortality or morbidity rates for the diseases the equipment diagnoses. In Buffalo, NY, there is a PET scanner for every 74,000 people, while in Rochester, NY, there are 215,000 people per PET scanner. In areas where there is high machine capacity, there is a tendency to use it, for reasons discussed below.

- **Duplication of procedures:** There is frequent duplication of diagnostic imaging procedures when they add little or no value. For example, while PET presents some clear medical benefit, its use after CT often only confirms a

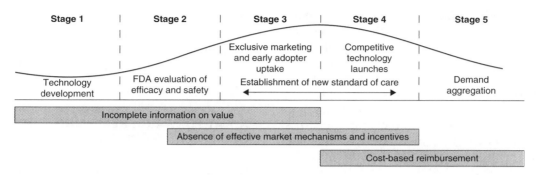

Exhibit 5   Medical Technology Life Cycle. *Source:* Booz Allen Hamilton analysis

diagnosis the physician has already reached before. While it is difficult to estimate the extent of low value PET scans, recent experience with benefit plans that have a coinsurance feature for diagnostic testing (10 percent coinsurance capped at $75 per scan) suggests reductions in procedures in the vicinity of 20 to 30 percent. On a market-wide basis, this equates to $10B per year for diagnostic scans.

- **Overuse of high-end procedures:** Technologies that deliver significant medical benefits in some cases are sometimes used in low value-added situations. For example, studies have shown that the value of ICDs (implantable cardioverter defibrillators), with all-in procedure costs of approximately $35,000, is very high in some patients. Death rates decline dramatically for patients with long QRS intervals. Nevertheless, in other patients an ICD provides more limited benefits.

At issue are why variations in capacity and medical practice exist, and how they affect health care value. We believe there are four key and interrelated reasons operating across the technology life cycle:

- **Incomplete information on value:** As described in Exhibit 5, most innovative medical technologies create value—but most often in a subset of diagnostic and therapeutic situations. Understandably, innovators focus their studies of value and cost-effectiveness during product development on the clinical situations where maximum value is created. The information they generate is focused, appropriately, on gaining regulatory approval and reimbursement: Most evaluations of medical technology address the efficacy and safety criteria that are the primary basis for regulatory approval, adoption by physicians, and reimbursement by health plans. The subtleties of defining clinical situations where the innovation may be less valuable are not typically addressed, particularly early in the product life cycle. To date, this has resulted in limited information on which to develop standards of care and reimbursement practices where value-based distinctions can be made by patient segment.

- **Absence of Effective Market Mechanisms and Incentives:** Two critical prerequisites for markets to assess value are missing in the case of innovative medical technology. As stated above, information on the value of innovative medical technology is often incomplete, particularly as standards of care are being established. In addition, the physicians and patients who select treatment options have little or no stake in the financial outcomes of their decisions.

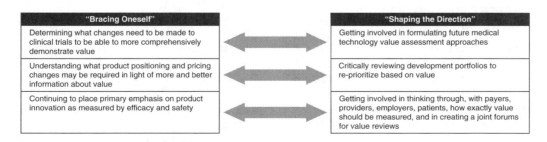

For manufacturers, this could mean thinking about: *Source:* Booz Allen Hamilton analysis

One result is that patients often ask their physicians for the latest and "best" technology whether or not it is appropriate in their situation.

That market mechanisms are absent in many areas of health care is of course an old story; at issue is what takes the place of the market. With respect to medical technology in particular, a number of approaches have been tried, each with limited success. For example, certificates of need (CONs) were introduced over 30 years ago in order to guarantee access to quality care while at the same time managing capacity and costs. They certainly had the right objective, but CONs failed to meet their goal, mostly because they attacked only a sub set of the costs, but also because they were often circumvented or overpowered by political pressure and lobbying. Given how unevenly they were used across states, CONs often established a differential competitive situation for neighboring hospital systems that were close to a state border. As a result, many states have abolished them, only to find that the move left them without any control of medical infrastructure, leading to overcapacity and spiraling costs. So today neither a set of functioning market mechanisms nor an effective substitute exists that is effective in addressing the value of medical technology.

- **Cost-based reimbursement:** In the absence of good measures of value and a market-based pricing system, medical technology is paid for (reimbursed) on the basis of its cost.

  There have been a number of attempts to create measures of value for reimbursement purposes in the absence of market mechanisms. These include various types of benefit and utility measures such as QALYs (Quality Adjusted Life Years), but they are not commonly used. Nevertheless, some standard measure of value/outcome must be used consistently if there is to be a fact-based prioritization of medical technology spending in the absence of a market mechanism in a resource-constrained world.

- **Litigation concerns:** There is little question that litigation concerns affect the cost of medical technology, and contribute to regional variations in costs. By comparing patterns in states with liability laws, Stanford researchers Daniel P. Kessler and Mark B. McClellan found that defensive medicine can increase costs by 6 to 9 percent in heart patients. There

is, of course, a debate about whether litigation serves a valuable purpose in maintaining the integrity of health care delivery, but that it has a significant impact on the cost of health care is clear.

A WAY FORWARD: REALIZING THE VALUE OF MEDICAL TECHNOLOGY

Payers, physicians, and patients have been struggling to balance the benefits and costs of medical technology for years. The fundamental underlying issue of an imperfect market, with third parties involved in reimbursement, is unlikely to go away in the near term. Concentration of provider power, imperfect information about the impact of innovation, concentration of payer power, and other factors will make purely market-based solutions impractical in the foreseeable future. So what is the practical and likely way forward, and what are the implications for all stakeholders?

Our view is that the next several years will see a variety of interrelated solutions, each of which will contribute to realizing the value of medical technology, but none of which will be a magic wand that solves the problem. The solutions will be a "combination of therapies" targeted at:

More and Better Information on Value

Value assessments of technology are performed only selectively in the U.S. today. Most assessments are focused on safety and clinical value of a new technology to provide input to reimbursement decisions. Cost-effectiveness studies, to the extent that they are done, focus on the clinical situations where new technology delivers the greatest value. A key difficulty is that relevant data around outcomes in a variety of clinical situations is generally not available when the technology is launched and standards of care as well as reimbursement policies are set. After that, it is generally much more difficult to modify standards of care, so it rarely happens.

Another difficulty is to establish a commonly accepted value definition. While a range of approaches such as QALYs exist, a widely agreed-upon standard or best practice has yet to be established.

In our view, payers and health plans will address these difficulties over the next few years, and more timely and detailed information about the value of new medical technologies will be required. An important question will concern the source for value assessments. Candidates include a public body and/or private institutions.

Other countries show how a public body could work. In the U.K., NICE provides the National Health Service with technology appraisals and guidance, clinical guidelines, and audits. Participation includes health economists, physicians, statisticians, patient advocates and ad hoc experts. Stakeholder groups make decisions, primarily about reimbursement, in a "partners' committee," and reimbursement decisions are mandatory. France (CEDIT), Spain (AETS) and Canada (CCOHTA) have similar forums. The drawback for all of them is the limited volume of value assessments being performed and that the payer perspective tends to dominate the outcomes.

In the U.S., a public/private partnership exists that has done evaluations of medical technology, but its focus has not been on cost effectiveness, and its findings do not have regulatory standing. The partnership includes 13 evidence-based practice centers of the Agency for Health Care Research and Quality (AHRQ), the federal agency charged with promoting the quality, safety, and cost-effectiveness of health care—The Emergency Care Research Institute (ECRI), the BlueCross BlueShield Technology Evaluation Center BCBSA TEC, and the Research Triangle Institute in NC are accredited members of AHRQ. Their focus has traditionally been on improving health outcomes rather than cost-effectiveness and reimbursement, and on evidence-based reviews that require a significant amount of clinical experience. The types of evaluations they currently undertake are unlikely to provide the early input necessary to guide the development of standards of care early in the product life cycle, or to support reimbursement decision-making. On that front, the practice has been for the private sector to follow CMS's lead.

The role of AHRQ itself in developing evidence-based practice guidelines is unclear, but nevertheless the members of AHRQ can and are expanding their efforts on earlier cost-effectiveness studies, and on setting common standards for assessment of the value of medical technology. It is particularly important that these evaluations take place early in the product life cycle, preferably before launch and before standards of practice are established.

Other options include making value part of the FDA approval process, or involving the National Institutes of Health in value assessments, but each has major political ramifications.

Aligning Decision-Makers and Financial Responsibility

There are a number of potential approaches to alignment. One strategy that is likely to be tried is the introduction of different benefit designs. A few health plans have already started experimenting with them and have introduced different level co-pays for various diagnostic imaging techniques and procedures. This seems to be an obvious choice given the success that co-pays, co-insurance, and deductibles have made possible in controlling drug costs. The challenge will be to establish medical equivalence, which is much more difficult for those medical technologies that are not tailored to one indication only and that are certainly less equivalent than different drugs with a similar mechanism of action.

Patient education will be an important supporting element to making alignment work in practice. BlueCross BlueShield of Tennessee has launched a campaign to make patients aware of asking their doctor if an MRI is necessary or whether an X-ray will suffice, although as yet there is no patient financial incentive in place.

Other potential strategies could focus on aligning the incentives with providers more closely so that over-utilization can be held in check; to "counter detail"; and to manage the installed based more closely. Setting targets together with physician groups and tying compensation to target volumes could provide an innovative way of aligning incentives.

More Active Third-Party Payer Involvement

One example of effective third-party payer involvement is regional business coalitions, which can be an important avenue for coming to agreement around necessary capacity increases. In Rochester, NY, for example, the Community Technology Assessment Advisory Board (CTAAB) reviews new technologies as well as capacity increases. The acceptance of the CTAAB's decisions by all stakeholders is a prerequisite for a functioning system that is geared to providing sufficient access to a local community while ensuring quality of care.

Sound, fact-based decision-making by third party payers will require good cost effectiveness analysis or value screens as a prerequisite. It is therefore likely that the approaches described above—better information, aligned incentives, and more active third-party involvement—will be pursued in parallel.

SOME IMPLICATIONS FOR STAKEHOLDERS

Some manufacturers have already started thinking about ways to more fully document the value of their technology. Some physicians and hospitals already have exposure to cost-management strategies, most notably linked to quality evaluations, which in turn are linked to reimbursement levels or bonuses. Health plans are actively reviewing the way they conduct medical technology assessments, and the role value plays in those assessments.

While the timing and the exact outcome of the medical technology value assessment process is uncertain, there will be changes. It is highly likely that value assessments will take place more often, more comprehensively, and earlier in the product life cycle. The change will be driven as much by the private sector as by government. Medical technology manufacturers, as well as other stakeholders, need to determine the right combination of actions to brace themselves for change, and to shape the direction of the change.

For health plans and providers, many of the same initiatives are relevant, including building the capability to undertake value assessments early in the product life cycle, designing benefit plans that provide patients with a financial stake in outcomes, and developing education programs for patients and physicians in partnership with medical technology innovators. It is also critical for health plans to engage with regional and national employer coalitions to help shape investments in health care infrastructure.

It is clear that manufacturers, health plans, and health care providers can play an important role in shaping the future medical technology environment. Manufacturers can help develop the information that technology assessment bodies and payers need. Manufacturers and health plans can help ensure appropriate use by working with payers to address value as well as safety and efficacy, rather than waiting and subjecting themselves to cost control based on imperfect information. Setting standards of care requires a collaborative solution, with all stakeholders involved. Successes in collaboration, such as those in Rochester, demonstrate the point.

The ultimate goals are the best care for each individual patient and continuing innovation in care. Channeling health care dollars to their best use will foster innovation and progress in medical technology that is sustainable in the long run.

3

Pharmaceutical Price Controls in OECD Countries

Source: U.S. Department of Commerce. 2004. Executive Summary. *Pharmaceutical Price Controls in OECD Countries: Implications for U.S. Consumers, Pricing, Research and Development, and Innovation.* Washington, DC: U.S. Department of Commerce. (pp. vii-xii)

EXECUTIVE SUMMARY

Improvements in health care and life sciences are an important source of gains in health and longevity globally. The development of innovative pharmaceutical products plays a critical role in ensuring these continued gains. To encourage the continued development of new drugs, economic incentives are essential. These incentives are principally provided through direct and indirect government funding, intellectual property laws, and other policies that favor innovation. Without such incentives, private corporations, which bring to market the vast majority of new drugs, would be less able to assume the risks and costs necessary to continue their research and development (R&D).

In the United States, government action has focused on creating the environment that would best encourage further innovation and yield a constant flow of new and innovative medicines to the market. The goal has been to ensure that consumers would benefit both from technological break-throughs and the competition that further innovation generates. The United States also relies on a strong generic pharmaceutical industry to create added competitive pressure to lower drug prices. Recent action by the Administration and Congress has accelerated the flow of generic medicines to the market for precisely that reason.

By contrast, in the Organization for Economic Cooperation and Development (OECD) countries studied in this report, governments have relied heavily on government fiat rather than competition to set prices, lowering drug spending through price controls applied to new and old drugs alike. Such controls, when applied to new drugs, reduce company compensation to levels closer to direct production costs, leaving less revenue for R&D. As OECD countries individually seek to reduce spending on drugs through price controls, their collective actions reduce R&D that would provide substantial health benefits to all.

The OECD countries examined in the study also employ a number of other regulatory practices that have the effect of limiting the competition that would otherwise accrue from generic pharmaceuticals. Perhaps the most glaring example is the bar imposed by a number of countries on the ability of generic pharmaceutical manufacturers to provide information on prices and therapeutic benefit directly to physicians and consumers. In short, the systems examined here rely heavily on government fiat to set prices rather than competition in the marketplace.

To examine the effect of such practices on prices, revenues, innovation and, ultimately, on consumers, Congress (in section 1123 of the Medicare Prescription Drug, Improvement, and Modernization Act of 2003, P.L. 108-173) instructed the Secretary of Commerce—with the assistance and support of the U.S. International Trade Commission, the Department of Heath and Human Services, and the Office of the U.S. Trade Representative—to conduct a study on OECD drug price controls and the implications for U.S. consumers.

Specifically, the Conference Report (House Report 108-391) requested that the study include the following:

- Identification of the countries that use price controls or other such practices with respect to pharmaceutical trade.

- Assessment of the price controls and other such practices that the identified countries use.

- Estimates of additional costs to U.S. consumers because of such price controls, and the extent to which additional costs would be reduced for U.S. consumers if price controls and other such practices are reduced or eliminated.

- Estimates of the impact that price controls, intellectual property laws, and other such measures have on fair pricing, innovation, generic competition, and R&D in the United States and each identified country.

This report responds to Congress' request. It details the effect of price controls imposed by various U.S. trade partners on pharmaceutical prices, R&D, innovation, and U.S. consumers. The study examined the drug price regulatory systems of 11 OECD countries.[1] A quantitative analysis of prices, revenues, and R&D effects based on available data was also conducted for nine OECD countries.[2] For reasons explained in the report, two of these nine countries were excluded from further consideration. The results from the remaining six countries[3] were then extrapolated to the total patented markets of five additional OECD countries. Thus, the final estimates of the impact of price controls on R&D and

innovation are based on an analysis of 11 OECD countries.[4]

SUMMARY OF THE REPORT'S CONCLUSIONS

Price Controls Are Widespread

The study examined the drug price regulatory systems of 11 OECD countries and found that all rely on some form of price controls to limit spending on pharmaceuticals. The principal methods these governments employ are reference pricing, approval delays and procedural barriers, restrictions on dispensing and prescribing, and reimbursement. These methods prevent companies from charging a market-based price for their products. They also tend to be nontransparent, as the criteria and rationale for certain pharmaceutical prices or reimbursement amounts are not fully disclosed even to the pharmaceutical companies seeking to market their drugs.

The most direct method the OECD governments we examined use to control prices is to set the sales price and make sales at any other price illegal. Governments often are the dominant market participant and may negotiate favorable prices with manufacturers by leveraging this monopsonistic power. Such negotiations generally result in prices lower than they would be in a free market. Another method the OECD governments we examined use is to set the reimbursement price of a new drug at levels well below the free market price. Since any price above the regulated price is borne by consumers, the reimbursement price often functions as the de facto market price where such mechanisms are employed. Finally, some OECD governments regularly cut the prices of drugs already on the market.

Intellectual Property Rights Are Adequately Enforced

Intellectual property rights (IPR) confer on innovators certain exclusive rights over inventions, trademarks, and other works. In the case of patents, which provide the IPR protection for pharmaceutical innovations, rights exist for 20 years. After this time the invention falls into the public domain. In this way, a balance is struck between rewarding innovation and maximizing scientific progress and access to technologies.

This balance ensures that pharmaceutical companies can recoup their enormous R&D expenses

---

[1]The overview of drug price regulatory systems corresponds to Australia, Canada, France, Germany, Greece, Japan, South Korea, Mexico, Poland, Switzerland, and the United Kingdom.
[2]The prices effects analysis corresponds to Australia, Canada, France, Germany, Greece, Japan, Poland, Switzerland, and the United Kingdom.
[3]Due to data limitations and methodology constraints, Poland, Greece, and Switzerland were excluded from the extrapolation.

---

[4]The final estimates of the impact of price controls on R&D and innovation correspond to France, Germany, Canada, the United Kingdom, Australia, Japan, Italy, Spain, Belgium, Netherlands, and Sweden.

and earn a return commensurate with the risks of their investment, while promoting generic competition after the expiration of the patent term. In short, intellectual property protection is a necessary prerequisite to ensure that innovative companies can continue to develop new drugs, which will eventually be available on the generic market. Conversely, poor enforcement or lack of intellectual property protection discourages the development of new medicines and results in a stagnant generic drug market.

The study did not find that a lack of intellectual property laws or enforcement of IPR in the selected countries (which generally have strong and effective intellectual property regimes) had a significant impact on prices. The existence of strong IPR and other incentives for innovation do not prevent robust generic competition. Indeed, the United States has the largest and most competitive generic market of the countries reviewed in this report.

Patented Drug Prices Are Below U.S. Levels

The study found that, for patented drugs that were best sellers in the United States, the prices in other OECD countries are below those in the United States. For the countries analyzed, the study showed that aggregate pharmaceutical prices were 18 to 67 percent less than U.S. prices, depending on the country. These results are consistent with recent academic research in this area.

It must be noted that since generic drugs account for more than half of all prescription drugs consumed in the United States, prices of patented and branded pharmaceuticals cannot be used to draw a comprehensive picture of relative aggregate prices among the various countries examined in this study.

Importantly, this study does not incorporate the reductions in price expected as a result of implementing provisions of the Medicare Modernization Act (for example, drug discount cards). This Act, when fully implemented, could have the potential to significantly lower drug prices for seniors who are eligible for Medicare and lack insurance for drugs.

Without Price Controls, Revenues Available for R&D Could Be Significantly Higher

The study found that by depressing prices of patented pharmaceuticals, the price controls maintained by OECD countries yield lower revenues for patented products than would otherwise exist in a competitive market. The study estimates that, after extrapolating to a broader set of OECD countries, the diminished returns are in the range of $18 billion to $27 billion

annually. This represents a 25 to 38 percent increase in revenues over actual 2003 revenues from sales of patented drugs in the OECD countries considered.

Higher Utilization Rates of Generic Drugs at Lower Prices in OECD Countries Offer Potential Savings

Analysis by the Department of Commerce and HHS found that higher utilization of generic drugs at lower prices could result in significant savings to OECD countries. The estimated savings, after extrapolating to a broader set of OECD countries, range from $5 billion to $30 billion annually. This range of potential savings suggests that if prices of on-patent drugs were to rise to competitive market levels, then the additional cost to OECD countries could be significantly or fully offset by a more competitive generic market.

Higher Revenues Would Mean More Research and Development and New Drugs

Based on published academic research, the study estimates the impact of increased revenues on pharmaceutical R&D. In limiting the return that would otherwise accrue to companies for undertaking the risk and expense of developing new drugs and bringing them to market, the price controls maintained by the OECD countries in the study also reduce the amount of global pharmaceutical R&D below what it would otherwise be under market conditions similar to those in the United States. The study estimates that this reduction falls in the range of $5 billion to $8 billion annually, once prices were fully adjusted. This represents between 11 and 16 percent of current private worldwide R&D, based on figures from the Center of Medicines Research (CMR) International Worldwide.

Based on an estimated cost of developing a new drug, an increase in R&D of $5 billion to $8 billion could lead to three or four new molecular entities annually once markets fully adjust. The U.S. Food and Drug Administration approved, on average, 30 new molecular entities between 2000 and 2003.[5]

---

[5]This estimate also includes FDA approvals of new biologics. See U.S. Food and Drug Administration, "Approval Times for Priority and Standard NMEs: Calendar Years 1993-2003" (created January 21, 2004), available at www.fda.gov/cder/rdmt/NMEapps93-03.htm; see also Pharmaceutical Research and Manufacturers of America, "New Drug Approvals In 2003" (January 2004), available at www.phrma.org/newmedicines/resources/2004-01-22.123.pdf.

U.S. Consumers Would Benefit from the Elimination of Price Controls Abroad

The benefit to U.S. drug purchasers from the new drugs that would be developed and marketed if there were no price controls is in the range of $5 billion to $7 billion per year. In the short term, the deregulation of OECD prices is not likely to have any impact on U.S. drug prices. The "increased competition" in the U.S. market resulting from price deregulation abroad could have some effect on U.S. prices in the long term. Relaxation of foreign price controls, if coupled with appropriate reform of foreign generic markets, could potentially bring about much of these gains from the flow of new drugs, even without increasing foreign spending on prescription drugs.

HOW THE DETAILED ANALYSIS OF PRICES AND REVENUES WAS CONDUCTED

In order to address the question of the impact of price controls, a detailed study of pharmaceutical prices for nine OECD countries was conducted, representing the largest OECD markets as well as OECD countries with a range of income levels. Price and related data for all products containing the active ingredient in the 60 best-selling products in the United States were purchased for each of the nine OECD countries from IMS Health, virtually the only source for detailed data on pharmaceutical prices and sales.

The analysis focused specifically on innovative pharmaceuticals, which are produced by research-based pharmaceutical companies and biotechnology companies. The study assumed that, in the absence of drug price controls, average prices in the OECD countries for innovative pharmaceuticals would be equal to U.S. prices adjusted for differences in per capita income. These adjusted prices were used to estimate revenues in the absence of drug price controls.

CONSTRAINTS AND CAVEATS

Given the resource and time constraints, it was necessary to make a number of significant simplifying assumptions that should be considered when reviewing the study's results, including:

- That subject to disparities in per capita income, U.S. prices could serve as a benchmark for deregulated prices;
- That the selected 54 molecules in the nine countries studied, as well as the United States (which represent 26 percent of world revenues in 2003[6]) are indicative of price differences for innovative drugs;
- That increased drug prices would not affect sales volumes;
- That funds would be available to pay the higher prices;
- That there would be no interplay between patented and generic drugs that might have affected the study's results.

Throughout this report, an effort has been made to use conservative assumptions regarding the effects of drug price regulations. Given the assumptions inherent in any analysis of this type, the results should necessarily be read with care and would not preclude other findings.

One further point bears emphasis. This assessment of the effects of foreign governments' policies regarding the pricing and use of drugs in their markets should not be construed to be an assessment of the impact of possible federal controls on the prices of drugs sold elsewhere, including the United States. This report does not address that question even indirectly. As the analysis reflects, both the economics of pharmaceutical production and the roles played by the private sector and government institutions in the United States vary significantly from those of its trading partners, rendering efforts to apply the results of this research to the U.S. context without merit.

---

[6] U.S. Department of Commerce calculations based on data from IMS Health, IMS MIDAS (TM), Q4/2003 and IMS Health, *IMS World Review* (TM), Country Profiles, 2004.

Some Unintended Consequences of Information Technology in Health Care: The Nature of Patient Care Information System-Related Errors

Source: Reprinted from Ash, J.S., M. Berg, and E. Coiera. 2004. Some Unintended Consequences of Information Technology in Health Care: The Nature of Patient Care Information System-related Errors. *Journal of the American Medical Informatics Association* 11 (2): 104-112. Copyright 2004, with permission from Elsevier.

ABSTRACT

Medical error reduction is an international issue, as is the implementation of patient care information systems (PCISs) as a potential means to achieving it. As researchers conducting separate studies in the United States, The Netherlands, and Australia, using similar qualitative methods to investigate implementing PCISs, the authors have encountered many instances in which PCIS applications seem to foster errors rather than reduce their likelihood. The authors describe the kinds of silent errors they have witnessed and, from their different social science perspectives (information science, sociology, and cognitive science), they interpret the nature of these errors. The errors fall into two main categories: those in the process of entering and retrieving information, and those in the communication and coordination process that the PCIS is supposed to support. The authors believe that with a heightened awareness of these issues, informaticians can educate, design systems, implement, and conduct research in such a way that they might be able to avoid the unintended consequences of these subtle silent errors.

Medical error reduction is an international issue. The Institute of Medicine's report on medical errors[1] dramatically called attention to dangers inherent in the U.S. medical care system that might cause up to 98,000 deaths in hospitals and cost approximately $38 billion per year. In the United Kingdom, the chief medical officer of the newly established National Patient Safety Agency estimates that "850,000 incidents and errors occur in the NHS each year."[2] In The Netherlands, the exact implications of the U.S. figures for the Dutch health care scene are much debated. There as well, however, patient safety is on its way to becoming a political priority. Medication errors alone have been estimated to cause 80,000 hospital admissions per year in Australia, costing $350 million.[3]

In much of the literature on patient safety, patient care information systems (PCISs) are lauded as one of the core building blocks for a safer health care system.[4] PCISs are broadly defined here as applications that support the health care process by allowing health care professionals or patients direct access to order entry systems, medical record systems, radiology information systems, patient information systems, and so on. With fully accessible and integrated electronic patient records, and with instant access to up-to-date medical knowledge, faulty decision making resulting from a lack of information can be significantly reduced.[5] Likewise, computerized provider order entry (CPOE) systems and automated reminder systems can reduce errors by eliminating illegible orders, improving communication, improving the tracking of orders, checking for inappropriate orders, and reminding professionals of actions to be undertaken. In this way, these systems can contribute to preventing under-, over-, or misuse of diagnostic or therapeutic interventions.[6-8] Among the broad array of health informatics applications, CPOE systems, and especially medication systems, have received the most attention.[9-12]

PCISs are complicated technologies, often encompassing millions of lines of code written by many different individuals. The interaction space[13] within which clinicians carry out their work can also be immensely complex, because individuals can execute their tasks by communicating across rich social networks. When such technologies become an integral part of health care work practices, we are confronted with a large sociotechnical system in which many behaviors emerge out of the sociotechnical coupling, and the behavior of the overall system in any new situation can never be fully predicted from the individual social or technical components.[13-17]

It is not surprising, therefore, that authors have started to describe some of the unintended consequences that the implementation of PCISs can trigger.[18] For instance, professionals could trust the decision support suggested by the seemingly objective computer more than is actually called for.[15,19] Also, PCISs could impose additional work tasks on already heavily burdened professionals,[20,21] and the tasks are often clerical and therefore economically inefficient.[17] They can upset smooth working relations and communication routines.[13,22] Also, given their complexity, PCISs could themselves contain design flaws "that generate specific hazards and require vigilance to detect."[23(p.511),24] As a consequence, PCISs might not be as successful in preventing errors as is generally hoped. Worse still, PCISs could actually generate new errors.[25-27]

It is obvious that PCISs will ultimately be a necessary component of any high-quality health care delivery system. Yet, in our research in three different countries, we have each encountered many instances in which PCIS applications seemed to *foster* errors rather than *reduce* their likelihood. In health care practices in the United States, Europe, and Australia alike, we have seen situations in which the system of people, technologies, organizational routines, and regulations that constitutes any health care practice seemed to be *weakened* rather than *strengthened* by the introduction of the PCIS application. In other words, we frequently observed instances in which the intended strengthening of one link in the chain of care actually leads unwittingly to a deletion or weakening of others.

We argue that many of these errors are the result of highly specific failures in PCIS design and/or implementation. We do not focus on errors that are the result of faulty programming or other technical dysfunctions. Hardware problems and software bugs are more common than they should be, especially in a high-risk field such as medicine. However, these problems are well known and can theoretically be dealt with through testing before implementation. Similarly, we do not discuss errors that are the result of obvious individual or organizational dysfunctioning such as a physician refusing to seek information in the computer system "because that is not his task," or a health care delivery organization cutting training programs for a new PCIS for budgetary reasons.

We do focus on those often latent or silent errors that are the result of a mismatch between the functioning of the PCIS and the real-life demands of health care work. Such errors are not easily found by a technical analysis of the PCIS design, or even suspected after the first encounter with the system in use. They can only emerge when the technical system is embedded into a working organization and can vary from one organization to the next. Yet, in failing to take seriously some by now well-recognized features of health care work, *some PCISs are designed or implemented in such a way that error can arguably be expected to result.* Only when thoughtful consideration is given to these issues, we argue, will PCISs be able to fulfill their promise.

BACKGROUND AND METHODS

This study draws on a literature review and a series of qualitative research studies in the United States, The Netherlands, and Australia. These studies are based on standard qualitative methods such as ethnographic observation in health care delivery settings and semistructured interviews with professionals.[28] All of the studies focused on the impact of PCISs in health care, yet none of the researchers set out to study error prevention. We did not focus especially on problematic PCIS implementations; on the contrary, most of our studies were done at sites that were recognized as highly successful. While discussing our different research projects, however, we realized that we had all gathered data that indicated the possibility of, fear about, or awareness of PCIS-related errors. In our view, the importance of this topic, and the relevance of the lessons these data can teach us, warrants a blended international treatment of this issue. Briefly, our reflections are based on U.S. data about CPOE from four hospitals, including 340 hours of observation and 59 formal interviews, Australian data about CPOE from 18 semistructured interviews with stakeholders at several public hospital sites, and Dutch data from electronic medical records, CPOE, and medication system studies involving participant observations and interviews from two hospitals and other settings in The Netherlands. All of the sites had patient care information systems in place; the four U.S. hospitals and one each of the Australian and Dutch sites also had CPOE. Interview transcripts and all field notes in the U.S. and Australian studies were analyzed with the assistance of qualitative data analysis software. (For detailed descriptions of these studies, see references.[29-35])

Because these were qualitative studies, they do not offer estimates of how *often* certain errors occurred or whether PCISs overall result in more or fewer medication errors, for example. The power of qualitative work is in the richness of its detailed descriptions.[28] We include results from the underlying studies, from diverse fields in diverse contexts, to emphasize the ubiquity of the issues we are addressing here. We offer an interpretation of the *nature* of health care work, the role of information and information technology, and the risks of an improper interrelation or fit between PCISs and health care work. Our goal is to present an argument, supported by extensive literature, and illustrated by prototypical examples from our studies, that will lead to more quantitative work that can track the "epidemiology" of these information system pathologies, as well as convince decision makers to be cautiously realistic about the benefits of PCISs.

The following discussion includes verbatim quotes from interviewees or field notes that illustrate patterns seen across the studies. The quotes were selected because they are both representative and well stated. Words in brackets are ours and have been added to clarify meanings. All studies received appropriate human subject approval from our universities. Finally, it is important to emphasize that, as far as we are aware, the examples given here never led to actual harm of patients.

RESULTS: CATEGORIZATION OF ERRORS

The complex nature of health care work both creates and hides errors, which can be nearly invisible or silent. Health care work can be characterized as the managing of patients' trajectories; under continuous time pressure, and in constant interaction with colleagues and the patient, health care professionals have to try to keep a patient's problem on track. This implies simultaneously acting on a whole range of dimensions, including interpreting physical signs and diagnostic tests, and dealing with organizational policies and the patient's individual needs. However, standardizing diagnostic and/or therapeutic care paths, individual trajectories always follow their own, unique course. Contingencies are the rule; smoothly molding such continuous lapses of order into events to be handled with "standard operating procedures" is the true skill of experienced health care professionals.[13,33,36] Computer applications are best when they automate routine work, but the complexities of the health care process often make it anything but routine.

In outpatient settings, the interaction with colleagues could be less pronounced than in inpatient settings, although there as well, the professional is connected through other health care professionals' opinions and needs through progress reports and referrals. This social organization of medical work, as the sociologist Strauss called it, is now widely recognized as an important feature to consider in the design of health care information technologies.[36-40]

In this section, we discuss two main categories of errors that occur at the interface of the information system and work practice that are the result of a failure to grasp this nature of health care work. First, we discuss errors in the process of *entering and retrieving* information in or from the system. Second, we discuss errors in the *communication and coordination* processes that the PCIS is supposed to support. As the examples will illustrate, such failures are the result of mistaken assumptions about health care work that are built into PCIS applications, creating dysfunctional interactions with users and, sometimes, leading to actual errors in the delivery of health care.

Errors in the Process of Entering and Retrieving Information

Increasingly, the entry and retrieval of information into and from a PCIS are a core activity in health care work. Given the characteristics of this work, these PCIS applications have to fulfill specific demands. Many of these are well known; PCIS applications have to have fast response times, have negligible downtime, be easily accessible, and have interfaces that are easy to understand and navigate.[5,30] Also, the software and hardware have to be designed to optimally fit the ecology of the work practice: mobile when necessary, robust, small but ergonomically suitable.[13,41] Although such requirements are widely known and accepted, they are often not met. Many system interfaces are still so impractical that using the systems takes a great deal of costly time on the part of busy professionals. Some systems in use in medical work practices today have interfaces that are outdated, with no windows, no intuitive graphic navigation aids, and endless lines of identical-looking text. In such cases, even when the information is there, it could be exceedingly hard to find. We discuss two problems in detail: (1) PCISs that have human-computer interfaces that are not suitable for this highly interruptive use context, and (2) PCISs that cause cognitive overload by overemphasizing structured and complete information entry or retrieval.

A Human-Computer Interface That Is Not Suitable for a Highly Interruptive Use Context

Working on the computer is rarely an isolated task; health care professionals are always communicating with others, including patients in outpatient settings, but primarily with other health care professionals. More often than not, different tasks are executed simultaneously, and interruptions by beepers, telephones, and colleagues are endless.[42,43] Many human-computer interfaces, however, seem to have been designed for workers doing their work by themselves, fully and extensively concentrating on the computer screens. This single-task assumption is aggravated by the fact that so many existing screen designs are already suboptimal by current office standards.

This mismatch between interface and use context often results in a *juxtaposition* error, the kind of error that can result when something is close to something else on the screen and the wrong option is too easily clicked in error. The following are typical quotations from physicians; note the allusions to the "interruptive" use context: "I have ordered the test that was right next to the one I thought I ordered, you know, right below it that my little thingie had come down and I clicked and I'm lookin' at this one but I in fact clicked on the thing before. By that time I turned my head and I'm hitting return and

typing my signature and not seeing it" [physician, U.S. hospital]. "I was ordering Cortisporin, and Cortisporin solution and suspension comes up. The patient was talking to me, I accidentally put down solution, realized that's not what I wanted . . . . I would not have made that mistake, or potential mistake, if I had been writing it out because I would have put down what I wanted" [physician, U.S. outpatient setting].

Likewise, there were many instances of patient or physician confusion when *orders were entered for or on behalf of the wrong person*. Again, in a context of many co-occurring activities and interruptions, a suboptimal interface becomes rapidly unforgiving: "Patients were getting the wrong orders for medications. You would order it on one patient and it would, cause of the vagaries of the light pen system, you thought you were ordering it on one, and it was really ordered on somebody else and somebody got the wrong medication and that sort of thing" [physician, U.S. hospital]. "She looked up the patient's diet and was trying to order a regular diet. At the fifth screen she saw that the patient was getting tube feeding. This clued her that this was the wrong patient" [field notes, observation of a nurse, U.S. hospital].

Causing Cognitive Overload by Overemphasizing Structured and "Complete" Information Entry or Retrieval

Professionals need fast access to data that are relevant to the case at hand. Simultaneously, they need to be able to record a maximum amount of information in a minimum amount of time and in such a way that it is most useful to other health care professionals involved in the handling of this patient's trajectory. Psychologic and sociologic studies have shown that in a shared context, concise, unconstrained, free-text communication is most effective for coordinating work around a complex task.[44-46] Attempting to require professionals to encode data, or enter data in more structured formats, can be fruitful and is necessary for research or managerial purposes but does not come without a cost. Such formats are generally more time-consuming to complete and read. When the information relevancy to the primary task is lessened through the structuring of the information, and/or when the time spent writing or reading this information increases significantly, the information ends up being *less* useful for the primary task at hand.[20]

Structure Some PCIS systems require data entry that is so elaborate that the time spent recording patient data is significantly greater than it was with its paper predecessors. What is worse, on several occasions during our studies, overly structured data entry led to a loss of cognitive focus by the clinician. Having to go to many different fields, often using many different screens to enter many details, physicians reported a *loss of overview*. When professionals are working through a case, determining a differential diagnosis, for example, the act of *writing* the information is integral to the cognitive processing of the case.[32,47] This act of writing-as-thinking can be aided greatly by *some* structure such as the grouping of similar types of information or sequencing to guide elucidating a history but is inevitably hampered by an excess of structure. Rather than helping the physician build a cognitive pattern to understand the complexities of the case, such systems over-load the user with details at odds with the cognitive model the user is trying to develop.

Fragmentation Similarly, the need to switch between different screens can result in a loss of overview. Physicians and nurses in an intensive care unit, for example, reported that the large paper daysheets they used to work with would include an order list, problem list, vital signs graphs, and medication lists, all on a single large sheet of paper. The graphic user interface software they used allowed all of these functions and more, but the user had to switch among multiple windows to get all of the information. Doing so, several professionals argued, worked against their ability to acquire, maintain, and refine a mental overview of the case. Some reported that they felt insecure about identifying emerging problems because the activity of clicking through the different screens inevitably fragmented the cognitive "images" they were constructing.

Likewise, records might overly separate the information flows according to work task or responsibility. In everyday practice, doctors can gather information from nurses' notes, or those of other specialists, that relate to the problem. Information systems could limit this easy access to other people's notes or other parts of the record, and thereby severely hamper the professional's ability to be optimally informed.[48] "... [R]egarding interpretation of results, currently this is often in the notes so [you] can see the results and the interpretation. On an order entry, results reporting may only get the raw data and not the interpretation, which could affect clinical work. This separation may also lead to clinicians being too specialty focused [and] not seeing what others have written—now [we] have to flick through notes so we see other information. On this system, if [we] only go to [our] own information, this may not happen and information may be missed" [allied health professional, Australia].

Overcompleteness Results reporting systems can also mistake completeness for efficacy. In several instances, physicians stated that systems that produced standard, "complete" reports actually reduced the usability and the transparency of these reports or discharge letters. The physicians explained: "There are so many standard phrases in the ordinary reports, I don't think that's good . . . you have to really search for the usable information. . . . Many others use the [standard templates] and then you often see a discussion with standard phrases, one or two added phrases, and then more standard phrases. You then have to really search what the considerations were. . . . In my reports the text is mine, it doesn't come from the computer, I make it up myself. . . . Everyone should do that. If you have so much standard text, it becomes too easy to just push that button and add some more" [insurance physician, The Netherlands]. "You'll have to write the largest part yourself. You can standardize only so much, since otherwise you get an empty report with only standard phrases that could be true for anyone" [insurance physician, The Netherlands].

Too many standard phrases, these physicians argued, actually decreased the readability and information value of the reports. From the point of view of the professional, overly "complete" reports could end up becoming "empty" and stand in the way of actual communication. The similarity of the phrases, and the impossibility of judging whether a sentence is part of the template or a result of a thoughtful weighing of words, threatens to obscure the transparency that such systems attempt to introduce.

Here, of course, ease of use can also lure users into learning new but poor recording practices. The ability to cut and paste or, more often, copy and paste, affords users the opportunity to exacerbate the data overload problem. As an attending physician stated: "Just before I came up here, I looked at a discharge summary that was an absolute disaster, because not only had she cut and pasted the progress note, but she had cut and pasted the whole thing, so the intern's signature and the whole thing was on it. [The system] is inherently error prone . . . people have the tendency to cut and paste . . . and instead of taking the pertinent facts from a laboratory report or from another clinician's progress note, they will cut and paste a whole laboratory report, cut and paste somebody else's thinking process into their own note and sign it" [physician, U.S. hospital].

Errors in the Communication and Coordination Process

In the previous section, we discussed errors related to the processes of entering and retrieving information in PCISs. In this section, we focus on the way computers can undermine communication about and coordination of events and activities. Here we encounter the truly interactive and contingent nature of health care work and the consequences of not taking these characteristics into account. Although the issues discussed here are highly interrelated, we have subdivided them in two overarching problems: (1) misrepresenting collective, interactive work as a linear, clear-cut, and predictable workflow; and (2) misrepresenting communication as information transfer.

Misrepresenting Collective, Interactive Work as a Linear, Clearcut, and Predictable Workflow

PCIS systems often appear to be imbued with a formal, stepwise notion of health care work: a doctor orders an intervention, a nurse subsequently arranges for or carries out the intervention, and then the doctor obtains the information about the result. As a chain of independent actions, an order is executed and reported on, or a piece of information is generated, processed, and stored.[49-51] Yet it has become common knowledge that it is inherently difficult for formal systems to accurately handle or anticipate the highly flexible and fluid ways in which professional work is executed in real life.[13,52,53] Carepath or workflow systems are plagued by the ubiquity of exceptions.[54] Similarly, decision support systems are in constant need of "supervision" to determine whether their suggestions fit a given case.[18] Systems cannot handle all potential exceptions; very soon, the number of branching points becomes too great, and the system becomes impossible to maintain and to use.[55]

Support of work processes is one of the main benefits of PCISs, yet it has its problems. Finding the proper balance between formalizing work activities so that the information technology application can fulfill its promise and respecting this fluid and contingency-driven nature of health care work is no easy task for system designers.[34] However, it is necessary if PCIS systems are to contribute to the overall quality improvement required in western health care.

Inflexibility These systems often fail to reflect some of the basic real-life exigencies of care work, thus resulting in problems for the user and potentially faulty reporting and/or actions. Seemingly easy and clearcut on paper, the real-time intricacies of treatment protocols, for example, could baffle the system's preconceptions of these processes. In one

instance, for example, a drug ordered three times a day had been discontinued, but one dose had already been given. The computer system would not allow the nurse to chart the one dose, because the system considered it an incomplete execution of the task [as told by a pharmacist, U.S. hospital, recorded in field notes].

Urgency In the case of urgent medication orders, nurses could already give a medication before the physician formally activates the order. There is a familiar category of errors here that has to do with the informal realities of medication handling in health care. In everyday health care work, experienced nurses often have more practical knowledge about what medications to give when, and what contraindications could be relevant, than many of the junior physicians who populate the wards.[56] For example, during nightly routine medication administration, nurses could initiate distribution without waking up the junior doctor who is formally responsible for signing the order. There is a rather large gray zone of informal management of these responsibilities and tasks, which can be entirely rational given the everyday organization and exigencies of health care work. Within this same gray zone, there could lie many practices that would contribute to unsafe medication routines such as doctors actively discouraging nurses to call them for medication requests or nurses taking too many liberties with dosing. All of these practices exist within the current paper medication systems, but many computerized medication systems all too radically *cut off* such practices. Many medication systems have been rejected by their users because they strictly demanded a physician's authorization before any drug could be distributed or because they made any alternative route (such as the nurse ordering the medication through an "agent-for" procedure) much too cumbersome. In the last example, nurses had to bear the consequences of physicians' not wanting to have to enter every medication order before anything could be given or changed. Understandably, both professional groups refused to fulfill these demands.[57]

Workarounds When such systems do remain in practice, workarounds, which are clever alternative approaches, are artfully developed by the users. Workarounds allow users to live with the system while avoiding some of the demands that are deemed to be unrealistic or harmful.[58,59] Such situations could undermine patient safety, however. In urgent situations, physicians could enter medication orders after the medication has already been administered, for example. Alternatively, the order might have been entered by the nurse but would have to be activated by the physician post hoc. A nurse remarked that in such situations, near the change of her shift, she often "worries that the [urgently given] medication could be given again when the order is 'activated' [critical care nurse, U.S. hospital].

Transfers Similar problems abound when transferring patients between wards or when admitting new patients. Here again, the real patient flow does not always match the clearcut, formal model of the patient flow in which you start with the completion of the required administrative data after which the clinical content can be accessed and entered. This ensures that the patient record is not accidentally fragmented over different electronic patient identities. In real-life health work, however, information can be required or activities will have to be started or planned *before* the proper administrative details are entered or even known. Problems such as this are familiar to everyone with some clinical experience, yet there are still systems that very poorly support this, as we have witnessed in all three countries. For example, during transfers between the emergency department and a patient ward, orders would not be transferred or new orders could not be entered in the system because the patient was not yet "in the system." "If they don't remember or know their social security number, it's tough," a U.S. hospital nurse remarked. In another example, we were told that once an order had been entered by a physician, that person expected it to be carried out but, if the administrative data had not yet been entered, the physician's orders might never be executed. "The doctors liked to be able to write orders and hold them pending an admission and the software was dropping off the orders you know . . . that was just incredible" [nurse, U.S. hospital].

A similar issue is "the midnight problem." It does not make a large difference for ongoing practical work or for a patient's health whether it is just before or just after midnight, but some systems create a difference. This could make sense from a purely administrative perspective, but not from a clinical one. "If the patient has a while to wait in the ER [Wednesday night] for a bed, or some other delay and doesn't get on the floor until 12:01 AM [Thursday], the order [for tomorrow's medications] effectively means Friday morning. [This is a] big problem from his perspective and I heard this from two other docs as well." This would cause there to be no orders in the system for Thursday [field notes, observation of U.S. physician].

Misrepresenting Communication as Information Transfer Loss of Communication

In a work practice such as health care, which is characterized by contingencies and constantly developing definitions of the situation, proper communication among the involved professionals is crucial. However, "physicians may assume that 'entry' into the computer system replaces their previous means of initiating and communicating their plans, and that orders will be carried out without further action on their part. The result is reduced direct interaction among physicians, nurses, and pharmacy, and increased overall reliance on the computer system."[60(p.380)] The entry of information into the system, in other words, is not the same as completing a successful *communication act*. When a U.K. hospital supplanted the telephoning of results by laboratory staff with installation of a results-reporting system in an emergency department and on the medical admissions ward, the results were devastating: "The results from 1,443/3,228 (45%) of urgent requests from accident and emergency and 529/1836 (29%) from the admissions ward were never accessed via the ward terminal. . . . In up to 43/1,443 (3%) of the accident and emergency test results that were never looked at, the findings might have led to an immediate change in patient management."[61(p.1101)]

In this case, the designers had overlooked the fact that in the previous work process, laboratory personnel called doctors when the results were in. In the new situation, doctors would have to actively log into the system to see whether the results were already available. In the hectic environment of these wards, this is a highly inefficient mode of communication for these professionals.[13]

Loss of Feedback We encountered many variations on this theme; nurses are often alerted to new orders by the printer, but this assumes the nurse is nearby and that the printer functions correctly: "There is a printer problem, for example, you know, something prints out or that piece of paper that gets printed out at the nurses' station somehow gets lost or not seen. I've seen a couple of antibiotics get missed" [physician, U.S. hospital]. Likewise, a typical complaint is that "he was totally unaware of this new order—he had heard no mention of it previously and there had not been a notification of the order by the ordering physician" [field notes, observing nurse, U.S. hospital]. Here again, the sender of the information mistakenly assumes that the computer will take care of notifying the receiver, the nurse. Similarly, a common problem is that physicians cannot tell if an order has been carried out, or that someone else has entered a similar order, without gaining feedback. In one U.S. hospital, we discovered that nurses put their initials into the computer when they take the order off rather than, for example, when they have completed the order. The latter might be more correct, but it would require yet another separate computer session. Although logical from the nurses' point of view, the system did not make a distinction between an order that was accepted and an order that was executed. This was problematic, because doctors then often do not know the true status of orders [field notes, observing nurses and physicians, U.S. hospital].

As a result of miscommunication, orders or appointments are missed, diagnostic tests are delayed, and medication is not given. Communication involves more than transferring information. Communication is about generating effect—the laboratory personnel wanted to make sure that the doctors would act on their data. Similarly, communication is about testing out assumptions regarding the other person's understanding of the situation and willingness to act on your information.[62-64] In addition, communication is always also about establishing, testing, or maintaining relationships.[65]

Decision Support Overload Decision support systems suffer from the same problem. They could trigger an overdose of reminders, alerts, or warning messages. These messages can be sent to the computer user even if the message is not relevant for that user at that moment, or if the *intended* recipient of the message is not even the one entering the data. From a communication perspective, it is crucial to realize that it is not just a simple data overload that such messages could generate.[18] Even worse, the user could feel supervised, treated as "stupid," distrusted, or resentful of being constantly interrupted. As a result, health care professionals disregard the messages, click them away, or turn the warning systems off when they have an opportunity. It is common to blame these professionals for such seemingly irresponsible behavior. However, in too many systems, too little attention is paid to ensuring the judicious use of alerts and to working on the problem of *contextual relevancy* for the alerts the system generates during actual use. When time is a scarce resource, and too many of the warnings or reminders are either irrelevant or overly predictable, irritated physicians who disregard these alerts are quite rational.

Catching Errors Appropriate and well-supported communication is also *part and parcel* of a safe work practice. In this sense, the systems we describe in this subsection could actually *hamper* safer working practices rather than stimulate them. In the hierarchies and task divisions of manual ordering, for example, many error prevention mechanisms are built in, often informally. For example, pharmacists routinely correct the medication orders given by physicians. Restructuring the medication ordering process might unwittingly eliminate these important mechanisms. "POE systems founded on notions of individual cognition are likely to be constrained by this model and be unable to take advantage of the distributed processing, fault tolerance, and resilience that obtains in settings characterized by distributed cooperative problem solving."[60(p.380)] Errors are caught constantly, and not necessarily by those formally responsible for them.[66]

The *redundancy* that is built into the system of people and technologies constituting the medication management chain is partly responsible for the fact that of the many *prescription* mistakes, only a minute fraction results in actual medication *administration* mistakes. Similarly, in practice, orders often come into being during patient rounds, during discussions among senior and junior physicians and nurses. A case is discussed, a suggestion is made and elaborated on, and it becomes an order. It can also be transformed, renegotiated, or ignored. When details remain unclear, those involved can ask for elaboration, or smoothly "repair" interpretations of junior members of the team. In most clinical order-entry systems, however, the entering of orders is the task of the junior resident, who only does ordering *after* the patient rounds. This is because systems are rarely mobile, so they are not available during rounds. Alone at a computer, the resident enters a series of orders on a series of patients, copying from the notes made during rounds. In such a setting, outside of the actual context in which the patient was discussed, and away from those who could correct his misinterpretations, order entry can be prone to errors.

DISCUSSION AND CONCLUSION

We have outlined a number of issues within a framework describing two major kinds of silent errors caused by health care information systems: those related to entering and retrieving information and those related to communication and coordination. Because the potential causes of these errors are subtle but insidious, the problems need to be addressed in a variety of ways through improvements in education, systems design, implementation, and research.

Education

Health professionals need to be educated with a critical perspective toward what PCISs can do for them. People tend to project "intelligence" and "objectivity" onto computers, [15,67,68] and physicians and nurses are no exception. In the classic case of the Therac-25 system, a computer-controlled radiation machine that was the cause of radiation overdoses in six patients, the operators trusted the "all is normal" messages the machine was delivering. They disregarded disturbing clinical signs because they had faith in the machine.[69] In a study of computer decision support in health care, users were unduly influenced by incorrect advice.[70] Medical education, and indeed the education of all health care professionals, should involve consideration of both the positives and negatives of using information systems. The outcome of these educational efforts should be a workforce that practices appropriate diligence when using a PCIS. Informatics education has a role to play in preventing these errors by educating individuals who can make sure that clinical systems are designed, implemented, and evaluated with unintended consequences in mind. It is imperative that we educate an increasing number of clinical informaticians: people who can bridge the gap between the clinical and technologic worlds, who can speak the language of both and therefore act as translators.

Systems Design

Systems developers and vendors should be clearer about the *limitations* of their technologies. When speaking of "order entry" and "intelligent" systems, and building on overly rationalist models of health care work, they can too readily lure users into expecting much more from a computer system than it can actually deliver. Systems should be designed to support *communication*[13] and provide the flexibility that is needed for systems to better fit real work practices. There are many lessons to be learned from proponents of good systems design, and although the technology is rapidly improving, known design principles are still not evident in today's systems. Increasing involvement of experienced clinicians who know what the work is truly like should improve designs in the future. The hiring of more clinical informaticians by vendors and health care organizations to design and customize systems is a positive trend. In addition, even systems designers with no clinical experience should seek to spend some time simply observing clinical activities so that the nature of these activities can be experienced first hand.

Systems should be able to help clinicians manage interruptions, perhaps by reminding them about what they were doing when last using the system. The systems also need more effective feedback mechanisms so clinicians know if and when the orders are being received and carried out. Mobile systems hold promise for assisting with overcoming problems related to both interruptions and lack of feedback, and further development efforts should focus on them.

Prevention of silent errors is preferable to fixing them after the fact. Repairing these errors by adding safety features that are not thoroughly designed could very well make things worse. Introducing safety devices is an artful process in its own right, requiring thorough insight into the communication space. For example, an observer wrote in his field notes: "We were told that the answer to this problem was then they inserted a safety level which is yet another screen so that when you press on the patient then there's five lines of information about this person and you have to verify each one . . . at what point are safety levels (more screens to make sure it's the right patient) more disruptive than helpful—similar problem to having too many alerts or too much information to take in" [field notes, observation of house officers, U.S. hospital].

Systems designers are not to be blamed for silent errors. Sometimes, a problem could really have been anticipated, but some problems are so subtle that you can only find them by closely monitoring practice. Constant vigilance is crucial. Information systems are on their own not a sufficient fix for the safety problem. A rush toward implementing systems might ultimately endanger the quality of care more than help it.

Implementation

During the implementation process, clinical informaticians need to assure not only that clinicians are heavily involved so that the implementation goes more smoothly, but also that clinicians are able to continue the social processes that the system could supplant. For example, luncheon meetings for the purpose of discussing new functions of the system might replace some of the communication loss caused by a CPOE system. During and following the implementation process, organizational systems should be in place to provide ongoing monitoring of the safety of clinical systems. As recommended by a consortium of health information technology organizations, clinical systems software oversight committees should be formed at the local level.[71,72]

Research

In practice, then, the flow of health care work activities is often much less linear than it is in other arenas, with roles much more flexibly defined and overlapping, and distinctions between steps much more fuzzy than the formalized PCIS models would have it.[60,73,74] Because of this complexity, standard quantitative research methods such as surveys fail to expose the subtle problems. Qualitative research techniques, on the other hand, can provide deep insight and can both identify problems and answer the "why" and "how" questions that quantitative studies cannot answer.[75] This research needs to be multidisciplinary and must consider the multiple perspectives of all stakeholder groups.

Finally, all of us involved in information technology in health care need to practice heightened vigilance. We must be aware of the issues described in this article through education and training, be alert to the problems identified through further research, be cautious when making major changes that might have unintended consequences, and be prepared to deal with the inevitability of such consequences. We should also be optimistic; if we can identify the presence of unintended negative consequences early enough, we can do something about them. If we can reach a high enough level of vigilance, we might be able to completely avoid many of the subtle silent errors described here.

About the Authors

Affiliations of the authors: Oregon Health & Science University, Portland, OR (JSA); Erasmus University, Rotterdam, The Netherlands (MB); University of New South Wales, Sydney, Australia (EC).

This work was supported in part by grant LM06942-02 from the National Library of Medicine. The authors appreciate the valuable contributions of Sophie Gosling and Johanna Westbrook from the Center for Health Informatics, University of New South Wales, who shared their Australian data, and Richard Dykstra, Lara Fournier, and Veena Seshadri of Oregon Health & Science University for analysis of U.S. data.

Correspondence and reprints: Joan S. Ash, PhD, Department of Medical Informatics and Clinical Epidemiology, School of Medicine, Oregon Health & Science University, 3181 SW Sam Jackson Park Road, Portland, OR 97201-3098; e-mail: ash@oshu.edu.

Received for publication: 10/03/03; accepted for publication: 10/27/03.

● ● ● References

1. Committee on Quality of Health Care in America. *To Err Is Human: Building a Safer Health System.* Washington, DC: National Academy Press, 2000.

2. NHS Magazine. Available at: http://www.nhs.uk/nhsmagazine/story316.asp. Accessed Sept 16, 2003.

3. Roughead E. The nature and extent of drug-related hospitalizations in Australia. *J Qual Clin Pract.* 1999;19:19-22.

4. Committee on Quality of Health Care in America. *Crossing the Quality Chasm: A New Health System for the 21st Century.* Washington, DC: National Academy Press, 2001.

5. Dick RS, Steen EB, Detmer DE (eds). *The Computer-Based Patient Record: An Essential Technology for Health Care.* Washington, DC: National Academy Press, 1997.

6. Bates DW, Pappins E, Kuperman GJ, et al. Using information systems to measure and improve quality. *Int J Med Inf.* 1999;53:115-24.

7. McDonald CJ, Hui SL, Smith DM, et al. Reminders to physicians from an introspective computer medical record. A two-year randomized trial. *Ann Intern Med.* 1984;100:130-8.

8. van Wijk M, Van der Lei J, Mosseveld M, Bohnen A, van Bemmel JH. Assessment of decision support for blood test ordering in primary care. A randomized trial. *Ann Intern Med.* 2001;134:274-81.

9. Sittig DF, Stead WW. Computer-based physician order entry: the state of the art. *J Am Med Inform Assoc.* 1994;1:108-23.

10. Bates DW, Leape LL, Cullen DJ, et al. Effect of computerized physician order entry and a team intervention on prevention of serious medication errors. *JAMA.* 1998;280:1311-6.

11. Dexter PR, Perkins S, Overhage JM, Maharry K, Kohler RB, McDonald CJ. A computerized reminder system to increase the use of preventive care for hospitalized patients. *N Engl J Med.* 2001;345:965-70.

12. Teich JM, Merchia PR, Schmiz JL, Kuperman GJ, Spurr CD, Bates DW. Effects of computerized physician order entry on prescribing practices. *Arch Intern Med.* 2000;160:2741-7.

13. Coiera E. When conversation is better than computation. *J Am Med Inform Assoc.* 2000;7:277-86.

14. Perrow C. *Normal Accidents. Living With High Risk Technologies.* New York, NY: Basic Books, 1984.

15. Weizenbaum J. *Computer Power and Human Reason. From Judgment to Calculation.* San Francisco, CA: W.H. Freeman and Co., 1976.

16. Berg M. Implementing information systems in health care organizations: myths and challenges. *Int J Med Inf.* 2001;64:143-56.

17. Tenner E. *Why Things Bite Back: Technology and the Revenge of Unintended Consequences.* New York, NY: Vintage Books, 1996.

18. Goldstein MK, Hoffman BB, Coleman RW, et al. Patient safety in guideline-based decision support for hypertension management: ATHENA DSS. *J Am Med Inform Assoc.* 2002;9(Nov-Dec suppl):S11-S16.

19. Burnum JF. The misinformation era: the fall of the medical record. *Ann Intern Med.* 1989;110:482-4.

20. Berg M, Goorman E. The contextual nature of medical information. *Int J Med Inform.* 1999;56:51-60.

21. Massaro TA. Introducing physician order entry at a major academic medical center. I. Impact on organizational culture and behavior. *Acad Med.* 1993;68:20-5.

22. Dykstra R. Computerized physician order entry and communication: reciprocal impacts. *AMIA Proc.* 2002:230-4.

23. Shojania KG, Duncan BW, McDonald KM, Wachter RM. Safe but sound: patient safety meets evidence-based medicine. *JAMA.* 2002;88:508-13.

24. Effken JA, Carty B. The era of patient safety: implications for nursing informatics curricula. *J Am Med Inform Assoc.* 2002;9(suppl):S120-3.

25. Weiner M, Gress T, Thiemann DR, et al. Contrasting views of physicians and nurses about an inpatient computer-based provider order-entry system. *J Am Med Inform Assoc.* 1999;6:234-44.

26. Bates DW, Cohen MS, Leape LL, Overhage JM, Shabot MM, Sheridan T. Reducing the frequency of errors in medicine using information technology. *J Am Med Inform Assoc.* 2001;8:299-308.

27. McNutt RA, Abrams R, Arons DC. Patient safety efforts should focus on medical errors. *JAMA.* 2002;287:1997-2001.

28. Strauss AL. *Qualitative Analysis for Social Scientists.* Cambridge, MA: Cambridge University Press, 1987.

29. Ash JS, Stavri PZ, Dykstra R, Fournier L. Implementing computerized physician order entry: the importance of special people. *Int J Med Inf.* 2003;69:235-50.

30. Ash JS, Gorman PN, Lavelle M, et al. A cross-site qualitative study of physician order entry. *J Am Med Inform Assoc.* 2003;10:188-200.

31. Ash JS, Gorman PN, Lavelle M, et al. Perceptions of physician order entry: results of a cross-site qualitative study. *Methods Inf Med.* 2003;42:313-23.

32. Berg M. Practices of reading and writing: the constitutive role of the patient record in medical work. *Sociol Health Illness.* 1996;18:499-524.

33. Berg M. Medical work and the computer-based patient record: a sociological perspective. *Methods Inf Med.* 1998;37:294-301.

34. Berg M. Search for synergy: interrelating medical work and patient care information systems. *Methods Inf Med.* 2003;42:337-44.

35. Gosling S, Westbrook JI, Coiera EW. Variation in the use of online clinical evidence: a qualitative analysis. *Int J Med Inf.* 2003;69:1-16.

36. Strauss A, Fagerhaugh S, Suczek B, Wieder C. *Social Organization of Medical Work.* Chicago, IL: University of Chicago Press, 1985.

37. Drazen EL, Metzger JB, Ritter JL, Schneider MK. Patient Care Information Systems: *Successful Design and Implementation.* New York, NY: Springer, 1995.

38. Kaplan B. Objectification and negotiation in interpreting clinical images: implications for computer-based patient records. *Artif Intell Med.* 1995;7:439-54.

39. Kuhn KA, Guise DA. From hospital information systems to health information systems: problems, challenges, perspectives. *Methods Inf Med.* 2001;40:275-87.

40. Forsythe DE. Studying *Those Who Study Us. An Anthropologist in the World of Artificial Intelligence.* Stanford, CA: Stanford University Press, 2001.

41. Luff P, Heath C, Greatbatch D. Tasks-in-interaction: paper and screen-based documentation in collaborative activity. In: Turner J, Kraus R (eds). *Proceedings of the Conference on Computer Supported Cooperative Work.* New York, NY: ACM Press, 1992; pp 163-70.

42. Coiera E, Jayasuriya R, Hardy J, Bannan A, Thorpe MEC. Communication loads on clinical staff in the emergency department. *Med J Aust.* 2002;176:415-8.

43. Tellioglu H, Wagner I. Work practices surrounding PACS: the politics of space in hospitals. *Computer Supported Cooperative Work.* 2001;10:163-88.

44. Patel VL, Kushniruk AW. Understanding, navigating and communicating knowledge: issues and challenges. *Methods Inf Med.* 1998;37:460-70.

45. Garfinkel H. *Studies in Ethnomethodology.* Englewood Cliffs, NJ: Prentice-Hall, 1967.

46. Garrod S. How groups co-ordinate their concepts and terminology: implications for medical informatics. *Methods Inf Med.* 1998;37:471-6.

47. Hutchins E. *Cognition in the Wild.* Cambridge, MA: MIT Press, 1995.

48. Faber MG. Design and introduction of an electronic patient record: how to involve users? *Methods Inf Med.* 2003;42:371-5.

49. Suchman L. Working relations of technology production and use. *Computer Supported Cooperative Work.* 1994;2:21-39.

50. Siddiqi J, Shekaran MC. Requirements engineering: the emerging wisdom. *IEEE Software.* 1996; 13:15-9.

51. Reddy M, Pratt W, Dourish P, Shabot MM. Sociotechnical requirements analysis for clinical systems. *Methods Inf Med.* 2003;42:437-44.

52. Star SL (ed). *The Cultures of Computing.* Oxford: Blackwell; 1995.

53. Zuboff S. *In the Age of the Smart Machine. The Future of Work and Power.* New York, NY: Basic Books, 1988.

54. Panzarasa S, Madde S, Quaglini S, Pistarini C, Stefanelli C. Evidence-based careflow management systems: the case of post-stroke rehabilitation. *J Biomed Inform.* 2002;35:123-39.

55. Collins HM. Artificial Experts. *Social Knowledge and Intelligent Machines.* Cambridge, MA: MIT Press, 1990.

56. Hughes D. When nurse knows best: some aspects of nurse/doctor interaction in a casualty department. *Sociol Health Illness.* 1988;10:1-22.

57. Goorman E, Berg M. Modelling nursing activities: electronic patient records and their discontents. *Nurs Inquiry.* 2000;7:3-9.

58. Gasser L. The integration of computing and routine work. *ACM Transactions on Office Information Systems.* 1986;4:205-25.

59. Schmidt K, Bannon L. Taking CSCW seriously: supporting articulation work. *Computer Supported Cooperative Work.* 1992;1:7-40.

60. Gorman PN, Lavelle M, Ash JS. Order creation and communication in healthcare. *Methods Inf Med.* 2003;42:376-84.

61. Kilpatrick ES, Holding S. Use of computer terminals on wards to access emergency test results: a retrospective audit. *BMJ.* 2001;322:1101-3.

62. Suchman L. *Plans and Situated Actions. The Problem of Human-Machine Communication.* Cambridge, MA: Cambridge University Press, 1987.

63. Kay S, Purves IN. Medical records and other stories: a narratological framework. *Methods Inf Med.* 1996;35:72-87.

64. Bardram J. Temporal coordination: on time and co-ordination of collaborative activities at a surgical department. *Computer Supported Cooperative Work.* 2000;9:157-87.

65. Hartswood M, Procter R, Rouncefield M, Sharpe M. Making a case in medical work: implications for the electronic medical record. *Computer Supported Cooperative Work.* 2004. In press.

66. Svenningsen S. Electronic Patient Records and Medical Practice. Reorganization of Roles, Responsibilities, and Risks. Copenhagen: Copenhagen Business School Thesis, 2002.

67. Kling R (ed). *Computerization and Controversy: Value Conflicts and Social Choices.* San Diego, CA: Academic Press, 1996.

68. Turkle S. *The Second Self: The Human Spirit in a Computer Culture.* New York, NY: Simon & Schuster, 1984.

69. Leveson NG, Turner CS. An investigation of the Therac-25 accidents. *Computer.* 1993;July:18-41.

70. Tsai TL, Fridsma DB, Gatti G. Computer decision support as a source of interpretation error: the case of electrocardiograms. *J Am Med Inform Assoc.* 2003;10:478-83.

71. Miller RA, Gardner RM. Summary recommendations for responsible monitoring and regulation of clinical software systems. *Ann Intern Med.* 1997;127:842-5.

72. Miller RA, Gardner RM. Recommendations for responsible monitoring and regulation of clinical software systems. *J Am Med Inform Assoc.* 1997;4:442-57.

73. Brown JS, Duguid P. *The Social Life of Information.* Cambridge, MA: Harvard Business School Press, 2000.

74. Lave J. *Cognition in Practice.* Cambridge, MA: Cambridge University Press, 1988.

75. Ash J, Berg M. Report of conference track 4: socio-technical issues of HIS. *Methods Inf Med.* 2003;69:305-6.

IV

MEDICAL HEALTH DETERMINANTS: THE CONTINUUM OF CARE

The continuum of care reflects of the infrastructure for health care delivery. Without an adequate infrastructure, even insured people cannot get timely access to needed health care services that also meet at least certain minimum standards of quality.

Apart from the physical infrastructure, a health care system must also have some mechanism to integrate the financing, insurance, delivery, and payment functions. In countries with national health insurance, the government plays a dominant role in integrating these four functions. The system is tightly controlled and access to various services is determined by government policy. In the United States, which does not have a centrally controlled system, managed care has stepped in to undertake the key functions of health care delivery. However, over time managed care's role has been diluted quite significantly mainly as a result of opposition from consumers, providers, and the media, a phenomenon that occurred during the 1990s and has been commonly referred to as *managed care bashing*. Government intervention through various laws followed to further restrict managed care's growing power. Regardless of these developments, today the vast majority of enrollees in both private and public plans receive health care services through a managed care organization, of which there are hundreds across the country.

Chapter 9 highlights the general organization of health care delivery from the perspectives of both insured and uninsured consumers. For the most part, the same organizational network of hospitals and outpatient clinics serves both the insured and the uninsured. The chapter also discusses *patient activation*, which is a relatively new concept that will see increased emphasis as health care delivery is increasingly viewed as a partnership between the patient and provider.

In the United States, a dichotomy exists between public health and the rest of the health care system, which is predominantly in private hands. A downside of this dichotomy is a lack of emphasis on prevention and community health. The public health infrastructure has also been charged with new responsibilities on preparedness for bioterrorism and natural disasters, yet the funding remains inadequate. These and other issues are presented in Chapter 10.

Chapter 11 addresses primary care from both global and U.S. perspectives. The health care infrastructure in the United States reflects an overemphasis on specialty care at the expense of primary care. This is a significant weakness particularly because the prevalence of chronic diseases has been on the rise with the aging of the population and primary care is best equipped to handle this.

Chapter 12 discusses the role of hospitals in the delivery of general inpatient care, tertiary care, and trauma services. Although these areas of inpatient care have been well-established and well-known, the emergence and growth of physician-owned hospitals have been a recent development in the hospital landscape. The chapter addresses controversies surrounding these hospitals. Certain challenges in the delivery of critical care in rural areas are also covered. The chapter concludes with a case study that demonstrates the incorporation of patients and families as community partners in the governance of intensive care units of hospitals.

Long-term care is multidimensional. As pointed out in Chapter 13, a variety of services must be made available to meet the needs of people of all ages who need assistance because of functional limitations. Housing is a critical component of long-term care, but adequate community-based support and clinical services are not always available. Worker shortages, financing, and availability of services to meet a variety of needs present some daunting challenges in an era of increasing demand and decreasing resources. The chapter concludes with a comprehensive overview of the quality of care provided in the nation's nursing homes.

As discussed in Chapter 14, mental illness, comorbid mental disorders, and substance abuse present significant challenges for the nation's health care resources. Thanks to the discovery and use of psychotropic drugs, significant progress has been made in the delivery of mental health care, and managed care carve-outs continue to play a significant role in cost-effective delivery of mental health services. Today, mental health services are provided in a variety of institutional and community-based settings, but the system does not adequately address the problems of people with the most complex needs and fewest resources. Issues pertaining to race, culture, and ethnicity persist. The chapter includes recommendations to improve the system.

9

Organization of Health Care

The U.S. health care delivery system is vast and complex. A variety of inpatient and outpatient providers are involved in the delivery of health care services. These providers differ by ownership: for-profit, nonprofit (tax-exempt), and public (government-owned). The consumer must navigate this complex system. Insurance status often determines when and where the consumer obtains available services. The vast majority of consumers who are covered under employer-sponsored health insurance programs are enrolled in managed care plans; only 1% of them were still covered under conventional insurance plans in 2009 (Claxton et al. 2009). In addition, 23% of Medicare beneficiaries in 2009 were enrolled in managed care (Henry J. Kaiser Family Foundation 2009), and about 70% of Medicaid enrollees received some or all of their services through managed care (Henry J. Kaiser Family Foundation 2010). Hence, managed care plays a dominant role in how insured consumers access health care services. Consumers may also wonder whether for-profit or nonprofit organizations deliver better quality of care, or whether managed care has negatively affected the quality of care.

From an organizational viewpoint, an adequate supply of health care services, the mix or balance between primary care and specialized services, and the distribution and availability of services according to population size and other characteristics can be important determinants of health. Primary care is a basic unit of health care organization. In a rationally organized health care system, primary care focuses on prevention, chronic care management, and coordination of care. It also serves as the point of entry to other services. Changing disease patterns and increased amounts of chronic care has raised the importance of primary care (Rushton 2009). In the United States, however, the health care delivery system did not evolve around a nucleus of primary care. For various reasons, American physicians have chosen to specialize rather than deliver primary care. Fewer medical school graduates are entering primary care specialties such as pediatrics, family medicine and internal medicine, and the existing workforce is diminishing as primary care physicians retire (Rushton 2009). Primary care workforce shortages are particularly pronounced in areas serving uninsured and underserved populations.

Although access to medical care in the United States is mainly through health insurance, the system also delivers certain medical services to the uninsured through a variety of sources that are mentioned in Chapter 7. Apart from voluntary free clinics and federally funded health centers, the same organizational network of hospitals and outpatient clinics serves both the insured and the uninsured. Health care for the latter group, of course, is uneven and sporadic.

Apart from the hospitals, clinics, and other facilities operated by the Veterans Health Administration, the Department of Defense, and the Indian Health Service, the health care infrastructure is largely privately owned and operated. Managed care organizations (MCOs) negotiate payment and delivery arrangements with these private providers so the MCO enrollees can obtain needed health care services.

The United States has pursued policies to reduce the number of hospital inpatient admissions and days of care as a method of containing costs. In comparison, many OECD countries have maintained a hospital-centric health care system. The U.S. places more emphasis on outpatient care than most other OECD countries (Anderson et al. 2007), yet the spending levels in the U.S. are much higher than those in OECD countries. The higher spending indicates innovation, adoption, and utilization of new technology and prices that are much higher than in other countries. It reflects a greater emphasis by Americans on specialized care.

Systematic reviews of research studies do not point to differences between nonprofit and for-profit hospitals in quality of care defined as mortality or other adverse events. Studies that did show that ownership had an impact on quality of care were influenced by their institutional context, such as differences across regions, markets, and time period (Eggleston et al. 2008). Generally, health outcomes evaluated for a wide range of conditions, diseases, and interventions demonstrated that there was little or no measurable difference in the quality of care delivered under managed care and traditional insurance plans. Although private insurance coverage has now shifted almost entirely to managed care, differences in quality may still be studied for the Medicare population because Medicare allows beneficiaries a choice to either remain in the traditional fee-for-service program or enroll in managed care under the Medicare Advantage program. Based on beneficiaries' responses on a survey, a study by Keenan and colleagues (2009) showed that beneficiaries in managed care plans reported less favorable care experiences than those in fee-for-service, particularly among the sick, but preventive

service measures were higher in managed care plans. The study, of course, has severe limitations in that it does not evaluate actual clinical outcomes. On the other hand, Medicaid managed-care enrollees in some instances may receive lower quality of care compared to enrollees in managed care plans that insure only non-Medicaid populations (Landon et al. 2007).

Health insurance and organizational aspects of the health care system are significant factors. However, patient activation also plays a critical role in health outcomes. *Patient activation* refers to a partnership between the patient and the health care providers in which the patient is actively involved in his or her own health. The level of activation can be measured using a standardized scale, the Patient Activation Measure (PAM). Higher scores on the PAM are associated with higher rates of self-care behaviors (Rask et al. 2009), improved adherence to treatment regimens (Skolasky et al. 2008), and improved outcomes (Mosen et al. 2007).

The four reading selections in this chapter shed further light on the themes discussed above. In the first reading, **Coordinating Care—A Perilous Journey through the Health Care System,** Bodenheimer points out that the most efficient structure for coordinating care among multiple providers is a system with a strong primary care foundation. The report cites several examples pointing out common flaws in care coordination that occur in health care delivery. Primary care physicians, however, are already overburdened and cannot adequately address care coordination for which they also do not get reimbursed. The author describes several models to improve care coordination. Different models apply to patient referrals to specialists, continuity of care after discharge from a hospital, and care coordination within primary care practices. These models are already being tried and their effectiveness needs to be evaluated. A patient-centered *medical home* has been promoted by primary care organizations. However, many patients do not have a usual source of primary care and 36% of primary care physicians still work in small practices of one or two physicians. These factors along with inadequate reimbursement are major deterrents to care coordination.

Community health centers are the backbone of preventive and primary for the uninsured and underserved populations. As Hurley and colleagues point out in their report, **Community Health Centers Tackle Rising Demands and Expectations,** these centers are facing many challenges despite a doubling of federal funding between 2000 and 2006. Rising demand for services, difficulties in recruitment and retention of staff, and regulatory stipulations have resulted in stressed capacity and long waits for appointments. The authors provide a detailed discussion of the challenges and how some centers are responding to the challenges. Community health centers have the potential to serve as patient-centered medical homes by using team-based care models that others could emulate.

In **Managed Care and Cancer Outcomes for Medicare Beneficiaries with Disabilities,** Roetzheim and colleagues evaluate whether the type of Medicare insurance—HMO or fee for service (FFS)—affects cancer outcomes for beneficiaries with disabilities. People with disabilities are a special population group covered by Medicare, and past studies comparing quality of care under Medicare Advantage and fee for service programs have shown mixed results. The study uses a large sample of disabled adults who had pathologically confirmed first diagnosis of breast cancer or lung cancer, thus excluding those who were disabled by cancer. The study evaluated cancer treatment as well as mortality rates by insurance status. Also included in the study were two secondary outcomes related to quality of care (receipt of axillary lymph node dissection and radiation therapy for women who underwent breast-conserving surgery). The study found that compared to FFS, disabled women with breast cancer who were covered by HMO plans were diagnosed at an earlier stage, were more likely to receive radiation therapy following breast-conserving surgery, and had higher breast cancer survival rates. In case of disabled people with lung cancer, the type of insurance coverage had few statistically significant associations. A greater focus on primary care contributes to higher rates of cancer screening for patients receiving services through an HMO. The study also confirms previous findings that Medicare beneficiaries covered by HMOs are more likely to undergo breast-conserving surgery, receive radiation therapy following breast-conserving surgery, and experience improved survival rates. On the other hand, patients with lung cancer did not fare any better in HMO plans than they did in FFS. In a small sample of patients with lung cancer, those who changed from HMO to FFS had better likelihood of undergoing surgery and better survival.

In the research brief, **How Engaged Are Consumers in Their Health and Health Care, and Why Does It Matter?,** Hibbard and Cunningham describe the four levels of patient activation derived from a nationally representative survey, according to which only 41% of American adults are at the highest level of activation. The activation levels vary by demographic factors, type of health insurance, and health status. People with lower levels of activation are more likely to have unmet medical needs, delay medical care, and not be able to get prescription drugs as needed. These differences remain after controlling for socioeconomic and health status. In addition to these findings, higher levels of activation enable people to get support for self-management from their health care providers. Because a person's activation level is changeable, the authors propose that policy interventions could be based on incentives and accountability for support from providers. The medical home model of care is particularly amenable to supporting patient activation.

● ● ● References

Anderson, G.F. et al. 2007. Health spending in OECD countries in 2004: An update. *Health Affairs* 26 (5): 1481–1489.

Claxton, G. et al. 2009. *Employer Health Benefits: 2009 Annual Survey.* Menlo Park, CA: Henry J. Kaiser Family Foundation, and Chicago: Health Research & Educational Trust.

Eggleston, K. et al. 2008. Hospital ownership and quality of care: what explains the different results in the literature? *Health Economics* 17 (12): 1345–1362.

Henry J. Kaiser Family Foundation. 2009. *Fact Sheet: Medicare, Medicare Advantage.* Retrieved February 2010 from http://www.kff.org/medicare/upload/2052–13.pdf.

Henry J. Kaiser Family Foundation. 2010. *Medicaid and Managed Care: Key Data, Trends, and Issues.* Retrieved February 2010 from http://www.kff.org/medicaid/upload/8046.pdf.

Keenan, P.S. et al. 2009. Quality assessments by sick and health beneficiaries in traditional Medicare and Medicare managed care. *Medical Care* 47 (8): 882–888.

Landon, B.E. et al. 2007. Quality of care in Medicaid managed care and commercial health plans. *Journal of the American Medical Association* 298 (14): 1674–1681.

Mosen, D.M. et al. 2007. Is patient activation associated with outcomes of care for adults with chronic conditions? *The Journal of Ambulatory Care Management* 30 (1): 21–29.

Rask, K.J. et al. 2009. Patient activation is associated with healthy behaviors and ease in managing diabetes in an indigent population. *The Diabetes Educator* 35 (4): 622–630.

Rushton, F.E. 2009. US health-care crisis. *Pediatrics International* 51 (5): 603–605.

Skolasky, R.L. et al. 2008. Patient activation and adherence to physical therapy in persons undergoing spine surgery. *Spine* 33 (21): E784–E791.

1

Coordinating Care—
A Perilous Journey through the Health
Care System

Source: Bodenheimer, T. 2008. Coordinating Care—A Perilous Journey through the Health Care System. *New England Journal of Medicine* 358 (10): 1064-1071.

In the United States, 125 million people are living with chronic illness, disability, or functional limitation.[1] The nature of modern medicine requires that these patients receive assistance from a number of different care providers. Between 2000 and 2002, the typical Medicare beneficiary saw a median of two primary care physicians and five specialists each year, in addition to accessing diagnostic, pharmacy, and other services. Patients with several chronic conditions may visit up to 16 physicians in a year.[2] Care among multiple providers must be coordinated to avoid wasteful duplication of diagnostic testing, perilous polypharmacy, and confusion about conflicting care plans.

The particularities of American health care, with its pluralistic delivery system that features large numbers of small providers, magnify the number of venues such patients need to visit. Care must be coordinated among primary care physicians, specialists, diagnostic centers, pharmacies, home care agencies, acute care hospitals, skilled nursing facilities, and emergency departments. Within each of these centers, a patient may be touched by a number of physicians, nurses, medical assistants, pharmacists, and other caregivers, who also need to coordinate with one another. Given this level of complexity, the coordination of care among multiple independent providers becomes an enormous challenge.

Care coordination has been defined as "the deliberate integration of patient care activities between two or more participants involved in a patient's care to facilitate the appropriate delivery of health care services."[3] Not only is care coordination needed among multiple providers, but coordination is also required between providers and patients and their families. Particularly for young children and elderly patients, the number of coordination relationships can multiply geometrically in the not-unusual case of three different provider organizations (with several caregivers in each organization) having to interact with a patient plus three distinct family members.

Care coordination is required when traditional continuity of care—the relationship between a single practitioner and a patient that extends beyond specific episodes of illness or disease[4]—is lacking. Continuity and fragmentation of care can be viewed as opposite ends of a spectrum. In unusual cases in which continuity is nearly total, coordination is rarely needed. In the most common situation in which continuity is limited and care is fragmented, coordination is essential. This report assesses the quality of care coordination, lists barriers to coordinated care, and discusses some solutions to improve care coordination.

COORDINATING CARE— HOW ARE WE DOING?

Recent research strongly suggests that failures in the coordination of care are common and can create serious quality concerns. Table 1 lists several studies documenting some of these problems. For example, referrals from primary care physicians to specialists often include insufficient information, and consultation reports from specialists back to primary care physicians are often late and inadequate.[5,6] When patients are hospitalized, their primary care physicians may not be notified at the time of discharge, and discharge summaries may contain insufficient information or never reach the primary care practice at all.[11] The studies listed in Table 1 do not comprise a rigorous review of the literature but provide examples of the kinds of difficulties in care coordination that patients and their families and caregivers face. In addition to research studies, the voices of patients and their families remind us that the coordination of their care among multiple providers is often flawed.[17]

BARRIERS TO SEAMLESS COORDINATION

Overstressed Primary Care

Care coordination is virtually impossible without a strong primary care foundation to the health care system. This foundation may be crumbling. U.S. medical graduates rarely choose careers in primary care.[18] With large panels of patients and a growing number of tasks to perform, primary care physicians can no longer provide high-quality short-term, long-term, and preventive care during a 15-minute visit, let alone perform care-coordination functions for which they are not reimbursed.[19]

The tasks that primary care physicians must accomplish are far more complex and time-consuming than they were a decade ago.[20] It has been estimated that it would take a physician 7.4 hours per working day to provide all recommended preventive services to a typical patient panel, plus 10.6 hours per day to provide high-quality long-term care.[21,22] Forty-two percent of primary care physicians reported not having sufficient time with their patients.[23] Providing information to patients and engaging in shared decision making take more time and thus are insufficiently done in the primary care visit.[24,25] The addition of care coordination to an impossible schedule cannot work

Lack of Interoperable Computerized Records

In 2005, only 15 to 20% of physician offices and 20 to 25% of hospitals had implemented electronic medical-record systems.[26] Rarely can health facilities access electronic information from all other facilities in the same geographic area.[27] The only advanced regional health-information system is the Indiana Network for Patient Care, which allows physicians, hospitals, and emergency departments to obtain rapid access to clinical information from many provider organizations in central Indiana.[28]

Analysis of the benefits of regional health-information systems is in its infancy. In one randomized study, patients in emergency departments whose emergency physician had access to their clinical data were compared with patients for whom the data were not provided. Costs for the intervention group were lower than for the control group at the emergency department of one hospital (which featured a well-organized work flow) but not at another hospital (whose emergency department was less well organized). No differences were found in rates of admission or repeat emergency-department visits. This study suggested that interoperable computerized records have the potential to reduce costs if the entity receiving the information is organized to make use of the data; the effect on quality or medical errors was not measured.[29]

Dysfunctional Financing

Most dollars are paid to physicians on the basis of quantity rather than quality and on face-to-face visit time rather the between-visit time required for care coordination.[30] Neither hospitals nor primary care physicians have a financial incentive to offer the discharge care needed to smooth the transition between hospital and home. Pay-for-performance systems, which provide a small percent of physician revenues, are generally based on specific measures that are less relevant for patients with multiple diagnoses, those most in need of care coordination.[31]

Lack of Integrated Systems of Care

Care coordination is more challenging when health care is delivered in many small practices. Forty-seven percent of private physicians work in practices of 1 or 2 physicians; the percentage of physicians in groups of 20 or more did not increase between 1996 and 2001.[32] Continuity of care may be deteriorating, which requires more care coordination, with

Table 1	Problems with Care Coordination

Domain of Care Coordination	Research Findings
Among providers	
Coordination between primary care physicians and specialists	A study of referrals by 122 pediatricians found that no information was sent to the specialist in 49% of referrals. The referring physician received feedback from the specialist 55% of the time.[5]
	In a study of the adult referral process at an academic medical center, 28% of primary care physicians and 43% of specialists were dissatisfied with the quality of information they received from each other; 25% of the time, specialist consultation reports had not reached the primary care physician 4 weeks after the specialty visit.[6]
Coordination between primary care physicians and emergency departments	In almost 33% of emergency department visits studied, information that included medical history and laboratory results was absent.[7]
	In 2004, 30% of adults seen in the emergency department reported that their regular physician was not informed about the care they received there.[8]
Coordination between physicians and sources of diagnostic data	Among patients who had visited at least one physician in the previous 2 years, 17% reported that test results or medical records were not available at the time of a scheduled appointment.[8]
	Adults with chronic illness who had seen a physician in the previous 2 years reported that either test results or medical records were not available at the time of a scheduled visit or the physician unnecessarily ordered a duplicate test 22% of the time for patients seeing one physician and 43% of the time for patients seeing four or more physicians.[9]
Coordination between hospital-based physicians and primary care physicians	A 2005 survey of U.S. adults with chronic illness or with a recent acute illness showed that one third of those who had been hospitalized in the previous 2 years reported that no follow-up arrangements had been made after hospital discharge.[9]
	One study found that fewer than half of primary care physicians were provided information about the discharge plans and medications of their recently hospitalized patients.[10]
	A literature review of information transfer between hospital-based and primary care physicians found that only 3% of primary care physicians were involved in discussions with hospital physicians about patients' discharge plans; 17 to 20% were always notified that the patient had been discharged; and fewer than 20% had received a discharge summary at 1 week after discharge. In addition, 25% of discharge summaries never reached the primary care physician, 38% of discharge summaries did not include reports of laboratory results, and 21% did not list discharge medications. In 66% of cases, primary care physicians contacted or treated patients after hospital discharge before receiving a discharge summary.[11]
Between providers and patients and their families	
Coordination between physicians and patients and their families	A study showed that 75% of physicians do not routinely contact patients about normal diagnostic test results, and up to 33% do not consistently notify patients about abnormal results.[7]
	In a 2004 survey, 18% of people who had visited a physician during the previous 2 years reported receiving conflicting information from various doctors; 24% reported leaving a physician visit with important questions unanswered, and 41% of those receiving regular prescriptions reported that their physician had not reviewed their medications and had not explained side effects.[8]
	In one study, 50% of patients left the office visit not understanding what they were told by the physician.[12]
	In another study, when physicians asked patients to restate the physician's instructions, the patients responded incorrectly 47% of the time, indicating a lack of clarity by the physician.[13]
	According to a study of more than 1000 audiotaped visits with 124 physicians, patients participated in medical decisions only 9% of the time.[14] Active participation in care is associated with healthier behaviors, better treatment of chronic disease and medication adherence, and better care coordination.[15,16]
Coordination between hospitals and patients and their families	In 2005, only 33% of adults who had been hospitalized in the previous 2 years and who were prescribed a new medication received information as to whether they should take their prehospital medications; 48% reported not routinely getting information about the side effects of drugs.[9]

many patients receiving fragmented care in emergency departments or "minute clinics" because they are unable to obtain prompt access to primary care.

Care coordination is more difficult for small, independent providers who cannot easily access patient records from other independent providers.

MODELS FOR IMPROVED CARE COORDINATION

A number of proposals seek to improve care coordination. Several of these proposals are at the innovation stage and have not been rigorously evaluated; others are structured interventions tested in controlled trials. What follows is a review of a few of these proposals in the domains of primary care and discharge after hospitalization.

Coordination Between Primary Care and Specialty Care

Electronic Referral

Many specialty consultations can be conducted without the need for a patient to see the specialist. For example, an endocrinologist who receives laboratory data and a medication history may be able to provide advice about the care of a patient with diabetes. A nephrologist who is given proper information may be able to answer a primary care request about an abnormality in electrolytes or renal function. A dermatologist who receives a patient's history plus a digital photo can often diagnose a skin condition. Electronic referral (e-referral) has a number of advantages: it can hasten access to specialists, reduce costs, and improve care coordination.

Some practices have implemented e-referral systems in which primary care physicians e-mail data regarding the patient's medical history, physical examination, laboratory tests, and radiographic results to specialists, asking specific questions about the patient. If those questions can be answered without the need to see the patient, the specialist e-mails back the response. E-referrals with specialists have been found to improve care coordination in the GreenField Health primary care practice in Portland, Oregon.[33] The implementation of e-referral systems for gastroenterology, cardiology, and other specialties at San Francisco General Hospital has markedly reduced waiting times for specialty appointments. Group Health Cooperative of Puget Sound uses a secured-messaging system through its electronic medical record in which primary care physicians can send nonurgent electronic consult requests to specialists and receive a response within 24 hours. This system appears to reduce unnecessary face-to-face specialty visits while improving the coordination of care.

E-referral can be successfully implemented in integrated systems, community health centers, and academic health centers—organized systems in which specialists are often salaried. In the private fee-for-service context, the loss of specialist income is a powerful barrier to e-referral, a barrier that might be overcome if health plans compensated specialists for the time spent handling e-referrals.

Referral Agreements

Some organizations are adopting referral agreements between primary care physicians and specialty practices that specify the responsibilities of each party. Referral agreements outline which clinical conditions are best managed within primary care and which conditions are best referred, specify which studies should be performed before specialty referral, and obligate the specialist to see the patient promptly, answer the questions posed by primary care, and report back to primary care in a timely fashion.[34] Although referral agreements are not in common use, they have been implemented in both dispersed and integrated delivery environments.

The dispersed Family Care Network, with 48 family physicians at 12 sites in northwest Washington State, negotiated an agreement with a cardiology practice that improved the referral process for all parties. The agreement specified the diagnoses that warranted referral, the studies that primary care needed to provide, and the timeliness of specialty appointments and written specialty consults. The agreement addressed whether the referral was a one-time-only consult, a permanent transfer of cardiac care to the cardiologist, or comanagement by primary care and cardiology. The Family Care Network is negotiating similar agreements with other specialties. Referral agreements have been developed in the integrated Veterans Health Administration system, facilitated by the systemwide electronic medical record. Diagnosis-specific templates make the referral process quick and easy for primary care physicians and specialists.

For both e-referral and referral agreements, anecdotal information shows improvements, such as shorter waiting times for specialty consultation, better information flow between primary care physicians and specialists, and more timely feedback from specialty practices to primary care. More systematic study is needed to rigorously evaluate the merit of these innovations.

Care After Hospital Discharge

Hospitalist-Initiated Projects

In the past, many patients were attended by the same physician in ambulatory and inpatient settings. The hospitalist movement, which separated the outpatient physician from the inpatient hospitalist, created discontinuity at a critical juncture of the patient's life. Hospitalist leaders are seeking remedies for this "voltage drop" in information after discharge. Working with surrounding community health centers, Boston Medical Center has reengineered the discharge process with the adoption of a comprehensive discharge plan that includes medications, lifestyle changes, follow-up care, intensive patient education geared to the patient's language and literacy level, and timely information flow to and from primary care.[35] The Hospital Patient Safe D(ischarge) project has developed a "discharge bundle" of three patient-safety interventions—a reconciliation of medication, discharge education, and a post-discharge continuity check by a clinician—to improve the transition period after discharge.[36]

Advanced-Practice Nursing

Mary Naylor at the University of Pennsylvania School of Nursing has developed a program for improving the coordination of care for older adults who have been hospitalized for heart failure complicated by other chronic health conditions. The intervention involves having advanced-practice nurses make in-hospital visits, post-discharge home visits, and phone consultations. Rehospitalizations, deaths, and total costs were significantly lower for the intervention group than for the group providing usual care.[37] Translating these findings into the real world, Naylor is collaborating with Aetna and Kaiser Permanente to develop, evaluate, and institutionalize the program in both dispersed (Aetna) and integrated (Kaiser Permanente) medical environments.

Care Transitions Program

Eric Coleman has developed the Care Transitions Program to address the problems of patients who are discharged from hospital to home. Coleman proposed that two things are needed to improve care coordination: patient activation and coaches. Many problems in care coordination can be solved only by the parties who are present both before and after a handoff: the patients and their families. Moreover, since a busy clinician cannot manage care coordination, a coach can assume care-coordination responsibilities. In Coleman's model, coaches do not actually perform post-hospital care; rather, the coach's role is to train patients and their families to coordinate care for themselves, which fosters independence. For example, if a dressing needs to be changed on a leg that is draining fluid, coaches instruct the family how to change the dressing rather than changing it themselves. If the patient needs to contact the primary care physician, coaches teach the patient how to approach the physician rather than calling the physician on the patient's behalf.

In the Care Transitions Program, advanced-practice nurses are trained as coaches, assisting patients and their families in self-care skills. In Coleman's studies, rates of rehospitalization for the same condition and total costs were significantly reduced at 6 months after discharge, as compared with controls.[16,38] Moving the program into practice, Coleman is partnering with 77 organizations, including health plans, hospitals, home care agencies, and physician groups, that have adopted the model in a variety of practice settings.

Assisting Primary Care Practices

Practice improvements often fail because they rely on the willingness of physicians, who are already too busy, to take on additional work. As described above, the primary care physician can no longer provide short-term, long-term, and preventive care in a 15-minute visit. The addition of care coordination to this list of tasks guarantees failure.

"Teamlet" Model

The primary care "teamlet" model addresses the inadequacy of the 15-minute visit by changing the care provider from the lone physician to a two-person team for patients needing support for self-management of long-term care and care coordination and by extending the 15-minute visit into care that is provided before the visit, during the visit, after the visit, and between visits for those patients. Because some practices have larger teams, the teamlet model recognizes that the two-person dyad is part but not all of the larger team. With a two-person teamlet that works together every day, the disadvantages of larger teams, which require multiple person-to-person interactions, are minimized.

The nonphysician teamlet member, who can be called a coach or another suitable name, would ideally be a registered nurse or an advanced-practice clinician but in small private practices is more likely to be a retrained medical assistant. The coach handles care before visits, after visits, and between visits and may accompany the physician during the visit. Details of this extended encounter are described elsewhere.[39] Pertinent to care coordination, the coach can assist with paperwork and authorizations and can help patients obtain necessary tests and appointments needed before referrals. Using reminder systems and checklists, the coach makes sure that consultation reports come back from specialists and that results are transmitted to patients. Each clinician-coach teamlet works out which functions the coach is adequately trained to perform; the clinician must be confident in the coach's competence before delegating any task.

Variations of the teamlet model are being tried at several primary care practices. In two fee-for-service practice settings that assign medical assistants as teamlet coaches, the model has been financially viable because physicians, whose duties in some routine functions are handled by the coaches, can see one or two more patients per day, thereby increasing revenues.[40]

Paying for Care Coordination

Most primary care practices receive fee-for-service payment, which covers visits but does not reimburse between-visit services. A study of 11 family physicians in different regions of the United States found that 13% of the workday was spent coordinating care.[41] In a separate study involving 16 geriatricians, the physicians spent 14% of the workday on uncompensated between-visit care coordination.[42] If primary care visits were reimbursed at an adequate level to cover work that was performed between visits, the uncompensated time would not be such a problem; however, primary care payment does not provide reasonable compensation for the between-visit work.

A payment reform that has received substantial attention is the institution of payment for care coordination, paid over and above the existing fee schedule and adjusted to the complexity of the patients' conditions requiring substantial care coordination. Such a payment would create an incentive for primary care practices to improve between-visit coordination of care for their patients.[43] The American College of Physicians and the American Academy of Family Physicians have strongly advocated for a care-coordination payment under Medicare, and the Medicare Payment Advisory Commission, an important body advising Congress on Medicare policy, has reported favorably on this new payment idea, citing evidence that care coordination improves quality and may reduce costs.[44]

ORGANIZATION OF HEALTH SERVICES

Although specific innovations may contribute to better coordination of care, consideration must also be given to how the overall organization of health services could facilitate or impede improvement in coordinating care. The most efficient structure for coordinating care is a system with a strong primary care foundation in which the primary care practice, in partnership with its patients, consciously assumes the responsibility for coordinating care throughout the health care system. With a primary care hub, all information resides at the hub and with the patient, and communications flow in and out of the hub. The alternative, multiple independent providers without a primary care center, fails to assign responsibility to anyone and, if all providers receive all clinical information about their patients, necessitates many more separate communications. Moreover, the practice of generalism—concern with everything about a patient—requires a different set of skills and expectations from those of the practice of specialism or "partialism," which calls on equally important but distinct skills and responsibilities for one part of a patient's health. Thus, the strengthening of primary care may be the most significant macro health policy capable of improving care transitions.

During the past year, the patient-centered "medical home," which has been promoted by primary care organizations, has become a prominent concept in health care reform. A set of general principles describing the ideal medical home were promulgated in February 2007 by the American Academy of Family Physicians, the American Academy of Pediatrics, the American College of Physicians, and the American Osteopathic Association.[45]

The medical home envisions a medical practice that is based on the same concepts put forth 40 years ago by primary care advocates: first-contact care, continuity of care over time, comprehensiveness, and responsibility to coordinate care throughout the health system. In the current iteration of this venerable idea, practices would be designated as a medical home if they conform to a set of standards (not yet established) that are considerably more specific than the general principles. Medical practices that meet the criteria would receive higher levels of reimbursement, including payment for care coordination.[46] The additional payment would finance increased staff support, such as that proposed in the teamlet model. Alternatively, the medical home could be reimbursed through a comprehensive per-patient payment that eliminates fee-for-service altogether.[47] The medical home is expected to contain health care costs by reducing unnecessary hospital admissions and emergency department visits.[20]

In 2005, 36% of primary care physicians were working in practices of one or two physicians.[48] It is difficult to imagine that such small practices could meet the challenging criteria for becoming a certified medical home. Nor is it easy to envision small primary care offices having the resources to successfully coordinate care; the effort required to coordinate with specialists, hospitals, home care agencies, and multiple insurers is overwhelming. Integrated delivery systems such as the Veterans Health Administration system and Kaiser Permanente have substantial advantages over smaller, independent practices in achieving the standards for a medical home and in coordinating care.

The adoption of electronic medical record systems, which will undoubtedly be a feature of the medical home, is higher in integrated medical groups,[49] simplifying and speeding information flow critical to care coordination. Integrated systems can accumulate financial, personnel, and other resources to plan and implement the improvements needed to qualify as a medical home. The financial incentives of globally budgeted systems favor the development of teams or teamlets, which are a feature of the medical home and essential in helping physicians to coordinate their services. Electronic portals for patients that are common in integrated systems assist in coordination with patients and their families, whereas internal messaging makes possible immediate handoffs among primary care services, specialists, hospitalists, and other services. Evidence suggests that integrated systems provide higher quality care than dispersed practices and also outperform loose networks of physician practices.[49-51] Perhaps the successful implementation of the medical-home vision requires the movement of ambulatory care delivery in the direction of larger, integrated systems organized as multispecialty groups.

As continuity of care diminishes with fewer primary care physicians, more part-time physicians, and the divorce of inpatient and outpatient practitioners, coordination of care assumes an increasingly central role. Addressing the flaws in care coordination is more difficult than the usual quality-improvement work that takes place within a hospital service or ambulatory care site. Improvement in care coordination requires that different health care entities, sometimes working in competition, perform together. Only then can all care be coordinated for every patient every day.

• • • References

1. Anderson G, Knickman JR. Changing the chronic care system to meet people's needs. *Health Aff (Millwood)* 2001;20(6):146-60.

2. Pham HH, Schrag D, O'Malley AS, Wu B, Bach PB. Care patterns in Medicare and their implications for pay for performance. *N Engl J Med* 2007;356: 1130-9.

3. McDonald KM, Sundaram V, Bravata DM, et al. Care coordination. Vol. 7. In: Shojania KG, McDonald KM, Wachter RM, Owens DK, eds. *Closing the quality gap: a critical analysis of quality improvement strategies.* Stanford, CA: Stanford University-UCSF Evidence-based Practice Center, Agency for Health-care Research and Quality, 2007.

4. Haggerty JL, Reid RJ, Freeman GK, Starfield BH, Adair CF, McKendry R. Continuity of care: a multidisciplinary review. *BMJ* 2003;327:1219-21.

5. Forrest CB, Glade GB, Baker AE, Bocian A, von Schrader S, Starfield B. Coordination of specialty referrals and physician satisfaction with referral care. *Arch Pediatr Adolesc Med* 2000;154:499-506.

6. Gandhi TK, Sittig DF, Franklin M, Sussman AJ, Fairchild DG, Bates DW. Communication breakdown in the outpatient referral process. *J Gen Intern Med* 2000;15:626-31.

7. Gandhi TK. Fumbled handoffs: one dropped ball after another. *Ann Intern Med* 2005;142:352-8.

8. Schoen C, Osborn R, Huynh PT, et al. Primary care and health system performance: adults' experiences in five countries. *Health Aff (Millwood)* 2004;Suppl Web Exclusives:W4-487-W4-503.

9. Schoen C, Osborn R, Huynh PT, et al. Taking the pulse of health care systems: experiences of patients with health problems in six countries. *Health Aff (Millwood)* 2005; Suppl Web Exclusives:W5-509-W5-525.

10. Moore C, Wisnivesky J, Williams S, McGinn T. Medical errors related to discontinuity of care from an inpatient to an outpatient setting. *J Gen Intern Med* 2003;18:646-51.

11. Kripalani S, LeFevre F, Phillips CO, Williams MV, Basaviah P, Baker DW. Deficits in communication and information transfer between hospital-based and primary care physicians. *JAMA* 2007;297: 831-41.

12. Roter DL, Hall JA. Studies of doctor-patient interaction. *Annu Rev Public Health* 1989;10:163-80.

13. Schillinger D, Piette J, Grumbach K, et al. Closing the loop: physician communication with diabetic patients who have low health literacy. *Arch Intern Med* 2003;163:83-90.

14. Braddock CH III, Edwards KA, Hasenberg NM, Laidley TL, Levinson W. Informed decision making in outpatient practice: time to get back to basics. *JAMA* 1999;282:2313-20.

15. Heisler M, Bouknight RR, Hayward RA, Smith DM, Kerr EA. The relative importance of physician communication, participatory decision making, and patient understanding in diabetes self-management. *J Gen Intern Med* 2002;17:243-52.

16. Coleman EA, Parry C, Chalmers S, Min S. The care transitions intervention: results of a randomized controlled trial. *Arch Intern Med* 2006;166:1822-8.

17. Levine C. *Rough crossings: family caregivers' odysseys through the health care system.* New York: United Hospital Fund, 1998.

18. Bodenheimer T. Primary care-will it survive? *N Engl J Med* 2006;355:861-4.

19. McGlynn EA, Asch SM, Adams J, et al. The quality of health care delivered to adults in the United States. *N Engl J Med* 2003;348:2635-45.

20. Grumbach K, Bodenheimer T. A primary care home for Americans: putting the house in order. *JAMA* 2002;288:889-93.

21. Yarnell KS, Pollak KI, Østbye T, Krause KM, Michener JL. Primary care: is there enough time for prevention? *Am J Public Health* 2003;93:635-41.

22. Østbye T, Yarnall KS, Krause KM, et al. Is there time for management of patients with chronic diseases in primary care? *Ann Fam Med* 2005;3: 209-14.

23. Center for Studying Health System Change. CTS Physician Survey. (Accessed February 14, 2008, at http://www.hschange.com/index.cgi?data504.)

24. Kaplan SH, Greenfield S, Gandek B, Rogers WH, Ware JE Jr. Characteristics of physicians with participatory decision-making styles. *Ann Intern Med* 1996;124:497-504.

25. Deveugele M, Derese A, De Bacquer D, van den Brink-Muinen A, Bensing J, De Maeseneer J. Consultation in general practice: a standard operating procedure? *Patient Educ Couns* 2004;54: 227-33.

26. Hillestad R, Bigelow J, Bower A, et al. Can electronic medical record systems transform health care? Potential health benefits, savings, and costs. *Health Aff (Millwood)* 2005;24:1103-17.

27. Halamka J, Overhage JM, Ricciardi L, Rishel W, Shirky C, Diamond C. Exchanging health information: local distribution, national coordination. *Health Aff (Millwood)* 2005;24:1170-9.

28. McDonald CJ, Overhage JM, Barnes M, et al. The Indiana Network for Patient Care: a working local health information infrastructure. *Health Aff (Millwood)* 2005;24:1214-20.

29. Overhage JM, Dexter PR, Perkins SM, et al. A randomized, controlled trial of clinical information shared from another institution. *Ann Emerg Med* 2002;39:14-23.

30. A system in need of change: restructuring payment policies to support patient-centered care. American College of Physicians position paper. Philadelphia: American College of Physicians, 2006.

31. Casalino LP, Elster A, Eisenberg A, Lewis E, Montgomery J, Ramos D. Will pay-for-performance and quality reporting affect health care disparities? *Health Aff (Millwood)* 2007;26(3):w405-w414.

32. Casalino LP, Devers KJ, Lake TK, Reed M, Stoddard JJ. Benefits of and barriers to large medical group practice in the United States. *Arch Intern Med* 2003;163:1958-64.

33. Kilo CM. Transforming care: medical practice design and information technology. *Health Aff (Millwood)* 2005;24:1296-301.

34. Murray M. Reducing waits and delays in the referral process. *Fam Pract Manag* 2002;9:39-42.

35. Anthony D, Chetty VK, Kartha A, McKenna K, DePaoli MR, Jack B. Re-engineering the hospital discharge: an example of a multifaceted process evaluation. In: *Advances in patient safety: from research to implementation.* Vol. 2. Rockville, MD: Agency for Healthcare Research and Quality, 2005. (AHRQ publication no. 05-0021-2.)

36. AHRQ partnerships in implementing patient safety. Rockville, MD: Agency for Healthcare Research and Quality, 2005. (Accessed February 14, 2008, at http://www.ahrq.gov/qual/pips.htm.)

37. Naylor MD, Brooten DA, Campbell RL, Maislin G, McCauley KM, Schwartz JS. Transitional care of older adults hospitalized with heart failure: a randomized, controlled trial. *J Am Geriatr Soc* 2004; 52:675-84. [Erratum, *J Am Geriatr Soc* 2004;52: 1228.]

38. Coleman EA, Smith JD, Frank JC, Min S, Parry C, Kramer AM. Preparing patients and caregivers to participate in care delivery across settings: the care transitions intervention. *J Am Geriatr Soc* 2004;52:1817-25.

39. Bodenheimer T, Laing BY. The teamlet model of primary care. *Ann Fam Med* 2007;5:457-61.

40. Bodenheimer T. *Building teams in primary care: 15 case studies.* Oakland, CA: California HealthCare Foundation, July 2007.

41. Gottschalk A, Flocke SA. Time spent in face-to-face patient care and work outside the examination room. *Ann Fam Med* 2005;3:488-93.

42. Farber J, Siu A, Bloom P. How much time do physicians spend providing care outside of office visits? *Ann Intern Med* 2007;147:693-8.

43. Davis K. Paying for care episodes and care coordination. *N Engl J Med* 2007;356:1166-8.

44. Medicare Payment Advisory Commission. *Increasing the value of Medicare: report to the Congress.* Washington, DC: MedPAC, June 2006.

45. American Academy of Family Physicians, American Academy of Pediatrics, American College of Physicians, American Osteopathic Association. Joint principles of the patient-centered medical home. March 2007. (Accessed February 14, 2008, at http://www.medicalhomeinfo.org/Joint%20 Statement.pdf.)

46. Davis K, Schoenbaum SC, Audet A-M. A 2020 vision of patient-centered primary care. *J Gen Intern Med* 2005;20:953-7.

47. Goroll AH, Berenson RA, Schoenbaum SC, Gardner LB. Fundamental reform of payment for adult primary care: comprehensive payment for comprehensive care. *J Gen Intern Med* 2007;22:410-5.

48. Liebhaber A, Grossman JM. *Physicians moving to mid-sized, single-specialty practices. Tracking report no. 18.* Washington, DC: Center for Studying Health System Change, August 2007.

49. Mehrotra A, Epstein AM, Rosenthal MB. Do integrated medical groups provide higher-quality medical care than individual practice associations? *Ann Intern Med* 2006;145:826-33.

50. Gillies RR, Chenok KE, Shortell SM, Pawlson G, Wimbush JJ. The impact of health plan delivery system organization on clinical quality and patient satisfaction. *Health Serv Res* 2006;41:1181-99.

51. Crosson FJ. The delivery system matters. *Health Aff (Millwood)* 2005;24:1543-8.

Community Health Centers Tackle Rising Demands and Expectations

Source: Hurley, R., L. Felland, and J. Lauer. 2007. *Community Health Centers Tackle Rising Demands and Expectations.* Issue Brief No. 116. Washington, DC: Center for Studying Health System Change. Used with permission.

As key providers of preventive and primary care for underserved people, including the uninsured, community health centers (CHCs) are the backbone of the U.S. health care safety net. Despite significant federal funding increases, community health centers are struggling to meet rising demand for care, particularly for specialty medical, dental and mental health services, according to findings from the Center for Studying Health System Change's (HSC) 2007 site visits to 12 nationally representative metropolitan communities. Health centers are responding to these pressures by expanding capacity and adding services but confront staffing, resource and other constraints. At the same time, CHCs are facing other demands, including increased quality reporting expectations, addressing racial and ethnic disparities, developing electronic medical records, and preparing for public health emergencies.

COMMUNITY HEALTH CENTERS STRIVE TO MEET DEMAND

Since 2000, federal funding for federally qualified community health centers—key providers of preventive and primary care for underserved people—has doubled to nearly $2 billion annually in 2006,

according to the Health Resources and Services Administration (HRSA). More than 16 million patients—primarily racial or ethnic minorities, low income, uninsured or covered by Medicaid—received care at more than 1,100 federally qualified and lookalike CHCs in 2006, up from just over 10 million patients in 2001.

Much of the recent federal investment has gone to building health centers in additional communities, while support for existing CHCs has not kept pace with operating expense increases and patient growth.[1] At the same time, recruiting and retaining staff members in a competitive labor market has grown more difficult, and external entities have increased requirements that CHCs must meet to stay in operation and to provide state-of-the-art clinical care, as well as to address racial and ethnic disparities and public health issues.

HSC's 2007 site visits to 12 nationally representative metropolitan communities—home to more than 100 federally qualified health centers (FQHCs) and lookalike facilities—explored how CHCs are responding to rising demand for services, funding challenges, and other new responsibilities. Many communities have other types of health centers, such as free clinics or public clinics, but results presented here focus on federally qualified and lookalike community health centers.

More Patients

Virtually all CHC directors reported treating more patients—mainly uninsured—over the last two years, leading to stressed capacity and, in some cases, longer waits for appointments. Observers attributed the increase in uninsured people to declining employer-based insurance, growing numbers of immigrants who lack coverage, and Medicaid cutbacks. While the number of uninsured patients treated at FQHCs increased from 4 million in 2001 to 6 million in 2006, according to HRSA,[2] the overall proportion of uninsured patients remained steady at about 40 percent in 2006. CHCs also serve a significant number of Medicaid patients—about 35 percent of all FQHC patients have Medicaid coverage. CHCs benefit from serving Medicaid patients because their Medicaid payment rates typically are higher than rates paid by private insurers or directly by patients. Changes in Medicaid physician payment rates affect CHCs indirectly. Reductions in payment rates to private physicians in some states, such as Michigan and California, made access to private providers more difficult for people with Medicaid coverage, increasing demand for care at CHCs. Conversely, in some cases, increased Medicaid payment rates may reduce a health center's proportion of Medicaid patients. In Orange County, Phoenix and Greenville, CHCs have faced new competition for Medicaid patients when rates increased to selected providers, such as obstetricians.

Additionally, new documentation requirements under the Deficit Reduction Act of 2005 adversely affected Medicaid coverage in some states, resulting in more uninsured CHC patients. Increased numbers of immigrants, without access to either employer-sponsored or publicly supported coverage, have grown increasingly reliant on CHCs, in part because centers are exempted from any obligation to ask an individual's legal status.

Fewer Care Alternatives

The growth in uninsured people seeking care at CHCs also reflects a decline in alternative sites of care. In the last decade, the amount of charity care provided by physicians has declined significantly.[3] Though many physicians donate time to free clinics and to specialty care banks, such as Project Access in Seattle and Little Rock or MedWell Access in Greenville, demand outstrips supply.

CHCs face serious challenges referring both uninsured and Medicaid patients to specialists; one veteran Seattle observer noted CHCs are "back to begging for specialty care almost like the 1970s," when there were fewer specialists relative to the population. In other markets, such as Orange County, academic health centers—often cornerstones of the safety net—have undertaken initiatives to shift uninsured patients in

their emergency departments (EDs) and outpatient clinics to community providers. In Greenville and Little Rock, as in many communities, the local health department has been phasing out direct primary care services, creating new demands for CHC services.

In several states, reductions in funding for mental health services have led to dramatic increases in patients with mental health conditions seeking care at CHCs. Dental care for low-income adults is another service that in a number of communities, such as Orange County and Little Rock, is available primarily at CHCs and often is limited to basic services. Nationally, the number of patients receiving mental health care at CHCs grew by almost 170 percent between 2001 and 2006, according to HRSA, while the number of patients receiving dental services grew by more than 80 percent during the same period.[4]

Recruiting and Retaining Staff

CHCs offer comprehensive services that are important in caring for persons with chronic conditions. In addition to clinical teams, many CHCs offer on-site diagnostic testing, subsidized pharmacies, transportation and patient education programs. To offer this range of services, CHCs rely on physicians, nurse practitioners, physician assistants and other clinical and administrative staff. CHC directors reported increased difficulty recruiting and retaining clinical staff because they must compete with other health care providers, especially hospitals, that offer comparatively better salaries and benefits.

Attracting bilingual staff is becoming more challenging for CHCs as other providers also attempt to improve cultural and linguistic competencies. Further, the general shortage of primary care physicians in many communities presents serious recruitment problems. In Boston, CHCs reported sharply increasing starting salaries for primary care physicians to better compete with hospitals and medical groups.

Many CHCs continue to rely on National Health Service Corps physicians who receive federal assistance in repaying medical school loans in exchange for working in medically underserved areas. Few centers attempt to recruit specialists, given restrictions on use of federal grant funds for hiring specialists, and most centers cannot generate sufficient revenue from other sources to fully support specialists.

Increased Emphasis on Accountability, Disparities and Public Health

While CHCs have been subject to federal monitoring and reporting requirements for many years, they now face increasing expectations from grantmakers and public and private payers. Some CHCs reported demands to more formally demonstrate their need for funds and how they will use them. One CHC director characterized the attitudes of philanthropies as, "Before they would say, 'Let's give money to people who do good things;' now they want outcome measures, logic models and more accountability." Though hardly a new phenomenon for CHCs, Medicaid managed care also is being extended to new populations in a number of markets, and these plan contracts carry new terms, relationships and reporting obligations. Reporting on clinical performance measures also is on the rise from public and private sources, though reporting is typically neither coordinated nor uniform. Community-wide public reporting and quality improvement collaborations are underway in Seattle, Cleveland and Little Rock, presenting new expectations for integration of CHC performance improvement efforts with those of private providers.

Since almost two-thirds of CHC patients are members of racial or ethnic minorities and nearly 30 percent of patients require interpretation services, health centers are on the front lines in trying to reduce racial and ethnic disparities.[5] In 1998, HRSA began sponsoring Health Disparities Collaboratives to bring federally qualified health centers together to learn quality improvement approaches developed by the Institute for Healthcare Improvement.[6] Most

health centers in the 12 HSC communities are now veterans of the collaboratives, and CHC directors reported these activities have not only helped improve delivery systems and processes of care for all of their patients, but also promoted a culture of continuous quality improvement.

Additionally, CHCs are preparing for potential public health emergencies in their communities. In some cases, this has been a challenge for CHCs that until recently were overlooked by state and local agencies developing preparedness plans. This situation is beginning to change, however, as one respondent from Phoenix remarked, "I guess they finally realized that the neediest population will probably show up at the clinics in the case of a disaster." Several CHCs are coordinating with community providers, stockpiling supplies and applying for grants for communication equipment and generators. A Boston CHC even hired a full-time employee to work with community agencies and providers on emergency preparedness.

CHCs also have other new public health responsibilities and priorities. A health center in northern New Jersey has been given responsibility for taking over tuberculosis testing from the county health department. A number of health centers have expanded their mission to include participating in or developing various wellness campaigns, which can require more staff and funding.

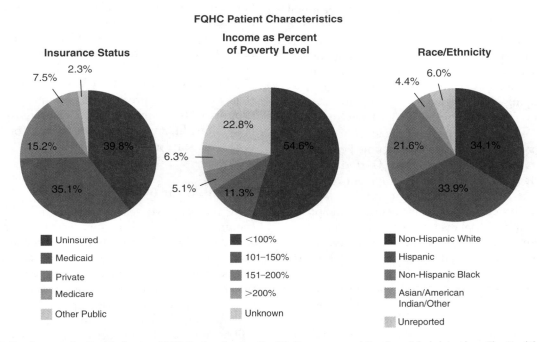

Figure 1 Key Community Health Center (CHC) Facts. *Source:* Health Resources and Services Administration, The Health Center Program, 2006 National Aggregate UDS Data

CHCs Respond to Mounting Challenges

In the past two years, new health centers have opened in three of the 12 communities, and CHCs in all but four communities added additional practice sites. Growth was particularly pronounced in Miami and northern New Jersey—communities that also benefited from increased state support. Boston, with the largest concentration of health centers in the country, also saw two new sites open. Other centers have expanded hours to include Saturdays and evenings to treat more patients and help improve access for people who cannot take time off from work to seek care. In some communities, CHCs are expanding hours to provide alternatives to hospital emergency department use.

Broadening of services at existing facilities is also evident, with centers in northern New Jersey and Phoenix expanding mental health services. Other health centers are adding pharmacies and dental services to meet patient needs. The largest health center in Indianapolis has developed an obstetric hospitalist program to meet the inpatient needs of maternity patients.

A number of health centers report major steps in developing new infrastructure, particularly information technology (IT). In Boston, most health centers have electronic medical records (EMRs) and are electronically connected to their affiliated safety net hospitals. A similar approach is under development with three Cleveland health centers and the public hospital. In Miami, the CHCs have organized a regional health information organization to create a shared medical record, and Seattle CHCs have a similar partnership for IT services. Despite these activities, there is significant variation in IT and EMR adoption across communities and health centers, with the costs of developing such systems often prohibitive.[7]

In several communities, CHCs have forged relationships with other parts of the local health care delivery system to improve low-income people's access to appropriate care. The United Way in Greenville is supporting the development of formal referral mechanisms between hospitals and community health centers. In other cases, public policy makers and health plans have been instrumental in encouraging CHCs to be effective, available alternatives to more costly sites of care, such as hospital emergency departments.

Many health centers are collaborating with their safety net hospital counterparts and other organizations to expand access to needed services. Enhanced financial screening systems for public hospital patients in Phoenix and Cleveland have made free or deeply discounted specialty and ancillary care more readily accessible to CHC patients. In Miami, CHCs are working with the school system to expand school-based services, with the added potential of freeing up appointments at CHC sites because children can now be treated at school. In Phoenix, health centers have partnered with new dental schools to provide teaching sites, volunteer opportunities, and, ultimately, post graduation employment as a means to "grow their own" future clinicians.

A major aim in some communities has been to pursue federal qualification or lookalike status for community clinics supported only with private donations and fees. In Orange County, a community with only two federally qualified health centers for a population of approximately 3 million, as many as five community clinics are now seeking or have obtained federally qualified or lookalike health center status. In Phoenix, obtaining lookalike status for the 11 centers sponsored by the county health authority meant a substantial infusion of new revenue.

Attracting more Medicare and privately insured patients also is a goal for some centers, including those in Boston, northern New Jersey, Greenville and Cleveland. However, payment for care of these patients is typically less than what CHCs receive for patients with Medicaid coverage.

A number of health centers have bolstered relationships with philanthropic organizations to obtain needed capital for new initiatives. One Phoenix CHC obtained a major grant from the Diamondbacks baseball team foundation to acquire a mobile health unit that now serves 10 school clinics and migrant and farm workers. United Way and Duke Endowment funds have supported a new dental initiative in the Greenville area at the CHC and other sites of care.

Many of the CHCs have longstanding relationships with not-for-profit local hospital systems that support CHCs as part of their community benefit obligations, an area of increased scrutiny on the part of federal, state and local policy makers.

Future Risks and Opportunities

Over the past two years, many community health centers have responded to increasing demands for services and new responsibilities in the face of serious financial constraints. Beyond the usual concerns of ensuring adequate funding to meet their missions, many CHC directors are anxious about how strategies aimed at universal coverage underway in several states will affect them and whether reformers will be mindful of the issues facing health centers.

CHCs are likely to benefit from caring for previously uncovered persons who bring additional revenue, if CHCs can make or keep themselves attractive to these patients. Whether that revenue will be adequate to compensate CHCs for the range of services they now provide is uncertain. Also unclear is how care will be financed for people who remain uninsured and for services that will be needed but either not covered or extremely restricted by payers.

At the same time, CHCs appear well positioned to inform the growing call for renewed emphasis on "patient-centered medical homes."[8] CHCs' model of care closely approximates the ideal type being advanced by proponents, and the fact that CHCs have been reimbursed for the comprehensive care they provide has enabled them to play this role. CHCs have established team-based care models that others could examine and emulate, and their progress in recent years in service expansions, infrastructure development and quality improvement initiatives underscores the potential yield from investing in such arrangements.

Data Source

Approximately every two years, HSC conducts site visits to 12 nationally representative metropolitan communities as part of the Community Tracking Study to interview health care leaders about the local health care market, how it has changed and the effect of those changes on people. The communities are Boston; Cleveland; Greenville, S.C.; Indianapolis; Lansing, Mich.; Little Rock, Ark.; Miami; northern New Jersey; Orange County, Calif.; Phoenix; Seattle; and Syracuse, N.Y. The sixth round of site visits was conducted between February and June 2007 with more than 500 interviews. This Issue Brief is based primarily on responses from community health center and safety net hospital executives, state policy makers, local health department directors and consumer advocates. In each community, the one or two largest community health centers were typically targeted for interview.

● ● ● References

1. National Association of Community Health Centers, Inc. (NACHC), *A Sketch of Community Health Centers: Chart Book 2006, www.nachc.com/research/Files/ChartBook2006.pdf* (Accessed Oct. 18, 2007).

2. Health Resources and Services Administration, The Health Center Program, 2006 National Aggregate UDS Data, *www.bphc.hrsa.gov/uds/2006data/National/NationalTable4Universal.htm.* (Accessed Nov. 7, 2007).

3. Cunningham, Peter J., and Jessica H. May, *A Growing Hole in the Safety Net: Physician Charity Care Declines Again,* Tracking Report No. 13, Center for Studying Health System Change, Washington, D.C. (March 2006).

4. Health Resources and Services Administration, The Health Center Program, The President's Health Center Initiative, *www.bphc.hrsa.gov/presidentsinitiative/* (Accessed Nov. 5, 2007).

5. Health Resources and Services Administration, The Health Center Program, 2006 National Aggregate UDS Data, www.bphc.hrsa.gov/uds/2006data/National/NationalTable4Universal.htm. (Accessed Nov. 7, 2007).

6. Landon, Bruce E., et al., "Improving the Management of Chronic Disease at Community Health Centers," *New England Journal of Medicine*, Vol. 356, No. 9 (March 1, 2007).

7. Shields, Alexandra, et al., "Adoption Of Health Information Technology In Community Health Centers: Results Of A National Survey" *Health Affairs*, Vol. 26, No. 5 (September/October 2007).

8. "Joint Principles of the Patient-Centered Medical Home" issued by the American Academy of Family Physicians, the American Academy of Pediatrics, the American College of Physicians and the American Osteopathic Association (February 2007).

Managed Care and Cancer Outcomes for Medicare Beneficiaries with Disabilities

Source: Roetzheim, R.G., T.N. Chirikos, K.J. Wells, et al. 2008. Managed care and cancer outcomes for Medicare beneficiaries with disabilities. *American Journal of Managed Care* 14(5):287-296.

In 2005, 1 in 6 Medicare beneficiaries (6.5 million persons) was entitled to receive Medicare benefits because of disability.[1] Medicare beneficiaries with disabilities seem to be at risk for increased cancer mortality,[2] even when diagnosed at the same stage or at an earlier stage, compared with persons without disabilities.[3] In addition, persons with disabilities may receive different cancer treatment than persons without disabilities.[2,4]

Medicare beneficiaries may receive care within a health maintenance organization (HMO) or within the fee-for-service (FFS) sector. It is uncertain whether the type of health insurance arrangement (HMO vs FFS) affects the quality of care for Medicare beneficiaries with disabilities.[5] In some studies,[6,7] beneficiaries with disabilities were less satisfied with managed care plan performance and were more likely to disenroll. However, other evidence indicates that beneficiaries with disabilities receiving care in HMO plans perceive better access to primary care services and greater affordability of health services than those with traditional Medicare coverage.[8] Medicare beneficiaries who are enrolled in HMO plans are more likely to undergo cancer screening,[9-12] generally have cancers diagnosed at an earlier stage,[13-16] and may have improved survival.[14]

The Surveillance, Epidemiology, and End Results (SEER) cancer registries merged with Medicare data have been used to study health disparities among persons with disabilities.[2,3] We used merged SEER-Medicare data to evaluate whether the type of Medicare insurance arrangement (HMO or FFS) affects cancer outcomes for Medicare beneficiaries with disabilities. We studied two high-volume cancers, breast cancer and lung cancer. We chose breast cancer because it is amenable to screening and because experiences of these patients would capture potential disparities in early detection and treatment. In contrast, screening is not recommended to detect lung cancer, although surgery and radiation treatment may improve survival.[17,18]

METHODS

Data Sources

We used the SEER-Medicare dataset, which links SEER registry information to Medicare claims data.[19,20] SEER consists of 11 population-based tumor registries representing approximately 14% of the US population.[20] SEER collects patient information on demographic characteristics, primary tumor site, stage at diagnosis, tumor size, histologic findings, tumor grade, hormone receptor status, initial course of treatment, and vital status.

SEER tracks vital status annually, and death certificates are used to capture underlying cause of death.

Study Sample

We identified all persons 21 years and older within the SEER-Medicare dataset having a pathologically confirmed first diagnosis of breast cancer (n = 62,315) or non-small cell lung cancer (n = 55,770) from January 1, 1988, through December 31, 1999. We then restricted our sample to those persons who originally qualified for Medicare coverage because of Social Security Disability Insurance (6,839 with breast cancer and 10,229 with lung cancer). Therefore, our sample includes persons younger than 65 years who have Social Security Disability Insurance and persons 65 years and older whose Social Security Disability Insurance has been automatically converted to Old Age Survivors Insurance. As described elsewhere, we focused exclusively on individuals with Medicare when newly diagnosed with cancer, eliminating persons disabled by cancer.[3]

Medicare data indicate for each month whether persons were eligible for Part A and Part B and whether they were enrolled in an HMO insurance arrangement. To examine possible effects of insurance structure on early detection of cancer, we constructed a variable that defined insurance arrangement before diagnosis. We determined the type of insurance arrangement during the month of diagnosis and the previous 12 months. For this period, we assigned cases to 1 of the following 3 insurance categories: FFS for persons continuously enrolled in traditional FFS Medicare, HMO for persons continuously enrolled in HMO plans, and mixed FFS/HMO for persons enrolled in both FFS and HMO plans during the period. To examine treatments following diagnosis, we designated similar postdiagnosis insurance variables for persons continuously eligible for Medicare Part A and Part B during the month of diagnosis and the 6 months after diagnosis (or until death if survival was <6 months). For analyses of survival, we assigned cases to similar insurance categories covering the prediagnosis and postdiagnosis periods combined.

Stage at Diagnosis

SEER determines stage at diagnosis based on a combination of pathologic surgical and clinical assessments available within 2 months of diagnosis.[21] Stage at diagnosis is recorded using the American Joint Committee on Cancer (AJCC) staging system (stage 0, I, II, III, or IV). In our analysis of stage at diagnosis, we excluded persons whose cancers were unstaged (346 with breast cancer and 1,182 with lung cancer).

Cancer-Directed Treatments

SEER collects information on the initial course of treatment, which was defined as all cancer-directed treatments within 4 months of diagnosis from 1973 through 1998 and within 12 months of diagnosis after 1998. Ascertainment of surgery and radiation therapy by SEER is generally complete.[22,23] However, ascertainment of chemotherapy is incomplete and is not included in the SEER-Medicare-linked dataset. SEER does not collect information on prediagnosis screening tests such as mammography. We relied solely on SEER information to define cancer-directed treatments because Medicare claims are unavailable for persons having HMO insurance.

We defined breast-conserving surgery as segmental mastectomy, lumpectomy, quadrantectomy, tylectomy, wedge resection, nipple resection, excisional biopsy, or partial mastectomy that was not otherwise specified. We defined mastectomy as subcutaneous, total (simple), modified radical, radical, extended radical mastectomy, or mastectomy that was not otherwise specified. We examined frequency of breast-conserving surgery among women having AJCC stage I, II, or IIIA cancers. We further examined the following 2 secondary outcomes related to quality of care: (1) receipt of axillary lymph node dissection and (2) receipt of radiation therapy among women who undergo breast-conserving surgery. Sentinel lymph node biopsies, a recent innovation, are not reported in our database.

Depending on tumor size, histologic findings, and location, surgery can provide definitive treatment for non-small cell lung cancer.[17,18] Radiation therapy may be curative for persons with resectable tumors who do not undergo surgery.[24,25] We examined the frequencies of surgical resection and radiation therapy among persons having early-stage lesions (AJCC stage I) for whom treatment can be curative. Similar to the classification by Bach and colleagues,[26] we categorized surgical resection with curative intent as follows: radical or partial pneumonectomy, lobectomy, bilobectomy, sleeve resection, segmentectomy, wedge resection, and local resection. For persons who did not undergo surgery, we used SEER data to determine if surgery was contraindicated or was not recommended.

Survival

We examined survival (all-cause and cancer-specific mortality) following diagnosis. We measured survival time as the number of days from diagnosis until death or December 31, 2001, whichever came first. For all-cause mortality analyses, we censored observations of persons alive at the end of followup. We studied breast cancer-specific and lung cancer-specific deaths, censoring observations of subjects alive at the end of follow-up or who died from causes other than breast cancer or lung cancer.

Statistical Analysis

We conducted bivariate analyses to compare demographic and tumor characteristics of our study sample by HMO status vs FFS status at diagnosis. Because this was an observational study that did not randomize subjects to HMO insurance vs FFS insurance, patient characteristics were expected to differ between the 2 groups. We used the method of propensity scoring to control for these differences.[27,28]

Propensity scores reflect the likelihood that a patient had HMO insurance at diagnosis based on his or her observed characteristics. We used multivariate logistic regression analysis with stepwise variable selection to calculate propensity scores (performed separately for patients with breast cancer and for patients with lung cancer). Having HMO insurance at diagnosis was the outcome, with the following variables as potential predictors: age at diagnosis, race/ethnicity, marital status at diagnosis, census-derived measures of median household income and percentage of households without high school education, SEER tumor registry, year of diagnosis, and tumor characteristics (grade, histologic findings, and hormone receptor status). We then used propensity scores to group patients into quintiles according to their probability of having HMO insurance at diagnosis derived from observed characteristics. We then added propensity scores (quintiles) as a covariate in all multivariate analyses. This process has been estimated to eliminate more than 90% of the bias resulting from differences in observed covariates.[29]

We conducted multivariate polychotomous logistic regression analysis to examine associations between HMO insurance vs FFS insurance arrangement and AJCC stage at diagnosis (stage 0, I, II, III, or IV). Odds ratios less than 1 indicate earlier stage at diagnosis. Logistic models adjusted for age at diagnosis (continuous), race/ethnicity (non-Hispanic white, non-Hispanic black, Hispanic, Asian American/ Pacific Islander, or other), marital status at diagnosis (married, widowed, never married, or other),

census-derived measures of median household income and percentage of households without high school education, SEER tumor registry, year of diagnosis, grade (well differentiated, moderately differentiated, or poorly/undifferentiated), and propensity scores. For persons with lung cancer, logistic models also adjusted for sex. For women with breast cancer, logistic models also adjusted for estrogen receptor status (positive, negative, or unknown), progesterone receptor status (positive, negative, or unknown), and histologic findings (unfavorable subtypes [inflammatory or Paget disease] or ductal or lobular/mixed favorable subtypes [medullary carcinoma or papillary, villous, or mucinous adenocarcinomas]). We converted odds ratios to relative risks with 95% confidence intervals for each treatment outcome.[30]

We plotted survival curves for all-cause mortality and for cancer-specific mortality separately. Survival differences between subjects having HMO insurance vs FFS insurance were tested using the log-rank test. We excluded persons with in situ cancers from survival analyses.

We conducted multivariate Cox proportional hazards regression analyses to estimate adjusted relative hazard rates for each mortality outcome (all cause and cancer specific). Hazard rates less than 1 indicate lower mortality and more favorable survival relative to the referent group. We fit 2 sets of Cox proportional hazards models for each mortality outcome. In the initial models, hazard rates were adjusted for age, sex (for lung cancer only), marital status (married, single, separated/divorced, widowed, or unknown), race/ethnicity (non-Hispanic white, non-Hispanic black, Hispanic, Asian, or other), census-derived measures of median household income and percentage of households without high school education, tumor grade (well differentiated, moderately differentiated, poorly differentiated, undifferentiated, or unknown), and propensity scores. For women with breast cancer, initial models also adjusted hazard rates for estrogen receptor status (negative, positive, or unknown), progesterone status (negative, positive, or unknown), and histologic findings (ductal, lobular/mixed, favorable subtypes, unfavorable subtypes, or other). Subsequent models also adjusted hazard rates for AJCC stage at diagnosis (stage I, II, III, IV, or unstaged).

As a sensitivity analysis, we repeated multivariate models excluding patients with missing data on tumor characteristics (tumor grade, estrogen receptor status, or progesterone receptor status). To gauge the public health effect of our findings, we calculated attributable fractions using the following formula: Attributable Fraction = pd (RR − 1)/RR, where pd indicates the proportion of cases exposed to the risk factor; and RR, the adjusted hazard rate.[31] The institutional review boards at our institutions approved this study. All statistical analyses used SAS version 9.1 (SAS Institute, Cary, North Carolina).

RESULTS

Table 1 lists the characteristics of our sample. Persons having HMO insurance at diagnosis tended to be older and more likely to reside in census tracts having higher median household income. Consistent with market penetration of HMOs, patients having HMO insurance were more likely to originate from SEER registries in California and in Seattle, Washington. Among patients with breast cancer, those having FFS insurance were more likely to have missing information on tumor grade and on estrogen receptor status and progesterone receptor status.

Table 2 summarizes the likelihood of earlier stage at diagnosis according to insurance arrangement during 12 months before diagnosis. For women with breast cancer, those having HMO insurance were diagnosed at earlier stages relative to those having FFS insurance. There was some evidence of earlier stage at diagnosis for women with mixed FFS/HMO insurance (i.e., the odds ratio was statistically significant in the unadjusted model but not in the model that controlled for age, race/ethnicity, and other covariates). Health maintenance organization insurance vs FFS insurance was not associated with stage at diagnosis for persons with lung cancer.

Insurance type was sometimes statistically significantly associated with cancer-directed treatments for breast cancer and for lung cancer (Table 3). Women having HMO insurance were more likely to receive radiation therapy following breast-conserving surgery. There was a statistically nonsignificant trend for women having HMO insurance to receive breast-conserving surgery rather than mastectomy. Insurance status had no effect on the likelihood of axillary lymph node dissection. Among persons diagnosed as having non-small cell lung cancer, those having mixed FFS/HMO insurance were more likely to receive definitive surgery for early-stage tumors.

eFigure 1 through eFigure 4 (available at http://www. ajmc.com) show all-cause and cancer-specific survival curves. Among women with breast cancer, those having HMO insurance had better breast cancer survival compared with those having FFS insurance. Among persons with lung cancer, there was a statistically nonsignificant trend for improved survival among persons having mixed FFS/HMO insurance.

Breast cancer mortality rates were lower for women having HMO insurance (Table 4). Lower breast cancer mortality rates persisted after adjustment for patient characteristics and for tumor characteristics but were no longer present after further adjustment for stage at diagnosis. Among patients with non-small cell lung cancer, those with mixed FFS/HMO insurance had better overall survival (with trends toward better lung cancer survival) in unadjusted analysis and in analysis adjusted for covariates.

Results were similar when subjects having missing information on tumor characteristics were excluded from the sample and multivariate analysis was repeated (data not shown). To examine the possibility that the effects of HMO insurance varied over time, we repeated our analyses separately for 2 periods, persons diagnosed from 1989 through 1994 and persons diagnosed from 1995 through 1999. Results were similar for both periods. We calculated an attributable fraction for the 831 breast cancer deaths observed in the cohort (769 with FFS insurance and 62 with HMO insurance). We estimated that 17% (144 deaths) would theoretically have been prevented if patients having FFS insurance had a mortality experience comparable to that of patients having HMO insurance.

DISCUSSION

Insurance type (FFS vs HMO) sometimes was statistically significantly associated with treatment outcomes for Medicare beneficiaries with disabilities diagnosed as having breast cancer or lung cancer. Patients with disabilities having HMO insurance coverage were more likely to be diagnosed as having earlier-stage breast cancer and were more likely to undergo radiation therapy after breast-conserving surgery. Health maintenance organization insurance coverage was associated with longer breast cancer survival primarily because of earlier-stage diagnosis. Insurance status had fewer statistically significant associations for patients with disabilities diagnosed as having lung cancer (e.g., no association with stage).

Among Medicare beneficiaries, patients belonging to HMOs are more likely to be screened for cancer[9-12] and are more likely to have cancers diagnosed at an earlier stage.[13-16] This may in part explain our finding of earlier breast cancer diagnosis and improved survival. Higher rates of cancer screening within HMOs may result from greater emphasis on delivery of preventive care[32] and from increased

Table 1	Demographic and Clinical Characteristics by Insurance Statusa

	Insurance Type at Breast Cancer Diagnosis			Insurance Type at Lung Cancer Diagnosis		
Characteristic	HMO (n = 878)	FFS (n = 5316)	P	HMO (n = 1491)	FFS (n = 7896)	P
Age, mean, y	63.9	61.4	<.001	66.9	64.4	<.001
Age, y, %						
<60	24.0	35.9	<.001	10.4	21.9	<.001
60–64	21.1	19.2		18.3	22.7	
65–69	29.4	22.6		35.5	29.0	
≥70	25.5	22.3		35.7	26.4	
Sex, %						
Female	—	—	—	29.2	28.0	.35
Male	—	—		70.8	72.0	
Race/ethnicity, %						
Non-Hispanic white	68.8	69.2	<.001	72.8	74.8	<.001
Non-Hispanic black	14.9	20.0		15.8	19.3	
Hispanic	10.1	6.9		7.7	3.5	
Asian	5.1	2.9		3.3	2.0	
Other	1.0	1.0		0.4	0.5	
Marital status, %						
Married	42.1	29.2	<.001	55.3	49.3	<.001
Single	11.9	24.2		10.8	14.6	
Separated/divorced	18.5	18.2		15.0	17.0	
Widowed	24.5	24.8		16.3	15.6	
Unknown	3.1	3.7		2.6	3.6	
Census-derived median household income, $	36,573	32,488	<.001	34,210	31,361	<.001
Percentage of ZIP code/ census tract without high school education	22.9	25.3	<.001	26.1	26.2	.84
Registry site, %						
San Francisco/Oakland, California	22.4	11.1	<.001	20.4	10.4	<.001
Connecticut	4.1	12.9		4.8	12.6	
Detroit, Michigan	4.6	19.8		10.4	22.3	
Hawaii	3.5	2.7		3.6	2.0	
Iowa	2.6	10.3		4.1	13.7	
New Mexico	4.4	4.4		5.2	4.0	
Seattle, Washington	14.4	10.5		12.3	11.8	
Utah	1.7	3.4		1.5	2.3	
Atlanta, Georgia	2.9	7.6		1.5	8.8	
San Jose/Monterey, California	5.5	3.4		3.3	2.2	
Los Angeles, California	33.9	14.0		33.1	9.9	
American Joint Committee on Cancer stage, %						
In situ	13.8	12.3	<.001	—	—	—
I	46.1	37.6		23.8	23.9	.30
II	29.3	32.9		4.7	4.4	
III	4.9	7.0		28.3	28.6	
IV	3.0	4.7		30.0	31.8	
Unstaged/unknown	3.0	5.6		13.2	11.4	
Tumor grade, %						
Well differentiated	16.6	11.4	<.001	3.9	3.8	.34
Moderately differentiated	30.0	27.7		16.3	17.2	
Poorly differentiated	27.2	24.7		38.2	35.4	
Undifferentiated	3.1	2.5		6.4	6.9	
Unknown	23.1	33.7		35.2	36.6	

(Continued)

| Table 1 | Demographic and Clinical Characteristics by Insurance Status[a] (continued) |

Characteristic	Insurance Type at Breast Cancer Diagnosis			Insurance Type at Lung Cancer Diagnosis		
	HMO (n = 878)	FFS (n = 5316)	P	HMO (n = 1491)	FFS (n = 7896)	P
Histologic findings, %						
Ductal	73.1	76.4	.25	—	—	—
Lobular/mixed	13.4	11.8		—	—	
Favorable subtypes[b]	7.4	6.2		—	—	
Unfavorable subtypes[c]	2.5	2.1		—	—	
Other	3.5	3.6		—	—	
Estrogen receptor status, %						
Positive	61.6	52.4	<.001	—	—	—
Negative	17.2	16.6		—	—	
Unknown	21.2	31.0		—	—	
Progesterone receptor status, %						
Positive	48.6	44.5	<.001	—	—	—
Negative	26.0	22.7		—	—	
Unknown	25.4	32.8		—	—	

[a] FFS indicates fee-for-service; HMO, health maintenance organization. Percentages may not sum to 100% due to rounding.
[b] Include papillary, mucinous, tubular, and medullary.
[c] Include inflammatory and Paget's disease.

| Table 2 | Likelihood of Earlier Stage at Diagnosis by Insurance Status[a] |

Insurance Type[b]	Unadjusted OR (95% CI)	Adjusted OR (95% CI)
Breast cancer (n = 5772)		
FFS (n = 4924)	1 [Reference]	1 [Reference]
HMO (n = 664)	**0.73 (0.63 – 0.85)**	**0.77 (0.65 – 0.91)**
Mixed FFS/HMO (n = 184)	**0.73 (0.56 – 0.96)**	0.78 (0.59 – 1.04)
Lung cancer (N = 7804)		
FFS (n = 6758)	1 [Reference]	1 [Reference]
HMO (n = 811)	0.97 (0.85 – 1.11)	0.96 (0.83 – 1.11)
Mixed FFS/HMO (n = 235)	1.02 (0.81 – 1.30)	1.01 (0.79 – 1.29)

CI indicates confidence interval; FFS, fee-for-service, HMO, health maintenance organization; OR, odds ratio.
[a] Results of polychotomous logistic regression analysis examining American Joint Committee on Cancer stage (0, I, II, III, or IV). Outcomes in boldface are statistically significant at $P < .05$.
[b] During 12 months before diagnosis.

focus on primary care rather than on subspecialty care.[33] In some studies, beneficiaries with disabilities in HMOs perceived better access to primary care services[8] and were more likely to undergo cancer screening tests.[34] Greater use of preventive services in HMOs may be the result in part of favorable selection in which healthier patients are differentially enrolled in HMOs.[35]

There was some evidence that Medicare beneficiaries with disabilities enrolled in HMOs were more frequently treated with breast-conserving surgery as shown by a statistically significant odds ratio in the unadjusted model but not in the adjusted model. These HMO enrollees were more often treated with radiation therapy following breast-conserving surgery (the treatment combination recommended by

Table 3	Cancer Treatments by Insurance Status[a]			
Insurance Type		**%**	**Unadjusted OR (95% CI)**	**Adjusted OR (95% CI)**
Breast cancer				
Receipt of breast-conserving surgery[b]				
FFS		40.2	1 [Reference]	1 [Reference]
HMO		47.2	**1.33 (1.13 − 1.58)**	0.97 (0.87 − 1.07)
Mixed FFS/HMO		44.9	1.22 (0.75 − 1.96)	1.04 (0.80 − 1.34)
Receipt of radiation therapy after breast-conserving surgery[c]				
FFS		70.7	1 [Reference]	1 [Reference]
HMO		79.4	**1.60 (1.18 − 2.16)**	**1.11 (1.03 − 1.19)**
Mixed FFS/HMO		83.3	2.07 (0.79 − 5.45)	**1.21 (1.06 − 1.39)**
Receipt of lymph node dissection[d]				
FFS		86.2	1 [Reference]	1 [Reference]
HMO		85.0	0.91 (0.72 − 1.15)	1.01 (0.98 − 1.04)
Mixed FFS/HMO		87.0	1.07 (0.53 − 2.17)	1.01 (0.92 − 1.11)
Lung cancer				
Receipt of surgery[e]				
FFS		63.1	1 [Reference]	1 [Reference]
HMO		69.3	**1.10 (1.01 − 1.20)**	1.06 (0.97 − 1.16)
Mixed FFS/HMO		80.0	**1.27 (1.04 − 1.54)**	**1.23 (1.02 − 1.49)**
Receipt of radiation therapy[f]				
FFS		28.7	1 [Reference]	1 [Reference]
HMO		22.9	0.79 (0.63 − 1.00)	0.93 (0.77 − 1.12)
Mixed FFS/HMO		20.0	0.69 (0.31 − 1.53)	1.11 (0.66 − 1.84)
Receipt of surgery or radiation therapy[f]				
FFS		88.6	1 [Reference]	1 [Reference]
HMO		88.8	1.00 (0.96 − 1.05)	1.00 (0.95 − 1.05)
Mixed FFS/HMO		96.0	1.09 (1.00 − 1.18)	**1.09 (1.02 − 1.17)**

CI indicates confidence interval; FFS, fee-for-service, HMO, health maintenance organization; OR, odds ratio.

[a] During 12 months before diagnosis and during 6 months after diagnosis. Outcomes in boldface are statistically significant at $P < .05$.
[b] Among women having American Joint Committee on Cancer (AJCC) stage I, II, or IIIA lesions and undergoing breast-conserving surgery or mastectomy (n = 4480).
[c] Among women having AJCC stage I, II, or IIIA lesions and undergoing breast-conserving surgery (n = 1775).
[d] Among women having AJCC stage I, II, or IIIA lesions (n = 4480).
[e] Among persons having AJCC stage I cancers (n = 2240).
[f] Among persons having AJCC stage I cancers (n = 2240). Adjusted models also controlled for concomitant lung cancer surgery.

National Institutes of Health consensus panels) and had better breast cancer survival. Persons having HMO insurance were more likely to have tumor grade and hormone receptor status documented for their cancers. Findings from previous studies suggest that in general Medicare beneficiaries belonging to HMOs are more likely to undergo breast-conserving surgery,[36] to receive adjuvant radiation therapy following breast-conserving surgery,[16] and to have improved breast cancer survival.[36,37] Our study extends these findings to Medicare beneficiaries with disabilities.

The reasons for treatment differences among patients having HMO insurance vs FFS insurance could not be ascertained in this study but may result from variations in practice structure. Health maintenance organizations, especially staff-model and group-model forms, have resources and organizational structures that can disseminate standards of care and ensure that current practice patterns are consistent with these standards.[38,39] Improved breast cancer survival among HMO recipients seemed to be primarily the result of earlier stage at diagnosis.

| Table 4 | Mortality Rates by Insurance Statusa Unadjusted |

Insurance Type	Unadjusted HR (95% CI)	Adjusted HR (95% CI)	Stage-adjusted HR (95% CI)[b]
Breast cancer (n = 4877)			
All-cause mortality			
FFS	1 [Reference]	1 [Reference]	1 [Reference]
HMO	0.87 (0.75 – 1.01)	**0.81 (0.69 – 0.95)**	0.91 (0.78 – 1.07)
Mixed FFS/HMO	0.94 (0.76 – 1.17)	0.92 (0.74 – 1.15)	0.97 (0.78 – 1.21)
Breast cancer mortality			
FFS	1 [Reference]	1 [Reference]	1 [Reference]
HMO	**0.67 (0.52 – 0.87)**	**0.75 (0.57 – 0.98)**	0.97 (0.73 – 1.27)
Mixed FFS/HMO	0.77 (0.54 – 1.11)	0.88 (0.61 – 1.28)	0.97 (0.67 – 1.41)
Lung cancer (n = 8834)			
All-cause mortality			
FFS	1 [Reference]	1 [Reference]	1 [Reference]
HMO	0.99 (0.92 – 1.06))	0.95 (0.88 – 1.03)	0.97 (0.90 – 1.05)
Mixed FFS/HMO	**0.88 (0.79 – 0.99)**	**0.89 (0.79 – 0.996)**	**0.87 (0.78 – 0.98)**
Lung cancer mortality			
FFS	1 [Reference]	1 [Reference]	1 [Reference]
HMO	1.01 (0.93 – 1.09)	0.99 (0.91 – 1.09)	1.01 (0.93 – 1.11)
Mixed FFS/HMO	**0.87 (0.77 – 0.99)**	0.89 (0.78 – 1.02)	0.88 (0.77 – 1.01)

CI indicates confidence interval; HR, hazard rate; OR, odds ratio.
[a] During 12 months before diagnosis and during 6 months after diagnosis for subjects with breast cancer (4118 for fee-for-service [FFS], 542 for health maintenance organization [HMO], and 217 for mixed FFS/HMO) and for subjects with non–small cell lung cancer (7568 for FFS, 916 for HMO, and 350 for mixed FFS/HMO). Outcomes in boldface are statistically significant at P< .05.
[b] Also adjusted for American Joint Committee on Cancer stage (I, II, III, IV, or unstaged). Persons with in situ cancers excluded.

While HMO insurance vs FFS insurance arrangement was statistically significantly associated with breast cancer outcomes, lung cancer outcomes showed few effects. The subset of persons changing between HMO and FFS plans seemed to have better lung cancer outcomes. Among 137 patients with lung cancer who changed insurance type between diagnosis and 6-month follow-up, most (65%) changed from HMO insurance to FFS insurance. This group had a greater likelihood of undergoing surgery for early-stage disease and had better overall survival, with a statistically nonsignificant trend toward better lung cancer survival.

Changing between HMO and FFS Medicare plans might indicate problems in accessing care or dissatisfaction with care. Patients having disabilities are generally more likely to report dissatisfaction or problems with their healthcare plan[6,7,40-42] and are more likely to disenroll from their HMO, often changing to an FFS plan.[43] Forced disenrollment from a Medicare HMO plan has been associated with problems in accessing needed care.[44-46]

In our study, Medicare beneficiaries with disabilities had remarkably stable HMO and FFS insurance status during their follow-up, similar to other studies.[47,48] Among persons continuously eligible for Medicare and followed up until their death, 95% of persons with lung cancer and 92% of persons with breast cancer had continuous coverage within FFS or HMO arrangements from the 12 months before diagnosis until their death. In addition, patients who changed between HMO and FFS plans generally had similar or better outcomes compared with persons continuously enrolled in FFS.

Our study had several important limitations. We did not have Medicare claims data for persons enrolled in HMOs and were unable to examine cancer screening or to supplement SEER information on treatment using Medicare claims. Our lack of Medicare claims for persons in HMOs prevented us from assessing comorbidity. SEER does not release data on chemotherapy, so we were unable to evaluate this aspect of cancer treatment, which is especially critical in breast cancer. Medicare data did not include details about the specific HMO plan, so we were unable to assess the particular financial arrangements for the HMO plan, nor could we capture patient movement between HMO plans. Our sample was restricted to persons who originally qualified for Medicare coverage because of Social Security Disability Insurance, and our results may not generalize to the greater population of persons having disabilities. We studied persons who were diagnosed as having cancer through the end of 1999, and it is possible that trends may have changed since that time. Finally, this was an observational study that did not randomize subjects to insurance types. Statistical methods, such as propensity scores, can only adjust for measured characteristics within the cohort. As a result, it is possible that our results were in part due to unmeasured patient characteristics that differed between HMO patients and FFS patients and not because of the specific insurance arrangement.

In conclusion, Medicare beneficiaries with disabilities diagnosed as having breast cancer generally had more favorable outcomes within HMO arrangements. Health maintenance organization vs FFS insurance status had little effect on lung cancer outcomes. Changes between HMO and FFS insurance types were not associated with poor cancer outcomes.

ACKNOWLEDGMENTS

This study used the linked SEER-Medicare database. The interpretation and reporting of these data are the sole responsibility of the authors. The authors acknowledge the efforts of several groups responsible for the creation and dissemination of the linked database, including the Applied Research Branch, Division of Cancer Control and Population Sciences, National Cancer Institute; the Office of Information Services and the Office of Strategic Planning, Centers for Medicare and Medicaid Services; Information Management Services, Inc; and the SEER Program Tumor Registries.

Author Affiliations:

Department of Family Medicine, University of South Florida (RGR), and H. Lee Moffitt Cancer Center & Research Institute (RGR, TNC, KJW), Tampa; and Divisions of General Medicine and Primary Care (EPM, LHN, DL) and Hematology and Oncology (RED), Beth Israel Deaconess Medical Center, Department of Medicine, Harvard Medical School (EPM, LHN, RED, LII), and Institute for Health Policy, Division of General Medicine, Massachusetts General Hospital (LII), Boston.

Funding Source:

This study was supported by grant R01 CA100029 from the National Cancer Institute.

Author Disclosures:

The authors (RGR, TNC, KJW, EPM, LHN, DL, RED, LII) report no relationship or financial interest with any entity that would pose a conflict of interest with the subject matter of this article.

Authorship Information:

Concept and design (RGR, TNC, EPM); acquisition of data (TNC, EPM, DL, LII); analysis and interpretation of data (RGR, TNC, KJW, EPM, DL, RED, LII); drafting of the manuscript (RGR, TNC, KJW, RED); critical revision of the manuscript for important intel-lectual content (RGR, TNC, EPM, RED, LII); statistical analysis (RGR, TNC, KJW, LHN, DL); and obtaining funding (TNC, LII).

Address correspondence to:

Richard G. Roetzheim, MD, MSPH, Department of Family Medicine, University of South Florida, 12901 Bruce B. Downs Blvd, MDC 13, Tampa, FL 33612. E-mail: rroetzhe@hsc.usf.edu.

Takeaway Points

It is unknown whether the type of Medicare insurance arrangement, specifically health maintenance organization (HMO) vs fee-for-service (FFS), affects cancer outcomes for Medicare beneficiaries with disabilities, a vulnerable population. We found that Medicare beneficiaries with disabilities had better breast cancer outcomes if they were continuously enrolled in HMOs.

- Improved outcomes among HMO enrollees included earlier-stage breast cancer diagnosis, greater likelihood of receiving radiation therapy following breast-conserving surgery, and better breast cancer survival.
- The HMO vs FFS insurance arrangement had little effect on the care and outcomes of lung cancer among Medicare beneficiaries with disabilities.

• • • REFERENCES

1. Centers for Medicare and Medicaid Services Web site. Medicare enrollment: disabled beneficiaries: as of July 2005. http://www.cms.hhs.gov/Medicare EnRpts/Downloads/05Disabled.pdf. Accessed January 21, 2008.

2. McCarthy EP, Ngo LH, Roetzheim RG, et al. Disparities in breast cancer treatment and survival for women with disabilities. *Ann Intern Med.* 2006;145(9):637-645.

3. McCarthy EP, Ngo LH, Chirikos TN, et al. Cancer stage at diagnosis and survival among persons with Social Security Disability Insurance on Medicare. *Health Serv Res.* 2007;42(2):611-628.

4. Caban ME, Nosek MA, Graves D, Esteva FJ, McNeese M. Breast carcinoma treatment received by women with disabilities compared with women without disabilities. *Cancer.* 2002;94(5):1391-1396.

5. Tanenbaum SJ, Hurley RE. Disability and managed care frenzy: a cautionary note. *Health Aff (Millwood).* 1995;14(4):213-219.

6. Mobley L, McCormack L, Booske B, et al. Voluntary disenrollment from Medicare managed care: market factors and disabled beneficiaries. *Health Care Financ Rev.* 2005;26(3):45-62.

7. Robins CS, Heller A, Myers MA. Financial vulnerability among Medicare managed care enrollees. *Health Care Financ Rev.* 2005;26(3):81-92.

8. Beatty PW, Dhont KR. Medicare health maintenance organizations and traditional coverage: perceptions of health care among beneficiaries with disabilities. *Arch Phys Med Rehabil.* 2001;82(8): 1009-1017.

9. Baker LC, Phillips KA, Haas JS, Liang SY, Sonneborn D. The effect of area HMO market share on cancer screening. *Health Serv Res.* 2004;39 (6, pt 1):1751-1772.

10. Carrasquillo O, Lantigua RA, Shea S. Preventive services among Medicare beneficiaries with supplemental coverage versus HMO enrollees, Medicaid recipients, and elders with no additional coverage. *Med Care.* 2001;39(6):616-626.

11. Gordon NP, Rundall TG, Parker L. Type of health care coverage and the likelihood of being screened for cancer. *Med Care.* 1998;36(5):636-645.

12. Potosky AL, Breen N, Graubard BI, Parsons PE. The association between health care coverage and the use of cancer screening tests: results from the 1992 National Health Interview Survey [published correction appears in *Med Care.* 1998;36(10):1470]. *Med Care.* 1998;36(3):257-270.

13. Lee-Feldstein A, Feldstein PJ, Buchmueller T, Katterhagen G. Breast cancer outcomes among older women: HMO, fee-for-service, and delivery system comparisons. *J Gen Intern Med.* 2001;16(3):189-199.

14. Lee-Feldstein A, Feldstein PJ, Buchmueller T. Health care factors related to stage at diagnosis and survival among Medicare patients with colorectal cancer. *Med Care.* 2002;40(5):362-374.

15. Riley GF, Potosky AL, Lubitz JD, Brown ML. Stage of cancer at diagnosis for Medicare HMO and fee-for-service enrollees. *Am J Public Health.* 1994; 84(10):1598-1604.

16. Riley GF, Potosky AL, Klabunde CN, Warren JL, Ballard-Barbash R. Stage at diagnosis and treatment patterns among older women with breast cancer: an HMO and fee-for-service comparison. *JAMA.* 1999; 281(8):720-726.

17. National Comprehensive Cancer Network Web site. NCCN Clinical Practice Guidelines in Oncology: non-small cell lung cancer, V.2.2008. http://www. nccn.org/professionals/physician_gls/PDF/nscl.pdf. Accessed February 29, 2008.

18. Manser R, Wright G, Hart D, Byrnes G, Campbell DA. Surgery for early stage non-small cell lung cancer. *Cochrane Database Syst Rev.* 2005;1:CD004699.

19. Potosky AL, Riley GF, Lubitz JD, Mentnech RM, Kessler LG. Potential for cancer related health services research using a linked Medicare-tumor registry database. *Med Care.* 1993;31(8):732-748.

20. Warren JL, Klabunde CN, Schrag D, Bach PB, Riley GF. Overview of the SEER-Medicare data: content, research applications, and generalizability to the United States elderly population. *Med Care.* 2002;40(8)(suppl):IV-3-IV-18.

21. Shambaugh E, Weiss M. *Summary Staging Guide: Cancer Surveillance, Epidemiology, and End Results Reporting.* Bethesda, MD: Public Health Service, US Dept of Health and Human Services, National Institutes of Health; 1977. Publication 86-2313.

22. Cooper GS, Virnig B, Klabunde CN, Schussler N, Freeman J, Warren JL. Use of SEER-Medicare data for measuring cancer surgery. *Med Care.* 2002;40(8)(suppl):IV-43-IV-48.

23. Virnig BA, Warren JL, Cooper GS, Klabunde CN, Schussler N, Freeman J. Studying radiation therapy using SEER-Medicare-linked data. *Med Care.* 2002;40(8)(suppl):IV-49-IV-54.

24. Rowell NP, Williams CJ. Radical radiotherapy for stage I/II non-small cell lung cancer in patients not sufficiently fit or declining surgery (medically inoperable) [update of *Cochrane Database Syst Rev.* 2001;1:CD002935]. *Cochrane Database Syst Rev.* 2001;2:CD002935.

25. Rowell NP, Williams CJ. Radical radiotherapy for stage I/II non-small cell lung cancer in patients not sufficiently fit or declining surgery (medically inoperable): a systematic review. *Thorax.* 2001;56(8): 628-638.

26. Bach PB, Cramer LD, Warren JL, Begg CB. Racial differences in the treatment of early-stage lung cancer. *N Engl J Med.* 1999;341(16):1198-1205.

27. Rosenbaum PR, Rubin DB. Reducing bias in observational studies using subclassification on the propensity score. *J Am Stat Assoc.* 1984;79:516-524.

28. Rubin DB. Estimating causal effects from large data sets using propensity scores. *Ann Intern Med.* 1997;127(8, pt 2):757-763.

29. Cochran WG. The effectiveness of adjustment by subclassification in removing bias in observational studies. *Biometrics.* 1968;24(2):295-313.

30. Flanders WD, Rhodes PH. Large sample confidence intervals for regression standardized risks, risk ratios, and risk differences. *J Chronic Dis.* 1987; 40(7):697-704.

31. Rockhill B, Newman B, Weinberg C. Use and misuse of population attributable fractions. *Am J Public Health.* 1998;88(1):15-19.

32. Landon BE, Zaslavsky AM, Bernard SL, Cioffi MJ, Cleary PD. Comparison of performance of traditional Medicare vs Medicare managed care. *JAMA.* 2004;291(14):1744-1752.

33. Phillips KA, Haas JS, Liang SY, et al. Are gatekeeper requirements associated with cancer screening utilization? *Health Serv Res.* 2004;39(1):153-178.

34. Chan L, Doctor JN, MacLehose RF, et al. Do Medicare patients with disabilities receive preventive services? a population-based study. *Arch Phys Med Rehabil.* 1999;80(6):642-646.

35. Morgan RO, Virnig BA, DeVito CA, Persily NA. The Medicare-HMO revolving door: the healthy go in and the sick go out. *N Engl J Med.* 1997;337(3):169-175.

36. Potosky AL, Merrill RM, Riley GF, et al. Breast cancer survival and treatment in health maintenance organization and fee-for-service settings. *J Natl Cancer Inst.* 1997;89(22):1683-1691.

37. Kirsner RS, Ma F, Fleming L, et al. The effect of Medicare health care delivery systems on survival for patients with breast and colorectal cancer. *Cancer Epidemiol Biomarkers Prev.* 2006; 15(4):769-773.

38. Clancy CM, Brody H. Managed care: Jekyll or Hyde? *JAMA.* 1995;273(4):338-339.

39. Wagner EH, Austin BT, Von Korff M. Organizing care for patients with chronic illness. *Milbank Q.* 1996;74(4):511-544.

40. Jha A, Patrick DL, MacLehose RF, Doctor JN, Chan L. Dissatisfaction with medical services among Medicare beneficiaries with disabilities. *Arch Phys Med Rehabil.* 2002;83(10):1335-1341.

41. Iezzoni LI, Davis RB, Soukup J, O'Day B. Satisfaction with quality and access to health care among people with disabling conditions. *Int J Qual Health Care.* 2002;14(5):369-381.

42. Gold M, Nelson L, Brown R, Ciemnecki A, Aizer A, Docteur E. Disabled Medicare beneficiaries in HMOs. *Health Aff (Millwood).* 1997;16(5): 149-162.

43. Laschober M. Estimating Medicare Advantage lock-in provisions impact on vulnerable Medicare beneficiaries. *Health Care Financ Rev.* 2005;26(3):63-79.

44. Schoenman JA, Parente ST, Feldman JJ, Shah MM, Evans WN, Finch MD. Impact of HMO withdrawals on vulnerable Medicare beneficiaries. *Health Care Financ Rev.* 2005;26(3):5-30.

45. Parente ST, Evans WN, Schoenman JA, Finch MD. Health care use and expenditures of Medicare HMO disenrollees. *Health Care Financ Rev.* 2005;26(3):31-43.

46. Booske BC, Lynch J, Riley G. Impact of Medicare managed care market withdrawal on beneficiaries. *Health Care Financ Rev.* 2002;24(1):95-115.

47. Field TS, Cernieux J, Buist D, et al. Retention of enrollees following a cancer diagnosis within health maintenance organizations in the Cancer Research Network. *J Natl Cancer Inst.* 2004;96(2):148-152.

48. Riley GF, Feuer EJ, Lubitz JD. Disenrollment of Medicare cancer patients from health maintenance organizations. *Med Care.* 1996;34(8):826-836.

How Engaged Are Consumers in Their Health and Health Care, and Why Does It Matter?

Source: Hibbard, J.H. and P.J. Cunningham. 2008. *How Engaged Are Consumers in Their Health and Health Care, and Why Does It Matter?* Research Brief No. 8. Washington, DC: Center for Studying Health System Change. Used with permission.

Patient activation refers to a person's ability to manage their health and health care. Engaging or activating consumers has become a priority for employers, health plans and policy makers. The level of patient activation varies considerably in the U.S. population, with less than half of the adult population at the highest level of activation, according to a new study by the Center for Studying Health System Change (HSC) (see Figure 1). Activation levels are especially low for people with low incomes, less education, Medicaid enrollees, and people with poor self-reported health. Higher activation levels are associated with much lower levels of unmet need for medical care and greater support from health care providers for self-management of chronic conditions.

CONSUMERS KEY TO HEALTH CARE REFORM EFFORTS

There is a growing consensus that activating and engaging consumers is an essential component to health care reform in the United States. The health care choices of individual consumers and daily management of their own health can profoundly affect health care utilization, costs and outcomes. While there are sharp differences between advocates of a strong government role in health care reform and those who believe reform should be achieved primarily through the private sector, most health care reformers at least acknowledge that improvements in quality, cost containment and reductions in low-value care will not occur without more informed and engaged consumers and patients. Payment reform and structural changes to care delivery only address one side of the equation. The other side is consumers and patients becoming more informed decision-makers and managers of their health.

From a policy perspective, this represents a serious challenge, with limited evidence and few strategies available to achieve this end. A first step is to understand what it means to be activated and engaged and the current extent of activation in the U.S. population. This Research Brief examines patient activation, how it varies by key socioeconomic characteristics, and how activation is related to other aspects of patients' experiences with the health care system.

MEASURING PATIENT ACTIVATION

Activation refers to people's ability and willingness to take on the role of managing their health and health care. The Patient Activation Measure (PAM) was designed to assess an individual's knowledge, skill and

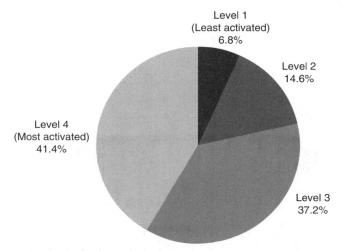

Note: Four levels of patient activation have been identified through the Patient Activation Measure (PAM)· At Level 1, the least-activated level, people tend to be passive and may not feel confident enough to play an active role in their own health. At Level 2, people may lack basic knowledge and confidence in their ability to manage their health. At Level 3, people appear to be taking some action but may still lack confidence and skill to support all necessary behaviors. At Level 4, the most-activated level, people have adopted many of the behaviors to support their health but may not be able to maintain them in the face of life stressors.

Figure 1 Level of Activation of U.S. Adults, 18 and Older, 2007 *Source:* HSC 2007 Health Tracking Household Survey

confidence in managing their health.[1] The PAM consists of a 13-item scale that asks people about their beliefs, knowledge and confidence for engaging in a wide range of health behaviors. Based on responses to the 13-item scale, each person is assigned an "activation score."

The PAM has been shown to be a valid measure of activation. For example, individuals identified as highly activated according to the measure are more likely to obtain preventive care, such as health screenings and immunizations, and to exhibit other behaviors known to be beneficial to health. These include maintaining good diet and exercise practices; self-management behaviors, such as monitoring their condition and adherence to treatment protocols; and health information seeking behaviors, such as asking questions in the medical encounter and using quality information to select a provider.[2]

Most importantly, studies show that activation is changeable over time. One study showed that gains in activation over a six-month period were followed by improvements in several health-related behaviors.[3] Another study showed that consumers who get support for being proactive about their health from their care team, from their coworkers and supervisors, and from friends and family tend to be more activated and to engage in healthier behaviors and choices.[4]

ACTIVATION LEVELS IN THE U.S. POPULATION

Prior research using the PAM has relied on relatively small samples or groups, such as health plan enrollees, Medicaid enrollees in several local areas, and older adults with chronic conditions. HSC's 2007 Health Tracking Household Survey is the first large nationally representative survey to include the PAM to assess the level of activation in the U.S. population (see Data Source).

Research on patient activation suggests that individuals go through phases or levels on their way to becoming effective self-managers. These levels are also useful for designing interventions to help people improve their ability to self-manage. Four levels of activation based on the individual's overall activation score have been identified. At the first or lowest level, people tend to be passive and may not feel confident enough to play an active role in their own health. At the second level, people may lack basic knowledge and confidence in their ability to manage their health. At the third level, people appear to be taking some action but may still lack confidence and skill to support all necessary behaviors. At the fourth level, people have adopted many of the behaviors to support their health but may not be able to maintain them in the face of life stressors.

Less than half of all adults in the United States (41.4%) are in the highest level of activation, according to findings from HSC's 2007 Health Tracking Household Survey. Even at this level, people still struggle to maintain healthy behaviors but tend to have the skills and confidence to manage their health in a more proactive way. On the other hand, relatively few people (21%) are in the lowest levels of activation (Levels 1 and 2), where basic skills and knowledge are lacking.[5]

ACTIVATION LEVELS VARY BY POPULATION AND HEALTH STATUS CHARACTERISTICS

There is a substantial amount of variation in activation levels across the U.S. population. Those who are younger, more educated and have higher incomes tend to be more activated (see Table 1). Similarly, those with private health insurance tend to have higher activation than those with Medicaid or those with only Medicare. Racial and ethnic differences in activation

Table 1	Level of Activation, U.S. Adults 18 and Older, by Selected Characteristics, 2007				
	LEVEL 1 (LEAST ACTIVATED)	LEVEL 2	LEVEL 3	LEVEL 4 (MOST ACTIVATED)	OVERALL ACTIVATION SCORE (ADJUSTED)
ALL ADULTS	6.8%	14.6%	37.2%	41.4%	
AGE					
18 – 34	6.0#	14.0#	39.3	40.7#	66.1#
35 – 44	7.8	14.2	36.0#	42.0#	65.0
45 – 64	6.8#	14.7	34.0#	44.6#	65.0
65 – 74	5.2#	14.8	40.4	39.6#	66.9#
75 + (R)	9.2	17.6	42.9	30.4	63.7
GENDER					
MALE (R)	6.8	14.3	38.6	40.3	64.8
FEMALE	6.8	14.9	36.0#	42.4	65.9#
FAMILY INCOME					
< 100% OF POVERTY (R)	8.9	19.6	43.6	27.9	65.0
100 – 199% OF POVERTY	10.5	19.4	38.0	32.2#	64.2
200 – 399% OF POVERTY	6.7	14.6#	38.2#	40.5#	65.0
400% OF POVERTY AND HIGHER	5.0#	11.6#	34.6#	48.9#	66.2#
EDUCATIONAL ATTAINMENT					
0 – 11 YEARS	9.7#	21.3#	45.8#	23.2#	62.3#
12 YEARS	8.5#	15.4#	39.3#	36.9#	64.1#
13 – 15 YEARS	5.2	13.9#	35.9#	45.0#	66.0#
16 + YEARS (R)	4.7	10.5	31.0	53.9	68.2
HEALTH INSURANCE COVERAGE					
AGE 65+					
MEDICARE ONLY	9.0	18.3	43.9#	28.8	63.4
MEDICARE AND OTHER INSURANC	6.6#	15.5#	41.0	36.9	63.9
LESS THAN AGE 65					
PRIVATE INSURANCE	4.4#	11.9#	36.0	47.7#	66.6#
MEDICAID/OTHER STATE COVERAGE	12.5	17.0	40.6	29.9	63.5
OTHER COVERAGE	7.8	20.2	35.4	36.7	64.2
UNINSURED (R)	10.8	19.9	36.6	32.8	63.9
RACE/ETHNICITY					
WHITE (R)	5.7	13.1	36.0	45.3	66.2
BLACK	9.8#	15.2	35.5	39.5#	65.0
HISPANIC	8.6#	21.3#	45.2#	24.8#	62.6#
OTHER	10.0#	16.2	36.4	37.5#	63.2#

Difference with reference group as designated by (R) is statistically significant at *p* < .05 level.

Note: Adjusted estimates of overall activation based on OLS regression, with PAM score as the dependent variable and all variables in the table included as independent variables.

Source: HSC 2007 Health Tracking Household Survey

are also apparent, with Hispanics having much lower activation levels compared with other groups.

Most of the differences in activation by education, race/ethnicity, age and insurance coverage remain after controlling for other characteristics. The one exception is that income differences narrow considerably after controlling for education, meaning that most of the income difference in activation reflects differences in educational attainment that are correlated with income.

Activation also varies by the type and number of chronic conditions, as well as other measures of health status. Overall, people with chronic conditions are more likely to have lower levels of activation—about 26% in Level 1 or 2—compared with people without any chronic conditions—about 18% in Level 1 or 2 (findings not shown).

However, among people with chronic conditions, there are considerable differences by condition and other health characteristics. For example, people with depression tend to be the least activated, while those with cancer tend to have higher activation (see Table 2). People with multiple chronic conditions, who report their health as fair or poor and who are obese are less activated than people with a single condition or those with better health indicators.

However, the adjusted activation scores indicate that after accounting for differences in health status, obesity and other characteristics, people with multiple chronic conditions tend to have higher activation scores compared with those with only a single chronic condition. All other things being equal, having multiple conditions may necessitate greater self-management and more careful moni-

Table 2	Level of Activation, U.S. Adults with Chronic Conditions, 2007				
	LEVEL 1 (LEAST ACTIVATED)	LEVEL 2	LEVEL 3	LEVEL 4 (MOST ACTIVATED)	OVERALL ACTIVATION SCORE (ADJUSTED)
ALL PERSONS WITH CHRONIC CONDITIONS	8.6%	17.3%	33.9%	40.1%	64.2
SELECTED CONDITIONS					
DIABETES	7.9	18.9	35.3	37.9	65.3*
ARTHRITIS	11.2*	19.1	32.2	37.5*	63.2*
ASTHMA	8.1	16.8	32.5	42.7	64.8
HYPERTENSION	9.6	18.5	34.2	37.7*	63.5*
HEART DISEASE	11.6	18.9	34.0	35.5*	64.0
CANCER	7.8	12.2*	34.5	45.5*	65.8
DEPRESSION	12.6*	21.1*	29.4*	36.8*	62.1*
MULTIPLE CONDITIONS					
1 CONDITION (R)	7.0	16.1	35.1	41.8	63.2
2 CONDITION	9.0	18.4	33.0	39.6	64.9#
3 OR MORE CONDITIONS	11.7#	19.8	32.6	35.9#	66.0#
PERCEIVED HEALTH STATUS					
EXCELLENT, VERY GOOD	3.3#	11.7#	32.6	52.4#	68.1#
GOOD	7.1#	17.7#	37.8#	37.5#	63.6#
FAIR OR POOR (R)	15.4	22.7	31.6	30.2	61.0
CURRENT SMOKER					
YES	14.7#	17.4	33.3	34.6#	63.4
NO (R)	6.9	17.3	34.0	41.8	64.5
BODY MASS INDEX					
NORMAL WEIGHT OR UNDERWEIGHT (<25)	8.9	15.4#	32.7	43.0#	64.9#
OVERWEIGHT (25–29.9)	6.7#	16.3	35.7	41.3#	64.8#
OBESE (30 AND OVER) (R)	10.1	19.6	32.9	37.4	63.3

*Difference with person who does not have condition is statistically significant at $p < .05$ level.

#Difference with reference group as designated by (R) is statistically significant at $p < .05$ level.

Note: Adjusted estimates of overall activation based on OLS regression, with PAM score as the dependent variable and all chronic condition and health status variables in the table included as independent variables, in addition to demographic and socioeconomic characteristics (from Table 1).

Source: HSC 2007 Health Tracking Household Survey

toring of one's own health. Moreover, health care providers may be more proactive about teaching self-management skills to patients with multiple conditions.

To some extent, activation reflects the degree to which one feels "in charge" of one's own health. People with more resources in the form of education and income score higher on the activation measure, while people who have experienced repeated failures in their ability to manage their health, such as those who are obese or who smoke, score lower.

It is important to note that it is difficult to discern the direction of causality in the observed relationships as the data were collected at a single moment in time. Longitudinal data are needed to determine whether poor health status causes lower activation, or whether low activation and passivity contribute to poorer health. Likely the causality operates in both directions, although low activation resulting from poor health may lead to a vicious cycle that precludes behaviors that could improve health.

Data Source

The data for this report are from the HSC 2007 Health Tracking Household Survey, a nationally representative telephone survey of the civilian noninstitutionalized U.S. population sponsored by the Robert Wood Johnson Foundation. The sample includes about 17,800 persons, including about 15,500 adults age 18 and over. The response rate for the survey was 43 percent. Population weights adjust for probability of selection and differences in nonresponse based on age, sex, race/ethnicity and education. Information was obtained on all adults in the family as well as a randomly selected child.

The 13-item Patient Activation Measure (PAM) was asked of all adults age 18 and over and was self-reported. Although the PAM was originally designed to be used for persons with chronic conditions, a slightly modified version was developed for persons with no chronic conditions. Persons in the survey were asked whether they had one or more of 10 common chronic conditions, including diabetes, arthritis, asthma, chronic obstructive pulmonary disease, hypertension, other heart disease, cancer, skin cancer, depression or uterine bleeding. Persons who reported one or more of these conditions were asked the original PAM version (i.e., for persons with chronic conditions), while those who did not have any of the 10 conditions were asked the modified PAM questions (i.e., for persons with no chronic conditions).

Both versions of the PAM questions use Likert-type response categories, including strongly agree, agree, disagree and strongly disagree. Persons who reported "not applicable," "don't know" or "refused" on more than half of the PAM scale items (7 or more) were dropped from the analysis. In addition, persons who replied "strongly agree" or "strongly disagree" on all 13 items were considered outliers and also excluded from the analysis. After these omissions, responses for about 13,500 adults were used to construct the PAM scale. Construction of the scale involved computing a "raw score" by summing the responses to all 13 questions. For persons who were missing one or more PAM items, the raw score was obtained by dividing the sum of the scores for the non-missing items by the number of non-missing items. Using the established methodology for the PAM, an activation score from 0-100 was assigned to each person based on their raw score.

Identifying levels of activation is based on whether an activation score falls within a previously determined range of scores. Level 1, the lowest level of activation, includes activation scores of 47 or lower; Level 2 includes scores of 47.1 to 55.1; Level 3 includes scores of 55.2 to 67.0; and Level 4 (the highest activation level) includes scores of 67.1 or above.

Moreover, while there are significant associations between demographic and health status characteristics and activation levels, there is also considerable variation in activation within categories of education, income and health status. For example, while there is a strong correlation between education level and activation, 15 percent of college graduates are in the lowest two levels of activation, while 23 percent of those with less than a high school education are in the highest level of activation. This suggests both that lower educational attainment need not be a barrier to higher activation and that knowing the socioeconomic characteristics of a population is insufficient to identify their activation level.

ACTIVATION LEVELS AND HEALTH CARE SYSTEM EXPERIENCES

Ultimately, the value of more highly activated patients is that it will lead to better health outcomes and health practices. For example, prior research has shown that higher levels of activation are associated with higher levels of preventive health behaviors and preventive care, as well as increased self-management of health conditions.[6] Part of being more activated is seeking and using relevant health information. For example, those who are more activated are more likely to report that they read about possible side effects when they get a new prescription drug. Ninety-four percent of those at the highest level of activation read about possible side effects, compared with 74 percent of the least activated (findings not shown).

Crucial to positive health outcomes is the ability to obtain needed health care services. While health policy often focuses on the financial and health insurance coverage barriers to obtaining needed medical care, it is likely that more highly activated patients have greater success in navigating a highly complex and often confusing health care system. For example, people with chronic conditions who are at lower levels of activation are much more likely to report unmet medical needs, to delay care and to have unmet prescription drug needs (see Table 3). Less activated people are also somewhat less likely to have a usual source of care. These differences remain even after controlling for socioeconomic and health status and likely reflect the more passive approach that people at lower levels of activation often take in managing their health. These findings also may indicate that those who are less activated are more vulnerable to barriers to care and are more easily dissuaded from taking action when faced with financial or health system barriers.

At the same time, people with chronic conditions who are more activated appear to get more support from their providers in managing their health. For example, 83.6 percent of those at the highest activation level reported that their health care provider helped them set goals to improve their diet, compared with 48.3 percent at the lowest activation level (see Table 4). Highly activated patients also were more likely to report that their provider helped them

set goals for exercise and taught them how to self-monitor their condition. In sum, more activated patients appear to have more positive and supportive health care experiences. As the direction of causality is unclear, this may either reflect highly activated people being more adept at choosing more supportive health care providers that will give them the care they need, or that greater support from providers contributes to higher activation levels in patients.

DISCUSSION AND POLICY IMPLICATIONS

Activated consumers take a proactive approach to managing their health and health care. Activation level is a reflection of the individual's beliefs about their role in managing their health, as well as their knowledge and confidence for doing so.

This is a much broader view of consumer activation than is often the focus of consumer-directed health plans, which primarily seek to increase consumer cost sensitivity. From a policy perspective, cost sensitivity by itself may be a necessary but not sufficient condition for greater consumer engagement. Indeed, increased cost sensitivity is but one manifestation of a more activated consumer, in which personal resourcefulness, education and motivation are necessary preconditions for seeking information on cost, quality and other important aspects of health care. A particularly striking finding is that higher activation levels are associated with much fewer problems with access to care, even when controlling for insurance coverage and income, which may reflect greater resourcefulness among more highly activated people in navigating the complexities of the health care system and overcoming barriers.

The findings indicate that activation levels differ considerably across socioeconomic and health sta-

| Table 3 | Access to Care by Activation Level, U.S. Adults with Chronic Conditions, 2007 All adults with chronic conditions Level 1 (least activated) Level |

	ALL ADULTS WITH CHRONIC CONDITIONS	LEVEL 1 (LEAST ACTIVATED)	LEVEL 2	LEVEL 3	LEVEL 4 (MOST ACTIVATED)
REGULAR SOURCE OF CARE	91.0%	88.4%	88.5%*	91.3%	92.4%
UNMET MEDICAL NEED	12.2	26.8*	15.2*	10.2	9.4
DELAYED CARE	15.5	47.1*	39.1*	30.2*	25.2
DID NOT GET PRESCRIPTION DRUGS DUE TO COST	21.0	37.4*	26.3*	19.9	20.0

*Difference with Level 4 is statistically significant at p < .05 level.

Note: All estimates are based on regression-adjusted means that control for the following variables: age, gender, family income, education, health insurance coverage, race/ethnicity, number of chronic conditions, perceived health status, body mass index, urban vs. rural residence, and census region.

Source: HSC 2007 Health Tracking Household Survey

| Table 4 | Self-Management Support from Health Care Providers by Activation Level, U.S. Adults with Chronic Conditions, 2007 |

	ALL ADULTS WITH CHRONIC CONDITIONS	LEVEL 1 (LEAST ACTIVATED)	LEVEL 2	LEVEL 3	LEVEL 4 (MOST ACTIVATED)
HEALTH CARE PROVIDER HELPED THEM TO SET GOALS TO IMPROVE THEIR DIET	75.7%	48.3%*	65.3%*	78.6%*	83.6%
HEALTH CARE PROVIDER HELPED THEM TO SET GOALS FOR EXERCISE	70.5	43.5*	61.6*	73.6*	77.7
HEALTH CARE PROVIDER TAUGHT THEM HOW TO SELF-MONITOR THEIR CONDITION	76.6	42.2*	66.5*	80.9*	84.7

*Difference with Level 4 is statistically significant at $p < .05$ level.

Note: All estimates are based on regression-adjusted means that control for the following variables: age, gender, family income, education, health insurance coverage, race/ethnicity, number of chronic conditions, perceived health status, body mass index, urban vs. rural residence, and census region.

Source: HSC 2007 Health Tracking Household Survey

tus characteristics. Because activation levels are linked to important outcomes, such as seeking care, seeking information and health behaviors, and because it is a changeable attribute, it is a potentially important lever for change.

Other research indicates that people who live, get their health care and work in supportive environments that enable proactive health behaviors tend to be more activated.[7] Although it is not possible to determine the direction of causality, one interpretation of the findings in this study is that support from physicians—teaching patients how to monitor or set up an exercise plan—stimulates patient activation. If this is correct, then encouraging this type of physician support may be a productive pathway for increasing activation. This may be particularly important for those at lower levels of activation, who not only engage in fewer health promoting behaviors, but also tend to be passive with regard to their health care. These individuals are particularly at risk for declines in health and inadequate health care. That less-activated individuals are disproportionately represented in racial and ethnic minority groups suggests that attention to this attribute is a possible avenue to closing some of the racial and ethnic disparities in health.

Perhaps the main question for policy makers is what—if anything—can be done from a policy perspective to increase levels of patient activation. Because activation is changeable and provider support appears to be a factor, incentivizing or holding health care delivery systems and providers accountable for patient gains in activation is a possible policy direction.

In particular, some models of delivery are more amendable to supporting patient activation than others. For example, the medical home model, where patient-centered care is the focus and where a functioning medical team provides coordinated care, customizing care to support activation is possible. Similarly, in community health centers, where there are dedicated staff for supporting patient self-management, explicit support for activation could be provided.

On the other hand, the study results should give pause to policy makers who are promoting consumer-directed health care in the Medicaid program. For example, Indiana became the first state in 2008 to implement a high-deductible plan and health savings account program for some uninsured and Medicaid enrollees under the President's Affordable Choices Initiative. Other states, including Florida, West Virginia, Kentucky and South Carolina, also have experimented with various types of consumer-directed care models in their Medicaid programs, with the objective of incentivizing enrollees to take more responsibility—and risks—for their health care utilization.

However, people enrolled in Medicaid are among the least-activated patients among all insurance groups, which reflects both lower educational levels and lower socioeconomic status. The findings suggest that efforts to increase patient responsibility in the Medicaid program will only succeed if they are accompanied by vigorous efforts to educate enrollees and increase their levels of activation.

• • • **References**

1. Hibbard, Judith H., et al., "Consumer Activation and Racial and Ethnic Health Disparities," *Health Affairs*, Vol. 27, No. 5 (September/October, 2008).

2. Hibbard, Judith H., et al., "Development of the Patient Activation Measure (PAM): Conceptualizing and Measuring Activation in Patients and Consumers," *Health Services Research*, Vol. 39, No. 4 (2004); Hibbard, Judith H., et al., "Development

and Testing of a Short Form of the Patient Activation Measure," *Health Services Research*, Vol. 40, No. 6 (2005); Mosen, David M., et al., "Is Patient Activation Associated with Outcomes of Care for Adults with Chronic Conditions?" *Journal of Ambulatory Care Management*, Vol. 30, No. 1 (2007); Hibbard, Judith H., "Assessing Activation Stage and Employing a 'Next Steps' Approach to Supporting Patient Self-Management," *Journal of Ambulatory Care Management*, Vol. 30, No. 1 (2007); and Becker, Edmund R., and Douglas W. Roblin, "Translating Primary Care Practice Climate into Patient Activation: The Role of Patient Trust in Physician," *Medical Care*, Vol. 46, No. 8 (2008).

3. Hibbard, Judith H., et al., "Do Increases in Patient Activation Result in Improved Self-Management Behaviors?" *Health Services Research*, Vol. 42, No. 4 (2007).

4. Becker, Edmund R., and Douglas Roblin, "Survey of Health and Healthy Behaviors Among Working Age Kaiser Permanente Adults in 2005," presented at the Annual Research Meeting of AcademyHealth, Orlando Fla., (June 2007); Becker and Roblin (2008).

5. Because there is a large range of scores represented in Level 4 activation, Hibbard and colleagues are examining a 5-level model, which would add more precision to the higher end of the activation dimension.

6. Hibbard, et al. (2004); Hibbard, et al. (2005); Mosen, et al. (2007); Hibbard (20007); and Becker and Roblin (2008).

7. Becker and Roblin (2007) and Becker and Roblin (2008).

10

The Public Health System

The growing importance of public health is evidenced by its increasing responsibilities. Public health was historically known for its contribution toward reduction and control of infectious diseases through such efforts as environmental sanitation (by securing safe air and water), hygienic practices, the elimination of smallpox and polio (through immunization), and reduction of overcrowding. As chronic diseases replaced infectious diseases as the leading causes of death, public health shifted its focus toward health promotion programs such as lifestyle changes in diet, tobacco, and exercise, to prevent contemporary health threats including cardiovascular disease, type-2 diabetes, and obesity. In recent years, as a result of a series of natural calamities such as Hurricanes Katrina and Rita and the spread of severe acute respiratory syndrome (SARS), and human created threats such as the 9-11 attacks and the possibility of terrorist attacks involving chemical, biological, radiological, or nuclear weapons, public health has again assumed center stage and been called upon to handle these emerging threats.

However, little is known about how the public health system can be organized to effectively and efficiently handle the modern-day threats of infectious and chronic diseases and environmental disruptions, both natural and human-created. Moreover, public health remains marginal in many countries' health care system, particularly the United States, where public policy has rarely emphasized public health. There remains a deep lack of appreciation of what public health can accomplish toward improving population health.

Although the USDHHS and CDC provide guidance and major funding to state (and sometimes local) health departments, the authority for public health matters constitutionally resides with state governments. State health departments craft policy and entrust the operational component to local health departments.

Based on a 2005 survey conducted by the Association of State and Territorial Health Officials (ASTHO) and another 2005 survey by the National Association of County and City Health Officials (NACCHO), total per capita state and local public health spending for 2004–05 from all sources was $149.[1] Another estimate put the public health annual per capita spending to be about $37–$102 among local agencies and $86–$232 in state agencies. On average, state public health agencies employed

1,924 full-time equivalent (FTE) workers (median of 1,145) whereas local public health agencies employed 66 FTE workers (median of 16).

At the state level, 58 percent of state public health agencies were free-standing, independent departments and 42 percent were part of an umbrella agency.[23] In terms of the form of organizational control between state and local public health agencies, the decentralized configuration was most common (42%), followed by mixed/shared (32%), and centralized (26%). State boards or councils existed in 48 percent of the states and had public health policy making and regulation power in 75 percent of the states with their presence. The state health officer was appointed by the governor in 66 percent of the states and by the secretary of health and human services 24 percent of the time.

The top programs and functions of state public health agencies included preparedness (100%); vital statistics (98%); tobacco prevention and control (96%); public health laboratories (96%); women, infants, and children (WIC) program (96%); environmental health (92%); food safety (92%); health facility regulation (90%); drinking water regulation (80%); environmental regulation (74%); health professional licensing (70%); substance abuse prevention (52%); medical error reporting (50%); mental health (34%); and Medicaid (32%).

At the local level, county was the most predominant jurisdiction providing public health services (59%), followed by city/county (14%), district (10%), township (8.8%), and city (7.1%). Local boards of health were present in 74.4 percent of all local jurisdictions and served the role of governing (55%), policy making (58%), and advising (62%).

The top programs and functions of local public health agencies included adult immunization (88%), communicable disease epidemiology (87%), child immunization (87%), tuberculosis screening (83%), food service inspection (74%), tobacco control (67%), WIC program (64%), septic tanks (64%), HIV/AIDS screening (59%), STD treatment (57%), obesity (55%), family planning (55%), early and periodic screening, diagnosis, and treatment (EPSDT) (44%), school health (40%), injury prevention (39%), prenatal care (37%), syndromatic surveillance (33%), public water supply monitoring (29%), oral health (27%), home health (25%), hazardous materials handling (19%), primary care (12%), and mental health (10%).

Recent literature (see, for example, notes 1–3) identifies a series of challenges facing the nation's public health system infrastructure as summarized below.

DISCREPANCIES BETWEEN MISSIONS AND FUNDING LEVEL

In the wake of the 9-11 terrorist attack and hurricane Katrina, public health assumed the new responsibility of preparing for and responding to bioterrorism and natural disasters. At the same time, the old responsibilities of health protection, health promotion, and disease prevention remain. Meanwhile, population-based core public health activities such as disease monitoring, surveillance, outbreak investigation, and response receive little funding. Funding for public health remains dismally low at less than $150 per capita (less than 2.5% of the overall health care spending), causing severe resource constraints. In contrast, Canada spent 5.5 percent of its total health expenditure on public health.[4] In the U.S., public health is an undervalued sector: little investment is made in technology, workforce training and recruitment, facility build-out or renovation.

Within the United States, spending on public health also varies widely across communities, raising concerns about how these differences may affect the availability of essential public health services. May and colleagues examined the association between public health spending and the performance of essential public health services and noted that performance of essential public health services is significantly associated with public health spending levels (particularly local funds), even after controlling for system and community characteristics.[5]

CATEGORICAL FUNDING

In addition to inadequate funding, the categorical nature of public health funding also presents a challenge. Public health funding is typically based on categorical programs and must be spent in specific ways, thereby reducing flexibility and efficiency. Categorical funding at the federal and state levels may limit the ability of local agencies to maintain core public health infrastructure and activities that fall outside of these categories.

LACK OF LEADERSHIP AND SHARED VISION

In the United States there is no single entity that has overall authority and responsibility for creation, maintenance, and oversight of the nation's public health infrastructure. Policymakers across jurisdictions and levels of government have not developed a shared, realistic vision of what public health should accomplish and who in the public health hierarchy should be held accountable.

This is not the case in other industrialized countries. For example, in Sweden, the National Institute of Public Health has the role of monitoring Sweden's national objectives for public health activities, formulating interim targets, and developing indicators of how well objectives are being met.[6]

In Canada, the creation of the Public Health Agency of Canada (PHAC) marks the beginning of a new approach to federal leadership and collaboration with provinces and territories on efforts to renew the public health system in Canada and support a sustainable health care system. Focusing on more effective efforts to prevent chronic diseases and injuries, and respond to public health emergencies and infectious disease outbreaks, PHAC works closely with provinces and territories to keep Canadians healthy and help reduce pressures on the health care system.[7] PHAC serves as the nerve center for Canada's expertise and research in public health, effectively coordinating efforts with other partners to identify, reduce, and respond to public health risks and threats.[8]

DISCREPANCIES BETWEEN EXPANDING ROLES AND OLD INFRASTRUCTURE

The organizational infrastructure that supports public health services is largely a remnant of the previous century when infectious diseases were the main target. Systematic failure of this infrastructure due to conflicting priorities, diffuse responsibilities, and inadequate resources are made readily apparent in numerous live tests of public health capabilities (such as Hurricane Katrina, the outbreak of SARS, and the anthrax attacks). Even though recent preparedness funding may be used to update and strengthen certain aspects of public health infrastructure, the funding is widely believed to be inadequate. In addition to the expanded preparedness role, public health, especially at the local levels, has been increasingly depended on as a medical provider of last resort. Serving as a safety net for medical services otherwise unobtainable by some populations (particularly the medically disenfranchised) has been a major impediment to investing in a stronger public health protection role.

STRUCTURAL VARIABILITY

There are significant variations in the structure of health departments across the country. State health departments craft policy and entrust the operational component to local health departments. The result is a nationally fragmented public health enterprise characterized by diverse practices across about 3,000 local agencies charged with meeting varying missions under 50 state health departments. The absence of nationally consistent systems leads to profound operational disconnects across public health authorities and hampers the public health effort to coordinate with other responder sectors, especially during disasters that cross geopolitical borders.

INADEQUATE WORKFORCE

The public health workforce is faced with a shortage and competence challenge. On the one hand, there is a shortage of public health workforce. The ratio of public health workers to US residents fell from 1:457 to 1:635 between 1970 and 2000.[2] A recent survey by ASTHO revealed a rapidly aging state agency workforce, high retirement eligibility rates, high vacancy rates, and high annual staff turnover rates.[9] The average tenure of a state health department's chief executive is two years. Nurses represent the largest professional group among public health workers, but they are rapidly retiring and in short supply. Given the rising challenge of chronic diseases and emerging threats, the decline in workforce represents a serious erosion of public health system capacity.

On the other hand, the current public health workforce may not have the competency to handle today's challenges that require new expertise for preparedness such as informatics, epidemiology, logistics, and risk communications. Self-assessment of public health competency by public health workers consistently shows gaps between mastery and what is needed for effective practice. Only 44 percent of public health workers had any formal, academic training in public health. Moreover, a sizable proportion of current public health workforce who have learned primarily on the job obtain higher-paying positions in hospitals, private laboratories, industry, and academia. The graduates of schools and programs of public health tend to find employment in academic and research careers, rather than in relatively low-paying state and local public health agencies. The compensation packages for public health cannot ensure the hiring of the brightest and best-trained workforce.

INCONSISTENT INFORMATION TECHNOLOGY

Throughout the country, there lacks a comprehensive electronic health intelligence and information system, to detect unusual disease events, trace vulnerable populations, monitor cases of diseases, catalog adverse event reports, track the course of outbreaks, resupply critical resources, deploy personnel during an epidemic, and scrutinize spending.

Across states, the infrastructure for information and data systems is inconsistent. Many public health surveillance systems have been late to replace the paper-based or telephone-based reporting system. In a survey conducted by CDC,[2] only 45 percent of local health departments had the capacity to broadcast alerts via facsimile to labs, physicians, state health agencies; fewer than half had high speed continuous internet access; and 20 percent lacked e-mail capability.

LACK OF EVIDENCE BETWEEN PUBLIC HEALTH PERFORMANCE AND GOVERNANCE STRUCTURE

There is a clear agreement that public health performance is related to the governance structure. However, it is less clear how that relationship works. The public health system's literature tends to focus on the deficiencies of the current US public health system including discrepancies between missions and funding level, categorical funding, lack of leadership and shared vision, discrepancies between expanding roles and old infrastructure, structural variability, inadequate workforce, and inconsistent information technology.

Further studies are needed to examine how the public health system (including its structure, process, and performance) can be designed to fulfill the mission of improving population health and reducing health disparities at the national, regional, state, and local levels. Specifically, studies need to develop indicators that measure achievements in the improvement of population health and the reduction of health disparities; develop and assess the essential services needed to lead to the intended performance; and develop and assess the structure (including governance, organization, financing, workforce, and information system) necessary to accomplish the essential services. These studies need to be performed at the national, regional, state, and local levels. Moreover, these studies should standardize common features that all levels can embrace as well as identify unique features that fit specific levels or types of communities.

The following course of action is recommended to address aforementioned deficiencies and advance public health systems research.

1. *Develop logic models on how public health improves population health and reduces health disparities*

   Even though there is large evidence that public health contributes to population health and that it often does so by influencing social determinants of health, we know very little about how public health can be called upon to address health disparities. We also have little knowledge about the roles of public health at the federal, state, and local levels, respectively. A clear conceptual understanding of these issues is critical and serves as a foundation for concerted efforts toward further research and practice. Therefore, logic models need to be developed about how public health improves population health and reduces health disparities at the national, state, and local levels. One way to accomplish this is to convene a joint expert panel and stakeholders meeting where draft logic models are proposed, discussed, and refined after incorporating inputs from all participants. The refined models are then circulated within the public health community and among public health systems researchers for further comments and refinement. These models may be updated periodically as new evidence is gathered.

2. *Develop indicators to measure public health performance at the national, state, and local levels*

   Once consensus is reached regarding the role of public health and the related logic models formulated, we need to develop indicators at the national, state, and local levels that measure public health performance that improves population health and reduces health disparities. A comprehensive national surveillance system of tracking these indicators consistently needs to be developed. Eventually, the system will also include measures of inputs (resources, capacity, etc.), core function-related processes (public health practices and services) as well as outcome. One way to accomplish this is to use the same joint expert panel and stakeholders meeting where draft indicators (tied to the logic models) are proposed, discussed, and refined after incorporating inputs from all participants. The refined indicators along with the logic models are then circulated within the public health community for further comments and refinement. The indicators may be updated periodically as new evidence is gathered. States are likely to be primarily responsible for developing and implementing a tracking system that captures the public health performance indicators. Since not all states are equal in terms of readiness, technical assistance is needed that enables states to learn from each other and collect comparable information.

3. *Conduct international studies that draw lessons from other industrialized countries*

Case studies of other industrialized countries that have similar political and economic systems and comparable cultural values would help the US learn from the experiences and lessons of successful and unsuccessful attempts to improve public health systems performance. Indeed, many of the topics identified in the research priority areas can benefit from an international perspective. For example, international studies can help address research topics including public health and population health determinants (e.g., how public health strategies can be developed to influence the socioeconomic determinants of population health, and how policies and strategies can be developed to reduce SES disparities among subpopulations), public policy and public health (e.g., examples of broad public policies that focus on population health, facilitators and barriers toward broad public policies that focus on population health), and public health performance and governance structure (e.g., what public health strategies, efforts, services, and programs are needed to fulfill the mission of improving population health and reducing health disparities, and how the public health system can be designed to carry out these services and programs). One way to accomplish this is through commissioned studies that explore these issues for selected countries (e.g., Sweden, UK, Canada, Australia). Public health professionals and experts from these countries could also be invited to attend an international symposium on public health systems performance and research. The commissioned studies, presentations by local experts, and the discussions that follow could result in a systematic understanding of other countries' experiences and lessons.

4. *Advocate state innovations to improve public health performance*

Due to the political and institutional structures of the US as well as the diversity of local needs and resources, significant and meaningful reforms are likely to happen at the state level. We need to encourage state innovations that try to improve public health infrastructure and performance. One way to accomplish this is to fund evaluations of states' innovative efforts at improving their public health systems infrastructure, practices, and performance. In refining structure and practices based on lessons learned from existing infrastructure, it is important to address the major determinants of population health and health disparities, by focusing on social and community factors, not just access to public health and medical care services for selected individuals. While it is much more difficult to influence social and economic determinants, it is necessary to examine and intervene, when possible, much earlier in the process of poor health development. Since many of these social factors are the root causes of poor health, addressing them will be paramount to improving population health and resolving health disparities in the US. To promote and protect society's interest in health and well-being, public health must influence the social, economic, political, and medical care factors that affect health and illness.

Turning Point is an initiative of The Robert Wood Johnson Foundation to transform and strengthen the public health system. The 21 states participating in this initiative developed multi-sector partnerships to produce public health improvement plans and chose one or more priorities for implementation. Strategies employed for transforming public health systems include institutionalization within government, establishing 'third-sector' institutions, cultivating relationships with significant allies, and enhancing communication and visibility among multiple communities.

5. *Advance community based projects that integrate research and practice*

A major initiative to address the research priorities developed earlier is to encourage community-based projects that integrate research with practice. Community has been defined as individuals with a shared affinity, and perhaps geography, who organize around an issue, with collective discussion, decision making, and action,[10] or as a group of people who have common characteristics, defined by location, race, ethnicity, age, occupation, interest in particular problems or outcomes, or other common bonds.[11] For the purpose of promoting a broad public health perspective, community could be broadly defined as including all those (individuals, organizations) residing in a defined geographic area with close political, social, or economic interactions. Community-based projects should adhere to the following principles.

Community-based projects should foster collaboration between public health agencies and other entities that can make a contribution toward improving health. Improving the health of populations and reducing health disparities will require the participation of traditional health agencies, and involvement from education, housing, environmental, criminal justice, and economic agencies. To achieve cross-agency collaboration, these agencies should create standing mechanisms for policy development among sectors and promote interdepartmental collaboration, and create networks among public and private agencies and particularly with advocates to openly study, evaluate, and disseminate policy options.

Community-based projects should stress multi-level integration of interventions. Invariably, for some vulnerable groups there are gaps in service provision and for others there are major duplications. Building on the focus on multiple risk factors, efforts could be made toward unifying services across agencies and organizations with common goals. Domestic and foreign public health initiatives have shown greater promise when utilizing the collective resources of public and private advocates. Recognizing common goals encourages multi-sector alliances and minimizes partisan or other political barriers.

Community-based projects should stress participation and empowerment, which are critical components of acceptance, success, and continuation of any set of interventions. Greater community involvement and leadership in priority-setting and policy development is critical for the project's ultimate success. Perhaps one of the best ways to include communities in decision-making is to

focus on community strengths and resources rather than community deficits or problems. Communities should be seen as action centers for development, progress, and change. Community members and community leaders should have a central role in planning and managing initiatives. Through community mobilization, skill building, and resource sharing, communities can be empowered to identify and meet their own needs, making them stronger advocates in supporting the vulnerable populations within and across their community boundaries.

Community-based projects should ensure feasibility. Making sure an intervention is feasible is critical to its success. Areas of feasibility to be considered include: technical feasibility (i.e., can the intervention plausibly solve or reduce the problem as defined?), economic feasibility (i.e., what are the costs and benefits of given intervention from an economic standpoint?), political feasibility (i.e., a proposed intervention must survive the test of political acceptability. This depends on support from key officials, other stakeholders inside and outside of government, and ultimately voters.), and administrative feasibility (i.e., assess how possible it would be to implement any given intervention given a variety of social, political, and administrative constraints.).

Community-based projects should apply strategies. An approach that has been successful in Europe—restating the public health issue using different language—may attract new attention to an issue not previously compelling to the public or policymakers. In the past, advocates have used the social justice argument to persuade the public that inequality in the US needed to be eliminated. Politicians in the Netherlands were more impressed by a discussion centering on "lost human potential" than inequality. Perhaps the same effect would be seen among Americans if the national conversation focused less on social justice.

Community-based projects should include a systematic evaluation component to allow feedback and refinement. Programs that are comprehensive in scope (addressing multiple risks) should be evaluated along multiple dimensions, but should be appropriately evaluated against criteria that are feasible to obtain. In too many circumstances, health and social programs are judged on whether they directly impact the health of their consumers, even though the program is funded for short-term cycles (e.g., just two or three years). If these projects are possible over a longer period, programs must be held accountable to meeting their goals to improve health.

6. *Search for innovative ways of funding public health systems research*

Funding for public health systems research ought to come from a variety of sources. In addition to traditional federal funding sources such as CDC, NIH, HRSA, and AHRQ, foundations can play a major role in shaping and fostering public health systems research. Foundations provide a unique avenue for promoting scientific and policy discussion of a public health issue. In addition to providing the necessary financial resources to further explore issues such as disparity, foundations are able to influence public opinion through publications and media and the discourse it inspires. In addition, the private sector should also be engaged especially in funding community based projects that aim at improving community health and benefit all those residing in the community including private business.

7. *Develop new methodologies and analytic tools*

Much of the research and evaluation in this field will not be like traditional medical research that relies on control groups, a large sample size, and a limited number of variables. In contrast, public health systems research typically involves single community and multiple layers of variables. New methodologies and analytic tools need to be developed to further this line of inquiry and advance the field. One way to facilitate this could be through a research retreat where experts in related field (e.g., social scientists, health services researchers, public health researchers, methodologists, qualitative researchers, and practitioners) gather and discuss challenges and solutions. As a result, suggested approaches (methodological and analytic) to carry out public health systems research could be summarized and promoted.

8. *Educate the public and enhance dissemination*

Education can be used as a tool to raise awareness about population health problems and challenges such as health disparities and to promote a climate of outrage and support for programmatic changes to eliminate such disparities. Technology has provided innumerable means for distributing information. A media campaign incorporating internet, television, radio and print ads with a simple, readable, and galvanizing message could reach and motivate a broad segment of the population. Policy alternatives, goals and research, in particular, should also be well published in highly regarded academic publications in order to ensure consistent political pressure on policymakers. In addition to enhancing awareness, it is critical that the public and policymakers understand the severity of the problem we face. Policymakers are more likely to act when there is a clear public demand and when there is a perceived crisis. One way to demonstrate severity is the publication of international rankings on key health and health care indicators. Taking advantage of national pride by highlighting a public health issue for which the US performs poorly compared to other countries may motivate the public to take steps to improve their national ranking. This strategy has often been invoked to garner support for infant mortality interventions. The US's abominable ranking among OECD countries as the 7th highest in infant mortality continues to inspire outrage that a country with so many resources does not ensure adequate care for vulnerable citizens.

Education can also be used to establish relevance. Although most Americans are concerned about the plights of the vulnerable populations, relatively few have considered these to be their own problems. Fewer have the understanding that it is actually to their economic advantage to address the plights of vulnerable populations. A rational review of the costs and benefits associated with improving the health of vulnerable populations reveals the advantage of making such an investment. The consideration of costs to the nation resulting from poor health status among the vulnerable cannot evade the public's attention much longer.

9. *Engage the policy community*

To elevate public health and public health systems research, ultimately, the policy community must be engaged. In the US, there is a lack of political conviction about improving population health and reducing health disparities. This is reflected in the absence of a coherent public policy agenda toward population health and in the lack of authority and funding for public health. The federal government has six main areas in which it plays a role in population health: policy making, financing, public health protection, collecting and disseminating information about health and healthcare delivery systems, capacity building for population health, and direct management of services.[12] Events in recent years such as preparedness against natural or human created disasters present a unique opportunity to strengthen the core capacity to deliver the essential public health services and strengthen public health. As stated by McGinnis, "public policymakers need to begin thinking in terms of a health agenda rather than a health care agenda or—even more narrowly—a health care financing agenda".[13]

The US needs to begin to develop a health policy agenda that reflects not just the impact of medical care services on health, but more importantly the impact of social and environmental factors. An examination of current health policy debates reveals that most debates center primarily on financing of health care rather than health outcomes or social determinants of health. The US should expand this focus on financing and issues of cost containment to include "health impact assessment," which would estimate the influence of social, economic, and health care policies on population health, not just cost-savings.

10. *Form a national center for public health excellence that coordinates national efforts to improve public health performance*

A national center for public health excellence could be formed to facilitate many of the research, evaluation, and services activities associated with promoting the public health systems research agenda. For example, the center could provide technical assistance to state and community based projects including designing and collecting standard measures and providing training on models commonly used in community health development and evaluation projects. Examples of these models include the health belief model, the transtheoretical model (stages of change), the planned approach to community health (PATCH), predisposing, reinforcing and enabling constructs in education/environmental diagnosis and evaluation, with its implementation phase: policy, regulatory and organizational constructs in education and environmental development (PRECEDE-PROCEED), and multilevel approach to community health (MATCH).[14] The center can also help with the evaluation of the projects.

The readings included in this chapter address a range of areas related to public health, including its importance, implementation strategies, and assessment. In the **Declaration of Alma-Ata International Conference on Primary Health Care**, the World Health Organization (WHO) declares that health, which is a state of complete physical, mental, and social well-being, and not merely the absence of disease or infirmity, is a fundamental human right and that the attainment of the highest possible level of health is a most important world-wide social goal whose realization requires the action of many other social and economic sectors in addition to the health sector. Governments have a responsibility for the health of their people, which can be fulfilled only by the provision of adequate health and social measures. Primary health care is essential health care based on practical, scientifically sound and socially acceptable methods and technology made universally accessible to individuals and families in the community through their full participation and at a cost that the community and country can afford to maintain at every stage of their development in the spirit of self reliance and self-determination. The International Conference on Primary Health Care calls for urgent and effective national and international action to develop and implement primary health care throughout the world and particularly in developing countries in a spirit of technical cooperation and in keeping with a New International Economic Order.

In **Political Will: A Bridge Between Public Health Knowledge and Action**, Lezine and Reed introduced the Bridges from Knowledge to Action model for developing and implementing public health policy. This approach stresses the development of political will and seeks to develop and implement public health policy on the basis of scientific evidence and community participation. It uses new information and ongoing public health support to push for preventive action, while applying political will to push health policy. Political will is described as "society's desire and commitment to support or modify old programs to develop new programs" and is largely based on "public understanding and support."

The process is described to be cyclical rather than linear. Community groups will use data to convince policymakers to fund studies that will increase the knowledge base, which can be used to evaluate future policies. The process begins with the collection of data. When interest groups have agreed that their knowledge base is sufficient to develop a strategy, they can begin to design a comprehensive plan to balance collected evidence with feasible interventions. Political will is used during this step in order to secure resources to develop the strategy. Developing political will early in the process will help implement the goals for a longer duration. Once the program has been put into play, the experience gathered from its duration goes into the knowledge base for the next cycle. Studies have shown that devoting time and attention to developing political will improves the chances of a program's success because it has society's support to continue, rather than its protests.

In **Improving the Effectiveness of Health Care and Public Health: A Multiscale Complex Systems of Analysis,** Bar-Yam introduced a systems analysis tool that can be used to evaluate the effectiveness of health care and public health. According to the authors, part of the reason that the US health care system is ineffective and inefficient is due to charging a system structured to meet individual needs with carrying out preventive care and community health, which deals with population needs. In order to develop a more efficient system, the US needs to look at creating a separate system, or a subsystem, that deals with prevention and community health. Effective organization of the health care system depends on matching its structures with the demands.

Separation opens up the possibility of more organizational forms. It could design systems that are more transparent and allow individuals to perform more appropriate roles. A public health system could be established that promotes private organizations or publicly supported organizations that are effective at prevention and population care, which is health care at a broader level, such as national vaccine programs as well as screening programs. These services can be separated from individual patient care, which requires more decision making based on the unique circumstances of a patient. The health care system needs to recognize that there is a distinction between individual and population health, and should organize itself according to this separation.

In **Public Health Services and Cost-Effectiveness Analysis,** Banta and de Wit showed how cost-effectiveness analysis may be used in assessing public health services. Cost-effectiveness analysis is an important tool to evaluate health programs, yet it is seldom used in establishing public health policies, programs, and interventions. It is seldom taken into consideration when proposing priority settings that establish rules that determine which groups of patients or disease areas should be favored to access limited resources. The cost-effectiveness of preventive services is also largely unknown. Childhood vaccination has the most data regarding its cost-effective and cost-saving nature, though more expensive modern vaccines (i.e., human papilloma virus, varicella) may impact the cost-effectiveness of immunization plans in the future. To determine insurance coverage, cost-effective analysis is important in deciding whether to include an intervention as a health benefit. This decision is not just based on cost-effectiveness, but also needs and safety. In Europe, pharmaceutical coverage has a transparent process in determining which pharmaceuticals are covered in their health care systems. Member states of the European Union often use an economic evaluation to decide on coverage, and rely on safety and efficacy of the drug to make any final determinations. The authors advocated that an economic analysis of cost-effectiveness should be used to determine how public health programs are implemented, but it should not be the only criteria involved. There are also politics and equity and ethical issues to contend with when trying to assess these programs. Cost-effectiveness should be a single aspect in a complex decision-making process.

● ● ● **References**

1. Beitsch LM, Brooks RG, Menachemi N, Libbey PM. Public health at center stage: New roles, old props. *Health Affairs* 2006; 25:911–922.

2. Baker EL, Potter MA, Jones DL, et al. The public health infrastructure and our nation's health. *Annual Review Public Health* 2005;26:303–18.

3. Salinsky E, Gursky EA. The case for transforming governmental public health. *Health Affairs* 2006; 25:1017–28.

4. Canadian Institute for Health Information. National Health Expenditure Trends 1975–2005. Table C.1.2.7 December 2005.

5. May GP, McHugh MC, Shim K, et al. *J of Public Health Management Practice* 2004; 10:435–43.

6. Sweden's new public health policy: National public health objectives for Sweden. Retrieved March 24,

2007 at http://www.fhi.se/shop/material_pdf/newpublic0401.pdf.

7. Public Health Agency of Canada. Retrieved March 24, 2007 at http://www.phac-aspc.gc.ca/about_apropos/index.html.

8. Evans R, Law M. The Canadian health care system: where are we and how did we get there. An *International Assessment of Health Care Financing*. Economic Development Institute of the World Bank, 1995.

9. ASTHO. *State public health employee worker shortage report: A civil service recruitment and retention crisis*. Washington DC, ASTHO, 2004.

10. Labonte R. Health promotion: From concepts to strategies. *Healthcare Magt Forum* 1988; 1 (3):24–30.

11. Turnock BJ. *Public Health: What It Is and How It Works*. Boston: Jones & Bartlett, 2004.

12. Lister SA. CRS Report for Congress—An Overview of the U.S. Public Health System in the Context of Emergency Preparedness. 2005.

13. McGinnis JM. National priorities in disease prevention. *Issues Sci Technol* 1989; 5(2):46–52.

14. Brownson RC, et al. *Evidence-Based Public Health*. New York, NY: Oxford University Press. Chapter 8: Developing an action plan and implementing interventions. 2003:169–93.

Declaration of Alma-Ata: International Conference on Primary Health Care, Alma-Ata, USSR, 6-12 September 1978

Source: Declaration of Alma-Ata International Conference on Primary Health Care, Alma-Ata, USSR, 6-12 September 1978 (http://www.who.int/ publications/almaata_declaration_en.pdf). Courtesy of the World Health Organization.

The International Conference on Primary Health Care, meeting in Alma-Ata this twelfth day of September in the year Nineteen hundred and seventy-eight, expressing the need for urgent action by all governments, all health and development workers, and the world community to protect and promote the health of all the people of the world, hereby makes the following

DECLARATION:

I

The Conference strongly reaffirms that health, which is a state of complete physical, mental and social well-being, and not merely the absence of disease or infirmity, is a fundamental human right and that the attainment of the highest possible level of health is a most important world-wide social goal whose realization requires the action of many other social and economic sectors in addition to the health sector.

II

The existing gross inequality in the health status of the people particularly between developed and developing countries as well as within countries is politically, socially and economically unacceptable and is, therefore, of common concern to all countries.

III

Economic and social development, based on a New International Economic Order, is of basic importance to the fullest attainment of health for all and to the reduction of the gap between the health status of the developing and developed countries. The promotion and protection of the health of the people is essential to sustained economic and social development and contributes to a better quality of life and to world peace.

IV

The people have the right and duty to participate individually and collectively in the planning and implementation of their health care.

V

Governments have a responsibility for the health of their people which can be fulfilled only by the provision of adequate health and social measures. A main social target of governments, international organizations and the whole world community in the coming decades should be the attainment by all peoples of the world by the year 2000 of a level of health that will permit them to lead a socially and economically productive life. Primary health care is the key to attaining this target as part of development in the spirit of social justice.

VI

Primary health care is essential health care based on practical, scientifically sound and socially acceptable methods and technology made universally accessible to individuals and families in the community through their full participation and at a cost that the community and country can afford to maintain at every stage of their development in the spirit of self-reliance and self-determination. It forms an integral part both of the country's health system, of which it is the central function and main focus, and of the overall social and economic development of the community. It is the first level of contact of individuals, the family and community with the national health system bringing health care as close as possible to where people live and work, and constitutes the first element of a continuing health care process.

VII

Primary health care:

1. reflects and evolves from the economic conditions and sociocultural and political characteristics of the country and its communities and is based on the application of the relevant results of social, biomedical and health services research and public health experience;

2. addresses the main health problems in the community, providing promotive, preventive, curative and rehabilitative services accordingly;

3. includes at least: education concerning prevailing health problems and the methods of preventing and controlling them; promotion of food supply and proper nutrition; an adequate supply of safe water and basic sanitation; maternal and child health care, including family planning; immunization against the major infectious diseases; prevention and control of locally endemic diseases; appropriate treatment of common

diseases and injuries; and provision of essential drugs;

4. involves, in addition to the health sector, all related sectors and aspects of national and community development, in particular agriculture, animal husbandry, food, industry, education, housing, public works, communications and other sectors; and demands the coordinated efforts of all those sectors;

5. requires and promotes maximum community and individual self-reliance and participation in the planning, organization, operation and control of primary health care, making fullest use of local, national and other available resources; and to this end develops through appropriate education the ability of communities to participate;

6. should be sustained by integrated, functional and mutually supportive referral systems, leading to the progressive improvement of comprehensive health care for all, and giving priority to those most in need;

7. relies, at local and referral levels, on health workers, including physicians, nurses, midwives, auxiliaries and community workers as applicable, as well as traditional practitioners as needed, suitably trained socially and technically to work as a health team and to respond to the expressed health needs of the community.

VIII

All governments should formulate national policies, strategies and plans of action to launch and sustain primary health care as part of a comprehensive national health system and in coordination with other sectors. To this end, it will be necessary to exercise political will, to mobilize the country's resources and to use available external resources rationally.

IX

All countries should cooperate in a spirit of partnership and service to ensure primary health care for all people since the attainment of health by people in any one country directly concerns and benefits every other country. In this context the joint WHO/ UNICEF report on primary health care constitutes a solid basis for the further development and operation of primary health care throughout the world.

X

An acceptable level of health for all the people of the world by the year 2000 can be attained through a fuller and better use of the world's resources, a considerable part of which is now spent on armaments and military conflicts. A genuine policy of independence, peace, détente and disarmament could and should release additional resources that could well be devoted to peaceful aims and in particular to the acceleration of social and economic development of which primary health care, as an essential part, should be allotted its proper share.

The International Conference on Primary Health Care calls for urgent and effective national and international action to develop and implement primary health care throughout the world and particularly in developing countries in a spirit of technical cooperation and in keeping with a New International Economic Order. It urges governments, WHO and UNICEF, and other international organizations, as well as multilateral and bilateral agencies, nongovernmental organizations, funding agencies, all health workers and the whole world community to support national and international commitment to primary health care and to channel increased technical and financial support to it, particularly in developing countries. The Conference calls on all the aforementioned to collaborate in introducing, developing and maintaining primary health care in accordance with the spirit and content of this Declaration.

Political Will: A Bridge Between Public Health Knowledge and Action

Lezine DA, Reed GA. Political will: a bridge between public health knowledge and action. *Am J Public Health* 2007;97:2010. Reprinted with permission of the American Public Health Association.

Most population-based public-health approaches that could prevent death and disability require social and political support to have a lasting effect. That support is often reflected in policy, the "laws, regulations, formal and informal rules and understandings that are adopted on a collective basis to guide individual and collective behavior."[1(p1207)] For example, policy initiatives contributed to the control of infectious diseases,[2] declines in smoking,[3] reductions in heart disease and stroke,[4] safer motor vehicles and highways,[5] and safer worksites.[6] We present a health policy model intended to harness social and political support (i.e., political will) to improve public health.

We propose a new model of the public health policy cycle: the Bridges from Knowledge to Action model. Many prevention initiatives require policy change to achieve broad implementation. Political will, society's commitment to support or alter prevention initiatives, is essential for securing the resources for policy change. We focus on the role of political will in developing and implementing public health policy that integrates scientific evidence and community participation. (*Am J Public Health.* 2007;97:2010-2013. doi:10.2105/AJPH.2007.113282)

METHODS

Richmond and Kotelchuck[7,8] identified 3 essential components for advancing public health policy: knowledge base, social strategy, and political will. Although many reports recognize the importance of a knowledge base and strategy for action, political will has garnered less attention.

Political will is "society's desire and commitment to support or modify old programs or to develop new programs. It may be viewed as the process of generating resources to carry out policies and programs."[8(p388)] Political will is based on "public understanding and support."[7(p451)] Here, *public* refers to both government leadership and the broader community.[9] Public support can influence public health outcomes when economic, social, and intellectual resources are committed to address an issue. The following model presents possibilities for applying political will to advance health policy.

RESULTS

The goal of the Bridges From Knowledge to Action model is to develop and implement public health policy on the basis of scientific evidence and community participation. We conceptualize the health policy process as a cycle that uses new information and ongoing public support to sustain preventive action. Each phase within the cycle of the Bridges from Knowledge to Action model attempts to integrate processes from previous public health frameworks (Table 1) with the 3 essential components[7-9] described earlier. We focus on the role of political will.

Gathering Information

The knowledge base about a public health issue can help guide policy formation, and political will expedites the development of a knowledge base (Table 2). The process is cyclical; community groups use data to convince policymakers to appropriate more resources for studies that might produce new data for community groups to use.

Preparing to Develop a Strategy

The groups concerned with an issue must develop a consensus about when the knowledge base is sufficient to develop a strategy for action. Although consensus building is difficult, several approaches foster the political will necessary to gather groups together and decide on appropriate actions (Table 2).

Drafting the Strategy

To design a comprehensive strategy, many stakeholders (e.g., basic and applied scientists, public health practitioners, community members) must collaborate to balance scientific evidence with the feasibility of potential interventions. Political will is applied to secure resources for the strategy process (Table 2).

Preparing for Action

With a strategy in hand, the goal is to prepare for sustained action by further developing political will. Again, community groups can work with scientists to assess and develop the political will for policy implementation (Table 2). Collaborative workgroups might consider using economic analysis,[18-20] community readiness assessment,[12] social marketing approaches,[21] environmental scans,[22,23] or implementation climate assessment.[13,24]

Taking Action

By first developing political will, communities might be able to implement appropriate goals from the strategy for a longer duration. Public officials and legislative bodies can adopt or renew initiatives, appropriate resources, and shift public opinion.[14,25] Later, the support of people who enact initiatives (e.g., public health practitioners, health providers) and the affected populations will determine implementation outcomes.[13] If all stakeholders are collaborating to address a health issue (Table 2), then the strategy is more likely to succeed.

Evaluation

After taking action, community-based experiences can be incorporated into the knowledge base for the next iteration of the cycle (Table 2). In addition to tracking health outcomes, ongoing evaluation could document process results such as growth of political will, levels of implementation, and policy change.[26–28]

DISCUSSION

Many efforts to create broad and sustained prevention initiatives will require policy change. The Bridges from Knowledge to Action model suggests that attention to specific phases in the development and implementation of public health policy might improve the chances of success. We argue that it is particularly important to devote time and attention to developing political will. Although political will is an "essential component" for advancing public health policy,[7-9] the concept has been understudied.

The Bridges from Knowledge to Action model and many applications of political will are based on reviews of previous literature and anecdotal experience but have yet to be tested. Although this is a preliminary model, it can contribute to the ongoing dialogue about bridging public health knowledge and action.

About the Authors

DeQuincy A. Lezine is with the Department of Psychiatry, University of Rochester School of Medicine, Rochester, NY. Gerald A. Reed is with the Suicide Prevention Action Network USA, Washington, DC.

Requests for reprints should be sent to DeQuincy A. Lezine, PhD, University of Rochester School of Medicine, Department of Psychiatry, 300 Crittenden Blvd, Box Psych, Rochester, NY 14642 (e-mail: dequincy_lezine@ urmc.rochester.edu).

This article was accepted May 25, 2007.

Contributors

Both authors jointly developed the concept and wrote and reviewed drafts of the article, and contributed to the final revision.

Table 1 Conceptual Frameworks Used to Develop and Implement Public Health Initiatives

Bridges From Knowledge to Action model	Phase 1: Gathering Information	Phase 1.5: Preparing to Develop a Strategy	Phase 2: Drafting the Strategy	Phase 2.5: Preparing for Action	Phase 3: Taking Action	Phase 3.5: Evaluation
(grouping)	Information	Strategy		Action		
Public health advocacy process[10]	Needs assessment	Initial mobilization	Prioritize needs; formal plan	Build capacity for action	Plan implementation	Tracking actions; evaluating effect
Community capacity and ecological assessment[11]	Local information; awareness	Collective efficacy	Concrete ideas; develop strategies	Develop leader support; costs vs benefits; resources	Training; events; policy change	Evaluation; recognition events; reports of progress
Community readiness[12]	(no awareness or denial)	(vague awareness)	(planning)	(preparation or initiation)	(stabilization or expansion)	(confirmation or professionalization)
Innovation implementation[13]	Innovation development; awareness	Awareness of innovations; select and adopt innovations; improve values fit		Implementation climate	Implementation effectiveness	Innovation effectiveness
Evidence-based policy development[14]	Health risks and intervention development	Prioritize intervention options; policy development		Policymaker and community	Policy enactment support; mobilizing coalitions; capacity	Evaluation loop
Diffusion of innovations[15]	Innovation development	Dissemination; diffusion; communication channels		Adoption; self-efficacy	Implementation and maintenance	
Organizational change/ organizational development[16]	Diagnosis; awareness of unsatisfied demands	Action planning; identify and evaluate alternative solutions	Action planning; adopt strategy; set policy	Process consultation; acquire and allocate resources	Intervention implementation; institutionalization	Evaluation
PRECEDE–PROCEED planning model[17]	Social, epidemiological, behavioral, environmental, educational, and organizational diagnosis		Administrative and policy diagnosis; selection of interventions; goals and measurable objectives	Community values; availability and allocation of resources	Implementation	Data collection; process, effect, and outcome evaluation

Table 2	Political Will in the Bridges from Knowledge to Action Model	
Bridges from knowledge to Action Model Phase	Primary Role of Political Will	Examples
Phase 1: Gathering Information	Apply political will to increase knowledge base	Legislatures request hearings on issue Policymakers request report on a health issue Government establishes a surveillance system Request increased research funding Community agrees to participate in research and dialogue about issue
Phase 1.5: Preparing to Develop a Strategy	Build political will to make an actionable strategy on the basis of scientific evidence	Identify influential "champions" for prevention Establish coalition or task force to address issue Use media interviews and opinion editorials to increase public awareness Hold public forums inviting citizen comment Lobby or testify on issue
Phase 2: Drafting the Strategy	Apply political will to craft the social strategy	Government and citizen groups join a coalition Identify leadership with conflict resolution skills, to facilitate participatory process Secure financial and social resources for process Policy entrepreneurs fit the strategy into political and economic context Groups take ownership and responsibility for strategy implementation
Phase 2.5: Preparing for Action	Assess and develop the political will necessary for implementation	Environmental scans and community analysis to identify needs, assets, and local opinion leaders (formal and informal) Assess community readiness and capacity Educate decisionmakers about the need for a long-term perspective on changing public health Preimplementation feedback from key stakeholders (target population, health professionals, public health practitioners)
Phase 3: Taking Action	Apply political will to implement plans	Cultivate interagency cooperation, community coalition, or advisory board Use media campaigns for public education and supporting prevention initiatives Citizens volunteer as peer providers or health educators Legislation or adoption of new policies and regulations Ongoing support by funding, training, and technical assistance
Phase 3.5: Evaluation	Develop political will for sustaining programs by using new knowledge	Community demand for accountability Disseminate information about process and outcome results in professional and lay outlets Funders request plans for sustainability Policymakers consider effect of recent policies and possible amendments

ACKNOWLEDGMENTS

DeQuincy A. Lezine was supported by the National Institute of Mental Health (grants T32MH020061 and P20MH071897).

The authors would like to thank Lucy Davidson, Gerald Weyrauch, Elsie Weyrauch, Yeates Conwell, and Kerry Knox for their critical review of and comments on earlier versions of the article.

Human Participant Protection
No institutional review board approval was required for this study because no human participants were involved.

● ● ● **References**

1. Schmid TL, Pratt M, Howze E. Policy as intervention: environmental and policy approaches to the prevention of cardiovascular disease. *Am J Public Health*. 1995;85:1207-1211.

2. Centers for Disease Control and Prevention. Achievements in public health, 1900-1999: control of infectious diseases. *MMWR Morb Mortal Wkly Rep*. 1999;48:621-629.

3. Centers for Disease Control and Prevention. Achievements in public health, 1900-1999: tobacco use—United States, 1900-1999 [published erratum appears in *MMWR Morb Mortal Wkly Rep*. 1999;48:1027]. *MMWR Morb Mortal Wkly Rep*. 1999;48:986-993.

4. Centers for Disease Control and Prevention. Achievements in public health, 1900-1999: decline in deaths from heart disease and stroke—United States, 1900-1999. *MMWR Morb Mortal Wkly Rep*. 1999;48:649-656.

5. Centers for Disease Control and Prevention. Achievements in public health, 1900-1999: motor-vehicle safety: a 20th century public health achievement [published erratum appears in *MMWR Morb Mortal Wkly Rep*. 1999;48:473]. *MMWR Morb Mortal Wkly Rep*. 1999;48:369-374.

6. Centers for Disease Control and Prevention. Achievements in public health, 1900-1999: improvements in workplace safety—United States, 1900-1999. *MMWR Morb Mortal Wkly Rep*. 1999;48:461-469.

7. Richmond JB, Kotelchuck M. Co-ordination and development of strategies and policy for public health promotion in the United States. In: Holland WW, Detels R, Knox G, eds. *Oxford Textbook of Public Health*. Oxford, England: Oxford Medical Publications; 1991:441-454.

8. Richmond JB, Kotelchuck M. Political influences: rethinking national heath policy. In: Mcquire C, Foley R, Gorr A, Richards R, eds. *Handbook of Health Professions Education*. San Francisco, Calif: Jossey-Bass Publishers; 1993:386-404.

9. Atwood K, Colditz GA, Kawachi I. From public health science to prevention policy: placing science in its social and political contexts. *Am J Public Health*. 1997;87:1603-1606.

10. Christoffel KK. Public health advocacy: process and product. *Am J Public Health*. 2000;90:722-726.

11. Goodman RM, Wandersman A, Chinman M, Imm P, Morrissey E. An ecological assessment of community-based interventions for prevention and health promotion: approaches to measuring community coalitions. *Am J Community Psychol*. 1996;24:33-61.

12. Edwards RW, Jumper-Thurman P, Plested BA, Oetting ER, Swanson L. Community readiness: research to practice. *J Community Psychol*. 2000;28:291-307.

13. Klein KJ, Sorra JS. The challenge of innovation implementation. *Acad of Manage Rev*. 1996;21:1055-1080.

14. Brownson RC, Newschaffer CJ, Ali-Abarghoui F. Policy research for disease prevention: challenges and practical recommendations. *Am J Public Health*. 1997; 87:735-739.

15. Oldenburg B, Hardcastle DM, Kok G. Diffusion of innovations. In: Glanz K, Lewis FM, Rimer BK, eds. *Health Behavior and Health Education: Theory, Research, and Practice*. 2nd ed. San Francisco, Calif: Jossey-Bass Publishers; 1997:270-286.

16. Goodman RM, Steckler A, Kegler MC. Mobilizing organizations for health enhancement. In: Glanz K, Lewis FM, Rimer BK, eds. *Health Behavior and Health Education: Theory, Research, and Practice*. 2nd ed. San Francisco, Calif: Jossey-Bass Publishers; 1997:287-312.

17. Gielen AC, McDonald EM. The PRECEDEPROCEED planning model. In: Glanz K, Lewis FM, Rimer BK, eds. *Health Behavior and Health Education: Theory, Research, and Practice*. 2nd ed. San Francisco, Calif: Jossey-Bass Publishers;1 997:359-387.

18. Ganiats TG. Prevention, policy, and paradox: what is the value of future health? *Am J Prev Med*. 1997;13:12-17.

19. Phillips KA, Hotlgrave DR. Using cost-effectiveness/ cost-benefit analysis to allocate health resources: a level playing field for prevention? *Am J Prev Med*. 1997;13:18-25.

20. Ramsey SD. Methods for reviewing economic evaluations of community preventive services: a cart without a horse? *Am J Prev Med*. 2000;18:15-17.

21. Lefebvre RC, Rochlin L. Social marketing. In: Glanz K, Lewis FM, Rimer BK, eds. *Health Behavior and Health Education: Theory, Research, and Practice*. 2nd ed. San Francisco, Calif: Jossey-Bass Publishers; 1997:384-402.

22. Choo CW. Environmental scanning as information seeking and organizational learning. *Inf Res* [serial online]. 2001;7(1). Available at: http://InformationR.net/ir/7-1/paper112.html. Accessed February 18, 2007.

23. Rowel R, Moore ND, Nowrojee S, Memiah P, Bronner Y. The utility of the environmental scan for public health practice: lessons from an urban pro-

gram to increase cancer screening. *J Natl Med Assoc.* 2005;97:527-534.

24. Cheadle A, Wagner E, Koepsell T, Kristal A, Patrick D. Environmental indicators: a tool for evaluating community-based health-promotion programs. *Am J Prev Med.* 1992;8:345-350.

25. Oliver TR. The politics of public health policy. *Annu Rev Public Health.* 2006;27:195-233.

26. Hancock T. The evolution, impact and significance of the healthy cities/healthy communities movement. *J Public Health Policy.* 1993;14:5-18.

27. Merzel C, D'Afflitti J. Reconsidering community-based health promotion: promise, performance, and potential. *Am J Public Health.* 2003;93:557-574.

28. Mittelmark MB, Hunt MK, Heath GW, Schmid TL. Realistic outcomes: lessons from community-based research and demonstration programs for the prevention of cardiovascular diseases. *J Public Health Policy.* 1993;14:437-462.

3

Improving the Effectiveness of Health Care and Public Health: A Multiscale Complex Systems Analysis

Source: Bar-Yam Y. Improving the effectiveness of health care and public health: a multiscale complex systems analysis. *Am J Public Health* 2006;96:459-66. Reprinted with permission of the American Public Health Association.

The U.S. health care system is struggling with a mismatch between the large, simple (low-information) financial flow and the complex (high-information) treatment of individual patients. Efforts to implement cost controls and industrial efficiency that are appropriate for repetitive tasks but not high-complexity tasks lead to poor quality of care.

Multiscale complex systems analysis suggests that an important step toward relieving this structural problem is a separation of responsibility for 2 distinct types of tasks: medical care of individual patients and prevention/population health. These distinct tasks require qualitatively different organizational structures. The current use of care providers and organizations for both purposes leads to compromises in organizational process that adversely affect the ability of health care organizations to provide either individual or prevention/population services.

Thus, the overall system can be dramatically improved by establishing 2 separate but linked systems with distinct organizational forms: (a) a high-efficiency system performing large-scale repetitive tasks such as screening tests, inoculations, and generic health care, and (b) a high-complexity system treating complex medical problems of individual patients. (*Am J Public Health.* 2006;96:459-466. doi:10.2105/ AJPH.2005. 064444)

The structure and processes of the existing U.S. health care system have been designed around the need to respond to the medical needs of a self-presenting individual. Widespread recognition of the importance of prevention and of population health[1-3] has led to efforts to charge the health care system to respond to these needs. There is, however, limited recognition that imposing on the same organization the need to respond to such radically different tasks leads to ineffectiveness and inefficiency. Instead, it should be understood that a distinct system (or subsystem) that is well adapted to the task of prevention and population health services can be much more effective and efficient at those tasks and, by serving these needs, help to solve many of the existing difficulties of the health care system. Thus, the imperatives of public health, which are concerned with prevention and population health, may be better served by developing organizations that serve these needs directly.

This is an organizational approach to the separation of tasks rather than an approach based on questions of public or private financing or delivery. A precise analysis distinguishes tasks that are numerous and repetitive (and thus "large scale") from those that are numerous and variable (and thus "fine scale" or "highly complex"). Distinct organizational structures are effective at these distinct types of tasks. Separating medical care for individual patients from preventive and population health services provides a first and important line of distinction between highly complex and large-scale health care services.

The concepts of scale and complexity can be used to analyze various aspects of organizational structure. A formal multi-scale analysis implies that for an organization to be effective, there must be a match between the scale and complexity of the functional capabilities of the organization and the scale and complexity of the tasks to be performed. My analysis implies that (1) the serial coupling of large-scale financial flows and complex medical decision-making is largely responsible for organizational turbulence and ineffectiveness in the health care system, and (2) development of separate organizational forms for tasks at different scales is an essential step toward resolving the structural problems of the health care system and will both relieve the financial and organizational turbulence of the health care system and lead to greater effectiveness of complex medical care and large-scale prevention and population health services.

STRUCTURE OF THE HEALTH CARE SYSTEM

Today, it is widely understood that the health care system suffers from low quality and high medical error rates.[4,5] Measures of the quality of care as a return on expenses[4] and the incidence of medical errors[5] depict a severely underperforming system despite the expansion of medical knowledge and the use of increasingly sophisticated technology and training.

Insight into the role of complexity and scale in the health care system can be gained by considering the role of insurance and the financial flows that exercise increasing control over the services provided. The development of health insurance and the trend toward managed care have affected the structure of the health care system in significant ways, separating the flow of money from the interaction between physician and patient. As is well known, the primary financial flow in health care consists of regular payments by employers (or, less often, individuals) to insurance companies, other health plans, or Medicare (or, through a variety of taxes, to Medicaid)—payments that are not directly dependent upon the actual services provided during the same time period. Practically speaking, the payment is often an electronic bank transfer once a month. Part of the money may be deducted from employee salaries, while the other part comes directly from the employer. Either way, the payment amounts are decided upon in advance and are the same from month to month until rate changes take place, typically on a yearly basis. With respect to the nature of the actual care provided, this sum is essentially featureless: large scale

and simple, having no information encoded into it about the services it will eventually fund. The insurance company, managed care organization, Medicare, or Medicaid divides this large-scale flow of money into smaller financial flows allocated to medical costs.[6]

Figure 1 represents the flow of information, services, and money in the existing health care system. Information and medical care are exchanged in the transactions between physicians and patients, whereas the flow of money is largely from employers to health care insurers and thence to health care provider systems and individual practitioners. The difficulties in imposing efficiency and improving quality of care have their origins in the structure of these flows.

MULTISCALE ANALYSIS

Using recent fundamental advances in complex systems research,[7,8] specifically multiscale analysis,[9,10] we can identify the functional effectiveness of a system by comparing the set of actions a system *can* perform at different scales with the same analysis of its designated tasks. Here, scale refers not to size but to the redundancy, coherence, or coordination of a task. Large-scale tasks involve multiple individuals working as a coordinated unit, or multiple individuals performing the same task (e.g., mass immunizations). In contrast, fine-scale tasks involve the attention of a number of individuals each performing

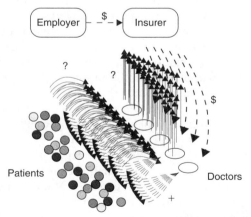

Note: Information (?) flows from patient to physician. Care and information (+) flow back to the patient. Financial flows ($) proceed from employers (employer) to insurers (insurer; private or public) and thence to care providers (doctors), who provide to insurers information (?) about the care being provided to individual patients (patients). Insurers receive lump sum payments, which are distributed in much smaller amounts to care providers for specific services.

Figure 1 The structure of the U.S. health care system today.

a unique task (e.g., one doctor diagnosing and treating an individual patient for a particular condition). To contrast two extreme possibilities, a system containing many individuals can be organized to perform a large number of unique (fine-scale) tasks, or a single largescale task. This illustrates a fundamental trade-off in organizational structure and function.

There are more subtle tradeoffs that can be achieved in the organization of a system and the nature of the tasks that can be performed. These trade-offs can be characterized by the "complexity profile" of a system: the complexity of possible actions as a function of scale. This mathematical construct specifies the number of distinct tasks that can be performed at each scale. It can serve as an analytic tool to provide an understanding of the role of organizational structure in organizational effectiveness.

Multiscale analysis and the complexity profile[9,10] decompose the capability of a system according to scale. They are an extension of information theory[11,12] designed to capture the relationship between the set of possible behaviors of a system on the one hand and its interdependencies and communication channels on the other. The subject of this analysis is not the same as information asymmetry, incentive analysis, or game theoretic analysis.[13-18] Instead, it is a new formalism that can characterize the function and desirability of organizational forms.[19-24]

In a sense, multiscale analysis is a generalization of statistical analysis that incorporates correlations of multiple variables rather than pairs of variables. Multiscale analysis considers the degree to which k-fold correlations between components of a system are present, where k ranges over the full set of values from 1 to N, the total number of components of the system. Correlations may be equivalently described by mutual information[11,12] (when multiple variables are correlated, the same information can be obtained from measurements of any of the variables), and the multiscale analysis quantifies the number of variables of the system from which the same information can be obtained. In effect, this determines how many components of the system are engaged in the same activity (i.e., are coupled in their actions).

As a simple example, consider N components that are coupled to each other in groups of q elements, and each group is tightly coupled so that only one action can be performed by each group so that the scale of action would be q, and the number of distinct actions at a particular time is the number of groups N/q. The complexity (or variety, or information), $C(k)$, as a function of scale, k, is defined as the effective number of actions that can be performed by a particular system at scale k or larger (more formally, it is defined as the logarithm of the number of possible states of the system). In the simple case just described, the number of actions is N/q for all values of k less than q and zero for larger values of k. Mathematical expressions that obtain $C(k)$ for systems with arbitrary probabilities of the set of states of the system can be found in the reference 9.

Figure 2 plots the response capabilities at each scale for the prototypical systems discussed in this section. Larger scales imply that many individuals are performing the same (or directly coupled) tasks, while fine scales imply independently acting individuals. Distinct curves illustrate the relationship between organizational forms and the tasks they can perform. A system in which individuals are independent, responding individually to distinct tasks (curve a), can perform many tasks, each of which draws the attention and efforts of one individual. This is quite different from a system in which all individuals are performing the same or coupled tasks (curve b) and which can only perform a single act in response to an environmental demand, whether the demand is for one or many individuals to perform that act. An organization that has various ways in which individuals coordinate activity into groups of different sizes can act at different scales to differing degrees in a manner that depends on the specific ways individuals are coordinated (curve c). The same analysis that describes the repetition of tasks among multiple individuals also can be used to describe the repetition of tasks over time, compared with its variation when tasks are distinct at different times.

A fundamental result of multiscale analysis[9] is that for a particular set of components, the area under the $C(k)$ curve is independent of organizational structure. This can be readily seen for the simple example earlier in this section, where the area is given by the product of the largest scale of action q—the width of the nonzero part of $C(k)$—and the number of such actions N/q—the height of the nonzero part of $C(k)$—which gives the structure-independent value N. The organizational structure therefore selects a trade-off in capability at different scales. This means that, fixing the number of individuals, an organization with the ability to respond at a larger scale is not able to respond at a fine scale, and vice versa.

Thus, different types of industries should be organized in different ways. For example, mass production is a large-scale task and an organization that is designed for mass production should be quite different from an organization that provides individualized care, as is generally understood to be the role of the existing health care system. Different parts of

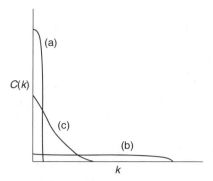

Note: Schematic illustration of complexity $C(k)$ (vertical axis) as a function of scale, k (horizontal axis). A system with the highest possible fine-scale complexity corresponds to a system with independent parts (curve a). When all parts act together, the system has the largest-scale behavior but the same low value of complexity at all scales (curve b). Complex systems have various possible scales of behavior, as illustrated by one example (curve c).

Figure 2 Complexity as a function of scale.

a system can also be analyzed in this way. Of particular relevance is an analysis of the financial flows of the health care system (larger scale) and the system of physicians that are performing the care (higher complexity at a finer scale of action).

TURBULENCE IN THE HEALTH CARE SYSTEM

This multiscale formalism can describe the coupling of a large-scale flow to a fine-scale flow, as is present in the financial flows of the health care system. An analogy to the phenomenon of fluid turbulence helps explain why this coupling, when used for health care, is ineffective. Our conclusions follow from the multiscale framework even without a fine-tuned, quantitative application because, in the language of multiscale formalism, the current situation is far from subtle. This should not be surprising, since the system failures are not subtle either. Turbulence occurs when a simple coherent flow is broken up into many smaller flows. It can be observed in the swirls and eddies in a fast-flowing river, or in the way a column of smoke rises from a camp fire. Although one can identify situations where turbulence will occur, it is very difficult to predict the resulting motions, which are irregular and can change rapidly.

In the health care system, we have an analogous situation. The large-scale financial flows that drive the system eventually have to be allocated as small payments to individual doctors treating individual patients for individual problems. The transition from large to fine scale is turbulent for financial flows just as it is for fluid motion. The idea that turbulence is

analogous to what occurs in the health care system will not surprise those who work in it, as they have experienced the turmoil over the past 20 to 30 years. The unpredictable rapid changes have not been in the relationships between doctors and patients, or in the relationships between employers and insurers (although sometimes they feel involved, at least as interested spectators); the main changes have been between insurers and the physicians. The growth of managed care, physician cooperatives, reporting and billing systems, and hospital mergers are all part of the interface between insurers and physicians. These changes in organizational structure, and particularly the consolidation (aggregation) of medical services, are a response to the flows that are disaggregating from large scale to fine scale. Many of the changes at the large scale that have occurred or are being considered to improve the system, including changes in the number of self-insured employers or degree of government involvement, do not significantly change the driving force or the structure of the turbulence.

What does this turbulence look like in human terms? The problem of large flows connected to highly complex flows is abstract, but the reality is quite easy to recognize. Eventually, the issue is related to the problem of controlling the flow, specifically: who is making the decisions that control the flow of money in this system? Increasingly, since the 1970s—or perhaps since the founding of Medicare in 1965—an effort has been made to control the flow at the large-scale end. Both government agencies and private insurers, frequently with the intervention of state and federal government organizations, negotiate the rate of flow of the money. They decide on changes in the rate from one year to the next.

Ultimately, the way these rate changes affect the system influences the character of the behavior and organization of the system.

Consider the effects of a simple action like changing the flow at the source, by increasing (or decreasing, although practically speaking the former is more likely) the amount by a certain percentage (e.g., 3%). The amount of increase reflects a decision about how much should be spent on health care. How does the health care industry implement this decision? At the opposite end of this flow, individual doctors treat individual patients with specific highly specialized care based on highly complex choices; their ultimate decisions are based on years of training and experience. The costs of individual treatments range widely—from tens of dollars to millions of dollars.

The consequence of this increase (so much and no more) must manifest itself in the decisions individual doctors make regarding the care of individual patients. They must decide what amount of time and attention to devote to a particular patient, as well as what medical tests and treatments are needed. Ultimately, these decisions must be based on tradeoffs in health and care that compare diverse treatments. Physicians faced with restrictions on expensive procedures and treatments, or incentives to lower their own expenses, have to decide whether the amount of time and effort devoted to a particular appointment or individual, or a particular diagnostic test or therapy, is "worth it"—that is, not only whether a successful outcome is likely but also whether it is cost-effective. Since this kind of judgment includes considerable uncertainties and is largely incompatible with their medical training, different organizations—and individual physicians—make this judgment in different ways, resulting in extremely unstable and variable quality of care overall.

What can those who want to control costs do? It is clearly impossible for those who "manage care" to make decisions about changes in care on an individual-by-individual basis in a way that will altogether correspond to the change in total flow specified from year to year. The only thing they can do is stipulate overall policies that act across the board. These policies typically restrict the set of options that are available for patients or physicians. Patients are restricted to certain physicians, hospitals, or other care providers. Physicians are restricted in what diagnostic tests or medications they can provide. The amount of time spent in hospitals might be limited, or incentives to reduce the amount of time or attention to individual patients could be implemented.

It is not surprising that limiting the options that a patient or physician can choose will have a negative impact on the quality of care that can be provided. Examples of detailed studies illustrating this principle include limitations on postpartum stays correlating with readmissions[25] and drug formularies (restrictive lists of prescription drugs) leading to increased costs and decreased quality of care.[26,27] The effectiveness of cost control strategies to achieve their objectives has been questioned on the basis of historical experience.[6] The more detailed studies challenge the idea that such actions actually save costs even when implemented according to plan, as indirect effects may ultimately lead to increased costs. Multiscale analysis provides a more general understanding that is based on the functional behaviors of complex systems, and this analysis does not require a specific mechanism in order to arrive at the same conclusion. Fundamentally, it is not a good idea to use across-the-board (large-scale) rules to try to control a highly complex system that is making careful (highly complex) decisions.

This discussion clarifies why recent efforts to increase efficiency have led to organizational turbulence and the current need for and difficulties with quality improvement. As the necessary treatment of individual patients has become progressively more complex and individualized, health maintenance organizations, managed care, Medicare, and Medicaid and other health insurance solutions have been acting in a way that makes the structure of health care more large scale and undifferentiated. Because of the complexity of the resulting allocation problem, unexpected "indirect" effects have resulted from these efficiency methods. According to the analysis presented here, these indirect effects arise from the reduction of fine-scale complexity of the organizations performing the tasks. When an organization becomes less effective overall at many different tasks, it is not necessarily less effective at the particular tasks or measures that management or regulators are focusing on. Indeed, one can expect that for those tasks or measures, the organization will improve, while for others its effectiveness will decline. This explains why problems appear as indirect effects.

Moreover, the more problems arise with quality, the greater are the efforts to regulate the actions of doctors, nurses, and other medical professionals. Uniform regulation, whether for cost containment or for quality, has the same effect on a system performing high-complexity tasks—diminishing overall effectiveness. It may seem that imposing uniform care in some context may be constructive; however, in the context of complex organizations, uniformity is in itself a limitation (exceptions do exist, but they must be understood within the framework of multiscale analysis rather than just assumed to exist). Since the resulting problems show up as indirect effects, it is difficult to discover their origins.

The problem is that the health care system is expected to behave efficiently with respect to financial flows at the large scale, but to exhibit the high complexity of individual patient care at the fine scale. If all patients were in roughly the same condition, requiring roughly the same treatment, an efficiency approach would be adequate, as this approach works well for streamlining low-complexity procedures. However, the medical treatment of patients is an extremely high-complexity fine-scale task. One-size-fits-all does not work in this case. Applying such methods can only result in poor-quality care. Although the current state of the health care system as presented here is grim, a fundamental approach to solving the problem does exist.

MATCHING SCALES

Multiscale analysis suggests that a key to organizational effectiveness is the matching of the scale of processes to the task. The current structure of the health care system inherently fails to do so. An important aspect of the solution to this problem is the recognition that some health care tasks are repeated many times and are thus large scale. Large-scale tasks *can* be performed with efficient processes, reducing expenses and improving the overall effectiveness of the system. Once we recognize which of the health care tasks are large scale, we can use them to improve the matching of tasks and financial flows. In this way, the current difficulties of financial control can also be relieved. The approach of identifying which tasks are large scale can be extended to identifying tasks that have intermediate scales. The development of organizations that perform tasks at various intermediate scales as appropriate would result in substantial additional efficiency. This article fouses on the largest-scale aspects of health care that should be addressed at a population level and are often identified with the field of public health.

How can we create a health care organization that is effective at large-scale tasks? The existing approach to health care organizations already has some separation of tasks, particularly in hospitals. Nevertheless, the patient-physician interaction continues to be used as an essential part of most health care tasks. The issue of a trade-off is manifest when we consider whether an individual (e.g., physician) is able to perform rapid repetitive tasks when they are needed and take enough time to perform careful complex tasks when these are needed. Is this possible, or does the speed become compromised in some cases while the need for time becomes compromised in others? Even more critical is the problem of coordination, since when there is a change in protocol of large-scale tasks, all individuals must change behavior. However, individuals must act independently for complex tasks. This creates a need for management structures that control the tasks being performed by the organization when it is necessary, but do not control tasks when it is not advisable. Thus, key demands on individuals and on organizational structures must be met.

We can contrast this to a strategy of separating the large-scale tasks from the fine-scale tasks, creating mostly separate organizations involving different people for doing them. Let's call the separated organizational structure a heterogeneous organization, and the single organizational structure for all tasks a homogeneous organization. We can think of the task requirements as a complexity profile, $C(k)$, of things to do, and the objective is to cover this area with the complexity profiles of individual people. Stacking individual profiles vertically means having them work independently, and stacking them horizontally means having them work in a coordinated way. In a heterogeneous organization, some individuals stack vertically and others stack horizontally, while in a homogeneous organization all individuals contribute equally to tasks at all scales (so that each individual has the profile $C(k)/N$).

The following observations support the choice of a heterogeneous organization: (1) The use of a homogeneous organization is a severe restriction on the types of organization that are possible. Heterogeneity opens many more possible organizational forms. (2) Not all organizations can achieve all forms of coordination. For example, it has been proven that hierarchical organizations cannot achieve high complexity at intermediate scales.[9] (3) Organizational structures that are designed for a restricted set of scales are both better known and more transparent than organizational structures requiring various levels of coordination of individuals at multiple scales. Thus, where tasks can be separated, a heterogeneous organization can be more easily understood, planned, and designed than a homogeneous structure. (4) Individuals may be quite different from each other in their individual scale and complexity trade-off. Thus, a person who intrinsically performs simple tasks repetitively is distinct from a person who intrinsically performs careful decision-making about high-complexity tasks. A heterogeneous organization allows different individuals to perform individually appropriate roles. (5) Organizational specialization (i.e., the formation of a heterogeneous organization) is a larger version of individual specialization, a well-established concept.

There are many examples of organizations, both biological and social, that separate distinct kinds of tasks and thus provide phenomenological support for these formal conclusions. Human physiology provides several illustrations: legs for walking are designed differently than hands that can manipulate finer-scale entities. The immune system is designed differently from muscles, the former for more complex finer-scale challenges than the latter. Similarly, the military is separated into a variety of forces: tank divisions, infantry, marines, and special forces for different trade-offs in scale and complexity. Even supermarkets have different sections for purchasing cheese—for example, the dairy and the deli, one for larger-scale and the other for more complex products.

These examples illustrate the fundamental principles revealed by the multiscale analysis and the theorem that implies a tradeoff in a system's effectiveness on the basis of organizational structure. They also show how, by creating distinct parts of the system to address different types of tasks, it is possible to effectively perform these different tasks.

SEPARATING LARGE-SCALE CARE FROM COMPLEX CARE

Intuitively, we can recognize that preventive care and population health services are frequently large-scale tasks. Indeed, we can consider the concept of large scale as defined by the multiscale analysis to provide a possible formal framework for understanding the domain of public health as an organizational imperative. The public health system works through many channels to achieve improved prevention and population health. Moreover, it also frequently serves as a palliative to the failings of the health care system by providing health care services. Still, one of the main channels for action is the health care system. The analysis presented here suggests that a public health system that promotes private organizations or publicly supported organizations (or both) that are effective at large-scale prevention and population care will be more effective in the long term.

The role of such organizations should include performance of a variety of tasks that are intrinsically large scale. In health care, these include wellness services (such as nutrition programs), the management of some widespread chronic problems, prenatal care, the treatment of common minor health issues (allergies, stress, the common cold), and preventive procedures (such as immunizations and screening through diagnostic tests). Many of these services can be made highly efficient when performed on populations, as they do not require decision-making on an individual basis. They can be separated from those aspects of health care that require decision-making on an individual basis. While the general principle is clear, the specific services to be separated should be determined by a more detailed quantitative analysis of complexity and scale as well as pilot programs that are properly focused on the issue of efficiency and effectiveness as articulated by the analysis. The degree of separation may also be explored. Some solutions might place prevention and population services as divisions or units within health care organizations, and others might have them associated with other types of organizations, such as pharmacies and supermarkets, that have more experience with efficient services. While the separation could also be done through government delivery, this is not necessary even if government oversight is desirable.

The high-efficiency prevention and population care system pictured in Figure 3 would function in some ways analogously to a traditional mass production factory model, or a mass market service organization like a fast food provider. There are ample precedents for such activities in health care in the United States and internationally, from historical and current public vaccination programs[28,29] to modern supermarket delivery[30,31] and mass screening programs.[32] Such programs administer vaccinations and diagnostic tests on groups rather than through individual appointment. The purpose is to ensure a high level of health in the population and to identify those who will need individual medical attention. Exceptions are referred to the medical system. The objective is large-scale efficiency, but once a problem is identified, individual attention can be personal and effective.

Separating large-scale tasks from complex tasks enables efficient and effective organizations to be formed around these distinct tasks. A system for population health can be made efficient on a large scale. A system designed for the complexities of individual medical care must be error free in individual tasks. Separating large-scale "prevention and population care" from complex "individualized care" relieves physicians of tasks that can be addressed with a much higher efficiency, enabling them to focus their

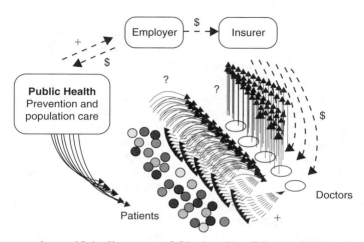

Note: The proposed new public health component (left box) provides efficient population-based care (+) to its customers, including employers (as shown by the upper left arrows), private insurers, government agencies, or individuals (similar to high-efficiency fast food and other mass market products or services); arrows are not shown for the latter cases. Moreover, it refers (gray arrows) those who need individualized care to the other part of the healthcare system (with interactions and symbols as in Figure 1) that is focused on individualized care.

Figure 3 A proposed structure for a new health care system.

attention on the complex tasks for which they are uniquely trained. Overall, this enables the system to be more efficient as well as more effective.

The idea of separate systems reasonably evokes concerns about reciprocal communication. Moreover, the need for communication often suggests the adoption of centralized databases, which raises concerns over privacy. Without engaging in a full discussion, I can suggest at least one potential solution: having individuals carry personal health information with them in portable storage media such as memory cards, which are a simple and relatively inexpensive technology.

The development of an efficient system for prevention and population health also would help to fundamentally address many of the other problems with the health care system. Highly efficient services would make such care much more widely available, with the potential of radically reducing disparities. Perhaps even more important, the fundamental role of prevention and population health in reducing the need for medical care (which is what prevention is about) could be realized. The benefits of the "virtuous cycle" of prevention—which reduces the costs of health care and frees resources for more careful medical care where it is needed, as well as for more preventive and population care—is the converse of the current "vicious cycle" of reduced prevention—which leads to the need for more medical care and the availability of fewer resources for each individual

that requires care. This virtuous cycle—along with the intrinsic value of improved health—is recognized as the reason prevention is needed, but it can only be realized when prevention is performed efficiently and effectively.

The principle of separation of tasks at different scales can be applied also to many other aspects of health care. For example, some surgical procedures may be performed as efficient mass production processes if there are many individuals with similar conditions requiring similar procedures. This may be true even if the decision to perform the surgery is highly complex. Other forms of surgery are clearly highly complex. Such examples abound within the health care system. Understanding the concepts of scale and complexity and how to apply them to specific tasks may be helpful in determining the details of organizational structures. A more detailed discussion is beyond the scope of this article.

The development of a highly efficient system for administering screening tests may also broaden their utility, making some that are not cost-effective become so through economy of scale. Moreover, more frequent testing may allay some of the concerns about false positives. Frequent testing allows the tracking of conditions over time, which provides greater certainty in diagnosis and care. Finally, high-efficiency processes, when widely applied, increase dramatically the availability of data that can improve knowledge of how to use this information.

CONCLUSIONS

A multiscale analysis of information flow in the health care system demonstrates that efforts to lower costs through managed care must lead to ineffectiveness, as is manifest in medical errors and low quality of care. Moreover, while there has been significant debate about whether the payer system should be public or private, this dichotomy does not address the essential failings of the system, and either choice (public or private) can be well or poorly executed.

A public health system should recognize key distinctions between individual and population care, and develop systems that are well designed for delivering distinct types of services. The need for increased investment in prevention and population-based services must be married to a recognition of the organizational needs for such tasks. Among the changes in the health care system that can contribute to improvement is a separation of complex tasks from large-scale tasks. The current health care system is an individualized system, and even when it provides care relevant to populations it typically provides them through a one-to-one physician-patient model. Individualized care should be entrusted to a fine-scale, individual-care medical system, while a distinct system should be created for large-scale and efficient prevention and population health programs.

With such a separation, we will no longer expect one organizational structure to provide both financially efficient population and preventative care that can be performed in a repetitive way and complex medical care that requires careful decision making in each case. Attempts by the same organization to perform both will create conflict between the short-term response to immediate needs of individual patients and the long-term benefits of prevention and population care. Just as having physicians doing the laundry at hospitals would be ineffective and inefficient, such a dual-purpose system can only be expected to provide mediocre response to both tasks. An efficient prevention and population-based care delivery system will improve this aspect of care and health care as a whole by helping to relieve the stresses on care provided to individuals.

A system that delivers effective population-based care can demonstrate clearly the importance of prevention and population care in the overall health care system. In this context, the traditional expectations of the benefit of prevention can be realized. The well-understood cost-effectiveness of prevention in the long term implies that even a small proportion of the overall costs, though not small in absolute terms, devoted to public health can enable the larger proportion, which is devoted to individual medical care, to be allocated to needed individual services that are not provided by the current overburdened system. The result is a relief of financial pressure, a better balance between prevention/population care and individualized medical care, and systems that are separately effective at both, leading ultimately to a healthier population.

A full discussion of specific practical transitional steps to achieve such a system is beyond the scope of this article. However, it should be understood that the benefit of a multiscale understanding of the health care system is the recognition that changes in organization can be of widespread benefit, and this understanding should promote the adoption of change. Specifically, a wide range of players should recognize that changes that promote adoption of a prevention- and population-based care system will serve their goals and interests.

A more complete solution for the problems of the health care system would also require other concepts essential to the development of highly complex organizational structures. These concepts, which can be obtained from multiscale analysis, include (1) recognition of the limitations of centralized control in the management of complex medical care; (2) recognition of both the possible constructive role and the limitations of automation in improving health care; (3) analysis of structures of information flow associated with medical errors, which may suggest structures that eliminate medical errors; and (4) the understanding of how to induce organizational change and improvement in highly complex organizations for high-complexity medical tasks, including the role of competition and cooperation in systems that may or may not be market driven. Such issues are relevant to the role of payment and reward systems. A discussion of these ideas can be found elsewhere.[10]

About the Author

The author is with the New England Complex Systems Institute, Cambridge, Mass.

Requests for reprints should be sent to Yaneer Bar-Yam, PhD, New England Complex Systems Institute, Cambridge, MA 02138 (e-mail: yaneer@necsi.org).

This article was accepted August 8, 2005.

ACKNOWLEDGMENTS
This work was supported in part by the Centers for Medicare and Medicaid Services and the Centers for Disease Control and Prevention.

Transcription and editing of early versions of the manuscript were performed by Chitra Ramalingam and Laurie Burlingame. Acknowledgments are due to my students and colleagues who read and commented on previous versions. In particular, I thank Michael Ganz for comments on the manuscript and the referees for helpful remarks.

Human Participant Protection
No protocol approval was needed for this study.

● ● ● References

1. Institute of Medicine. *The Future of Public Health.* Washington, DC: National Academies Press; 1989.

2. Institute of Medicine. *Future of the Public's Health in the 21st Century.* Washington, DC: National Academies Press; 2003.

3. Declaration of Alma-Ata. International Conference on Primary Health Care, Alma-Ata, USSR. Geneva, Switzerland: World Health Organization;1978.

4. *World Health Report 2000.* Geneva, Switzerland: World Health Organization; 2001.

5. Institute of Medicine. Crossing the Quality Chasm: A New Health System for the Twenty-First Century. Washington, DC: National Academy Press; 2001.

6. Altman D, Levitt L. The sad story of health care cost containment as told in one chart. *Health Aff.* January 23, 2003. Available at: http://content. healthaffairs.org/cgi/content/full/hlthaff. w2.83v1/DC1. Accessed January 25, 2006.

7. Bar-Yam Y. *Dynamics of Complex Systems.* Cambridge, Mass: Perseus Press; 1997.

8. Bar-Yam Y. General features of complex systems. In: Keil LD, ed. *Knowledge Management, Organizational Intelligence and Learning, and Complexity. Encyclopedia of Life Support Systems* [online publication]. Oxford, England: UNESCO EOLSS Publishers; 2002. Available at: http://www. eolss.net. Accessed January 26, 2006.

9. Bar-Yam Y. Multiscale variety in complex systems. *Complexity.* 2004;9:37-45.

10. Bar-Yam Y. Making Things Work: Solving Complex Problems in a Complex World. Cambridge, Mass: NECSI Knowledge Press; 2005.

11. Shannon CE. A mathematical theory of communication. In: Shannon CE, Weaver W. *The Mathematical Theory of Communication.* Urbana: University of Illinois Press; 1963:29-125.

12. Cover TM, Thomas JA. *Elements of Information Theory.* New York, NY: Wiley; 1991.

13. Arrow KJ. Uncertainty and the welfare economics of medical care. *Am Econ Rev.* 1963;53:941-969.

14. Rothschild M, Stiglitz J. Equilibrium in competitive insurance markets: an essay on the economics of imperfect information. *Q J Econ.* 1976;90:629-650.

15. Akerlof G. The market for lemons: qualitative uncertainty and the market mechanism. *Q J Econ.* 1970;84:488-500.

16. Ma CA. Health care payment systems: cost and quality incentives. *J Econ Manage Strategy.* 1994;3:93-112.

17. Ellis RP. Creaming, skimping, and dumping: provider competition on the intensive and extensive margins. *J Health Econ.* 1998;17:537-555.

18. Glazer J, McGuire TG. Optimal risk adjustment in markets with adverse selection: an application to managed care. *Am Econ Rev.* 2000;90:1055-1071.

19. March JG, Simon HA. *Organizations.* 2nd ed. New York, NY: John Wiley & Sons; 1958.

20. Galbraith J. *Designing Complex Organizations.* Reading, Mass: Addison-Wesley; 1973.

21. Mintzberg H. *The Structuring of Organizations.* Englewood Cliffs, NJ: Prentice-Hall; 1979.

22. Weick K. *The Social Psychology of Organizing.* 2nd ed. New York, NY: McGraw-Hill; 1979.

23. Robbins SP. *Organization Theory.* 3rd ed. Englewood Cliffs, NJ: Prentice-Hall; 1990.

24. Daft RL. *Organization Theory and Design.* 8th ed. Cincinnati, Ohio: South-Western; 2004.

25. Malkin JD, Broder MS, Keeler E. Do longer postpartum stays reduce newborn readmissions? Analysis using instrumental variables. *Health Serv Res.* 2000;35:1071-1091.

26. Horn SD, Sharkey PD, Tracy DM, Horn CE, James B, Goodwin F. Intended and unintended consequences of HMO cost-containment strategies: results from the Managed Care Outcomes Project. *Am J Manag Care.* 1996;2:253-264.

27. Horn SD, Sharkey PD, Phillips- Harris C. Formulary limitations and the elderly: results from the Managed Care Outcomes Project. *Am J Manag Care.* 1998;4:1104-1113.

28. Plotkin SA, Orenstein WO, eds. *Vaccines.* 3rd ed. Philadelphia, Pa: WB Saunders; 1999:112.

29. Bland J, Clements J. Protecting the world's children: the story of WHO's immunization programme. *World Health Forum.* 1998;19:162-173.

30. Weitzel KW, Goode JV. Implementation of a pharmacy-based immunization program in a supermarket chain. *J Am Pharm Assoc (Wash).* 2000;40:252-256.

31. Glezen WP, Mostow SR, Schaffner W. The revolution in influenza care. *Patient Care.* 2000;34:22-24.

32. Sone S, Takashima S, Li F, et al. Mass screening for lung cancer with mobile spiral computed tomography scanner. *Lancet.* 1998;351:1242-1245.

4

Public Health Services and Cost-Effectiveness Analysis

Source: Banta HD, de Wit GA. Public health services and cost-effectiveness analysis. Annu Rev Public Health 2008;29:383-97.

INTRODUCTION

The rationale for cost-effectiveness analysis is simple: Resources are always limited. Not everything worth doing can be done, and not everything that can be done is worth doing. This argument applies to every sector of society, including health care. Choices must be made. Advocates of cost-effectiveness analysis say that economic studies are essential to making rational choices. However, what is today's reality? How has cost-effectiveness analysis developed in relation to public health? What is needed for the future?

In the 2007 issue of the *Annual Review of Public Health*, Grosse et al.[35] described the status quo of the use of cost-effectiveness analysis in public health. Agreeing with their general assessment, we here examine the use of cost-effectiveness analysis in the planning and execution of public health activities. Public health is the art and science of preventing disease, prolonging life, and promoting health through organized community efforts. It is made up of systematic efforts to identify health needs and to organize comprehensive health services within a well-defined population base.[2] Thus, planning of and priority setting between clinical services are integral

parts of public health. An important area where economic evaluation seems to be playing a major role is in insurance coverage decisions, especially those concerning pharmaceutical coverage. We therefore pay considerable attention to this evolving field of inquiry and policy.

THE BODY OF ECONOMIC RESEARCH RELATED TO PUBLIC HEALTH

The Health Economics Evaluations Database had more than 34,000 references in early 2007.[38] The National Health Service (NHS) economic evaluation database adds ,70 studies per month.[31] However, Goldsmith et al.[33] searched for economic studies on 290 recommended preventive interventions and found no study mentioned in 159 of these interventions. We then considered the presence of high-quality studies. Clear standards have been developed by a number of groups on the basis of good analysis practice.[21,32] A vast literature lies behind this information. However, we pay only limited attention to questions of methods because this is not the theme of our review.

Sonnad et al.[56] systematically reviewed the literature published from 1976 to 2001. Using as inclusion criteria the guidelines of the Panel on Cost-Effectiveness Analysis in Health and Medicine[32] for cost-utility analyses, they found only 539 studies that adhered to these guidelines. If we consider the annual number of 10,000 new randomized controlled trials (RCTs) that are added to the Cochrane Collaboration database, which contains as many as 1 million RCTs, we could conclude that economic evaluation is of minor importance.[8] The relatively small number of studies that incorporate high-quality cost-effectiveness analyses may explain the relative lack of use of such cost-effectiveness analyses in the health care sector. Furthermore, economic studies are carried out in only a few countries. For example, in Latin America, Iglesias et al.[40] found few such studies and no tradition for relying on economic evidence in decision making. In addition, economic evaluations have been conducted and used in only some, certainly not all, Western countries.

Hence, high-quality economic evaluation studies are relatively rare. But defining the minimum content of a good-quality study remains under debate because key methodological problems have not been definitively solved and guidelines may differ between countries. According to Goddard et al.,[31] key methodologic problems in economic evaluation include the following:

- Choice of summary measures of health outcome [quality-adjusted life year (QALY), disability-adjusted life year (DALY), healthy years equivalent (HYE)]
- Ability of summary measures to capture other benefits important to patients and the public
- Noncomparability of the values elicited with the different health state value elicitation instruments
- Generalizability of the studies beyond the study setting or country
- Choice of target populations receiving the intervention
- Accounting for uncertainty in measuring costs and outcomes
- Inability to account for the opportunity costs of pricey new interventions
- The need to consider portfolios of programs rather than individual technologies

Implementing research evidence into public health practice also raises additional problems.

A key problem is that studies are mostly carried out at the local or, sometimes, national level. Context becomes an issue when attempting to interpret these studies in another setting. The essence of the argument is that propositions cannot simply be stated in terms of what works as measured by means of one particular scientific standard. "For whom" and "in which circumstances" must also be considered to evaluate effectiveness. As such, Leichter[43] has stressed the importance of contextual factors. Without considering a specific situation's context, determining the applicability and generalizability of research evidence may be impossible. Cost-effectiveness studies are not often generalizable for many reasons, including differences in availability of health care resources, clinical practice patterns, and relative prices. Drummond & Pang[20] and Drummond et al.[19] have given some suggestions for improving generalizability so that studies could be used away from the site of origin.

The World Health Organization (WHO) has attacked this problem head on by suggesting "generalized cost-effectiveness analysis" as a course of action.[26] In brief, WHO proposes that the costs and benefits of a set of related interventions should be evaluated with respect to a "null set" of interventions (i.e., doing nothing), and the results should be presented in a single league table as the first step in policy analysis. WHO acknowledges that this method can be useful only within a set of similar countries or regions: "Clearly, global comparisons of the cost-effectiveness of interventions with respect to the null set, even if input costs and effectiveness parameters are adjusted, are unlikely to be useful."[26] Whether such a method can ever be useful remains to be determined.

PRIORITY SETTING

Priority setting addresses the problems of high demands for health care despite limited resources allocated for this purpose.[31,36] As Goddard et al.[31] observe, "Priority setting seeks to address these problems by proposing rules to decide which groups of patients or disease areas should secure favored access to limited health care resources" (p. 79). Priority setting, then, should address relative efficiency: how to buy as much health care as possible for the monetary unit. An economic approach to priority setting is often proposed by economists and others. In some areas of health care, for example, new vaccines for a national immunization program or a screening procedure for nationwide screening, formal cost-effectiveness studies play a role in decision making, but even then, coseffectiveness is never used as the main issue in policy making. Alas, policy makers seldom take cost-effectiveness considerations into account when making decisions,[14,23,36,53,54] as discussed below.

Baltussen et al.[1] have proposed to address these problems by a "shift away from present economic evaluation activities . . . toward a more systematic approach to economic evaluation research" (p. 532). They consider the main problem to be the lack of central guidance in present economic evaluation research, which results in a plethora of studies of individual interventions. They further propose the joint evaluation of new and existing preventive and curative intervention portfolios, e.g., for one specific disease area in one single exercise. However, this proposal, which could lead to potentially more useful studies, overlooks many of the problems raised by Goddard, as mentioned above. But even more critically, there is no single body, nor any potential body, that could steer all economic studies, not even within one country. Therefore, the most realistic option is to continue to encourage the use of guidelines to systematize evaluation of interventions while debating issues such as the outcome measures used in cost-effectiveness analysis.

PREVENTIVE SERVICES

As in most other areas of public health, the cost-effectiveness of preventive services is often unknown. As the U.S. Prevention Task Force observed,[61]

> Cost-effectiveness studies are currently available on many health care services. . . . A much larger group of services remains for which cost-effectiveness is not yet established. Information on costs and outcomes is inadequate for many interventions. For others, the cost-effectiveness analyses have not been done, or their quality is insufficient to provide conclusive evidence. Finally, the variation in cost-effectiveness methodology often makes it difficult to take costeffectiveness results at face value. (p. xci)

Similar comments can be found in reports from the United Kingdom[50,51] and Canada,[33] which note the disappointing lack of comparable studies of cost-effectiveness of preventive interventions.

In 2002, a group funded by the European Commission systematically reviewed the status of the literature of prevention cost-effectiveness.[2] Taking into account the two above-mentioned reports as well as others, the group identified more than 70 effective prevention interventions. Upon further review of the literature on the cost-effectiveness of these interventions, researchers found relatively little reliable economic evidence.

An interesting approach to this issue was presented by a group associated with the U.S. Prevention Task Force.[9,44,45] These investigators also pointed to the small number of high-quality cost-effectiveness analyses. The group ranked the priority of 30 interventions using burden of disease (preventable disease burden) and level of cost-effectiveness in the U.S. population. The following list shows the highest ranked services in order in 2001[45]:

1. Providing tobacco cessation counseling in adults
2. Screening older adults for undetected vision impairments
3. Offering adolescents an antitobacco message or advice to quit
4. Counseling adolescents on alcohol and drug abstinence
5. Screening adults for colorectal cancer
6. Screening young women for chlamydial infection
7. Screening adults for problem drinking
8. Vaccinating older adults against pneumococcal disease

The study was updated in 2006,[44] at which point the three highest ranking services were addressing aspirin use with high-risk adults, immunizing children, and tobacco use screening and brief intervention. Currently in the United States, multiple high-ranking services are not often used: These include smoking and tobacco interventions, colorectal cancer screening, immunization of adults against pneumococcal disease, and the screening of women for *Chlamydia* infection.

Of the many services offered, childhood immunization has been shown to be not only cost effective, but also cost saving. Despite such findings, childhood immunization is not fully implemented in several countries, including the United States and the United Kingdom. However, there is a difference between the classical childhood vaccines, such as those against diphtheria, tetanus, and pertussis, and the more recently launched, highly technological vaccines, such as varicella vaccine, rotavirus vaccine, and human papillomavirus vaccine. These modern vaccines are often very costly, which may severely impact the budgets of national immunization plans. This situation may stimulate the early conduct of economic evaluation studies in the field of newly developed vaccines. Indeed, vaccines have been a rapidly growing area of economic evaluation research. But are the study results used by those making decisions regarding the implementaton of vaccines? This was the focus of an interesting study regarding the decision making for the meningococcal group C vaccine in 21 different developed countries.[62] Only 6 of those 21 countries had published economic evaluations, and in 4 countries, the study outcomes offered guidance about the most efficient way to add meningococcal vaccine to the routine infant immunization schedule. In 3 countries, this guidance was actually used by decision makers. Most countries made their decisions whether to implement the meningococcal vaccine without economic evidence.

As identified by Welte et al.[62] the Netherlands was one of the countries that used economic evidence to design the most appropriate vaccination strategy for meningococcal group C disease. However, also in the Netherlands, no formal assessment system to support informed decision making and prioritization was available until recently, when the Health Council launched such a system.[37] The Health Council defined seven criteria for how to provide a certain form of vaccination for a given group, and these seven criteria must all be met before a new vaccine can be introduced into the national immunization program. One of these criteria is cost-effectiveness: "The ratio between the cost of vaccination and the associated health benefit compares favourably to the cost-benefit ratio associated with other means of reducing the relevant disease burden."[37,p25] In the Netherlands, (preventive) interventions with a cost-effectiveness ratio below £20,000 per QALY are generally perceived to be cost effective. However, the critera as defined above require the availability of cost-effectiveness analyses of other possible investments for a specific health problem because cost-effectiveness should not be assessed in relation to this absolute threshold but rather to alternative investments for the same health problem. As noted above, this information is rarely available.

Screening is a popular strategy in preventive services. In 1998, the National Screening Committee of the United Kingdom carried out a national inventory, identifying more than 300 screening programs in use and in development.[17] The key issue identified by the Committee was the need to assure the effectiveness of screening. The U.S. Prevention Task Force has reviewed many screening methods on the basis of effectiveness and has recommended relatively few methods for general use, including mammography screening, Pap screening for cervical cancer, and fecal occult blood test for colon cancer. Then in 2001, the HTA database[52] was examined to characterize the reports on prevention in terms of cost-effectiveness.[2] Of the 753 reports, 156 addressed prevention. These reports included 18 on screening in general, 38 on cancer screening, and 6 on prenatal screening. The quality of the economic evidence in these cases was generally poor.

COVERAGE OF SERVICES

Coverage refers to the benefits available to eligible beneficiaries or the promise by a third party to pay for all or a portion of the expenses incurred for specified health care services.[15] The main philosophy of coverage states that decisions to include an intervention in a health benefits package should be based on sound information about needs, effectiveness, safety, and costs. Although this idea can be applied to all types of health care systems, it has been most visible in systems based on social insurance, where payment can be withheld for defined services (or technologies) or levels of payment increased or decreased to encourage or discourage certain technologies.

The issue of health benefits coverage has gained increasing attention during the past 30 years. Historically, insurance covered services provided by physicians without question. However, rising costs of care, limited resources, and evidence of overuse and inappropriate use of health care technology have led to increasing attempts to limit services on the basis of health benefits and cost-effectiveness.[15] This process is usually performed through HTA.[15]

One of the most widely used methods is to pay only for care that has been proven successful and cost effective and not to pay for experimental and unproven interventions. One important result of this method is the delay of decisions until evidence is available. Simply put, insurance programs and other payers do not cover costs for new interventions until they are proven by clinical research. Once proven, these interventions can be entered into the standard benefit package of care resulting in coverage. However, those interventions already reimbursed have not been assessed using stricter criteria, implying that large parts of the insurance package lack evidence of efficacy and cost-effectiveness.

Efforts to base coverage decisions on assessment were begun by the national Blue Cross/Blue Shield Organization (BC/BS) in the United States in the mid-1970s and were quickly picked up by the national Medicare program, which covers care for the elderly.[29] The first motion was to stop covering procedures, for instance some diagnostic tests, that did not seem to provide any benefit, on the basis of simple efficacy studies. Later, BC/BS also began to evaluate new technologies for coverage. BC/BS established a Technology Evaluation Center, in conjunction with the Kaiser health plan, to carry out these evaluations.[3,4,29] Many organizations in the United States followed the lead of BC/BS, including the Medicare program,[60] health maintenance organizations, and private insurance companies.[59] Analyzing the U.S. experience, as expressed in a consensus meeting of insurers, Eddy[24,25] observed that it was appropriate for a health plan to try to limit services provided. However, he added, clear and simple language was key so that both parties would know their rights and responsibilities. He stated that using such terms as "necessary," "appropriate," and "investigational" was insufficient.

The most important point here is that coverage language must be precise and must be based on clear standards, such as proven effectiveness. This point is particularly important because a number of countries have vague language in their health insurance laws, which makes establishing sound coverage practices challenging. For example, U.S. Medicare policy refers to covered treatments as "reasonable and necessary." This wording has hampered development of coverage policies in the United States.[30,59] The Netherlands uses similar language in its health insurance act. In Switzerland, the law was changed in 1999 to put a basis of coverage on criteria such as "effectiveness" and "cost-effectiveness."

These ideas concerning coverage spread to Europe in the 1980s and 1990s. For example, a much-publicized report in the Netherlands by the Dunning Committee in 1991 examined the question of how to make difficult choices in health care.[22] The committee acknowledged serious problems regarding the use of ineffectual and cost-ineffective technologies and overuse of effective technologies in the Dutch health care system. As part of health care reforms, the committee proposed that a basic benefit package for the population be defined using formal studies of efficacy and cost-effectiveness. The Dutch public health insurance system gradually implemented some of the recommendations, especially the recommendation to base its pharmaceutical coverage decisions on formal cost-effectiveness studies. The Dutch government also funds a considerable number of prospective clinical trials through ZonMw, the Netherlands Organization for Health Research and Development. These prospective trials usually include a cost-effectiveness component used mainly to guide coverage decisions. However, the recommendations of the Dunning Committee concerning cost-effectiveness have not been fully implemented in part because of the relative paucity of such studies outside the area of pharmaceuticals.

This basic decision has been mimicked in many other countries. The literature on these policies is not extensive, but it is known that most members of the European Union, including new members such as Poland and Hungary, have tried and are trying to implement such steps in their health care systems. In other countries such as Argentina and Malaysia, a similar course is being followed. Nonetheless, formal cost-effectiveness studies have played only a limited role in these moves, except in the area of pharmaceuticals. The United Kingdom, with its NICE program, is an exception: Most NICE evaluations examine cost-effectiveness in some way (see below).

COVERAGE AND PHARMACEUTICALS

The question of pharmaceutical coverage is complex and must take into account the execution of studies, the sources of information, including pharmaceutical regulation, and the different actions taken by governments to control pharmaceutical use and costs. We summarize the situation here, whereas Kanovos[42] and Mossialos et al.[47] give a comprehensive overview of the European position.

No European regulations or directives address provision of health care in general or pharmaceutical coverage specifically. Many issues have encouraged European countries to make more explicit decisions concerning pharmaceutical coverage:

1. The visibility and cost of pharmaceuticals, which make up ~15% of health care expenditures in EU countries

2. Ongoing problems of efficacy and safety with many drugs

3. Extensive evidence of overuse and misuse of pharmaceuticals

4. The relative ease of identifying and assessing pharmaceuticals, compared with many other areas of health technology

Therefore, coverage decisions concerning pharmaceuticals have been made explicit in nearly all member states of the European Union. This area is considered by the European Commission to fall within the competence of each member state. Pharmaceuticals can be placed on a positive list, a negative list, or both. The European court has explicitly stated that pharmaceuticals on negative lists, although not to be reimbursed in particular member states, are legal because member states have a legitimate interest to control their health budgets. However, evolving European law requires that the basis for such decisions must be transparent, objective, and verifiable.

Member states of the European Union also retain substantial autonomy in the areas of pricing, reimbursement, and user charges. Because all member states wish to control pharmaceutical expenditure, a variety of mechanisms have been adopted. Among these mechanisms is cost-sharing (copayments), which is intended to influence patients' behavior. Attempts to influence physicians' behavior include using positive and negative lists, encouraging generic prescriptions, monitoring doctors' prescribing patterns, and giving budgets to each doctor. Finally, regulating or influencing prices, for instance with a reference-pricing system, operates at the industry level. Such mechanisms have stimulated the development of pricing and cost-effectiveness studies in HTA in the field generally referred to as pharmacoeconomics.[41] Since the mid-1980s, studies to determine the cost-effectiveness of drugs has far out numbered those considering other types of technologies because industry is supporting these studies, which are increasingly required for decision making.

The issue of paying for new, expensive pharmaceutical products has generated significant controversy in Europe: Whereas the European Commission is concerned mainly with innovation, the pharmaceutical industry is concerned with innovation as linked to profits. Entry of new drugs to the market is increasingly determined by one central institution. However, the price of new products is often high, and countries wish to control these costs. Several countries have developed special pricing, reimbursement, and delivery policies for new drugs, e.g., a system in which only specialized doctors in some hospitals are allowed to prescribe a certain type of drug.

SWITZERLAND

In Switzerland, as well as the Netherlands and the United Kingdom, economic evaluation is used in decision making. The Swiss system of defining the health benefits package using HTA is extensive, requiring data on effectiveness.[15,34] The system for defining pharmaceutical benefits has some additional organizations and principles.

The federal commission on health insurance benefits (ELK) makes the final coverage decisions after documents developed under the leadership of the Swiss Federal Office of Social Security (SFOSS) have been presented. Drugs that the SFOSS considers for coverage have already been examined for efficacy and safety and admitted to the market by the Swiss pharmaceutical regulatory agency (IOCM). The SFOSS is also advised by the Federal Drug Commission (FDC) in the choice of pharmaceuticals to be reimbursed. The FDC is composed of 28 members representing physicians, pharmacists, sickness funds, compulsory accident insurers, laboratories, and hospitals. The FDC is split into two subcommittees: One addresses scientific matters and consists of scientific experts, and the other addresses economic matters.[16]

The following criteria are used to determine if a pharmaceutical is cost effective[16]:

1. Therapeutic efficacy in relation to other drugs for the same indication or with a similar mode of action

2. Cost per day or per course of treatment, in comparison with the costs of drugs for the same indication or with a similar mode of action

3. Cost for research work, clinical trials, and introduction to the domestic market, in the case of a new preparation

4. Price structuring in Switzerland and abroad

The FDC classifies each pharmaceutical into one of four categories, according to the medical need it meets, its therapeutic value, and the guarantees it offers in terms of efficacy and composition: (*a*) indispensible, (*b*) important, (*c*) conditionally necessary, and (*d*) unnecessary. If a drug is classified in category *a* or *b*, the price is of little importance because access by patients with serious health conditions is the priority. Preparations in category *d* are not placed on the reimbursement list. A plenary assembly of the FDC, which transmits its recommendation to the SFOSS, provides final advice on reimbursement. The Swiss experience shows how principles concerning coverage can be put into operation.

THE NETHERLANDS

Coverage of pharmaceuticals is similar to general coverage in the Netherlands but is further developed and requires formal economic analysis for cases when the pharmaceutical industry wants to settle a price outside the existing reference pricing system.

In the Netherlands, the Medicines Evaluation Board [*College ter Beoordeling van Geneesmiddelen*

(CBG)] is responsible for registering all pharmaceutical products. The CBG registers drugs only on the basis of safety and efficacy; cost-effectiveness plays no role in these decisions. Approval of pharmaceutical products by the Medicines Evaluation Board leads to an almost automatic reimbursement by health insurance companies and sickness funds. However, the inclusion of pharmaceuticals for reimbursement is becoming increasingly based on efficacy and cost-effectiveness.[5,10,12,57]

In 1997, the Minister of Health asked the Health Care Insurance Board to formulate guidelines for pharmacoeconomic evaluation. Pharmacoeconomic research, they advised, should provide reliable, producible, and verifiable insight into the therapeutic value of a drug, the cost of using the drug, and possible cost-savings compared with other drugs and/or treatments. The resulting 19 guidelines[11] are based on Canadian pharmacoeconomic guidelines[7] and focus on target groups, study perspectives, indications, analytical methods, definition of costs, methods for measuring costs, determination and valuation of quality of life, the reference treatment to be used, outcome measures, reliability, validity, and results.[11] According to these guidelines, a cost-effectiveness analysis should be performed on those pharmaceuticals for which the manufacturer claims added value compared with existing treatment options. The responsibility of performing pharmacoeconomic research lies with the manufacturer, which means a manufacturer needs to demonstrate information on cost-effectiveness of the new pharmaceutical before claiming additional value of this new pharmaceutical compared with existing interventions. The new system was implemented on a voluntary basis before it came into full use in 2005.[18,58] Hence, economic evaluations play a role in decision making on these new and innovative drugs. However, for "me too" drugs, the reference pricing system, guaranteeing a set upper price for most drugs, does not include any incentive to make the pharmaceutical market more efficient. Therefore, the Dutch government's attempts to control pharmaceutical spending have been only partially successful.[18]

THE UNITED KINGDOM: THE NICE PROGRAM

One of the most extensive and transparent HTA programs worldwide is based in the United Kingdom. Since 1999, the National Institute of Clinical Excellence (NICE) has issued guidance on public health, health technologies, and clinical practice, with the underlying policy target to maximize health gain within the National Health Service (NHS) budget.[49] Each guidance area has a center of excellence responsible for the production of guidelines relevant to that center's scope. The Center for Public Health Excellence develops public health guidance on the promotion of good health and the prevention of ill health. The Center for Health Technology Evaluation develops technology appraisals and interventional procedure guidance. Technology appraisals are recommendations on the use of new and existing medicines and treatments within the NHS. Interventional procedure guidance evaluates the safety and efficacy of such procedures where they are used for diagnosis or treatment. The Center for Clinical Practice develops clinical guidelines. These are recommendations, based on the best available evidence, on the appropriate treatment and care of people with specific diseases and conditions. Stakeholders, including patient groups, participate in all stages of the technology appraisal process.

For public health guidance and technology appraisals, the existing body of economic evidence is checked by independent academic centers. So far, economic evidence has not been considered during the development of either new interventional procedures or clinical guidelines.[6] The aim of the economic evidence study is to develop an estimate of the relative efficiency of health care budget spending on the specific preventive or therapeutic intervention under study, in the form of a cost per QALY estimate. NICE considers two different QALY thresholds, which guide the reimbursement of technology within the NHS.[6,48] If the best estimate of the cost per QALY stays below £20,000, the intervention is implemented in the NHS. If the incremental cost-effectiveness ratio lies between £20,000 and £30,000, additional evidence is needed before a reimbursement decision can be made. Above a threshold value of £30,000 per QALY, additional evidence regarding the benefits of the intervention should be strong and provide explicit reasoning for the decision to support the technology.[6,48]

The NICE process has been criticized for not sufficiently influencing the everyday practice within the NHS because guidance issued is not fully implemented.[55] Here, the main problem is that the centralized decision-making process is not reflected within the local NHS situation; the NHS is organized into regions that have responsibilities pertaining to their own regional budget spending. An acceptable cost-effectiveness ratio at a national level could be overruled on the basis of the budget impact that interventions would have when implemented at the local level, such as within an NHS region or a hospital. Buxton[6] addresses the additional problem of the necessity of disinvestments in cost-ineffective technologies to make a budget available for the implementation of new cost-effective interventions. NICE must invest in the identification of such cost-ineffective measures and NHS needs the political strength to communicate disinvestments to the public. Although economic evaluation plays a large role in NICE guidance, the actual provision of health and preventive services is a result of many forces in addition to economic ones, even within the centralized health care system of the United Kingdom.

THE COVERAGE ISSUE

From the study of countries' systems, some findings emerge: HTA information on pharmaceuticals is more complete than that for other health technologies. The main reason for this is that societal concerns about pharmaceuticals preceded by some years serious concerns about other health technologies. Pharmaceuticals have been increasingly regulated for efficacy and safety since the early 1960s, whereas general HTA began in the mid-1970s.

Fostered by problems of safety and efficacy of drugs, governmental regulation has developed to assure a favorable benefit/risk ratio in pharmaceutical use. The special status of drugs as a product fostered this development. The public, in general, and government policy makers, in particular, have been favorable to the idea that industry products must be regulated in the public's interest. It has been more difficult to develop analogous approaches to physician practice because physicians are prestigious professionals, generally trusted by the public and by policy makers. Also, their "product" is not as easily definable as a pharmaceutical product because it is customized to specific patients' individual needs. This hampers the evaluation of medical interventions as compared with the evaluation of pharmaceuticals.

With increasingly visible problems in all health technologies and rising costs of care, other policies have been sought. Reimbursement has been seen as an important tool since 1980. Here, again, pharmaceuticals have led the way. The defined list of pharmaceuticals on the market, and the information available on their safety and efficacy, has stimulated use of reimbursement mechanisms, especially coverage decisions.[64]

In contrast, broad public health programs and their implementation are more complex to evaluate.[39] Because public health programs take longer to debate and define their means and ends, evaluating their future effectiveness is also difficult. Also, public health programs, more specifically those directed

at the improvement of lifestyle, are often directed at risk factors such as smoking. Here, effect is often measured in intermediate outcomes, such as the number of quitters, and economic evaluation in terms of cost per QALY is therefore relatively rare. In addition, as Holland[39] says, public health is often made up of polarized decision areas, such as cigarette smoking, where tobacco industry tries to influence health-care policy making. However, despite the power of the pharmaceutical industry, it has not been able to prevent the spread of coverage based on cost-effectiveness analysis. And yet, even with a large array of policy measures to reduce or decelerate public expenditure on pharmaceuticals, European countries have not been successful in containing drug costs at a national level.[28]

The main criterion in coverage decisions is effectiveness,[34] but outside of pharmaceuticals, economic analysis is not often used to determine coverage. The controversy arises on the use of cost-effectiveness information in coverage decisions, especially in cases where certain patient groups were denied access to pharmaceuticals that were perceived to be beneficial. The pharmaceutical industry refers to the fact that the European pharmaceutical market is more restricted and less profitable than the U.S. market and points to a resulting (future) lack of innovation. At this time, however, the main problem continues to be overuse and misuse of drugs.[63] Equity concerns have been discussed, but no examples have been given to indicate that equity is a problem. This may be because the use of cost-effectiveness analysis is limited, as new drugs are reimbursed at relatively high rates.

GENERAL DISCUSSION

Overall, the paucity of relevant studies may be the strongest argument for the use of cost-effectiveness analysis in public health programs. The fact that results of cost-effectiveness studies cannot be generalized has also prevented the use of studies acros countries.[46] Furthermore, the economic analysis of portfolios of different curative and preventive interventions for one health care problem, rather than of individual treatments compared with their best alternatives, would enhance the use of health economics study results because policy makers are often concerned with the issue of choosing the best approaches to a disease problem.

As discussed above, some countries use cost-effectiveness to make coverage decisions. Traditionally, pharmaceuticals, expensive screening programs, and other defined technologies have been subject to economic evaluations, and the results have been used in decision making. Other "softer" types of technologies, such as health promotion, have been evaluated less thoroughly. Much work remains to be done, both for health economists and for policy makers, who are not always trained to use economic information as a basis for their decisions. The use of cost-effectiveness analysis to guide medical device regulation is another area of potential growth. In fact, in the United Kingdom, the MATCH program is already engaging with regulators to discover if different economic approaches can improve the regulatory process.[27] Also, in the Netherlands, first attempts are now being made to require economic information in decisions regarding medical device coverage.[13]

However, difficulties remain. There is no consensus as to the place of economic analysis in public health decision making. Professional economists often ignore the situations of the real world, seeking to maximize outcomes or outputs within a fixed budget restraint (limited resources). This limitation implies that policy makers should use some measure of incremental health outcome in relation to resources. Such displays as "league tables" or the WHO statements on priority services are based on this assumption.[26] However, economic analysis cannot be more than one element used to set priorities or determine which public health program should be implemented and how.[36] Political issues will also play a role. Equity and ethical issues seem certain to play an increasing part in decision making. Thus the question should not be, how is the use of cost-effectiveness analysis assured? Instead, the appropriate question is, how are the findings of such studies integrated into the rich and complicated decision-making processes that exist worldwide? We have little option but to work through this via discussion and debate in our democratic systems.

Disclosure Statement

The authors are not aware of any biases that might be perceived as affecting the objectivity of this review.

Annu. Rev. Public Health 2008. 29:383–97. First published online as a Review in Advance on January 3, 2008. The Annual Review of Public Health is online at http://publhealth.annualreviews.org. This article's doi: 10.1146/annurev.publhealth.29.020907.090808.

● ● ● **References**

1. Baltussen R, Brouwer W, Niessen L. 2005. Cost-effectiveness analysis for priority setting in health: penny-wise but pound-foolish. *Int. J. Technol. Assess. Health Care* 21:532-34.

2. Banta HD, Hatziandreu E, Dauben HP, Forde OH, Loud ML, et al. 2002. Health promotion and disease prevention as a complement to community health indicators. Working Group 1. ECHTA/ECAHI project. *Int. J. Technol. Assess. Health Care* 18:218-37.

3. Blue Cross/Blue Shield Assoc. 2000. TEC Bull. 17:No. 4. http://www.bluecross.com.

4. Blue Cross/Blue Shield Assoc. 1994. *The Decision Maker's Guide to the Technology Evaluation Center.* Chicago: Blue Cross/Blue Shield Assoc.

5. Bos M. 2000. Health technology assessment in The Netherlands. *Int. J. Technol. Assess. Health Care* 16:485-519.

6. Buxton MJ. 2006. Economic evaluation and decision making in the UK. *Pharmacoeconomics* 24:1133-42.

7. Can. Coord. Off. Health Technol. Assess. 1997. *Guide for Economic Evaluation of Pharmaceuticals.* Ottawa: Can. Coord. Off. Health Technol. Assess. 2nd ed.

8. Cochrane Collab. http://www.cochrane.org.

9. Coffield A, Maciosek M, McGinnis M. 2001. Priorities among recommended clinical preventive services. *Am. J. Prev. Med.* 21:1-9.

10. Coll. voor Zorgverzekeringen (Health Care Ins. Board). 1997.*Toetsing geneesmiddelenpakket [Assessment of the benefits package regarding pharmaceuticals].* Amstelveen: Ziekenfondsraad.

11. Coll. voor Zorgverzekeringen (Health Care Ins. Board). 1999. *Richtlijnen voor farmacoeconomische onderzoek [Dutch guidelines for pharmacoeconomic research].* Amstelveen: Coll. voor Zorgverzekeringen.

12. Coll. voor Zorgverzekeringen (Health Care Ins. Board). 2000. *Procedure aanvraag vergoeding geneesmiddel (Procedure for reimbursement of pharmaceuticals).* Amstelveen: Coll. voor Zorgverzekeringen. http://www.cvz.nl.

13. Coll. voor Zorgverzekeringen (Health Care Ins. Board). 2007. *Rapport pakketadvies 2007* (Report on health care basket 2007). Diemen: Coll. voor Zorgverzekeringen, Rep. 248.

14. Cox ER, Motheral BR, Griffis D. 2000. Relevance of pharmacoeconomics and health outcomes information to health care decisionmakers in the United States. *Value Health* 3:162 (Abstr.).

15. Cranovsky R, Matillon Y, Banta HD. 1997. EUR-ASSESS project subgroup report on coverage. *Int. J. Technol. Assess. Health Care* 13:287-332.

16. Cranovsky R, Schilling J, Faisst K. 2000. Health technology assessment in Switzerland. *Int. J. Technol. Assess. Health Care* 16:576-90.

17. Dep. Health. 1998. *The First Report of the National Screening Committee.* London: Dep. Health.

18. De Wolf P, Brouwer WBF, Rutten FFH. 2005. Regulating the Dutch pharmaceutical market: im-

proving efficiency or controlling costs? *Int. J. Health Plan. Manag.* 20:351-74.

19. Drummond M, Manca A, Sculpher M. 2000. Increasing the generalizability of economic evaluations: recommendations for the design, analysis, and reporting of studies. *Int. J. Technol. Assess. Health Care* 16:165-71.

20. Drummond M, Pang F. 2001. Transferability of economic evaluation results. In *Economic Evaluation in Health Care: Merging Theory with Practice*, ed. M Drummond, A McGuire, pp. 256-76. Oxford: Oxford Univ. Press.

21. Drummond MF, Sculpher MJ, Torrance GW, O'Brien BJ, Stoddart GL. 2005. *Methods for the Economic Evaluation of Health Care Programmes*. Oxford: Oxford Univ. Press. 3rd ed.

22. Dunning A. 1991. *Kiezen en delen (Choices in health care)*. Rijswijk: Minist. Health Neth.

23. Duthie T, Trueman P, Chancellor J, Diez L. 1999. Research into the use of health economics in decisionmaking in the United Kingdom. *Health Policy* 46:143-57.

24. Eddy D. 1992. *A Manual for Assessing Health Practices and Designing Practice Policies*. Philadelphia: Am. Coll. Physicians.

25. Eddy D. 1996. Benefit language, criteria that will improve quality while reducing costs. *JAMA* 275:650-57.

26. Edejer T, Baltussen R, Adam T, Hutubessy R, Acharya A, et al. 2003. *WHO Guide to Cost-Effectiveness Analysis*. Geneva: WHO.

27. Eng. Phys. Sci. Res. Counc. (EPSRC). 2007. *Match Renewal Review*. Swindon, UK: EPSRC.

28. Ess SM, Schneeweiss S, Szucs TD. 2003. European healthcare policies for controlling drug expenditure. *Pharmacoeconomics* 21:89-103.

29. Garber A. 2001. Evidence-based coverage policy. *Health Aff.* 20:62-82.

30. Gen. Account. Off. 2003. *Medicare: Divided Authority for Policies on Coverage of Procedures and Devices Results in Inequities*.Washington, DC: Gen. Account. Off.

31. Goddard M, Hauck K, Preker A, Smith P. 2005. Priority setting in health—a political economy perspective. *Health Econ. Policy Law* 1:79-90.

32. Gold MR, Siegel JE, Russel LB, Weinstein MC. 1996. *Cost-Effectiveness in Health and Medicine*. Oxford: Oxford Univ. Press.

33. Goldsmith L, Henderson B, Hurley J. 2004. *Economic Evaluation across the Four Faces of Prevention: A Canadian Perspective*. Hamilton, Ont.: McMaster Univ., Cent. Health Econ. Policy Anal.

34. Gress S, Niebuhr D, Rothgang H,Wasem J. 2005. Criteria and procedures for determining benefit packages in health care. A comparative perspective. *Health Policy* 73:78-91.

35. Grosse SD, Teutsch SM, Haddix AC. 2007. Lessons from cost-effectiveness research for United States Public Health Policy. *Annu. Rev. Public Health* 28:19-31.

36. Hauck K, Smith P, Goddard M. 2003. *The Economics of Priority Setting for Health Care: A Literature Review*.Washington, DC: The World Bank.

37. Health Counc. Neth. 2007. *The Future of the National Immunisation Programme: Towards a Programme for All Age Groups*. The Hague: Health Counc. Neth., Publ. No. 2007/02.

38. Health Econ. Eval. Database (HEED). 2007. http://www.ihe-heed.com.

39. Holland W. 2004. Health technology assessment and public health: a commentary. *Int. J. Technol. Assess. Health Care* 20:77-80.

40. Iglesias C, Drummond M, Rovira J. 2005. Healthcare decision-making processes in Latin America: problems and prospects for the use of economic evaluation. *Int. J. Technol. Assess. Health Care* 21:1-15.

41. Kanovos P, ed. 1989. *Pharmacoepidemiology*. London: Churchill-Livingstone.

42. Kanovos P. 2001. *Overview of Pharmaceutical Pricing and Reimbursement Regulation in Europe*. London: London Sch. Econ.

43. Leichter H. 1991. *Politics and Health Promotion in the United States and Great Britain*. Princeton, NJ: Princeton Univ. Press.

44. Maciosek M, Coffield A, Edwards W. 2006. Priorities among effective clinical preventive services. *Am. J. Prev. Med.* 31:52-61.

45. Maciosek M, Coffield A, McGinnis M. 2001. Methods for priority setting among clinical preventive services. *Am. J. Prev. Med.* 21:10-19.

46. Marino P, Siani C, Roche H. 2005. Impact of uncertainty on cost-effectiveness analysis of medical strategies: the case of high-dose chemotherapy for breast cancer patients. *Int. J. Technol. Assess. Health Care* 21:342-50.

47. Mossialos E, Mrazek M,Walley T, eds. 2004. *Regulating Pharmaceuticals in Europe: Striving for Efficiency, Equity and Quality*. Berkshire: Open Univ. Press.

48. Natl. Inst. Clin. Excell. (NICE). 2004. *Guide to the Method of Technology Appraisal (Ref. N0515)*. http://www.nice.org.uk.

49. Natl. Inst. Clin. Excell. (NICE). 2005. Social value judgements—principles for the development of NICE guidance. http://www.nice.org.uk.

50. NHS Cent. Rev. Dissem., Univ. York. 1995. *Review of the research on the effectiveness of health services*

interventions to reduce variations in health. CRD Rep. 3. York: NHS Cent. Rev. Dissem.

51. NHS Cent. Rev. Dissem., Univ. York. 2000. *Evidence from systematic reviews of research relevant to implementing the "wide public health" agenda.* York: NHS Cent. Rev. Dissem.

52. NHS Cent. Rev. Dissem. 2001. HTA database. http://www.nhscrd.co.uk.

53. Nyborg K. 1998. Some Norwegian politicians use of cost-benefit studies. *Publ. Choice* 95:381-401.

54. Ross J. 1995. The use of economic evaluation in health care: Australian decisionmakers perceptions. *Health Policy* 31:103-10.

55. Sheldon TA, Cullum N, Dawson D, Lankshear A, Lowson K, et al. 2004. What's the evidence that NICE guidance has been implemented? Results from a national evaluation using time series analysis, audit of patients' notes, and interviews. *Br. Med. J.* 329:999-1003.

56. Sonnad S, Greenberg D, Rosen A, Neumann P. 2005. Diffusion of published cost-utility analyses in the field of health policy and practice. *Int. J. Technol. Assess. Health Care* 21:399-402.

57. Stolk EA, Rutten FFH. 2005. The "Health Benefit Basket" in the Netherlands. *Eur. J. Health Econ.* 6(Suppl. 1):53-57.

58. Toenders WGM. 2001. *Breedte geneesmiddelenpakket [Width of the benefits package regarding pharmaceuticals].* Amstelveen: Coll. voor Zorgverzekeringen.

59. Tunis SR. 2002. Why Medicare has not established criteria for coverage decisions. *N. Engl. J. Med.* 350:2196-98.

60. Tunis SR, Kang JL. 2001. Improvements in Medicare coverage of new technology. *Health Aff. (Millwood)* 20(5):83-85.

61. US Prev. Task Force. 1996. *Guide to Clinical Preventive Services.* Baltimore, MD:Williams &Wilkins. 2nd ed. http://www.ahrq.gov.

62. Welte R, Trotter CL, Edmunds WJ, Postma MJ, Beutels P. 2005. The role of economic evaluation in vaccine decision making. Focus on meningococcal groupCconjugate vaccine. *Pharmacoeconomics* 23:855-74.

63. WHO. 2004. *World Medicines Situation.* Geneva: WHO.

64. WHO, Eur. Off. 2000. *Policies on Pricing and Reimbursement of Medicines in Europe.* Copenhagen: WHO.

11

Primary Care

Primary care may be distinguished from specialty care by the time, focus, and scope of the services provided to the patients. Primary care is first contact care or the portal to the healthcare system,[1] whereas specialty care, if needed, generally follows primary care. In a managed care environment where financing and provision of services are integrated, primary care providers serve as "gatekeepers," an important role in controlling cost, utilization, and the rational allocation of resources. Primary care is also longitudinal.[2] Primary care providers follow through the course of treatment and coordinate various activities including initial diagnosis, treatment, referral, consultation, monitoring, and follow-up. This coordinating role is especially important in the provision of continuing care for chronic conditions.

Primary care focuses on the person as a whole whereas specialty care centers on diseases or organ systems (e.g., infectious disease specialist, cardiologist).[3] Primary care providers see patients at their initial interface with the healthcare system. Patients present with a variety of illnesses and concerns that represent early stages of disease that are not easily classified by organ system

or diagnostic label. Often patients have multiple problems, and the provision of specialty care to one problem may make another worse. Primary care thus provides an integrating function, balancing the multiple requirements of the patient's problem(s) and referring patients to appropriate specialty care when needed.

Primary care is comprehensive in scope and includes health promotion, disease prevention, health maintenance, counseling, patient education, diagnosis and treatment of acute and chronic illnesses.[1] Primary care providers serve the role of patient adviser, advocate, as well as system gatekeeper.[4] Specialty care, in contrast, tends to be limited to illness episodes, the organ system, or disease process involved.

Over thirty years ago, the Declaration of Alma-Ata was created by high-level national leaders and United Nation agencies pushing for a primary care revolution that could improve the health of the global community. Alma-Ata envisioned primary care that focused on preventive and curative interventions to improve social well-being as well as a comprehensive process that involved the community. Progress toward improved primary care has varied from country to country. Integration of services and coordination of care have been significant challenges for improving the health systems.[5]

In the United States, primary care providers are predominantly trained in family medicine/general practice, general internal medicine, and general paediatrics.[6] These primary care physicians are often called generalists. Physicians in non-primary care specialties are referred to as specialists.

The principal determinant of need for primary care physicians is the demographics of the general population. The major driving force behind specialists is the development of medical technology. The rapid advances in medical technology continuously expanded the diagnostic and therapeutic options at the disposal of physician specialists. The majority of patients, significantly freed from financial constraints thanks to third-party payment, turned to physicians who could provide them with the most up-to-date, sophisticated treatment. Since population has increased significantly more slowly than technological advancement, there is a growing gap between primary and specialty care in the physician workforce. The rapid advance of medical technology expands the demand for specialty services and provides an impetus for specialty development.

In addition to these factors, higher reimbursement for specialists relative to primary care physicians also contributes to the current imbalance. Despite the implementation of resource-based relative value scale (RBRVS) to reimburse physicians, primary care physicians continue to receive lower payments than specialists for comparable work because physician payments are based on historically determined, estimated practice costs as well as total work effort.[7-8] Moreover, many insurance companies would pay for hospital-based complex diagnostic and invasive procedures using high technology, but not for routine preventive visits and consultations. Such a practice not only encourages career choices in subspecialties and the delivery of intensive specialty services, but discourages potentially important primary care services as well as deterring patients from early care-seeking behavior.

Specialists not only earn higher incomes, they have more predictable work hours, and enjoy higher prestige both among their colleagues and from the public at large.[9-10] Several problems contribute to the difficulty in recruiting physicians to rural areas. They include longer working hours, on-call hours, less financial reward for services performed, and professional isolation. Rural physicians have less direct access to high technology that is typically located in medical centers.[11] Among factors affecting medical students' career choice, society's perception of value, intellectual challenge, and lifestyle factors (hours worked, community amenities, for example) were ranked as very important along with financial rewards.[12-14] Medical education environment—organized according to specialties and controlled by those who have achieved their leadership positions by demonstrating their ability in narrow scientific or clinic areas—emphasizes technology-intensive procedures and tertiary care settings, and may deter students from choosing the field of primary care.[15-16] As a result, there is currently an uneven balance of specialists and primary care physicians among the U.S. healthcare workforce. Medical students often abandon primary care for "ROAD" specialties (radiology, opthalmology, anesthesiology, and dermatology) due to the wide income gap and need for prestige.

One consequence of having too many specialists is that they have been regarded as the major force in driving up the volume of intensive, expensive, and invasive medical services and therefore the costs of healthcare.[17-20] Higher surgeon supply increases the demand for initial contact with surgeons.[21] Many now frequently performed operations, such as coronary artery bypass, hip replacements, carotid endarterectomy, arthroscopy, laparoscopy, and heart and liver transplantation, were little known 40 years ago. Technological developments also include new drugs for treating ulcers, depression, and heart disease, new diagnostic tests based on genetic engineering, new imaging advances like magnetic resonance imaging, the increased application of computers to diagnosis and treatment, new endoscopic equipment and technique, and breakthroughs in the field of micro-, minimal-incision, and laser-assisted surgery.[22] Systematic comparison across industrialized countries shows that the United States has higher rates of coronary surgery, diagnostic imaging, neurosurgery, treatment for end-stage renal disease, and cancer chemotherapy than any other countries.[23-24] As the disease prevalence is too low to support all the specialists, many of the procedures performed might be unnecessary. The Congressional Subcommittee on Oversight and Investigations estimated that nationwide there were 2.4 million unnecessary operations performed annually, resulting in a cost of $3.9 billion and 11,900 deaths.[25-26] Primary care services are less costly than specialty services because they are less technology-intensive.

In addition to cost, seeking care directly from specialists is often less effective whereas primary care makes it possible for people to obtain services before their illness becomes severe.[2,27] While higher levels of primary care manpower are associated with lower overall mortality, and lower death rates due to diseases of the heart and cancer, in contrast, the number of specialty physicians is positively and significantly related to higher mortality rates.[28–29] Primary care physicians have been the major providers of care to minorities, the poor, and people living in underserved areas such as rural towns and inner cities.[30–32] The continual shortage of primary care physicians could exacerbate access to care particularly for the underserved.

To achieve a better balance in the proportion of primary care physicians and specialists, continual efforts are needed to improve the geographic and specialty distribution of physician labor forces. Medical schools should strive to develop students' competencies in skills, values, and attitudes relevant to the practice of primary care. Their curricula should be oriented toward issues of special concern to generalists such as outpatient experience, public health concepts and disease prevention, and cultural, ethnic, and population-specific knowledge, and provide students with opportunities to work with the poor, minorities, uninsured, and practice in rural or underserved areas.[16] Clinical skills must be current and practitioners should be capable of managing the large volume of information and continue lifelong learnings.[33]

The means of financing medical training and physician services should be improved. The current system of graduate medical education payments through Medicare is the largest source of funds for residency programs (exceeds $3 billion annually) and bases its payments on the number of trainees contributes to specialty-oriented training and creates disincentives for primary care training.[17,34–35] The National Institutes of Health further contributes billions of dollars annually for basic research, much of which is carried out under the auspices of specialty departments.[36] A possible solution is to encourage and provide priority funding for primary care residency slots and primary care–related research. Hospitals whose graduates actually went into primary care in underserved areas should be rewarded. Since fee-for-service reimbursement favors the practice of specialists, who employ more technology and perform more procedures than generalists, its predominance will continue to act as a deterrent to the entrance of physicians into primary care. Reimbursement to providers and patients should emphasize preventive, primary care services, and stress the attributes of primary care (i.e., first contact, longitudinal, person focused, comprehensive, and coordinated). Deductibles and co-payments should not apply to primary care services, since reduced access to primary care is associated with higher costs and poorer outcomes.[37–38] Since physicians tend to practice in affluent urban areas, it is necessary to differentially reward providers who practice in less desirable areas or care for socially disadvantaged populations.

A more rational referral system should be established that achieves a reasonable division of work based on the frequency and severity of health problems in the populations.[2] In general, primary care physicians provide preventive services (e.g., health examination, immunization, mammograms, Papanicolaou's smears), treat frequently occurring and less severe problems. Problems that occur less frequently, or require complex diagnostic or therapeutic approaches may be referred to specialists. The medical team that comprises both primary care physicians and specialists should discuss and decide upon the specific division of labor. The formulation of new practice guidelines based on patient-oriented clinical research and their dissemination should contribute to updating and improving the diagnostic and therapeutic practices of practicing physicians. Disincentives for non-referred specialist care should be established.

There have been attempts to balance physician supply and distribution though monetary incentives such as scholarships and loan-forgiveness programs for medical students interested in primary care, but it has not been enough to offset the larger interest for specialties.[39] The shortage has also led to a reliance on international medical students to become primary care physicians, as they are more likely to serve as general practitioners, general internists, and pediatricians than their U.S.-trained counterparts. Currently, 57% of international physicians serving in the U.S. work in primary care. New and better tactics are needed to recruit U.S. graduates into primary care. Rather than focusing on monetary incentives, which have not worked as well as intended, other factors that influence the decision to choose primary care should be examined as a possible tool for increasing the primary care workforce. Studies have shown that students who have grown up in rural areas or demonstrated interest in care for the underserved are more likely to choose a primary care specialty. In addition, public medical schools and medical schools located in rural regions place more students in primary care than private institutions. Investing in these medical schools as well as in primary care clerkships could influence more physicians to choose primary care.[40]

A number of federal programs have demonstrated success in increasing the supply of primary care services available to underserved populations, and should be continued. These programs include the National Health Service Corps (which conditions scholarship support on a commitment to future service in an underserved area), the Migrant and Community Health Programs (designated to provide primary care services to the poor and underserved using federal grants), support of primary care training programs, and support of Area Health Education Centers. Research indicates physicians' personal characteristics play a significant role in their practice location decision.[9,41–42] Physicians are more likely to be attracted to rural practice if they have a rural background or exposure to rural practice settings in their clinical training. To ensure a sufficient supply of rural physicians, one comprehensive approach would be to assist rural persons in the competition for admission to medical school, foster premedical training in rural settings, emphasize rural background in the admission policies of medical schools,[43] and use rural preceptorships or externships by medical schools and rural residency training programs to expose students to medical practice in small towns and rural areas.

The shortage of providers in primary care is only one issue. The U.S. also lags behind in information technology whereas countries like the United Kingdom, New Zealand, and Australia have widespread use of electronic medical records that allow primary care doctors to better coordinate the care of their patients. Payment plans in the U.S. also lack a primary care focus with its fee-for-service structure that pays physicians more to treat than to prevent disease. In the United Kingdom, financial incentives are provided for physicians to meet performance targets. In Australia and New Zealand, quality-related incentives are also in place, which reflects the countries' decision to invest in primary care. While the U.S. spends more than all other countries on healthcare, it has the largest number of patients who have difficulty paying for care and worse health outcomes than other industrialized countries—a discrepancy that needs a solution.[5]

Fixing primary care in the U.S. is important for community health as studies have shown that utilization of primary care services leads to better health outcomes and lower healthcare costs. A higher proportion of primary care physicians in an area has been shown to lead to lower levels of spending.[44] Having a regular source of care also leads to reductions in hospital admissions, emergency department visits, and inappropriate specialty consults. It also provides a setting to manage chronic conditions so that individuals can stay healthier over time.[45]

A step toward improving primary care would be to prioritize clinical preventive services, which are not utilized heavily despite a significant amount of evidence that demonstrates the effectiveness of primary care in keeping a community healthy. In 2005, 70% of smokers and problem drinkers surveyed said that no clinician offered them assistance for the cessation of these risky behaviors that lead to preventable diseases. Preventive services should address diseases causing the greatest burden, such as preventable diseases that are the leading cause of death, or diseases that cost the most when left unmanaged. Preventive services proven to be cost-effective and cost-beneficial should be utilized in clinical settings. A framework for prevention with these points would be a good starting point for prioritizing these essential primary care services.[46]

Currently, the medical home seems to be the potential solution to revitalizing primary care. The term "medical home" was first coined in 1967 and established for special-needs children whose healthcare needs required constant coordination. The medical home began to evolve in the primary care realm after the Declaration of Alma-Ata as managed care programs began to use primary care providers to coordinate patient care. Medical homes carry the potential to fix problems found in the current organization of primary care, if they are established properly. They could provide patient-centered care to the community, providing patients with a "home" that is accessible and will coordinate their care. A cross-national survey of seven countries with medical homes have all had positive feedback from patients. The medical home could be a better setting to manage chronic care, especially if the chronic care model (CCM) is used within the home. CCM is based on the idea that chronic conditions are best managed through productive interaction between multidisciplinary teams and patients who are well-informed and motivated. Both demonstration projects and research point to the effectiveness of this model. Finally, the medical home could provide a setting to support primary care activities that are not recognized or supported in the current payment system. Medical homes could be given supplemental payments to make up for poor compensation if health targets are met. Despite all this potential, the idea of a medical home is still met with much hesitancy, even from physicians, who balk at the system because the fee-for-service structure still pays them more for acute care than preventive care.[47]

This chapter includes readings that describe primary care from both a global and U.S. perspective. In **Primary Health Care: Making Alma-Ata a Reality,** Waley et al. described the evolution of primary care since the Alma-Ata Declaration more than thirty years ago. The Alma-Ata Declaration focuses on primary care with the idea of "health for all," but its basic tenets have still not been achieved. In 2000, the Millennium Development Goals (MDGs) was an attempt to revisit the idea of "health for all" through primary care with narrower target points that included reduction in maternal and child mortality, burden of HIV, malaria, and tuberculosis, and education and gender equity.

Achieving these health goals has been variable from country to country. And, despite the general lack of support and resource to improve primary care, some countries have seen marked gains toward the MDGs as a result of the willingness to try innovative means of care and the country's political and social commitment to health. For example, Thailand, a low-income country, has had success in lowering child mortality as well as reach equity in mental health.

In order to push for further progress and uphold the principles of Alma-Ata, the article keys in on seven areas that would help improve primary healthcare. First is the need to maintain health and health equity, with health defined as physical and emotional well-being and not merely the absence of disease and death. It calls for the integration of healthcare in order to better manage the growing rates of chronic disorders. While a short time frame would require vertical implementation of services, better primary care can only be achieved with the eventual turn to integrated care. Primary care should attempt to ensure that care is equal. Proper attention must be focused on vulnerable and underserved populations in order to prevent disparities. The community served should be engaged such that they feel empowered to take an active role in keeping themselves healthy. There must also be an investment in the innovation of new drugs and the latest technology. While remarkable progress has been made with better medicine for children and affordable drugs for all, innovation for health technology targeted at poor populations has disappeared from the global agenda. The latest medical technology is often aimed at higher income brackets who can afford the services. Development must also be tied with health, resulting in an "intersectoral collaboration" so that all entities that affect an individual's health work together for the same common goal. Finally, progress must be measured quantitatively in order to evaluate improvement. In order to revitalize primary care as stated in the Alma-Ata Declaration, all agencies—whether governments, international agencies, and civil societies—must work together.

In **The World Health Report 2008: Primary Health Care—Now More than Ever,** the World Health Organization further clarified what primary care ought to be. Good primary care means placing people first. For example, an Alaskan medical center reorganized itself so that the staff had more personal contact with patients. It resulted in a reduction of ER visits by 50% and referrals by 30% as well as shortened waiting times. People's experience of the healthcare system is influenced first and foremost by how they are treated, yet the effectiveness and safety of ambulatory care is given little attention.

Primary care requires a degree of person-centeredness, in which clinicians engage patients and encourage them to be active participants in maintaining their health rather than giving treatments without addressing a patient's concerns and beliefs, the more common practice among health professionals now. It also needs a comprehensive set of services that includes prevention and screening. Primary care must take the initiative in running health promotions as well as addressing the social determinants that put an individual's well-being at risk. In order for healthcare to make an impact, it must find a way to interact with the community outside of the office. Care cannot stop once the consult is over. There must also be a consistent and coherent approach in managing a patient through the years. In Canada, 1 in 7 patients arriving at the emergency room have medical information missing, which could often lead to patient harm. Missing information in the United States has been attributed to 15.6% of all errors in ambulatory care. While primary care cannot solve all the health problems, it serves as an excellent entry point into a healthcare system, especially if clinicians within this setting were given the responsibility to coordinate the care of their patients.

Better health outcomes can result in providing primary care that is comprehensive, continuous, and person-centered, and one where there is a long, stable relationship between health professionals and the community it serves. Currently, ambulatory care is not structured for person-centered care. The reorganization of the system is necessary, similar to the one that took place in the Alaskan medical center in which healthcare is provided at a more personal level and mindful of reaching out to the community to build closer ties.

In **Quantifying the Health Benefits of Primary Care, in the United States,** Macinko and colleagues provided evidence of the effect of primary care on population health. The United States health workforce changed during the 20th century. Primary care physicians made up more than half of the physician workforce in the 1940s and 1950s, but this proportion drastically decreased in the 1960s when the specialist supply increased at a much faster rate. By 1975, primary care physicians made up approximately 35% of all physicians, and has stayed at that level ever since.

Reviewing articles on the health workforce of the United States from 1985 to 2005 has found a positive association between an increase in the supply of primary care physicians and better health outcomes. Increasing the number of primary care providers serving a population predicted a reduction in mortality, as well as reductions in low birth weight, infant mortality, and stroke mortality. Improved health outcome was more pronounced in areas suffering from health inequities. Black populations saw a reduction in mortality four times greater than that of white populations with the increase of primary care providers.

The association between better health outcome and primary care providers implies a need to strengthen the primary care workforce. Results also imply that primary care resources should be targeted in communities with the greatest need since the effect is much greater in these areas.

Better population health and an increase in primary care could be associated for several reasons. First of all, primary care has been shown to improve primary prevention in the U.S. with higher primary care physician to population ratios linked to areas with lower smoking and obesity rates. Primary care also leads to early detection of disease since screenings often take place in primary care settings. Early detection improves when there are more primary care providers offering the services. Finally, access to primary care leads to a more efficient healthcare system. Patients who have and utilize a constant source of care rely less on emergency departments and have better compliance and improved satisfaction with their care.

In **America's Health Centers,** the National Association of Community Health Centers provided a snapshot of the nation's primary care safety-net provider—community health centers. Health centers are "non-profit, community-directed healthcare providers" who serve vulnerable populations, such as low-income groups, minorities, and the uninsured, offering primary and preventive care. Currently, health centers serve 20 million people, nearly all of them belonging to the low-income bracket and either

uninsured or on Medicaid. Because they serve vulnerable populations, health centers carry the potential to reduce health disparities seen in these subgroups. Studies have shown that patients served by health centers are absent of the disparities seen in the general population. They are located in areas that have an inadequate supply of healthcare services, such as remote rural areas or inner city neighborhoods The presence of health centers in these regions increase accessibility to healthcare and provide much-needed services at an affordable price. Since these locations are also often economically depressed, health centers provide a boost in the local economy through the production of jobs. It is important to expand on the health centers across the country so they can continue to serve vulnerable populations and improve overall community health.

• • • References

1. Kahn NB, Ostergaard DJ, Graham R. AAFP constructs definitions related to primary care. *Am Fam Physic* 1994;50:1211–15.

2. Starfield B, Simpson L. Primary care as part of U.S. health services reform. *JAMA* 1993;269:3136–39.

3. Hibbard H, Nutting PA. Research in primary care: a national priority. In: Grady ML, ed. *AHCPR Conference Proceedings: Primary Care Research: Theory and Methods.* Washington, DC: U.S. Department of Health and Human Services, September 1991.

4. Williams SJ. Ambulatory health care services. In: Williams SJ, Torrens PR eds. *Introduction to Health Services.* Albany, NY: Delmar, 1994:108–33.

5. Lawn, Joy E.; Rhode, Jon; Rikin, Susan; Were, Miriam; Paul, Vinod K.; Chopra, Mickey. "Alma-Ata 30 years on: revolutionary, relevant, and time to revitalise." *Lancet,* 2008:372:917–27.

6. Rich EC, Wilson M, Midtling J, Showstack J. Preparing generalist physicians: the organizational and policy context. *J Gen Intern Med* 1994;9(suppl 1):Sl 15–Sl 22.

7. Physician Payment Review Commission. *Annual Report to Congress.* Washington, DC: Physician Payment Review Commission, 1993.

8. Hsiao W, Dunn D, Verrilli D. Assessing the implementation of physician-payment reform. *N Engl J Med* 1993;328:928–33.

9. Samuels ME, Shi L. *Physician Recruitment and Retention: A Guide for Rural Medical Group Practice.* Englewood, CO: Medical Group Management Association Press, 1993.

10. Rosenblatt RA, Lishner DM. Surplus or shortage? Unraveling the physician supply conundrum. *West J Med* 1991;154:43–50.

11. Kohler PO. Specialists/primary care professionals: striking a balance. *Inquiry* 1994;31:289–95.

12. Kassebaum D. Factors influencing the specialty choices of 1993 medical school graduates. *Acad Med* 1994;69:164–70.

13. Steinbrook R. Money and career choice. *N Engl J Med* 1994;330:1311–12.

14. Rosenthal MP, Diamond JJ, Rabinowitz HK. Influence of income, hours worked, and loan repayment on medical students' decision to pursue a primary care career. *JAMA* 1994;271:914–47.

15. Medical education may deter grads from choosing primary care careers. *AAMC Wkly Rep* 1990; March 5: 1.

16. Verby JE, Newell JP, Andersen SA, Swentko WM. Changing the medical school curriculum to improve patient access to primary care. *JAMA* 1991;266: 110–13.

17. Wennberg JE, Goodman DC, Nease RF, Keller RB. Finding equilibrium in U.S. physician supply. *Hlth Affairs* 1993; Summer:89–103.

18. Schroeder S, Sandy LG. Specialty distribution of U.S. physicians: the invisible driver of health care costs. *N Engl J Med* 1993;328:961–3.

19. Rosenblatt RA. Specialists or generalists: on whom should we base the American health care system? *JAMA* 1992;267:1665–6.

20. Schroeder SA, Sandy LG. Specialty distribution of U.S. physicians: the invisible driver of health care costs. *N Engl J Med* 1993;328:961–3.

21. Escarce JJ. Explaining the association between surgeon supply and utilization. *Inquiry* 1992;29: 403–15.

22. Weiner JP. The demand for physician services in a changing health care system: a synthesis. *Med Care Rev* 1993;50:411–49.

23. Schroeder SA. Physician supply and the U.S. medical marketplace. *Hlth Affairs* 1992;Spring:235–43.

24. Banta HD, Kemp KB. *The Management of Health Care Technologies in Ten Countries, Background Paper 4.* Washington DC: U.S. Congress Office of Technology Assessment, 1980.

25. US Congressional House Subcommittee Oversight Investigation. *Cost and Quality of Health Care: Unnecessary Surgery.* Washington, DC: GPO, 1976.

26. Leape LL. Unnecessary surgery. *Ann Rev Pub Hlth* 1992;13:363–83.

27. Starfield B. *Primary Care: Concepts, Evaluation, and Policy.* New York, NY: Oxford University Press, 1992.

28. Shi L. The relation between primary care and life chances. *J Hlth Care Poor Underserved* 1992;3: 321–335.

29. Shi L. Primary care, specialty care, and life chances. *Int J Hlth Serv* 1994;24:431–58.

30. Ginzberg E. Improving health care for the poor. *JAMA* 1994;271:464–47.

Politzer RM. Primary care physician supply and the medically underserved. *JAMA* 1991;266:104–9.

31. Starr P. *The Social Transformation of American Medicine: The Rise of a Sovereign Profession and the Making of a Vast Industry.* New York, NY: Basic Books Inc 1982.

32. US Bureau of Census. Current Population Reports. Series P25, No. 997. Washington DC. U.S. Bureau of Census, 1986.

33. Grandin J. Coordinating efforts to remove barriers to workforce balance. *Inquiry* 1994;31:338–41.

34. Budetti PP. Achieving a uniform federal primary care policy: opportunities presented by national health reform. *JAMA* 1993;269:498–501.

35. Institute of Medicine. *Primary Care Physicians: Financing Their GME in Ambulatory Settings.* Washington, DC: National Academy Press, 1989.

36. Ginzberg E, Dutka AL. *The Financing of Biomedical Research.* Baltimore, Md: Johns Hopkins University, 1989.

37. Roemer M, Hopkins C, Carr L, Gartside F. Copayments for ambulatory care: penny-wise and pound foolish. *Med Care* 1975;13:457–66.

38. Lurie N, Ward N, Shapiro M, Gallego C, Vahaiwalla R, Brook R. Termination of medical benefits: a follow-up study one year later. *N Engl J Med* 1986;314:1266–8.

39. Sandy, Lewis G.; Bodenheimer, Thomas; Pawlson, L. Gregory; Starfield, Barbara. "The Political Economy of U.S. Primary Care." *Health Affairs,* 2009;28:1136–1144.

40. Steinbrook, Robert. "Easing the Shortage in Adult Primary Care—Is It All about Money?" *New England Journal of Medicine,* 2009;360:2696–99.

41. Crandall LA, Dwyer JW, Duncan RP. Recruitment and retention of rural physicians: issues from the 1990s. *J Rural Hlth* 1990;6:19–38.

42. Eisenberg JM. Physician utilization: the state of research about physician's practice patterns. *Med Care* 1985;23:461–83.

43. Schoen, Cathy; Osborn, Robin; Huynh, Phuong Trang; Doty, Michelle; Peugh, Jordon; Zapert, Kinga. "On the Front Lines of Care: Primary Care Doctors' Office Systems, Experiences, and Views in Seven Countries." *Health Affairs,* 2006;25: w555–w571.

44. Chernew, Michael E.; Sabik, Lindsay; Chandra, Amitabh; Newhouse, Joseph P. "Would Having More Primary Care Doctors Cut Health Spending Growth?" *Health Affairs,* 2009; 28:1327–35.

45. Sepulveda, Martin-J.; Bodenheimer, Thomas; Grundy, Paul. "Primary Care: Can It Sold Employers' Health Care Dilemma?" *Health Affairs*, 2008;27:151–58.

46. Maciesek, Michael V.; Coffield, Ashley B.; Edwards, Nichol M.; Flottemesch, Thomas J.; Solberg, Leif I. "Prioritizing Clinical Preventive Services: A Review and Framework with Implications for Community Preventive Services." *Annual Review of Public Health*, 2009;30:341–55.

47. Berenson, Robert A.; Hammons, Terry; Gans, David N.; Zuckerman, Stephen; Merrel, Katie; Underwood, William S.; Williams, Aimee F. "A House is Not a Home: Keeping Patients At the Center of Practice Redesign." *Health Affairs*, 2008; 1219–1230.

1

Primary Health Care: Making Alma-Ata a Reality

Source: Reprinted from The Lancet, 372:1001-7. Walley J, Lawn JE, Tinker A, et al. Primary health care: making Alma-Ata a reality, Copyright 2008, with permission from Elsevier.

The principles agreed at Alma-Ata 30 years ago apply just as much now as they did then. "Health for all" by the year 2000 was not achieved, and the Millennium Development Goals (MDGs) for 2015 will not be met in most low-income countries without substantial acceleration of primary health care. Factors have included insufficient political prioritisation of health, structural adjustment policies, poor governance, population growth, inadequate health systems, and scarce research and assessment on primary health care. We propose the following priorities for revitalising primary health care. Health-service infrastructure, including human resources and essential drugs, needs strengthening, and user fees should be removed for primary health-care services to improve use. A continuum of care for maternal, newborn, and child health services, including family planning, is needed. Evidence-based, integrated packages of community and primary curative and preventive care should be adapted to country contexts, assessed, and scaled up. Community participation and community health workers linked to strengthened primary-care facilities and first-referral services are needed. Furthermore, intersectoral action linking health and development is necessary, including that for better water, sanitation, nutrition, food security, and HIV control. Chronic diseases, mental health, and child development should be addressed. Progress should be measured and accountability assured. We prioritise research questions and suggest actions and measures for stakeholders both locally and globally, which are required to revitalise primary health care.

REVISITING ALMA-ATA

Thirty years after the Alma-Ata Declaration for primary health care, "health for all"[1] remains a long way off for many countries, even those that are on track for mortality reduction goals, yet it remains the ultimate vision. The Millennium Development Goals (MDGs), which were adopted in 2000 as the next generation of the "health for all goals", specify eight aims and measurable targets, including reduction in maternal and child mortality and in the burden of HIV, malaria, and tuberculosis, and associated development targets for education and gender equity.[2] These goals have been accepted by the widest constituency of any set of health and development goals in history. The health targets correctly aim at reducing deaths as the first priority, yet reducing nonfatal diseases and improving quality of life are also important.

Primary health care is an approach to achieve both the MDGs and the wider goal of universal access to health through acceptable, accessible, appropriate, and affordable health care. Thus primary health care, if implemented, would advance health equity in all countries rich and poor and, as a result, promote human and national development.[3] Effective primary health care strengthens the integration of community, primary, and district health-care and prevention services.[4] Health depends on more than the health-care sector alone, and primary health care has from the beginning stressed the importance of intersectoral collaboration, social justice with community participation, and empowerment. Finally, the broad range of preventive and curative services provided within primary health care makes it a particularly cost-effective approach to address the large population health challenges in low-income and middle-income countries.

In retrospect, one concern with the primary health-care approach was the scarcity of a proposed strategy for implementation and its monitoring for accountability and scale-up purposes.[3] Furthermore, the ideals adopted in Alma-Ata and the energy created by the declaration lost their initial power in arguments between comprehensive or selective approaches. This tension is now being resolved in many countries by integration of vertical approaches (programmes for priority diseases) with horizontal approaches (to strengthen services for all health problems), thus developing integrated primary health-care services in a phased or step-wise manner. Recognition of the need to train and retain competent staff is also leading to more effective implementation.[5]

The variability of progress in the primary health-care approach, and the move towards integration, are well shown in the area of maternal, newborn, and child health.[3] Substantial progress is being made for child survival, whereas maternal and newborn health have been comparatively neglected until recently. The emphasis has shifted to provision of a continuum of care—including skilled attendance at birth for mothers and neonates and strengthening early postnatal care—as well as maternal, newborn, and child health, but most countries with high burden of disease still have very low coverage of such services.[3,6] Access to family planning, previously a priority, has fallen off the global priority list, despite it being one of the most cost-effective interventions for maternal, newborn, and child health.[7] Newer disease burdens, such as chronic diseases[8] and mental health,[9] are becoming more apparent. Hunger is an enduring threat, and an unacceptably high proportion of children and mothers remain undernourished, mainly in south Asia and Africa.[10] Integration of nutrition services within primary health care and improved links to other relevant non-health sectors remain as important now as they were 30 years ago.

Over the past decade, assistance agencies have substantially increased funding through global funds to address specific diseases, particularly HIV/AIDS, tuberculosis, and malaria. Even for these diseases much still remains to be done—e.g., coverage for HIV prevention interventions is only around 20%.[11] The challenge is to implement an achievable but comprehensive integrated approach to primary health care together with phased, long-term health-system building.[3]

WHERE ARE WE NOW, AND WHAT ARE THE GAPS?

Despite the ideals and enthusiasm after Alma-Ata, primary health care continues to be inadequately supported and resourced.[12] The coverage and quality of services in some countries has deteriorated because of conflict, poor governance, structural adjustment, population growth, and disinvestment in health.[13,14]

There are notable exceptions, as shown by the 30 low-income countries that have made steady progress to reduce deaths in children younger than 5 years and, in some cases, also newborn and maternal deaths.[15] For instance, Thailand, with a gross per-head income less than U.S. $3000 a year, has achieved remarkable progress and is at the top of the list of 30 low-income countries making rapid progress for child mortality reduction and equity in facility-based maternal-health services.[15] Success in progress towards health goals is affected by a country's political and social commitment to health and development. When stability, good governance, and stewardship for primary health care and other health services has been exhibited, progress is obvious.[15] However, even in countries with major challenges, a sustained political commitment makes a difference. In Malawi, for example, primary health-care services have been maintained despite the additional burden from HIV/AIDS. Sri Lanka and Haiti provide good examples of successful sociopolitical commitment despite political instability. In Haiti, this commitment has largely been through non-governmental and faith-based organisations.[15] Progress is possible with a willingness to innovate—e.g., with different types of partners and health workers used to access hard to reach populations.

Community care, empowerment, and active social participation in improvement of health services might be the most neglected part of Alma-Ata.[3,16] Chronic diseases and mental-health disorders are emerging health problems. Key aspects of primary

Table 1   Implementation and measurement of primary health care at scale by level of responsibility

	Action: implementation of PHC at scale	Measurement: measuring markers, progress, and accountability
Community, family, individuals	• Select and support CHWs • Actively participate in community health-promotion activities and development programmes (income generation, water and sanitation, self-reliance)	• Funding, training, and supervision for CHWs that is established and tracked, including attrition rates • Community mobilisation for health promotion and poverty eradication programmes which are established and have trackable indicators
Health centres, hospitals, practitioners	• Train, supervise, and use packages of care, guidelines, and management methods—e.g., IMCI, IMAI, IMPAC • Provide outreach activities and links with CHWs and private sector to improve coverage of interventions and strengthen referral • Support community health promotion	• Health facility capability to provide services that are assessed regularly • Regular assessment of client satisfaction in place with use of available methods to measure quality • Effective functional plans to register and link public and private providers
District, subdistrict	• Plan and budget according to disease burden and related cost-effective packages of care and prevention • Build CHW, MNCH, and FP delivery, and strengthen referral strategies • Ensure equitable distribution and quality of health workers	• District level methods used for planning, linking burden with budget allocation, procurement, and management • District plan in place to integrate MNCH and FP interventions at community, health centre, hospital levels, and referral system • Track health worker knowledge, skills, performance, and the rate that they leave their place of work
National, state, or provincial	• Integrate health sector plans and use of methods for planning • Scale up proven health systems approaches on the basis of evidence • Coordinate funding with agriculture, food security, climate change, and population policies • Introduce phased removal of user fees for PHC services, at least for vulnerable populations and poor people	• One national health plan and national legislation for health promotion and sex equality in place • Documentation of content and process for programme priority setting to develop and refine integrated high-impact interventions adapted to context on the basis of local epidemiology and evidence • One national monitoring plan including coverage and quality of key interventions assessed, and disaggregated by equity, sex, or ethnic origin • One national general budget with a section with health allocations specified • User fees removed for PHC (or at least exemptions for MNCH and vulnerable populations)
Global	• Prioritise funding by burden of disease, cost-effective interventions, and health systems building over time • Provide predictable long-term financing for health • Provide budget support for sector-wide approaches in countries with good governance and where equity goals are pursued • Increase investment in implementation research for PHC and building local research capacity	• Coordination of development partners and national funds for health in accordance with the Paris Declaration (OECD tracking) • Unified or harmonised assessment frameworks available for MNCH and PHC, with funds allocated for continued assessment at scale • Methods for programme priority setting for programmes on the basis of peer-reviewed effectiveness and cost inputs, and which are user friendly for country use • Research funding on the basis of transparent priority setting methods

PHC = primary health care. CHW = community health worker. IMCI = Integrated Management of Childhood Illness. IMAI = Integrated Management of Adolescent and Adult Illness. IMPAC = Integrated Management of Pregnancy and Childbirth. MNCH = maternal, newborn, and child health. FP = family planning. OECD = Organization for Economic Co-operation and Development.

Table: Implementation and measurement of primary health care at scale by level of responsibility health-care services that need to be strengthened include district health management systems with local use of data for decision making and coherent use of community health workers and other primary health-care personnel. The reality of intersectoral linkage between health and development is variable, with some countries achieving great progress in education, water and sanitation, and nutrition, and others not progressing and continuing to dichotomise development and health.[15]

Despite the challenges and restrictions in implementation so far, the ideals expressed at Alma-Ata and the primary health-care approach are as valid now as ever. We also now have evidence for a much greater range of cost-effective interventions than we did 30 years ago.[17] Unlike at Alma-Ata, specific health targets have now been set for 2015 and progress is being monitored. However, only 7 years remain in which to achieve the MDGs. Should we be considering a further set of goals for an extended timeframe, such as over the coming 20 years, which would go beyond mortality reduction and help to sustain action for health after 2015? If so, now is the time to start, since such goals would take time to develop as measurable targets owned by countries and the global health community.

REVITALISATION OF PRIMARY HEALTH CARE AT SCALE

All levels—individual, family, community, facility, district, provincial, national, and global—have a role and responsibility if health for all is to be achieved. To deliver results with a primary health-care approach will need partnerships, links, and an enabling environment including bottom-up support from empowered communities, top-down support from responsible governments and across municipal and state levels, and external support with technical and financial resources, when needed and appropriate.[5,18] Primary-care services and facilities need to be strengthened and linked to the communities that they serve. But primary health care is wider than the health system, and needs greater action. The emphasis on community participation and intersectoral collaboration given by the Alma-Ata Declaration is even more relevant now with increasing complexity of the development architecture. We need pragmatic and measurable approaches that build evidence on how these strategies can best be implemented in various settings. The table outlines some priority actions that can be taken and their measurement at each level.

The seven priorities for revitalisation of the Alma-Ata commitment to a primary health-care approach are described below.

(1) Making and Keeping Health and Health Equity a Priority

Although mortality is an important indicator, the vision that health is a state of wellness, not solely an absence of death or disease, should not be lost.[19] The MDGs, which have measurable outcomes and build on health and development for all, will continue to be valid and relevant for many countries beyond 2015 and need to be held as a benchmark of success. However, measurable targets are also needed to extend beyond the MDGs' target date of 2015 and cover the broader health agenda as envisioned in Alma-Ata.

(2) Implementation of Integrated Primary Health Care at Scale

When unified national health plans, including those for maternal, newborn, and child health and wider components of primary health care do not exist, investments of time, expertise, and funds are urgently needed to put them into place. Even more important than national strategic plans are specific implementation planning processes, leading to district action. National to district planning and management systems need to be systematic, and human and material resources strengthened.[5] Good governance has to be fostered and, where it exists, an increased proportion of donor funds should be channelled through budget support and sector-wide approaches, while partnerships with civil society are strengthened. Public, non-governmental, faith-based, and private providers need to be linked into a coherent health system under responsible government stewardship. Countries with such frameworks in place are over-performing for health outcomes despite major challenges—e.g., Malawi has an essential health package and a national agreement with Christian Health Association of Malawi, which provides 40% of health-care services.[15]

Selection of a set of key evidence-based interventions for implementation in primary health-care settings is crucial.[4] Packages of care for maternal, newborn, and child health can be expanded to include interventions that address mental health, child development, and other long-term outcomes.[6] An integrated approach to the management of chronic disorders, irrespective of the cause, is not only feasible but desirable within primary health care.[8] Experience and evidence from successes of this approach need to be applied to other disease groups. For example, the systematic package for tuberculosis care has been successfully adapted to deliver HIV antiretroviral services within the general health services of Malawi.[20] This approach could be applied to other chronic diseases such as diabetes, epilepsy, and mental illness, and to a continuum of care approach to maternal, newborn, and child health at a district level. All innovations should be designed so as to be replicable and sustainable with available or realistically attainable human and material resources. Assessment embedded within early district implementation can be the basis for refining guidelines and other methods for implementation to ensure effective scale-up nationally and to learn from what works and why, or why not.[21]

When health systems are weak or the timeframe is short, interventions have been implemented vertically. This approach can be either to achieve important benefits at scale in as short a time as possible—e.g., since 2000 for HIV antiretroviral services—or because donors are focused on short-term goals. However, even if the start is vertical, over time interventions should be integrated and delivered by coordinated cadres of multipurpose and more specialised health workers within district management systems and with participation from communities.[3,5,15] As new evidence for an intervention becomes available, the feasibility and effectiveness of adding the intervention to primary health-care services should be assessed locally.[4] Some leading advocates of primary health care have suggested that 15% of all funds from vertical interventions should be invested in comprehensive primary health-care systems.[12]

To achieve quality and safety in primary healthcare services, suficient numbers of appropriately trained and supported health workers are needed. Properly supervised task shifting is required, as proposed by WHO in the context of HIV care.[22] Although evidence for task shifting from doctors to nurse practitioners and from health professionals to lay health workers does exist, the evidence base needs to be strengthened.[23] Pakistan provides an example of an effective national programme for community health workers.[24] There is a real danger of overloading health workers with too many tasks, hence careful and systematic tailoring of tasks to local health needs and available resources will be necessary.[3] Effective and supportive supervision is key to improvement of service delivery, and educational outreach visits have improved prescribing.[23]

The quality of care rests on the use of high-quality guidelines. Essential care and prevention packages have been developed for the major health disorders affecting children; for maternal, newborn, and child health; and for adults.[23] These packages include the integrated management of childhood illness; an essential practice guide for pregnancy, childbirth, post-partum, and newborn care;[25] and the integrated management of adolescent and adult illness,[26] which already includes chronic HIV and antiretroviral treatment guidelines, but diabetes and other chronic diseases could be added.[8] These technical interventions need to be designed in the broader context of primary health care and community development, including education, nutrition, water, and sanitation. Together with access to basic primary health care and prevention measures, essential drug lists and formularies remain important in implementation of primary healthcare services.

(3) Ensuring Equity and Sex Equality

Since the burden of disease is greatest for the poorest people, we must consider their needs first. Evidence shows that use of services by poor people is improved when user fees are reduced or withdrawn, providing that the resources are replaced,[23] or if incentives for care are provided through conditional cash transfers.[27] Services should specifically target and reach deprived rural and urban areas, with particular attention to women, children, and other disadvantaged and vulnerable groups (e.g., indigenous people, inmates, elderly people, people with disabilities, refugees, and internally displaced populations). For example, working directly with women's groups can help address sex inequities and increase cultural acceptance and sustainability, while indirectly benefiting other family and community members. Community health workers can reach and serve populations that have limited access to facility care.[28]

(4) Facilitating Community Participation and Empowerment

Active community participation is essential for effective community interventions such as those for maternal, newborn, and child health and environment-related diseases.[16] Community participation is not merely mobilising people to accept a health intervention.[29] Experience has shown the need for a shift from health education (provision of information) to health promotion (transformation of attitudes and behaviour) to empower people to have a more active role in their health.[30,31] Health promotion messages are not static—the epidemiological transition and a rise in chronic, non-communicable diseases related to ageing populations, changing diets, tobacco use, and more sedentary lifestyles will need appropriate messages and dissemination. Through education in schools and health promotion, communities can take control over their health.

One trial has shown that mobilisation of women and other community-based groups in Nepalese villages can lead to decreases in newborn and probably maternal mortality.[32] The challenge for the community mobilisation approach is to effectively replicate it at scale. Previously, the emphasis on community participation has been focused on poor people in rural areas. However, since a majority of the world's population now live in cities, the need is for community engagement for poor people living in urban areas and requires functional models of care. For example, the BRAC (formerly the Bangladesh Rural Advancement Committee) programme in Bangladesh delivers maternal and child health and family planning interventions in urban areas with good results.[33] Participatory research should be embedded within implementation projects, as with the tuberculosis public-private doctors' partnership in Nepal.[34]

(5) Linking Health and Development

Health professionals can easily overlook that health is affected by much more than health services, and conversely the development community can view health as a separate entity.[3] Both the Alma-Ata declaration and the MDGs have helped broaden this view by emphasising the importance of intersectoral approaches to poverty reduction and development. In practice, intersectoral collaboration is difficult to achieve since sectors tend to operate in isolation—e.g., persuasion of the health and agricultural sectors to prioritise nutrition and food security is difficult, yet this need is greater than ever. That investment in education, especially of girls, greatly affects health is well known. The WHO Commission on Social Determinants for Health recommends that countries address and monitor the inequitable distribution of resources, living and working conditions, and child development.[35] They should provide universal health-care coverage on the basis of the primary health-care model with "locally appropriate action for prevention and promotion in balance with investment in curative interventions, and an emphasis on the primary level of care".[35] It recommends ending user fees and financing the health-care system through general taxation or mandatory universal insurance. Generally, although intersectoral collaboration is difficult to

measure, such evidence (or at least more assessment of experiences at scale in countries) will be crucial for the development of sound strategies to affect the health of this generation and the next.

(6) Measurement of Change and Ensuring Accountability

Statements such as "health for all" are inspirational, yet difficult to measure. Effective tracking of primary health-care implementation needs definite outcome and process measures, including mortality measurement and measures of coverage of high-impact interventions, health systems functioning, and community action. A key challenge for primary health-care implementation is that of monitoring progress towards clearly defined and realistic targets. Such monitoring needs process indicators, including those reflecting health-system performance (human resources and management, infrastructure and maintenance, regulatory procedures, transparency and democratic governance arrangements, levels of sustained financing, budgeting, and planning). Measurement of equity is key to assessment of progress towards the MDGs and primary health care, particularly the way in which we are reaching people who are underserved. This approach should include monitoring process measures, such as vulnerable populations' access to services, service coverage, and health-care practices.

(7) Investment in Innovation for Drugs and Technologies, and in Implementation Research

The early days after Alma-Ata resulted in innovation for drugs and technologies (such as oral rehydration solution), which was driven by need and feasibility in low-resource settings. Essential drugs policies advanced the use of appropriate and low-cost generic drugs. However, innovation for health technologies for poor people has again fallen off the global agenda, apart from some encouraging signs in specific initiatives: better medicines for children and affordable medicines for all, and drugs for neglected diseases. Strategic prioritisation for new drugs and technologies and effective partnerships are needed to address the gaps and make sure that the solutions reach poor people, as has been achieved very effectively for pneumococcal vaccines through the accelerated development and introduction plan.[3]

Research and innovation are needed to improve health status, and the interaction between researchers, policy makers, and other stakeholders is essential to design, undertake, and use the results of research.[36] Implementation research and assessment should be embedded within new primary health-care services and approaches, so that locally produced evidence can support effective national scale-up.[21,37] Health policy and decision makers need to commission implementation research, and apply innovative and empirically supported approaches.[32] Policy makers also need to know the extent to which interventions are based on evidence. Research findings need to be disseminated widely and beyond the research community, in ways that non-academic people can understand.

RESEARCH PRIORITIES FOR PRIMARY HEALTH CARE

The so-called 10/90 gap indicates the imbalance of having a small proportion (10%) of research fund-

ing addressing the health needs of most of the population (90%) worldwide.[38] Identification of research priorities for primary health care is important for optimising the effective use of scarce resources. Reviews have established the scarcity of rigorous evidence for implementation and delivery of services generally and for human resources particularly, especially in low-income and middle-income countries.[39]

The child health and nutrition research initiative (CHNRI) has developed a systematic method for setting priorities for health research investments that can be applied globally and nationally and for different purposes.[40] We used this method, which has previously been used in several areas,[41] to identify research priorities for primary health care, with the following criteria: the likelihood that the research option would (1) be answerable, (2) be feasible to undertake, (3) fill a crucial gap in knowledge, and that the resulting intervention would (4) improve deliverability of interventions in primary health care, (5) improve equity, and (6) have an important effect on disease burden.

The rationale, conceptual framework, and application guidelines have all been described in greater detail elsewhere.[40,41]

Panel 1 shows the top five research options addressing overall primary health-care questions with the highest scores, along with the top questions for delivery of services for maternal, newborn, and child health. Research priorities for chronic diseases have been defined in a previous paper in this issue.[8] In each of the categories, a list of important research issues was identified by the *Lancet* Alma-Ata Working Group. In commissioning research to address these issues, local stakeholders and researchers (both clinical and health-service researchers) should be involved in further refining the research questions to develop effectiveness studies that are locally relevant. One opportunity is when the Global Ministerial Forum on Research for Health, in Bamako, Mali, November 2008, brings together policy makers and researchers to promote and support research on priorities identified to improve health in developing countries. As with clinical services, delivery of high-quality research, especially with an equity focus, first needs development and nurturing of local capacity.[42]

RENEWING COMMITMENT AND INVESTMENT IN PRIMARY HEALTH CARE

We call for the global health community, governments, national authorities, international agencies, and civil society to revitalise primary health care according to the original tenets of Alma-Ata and to

Panel 2: Actions to increase commitment and resources for primary health care

- Join with other calls for global commitment to allocate more development assistance to health for the countries with the least favourable health indicators and most diffcult health challenges, investing in comprehensive and selective primary health care to build strong health systems over time
- Mobilise strategic, consistent, and long-term investment from Ministries of Finance, linking with Ministries of Health in primary health care within health-sector planning with evidence of the cost-effectiveness and economic and development benefits of primary health care
- Develop a comprehensive human resource plan for primary health care that is tailored to every country, linking with existing national planning and targeting high-impact interventions for maternal, newborn, and child health, adult infections, and chronic diseases, especially in areas that are dificult to serve, delegating tasks when appropriate and strengthening team work, supervision, and coordination, and addressing staff retention issue for hard-to-serve settings
- Rationalise the use of drugs, because of their large budget requirements, with generic drugs and public funding for essential drugs, and promote innovation for development of essential dugs and appropriate technology that is needed for crucial primary health-care services
- Increase local capacity for collecting and using data for action to improve the coverage, quality, and equity of primary health-care services
- Promote community and civil society participation in the primary health-care process towards health and development for all

coverage for underserved people in rural and urban communities is essential and is the real test of social justice and sex equity. Resources should be increased and targeted towards evidence-based and integrated packages of care and towards the least served countries and communities. These resources can be delivered through strengthened primary and community care, together with community mobilisation and intersectoral collaboration for health. Individuals must be seen as active participants in their health, not passive recipients of supply-driven interventions. The emphasis has to shift from showing immediate results from single interventions to creating integrated, long-term, sustainable health systems, which can be built from a more selective primary health-care start. Research needs to be embedded within primary health-care activities, especially to be able to compare varying delivery approaches.

Margaret Chan, Director-General of WHO, has recently said "When I took office at the start of last year, I called for a return to primary health care as an approach to strengthening health systems. My commitment has deepened. If we want to reach the health-related goals, we must return to the values, principles, and approaches of primary health care."[43] What is needed is for all stakeholders to renew their commitment to the principles of primary health care so that we do, after all, achieve health for all.

Conflict of Interest Statement

We declare that we have no conflict of interest.

ACKNOWLEDGMENTS

The contents are the responsibility of the authors. The work was not funded by any agency. We thank Lynn Auty for editing assistance.

Lancet 2008; 372: 1001–07. See Editorial page 863. This is the eighth in a Series of eight papers about Alma-Ata: rebirth and revision. Members listed at end of paper Nuffield Centre for Health and Development, Leeds Institute of Health Sciences, University of Leeds, Leeds, UK (Prof J Walley FFPH); Save the Children, Washington DC, USA (J E Lawn MPH, A Tinker MPH); Saving Newborn Lives, Cape Town, South Africa (J E Lawn, A Tinker); Partnership for Maternal, Newborn and Child Health, Geneva, Switzerland (A de Francisco MD); Health Systems Research Unit, Medical Research Council, Cape Town, South Africa (M Chopra MSc); Croatian Centre for Global Health, University of Split Medical School, Split, Croatia (Prof I Rudan MD); Department of Public Health Sciences, The University of Edinburgh Medical School, Teviot Place, Edinburgh, UK (I Rudan); Department of Paediatrics and Child Health, Aga Khan University Hospital, Karachi, Pakistan (Prof Z A Bhutta PhD); and Department of International Health, Johns Hopkins Bloomberg School of Public Health, Baltimore, MD, USA (Prof R E Black MD).

Correspondence to: Prof John Walley Nuffield Centre for Health and Development, Leeds Institute of Health Sciences, University of Leeds, 101 Clarendon Road, Leeds LS2 9LJ, UK j.d.walley@leeds.ac.uk.

monitor progress. We propose the establishment of a process to set new measurable targets that build on, yet go beyond, the MDGs to reflect the broader primary health-care agenda and to ensure continued momentum towards health for all after 2015. A possibility for one such goal could be a specified increase in average life expectancy in all countries, with defined targets for equity and quality of life.

We propose several actions to increase commitment and resources for primary health care (Panel 2). The biggest challenge is implementation with community participation, especially scaling up known, cost-effective interventions for prevention and essential care. Priorities continue to be maternal, newborn, and child health; family planning; and the high burden of communicable diseases in many countries. However, there is also a growing need to address chronic, non-communicable diseases. Reaching high

• • • References

1. Alma-Ata. *Declaration of Alma-Ata: international conference on primary health care.* USSR; Sept 6-12, 1978.

2. UN. *Road Map towards the implementation of the United Nations Millennium Declaration.* New York: United Nations, 2001.

3. Lawn JE, Rohde J, Rifkin S, Were M, Paul VK, Chopra M. Alma-Ata 30 years on: revolutionary, relevant, and time to revitalise. *Lancet* 2008; 372: 917-27.

4. Bhutta ZA, Ali S, Cousens S, et al. Interventions to address maternal, newborn, and child survival: what difference can integrated primary health-care strategies make? *Lancet* 2008; 372: 972-89.

5. Ekman B, Pathmanathan I, Liljestrand J. Integrating health interventions for women, newborn babies, and children: a framework for action. *Lancet* 2008; 372: 990-1000.

6. Kerber KJ, de Graft-Johnson JE, Bhutta ZA, Okong P, Starrs A, Lawn JE. Continuum of care for maternal, newborn, and child health: from slogan to service delivery. *Lancet* 2007; 370: 1358-69.

7. Cleland J, Bernstein S, Ezeh A, Faundes A, Glasier A, Innis J. Family planning: the unfinished agenda. *Lancet* 2006; 368: 1810-27.

8. Beaglehole R, Epping-Jordan JA, Patel V, et al. Improving the prevention and management of chronic disease in low-income and middle-income countries: a priority for primary health care. *Lancet* 2008; 372: 940-49.

9. Prince M, Patel V, Saxena S, et al. No health without mental health. *Lancet* 2007; 370: 859-77.

10. Black RE, Allen LH, Bhutta ZA, et al. Maternal and child undernutrition: global and regional exposures and health consequences. *Lancet* 2008; 371: 243-60.

11. UNAIDS. *Report on the global AIDS epidemic: executive summary.* Geneva: UNAIDS, 2006.

12. De Maeseneer J, van Weel C, Egilman D, et al. Funding for primary health care in developing countries. *BMJ* 2008; 336: 518-19.

13. Bhutta ZA, Belgaumi A, Abdur RM, Karrar Z, Khashaba M, Mouane N. Child health and survival in the Eastern Mediterranean region. *BMJ* 2006; 333: 839-42.

14. Simms C, Rohson M, Peattie S. *The bitterest pill of all: the collapse of Africa's health systems.* London: Save the Children and Medact, 2001.

15. Rohde J, Cousens S, Chopra M, et al. 30 years after Alma-Ata: has primary health care worked in countries? *Lancet* 2008; 372: 950-61.

16. Rosato M, Laverack G, Howard Grabman L, et al. Community participation: lessons for maternal, newborn, and child health. *Lancet* 2008; 372: 962-71.

17. Jamison DT, Breman JG, Measham AR, et al, eds. *Disease control priority project in developing countries, 2 edn.* Washington DC: The International Bank for Reconstruction and Development/The World Bank, 2006.

18. Taylor-Ide D, Taylor CE. *Just and lasting change: when communities own their own futures.* Baltimore, JHU: 2002.

19. WHO. *Preamble to the Constitution of the World Health Organization International Health Conference, New York, June 19-22, 1946.* Official Records of the World Health Organization, number 2. Geneva: World Health Organization, 1948.

20. Harries AD, Libamba E, Schouten EJ, Mwansambo A, Salaniponi FM, Mpazanje R. Expanding anti-retroviral therapy in Malawi: drawing on the country's experience with tuberculosis. *BMJ* 2004; 329: 1163-66.

21. Walley J, Khan MA, Shah SK, Witter S, Wei X. How to get research into practice: first get practice into research. *Bull World Health Organ* 2007; 85: 424.

22. Wiler G, Dreesch N, Dal Poz M. *Planning human resources development to achieve priority health programme goals.* Human resources for Health Development. Geneva: World Health Organization, 2008.

23. Lewin S, Lavis JN, Oxman AD, et al. Supporting the delivery of cost-effective interventions in primary health-care systems in low-income and middle-income countries. *Lancet* 2008; 372: 928-39.

24. Oxford Policy Management. *Evaluation of the Prime Minister's Lady Health Worker Programme.* Islamabad: Oxford Policy Management/Ministry of Health, 2002.

25. WHO. *Pregnancy, childbirth, postpartum and newborn care: a guide for essential practice.* Geneva: World Health Organization, 2006.

26. WHO. *IMAI/IMCI heath centre/primary care guideline modules.* Geneva: World Health Organization, 2007. *http://www.who.int/hiv/ pub/imai/primary/en/ index.html* (accessed Aug 24, 2008).

27. Lagarde M, Haines A, Palmer N. Conditional cash transfers for improving uptake of health interventions in low- and middle-income countries: a systematic review. *JAMA* 2007; 298: 1900-10.

28. Haines A, Sanders D, Lehmann U, et al. Achieving child survival goals: potential contribution of community health workers. *Lancet* 2007; 369: 2121-31.

29. McPake B, Hansen K, Mills A. *Implementing the Bamako initiative in Africa: a review and five case studies.* London: London School of Hygiene and Tropical Medicine, 1992.

30. Laverack G. *Health promotion and practice: power and empowerment.* London: Sage Publications, 2008.

31. WHO. *The Bangkok Charter for Health Promotion in a Globalized World.* Geneva: World Health Organization, 2005.

32. Manandhar DS, Osrin D, Shrestha BP, et al. Effect of a participatory intervention with women's groups on birth outcomes in Nepal: cluster-randomised controlled trial. *Lancet* 2004; 364: 970-79.

33. Mustaque A, Chowdhury R, Aminul Alam M, Ahmed J. Development knowledge and experience-from Bangladesh to Afghanistan and beyond. *Bull World Health Organ* 2006; 84: 677-81.

34. Newell JN, Pande SB, Baral SC, Bam DS, Malla P. Control of tuberculosis in an urban setting in Nepal: public-private partnership. *Bull World Health Organ* 2004; 82: 92-98.

35. Commission on Social Determinants of Health. *Closing the gap in a generation: health equity through action on the social determinants of health.* Final Report of the Commission on Social Determinants of Health. Geneva: World Health Organization, 2008.

36. Lavis JN, Posada FB, Haines A, Osei E. Use of research to inform public policymaking. *Lancet* 2004; 364: 1615-21.

37. Sanders D, Haines A. Implementation research is needed to achieve international health goals. *PLoS Med* 2006; 3: e186.

38. de Francisco A, Matlin A, eds. *Monitoring financial flows for health research, 2006: the changing landscape of health research for development.* Geneva: Global Forum for Health Research, 2006.

39. Chopra M, Munro S, Lavis JN, Vist G, Bennett S. Effects of policy options for human resources for health: an analysis of systematic reviews. *Lancet* 2008; 371: 668-74.

40. Rudan I, Chopra M, Kapiriri L, et al. Setting priorities in global child health research investments: universal challenges and conceptual framework. *Croat Med J* 2008; 49: 307-17.

41. Tomlinson M, Chopra M, Sanders D, et al. Setting priorities in child health research investments for South Africa. *PLoS Med* 2007; 4: e259.

42. Victora CG. Measuring progress towards equitable child survival: where are the epidemiologists? *Epidemiology* 2007; 18: 669-72.

43. Margaret Chan, Director-General. *Address to the 61st World Health Assembly.* Geneva: World Health Organization, 2008.

2

Primary Care: Putting People First

Source: World Health Organization. Chapter 3: Primary care: putting people first. In: World Health Organization, eds. *The World Health Report 2008: Primary Health Care—Now More than Ever*. Geneva, Switzerland: World Health Organization, 2008:41-60.

This chapter describes how primary care brings promotion and prevention, cure and care together in a safe, effective and socially productive way at the interface between the population and the health system. In short, what needs to be done to achieve this is "to put people first": to give balanced consideration to health and well-being as well as to the values and capacities of the population and the health workers[1]. The chapter starts by describing features of health care that, along with effectiveness and safety, are essential in ensuring improved health and social outcomes.

These features are person-centredness, comprehensiveness and integration, and continuity of care, with a regular point of entry into the health system, so that it becomes possible to build an enduring relationship of trust between people and their health-care providers. The chapter then defines what this implies for the organization of health-care delivery: the necessary switch from specialized to generalist ambulatory care, with responsibility for a defined population and the ability to coordinate support from hospitals, specialized services and civil society organizations.

GOOD CARE IS ABOUT PEOPLE

Biomedical science is, and should be, at the heart of modern medicine. Yet, as William Osler, one of its founders, pointed out, "it is much more important to know what sort of patient has a disease than what sort of disease a patient has"[2]. Insufficient recognition of the human dimension in health and of the need to tailor the health service's response to the specificity of each community and individual situation represent major shortcomings in contemporary health care, resulting not only in inequity and poor social outcomes, but also diminishing the health outcome returns on the investment in health services.

Putting people first, the focus of service delivery reforms is not a trivial principle. It can require significant—even if often simple—departures from business as usual. The reorganization of a medical centre in Alaska in the United States, accommodating 45,000 patient contacts per year, illustrates how far-reaching the effects can be. The centre functioned to no great satisfaction of either staff or clients until it decided to establish a direct relationship between each individual and family in the community and a specific staff member[3]. The staff were then in a position to know "their" patients' medical history and understand their personal and family situation. People were in a position to get to know and trust their health-care provider: they no longer had to deal with an institution but with their personal caregiver. Complaints about compartmentalized and fragmented services abated[4]. Emergency room visits were reduced by approximately 50% and referrals to specialty care by 30%; waiting times shortened significantly. With fewer "rebound" visits for unresolved health problems, the workload actually decreased and staff job satisfaction improved. Most importantly, people felt that they were being listened to and respected—a key aspect of what people value about health care[5,6]. A slow bureaucratic system was thus transformed into one that is customer-responsive, customer-owned and customer-driven[4].

In a very different setting, the health centres of Ouallam, a rural district in Niger, implemented an equally straightforward reorganization of their way of working in order to put people first. Rather than the traditional morning curative care consultation and specialized afternoon clinics (growth monitoring, family planning, etc.), the full range of services was offered at all times, while the nurses were instructed to engage in an active dialogue with their patients. For example, they no longer waited for women to ask for contraceptives, but informed them, at every contact, about the range of services available. Within a few months, the very low uptake of family planning, previously attributed to cultural constraints, was a thing of the past (Figure 3.1, not included)[7] .

People's experiences of care provided by the health system are determined first and foremost by the way they are treated when they experience a problem and look for help: by the responsiveness of the health-worker interface between population and health services. People value some freedom in choosing a health provider because they want one they can trust and who will attend to them promptly and in an adequate environment, with respect and confidentiality[8].

Health-care delivery can be made more effective by making it more considerate and convenient, as in Ouallam district. However, primary care is about more than shortening waiting times, adapting opening hours or getting staff to be more polite. Health workers have to care for people throughout the course of their lives, as individuals and as members of

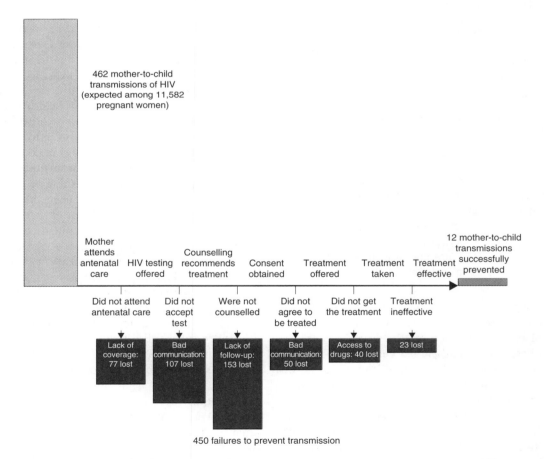

Figure 3.2 Lost opportunities for prevention of mother-to-child transmission of HIV (MTCT) in Côte d'Ivoire[29]: only a tiny fraction of the expected transmissions are actually prevented

a family and a community whose health must be protected and enhanced[9], and not merely as body parts with symptoms or disorders that require treating[10].

The service delivery reforms advocated by the PHC movement aim to put people at the centre of health care, so as to make services more effective, efficient and equitable. Health services that do this start from a close and direct relationship between individuals and communities and their caregivers. This, then, provides the basis for person-centredness, continuity, comprehensiveness and integration, which constitute the distinctive features of primary care. Table 3.1 summarizes the differences between primary care and care provided in conventional settings, such as in clinics or hospital outpatient departments, or through the disease control programmes that shape many health services in resource-limited settings. The section that follows reviews these defining features of primary care, and describes how they contribute to better health and social outcomes.

THE DISTINCTIVE FEATURES OF PRIMARY CARE

Effectiveness and Safety Are Not Just Technical Matters

Health care should be effective and safe. Professionals as well as the general public often over-rate the performance of their health services. The emergence of evidence-based medicine in the 1980s has helped to bring the power and discipline of scientific evidence to health-care decision-making[11], while still taking into consideration patient values and preferences[12]. Over the last decade, several hundred reviews of effectiveness have been conducted[13], which have led to better information on the choices available to health practitioners when caring for their patients.

Evidence-based medicine, however, cannot in itself ensure that health care is effective and safe. Growing awareness of the multiple ways in which care may be compromised is contributing to a gradual rise in standards of quality and safety (Box 3.1). Thus far, however, such efforts have concentrated disproportionately on hospital and specialist care, mainly in high- and middle-income countries. The effectiveness and safety of generalist ambulatory care, where most interactions between people and health services take place, has been given much less attention[14]. This is a particularly important issue in the unregulated commercial settings of many developing countries where people often get poor value for money (Box 3.2)[15].

Technical and safety parameters are not the only determinants of the outcomes of health care. The disappointingly low success rate in preventing mother-to-child transmission (MTCT) of HIV in a study in the Côte d'Ivoire (Figure 3.2) illustrates that other features of the organization of health care are equally critical—good drugs are not enough. How services deal with people is also vitally important. Surveys in Australia, Canada, Germany, New Zealand, the United Kingdom and the United States show that a

Table 3.1	Aspects of care that distinguish conventional health care from people-centred primary care

Conventional ambulatory medical care in clinics or outpatient departments	Disease control programmes	People-centred primary care
Focus on illness and cure	Focus on priority diseases	Focus on health needs
Relationship limited to the moment of consultation	Relationship limited to programme implementation	Enduring personal relationship
Episodic curative care	Programme-defined disease control interventions	Comprehensive, continuous and person-centred care
Responsibility limited to effective and safe advice to the patient at the moment of consultation	Responsibility for disease-control targets among the target population	Responsibility for the health of all in the community along the life cycle; responsibility for tackling determinants of ill-health
Users are consumers of the care they purchase	Population groups are targets of disease-control interventions	People are partners in managing their own health and that of their community

Box 3.1 Towards a science and culture of improvement: evidence to promote patient safety and better outcomes

The outcome of health care results from the balance between the added value of treatment or intervention, and the harm it causes to the patient[16]. Until recently, the extent of such harm has been underestimated. In industrialized countries, approximately 1 in 10 patients suffers harm caused by avoidable adverse events while receiving care[17]: up to 98,000 deaths per year are caused by such events in the United States alone[18]. Multiple factors contribute to this situation[19], ranging from systemic faults to problems of competence, social pressure on patients to undergo risky procedures, to incorrect technology usage[20]. For example, almost 40% of the 16 billion injections administered worldwide each year are given with syringes and needles that are reused without sterilization[14]. Each year, unsafe injections thus cause 1.3 million deaths and almost 26 million years of life lost, mainly because of transmission of hepatitis B and C, and HIV[21].

Especially disquieting is the paucity of information on the extent and determinants of unsafe care in low- and middle income countries. With unregulated commercialization of care, weaker quality control and health resource limitations, healthcare users in low-income countries may well be even more exposed to the risk of unintended patient harm than patients in high-income countries. The World Alliance for Patient Safety[22], among others, advocates making patients safer through systemic interventions and a change in organizational culture rather than through the denunciation of individual health-care practitioners or administrators[23].

Box 3.2 When supplier-induced and consumer-driven demand determine medical advice: ambulatory care in India

"Ms. S is a typical patient who lives in urban Delhi. There are over 70 private-sector medical care providers within a 15-minute walk from her house (and virtually any household in her city). She chooses the private clinic run by Dr. SM and his wife. Above the clinic a prominent sign says "Ms. MM, Gold Medalist, MBBS", suggesting that the clinic is staffed by a highly proficient doctor (an MBBS is the basic degree for a medical doctor as in the British 2 system). As it turns out, Ms. MM is rarely at the clinic. We were told that she sometimes comes at 4 a.m. to avoid the long lines that form if people know she is there. We later discover that she has "franchised" her name to a number of different clinics. Therefore, Ms. S sees Dr. SM and his wife, both of whom were trained in traditional Ayurvedic medicine through a six-month long-distance course. The doctor and his wife sit at a small table surrounded, on one side, by a large number of bottles full of pills, and on the other, a bench with patients on them, which extends into the street. Ms. S sits at the end of this bench. Dr. SM and his wife are the most popular medical care providers in the neighbourhood, with more than 200 patients every day. The doctor spends an average of 3.5 minutes with each patient, asks 3.2 questions, and performs an average of 2.5 examinations. Following the diagnosis, the doctor takes two or three different pills, crushes them using a mortar and pestle, and makes small paper packets from the resulting powder which he gives to Ms. S and asks her to take for two or three days. These medicines usually include one antibiotic and one analgesic and anti-inflamatory drug. Dr. SM tells us that he constantly faces unrealistic patient expectations, both because of the high volume of patients and their demands for treatments that even Dr. SM knows are inappropriate. Dr. SM and his wife seem highly motivated to provide care to their patients and even with a very crowded consultation room they spend more time with their patients than a public sector doctor would. However, they are not bound by their knowledge [...] and instead deliver health care like the crushed pills in a paper packet, which will result in more patients willing to pay more for their services"[24].

high number of patients report safety risks, poor care coordination and deficiencies in care for chronic conditions[25]. Communication is often inadequate and lacking in information on treatment schedules. Nearly one in every two patients feels that doctors only rarely or never asked their opinion about treatment. Patients may consult different providers for related or even for the same conditions which, given the lack of coordination among these providers, results in duplication and contradictions[25]. This situation is similar to that reported in other countries, such as Ethiopia[26], Pakistan[27] and Zimbabwe[28].

There has, however, been progress in recent years. In high-income countries, confrontation with chronic disease, mental health problems, multi-morbidity and the social dimension of disease has focused attention on the need for more comprehensive and person-centred approaches and continuity of care. This resulted not only from client pressure, but also from

professionals who realized the critical importance of such features of care in achieving better outcomes for their patients. Many health professionals have begun to appreciate the limitations of narrow clinical approaches, for example, to cardiovascular disease. As a result there has been a welcome blurring of the traditional boundaries between curative care, preventive medicine and health promotion.

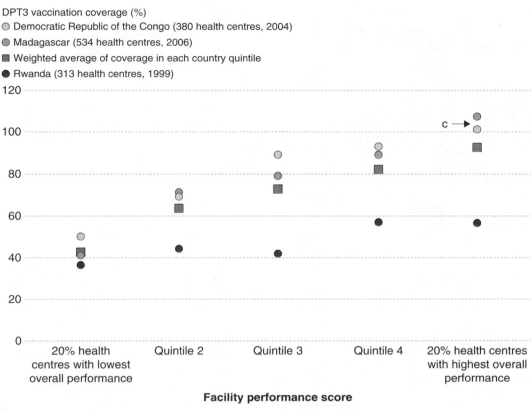

DPT3 vaccination coverage (%)
○ Democratic Republic of the Congo (380 health centres, 2004)
● Madagascar (534 health centres, 2006)
■ Weighted average of coverage in each country quintile
● Rwanda (313 health centres, 1999)

Figure 3.3 More comprehensive health centres have better vaccination coverage[a,b]

[a] Total 1227 health centres, covering a population of 16 million people.
[b] Vaccination coverage was not included in the assessment of overall health-centre performance across a range of services.
[c] Includes vaccination of children not belonging to target population.

In low-income countries, this evolution is also visible. In recent years, many of the programmes targeting infectious disease priorities have given careful consideration to comprehensiveness, continuity and patient-centredness. Maternal and child health services have often been at the forefront of these attempts, organizing a continuum of care and a comprehensive approach. This process has been consolidated through the joint UNICEF/WHO Integrated Management of Childhood Illness initiatives[30]. Their experience with programmes such as the WHO's Extended Programme for Immunization has put health professionals in many developing countries a step ahead compared to their high-income country colleagues, as they more readily see themselves responsible not just for patients, but also for population coverage. More recently, HIV/AIDS programmes have drawn the attention of providers and policy-makers to the importance of counselling, continuity of care, the complementarity of prevention, treatment and palliation and critically, to the value of empathy and listening to patients.

UNDERSTANDING PEOPLE: PERSON-CENTRED CARE

When people are sick they are a great deal less concerned about managerial considerations of productivity, health targets, cost-effectiveness and rational organization than about their own predicament. Each individual has his or her own way of experiencing and coping with health problems within their specific life circumstances[31]. Health workers have to be able to handle that diversity. For health workers at the interface between the population and the health services, the challenge is much more complicated than for a specialized referral service: managing a well-defined disease is a relatively straightforward technical challenge. Dealing with health problems, however, is complicated as people need to be understood holistically: their physical, emotional and social concerns, their past and their future, and the realities of the world in which they live. Failure to deal with the whole person in their specific familial and community contexts misses out on important aspects of

Box 3.3 The health-care response to partner violence against women

Intimate partner violence has numerous well-documented consequences for women's health (and for the health of their children), including injuries, chronic pain syndromes, unintended and unwanted pregnancies, pregnancy complications, sexually transmitted infections and a wide range of mental health problems[32,33,34,35,36,37]. Women suffering from violence are frequent health-care users[38,39].

Health workers are, therefore, well placed to identify and provide care to the victims of violence, including referral for psychosocial, legal and other support. Their interventions can reduce the impact of violence on a woman's health and well-being, and that of her children, and can also help prevent further violence.

Research has shown that most women think health-care providers should ask about violence[40]. While they do not expect them to solve their problem, they would like to be listened to and treated in a non-judgemental way and get the support they need to take control over their decisions. Health-care providers often find it difficult to ask women about violence. They lack the time and the training and skills to do it properly, and are reluctant to be involved in judicial proceedings.

The most effective approach for health providers to use when responding to violence is still a matter of debate[41]. They are generally advised to ask all women about intimate partner abuse as a routine part of any health assessment, usually referred to as "screening" or routine enquiry[42]. Several reviews found that this technique increased the rate of identification of women experiencing violence in antenatal and primary-care clinics, but there was little evidence that this was sustained[40], or was effective in terms of health outcomes[43]. Among women who have stayed in shelters, there is evidence that those who received a specific counselling and advocacy service reported a lower rate of re-abuse and an improved quality of life[44]. Similarly, among women experiencing violence during pregnancy, those who received "empowerment counselling" reported improved functioning and less psychological and non-severe physical abuse, and had lower postnatal depression scores[45].

While there is still no consensus on the most effective strategy, there is growing agreement that health services should aim to identify and support women experiencing violence[46], and that health-care providers should be well educated about these issues, as they are essential in building capacity and skills. Health-care providers should, as a minimum, be informed about violence against women, its prevalence and impact on health, when to suspect it and how to best respond. Clearly, there are technical dimensions to this. For example, in the case of sexual assault, providers need to be able to provide the necessary treatment and care, including provision of emergency contraception and prophylaxis for sexually transmitted infections, including HIV where relevant, as well as psychosocial support. There are other dimensions too: health workers need to be able to document any injuries as completely and carefully as possible[47,48,49] and they need to know how to work with communities—in particular with men and boys—on changing attitudes and practices related to gender inequality and violence.

health that do not immediately fit into disease categories. Partner violence against women (Box 3.3), for example, can be detected, prevented or mitigated by health services that are sufficiently close to the communities they serve and by health workers who know the people in their community.

People want to know that their health worker understands them, their suffering and the constraints they face. Unfortunately, many providers neglect this aspect of the therapeutic relation, particularly when they are dealing with disadvantaged groups. In many health services, responsiveness and person-centredness are treated as luxury goods to be handed out only to a selected few.

Over the last 30 years, a considerable body of research evidence has shown that person-centredness is not only important to relieve the patient's anxiety but also to improve the provider's job satisfaction[50]. The response to a health problem is more likely to be effective if the provider understands its various dimensions[51]. For a start, simply asking patients how they feel about their illness, how it affects their lives, rather than focusing only on the disease, results in measurably increased trust and compliance[52] that allows patient and provider to find a common ground on clinical management, and facilitates the integration of prevention and health promotion in the therapeutic response[50,51]. Thus, person-centredness becomes the "clinical method of participatory democracy"[53], measurably improving the quality of care, the success of treatment and the quality of life of those benefiting from such care (Table 3.2).

In practice, clinicians rarely address their patients' concerns, beliefs and understanding of illness, and seldom share problem management options with them[58]. They limit themselves to simple technical prescriptions, ignoring the complex human dimensions that are critical to the appropriateness and effectiveness of the care they provide[59].

Thus, technical advice on lifestyle, treatment schedule or referral all too often neglects not only

Table 3.2	Person-centredness: evidence of its contribution to quality of care and better outcomes
Improved treatment intensity and quality of life—Ferrer (2005)[54]	
Better understanding of the psychological aspects of a patient's problems—Gulbrandsen (1997)[55]	
Improved satisfaction with communication—Jaturapatporn (2007)[56]	
Improved patient confidence regarding sensitive problems—Kovess-Masféty (2007)[57]	
Increased trust and treatment compliance—Fiscella (2004)[52]	
Better integration of preventive and promotive care—Mead (1982)[50]	

the constraints of the environment in which people live, but also their potential for self-help in dealing with a host of health problems ranging from diarrhoeal disease[60] to diabetes management[61]. Yet, neither the nurse in Niger's rural health centre nor the general practitioner in Belgium can, for example, refer a patient to hospital without negotiating[62,63]: along with medical criteria, they have to take into account the patient's values, the family's values, and their lifestyle and life perspective[64].

Few health providers have been trained for person-centred care. Lack of proper preparation is compounded by cross-cultural conflicts, social stratification, discrimination and stigma[63]. As a consequence, the considerable potential of people to contribute to their own health through lifestyle, behaviour and self-care, and by adapting professional advice optimally to their life circumstances is underutilized. There are numerous, albeit often missed, opportunities to empower people to participate in decisions that affect their own health and that of their families (Box 3.4). They require health-care providers who can relate to people and assist them in making informed choices. The current payment systems and incentives in community health-care delivery often work against establishing this type of dialogue[65]. Conflicts of interest between provider and patient, particularly in unregulated commercial settings, are a major disincentive to person-centred care. Commercial providers may be more courteous and client-friendly than in the average health centre, but this is no substitute for person-centredness.

Box 3.4 Empowering users to contribute to their own health

Families can be empowered to make choices that are relevant to their health. Birth and emergency plans[66], for example, are based on a joint examination between the expectant mother and health staff—well before the birth—of her expectations regarding childbirth. Issues discussed include where the birth will take place, and how support for care of the home and any other children will be organized while the woman is giving birth. The discussion can cover planning for expenses, arrangements for transport and medical supplies, as well as identification of a compatible blood donor in case of haemorrhage. Such birth plans are being implemented in countries as diverse as Egypt, Guatemala, Indonesia, the Netherlands and the United Republic of Tanzania. They constitute one example of how people can participate in decisions relating to their health in a way that empowers them[67]. Empowerment strategies can improve health and social outcomes through several pathways; the condition for success is that they are embedded in local contexts and based on a strong and direct relationship between people and their health workers[68]. The strategies can relate to a variety of areas, as shown below:

- developing household capacities to stay healthy, make healthy decisions and respond to emergencies—France's self-help organization of diabetics[69], South Africa's family empowerment and parent training programmes[70], the United Republic of Tanzania's negotiated treatment plans for safe motherhood[71], and Mexico's active ageing programme[72];
- increasing citizens' awareness of their rights, needs and potential problems—Chile's information on entitlements[73] and Thailand's Declaration of Patients' Rights[74];
- strengthening linkages for social support within communities and with the health system—support and advice to family caregivers dealing with dementia in developing country settings[75], Bangladesh's rural credit programmes and their impact on care-seeking behaviour[76], and Lebanon's neighbourhood environment initiatives[77].

COMPREHENSIVE AND INTEGRATED RESPONSES

The diversity of health needs and challenges that people face does not fit neatly into the discrete diagnostic categories of textbook promotive, preventive, curative or rehabilitative care[78,79]. They call for the mobilization of a comprehensive range of resources that may include health promotion and prevention interventions as well as diagnosis and treatment or referral, chronic or long-term home care, and, in some models, social services[80]. It is at the entry point of the system, where people first present their problem, that the need for a comprehensive and integrated offer of care is most critical.

Comprehensiveness makes managerial and operational sense and adds value (Table 3.3). People take up services more readily if they know a comprehensive spectrum of care is on offer. Moreover, it maximizes opportunities for preventive care and health promotion while reducing unnecessary reliance on specialized or hospital care[81]. Specialization has its comforts, but the fragmentation it induces is often visibly counterproductive and inefficient: it makes no sense to monitor the growth of children and neglect the health of their mothers (and vice versa), or to treat someone's tuberculosis without considering their HIV status or whether they smoke.

That does not mean that entry-point health workers should solve all the health problems that are presented there, nor that all health programmes always need to be delivered through a single integrated service-delivery point. Nevertheless, the primary-care team has to be able to respond to the bulk of health problems in the community. When it cannot do so, it has to be able to mobilize other resources, by referring or by calling for support from specialists, hospitals, specialized diagnostic and treatment centres, public-health programmes, long-term care services, home-care or social services, or self-help and other

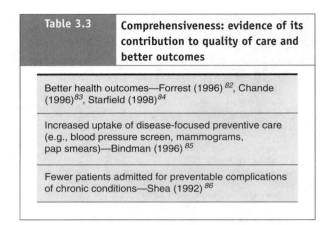

Table 3.3	Comprehensiveness: evidence of its contribution to quality of care and better outcomes
Better health outcomes—Forrest (1996)[82], Chande (1996)[83], Starfield (1998)[84]	
Increased uptake of disease-focused preventive care (e.g., blood pressure screen, mammograms, pap smears)—Bindman (1996)[85]	
Fewer patients admitted for preventable complications of chronic conditions—Shea (1992)[86]	

community organizations. This cannot mean giving up responsibility: the primary-care team remains responsible for helping people to navigate this complex environment.

Comprehensive and integrated care for the bulk of the assorted health problems in the community is more efficient than relying on separate services for selected problems, partly because it leads to a better knowledge of the population and builds greater trust. One activity reinforces the other. Health services that offer a comprehensive range of services increase the uptake and coverage of, for example, preventive programmes, such as cancer screening or vaccination (Figure 3.3). They prevent complications and improve health outcomes.

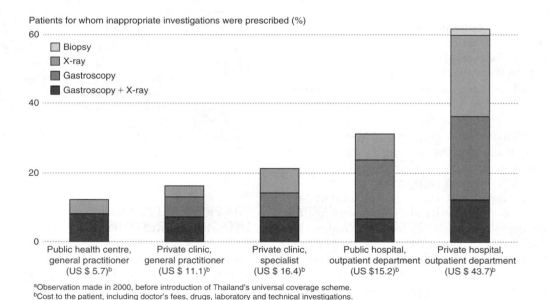

Patients for whom inappropriate investigations were prescribed (%)

- Biopsy
- X-ray
- Gastroscopy
- Gastroscopy + X-ray

Public health centre, general practitioner (US $ 5.7)[b]
Private clinic, general practitioner (US $ 11.1)[b]
Private clinic, specialist (US $ 16.4)[b]
Public hospital, outpatient department (US $15.2)[b]
Private hospital, outpatient department (US $ 43.7)[b]

[a]Observation made in 2000, before introduction of Thailand's universal coverage scheme.
[b]Cost to the patient, including doctor's fees, drugs, laboratory and technical investigations.

Figure 3.4 Inappropriate investigations prescribed for simulated patients presenting with a minor stomach complaint, Thailand[a,b,162]

Comprehesive services also facilitate early detection and prevention of problems, even in the absence of explicit demand. There are individuals and groups who could benefit from care even if they express no explicit spontaneous demand, as in the case of women attending the health centres in Ouallam district, Niger, or people with undiagnosed high blood pressure or depression. Early detection of disease, preventive care to reduce the incidence of poor health, health promotion to reduce risky behaviour, and addressing social and other determinants of health all require the health service to take the initiative. For many problems, local health workers are the only ones who are in a position to effectively address problems in the community: they are the only ones, for example, in a position to assist parents with care in early childhood development, itself an important determinant of later health, well-being and productivity[87]. Such interventions require proactive health teams offering a comprehensive range of services. They depend on a close and trusting relationship between the health services and the communities they serve, and, thus, on health workers who know the people in their community[88].

CONTINUITY OF CARE

Understanding people and the context in which they live is not only important in order to provide a comprehensive, person-centred response, it also conditions continuity of care. Providers often behave as if their responsibility starts when a patient walks in and ends when they leave the premises. Care should not, however, be limited to the moment a patient consults nor be confined to the four walls of the consultation room. Concern for outcomes mandates a consistent and coherent approach to the management of the patient's problem, until the problem is resolved or the risk that justified follow-up has disappeared. Continuity of care is an important determinant of effectiveness, whether for chronic disease management, reproductive health, mental health or for making sure children grow up healthily (Table 3.4).

Continuity of care depends on ensuring continuity of information as people get older, when they move from one residence to another, or when different professionals interact with one particular individual or household. Access to medical records and discharge summaries, electronic, conventional or client-held, improves the choice of the course of treatment and of coordination of care. In Canada, for example, one in seven people attending an emer-

Table 3.4	Continuity of care: evidence of its contribution to quality of care and better outcomes
	Lower all-cause mortality—Shi (2003)[90], Franks (1998)[91], Villalbi (1999)[92], PAHO (2005)[93]
	Better access to care—Weinick (2000)[94], Forrest (1998)[95]
	Less re-hospitalization—Weinberger (1996)[96]
	Fewer consultations with specialists—Woodward (2004)[97]
	Less use of emergency services—Gill (2000)[98]
	Better detection of adverse effects of medical interventions—Rothwell (2005)[99], Kravitz (2004)[100]

gency department had medical information missing that was very likely to result in patient harm[101]. Missing information is a common cause of delayed care and uptake of unnecessary services[102]. In the United States, it is associated with 15.6% of all reported errors in ambulatory care[103]. Today's information and communication technologies, albeit underutilized, gives unprecedented possibilities to improve the circulation of medical information at an affordable cost[104], thus enhancing continuity, safety and learning (Box 3.5). Moreover, it is no longer the exclusive privilege of high-resource environments, as the Open Medical Record System demonstrates: electronic health records developed through communities of practice and open-source software are facilitating continuity and quality of care for patients with HIV/AIDS in many low-income countries[105].

Better patient records are necessary but not sufficient. Health services need to make active efforts to minimize the numerous obstacles to continuity of care. Compared to payment by capitation or by fee-for-episode, out-of-pocket fee-for-service payment is a common deterrent, not only to access, but also to continuity of care[107]. In Singapore, for example, patients were formerly not allowed to use their health savings account (Medisave) for outpatient treatment, resulting in patient delays and lack of treatment compliance for the chronically ill. This had become so problematic that regulations were changed. Hospitals are now encouraged to transfer patients with diabetes, high blood pressure, lipid disorder and stroke to registered general practitioners, with Medisave accounts covering ambulatory care[108].

Box 3.5 Using information and communication technologies to improve access, quality and efficiency in primary care.

Information and communication technologies enable people in remote and underserved areas to have access to services and expertise otherwise unavailable to them, especially in countries with uneven distribution or chronic shortages of physicians, nurses and health technicians or where access to facilities and expert advice requires travel over long distances. In such contexts, the goal of improved access to health care has stimulated the adoption of technology for remote diagnosis, monitoring and consultation. Experience in Chile of immediate transmission of electrocardiograms in cases of suspected myocardial infarction is a noteworthy example: examination is carried out in an ambulatory setting and the data are sent to a national centre where specialists confirm the diagnosis via fax or e-mail. This technology-facilitated consultation with experts allows rapid response and appropriate treatment where previously it was unavailable. The Internet is a key factor in its success, as is the telephone connectivity that has been made available to all health facilities in the country.

A further benefit of using information and communication technologies in primary-care services is the improved quality of care. Healthcare providers are not only striving to deliver more effective care, they are also striving to deliver safer care. Tools, such as electronic health records, computerized prescribing systems and clinical decision aids, support practitioners in providing safer care in a range of settings. For example, in a village in western Kenya, electronic health records integrated with laboratory, drug procurement and reporting systems have drastically reduced clerical labour and errors, and have improved follow-up care.

As the costs of delivering health care continue to rise, information and communication technologies provide new avenues for personalized, citizen-centred and home-centred care. Towards this end, there has been significant investment in research and development of consumer-friendly applications. In Cape Town, South Africa, an "on cue compliance service" takes the names and mobile telephone numbers of patients with tuberculosis (supplied by a clinic) and enters them into a database. Every half an hour, the on cue server reads the database and sends personalized SMS messages to the patients, reminding them to take their medication. The technology is low-cost and robust. Cure and completion rates are similar to those of patients receiving clinic-based DOTS, but at lower cost to both clinic and patient, and in a way that interferes much less with everyday life than the visits to the clinic[106]. In the same concept of supporting lifestyles linked to primary care, network devices have become a key element of an innovative community programme in the Netherlands, where monitoring and communication devices are built into smart apartments for senior citizens. This system reduces clinic visits and facilitates living independently with chronic diseases that require frequent checks and adjustment of medications.

Many clinicians who want to promote health and prevent illness are placing high hopes in the Internet as the place to go for health advice to complement or replace the need to seek the advice of a health professional. New applications, services and access to information have permanently altered the relationships between consumers and health professionals, putting knowledge directly into people's own hands.

Other barriers to continuity include treatment schedules requiring frequent clinic attendance that carry a heavy cost in time, travel expenses or lost wages. They may be ill-understood and patient motivation may be lacking. Patients may get lost in the complicated institutional environment of referral hospitals or social services. Such problems need to be anticipated and recognized at an early stage. The effort required from health workers is not negligible: negotiating the modalities of the treatment schedule with the patients so as to maximize the chances that it can be completed; keeping registries of clients with chronic conditions; and creating communication channels through home visits, liaison with community workers, telephonic reminders and text messages to re-establish interrupted continuity. These mundane tasks often make the difference between a successful outcome and a treatment failure, but are rarely rewarded. They are much easier to implement when patient and caregiver have clearly identified how and by whom follow-up will be organized.

A REGULAR AND TRUSTED PROVIDER AS ENTRY POINT

Comprehensiveness, continuity and person-centredness are critical to better health outcomes. They all depend on a stable, long-term, personal relationship (a feature also cal led "longitudinality"[84]) between the population and the professionals who are their entry point to the health system.

Most ambulatory care in conventional settings is not organized to build such relationships. The busy, anonymous and technical environment of hospital outpatient departments, with their many specialists and sub-specialists, produce mechanical interactions between nameless individuals and an institution—not people-centred care. Smaller clinics are less anonymous, but the care they provide is often more akin to a commercial or administrative transaction that starts and ends with the consultation than to a responsive problem-solving exercise. In this regard, private clinics do not perform differently than public health centres[64]. In the rural areas of low-income countries, governmental health centres are usually designed to work in close relationship with the community they serve. The reality is often different. Earmarking of resources and staff for selected programmes is increasingly leading to fragmentation[109], while the lack of funds, the pauperization of the health staff and rampant commercialization makes building such relationships difficult[110]. There are many examples to the contrary, but the relationship between providers and their clients, particularly the poorer ones, is often not conducive to building relationships of understanding, empathy and trust[62].

Building enduring relationships requires time. Studies indicate that it takes two to five years before its full potential is achieved[84] but, as the Alaska health centre mentioned at the beginning of this chapter shows, it drastically changes the way care is being provided. Access to the same team of healthcare providers over time fosters the development of a relationship of trust between the individual and their health-care provider[97,111,112]. Health professionals are more likely to respect and understand patients they know well, which creates more positive interaction and better communication[113]. They can more readily understand and anticipate obstacles to continuity of care, follow up on the progress and assess how the experience of illness or disability is affecting the individual's daily life. More mindful of the circumstances in which people live, they can tailor care to the specific needs of the person and recognize health problems at earlier stages.

This is not merely a question of building trust and patient satisfaction, however important these [114,115]. It is worthwhile because it leads to better quality and better outcomes (Table 3.5). People who use the same source of care for most of their health-care needs tend to comply better with advice given, rely less on emergency services, require less hospitalization and be more satisfied with care[98,116,117,118]. Providers save consultation time, reduce the use of laboratory tests[95,119,120], and increase uptake of preventive care[121]. Motivation improves through the social recognition built up by such relationships. Still, even dedicated health professionals will not seize all these opportunities spontaneously[122,123]. The interface between the population and their health services needs to be designed in a way that not only makes this possible, but also the most likely course of action.

Table 3.5	Regular entry point: evidence of its contribution to quality of care and better outcomes

Increased satisfaction with services—Weiss (1996)[116], Rosenblatt (1998)[117], Freeman (1997)[124], Miller (2000)[125]

Better compliance and lower hospitalization rate—Weiss (1996)[116], Rosenblatt (1998)[117], Freeman (1997)[124], Mainous (1998)[126]

Less use of specialists and emergency services—Starfield (1998)[82], Parchman (1994)[127], Hurley (1989)[128], Martin (1989)[129], Gadomski (1998)[130]

Fewer consultations with specialists—Hurley (1989)[128], Martin (1989)[129]

More efficient use of resources—Forrest (1996)[82], Forrest (1998)[95], Hjortdahl (1991)[131], Roos (1998)[132]

Better understanding of the psychological aspects of a patient's problem—Gulbrandsen (1997)[55]

Better uptake of preventive care by adolescents—Ryan (2001)[133]

Protection against over-treatment—Schoen (2007)[134]

ORGANIZING PRIMARY-CARE NETWORKS

A health service that provides entry point ambulatory care for health and health-related problems should, thus, offer a comprehensive range of integrated diagnostic, curative, rehabilitative and palliative services. In contrast to most conventional health-care delivery models, the offer of services should include prevention and promotion as well as efforts to tackle determinants of ill-health locally. A direct and enduring relationship between the provider and the people in the community served is essential to be able to take into account the personal and social context of patients and their families, ensuring continuity of care over time as well as across services.

In order for conventional health services to be transformed into primary care, i.e., to ensure that these distinctive features get due prominence, they must reorganized. A precondition is to ensure that they become directly and permanently accessible, without undue reliance on out-of-pocket payments and with social protection offered by universal coverage schemes. But another set of arrangements is critical for the transformation of conventional care-ambulatory—and institution-based, generalist and specialist—into local networks of primary-care centres[135,136,137,138,139,140].

- bringing care closer to people, in settings in close proximity and direct relationship with the community, relocating the entry point to the health system from hospitals and specialists to close-to-client generalist primary-care centres;

- giving primary-care providers the responsibility for the health of a defined population, in its entirety: the sick and the healthy, those who choose to consult the services and those who choose not to do so;

- strengthening primary-care providers' role as coordinators of the inputs of other levels of care by giving them administrative authority and purchasing power.

BRINGING CARE CLOSER TO THE PEOPLE

A first step is to relocate the entry point to the health system from specialized clinics, hospital outpatient departments and emergency services, to generalist ambulatory care in close-to-client settings. Evidence has been accumulating that this transfer carries measurable benefits in terms of relief from suffering, prevention of illness and death, and improved health equity. These findings hold true in both national and cross-national studies, even if all of the distinguishing features of primary care are not fully realized[31].

Generalist ambulatory care is more likely or as likely to identify common life-threatening conditions as specialist care[141,142]. Generalists adhere to clinical practice guidelines to the same extent as specialists[143], although they are slower to adopt them[144,145]. They prescribe fewer invasive interventions[146,147,148,149], fewer and shorter hospitalizations[127,133,149] and have a greater focus on preventive care[133,150]. This results in lower overall health-care costs[82] for similar health[146,151,152,153,154,155] and greater patient satisfaction[125,150,156]. Evidence from comparisons between high-income countries shows that higher proportions of generalist professionals working in ambulatory settings are associated with lower overall costs and higher quality rankings[157]. Conversely, countries that increase reliance on specialists have stagnating or declining health outcomes when measured at the population level, while fragmentation of care exacerbates user dissatisfaction and contributes to a growing divide between health and social services[157,158,159]. Information on low- and middle-income countries is harder to obtain[160], but there are indications that patterns are similar. Some studies estimate that in Latin America and the Caribbean more reliance on generalist care could avoid one out of two hospital admissions[161]. In Thailand, generalist ambulatory care outside a hospital context has been shown to be more patient-centred and respon-

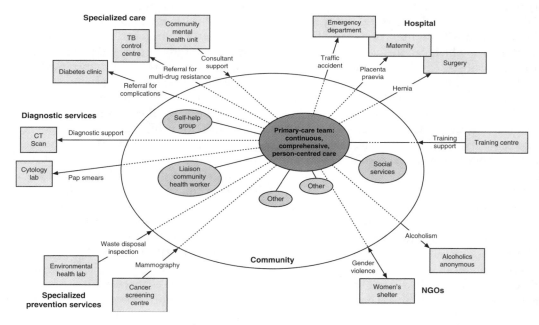

Figure 3.5 Primary care as a hub of coordination: networking within the community served and with outside partners[173,174]

sive as well as cheaper and less inclined to over-medicalization[162] (Figure 3.4).

The relocation of the entry point into the system from specialist hospital to generalist ambulatory care creates the conditions for more comprehensiveness, continuity and person-centredness. This amplifies the benefits of the relocation. It is particularly the case when services are organized as a dense network of small, close-to-client service delivery points. This makes it easier to have teams that are small enough to know their communities and be known by them, and stable enough to establish an enduring relationship. These teams require relational and organizational capacities as much as the technical competencies to solve the bulk of health problems locally.

RESPONSIBILITY FOR A WELL-IDENTIFIED POPULATION

In conventional ambulatory care, the provider assumes responsibility for the person attending the consultation for the duration of the consultation and, in the best of circumstances, that responsibility extends to ensuring continuity of care. This passive, response-to-demand approach fails to help a considerable number of people who could benefit from care. There are people who, for various reasons, are, or feel, excluded from access to services and do not take up care even when they are in need. There are people who suffer illness but delay seeking care. Others present risk factors and could benefit from screening or prevention programmes (e.g., for cervical cancer or for childhood obesity), but are left out because they do not consult: preventive services that are limited to service users often leave out those most in need[163]. A passive, response-to-demand approach has a second untoward consequence: it lacks the ambition to deal with local determinants of ill-health—whether social, environmental or work-related. All this represents lost opportunities for generating health: providers that only assume responsibility for their customers concentrate on repairing rather than on maintaining and promoting health.

The alternative is to entrust each primary-care team with the explicit responsibility for a well-defined community or population. They can then be held accountable, through administrative measures or contractual arrangements, for providing comprehensive, continuous and person-centred care to that population, and for mobilizing a comprehensive range of support services—from promotive through to palliative. The simplest way of assigning responsibility is to identify the community served on the basis of geographical criteria—the classic approach in rural areas. The simplicity of geographical assignment, however, is deceptive. It follows an administrative, public sector logic that often has problems adapting to the emergence of a multitude of other providers. Furthermore, administrative geography may not coincide with sociological reality, especially in urban areas. People move around and may work in a different area than where they live, making the health unit closest to home actually an inconvenient source of care. More importantly, people value choice and may resent an administrative assignment to a particular health unit. Some countries find geographical criteria of proximity the most appropriate to define who fits in the population of responsibility, others rely on active registration or patient lists. The important point is not how but whether the population is well identified and mechanisms exist to ensure that nobody is left out.

Once such explicit comprehensive responsibilities for the health of a well-identified and defined population are assigned, with the related financial and administrative accountability mechanisms, the rules change.

- The primary-care team has to broaden the portfolio of care it offers, developing activities and programmes that can improve outcomes, but which they might otherwise neglect[164]. This sets the stage for investment in prevention and promotion activities, and for venturing into areas that are often overlooked, such as health in schools and in the workplace. It forces the primary-care team to reach out to and work with organizations and individuals within the community: volunteers and community health workers who act as the liaison with patients or animate grassroots community groups, social workers, self-help groups, etc.

- It forces the team to move out of the four walls of their consultation room and reach out to the people in the community. This can bring significant health benefits. For example, large-scale programmes, based on home-visits and community animation, have been shown to be effective in reducing risk factors for neonatal mortality and actual mortality rates. In the United States, such programmes have reduced neonatal mortality by 60% in some settings[165]. Part of the benefit is due to better uptake of effective care by people who would otherwise remain deprived. In Nepal, for example, the community dynamics of women's groups led to the better uptake of care, with neonatal and maternal mortality lower than in control communities by 29% and 80%, respectively[166].

- It forces the team to take targeted initiatives, in collaboration with other sectors, to reach the excluded and the unreached and tackle broader determinants of ill-health. As Chapter 2 (not included) has shown, this is a necessary complement to establishing universal coverage and one where local health services play a vital role. The 2003 heatwave in western Europe, for example, highlighted the importance of reaching out to the isolated elderly and the dramatic consequences of failing to do so: an excess mortality of more than 50,000 people[167].

For people and communities, formal links with an identifiable source of care enhance the likelihood that long-term relationships will develop; that services are encouraged to pay more attention to the defining features of primary care; and that lines of communication are more intelligible. At the same time, coordination linkages can be formalized with other levels of care—specialists, hospitals or other technical services—and with social services.

THE PRIMARY-CARE TEAM AS A HUB OF COORDINATION

Primary-care teams cannot ensure comprehensive responsibility for their population without support from specialized services, organizations and institutions that are based outside the community served. In resource-constrained circumstances, these sources of support will typically be concentrated in a "first referral level district hospital". Indeed, the classic image of a health-care system based on PHC is that of a pyramid with the district hospital at the top and a set of (public) health centres that refer to the higher authority.

In conventional settings, ambulatory care professionals have little say in how hospitals and specialized services contribute—or fail to contribute—to the health of their patients, and feel little inclination to reach out to other institutions and stakeholders that are relevant to the health of the local community. This changes if they are entrusted with responsibility for a defined population and are recognized as the regular point of entry for that population. As health-care networks expand, the health-care landscape becomes far more crowded and pluralistic. More resources allow

for diversification: the range of specialized services that comes within reach may include emergency services, specialists, diagnostic infrastructure, dialysis centres, cancer screening, environmental technicians, long-term care institutions, pharmacies, etc. This represents new opportunities, provided the primary-care teams can assist their community in making the best use of that potential, which is particularly critical to public health, mental health and long-term care[168].

The coordination (or gatekeeping) role this entails effectively transforms the primary-care pyramid into a network, where the relations between the primary-care team and the other institutions and services are no longer based only on top-down hierarchy and bottom-up referral, but on cooperation and coordination (Figure 3.5). The primary-care team then becomes the mediator between the community and the other levels of the health system, helping people navigate the maze of health services and mobilizing the support of other facilities by referring patients or calling on the support of specialized services.

This coordination and mediation role also extends to collaboration with other types of organizations, often nongovernmental. These can provide significant support to local primary care. They can help ensure that people know what they are entitled to and have the information to avoid substandard providers[169,170]. Independent ombudsman structures or consumer organizations can help users handle complaints. Most importantly, there is a wealth of self-help and mutual support associations for diabetics, people living with handicaps and chronic diseases that can help people to help themselves[171]. In the United States alone, more than five million people belong to mutual help groups while, in recent years, civil society organizations dealing with health and health-related issues, from self-help to patient's rights, have been mushrooming in many low- and middle-income countries. These groups do much more than just inform patients. They help people take charge of their own situation, improve their health, cope better with ill-health, increase self-confidence and diminish over-medicalization[172]. Primary-care teams can only be strengthened by reinforcing their linkages with such groups.

Where primary-care teams are in a position to take on this coordinator role, their work becomes more rewarding and attractive, while the overall effects on health are positive. Reliance on specialists and hospitalization is reduced by filtering out unnecessary uptake, whereas patient delay is reduced for those who do need referral care, the duration of their hospitalization is shortened, and post-hospitalization follow-up is improved[83,128,129].

The coordination function provides the institutional framework for mobilizing across sectors to secure the health of local communities. It is not an optional extra but an essential part of the remit of primary-care teams. This has policy implications: coordination will remain wishful thinking unless the primary-care team has some form of either administrative or financial leverage. Coordination also depends on the different institutions' recognition of the key role of the primary-care teams. Current professional education systems, career structure and remuneration mechanisms most often give signals to the contrary. Reversing these well-entrenched disincentives to primary care requires strong leadership.

MONITORING PROGRESS

The switch from conventional to primary care is a complex process that cannot be captured in a single, universal metric. Only in recent years has it been possible to start disentangling the effects of the various features that define primary care. In part, this is because the identification of the features that make the difference between primary care and conventional health-care delivery has taken years of trial and error, and the instruments to measure them have not been generalized. This is because these features are never all put into place as a single package of reforms, but are the result of a gradual shaping and transformation of the health system. Yet, for all this complexity, it is possible to measure progress, as a complement to the follow-up required for measuring progress towards universal coverage.

The first dimension to consider is the extent to which the organizational measures required to switch to primary care are being put into place.

- Is the predominant type of first-contact provider being shifted from specialists and hospitals to generalist primary-care teams in close proximity to where the people live?

- Are primary-care providers being made responsible for the health of all the members of a well-identified population: those who attend health services and those who do not?

- Are primary-care providers being empowered to coordinate the various inputs of specialized, hospital and social services, by strengthening their administrative authority and purchasing power?

The second dimension to consider is the extent to which the distinctive features of primary care are gaining prominence.

- Person-centredness: is there evidence of improvement, as shown by direct observation and user surveys?

- Comprehensiveness: is the portfolio of primary-care services expanding and becoming more comprehensive, reaching the full essential benefits package, from promotion through to palliation, for all age groups?

- Continuity: is information for individuals being recorded over the life-course, and transferred between levels of care in cases of referral and to a primary-care unit elsewhere when people relocate?

- Regular entry point: are measures taken to ensure that providers know their clients and vice versa?

This should provide the guidance to policy-makers as to the progress they are making with the transformation of health-care delivery. However, they do not immediately make it possible to attribute health and social outcomes to specific aspects of the reform efforts. In order to do so, the monitoring of the reform effort needs to be complemented with a much more vigorous research agenda. It is revealing that the Cochrane Review on strategies for integrating primary-health services in low-and middle-income countries could identify only one valid study that took the user's perspective into account[160]. There has been a welcome surge of research on primary care in high-income countries and, more recently, in the middle-income countries that have launched major PHC reforms. Nevertheless, it is remarkable that an industry that currently mobilizes 8.6% of the world's GDP invests so little in research on two of its most effective and cost-effective strategies: primary care and the public policies that underpin and complement it.

● ● ● **References**

1. *People at the centre of health care: harmonizing mind and body, people and systems.* New Delhi, World Health Organization Regional Office for South-East Asia, Manila, World Health Organization Regional Office for the Western Paciicc, 2007.

2. Osler W. *Aequanimitas*. Philadelphia PA, Blakiston, 1904.

3. Eby D. Primary care at the Alaska Native Medical Centre: a fully deployed "new model" of primary care. *International Journal of Circumpolar Health,* 2007, 66(Suppl. 1):4-13.

4. Eby D. Integrated primary care. *International Journal of Circumpolar Health*, 1998, 57(Suppl. 1):665-667.

5. Gottlieb K, Sylvester I, Eby D. Transforming your practice: what matters most. *Family Practice Management*, 2008, 15:32-38.

6. Kerssens JJ et al. Comparison of patient evaluations of health care quality in relation to WHO measures of achievement in 12 European countries. *Bulletin of the World Health Organization*, 2004 82:106-114.

7. Bossyns P, Miye M, Van Lerberghe W. Supply-level measures to increase uptake of family planning services in Niger: the effectiveness of improving responsiveness. *Tropical Medicine and International Health*, 2002, 7:383-390.

8. *The World Health Report 2000-Health systems: improving performance.* Geneva, World Health Organization, 2000.

9. Mercer SW, Cawston PG, Bikker AP. Quality in general practice consultations: a qualitative study of the views of patients living in an area of high socio-economic deprivation in Scotland. *BMC Family Practice*, 2007, 8:22.

10. Scherger JE. What patients want. *Journal of Family Practice*, 2001, 50:137.

11. Sackett DL et al. Evidence based medicine: what it is and what it isn't. *British Medical Journal*, 1996, 312:71-72.

12. Guyatt G, Cook D, Haynes B. Evidence based medicine has come a long way: The second decade will be as exciting as the first. *BMJ*, 2004, 329:990-991.

13. Cochrane database of systematic reviews. The Cochrane Library, 2008 (http://www. cochrane .org, accessed 27 July 2008).

14. Iha A, ed. *Summary of the evidence on patient safety: implications for research.* Geneva, World Health Organization, The Research Priority Setting Working Group of the World Alliance for Patient Safety, 2008.

15. Smith GD, Mertens T. What's said and what's done: the reality of sexually transmitted disease consultations. *Public Health*, 2004, 118:96-103.

16. Berwick DM. The science of improvement. *JAMA*, 2008, 299:1182-1184.

17. Donaldson L, Philip P. Patient safety: a global priority. *Bulletin of the World Health Organization*, 2004, 82:892−893.

18. Kohn LT, Corrigan JM, Donaldson MS, eds. *To err is human: building a safer health system.* Washington, DC, National Academy Press, Committee on Quality of Health Care in America, Institute of Medicine, 1999.

19. Reason J. Human error: models and management. *BMJ*, 2000, 320:768−770.

20. Kripalani S et al. Deficits in communication and information transfer between hospital-based and primary care physicians: implications for patient safety and continuity of care. *JAMA*, 2007, 297: 831−841.

21. Miller MA, Pisani E. The cost of unsafe injections. *Bulletin of the World Health Organization*, 1999, 77:808-811.

22. *The purpose of a world alliance.* Geneva, World Health Organization, World Alliance for Patient Safety, 2008 (http://www.who.int/patientsafety/ worldalliance/alliance/en/, accessed 28 July 2008).

23. Shortell SM, Singer SJ. Improving patient safety by taking systems seriously. *JAMA* 2008, 299:445−447.

24. Das J, Hammer JS, Kenneth LL. *The quality of medical advice in low-income countries.* Washington DC, The World Bank, 2008 (World Bank Policy Research Working Paper No. 4501; http://ssrn.com/abstract51089272, accessed 28 Jul 2008).

25. Schoen C et al. Taking the pulse of health care systems: experiences of patients with health problems in six countries. *Health Affairs*, 2005 (web exclusive W 5-5 0 9 DOI 10.1377/hlthaff.W5.509).

26. Mekbib TA, Teferi B. Caesarean section and foetal outcome at Yekatit 12 hospital, Addis Abba, Ethiopia, 1987-1992. *Ethiopian Medical Journal*, 1994, 32:173−179.

27. Siddiqi S et al. The effectiveness of patient referral in Pakistan. *Health Policy and Planning*, 2001, 16: 193−198.

28. Sanders D et al. Zimbabwe's hospital referral system: does it work? *Health Policy and Planning*, 1998, 13:359−370.

29. Data reported at World Aids Day Meeting, Antwerp, Belgium, 2000.

30. *The World Health Report 2005—Make every mother and child count.* Geneva, WorHealth Organization, 2005. ld

31. Starfield B, Shi L, Macinko J. Contributions of primary care to health systems and health. *The Milbank Quarterly*, 2005, 83:457−502.

32. Heise L, Garcia-Moreno C. Intimate partner violence. In: Krug EG et al, eds. *World report on violence and health.* Geneva, World Health Organization, 2002.

33. Ellsberg M et al. Intimate partner violence and women's physical and mental health in the WHO multi-country study on women's health and domestic violence: an observational study. *Lancet*, 2008, 371:1165−1172.

34. Campbell JC. Health consequences of intimate partner violence. *Lancet*, 2002, 359:1331−1336.

35. Edleson JL. Children's witnessing of domestic violence. *Journal of Interpersonal Violence*, 1996, 14: 839-870.

36. Dube SR et al. Exposure to abuse, neglect, and household dysfunction among adults who wit-

nessed intimate partner violence as children: implications for health and social services. *Violence and Victims*, 2002, 17:3-17.

37. Åsling-Monemi K et al. Violence against women increases the risk of infant and child mortality: a case-referent study in Nicaragua. *Bulletin of the World Health Organization*, 2003, 81:10–18.

38. Bonomi A et al. Intimate partner violence and women's physical, mental and social functioning. *American Journal of Preventive Medicine*, 2006, 30:458-466.

39. National Centre for Injury Prevention and Control. *Costs of intimate partner violence against women in the United States*. Atlanta GA, Centers for Disease Control and Prevention, 2003.

40. Ramsay J et al. Should health professionals screen women for domestic violence? Systematic review. *BMJ*, 2002, 325:314–318.

41. Nelson HD et al. Screening women and elderly adults for family and intimate partner violence: a review of the evidence for the U.S. Preventive Services Task force. *Annals of Internal Medicine*, 2004, 140:387–403.

42. Garcia-Moreno C. Dilemmas and opportunities for an appropriate health-service response to violence against women. *Lancet*, 2002, 359:1509–1514.

43. Wathan NC, MacMillan HL. Interventions for violence against women. Scientific review. *JAMA*, 2003, 289:589–600.

44. Sullivan CM, Bybee DI. Reducing violence using community-based advocacy for women with abusive partners. *Journal of Consulting and Clinical Psychology*, 1999, 67:43–53.

45. Tiwari A et al. A randomized controlled trial of empowerment training for Chinese abused pregnant women in Hong Kong. *British Journal of Obstetrics and Gynaecology*, 2005, 112:1249–1256.

46. Taket A et al. Routinely asking women about domestic violence in health settings. *BMJ*, 2003, 327:673–676.

47. MacDonald R. Time to talk about rape. *BMJ*, 2000, 321:1034–1035.

48. Basile KC, Hertz FM, Back SE. *Intimate partner and sexual violence victimization instruments for use in healthcare settings*. 2008. Atlanta GA, Centers for Disease Control and Prevention, 2008.

49. *Guidelines for the medico-legal care of victims of sexual violence*. Geneva, World Health Organization, 2003.

50. Mead N, Bower P. Patient-centredness: a conceptual framework and review of the empirical literature. *Social Science and Medicine*, 51:1087–1110.

51. Stewart M. Towards a global definition of patient centred care. *BMJ*, 2001, 322:444–445.

52. Fiscella K et al. Patient trust: is it related to patient-centred behavior of primary care physicians? *Medical Care*, 2004, 42:1049–1055.

53. Marincowitz GJO, Fehrsen GS. *Caring, learning, improving quality and doing research: Different faces of the same process*. Paper presented at: 11th South African Family Practice Congress, Sun City, South Africa, August 1998.

54. Ferrer RL, Hambidge SJ, Maly RC. The essential role of generalists in health care systems. *Annals of Internal Medicine*, 2005, 142:691–699.

55. Gulbrandsen P, Hjortdahl P, Fugelli P. General practitioners' knowledge of their patients' psychosocial problems: multipractice questionnaire survey. *British Medical Journal*, 1997, 314: 1014-1018.

56. Jaturapatporn D, Dellow A. Does family medicine training in Thailand affect patient satisfaction with primary care doctors? *BMC Family Practice*, 2007, 8:14.

57. Kovess-Masféty V et al. What makes people decide who to turn to when faced with a mental health problem? Results from a French survey. *BMC Public Health*, 2007, 7:188.

58. Bergeson D. A systems approach to patient-centred care. *JAMA*, 2006, 296:23.

59. Kravitz RL et al. Recall of recommendations and adherence to advice among patients with chronic medical conditions. *Archives of Internal Medicine*, 1993, 153:1869–1878.

60. Werner D et al. *Questioning the solution: the politics of primary health care and child survival, with an in-depth critique of oral rehydration therapy*. Palo Alto CA, Health Wrights, 1997.

61. Norris et al. Increasing diabetes self-management education in community settings. A systematic review. *American Journal of Preventive Medicine*, 2002, 22:39–66.

62. Bossyns P, Van Lerberghe W. The weakest link: competence and prestige as constraints to referral by isolated nurses in rural Niger. *Human Resources for Health*, 2004, 2:1.

63. Willems S et al. Socio-economic status of the patient and doctor-patient communication: does it make a difference. *Patient Eucation and Counseling*, 2005, 56:139–146.

64. Pongsupap Y. *Introducing a human dimension to Thai health care: the case for family practice*. Brussels, Vrije Universiteit Brussel Press. 2007.

65. *Renewing primary health care in the Americas. A Position paper of the Pan American Health Organization*. Washington DC, Pan American Health Organization, 2007.

66. Penny Simkin, PT. Birth plans: after 25 years, women still want to be heard. *Birth*, 34:49-51.

67. Portela A, Santarelli C. Empowerment of women, men, families and communities: true partners for improving maternal and newborn health. *British Medical Bulletin*, 2003, 67:59–72.

68. Wallerstein N. *What is the evidence on effectiveness of empowerment to improve health?* Copenhagen, World Health Organization Regional Office for Europe 2006 (Health Evidence Network report; (http://www.euro.who.int/Document/E88086.pdf, accessed 21-11-07).

69. Diabète-France.com-portail du diabète et des diabetiques en France, 2008 (http:// www.diabete-france.com, accessed 30 July 2008).

70. Barlow J, Cohen E, Stewart-Brown SSB. Parent training for improving maternal psychosocial health. *Cochrane Database of Systematic Reviews*,2003, (4):CD002020.

71. Ahluwalia I. An evaluation of a community-based approach to safe motherhood in northwestern Tanzania. *International Journal of Gynecology and Obstetrics*, 2003, 82:231.

72. De la Luz Martínez-Maldonado M, Correa-Muñoz E, Mendoza-Núñez VM. Program of active aging in a rural Mexican community: a qualitative approach. *BMC Public Health*, 2007, 7:276 (DOI:10.1186/1471-2458-7-276).

73. Frenz P. *Innovative practices for intersectoral action on health: a case study of four programs for social equity.* Chilean case study prepared for the CSDH. Santiago, Ministry of Health, Division of Health Planning, Social Determinants of Health Initiative, 2007.

74. Paetthayasapaa. Kam Prakard Sitti Pu Paui, 2003? (http://www.tmc.or.th/, accessed 30 July 2008).

75. Prince M, Livingston G, Katona C. Mental health care for the elderly in low-income countries: a health systems approach. *World Psychiatry*, 2007, 6:5–13.

76. Nanda P. Women's participation in rural credit programmes in Bangladesh and their demand for formal health care: is there a positive impact? *Health Economics*, 1999, 8:415–428.

77. Nakkash R et al. The development of a feasible community-specific cardiovascular disease prevention program: triangulation of methods and sources. *Health Education and Behaviour*, 2003, 30:723–739.

78. Stange KC. The paradox of the parts and the whole in understanding and improving general practice. *International Journal for Quality in Health Care*, 2002, 14:267–268.

79. Gill JM. The structure of primary care: framing a big picture. *Family Medicine*, 2004, 36:65–68.

80. *Pan-Canadian Primary Health Care Indicator Development Project. Pan-Canadian primary health care indicators, Report 1, Volume 1.* Ottawa, Canadian Institute for Health Information 2008 (http://www.cihi.ca).

81. Bindman AB et al. Primary care and receipt of preventive services. *Journal of General Internal Medicine*, 1996, 11:269–276.

82. Forrest CB, Starfield B. The effect of first-contact care with primary care clinicians on ambulatory health care expenditures. *Journal of Family Practice*, 1996, 43:40-48.

83. Chande VT, Kinane JM. Role of the primary care provider in expediting children with acute appendicitis. *Archives of Pediatrics and Adolescent Medicine*, 1996, 150:703–706.

84. Starfield B. *Primary care: balancing health needs, services, and technology.* New York, Oxford University Press 1998.

85. Bindman AB et al. Primary care and receipt of preventive services. *Journal of General Internal Medicine*, 1996, 11:269-276.

86. Shea S et al. Predisposing factors for severe, uncontrolled hypertension in an inner-city minority population. *New England Journal of Medicine*, 1992, 327:776-781.

87. Galobardes B, Lynch JW, Davey Smith G. Is the association between childhood socioeconomic circumstances and cause-specific mortality established? Update of a systematic review. *Journal of Epidemiology and Community Health*, 2008, 62:387–390.

88. *Guide to clinical preventive services, 2007* . Rockville MD, Agency for Healthcare Research and Quality, 2007 (AHRQ Publication No. 07-05100; http://www.ahrq.gov/clinic/pocketgd.htm).

89. Porignon D et al. *Comprehensive is effective: vaccination coverage and health system performance in Sub-Saharan Africa*, 2008 (forthcoming).

90. Shi L et al. The relationship between primary care, income inequality, and mortality in the United States, 1980-1995. *Journal of the American Board of Family Practice*, 2003, 16:412-422.

91. Franks P, Fiscella K. Primary care physicians and specialists as personal physicians. Health care expenditures and mortality experience. *Journal of Family Practice*, 1998, 47:105-109.

92. Villalbi JR et al. An evaluation of the impact of primary care reform on health. *Atención Primaria*, 1999, 24:468-474.

93. *Regional core health data initiative.* Washington DC, Pan American Health Organization, 2005 (http://www.paho.org/English/SHA/coredata/tabulator/newTabulator.htm).

94. Weinick RM, Krauss NA. Racial/ethnic differences in children's access to care. *American Journal of Public Health*, 2000, 90:1771-1774.

95. Forrest CB, Starfield B. Entry into primary care and continuity: the effects of access. *American Journal of Public Health*, 1998, 88:1330-1336.

96. Weinberger M, Oddone EZ, Henderson WG. Does increased access to primary care reduce hospital readmissions? For The Veterans Affairs Cooperative Study Group on Primary Care and Hospital Readmission. *New England Journal of Medicine*, 1996, 334:1441-1447.

97. Woodward CA et al. What is important to continuity in home care? Perspectives of key stakeholders. *Social Science and Medicine*, 2004, 58:177-192.

98. Gill JM, Mainous AGI, Nsereko M. The effect of continuity of care on emergency department use. *Archives of Family Medicine*, 2000, 9:333–338.

99. Rothwell P. Subgroup analysis in randomised controlled trials: importance, indications, and interpretation, *Lancet*, 2005, 365:176–186.

100. Kravitz RL, Duan N, Braslow J. Evidence-based medicine, heterogeneity of treatment effects, and the trouble with averages. *The Milbank Quarterly*, 2004, 82:661-687.

101. Stiell A. et al. Prevalence of information gaps in the emergency department and the effect on patient outcomes. *Canadian Medical Association Journal*, 2003, 169:1023–1028.

102. Smith PC et al. Missing clinical information during primary care visits. *JAMA*, 2005, 293:565–571.

103. Elder NC, Vonder Meulen MB, Cassedy A. The identification of medical errors by family physicians during outpatient visits. *Annals of Family Medicine*, 2004, 2:125–129.

104. Elwyn G. Safety from numbers: identifying drug related morbidity using electronic records in primary care. *Quality and Safety in Health Care*, 2004, 13:170–171.

105. Open Medical Records System (OpenMRS) [online database]. Cape Town, South African Medical Research Council, 2008 (http://openmrs.org/wiki/OpenMRS, accessed 29 July 2008).

106. Hüsler J, Peters T. *Evaluation of the On Cue Compliance Service pilot: testing the use of SMS reminders in the treatment of tuberculosis in Cape Town, South Africa. Prepared for the City of Cape Town Health Directorate and the International Development Research Council (IDRC).* Cape Town, Bridges Organization, 2005.

107. Smith-Rohrberg Maru D et al. Poor follow-up rates at a self-pay northern Indian tertiary AIDS clinic. *International Journal for Equity in Health*, 2007, 6:14.

108. Busse R, Schlette S, eds. *Focus on prevention, health and aging, and health professions.* Gütersloh, Verlag Bertelsmann Stiftung, 2007 (Health policy developments 7/8).

109. James Pfeiffer International. NGOs and primary health care in Mozambique: the need for a new model of collaboration. *Social Science and Medicine*, 2003, 56:725-738.

110. Jaffré Y, Olivier de Sardan J-P. *Une médecine inhospitalière. Les difficiles relations entre soignants et soignés dans cinq capitales d'Afrique de l'Ouest.* Paris, Karthala, 2003.

111. Naithani S, Gulliford M, Morgan M. Patients' perceptions and experiences of "continuity of care" in diabetes. *Health Expectations*, 2006, 9: 118–129.

112. Schoenbaum SC. The medical home: a practical way to improve care and cut costs. *Medscape Journal of Medicine*, 2007, 9:28.

113. Beach MC. Are physicians' attitudes of respect accurately perceived by patients and associated with more positive communication behaviors? *Patient Education and Counselling*, 2006, 62:347–354 (Epub 2006 Jul 21).

114. Farmer JE et al. Comprehensive primary care for children with special health care needs in rural areas. *Pediatrics*, 2005, 116:649–656.

115. Pongsupap Y, Van Lerberghe W. Patient experience with self-styled family practices and conventional primary care in Thailand. *Asia Pacific Family Medicine Journal*, 2006, Vol 5.

116. Weiss LJ, Blustein J. Faithful patients: the effect of long term physician-patient relationships on the costs and use of health care by older Americans. *American Journal of Public Health*, 1996, 86:1742-1747.

117. Rosenblatt RL et al. The generalist role of specialty physicians: is there a hidden system of primary care? *JAMA*,1998, 279:1364–1370.

118. Kempe A et al. Quality of care and use of the medical home in a state-funded capitated primary care plan for low-income children. *Pediatrics*, 2000, 105:1020–1028.

119. Raddish MS et al. Continuity of care: is it cost effective? *American Journal of Managed Care*, 1999, 5:727–734.

120. De Maeseneer JM et al. Provider continuity in family medicine: does it make a difference for total health care costs? *Annals of Family Medicine*, 2003, 1:131–133.

121. Saver B. Financing and organization findings brief. *Academy for Research and Health Care Policy*, 2002, 5:1–2.

122. Tudiver F, Herbert C, Goel V. Why don't family physicians follow clinical practice guidelines for cancer screening? *Canadian Medical Association Journal*, 1998, 159:797–798.

123. Oxman AD et al. No magic bullets: a systematic review of 102 trials of interventions to improve

professional practice. *Canadian Medical Association Journal*, 1995, 153:1423–1431.

124. Freeman G, Hjortdahl P. What future for continuity of care in general practice? *British Medical Journal*, 1997, 314:1870–1873.

125. Miller MR et al. Parental preferences for primary and specialty care collaboration in the management of teenagers with congenital heart disease. *Pediatrics*, 2000, 106:264–269.

126. Mainous AG III, Gill JM. The importance of continuity of care in the likelihood of future hospitalization: is site of care equivalent to a primary clinician? *American Journal of Public Health*, 1998, 88:1539–1541.

127. Parchman ML, Culler SD. Primary care physicians and avoidable hospitalizations. *Journal of Family Practice*, 1994, 39:123–128.

128. Hurley RE, Freund DA, Taylor DE. Emergency room use and primary care case management: evidence from four medicaid demonstration programs. *American Journal of Public Health*, 1989, 79: 834–836.

129. Martin DP et al. Effect of a gatekeeper plan on health services use and charges: a randomized trial. *American Journal of Public Health*, 1989, 79:1628-1632.

130. Gadomski A, Jenkins P, Nichols M. Impact of a Medicaid Primary Care Provider and Preventive Care on pediatric hospitalization. *Pediatrics*, 1998, 101:E1 (http:// pediatrics.aappublications.org/cgi/reprint/101/3/e1, accessed 29 July 2008).

131. Hjortdahl P, Borchgrevink CF. Continuity of care: influence of general practitioners' knowledge about their patients on use of resources in consultations. *British Medical Journal*, 1991, 303: 1181-1184.

132. Roos NP, Carriere KC, Friesen D. Factors influencing the frequency of visits by hypertensive patients to primary care physicians in Winnipeg. *Canadian Medical Association Journal*, 1998, 159:777-783.

133. Ryan S et al. The effects of regular source of care and health need on medical care use among rural adolescents. *Archives of Pediatric and Adolescent Medicine*, 2001, 155:184-190.

134. Schoen C et al. Towards higher-performance health systems: adults' health care experiences in seven countries, 2007. *Health Affairs*, 2007, 26:w717–w734.

135. Saltman R, Rico A, Boerma W, eds. *Primary care in the driver's seat? Organizational reform in European primary care*. Maidenhead, England, Open University Press, 2006 (European Observatory on Health Systems and Policies Series).

136. Nutting PA. Population-based family practice: the next challenge of primary care. *Journal of Family Practice*, 1987, 24:83–88.

137. *Strategies for population health: investing in the health of Canadians*. Ottawa, Health Canada, Advisory Committee on Population Health, 1994.

138. Lasker R. *Medicine and public health: the power of collaboration*. New York, New York Academy of Medicine, 1997.

139. Longlett SK, Kruse JE, Wesley RM. Community-oriented primary care: historical perspective. *Journal of the American Board of Family Practice*, 2001,14:54–563.

140. *Improving health for New Zealanders by investing in primary health care*. Wellington, National Health Committee, 2000.

141. Provenzale D et al. Gastroenterologist specialist care and care provided by generalists—an evaluation of effectiveness and efficiency. *American Journal of Gastroenterology*, 2003, 98:21-8.

142. Smetana GW et al. A comparison of outcomes resulting from generalist vs specialist care for a single discrete medical condition: a systematic review and methodologic critique. *Archives of Internal Medicine*, 2007, 167:10-20.

143. Beck CA et al. Discharge prescriptions following admission for acute myocardial infarction at tertiary care and community hospitals in Quebec. *Canadian Journal of Cardiology*, 2001, 17:33–40.

144. Fendrick AM, Hirth RA, Chernew ME. Differences between generalist and specialist physicians regarding Helicobacter pylori and peptic ulcer disease. *American Journal of Gastroenterology*, 1996, 91:1544–1548.

145. Zoorob RJ et al. Practice patterns for peptic ulcer disease: are family physicians testing for H. pylori? *Helicobacter*, 1999, 4:243–248.

146. Rose JH et al. Generalists and oncologists show similar care practices and outcomes for hospitalized late-stage cancer patients. For SUPPORT Investigators (Study to Understand Prognoses and Preferences for Outcomes and Risks for Treatment). *Medical Care*, 2000, 38:1103–1118.

147. Krikke EH, Bell NR. Relation of family physician or specialist care to obstetric interventions and outcomes in patients at low risk: a western Canadian cohort study. *Canadian Medical Association Journal*, 1989, 140:637–643.

148. MacDonald SE, Voaklander K, Birtwhistle RV. A comparison of family physicians' and obstetricians' intrapartum management of low-risk pregnancies. *Journal of Family Practice*, 1993, 37:457-462.

149. Abyad A, Homsi R. A comparison of pregnancy care delivered by family physicians versus obstetricians in Lebanon. *Family Medicine*, 1993, 25: 465–470.

150. Grunfeld E et al. Comparison of breast cancer patient satisfaction with follow-up in primary care versus specialist care: results from a randomized

controlled trial. *British Journal of General Practice*, 1999, 49:705–710.

151. Grunfeld E et al. Randomized trial of long-term follow-up for early-stage breast cancer: a comparison of family physician versus specialist care. *Journal of Clinical Oncology*, 2006, 24:848–855.

152. Scott IA et al. An Australian comparison of specialist care of acute myocardial infarction. *International Journal for Quality in Health Care*, 2003, 15:155–161.

153. Regueiro CR et al. A comparison of generalist and pulmonologist care for patients hospitalized with severe chronic obstructive pulmonary disease: resource intensity, hospital costs, and survival. For SUPPORT Investigators (Study to Understand Prognoses and Preferences for Outcomes and Risks of Treatment). *American Journal of Medicine*, 1998, 105:366–372.

154. McAlister FA et al. The effect of specialist care within the first year on subsequent outcomes in 24,232 adults with new-onset diabetes mellitus: population-based cohort study. *Quality and Safety in Health Care*, 2007, 16:6–11.

155. Greenfield S et al. Outcomes of patients with hypertension and non-insulin dependent diabetes mellitus treated by different systems and specialties. Results from the medical outcomes study. *Journal of the American Medical Association*, 1995, 274:1436–1444.

156. Pongsupap Y, Boonyapaisarnchoaroen T, Van Lerberghe W. The perception of patients using primary care units in comparison with conventional public hospital outpatient departments and "prime mover family practices": an exit survey. *Journal of Health Science*, 2005, 14:3.

157. Baicker K, Chandra A. Medicare spending, the physician workforce, and beneficiaries' quality of care. *Health Affairs*, 2004 (Suppl. web exclusive: W4-184–197).

158. Shi, L. Primary care, specialty care, and life chances. *International Journal of Health Services*, 1994, 24:431–458.

159. Baicker K et al. Who you are and where you live: how race and geography affect the treatment of Medicare beneficiaries. *Health Affairs*, 2004 (web exclusive: VAR33–V44).

160. Briggs CJ, Garner P. Strategies for integrating primary health services in middle and low-income countries at the point of delivery. *Cochrane Database of Systematic Reviews*, 2006, (3):CD003318.

161. *Estudo regional sobre assistencia hospitalar e ambulatorial especializada na America Latina e Caribe*. Washington DC, Pan American Health Organization, Unidad de Organización de Servicios de Salud, Area de Tecnología y Prestación de Servicios de Salud, 2004.

162. Pongsupap Y, Van Lerberghe W. Choosing between public and private or between hospital and primary care? Responsiveness, patient-centredness and prescribing patterns in outpatient consultations in Bangkok. *Tropical Medicine and International Health*, 2006, 11:81–89.

163. *Guide to clinical preventive services, 2007*. Rockville MD, Agency for Healthcare Research and Quality, 2007 (AHRQ Publication No. 07-05100; http://www.ahrq.gov/clinic/pocketgd.htm).

164. Margolis PA et al. From concept to application: the impact of a community-wide intervention to improve the delivery of preventive services to children. *Pediatrics*, 2001, 108:E42.

165. Donovan EF et al. Intensive home visiting is associated with decreased risk of infant death. *Pediatrics*, 2007, 119:1145–1151.

166. Manandhar D et al. Effect of a participatory intervention with women's groups on birth outcomes in Nepal: cluster-randomised controlled trial. *Lancet*, 364:970–979.

167. Rockenschaub G, Pukkila J, Profili MC, eds. *Towards health security. A discussion paper on recent health crises in the WHO European Region*. Copenhagen, World Health Organization Regional Office for Europe, 2007

168. *Primary care. America's health in a new era*. Washington DC, National Academy Press Institute of Medicine, 1996.

169. Tableau d'honneur des 50 meilleurs hôpitaux de France. Palmarès des Hôpitaux. *Le Point*, 2008 (http://hopitaux.lepoint.fr/tableau-honneur.php, accessed 29 July 2008).

170. Davidson BN, Sofaer S, Gertler P. Consumer information and biased selection in the demand for coverage supplementing Medicare. *Social Science and Medicine*, 1992, 34:1023–1034.

171. Davison KP, Pennebaker JW, Dickerson SS. Who talks? The social psychology of illness support groups. *American Psychology*, 2000, 55:205–217.

172. Segal SP, Redman D, Silverman C. Measuring clients' satisfaction with self-help agencies. *Psychiatric Services*, 51:1148–1152.

173. Adapted from Wollast E, Mercenier P. Pour une régionalisation des soins. In: Groupe d'Etude pour une Réforme de la Médecine. *Pour une politique de la santé*. Bruxelles, Editions Vie Ouvrière/La Revue Nouvelle, 1971.

174. Criel B, De Brouwere V, Dugas S. *Integration of vertical programmes in multi-function health services*. Antwerp, ITGPress, 1997 (Studies in Health Services Organization and Policy 3).

3

Quantifying the Health Benefits of Primary Care Physician Supply in the United States

Source: Macinko, James, Starfield, Barbara, Shi, Leiyu. "Quantifying the Health Benefits of Primary Care, in the United States." *International Journal of Health Services*, 37(1):111-126, 2007.

This analysis addresses the question, Would increasing the number of primary care physicians improve health outcomes in the United States? A search of the PubMed database for articles containing "primary care physician supply" or "primary care supply" in the title, published between 1985 and 2005, identified 17 studies, and 10 met all inclusion criteria. Results were reanalyzed to assess primary care effect size and the predicted effect on health outcomes of a one-unit increase in primary care physicians per 10,000 population. Primary care physician supply was associated with improved health outcomes, including all-cause, cancer, heart disease, stroke, and infant mortality; low birth weight; life expectancy; and self-rated health. This relationship held regardless of the year (1980-1995) or level of analysis (state, county, metropolitan statistical area [MSA], and non-MSA levels). Pooled results for all-cause mortality suggest that an increase of one primary care physician per 10,000 population was associated with an average mortality reduction of 5.3 percent, or 49 per 100,000 per year.

Forecasting the need for physicians is generally based on task and time projections[1] and benchmarking with health maintenance organizations rather than on assessments of the likely contributions to improving health.[2] In the 1990s, these approaches predicted physician surpluses in the 2000s. However, recent analyses using macroeconomic projections of demand for health services predict physician deficits of as many as 200,000 by 2025.[3] As a consequence, the Council on Graduate Medical Education reversed its position that the United States is producing too many physicians, and it has now endorsed the view that the nation may, in fact, be producing too few.[4] The purpose of this article is to summarize existing studies of the likely effect of primary care physician supply on a variety of health outcomes. It addresses the question, Would increasing the number of primary care physicians improve health outcomes in the United States?

METHODS

Our analysis draws its data from published studies that measure the impact of primary care physician supply on health outcomes in the United States. Articles were obtained by searching the PubMed database in January 2005 for titles including the terms "primary care physician supply" or "primary care supply" for articles published between 1985 and 2005. This search revealed 86 potential articles. Hand searching of references revealed an additional 20 potential articles.

Inclusion criteria for studies were that the study must be based in the United States; address the association of primary care supply with health outcomes; control for relevant ecological variables (e.g., income, education, poverty, income inequality, or unemployment); assess effects in more than one state; and present sufficient data to establish the effect of primary care on the health outcomes in question. Based on these criteria, the final selection of articles included 17 peer-reviewed studies. Seven of these were excluded from the analyses either because the analytical techniques did not lend themselves to reanalysis or because inadequate data were presented to allow the calculation of effect size.[5-11] We do include these seven studies in the discussion section.

For the remaining 10 studies, we reanalyzed the data to estimate the effect of increases in primary care physician supply at the various geographic levels. Regression coefficients, after controlling for potentially confounding characteristics (e.g., unemployment levels, average income levels, educational attainment, percentage minority population, or income inequality in the area), were used to estimate the effect of increasing the primary care physician supply variable on the health outcomes in question.

We report results as the primary care effect (percentage change in outcome associated with one more primary care physician per 10,000 population) and as the absolute change in existing outcome measures associated with this one-unit increase in primary care physicians. All results are presented with 95 percent confidence intervals (95% CI).

RESULTS

The composition of the U.S. health care workforce has changed considerably in the past 50 years. In the 1940s and 1950s, more than 50 percent of all physicians practiced primary care. Beginning in 1960, increases in specialist supply outpaced increases in primary care physician supply. Since 1975, the proportion of active physicians in primary care has been relatively stable at just below 35 percent. The composition of the primary care physician supply has fluctuated, with a declining proportion in general or family practice (currently about 12% of total physician supply) and an increasing proportion in general internal medicine (about 15%). The percentage in general pediatrics increased from about 6 percent in 1960 to about 7.5 percent in 2002 (Figure 1).

The state mean for active, nonfederal, office-based primary care physicians per 10,000 population (hereafter, PCP/10,000) steadily increased from about 5 PCP/10,000 in 1980 to 8 PCP/10,000 in 2000, with a considerable increase in 1995. The average ratio for counties was about 5 PCP/10,000 in the 1990s and has steadily increased over time to about the same level as state averages (Figure 2).

Table 1 provides a summary of the 20 analyses of the 10 studies. Analyses 1 through 5 cover two different studies[12,13] that assess the relationship between ratios of primary care physician to population and all-cause mortality at the state level, for each of the specified years between 1980 and 1995. Analyses

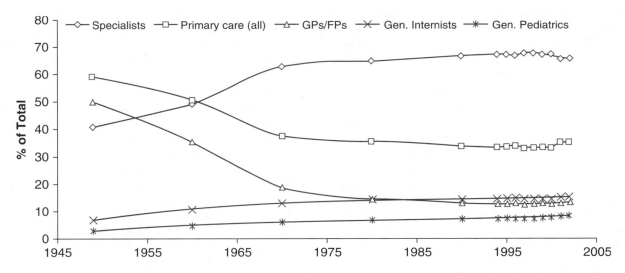

Figure 1 Composition of U.S. physician supply as proportion of total, 1945–2005. Total includes active physicians only; figures include federal physicians, who are generally excluded from most analyses. GPs, general practice; FPs, family practice. *Source:* National Center for Health Statistics, Health, United States, 2004, Hyattsville, MD, 2004.

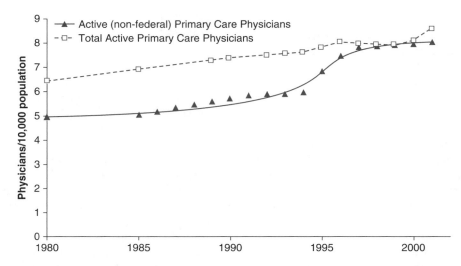

Figure 2 Active, nonfederal, office-based primary care physicians per 10,000 population, United States, 1980–2001. Data for total primary care physicians for 1985 and 1989 were modeled based on average rates of increase. *Source:* Authors' calculations from AMA Master Files.

6 through 10 are longitudinal analyses at the state level that pool data over a 10-year period (1985-1995). The total sample size is 549 (one data point—Delaware in 1991—was dropped from these studies because of incomplete data). These studies assess the effect of primary care supply on mortality for black and for white populations,[14] on low birth weight and infant mortality,[15] and on stroke mortality.[16] Analyses 11 through 13 assess the effects of county-level primary care supply on heart disease, cancer, and total mortality rate,[17] and analyses 14 through 16 assess the same relationships but restricted to rural areas (defined as non-metropolitan statistical areas, or non-MSAs).[18] Analyses 17 and 18 compare mortality between black and white populations in metropolitan statistical areas (MSAs) in 1990.[19] Finally, analyses 19 and 20 examine self-rated health and state-level primary care supply.[20,21]

Primary care supply was measured in two different but related ways. The most common method is a continuous measure of number of primary care physicians per 10,000 population. This measure is calculated at the state, county, or MSA level. The second method uses the PCP/10,000 measure to divide counties into quartiles of increasing primary care physician density. The measure compares counties in the lowest three quartiles with counties having the highest PCP/10,000. In every study, "primary care physicians" was defined as doctors of allopathic medicine working in family medicine, general practice, general internal medicine, and general pediatrics who are in active, nonfederal, office-based patient care.[22] Analyses conducted at the state level generally

exclude Washington, DC, but county and MSA-level analyses do include Washington, DC.

Table 1 also presents predicted improvements in health outcomes associated with an increase of one PCP/10,000. For every health outcome, the PCP/10,000 measure was found to be associated with improved outcome. In state-level analyses, reductions in all-cause mortality ranged from 1.30 to 9.08 percent, depending on the year analyzed and the study source.

For state-level all-cause mortality, an increase in primary care supply is predicted to reduce mortality by 41 to 85 per 100,000, averaging about 68 per 100,000. One additional primary care physician per 10,000 population is estimated to result in a fourfold greater reduction in mortality for black populations than for white populations.

In 1990, reductions in all-cause mortality associated with increased primary care supply were higher when analyzed at the county level (10.8%) than at the state level (4.4% to 9%, depending on the study). Reductions were lower in rural counties (2.3%). On the other hand, expected changes in mortality rates were actually higher in rural counties (24.64 per 100,000) than in all counties (17.60 per 100,000) because mortality rates are generally higher in rural areas, so even a small percentage decrease translates to a larger change in overall rates.

Cause-specific mortality showed a similar pattern. At the state level, over the period 1985-1995, an increase in primary care physician supply was associated with moderate decreases in low birth weight, infant mortality, and stroke mortality rates. At the

Table 1 Predicted effects of a one-unit change in primary care physician (PCP) supply on health outcomes

Analysis number (reference)	Unit of analysis	N	PCP[a]	Year	Outcome	Percent improvement in outcome with PCP increase	Absolute change in outcome with PCP increase[b]
1 (12)	States (all)	50	A	1980	Mortality, all-cause, per 100,000	7.07 (6.33–7.81)	84.57 (75.74–93.41)
2 (12)	States (all)	50	A	1985	Mortality, all-cause, per 100,000	8.14 (7.29–8.99)	69.91 (62.59–77.23)
3 (12)	States (all)	50	A	1990	Mortality, all-cause, per 100,000	9.08 (7.89–10.26)	85.19 (74.11–96.28)
4 (12)	States (all)	50	A	1995	Mortality, all-cause, per 100,000	6.41 (5.83–6.98)	58.28 (53.04–63.52)
5 (13)	States (all)	50	A	1990	Mortality, all-cause, per 100,000	4.43 (3.99–4.86)	41.54 (37.42–45.66)
6 (14)	States (all)	549	A	1985–95	Mortality, whites, per 100,000	1.30 (1.28–1.32)	11.81 (11.66–11.97)
7 (14)	States (all)	549	A	1985–95	Mortality, blacks, per 100,000	3.81 (3.75–3.87)	47.59 (46.85–48.33)
8 (15)	States (all)	549	A	1985–95	Low birth weight, percent	3.17 (3.13–3.21)	0.22 (0.21–0.23)
9 (15)	States (all)	549	A	1985–95	Infant mortality, per 1,000 live births	2.45 (2.41–2.49)	0.22 (0.22–0.23)
10 (16)	States (all)	549	A	1985–95	Stroke mortality, per 100,000	1.52 (1.50–1.55)	0.82 (0.81–0.83)

(Continued)

Table 1	Predicted effects of a one-unit change in primary care physician (PCP) supply on health outcomes (continued)						
11 (17)	Counties (all)	3,075	B	1990	Heart disease mortality, per 100,000	1.74 (1.71–1.77)	14.26 (14.10–14.41)
12 (17)	Counties (all)	3,075	B	1990	Cancer mortality, per 100,000	0.66 (0.58–0.73)	4.34 (4.26–4.42)
13 (17)	Counties (all)	3,075	B	1990	Mortality, all-cause, per 100,000	10.79 (8.79–12.78)	17.60 (17.32–17.89)
14 (18)	Non-MSA	815	B	1990	Mortality, all-cause, per 100,000	2.29 (2.22–2.36)	24.64 (23.86–25.43)
15 (18)	Non-MSA	815	B	1990	Heart disease mortality, per 100,000	3.96 (3.87–4.05)	19.56 (19.11–20.01)
16 (18)	Non-MSA	815	B	1990	Cancer mortality, per 100,000	2.77 (2.68–2.87)	6.47 (6.25–6.68)
17 (19)	MSAs	273	B	1990	Mortality, whites, per 100,000	1.95 (1.92–1.99)	N.A.
18 (19)	MSAs	273	B	1990	Mortality, blacks, per 100,000	3.11 (3.07–3.14)	N.A.
19 (20)	Individuals	26,679	A	1996–97	Self-rated health, excellent/good,percent	3.00 (1.00–1.05)	2.65 (N.A.)
20 (21)	Individuals	60,446	A	1996–97	Self-rated health excellent/good, percent	2.00 (1.01–1.04)	1.76 (N.A.)

Note: MSA, metropolitan statistical area; N.A., authors do not provide sufficient data to calculate.
[a] Primary care physician supply: A = PCP/10,000 population); B = counties in the lowest 75th percentile based on PCP/10,000 population.
[b] Absolute values. All figures represent improvements in health, based on the health indicator and the primary care measured used; 95% confidence in tervals inparentheses.

county level, primary care supply was associated with moderate reductions in heart disease and cancer mortality. At the county level, an increase of one PCP/10,000 would result in an estimated decrease in heart, cancer, and all-cause mortality of between 0.66 and 10.79 percent. At the rural level, improvements in all outcomes except all-cause mortality were higher than those for counties. Self-rated excellent/good health would be expected to improve between 2 and 3 percent overall.

Figure 3 compares estimated percentage reductions in all-cause mortality associated with an increase of one PCP/10,000. State-level estimates for 1980, 1985, and 1995 all exceed 6 percent. Estimates for 1990 vary by study and unit of analysis. Combining all 11 results, the mean percentage reduction in all-cause mortality was 5.31 percent (95% CI, 4.76-5.85). Values for MSAs and pooled years

(1985-1995) were generally below the average. Health improvements for black populations (at both the state and county levels) were higher than those for white populations.

Figure 4 compares estimated reductions in all-cause mortality rates associated with the percentage improvements presented above. State-level analyses show an overall declining trend in predicted mortality rate reductions from about 85 per 100,000 in 1980 to about 58 per 100,000 in 1995. Insufficient data were available to calculate the rate reductions for studies conducted at the MSA level. Combining all nine results presented in the graph, the average reduction in all-cause mortality rates associated with a one-unit increase in PCP/10,000 was 49 per 100,000 (95% CI, 44.73-53.97). Mortality rate reductions for black populations were higher than those for white populations.

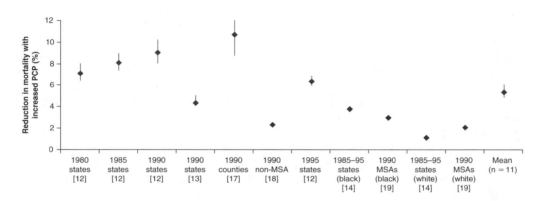

Figure 3 Estimated improvements in all-cause mortality rates associated with increased primary care physician (PCP) supply (percentage reduction in mortality, with 95% confidence intervals). Mean is calculated from all results included in the graph. MSA, metopolitan statistical area. *Source:* reference sources in brackets.

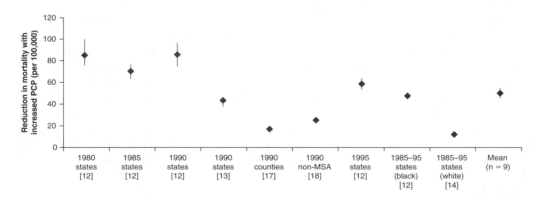

Figure 4 Estimated improvements in all-cause mortality rates associated with increased primary care physician (PCP) supply (absolute reduction in mortality per 100,000, with 95% confidence intervals). Mean is calculated from all results included in the graph. MSA, metropolitan statistical area. *Source:* reference sources in brackets.

DISCUSSION

The studies reviewed here suggest that ecological measures of primary care physician supply are consistently associated with improved health outcomes, regardless of the year, level of analysis, or type of outcome studied. A one-unit increase in primary care supply (one PCP/10,000) resulted in improvements in all health outcomes studied, with a range of 0.66 to 10.8 percent improvement, depending on the outcome and the geographic unit of analysis. Limiting results to all-cause mortality, predicted reductions averaged 5.31 percent, with a corresponding average decrease in mortality rate of 49 per 100,000. Race-stratified analyses suggest that potential reductions in mortality would be greater for blacks than for whites.

The policy impact of these findings is considerable. At the national level, a 5.31 percent reduction in all-cause mortality in 2000 would translate into 127,617 deaths potentially averted.

An increase of one PCP/10,000 would necessitate a 12.6 percent overall increase in primary care physician supply, or an absolute increase of 28,726 physicians, based on the supply in 2000. If there is indeed a physician shortage in the United States, these results suggest that considerable health gains could be obtained by creating incentives to train more physicians in primary care.

The estimate of effect presented here is likely to be conservative, because it does not include the impact of increased primary care supply on morbidity and quality of life. The data do not allow the calculation of quality-adjusted life years or other measures that would better capture the contribution of primary care to reducing death and disability over the life course, nor do they allow calculation of the average cost savings associated with reduced use of emergency room and other inappropriate and expensive services required by individuals who lack a primary care physician as their usual source of care. It is therefore likely that increasing primary care supply in the United States represents an effective strategy to improve population health, especially if it is compared with the likely impact of expanding the supply of specialists. The health effects of expanding specialist supply are unknown, but, at the very least, expanding supply would lead to increased costs, perhaps even with no commensurate benefits for the health of the population.[23]

Another implication of these results is that primary care resources could be better targeted to regions with higher levels of social inequality. The studies reviewed here indicate that although primary care supply has a positive effect on the entire population, the magnitude of this effect is greater in areas with higher levels of income inequality (which in general are also areas with higher levels of poverty) and on outcomes for African Americans.[14] Expanding community health centers, for example, might be one way to improve the supply of primary care in areas with particularly vulnerable populations.[24,25]

These findings are generally consistent with evidence from other countries. A series of studies that estimated the contribution of primary care systems (not just primary care physicians) to population health in 19 wealthy countries found that better primary care was associated with a 6.5 to 15 percent improvement in health outcomes, depending on the degree to which the outcome was amenable to primary care.[26,27] Similar evidence from Spain showed that primary care reforms were associated with a significant reduction in mortality rates for several major causes of death.[28] A study in England also found primary care physician supply to be associated with lower mortality; each unit of increase in general practitioners per 10,000 population was associated with a five-unit (about 6%) decrease in mortality.[29]

The finding of a positive impact of primary care physician supply is supported by several studies that could not be included in our meta-analysis because of the analytical techniques used in the study or the lack of information necessary to calculate primary care effects. For example, Vogel and Ackermann[6] found that state-level primary care supply was associated with reduced low birth weight, lower neonatal mortality, and higher life expectancies.

Only two of the studies we identified found no evidence of a positive impact of primary care physician supply, and these were studies of hospitalizations rather than health outcomes. Both assessed the relationship between ambulatory care sensitive hospitalization (ACSH) and primary care physician supply in specific U.S. state. The first found that primary care supply had no relationship to ACSH conditions in North Carolina.[10] The second study, conducted in New York State, found a positive relationship; the number of primary care physicians per 1,000 population was associated with increased ACSH rates.[11] These findings are not consistent with other studies of ACSH, and their results may be at least partially explained by the peculiarities of the health care markets in the two states examined.

There are several reasons why primary care physician supply might be associated with better population health. First, considerable evidence suggests that primary care improves primary prevention. In the United States, the states with higher ratios of primary care physicians to population have lower smoking rates, less obesity, and higher seatbelt use than states with lower ratios.[21] Continuity of care with a single provider is positively associated with primary preventive care, including smoking cessation and influenza immunization.[21,30]

Second, several state-specific studies illustrate the effectiveness of primary care in early detection of disease. Early detection of breast cancer,[31,32] colorectal cancer,[33] cervical cancer,[34] and melanoma[35,36] is enhanced when the supply of primary care physicians is greater. Many regular screening activities take place through primary care. Most mammograms are ordered by primary care physicians,[37] and people with an adequate primary care source are more likely to receive blood pressure screening and Pap smears.[38]

Finally, availability of good primary care can influence the efficiency of the health system as a whole. Geographic areas with more general and family physicians per population have lower hospitalization rates for conditions that should be preventable or detected early with good primary care (including diabetes mellitus or pneumonia in children and congestive heart failure, hypertension, pneumonia, and diabetes mellitus in adults).[8] Rates of hospital admission are lower in U.S. communities where primary care physicians are more involved in the care of children both before and during hospitalization.[39] Adolescents with the same regular source of primary care are much more likely to receive indicated preventive care and less likely to seek care in emergency rooms.[40] Individuals who use their primary source of care over time for most health care needs have improved satisfaction, better compliance, lower hospitalization rates, and less emergency room use than those who do not.[41-43]

LIMITATIONS OF THE STUDY

The different modes of analysis, different years studied, and consistency of results in terms of sign and relative magnitude indicate how robust these findings are. Yet there may be some limitations to generalizability. Two of the studies included here produced different results for similar years and units of analysis.[12,13] This could be because the studies employed different sets of covariates. The highest primary care supply effects were seen in studies that also controlled for specialist supply,[12] suggesting that these analyses may have been more successful in isolating the primary care physician effect from that of other physicians.

Although our analysis was based on a review of the available literature, there is the possibility of bias, because most of the studies analyzed were by the same authors. It is important to note, however, that the few studies performed by other authors generally had similar results.

There is also research to suggest that increasing physician supply may have the effect of improving the health of those who already have access, rather than actually increasing access.[44,45] This hypothesis cannot be tested from the studies presented here, since they are primarily at the ecological level, but increasing primary care physician supply would certainly not remove financial barriers to access in the absence of concomitant changes in health financing mechanisms.

Another potential limitation is that there is no guarantee that the relationship between primary care physician supply and health is linear; after a certain point there might be a threshold effect beyond which an increase in primary care supply would no longer result in the same rate of improvement in health outcomes. The studies analyzed here show a slight decrease in magnitude as the supply of primary care physicians increased over the 1990s, but there is no evidence to suggest that even if such a plateau does exist, the United States has reached it.

Another potential limitation is that improvements in health outcomes might be achievable by improving the effectiveness of primary care physicians without increasing their number. It is even possible that an increase in primary care supply would necessitate a shift in the type and number of specialist physicians in order to accommodate changing patterns of referrals. A recent analysis found that a selection of pre-paid group practices achieved better health outcomes with lower physician-to-population ratios than those found in the United States as a whole.[46] However, even in that study, there was a slightly higher proportion of primary than specialty care physicians than in the United States as a whole and a much higher percentage of non-physician providers of primary care (physician assistants and nurse-practitioners) than the U.S. average. All the organizations studied had specialist-to-population ratios considerably lower than U.S. averages.

CONCLUSIONS

Our analysis found consistent evidence that at the ecological level, the supply of primary care physicians is positively associated with better population health in the United States. The relationship holds at different units of analysis (state, county, and MSA levels) for various health outcomes (all-cause mortality; cancer, heart disease, stroke, and infant mortality; low birth weight; life expectancy; and self-rated health) and for various approaches to categorizing the primary care physician supply.

Previous studies have shown that countries with well-developed primary care systems have lower overall health system costs, better health outcomes, and higher levels of satisfaction than countries without.[26,27] These systems have better results not only because the relative roles of primary care physicians and specialists may be more clearly defined than in the United States, but also because the health system as a whole is more directed at the supply side than at the demand side. Greater use of evidence on the roles of primary care physicians and specialists, and on ways to most effectively deploy them, offers promise of more informed health policy.

ACKNOWLEDGMENTS
This work was supported in part by grant no. 6 U30 CS 00189-05 S1 R1 of the Bureau of Primary Health Care, Health Resources and Services Administration, Department of Health and Human Services, to the Primary Care Policy Center for the Underserved at the Johns Hopkins University. The funding source had no role in the collection, analysis, or interpretation of data, the writing of the report, or the decision to submit the article for publication.

● ● ● **References**

1. Council on Graduate Medical Education. *Third Report: Improving Access to Health Care Through Physician Workforce Reform.* Washington, DC, 1992. www.cogme.gov/rpt3.htm.

2. Weiner, J. Forecasting the effects of health reform on US physician workforce requirement: Evidence from HMO staffing patterns. *JAMA* 272:222-230, 1994.

3. Copper, R. A. Weighing the evidence for expanding physician supply. *Ann. Intern. Med.* 141:705-714, 2004.

4. Council on Graduate Medical Education. *Summary Report to Congress and Secretary Department of Health and Human Services.* Washington, DC, June 2002. www.cogme.gov/2002summary.htm.

5. Joines, J. D., et al. A spatial analysis of county-level variation in hospitalization rates for low back problems in North Carolina. *Soc. Sci. Med.* 56:2541-2553, 2003.

6. Vogel, R. L., and Ackermann, R. J. Is primary care physician supply correlated with health outcomes? *Int. J. Health Serv.* 28:183-196, 1998.

7. Laditka, J. N. Physician supply, physician diversity, and outcomes of primary health care for older persons in the United States. *Health Place* 10:231-244, 2004.

8. Parchman, M., and Culler, S. Primary care physicians and avoidable hospitalization. *J. Fam. Practice* 39:123-128, 1994.

9. Parchman, M. L., and Culler, S. D. Preventable hospitalizations in primary care shortage areas: An analysis of vulnerable Medicare beneficiaries. *Arch. Fam. Med.* 8:487-491, 1999.

10. Ricketts, T. C., et al. Hospitalization rates as indicators of access to primary care. *Health Place* 7:27-38, 2001.

11. Schreiber, S., and Zielinski, T. The meaning of ambulatory care sensitive admissions: Urban and rural perspectives. *J. Rural Health* 13:276-284, 1994.

12. Shi, L., et al. The relationship between primary care, income inequality, and mortality in US States, 1980-1995. *J. Am. Board Fam. Pract.* 16:412-422, 2003.

13. Shi, L., et al. Income inequality, primary care, and health indicators. *J. Fam. Pract.* 48:275-284, 1999.

14. Shi, L., et al. Primary care, race, and mortality in US states. *Soc. Sci. Med.* 61:65-75, 2005.

15. Shi, L., et al. Primary care, infant mortality, and low birth weight in the states of the USA. *J. Epidemiol. Community Health* 58:374-380, 2004.

16. Shi, L., et al. Primary care, income inequality, and stroke mortality in the United States: A longitudinal analysis, 1985-1995. *Stroke* 34:1958-1964, 2003.

17. Shi, L., et al. Primary care, social inequalities, and all-cause, heart disease, and cancer mortality in US counties, 1990. *Am. J. Public Health* 95:674-680, 2005.

18. Shi, L., et al. Primary care, social inequalities, and all-cause, heart disease, and cancer mortality in US counties: A comparison of urban and rural areas. *Public Health*, 2006, in press.

19. Shi, L., and Starfield, B. The effect of primary care physician supply and income inequality on mortality among blacks and whites in US metropolitan areas. *Am. J. Public Health* 91:1246-1250, 2001.

20. Shi, L., et al. Primary care, self-rated health, and reductions in social disparities in health. *Health Serv. Res.* 37:529-550, 2002.

21. Shi, L., and Starfield, B. Primary care, income inequalities, and self-rated health in the United States: A mixed-level analysis. *Int. J. Health Serv.* 30:541-555, 2000.

22. U.S. Centers for Disease Control and Prevention. Health status indicators: Definitions and national data. *Statistical Notes* 1:1-8, 1992.

23. Starfield, B., et al. The effects of specialist supply on populations' health: Assessing the evidence. *Health Aff. (Millwood)* Suppl. Web exclusives: W5-97-107, 2005.

24. Forrest, C. B., and Whelan, E. M. Primary care safety-net delivery sites in the United States: A comparison of community health centers, hospital out-

patient departments, and physicians' offices. *JAMA* 284:2077-2083, 2000.

25. Shi, L., et al. America's health centers: Reducing racial and ethnic disparities in perinatal care and birth outcomes. *Health Serv. Res.* 39(6, pt. 1):1881-1901, 2004.

26. Macinko, J., Starfied, B., and Shi, L. The contribution of primary care systems to health outcomes within OECD countries, 1970-1998. *Health Serv. Res.* 38:819-853, 2003.

27. Starfield, B., and Shi, L. Policy relevant determinants of health: An international perspective. *Health Policy* 60:201-216, 2002.

28. Villalbi, J. R., et al. Evaluacion del impacto de la reforma de la atencion primaria sobre la salud. *Atencion primaria* 24:468-474, 1999.

29. Gulliford, M. C. Availability of primary care doctors and population health in England: Is there an association? *J. Public Health Med.* 24:252-254, 2002.

30. Saver, B. Financing and organization findings brief. *Acad. Res. Health Care Policy* 5:1-2, 2002.

31. Ferrante, J. M., et al. Effects of physician supply on early detection of breast cancer. *J. Am. Board Fam. Pract.* 13:408-414, 2000.

32. Davidson, P. L., et al. Role of community risk factors and resources on breast carcinoma stage at diagnosis. *Cancer* 103(5), 2005.

33. Roetzheim, R. G., et al. The effects of physician supply on the early detection of colorectal cancer. *J. Fam. Pract.* 48:850-858, 1999.

34. Campbell, R. J., et al. Cervical cancer rates and the supply of primary care physicians in Florida. *Fam. Med.* 35:60-64, 2003.

35. Roetzheim, R. G., et al. Increasing supplies of dermatologists and family physicians are associated with earlier stage of melanoma detection. *J. Am. Acad. Dermatol.* 43(2, pt. 1):211-218, 2000.

36. Van Durme, D. J., et al. Effects of physician supply on melanoma incidence and mortality in Florida. *South. Med. J.* 96:656-660, 2003.

37. Schappert, S. M. National Ambulatory Medical Care Survey: 1992 summary. *Adv. Data* 253:1-20, 1994.

38. Bindman, A., et al. Primary care and receipt of preventive services. *J. Gen. Intern. Med.* 11:269-276, 1996.

39. Perrin, J. M., et al. Primary care involvement among hospitalized children. *Arch. Pediatr. Adolesc. Med.* 150:479-486, 1996.

40. Ryan, S., et al. The effects of regular source of care and health need on medical care use among rural adolescents. *Arch. Pediatr. Adolesc. Med.* 155:184-190, 2001.

41. Rosenblatt, R. A., et al. The effect of the doctor-patient relationship on emergency department use among the elderly. *Am. J. Public Health* 90:97-102, 2000.

42. Gill, J. M., Mainous, A. G. 3rd, and Nsereko, M. The effect of continuity of care on emergency department use. *Arch. Fam. Med.* 9:333-338, 2000.

43. Weiss, L. J., and Blustein, J. Faithful patients: The effect of long-term physician-patient relationships on the costs and use of health care by older Americans. *Am. J. Public Health* 86:1742-1747, 1996.

44. Grumbach, K., Vranizan, K., and Bindman, A. Physician supply and access to care in urban communities. *Health Aff. (Millwood)* 16:71-86, 1997.

45. Hendryx, M. S., et al. Access to health care and community social capital. *Health Serv. Res.* 37:87-103, 2002.

46. Weiner, J. P. Prepaid group practice staffing and U.S. physician supply: Lessons for workforce policy. *Health Aff. (Millwood)*, Suppl. Web exclusives: W4-43-59, 2004.

4

America's Health Centers

Source: America's Health Centers. Fact Sheet, October 2009, Washington DC. Courtesy of National Association of Community Health Centers.

WHAT ARE HEALTH CENTERS?

Community, Migrant, Homeless, and Public Housing Health Centers are **non-profit, community-directed health care providers serving low income and medically underserved communities**. For over 40 years, the national network of health centers has provided **high-quality, affordable primary and preventive care**, as well as dental, mental health and substance abuse, and pharmacy services. Also known as Federally Qualified Health Centers (FQHCs), they are located in areas where care is needed but scarce, and improve access to care for millions of Americans regardless of their insurance status or ability to pay. Their costs of care rank among the lowest, and they reduce the need for more expensive hospital-based and specialty care, saving billions of dollars for taxpayers. Currently, 1,200 health centers deliver care through over 7,500 service delivery sites in every state and territory.

WHO DO HEALTH CENTERS SERVE?

Health centers serve as the medical and health care home for **20 million people** nationally—a number that is quickly growing. Health center patients are among the nation's most vulnerable populations—people who even if insured would nonetheless remain isolated from traditional forms of medical care because of where they live, who they are, the language they speak, and their higher levels of complex health care needs. As a result, patients are disproportionately low income, uninsured or publicly insured, and minority.

Nearly all patients are low income, with 70% of health center patients having family incomes at or below poverty (Figure 1). Patients also tend to be **members of racial and ethnic minority groups,** as shown in Figure 2. At the same time, **38% of health**

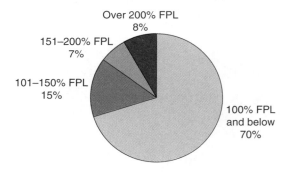

Figure 1 Health Center Patients By Income Level, 2008
Notes: Federal Poverty Level (FPL) for a family of three in 2008 was $17,600. (See http://aspe.hhs.gov/poverty/08poverty.shtml.) Based on percent known. Percents may not total 100% due to rounding. *Source:* Bureau of Primary Health Care, HRSA, DHHS, 2008 Uniform Data System.

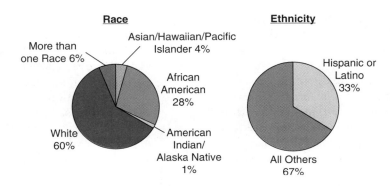

Race

Ethnicity

Note: Based on percent known. Percents may not total 100% due to rounding.

Figure 2 Health Center Patients By Race/Ethnicity, 2008 *Source:* Bureau of Primary Health Care, HRSA, DHHS, 2008 Uniform Data System

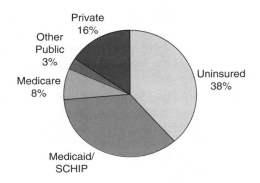

Figure 3 Health Center Patients By Insurance Status, 2008 *Note:* Other Public may include non-Medicaid SCHIP. Percents may not total 100% due to rounding. *Source:* Bureau of Primary Health Care, HRSA, DHHS, 2008 Uniform Data System

center patients are uninsured and another 36% depend on Medicaid (Figure 3). Additionally, about half of health center patients reside in rural areas, while the other half tend to live in economically depressed inner city communities.

HOW DO HEALTH CENTERS OVERCOME BARRIERS TO CARE?

Health centers remove common barriers to care by serving communities that otherwise confront financial, geographic, language, cultural and other barriers, making them different from most private, office-based physicians. They

- are **located in high-need areas** identified by the federal government as having elevated poverty, higher than average infant mortality, and where few physicians practice;

- are **open to all residents**, regardless of insurance status, and provide free or reduced cost care based on ability to pay;

- **offer services that help their patients access health care,** such as transportation, translation, case management, health education, and home visitation; and

- **tailor their services** to fit the special needs and priorities of their communities, and provide services in a linguistically and culturally appropriate setting. Nearly a third of all patients are best served in languages other than English, and nearly all patients report their clinician speaks the same language they do.

For many patients, the health center may be the only source of health care services available. In fact, the number of uninsured patients at health centers has doubled—from 3.9 million in 1998 to 7.8 million today.

HOW DO HEALTH CENTERS MAKE A DIFFERENCE?

Key to health centers' accomplishments is **patient involvement in service delivery.** Governing boards—the majority of which must be patients according to grant requirements—manage health center operations. Board members serve as community representatives and make decisions on services provided. Active patient management of health centers assures responsiveness to local needs, and helps guarantee that health centers improve the quality of life for millions of patients in the following ways.

- **Improve Access to Primary and Preventive Care.** Health centers provide preventive services to vulnerable populations that would otherwise not have access to certain services, such as immunizations, health education, mammograms, pap smears, and other screenings. Low income, uninsured health center patients are much *more likely to have a usual source of care* than the uninsured nationally. Moreover, uninsured people living within close proximity to a health center are *less likely to have an unmet medical need, less likely to visit the emergency room or have a hospital stay, and more likely to have had a general medical visit* compared to other uninsured.

- **Cost-Effective Care.** Care received at health centers is ranked among the most cost-effective. Two recent reports found that *total patient care costs are 24-50% lower than those served in other settings, producing up to $24 billion in annual health system savings. This includes $6.7 billion in savings for the federal share of the Medicaid program,* and is driven by lower utilization of costly specialty care, emergency departments, and hospitals. Furthermore, if avoidable visits to emergency rooms were redirected to health centers, an additional $18 billion in annual health care costs could be saved nationally.

- **High Quality of Care.** Studies have found that the quality of care provided at health centers is *equal to or greater* than the quality of care provided elsewhere. Moreover, 99% of surveyed patients report that they were satisfied with the care they receive at health centers.

- **Reduction of Health Disparities.** *Disparities in health status do not exist among health center patients,* even after controlling for sociodemographic factors. The absence of such disparities at health centers may be related to their culturally sensitive practices and community involvement—features that other primary care settings often lack. Moreover, as more of a state's low income population is served by health centers, racial and ethnic health disparities in key areas are reduced across the state.

- **Effective Management of Chronic Illness.** Health centers meet or exceed nationally accepted practice standards for treatment of chronic conditions. In fact, the Institute of Medicine and the Government Accountability Office have recognized health centers as models for screening, diagnosing, and managing chronic conditions such as diabetes, cardiovascular disease, asthma, depression, cancer, and HIV. Health centers' efforts have led to *improved health outcomes* for their patients, as well as *lowered the cost of treating patients* with chronic illness.

- **Improve Birth Outcomes.** Health centers also improve access to timely prenatal care. Communities served by health centers have *infant mortality rates at least 10% lower* than comparable communities not served by health centers. Women of low socioeconomic status seeking care at health centers experience *lower rates of low birth weight* compared to all such mothers. This trend holds for each racial/ethnic group.

- **Create Jobs and Stimulate Economic Growth.** In addition to health care savings, health centers also bring much needed economic benefits to the low income communities they serve. Their *overall economic impact reaches $12.6 billion annually,* while also producing 143,000 jobs some of the country's most economically deprived neighborhoods.

WHY IS INVESTING IN HEALTH CENTERS IMPORTANT?

Expanding and strengthening the Health Centers Program would further reduce health disparities, increase access to high quality and regular care, and boost more local economies. As a result, fewer Americans would rely on costly sources of care, such as the emergency room, thereby saving tax payers significantly and making the overall health care system more efficient. Health centers are therefore good public investments that generate substantial benefits for patients, communities, insurers, and governments. However, health center expansion should coincide with expansions in insurance coverage and the primary care workforce in order to most effectively achieve improved health outcomes for the entire population.

12

Inpatient and Tertiary Care

For well over a century now, hospitals have served as the central core of health care delivery. In many communities, hospitals are not only a source of needed medical care, but also major employers and contributors to the local economies. Hence, the benefits of hospitals to society extend far beyond the delivery of medical care. Over time, hospitals have evolved into many different types according to where they are located, the breadth of services they offer, specialization in a given field of medicine, specialization in serving a particular population, and their role in medical training. Generally, American hospitals provide the most technologically advanced diagnostic, therapeutic, and life-saving services available anywhere in the world in accordance with the latest scientific and medical knowledge. For example, a Level I trauma center is equipped to provide the highest level of emergency care 24-hours a day. The American College of Surgeons runs a verification process that trauma centers can participate in to ascertain that the center has the resources necessary for optimal delivery of care for severe and life-threatening trauma. Local governments or other agencies may label certain hospitals as "designated trauma centers" based on the capacity of these hospitals to treat trauma victims. Level I trauma centers are tertiary care hospitals that receive referrals from other medical facilities because the treatments they offer are not available elsewhere. Tertiary care centers provide additional high-tech services such as neonatal intensive care, invasive cardiac services, organ transplantations, and various high-risk procedures. In 2008, 242 tertiary care centers performed 16,517 kidney transplants—the most common type of organ transplant—with a 95.4% one-year patient survival rate (U.S. Census Bureau 2010, Table 175).

Hospitals interface with almost all other types of health care services. For example, physicians practicing in the community may refer their patients to a hospital for inpatient services, nursing homes transfer patients to hospitals when their patients develop acute symptoms that require hospitalization, and smaller hospitals with limited services render basic treatments and may transfer the patient to a larger hospital for more specialized care. Hospitals also collaborate with other community-based services, such as home health care, hospice, and long-term care, to ensure continuity of care to the patient following discharge from the hospital.

Most community hospitals offer emergency services as well as a range of inpatient and outpatient medical and surgical services. In 2006, there were 5,747 hospitals with 947,412 beds in the United States, which amount to 3.2 beds per 1,000 population (National Center for Health Statistics 2009, p. 403). Japan, on the other hand, has 14 beds per 1,000 population, the highest of any OECD country (OECD 2009). Hospital utilization among developed countries is actually not the lowest in the United States. For example, discharges per 100,000 population in 2006 were 12,632 in the U.S., compared with 8,429 in Canada, and the average length of stay of 5.6 days compared to 4.6 days in Sweden and 4.7 days in Finland (OECD 2009). In the United States, almost one-third of all health expenditures are incurred in the delivery of hospital care.

Rural communities have long struggled to maintain access to adequate health care services. Some of the problems that contribute to issues in rural health delivery include a declining population, economic stagnation, shortages of physicians and other health care professionals, and a disproportionate number of elderly, poor, and underinsured residents (Weisgrau 1995). Access to trauma centers has been a notable problem. For example, a study revealed that the 46.7 million Americans who had no access to a level I or II trauma center within 60 minutes lived mostly in rural areas (Branas et al. 2005). Closure of rural hospitals became an issue in the 1980s and 1990s. One policy initiative created under the 1997 Balanced Budget Act was to create the designation of Critical Access Hospital (CAH) as a safety net to assure Medicare beneficiaries access to health care services in rural areas. CAHs are required by law to have available 24-hour emergency care services 7 days per week.

In recent years, the number of physician-owned specialty hospitals has been on the rise. These hospitals primarily perform cardiac, orthopedic, or surgical procedures and are partially or fully owned by physician investors. As the number of these hospitals has increased, they have been surrounded by controversy. Four main issues have emerged (Guterman 2006): (1) physicians' clinical decisions may be distorted by financial considerations, (2) specialty hospitals may treat less complex, more profitable patients, (3) these hospitals may avoid uninsured and Medicaid patients, and (4) selection of more profitable patients by these hospitals may adversely affect full-service community hospitals. They may also have an adverse effect on the stability of safety net hospitals which provide essential services to vulnerable and uninsured populations. Another issue surrounds

the delivery of emergency care. If emergency services are inadequate or nonexistent in physician-owned specialty hospitals, those patients have to be treated by emergency departments in community hospitals. That will put further strains on the financial stability of full-service hospitals. The Office of Inspector General (2008) found that only 55% of all physician-owned specialty hospitals had an emergency department, which in many instances had only one or two beds. A few of these hospitals do not have nurses on duty and/or physicians on call at all times. Many of these hospitals rely on 9-1-1 as part of their medical emergency response procedures, to obtain medical assistance to stabilize a patient, or to transfer a patient. In addition, research does not support that specialty hospitals are more efficient than the full-service hospitals with which they compete. In particular, orthopedic and surgical specialty hospitals appear to have significantly higher levels of cost inefficiency (Carey et al. 2008). On the other hand, quality of care in specialty hospitals is at least comparable to that in general hospitals. Cram et al. (2005) found no significant differences in mortality for cardiac patients treated at specialty hospitals and general hospitals, after adjusting for lower severity of patients treated in specialty hospitals. For orthopedic patients, the odds of adverse outcomes were significantly lower in specialty hospitals (Cram et al. 2007).

The first reading for this chapter, **Physician-Owned Specialty Hospitals**, provides an overview of specialty hospitals in a testimony before the U.S. Senate by Mark E. Miller, Executive Director of the Medicare Payment Advisory Commission (MedPAC). The testimony confirmed some of the issues noted above, but it did not find that community hospitals competing with specialty hospitals had unfavorable financial performance.

In **General Hospitals, Specialty Hospitals and Financially Vulnerable Patients**, Tynan and colleagues examine the impact of specialty hospitals on the ability of general and safety net hospitals to care for financially vulnerable patients, including low-income and uninsured patients, in three U.S. cities. The data source for this study came from interviews with key stakeholders in the three communities. Based on their analysis, Tynan and colleagues reached six main conclusions. (1) General hospitals, rather than safety net hospitals, were more likely to be affected by specialty hospitals. When adversely affected, these hospitals were able to take steps to overcome the situations. (2) Specialty hospitals attracted physicians, nurses, and other staff, mainly from general hospitals. Loss of staff created challenges in providing emergency department on-call coverage. To overcome this situation, general hospitals took aggressive steps to align themselves with various specialists by accommodating their preferences. (3) Upon the entry of specialist hospitals in the marketplace, general hospitals experienced a drop in service volume. However, the loss in volume could only partially be attributed to specialty hospitals. Other market factors played a role. General hospitals used alignment with specialists, development of new service lines, and advertising campaigns to overcome volume shortfalls. (4) The rise in patient acuity levels in general and safety net hospitals could not be attributed to specialty hospitals, which have been accused of cream-skimming less complex patients and off-loading complicated patients to general and safety net hospitals. (5) An increase in financially vulnerable patients at general and safety net hospitals could not be fully attributed to specialty hospitals. Safety net hospitals particularly attributed the change in payer mix to an overall increase in the number of uninsured. (6) Specialty hospitals had little impact on the financial stability of general and safety net hospitals, and therefore did not significantly reduce the ability of these hospitals to serve financially vulnerable populations.

The study by Sutton and Eichner, **Experiences of Critical Access Hospitals in the Provision of Emergency Medical Services**, focuses on ambulance services operated by CAHs. The predominance of volunteer- or local-government based emergency medical services (EMS) in rural areas contributed to both financial and operational weaknesses. As these operators were forced to discontinue their services, in many instances, they were acquired by CAHs which regarded EMS as an important community service despite the fact that 92% of CAH-owned EMS providers did not qualify for Medicare's cost-based reimbursement. The hospitals claim that they benefit by making use of the down time their paramedics experience, and they gain goodwill in the community which increases business for the hospital. On the other hand, challenges remain that include staffing, difficulties integrating paramedics into the hospital, need for special management skills, and negative financial impact on the hospital.

In the final article for this chapter, **Partners in Critical Care**, Hynes and colleagues emphasize the importance of patient- and family-centered care

(PFCC), which is akin to the philosophies of family-focused care and patient-centered care. The concept revolves around consultation between patients and families (community partners) and the interdisciplinary team of critical care specialists in intensive care units of hospitals. The article cites a case study in which community partners were involved in the governance of the hospital's clinical units and PFCC was incorporated in the hospital's balanced scorecard. Hynes and colleagues offer guidelines for engaging community partners in unit governance. Family can also play an important supportive role in patient care and in performing certain low-risk tasks with the aim of improving patient care.

● ● ● **References**

Branas, C.C. et al. 2005. Access to trauma centers in the United States. *Journal of the American Medical Association* 293 (21): 2626–2633.

Carey, K. et al. 2008. Specialty and full-service hospitals: A comparative cost analysis. *Health Services Research* 43 (5): 1869–1887.

Cram, P. et al. 2005. Cardiac revascularization in specialty and general hospitals. *New England Journal of Medicine* 352 (14): 1454–1463.

Cram, P. et al. 2007. A comparison of total hip and knee replacement in specialty and general hospitals. *Journal of Bone and Joint Surgery* 89 (8): 1675–1684.

Guterman, S. 2006. Specialty hospitals: A problem or a symptom? *Health Affairs* 25 (1): 95–105.

National Center for Health Statistics. 2009. *Health, United States, 2008*. Hyattsville, MD: National Center for Health Statistics.

OECD. 2009. *Health At a Glance 2009*. Paris: Organisation for Economic Co-operation and Development.

Office of Inspector General. 2008. *Physician-owned Specialty Hospitals' Ability to Manage Medical Emergencies*. Washington, DC: Department of Health and Human Services.

U.S. Census Bureau. 2010. *Statistical Abstract of the United States, 2010*. Washington, DC: U.S. Census Bureau.

Weisgrau, S. 1995. Issues in rural health: access, hospitals, and reform. *Health Care Financing Review* 17 (1): 1–14.

1

Physician-Owned Specialty Hospitals

Source: Miller, M.E. 2005. *Physician-Owned Specialty Hospitals.* Testimony before the Subcommittee on Federal Financial Management, Government Information, and International Security Committee on Homeland Security and Governmental Affairs on May 24, 2005.

Chairman Coburn, Senator Carper, distinguished Subcommittee members. I am Mark Miller, executive director of the Medicare Payment Advisory Commission (MedPAC). I appreciate the opportunity to be here with you this morning to discuss physician-owned specialty hospitals.

Proponents claim that physician-owned specialty hospitals are the focused factory of the future for health care, taking advantage of the convergence of financial incentives for physicians and hospitals to produce more efficient operations and higher-quality outcomes than conventional community hospitals. Detractors counter that because the physician-owners can refer patients to their own hospitals they compete unfairly, and that such hospitals concentrate on only the most lucrative procedures and treat the healthiest and best-insured patients—leaving the community hospitals to take care of the poorest, sickest patients and provide services that are less profitable.

The Congress, in the Medicare Prescription Drug, Improvement, and Modernization Act of 2003 (MMA), imposed an 18-month moratorium that effectively halted the development of new physician-

owned specialty hospitals. That act also directed MedPAC and the Secretary of the Department of Health and Human Services to report to the Congress on certain issues concerning physician-owned heart, orthopedic, and surgical specialty hospitals.

To answer the Congress's questions, MedPAC conducted site visits, legal analysis, met with stakeholders, and analyzed hospitals' Medicare cost reports and inpatient claims from 2002 (the most recent available at the time). From its empirical analyses, MedPAC found that:

- Physician-owned specialty hospitals treat patients who are generally less severe cases (and hence expected to be relatively more profitable than the average) and concentrate on particular diagnosis-related groups (DRGs), some of which are relatively more profitable.

- They tend to have lower shares of Medicaid patients than community hospitals.

- In 2002, they did not have lower costs for Medicare inpatients than community hospitals, although their inpatients did have shorter lengths of stay.

- The financial impact on community hospitals in the markets where physician-owned specialty hospitals are located was limited in 2002. Those community hospitals competing with specialty hospitals demonstrated financial performance comparable to other community hospitals.

- Many of the differences in profitability across and within DRGs that create financial incentives for patient selection can be reduced by improving Medicare's inpatient prospective payment system (IPPS) for acute care hospitals.

These findings are based on the small number of physician-owned specialty hospitals that have been in operation long enough to generate Medicare data. The industry is in its early stage, but growing rapidly. Some of these findings could change as the industry develops and have ramifications for the communities where they are located and the Medicare program. We did not evaluate the comparative quality of care in specialty hospitals, because the Secretary is mandated to do so in a forthcoming report.

We found that physicians may establish physician-owned specialty hospitals to gain greater control over how the hospital is run, to increase their productivity, and to obtain greater satisfaction for them and their patients. They may also be motivated by the financial rewards, some of which derive from inaccuracies in the Medicare payment system.

Our recommendations concentrate on remedying those payment inaccuracies, which result in Medicare paying too much for some DRGs relative to others, and too much for patients with relatively less severe conditions within DRGs. Improving the accuracy of the payment system would help make competition more equitable between community hospitals and physician-owned specialty hospitals, whose physician-owners can influence which patients go to which hospital. It would also make payment more equitable among community hospitals that currently are advantaged or disadvantaged by their mix of DRGs or patients. Some community hospitals have invested disproportionately in services thought to be more profitable, and some non-physician-owned hospitals have specialized in the same services as physician-owned specialty hospitals.

We also recommend an approach to aligning physician and hospital incentives through gainsharing, which allows physicians and hospitals to share savings from more efficient practices and might serve as an alternative to direct physician ownership. Because of remaining concerns about self-referral; need for further information on the efficiency, quality, and effect of specialty hospitals; and the time needed to implement our recommendations, the Commission also recommends that the Congress extend the current moratorium on specialty hospitals until January 1, 2007.

HOW MANY AND WHERE?

We found 48 hospitals in 2002 that met our criteria for physician-owned specialty hospitals: 12 heart hospitals, 25 orthopedic hospitals, and 11 surgical hospitals. (Altogether there are now approximately 100 specialty hospitals broadly defined, but some opened after 2002 and did not have sufficient discharge data for our analysis; others are not physician-owned or are women's hospitals that do not meet our criteria for surgical hospitals.) Specialty hospitals are small: the average orthopedic specialty hospital has 16 beds and the average surgical specialty hospital has 14. Heart hospitals are larger, averaging 52 beds.

Many specialty hospitals do not have emergency departments (EDs), in contrast to community hospitals where the large majority (93 percent) do. Those that have EDs differ in how they are used, and that may influence how much control the hospital has over its schedule and patient mix. For example, 8 of the 12 heart hospitals we examined have EDs, and the heart hospitals we visited that had EDs were included in their area's emergency medical systems' routing of patients who required the services they could provide. In contrast, even when surgical and orthopedic specialty hospitals have EDs, they are often not fully staffed or included in ambulance routings.

Specialty hospitals are not evenly distributed across the country (Figure 1). Almost 60 percent of the specialty hospitals we studied are located in four states: South Dakota, Kansas, Oklahoma, and Texas. Many of the specialty hospitals that are under construction or have opened since 2002 are located in the same states and markets as the specialty hospitals we studied. As the map shows, specialty hospitals are concentrated in states without certificate-of-need (CON) programs.

MOTIVATIONS FOR FORMING PHYSICIAN-OWNED SPECIALTY HOSPITALS AND CRITICS' OBJECTIONS

Physician control over hospital operations was one motivation for many of the physicians we spoke with who were investing in specialty hospitals. In the physician-owned specialty hospitals we studied, the cardiologists and surgeons want to admit their patients, perform their procedures, and have their patients recover with minimal disruption. Physician control, they believe, makes this possible in ways community hospitals cannot match because of their multiple services and missions. Control allows

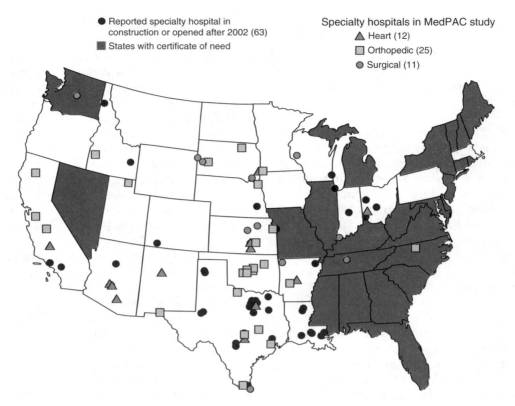

Figure 1 Speciality hospitals are geographically concentrated

physicians to increase their own productivity for the following reasons:

- fewer disruptions to the operating room schedule (for example, delays and canceling of cases that result from emergency cases),
- less "down" time between surgeries (for example, by cleaning the operating rooms more efficiently),
- heightened ability to work between two operating rooms during a "block" of operating room time, and
- more direct control of operating room staff.

The other motivation to form specialty hospitals is enhanced income. In addition to increased productivity resulting in more professional fees, physician investors also could augment their income by retaining a portion of the facility profits for their own and others' work. Although some specialty hospitals have not made distributions, the annual distributions at others frequently have exceeded 20 percent of the physicians' initial investment, and the specialty hospitals in our study had an average all-payer margin of 13 percent in 2002, well above the

3 to 6 percent average for community hospitals in their markets.

Critics contend that much of the financial success of specialty hospitals may revolve around selection of patients. Physicians can influence where their patients receive care, and physician ownership gives physician-investors a financial incentive to refer profitable patients to their hospital. If the payment system does not adequately differentiate among patients with different expected costs, and the factors determining cost, such as severity of illness, can be observed in advance, then the physician has an incentive to direct patients accordingly. At the extreme, some community hospitals claimed physicians sometimes transferred low complexity patients out of the community hospitals to specialty hospitals that the physicians owned, while transferring high complexity patients into the community hospitals. Referrals of healthier (more profitable) patients to limited-service specialty hospitals may not harm less complex patients. Nonetheless, critics argue that referral decisions should not be influenced by financial incentives, and therefore, they object to physician ownership of specialty hospitals. Critics also argue that eventually community hospitals' ability to provide less profitable services (which are often subsidized by more profitable services) would be undermined.

Restrictions on physician self-referral have a long history in the Medicare program. The anti-kickback statute, the Ethics in Patient Referrals Act (the Stark law), and their implementing regulations set out the basic limitations on self-referral and create exceptions. The primary concern was that physician ownership of health care providers would create financial incentives that could influence physicians' professional judgment and lead to higher use of services. In addition, self-referral could lead to unfair competition if one facility was owned by the referring physician, and competing facilities were not. Because hospitals provide many kinds of services, an exception was created that allowed physicians to refer patients to hospitals in which they invest. This is the "whole hospital" exception. Physician investors have a greater opportunity to influence profits at single-specialty hospitals—which generally provide a limited range of services—than at full-service hospitals.

DO PHYSICIAN-OWNED SPECIALTY HOSPITALS HAVE LOWER COSTS?

We compared physician-owned specialty hospitals to three groups of hospitals. *Community* hospitals are full service hospitals located in the same market. *Competitor* hospitals are a subset of community hospitals that provide at least some of the same services provided by specialty hospitals in that market. And *Peer* hospitals are specialized, but not physician-owned.

After controlling for potential sources of variation, including patient severity, we found that inpatient costs per discharge at physician-owned specialty hospitals are higher than the corresponding values for peer, competitor, and community hospitals. However, these differences were not statistically significant.

Lengths of stay in specialty hospitals were shorter, in some cases significantly so, than those in comparison hospitals. Other things being equal, shorter stays should lead to lower costs. The apparent inconsistency of these results raises questions about what other factors might be offsetting the effects of shorter stays. Such factors might include staffing levels, employee compensation, costs of supplies and equipment, initial start-up costs, or lack of potential economies of scale due to smaller hospital size. These results could change as the hospitals become more established and as the number of specialty hospitals reporting costs and claims increases.

WHO GOES TO PHYSICIAN-OWNED SPECIALTY HOSPITALS, AND WHAT HAPPENS TO COMMUNITY HOSPITALS IN THEIR MARKETS?

Critics of specialty hospitals contend that physicians have financial incentives to steer profitable patients to specialty hospitals in which they have an ownership interest. These physicians may also have an incentive to avoid Medicaid, uninsured, and unusually costly Medicare patients. Critics further argue that if physician-owned hospitals take away a large share of community hospitals' profitable patients, community hospitals would not have sufficient revenues to provide all members of the community access to a full array of services.

Supporters counter that the specialty hospitals are engaging in healthy competition with community hospitals and that they are filling unmet demand for services. They acknowledge that community hospital volumes may decline when they enter a market, but claim that community hospitals can find alternative sources of revenue and remain profitable even in the face of competition from physician-owned specialty hospitals. We found:

- Physician-owned heart, orthopedic, and surgical hospitals that did not focus on obstetrics tended to treat fewer Medicaid patients than peer hospitals and community hospitals in the same market. Heart hospitals treated primarily Medicare patients, while orthopedic and surgical hospitals treated primarily privately insured patients.

- The increases in cardiac surgery rates associated with the opening of physician-owned heart hospitals were small enough to be statistically insignificant for most types of cardiac surgery. It appears that specialty hospitals obtained most of their patients by capturing market share from community hospitals.

- Though the opening of heart hospitals was associated with slower growth in Medicare inpatient revenue at community hospitals, on average, community hospitals competing with physician-owned heart hospitals did not experience unusual declines in their all-payer profit margin.

Note that most specialty hospitals are relatively new, and the number of hospitals in our analysis is small. The impact on service use and community hospitals could change over time, especially if a large number of additional specialty hospitals are formed.

DO SPECIALTY HOSPITALS TREAT A FAVORABLE MIX OF PATIENTS?

Specialty hospitals may concentrate on providing services that are profitable, and on treating patients who are less sick—and therefore less costly. Under Medicare's IPPS, payments are intended to adequately cover the costs of an efficient provider treating an average mix of patients, some with more and some with less complex care needs. But if differences in payments do not fully reflect differences in costs across types of admissions (DRGs) and patient severity within DRGs, some mixes of services and patients could be more profitable than others. Systematic bias in any payment system, not just Medicare's, could reward those hospitals that selectively offer services or treat patients with profit margins that are consistently above average. We found:

- Specialty hospitals tend to focus on surgery, and under Medicare's IPPS, surgical DRGs are relatively more profitable than medical DRGs in the same specialty.

- Surgical DRGs that were common in specialty heart hospitals were relatively more profitable than the national average DRG, those in orthopedic hospitals relatively less profitable, and those in specialty surgical hospitals had about average relative profitability.

- Within DRGs, the least severely ill Medicare patients generally were relatively more profitable than the average Medicare patient. More severely ill patients generally were relatively less profitable than average, reflecting their higher costs but identical payments. Specialty hospitals had lower severity patient mixes than peer, competitor, or community hospitals.

- Taking both the mix of DRGs and the mix of patients within DRGs into account, specialty hospitals would be expected to be relatively more profitable than peer, competitor, or community hospitals if they exhibited average efficiency.

Table 1 shows the expected relative profitability for physician-owned specialty hospitals and their comparison groups. The expected relative profitability for a hospital is: the ratio of the payments for the mix of DRGs at the hospital to the costs that would be expected for that mix of DRGs and patients if the hospital had average costs—relative to the national average expected profitability over all cases. It is not the actual profitability for the hospital.

Heart specialty hospitals treat patients in financially favorable DRGs and, within those, patients who are less sick (and less costly, on average). Assuming that heart specialty hospitals have average costs, their selection of DRGs results in an expected relative profitability 6 percent higher than the average profitability. Heart hospitals receive an additional potential benefit (3 percent) from favorable selection among patient severity classes. As a result, their average expected relative profitability value is 1.09.

Reflecting their similar concentration in surgical cardiac cases, peer heart hospitals also benefit from favorable selection across DRGs, though not as much as specialty heart hospitals. However, peer heart hospitals receive no additional benefit from selection among more- or less-severe cases within DRGs. Both specialty heart and peer heart hospitals have a favorable selection of patients compared with community hospitals in the specialty heart hospitals' markets, as well as with all IPPS hospitals.

In contrast to the heart hospitals, neither orthopedic specialty hospitals nor their peers seem to have a favorable DRG selection. However, by treating a high proportion of low-severity patients within their mix of DRGs, specialty orthopedic hospitals show selection that appears to be slightly favorable overall (1.02). Surgical specialty hospitals show a very favorable selection of patients overall (1.15) because they also treat relatively low-severity patients within the DRGs.

PAYMENT RECOMMENDATIONS

The Congress asked the Commission to recommend changes to the IPPS to better reflect the cost of delivering care. We found changes are needed to improve the accuracy of the payment system and thus reduce opportunities for hospitals to benefit from selection. We recommend several changes to improve the IPPS.

The Commission recommends the Secretary should improve payment accuracy in the IPPS by:

- refining the current DRGs to more fully capture differences in severity of illness among patients,

- basing the DRG relative weights on the estimated cost of providing care rather than on charges, and

Table 2	Speciality hospitals have high expected relative profitability of inpatient care under Medicare because of the mix of cases they treat			
		Expected relative profitability due to selection of		
Type of hospital	Number of hospitals	DRGs	Patient severity	DRGs and patient severity
All nonspecialty IPPS hospitals	4,375	1.00	1.00	1.00
Heart hospitals				
Specialty	12	1.06	1.03	1.09[ab]
Peer	36	1.04	0.99	1.03[b]
Competitor	79	1.01	1.00	1.00
Community	315	0.99	1.01	1.01
Orthopedic hospitals				
Specialty	25	0.95	1.07	1.02[ab]
Peer	17	0.95	1.01	0.96
Competitor	305	1.00	1.00	1.00
Community	477	1.00	1.01	1.01
Surgical hospitals				
Specialty	11	0.99	1.16	1.15[ab]
Peer	25	1.00	1.06	1.06[b]
Competitor	237	0.99	1.01	1.01
Community	289	0.99	1.01	1.01

Note: IPPS (inpatient prospective payment system), APR–DRG (all-patient refined diagnosis-related group), DRG (diagnosis-related group). Expected relative profitability measures the financial attractiveness of the hospital's mix of Medicare cases, given the national average relative profitability of each patient category (DRG or APR–DRG severity class). The relative profitability measure is an average for each DRG category, based on cost accounting data. Thus, small differences (for example, 1 or 2 percent) in relative profitability may not be meaningful. Specialty hospitals are specialized and physician owned. Peer hospitals are specialized but are not physician owned. Competitor hospitals are in the same markets as specialty hospitals and provide some similar services. Community hospitals are all hospitals in the same market as specialty hospitals.

[a] Significantly different from peer hospitals using a Tukey mean separation test and a $p < .05$ criterion.

[b] Significantly different from nonpeer community hospitals using a Tukey mean separation test and a $p < .05$ criterion.

Source: MedPAC analysis of Medicare hospital inpatient claims and cost reports from CMS, fiscal year 2000–2002.

- basing the weights on the national average of hospitals' relative values in each DRG.

All of these actions are within the Secretary's current authority.

The commission also recommends the Congress amend the law to give the Secretary authority to adjust the DRG relative weights to account for differences in the prevalence of high-cost outlier cases.

Taken together, these recommendations will reduce the potential to profit from patient and DRG selection, and result in payments that more closely reflect the cost of care while still retaining the incentives for efficiency in the IPPS. Figure 2 shows that the share of IPPS payments in DRGs that have a relative profitability within 5 percent of the national average would increase from 35 percent under current policy to 86 percent if all of our recommendations were implemented. At the hospital group level, under current policy, heart hospitals' expected relative profitability from their combination of DRGs and patients is above the national average prof-

itability for all DRGs and patients. Following our recommendations, that ratio would be about equal to the national average. Physician-owned orthopedic and surgical hospitals would show similar results.

These payment system refinements would affect all hospitals—both specialty hospitals and community hospitals. Many hospitals would see significant changes in payments, and, although our recent analysis suggests that hospitals' inpatient profitability increases as selection becomes more favorable, a transitional period would mitigate those effects and allow hospitals to adjust to the refined payment system. Thus, the Commission recommends the Congress and the Secretary should implement the payment refinements over a transitional period.

Making these payment system improvements and designing the transition will not be simple tasks. We recognize that the Centers for Medicare & Medicaid Services (CMS) has many priorities and limited resources, and that the refinements will raise some difficult technical issues. These include the potentially large number of payment groups created,

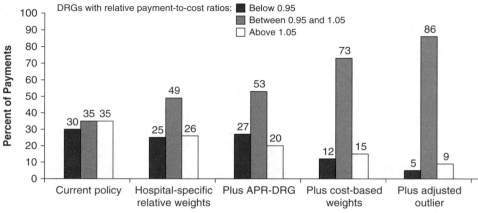

Figure 2 Improvement in payment accuracy from policy changes *Source:* MedPAC analysis of Medicare hospital inpatient claims and cost reports from CMS, fiscal year 2000-2002

possible increases in spending from improvements in coding, rewarding avoidable complications, and the burden and time lag associated with using costs rather than charges. Nevertheless, certain approaches that we discuss in this report, such as reestimating cost-based weights every several years instead of annually, could make these issues less onerous. The Congress should take steps to assure that CMS has the resources it needs to make the recommended refinements.

RECOMMENDATIONS ON THE MORATORIUM AND GAINSHARING

The Commission is concerned with the issue of self-referral and its potential for patient selection and higher use of services. However, removing the exception that allows physician ownership of whole hospitals would be too severe a remedy given the limitations of the available evidence, although we may wish to reconsider it in the future. Our evidence on physician-owned specialty hospitals raises some concerns about patient selection, utilization, and efficiency, but it is based on a small sample of hospitals, early in the development of the industry. We do not know yet if physician-owned hospitals will increase their efficiency and improve quality. We also do not know if, in the longer term, they will damage community hospitals or unnecessarily increase use of services. The Secretary's forthcoming report on specialty hospitals should provide important information on quality. Further information on physician-owned specialty hospitals' performance is needed before actions

are taken that would, in effect, entirely shut them out of the Medicare and Medicaid market. In addition, the Congress will need time during the upcoming legislative cycle to consider our recommendations and craft legislation, and the Secretary will need time to change the payment system. Therefore, the Commission recommends that the Congress extend the current moratorium on specialty hospitals until January 1, 2007. The current moratorium expires on June 8, 2005. Continuing the moratorium will allow time for efforts to implement our recommendations and time to gather more information.

Aligning financial incentives for physicians and hospitals could lead to efficiencies. Physician ownership fully aligns incentives; it makes the hospital owner and the physician one in the same, but raises concerns about self-referral. Similar efficiencies might be achieved by allowing the physician to share in savings that would accrue to the hospital from reengineering clinical care. Such arrangements have been stymied by provisions of law that prevent hospitals from giving physicians financial incentive to reduce or limit care to patients because of concerns about possible stinting on care and quality. Recently, the Office of Inspector General has approved some narrow gainsharing arrangements, although they have been advisory opinions that apply only to the parties who request them.

The Commission recommends that the Congress should grant the Secretary the authority to allow gainsharing arrangements between physicians and hospitals and to regulate those arrangements to protect the quality of care and minimize financial incentives that could affect physician referrals.

Gainsharing could capture some of the incentives that are animating the move to physician-owned specialty hospitals while minimizing some of the concerns that direct physician ownership raises. Permitting gainsharing opportunities might provide an alternative to starting physician-owned specialty hospitals, particularly if the incentives for selection were reduced by correcting the current inaccuracies in the Medicare payment system.

General Hospitals, Specialty Hospitals and Financially Vulnerable Patients

Source: Tynan, A., E. November, J. Lauer, et al. 2009. *General hospitals, specialty hospitals and financially vulnerable patients.* Research Brief No. 11. Washington, DC: Center for Studying Health System Change. Used with permission.

In the past decade, the rapid growth of specialty hospitals focused on profitable service lines, including cardiac and orthopedic care, has prompted concerns about general hospitals' ability to compete. Critics contend specialty hospitals actively draw less-complicated, more-profitable patients with Medicare and private insurance away from general hospitals, threatening general hospitals' ability to cross-subsidize less-profitable services and provide uncompensated care. A contentious debate has ensued, but little research has addressed whether specialty hospitals adversely affect the financial viability of general hospitals and their ability to care for low-income, uninsured and Medicaid patients. Despite initial challenges recruiting staff and maintaining service volumes and patient referrals, general hospitals were generally able to respond to the initial entry of specialty hospitals with few, if any, changes in the provision of care for financially vulnerable patients, according to a new study by the Center for Studying Health System Change (HSC) of three markets with established specialty hospitals—Indianapolis, Phoenix and Little Rock, Ark. In addition, safety net hospitals—general hospitals that care for a disproportionate share of financially vulnerable patients—reported limited impact from spe-

cialty hospitals since safety net hospitals generally do not compete for insured patients.

IS THE PLAYING FIELD LEVEL?

Amid concerns that specialty hospitals "cream-skim" more-profitable, less-complicated, well-insured patients from general hospitals, Congress in 2003 mandated an 18-month Medicare moratorium on physician self-referrals to new physician-owned specialty hospitals, effectively stalling their development (See Data Source box for more about specialty hospital pros and cons). Specialty hospitals and general hospitals typically compete for profitable service lines, such as cardiac and orthopedic care, which because of unintended payment rate distortions tend to be more lucrative.[1]

General hospitals often rely on profitable services and patients to subsidize unprofitable services and patients. Faced with the loss of profitable services and patients to specialty hospitals, some feared that general hospitals might curtail emergency services, close burn or psychiatric units or provide less uncompensated care. Whether specialty hospitals compromise general hospitals' financial viability and ability to cross-subsidize care for financially vulnerable populations—low-income, uninsured and Medicaid patients—remains a debated issue.[2]

Since the 2003 moratorium, a body of research has been conducted evaluating physician-owned specialty hospitals. Generally, the research indicates that specialty hospitals treat less-complex patients with lower acuity[3] and a higher proportion of patients with more generous insurance coverage.[4] In addition, physician ownership interests in specialty hospitals may result in referral patterns that shift patient volume from general to specialty hospitals.[5]

In 2007, in an effort to improve payment accuracy based on patient acuity and reduce cream skimming by all types of hospitals—which rely on Medicare for a significant portion of their revenue—the Centers for Medicare and Medicaid Services began phasing in severity-based adjustments and other changes to Medicare payments for inpatient care.

SPECIALTY HOSPITALS IN THREE COMMUNITIES

This study examines the impact of specialty hospitals—cardiac, surgical and orthopedic—on the ability of general and safety net hospitals to care for financially vulnerable patients in Indianapolis, Little Rock and Phoenix (see Data Source). While these markets are not nationally representative, and specialty hospitals represent a relatively limited share of the overall inpatient market, their experiences are useful in illustrating the range of hospital responses to the market entry of specialty hospitals. Each of the three communities has an established presence of specialty hospitals, general hospitals that provide care to financially vulnerable populations and a major safety net hospital that primarily serves low-income and uninsured patients.

The three communities vary in terms of ownership structures of specialty hospitals (see Table 1) and the level of specialty physician consolidation. However, all three markets lack certificate-of-need requirements that can restrict the growth of specialty hospitals.

In Indianapolis, where there are a few very large single-specialty medical groups,[6] cardiac specialty

Data Source

To examine the impact of specialty hospitals on the ability of general and safety net hospitals to care for vulnerable populations, HSC conducted key stakeholder interviews in three Community Tracking Study communities with an established presence of specialty hospitals. These communities are Indianapolis, Little Rock and Phoenix. In each of these communities, researchers interviewed representatives from physician practices, community health centers, emergency medical services, medical societies, hospital associations, state regulatory agencies, and other respondents who could provide a market-wide perspective. Interviews also were conducted with hospital executives of at least two general hospitals, two specialty hospitals and one safety net hospital in each community, with the exception of Little Rock. Researchers were unable to interview executives from the two specialty hospitals in Little Rock (because of ongoing litigation [heart hospital] and changes in leadership [surgical hospital]). The findings are based on semi-structured phone interviews with 43 respondents conducted by two-person interview teams between March and June 2008, and interveiw data were analyzed using Atlas.ti, a qualitative software package.

Table 1	Specialty Hospitals by Site, Primary Service Line and Ownership Structure

	NUMBER OF SPECIALTY HOSPITALS	PRIMARY SERVICE LINE		OWNERSHIP STRUCTURE		
SITE		CARDIAC	ORTHOPEDIC/ SURGICAL SPECIALTY	HOSPITAL	MIXED[1]	PHYSICIANS[2]
INDIANAPOLIS	4	3	1	1	2	1
LITTLE ROCK	2	1	1	0	0	2
PHOENIX	5	2	3	1	2	2

[1] Specialty hospitals with a mixed ownership structure are partially owned by a hospital and partially owned by physicians.
[2] Specialty hospitals that are physician-owned are owned by a group of independent physicians, a physician group, or a mix of physicians and a hospital management company, such as MedCath or National Surgical Hospitals.

hospitals began as joint ventures between local general hospital systems and physicians. Over time, they became majority-owned by the hospital systems. In Little Rock, which has large single-specialty medical groups,[7] the only stand-alone cardiac specialty hospital is owned by physicians affiliated in a medical group and MedCath, a corporation that operates specialty hospitals. In Phoenix, with fewer single-specialty medical groups than Little Rock,[8] one of the cardiac specialty hospitals also is owned by physicians and MedCath, while the surgical specialty hospital is wholly owned by physicians. Orthopedic specialty hospitals in the three communities are typically wholly owned by physicians.

Specialty hospitals in the three markets were established between 2000 and 2005, with the exception of a heart hospital in Little Rock in 1997 and a heart hospital in Phoenix in 1998. Across all three markets, general hospital systems lacking ownership interest in stand-alone specialty hospitals operate competing specialty-service lines, for example, through a center of excellence for cardiac care or orthopedics.

GENERAL HOSPITALS RESPOND AND ADAPT TO COMPETITION FROM SPECIALTY HOSPITALS

Study respondents identified several ways that specialty hospital competition affected the financial well-being of general and safety net hospitals through competition for physicians and other staff, new challenges in providing emergency department (ED) on-call coverage and decreases in service volume. Respondents reported little, if any, change in patient acuity in general hospitals. And respondents more often attributed changes in payer mix to the rising rate of uninsured people in the market generally, rather than the loss of patient volume to specialty hospitals. General hospitals were more likely than safety net hospitals to feel the impact of competition from specialty hospitals.

Competition for Staff and Emergency Call Coverage

Specialty hospitals initially attracted physicians and other staff from general hospitals and, to a lesser extent, safety net hospitals. An ownership stake in a specialty hospital enables physicians to have a larger role in hospital governance and share in the hospital's profits. A few general hospitals reported losing significant numbers of cardiologists, orthopedists or other specialists who left to start their own hospitals or enter joint ventures with a corporate entity.

For physicians, specialty hospitals can offer greater control over their work environment, such as more predictable scheduling and more access to operating rooms and diagnostic equipment. Respondents also noted that physicians may be drawn to specialty hospitals because of efficiencies associated with focusing on a single service line and the opportunity to see more patients at one location, reducing the inefficiency of traveling among hospitals.

Specialty hospitals also increased competition for other clinical staff, such as nurses and diagnostic technicians, by offering competitive compensation packages and more predictable work hours. As one specialty hospital respondent noted, "We have been very successful at recruiting full-time nurses. And nurses are in a shortage, so I imagine there is some withdrawal [from other hospitals]." Specialty hospitals also enable non-physician staff to focus on a particular specialty, potentially creating a less stressful and more predictable work environment compared with general hospitals where the demands of the patients and physicians change daily.

Safety net hospitals in two markets that also are academic medical centers reported being somewhat buffered from losing physicians, because physicians at these hospitals are often employees and would have to start or join a private practice to move to a specialty hospital. Also academic medical centers have complex case loads and teaching opportunities that attract physicians. Respondents also noted that their physicians, nurses and other staff may be attracted to the organizations' mission to serve the underserved in the community.

General and safety net hospitals also faced challenges getting specialists who retain admitting privileges at their facilities to take on-call coverage and this situation has worsened because of the entry of specialty hospitals, according to respondents. Physicians practicing at specialty hospitals with very small or no emergency departments have little or no obligation for ED call coverage. Specialists, particularly newly trained physicians with different lifestyle expectations—such as work-life balance, shorter work weeks—than previous generations, may prefer not to have on-call obligations and may choose to practice at a specialty hospital rather than a general hospital. Or they may threaten to move to a specialty hospital in negotiating for reduced call responsibilities at general hospitals.

According to one hospital association respondent, "Every hospital has a requirement in their bylaws that physicians will take ED call as part of having medical staff privileges. More and more physicians are saying 'I don't care what's in the bylaws, I'm not doing it. You can throw me off the medical staff.' Specialty hospitals have contributed to and exacerbated the problem [lack of ED call coverage] without a doubt, but the problem is beyond them."

General hospitals have responded to the increased competition for staff and call coverage in various ways. Some hospitals, particularly those that have lost specialist physicians to specialty hospitals, have employed specialists or aggressively aligned with specialists who practice at multiple facilities via contractual arrangements, encouraging them to concentrate their practice at a particular hospital. This strategy also helped general hospitals rebound from initial losses in service volume to specialty hospitals. General hospitals also reported adapting the hospital environment to better accommodate physicians' preferences, such as making more operating rooms available to them.

One Little Rock general hospital took a more aggressive approach, using economic credentialing for its medical staff, which bars physicians with admitting privileges or their family members from having financial interests in competing specialty hospitals. In recent years, there have been highly publicized court cases related to the general hospital's economic credentialing policy, as well as a lawsuit alleging that the general hospital aligned with the state's largest insurer to avoid competition by keeping physicians affiliated with specialty hospitals out of the insurer's network. Finally, general and safety net hospitals often have to pay significant money to ensure emergency call coverage and, in some cases, recruit specialists from outside of the market, which has resulted in increased costs.

Changes in Service Volume

General hospitals in all three communities and a safety net hospital in Little Rock observed a drop in service volume upon the entry of specialty hospitals. Some respondents suggested that the drop in service volume may have been caused at least in part by the loss of patients as physicians left the general hospital staff to join the specialty hospital staff. Additionally, specialists with privileges at both general and specialty hospitals may have begun preferentially referring patients to the specialty hospital. However, hospital executives acknowledged that other factors beyond specialty hospitals might have affected their service volumes.

According to hospital executives, some market factors may have shielded general hospitals from worse losses in service volume. Phoenix—which has experienced rapid population growth in recent years—had relatively low per-capita hospital capacity, which may have ensured sufficient patient demand to offset any noticeable drop in service volume at general hospitals when specialty hospitals entered the market. Respondents also noted that changes in medical technology may have prompted a decline in cardiac service volume at general hospitals—there has been a nationwide drop in cardiac surgeries because of increased use of stents and balloon angioplasty as alternatives to cardiac bypass surgery. According to a Little Rock hospital respondent, "There have been trends in technology offerings related to fewer bypass procedures and more procedures in the catheterization lab. So there's a definite decrease in surgical procedures that's not necessarily related to the heart hospital."

Safety net hospitals reported little impact on service volume because of the presence of specialty hospitals, since safety net hospitals generally do not compete intensely for patients with private insurance or Medicare. According to one safety net hospital respondent, "Our competitors don't want us to fail . . . they don't want us to compete, but don't want us to go away because then they'd have to deal with our patients."

General hospitals and a safety net hospital reported using various strategies to respond to the initial losses in service volume. As discussed earlier, general hospitals increased employment of specialists or more tightly aligned themselves with specialists as strategies to retain staff and to preserve, if not grow, service volume. General hospitals in Indianapolis and Little Rock, for example, reported developing new specialty-service lines, mainly for orthopedic services. Respondents noted that some general hospitals began advertising campaigns to promote cardiac services and facilities as a way to increase demand. A state insurance regulator explained, "General hospitals are doing a whole lot of advertising now. And the area of heart and cancer are two of the areas where they're doing a lot of heavy advertising and seeing they need to do that to compete."

Changes in Patient Acuity and Case-Mix Severity

General and safety net hospital respondents generally did not observe specialty hospitals as cream skimming less-complicated, lower-risk patients. General hospital respondents in Little Rock and Phoenix reported higher patient acuity since the entry of specialty hospitals but couldn't specifically attribute this to specialty hospitals. Moreover, respondents reported that transfers from specialty hospitals to general or safety net hospitals generally are rare in contrast to recent media reports that specialty hospitals off-load complicated patients to general and safety net hospitals.[9]

Changes in Payer Mix

A few general and safety net hospitals noted serving more financially vulnerable patients. In some cases, hospitals attributed these changes in payer mix to a loss of insured patients to specialty hospitals. More often, however, respondents, particularly safety net hospitals, attributed changes in payer mix to an overall increase in the number of uninsured in their respective markets. Further, the leading general hospitals likely were able to cost shift to private payers by negotiating increases in payment rates to cross-subsidize losses from charity care and Medicaid.

Respondents observed little impact on payer mix from the introduction of Medicare severity-adjusted diagnostic related groups that allow higher reimbursements for sicker patients. These reimbursement changes haven't yet had the leveling effect between general hospitals and specialty hospitals (boosting reimbursement to general hospitals and reducing reimbursement to specialty hospitals) anticipated by policy makers, assuming the presence of cream skimming by specialty hospitals. According to respondents, the changes helped all hospitals caring for a greater proportion of higher-severity patients. General and specialty hospitals that have a mix of patients with different levels of acuity reported seeing no change in payments.

OTHER CHALLENGES EMERGE

While specialty hospitals affected general hospitals' ability to attract and retain physicians and other staff and service volumes, general hospitals' responses limited the impact on their financial viability. In a 2006 study, the Medicare Payment Advisory Commission (MedPAC) similarly reported that, "While specialty hospitals took profitable surgical patients from the competitor community hospitals (slowing Medicare revenue growth at some hospitals), most competitor community hospitals appeared to compensate for this lost revenue."[10]

General and safety net hospital respondents did not report changes in the provision of care for fi-

nancially vulnerable patients as a result of specialty hospital competition. One general hospital each in Indianapolis and Little Rock reported that competition from specialty hospitals has strained their ability to cross-subsidize services but did not report limiting care to financially vulnerable patients. Many respondents noted that competition by specialty hospitals is only one of many factors that affect the financial stability of general and safety net hospitals, including cost increases outpacing payment rate increases from Medicare and Medicaid.

According to one Indianapolis general hospital executive, "Specialty hospitals definitely have an impact. At the same time you have to say the reimbursement levels and government programs aren't going up as fast as the cost is going up. Costs are going up double digits, but we get a single-digit increase on Medicare and things like that. You have that as another hurdle that is having an impact on your economic health." This assessment was echoed by a Phoenix general hospital executive, "If you asked me the three-to-five factors on financial performance [in general hospitals], specialty hospitals wouldn't be in that list."

IMPLICATIONS

To date, the entry of specialty hospitals to the Indianapolis, Little Rock and Phoenix markets has not had dramatic, adverse effects on the financial viability of general and safety net hospitals and their ability to provide care to financially vulnerable populations. However, this seems largely because of the ability of general hospitals to compensate for the competition in various ways. General hospitals likely have enjoyed sufficient market leverage in recent years to allow them to cost-shift to private payers without reducing unprofitable services that provide community benefit, such as burn units and psychiatric care.

In the context of the current economic recession, however, it is unclear whether general hospitals will be able to continue cost-shifting to private payers that must balance the demands for provider payment rate increases with employer-purchaser pressures to contain escalating health care costs and insurance premiums. General hospitals will likely experience an increased burden of uncompensated care as job losses in the worsening economy are accompanied by the loss of health insurance. According to one estimate, for every 1 percent increase in unemployment, the number of uninsured grows by 1.1 million.[11] Further, general hospitals' reserves and investment portfolios, which can help offset increases in the cost of uncompensated care, have likely lost significant value. As financial constraints tighten, general hospitals may seek alternative remedies to specialty hospital competition, such as economic credentialing. Consequently, pending court decisions could have significant policy implications for the ability of general hospitals to manage competition from specialty hospitals.

Broader market changes and the worsening economic recession—characterized by job loss, increased number of uninsured, more difficult debt financing, reduced or stagnant reimbursement by private payers—likely will adversely affect specialty hospitals as well. Specialty hospitals burgeoned in times of relative economic prosperity. How specialty hospitals in the three communities will cope with a shrinking base of privately insured patients and reductions in elective procedures already reported by hospitals around the country remains to be seen.

Severity adjustments to Medicare inpatient hospital payment rates haven't had a noticeable impact on the hospitals in the three communities; however, these payment changes haven't been fully phased in. Over time, it is possible that severity-adjusted payments may prove to do more to support general hospitals. The continued effort by Medicare to accurately price inpatient services based on patient acuity will be integral to future policy regarding specialty hospitals. Moreover, it will be important for policy makers to continue to track the impact of specialty hospitals on the ability of general hospitals—more so than safety net hospitals—to serve financially vulnerable patients and provide other less-profitable but needed services.

● ● ● References

1. Ginsburg, Paul B., and Joy M. Grossman, "When the Price Isn't Right: How Inadvertent Payment Incentives Drive Medical Care," *Health Affairs*, Web exclusive (Aug. 5, 2005).

2. Medicare Payment Advisory Commission (MedPAC), *Report to the Congress: Physician-Owned Specialty Hospitals*, Washington, D.C. (March 2005); Moore, Keith, and Dean Coddington, "Specialty Hospital Rise Could Add to Full-Service Hospital Woes," *Healthcare Financial Management* (July 2005).

3. Greenwald, Leslie, et al., "Specialty Versus Community Hospitals: Referrals, Quality, and Community Benefits," *Health Affairs*, Vol. 25, No. 1 (January/February 2006).

4. Cram, Peter, et al., "Insurance Status of Patients Admitted to Specialty Cardiac and Competing General Hospitals: Are Accusations of Cherry Picking Justified," *Medical Care*, Vol. 46, No. 5 (May 2008).

5. Greenwald, et al. (2006).

6. Devers, Kelly, Linda R. Brewster and Paul B. Ginsburg, *Specialty Hospitals: Focused Factories or Cream Skimmers?* Issue Brief No. 62, Center for Studying Health System Change, Washington, D.C. (April 2003).

7. Katz, Aaron, et al., *Little Rock Providers Vie for Revenues, As High Health Care Costs Continue*, Community Report No. 3, Center for Studying Health System Change, Washington, D.C. (July 2005).

8. Trude, Sally, et al., *Rapid Population Growth Outpaces Phoenix Health System Capacity*, Community Report No. 6, Center for Studying Health System Change, Washington, D.C. (September 2005).

9. "5 Investigates Hospitals Calling 911," KPHO (Julys 27, 2007) at http://www.kpho.com/iteam/13770265/detail.html.

10. MedPAC, *Report to Congress: Physician-Owned Specialty Hospitals, Revised*, Washington, D.C. (August 2006).

11. Holahan, John, and Bowen Garrett, *Rising Unemployment, Medicaid and the Uninsured*, prepared for the Kaiser Commission on Medicaid and the Uninsured (January 2009).

3

Experiences of Critical Access Hospitals in the Provision of Emergency Medical Services

Source: Sutton, J.P. and J. Eichner. 2008. *Experiences of Critical Access Hospitals in the Provision of Emergency Medical Services.* Policy Analysis Brief: W Series, No. 15. Walsh Center for Rural Health Analysis, NORC at University of Chicago.

This study was conducted to better understand the experiences of Critical Access Hospitals in operating an EMS unit. Using key informant interviews, we examine motivations for acquiring EMS services and the effect of these services on the level of emergency care available in a community. The benefits and challenges that CAH providers face in operating EMS services are discussed.

Our findings and analyses are based on a review of the literature on rural ambulance services and structured interviews, conducted in 2005 and 2006, with administrators and ambulance staff from five CAHs located across the country. Each of the hospital representatives contacted as part of this study indicated that Medicare was their largest single payer for EMS services and that they were reimbursed under the new ambulance fee schedule. These interviews served to confirm many of the findings from the literature review and provided valuable insights on the experiences of CAHs that acquire ambulance services and are reimbursed under the fee schedule.

Regardless of the fact that the CAH administrators that Walsh Center staff spoke with described similar experiences and generally supported information in the literature, the number of hospitals rep-

Policy Conclusions

- Reconsider elimination or relaxation of the 35-mile rule for cost-based reimbursement of EMS services;
- Consider funding research to determine the efficiencies achieved by direct involvement of EMS staff in hospital-based patient care (when not engaged in EMS-related activities);
- Evaluate state laws that may unnecessarily limit involvement of EMS staff in hospital-based patient care to determine the extent to which these laws also limit access to essential manpower in rural areas;
- Continuous monitoring of the financial performance of CAHs with EMS units is necessary to ensure access to hospital services in small rural, frontier, and isolated communities;
- Resources devoted to training EMS management and administrative staff may be necessary to ensure the continued operation and success of these programs.

resented was small. Therefore, findings from this study must be interpreted with caution.

BACKGROUND ON EMERGENCY MEDICAL SERVICES IN RURAL COMMUNITIES

Despite extensive need, rural areas have particular difficulties maintaining adequate Emergency Medical Service (EMS) capacity. Low call volumes contribute to higher costs per transport, and make it difficult for staff to retain specialized skills. In many cases, rural areas lack the resources to train and attract skilled personnel, and must rely on volunteers to staff EMS agencies.

For some time, the Government Accountability Office[1] has expressed concern that the EMS industry is excessively reliant on volunteers, particularly in rural areas of the country. Volunteers are often unavailable or difficult to recruit and they must financially support themselves. Commutes to and from EMS stations may also be long. Moreover, ambulance providers, particularly those that are volunteer- or local-government based, have historically been reluctant to bill patients. Volunteer services, for instance, "have considered patient billing as contrary to the community-service nature of their operation [and some providers] have had no expertise or infrastructure for collecting fees or maintaining the business function."[2]

The lack of predictable funding has made it difficult for many volunteer and private EMS agencies

---

Basics of the Ambulance Fee Schedule

Phase-in of the fee schedule began in 2002. With temporary provisions enacted by the Medicare Prescription Drug Improvement and Modernization Act (MMA), the phase-in period is expected to continue until the year 2010. In general, the ambulance fee schedule reimburses providers a base rate, adjusted for differences in case mix and mileage. Specific components of the ground ambulance fee schedule include the following:

- relative value unit (RVU) that ranges from 1.00 for basic life support to 3.25 for specialty care transport;
- conversion factor used to set a base rate for ground transportation;
- geographic adjustment factor to account for regional cost differences (based on location of beneficiary);
- mileage rate for loaded (beneficiary in the ambulance) mile; and
- rural adjustment factor (applicable until the end of calendar year 2008), equal to 25 percent of the ambulance fee schedule mileage rate, for transports exceeding 50 miles.

---

to upgrade equipment, furnish vehicles to respond to emergencies in a timely fashion, train staff in the provision of advanced life support services or even remain operational. Despite the importance of fundraising activities and financial support available from the community, resources are often insufficient to meet day-to-day operational needs. These factors place EMS agencies that depend on volunteer or financial support from the local community in a weak and unstable position.

MEDICARE REIMBURSEMENT TO RURAL PROVIDERS

Since Medicare began paying for ambulance transports under a prospectively determined national fee schedule, some policymakers have been advocating increased payments for small rural ambulance providers. The rationale for these payment increases is based on two factors—first, that per-transport cost of the rural low-volume provider may be higher than for the average provider because low-volume providers must spread the cost of emergency standby capacity over fewer transports and, second, because rural providers often incur higher costs associated with longer-distance transports. If not adequately addressed under the fee schedule, each of these factors may result in financial losses to hospitals. Particularly vulnerable are those CAHs that do not meet criteria for cost-based reimbursement for EMS; this includes EMS providers located in a 35-mile range of another EMS provider.

Although there is some speculation that the opportunity to receive cost-based reimbursement may encourage Critical Access Hospitals to acquire or operate an EMS unit, a CAH/FLEX National Tracking Project survey found that 92 percent of CAH-owned EMS providers did not qualify for cost-based reimbursement due to the 35-mile rule.

WHY DO CRITICAL ACCESS HOSPITALS CHOOSE TO ACQUIRE AN EMS UNIT?

Frequently, CAHs acquire an EMS unit from financially vulnerable community or private organizations. The prior organizations that operated the EMS or ambulance service often have a long history of unprofitable operations, despite government subsidies. In some cases, to ensure that an EMS unit exists to serve the community, local governments have requested that the hospital assume ownership of the unit. As one of the hospital administrators in-

---

[1] United States Government Accountability Office. Ambulance Services: Medicare Payments Can be Better Targeted to Trips in Less Densely Populated Rural Areas. GAO-03-986, Washington, DC: United States Government Accountability Office, September 2003.

[2] McGinnis KK. Rural and Frontier Emergency Medical Services: An Agenda for the Future" October 2004.

terviewed for this study stated, ". . . the county was pleased to find a reliable entity to fulfill the county's requirement that it have an ambulance service." However, financial difficulties were not the sole reason for the failure of these operations; problems in recruitment and retention of volunteer staff also contributed to problems in maintaining an EMS service.

Commitment to the community is a major reason why a CAH might acquire an ambulance service. Although many CAHs have no prior experience in the operation of emergency medical services, the decision to acquire an EMS unit is considered a benefit to the community. A number of our hospital respondents described the community's issues with the prior EMS owner, including long waits for transports to non-emergency facilities, lack of higher-level EMS staff, and unreliability of service. The hospital and the community believed that the CAH had systems in place and could better manage the EMS service. In some cases, the hospital received donations (such as a new ambulance from the city) to start up operations, and access to county-paid management fees, tax referendums, and state grants were frequently provided to the CAH to offset the cost of its services.

HOW IS THE LEVEL OF EMS SERVICE AFFECTED?

Acquisition or operation of an EMS unit typically increases the community's access to advanced emergency service levels. Prior to CAH acquisition, many of the community or volunteer EMS units only provided basic life support services. After acquisition by the CAH, many hospitals hired intermediate-level EMTs or additional paramedic personnel. Most hospital staff interviewed for this study indicated that they now provide the full range of services, from basic to advanced life support. As an unusual example, one of the hospital representatives that Walsh Center staff spoke with indicated that the CAH had acquired and used an EMS unit primarily, albeit not exclusively, for transport of patients to and from local nursing homes and to a regional hospital that served as part of the referral network. In fact, while this hospital rarely responded to 911 calls, it continued to staff EMS services using one paramedic, one cardiac technician (EMT-I) and two other intermediate EMTs.

WHAT IS THE RELATIONSHIP BETWEEN HOSPITAL-BASED AND LOCAL EMS PROVIDERS?

Hospital-based EMS units that operate within the same service area as other emergency providers often have an agreement that clarifies services and fosters cooperation when necessary. In some cases, these other providers are volunteers, whereas in others instances, they are paid, government employees, (e.g., fire fighters) or employees from neighboring hospitals. The hospital representatives interviewed for this study indicated that they desire to be respectful of volunteer EMS providers and are careful not to "step on toes." Perhaps the best example of this is the hospital (described above) that had limited itself to patient transports to nursing homes and referral hospitals. This hospital had signed a "mutual aid agreement" with a volunteer EMS agency in the community. As part of this arrangement, the hospital agreed to respond to 911 calls only when volunteer units were unavailable or could not be staffed.

DOES ACQUISITION OF EMS SERVICES PROVIDE ANY BENEFITS TO CAHS?

Integration of EMS Staff in Support of Hospital: The most frequently cited benefit of operating an EMS unit is the ability to ease staffing shortages by integrating EMS personnel into other hospital units. Typically, EMS personnel experience "down time," or a period in which they are neither responding to calls nor being used for routine EMS activities (e.g., stocking the ambulance). Although the amount of downtime varies by hospital, the staff we interviewed stated that their downtime ranged from 20 to 50 percent. Interviews with hospital administrators confirmed that hospitals make use of paramedic or EMT downtime to assist in moving patients for tests or to different hospital rooms, entering data into electronic medical record systems, and supporting emergency room physicians as needed.

Integration of Administrative Support Functions: Prior to acquisition by hospitals, private and government-run EMS units maintain human resource functions, billing departments and other support services that are typically necessary to run the organization. Hospital representatives that we interviewed indicated that they have been able to achieve some efficiencies, such as lower overhead costs, by integrating EMS administrative functions into the hospital's administrative functions. Although respondents acknowledged that training of administrative staff in these areas is still required, in the longer-term, some cost savings were anticipated.

Goodwill: Despite several challenges associated with operating an EMS unit (discussed below), managing an EMS unit, particularly with the hospital's name on the side of the ambulance or transport vehicle, creates goodwill among members of the community and is seen as an important marketing opportunity. As one administrator stated "(i)t's good PR to be first on the scene . . . many persons in the community know our paramedics. . ." This goodwill is believed to increase business to the hospital.

WHAT ARE THE CHALLENGES TO CAH OPERATION OF AN EMS UNIT?

CAHs with an EMS unit face many difficult challenges. Among these are the following:

Staffing: CAHs attempting to run an EMS unit are frequently confronted with staff recruitment and retention problems. To some extent, recruitment of health care professionals, such as nurses, physicians, ancillary hospital staff, as well as paramedics is a problem that is endemic to many small rural areas. However, with specific regard to paramedics and EMTs, a CAH may compete with physician offices for qualified staff. More than one of the hospital staff we interviewed said that, because EMS staff are paid less than nurses and are able to perform many of the same duties as nursing staff, physician practices often find that it is cost-effective to hire EMTs and paramedics rather than nurses. EMTs often prefer to work in physician offices or private practices because of the regular hours, higher salaries, and better benefits, relative to those offered by the CAH. To the extent that emergency personnel find physician offices or other private practices a more desirable work environment, the pool of candidates to staff the CAH's EMS unit is limited.

In addition to the challenges of recruitment and retention, CAHs often experience difficulties in locating appropriate educational and training services for EMS staff. While some hospitals indicated that EMS personnel receive training along with other hospital personnel, specific training necessary for EMS licensure and continuing education requirements may not be available within the area or may be very costly for the hospital to arrange.

Limits of Integration: There may be difficulties integrating EMS staff into the hospital. Although experiences working with paramedic and EMT staff in the hospital are generally positive, one hospital representative indicated that it has been difficult at times to use EMS staff in the hospital, in part because these professionals are not trained to practice in a hospital setting, as part of a patient care team.

The ability to integrate EMS staff into patient care activities varies across states. Two hospital representatives said they could not understand why state laws precluded paramedics and certain classes of EMTs from performing procedures or interventions in a hospital setting, even though by law they are permitted to perform the same procedures outside the hospital in the course of an emergency run.

Management of EMS Departments/Units: Special management skills may be required in order to effectively operate an EMS unit. According to one hospital administrator, "(o)versight of EMS operations carry a disproportionate amount of problems and issues relative to other hospital services." This same respondent was not well informed about the relationship between EMS revenues and costs at their facility, and cited the poor communication between the CAH billing office and EMS management staff for this lack of information. Respondents voiced the critical importance of recruiting administrative personnel who are trained in EMS management, financing and accounting.

Negative Financial Impact: Ownership of an EMS unit appears to be a financially unprofitable venture. None of the CAH hospital administrators we spoke with could make a strong business case for ownership of an EMS unit. Several respondents indicated that payments frequently failed to cover costs and that hospitals were forced to rely on county subsidies, management fees, tax levies, grants, donations or fund-raising activities to meet costs associated with service provision. The amount of subsidy received from cities and counties varied across hospitals; in one case subsidies were almost 70 percent of costs.

Several of the administrators interviewed indicated that these financial losses might have been averted had the hospital been eligible to receive cost-based reimbursement. In one instance, a CAH found it necessary to transfer their EMS unit to an affiliated network prospective payment system (PPS) hospital in order to improve the CAH's overall financial performance that resulted during the fee schedule phase-in period. Another hospital was also experiencing significant financial losses, but was unable to eliminate or transfer its EMS unit to another service because, by state law, the hospital was considered a district hospital and was required to assume responsibility for EMS services. Despite the fact that the hospital was incurring financial losses, the administrator indicated that the hospital was unable to "give EMS back. . . [since it was] not a viable political alternative." In this instance, the hospital operated with the support of a local government subsidy.

KEY POLICY ISSUES

Community Subsidies and Financial Support: The National Rural Health Association (NRHA) report "Rural and Frontier Emergency Medical Services: An Agenda for the Future"[3] recommends that "EMS should not only weave itself into the local health care system but into the fabric of the community itself." However, this report acknowledges that "(o)ther than reimbursement provisions for ambulance services attached to the hospital, there has been no federal, and limited state focus on maintaining a safety net of critical access ambulance services." Walsh Center findings indicate that CAH dependence on community subsidies and outside financial sources to maintain EMS services places these providers in a precarious financial position if, for any number of factors, these financial resources are unavailable or reduced. Loss of this revenue would not only affect the viability of the EMS unit but, in instances where the hospital is unable to divest itself from EMS responsibilities (e.g., due to state law or regulations), the viability of the hospital itself.

Hospital Efficiencies Resulting from EMS Staffing: Rural hospitals have long been recognized as facing challenges in the recruitment and retention of health care professionals. As noted in our discussions with hospital representatives, CAHs with an EMS unit have found opportunities to fill gaps in staffing and reduce downtime by integrating these emergency personnel in patient care, when not otherwise engaged in EMS duties. In addition to understanding how EMTs and paramedics may best be utilized to enhance patient care, research examining state laws governing activities of emergency medical professionals may be necessary to understand the opportunities that are available to CAHs to maximize staffing efficiencies.

Changes in Reimbursement to Critical Access Hospitals: As the Medicare ambulance fee schedule is fully implemented, it is necessary to monitor CAH performance to ensure that these facilities are able to remain financially viable under the existing fee schedule. The GAO[4] noted that between 2001 and 2004, the number of ambulance transports in "super-rural"[5] areas declined by 8 percent and concluded that "(d)eclining utilization coupled with potentially negative Medicare margins in super-rural areas, which could be exacerbated when the MMA temporary payment provisions expire, raise questions as to whether Medicare payments will be adequate to support beneficiary access in super-rural areas."

The GAO study included only ambulance providers that did not share costs with other institutions or those that shared costs but reported ambulance costs separately. As such, it is not possible to generalize these findings to all CAH-based EMS providers. Nevertheless, combined with the findings of our study, these analyses suggest that the 35-mile rule may need to be eliminated or relaxed in order to ensure access to emergency medical services in many small, rural communities.

Conclusions: Findings from this study suggest the need to continuously monitor CAH experiences with EMS units. The purpose of this monitoring is to ensure the continued availability of EMS resources in a community and that operation or acquisition of an EMS unit does not pose negative financial repercussions for CAHs. Moreover, hospitals and local governments must continue to collaborate in order to strengthen the EMS infrastructure, enhance levels of service availability, reduce service duplication and employ limited funds in the most cost-effective manner.

---

[3] McGinnis KK. "Rural and Frontier Emergency Medical Services: An Agenda for the Future" National Rural Health Association, October 2004.

[4] U.S. Government Accountability Office, Ambulance Providers: Costs and Expected Medicare Margins Vary Greatly, GAO-07-383, May 2007.

[5] A "super-rural" transport was defined in the GAO study as one that originated in the 25th percentile of rural areas; areas were designated as based on population density in a rural county.

4

Partners in Critical Care

Source: Hynes, P., P. Conlon, J. O'Neill, and S. Lapinsky. 2008. Partners in critical care. *Dynamics* 19 (1): pp. 12-17. Used with the permission of The Canadian Association of Critical Care Nurses.

ABSTRACT

Patient and family-centred care (PFCC) concepts are increasingly cited in the critical care literature and are a welcome addition to the vernacular of the intensive care unit (ICU). The implementation and maintenance of a supportive PFCC environment is challenging, however, and usual strategies for knowledge translation using guidelines and policies, no matter how articulate, have not yet resulted in sustained practice change at the point of care delivery. In this article, co-authored by community partners, the physician director and nurse leader of one tertiary care ICU, we describe an initiative in which patient and family representatives were included in the ICU interdisciplinary team membership. After two years and now, at the conclusion of the assignment, options for community partner participation in various activities related to unit governance are shared.

WHAT IS PFCC AND WHY IS IT IMPORTANT?

Opportunities to provide patient and family-centred care (PFCC) are increasing throughout health care and gaining momentum in a variety of settings. Embracing this concept requires that health providers enter into mutually beneficial partnerships with patients and those individuals who patients call family. PFCC embodies four core concepts: (1) dignity and respect, (2) information sharing, (3) participation, and (4) collaboration (Conway, Johnson, Edgman-Levitan, Schlucter, Ford, Sodomka, et al., 2006). Endorsement and commitment at the senior management level of the organization are essential in order to ensure that the infrastructure (resources and institutional culture) needed to facilitate PFCC is available, both at the point of care delivery, as well as more formally in policy development and other committee forums. This is important because, while PFCC has primarily been a focus in the clinical arena among patients, families and frontline caregivers, there is more involvement at the program and policy level as the concept matures (Conway et al.).

The purpose of this article is to provide an overview of our initial experience with patient and family representatives (community partners) as members of our intensive care unit (ICU) leadership team and to discuss some of the opportunities and possibilities for PFCC in the ICU, as we understand them currently. Our article is unique in that it is written collaboratively with community partners (JO & PC) who recently completed a two-year term on our adult critical care team (ACCT). While the partnership increased and elevated our understanding of PFCC and what it means to honour patient and family perspectives in the ICU setting, there are tangible outcomes also, that we refer to throughout the article and share in the form of tables. For example, a role description has been drafted to provide guidance on how the experience of community partners may be enhanced using strategies, such as early assignment of an ICU team member skilled to facilitate assigned project work over the course of a one-year term (see Table One). Background information includes the context out of which this article emerged and a brief overview of our ICU. A discussion of community partner participation in unit governance is situated in relevant literature.

WHAT DOES THE LITERATURE SAY ABOUT PFCC?

We continue to encounter helpful literature on various aspects of PFCC in the health care journals. Henneman & Cardin (2002) captured the essence of family-centred critical care in describing it as a philosophical approach that recognizes the needs of patients and families, and moves beyond theoretical acceptance to view the patient and family as the unit to be engaged in care planning and delivery. Recently, a task force was assembled by the Society of Critical Care Medicine and the American College of Critical Care Medicine and charged with developing guidelines to support family in the patient-centred ICU (Davidson et al., 2007). In preparation, the published literature was reviewed (CINAHL, Medline and the Cochrane library 1980-2003) with a yield of more than 300 related studies. Although evaluation using Cochrane methodology indicated a need for further research for most areas, from a theoretical perspective the issues associated with PFCC appear to be well represented.

What is needed now is implementation and evaluation so as to arrive on evidence informed practices in support of care delivery processes, as well as community partner involvement in governance. Interesting findings have already been reported from seemingly basic and inexpensive interventions at the clinical level, such as the use of music to enhance relaxation and decrease physiological demand in mechanically ventilated patients (Lee, Chung, Chan, & Chan, 2005). Similarly, the provision of bereavement literature, combined with structured conferencing to improve communication with families of dying patients resulted in fewer reported symptoms of anxiety and depression and a decrease in post-traumatic stress disorder-related symptoms at three months after the patient's death (Lautrette, Darmon, Megarbane, Joly, Chevret, Adrie, et al., 2007). With respect to involvement at the level of policy devel-

Table One	**Adult Critical Care Team Guidelines for Engagement of Community Partners**

1. We recommend that community partners be invited to join the team for a term of no more than one year, thus encouraging an annual rollover of fresh ideas from the community. Obviously, term extensions could be negotiated—but we suggest only for the purpose of concluding unfinished business and that the community partners are assigned to a team member who can facilitate timely completion.

2. We recommend that community partners be assigned specific tasks or projects that are consistent with the team's goals and objectives—and that their progress report is included as an agenda item at team meetings.

3. We recommend that a member of the ACCT be designated to serve as the team's active liaison with community partners throughout each term. This will give community partners a single go-to team resource, someone to call with ideas, questions or comments before full-team discussion.

4. We recommend that community partners' option and role be actively integrated into any policy or practice discussions that impact on families, including the current discussion about elective family presence at resuscitation efforts.

5. We recommend that team members be mindful of the fact that they often communicate casually with one another through the course of a workday, but that community partners are normally only present in the unit once a month. Therefore, they may feel out of the loop. They may feel like spectators instead of participants. Perhaps the team's designated liaison can make a point of touching base with partners every week, to keep them in the flow as to changes or developments.

Submitted by Jim O'Neill & Patrick Conlon, March 2007

opment, system evaluation and facility design, the PFCC core concepts referred to above embody opportunities for patient and family participation in governance, both unit-based and institution-wide (Conway et al., 2006) The importance of a team member who is knowledgeable of PFCC and prepared to act as a liaison to community partners involved in governance initiatives has been acknowledged (see Table One).

IMPLEMENTING PFCC AT MOUNT SINAI HOSPITAL

Background. The experience of having patient and family representatives included in the interdisciplinary team at the Mount Sinai Hospital (MSH) ICU in Toronto was in its early stages in 2005 when it was first introduced through Critical Thinking, which is a standing column the Canadian Association of Critical Care Nurses' (CACCN) national president contributes to in each of the quarterly publications of the **Dynamics** journal (Hynes, 2005). Later that year, more information was provided during a joint nursing social work presentation at the Dynamics 2005 conference in Ottawa, with a great deal of interest evident in the audience and many queries in the months that followed. As a philosophical approach to care, we appreciate the complexity that PFCC entails and invite readers to contact us if more information about our experiences is helpful.

Setting. The MSH ICU is a 16-bed academic, single-centre, intensivist-led, closed medical surgical unit that admits approximately 800 patients per year. We serve a variety of patient populations, including general medical patients (admitted from the wards, step-down unit and the emergency department), postoperative patients, high-risk obstetrical patients, and oncology patients from Princess Margaret Hospital (PMH). Although PMH is under a separate administration, we are their primary ICU intake centre due to their physical location, and we provide them with critical care services, including ICU consults, code blue and rapid response team availability for their inpatient areas. In addition, we accept transfers through CritiCall, which is an Ontario-wide referral service for critically ill patients who require an ICU bed or need to be transferred to a different ICU for specialized treatment. As an example, our ICU is reputable in the management of patients with severe acute respiratory distress syndrome (ARDS) and we receive referrals from around the province for therapies, such as high-frequency oscillation (HFO). One of the benefits of specialization is that we are gaining more expertise in managing ARDS patients and, as survival increases, so do the opportunities to explore longer term outcomes and understand their meaning for these patients (Herridge, Cheung, Tansey, Matte-Martyn, Diaz-Granados, Al-Saidi, et al., 2003). To illustrate the benefits of that work, we offer the following:

> Tom (Dr. Stewart) referred me . . . and she (Dr. Herridge) assessed me. I became part of her study. She gave me all the statistical data to show that I could recover from this. This was a time when I was feeling discouraged. . . . I benefited from hearing that. —Jim O'Neill, community partner, on ARDS outcomes research

To ensure the highest quality of service delivery, an interdisciplinary team of critical care specialists works together on a daily basis coordinating care for patients from all the services outlined above. There is a monthly meeting of the leadership team, including community partners, that is cochaired by the ICU medical site director (SL) and nursing unit administrator (PH). This is the ACCT forum where matters related to unit governance are tabled for discussion, priorities set, and progress monitored. In the attempt to mainstream our efforts while ensuring that the goals and objectives of the ICU are aligned with the strategic priorities of the organization, we revised our terms of reference this past year to capture ICU initiatives into hospital-wide balanced scorecard quadrants. The balanced scorecard is a strategic management system that organizes the business of an organization, including, but not restricted to financial performance, into metrics or quadrants so as to enable more comprehensive progress reporting (Kaplan & Norton, 1992). Those quadrants are (1) PFCC, (2) organizational safety, (3) organizational efficiency and growth, and (4) learning and innovation (see Table Two). Each quadrant functions under the leadership of one or more members of the ICU interdisciplinary team who provide a progress report at the monthly meetings. Upon considering that units most successful in adopting PFCC characteristically have strong leaders, caring staff and the support of a committed interdisciplinary team (Henneman & Cardin, 2002), we agree that a decentralized approach to unit governance is optimal.

Community Partners' Participation in Unit Governance. Prior to inviting community partners to participate in ICU governance, input from families was largely on an individual case basis, in addition to our ongoing commitment to regular meetings between the interdisciplinary team and family members of our patients. For the past several years, we have been fortunate to encounter more opportunities to learn from former patients as some return to visit us in the ICU and others for followup in outpatient clinics. We have also scheduled presentations by former ICU patients into our teaching program, for example, a respiratory therapist who was treated in another ICU for Guillain-Barré Syndrome and community partners Patrick Conlon (PC) and Jim O'Neill (JO) who presented during Nursing Week 2005. The need to understand critical care from the unique perspective of patients and families has increasingly come to focus in our ICU in recent years.

The invitation to join our ACCT followed an emotive presentation by PC and JO describing a view of the ICU from the patient and family perspective, much of which is captured in PC's recently published book called *No Need to Trouble the Heart* (Conlon, 2006). Once community partners, PC and JO attended our monthly ACCT meetings where they

Table Two	Adult Critical Care Team (ACCT) Terms of Reference

Responsible to: Acute and Chronic Medicine Centre of Excellence (COE)

Purpose: The ACCT exists to ensure that the MSH ICU fulfills its role, as a leading teaching and research critical care centre, in the provision of optimal care for critically ill patients and families within a framework of accountability and a commitment to interdisciplinary teamwork.

General statement: Consistent with the vision, mission, and strategic directions of MSH, the ACCT activity will be organized according to the balanced scorecard quadrants, specifically 1. Patient- and family-centred care, 2. Organizational safety, 3. Organizational efficiency and growth, and 4. Learning and innovation.

Each quadrant will have a designated leader(s) who is (are) members of the ACCT and responsible for reporting to the ACCT on their respective quadrants at each meeting.

Other functions include:
• To review and approve policies and procedures and ensure they comply with best practices and legislative requirements
• To provide a forum for the interdisciplinary team to voice concerns or commendations

Spectrum of functions of each quadrant subcommittee includes (for example):

Patient- and family-centred care: Develop guidelines for the role of community partners, define and enhance processes that facilitate family involvement.

Organizational safety: Identify opportunities for quality improvement, optimize infection control, develop transparency guidelines for non-punitive management of incidents

Organizational efficiency and growth: Establish processes for data capturing, reporting and analysis to enhance operational decision making, monitor critical care resource utilization, collaborate with COE co-leaders to optimize patient flow processes

Learning and innovation: Foster an environment that nurtures academic excellence and evidence informed practice.

Membership:

Co-Chairs: The ACCT is co-led by the ICU Physician Director (MSH Site) and the ICU Nursing Unit Administrator (NUA).

Ex-Officio: ICU Medical Director MSH/UHN; MSH Senior Director Acute and Chronic Medicine & Nursing

ACCT Representation: Chaplaincy, Community Partners, Infection Control, Medicine, Nursing, Nutritional Services, Pharmacy, Physiotherapy, Research/Data Collection, Respiratory Therapy, Social Work and Clerical Assistant (Recorder)

Tenure: The membership and terms of reference for the ACCT will be reviewed annually at the first meeting of the year.

Frequency of meetings: A minimum of eight meetings per year will be held.

---

provided valuable insights and observations on a variety of ICU routines and suggested practice changes, as well as leading specific projects themselves. For example, they drafted an insert for our ICU pamphlet with suggestions for how family members can contribute to the care of their loved one at the bedside (see Table Three). Another of their initiatives involved the promotion of a lip reading service to facilitate communication with patients who have a tracheotomy. A lip reader was described as invaluable during JO's hospitalization, as portrayed by the following:

> Niki had helped ease Jim out of his darkness simply by listening, by connecting to him. . . . This doctor would comprehend and value the legacy of her gift or not, and in his own time. . . . No matter. It was enough for now to witness the pale but unmistakable flickers of returning light in Jim's eyes. (Conlon, 2006, p. 168)

Community partner participation in the accreditation process included contributions to both the self-assessment document preparation and attending the ICU team interview. They alerted us to deficiencies in communication with families around ICU discharge, whether to do with transfer to a general ward bed or externally to another hospital. Despite the logic of transfer to a hospital closer to home, advance planning and preparing the family for repatriation are important. They proposed that a survey of families would help to identify other issues of concern.

RELATED LITERATURE

The needs of families of critically ill patients have been known for some time. They value information, reassurance and support and want to be near the patient (Molter, 1979). We have also heard from patients directly. For example, in a book called *Bed Number Ten*, Baier and Zimmeth Schomaker (1986) describe an experience over four months in an ICU with Guillain-Barré syndrome. Much of the infor-

Table Three	Opportunities for Care-Giving

FAMILY CAN HELP

First, we believe that family is who the patient says it is—but we rely on next-of-kin in cases where patients are unable to express their wishes.

Second, we believe that family can play an important supportive role in patient care, and we welcome willing and able family members who want to help us improve patient comfort and self-esteem.

FAMILY CAN ACT

It's normal for family members to feel anxious and even powerless while a loved one is in intensive care. But we suggest there are some practical low-risk tasks that can be undertaken by you after consultation with the team.

Some examples:

Grooming

Hair brushing, gentle oral care, nail care and application of unscented hand creams can all help restore the patient's personal connection to family.

Reading/Photos

If the patient's hearing is not impaired, reading passages from a favourite book or magazine in a calm voice can be beneficial and soothing. And family photos posted nearby can also help restore the patient's sense of connection to loved ones.

Physiotherapy

Physiotherapy is valuable to recovery, even in ICU.

If the patient's physiotherapy program involves repetitive movements, ask the physiotherapist or the nurse if you can assist with maintenance of the program to sustain continuity between the physiotherapist's visits.

Mobilization

Some patients will benefit from being raised to an upright position for short periods of time. Ask the nurse if you can assist by simply sitting with the patient while upright and being alert to any signs of distress or discomfort.

FAMILY CAN WATCH

You know the patient. We encourage you to report any unusual behavioural or mood changes that you observe in your loved one. This is particularly important with longer-stay patients who can sometimes become agitated or depressed.

What we learn from you about your loved one will help us meet our commitment to achieving the best possible outcome for everyone.

mation contained in both of these works is as true today as when they were first published, almost 30 and 20 years ago, respectively.

No Need to Trouble the Heart (Conlon, 2006) provides a sensitive account of critical care service delivery based on direct experience with two Ontario ICUs. Written by a community partner (PC), it ap-peals to a diverse readership, but offers health providers, in particular, an exercise in reflective practice. Those who accept the challenge will understand that the development of reflective practice and the implementation of sustained PFCC are synergistic. Rather than providing a synopsis of key points, we deferred to the author, community partner PC, who commented as follows:

No Need to Trouble the Heart—Commentary

It was an ICU nurse who inspired the book title. It was superb nursing care that energized its writing.

When my longtime partner, Jim O'Neill, was suddenly diagnosed with ARDS, we were both thrust into a nightmare of dread and uncertainty. My book chronicles the first 10 weeks of his 15-week hospital stay in two different settings, from early predictions of his death to his first unsteady steps away from a confining bed. Throughout, I successfully negotiated a place on various care teams, instinctively convinced that family would add value to the treatment plan. I reasoned that the alliance of clinical skills and intimate personal knowledge of the patient would combine to assure the best possible outcome.

Was there professional resistance to my persistent presence at the bedside? Occasionally there was. But any discomforts were worked out amicably because there was good will on both sides, as well as tacit agreement that the patient's needs, both clinical and personal, should always be paramount. One example of good clinical/family partnership took place a couple of weeks after Jim's transfer from the Trillium Health Centre ICU to Mount Sinai ICU for HFO therapy. Clinicians determined that he would benefit from a tracheotomy and Jim initially appeared to consent to the procedure, but then resisted. He and I discussed his ambivalence and it slowly became apparent that he assumed a tracheotomy was always an endstage procedure, his belief based on his experience with a much-loved older brother whose breathing had been eased by a tracheotomy during the final phase of a terminal illness many years before. Once I notified clinicians about the reasons for Jim's fear, they immediately stepped forward to reassure him that his condition was actually improving and that a tracheotomy was only indicated to increase his comfort. He then agreed to the procedure, was immediately more comfortable and the tracheotomy was removed a few weeks later. It was a stirring demonstration of PFCC at its best, with clinicians and family as true partners in care.

Jim's repatriation to Trillium Health Centre did not go as smoothly. I had called his duty nurse, as I did every day, to check on his overnight status and to confirm when I'd be arriving for my daily visit. I was notified that he was already on his way by ambulance to Trillium. It was a jarring piece of news. There had been no advance notice that his transfer was imminent, and I believe I was rightly angry at an appalling lapse in communication.

But most of our experience was essentially positive, which is why Jim and I quickly agreed to join Mount Sinai's ACCT as community partners and why we've promoted the tangible merits of family-inclusive care at hospitals and conferences all over North America. Those merits were best summarized by a veteran nurse who approached me late in Jim's hospital stay. "I want you to know something," she said. "Jim will go home sooner and get better quicker because you were here, because you were involved."

That, I submit, is what it's all about (Conlon, 2006).

DISCUSSION

While a number of different terms are in current clinical use and applied interchangeably to refer to care delivery models that are inclusive of patient and family partnerships, including patient and family-centred care (PFCC), family-focused care (FCC) and patient-centred care (PCC), a universal concept remains elusive. While some may think that this lack of consensus contributes to inconsistencies in how care is planned, organized and delivered, our experience so far has revealed nothing to suggest that absolute agreement on this point is prerequisite to meaningful engagement with patients and families. We appreciate the intellectual exercise that such a debate would entail and would welcome it, believing this to be a theory versus practice debate eventuality. In our ICU, we call it PFCC.

The manner in which health professionals engage with patients and families and how those relationships will be sustained is complex. This is particularly the case in the ICU setting where changing relevance and rapid intervention is routine. An understanding of the clinical profile that patient pop-

ulations share (typical responses, complications, and the illness trajectory) is essential, but clinical experts add to this what they call qualitative distinctions, referring to information that is based on knowing the patient and accounting for the meaning of patient and/or family responses (Benner, Hooper-Kyriakidis, & Stannard, 1999). For example, the benefits of a tracheotomy over endotracheal intubation for patients who require longer-term airway management are well understood by ICU clinicians and can be easily conveyed to patients and families by most, if not all, interdisciplinary team members. Patients are regularly assessed for this procedure in our ICU and, in most cases, it can be performed safely at the bedside. When the time came for community partner JO to have a tracheotomy, he regressed immediately once consulted about the procedure. Memories of his older brother who had a tracheotomy as a palliative measure years ago was the only context available to JO on learning that he was a candidate for the same intervention. This is what Benner et al. (1999) mean by qualitative distinction. In JO's case, the necessary information sat with community partner PC, whose need to situate the burden associated with providing consent on JO's behalf illuminates the important consideration of support for family, as follows:

> Did I say, go ahead and cut him because you guys know what you're doing, and I don't, not at all, but you're the only hope I've got . . . I need you to like me right now, need to feel I am a partner in this, need to feel I am one of you, need to feel not alone in this." (Conlon, 2006, p. 123)

We have emphasized the importance of a commitment to PFCC as a philosophical approach that encompasses involvement of patients and family in care planning, delivery and evaluation. It may be useful to differentiate between this commitment and the introduction of specific PFCC initiatives into clinical practice, which can be managed along a continuum as a strategy for implementation. One could argue that a staged approach to implementation is prudent in that it allows for more consultation with patients and families and the interdisciplinary team. Frontline staff at the point of care delivery may experience opportunities for formative evaluation that would be beneficial for sharing observations and experiences and for suggesting revisions where needed. A commitment to PFCC as the model of care delivery should be organization-wide, visible and unwavering.

In conclusion, we are aware that there are many examples of PFCC eloquently presented at conferences, seminars and in the published literature in the form of case illustrations and expert opinions. We recognize these as the lived experiences of our critical care colleagues, carefully extracted from their day-to-day work in much the same way that we have described our experience. There is intrinsic value that is associated with caring for the critically ill. In partnership with patients and families, we may extend the benefits of our good work beyond what we have been able to achieve through more traditional models of care delivery.

About the Authors

Patricia Hynes, RN, MA, CNCC(C), Nursing Unit Administrator, ICU, Mount Sinai Hospital, Toronto, ON. Patrick Conlon, Community Partner, Mount Sinai Hospital, Toronto, ON. Jim O'Neill, Community Partner, Mount Sinai Hospital, Toronto, ON. Stephen Lapinsky, MD, ICU Site Director, Mount Sinai Hospital, Toronto, ON. Contact for correspondence: Patricia Hynes, Email: phynes@mtsinai.on.ca.

ACKNOWLEDGMENTS
We would like to acknowledge the Mount Sinai Hospital ICU staff who all contributed to this initiative.

We are especially grateful to Dr. Tom Stewart and Lieve Verhaeghe, MSW, RSW.

• • • References

Baier, S., & Zimmeth Schomaker, M. (1986). *Bed number ten*. New York: CRC Press.

Benner, P., Hooper-Kyriakidis, P., & Stannard, D. (1999). *Clinical wisdom and interventions in critical care*. Philadelphia: Saunders.

Conlon, P. (2006). *No need to trouble the heart*. Vancouver: Raincoast Books.

Conway, J., Johnson, B., Edgman-Levitan, S., Schlucter, J., Ford, D., Sodomka, P., et al. (2006). *Partnering with patients and families to design a patient and family centred healthcare system. A roadmap for the future*. Retrieved July 4, 2007, from www.family centredcare.org

Davidson, J.E., Powers, K., Hedayat, K.M., Tieszem, M., Kon, A.A., Shepard, E., et al. (2007). Clinical practice guidelines for support of the family in the patient centred intensive care unit: American College of Critical Care Medicine task force 2004-2005. *Critical Care Medicine, 35*, 605–622.

Henneman, E.A., & Cardin, S. (2002). Family-centred critical care: A practical approach to making it happen. *Critical Care Nurse, 22*, 12–19.

Herridge, M.S., Cheung, A.M., Tansey, C.M., Matte-Martyn, A., Diaz-Granados, N., Al-Saidi, F., et al. for the Canadian Critical Care Trials Group. (2003). One-year outcomes in survivors of the acute respiratory distress syndrome. *New England Journal of Medicine, 348*, 683-693.

Hynes, P. (2005). Critical thinking. *Dynamics, 16*(3), 4–5.

Kaplan, R.S., & Norton, D.P. (1992). The balanced scorecard: Measures that drive performance. *Harvard Business Review, 70*(1), 71–79 .

Lautrette, A., Darmon, M., Megarbane, B., Joly, L.M., Chevret, S., Adrie, C., et al. (2007). A communication strategy and brochure for relatives of patients dying in the ICU. *New England Journal of Medicine, 356*, 469–478.

Lee, O.K.A., Chung, Y.F.L., Chan, M.F., & Chan, W.M. (2005). Music and its effect on the physiological responses and anxiety levels of patients receiving mechanical ventilation: A pilot study. *Journal of Clinical Nursing, 14*, 609–620.

Molter, N.C. (1979). Needs of relatives of critically ill patients: A descriptive study. *Heart & Lung, 8*, 332–339.

13

Long-Term and Community Care

Long-term care (LTC) encompasses a variety of services for those who need assistance because of functional deficits. The functional limitations can arise from complications associated with age-related chronic conditions; from disabilities related to birth defects, brain damage, or mental retardation in children; or from major illnesses or injuries suffered by adults. More than 10 million Americans are estimated to need LTC services. The majority (58%) are elderly, but a significant proportion (42%) are under the age of 65. Among those who need LTC, 14% are in nursing homes and 86% reside in the community (Kaiser 2007). Hence, informal care by family members and friends, and a variety of community-based services play a major role in the delivery of long-term care. The type of services needed can vary significantly from individual to individual. Deficits in the instrumental activities of daily living (IADLs) and/or some basic deficits in the activities of daily living (ADL), such as assistance with bathing and grooming, generally indicate a need for supportive and community-based services. Those who have significant functional deficits—evaluated by using the activities of daily living (ADL)

scale—may need to receive LTC services in an institution.

The majority of LTC services in the United States are provided informally by family, friends, and neighbors who receive no payment for their work. Although accurate numbers are difficult to come by, according to one estimate, there may be 22.4 million informal caregivers in the U.S., many of whom are between the ages of 50 and 64 (Scott 2006).

The majority of Americans prefer to receive care in their own home. Secondly, the majority of financing for LTC services flows through the Medicaid program. Hence, there are cost implications for the government. These factors have led to government policies to expand LTC service options in communities and, at the same time, deemphasize institutional care whenever it is appropriate to do so. The federal Home- and Community-Based Services (HCBS) program has been largely successful in providing community-based services in all 50 states to the elderly, and also to the nonelderly with disabilities, AIDS, and serious mental health problems. Community services include adult day care, home health care, Meals on Wheels, congregate meals and basic health services provided at senior centers, and support programs such as transportation and homemaker services. The availability of these services varies from community to community in accordance with available funding.

In long-term care, housing conditions are as essential as services. The place where people live, including the physical and social environment, can greatly enhance or impede a person's functional disability, independence, and quality of life (Stone 2000). Congregate housing units provide a basic supportive environment. There are two main types of housing categories: government-assisted housing and private-pay housing. Independent living housing generally does not have staff to provide any assistance. The clients must obtain informal and/or formal community-based services to address their LTC needs.

There is a range of institutional choices available to accommodate a variety of needs. Personal care homes generally provide light assistive care such as assistance with bathing and grooming in addition to a physically supportive environment. Assisted living facilities go a step beyond basic custodial care by delivering a higher level of assistance with ADLs such as transfer, toileting, and ambulating, and also rehabilitation services. Skilled nursing facilities care for those who require around-the-clock nursing care and supervision. At the upper end of the institutional continuum, there are facilities that specialize in delivering subacute care, services to Alzheimer's patients, and services for those who have other types of specialized needs such closed head trauma care, ventilator care, and care for serious psychiatric disorders.

About 10 to 11 million people in the United States receive community-based services and another 1.6 million are residents of long-term care institutions. It is estimated that 1.6 million community residents of all ages, mostly those needing assistance with ADLs, receive paid LTC services each month (Kaye et al. 2010). The majority of LTC services, both in the community and in nursing homes, are paid by Medicaid. To a lesser extent and for shorter durations, services for the elderly may be covered under Medicare, mainly after discharge from a hospital. In the absence of eligibility for payment under either of these two major government programs, services have to be paid for out of private funds or through private long-term care insurance. On an inflation-adjusted basis, in 2009, the median monthly payments for community-based LTC services amounted to $928, and $5,243 for institutional services. Total national spending on LTC services, from all public and private sources, was estimated to be $183 billion in 2003 (Allen 2005).

The impetus to improve quality of care in nursing homes came from the Nursing Home Reform Amendment to the 1987 Omnibus Budget Reconciliation Act. This policy intervention became necessary because of the government's heavy involvement in paying for nursing home care. For example, in 2006, of the $124.9 billion spent on nursing home care in the United States, 62.5% came from various public sources, mainly Medicaid and Medicare (National Center for Health Statistics 2009). During the past 25 years, nursing home populations have become older and the overall acuity levels have increased significantly. Hence, the need for accurate measurement of quality has also become more important than ever before.

Approximately 80% of the total spending for LTC services is for the elderly. As the proportion of the population 65 years and over climbs, federal spending on the elderly will absorb a larger and ultimately unsustainable share of the federal budget and economic resources. Federal spending for Medicaid, Medicare, and Social Security is expected to surge—nearly doubling by 2035—as people live longer and spend more time in retirement (Allen 2005).

In the first reading for this chapter, **Introduction to Where Old People Live: The Need for Affordability, Accessibility, and Acceptability**, Wilson points out that senior housing has emerged as a market niche in only the past 25 years as an increasing number of older people have chosen various types of senior housing living arrangements. Some of the arrangements are housing-with-services, which may include services such as housekeeping, grocery shopping, and meal preparation, while the majority of them do not provide any services. Conservation of financial resources and cultural norms that value personal autonomy are the two main reasons that most people choose not to obtain paid services. Some housing-with-services options include personal and health care services that resemble assisted living and for which various pricing models exist, from all-inclusive rates to separate pricing for housing and services based on type and use. For many consumers, the various models are difficult to understand and to budget for. Worker shortages, financing, and availability of housing to meet a variety of needs present some daunting challenges for the future. The notions of entitlement and dependence on public resources will be sorely tested in an era of increasing demands and decreasing resources.

The reading, **Consumer Preparedness for Long-Term Care**, is based on a 2007 colloquium sponsored by the Commonwealth Fund and Academy Health. In a survey conducted by the National

Academy of Social Insurance, more than 70% of the respondents favored a large role for the federal government to meet the costs of long-term care. The amount of LTC services needed varies greatly among different people; 26% may need more than $100,000 in paid assistance. Yet, few Americans plan ahead. Fewer than 10% of those over the age of 65 have purchased long-term care insurance. Social and cultural factors and a lack of understanding of the variety of care options in LTC are at least some factors that prevent people from obtaining long-term care insurance. The federal government's campaign called *Own Your Future* is intended to increase consumer awareness about LTC planning, but not all states have implemented the program. People have various options for financial planning, but each option has significant barriers. On the other hand, certain policy initiatives have been implemented under the premise of private-public partnerships in which individuals take at least part of the responsibility for their LTC planning.

In **Long-Term Care: Understanding Medicaid's Role for the Elderly and Disabled**, O'Brien highlights the role of Medicaid in paying for long-term care. Although Medicaid is the largest source of financing LTC services, its role is limited because eligibility is either through a welfare-related pathway or through exhaustion of one's financial assets while paying for one's care. Also, states decide on an optional basis which services to cover. In spite of these limitations, millions of people are served in both institutions and community-based care settings. Current policy is focused on slowing the growth of spending and improving service options for the community-dwelling elderly. The future growth of demand is expected to vary from state to state. Hence, the current federal-state structure of Medicaid financing may need to be reformed.

The report by Mor and colleagues, **Changes in the Quality of Nursing Homes in the US: A Review and Data Update**, is the most comprehensive report of its kind published to date. The report presents a thorough review of the extant literature on nursing home quality. The evaluation of nursing home quality and comparison of quality between facilities have both become challenging because of changes in the case mix acuity of the patients served and segmentation of the market which has changed the composition of nursing facilities. To date, research has shown that improvement in quality has been associated with increases in Medicaid reimbursement and web-based public reporting of nursing home quality. Staff-to-resident ratios have continued to improve. Substantial improvements have also been noted in various process measures such as use of restraints, immunization rates, pain management, and bladder training for incontinent patients. Outcome measures associated with functional decline and the prevalence of pressure ulcers have also shown improvement, but hospitalization of nursing home residents appears to show regional differences. Many of these hospitalizations are preventable. Of ongoing concern is the variability in the nursing home survey (inspection) process by the states. The extent of deficiencies cited on these surveys often does not reflect the independently assessed improvements in quality. Mor and colleagues furnish several recommendations for the future direction of research to evaluate nursing home quality. As a final word, nursing home quality is multidimensional. Specialization in care delivery requires the use of dimensions of quality that may be appropriate for one setting, but not for another. It is becoming increasingly clear that it is not appropriate to compare all nursing homes with one another.

• • • **References**

Allen, K.G. 2005. *Long-Term Care Financing: Growing Demand and Cost of Services are Straining Federal and State Budgets.* Testimony before the Subcommittee on Health, Committee on Energy and Commerce, House of Representatives on April 27, 2005. Washington, DC: Government Accountability Office.

Kaiser (Kaiser Commission on Medicaid and the Uninsured). 2007. *Medicaid Facts.* Menlo Park, CA: The Henry J. Kaiser Family Foundation.

Kaye, H.S. et al. 2010. Long-term care: Who gets it, who provides it, who pays, and how much? *Health Affairs* 29 (1): 11-21.

National Center for Health Statistics. 2009. *Health, United States, 2008.* Hyattsville, MD: National Center for Health Statistics.

Scott, J.A. 2006. *Informal Caregiving.* Retrieved February 2010 from http://www.umaine.edu/mainecenteronaging/documents/issuebriefinformal caregiving.pdf

Stone, R. I. 2000. *Long-Term Care for the Elderly with Disabilities: Current Policy, Emerging Trends, and Implications for the Twenty-First Century.* New York, NY: Milbank Memorial Fund.

1

Introduction to Where Old People Live: The Need for Affordability, Accessibility, and Acceptability

Source: Wilson, K.B. 2006. Introduction to where older people live: The need for affordability, accessibility, and acceptability. *Generations* 29 (4): 5-8. Reprinted with permission of The American Society on Aging.

INTRODUCTION

In tackling a topic as broad and complex as senior housing and the intersection of individual needs for housing and supportive services, with affordability, accessibility, and acceptability, the first challenge is defining the subject. Housing can be defined as a setting or location where people live- at any age, as opposed to where those roughly classified as "seniors" live.

The term *senior housing* typically is used to describe settings that use age as a criterion for entrance to that setting. Sometimes in "policy-speak" the term *age-segregated* housing is used. In relation to the total number of households headed by those over age 65, the number living in "senior housing" remains limited. For at least the past 100 years, a pattern of growth in size and cost of housing has continued through an individual's peak earning and child-rearing years, with older people then remaining in that setting as children left and spouses died. It is in the past twenty-five years that senior housing has emerged as a market niche, with some older people choosing to move to smaller places or to age-segregated environments. Although some worry

about ill effects of age-segregated housing, for example, isolation of one generation from others, the number of older adults living in such arrangements continues to grow, as does the number who move to smaller quarters after children have grown up and moved out. Be it in a gated community, low-income housing, "snow bird" mobile-home parks, or various versions of retirement communities, significant numbers of older people now select some form of senior housing and are likely to continue to make this choice. Thus, the continued evolution of senior housing and its impact on older people, on those specifically concerned about their well-being, and on the larger society is increasingly important.

Senior housing may also mean a location where concentrated numbers of older people live, with some needing various degrees of supportive services. Inventive names such as "naturally occurring retirement communities," "congregate housing," "continuing care retirement communities" and "cohousing" are used to describe senior housing with various ways of providing support, each with a different combination of ways of introducing supportive services. Such services might be the result of personal preference such as having a housekeeper to change the bed, clean the bathroom, or vacuum floors. For others the use of services might be result of inability to perform everyday tasks such as securing groceries and preparing meals.

In housing-with-services arrangements, services set up and paid for privately by an individual typically are not monitored unless the ring or the organization providing the services receives some form of government assistance, the degree of monitoring varying depending upon type and extent of government involvement.

For example, housing settings built with tax credits or tax-exempt bonds often establish eligibility criteria for residents and often require ongoing certification, and an investigation may occur if a specific complaint is made to an organization such as a professional standards board, protective services agency, or ombudsman's office. However, services arranged by organizations or individuals actually subsidized by any public dollars receive more oversight. Most of this oversight is not related to quality concerns, but rather has as its purpose prevention of use of the funds for individuals or services not authorized. Location or setting is only a concern if there is a possibility of the same service for an individual being paid for more than once.

The housing-with-services model constitutes a rapidly growing market. Part of this growth is the result of an effort to respond to consumers' demands for greater flexibility in meeting their changing needs. But it is also a reaction to increasing oversight of housing options that include some form of personal or nursing services. There is especially stiff resistance to such oversight among those consumers who are paying privately for services and among those who provide the services. Both groups want more control over what services are available and how they are provided. Efforts to use this same approach for those with inadequate resources to pay the full cost of shelter and service until death are proving significantly more challenging.

Fortunately, the majority of older people are able to live out their lives in housing without services, as is typically their first choice. When they need assistance, they rely on family members, friends, neighbors, and connections with local organizations like churches or temples with which they have an established voluntary association. Reaching beyond these resources to paid service providers of any kind typically occurs only in limited circumstances such as a significant health event or the loss of a primary caregiver.

The general reluctance to live in housing with services is partially related to the desire to conserve financial resources, but it is also related to cultural norms that value personal autonomy and a creed of reciprocity that demonstrates continuing ability to live independently in a setting of choice. Of course, this option does not always work. Individual resources often become stressed—especially when the need for assistance continues over a sustained period and requires hands-on care or unscheduled services that depend on the continued physical presence of another person.

Some older individuals seek options of housing-with-services arrangements sooner than others. Historically, such behavior has been assumed to be associated with such personal character traits as being a "planner." Such individuals reportedly have a higher need for personal control or to "not be a burden." But the experience of the past decade or so suggests that this behavior may also be associated with the choices actually available to older people. That is, some older people without resources would prefer housing with services if it were available to them but they cannot afford to make this choice. It is scarcity of resources that prevents them from "planning"; they are more likely to wait for a precipitating crisis that forces change. Other older individuals who do have financial resources have chosen to pay privately for packages housing and services that they view as suitable for them. Such behavior may indicate that limited choices affect housing decisions previously attributed solely to whether an older person was a planner. Indeed, it is likely that acceptable and affordability have more impact on planning for changing needs than is currently thought, and these factors require more consideration for many reasons, including efforts to encourage all older adults to be more proactive at planning for changing needs.

Regardless of whether planning for changing needs occurs or not, for some a time when the regular use of services, beyond what can be organized through informal networks or even episodic paid help, is not optional. In some cases, individuals may not obtain or use needed services, even though they are essential to maintenance of any semblance of a normal life or, in many cases, life itself.

While such needs can often be met in any number of settings, in cases where the individual's first choice simply no longer works, the questions quickly become, Where can I get the services I need? Is there a spot available for me? Is there a way to pay for what I need? Now the discussion is about housing *and* services.

Housing-and-services options typically come as a package deal, with a minimum set of basic services such as a meal plan, housekeeping, and laundry. Many include extensive personal and health-related services that vary according to individual need. In many housing-and-services settings, the cost of the housing and services is fixed, regardless of amenity level. In other settings, housing is priced separately and added to one of a number of service plans. Some settings use an approach with all-inclusive rates that vary according to whatever combination of type of housing and specific services are selected. Other settings set the price of housing according to size and amenity level and then charge for services as they are used, based on criteria such as episode of utilization, diagnosis, or minutes of service. While the availability of various pricing models is considered desirable, many consumers find it hard to understand the various models and harder still to budget for them.

These settings that combine housing and services typically have services available at any time, including nights, weekends, and holidays. Some staff members are always available on the premises, with a resulting capacity for unscheduled care. Some offer special services such as a secure setting, response to unscheduled care needs such as nighttime help with using the toilet, routine and skilled nursing services, therapies, respite, and end-of-life care. Those sites providing any kind of hands-on care directly are typically required to have some type of license in order to provide services and are inspected to review compliance with regulatory requirements. Such sites include congregate housing, adult foster-care settings, residential care homes, assisted living, and, of course, nursing facilities.

In the past decade, remarkable changes have occurred in these settings. Some of the changes are in the physical environment. Many in the boomer generation will live, for some portion of their lives, in new housing stock specifically built as senior housing ("purpose built"), much of which was created as a part of the senior housing building boom that occurred in the 1990s. These elders will benefit from significant improvements in the physical environment, including safety features, access for those with mobility problems, control over private living space, and common space to encourage community building. A more normal environment for those living in all specialized care settings, a hallmark of assisted living and taken up by some pioneers in the field, will no longer be novel concepts. People in the coming generation of elders will have more age-friendly housing of all types.

Finding ways to provide the care needed will continue to be a growing challenge. It is possible that some of the current issues, for example, those related to meeting cultural needs of clients, will have markedly improved in future years simply as our increasingly diverse culture evolves, but it is more likely that these crucial issues will remain central and will require significant amounts of resources and effort to address. Similarly, while the need to reward and respect those who care for others is beginning to gar-

ner some attention, it is not yet the focus of the major societal effort that is required. Initiatives for improved training and career development undoubtedly will help some in this regard, but the larger challenge lies in changing public perceptions of the work itself.

Moreover, while an influx of immigrant workers over the past twenty-five years has mitigated to some extent the impending crisis in finding adequate numbers of caregivers, the effects on the caregiver workforce of the turmoil currently surrounding immigration are not yet known. But, what is known is that in states like Florida and Texas, the use of nonlicensed facilities to provide care continues to grow unabated. This is particularly true for those who have inadequate resources to pay privately for care and who, in times of ever stringent eligibility criteria, do not qualify for financial assistance. While expanding the use of universal workers, nurse delegation, and client-employed providers will continue to provide some relief for growing worker shortages, these mitigating solutions may soon be swallowed by demands for ever greater skill levels. And for some areas, we are pinning our hopes on cheaper and better technology to help us in all settings.

We will need all the success we can get to make it through the next twenty-five years without declines in our ability to support well-being in later life. While we have seen the redistribution of where individuals needing supportive services live, the percentage of the population at any given time needing some sort of housing and services has not altered much in the past twenty-five years. If anything, as the result of increasing options for those with personal resources, those who live in designated housing-and-services settings are likely to need more services and to have fewer resources than ever before. We are, in fact, at a crossroads. Indeed, the United States faces a daunting task in meeting the housing and services needs of older adults over the next twenty-five years.

Much of the coming crisis is the result of a maladaptive system with a lack of viable options for financing long-term care. Some of this crisis is a result of the failure of policy to address issues of accessibility, affordability, and acceptability of existing housing options for older adults who have changing service needs. Simply put, we have increased expectations, both in terms of a sense of entitlement and of various types of standards that must be met. For a brief time, we managed to increase access for some who had inadequate personal resources by creative use of financing sources and by shifting shrinking dollars with clever initiatives such as waivers and reverse-annuity mortgages. In some cases we were able to introduce expanded notions that supported a broader view of quality. But we also ignored the cost of increasing expectations and failed to address the question of how, in the long run, they could be sustained.

For those whose resources are mainly in the value of a home and a pension, many are reduced to simply hoping that "nothing happens" that will require them to obtain any type of long-term care. This situation is a crisis waiting to happen—and the likelihood that it will happen is heightened by portfolio losses in the meltdown of the stock market in 2001-2002, collapsing pension plans, and the projected loss of living-wage jobs by older workers. Toss in talk of Social Security changes, increasing worries over healthcare coverage, growing needs of parents aged past "the golden years" and increasing numbers of adult children having difficulty successfully launching themselves economically, and you have a hint of what those heading into later life face. And with little time left to create a new game plan.

And yet it is precisely the current generation of boomers moving toward the outer ring of later life who expect the most and whose needs have always been addressed by government. Many hospitals, schools, loans for higher education, job training, federal insurance, mortgage programs, public health initiatives, and consumer protection programs arose in response to a cohort that reversed, at least tem-

porarily, declining birthrates in the United States. Many in this generation championed rights for everyone else and now believe they have "earned" the right to a comfortable retirement, which seemed likely in the economy of the eighties and nineties. That notion is now likely to be sorely tested. And those approaching traditional retirement age will need to make adjustments, as will those who work in the field of aging.

Now is no time for those who work in the field of aging to shrink from the larger challenges that lie ahead. Life can indeed be great after age 60, and it will be for many older people because of the many advances that have taken place in prevention and treatment of chronic disease and disability and in understanding about human development and modification of the life course to adjust to larger-scale social changes. But we still have our work cut out for us.

Thinking about how these changes will affect where older adults live, how they spend their time, and how needed care is provided is an area rich for exploration. And many of *Generations'* readers will be the ones doing that exploring.

2

Consumer-Preparedness for Long-Term Care

Source: Rogal, D.L. and R. Shiffrin. Undated. *Consumer-Preparedness for Long-Term Care.* Washington, DC and New York, NY: Academy Health/ The Commonwealth Fund.

INTRODUCTION

As Baby Boomers (those born between 1946 and 1964) age and medical advances result in more people living longer with chronic, often disabling, medical conditions, the need for long-term care services in America is growing. The U.S. Census Bureau predicts that the population over age 65 will double from 36 million in 2003 to 72 million in 2030, increasing from 12 percent to 20 percent of the population.[1] Eighty percent of seniors have at least one chronic health condition and 50 percent have at least two.[2] Chronic and disabling conditions often lead to declines in independent living and quality of life, imposing an economic burden on those requiring long-term care services.[3,4] Long-term care services are provided through a variety of care arrangements, including community-based paid or unpaid care, institutional care, self-care using assistive devices, or a combination of these. The majority of older adults with functional disabilities receive long-term care services in the community (71%), primarily from family and friends.[5]

Unfortunately, despite the population trends and the growing need for long-term care services, there is a significant discrepancy between consumer expectations and their actual long-term care needs. As a result, there is inadequate planning by many. To address this issue, the Commonwealth Fund and AcademyHealth brought together a panel of experts who have been thinking about the issues involved with long-term care planning to participate in the June 2007 colloquium on long-term care, *Building Bridges: Making a Difference in Long-Term Care.* Panelists included Lisa Alecxih, The Lewin Group, Brian Burwell, Thomson Healthcare, Robert Kane, M.D., University of Minnesota, and Brenda Spillman, Ph.D., Urban Institute. With the assistance of a facilitator, Len Fishman, Hebrew SeniorLife, the panelists shared their perspectives about issues of concern to policymakers and practitioners. Panelists addressed the current state of long-term care needs awareness and planning, barriers that dissuade individuals from adequate preparation (with the lack of practical financial planning options one of the greatest challenges), and possible strategies to encourage consumers to better prepare for their future long-term care needs.

CURRENT AWARENESS OF LONG-TERM CARE NEEDS

Setting the tone for the dialogue, Len Fishman reported that polling by the Long-Term Care Study Panel of the National Academy of Social Insurance found that 63 percent of respondents had personal experience with long-term care, most gained through a parent or spouse's parent, or a grandparent or spouse's grandparent. In addition, one-third indicated that they would rely on long-term care insurance, far more than actually have such insurance.[6] Fifty-three percent of respondents indicated that long-term care should be a high priority for the nation, with 34 percent indicating that it should be a very high priority.[7] More than 70 percent favored a larger role for the federal government in meeting the costs of long-term care.[8] Personal experience with long-term care was not necessary for concern about the issue.[9] Interestingly, the pollsters conclude that while many find increased policy focus on meeting individuals' long-term care needs important, "after listening to an extensive case for doing more to help people meet long-term care costs, the proportion that are concerned a great deal or fair amount . . . remains virtually unchanged from the outset of the survey." Fishman noted that this is an indicator of challenges ahead for public education about this issue.

MAKING THE CASE FOR LONG-TERM CARE PLANNING

The probability of needing assistance with activities of daily living[10] and instrumental activities of daily living[11] increases with age. As a result, an increasing proportion of elderly individuals require long-term care services. As noted above, the majority of those people receive services while continuing to live in the community, primarily through unpaid care from family and friends. Others in the community benefit from home and community based services, such as home health care, personal care, or adult day services. Still others receive care in institutional settings, including nursing homes, assisted living facilities, or other residential care facilities.[12]

Costs of long-term care services can be significant. As Alecxih notes, even when care is provided by family and friends there is a commitment of time and money for which they are often not prepared. For those relying on professional services in the community or in institutions, information from a Genworth Financial survey for 2007 shows that costs are substantial and vary widely. The average annual cost of nursing home care was $74,806, which varied from a low of $43,435 in Louisiana to a high of $196,735 in Alaska. Likewise average annual costs for assisted living were $32,573, ranging from $19,308 in Montana to $57,036 in Massachusetts. The average hourly rate for a home health aide from an agency was $25.47.[13] Someone turning 65 today can expect to need long-term care for three years prior to death.

However, the amount that a specific individual will need for long-term care services over the course of his or her life varies widely, with 26 percent needing more than $100,000 in paid assistance and 31 percent needing no long-term care services at all.[14]

There are a variety of sources of financial support for long-term care services. Medicaid is the largest source of financing (37%), followed by family resources (36%). While Medicare covers limited time in a skilled nursing facility following a hospitalization, it does not cover long-term care services. Long-term care insurance covers costs for some individuals (4%). Alecxih notes that even those with Medicaid coverage also incur out-of-pocket costs for long-term care. Those in nursing homes contribute the vast majority of their income to the facility, and some states also require cost-sharing under their Home and Community-Based Services waivers.[15]

PLANNING FOR LONG-TERM CARE IS INADEQUATE

Unfortunately, despite the likelihood of requiring long-term services and the significant costs of obtaining them, Alecxih concludes that few Americans plan ahead to meet these needs. Fewer than 10 percent of those over 65 years old own a long-term care insurance policy, and while older adults have a significant investment in home equity, few use it as a resource for obtaining long-term care services.

Agreeing with Alecxih that too few plan adequately, if at all, for their long-term care needs, Kane posited this was due to factors beyond poor financing options. He noted peoples' experience or exposure to long-term care is often negative. They associate the care with cognitive or physical declines in the person receiving services. In addition, they may have experienced services being provided in a negative, usually institutional, environment. In addition, people find confronting issues of long-term care forces them to face their own mortality, never an easy thing to do. Further, some individuals consider the prospect of needing long-term care services and being dependent on others worse than death. For these reasons, they avoid planning for their long-term care needs. Others, who are able to overcome the emotional barriers to adequate planning, may understand that long-term care is necessary but not find it worth the investment or they may believe all long-term care is the same, not understanding that there is variation in quality, as well in the location of service provision, which can make a difference.[16]

Burwell noted that poor planning for long-term care raises concern among policymakers and others that pressure on Medicaid and other publicly-financed systems may become overwhelming. As a result, there is increased interest in better understanding planning behavior among Americans, as well as motivators that would encourage better planning. Research and focus groups on long-term care planning have found variation in the propensity to plan for the future aligning with basic personality traits. To adequately plan for long-term care, one must accept the possibility of future functional decline and believe that one can exercise some control over future events. Failing this leads to denial or fatalism and ultimately to lack of future planning.[17]

Understanding that long-term care was perceived negatively, that there was denial about the possibility of the need for long-term care, and that dignity and control were major motivators for planning, the federal government launched the Long-Term Care Awareness Campaign *Own Your Future* in 2005. This national initiative[18] is designed to increase consumer awareness about planning for long-term care. Core activities include using the governor as a "trusted source" in state-based direct mail campaigns. Households with members between the ages of 45 and 70 are targeted and encouraged to consider long-term care needs in their overall retirement planning. They are provided with a planning guide that includes an audio CD with anecdotes about individuals' experiences with long-term care, as well as shopping tips for long-term care insurance. As of March 2007, 15 states had participated in the *Own Your Future* campaign.[19,20]

OPTIONS FOR BETTER LONG-TERM CARE FINANCIAL PLANNING

Recognizing the growing need for long-term care services, as well as consumers' lack of preparation for financing them, Brenda Spillman highlighted current options for long-term care financing, as well as barriers limiting their feasibility.[21] She noted that the policy concern over long-term care financing emanates from a fear of rising Medicaid costs on the part of states and the federal government, as well as the long time horizon and complexity that make personal planning difficult.

She stated that there are currently two primary approaches individuals can take to financial planning for long-term care: (1) pre-funded options, including long-term care insurance, hybrid products combining annuities or life insurance with long-term care benefits, accelerated death benefits as a life insurance option, and continuing care retirement communities; and (2) self-insurance and ad hoc solutions, including personal savings, life annuities, and reverse mortgages.

Each of these options has significant barriers. Long-term care insurance is relatively expensive, the cost rises with age, and affordable coverage may have benefits that provide insufficient protection. In addition, medical underwriting often precludes the purchase of long-term care insurance, either because the insurer excludes the individual or because risk-rated policies are too costly. While fewer younger individuals would be subject to medical underwriting exclusions, younger individuals typically have other spending and savings priorities. The difficulty in understanding the complex array of options for long-term care insurance may inhibit some individuals from purchasing it, since knowing whether the decision is the "right" one may not be obvious for twenty years after the purchase is made. The long-term care shopper's guide disseminated by the National Association of Insurance Commissioners suggests that buyers' have a high level of foreknowledge before purchasing a policy. For example, it mentions the importance of knowing whether your policy will cover new kinds of facilities that may be developed in the future and suggests one be aware of how much facilities and home health agencies will charge.[22]

Describing his elderly, financially independent (although not wealthy) mother's experience, Kane noted that when she was approached by a long-term care insurance salesperson, he advised her against purchasing the policy.[23] Citing its limited coverage (nursing home and formal home care) and the low statistical probability of her needing prolonged long-term care, he recommended that she invest her money instead. Five years later, Kane's mother had a stroke resulting in her spending 3.5 years in an assisted living facility with additional aides, followed by three months in a nursing home, prior to her death. The total cost of Kane's mother's care was $330,125. Four years of premiums for the long-term care insurance policy she was offered would have been $96,000 and Kane calculates that the policy would have covered only $90,500 of the costs incurred. Kane acknowledges that if she had purchased the policy at age 55, rather than at age 80, the premiums would have been significantly lower. However, it would have been impossible to estimate costs 25 years into the future, even with an inflation adjuster, and having invested the premiums for 30 years would have resulted in more funds available for long-term care services than purchasing the long-term care coverage.[24]

Kane concludes that if professionals working within the health care and long-term care systems are having serious problems getting desired care even when they can pay for it for themselves and their families, the system is failing. If the infrastructure is missing why would one save for such care? Noting that there is no advocacy group to support the needs of the elderly or those with chronic illness, Kane has taken the lead in forming the group Professionals with Personal Experience in Chronic Care (PPECC), whose mission is to draw upon the credentials of health care professionals as both recipients (directly or indirectly) and subject matter experts to promote the changes needed for aligning the medical system to better provide chronic illness care.[25]

Spillman notes that several policy approaches exist or have been proposed to address issues of long-term care financing, including incentives for increased private support and social insurance approaches.[26] Policy initiatives or proposals designed to provide incentives for private financing include:

Partnership for Long-Term Care: This initiative, originally limited to four states but available to more under the Deficit Reduction Act (DRA), allows purchasers to become Medicaid eligible when their private benefits (meeting program standards) have been exhausted, while retaining some or all of their remaining assets.

Tightening of Medicaid Eligibility: The DRA makes it more difficult to gain Medicaid eligibility through financial manipulations by lengthening the "look back" period for asset transfers. The DRA also requires disclosure of all annuities with the state named as remainder beneficiary to preclude the use of annuities to shelter assets.

Federalizing Medicaid Long-Term Care Benefits: Standardized federal Medicaid long-term care benefits would make it easier to understand what can be expected from Medicaid and might encourage offerings of private, portable long-term care insurance product innovations for those with modest means.

Tax Incentives: The Pension Protection Act of 2006 extended tax deductibility to include long-term care benefits offered as part of an annuity or life insurance contract. Policymakers have also discussed extending deductions to all taxpayers and using other tax-related vehicles, such as medical savings accounts or tax-free withdrawals from retirement accounts, for the purchase of long-term care insurance.

Social insurance options that have been discussed as tools for meeting the long-term care needs of Americans include:

- Linking a long-term care benefit to Social Security;

- Universal premium-funded federal social insurance with a cash benefit (automatic enrollment requiring enrollees to "opt out"); and

- The Community Living Assistance Services and Supports Act (CLASS Act) to establish a national long-term care benefit for workers and their dependents, introduced originally by Senator Edward Kennedy in 2005 and reintroduced in 2007.

WHAT DOES THE FUTURE HOLD?

As Baby Boomers age and the long-term care needs of society place increased stress on both private and public sources of funding, the challenges are great and their impact is widespread. There are no magic bullets to address the issues of long-term care provision or financing, but it is clear that as more individuals are affected it will become an increasingly important issue for society. Consumers need to continue to receive reliable information about available long-term care services, as well as alternative financing mechanisms. As Spillman concludes, the challenge for policymakers is deciding how important long-term care is and who will pay for it, while researchers continue to provide the evidence to support informed debate of the options.[27]

About the Authors
Deborah L. Rogal is a director at AcademyHealth and can be reached at 202.292.6700 or deborah.rogal@academyhealth.org. Rachel Shiffrin co-authored the brief while she was an intern with AcademyHealth.

● ● ● **References**

1. He, et al. *U.S. Census Bureau, Current Population Reports, P23-209, 65+ in the United States: 2005*, U.S. Government Printing Office, Washington, DC, 2005.

2. Centers for Disease Control, *Healthy Aging: Preventing Disease and Improving Quality of Life Among Older Americans 2003, At a Glance*, Department of Health and Human Services, 2003, as cited in He, et al. *U.S. Census Bureau, Current Population Reports, P23-209, 65+ in the United States: 2005*, U.S. Government Printing Office, Washington, DC, 2005.

3. Ibid.

4. National Center for Health Statistics, *Health, United States, 1999, with Health and Aging Chartbook*, Centers for Disease Control and Prevention/National Center for Health Statistics, Department of Health and Human Services, Publication No.99-1232, 1999 as cited in He, et al. *U.S. Census Bureau, Current Population Reports, P23-209, 65+ in the United*

States: 2005, U.S. Government Printing Office, Washington, DC, 2005.

5. The Lewin Group analysis of the 1999 National Long-Term Care Survey, 2002 Medicare Current Beneficiary Survey, and 2005 CMS Minimum Data Set as cited in *Why You Need to Plan for Potential Future Long-Term Support Needs* by Lisa Alecxih, prepared as background for *Building Bridges: Making a Difference in Long-Term Care:* 2007 Colloquium, Orlando, FL, June 2, 2007.

6. Peter D. Hart Research Associates, *Long-Term Care: The Public's View,* National Academy of Social Insurance, Health and Income Security Brief No. 8, November 2005.

7. Ibid.

8. Ibid.

9. National Academy of Social Insurance, *Developing a Better Long-Term Care Policy: A Vision and Strategy for America's Future,* Report of the Long-Term Care Study Panel, November 2005.

10. Activities of daily living are activities related to personal care and include bathing or showering, dressing, getting in or out of bed or a chair, using the toilet, and eating. http://www.cdc.gov/NCHS/datawh/nchsdefs/adl.htm.

11. Instrumental activities of daily living are activities related to independent living and include preparing meals, managing money, shopping for groceries or personal items, performing light or heavy housework, and using a telephone. http://www.cdc.gov/NCHS/datawh/nchsdefs/iadl.htm.

12. Alecxih, L., *Why You Need to Plan for Potential Future Long-Term Support Needs, background and slide presentation for Building Bridges: Making a Difference in Long-Term Care*: 2007 Colloquium, Orlando, FL, June 2, 2007.

13. The Genworth Financial 2007 Cost of Care Survey, http://longtermcare.genworth.com/overview/cost_of_care.jsp, as cited in Why *You Need to Plan for Potential Future Long-Term Support Needs* by Lisa Alecxih, prepared as background for *Building Bridges: Making a Difference in Long-Term Care*: 2007 Colloquium, Orlando, FL, June 2, 2007.

14. Kemper, P., H. Komisar, and L. Alecxih, *Long-Term Care Over an Uncertain Future: What Can Current Retirees Expect?, Inquiry,* Vol. 42, 2005.

15. Alecxih, L., *Why You Need to Plan for Potential Future Long-Term Support Needs,* background and slide presentation for *Building Bridges: Making a Difference in Long-Term Care:* 2007 Colloquium, Orlando, FL, June 2, 2007.

16. Kane, R. L., *A Consumer's View of Long-Term Care,* slide presentation at *Building Bridges: Making a Difference in Long-Term Care:* 2007 Colloquium, Orlando, FL, June 2, 2007.

17. Burwell, B., *Long-Term Care Planning Research: A Brief Overview,* background and slide presentation for *Building Bridges: Making a Difference in Long-Term Care:* 2007 Colloquium, Orlando, FL, June 2, 2007.

18. The Own Your Future Campaign is a collaboration of the Centers for Medicare & Medicaid Services (CMS), the Office of the Assistant Secretary for Planning & Evaluation (ASPE), and the Administration on Aging (AoA), and has support from the National Governors Association (NGA).

19. U.S. Department of Health and Human Services, National Clearinghouse for Long-Term Care Information, Own Your Future Campaigns, http://www.longtermcare.gov/LTC/Main_Site/Planning_LTC/Campaign/index.aspx.

20. Burwell, B., *Long-Term Care Planning Research: A Brief Overview,* background and slide presentation for *Building Bridges: Making a Difference in Long-Term Care:* 2007 Colloquium, Orlando, FL, June 2, 2007.

21. Spillman, B., *Consumer Preparedness for Long-Term Care: Personal Financing Options for Long-Term Care,* background and slide presentation for *Building Bridges: Making a Difference in Long-Term Care:* 2007 Colloquium, Orlando, FL, June 2, 2007.

22. National Association of Insurance Commissioners, Shopper's Guide to Long-Term Care, http://www.naic.org/index_ltc_section.htm.

23. Kane, R.L. and West, J., *It Shouldn't Be This Way,* Nashville, TN, 2005.

24. Kane, R. L., *A Consumer's View of Long-Term Care,* slide presentation at *Building Bridges: Making a Difference in Long-Term Care:* 2007 Colloquium, Orlando, FL, June 2, 2007.

25. Kane, R. L., *A Consumer's View of Long-Term Care,* slide presentation at *Building Bridges: Making a Difference in Long-Term Care:* 2007 Colloquium, Orlando, FL, June 2, 2007.

26. Spillman, B., *Consumer Preparedness for Long-Term care: Personal Financing Options for Long-Term Care,* background and slide presentation for *Building Bridges: Making a Difference in Long-Term Care:* 2007 Colloquium, Orlando, FL, June 2, 2007.

27. Spillman, B., *Consumer Preparedness for Long-Term care: Personal Financing Options for Long-Term Care,* background and slide presentation for *Building Bridges: Making a Difference in Long-Term Care:* 2007 Colloquium, Orlando, FL, June 2, 2007.

Long-Term Care: Understanding Medicaid's Role for the Elderly and Disabled

Source: "Long-Term Care: Understanding Medicaid's Role for the Elderly and Disabled—Executive Summary", The Henry J. Kaiser Family Foundation, November 2005. This information was reprinted with permission from the Henry J. Kaiser Family Foundation. The Kaiser Family Foundation is a non-profit private operating foundation, based in Menlo Park, California, dedicated to producing and communicating the best possible analysis and information on health issues.

EXECUTIVE SUMMARY

Medicaid today plays a critical role for people with long-term care needs. With expenditures of $86.3 billion in 2003, Medicaid is the single largest source of financing for long-term care, providing services to the elderly, working age adults and children with disabilities. Despite Medicaid's importance to people who need long-term care, Medicaid also has significant limitations. Medicaid's benefits are provided unevenly across the nation and stringent means-testing forces people who need care to impoverish themselves to receive assistance. This paper provides a review of how Medicaid works for people with long-term care needs and describes the fiscal challenges that states currently face and that Medicaid may face in the future as the population ages.

Key facts about Medicaid and long-term care include the following:

Medicaid is the Nation's Primary Source of Financing for Long-Term Care

- **Medicaid is the single largest source of financing for long-term care.** With payments of $86.3 billion in 2003, Medicaid accounted for nearly half (47.4 percent) of the nation's spending on long-term care services.

- **Medicaid is an important source of payment for both the elderly and the nonelderly with long-term care needs.** Estimates of long-term care spending for different age groups are hard to come by, but the Congressional Budget Office estimates that Medicaid paid for about a third of the long-term care spending on the elderly in 2004, including a third of all nursing home costs. The CBO also reports that Medicaid paid for a much larger share, an estimated 60 percent, of the long-term care spending of nonelderly persons with disabilities in 1998.

- **People who need long-term care services are diverse.** They include the elderly with physical and cognitive impairments, as well as children and nonelderly adults. People with disabilities in Medicaid include children and adults with mental retardation and developmental disabilities, the severely mentally ill, people with traumatic brain injuries and spinal cord injury, adults with debilitating illness such as Parkinson's disease and multiple sclerosis, people with AIDS, and children born with severe physical and cognitive impairments (mental retardation, cerebral palsy, multiple sclerosis, epilepsy, muscular dystrophy, hearing loss or deafness, and blindness, for example).

Medicaid Eligibility Is Limited

- **Medicaid is limited to poor and low-income people and those who become poor paying for care.** With limited exceptions, states must cover the elderly and people with disabilities who receive income support through the SSI program. However, states can extend benefits to higher income people who would otherwise qualify for SSI, and states can also expand eligibility through medically needy programs and special income rules for people residing in institutions. Most elderly and disabled people who qualify for Medicaid become eligible through a mandatory, welfare-related pathway. In 2001, 85 percent of disabled children in Medicaid were part of a mandatory eligibility group, as were roughly three quarters of disabled adults. The elderly are more likely to apply for Medicaid when they need nursing home care. Consequently, a somewhat larger share of the elderly qualifies through an optional category such as the special income rule.

Medicaid Provides a Wide Range of Long-Term Care Benefits

- **State Medicaid programs provide a wide range of long-term care services needed by people of all ages.** These include comprehensive long-term care services provided in institutions—nursing homes and intermediate care facilities for the mentally retarded—as well as a wide range of services and supports needed by people to live independently in the community—home health care, personal care, medical equipment, rehabilitative therapy, adult day care, case management, home modifications, transportation, and respite for caregivers. Through these varied long-term care benefits, states provide services to millions of people annually. In 2002, more than 1.8 million Medicaid beneficiaries received long-term care services while living in institutional facilities during the year, including nursing homes (1.7 million) and ICFs-MR (129,000), about 920,000 received care under HCBS waivers, 722,000 received home health care services, and 683,000 received services under Medicaid's optional personal care benefit.

- **Medicaid has long been accused of having an "institutional bias," but there has been substantial growth in Medicaid spending on community-based long-term care services over the past decade, and a significant shift in the distribution of Medicaid long-term care resources from institutional to home- and community-based services.** Between 1994 and 2004, spending on home and community-based services increased from $8.4 billion to $31.6 billion, rising from 19 percent to 36 percent of Medicaid long-term care spending. The shift was primarily due to the rapid growth in HCBS waiver spending which today accounts for nearly two-thirds of all Medicaid long-term care spending in the community.

Medicaid Spending on Long-Term Care Varies by State

- **States vary widely in the resources they devote to long-term care.** Medicaid spending on long-term care in 2004 ranged from a high of $833 per state resident in New York to just about $100 per resident in Utah and Nevada. Similarly, Medicaid spending per enrollee varies widely. Medicaid nursing home spending per elderly beneficiary varied from a high of nearly $15,000 in Connecticut to about $2,600 in California and Maine in 2001. Spending on home and personal care ranged from a high of $7,145 per disabled enrollee in Connecticut to less than $250 in the District of Columbia, Hawaii, and Mississippi in 2001.

- **Inequities in access to long-term care services have profound impacts on the health and well-being of the frail elderly and nonelderly people with disabilities.** Waiting lists for home and community-based services prevent financially eligible individuals from receiving services, leading to inappropriate institutionalization and unmet needs. One recent study of frail elderly applicants for a Medicaid HCBS waiver in Connecticut found that the elderly applicants who did not participate in the waiver program "appear to get by in the community" through a combination of informal care, use of Medicare home care, and going without needed services. Their ability to manage in the community, however, was limited. The elderly who applied for but did not receive waiver services were far more likely than those who received HCBS to enter a nursing home within six months following their assessment for waiver services.

Policymakers Are Seeking Strategies to Reduce Medicaid Spending Growth

- **Long-term care spending has grown slowly in recent years, but remains a target for efforts to close state and federal budget gaps.** Spending on long-term care ($91 billion in 2003) accounts for about a third of all Medicaid spending nationally. Spending on nursing home care represents the single largest category of Medicaid spending (about 17 percent), surpassing spending on inpatient hospital care and payments to managed care plans. In theory, states have significant flexibility to reduce spending on long-term care services in Medicaid. Unlike acute care, where the majority of Medicaid spending is for mandatory services for mandatory groups, the vast majority of all Medicaid spending for long-term care (85 percent) is "optional"— payments for optional services or enrollees. Although states have sought to reduce payments to providers, limit optional benefits and reduce eligibility for the elderly and people with disabilities, long-term care has not been the primary target of cost containment efforts. Long-term care for the elderly may be targeted for reductions in the current federal budget debate which seeks $10 billion in Medicaid savings to help address the growing federal budget deficit.

- **Medicaid is at the center of discussions about how to address future long-term care challenges, but opinions differ sharply about what Medicaid's role should be.** Continuing increases in health care costs, population aging, and growing demands for longterm care are expected to contribute to growing, and, some argue, "unsustainable" public spending burdens. An older but more affluent nation will be able to afford to spend some share of increased national income to maintain and expand Medicaid's (and Medicare's) benefits for people who need long-term care. However, current policy debates focus on slowing the growth of entitlement spending rather than on improving long-term care protections.

- **If Medicaid is to remain the nation's long-term care safety net, pressing financing, service delivery, and quality challenges will need to be addressed.** Because the future growth in demand for Medicaid services is likely to be unevenly distributed across states, long-term care financing may pose a serious challenge to the current federal-state structure in Medicaid. A number of program and policy initiatives implemented over the past decade seek to enhance the cost-effective delivery of long-term care services and improve the quality and satisfaction with services. These include efforts to reform Medicaid long-term care by "rebalancing" long-term care services, implementing consumer-directed service delivery models, and "integrating" acute and long-term care services in Medicare and Medicaid. Improving service delivery models especially for the community-dwelling elderly, for whom options are lacking in many states, will remain a priority. However, savings from more cost effective approaches may not be sufficient to offset the gap in states' abilities to finance future long-term care needs. Another option would be to federalize home and community-based services by expanding the federal financing to cover 100 percent of all community-based long-term care. This policy would go a long way toward relieving burdens on states, improving equity, and addressing unmet needs for care. Another option would be to expand Medicare's role in long-term care. Medicare already provides universal health coverage to the elderly and has large expenditures for skilled nursing and home health care.

Medicaid's long-term care services are a critical source of support for millions of poor and low income people. The long-term care system we have today is primarily financed by Medicaid, and without significant policy changes, Medicaid is likely to be the major source of long-term care coverage in the future. In the absence of a universal, social insurance program for long-term care, expanded private insurance and savings will not be adequate to address all long-term care risks and needs for all people. The low- and modest-income elderly will remain at risk of impoverishment due to long-term care needs, and private insurance will not likely address the needs of either nonelderly persons with disabilities or the low- and modest-income elderly. Medicaid will likely remain the nation's safety net for the poor and the middle class with long-term care needs, but Medicaid has important gaps and inequities that should be addressed to assure that elderly and nonelderly people with disabilities have access to the long-term care services that are needed to assure their health and well-being.

Changes in the Quality of Nursing Homes in the U.S.: A Review and Data Update

Source: Mor, V., C. Caswell, S. Littlehale, et al. 2009. *Changes in the quality of nursing homes in the U.S.: A review and data update.* 2009 Annual Quality Report: American Health Care Association/The Alliance for Quality Nursing Home Care. Used with the permission of the American Health Care Association and The Alliance for Quality Nursing Home Care.

This report summarizes the literature and presents syntheses of data from over the last half decade on changes in nursing home quality as measured by staffing, process and outcome quality as well as the results of regulators' inspections. Since these changes in quality occurred within the context of substantial changes in the role of U.S. nursing homes, changes that resulted in large increases in the acuity and complexity of those being served, we also summarize changes in case-mix acuity and in the "segmentation" of the nursing home market as facilities increasingly specialized in caring for different groups of residents. In reviewing the literature, we've focused on the manner in which policies ranging from state Medicaid reimbursement to federal public reporting efforts have influenced nursing home quality since provider efforts to improve quality have not occurred in a vacuum. The report closes with recommendations made in the light of the changing role and composition of U.S. nursing homes and the need for measures of quality that more precisely reflect the different reasons people use nursing homes and in light of impending policy changes.

We examined structural, process and outcome measures of quality. Literature and data summaries indicate that nurse staffing has increased, although this has been primarily at the low skill level. Indeed, using existing data we observe both an increase in the proportion of homes achieving high levels of nurse staffing as well as an increase in the proportion falling below minimum levels. At the same time, most existing staffing measures ignore the fastest growing segment of facility staff-therapists who are concentrated in high Medicare facilities. Process quality measures like the use of physical restraints continued to improve with increases in both the number of "restraint"-free homes and the number with high proportions of residents restrained. While use of psychotropic drugs seems to have increased, most of this is attributable to ongoing increases in anti-depressant use; growth in anti-psychotic use has leveled off. Most of the CMS-reported outcome measures, particularly for the long stay population, have improved over time from ADL decline to facility acquired pressure ulcers. In contrast, incontinence among long stay residents has worsened in spite of the fact that there is evidence that toileting programs can be effective. The results of state regulators' inspections of nursing homes are not consistent with the measured outcomes; both the number and severity of deficiencies levied against nursing homes tended to increase. However, there is so much inter and intra-state variation in how the survey guidelines are apparently applied, it is difficult to understand precisely what those mean. Finally, while there is no agreement as to what the appropriate rate of hospitalization is, the outcomes of re-hospitalization of post-acute Medicare patients and hospitalization of long stay residents increased substantially, becoming a major policy concern.

These improvements in process and outcome quality were observed in spite of substantial evidence of increasing case-mix acuity and specialization amongst U.S. nursing homes. The clinical complexity and functional impairment of both admitted and long stay residents has increased virtually across the board and since 2002 there was almost a doubling of the proportion of free-standing facilities serving more than 20% of Medicare patients on any given day, a phenomenon that more than offset losses in the number of hospital based facilities. Other more challenging forms of segmentation are also underway, with some facilities increasingly "specializing" in psychiatric patients and the concentration of Medicaid patients in selected facilities.

Nursing home policies that affect quality have achieved their intended effect, although not as completely as many would desire. Medicaid case mix reimbursement has improved access to many very sick patients residents and rising Medicaid payment rates appear to be associated with greater improvements in quality and lower rates of hospitalization. Public reporting of nursing homes' quality performance has clearly stimulated many providers to institute quality improvement efforts which appear to have resulted in greater improvements in both measured and some unmeasured quality scores but there is also evidence suggesting that public reporting has begun to "steer" those seeking nursing home care to better-performing facilities, at least in the post-acute care arena.

Many challenges remain. The mixed picture of findings is at least partly related to the fact that our measures of the structure, process and outcomes of quality nursing home care continue to be very crude, uncorrelated and, therefore, seem to confuse both providers and consumers. Regulators' inspection results don't seem to resolve the confusion amongst the other measures and indeed, appear to be responsive to political influences at both the local and the national levels. Clearly we need better measures if we are to understand how we are making improvements and where else there are gaps to be filled. Even more importantly, if we are to respond to the growing specialization of nursing home care in the United States, we must develop measures that are appropriate to the different populations of people using nursing homes for different purposes. All of this important measure development work to guide quality improvement efforts will have to be made while the industry, regulators, policy makers and researchers are struggling with the scheduled introduction of MDS 3.0 with its new emphasis on hearing the voice of the resident so that clinical care planning can be even more individualized.

I. INTRODUCTION AND PURPOSE

In an effort to review how nursing home quality has changed over the last decade and to place those changes within the context of broader changes in how nursing home care is rendered in the United States, this paper reviews the literature on nursing home quality, identifies the policies and other trends that have influenced nursing home quality over the past decade and presents data documenting recent progress in quality. Since the role nursing homes play in providing post-acute care has expanded greatly and nursing homes appear to be increasingly "specializing" in serving certain types of residents and providing certain types of services, we characterize quality performance by these emerging specialized nursing home categories. While there are numerous types of measures of nursing home quality, this paper draws upon the published literature and presents new data based only upon publicly available information; staffing, nationally reported quality measures and selected summary deficiency information from regulatory inspections. Other measures capturing residents' and families' satisfaction with their experience are not included here. Finally, the paper concludes with a series of recommendations regarding future directions and challenges for better understanding how to improve nursing home quality of care.

II. BACKGROUND OF POLICY CHANGES IN THE NURSING HOME ARENA SINCE OBRA '87

Concerns about inadequate quality provided to nursing home residents have been discussed in the lay media and the professional literature for decades (U.S. Senate 1974). In 1986, the Institute of Medicine (IOM) published its landmark report that called for major revisions in the way nursing home quality is monitored (Vladeck 1982; (IOM) 1986). It recommended the continuation of the existing system that periodically monitors quality through a survey process with deficiency citations but called for more emphasis on quality of life as well as quality of care and encouraged the use of outcome indicators to assess quality. Implementation of many of the IOM recommendations began in 1987 with the passage of the Nursing Home Reform Amendment to the Omnibus Budget Reconciliation Act (OBRA). This mandated a new system of standards of care, including increased minimum staffing regulations, and quality of care monitoring (Harrington & Carrillo, 1999). These efforts culminated in the 1991 nationwide implementation of the Resident Assessment Instrument (RAI) system, which is the corner stone of the CMS (Centers for Medicare & Medicaid Services) Health Care Quality Improvement Program (HCQIP) for nursing homes. The RAI was designed to improve quality by requiring nursing homes to develop individual care plans, protocols for follow-up care and algorithms to "trigger" residents' potential care needs. The Minimum Data Set (MDS), a component of the RAI, is used to collect information about patients' physical and mental health status as well as specific treatments at regular time intervals. In addition to structuring resident care planning, the MDS made it possible to compare health outcomes of nursing home residents across facilities and to compare trends over time using more detailed resident level data rather than relying upon the cruder facility level reports.

Despite documented improvements in various aspects of nursing home quality following passage of OBRA, including reductions in the use of physical restraints (Phillips, Hawes et al. 1996; Castle, Fogel et al. 1997; Hawes, Mor et al. 1997; Mor 2002), psychotropic drug use (Rovner, 1992; Shorr, 1994), catheter use (Hawes, Mor et al. 1997; Harrington, Swan et al. 1999) and pressure ulcers (Fries, Hawes et al. 1997), opportunities for improvement remained (IOM 2001). The literature from that period documented quality problems ranging from malnutrition, (Abbasi & Rudman, 1994; Crogan, Shultz, Adams, & Massey, 2001) and dehydration, (Kayser-Jones, Schell, Porter, Barbaccia, & Shaw, 1999) to medication errors (Gurwitz, Field, Avorn, et al. 2000) and pain (Teno, Weitzen et al. 2001). These mixed findings related to nursing home quality have been attributed to many different phenomenon including small samples drawn from different parts of the country, poor and inconsistent measurement and inadequate controls for the variation in resident acuity.

One factor underlying the inconsistent findings regarding changes in nursing home quality over the last several decades has been the growing heterogeneity of U.S. nursing homes. First, due to federal and state policy changes in reimbursement as well as the emergence of community-based services, particularly the rise of assisted living, the acuity of the nursing home resident population has increased dramatically and the length of stay of most patients is now less than 90 days (Decker 2005; Feng, Grabowski et al. 2006; Mor, Zinn et al. 2007). Secondly, there is considerable heterogeneity among facilities with respect to the mix of residents they serve, for example how many are short-stay, post-acute, Medicare patients, and even their location in poor communities appears to have a significant impact on staffing, deficiencies and the outcomes residents experience (Grabowski and Castle 2004; Mor, Zinn et al. 2004; Smith, Feng et al. 2007; Zinn, Mor et al. 2009). Regional variation in medical practice as well as the availability of alternative long-term care resources also appears to affect who enters nursing homes and their likelihood of hospitalization (Baicker, Chandra et al. 2004; Mor, Zinn et al. 2007; Teno, Feng et al. 2008). Finally, states' policies, ranging from Medicaid payment rates to Medicaid reimbursement models and rules clearly affect the composition of patients served, the services facilities offer and the rate of outcomes like hospitalization and selected indicators of care quality (Grabowski, Angelelli et al. 2004; Intrator and Mor 2004; Intrator, Feng et al. 2005; Feng, Grabowski et al. 2006; Gruneir, Mor et al. 2007). Throughout this report, we emphasize that findings regarding changes in the quality of care of U.S. nursing homes must be considered in light of both the changing heterogeneity of facilities as well as changes in the overall composition of the nursing home population. Furthermore, these changes have occurred relatively quickly, making it all the more important to consider these influential factors.

III. CHANGING ROLES OF NURSING HOMES IN THE LAST DECADES

Since the introduction of Medicare's hospital prospective payment policy in the early 1980s, nursing homes in the United States have increasingly served as a "release valve" for hospitals, permitting more rapid discharge into a setting where patients could recuperate in controlled circumstances. Initially this phenomenon was largely restricted to hospital based skilled nursing facilities, but by the early

1990s, free-standing facilities began investing in the staff expertise allowing them to specialize in post-acute care. At around the same time, assisted living facilities began to emerge throughout the country, providing an alternative residential care setting to nursing homes. Finally, as a new generation of elderly persons began requiring long-term care, their preferences for home care were increasingly met by states' investments in home and community based services. In the following paragraphs, we briefly summarize each of these developments and their implications for assessing improvements in the quality of nursing home care.

a. Increasing Case Mix Acuity

Numerous studies have documented the increasing acuity of nursing home residents over the last several decades (Davis, Freeman et al. 1998; IOM 2001; Grabowski 2002; Decker 2005; Feng, Grabowski et al. 2006). The Institute of Medicine 2001 report examining long-term care quality summarized changes in the mix of individuals using nursing homes as part of a comprehensive effort to understand whether quality had improved since the passage of OBRA 1987. Decker and colleagues, using data collected from the National Nursing Home surveys between 1977 and 1999, found that the number of discharges per bed rose from 86 per 100 to 134 per 100, (a 56% increase) between 1985 and 1999 (Decker 2005). In addition to the rising number of admissions, the composition of those residents changed to an older population more dependent in activities of daily living, with the proportion of residents able to walk independently declining from nearly 40% to under 20%. Using OSCAR data from the 1990s, Grabowski examined changes in resident acuity attributable to different state policies, and found that "management minutes", a measure of resident dependence translated into estimated care time, increased significantly during the same period and even more so in states with case mix reimbursement (Grabowski 2002). Feng and colleagues extended these analyses both in time and by examining changes in the acuity of residents as well as of all admissions to nursing homes between 1996 and 2002. They observed a strong secular trend in the rising rate of acuity for both admissions and residents, averaging nearly a 1% per year increase in case mix acuity (using the RUGS nursing case mix index) among admissions and somewhat less than that for residents (Feng, Grabowski et al. 2006).

The importance of taking increasing case mix into consideration is that case mix affects virtually all of our measures of quality, both those based upon person level measures like the MDS quality measures, and also many of the deficiencies levied by inspectors since these are predicated upon the likelihood that residents will experience a clinical problem, clearly a more likely outcome for the sicker residents.

b. Changing Composition of Facilities

Not only has the overall acuity of nursing home residents been increasing, there has been an increasing concentration of different types of residents in certain facilities. That is, in most markets some facilities have ended up caring for a disproportionate share of certain types of residents, be they post-acute Medicare reimbursed residents or those with dementing disorders or psychiatric histories. There is considerable evidence that specialization in Medicare post-acute care patients has emerged as a result of a strategic focus. Zinn and colleagues found that following the introduction of the Balanced Budget Act (BBA) and the introduction of Medicare case mix reimbursement, there was a tremendous change in the industry resulting in the closure of many hospital based facilities and the bankruptcy of a number of nursing home systems (Zinn, Mor et al. 2003; Stevenson and Grabowski 2008; Zinn, Feng et al. 2008). Evidence suggests that those facilities able to anticipate and respond to policy changes and/or who adopted service innovations earlier than their local competition performed better viz. occupancy rate and payer mix (Zinn, Mor et al. 2009). The net result has been a growing segmentation of the market, with an increasing share of all post-acute patients served in a minority of facilities specializing in that type of care. In contrast, "lower tier" facilities in all markets end up with high concentrations of Medicaid patients or patients with long-term psychiatric histories or minority patients. These facilities are much more likely to fail and to have chronic quality problems (Mor, Zinn et al. 2004; Smith, Feng et al. 2007; Zinn, Mor et al. 2009).

The substantial differences among these types of nursing facilities make it very difficult to compare their quality performance. Current quality measures are only minimally risk-adjusted and even were there to be more complete risk adjustment (a significant challenge both technically and conceptually), the fact that the different types of facilities select their residents from very different patient populations means that there are likely to be many unmeasured confounders that undermine the validity of many comparisons (Mor, Berg et al. 2003).

c. The Effect of State and Federal Policies on Quality

As noted, over the past decade there have been a number of policy changes associated with changes in the acuity of those using nursing homes. However, these policies have also had an impact on the level and type of staffing as well as on selected indicators of quality.

The policy that has been most extensively studied is the introduction of case-mix reimbursement, either at the federal or state level. Feng and his colleagues definitively demonstrated that the introduction of state-based (as well as federal) case mix reimbursement was associated with a 1% (for long-stay residents) or 2% (for admissions) increase in RUGS-based nursing case mix index over the period from 1996 to 2002 (Feng, Grabowski et al. 2006). Since that time, additional states have adopted this form of Medicaid reimbursement and the evidence continues to support an immediate and sustained increase in acuity (Miller, Mor et al. 2009). One fear often voiced by opponents of case mix reimbursement is that patients will be treated so as to maximize reimbursement levels, through the use of feeding tubes or even intravenous therapy. Rapid increases in the proportion of nursing home residents with feeding tubes during the 1990s appeared to confirm this "common wisdom" (Teno, Mor et al. 2002). However, careful analysis of the impact of the introduction of state-based case mix reimbursement clearly revealed that there was no policy effect after controlling for general secular trends present in all states, but which apparently began to slow around 2002 (Teno, Feng et al. 2008). Indeed, recent research clearly reveals that most feeding tubes are inserted during hospitalizations and that regional variation in medical practice is highly correlated with this phenomenon which is most prevalent (and of questionable benefit) among severely demented nursing home residents (Teno, Mitchell et al. 2009).

On the other hand, staffing levels have not been so positively affected by case mix reimbursement. Konetzka and colleagues found that the introduction of Medicare case mix reimbursement under BBA was associated with significant reductions in professional staffing (Konetzka, Yi et al. 2004), while Feng reported that the level of professional staffing dropped with the introduction of state-based case mix reimbursement, accompanied by large increases in lower skilled aides (Feng, Grabowski et al. 2008). Closer analyses of these data by Zinn and colleagues suggest that some of this drop in professional direct care staffing may have occurred by the hiring of additional administrative staff, presumably needed to document patients' clinical needs and care processes under most case mix reimbursement schemes, or by switching how nursing staff are classified (Zinn, Feng et al. 2008). Still not accounted for in the examination of the impact of case mix reimbursement on direct care staffing levels is the widespread use of therapy staff needed to meet the needs of the increasing number of post-acute Skilled Nursing Facility (SNF) residents. Because most research to date hasn't included these individuals in the calculation of direct care staff, it is difficult to fully appreciate the impact of case mix reimbursement since this critical staffing resource has remained uncounted.

There is a long history of research on the impact that Medicaid payment rates have on quality. The health economics literature on nursing home quality of care in the 1980s and 1990s was largely based on Scanlon's model in which nursing homes face two markets (Scanlon 1980); one for private residents with downward-sloping demand, and the other for Medicaid residents who are insensitive to price. The existence of supply constraints in the form of Certificate of Need (CON) were consistent with the economists' perception that excess demand blunts any impact of payment increases on quality (Grabowski 2001). Some empirical research, largely based upon cross-sectional data from the 1980s were consistent with this theoretical perspective (Nyman 1988; Gertler 1989).

Perhaps because of the recent decline in nursing home occupancy rates, repeal of CON laws in certain states, and the emergence of improved data and methods, results from more recent studies, generally relying upon longitudinal data and more detailed outcome measurements, have by and large found a modest positive relationship between state Medicaid payment rates and nursing home quality. Higher payment rates have been found to be associated with fewer pressure ulcers (Grabowski and Angelelli 2004), more staffing (Cohen and Spector 1996; Grabowski 2001), fewer hospitalizations (Intrator and Mor 2004; Intrator, Grabowski et al. 2007), fewer physical restraints and feeding tubes (Grabowski 2004; Grabowski, Angelelli et al. 2004), and fewer government-cited deficiencies (Grabowski 2004). In terms of the size of the effect, these studies typically indicate a payment-quality elasticity in the range 0.1 to 0.7 (i.e., a 10% increase in payment improves quality by 1%-7%), depending upon the quality measure. For example, a 10% increase in Medicaid payment reduced pressure ulcers by roughly 2% (Grabowski 2004; Grabowski and Angelelli 2004). Importantly, across all recent studies, there is virtually no support for a negative relationship between the Medicaid payment level and quality.

d. Impact of Public Reporting on Quality

Public reporting of nursing home quality has been in place since 2002 with the advent of the CMS "Nursing Home Compare" website (Harris and Clauser 2002). In actuality, data on facilities' staffing levels and inspection results had been publicly reported for some time prior to 2002, and this information was supposed to have been prominently displayed and available to any consumer on all Medicare/Medicaid certified facilities for decades before MDS based clinical quality measures were publicly reported on the CMS website. Public reporting may have an effect on quality because consumers (or their advocates) use the information to select facilities that appear superior viz. quality performance and/or by inducing providers to institute quality improvement efforts to compensate for poor performance reports. While early research on the topic suggested that consumers weren't using the sites, or at least providers didn't believe they were, more recent research suggests that the publication of quality measures on Nursing Home Compare is associated with independent improvements in outcomes, both reported as well as unreported (Mor 2005; Mukamel, Weimer et al. 2008; Zinn, Spector et al. 2008; Werner, Konetzka et al. 2009a; Werner, Konetzka et al. 2009b).

More recently, Werner and her colleagues examined the effect of public reporting of post-acute measures on the patterns of admissions to skilled nursing facilities. They found significant reduction in pain, improvements in walking and in delirium associated with both nursing home specific improvements as well as changes in the market share of post-acute admissions entering higher quality facilities. Depending upon the post-acute measure, they estimate that as much as half of the improvement observed across all three quality measures is attributable to patients' selecting higher-quality facilities and the rest was associated with facility specific improvements (Werner and Konetzka 2009).

IV. EXAMINING CHANGES IN NURSING HOME QUALITY

The literature cited above, particularly that covering the period of the last decade strongly suggests a general pattern of improvement in quality, partly associated with increases in Medicaid payment rates but also associated with public reporting. In the section below, we present data on changes in staffing, in various MDS-based quality measures and deficiencies emanating from the federal inspection process. In some instances the data are presented separately from the earlier to the later part of the current decade and although we find that the trends are not always consistent, these data directly reflect the three different ways to think about quality structure (staffing); processes (deficiencies and selected aggregated MDS measures), and outcomes (measures like ADL decline or pain).

a. Staffing Changes

Staffing levels are often thought of as the sine quo non of nursing home quality since without adequate staff it is not possible to care for the frail population (Harrington, Kovner et al. 2000; Schnelle, Bates-Jensen et al. 2004). In keeping with the substantial heterogeneity of case mix acuity across U.S. nursing homes, there is great heterogeneity in the level of staffing, in spite of the existence of state specific mandated staffing levels (Feng, Grabowski et al. 2008). While there have been numerous complaints about the inadequacy of the OSCAR staffing data since they are self-reported by administrators around the time of their certification inspection, these data are the only consistent national source of information regarding staffing levels and composition. Feng and colleagues documented changes in direct care staffing levels between 1996 and 2004 in terms of the proportion of facilities that met selected minimum and recommended staffing levels and recently updated these data (see Figure 1). They found increases in total direct care staffing as an increasingly high proportion of facilities achieved the benchmark of 3.0 or more FTEs per resident (Feng, Grabowski et al. 2008). In more recent years, there appears to have been a simultaneous increase in number of highly staffed and poorly staffed facilities, presumably reflecting continuing specialization in certain types of residents.

Figure 2 presents summary data on the number of hours of staff time per resident day by type of staff person from the period 2005 through 2009, looking at all facilities whose most recent inspection occurred in Quarter 1 of each of those years. As is evident, when all facilities are averaged, we see growth in the number of aides per resident day, the number of licensed practical nurses per day and stability in the number of RNs per resident day. As noted above, missing in these figures were therapy staff, particularly important for facilities concentrating in

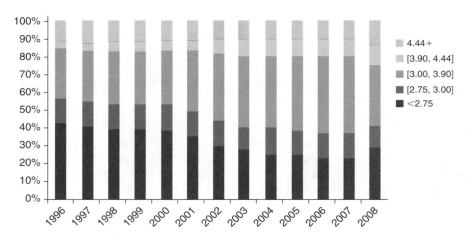

Figure 1 Total Direct Care Staff (RN+LPN+CNA) HPRD, 1996-2008

postacute care; nor were "administrative" nurses, a group that has grown substantially in the last decade, included in the figures summarized here.

b. Quality Measures

i. Process Indicators

As noted above, the literature is consistent in documenting reduced rates of physical restraints since OBRA '87. Using MDS data from all certified U.S. nursing homes aggregated to the level of the facility, Brown investigators documented the continuing rate of decline in restraint use between 1999 and 2005. Figure 3 presents the "box and whisker plots" of these data by quarter, indicating the median facility restraint rate as well as the 10th and 90th percentile. Of note is that both the median and the 90th percentile have been dropping over the same time period.

More recent national data (2005-09) from the OSCAR which is based upon annual inspections is presented below in Table 1 standardized by the quarter in which the inspection occurred. As can be seen, the downward trend in the proportion of residents restrained has continued to the point that by the first quarter of 2009, in the average U.S. nursing home, only 3.5% of residents were restrained. While there was a slight increase in the proportion of residents receiving any psychoactive drugs, this was largely attributable to an increase in the proportion of residents taking antidepressants and anti-anxiety agents so that the proportion of residents taking antipsychotics dropped from 26.1% to 24.6% between 2005 and 2009. Other process quality measures have also improved substantially over the last five years including improvements in immunization rates for both influenza and pneumonia. Small improvements were also noted

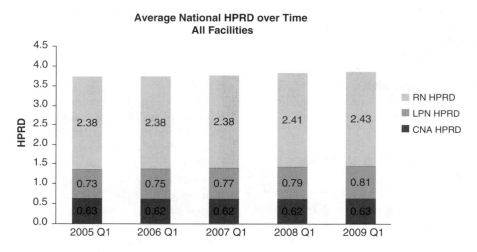

Figure 2 Trends in Nursing Home Staffing

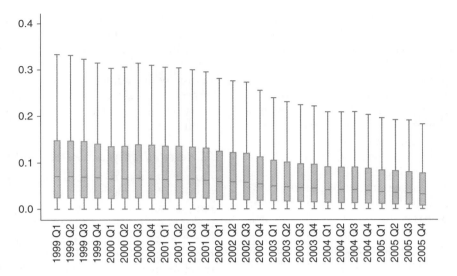

Figure 3 Restraints

for process measures such as providing pain management programs for residents in pain or providing bladder training programs for those who are incontinent.

ii. Outcome Indicators

The availability of the MDS provides numerous opportunities to measure changes in patients' condition which, if properly constructed, risk adjusted, and averaged, while accounting for patient selection, can provide insight into the variation in the outcomes of care that short-stay and long-stay residents experience due to differences in the providers caring for them. Most existing measures in common use fall short of the ideal either because of inadequate risk adjustment,

	Table 1	Process Measures and Outcomes					
↑	Statistically Significant Improvement						
↓	Statistically Significant Decline						
—	No Significant Change	Process Measures and Outcomes	2005 Q1	2006 Q1	2007 Q1	2008 Q1	2009 Q1
↑		Percent of Residents with Facility-Acquired Pressure Ulcers	3.5%	3.3%	3.2%	3.1%	3.1%
↑		Percent of Residents with Facility-Acquired Restraints	5.7%	5.3%	4.8%	4.2%	3.5%
↑		Percent of Residents with Facility-Acquired Catheters	1.9%	1.8%	1.8%	1.7%	1.7%
↑		Percent of Residents with Pneumonia Immunization	32.2%	39.1%	53.0%	58.9%	61.8%
↑		Percent of Residents with Influenza Immunization	60.5%	64.0%	68.5%	70.4%	70.7%
—		Percent of Residents with Advanced Directives	62.2%	62.5%	62.5%	62.6%	62.3%
↑		Percent of Residents with Pain Management	24.6%	25.5%	26.6%	27.0%	27.6%
↑		Percent of Residents with Bladder Training	5.7%	6.0%	6.6%	6.7%	6.4%
↑		Percent of Residents Receiving any Psychoactive Medications	63.4%	64.1%	65.1%	65.4%	65.4%
↑		Percent of Residents Receiving any Antipsychotic Medications	26.1%	25.8%	25.5%	25.0%	24.6%
↓		Percent of Residents Receiving Anti-anxiety Medications	17.3%	17.9%	18.6%	19.3%	20.1%
*		Percent of ResidentsReceiving Antidepressant Medications	45.0%	46.0%	47.0%	48.0%	48.2%

selection or sample size (Wu, Miller et al. 2005; Mor 2007). Nonetheless, as long as one doesn't attempt to explicitly compare the performance of facilities, it is very useful to track MDS-based outcome measures over time to get a sense of the trends in the industry altogether. Using a risk adjusted measure of ADL decline among long-stay residents, Brown investigators examined changes in the rates of ADL change across all non-hospital based facilities in the country having a minimum of 30 observations per quarter.

As can be seen in Figure 4, the likelihood that long-stay residents decline at least 4 points on the MDS-based ADL scale dropped between 1999 and 2005. These declines might appear small, but it is clear that both the median and the 90th percentile homes are experiencing lower rates of ADL decline. Using the CMS publicly reported measure of ADL decline among the long-stay residents, we find that between 2005 and 2008 the pattern of improvements in ADL decline continued with the average facility reducing the rate of decline by about one half of a percentage point. Consistent with the ADL decline measure, as can be seen in Table 2, worsening mobility declined as well over the last five years, suggesting a more generalized improvement in nursing facilities' ability to maintain their residents' functional status.

Again, as can be seen in Table 2, even larger declines are observed for pain, a finding consistent with Brown investigators' for the period 1999-2004, using a measure based upon more extensive case mix adjustment and which appeared responsive to public reporting in a recently published paper (Werner, Konetzka et al. 2009a). Table 2 also reveals almost

a 2 percentage point reduction in the prevalence of pressure ulcers among high-risk nursing home residents between 2004 and 2005. Since even the measures Brown investigators have been using are not optimally risk adjusted, these reductions must be interpreted in light of the substantial year to year increase in case mix acuity in the resident nursing home population.

iii. Hospitalization and Re-Hospitalization

Hospitalization of those in nursing homes is another marker of nursing home care quality that is increasingly being examined due to the high cost as well as the implications for continuity of care. High rates of hospitalization and re-hospitalization from SNFs have been documented, calling into question the practice of rapidly discharging Medicare patients from the hospital to be cared for in nursing homes (Coleman, Min et al. 2004; Ma, Coleman et al. 2004; Gruneir, Miller et al. 2008). Researchers at Brown, PointRight, and elsewhere have been studying the determinants of hospitalization of long-stay residents and the re-hospitalization of those admitted to SNF for short stays (Mor, Intrator et al. 1997; Intrator, Castle et al. 1999; Miller, Gozalo et al. 2001; Gruneir, Miller et al. 2007). As many have noted, a significant, but imprecise, number of these hospitalizations are avoidable. First, a failure of advanced care planning, either in the hospital or in the SNF, often leads to hospitalizations that are of no benefit to patients who are terminal (Teno, Mitchell et al. 2009). Secondly, inadequate communication and transfer of clinically important information between the discharging hospital and the receiving nursing

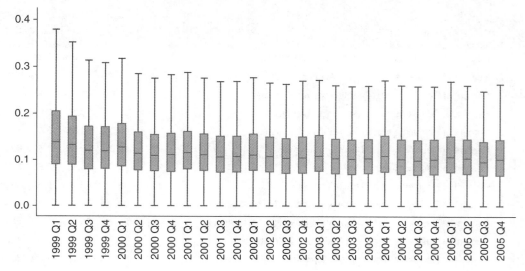

Figure 4 ADL Decline

| Table 2 | National Trends – CMS Quality Measures | | | | | |

	Quality Measures	2004	2005	2006	2007	2008
↑ Statistically Significant Improvement						
↓ Statistically Significant Decline						
— No Significant Change						
↑	ADL Decline	15.7%	15.8%	15.9%	15.3%	15.2%
↑	Pain in Long-Stay Residents	6.3%	6.2%	5.1%	4.4%	4.0%
↑	Pressure Ulcers in High-Risk Residents	13.7%	13.4%	12.8%	12.3%	12.0%
↓	Incontinence in Low-Risk Residents	46.9%	47.6%	48.1%	49%	49.8%
↑	Adjusted Prevalence of Indwelling Catheter Use	5.9%	6.0%	5.8%	5.7%	5.5%
—	Worsening Mobility	12.5%	12.7%	12.8%	12.2%	11.9%
↓	Urinary Tract Infection	8.5%	8.7%	8.8%	9.0%	9.1%
↑	Delirium in Short-Stay Patients	3.2%	2.8%	2.4%	2.0%	1.8%
↑	Pain in Short-Stay Residents	22.7%	22.5%	21.4%	20.7%	20.0%

home facility has been shown to increase "bounce back" re-hospitalizations (Coleman, Min et al. 2004). Thirdly, the availability of a cohesive medical staff and physician extenders such as nurse practitioners and physician assistants is consistently associated with reduced likelihood of hospitalization (Intrator, Castle et al. 1999; Intrator, Grabowski et al. 2007; Konetzka, Spector et al. 2008). Finally, there are substantial regional differences in the rates of hospitalization of nursing home residents and re-hospitalization of post-acute patients in the same way that Wennberg and his colleagues have observed large regional variation in all manner of health care utilization (Fisher, Wennberg et al. 2000).

Brown investigators have prepared data on state variations in the rates of hospitalization and rehospitalization of persons in nursing homes for use in the Commonwealth Fund Chartbook on High Performing Health Care systems which compares the performance of states' "health care systems" on a variety of different parameters.[3] Using Medicare claims matched to MDS records of all "fee for service" Medicare beneficiaries ever using a nursing home between 1999 and 2006, Brown investigators identified two cohorts of Medicare nursing home users: (1) those who'd been in a facility continuously for at least 6 months; and, (2) those who had, based upon the available data, never been in a nursing home before. For the first group, we calculated the probability of hospitalization during the subsequent 6 months whereas for the second group, we calculated the likelihood that the patient was rehospitalized at least once within 30 days of hospital discharge. For both groups we aggregated the person level hospitalization rates to the state in which the nursing home was located and examined how these rates changed between 2000 and 2006.

Figure 5 below presents the 6 month hospitalization rates of long-stay residents by year, based upon the inter-state distribution. The median state's rate of hospitalization increased from 16% to 20% between 2000 and 2006, while the state with the highest rate of hospitalization increased to over 30%. Consistent with our observation about the importance of regional variations in patterns of medical care use, in examining changes in the rates of hospitalization of long-stay residents, we observed consistency among those states which were "high users" and those states classified as "low users." The lowest using states, Oregon, Utah and Arizona remained under 10% over the seven year period, while the highest using states, Mississippi and Louisiana, ended up exceeding a 30% hospitalization rate over the 6 month period. It is important to note that this definition of hospitalization excludes those individuals who experience multiple hospitalizations within a 6 month period, a proportion that also appears to vary substantially by state.

[3]http://www.commonwealthfund.org/Content/Publications/ Fund-Reports/2009/Feb/The-Path-to-a-High-Performance-USHealth-System.aspx

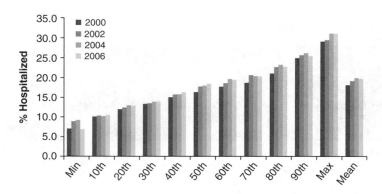

Figure 5 2000, 2002, 2004, and 2006

Findings for the newly admitted residents are remarkably similar even though all the individuals are very different and tend to be concentrated in facilities that specialize in providing post-acute care. Rehospitalization has increased each year and the inter-state differences are large, ranging from around 13% to 28% in 2006. As noted, we calculate the percentage of residents re-hospitalized within 30 days of admission to a SNF. It should be noted that in terms of calculating the "true" rate of rehospitalization, the proportion re-hospitalized is an underestimate since some of these individuals were re-hospitalized on more than one occasion during the 30 day period following their originating hospitalization. Obviously, those individuals who have never before used a SNF for post-acute care are less likely to be among the "frequent flyers" so often noted in the literature (Coleman 2007). What is most surprising about these data is that in spite of the presumably "healthier" selected residents included in these analyses, the median state re-hospitalizes about one fifth (and growing) of Medicare beneficiaries' first time "fee for service" SNF post-acute users. The highest using state is the same as for the long stay population, Louisiana. However, New Jersey has a rate of about 25% as well, suggesting another dynamic is operating here. The lowest use rate states again include Utah and Oregon, states that, according to the Dartmouth Atlas of Health Care, have low aggregate Medicare expenditures per capita.

iv. Quality Reflected in the Nursing Home Survey Process

Medicare/Medicaid certified nursing homes are inspected at least once every 15 months by state officials following centrally established guidelines. The surveyor guidelines provide detailed review processes for inspectors to follow as they review patient care processes based upon a sample of residents' records, observation of residents, and the interaction between residents and care staff. Emerging from the inspection are findings regarding the number and severity of deficiencies which are violations of the clinical care guidelines. In spite of the detailed guidelines, the literature clearly documents large inter-state variation in the number and severity of deficiencies (Angelelli, Mor et al. 2003; Mor 2007; Kelly, Liebig et al. 2008). Kelly and colleagues found that state funding levels, the "professionalism" of the state's bureaucracy and even the character of the state's legislature is related to the regulatory stringency applied to nursing homes by state inspectors. Indeed, these authors and Brown investigators note that some states are prone to levy a higher average number of deficiencies while other states are much more likely to identify deficiencies that are viewed as more severe, placing residents' lives at risk. In addition to interstate variation, historically there has also been substantial variation in the propensity of state officials to levy deficiencies.

Figure 6 reveals changes over time as well as inter-state variation in the percentage of facilities cited for actual harm or immediate jeopardy to residents of U.S. nursing homes. As can be seen, in 1997 and 98, there was considerable inter-state variation around a national median of 30% whereas by 2004 there was much less variation around a much lower proportion.

A more recent analysis performed for CMS as part of an examination of how the Five-Star rating system might be revised, reveals continued increases in the number of severity weighted deficiencies. As can be seen in Figure 7, these increases were apparently occurring in response to policy initiatives emanating from CMS, which is one reason we can see periodic shifts in the volume and severity of deficiencies.

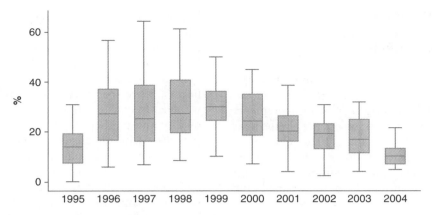

Figure 6 Trends and Inter-State Variations in the Percentage of Facilities Cited for Actual Harm or Immediate Jeopardy to Residents, 1995-2004 *Source:* OSCAR

According to CMS staff, the period of the late 1990s coincided with directives requiring less predictable survey scheduling and greater focus on complaint investigations. No new quality review initiatives were instituted outside of the introduction of public reporting and providing quality measures to the survey teams until 2004 when additional surveyor guidance directives were released and the trend toward more deficiency citations resumed.

During the period 2003 through 2008, the proportion of nursing facilities in the U.S. that were cited for pressure ulcer clinical care problems increased from around 15% to around 18% during a period of time when, as we've just seen, the prevalence of pressure ulcers among high risk patients was actually declining. This is quite consistent with the national finding that there is relatively little correlation between the measures of nursing home quality that emanate from the survey and inspection process and those which pertain to the reported and unreported measures of clinical quality created from the MDS. While this is not to say that there is no validity to the survey results, it does mean that these two sources of information are capturing very different aspects of quality.

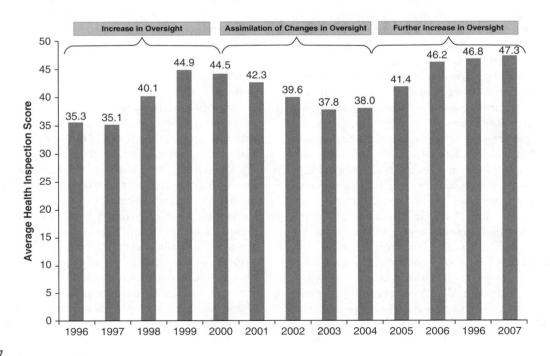

Figure 7

V. FUTURE DIRECTIONS AND RECOMMENDATIONS FOR ADDITIONAL RESEARCH

There are numerous unanswered questions about the changing nature and role of nursing homes in the U.S. context and how to improve the measurements of the outcomes that patients experience. In the next few paragraphs we discuss some of the challenges that need to be addressed in order to better understand the determinants of nursing home quality and how to best measure and think about nursing home quality for the increasingly heterogeneous groups of nursing home residents.

First, we need to better understand the current process of nursing home specialization that is underway since it is crucial to our understanding of whether quality is improving and in which sector(s) it is and is not improving. This is particularly important in light of the recent study suggesting that consumers and their advocates appear to be selectively "choosing" post-acute nursing homes with superior quality measures (Werner and Konetzka 2009). If one consequence of public reporting is, as was originally hypothesized, to "steer" patients to superior facilities, given the heterogeneous long-term care needs nursing homes meet, it is incumbent upon us to better understand which types of homes appear to best meet the needs of which types of residents. The increasing use of the nursing home as a post-acute care setting following hospitalization for serious surgeries, medical infections and complications means that a subset of nursing homes will increasingly resemble the general medical hospital wards of yesterday. Hospital-based facilities have traditionally served this population but now nearly 20% of free-standing nursing homes have 20% of their patient days covered by Medicare, a number that has been growing almost annually. Another area of specialization that has arisen is care of the seriously demented, long-stay resident; and nearly 30% of nursing homes now care for over 50% of residents with dementia, whether within or outside of dementia special care units (Gruneir, Lapane et al. 2008). An emerging trend, perhaps arising by default, is one of serving the growing number of young old, relatively recent Medicare beneficiaries with a long-standing serious psychiatric disorder who are entering nursing homes and staying there. (Fullerton, McGuire et al. 2009; Grabowski, Aschbrenner et al. 2009) While there is still much to be learned, there are indications that facilities with a disproportionate share of residents with serious mental illness diagnoses have more serious quality problems, have lower staffing levels and very high proportions of Medicaid residents. (Mor, Zinn et al. 2004) In light of the different types of individuals being served, it is difficult to imagine that the same set of quality measures are appropriate for these different types of homes. Since specialization is obviously occurring, we need to consider the implications for measuring quality and publicly reporting those results so that they are useful to consumers and their advocates.

Nursing home quality is currently being measured using a multiplicity of different "instruments" and approaches. Survey and certification results along with complaints vary between states (and even within states as a function of inspection team districts) and seem quite responsive to political and policy initiatives. As importantly, they are not correlated with quality measures purportedly measuring a similar concept. Quality measures focus on clinical outcomes but have been shown to be strongly correlated with facility acuity and so are inadequately case mix adjusted (Mukamel, Glance et al. 2008). Structural measures such as staffing levels are widely acknowledged to be important, but the level of staffing should clearly be related to the mix of patients being served and the specific types of needs that they have. While the new CMS Five-Star rating system takes resident acuity into account, there are some types of clinical staff like therapists and nurse practitioners that aren't counted and there appears to be great variation in how the staffing data are reported. Finally, other measures like rehospitalization, satisfaction, patients' experience and a host of other possible process quality measures have not been examined in relation to the existing set of measures nor in terms of which types of patients and homes they matter for the most. It is clear that nursing home quality is multi-dimensional; what is also becoming clear is that it is no more appropriate to compare all nursing homes with one another than it would be appropriate to compare an Obstetrics hospital with an Oncology hospital.

One corollary to both the heterogeneity of facilities and the different types of quality measures is the need to greatly enhance our measures of quality for the post-acute patients using nursing homes. Presently, there are only three measures and these are only possible for that group of SNF residents who are in the facility long enough to have at least two measures—generally the 5-day Medicare assessment and the 14-day admission assessment. One of the main goals of post-acute care, whether it is for residents undergoing rehabilitation or those recovering from a serious medical problem, is recovery to pre-morbid functioning, or at least improvement from their level of functioning at the time of admission. The alternatives to post-acute nursing home care, home health and rehabilitation hospitals, both have outcome measurements that are clearly calculated as the difference between patients' condition upon entry and upon discharge. It is imperative that nursing homes adopt a discharge assessment that can be used to calculate improvement in functioning, as well. As it is, too many post-acute patients are being treated and returned to their pre-hospital living situations without an opportunity to contribute to the performance evaluation of the nursing home. Furthermore, the array of possible quality measures for post-acute nursing home residents is greatly restricted without the benefit of having a discharge assessment with which to calculate a change score.

Finally, implementation of the MDS 3.0 is rapidly approaching. It will introduce even more complex conceptual and empirical measurement problems than currently face us for interpreting outcome measures based upon staff input and assessment (Mor, Berg et al. 2003). Currently, small facilities or facilities with very short lengths of stay may not have enough observations to be able to generate a quality measure. Under MDS 3.0, efforts to appropriately hear the residents' voice by asking staff to determine which residents can be interviewed will greatly complicate any quality of life measures, since it will require an understanding of the fact that the proportion of residents that may actually be interviewed will vary by type of resident. For example, a higher proportion of those who have experienced declines in locomotion or in other areas of physical functioning will be interviewed compared with those who have experienced cognition loss, aphasia or other disorders that may prevent them from providing coherent responses. Furthermore, measures relying upon the residents' voice cannot reasonably be combined with measures of the same concept that are based upon staff observation. Beyond the obvious advantages and complications that interviewing the resident brings to the situation, almost all of the existing quality measures have to be revised, making comparisons over time unlikely, if not utterly impossible. Thus, the pending changes will be of sufficient magnitude to require a complete reconstruction of much of the measurement research that has developed around the MDS 2.0 over the last decade.

If this review has done anything it is to underscore the heterogeneity of U.S. nursing homes and the need to explicitly take that heterogeneity into account in describing their performance and staffing, in comparing the manner in which they serve their distinct populations and in comparing the outcomes experienced by their residents. It is perhaps time to begin thinking explicitly about this heterogeneity in considering how CMS sets policy governing nursing homes in the United States.

• • • References

Angelelli, J., V. Mor, et al. (2003). "Oversight of nursing homes: pruning the tree or just spotting bad apples?" *Gerontologist* 43 Spec No 2: 67-75.

Baicker, K., A. Chandra, et al. (2004). "Who you are and where you live: how race and geography affect the treatment of medicare beneficiaries." *Health Aff (Millwood)* Suppl Web Exclusives: VAR33-44.

Castle, N. G., B. Fogel, et al. (1997). "Risk factors for physical restraint use in nursing homes: pre- and postimplementation of the Nursing Home Reform Act." *Gerontologist* 37(6): 737-47.

Cohen, J. and W. Spector (1996). "The effect of Medicaid reimbursement on quality of care in nursing homes." *J Health Econ* 15(1): 23-48.

Coleman, E. A. (2007). "How can we ground the "frequent fliers"?" *J Am Geriatr Soc* 55(3): 467-8.

Coleman, E. A., S. J. Min, et al. (2004). "Post-hospital care transitions: patterns, complications, and risk identification." *Health Serv Res* 39(5): 1449-65.

Davis, M. A., J. W. Freeman, et al. (1998). "Nursing home performance under case-mix reimbursement: responding to heavy-care incentives and market changes." *Health Serv Res* 33(4 Pt 1): 815-34.

Decker, F. (2005). *Nursing Homes 1977-1999: What has changed, what has not?* Hyattsville, Md., National Center for Health Statistics.

Feng, Z., D. C. Grabowski, et al. (2006). "The effect of state medicaid case-mix payment on nursing home resident acuity." *Health Serv Res* 41(4 Pt 1): 1317-36.

Feng, Z., D. C. Grabowski, et al. (2008). "Medicaid payment rates, case-mix reimbursement, and nursing home staffing- 1996-2004." *Med Care* 46(1): 33-40.

Fisher, E. S., J. E. Wennberg, et al. (2000). "Associations among hospital capacity, utilization, and mortality of US Medicare beneficiaries, controlling for sociodemographic factors." *Health Serv Res* 34(6): 1351-62.

Fries, B. E., C. Hawes, et al. (1997). "Effect of the National Resident Assessment Instrument on selected health conditions and problems." *J Am Geriatr Soc* 45(8): 994-1001.

Fullerton, C. A., T. G. McGuire, et al. (2009). "Trends in mental health admissions to nursing homes, 1999-2005." *Psychiatr Serv* 60(7): 965-71.

Gertler, P. J. (1989). "Subsidies, quality, and the regulation of nursing homes." *Journal of Public Economics* 38(1): 33-52.

Grabowski, D. C. (2001). "Medicaid reimbursement and the quality of nursing home care." *J Health Econ* 20(4): 549-69.

Grabowski, D. C. (2002). "The economic implications of case-mix Medicaid reimbursement for nursing home care." *Inquiry* 39(3): 258-78.

Grabowski, D. C. (2004). "A longitudinal study of Medicaid payment, private-pay price and nursing home quality." *Int J Health Care Finance Econ* 4(1): 5-26.

Grabowski, D. C. and J. J. Angelelli (2004). "The relationship of Medicaid payment rates, bed constraint policies, and risk-adjusted pressure ulcers." *Health Serv Res* 39(4 Pt 1): 793-812.

Grabowski, D. C., J. J. Angelelli, et al. (2004). "Medicaid payment and risk-adjusted nursing home quality measures." *Health Aff (Millwood)* 23(5): 243-52.

Grabowski, D. C., K. A. Aschbrenner, et al. (2009). "Mental illness in nursing homes: variations across States." *Health Aff (Millwood)* 28(3): 689-700.

Grabowski, D. C. and N. G. Castle (2004). "Nursing homes with persistent high and low quality." *Med Care Res Rev* 61(1): 89-115.

Gruneir, A., K. L. Lapane, et al. (2008). "Is dementia special care really special? A new look at an old question." *J Am Geriatr Soc* 56(2): 199-205.

Gruneir, A., S. C. Miller, et al. (2007). "Hospitalization of nursing home residents with cognitive impairments: the influence of organizational features and state policies." *Gerontologist* 47(4): 447-56.

Gruneir, A., S. C. Miller, et al. (2008). "Relationship between State Medicaid Policies, Nursing Home Racial Composition, and the Risk of Hospitalization for Black and White Residents." *Health Serv Res* 43(3): 869-81.

Gruneir, A., V. Mor, et al. (2007). "Where people die: a multilevel approach to understanding influences on site of death in america." *Med Care Res Rev* 64(4): 351-78.

Harrington, C., C. Kovner, et al. (2000). "Experts recommend minimum nurse staffing standards for nursing facilities in the United States." *Gerontologist* 40(1): 4-16.

Harrington, C., J. H. Swan, et al. (1999). *1998 State Data Book on Long Term Care Program and Market Characteristics*. San Francisco, CA, Department of Social and Behavioral Sciences, University of California.

Harris, Y. and S. B. Clauser (2002). "Achieving improvement through nursing home quality measurement." *Health Care Financ Rev* 23(4): 5-18.

Hawes, C., V. Mor, et al. (1997). "The OBRA-87 nursing home regulations and implementation of the Resident Assessment Instrument: effects on process quality." *J Am Geriatr Soc* 45(8): 977-85.

Intrator, O., N. G. Castle, et al. (1999). "Facility characteristics associated with hospitalization of nursing home residents: results of a national study." *Med Care* 37(3): 228-37.

Intrator, O., Z. Feng, et al. (2005). "The employment of nurse practitioners and physician assistants in U.S. nursing homes." *Gerontologist* 45(4): 486-95.

Intrator, O., D. C. Grabowski, et al. (2007). "Hospitalization of nursing home residents: the effects of states' Medicaid payment and bed-hold policies." *Health Serv Res* 42(4): 1651-71.

Intrator, O. and V. Mor (2004). "Effect of state Medicaid reimbursement rates on hospitalizations from nursing homes." *J Am Geriatr Soc* 52(3): 393-8.

IOM (1986). Improving the quality of care in nursing homes. Wash. DC, National Academy Press.

IOM (2001). *Improving the quality of long-term care*. Wash., DC, National Academy Press.

Kelly, C. M., P. S. Liebig, et al. (2008). "Nursing home deficiencies: an exploratory study of interstate variations in regulatory activity." *J Aging Soc Policy* 20(4): 398-413.

Konetzka, R. T., W. Spector, et al. (2008). "Reducing hospitalizations from long-term care settings." *Med Care Res Rev* 65(1): 40-66.

Konetzka, R. T., D. Yi, et al. (2004). "Effects of Medicare payment changes on nursing home staffing and deficiencies." *Health Serv Res* 39(3): 463-88.

Ma, E., E. A. Coleman, et al. (2004). "Quantifying posthospital care transitions in older patients." *J Am Med Dir Assoc* 5(2): 71-4.

Miller, E. A., V. Mor, et al. (2009). "The devil's in the details: trading policy goals for complexity in medicaid nursing home reimbursement." *J Health Polit Policy Law* 34(1): 93-135.

Miller, S. C., P. Gozalo, et al. (2001). "Hospice enrollment and hospitalization of dying nursing home patients." *Am J Med* 111(1): 38-44.

Mor, V. (2002). "Persistent restraints: a performance marker and a call for action." *Med Care* 40(10): 851-2.

Mor, V. (2005). "Improving the quality of long-term care with better information." *Milbank Q* 83(3): 333-64.

Mor, V. (2007). "Defining and measuring quality outcomes in long-term care." *J Am Med Dir Assoc* 8(3 Suppl 2): e129-37.

Mor, V., K. Berg, et al. (2003). "The quality of quality measurement in U. S. nursing homes." *Gerontologist* 43: 37-46.

Mor, V., K. Berg, et al. (2003). "The quality of quality measurement in U.S. nursing homes." *Gerontologist* 43 Spec No 2: 37-46.

Mor, V., O. Intrator, et al. (1997). "Changes in hospitalization associated with introducing the Resident

Assessment Instrument." J *Am Geriatr Soc* 45(8): 1002-10.

Mor, V., J. Zinn, et al. (2004). "Driven to tiers: socioeconomic and racial disparities in the quality of nursing home care." *Milbank Q* 82(2): 227-56.

Mor, V., J. Zinn, et al. (2007). "Prospects for transferring nursing home residents to the community." *Health Aff (Millwood)* 26(6): 1762-71.

Mukamel, D. B., L. G. Glance, et al. (2008). "Does risk adjustment of the CMS quality measures for nursing homes matter?" *Med Care* 46(5): 532-41.

Mukamel, D. B., D. L. Weimer, et al. (2008). "Publication of quality report cards and trends in reported quality measures in nursing homes." *Health Serv Res* 43(4): 1244-62.

Nyman, J. A. (1988). "Excess demand, the percentage of Medicaid patients, and the quality of nursing home care." *Journal of Human Resources* 23(1): 76-92.

Phillips, C. D., C. Hawes, et al. (1996). "Facility and area variation affecting the use of physical restraints in nursing homes." *Med Care* 34(11): 1149-62.

Scanlon, W. J. (1980). "A theory of the nursing home market." *Inquiry* 17(1): 25-41.

Schnelle, J. F., B. M. Bates-Jensen, et al. (2004). "Accuracy of nursing home medical record information about care-process delivery: implications for staff management and improvement." *J Am Geriatr Soc* 52(8): 1378-83.

Smith, D. B., Z. Feng, et al. (2007). "Separate and unequal: racial segregation and disparities in quality across U.S. nursing homes." *Health Aff (Millwood)* 26(5): 1448-58.

Stevenson, D. G. and D. C. Grabowski (2008). "Private equity investment and nursing home care: is it a big deal?" *Health Aff (Millwood)* 27(5): 1399-408.

Teno, J. M., Z. Feng, et al. (2008). "Do financial incentives of introducing case mix reimbursement increase feeding tube use in nursing home residents?" *J Am Geriatr Soc* 56(5): 887-90.

Teno, J. M., S. L. Mitchell, et al. (2009). "Churning: the association between health care transitions and feeding tube insertion for nursing home residents with advanced cognitive impairment." *J Palliat Med* 12(4): 359-62.

Teno, J. M., V. Mor, et al. (2002). "Use of feeding tubes in nursing home residents with severe cognitive impairment." *Jama* 287(24): 321-2.

Teno, J. M., S. Weitzen, et al. (2001). "Persistent pain in nursing home residents." *Jama* 285(16): 2081.

U.S. Senate (1974). *Nursing home care in the United States: Failure in public policy. Senate Special Committee on Aging, Subcommittee on Long-term Care.* Washington, D.C., U.S. Government Printing Office.

Vladeck, B. (1982). "Understanding Long Term Care." *NEJM* 307(14): 889-90.

Werner, R. M., R.T. Konetzka (2009). *What drives nursing home quality improvement under public reporting? An examination of post-acute care.* AcademyHealth. Chicago, Ill.

Werner, R. M., R. T. Konetzka, et al. (2009a). "Impact of Public Reporting on Quality of Postacute Care." *Health Serv Res.*

Werner, R. M., R. T. Konetzka, et al. (2009b). "Impact of public reporting on unreported quality of care." *Health Serv Res* 44(2 Pt 1): 379-98.

Wu, N., S. C. Miller, et al. (2005). "The quality of the quality indicator of pain derived from the minimum data set." *Health Serv Res* 40(4): 1197-216.

Zinn, J., Z. Feng, et al. (2008). "Restructuring in response to case mix reimbursement in nursing homes: a contingency approach." *Health Care Manage Rev* 33(2): 113-23.

Zinn, J., V. Mor, et al. (2009). "Determinants of performance failure in the nursing home industry." *Soc Sci Med* 68(5): 933-40.

Zinn, J. S., V. Mor, et al. (2003). "The impact of the prospective payment system for skilled nursing facilities on therapy service provision: a transaction cost approach." *Health Serv Res* 38(6 Pt 1): 1467-85.

Zinn, J. S., W. D. Spector, et al. (2008). "Strategic orientation and nursing home response to public reporting of quality measures: an application of the miles and snow typology." *Health Serv Res* 43(2): 598-615.

14

Mental Health Care

Mental health is defined as a state of successful performance of mental function, resulting in productive activities, fulfilling relationships with other people, and the ability to adapt to change and cope with adversity (Department of Health and Human Services [DHHS] 1999). Virtually everyone has experienced mental health problems to some degree. For example, under stress, anyone can exhibit behaviors that resemble some symptoms of mental disorders (LaVeist & Thomas 2005). Although an estimated 26.2 percent of American adults suffer from a diagnosable mental disorder in a given year, the main burden of illness is concentrated in a much smaller proportion—about 6 percent, or 1 in 17—who suffer from a serious mental illness. *Serious mental illness* is a term used in federal regulations to refer to a mental disorder that interferes with at least one area of social functioning (Goldman and Grob 2006). The phrase *severe and persistent mental illness* (SPMI) refers to mental illness that manifests itself in recurrent relapses necessitating periodic restabilization and rehospitalization over more than one year and that is accompanied by major functional disabilities (Ruggeri et al. 2000). This category includes schizophrenia, bipolar disorder, severe forms of depression, panic disorder, and obsessive-compulsive disorder (DHHS 1999). Among those who have mental disorders, approximately 45% have two or more disorders (Kessler et al. 2005). In addition, mental disorders are the leading cause of disability in the United States and Canada for ages 15-44 (World Health Organization 2004). In the U.S., mental disorders are diagnosed based on the *Diagnostic and Statistical Manual of Mental Disorders, fourth edition (DSM-IV)*.

According to the Substance Abuse and Mental Health Services Administration (SAMHSA), in 2006, an estimated 20.4 million Americans aged 12 or older, or 8.3% of the population, were using illicit drugs (SAMHSA 2007). It is also estimated that six out of ten people with a substance use disorder also suffer from another form of mental illness, but the high prevalence of these comorbidities (or co-occurring disorders) does not mean that one condition causes the other (National Institute on Drug Abuse 2007).

Like adults, children and adolescents can have mental health disorders that interfere with normal functioning. When untreated, mental health disorders can lead to school failure, family conflicts, drug abuse, violence, and even suicide. One in five children and adolescents may have a mental health disorder and at least one in 10 has a serious emotional disturbance (DHHS 1999).

Until the mid-1940s, understanding of the causes, treatment, and prevention of mental illness lagged behind other fields of medical science. The National Mental Health Act of 1946 created the National Institute of Mental Health (NIMH) for developing a broad program to improve the mental health of the nation through: (1) training mental health personnel, (2) research in the problems of mental illness, and (3) development by the states of preventive mental health programs in their communities (Carter 1950). A decade later, the discovery of modern psychotropic (also called antipsychotic) drugs provided new ways to control and treat mental illness. Prior to this, people with mental illnesses were mainly confined to state mental hospitals or asylums. The federal government has had a long-standing policy that long-term psychiatric care, primarily for adults, is the responsibility of the states. Hence, the states operated mental institutions. Later, the Community Mental Health Centers Act of 1963 started a trend toward deinstitutionalization. From 1970 to 2000, state-run psychiatric hospital beds dropped from 207 to 21 beds per 100,000 persons (Manderscheid 2004). The deinstitutionalization movement further intensified after the 1999 U.S. Supreme Court decision in *Olmstead v. L.C.* that directed the states to provide community-based services to people with mental illness, among others.

With the creation of Medicare and Medicaid in 1965, the federal government became responsible for an increasing share of the cost of mental health services. Later, private health plans started including coverage for mental health services. In spite of these developments, the physical and mental health services have remained fragmented although policy efforts continue to take aim at reconciling the two. The Mental Health Parity Act of 1996 required employers with 50 or more employees to offer the same annual or lifetime dollar coverage on mental health as for general medical care. Many states passed their own parity legislation that went beyond the requirements of the federal legislation. The federal law, for example, did not apply to benefits for substance abuse or chemical dependency. The Mental Health Parity and Addiction Equity Act of 2008 closed the gaps in insurance coverage for mental health and substance abuse (MH/SA) conditions. This law establishes new coverage requirements for 113 million Americans in group health plans. It also extends par-

ity benefits to Medicaid managed care plans that will greatly expand coverage for the poor and for underserved children (Shern et al. 2009).

Today, MH/SA treatments are rendered in a variety of settings. These settings include general hospitals, specialty units in general hospitals, specialty hospitals, private practices of psychiatrists and psychologists, primary care clinics, multi-service mental health organizations, specialty substance abuse centers, and nursing facilities. In 2003, national expenditures for mental health services amounted to $100.3 billion and another $20.7 billion for substance abuse treatments (National Center for Health Statistics 2010, Tables 129 and 130). Medicaid is the primary source of federal funding for MH/SA services.

To control rising costs, many health plans use carve-out arrangements to outsource mental health contracts to providers who specialize in the management of mental health benefits. These specialized providers or managed behavioral healthcare (MBHC) programs employ cost-control methods such as contracted networks of providers, utilization management and case management (Dixon 2009). Cost savings have also been realized as new, more effective technologies have replaced previous, more expensive treatments. For example, the quality-adjusted prices for treating the three most costly disorders—depression, schizophrenia, and bipolar disorder—have been declining (Berndt et al. 2005).

The first reading in this chapter, **Trends in Mental Health Care,** gives an overview of mental healthcare delivery. It points to some of the shortcomings of the existing system, such as a lack of integration between primary care and mental health delivery. Some social ills such as the rise in homelessness and incarceration could be attributed to the policy of deinstitutionalization, but that remains mainly a conjecture. While the growth in overall mental healthcare spending has slowed, mainly because of decreased institutionalization and cost control in managed care plans, coverage for psychotropic drugs has been quite generous and has resulted in increased expenditures. The report points to other issues such as stigma associated with mental health, some effects of the federal Welfare-to-Work and Ticket-to-Work programs, placement of children in welfare or juvenile justice systems by their parents, and barriers to the delivery of mental health services. Disparities in mental health services present an ongoing issue. It is further explored in the next reading.

Culture Counts: The Influence of Culture and Society on Mental Health, Mental Illness, a report produced by the Department of Health and Human

Services, explores the role of culture in whether people seek help, the types of coping styles they use, and the availability of social support. In addition to the patient's own cultural background, the culture of Western medicine in which most clinicians are trained can lead to differences in how illness is perceived and treated. For example, clinicians may ignore symptoms that the patient may deem important. Cultural differences can impede verbal communication and rapport between the patient and clinician. Bias and stereotyping can hinder proper diagnosis and treatment, and may even lead to discrimination in the practice of medicine. Finally, societal culture determines how services are organized and financed. Although a range of choices in treatment settings is available, the current mental healthcare system does not adequately address the problems of people with the most complex needs and fewest resources. As the focus of healthcare delivery increasingly shifts to the use of evidence-based treatments, race and ethnicity are underrepresented in clinical trials. Hence, treatment guidelines derived mainly from clinical trials using white populations have been proposed as best available treatments for everyone, regardless of race or ethnicity. Utilization and outcomes can be improved through culturally competent services.

Frank and Garfield evaluate the trends in MBHC carve-outs in the article, **Managed Behavioral Health Carve-Outs: Past Performance and Future Prospects.** Despite some reports to the contrary, MBHC delivered by managed behavioral health organizations (MBHOs) has continued to grow. The article begins with a historical background of carve-outs and describes the two types of carve-outs, payer carve-outs and health plan carve-outs. The MBHC industry has been built on four main economic principles: economics of specialization, economies of scale, price negotiation, and selection in insurance markets. Frank and Garfield evaluate the body of literature to arrive at three main conclusions on the performance of carve-outs. (1) Carve-outs have led to overall cost savings for behavioral health services as well as overall healthcare spending. The latter indicates that costs have not been shifted from one type of service to another. (2) Overall access to behavioral healthcare does not decline under carve-outs. Access may actually increase, but the intensity of service use is lessened. (3) In spite of the difficulties in evaluating the quality of care across studies, there is at least no indication that quality has decreased under carve-outs. On the other hand, there is always a potential that certain high-need groups such as those in poorest health and highest risk may not find their needs

adequately met. Carve-outs are evolving to address some longstanding policy and management challenges such as coordination of care with primary care physicians, misalignment between pharmacy benefit management and MBHC carve-out which had raised concerns about possible cost shifting, and market fragmentation. Thus, carve-outs have made some important contributions in solving problems in MH/SA delivery.

The New Freedom Initiative was launched by President George W. Bush in 2001 with the aim to promote full access to community life by people with disabilities, including those with psychiatric disabilities. The president appointed a commission to study the problems and gaps in the mental health system and to make recommendations for improvement. The final reading in this chapter, **Achieving the Promise: Transforming Mental Health Care in America,** is the executive summary of the commission's report to the president. The commission uncovered unmet needs and barriers that impede care for people with mental illnesses. Disability and suicide have been under-recognized as public health challenges. In addition, mental illnesses impose a huge burden on the nation's economy through loss of productivity. There is an ongoing time lag in transferring research findings to their actual application in improving care. There is a need to provide effective services in communities and a need to integrate programs that are fragmented across levels of government and among many agencies. A successful transformation of the mental health services delivery system requires that services and treatments are consumer and family centered, and that the services and treatments focus on the people's ability to successfully cope with life's challenges, and that they facilitate recovery, and build resilience. The report concludes with five goals to transform the mental health system.

• • • References

Berndt, E.R. et al. 2005. *Real output in mental health care during the 1990s. NBER Working Paper no. 11557.* Cambridge, MA: National Bureau of Economic Research.

Burnam, M.A. and J.J. Escarce. 1999. Equity in managed care for mental disorders. *Health Affairs* 18 (5): 22-31.

Carter, J.W. 1950. The community services program of the national institute of mental health, U.S. Public Health Service. *Journal of Clinical Psychology* 6 (2): 112-117.

Department of Health and Human Services. 1999. *Mental Health: A Report of the Surgeon General.* Washington, DC: Department of Health and Human Services.

Dixon, K. 2009. Implementing mental health parity: The challenge for health plans. *Health Affairs* 28 (3): 663-665.

Goldman, H.H. and G, N. Grob. 2006. Defining 'mental illness' in mental health policy. *Health Affairs* 25 (3): 737-749.

Kessler R.C. et al. 2005. Prevalence, severity, and comorbidity of twelve-month DSM-IV disorders in the National Comorbidity Survey Replication (NCS-R). *Archives of General Psychiatry* 62(6): 617-27.

LaVeist, T. and D. Thomas. 2005. Mental health. In *Minority Populations and Health: An Introduction to Health Disparities in the United States*, T. LaVeist. San Francisco: Jossey-Bass Publishers.

Manderscheid, R.W. et al. 2004. Highlights of organized mental health services in 2000 and major national and state trends. In R. W. Manderscheid and M. J. Henderson (eds.). *Mental Health, United States, 2002* (pp. 243–279). Washington, DC: U.S. Government Printing Office.

National Center for Health Statistics. 2010. *Health, United States, 2009.* Hyattsville, MD: National Center for Health Statistics.

National Institute on Drug Abuse. 2007. *Topics in Brief: Comorbid Drug Abuse and Mental Illness.* Department of Health and Human Services. Retrieved February 2010 from http://www.drug abuse.gov/pdf/tib/comorbid.pdf

Ruggeri, M. et al. (2000). Definition and prevalence of severe and persistent mental illness. *The British Journal of Psychiatry 177*: 149–155.

Shern, D.L. et al. 2009. Perspective: After parity—what's next. *Health Affairs* 28 (3): 660-662.

Substance Abuse and Mental Health Services Administration (SAMHSA). 2007. *Results from the 2006 National Survey on Drug Use and Health: National Findings.* Rockville, MD: Department of Health and Human Services.

World Health Organization. 2004. *The World Health Report 2004: Changing History, Annex Table 3: Burden of disease in DALYs by cause, sex, and mortality stratum in WHO regions, estimates for 2002.* Geneva: WHO.

1

Trends in Mental Health Care

Source: Barry, C.L. 2004. *Trends in Mental Health Care.* Issue Brief. New York, NY: The Commonwealth Fund. Used with the permission of The Commonwealth Fund.

INTRODUCTION

In the last few years, a number of major government reports have placed mental health care at the center of health policy and public health. *Mental Health: A Report of the Surgeon General,* released in December 1999, summarized the findings of a vast body of scientific literature on the prevalence and treatment of mental disorders.[1] Evidence amassed in this report indicated that a variety of efficacious treatments are available for most mental disorders. The Surgeon General's office also released a supplement to this report entitled *Mental Health: Culture, Race and Ethnicity,* addressing the disparities in access to mental health services and their toll on overall health and productivity, and *A Call to Action to Prevent Suicide,* providing a blueprint for reducing suicides in the United States.[2] Most recently, the New Freedom Commission appointed by President Bush to study the mental health delivery system released its final report, *Achieving the Promise: Transforming Mental Health Care in America,* in July 2003.[3] The report recommended a fundamental transformation in mental health care delivery. Together with prior research, these four publications provide a valuable framework for assessing how public policies affect care for those with mental illnesses.

DELIVERY OF MENTAL HEALTH CARE

Striking changes have occurred in the delivery of mental health care over the past few decades. Fifty years ago, most individuals receiving care for mental disorders obtained treatment from a specialty provider in an inpatient setting. Of the 1.7 million psychiatric patient-care episodes in 1955, 77 percent were in 24-hour hospital services.[4] At that time, government-owned psychiatric hospitals and specialty mental health clinics accounted for 84 percent of mental health spending.[5] Today, most individuals receive mental health care on an outpatient basis and live in a community setting. Services delivered in public psychiatric hospitals account for less than 15 percent of total spending.[6] Instead, delivery of mental health care in general hospitals and nursing homes, and by primary care clinicians, psychologists, psychiatrists, and social workers provides a broader array of treatment options. Likewise, the development of insurance-based financing (including Medicaid and Medicare) has fostered the emergence of markets providing greater autonomy and choice to individuals with mental illnesses as consumers of health care. Even the most severely ill individuals are able receive community-based care financed through public insurance. However, this transformation has also fragmented care across a patchwork of public and private insurance programs and delivery settings. New policy concerns have also emerged through enhanced civil rights to individuals with mental disorders. Advocates view the dramatic rise in homelessness and incarceration of individuals with mental disorders as unintended, troubling consequences of the evolution of the mental health system.

PREVALENCE, SERVICE USE, AND SOCIAL COSTS

The National Comorbidity Survey (NCS) constitutes the primary source of data on prevalence of mental disorders in the United States.[7] The NCS reported that about 19 percent of the population have a diagnosable mental disorder.[8] About 15 percent of Americans use mental health services each year, yet only half of these individuals have a specific disorder. Therefore, only about 37 percent of individuals with a disorder actually receive mental health treatment. These data signal that problems of both under- and over-treatment for mental disorders exist.[9] Diagnosis might not always be an appropriate measure of need for services. Mental health experts suggest that treatment decisions should be made on the basis of diagnosis in conjunction with other indicators of need, such as persistent or recurring symptoms, comorbidity, and impaired functioning.

Untreated mental disorders can lead to decreased work productivity, family disruptions, significant personal distress, and disability. Mental disorders constitute a major cause of disability in the United States and one of the top ten leading causes of disability worldwide.[10] Anxiety and mood disorders are the most prevalent diagnoses.[11] Poor mental health is more common among the poor than among higher-income individuals, though causality may run in both directions.[12]

The indirect costs of mental illness represented a $112.3 billion loss to the U.S. economy in 1994.[13] This estimate included $88 billion in morbidity costs reflecting loss of productivity in usual activities due to illness, as well as $16.5 million in mortality costs from lost productivity due to premature death and $7.8 billion in productivity losses for incarcerated individuals and care-giving family members.[14] Suicide also constitutes a major, preventable public health problem and is a consequence of under-diagnosed and undertreated mental illnesses. In the United States, suicide results in 30,000 deaths each year. It ranked as the eleventh leading cause of death in 2000 and the fourth leading cause of death among those 25 to 44 years of age.[15]

EFFICACY OF TREATMENTS FOR MENTAL DISORDERS

Mental Health: A Report of the Surgeon General highlighted the extraordinary pace and productivity of scientific research on the etiology and treatment of mental illness with particular focus on the brain and behavior. Significant gains in pharmaceutical technology have led to the development of a range of effective treatments with fewer side effects. Both the pace of medical discovery and faster approvals of new drugs in recent years by the U.S. Food and Drug Administration have contributed to the increasing use of these therapies. Various psychotherapies, such as psychodynamic, interpersonal, and cognitive-behavioral therapy also are available.

Many Americans with disorders do not benefit from the effective treatments now offered.[16] The Institute of Medicine report, *Crossing the Quality Chasm: A New Health System for the 21st Century,* noted that the lag between treatment discovery and incorporation into routine patient care tends to be unnecessarily long across health diagnoses.[17] The Surgeon General's report specifically highlighted the challenges associated with translating the best scientific knowledge about mental health treatment into everyday clinical practice. In an effort to improve quality, the mental health field has developed evidence-based practices defined as treatments and services where effectiveness is well documented. In contrast, emerging best practices are mental health treatments and services that are promising but less thoroughly documented.

Given the complexity of mental health care delivery and financing, a primary challenge involves disseminating evidence on treatment efficacy and coordinating care across a range of service settings. For example, most people suffering from depression seek care in primary care settings, so it is helpful to create linkages between primary and special mental health care providers. Furthermore, the delivery system for dispensing psychotropic drugs has expanded. Currently, psychiatrists prescribe only a third of psychotropic medications, while primary care physicians and other specialists prescribe the remaining two-thirds.[18] Yet, evidence has shown that primary care clinicians often lack the necessary training, time or financial incentives for appropriate detection and treatment of mental conditions.[19] Diffusion also appears hampered by uncertainty among private and public payers regarding how to cover evidence-based services.

SPENDING ON MENTAL HEALTH CARE

National expenditures for the treatment of mental health and substance abuse totaled $82.2 billion in 1997, with 86 percent ($70.8 billion) spent on treating mental illness and 14 percent ($11.4 billion) spent on treating substance abuse.[20] Mental health and substance abuse expenditures constitute about 8 percent of the more than 1 trillion dollars spent on all U.S. health expenditures in 1997. Specialty mental health providers received 71 percent of mental health and substance abuse expenditures, while general health care providers received 14 percent. The remaining 15 percent covered prescription drug costs and administrative expenses of insurers.

Mental health care spending grew more slowly than overall health expenditures over the last decade. While real health care spending increased by 5 percent annually between 1987 and 1997, real mental health spending grew by only 4 percent.[21] Notably, these trends are reversed for prescription drug spending. The annual 9 percent inflation-adjusted increase in spending for prescription drugs to treat mental illness exceeds the annual 8 percent increase in spending on drugs for all health-related diagnoses. Outpatient psychotropic drugs now constitute the fastest growing mental health care cost. Prescription drug use grew from 22 percent of total behavioral health spending in 1992 to 48 percent in 1999 among people with employer-based health insurance.[22] Growth in the use of psychotropic drugs is attributable both to the increased availability of effective medications to treat mental disorders and to the comparatively generous coverage for this portion of the mental health benefit.

The primary explanation for lower relative growth in overall mental health and substance abuse spending is the reduction in hospital expenditures, which in turn resulted from widespread adoption of specialty managed behavioral health carve-outs in part due to price competition among health plans. Carve-out companies use specialized expertise to establish networks of mental health providers (including psychiatrists, psychologists, social workers, and psychiatric nurses), negotiate volume-related discount contracts, identify evidence-based treatment protocols, and develop other incentive programs to manage use of services and costs. According to an annual survey, the managed behavioral health care industry has experienced a substantial increase in enrollment over the decade, from 70 million in 1993 to 164 million in 2002.[23] Studies have produced relatively consistent evidence that contracting with behavioral health carve-out companies reduces mental health and substance abuse costs by around 30 to 48 percent in the private sector.[24] Most of these savings result from decreases in use and spending for inpatient care. Most often, the proportion of enrollees using outpatient care increased while the number of outpatient visits decreased under carve-outs. Fewer studies have examined the effects of carve-outs on quality of care. Carve-outs do not appear to increase rates of re-hospitalization,[25] however studies have produced mixed results on their effects on continuity of care,[26] adherence to treatment guidelines,[27] and clinical outcomes.[28]

DISPARITIES IN MENTAL HEALTH SERVICES

Substantial disparities exist in access to mental health services. According to the Surgeon General's report, *Mental Health: Culture, Race and Ethnicity*, racial and ethnic minorities are less likely than whites to seek out or access services, and they receive poorer quality mental health care despite having similar community rates of mental disorders.[29] While use of mental health care among Asian American groups has been difficult to accurately measure, a number of studies found that they use fewer services per capita than other groups.[30] After controlling for sociodemographic characteristics and differences in need, another study found that African Americans receiving mental health treatment from any sources was about half that of whites.[31] Most studies of Latino mental health care access also reported low service use.[32] Also, in geographically remote areas, people with mental illness encounter more trouble accessing services due to limited availability of providers, lower family income, and possibly greater social stigma.[33]

THE ROLE OF THE PUBLIC SECTOR

Federal, state, and local governments contribute substantially to the financing and delivery of mental health care. Public payers funded 58 percent of mental health and substance abuse spending in 1997, a much larger share than the 46 percent of total health expenditures paid for through the public sector.[34] Historically, state and local governments have assumed a particularly large role in financing mental health services. In 1997, state and local governments provided 28 percent of all mental health and substance abuse expenditures, while funding only about 13 percent of health care services overall.[35]

Among all payers, Medicaid is currently the largest single payer for mental health services. In 1971, Medicaid represented only about 12 percent of national spending for mental health treatment. By 1997, this share had increased to nearly 20 percent, totaling $14 billion.[36] Expenditures through the Medicaid and Medicare programs constitute 35 and 21 percent, respectively, of total public sector expenditures on mental health services.[37]

Medicaid pays for mental health care primarily for two distinct populations: people enrolled in Temporary Assistance to Needy Families (TANF) and in Supplemental Security Income (SSI). TANF recipients have somewhat higher rates of treatment for mental disorders than the general population[38] and an estimated 28 percent of enrolled adults report very poor mental health scores.[39] With regard to depression, Medicaid provides a vital source of access to services given that rates are particularly high among low-income women. For example, a recent study found that mothers of young children experience rates of depression ranging from 12 to 50 percent, with the highest levels among women who are poor or homeless or have a chronic health problem. Their children are at increased risk of developmental, behavioral, and emotional problems.[40] Adolescent girls also experience high rates of depression and report relatively high rates of suicidal ideation.[41]

In addition to Medicaid and Medicare, the federal government provides resources through the Community Mental Health Block Grant, community support programs, the PATH program for services to the homeless mentally ill, and Comprehensive Community Mental Health Services for Children. Income supports for individuals unable to work due to mental illness include SSI, TANF, and Social Security Disability Insurance (SSDI). Thirty-five percent of SSI beneficiaries and 27 percent of SSDI beneficiaries were disabled by mental illnesses in 2001, including a large proportion with schizophrenia.[42]

STIGMA AND MENTAL HEALTH

The New Freedom Commission Report and Surgeon General's Report both emphasized the importance of changing public attitudes to eliminate the stigma associated with mental illness. Advocates for the mentally ill identify stigma and discrimination as major impediments to treatment. Stigma prevents individuals from acknowledging these conditions and erodes public confidence that mental disorders are

treatable. A plurality of Americans believe that mental illnesses are just like any other illness; however, 25 percent of survey respondents would not welcome into their neighborhoods facilities that treat or house people with mental illnesses, suggesting that some level of lingering stigma persists.[43] Sixty-one percent of Americans think that people with schizophrenia are likely to be dangerous to others[44] despite research suggesting that these individuals are rarely violent.[45]

The Surgeon General's report viewed increasingly efficacious treatments for mental disorders as the most effective long-range antidote to stigma, noting that "effective interventions help people to understand that mental disorders are not character flaws but are legitimate illnesses that respond to specific treatments, just as other health conditions respond to medical interventions."[46]

MENTAL HEALTH INSURANCE COVERAGE

Under most health insurance plans, coverage for mental disorders is more limited than coverage for general medical care. Plans commonly require higher cost sharing and more stringent limits on inpatient hospital days and outpatient visits for mental health treatment. Until recently, special lifetime and annual dollar limits were often used. A recent study reported that 74 percent of privately insured workers were subject to special annual outpatient mental health visit limits and 64 percent were subject to special annual inpatient mental health day limits in 2002.[47] In the Medicare program, outpatient psychotherapy services are covered with a 50 percent beneficiary co-payment requirement, compared with 20 percent enrollee cost-sharing on other Medicare outpatient services.[48] A 1998 survey by the Robert Wood Johnson Foundation reported that 83 percent of uninsured and 53 percent of privately insured individuals listed cost concerns as the principal reason for not seeking mental health care.[49]

In the 1990s, states began to enact parity laws as a policy response to mental health coverage limitations. The objective of parity is to require insurers to provide the same level of benefits for mental health (and sometimes substance abuse) as general medical care. Thirty-four states have enacted some form of parity legislation. In 1996, Congress passed a law addressing one aspect of mental health coverage limits. The Mental Health Parity Act (P.L. 104-204) took effect in 1998 and prohibits the use of annual or lifetime dollar limits on coverage for mental illnesses. Unlike state parity laws, it extends to all self-insured companies exempt from state mandates under ERISA. The law does not apply to other kinds of benefit limits, such as special day or visit limits and higher cost sharing. Companies with fewer than 50 employees and those that offer no mental health benefit are exempt from the federal parity law. Payers experiencing more than a 1 percent increase in premiums as a result of federal parity can apply for an exemption. In 2000, the General Accounting Office reported that two-thirds of compliant employers had made at least one other aspect of their mental health benefits more restrictive, raising concerns about circumvention of this law.[50]

Insurers have traditionally limited coverage for mental disorders out of concern that generous benefits could lead to high costs due to long-term or intensive psychotherapy and lengthy hospital stays. In fact, there is evidence that in fee-for-services settings consumers are more sensitive to changes in the price of mental health services than other health care services. The RAND Health Insurance Experiment demonstrated that increased use of services by consumers in response to decreased out-of-pocket costs was twice as great for outpatient mental health services than for ambulatory health services as a whole under indemnity insurance.[51]

However, contracting with carve-out companies eases these concerns since cost-control efforts no longer rely exclusively on limiting benefits. Importantly, some evidence suggests that plans may structure mental health benefits to avoid selection of unfavorable or high-risk consumers.[52] Mental health is an area where economic research has also identified particularly strong selection incentives. Inefficiently low levels of insurance coverage may result if health plans narrowly limit benefits to discourage enrollment by consumers with high expected mental health use.

In the 108th Congress, Senator Pete Domenici and Representative Patrick Kennedy have introduced the Senator Paul Wellstone Mental Health Equitable Treatment Act of 2003 (S. 486/H.R. 953) to provide more comprehensive parity for mental health benefits. This legislation is patterned on an executive order issued in 1999 mandating comprehensive mental health and substance abuse benefit parity for the nine million enrollees of the Federal Employees Health Benefits Program (FEHBP).[53] The Office of Personnel Management and the Department of Health and Human Services are evaluating the impact of the FEHBP benefit change on cost, access, and quality. Like the FEHBP parity policy, this legislation would prohibit the use of special mental health day or visit limits and higher cost sharing. Employers remain concerned about the cost of en-

acting broader federal parity. The Congressional Budget Office estimated in 2001 that an identical version of the bill introduced in the prior Congress would increase premiums for group health plans by 0.4 percent after accounting for the responses of health plans, employers and workers.[54]

In addition, Sen. Jon Corzine and Rep. Pete Stark introduced the Medicare Mental Health Modernization Act of 2003 (S. 646/H.R. 1340). This legislation would eliminate the lifetime limit on inpatient mental health services and require parity in coverage for outpatient mental health services in the Medicare program. S. 853 introduced by Senator Olympia Snowe specifically addresses the issue of reducing the outpatient coinsurance rates for mental health services in the Medicare program from 50 percent to the 20 percent level for general outpatient medical services.

OTHER CURRENT MENTAL HEALTH POLICY ISSUES

Recent federal policies encourage those with mental disorders to re-enter the workforce. People disabled by mental illness have the lowest rates of employment among all disabled groups. Only one in three mentally disabled individuals has a job.[55] The federal Welfare-to-Work initiative created a strong financial incentive for beneficiaries to obtain training and employment by placing time limits on income support. Likewise, the Ticket to Work Incentives Improvement Act of 1999 (P.L. 106-170) sought to encourage SSI and SSDI beneficiaries to enroll in employment training and obtain jobs. However, the New Freedom Commission Report raised a concern that its rules do not create enough of an incentive for vocational rehabilitation providers to take on clients with more severe mental illnesses.[56]

Through the Balanced Budget Act (BBA) of 1997 (P.L. 105-33) and the Ticket to Work Act, the Congress has addressed the related issue of loss of Medicaid as a disincentive to employment. Under the BBA, states are permitted to extend Medicaid coverage to disabled individuals with incomes up to 250 percent of poverty. Under the Ticket to Work program, states can set higher income and resources levels for receiving Medicaid coverage, including for those whose health and functioning has improved enough through the use of psychotropic medications to enable a return to work. Most states have not opted to implement these Medicaid buy-in programs. Increasing attention has focused on the troubling issue of trading custodial rights for access to children's mental services. The General Accounting Office examined the issue of parents placing children with mental health issues in welfare or juvenile justice systems solely to obtain treatment after exhausting savings and health insurance.[57] The GAO reported that state child welfare officials in 19 states and juvenile justice officials in 30 counties estimated that parents placed over 12,700 children in welfare or juvenile justice systems to receive mental health care treatment in 2001. Nationwide, this estimate is likely to be higher since 32 states, including the five largest states, and many counties were unable to provide data on the number of affected children. No formal federal or state tracking of these placements occurs.

In the 1999 *Olmstead v. L.C.* decision, the U.S. Supreme Court held that unnecessary institutionalization of people with disabilities is discriminatory under the Americans with Disabilities Act (ADA).[58] This decision requires that services to those disabled by mental illness be delivered in the most integrated setting possible. While states are required to develop comprehensive work plans for placing disabled people in appropriate treatment settings and to "maintain a waiting list that moves at a reasonable pace," some have been slow to comply.[59] Four years after the Olmstead ruling, 42 states and the District of Columbia have set up task forces, commissions or state agency working groups to develop implementation plans.[60]

Finally, President Bush appointed the New Freedom Commission to study the mental health delivery system citing major barriers to the provision of high quality mental health care including stigma, inadequate insurance coverage, and a fragmented service delivery system. Noting problems with the evolution of community mental health care over the intervening decades since deinstitutionalization, Commission members proposed six goals aimed at fundamentally transforming mental health care delivery:

- Americans should understand that mental health is essential to overall health. The report recommended developing national campaigns to reduce stigma and prevent suicide. It noted that mental health should be addressed with the same urgency as physical health.

- Mental health care should be consumer- and family-driven. The report urged patient and family-centered care through the development of individualized treatment planning, improved care integration and accountability, and a focus on consumer rights and protections.

- Disparities in mental health services should be eliminated through improving access to culturally competent care and increasing services to geographically remote areas.

- Early mental health screening, assessment and referral to services should become common practice. The report stressed the importance of screening by primary care clinicians, expanding school mental health programs, and improving detection and treatment of co-occurring mental health and substance abuse disorders.

- Excellent mental health care should be delivered and research should be accelerated. Specific understudied areas include developing a knowledge base in mental health disparities, long-term effects of medication, and trauma and acute services for those in crisis.

- Technology should be used to better access mental health information and coordinate service delivery. Information technology can minimize mental health delivery problems in rural and other underserved areas, and electronic medical records can facilitate the adoption of and adherence to evidence-based practices.

CONCLUSION

Dramatic changes have occurred in mental health over the last 50 years, including significant advances in the diagnosis and treatment of mental illness, positive shifts in public attitudes about mental disorders, and a transformation in the delivery of mental health services. Yet, fragmented systems of care, insurance and reimbursement issues, and barriers to evidence-based treatments prevent some Americans from receiving quality care for mental disorders.

For More Information
Please contact: Mary Mahon, Public Information Officer, The Commonwealth Fund,
   One East 75th Street, New York, NY 10021-2692. Tel 212.606.3853. Fax 212.606.3500. E-mail mm@cmwf.org.

● ● ● **References**

1. U.S. Department of Health and Human Services. 1999. *Mental Health: A Report of the Surgeon General.* Rockville, MD: U.S. Department of Health and Human Services, Substance Abuse and Mental Health Services Administration, Center for Mental Health Services, National Institutes of Health, National Institute of Mental Health.

2. U.S. Department of Health and Human Services. 2001. *Mental Health: Culture, Race and Ethnicity.* Rockville, MD: U.S. Department of Health and Human Services, Public Health Service, Office of the Surgeon General and U.S. Public Health Services. 1999. *Surgeon General's Call to Action to Prevent Suicide.* Washington, D.C.

3. New Freedom Commission on Mental Health. 2003. *Achieving the Promise: Transforming Mental Health Care in America. Final Report.* Rockville, MD: DHHS Pub. No. SMA-03-3832.

4. Center for Mental Health Services. 1999. *Mental Health United States, 1998.* Manderscheid, R.W. and M.J. Henderson, Eds., U.S. Department of Health and Human Services. Washington, D.C.: DHHS Pub. SMA-99-3285.

5. Fein, R. 1958. *Economics of Mental Illness.* Joint Commission on Mental Illness and Health no. 2. New York: Basic Books, Inc.

6. Coffey R. et al. 2000. *National Estimates of Expenditures for Mental Health and Substance Abuse Treatment, 1997.* U.S. Department of Health and Human Services, Substance Abuse and Mental Health Services Administration: SAMHSA Pub. SMA-00-3499.

7. Kessler, R.C. et al. 1994. Lifetime and 12-Month Prevalence of DSM-III-R Psychiatric Disorders in the U.S: Results from the National Comorbidity Survey. *Archives of General Psychiatry* 51 (1): 8-19.

8. In addition, 3 percent of the population have both mental and addictive disorders, and 6 percent have addictive disorders, alone in a given year.

9. U.S. DHHS. 1999. *Mental Health: A Report of the Surgeon General.*

10. Murray, C.J., and A.D. Lopez. 1996. *The Global Burden of Disease: A Comprehensive Assessment of Mortality and Disability from Diseases, Injuries, and Risk Factors in 1990 and Projected to 2020.* Cambridge, MA: Harvard University Press.

11. U.S. DHHS. 1999. *Mental Health: A Report of the Surgeon General.* This report developed conservative best-estimate 1-year prevalence rates by diagnosis from two studies: the Epidemiologic Catchment Area Study (ECA) and the National Comorbidity Survey (NCS). Anxiety disorders include simple phobia, social phobia, agoraphobia, generalized anxiety disorder, panic disorder, obsessive compulsive disorder (OCD), and post traumatic stress disorder (PTSD). Mood disorders include unipolar major depressive disorder, dysthymia, bipolar I and bipolar II.

12. Muntaner, C. et al. 1998. Social Class, Assets, Organizational Control and the Prevalence of Common Groups of Psychiatric Disorders. *Social Science and Medicine* 47 (12): 2043-53; Adler, N.E. et al. 1994. Socioeconomic Status and Health: The Challenge of the Gradient. *American Psychologist* 49 (1): 15-24; Regier, D.A. et al. 1993.The De Facto U.S. Mental and Addictive Disorders Service System: Epidemiological Catchment Area Prospective One Year Prevalence Rates of Disorders and Services. *Archives of General Psychiatry* 50 (2): 85-94; Holzer, C.E. et al. 1986.The Increased Risk for Specific Psychiatric Disorders Among Persons of Low Socioeconomic Status: Evidence from the Epidemiologic Catchment Area Surveys. *American Journal of Social Psychiatry* 6 (4): 259-71.

13. Rice, D.P. 1994. *Costs of Mental Illness* (unpublished manuscript). These estimates are based on projections of socioeconomic indices applied from 1985 estimates published in Rice, D.P. et al. 1990. *The Economic Costs of Alcohol and Drug Abuse and Mental Illness, 1985.* San Francisco: Institute for Health and Aging.

14. Ibid.

15. See Institute of Medicine. 2002. *Reducing Suicide: A National Imperative.* Washington, DC: National Academies Press; and National Center for Health Statistics, *Health, United States. 2003.* DHHS Pub. No. 2003-1232,Table 32.

16. Wang, P.S. et al. 2002.Adequacy of Treatment for Serious Mental Illness in the United States. *American Journal of Public Health* 92 (1): 92-98.

17. Institute of Medicine. 2001. *Crossing the Quality Chasm: A New Health System for the 21st Century.* Washington D.C.: National Academies Press.

18. Pincus, H. et al. 1998. Prescribing Trends in Psychotropic Medications: Primary Care, Psychiatry and Other Medical Specialties. *Journal of the American Medical Association* 279 (7): 526-31.

19. See, for example, Pincus, H. (note 18); Simon, G.E. 1998. Can Depression Be Managed Appropriately in Primary Care? *Journal of Clinical Psychiatry* 59 (2): 3-8; Unutzer, J. et al. 2002. Collaborative Care Management of Late-Life Depression in Primary Care Setting: A Randomized Controlled Trial. *Journal of the American Medical Association* 288 (22): 2836-45; Hunkeler, E.M. et al. 2000. Efficacy of Nurse Telehealth Care and Peer Support in Augmenting Treatment of Depression in Primary Care. *Archives of Family Medicine* 9 (8): 700-708; Katzelnick, D.J. 2000. Randomized Trial of a Depression Management Program in High Utilizers of Medical Care. *Archives of Family Medicine* 9 (4): 345-51.

20. Coffey, R. et al., 2000. *National Estimates of Expenditures for Mental Health and Substance Abuse Treatment, 1997.* U.S. Department of Health and Human Services, Substance Abuse and Mental Health Services Administration: SAMHSA Pub. SMA-00-3499. This report produces estimates according to a methodology equivalent to the National Health Expenditures (NHE) reports

produced annual by the Office of the Actuary, HCFA. This methodology specifically excludes expenditures for social services totaling about 3 million in 1997. This 1997 data constitutes the most up-to-date information available on mental health and substance abuse spending.

21. Ibid.

22. Mark, T. and R. Coffey. 2003. What Drove Private Health Insurance Spending on Mental Health and Substance Abuse Care, 1992-1999? *Health Affairs* 22 (1): 165-72.

23. Oss M., et al. 2003. *Open Minds Yearbook of Managed Behavioral Health and Employee Assistance Program Market Share in the U.S. 2002-2003.* Gettysburg, PA: Open Minds Publication.

24. See, for example, C.A. Ma and T.G. McGuire. 1998. Costs and Incentives in a Behavioral Health Care Carve Out. *Health Affairs* 17 (2): 53-69; Goldman, W.J. et al. 1998. Costs and Use of Mental Health Services Before and After Managed Care. *Health Affairs* 17 (3): 40-52; Grazier, K.L. et al. 1999. Effects of a Mental Health Carve-out on Use, Costs and Payers: A Four-year Study. *Journal of Behavioral Health Services and Research* 26 (4): 381-89. Sturm R. 1999. Tracking Changes in Behavioral Health Services: How Have Carve-outs Changed Care? *Journal of Behavioral Health Services and Research* 26 (4): 360-71; and Brisson, A.S. et al. 2000. *Changes in a MBHC Carve-out: Impact on MH/SA Spending and Utilization* (unpublished working paper).

25. For evidence on re-hospitalization rates, see Merrick E. 1998. Treatment of Major Depression Before and After Implementation of a Behavioral Health Carve-out Plan. *Psychiatric Services* 49 (11): 1563-67; Sturm R. 1999. Tracking Changes in Behavioral Health; and Dickey, B. et al. 1998. Managed Mental Health Experience in Massachusetts, in D. Mechanic (ed.), *Managed Behavioral Health Care: Current Realities and Future Potential.* San Francisco: Jossey-Bass, 115-22.

26. For evidence on continuity of care, see Merrick, E. (note 25); Dickey, B. (note 25); and Ray, W.A. et al. 2003. Effect of a Mental Health "Carve-out" Program on the Continuity of Antipsychotic Therapy. *New England Journal of Medicine* 348 (19): 1885-94.

27. For evidence on adherence to treatment guidelines, see Busch, S.H. 2002. Specialty Health Care, Treatment Patterns and Quality: A Case Study of Treatment for Depression. *Health Services Research* 37 (6): 1583-1601.

28. For evidence on clinical outcomes, see Cuffel, B.J. et al. 2002. Two-year Outcomes of Fee-for-Service and Capitated Medicaid Programs for People with Severe Mental Illness. *Health Services Research* 37 (2): 341-59; and Manning. W.G. et al. 1999.

Outcomes for Medicaid Beneficiaries with Schizophrenia Under a Pre-paid Mental Health Carve-out. *Journal of Behavioral Health Services and Research* 26 (4): 442-50.

29. U.S. DHHS. 2001. *Mental Health: Culture, Race and Ethnicity.*

30. See, for example, Matsuoka, J.K. et al. 1997. National Utilization of Mental Health Services by Asian Americans/Pacific Islanders. *Journal of Community Psychology* 25 (2): 141-46; Snowden, L.R. and F.K. Cheung. 1990. Use of Inpatient Mental Health Services by Members of Ethnic Minority Groups. *American Psychologist* 45 (3): 347-55.

31. Swartz, M.S. et al. 1998. Comparing Use of Public and Private Mental Health Services: The Enduring Barriers of Race and Age. *Community Mental Health Journal* 34 (2): 133-44.

32. See, for example, Snowden, L.R. (note 30); Breaux, C. and D. Ryujin. 1999. Use of Mental Health Services by Ethnically Diverse Groups Within the U.S. *Clinical Psychologist* 52 (3): 4-15.

33. Rost, K. et al. 2002. Use, Quality, and Outcomes of Care for Mental Health: The Rural Perspective. *Medical Care Research and Review* 59 (3): 231-65.

34. Coffey, R. 2000. *National Estimates of Expenditures, 1997*

35. Ibid.

36. Ibid; and Levine, D.S. and D.R. Levine. 1975. *The Costs of Mental Illness, 1971.* National Institute of Mental Health, Report Series B (7): Table 1.

37. Ibid.

38. Frank, R.G., H.H. Goldman, and M. Hogan. 2003. Medicaid and Mental Health: Be Careful What You Ask For. *Health Affairs* (22) 1: 101-13.

39. Loprest, P.J. and S.R. Zedlewski. 1999. *Current and Former Welfare Recipients: How Do They Differ?* Washington, D.C.: The Urban Institute.

40. 2003. Family Pediatrics: Report of the Task Force on the Family. *Pediatrics* [Family Pediatrics Suppl.] 111 (6): 1541-71.

41. Schoen, C. et al. 1997. *The Commonwealth Fund Survey of the Health of Adolescent Girls.* The Commonwealth Fund.

42. U.S. Social Security Administration. 2001. *Statistical Supplement of the Social Security Bulletin.* Washington, D.C.: U.S. Government Printing Office.

43. Borinstein, A.B. 1992. Public Attitudes Toward Persons with Mental Illness. *Health Affairs* 11 (3): 186-96.

44. Pescosolido, B. et al. 2000. Americans' Views of Mental Health and Illness at the Century's End: Continuity and Change. *Public Report on the*

MacArthur Mental Health Module, 1996 General Social Survey. Bloomington, Indiana.

45. Steadman, H.J. et al. 1998.Violence by People Discharged from Acute Psychiatric Inpatient Facilities and by Others in the Same Neighborhoods. *Archives of General Psychiatry 55* (5): 393-401.

46. U.S. DHHS. 1999. *Mental Health: A Report of the Surgeon General.*

47. Barry, C.B. et al. 2003. Design of Mental Health Benefits: Still Unequal After All These Years. *Health Affairs* 22 (5): 127-37.

48. 1998. *A Profile of Medicare: Chartbook.* Office of Strategic Planning and Health Care Financing Administration, U.S. Department of Health and Human Services.

49. Sturm, R. and C.D. Shelborne. 1999. *Are Barriers to Mental Health and Substance Abuse Still Rising* (unpublished manuscript).

50. U.S. General Accounting Office. 2000. *Mental Health Parity Act: Despite New Federal Standards, Mental Health Benefits Remain Limited.* GAO/HEHS-00-05.

51. Newhouse, J.P. 1993. *Free for All? Lessons from the RAND Health Insurance* Experiment. Cambridge: Harvard University Press.

52. See, for example, a discussion on evidence of selection in mental health and substance abuse in Frank, R.G. and T.G. McGuire. 2000. *Economics and Mental Health. Handbook of Health Economics.* A.J. Culyer and J.P. Newhouse (eds.). Amsterdam: Elsevier.

53. U.S. Office of Personnel Management. 1999. *Executive Order: Amending the Civil Service Rules Related to Federal Employees with Psychiatric Disabilities.*

54. U.S. Congressional Budget Office. 2001. *Cost Estimate: Mental Health Equitable Treatment Act of 2001.* On. S. 543 on 107th U.S. Congress ordered by the U.S. Senate Committee on Health, Education, Labor and Pensions.

55. Social Security Administration, 2002. *Annual Statistical Supplement.*

56. New Freedom Commission. 2003. *Achieving the Promise.*

57. U.S. General Accounting Office. 2003. *Federal Agencies Could Play a Stronger Role in Helping States Reduce the Number of Children Placed Solely to Obtain Mental Health Services.* Pub. GAO-03-397.

58. *Olmstead v. L.C.,* 527 U.S. 581, 610 (1999) (Kennedy, J., concurring in judgment).

59. Health Care Financing Administration, Letter to State Medicaid Directors.

60. Fox-Grage, W. et al. 2003. *The States' Response to the Olmstead Decision: How Are States Complying?* Washington, D.C.: National Conference of State Legislatures. A major strategy for complying with the Olmstead decision is to use a task force or commission for planning and coordination purposes. To date, eight states—Kansas, Michigan, Minnesota, Nebraska, Oregon, Rhode Island, South Dakota, and Tennessee—do not have a task force or similar group.

2

Mental Health: Culture, Race, and Ethnicity

Source: U.S. Department of Health and Human Services. (2001). *Mental Health: Culture, Race, and Ethnicity—A Supplement to Mental Health: A Report of the Surgeon General.* Rockville, MD: U.S. Department of Health and Human Services, Substance Abuse and Mental Health Services Administration, Center for Mental Health Services, pp. 25-49.

INTRODUCTION

To better understand what happens inside the clinical setting, this chapter looks outside. It reveals the diverse effects of culture and society on mental health, mental illness, and mental health services. This understanding is key to developing mental health services that are more responsive to the cultural and social contexts of racial and ethnic minorities.

With a seemingly endless range of subgroups and individual variations, culture is important because it bears upon what *all* people bring to the clinical setting. It can account for minor variations in how people communicate their symptoms and which ones they report. Some aspects of culture may also underlie *culture-bound syndromes*—sets of symptoms much more common in some societies than in others. More often, culture bears on whether people even seek help in the first place, what types of help they seek, what types of coping styles and social supports they have, and how much stigma they attach to mental illness. Culture also influences the *meanings* that people impart to their illness. Consumers of mental health services, whose cultures vary both between and within groups, naturally carry this diversity directly to the service setting.

The cultures of the clinician and the service system also factor into the clinical equation. Those cultures most visibly shape the interaction with the mental health consumer through diagnosis, treatment, and organization and financing of services. It is all too easy to lose sight of the importance of culture—until one leaves the country. Travelers from the United States, while visiting some distant frontier, may find themselves stranded in miscommunications and seemingly unorthodox treatments if they seek care for a sudden deterioration in their mental health.

Health and mental health care in the United States are embedded in Western science and medicine, which emphasize scientific inquiry and objective evidence. The self-correcting features of modern science—new methods, peer review, and openness to scrutiny through publication in professional journals—ensure that as knowledge is developed, it builds on, refines, and often replaces older theories and discoveries. The achievements of Western medicine have become the cornerstone of health care worldwide.

What follows are numerous examples of the ways in which culture influences mental health, mental illness, and mental health services. This chapter is meant to be illustrative, not exhaustive. It looks at the culture of the patient, the culture of the clinician, and the specialty in which the clinician works. With respect to the context of mental health services, the chapter deals with the organization, delivery, and financing of services, as well as with broader social issues—racism, discrimination, and poverty—which affect mental health.

Culture refers to a group's shared set of beliefs, norms, and values. Because common social groupings (e.g., people who share a religion, youth who participate in the same sport, or adults trained in the same profession) have their own cultures, this chapter has separate sections on the culture of the patient as well as the culture of the clinician. Where cultural influences end and larger societal influences begin, there are contours not easily demarcated by social scientists. This chapter takes a broad view about the importance of both culture and society, yet recognizes that they overlap in ways that are difficult to disentangle through research.

What becomes clear is that culture and social contexts, while not the only determinants, shape the mental health of minorities and alter the types of mental health services they use. Cultural misunderstandings between patient and clinician, clinician bias, and the fragmentation of mental health services deter minorities from accessing and utilizing care and prevent them from receiving appropriate care. These possibilities intensify with the demographic trends highlighted at the end of the chapter.

CULTURE OF THE PATIENT

The culture of the patient, also known as the consumer of mental health services, influences many aspects of mental health, mental illness, and patterns of health care utilization. One important cautionary note, however, is that general statements about cultural characteristics of a given group may invite stereotyping of individuals based on their appearance or affiliation. Because there is usually more diversity within a population than there is between populations (e.g., in terms of level of acculturation, age, income, health status, and social class), information in the following sections should not be treated as stereotypes to be broadly applied to any individual member of a racial, ethnic, or cultural group.

Symptoms, Presentation, and Meaning

The symptoms of mental disorders are found worldwide. They cluster into discrete disorders that are real and disabling (U.S. Department of Health and Human Services [DHHS], 1999). Mental disorders are defined in the *Diagnostic and Statistical Manual of Mental*

Disorders (American Psychiatric Association [APA], 1994). Schizophrenia, bipolar disorder, panic disorder, obsessive compulsive disorder, depression, and other disorders have similar and recognizable symptoms throughout the world (Weissman et al., 1994, 1996, 1997, 1998). Culture-bound syndromes, which appear to be distinctive to certain ethnic groups, are the exception to this general statement. Research has not yet determined whether culture-bound syndromes are distinct[1] from established mental disorders, are variants of them, or whether *both* mental disorders and culture-bound syndromes reflect different ways in which the cultural and social environment interacts with genes to shape illness.

One way in which culture affects mental illness is through how patients describe (or present) their symptoms to their clinicians. There are some well-recognized differences in symptom presentation across cultures. The previous chapter described ethnic variation in symptoms of somatization, the expression of distress through one or more physical (somatic) symptoms (Box 1-3, not included). Asian patients, for example, are more likely to report their somatic symptoms, such as dizziness, while not reporting their emotional symptoms. Yet, when questioned further, they do acknowledge having emotional symptoms (Lin & Cheung, 1999). This finding supports the view that patients in different cultures tend to selectively express or present symptoms in culturally acceptable ways (Kleinman, 1977, 1988).

Cultures also vary with respect to the *meaning* they impart to illness, their way of making sense of the subjective experience of illness and distress (Kleinman, 1988). The meaning of an illness refers to deep-seated attitudes and beliefs a culture holds about whether an illness is "real" or "imagined," whether it is of the body or the mind (or both), whether it warrants sympathy, how much stigma surrounds it, what might cause it, and what type of person might succumb to it. Cultural meanings of illness have real consequences in terms of whether people are motivated to seek treatment, how they cope with their symptoms, how supportive their families and communities are, where they seek help (mental health specialist, primary care provider, clergy, and/or traditional healer), the pathways they take to get services, and how well they fare in treatment. The consequences can be grave—extreme distress,

---

[1]In medicine, each disease or disorder is considered mutually exclusive from another (WHO, 1992). Each disorder is presumed, but rarely proven, to have unique pathophysiology (Scadding, 1996).

disability, and possibly, suicide—when people with severe mental illness do not receive appropriate treatment.

Causation and Prevalence

Cultural and social factors contribute to the causation of mental illness, yet that contribution varies by disorder. Mental illness is considered the product of a complex interaction among biological, psychological, social, and cultural factors. The role of any one of these major factors can be stronger or weaker depending on the disorder (DHHS, 1999).

The prevalence of schizophrenia, for example, is similar throughout the world (about 1 percent of the population), according to the *International Pilot Study on Schizophrenia,* which examined over 1,300 people in 10 countries (World Health Organization [WHO], 1973). International studies using similarly rigorous research methodology have extended the WHO's findings to two other disorders: The lifetime prevalence of bipolar disorder (0.3-1.5%) and panic disorder (0.4-2.9%) were shown to be relatively consistent across parts of Asia, Europe, and North America (Weissman et al., 1994, 1996, 1997, 1998). The global consistency in symptoms and prevalence of these disorders, combined with results of family and molecular genetic studies, indicates that they have high heritability (genetic contribution to the variation of a disease in a population) (National Institute of Mental Health [NIMH], 1998). In other words, it seems that culture and societal factors play a more subordinate role in causation of these disorders.

Cultural and social context weigh more heavily in causation of depression. In the same international studies cited above, prevalence rates for major depression varied from 2 to 19 percent across countries (Weissman et al., 1996). Family and molecular biology studies also indicate less heritability for major depression than for bipolar disorder and schizophrenia (NIMH, 1998). Taken together, the evidence points to social and cultural factors, including exposure to poverty and violence, playing a greater role in the onset of major depression. *In this context, it is important to note that poverty, violence, and other stressful social environments are not unique to any part of the globe, nor are the symptoms and manifestations they produce. However, factors often linked to race or ethnicity, such as socioeconomic status or country of origin can increase the likelihood of exposure to these types of stressors.*

Cultural and social factors have the most direct role in the causation of post-traumatic stress disorder (PTSD). PTSD is a mental disorder caused by exposure to severe trauma, such as genocide, war combat, torture, or the extreme threat of death or serious injury (APA, 1994). These traumatic experiences are associated with the later development of a long-standing pattern of symptoms accompanied by biological changes (Yehuda, 2000). Traumatic experiences are particularly common for certain populations, such as U.S. combat veterans, inner-city residents, and immigrants from countries in turmoil. Studies described in the chapters on Asian Americans and Hispanic Americans reveal alarming rates of PTSD in communities with a high degree of pre-immigration exposure to trauma. For example, in some samples, up to 70 percent of refugees from Vietnam, Cambodia, and Laos met diagnostic criteria for PTSD. By contrast, studies of the U.S. population as a whole find PTSD to have a prevalence of about 4 percent (DHHS, 1999).

Suicide rates vary greatly across countries, as well as across U.S. ethnic sub-groups (Moscicki, 1995). Suicide rates among males in the United States are highest for American Indians and Alaska Natives (Kachur et al., 1995). Rates are lowest for African American women (Kachur et al., 1995). The reasons for the wide divergence in rates are not well understood, but they are likely influenced by variations in the social and cultural contexts for each subgroup (van Heeringen et al., 2000; Ji et al., 2001).

Even though there are similarities and differences in the distribution of certain mental disorders across populations, the United States has an aggregate rate of about 20 percent of adults and children with diagnosable mental disorders (DHHS, 1999; Table 1-1, not included). The aggregate rate for the population as a whole does not have sufficient representation from most minority groups to permit comparisons between whites and other ethnic groups. The rates of mental disorder are not sufficiently studied in many smaller ethnic groups to permit firm conclusions about overall prevalence; however, several epidemiological studies of ethnic populations, supported by the NIMH, are currently in progress. Until more definitive findings are available, this Supplement concludes, on the basis of smaller studies, that overall prevalence rates for mental disorders in the United States are similar across minority and majority populations. This general conclusion applies to racial and ethnic minority populations living in the community, because high-need subgroups are not well captured in community household surveys.

Family Factors

Many features of family life have a bearing on mental health and mental illness. Starting with etiology, Chapter 1 highlighted that family factors can protect against, or contribute to, the risk of developing a mental illness. For example, supportive families and good sibling relationships can protect against the onset of mental illness. On the other hand, a family environment marked by severe marital discord, overcrowding, and social disadvantage can contribute to the onset of mental illness. Conditions such as child abuse, neglect, and sexual abuse also place children at risk for mental disorders and suicide (Brown et al., 1999; Dinwiddie et al., 2000).

Family risk and protective factors for mental illness vary across ethnic groups. But research has not yet reached the point of identifying whether the variation across ethnic groups is a result of that group's culture, its social class and relationship to the broader society, or individual features of family members.

One of the most developed lines of research on family factors and mental illness deals with relapse in schizophrenia. The first studies, conducted in Great Britain, found that people with schizophrenia who returned from hospitalizations to live with family members who expressed criticism, hostility, or emotional involvement (called *high expressed emotion*) were more likely to relapse than were those who returned to family members who expressed lower levels of negative emotion (Leff & Vaughn, 1985; Kavanaugh, 1992; Bebbington & Kuipers, 1994; Lopez & Guarnaccia, 2000). Later studies extended this line of research to Mexican American samples. These studies reconceptualized the role of family as a dynamic interaction between patients and their families, rather than as static family characteristics (Jenkins, Kleinman, & Good, 1991; Jenkins, 1993). Using this approach, a study comparing Mexican American and white families found that different types of interactions predicted relapse. For the Mexican American families, interactions featuring distance or lack of warmth predicted relapse for the individual with schizophrenia better than interactions featuring criticism. For whites, the converse was true (Lopez et al., 1998). This example, while not necessarily generalizable to other Hispanic groups, suggests avenues by which other culturally based family differences may be related to the course of mental illness.

Coping Styles

Culture relates to how people cope with everyday problems and more extreme types of adversity. Some Asian American groups, for example, tend not to dwell on upsetting thoughts, thinking that reticence or avoidance is better than outward expression. They place a higher emphasis on suppression of affect (Hsu, 1971; Kleinman, 1977), with some tending first to rely on themselves to cope with distress (Narikiyo & Kameoka, 1992). African Americans tend to take an active approach in facing personal problems, rather than avoiding them (Broman, 1996). They are more inclined than whites to depend on handling distress on their own (Sussman et al., 1987). They also appear to rely more on spirituality to help them cope with adversity and symptoms of mental illness (Broman, 1996; Cooper-Patrick et al., 1997; Neighbors et al., 1998).

Few doubt the importance of culture in fostering different ways of coping, but research is sparse. One of the few, yet well developed, lines of research on coping styles comes from comparisons of children living in Thailand versus America. Thailand's largely Buddhist religion and culture encourage self-control, emotional restraint, and social inhibition. In a recent study, Thai children were two times more likely than American children to report reliance on covert coping methods such as "not talking back," than on overt coping methods such as "screaming" and "running away" (McCarty et al., 1999). Other studies by these investigators established that different coping styles are associated with different types and degrees of problem behaviors in children (Weisz et al., 1997).

The studies noted here suggest that better understanding of coping styles among racial and ethnic minorities has implications for the promotion of mental health, the prevention of mental illness, and the nature and severity of mental health problems.

Treatment Seeking

It is well documented that racial and ethnic minorities in the United States are less likely than whites to seek mental health treatment, which largely accounts for their under-representation in most mental health services (Sussman et al., 1987; Kessler et al., 1996; Vega et al. 1998; Zhang et al., 1998). Treatment seeking denotes the pathways taken to reach treatment and the types of treatments sought (Rogler & Cortes, 1993). The pathways are the sequence of contacts and their duration once someone (or their family) recognizes their distress as a health problem.

Research indicates that some minority groups are more likely than whites to delay seeking treatment until symptoms are more severe. Further, racial and ethnic minorities are less inclined than whites to seek treatment from mental health specialists (Gallo et al., 1995; Chun et al., 1996; Zhang et al., 1998). Instead, studies indicate that minorities turn more often to primary care (Cooper-Patrick et al., 1999a; see later section on *Primary Care*). They also turn to informal sources of care such as clergy, traditional healers, and family and friends (Neighbors & Jackson, 1984; Peifer et al., 2000). In particular, American Indians and Alaska Natives often rely on traditional healers, who frequently work side-by-side with formal providers in tribal mental health programs. African Americans often rely on ministers, who may play various mental health roles as counselor, diagnostician, or referral agent (Levin, 1986). The extent to which minority groups rely on informal sources in lieu of, or in addition to, formal mental health services in primary or specialty care is not well studied.

When they use mental health services, some African Americans prefer therapists of the same race or ethnicity. This preference has encouraged the development of ethnic-specific programs that match patients to therapists of the same culture or ethnicity (Sue, 1998). Many African Americans also prefer counseling to drug therapy (Dwight-Johnson et al., 2000). Their concerns revolve around side effects, effectiveness, and addiction potential of medications (Cooper-Patrick et al., 1997).

The fundamental question raised by this line of research is: Why are many racial and ethnic minorities less inclined than whites to seek mental health treatment? Certainly, the constellation of barriers deterring whites also operates to various degrees for minorities-cost, fragmentation of services, and the societal stigma on mental illness (DHHS, 1999). But there are extra barriers deterring racial and ethnic minorities such as mistrust and limited English proficiency.

Mistrust

Mistrust was identified by the SGR as a major barrier to the receipt of mental health treatment by racial and ethnic minorities (DHHS, 1999). Mistrust is widely accepted as pervasive among minorities, yet there is surprisingly little empirical research to document it (Cooper-Patrick et al., 1999). One of the few studies on this topic looked at African Americans and whites surveyed in the early 1980s in a national study known as the Epidemiologic Catchment Area (ECA) study. This study found that African Americans with major depression were more likely to cite their fears of hospitalization and of treatment as reasons for not seeking mental health treatment. For instance, almost half of African Americans, as opposed to 20 percent of whites, reported being afraid of mental health treatment (Sussman et al., 1987).

What are the reasons behind the lack of trust? Mistrust of clinicians by minorities arises, in the broadest sense, from historical persecution and from present-day struggles with racism and discrimination. It also arises from documented abuses and perceived mistreatment, both in the past and more recently, by medical and mental health professionals (Neal-Barnett & Smith, 1997; see later section on "Clinician Bias and Stereotyping"). A recent survey conducted for the Kaiser Family Foundation (Brown et al., 1999) found that 12 percent of African Americans and 15 percent of Latinos, in comparison with 1 percent of whites, felt that a doctor or health provider judged them unfairly or treated them with disrespect because of their race or ethnic background. Even stronger ethnic differences were reported in the Commonwealth Fund Minority Health Survey: It found that 43 percent of African Americans and 28 percent of Latinos, in comparison with 5 percent of whites, felt that a health care provider treated them badly because of their race or ethnic background (LaVeist et al., 2000). Mistrust of mental health professionals is exploited by present day antipsychiatry groups that target the African American community with incendiary material about purported abuses and mistreatment (Bell, 1996).

Mistrustful attitudes also may be commonplace among other groups. While insufficiently studied, mistrust toward health care providers can be inferred from a group's attitudes toward government-operated institutions. Immigrants and refugees from many regions of the world, including Central and South America and Southeast Asia, feel extreme mistrust of government, based on atrocities committed in their country of origin and on fear of deportation by U.S. authorities. Similarly, many American Indians and Alaska Natives are mistrustful of health care institutions; this dates back through centuries of legalized discrimination and segregation.

Stigma

Stigma was portrayed by the SGR as the "most formidable obstacle to future progress in the arena of mental illness and health" (DHHS, 1999). It refers to a cluster of negative attitudes and beliefs that motivate the general public to fear, reject, avoid, and discriminate against people with mental illness (Corrigan & Penn, 1999).

Stigma is widespread in the United States and other Western nations (Bhugra, 1989; Brockington et al., 1993) and in Asian nations (Ng, 1997). In response to societal stigma, people with mental problems internalize public attitudes and become so embarrassed or ashamed that they often conceal symptoms and fail to seek treatment (Sussman et al., 1987; Wahl, 1999). Stigma also lowers their access to resources and opportunities, such as housing and employment, and leads to diminished self-esteem and greater isolation and hopelessness (Penn & Martin, 1998; Corrigan & Penn, 1999). Stigma can also be against family members; this damages the consumer's self-esteem and family relationships (Wahl & Harman, 1989). In some Asian cultures, stigma is so extreme that mental illness is thought to reflect poorly on family lineage and thereby diminishes marriage and economic prospects for other family members as well (Sue & Morishima, 1982; Ng, 1997).

Stigma is such a major problem that the very topic itself poses a challenge to research. Researchers have to contend with people's reluctance to disclose attitudes often deemed socially unacceptable. How stigma varies by culture can be studied from two perspectives. One perspective is that of the targets of stigma, i.e., the people with symptoms: If they are members of a racial or ethnic minority, are they more likely than whites to experience stigma? The other perspective is that of the public in their attitudes toward people with mental illness: Are members of each racial or ethnic minority group more likely than whites to hold stigmatizing attitudes toward mental illness? The answers to these cross-cultural questions are far from definitive, but there are some interesting clues from research.

Turning first to those who experience symptoms, one of the few cross-cultural studies questioned Asian Americans living in Los Angeles. The findings were eye-opening: Only 12 percent of Asians would mention their mental health problems to a friend or relative (versus 25 percent of whites). A meager 4 percent of Asians would seek help from a psychiatrist or specialist (versus 26 percent of whites). And only 3 percent of Asians would seek help from a physician (versus 13 percent of whites). The study concluded that stigma was pervasive and pronounced for Asian Americans in Los Angeles (Zhang et al., 1998).

Turning to the question of public attitudes toward mental illness, the largest and most detailed study of stigma in the United States was performed in 1996 as part of the General Social Survey, a respected, nationally representative survey being conducted by the National Opinion Research Center since the 1970s. In this study, a representative sample was asked in personal interviews to respond to different vignettes depicting people with mental illness. The respondents generally viewed people with mental illness as dangerous and less competent to handle their own affairs, with their harshest judgments reserved for people with schizophrenia and substance use disorders. Interestingly, neither the ethnicity of the respondent, nor the ethnicity of the person portrayed in the vignette, seemed to influence the degree of stigma (Pescosolido et al., 1999).

By contrast, another large, nationally representative study found a different relationship between race, ethnicity, and attitudes towards patients with mental illness. Asian and Hispanic Americans saw them as more dangerous than did whites. Although having contact with individuals with mental illness helped to reduce stigma for whites, it did not for African Americans. American Indians, on the other hand, held attitudes similar to whites (Whaley, 1997).

Taken together, these results suggest that minorities hold similar, and in some cases stronger, stigmatizing attitudes toward mental illness than do whites. Societal stigma keeps minorities from seeking needed mental health care, much as it does for whites. Stigma is so potent that it not only affects the self-esteem of people with mental illness, but also that of family members. The bottom line is that stigma does deter major segments of the population, majority and minority alike, from seeking help. It bears repeating that a majority of *all* people with diagnosable mental disorders do not get treatment (DHHS, 1999).

Immigration

Migration, a stressful life event, can influence mental health. Often called acculturative stress, it occurs during the process of adapting to a new culture (Berry et al., 1987). Refugees who leave their homelands because of extreme threat from political forces tend to experience more trauma, more undesirable change, and less control over the events that define their exits than do voluntary immigrants (Rumbaut, 1989; Meinhardt et al., 1986).

The psychological stress associated with immigration tends to be concentrated in the first three years after arrival in the United States (Vega & Rumbaut, 1991). According to studies of Southeast Asian refugees, an initial euphoria often characterizes the first year following migration, followed by a strong disenchantment and demoralization reaction during the second year. The third year includes a gradual return to well-being and satisfaction (Rumbaut, 1985, 1989). This U-shaped curve has been observed in Cubans and Eastern Europeans (Portes & Rumbaut, 1990). Similarly, Ying (1988) finds that Chinese immigrants who have been in the United States less than one year have fewer symptoms of distress than those residing here for several years. Korean American immigrants have been found to have the highest levels of depressive symptoms in the one to two years following immigration; after three years, these symptoms remit (Hurh & Kim, 1988).

Although immigration can bring stress and subsequent psychological distress, research results do not suggest that immigration *per se* results in higher rates of mental disorders (e.g., Vega et al., 1998). However, as described in the chapters on Asian Americans and Latinos, the traumas experienced by adults and children from war-torn countries before and after immigrating to the United States seem to result in high rates of posttraumatic stress disorder (PTSD) among these populations.

Overall Health Status

The burden of illness in the United States is higher in racial and ethnic minorities than whites. The National Institutes of Health (NIH) recently reported that compared with the majority populations, U.S. minority populations have shorter overall life expectancies and higher rates of cardiovascular disease, cancer, infant mortality, birth defects, asthma, diabetes, stroke, adverse consequences of substance abuse, and sexually transmitted diseases (DHHS, 2000; NIH, 2000). The list of illnesses is overpoweringly long.

Disparities in health status have led to high-profile research and policy initiatives. One longstanding policy initiative is *Healthy People,* a comprehensive set of national health objectives issued every decade by the Department of Health and Human Services. The most recent is *Healthy People 2010,* which contains both well defined objectives for reducing health disparities and the means for monitoring progress (DHHS, 2000).

Higher rates of physical (somatic) disorders among racial and ethnic minorities hold significant implications for mental health. For example, minority individuals who do not have mental disorders are at higher risk for developing problems such as depression and anxiety because chronic physical illness is a risk factor for mental disorders (DHHS, 1999; see also earlier section). Moreover, individuals from racial and ethnic minority groups who *already* have both a mental and a physical disorder (known as comorbidity) are more likely to have their mental disorder missed or misdiagnosed, owing to competing demands on primary care providers who are preoc-

cupied with the treatment of the somatic disorder (Borowsky, et al., 2000; Rost et al., 2000). Even if their mental disorder is recognized and treated, people with comorbid disorders are saddled by more drug interactions and side effects, given their higher usage of medications. Finally, people with comorbid disorders are much more likely to be unemployed and disabled, compared with people who have a single disability (Druss et al., 2000).

Thus, poor somatic health takes a toll on mental health. And it is probable that some of the mental health disparities described in this Supplement are linked to the poorer somatic health status of racial and ethnic minorities. The interrelationships between mind and body are inescapably evident.

CULTURE OF THE CLINICIAN

As noted earlier, a group of professionals can be said to have a "culture" in the sense that they have a shared set of beliefs, norms, and values. This culture is reflected in the jargon members of a group use, in the orientation and emphasis in their textbooks, and in their mindset, or way of looking at the world.

Health professionals in the United States, and the institutions in which they train and practice, are rooted in Western medicine. The culture of Western medicine, launched in ancient Greece, emphasizes the primacy of the human body in disease.[2] Further, Western medicine emphasizes the acquisition of knowledge through scientific and empirical methods, which hold objectivity paramount. Through these methods, Western medicine strives to uncover universal truths about disease, its causation, diagnosis, and treatment.

Around 1900, Western medicine started to conceptualize disease as affected by social, as well as by biological phenomena. Its scope began to incorporate wider questions of income, lifestyle, diet, employment, and family structure, thereby ushering in the broader field of public health (Porter, 1997).

Mental health professionals trace their roots to Western medicine and, more particularly, to two major European milestones—the first forms of biological psychiatry in the mid-19th century and the advent of psychotherapy (or "talk therapy") near the end of that century (Shorter, 1997). The earliest

---

[2]In very general terms, most other healing systems throughout history conceived of sickness and health in the context of understanding relations of human beings to the cosmos, including planets, stars, mountains, rivers, deities, spirits, and ancestors (Porter 1997).

forms of biological psychiatry primed the path for more than a century of advances in pharmacological therapy, or drug treatment, for mental illness. The original psychotherapy, known as psychoanalysis, was founded in Vienna by Sigmund Freud. While many forms of psychotherapy are available today, with vastly different orientations, all emphasize verbal communication between patient and therapist as the basis of treatment. Today's treatments for specific mental disorders also may combine pharmacological therapy and psychotherapy; this approach is known as multimodal therapy. These two types of treatment and the intellectual and scientific traditions that galvanized their development are an outgrowth of Western medicine.

To say that physicians or mental health professionals have their own culture does not detract from the universal truths discovered by their fields. Rather, it means that most clinicians share a worldview about the interrelationship among body, mind, and environment, informed by knowledge acquired through the scientific method. It also means that clinicians view symptoms, diagnoses, and treatments in a manner that sometimes diverges from their patients. "[Clinicians'] conceptions of disease and [their] responses to it unquestionably show the imprint of [a] particular culture, especially its individualist and activist therapeutic mentality," writes sociologist of medicine Paul Starr (1982).

Because of the professional culture of the clinician, some degree of distance between clinician and patient always exists, regardless of the ethnicity of each (Burkett, 1991). Clinicians also bring to the therapeutic setting their own personal cultures (Hunt, 1995; Porter, 1997). Thus, when clinician and patient do not come from the same ethnic or cultural background, there is greater potential for cultural differences to emerge. Clinicians may be more likely to ignore symptoms that the patient deems important, or less likely to understand the patient's fears, concerns, and needs. The clinician and the patient also may harbor different assumptions about what a clinician is supposed to do, how a patient should act, what causes the illness, and what treatments are available. For these reasons, *DSM-IV* exhorts clinicians to understand how their relationship with the patient is affected by cultural differences.

Communication

The emphasis on verbal communication is a distinguishing feature of the mental health field. The diagnosis and treatment of mental disorders depend to a large extent on verbal communication between patient and clinician about symptoms, their nature, intensity, and impact on functioning. While many mental health professionals strive to deliver treatment that is sensitive to the culture of the patient, problems can occur.

The emphasis on verbal communication yields greater potential for miscommunication when clinician and patient come from different cultural backgrounds, even if they speak the same language. Overt and subtle forms of miscommunication and misunderstanding can lead to misdiagnosis, conflicts over treatment, and poor adherence to a treatment plan. But when patient and clinician do not speak the same language, these problems intensify. The importance of cross-cultural communication in establishing trusting relationships between clinician and patient is just beginning to be explored through research in family practice (Cooper-Patrick et al., 1999) and mental health (see later section on "Culturally Competent Services").

Primary Care

Primary care is a critical portal to mental health treatment for ethnic and racial minorities. Minorities are more likely to seek help in primary care as opposed to specialty care, and cross-cultural problems may surface in either setting (Cooper-Patrick et al., 1999). Primary care providers, particularly under the constraints of managed care, may not have the time or capacity to recognize and diagnose mental disorders or to treat them adequately, especially if patients have co-existing physical disorders (Rost et al., 2000). Some estimates suggest that about one-third to one-half of patients with mental disorders go undiagnosed in primary care settings (Higgins, 1994; Williams et al., 1999). Minority patients are among those at greatest risk of nondetection of mental disorders in primary care (Borowsky et al., 2000). Missed or incorrect diagnoses carry severe consequences if patients are given inappropriate or possibly harmful treatments, while their underlying mental disorder is left untreated.

Clinician Bias and Stereotyping

Misdiagnosis also can arise from clinician bias and stereotyping of ethnic and racial minorities. Clinicians often reflect the attitudes and discriminatory practices of their society (Whaley, 1998). This institutional racism was evident over a century ago with the establishment of a separate, completely segregated mental hospital in Virginia for African American patients (Prudhomme & Musto, 1973).

While racism and discrimination have certainly diminished over time, there are traces today which are manifest in less overt medical practices concerning diagnosis, treatment, prescribing medications, and referrals (Giles et al., 1995; Shiefer, Escarce, & Schulman, 2000). One study from the mental health field found that African American youth were four times more likely than whites to be physically restrained after acting in similarly aggressive ways, suggesting that racial stereotypes of blacks as violent motivated the professional judgment to have them restrained (Bond et al., 1988). Another study found that white therapists rated a videotape of an African American client with depression more negatively than they did a white patient with identical symptoms (Jenkins-Hall & Sacco, 1991).

There is ample documentation shown that African American patients are subject to overdiagnosis of schizophrenia. African Americans are also underdiagnosed for bipolar disorder (Bell et al., 1980, 1981; Mukherjee, et al., 1983), depression, and, possibly, anxiety (Neal-Barnett & Smith, 1997; Baker & Bell, 1999; Borowsky et al., 2000). The problems extend beyond African Americans. Widely held stereotypes of Asian Americans as "problem free" may prompt clinicians to overlook their mental health problems (Takeuchi & Uehara, 1996). Also, minority patients are less likely than whites to receive the best available treatments for depression and anxiety (Wang et al., 2000; Young et al., 2001).

To infer a role for bias and stereotyping by clinicians does not prove that it is actually occurring, nor does it indicate the extent to which it explains disparities in mental health services. Some of the racial and ethnic disparities described in this Supplement are likely the result of racism[3] and discrimination by white clinicians; however, the limited research on this topic suggests that the issue is more complex. A large study of cardiac patients could not attribute African Americans' lower utilization of a cardiac procedure to the race of the physician. Lower utilization by African American versus white patients was independent of whether patients were treated by white or black physicians (Chen et al., 2001). The study authors suggested the possibility that institutional factors and attitudes that were common to black and white physicians contributed to lower rates of utilization by black patients. Some have suggested that what appears to be racial bias by clinicians might instead reflect biases of their socioeconomic status or their professional culture (Epstein & Ayanian, 2001). These biases, whether intentional or unintentional, may be more powerful influences on care than the influence of the clinician's own race or ethnicity.

CULTURE, SOCIETY, AND MENTAL HEALTH SERVICES

Every society influences mental health treatment by how it organizes, delivers, and pays for mental health services. In the United States, services are financed and delivered in vastly different ways than in other nations. That organization was shaped by and reflects a unique set of historical, economic, political, and social forces, which were summarized in the SGR (DHHS, 1999). The mental health service system is a fragmented patchwork, often referred to as the "*de facto* mental health system" because of its lack of a single set of organizing principles (Regier et al., 1993). While this hybrid system serves a range of functions for many people, it has not successfully addressed the problem that people with the most complex needs and the fewest financial resources often find it difficult to use. This problem is magnified for minority groups. To understand the obstacles that minorities face, this section provides background on mental health service settings, financing, and the concept of culturally competent services.

Service Settings and Sectors

Mental health services are provided by numerous types of practitioners in a diverse array of environments, variously called settings and sectors. Settings range from home and community to institutions, and sectors include public or private primary care and specialty care. This section provides a broad overview of mental health services, patterns of use, and trends in financing. Interested readers are referred to the SGR, which covers these topics in greater detail.

The burgeoning types of community services available today stand in sharp contrast to the institutional orientation of the past. Propelled by reform movements, advocacy, and the advent of managed care, today's best mental health services extend beyond diagnosis and treatment to cover prevention and the fulfillment of broader needs, including housing and employment. Services are formal (provided by professionals) or informal (provided by lay volunteers). The most fundamental shift has been in the

---

[3]Defined in the next section of this chapter as "beliefs, attitudes, and practices that denigrate individuals or groups because of phenotypic characteristics or ethnic group affilliation . . . . [which] can be perpetrated by institutions or individuals, acting intentionally or unintentionally."

setting for service delivery, from the institution to the community.

There are four major sectors for receiving mental health care:

1. The specialty mental health sector is designed solely for the provision of mental health services. It refers to mental hospitals, residential treatment facilities, and psychiatric units of general hospitals. It also refers to specialized agencies and programs in the community, such as community mental health centers, day-treatment programs, and rehabilitation programs. Within these settings, services are furnished by specialized mental health professionals, such as psychologists, psychiatric nurses, psychiatrists, and psychiatric social workers;

2. The general medical and primary care sector offers a comprehensive range of health care services including, but not limited to, mental health services. Primary care physicians, nurse practitioners, internists, and pediatricians are the general types of professionals who practice in a range of settings that include clinics, offices, community health centers, and hospitals;

3. The human services sector is made up of social welfare (housing, transportation, and employment), criminal justice, educational, religious, and charitable services. These services are delivered in a full range of settings-home, community, and institutions;

4. The voluntary support network refers to self-help groups and organizations devoted to education, communication, and support. Services provided by the voluntary support network are largely found in the community. Typically informal in nature, they often help patients and families increase knowledge, reduce feelings of isolation, obtain referrals to formal treatment, and cope with mental health problems and illnesses.

Consumers can exercise choice in treatment largely because of the range of effective treatments for mental illness and the diversity of settings and sectors in which these treatments are offered. Consumers can choose, too, between distinct treatment modalities, such as psychotherapy, counseling, pharmacotherapy (medications), or rehabilitation. For severe mental illnesses, however, all types are usually essential, as are delivery systems to integrate their services (DHHS, 1999).

Consumer preferences cannot necessarily be inferred from the types of treatment they actually use because costs, reimbursement, or availability of services—rather than preferences—may drive their utilization. For example, minority patients who wish to see mental health professionals of similar racial or ethnic backgrounds may often find it difficult or impossible, because most mental health practitioners are white. Because there are only 1.5 American Indian/Alaska Native psychiatrists per 100,000 American Indians/Alaska Natives in this country, and only 2.0 Hispanic psychiatrists per 100,000 Hispanics, the chance of an ethnic match between Native or Hispanic American patient and provider is highly unlikely (Manderscheid & Henderson, 1999).

Financing of Mental Health Serves and Managed Care

Mental health services are financed from many funding streams that originate in the public and private sectors. In 1996, slightly more than half of the $69 billion in mental health spending was by public payers, including Medicaid and Medicare. The remainder came mostly from either private insurance (27%) or out-of-pocket payments (17%) by patients and their families (DHHS, 1999).

One of the most significant changes affecting both privately and publicly funded services has been the striking shift to managed care. Relatively uncommon two decades ago, managed care in some form now covers the majority of Americans, regardless of whether their care is paid for through the public or the private sector (Levit & Lundy, 1998). The term "managed care" technically refers to a variety of mechanisms for organizing, delivering, and paying for health services. It is attractive to purchasers because it holds the promise of containing costs, increasing access to care, improving coordination of care, promoting evidence-based quality care, and emphasizing prevention. Attainment of these goals for all racial and ethnic groups is difficult to verify through research because of the breathtaking pace of change in the health care marketplace. Study in this area is also challenging because claims data are closely held by private companies and thus are often unavailable to researchers, and because insurers and providers often do not collect information about ethnicity or race (Fraser, 1997).

Almost 72 percent of Americans with health insurance in 1999 were enrolled in managed *behavioral* health organizations for mental or addictive disorders (OPEN MINDS, 1999). Managed care has far-reaching implications for mental health services in terms of access, utilization, and quality, yet there has been only a limited body of research on its effectiveness in these areas (DHHS, 1999).

Through lower costs, managed care was expected to boost access to care, which is especially critical for racial and ethnic minorities. However, there is preliminary evidence that managed care is perceived by some racial and ethnic minorities as imposing more barriers to treatment than does fee-for-service care (Scholle & Kelleher, 1997; Provan & Carle, 2000). Yet, improved access alone will not eliminate disparities. Other compelling factors curtail utilization of services by racial and ethnic minorities, and they need to be addressed to reduce the gap between minorities and whites.

In terms of quality of care, the SGR noted ongoing efforts within behavioral health care to develop quality reporting systems. It also pointed out that existing incentives within and outside managed care do not encourage an emphasis on quality of care (DHHS, 1999). While the SGR concluded that there is little direct evidence of problems with quality in well implemented managed care programs, it cautioned that "the risk for more impaired populations and children remains a serious concern."

Finally, managed care has been coupled with legislative proposals to impose parity in financing of mental health services. Intended to reverse decades of inequity, parity seeks coverage for mental health services on a par with that for somatic (physical) illness. Managed care's potential to control costs through various management strategies that prevent overuse of services makes parity more economically feasible (DHHS, 1999). Studies described in the SGR found negligible cost increases under existing parity programs within several States. Further, several studies have shown that racial and ethnic disparities in access to health care and in treatment outcomes are reduced or eliminated under equal access systems such as the Department of Defense health care system (Optenberg et al., 1995; Taylor et al., 1997), the VA medical system for some disease conditions, and in some health maintenance organizations (Tambor et al., 1994; Martin, Shelby, & Zhang, 1995; Clancy & Franks, 1997).

Evidence-Based Treatment and Minorities

The SGR documented a comprehensive range of effective treatments for many mental disorders (DHHS, 1999). These evidence-based treatments rely on consistent scientific evidence, from controlled clinical trials, that they significantly improve patients' out-comes (Drake et al., 2001). Despite strong and consistent evidence of efficacy, the SGR spotlighted the problem that evidence-based treatments are not being translated into community settings and are not being provided to everyone who comes in for care.

Many reasons have been cited as underlying the gap between research and practice. The most significant are practitioners' lack of knowledge of research results, the lag time between reporting of results and their translation into the practice setting, and the cost of introducing innovative services into health systems, most of which are operating within a highly competitive marketplace. There are also fundamental differences in the health characteristics of patients studied in academic settings where the research is conducted versus practice settings where patients are much more heterogeneous and often disabled by more than one disorder (DHHS, 1999).

The gap between research and practice is even worse for racial and ethnic minorities. Problems span both research and practice settings. A special analysis performed for this Supplement reveals that controlled clinical trials used to generate professional treatment guidelines did not conduct specific analyses for any minority group. Controlled clinical trials offer the highest level of scientific rigor for establishing that a given treatment works.

Several professional associations and government agencies have formulated treatment guidelines or evidence-based reports on treatment outcomes for certain disorders on the basis of consistent scientific evidence, across multiple controlled clinical trials. Since 1986, nearly 10,000 participants have been included in randomized clinical trials evaluating the efficacy of treatments for bipolar disorder, major depression, schizophrenia, and attention-deficit/hyperactivity disorder. However, for nearly half of these participants (4,991), no information on race or ethnicity is available.[4] For another 7 percent of participants (N = 656), studies only reported the designation "non-white," without indicating a specific minority group. For the remaining 47 percent of participants (N = 4,335), Table 2-1 shows the breakdown by ethnicity. In all clinical trials reporting data on ethnicity, very few minorities were included and not a single study analyzed the efficacy of the treatment by ethnicity or race.[5] A similar conclusion was reached by the American

---

[4]Researchers may have collected this information but did not report it in their published studies.
[5]One study of attention-deficit/hyperactivity disorder (AD/HD), the NIMH Multimodal Treatment Study of AD/HD, plans to conduct ethnic-specific analyses.

| Table 2 | Ethnic Specific Analyses in Clinical Trials for Developing Evidence Based Treatment Guidelines |

STUDIES	Total Number of Participants	NUMBER OF PARTICIPANTS FOR WHOM ETHNICITY IS REPORTED							Total Number of Ethnic Specific Analyses Conducted
		N (% of total sample)	White	Unspecified Non-White	Black	Hispanic	AA/PI	AI/AN	
Bipolar Disorder	921	305 (33%)	234	39	32	0	0	0	0
Schizophrenia	2813	2044 (73%)	1314	305	376	44	5	0	0
Depression	3860	1841 (48%)	1571	241	27	0	2	0	0
ADHD	1672	801 (48%)	545	71	126	55	4	0	0
Total	9266	4991 (54%)	3664	656	561	99	11	0	0

See Appendix A (not included)

Psychological Association in a careful analysis of all empirically validated psychotherapies: "We know of no psychotherapy treatment research that meets basic criteria important for demonstrating treatment efficacy for ethnic minority populations . . ." (Chambless et al., 1996).

The failure to conduct ethnic-specific analyses in clinical research is a problem that must be addressed. This problem is not unique to the mental health field; it affects all areas of health research. In 1993, Congress passed legislation creating the National Institute of Health's Office of Research on Minority Health to increase the representation of minorities in all aspects of biomedical and behavioral research (National Institutes of Health, 2001). In November 2000, the Minority Health Disparities Research and Education Act elevated the Office of Research on Minority Health to the National Center on Minority Health and Health Disparities. This gave NIH increased programmatic and budget authority for research on minority health issues and health disparities. The law also promotes more training and education of health professionals, the evaluation of data collection systems, and a national public awareness campaign.

Even though the treatment guidelines are extrapolated from largely white populations, they are, as a matter of public health prudence, the best available treatments for everyone, regardless of race or ethnicity. Yet evidence suggests that in clinical practice settings, minorities are less likely than whites to receive treatment that adheres to treatment guidelines (see also Lehman & Steinwachs, 1998; Sclar et al., 1999; Blazer et al., 2000; Young et al., 2001). Existing treatment guidelines should be used for all people with mental disorders, regardless of ethnicity or race. But to be most effective, treatments need to be tailored and delivered appropriately for individuals according to age, gender, race, ethnicity, and culture (DHHS, 1999).

Culturally Competent Services

The last four decades have witnessed tremendous changes in mental health service delivery. The civil rights movement, the expansion of mental health services into the community, and the demographic shift toward greater population diversity led to a growing awareness of inadequacies of the mental health system in meeting the needs of ethnic and racial minorities (Rogler et al., 1987; Takeuchi & Uehara, 1996). Research documented huge variations in utilization between minorities and whites, and it began to uncover the influence of culture on mental health and mental illness (Snowden & Cheung, 1990; Sue et al., 1991). Major differences were found in some manifestations of mental disorders, idioms for communicating distress, and patterns of help-seeking. The natural outgrowth of research and public awareness was self-examination by the mental health field and the advent of consumer and family advocacy. Major recognition was given to the importance of culture in the assessment of mental illness with the publication of the "*Outline for Culture Formulation*" in DSM-IV (APA, 1994).

Another innovation was to take stock of the mental health treatment setting. This setting is arguably unique in terms of its strong reliance on language, communication, and trust between patients and providers. Key elements of therapeutic success depend on rapport and on the clinicians' understanding of patients' cultural identity, social supports, self-esteem, and reticence about treatment due to societal stigma. Advocates, practitioners, and policymakers, driven by widespread awareness of treatment inadequacies for minorities, began to press for a new treatment approach: the delivery of services responsive to the cultural concerns of racial and ethnic minority groups, including their languages, histories, traditions, beliefs, and values. This approach to service delivery, often referred to as cultural competence, has been promoted largely on the basis of humanistic values and intuitive sensibility rather than empirical evidence. Nevertheless, substantive data from consumer and family self-reports, ethnic match, and ethnic-specific services outcome studies suggest that tailoring services to the specific needs of these groups will improve utilization and outcomes.

Cultural competence underscores the recognition of patients' cultures and then develops a set of skills, knowledge, and policies to deliver effective treatments (Sue & Sue, 1999). Underlying cultural competence is the conviction that services tailored to culture would be more inviting, would encourage minorities to get treatment, and would improve their outcome once in treatment. Cultural competence represents a fundamental shift in ethnic and race relations (Sue et al., 1998). The term *competence* places the responsibility on mental health services organizations and practitioners—most of whom are white (Peterson et al., 1996)—and challenges them to deliver culturally appropriate services. Yet the participation of consumers, families, and communities helping service systems design and carry out culturally appropriate services is also essential.

Many models of cultural competence have been proposed. One of the most frequently cited models was developed in the context of care for children and adolescents with serious emotional disturbance (Cross et al., 1989). At the Federal level, efforts have begun to operationalize cultural competence for applied behavioral healthcare settings (U.S. CMHS, 2000). Though

these and many other models have been proposed, few if any have been subject to empirical test. No empirical data are yet available as to what the key ingredients of cultural competence are and what influence, if any, they have on clinical outcomes for racial and ethnic minorities (e.g., Sue & Zane, 1987; Ramirez, 1991; Pedersen & Ivey, 1993; Ridley et al., 1994; Lopez, 1997; Szapocznik et al. 1997; Falicov, 1998; Koss-Chioino & Vargas, 1999; Sue & Sue, 1999). A common theme across models of cultural competence, however, is that they make treatment effectiveness for a culturally diverse clientele the responsibility of the system, not of the people seeking treatment.

The main point is that cultural competence is more than the sum of its parts: It is a broad-based approach to transform the organization and delivery of all mental health services to meet the diverse needs of all patients.

Medications and Minorities

There are overall genetic similarities across ethnic groups and it is noted that while there may be some genetic polymorphisms that show mean differences between groups, these variations cannot be used to distinguish one population from another. Observed group differences are outweighed by shared genetic variation and may be correlates of lifestyle rather than genetic factors (Paabo, 2001). For example, researchers are finding some racial and ethnic differences in response to a heart medication (Exner et al., 2001) that appear to reflect both genetic and environmental factors. It is nevertheless reasonable to assume that medications for mental disorders, in the absence of data to the contrary, are as effective for racial and ethnic minority groups as they are for whites. Therefore, this Supplement encourages people with mental illness, regardless of race or ethnicity, to take advantage of scientific advances and seek effective pharmacological treatments for mental illness. As part of the standard practice of delivering medicine, clinicians always need to individualize therapies according to the age, gender, culture, ethnicity, and other life circumstances of the patient.

There is a growing body of research on subtle genetic differences in how medications are metabolized across certain ethnic populations. Similarly, this body of research also focuses on how lifestyles that are more common to a given ethnic group affect drug metabolism. Lifestyle factors include diet, rates of smoking, alcohol consumption, and use of alternative or complementary treatments. These factors can interact with drugs to alter their safety or effectiveness.

The relatively new field known as ethnopsychopharmacology investigates ethnic variations that affect medication dosing and other aspects of pharmacology. Most research in this field has focused on gene polymorphisms (DNA variations) affecting drug metabolizing enzymes. After drugs are taken by mouth, they enter the blood and are circulated to the liver, where they are metabolized by enzymes (proteins encoded by genes). Certain genetic variations affecting the functions of these enzymes are more common to particular racial or ethnic groups. The variations can affect the pace of drug metabolism: A faster rate of metabolism leaves less drug in the circulation, whereas a slower rate allows more drug to be recirculated to other parts of the body. For example, African Americans and Asians are, on average, more likely than whites to be slow metabolizers of several medications for psychosis and depression (Lin et al., 1997). Clinicians who are unaware of these differences may inadvertently prescribe doses that are too high for minority patients by giving them the dose normally prescribed for whites. This would lead to more medication side effects, patient nonadherence, and possibly greater risk of long-term, severe side effects such as tardive dyskinesia (Lin et al., 1997; Lin & Cheung, 1999).

A key point is that this area of research looks for frequency differences across populations, rather than between individuals. For example, one research study reported on population frequencies for a polymorphism linked to the breakdown of neurotransmitters. It found the particular polymorphism in 15 to 31 percent of East Asians, compared with 7 to 40 percent of Africans, and 33 to 62 percent of Europeans and Southwest Asians (Palmatier et al., 1999). It is important to note that these differences become apparent across populations, but do not apply to an individual seeking treatment (unless the clinician has specific knowledge about that person's genetic makeup, or genotype, or their medication blood levels). The concern about applying research regarding ethnically based differences in population frequencies of gene polymorphisms is that it will lead to stereotyping and racial profiling of individuals based on their physical appearance (Schwartz, 2001). For any individual, genetic variation in response to medications cannot be inferred from racial or ethnic group membership alone.

RACISM, DISCRIMINATION, AND MENTAL HEALTH

Since its inception, America has struggled with its handling of matters related to race, ethnicity, and immigration. The histories of each racial and ethnic minority group attest to long periods of legalized discrimination—and more subtle forms of discrimination—within U.S. borders (Takaki, 1993). Ancestors of many of today's African Americans were forcibly brought to the United States as slaves. The Indian Removal Act of 1830 forced American Indians off their land and onto reservations in remote areas of the country that lacked natural resources and economic opportunities. The Chinese Exclusion Act of 1882 barred immigration from China to the United States and denied citizenship to Chinese Americans until it was repealed in 1952. Over 100,000 Japanese Americans were unconstitutionally incarcerated during World War II, yet none was ever shown to be disloyal. Many Mexican Americans, Puerto Ricans, and Pacific Islanders became U.S. citizens through conquest, not choice. Although racial and ethnic minorities cannot lay claim to being the sole recipients of maltreatment in the United States, legally sanctioned discrimination and exclusion of racial and ethnic minorities have been the rule, rather than the exception, for much of the history of this country.

Racism and discrimination are umbrella terms referring to beliefs, attitudes, and practices that denigrate individuals or groups because of phenotypic characteristics (e.g., skin color and facial features) or ethnic group affiliation. Despite improvements over the last three decades, research continues to document racial discrimination in housing rentals and sales (Yinger, 1995) and in hiring practices (Kirschenman & Neckerman, 1991). Racism and discrimination also have been documented in the administration of medical care. They are manifest, for example, in fewer diagnostic and treatment procedures for African Americans versus whites (Giles et al., 1995; Shiefer et al., 2000). More generally, racism and discrimination take forms from demeaning daily insults to more severe events, such as hate crimes and other violence (Krieger et al., 1999). Racism and discrimination can be perpetrated by institutions or individuals, acting intentionally or unintentionally.

Public attitudes underlying discriminatory practices have been studied in several national surveys conducted over many decades. One of the most respected and nationally representative surveys is the General Social Survey, which in 1990 found that a significant percentage of whites held disparaging stereotypes of African Americans, Hispanics, and Asians. The most extreme findings were that 40 to 56 percent of whites endorsed the view that African Americans and Hispanics "prefer to live off welfare" and "are prone to violence" (Davis & Smith, 1990).

Minority groups commonly report experiences with racism and discrimination, and they consider these experiences to be stressful (Clark et al., 1999). In a national probability sample of minority groups and whites, African Americans and Hispanic Americans reported experiencing higher overall levels of global stress than did whites (Williams, 2000). The differences were greatest for two specific types: financial stress and stress from racial bias. Asian Americans also reported higher overall levels of stress and higher levels of stress from racial bias, but sampling methods did not permit statistical comparisons with other groups. American Indians and Alaska Natives were not studied (Williams, 2000).

Recent studies link the experience of racism to poorer mental and physical health. For example, racial inequalities may be the primary cause of differences in reported quality of life between African Americans and whites (Hughes & Thomas, 1998). Experiences of racism have been linked with hypertension among African Americans (Krieger & Sidney, 1996; Krieger et al., 1999). A study of African Americans found perceived[6] discrimination to be associated with psychological distress, lower well-being, self-reported ill health, and number of days confined to bed (Williams et al., 1997; Ren et al., 1999).

A recent, nationally representative telephone survey looked more closely at two overall types of racism, their prevalence, and how they may differentially affect mental health (Kessler et al., 1999). One type of racism was termed "major discrimination" in reference to dramatic events like being "hassled by police" or "fired from a job." This form of discrimination was reported with a lifetime prevalence of 50 percent of African Americans, in contrast to 31 percent of whites. Major discrimination was associated with psychological distress and major depression in both groups. The other form of discrimination, termed "day-to-day perceived discrimination," was reported to be experienced "often" by almost 25 percent of African Americans and only 3 percent of whites. This form of discrimination was related to the development of distress and diagnoses of generalized anxiety and depression in African Americans and whites. The magnitude of the association between these two forms of discrimination and poorer mental health was similar to other commonly studied stressful life events, such as death of a loved one, divorce, or job loss.

While this line of research is largely focused on African Americans, there are a few studies of racism's impact on other racial and ethnic minorities. Perceived discrimination was linked to symptoms of depression in a large sample of 5,000 children of Asian, Latin American, and Caribbean immigrants (Rumbaut, 1994). Two recent studies found that perceived discrimination was highly related to depressive symptoms among adults of Mexican origin (Finch et al., 2000) and among Asians (Noh et al., 1999).

In summary, the findings indicate that racism and discrimination are clearly stressful events (see also Clark et al., 1999). Racism and discrimination adversely affect health and mental health, and they place minorities *at risk for* mental disorders such as depression and anxiety. Whether racism and discrimination can by themselves cause these disorders is less clear, yet deserves research attention.

These and related findings have prompted researchers to ask how racism may jeopardize the mental health of minorities. Three general ways are proposed:

1. Racial stereotypes and negative images can be internalized, denigrating individuals' self-worth and adversely affecting their social and psychological functioning;

2. Racism and discrimination by societal institutions have resulted in minorities' lower socioeconomic status and poorer living conditions in which poverty, crime, and violence are persistent stressors that can affect mental health (see next section); and

3. Racism and discrimination are stressful events that can directly lead to psychological distress and physiological changes affecting mental health (Williams & Williams-Morris, 2000).

POVERTY, MARGINAL NEIGHBORHOODS, AND COMMUNITY VIOLENCE

Poverty disproportionately affects racial and ethnic minorities. The overall rate of poverty in the United States, 12 percent in 1999, masks great variation. While 8 percent of whites are poor, rates are much higher among racial and ethnic minorities: 11 percent of Asian Americans and Pacific Islanders, 23 percent of Hispanic Americans, 24 percent of African Americans, and 26 percent of American Indians and Alaska Natives (U.S. Census Bureau, 1999). Measured another way, the per capita income for racial and ethnic minority groups is much lower than that for whites (Table 2-2).

---

[6]"Perceived discrimination" is the term used by researchers in reference to the self-reports of individuals about being the target of discrimination or racism. The term is not meant to imply that racism did not take place.

Table 2	Per Capita Income by Ethnicity in 1999	
		Per Capita Incomes
African Americans		$14,397
Hispanic Americans		$11,621
Asian Americans & Pacific Islanders		$21,134
American Indians/Alaska Natives		Not Available
White Americans		$24,109

Source: U.S. Census Bureau, Current Population Reports, Money Income in the U.S., 1999.

For centuries, it has been known that people living in poverty, whatever their race or ethnicity, have the poorest overall health (see reviews by Krieger, 1993; Adler et al., 1994; Yen & Syme, 1999). It comes as no surprise then that poverty is also linked to poorer mental health (Adler et al., 1994). Studies have consistently shown that people in the lowest strata of income, education, and occupation (known as socioeconomic status, or SES) are about two to three times more likely than those in the highest strata to have a mental disorder (Holzer et al., 1986; Regier et al., 1993; Muntaner et al., 1998). They also are more likely to have higher levels of psychological distress (Eaton & Muntaner, 1999).

Poverty in the United States has become concentrated in urban areas (Herbers, 1986). Poor neighborhoods have few resources and suffer from considerable distress and disadvantage in terms of high unemployment rates, homelessness, substance abuse, and crime. A disadvantaged community marked by economic and social flux, high turnover of residents, and low levels of supervision of teenagers and young adults creates an environment conducive to violence. Young racial and ethnic minority men from such environments are often perceived as being especially prone to violent behavior, and indeed they are disproportionately arrested for violent crimes. However, the recent Surgeon General's Report on Youth Violence cites self-reports of youth from both majority and minority populations *that indicate that differences in violent acts committed* may not be as large as arrest records suggest. The Report on Youth Violence concludes that race and ethnicity, considered in isolation from other life circumstances, shed little light on a given child's or adolescent's propensity for engaging in violence (DHHS, 2001).

Regardless of who is perpetrating violence, it disproportionately affects the lives of racial and ethnic minorities. The rate of victimization for crimes of violence is higher for African Americans than for any other ethnic or racial group (Maguire & Pastore, 1999). More than 40 percent of inner city young people have seen someone shot or stabbed (Schwab-Stone et al., 1995). Exposure to community violence, as victim or witness, leaves immediate and sometimes long-term effects on mental health, especially for youth (Bell & Jenkins, 1993; Gorman-Smith & Tolan, 1998; Miller et al., 1999).

How is poverty so clearly related to poorer mental health? This question can be answered in two ways. People who are poor are more likely to be exposed to stressful social environments (e.g., violence and unemployment) and to be cushioned less by social or material resources (Dohrenwend, 1973; McLeod & Kessler, 1990). In this way, poverty among whites and nonwhites is a risk factor for poor mental health. Also, having a mental disorder, such as schizophrenia, takes such a toll on individual functioning and productivity that it can lead to poverty. In this way, poverty is a consequence of mental illness (Dohrenwend et al., 1992). Both are plausible explanations for the robust relationship between poverty and mental illness (DHHS, 1999).

Scholars have debated whether low SES alone can explain cultural differences in health or health care utilization (e.g. Lillie-Blanton et al., 1996; Williams, 1996; Stolley, 1999, 2000; LaVeist, 2000;

Krieger, 2000). Most scholars agree that poverty and socioeconomic status do play a strong role, but the question is whether they play an exclusive role. The answer to this question is "no." Evidence contained within this Supplement is clearly contrary to the simple assertion that lower SES by itself explains ethnic and racial disparities. Mexican American immigrants to the United States, although quite impoverished, enjoy excellent mental health (Vega et al., 1998). In this study, immigrants' culture was interpreted as protecting them against the impact of poverty. In other studies of African Americans and Hispanics, more generous mental health coverage for minorities did not eliminate disparities in their utilization of mental health services. Minorities of the same SES as whites still used fewer mental health services, despite good access.

The debate separates poverty from other factors that might influence the outcome—such as experiences with racism, help-seeking behavior, or attitudes—as if they were isolated or independent from one another. In fact, poverty is caused in part by a historical legacy of racism and discrimination against minorities. And minority groups have developed coping skills to help them endure generations of poverty. In other words, poverty and other factors are overlapping and interdependent for different ethnic groups and different individuals. As but one example, the experience of poverty for immigrants who previously had been wealthy in their homeland cannot be equated with the experience of poverty for immigrants coming from economically disadvantaged backgrounds.

An important caveat in reviewing this evidence is that while most researchers measure and control for SES they do not carefully define and measure aspects of culture. Many studies report the ethnic or racial backgrounds of study participants as a shorthand for their culture, without systematically examining more specific information about their living circumstances, social class, attitudes, beliefs, and behavior. In the future, defining and measuring different aspects of culture will strengthen our understanding of ethnic differences that occur, beyond those explained by poverty and socioeconomic status.

DEMOGRAPHIC TRENDS

The United States is undergoing a major demographic transformation in racial and ethnic composition of its population. In 1990, 23 percent of U.S. adults and 31 percent of children were from racial and ethnic minority groups (Hollmann, 1993). In 25 years, it is projected that about 40 percent of adults and 48 percent of children will be from racial and ethnic minority groups (U.S. Census Bureau, 2000; Lewit & Baker, 1994). While these changes bring with them the enormous richness of diverse cultures, significant changes are needed in the mental health system to meet the associated challenges.

Diversity within Racial and Ethnic Groups

The four most recognized racial and ethnic minority groups are themselves quite diverse. For instance, Asian Americans and Pacific Islanders include at least 43 separate subgroups who speak over 100 languages. Hispanics are of Mexican, Puerto Rican, Cuban, Central and South American, or other Hispanic heritage (U.S. Census Bureau, 2000). American Indian/Alaskan Natives consist of more than 500 tribes with different cultural traditions, languages, and ancestry. Even among African Americans, diversity has recently increased as black immigrants arrive from the Caribbean, South America, and Africa. Some members of these subgroups have largely acculturated or assimilated into mainstream U.S. culture, whereas others speak English with difficulty and interact almost exclusively with members of their own ethnic group.

Growth Rates

African Americans had long been the country's largest ethnic minority group. However, over the past decade, they have grown by just 13 percent to 34.7 million people. In contrast, higher birth and immigration rates led Hispanics to grow by 56 percent, to 35.3 million people, while the whites grew just 1 percent from 209 million to 212 million. According to 2000 census figures, Hispanics have replaced African Americans as the second largest ethnic group after whites (U.S. Census Bureau, 2001).

Hispanics grew faster than any other ethnic minority group in terms of the actual number of individuals and the rate of population growth. The group with the second highest rate of population growth was Asian Americans, who in the 2000 census were counted separately from Native Hawaiians and Other Pacific Islanders. Because of immigration, the Asian American population grew 40.7 percent to 10.6 million people, and this growth is projected to continue throughout the century (U.S. Census Bureau, 2001).

American Indians and Alaska Natives surged between 38 and 50 percent over each of the decades from the 1960s through the 1980s. However, during the 1990s, the rate of growth was slightly slower (19%). Even so, the rate is still greater than that for the general population. One factor accounting for this higher-than-average growth rate is an increase in the number of people who now identify themselves as American Indian or Alaska Native. The current size of the American Indian and Alaska Native population is just under 1 percent of the total U.S. population, or about 2.5 million people. This number nearly doubles, however, when including individuals who identify as being American Indian and Alaska Native as well as one or more other races (U.S. Census Bureau, 2001).

The numbers of ethnic minority children and youth are increasing most rapidly. Between 1995 and 2015, the numbers of black youth are expected to increase by 19 percent, American Indian and Alaska Native youth by 17 percent, Hispanic youth by 59 percent, and Asian and Pacific Islander youth by 74 percent. During the same period, the white youth population is expected to increase by 3 percent (Snyder & Sickmund, 1999).

Geographic Distribution

Until the 1960s, American Indians, Asian Americans, and Hispanic Americans were geographically isolated. Before then, American Indians lived primarily on reservations to which the government assigned them. Few Asian Americans lived outside California, Hawaii, Washington, and New York City. Latinos resided primarily in the southwestern border States, New York City, and a few midwestern industrial cities (Harrison & Bennett, 1995).

Today, although they are not evenly distributed, members of each of the four major racial and ethnic minority groups reside throughout the United States. The western States are the most ethnically diverse in the United States, and they are home to many Latinos, Asian Americans, and American Indians. In the Midwest, which is less ethnically diverse, over 85 percent of the population is white, and most of the remainder is black. This proportion has remained relatively unchanged since the 1970s.

Although the Nation as a whole is becoming more ethnically diverse, this diversity remains relatively concentrated in a few States and large metropolitan areas. In general, minorities are more likely than whites to live in urban areas. In 1997, 88 percent of minorities lived in cities and their surrounding areas, compared to 77 percent of whites. American Indians/Alaska Natives and African Americans are the only minority groups with any considerable rural population. (U.S. Census Bureau, 1999).

Impact of Immigration Laws

During the last century, U.S. immigration laws alternately closed and opened the doors of immigration to different foreign populations. For example, the 1924 Immigration Act established the National Origins System, which restricted annual immigration from any foreign country to 2 percent of that country's population living in the United States, as counted in the census of 1890. Since most of the foreign-born counted in the 1890 census were from northern and western European countries, the 1924 Immigration Act reinforced patterns of white immigration and staved off immigration from other areas, including Asia, Latin America, and Africa.

Until the 1960s, approximately two-thirds of all legal immigrants to the United States were from Europe and Canada. The Immigration Act of 1965 replaced the National Origins System and allowed an annual immigration quota of 20,000 individuals from each country in the Eastern Hemisphere. The Act also gave preference to individuals in certain occupations. The effect was striking: Immigration from Asia skyrocketed from 6 percent of all immigrants in the 1950s to 37 percent by the 1980s. Yet another provision of the Act supported family reunification and gave preference to people with relatives in the United States, one factor behind the growth in immigration from Mexico and other Latin American countries (U.S. Census Bureau, 1999). Over this same period of time, the percentage of immigrants from Europe and Canada fell from 68 percent to 12 percent (U.S. Immigration and Naturalization Service, 1999).

In the past 20 years, immigration has led to a shift in the racial and ethnic composition of the United States not witnessed since the late 17th century, when black slaves became part of the labor force in the South (Muller, 1993). Though this wave of immigration is similar to the surge of immigration that occurred in the early part of this century, a critical difference is in the countries of origin. In the early 1900s, immigrants primarily came from Europe and Canada, while recent immigration is primarily from Asian and Latin American countries.

Overall, the racial and ethnic makeup of the United States has changed more rapidly since 1965 than during any other period in history. The reform in immigration policy in 1965, the increase in self-identification by ethnic minorities, and the slowing of the country's birth rates, especially among non-Hispanic white Americans, have all led to an increasing, and increasingly diverse, racial and ethnic minority population in the United States.

CONCLUSIONS

1. Culture influences many aspects of mental illness, including how patients from a given culture express and manifest their symptoms, their style of coping, their family and community supports, and their willingness to seek treatment. Likewise, the cultures of the clinician and the service system influence diagnosis, treatment, and service delivery. Cultural and social influences are not the only determinants of mental illness and patterns of service utilization for racial and ethnic minorities, but they do play important roles.

2. Mental disorders are highly prevalent across all populations, regardless of race or ethnicity. Cultural and social factors contribute to the causation of mental illness, yet that contribution varies by disorder. Mental illness is considered the product of a complex interaction among biological, psychological, social, and cultural factors. The role of any one of these major factors can be stronger or weaker depending on the specific disorder

3. Within the United States, overall rates of mental disorders for most minority groups are largely similar to those for whites. This general conclusion does not apply to vulnerable, high-need subgroups, who have higher rates and are often not captured in community surveys. The overall rates of mental disorder for many smaller racial and ethnic groups, most notably American Indians, Alaska Natives, Asian Americans and Pacific Islanders are not sufficiently studied to permit definitive conclusions.

4. Ethnic and racial minorities in the United States face a social and economic environment of inequality that includes greater exposure to racism and discrimination, violence, and poverty, all of which take a toll on mental health. Living in poverty has the most measurable impact on rates of mental illness. People in the lowest stratum of income, education, and occupation are about two to three times more likely than those in the highest stratum to have a mental disorder.

5. Racism and discrimination are stressful events that adversely affect health and mental health. They place minorities at risk for mental disorders such as depression and anxiety. Whether racism and discrimination can by themselves cause these disorders is less clear, yet deserves research attention.

6. Stigma discourages major segments of the population, majority and minority alike, from seeking help. Attitudes toward mental illness held by minorities are as unfavorable, or even more unfavorable, than attitudes held by whites.

7. Mistrust of mental health services is an important reason deterring minorities from seeking treatment. Their concerns are reinforced by evidence, both direct and indirect, of clinician bias and stereotyping. The extent to which clinician bias and stereotyping explain disparities in mental health services is not known.

8. The cultures of ethnic and racial minorities alter the types of mental health services they use. Cultural misunderstandings or communication problems between patients and clinicians may prevent minorities from using services and receiving appropriate care.

● ● ● **References**

Adler, N. E., Boyce, T., Chesney, M. A., Cohen, S., Folkman, S., Kahn, R. L., & Syme, S. L. (1994). Socioeconomic status and health: The challenge of the gradient. *American Psychologist, 49,* 15-24.

American Psychiatric Association. (1994). *Diagnostic and statistical manual of mental disorders* (4th ed.). Washington, DC: Author.

Baker, F. M., & Bell, C. C. (1999). Issues in the psychiatric treatment of African Americans. *Psychiatric Services, 50,* 362-368.

Bebbington, P., & Kuipers, L. (1994). The predictive utility of expressed emotion in schizophrenia: An aggregate analysis. *Psychological Medicine, 24,* 707-718.

Bell, C. C. (1996). Pimping the African-American community. *Psychiatric Services, 47,* 1025.

Bell, C. C., & Jenkins, E. J. (1993). Community violence and children on Chicago's southside. *Psychiatry, 56,* 46-54.

Bell, C. C. & Mehta, H. (1980). The misdiagnosis of black patients with manic depressive illness. *Journal of the National Medical Association, 72,* 141-145.

Bell, C. C. & Mehta, H. (1981). The misdiagnosis of black patients with manic depressive illness: Second in a series. *Journal of the National Medical Association, 73,* 101-107.

Berry, J. W., Kim, U., Minde, T., & Mok, D. (1987). Comparative studies of acculturative stress. *International Migration Review, 21,* 491-511.

Bhugra, D. (1989). Attitudes towards mental illness: A review of the literature. *Acta Psychiatrica Scandinavia, 80,* 1-12.

Blazer, D. G., Hybels, C. F., Simonsick, E. G., et al. (2000). Marked differences in antidepressant use by race in an elderly community sample: 1986-1996. *American Journal of Psychiatry. 157,* 1089-1094.

Bond, C. F., DiCandia, C. G., MacKinnon, J. R. (1988). Responses to violence in a psychiatric setting: The role of patient's race. *Personality and Social Psychology Bulletin, 14,* 448-458.

Borowsky, S. J., Rubenstein, L. V., Meredith, L. S., Camp, P., Jackson-Triche, M., & Wells, K B. (2000). Who is at risk of nondetection of mental health problems in primary care? *Journal of General Internal Medicine, 15,* 381-388.

Brockington, I., Hall, P. Levings, J., & Murphy, C. (1993). The community's tolerance of the mentally ill. *British Journal of Psychiatry, 162,* 93-99.

Broman, C. L. (1996). Coping with personal problems. In H. W. Neighbors & J. S. Jackson (Eds.), *Mental health in black America* (pp. 117-129). Thousand Oaks, CA: Sage.

Brown, E. R., Ojeda, V. D., Wyn, R., & Levan, R. (2000). *Racial and ethnic disparities in access to health insurance and health care.* Los Angeles: UCLA Center for Health Policy Research and The Henry J. Kaiser Family Foundation.

Brown, J., Cohen, P., Johnson, J. G., & Smailes, E. M. (1999). Childhood abuse and neglect: Specificity of effects on adolescent and young adult depression and suicidality. *Journal of the American Academy of Child and Adolescent Psychiatry, 38,* 1490-1496.

Burkett, G. L. (1991). Culture, illness, and the biopsychosocial model. *Family Medicine, 23,* 287-291.

Chambless, D. L., Sanderson, W. C., Shoham, V., Bennett Johnson, S., Pope, K. S., Crits-Christoph, P., Baker, M., Johnson, B., Woody, S. R., Sue, S., Beutler, L., Williams, D. A., & McCurry, S. (1996). An update on empirically validated therapies. *The Clinical Psychologist, 49,* 5-18.

Chen, J., Rathore, S. S., Radford, M. J., Wang, Y., & Krumholz, H. M. (2001). Racial differences in the use of cardiac catheterization after acute myocardial infarction. *New England Journal of Medicine, 344,* 1443-1449.

Chun, C., Enomoto, K., & Sue, S. (1996). Health-care issues among Asian Americans: Implications of somatization. In P. M. Kata & T. Mann (Eds.),

Handbook of diversity issues in health psychology (pp. 347-366). New York: Plenum.

Clancy, C. M., & Franks, P. (1997). Utilization of specialty and primary care: The impact of HMO insurance and patientrelated factors. *Journal of Family Practice, 45,* 500-508.

Clark, R., Anderson, N. B., Clark, V. R., & Williams, D. R. (1999). Racism as a stressor for African Americans. A biopsychosocial model. *American Psychologist, 54,* 805-816.

Cooper-Patrick, L., Gallo, J. J., Gonzales, J. J., Vu, H. T., Powe, N. R., Nelson, C., & Ford, D. E. (1999). Race, gender, and partnership in the patient-physician relationship. *Journal of the American Medical Association, 282,* 583-589.

Cooper-Patrick, L., Gallo, J. J., Powe, N. R., Steinwachs, D. M., Eaton, W. W., & Ford, D. E. (1999). Mental health service utilization by African Americans and whites: The Baltimore Epidemiologic Catchment Area follow-up. *Medical Care, 37,* 1034-1045.

Cooper-Patrick, L., Powe, N. R., Jenckes, M. W., Gonzales, J. J., Levine, D. M., & Ford, D. E. (1997). Identification of patient attitudes and preferences regarding treatment of depression. *Journal of General Internal Medicine, 12,* 431-438.

Corrigan, P. W., & Penn, D. L. (1999). Lessons from social psychology on discrediting psychiatric stigma. *American Psychologist, 54,* 765-776.

Cross, T. L., Bazron, B. J., Dennis, K. W., & Isaacs, M. R. (1989). *Towards a culturally competent system of care.* Washington, DC: CAASP Technical Assistance Center.

Davis, J. A., & Smith, T. W. (1990). *General social surveys, 1972-1990.* Chicago: National Opinion Research Center.

Dinwiddie, S., Heath, A. C., Dunne, M. P., Bucholz, K. K., Madden, P. A., Slutske, W. S., Bierut, L. J., Statham, D. B., & Martin, N. G. (2000). Early sexual abuse and lifetime psychopathology: A co-twin-control study. *Psychology and Medicine, 30,* 41-52. *14,* 448-458.

Dohrenwend, B. P. (1973). Social status and stressful life events. *Journal of Personality and Social Psychology, 28,* 225-235.

Dohrenwend, B. P., Levav, I., Shrout, P. E., Schwartz, S., Naveh, G., Link, B. G., Skodol, A. E., & Stueve, A. (1992). Socioeconomic status and psychiatric disorders: The causation-selection issue. *Science, 255,* 946-952.

Drake, R. E., Goldman, H. H., Leff, H. S., Lehman, A. F., Dixon, L., Mueser, K. T., & Torrey, W. C. (2001). Implementing evidence-based practices in routine mental health service settings. *Psychiatric Services 52,* 179-182.

Druss, B. G., Marcus, S. C., Rosenheck, R. A., Olfson, M., Tanielian, T., & Pincus, H. A. (2000). Understanding disability in mental and general medical conditions. *American Journal of Psychiatry, 157,* 1485-1491

Dwight-Johnson, M., Sherbourne, C. D., Liao, D., & Wells, K. B. (2000). Treatment preferences among primary care patients. *Journal of General Internal Medicine, 15,* 527-534.

Eaton, W. W., & Muntaner, C. (1999). Socioeconomic stratification and mental disorder. In A. V. Horwitz & T. K. Scheid (Eds.), *A handbook for the study of mental health: Social contexts, theories, and systems* (pp. 259-283). New York: Cambridge University Press.

Epstein, A. M., & Ayanian, J. Z. (2001). Racial disparities in medical care. *New England Journal of Medicine, 344,* 1471-1473.

Exner, D. V., Dries, D. L., Domanski, M. J., & Cohn, J. N. (2001). Lesser response to angiotensin-converting-enzyme inhibitor therapy in black as compared with white patients with left ventricular dysfunction. *New England Journal of Medicine, 344,* 1351-1357.

Falicov, C. J. (1998). *Latino families in therapy: A guide to multicultural practice.* New York: Guilford Press.

Finch, B. K., Kolody, B., & Vega, W.A. (2000). Perceived discrimination and depression among Mexican origin adults in California. *Journal of Health and Social Behavior, 41,* 295-313.

Fraser, I. (1997). Introduction: Research on health care organizations and markets—the best and worst of times. *Health Services Research, 32,* 669-678.

Gallo, J. J., Marino, S., Ford, D., & Anthony, J. C. (1995). Filters on the pathway to mental health care, II. Sociodemographic factors. *Psychological Medicine, 25,* 1149-1160.

Giles, W. H., Anda, R. F., Casper, M. L., Escobedo, L. G., & Taylor, H. A. (1995). Race and sex differences in rates of invasive cardiac procedures in U.S. hospitals. Data from the National Hospital Discharge Survey. *Archives of Internal Medicine, 155,* 318-324.

Gorman-Smith, D., & Tolan, P. (1998). The role of exposure to community violence and developmental problems among inner-city youth. *Development and Psychopathology, 10,* 101-116.

Harrison, R. J., & Bennett, C. (1995). Racial and ethnic diversity. In R. Farley (Ed.), *State of the Union: America in the 1990s. Vol. 2, Social Trends.* New York: Russell Sage.

Herbers, J. (1986). *The new heartland: America's flight beyond the suburbs and how it is changing our future.* New York: Times Books.

Higgins, E. S. (1994). A review of unrecognized mental illness in primary care: Prevalence, natural history, and efforts to change the course. *Archives of Family Medicine, 3,* 908-917.

Hollmann, F. W. (1993). *U.S. population estimates, by age, sex, race, and Hispanic origin: 1980 to 1991* (U.S. Bureau of the Census, Current Population Reports Series P25, No. 1095). Washington, DC: U.S. Government Printing Office.

Holzer, C., Shea, B., Swanson, J., Leaf, P., Myers, J., George, L., Weissman, M., & Bednarski, P. (1986). The increased risk for specific psychiatric disorders among persons of low socioeconomic status. *American Journal of Social Psychiatry, 6,* 259-271.

Hsu, F. L. K. (1971). Psychosocial homeostasis and jen: Conceptual tools for advancing psychological anthropology. *American Anthropologist, 73,* 23-44.

Hughes, M., Thomas, M. E. (1998). The continuing significance of race revisited: A study of race, class and quality of life in America, 1972-1996. *American Sociological Review, 63,* 785-795.

Hunt, G. J. (1995). Social and cultural aspects of health, illness, and treatment. In H. H. Goldman (Ed.), *Review of general psychiatry.* Norwalk, CT: Appleton and Lange.

Hurh, W. M., & Kim, K. C. (1988). *Uprooting and adjustment: A sociological study of Korean immigrants' mental health* (Final report to the National Institute of Mental Health). Macomb, IL: Western Illinois University, Department of Sociology and Anthropology.

Jenkins, J. H. (1993). Too close for comfort: Schizophrenia and emotional overinvolvement among Mexicano families. In A. D. Gaines (Ed.), *Ethnopsychiatry* (pp. 203-221). Albany, NY: State University of New York Press.

Jenkins, J. H., Kleinman, A., & Good, B. J. (1991). Cross- cultural studies of depression. In J. Becker & A. Kleinman (Eds.), *Psychosocial aspects of depression* (pp. 67-99). Hillsdale, NJ: Erlbaum.

Jenkins-Hall, K. D., & Sacco, W. P. (1991). Effect of client race and depression on evaluations by white therapists. *Journal of Social and Clinical Psychology, 10,* 322-333.

Ji, J., Kleinman, A., & Becker, A. E. (2001). Suicide in contemporary China: A review of China's distinctive suicide demographics in their sociocultural context. *Harvard Review of Psychiatry, 9,* 1-12

Kachur, S. P., Potter, L. B., James, S. P., & Powell, K. E. (1995). *Suicide in the United States, 1980-1992* (Violence Surveillance Summary Series, No. 1). Atlanta, GA: Centers for Disease Control and Prevention.

Kavanaugh, D. (1992). Recent developments in expressed emotion and schizophrenia. *British Journal of Psychiatry, 160,* 601-620.

Kessler, R. C., Berglund, P. A., Zhao, S., Leaf, P. J., Kouzis, A. C., Bruce, M. L., Freidman, R. L.,

Grosser, R. C., Kennedy, C., Narrow, W. E., Kuehnel, T. G., Laska, E. M., Manderscheid, R. W., Rosenheck, R. A., Santoni, T. W., & Schneier, M. (1996). The 12-month prevalence and correlates of serious mental illness (SMI). In R. W. Manderscheid & M. A. Sonnenschein (Eds.), *Mental health, United States* (Pub. No. [SMA] 96-3098). Rockville, MD: Center for Mental Health Services.

Kessler, R. C., Mickelson, K. D., Williams, D. R. (1999). The prevalence, distribution, and mental health correlates of perceived discrimination in the United States. *Journal of Health and Social Behavior, 40,* 208-230.

Kirschenman, J., & Neckerman, K. M. (1991). "We'd love to hire them, but . . .": The meaning of race for employers. In C. Jencks and P.E. Peterson (Eds.), *The urban underclass* (pp. 203-234). Washington, DC: Brookings Institution.

Kleinman, A. (1977). Depression, somatization and the "new cross-cultural psychiatry." *Social Science and Medicine, 11,* 3-10.

Kleinman, A. (1988). *Rethinking psychiatry: From cultural category to personal experience.* New York: Free Press.

Koss-Chioino, J. D., & Vargas, L. A. (1999). *Working with Latino youth: Culture, development and context.* San Francisco: Jossey-Bass.

Krieger N. (1993). Epidemiologic theory and societal patterns of disease. *Epidemiology, 4,* 276-278.

Krieger, N. (2000). Refiguring "race": Epidemiology, racialized biology, and biological expressions of race relations. *International Journal of Health Services, 30,* 211-216.

Krieger, N., & Sidney, S. (1996). Racial discrimination and blood pressure: The CARDIA study of young black and white adults. *American Journal of Public Health, 86,* 1370-1378.

Krieger, N., Sidney, S., & Coakley, E. (1999). Racial discrimination and skin color in the CARDIA study: Implications for public health research. *American Journal of Public Health, 88,* 1308-1313.

LaVeist, T. A. (2000). On the study of race, racism, and health: A shift from description to explanation. *International Journal of Health Services, 30,* 217-219.

LaVeist, T. A., Diala, C., & Jarrett, N. C. (2000). Social status and perceived discrimination: Who experiences discrimination in the health care system, how, and why? In C. Hogue, M. Hargraves, & K. Scott-Collins (Eds.), *Minority health in America* (pp. 194-208). Baltimore, MD: Johns Hopkins University Press.

Leff, J., & Vaughn, C. (1985). *Expressed emotion in families: Its significance for mental illness.* New York: Guilford Press.

Lehman, A. F., & Steinwachs, D. M. (1998). Patterns of usual care for schizophrenia: Initial results from the Schizophrenia Patient Outcomes Research Team (PORT) Client Survey (Discussion 20-32). *Schizophrenia Bulletin, 24,* 11-20.

Levin, J. (1986). Roles for the black pastor in preventive medicine. *Pastoral Psychology, 35,* 94-103.

Levit, L., & Lundy, J. (1998). Trends and indicators in the changing health care market place: Chartbook. Menlo Park, CA: Henry J. Kaiser Family Foundation.

Lewit, E. M., & Baker, L. S. (1994). Children's health and the environment. *Future of Children, 5,* 8-10.

Lillie-Blanton, M., Parsons, P. E., Gayle, H., & Dievler, A. (1996). Racial differences in health: Not just black and white, but shades of gray. *Annual Review of Public Health, 17,* 411-448.

Lin, K. M., & Cheung, F. (1999). Mental health issues for Asian Americans. *Psychiatric Services 50,* 774-780.

Lin, K. M., Cheung, F., Smith, M., & Poland, R. E. (1997). The use of psychotropic medications in working with Asian patients. In E. Lee (Ed.), *Working with Asian Americans: A guide for clinicians* (pp.388-399). New York: Guilford Press.

Lopez, S. R. (1997). Cultural competence in psychotherapy: A guide for clinicians and their supervisors. In C. E. Watkins, Jr. (Ed.), *Handbook of psychotherapy supervision.* New York: Wiley.

Lopez, S. R., & Guarnaccia, P. J. (2000). Cultural psychopathology: Uncovering the social world of mental illness. *Annual Review of Psychology, 51,* 571-598.

Lopez, S. R., Nelson, K. A., Polo, J. A., Jenkins, J., Karno, M., & Snyder, K. (1998, August). *Family warmth and the course of schizophrenia of Mexican Americans and Anglo Americans.* Paper presented at the International Congress of Applied Psychology, San Francisco, CA.

Maguire, K., & Pastore, E. (Eds.). (1999). *Sourcebook of criminal justice statistics 1998.* Washington, DC: U.S. Government Printing Office.

Manderscheid, R. W., & Henderson, M. J., Eds. (1999). *Mental Health, United States: 1998.* Rockville, MD: Center for Mental Health Services.

Martin, T. L., Shelby, J. V., & Zhang, D. (1995). Physician and patient prevention practices in NIDDM in a large urban managed-care organization. *Diabetes Care, 18,* 1124-1132.

McCarty, C. A., Weisz, J. R., Wanitromanee, K., Eastman, K. L., Suwanlert, S., Chaiyasit, W., & Band, E. B. (1999). Culture, coping, and context: Primary and secondary control among Thai and American youth. *Journal of Child Psychology and Psychiatry, 40,* 809-818.

McLeod, J. D., & Kessler, R. C. (1990). Socioeconomic status differences in vulnerability to undesirable life events. *Journal of Health and Social Behavior, 31,* 162-172.

Meinhardt, K., Tom, S., Tse, P., & Yu, C. Y. (1986). Southeast Asian refugees in the "Silicon Valley": The Asian Health Assessment Project. *Amerasia Journal, 12,* 43-65.

Miller, L. S., Wasserman, G. A., Neugebauer, R., Gorman- Smith, D., & Kamboukos, D. (1999). Witnessed community violence and antisocial behavior in high-risk, urban boys. *Journal of Clinical Child Psychology, 28,* 2-11.

Moscicki, E. K. (1995). Epidemiology of suicide. *International Psychogeriatrics, 7,* 137-148.

Mukherjee, S., Shukla, S., Woodle, J., Rosen, A. M., & Olarte, S. (1983). Misdiagnosis of schizophrenia in bipolar patients: A multiethnic comparison. *American Journal of Psychiatry, 140,* 1571-1574.

Muller, T. (1993). *Immigrants and the American city.* New York: New York University Press.

Muntaner, C., Eaton, W. W., Diala, C., Kessler, R. C., & Sorlie, P. D. (1998). Social class, assets, organizational control and the prevalence of common groups of psychiatric disorders. *Social Science and Medicine, 47,* 2043-2053.

Narikiyo, T. A., & Kameoka, V. A. (1992). Attributions of mental illness and judgments about help seeking among Japanese-American and white American students. *Journal of Counseling Psychology, 39,* 363-369.

National Institute of Mental Health. (1998). *Genetics and mental disorders: Report of the National Institute of Mental Health's Genetics Workgroup.* Rockville, MD: Author.

National Institutes of Health. (2000). *Strategic research plan to reduce and ultimately eliminate health disparities, fiscal years 2002-2006.* Draft, October 6, 2000.

National Institutes of Health. (2001). *ORMH Mission.* Retrieved June 21, 2001, from www1.od.nih.gov/ormh/mission.html.

Neal-Barnett, A. M., & Smith, J. (1997). African Americans. In S. Friedman (Ed.), *Cultural issues in the treatment of anxiety* (pp. 154-174). New York: Guilford Press.

Neighbors, H. W., & Jackson, J. S. (1984). The use of informal and formal help: Four patterns of illness behavior in the black community. *American Journal of Community Psychology, 12,* 629-644.

Neighbors, H. W., Musick, M. A., & Williams, D. R. (1998). The African American minister as a source of help for serious personal crises: Bridge or barrier to mental health care? *Health Education and Behavior, 25,* 759-777.

Ng, C. H. (1997). The stigma of mental illness in Asian cultures. *Australian and New Zealand Journal of Psychiatry, 31,* 382-390.

Noh, S., Beiser, M., Kaspar, V., Hou, F., & Rummens, J. (1999). Perceived racial discrimination, depression and coping: A study of Southeast Asian refugees in Canada. *Journal of Health and Social Behavior, 40,* 193-207.

OPEN MINDS. (1999). Over 72% of insured Americans are enrolled in MBHOs: Magellan Behavioral Health continues to dominate the market. *OPEN MINDS Behavioral Health and Social Service Industry Analyst, 11,* 9.

Optenberg, S. A., Thompson, I. M., Friedrichs, P., Wojcik, B., Stein, C. R., Kramer, B. (1995). Race, treatment, and long-term survival from prostate cancer in an equalaccess medical care system. *Journal of the American Medical Association, 274,* 1599-1605.

Paabo, S. (2001). Genomics and society. The human genome and our view of ourselves. *Science, 291* (5507), 1219-1220.

Palmatier, M. A., Kang, A. M., & Kidd, K. K. (1999). Global variation in the frequencies of functionally different catechol-O-methyltransferase alleles. *Biological Psychiatry, 15,* 557-567.

Pedersen, P. B., & Ivey, A. (1993). *Culture-centered counseling and interviewing skills: A practical guide.* New York: Praeger.

Peifer, K. L., Hu, T. W., & Vega, W. (2000). Help seeking by persons of Mexican origin with functional impairments. *Psychiatric Services, 51,* 1293-1298.

Penn, D. L., & Martin, J. (1998). The stigma of severe mental illness: Some potential solutions for a recalcitrant problem. *Psychiatric Quarterly, 69,* 235-247.

Pescosolido, B. A., Monahan, J., Link, B. G., Stueve, A., & Kikuzawa, S. (1999). The public's view of the competence, dangerousness, and need for legal coercion of persons with mental health problems. *American Journal of Public Health, 89,* 1339-1345.

Peterson, J. L., Folkman, S., Bakeman, R. (1996). Stress, coping, HIV status, psychosocial resources, and depressive mood in African American gay, bisexual, and heterosexual men. *American Journal of Community Psychology, 24,* 461-487.

Porter, R. (1997). *The greatest benefit to mankind: A medical history of humanity.* New York: Norton.

Portes, A., & Rumbaut, R. G. (1990). *Immigrant America: A portrait.* Berkeley, CA: University of California Press.

Provan, K. G., & Carle, N. (2000). *A guide to behavioral health managed care for Native Americans.* Tucson, AZ: University of Arizona, Center for Native American Health.

Prudhomme, C., & Musto, D. F. (1973). Historical perspectives on mental health and racism in the United States. In C. V. Willie, B. M. Kramer, & B. S. Brown (Eds.), *Racism and mental health* (pp. 25-57). Pittsburgh, PA: University of Pittsburgh Press.

Ramirez, M. (1991). *Psychotherapy and counseling with minorities: A cognitive approach to individual and cultural differences.* New York: Pergamon Press.

Regier, D. A., Narrow, W.E., Rae, D. S., Manderscheid, R. W., Locke, B. Z., & Goodwin, F. K. (1993). The de facto U.S. mental and addictive disorders service system. Epidemiologic Catchment Area prospective 1-year prevalence rates of disorders and services. *Archives of General Psychiatry, 50,* 85-94.

Ren, X. S., Amick, B., & Williams, D. R. (1999). Racial/ethnic disparities in health: The interplay between discrimination and socioeconomic status. *Ethnicity & Disease, 9,* 151165.

Ridley, C. R., Mendoza, D. W., Kanitz, B. E., Angermeier, L., & Zenk, R. (1994). Cultural sensitivity in multicultural counseling: A perceptual schema model. *Journal of Counseling Psychology, 41,* 125-136.

Rogler, L. H., & Cortes, D. E. (1993). Help-seeking pathways: A unifying concept in mental health care. *American Journal of Psychiatry, 150,* 554-561.

Rogler, L. H., Malgady, R. G., Costantino, G., & Blumenthal, R. (1987). What do culturally sensitive mental health services mean? The case of Hispanics. *American Psychologist, 42,* 565-570.

Rost, K., Nutting, P., Smith, J., Coyne, J. C., Cooper-Patrick, L., & Rubenstein, L. (2000). The role of competing demands in the treatment provided primary care patients with major depression. *Archives of Family Medicine, 9,* 150-154.

Rumbaut, R. G. (1989). Portraits, patterns, and predictors of the refugee adaptation process. In D.W. Haines (Ed.), *Refugees as immigrants: Cambodians, Laotians and Vietnamese in America* (pp. 138-182). Totowa, NG: Rowman & Littlefield.

Rumbaut, R. G. (1994). The Crucible Within: Ethnic Identity, Self-Esteem, and Segmented Assimilation Among Children of Immigrants. *International Migration Review, 28,* 748-794.

Scadding, J. G. (1996). Essentialism and nominalism in medicine: Logic of diagnosis in disease terminology. *Lancet, 348* (9,027), 594-596.

Scholle, S., & Kelleher, K. (1998). *Managed care for seriously emotionally disturbed children.* Paper presented at a Substance Abuse and Mental Health Services Administration Managed Care Seminar, Washington, DC.

Schwab-Stone, M. E., Ayers, T. S., Kasprow, W., Voyce, C., Barone, C., Shriver, T., Weissberg, R. P. (1995). No safe haven: A study of violence exposure in an urban community. *Journal of the American Academy of Child and Adolescent Psychiatry, 34,* 1343-1352.

Schwartz, R. C. (2001). Racial profiling in medical research. *New England Journal of Medicine, 344,* 1392-1393.

Sclar, D. A., Robison, L. M., Skaer, T. L., & Galin, R. S. (1999). Ethnicity and the prescribing of antidepressant pharmacotherapy: 1992-1995. *Harvard Review of Psychiatry, 7,* 29-36.

Shiefer, S. E., Escarce, J. J., Schulman, K. A. (2000). Race and sex differences in the management of coronary artery disease. *American Heart Journal, 139,* 848-857.

Shorter, E. (1997). *A history of psychiatry.* New York: Wiley.

Snowden, L. R., & Cheung, F. K. (1990). Use of inpatient mental health services by members of ethnic minority groups. *American Psychologist, 45,* 347-355.

Snyder, H., & Sickmund, M. (1999). *Juvenile Offenders and Victims: 1999 National Report.* Washington, DC: Office of Juvenile Justice and Delinquency Prevention.

Starr, P. (1982). *The social transformation of American medicine.* New York: Basic Books.

Stolley, P. D. (1999). Race in epidemiology. *International Journal of Health Services, 29,* 905-909.

Stolley, P. D. (2000). Reply to commentaries by Drs. Krieger and LaVeist on "Race in epidemiology." *International Journal of Health Services, 30,* 221-222.

Sue, D. W., & Sue, D. (1999). *Counseling the culturally different: Theory and practice (3rd edition).* New York: Wiley.

Sue, S. (1998). In search of cultural competence in psychotherapy and counseling. *American Psychologist, 53,* 440-448.

Sue, S., Fujino, D., Hu, L. T., Takeuchi, D. T., & Zane, N. W. (1991). Community mental health services for ethnic minority groups: A test of the cultural responsiveness hypothesis. *Journal Of Consulting and Clinical Psychology, 59,* 533-540.

Sue, S., Kurasaki, K. S., & Srinivasan, S. (1998). Ethnicity, gender, and cross-cultural issues in research. In P. C. Kendall, J. N. Butcher, & G. N. Holmbeck (Eds.). *Handbook of research methods in clinical psychology* (2nd ed., pp. 51-71). New York: Wiley.

Sue, S., & Morishima, J. K. (1982). *The mental health of Asian Americans.* San Francisco: Jossey-Bass.

Sue, S., & Zane, N. (1987). The role of culture and cultural techniques in psychotherapy: A critique and reformulation. *American Psychologist, 42,* 37-45.

Sussman, L. K., Robins, L. N., & Earls, F. (1987). Treatment-seeking for depression by black and white Americans. *Social Science and Medicine, 24,* 187-196.

Szapocznik, J., Kurtines, W., Santisteban, D. A., Pantin, H., Scopetta, M., Mancilla, Y., Aisenberg, S., McIntosh, S., Perez-Vidal, A., & Coatsworth, J. D. (1997). The evolution of structural ecosystemic theory for working with Latino families. In J. G. Garcia & M. C. Zea (Eds.), *Psychological interventions and research with Latino populations* (pp. 166-190). Boston: Allyn & Bacon.

Takaki, R. (1993). *A different mirror: A history of multicultural America.* Boston: Little, Brown.

Takeuchi, D. T., & Uehara, E. S. (1996) Ethnic minority mental health services: Current research and future conceptual directions. In. B. L. Levin & J. Petrila (Eds.), *Mental health services: A public health perspective* (pp. 63-80). New York: Oxford University Press.

Tambor, E. S., Bernhardt, B. A., Chase, G. A., Faden, R. R., Geller, G., Hofman, K. J., & Holtzman, N. A. (1994). Offering cystic fibrosis carrier screening to an HMO population: Factors associated with utilization. *American Journal of Human Genetics, 55,* 626-637.

Taylor, A. J., Meyer, G. S., Morse, R. W., & Pearson, C. E. (1997). Can characteristics of a health care system mitigate ethnic bias in access to cardiovascular procedures? Experience from the Military Health Services System. *Journal of the American College of Cardiology, 30,* 901-907

U.S. Census Bureau. (1999). *Statistical Abstract of the United States: The National Data Book.* Washington, DC: Author.

U.S. Census Bureau. (2001) *Census 2000 Redistricting [Public Law 94-171] Summary File.* Washington, DC: Author.

U.S. Center for Mental Health Services. (2000). *Cultural competence standards in managed care mental health services: Four underserved/underrepresented racial/ethnic groups.* Rockville, MD: Author.

U.S. Department of Health and Human Services. (1999). *Mental health: A report of the Surgeon General.* Rockville, MD: Author.

U.S. Department of Health and Human Services. (2000). *Healthy People 2010* (2nd ed.). With *Understanding and improving health and Objectives for improving health* (2 vols.). Washington, DC: Author.

U.S. Department of Health and Human Services. (2001). *Youth violence: A report of the Surgeon General.* Rockville, MD: Author.

U.S. Immigration and Naturalization Service. (1999). *1999 Statistical Yearbook.* Washington, DC: Government Printing Office.

van Heeringen, K., Hawton, K., & Williams, J. M. G. (2000). Pathways to suicide: An integrative approach. In K. Hawton & K. van Heeringen (Eds.), *The international handbook of suicide and attempted suicide* (pp. 223-234). New York: Wiley.

Vega, W. A., Kolody, B., Aguilar-Gaxiola, S., Alderate, E., Catalano, R., & Carveo-Anduaga, J. (1998). Lifetime prevalence of DSM-III-R psychiatric disorders among urban and rural Mexican Americans in California. *Archives of General Psychiatry, 55,* 771-778.

Vega, W. A., & Rumbaut, R. G. (1991). Ethnic minorities and mental health. *Annual Review of Sociology, 17,* 351-383.

Wahl, O. F. (1999). Mental health consumers' experience of stigma. *Schizophrenia Bulletin, 25,* 467-478.

Wahl, O. F., & Harman, C. R. (1989). Family views of stigma. *Schizophrenia Bulletin, 15,* 131-139.

Wang, P. S., Berglund, P., & Kessler, R. C. (2000). Recent care of common mental disorders in the United States. *Journal of General Internal Medicine, 15,* 284-292.

Weissman, M. M., Bland, R. C., Canino, G. J., Faravelli, C., Greenwald, S., Hwu, H. G. et al. (1996). Cross-national epidemiology of major depression and bipolar disorder. *Journal of the American Medical Association, 276,* 293-299.

Weissman, M. M., Bland, R. C., Canino, G. J., Faravelli, C., Greenwald, S., Hwu, H. G. et al. (1997). The cross-national epidemiology of panic disorder. *Archives of General Psychiatry, 54,* 305-309.

Weissman, M. M., Bland, R. C., Canino, G. J., Greenwald, S., Hwu, H. G., Lee et al. (1994). The cross national epidemiology of obsessive compulsive disorder. The Cross National Collaborative Group. *Journal of Clinical Psychiatry, 55* (Suppl.), 5-10.

Weissman, M. M., Broadhead, W. E., Olfson, M., Sheehan, D. V., Hoven, C., Conolly, P. et al. (1998). A diagnostic aid for detecting (DSM-IV) mental disorders in primary care. *General Hospital Psychiatry, 20,* 1-11.

Weisz, J. R., McCarty, C. A., Eastman, K.L., Chaiyasit, W., Suwanlert, S. (1997). Developmental psychopathology and culture: Ten lessons from Thailand. In S. S. Luthar, J. A. Burack, D. Cicchetti, & J. R. Weisz (Eds.), *Developmental psychopathology: Perspectives on adjustment, risk, and disorder* (pp. 568-592). Cambridge, England: Cambridge University Press.

Whaley, A. L. (1997). Ethnic and racial differences in perceptions of dangerousness of persons with mental illness. *Psychiatric Services, 48,* 1328-1330.

Whaley, A. L. (1998). Issues of validity in empirical tests of stereotype threat theory. *American Psychologist, 5,* 679-680.

Williams, D. R. (1996). Race/ethnicity and socioeconomic status: Measurement and methodological issues. *International Journal of Health Services, 26,* 483-505.

Williams, D. R. (2000). Race, stress, and mental health. In C. Hogue, M. Hargraves, & K. Scott-Collins (Eds.). *Minority health in America* (pp. 209-243). Baltimore: Johns Hopkins University Press.

Williams, D. R. & Williams-Morris, R. (2000). Racism and mental health: The African American experience. *Ethnicity and Health, 5,* 243-268.

Williams, D. R., Yu, Y., Jackson, J. S., & Anderson, N.B. (1997). Racial Differences in Physical and Mental Health: Socio-Economic Status, Stress and

Discrimination. *Journal of Health Psychology, 2,* 335-351.

Williams, J. W., Jr., Rost, K., Dietrich, A. J., Ciotti, M. C., Zyzanski, S. J., & Cornell, J. (1999). Primary care physicians' approach to depressive disorders: Effects of physician specialty and practice structure. *Archives of Family Medicine, 8,* 58-67.

World Health Organization. (1973). *Report of the International Pilot Study on Schizophrenia.* Geneva, Switzerland: Author.

World Health Organization. (1992). *International statistical classification of diseases and related health problems* (10th revision, ICD-10). Geneva: Author.

Yehuda, R. (2000). The biology of post traumatic stress disorder. *Journal of Clinical Psychiatry, 61* (Suppl. 7), 14-21.

Yen, I. H., & Syme, S. L. (1999). The Social Environment and Health: A Discussion of the Epidemiologic Literature. *Annual Review of Public Health, 20,* 287-308.

Ying, Y. (1988). Depressive symptomatology among Chinese-Americans as measured by the CES-D. *Journal of Clinical Psychology, 44,* 739-746.

Yinger, J. (1995). Closed *doors, opportunities lost: The continuing costs of housing discrimination.* New York: Russell Sage Foundation.

Young, A. S., Klap, R., Shebourne, C. D., Wells, K.B. (2001). The quality of care for depressive and anxiety disorders in the United States. *Archives of General Psychiatry, 58,* 55-61.

Zhang, A. Y., Snowden, L. R., & Sue, S. (1998). Differences between Asian- and White-Americans' help-seeking and utilization patterns in the Los Angeles area. *Journal of Community Psychology, 26,* 317-326.

3

Managed Behavioral Health Care Carve-Outs: Past Performance and Future Prospects

Source: Frank, R.G. and R.L. Garfield. 2007. Managed Behavioral Health Care Carve-Outs: Past Performance and Future Prospects. *Annual Review of Public Health* 28: 303-320.

INTRODUCTION

Reports in the press over the past several years suggest that the managed behavioral health care industry is "in flux,"[8] leaving the accomplishments and future of the market unclear. Whereas some stories report new contract awards or positive outcomes stemming from managed behavioral health care arrangements, reports of provider frustration with companies, problems in managing care, and instability in the market are more common. A scan of stories over just the past year may lead one to question whether the industry will survive, as stories of trends toward "carve-ins" of behavioral health services or managed behavioral health organizations' (MBHOs) forays into new business areas dominate coverage. In 2005, several large insurers (most notably, Aetna) announced plans to cease carve-outs of behavioral health services. Some managed behavioral health care companies noted that the "mature" market and a trend toward in-sourcing were leading them to develop new product lines.[43,44]

The facts, however, present a somewhat different picture. Managed behavioral health care (MBHC) has con-

tinued to expand and develop in recent years. From 1999 to 2003, the share of health plans contracting with MBHOs grew from 58% to 72%, whereas the proportion managing behavioral health services internally decreased from 28% to 15% (C.M. Horgan, D.W. Garnick, E.L. Merrick, D. Hodgkin, unpublished manuscript). State Medicaid programs also continue to use or initiate behavioral health carve-outs: As of 2003, about one third of states used behavioral health carve-outs in their Medicaid programs (D.C. Ling, E.R. Berndt, R.G. Frank, unpublished manuscript).

The discrepancy between the news coverage and actual market trends likely reflects the ambivalence about carve-outs, which are alternatively hailed as a panacea to the problems in mental health care and maligned as destroying efforts to integrate and streamline mental health care. As has generally been the case with managed care backlash, the functions and performance of these organizations have frequently been misunderstood and mischaracterized by both the supporters and the opponents of MBHC. As the MBHC market has matured and more payers have gained experience with contracts, carve-outs have solved many problems facing the delivery of behavioral health services and evolved to take on new roles within the health system. However, they also have exacerbated existing difficulties or created new problems in the delivery of behavioral health care.

Although there have been many assessments of managed behavioral health care and carve-outs, much of the current literature on MBHOs does not examine how carve-outs have changed over time to fit with emerging policy issues and market trends. This review assesses the evolution of behavioral health carve-outs and examines their function in today's health system. It briefly traces the history of carve-outs, explains their underlying principles, and provides an overview of what is known about their performance in costs, access, and quality of care. The article then reviews how carve-outs have developed in recent years, given what is known about their impact and emerging health policy issues. Last, it evaluates the promise of carve-outs in light of experience to date.

BACKGROUND

Following the managed care revolution in the delivery of health services in the United States, the past decade has witnessed the growth of specialty managed care organizations to provide behavioral health care (mental health and substance abuse services) to insured individuals. Up from about 53 million in 1994,[50] today 170 million insured Americans receive their behavioral health coverage through an MBHO,[1] MBHOs contract with payers or health plans under "carve-out" arrangements, in which responsibility for management of (and sometimes financial risk for) behavioral health services is separated from general medical insurance. Carve-outs operate independently from enrollees' general medical insurance, maintaining their own provider networks, coverage rules, administrative services, and other insurance functions.

Carve-out contracts can take many forms and can be generally classified as payer carve-outs or

health plan carve-outs (see Figure 1).[64] In a payer carve-out, the purchaser of insurance (e.g., an employer or state Medicaid program) contracts separately with health plans for general medical care and with an MBHO for behavioral health care.[a] About 20% of privately insured individuals are covered under such arrangements, which are more likely to be used by large employers. Direct payer carve-outs are also used by 18 state Medicaid programs.[39] In the alternative, more widely used health plan carve-out, a health plan responsible for care of a population enters into a subcontract with an MBHO to manage the behavioral health services component of enrollees' care. Because the MBHC market is highly concentrated among a few large firms, it is common for more than one health plan to contract with the same MBHO, as shown on the right hand side of Figure 1.

Within both types of carve-outs, there is wide variation in the scope of services included, cost-sharing requirements, coordination with other coverage (such as employee assistance programs), and the assumption of financial risk.[62] For example, a carve-out may be at full risk for the cost of all behavioral health services for enrollees, may provide only administrative services and utilization review, or may have any combination of functions. Full risk contracts, although more commonly used by public payers and health plan carve-outs, cover a minority of enrollees in MBHOs.[62] MBHOs also vary in how they work with providers; for example, they may place providers at risk (through capitation contracts) or pay them a discounted fee-for-service, and they may have different rules for inclusion in networks. Although benefits covered by an MBHO vary by contract, carve-outs nearly always exclude prescription drugs, which continue to be provided through general medical insurance or through a separate carve-out contract with a pharmacy benefit manager (PBM).[39]

Most payers enter carve-out arrangements in hopes of cutting or restraining the cost of behavioral

---

[a]In another form of a carve-out, payers offering a range of plan options may carve out services only for enrollees in a traditional plan and keep behavioral health and medical care services integrated for enrollees in managed care plans.[27]

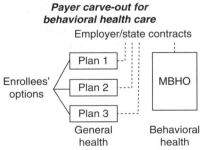

Payer carve-out for behavioral health care

Employer/state contracts

Enrollees' options — Plan 1, Plan 2, Plan 3 — MBHO

General health   Behavioral health

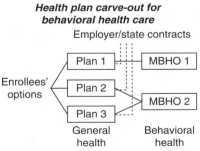

Health plan carve-out for behavioral health care

Employer/state contracts

Enrollees' options — Plan 1, Plan 2, Plan 3 — MBHO 1, MBHO 2

General health   Behavioral health

Figure 1 Types of behavioral health carve-outs

health care[35,55] either by passing on risk and limiting their own financial liability for behavioral health services or relying on the expertise and managed care techniques of the MCBO to manage costs. However, the potential of carve-outs is tempered by several concerns about their negative implications. Carve-outs are seen as aggravating the fragmentation in mental health delivery, which goes against recent calls for service integration.[39] There is widespread concern that the financial incentives in MBHC contracts and utilization management result in underuse of mental health services, reductions in quality of care, or cost-shifting to other sectors.[60,64] Increased administrative costs are an additional potential drawback of carve-out arrangements.[39]

HISTORY AND RATIONALE FOR MANAGED BEHAVIORAL HEALTH CARE CARVE-OUTS

The specialty MBHC industry has its origins in the 1980s, when state abandonment of certificate-of-need legislation led to an increase in private psychiatric beds. Between 1980 and 1990, the number of beds in private psychiatric hospitals more than doubled from 17,157 to 44,871.[45] The number of beds in specialty psychiatric units of general hospitals also expanded greatly (from 29,384 in 1980 to 53,479 in 1990). The increase in beds was accompanied by increases in spending: Mental health costs grew about four percentage points above general economic growth in the late 1980s,[15] and a substantial portion of the growth was traced to rising spending on inpatient psychiatric care. Thus, the private psychiatric hospital industry went from a $350 million activity in 1980 to a $1.2 billion enterprise in 1990. Spending on inpatient psychiatric care in general hospitals grew from about $342 million in 1980 to $913 million in 1990.[45]

The industry's growth presented many challenges to those concerned about the delivery and costs of behavioral health services. Much of the growth in utilization in the 1980s stemmed from hospitalization of children and adolescents[29] and reflected some unsavory practices such as inappropriate admission and excessive stays in hospitals.[30,63] At the same time that spending was increasing, private insurance for inpatient psychiatric care was strictly limited. The most common coverage limited inpatient psychiatric coverage to 30 days per year,[2] leaving little room to control costs by constraining coverage further. Finally, inpatient mental health care in private health insurance was reimbursed largely on a cost plus basis.

Thus the industry needed methods of rationing mental health care to control costs that did not rely on further curtailing limited insurance coverage. Organizations that could apply clinical expertise to redirect mental health care toward more appropriate use of inpatient care and alternative treatment settings offered a viable solution. The MBHC industry developed in response to this need. Given the context in which MBHOs arose, the first order of business for MBHC vendors was to control the use of inpatient care and rising costs.[b]

The MBHC industry was built on several key economic principles. The first is economics of specialization. MBHC carve-outs offer payers and health plans the opportunity to hire organizations that focus solely on mental health and substance abuse services. These organizations offer expertise in the clinical processes of modern treatment of mental and addictive disorders, as well as specialized information systems to track and manage services. They are also immersed in the specialty provider communities that have historically been quite separate from general medical care. The specialty MBHC carve-out may therefore be in a better position than integrated health plans would be to identify the most qualified and efficient providers, define appropriate utilization, measure performance, and develop care management protocols. These advantages offer the promise of more efficient contracting, cost and quality monitoring, and appropriate treatment management.

The second economic principle underlying MBHC carve-outs is economies of scale. Smaller to mid-size health plans may not have the capacity to organize and manage a network of specialty providers. Even if they did, their share of patients may be too small to affect provider behavior. MBHC carve-outs contract with multiple payers and health plans and thus aggregate potential patient populations. As a result, networks of providers and care management protocols can be efficiently brought to bear to manage behavioral health services.

The third principle involves price negotiation in periods of excess capacity. As noted earlier, the capacity to supply private inpatient psychiatric care in the United States expanded substantially during the 1980s. By implementing guidelines regarding the appropriate level of care and attempting to reduce psychiatric admissions, the MBHC carve-out industry

---

[b]Information on the origins of the managed behavioral health care carve-out industry is based on discussions with Dr. Saul Feldman.

translated this supply into excess capacity in inpatient psychiatric care. The presence of excess capacity, along with the ability of carve-out vendors to redirect patients toward preferred providers, creates bargaining power for MBHC carve-outs in fee negotiations. By being able to direct admissions to a subset of inpatient care providers, MBHC carve-outs are able to reward providers willing to grant price concessions with an increased volume of patients.

A final economic principle is selection in insurance markets. Markets for behavioral health have been especially vulnerable to inefficiencies stemming from adverse selection, or the tendency of people who anticipate using mental health care to enroll in health plans offering relatively generous coverage for such care.[28] Because people with mental and substance abuse disorders are more costly than other enrollees, adverse selection creates an incentive for insurers to compete to avoid enrolling high-risk/high-cost clients. One effective means of conducting such competition has been to limit coverage and availability of mental health care (thereby making a plan less attractive to people with mental health and substance abuse problems). In payer carve-outs, a single carve-out plan covers mental health and substance abuse services, even if multiple health plans exist (shown on the left-hand side of Figure 1), and mental health and substance abuse coverage and access are the subject of a direct contract between the employer and the carve-out vendor. Having a single insurer for mental health and substance abuse care removes these services from the competitive dynamics of the insurance markets. The result is a diminished tendency for competitive insurers to "race to the bottom" in mental health and substance abuse coverage.

PERFORMANCE

Nearly a decade of research on MBHC carve-outs has provided evidence on how these arrangements have operated in the market to date. Although studies are typically case studies of a particular payer, together the body of literature covers a broad range of carve-out models, from private firms carving out to a single large MBHO to public payers carving out to several community mental health centers. The focus of much of the literature has been on the impact of carve-outs on costs and utilization, but recent studies have also incorporated measures of quality and outcomes.

Many methodological challenges exist when assessing the impact of carve-outs. Each contract is intricate and unique in how benefits, payment, and populations are covered, making general conclusions sometimes difficult to draw.[17,25,51] Outcomes for which findings conflict may therefore be linked to either the particulars of the study or the nature of the contract. In addition, many carve-outs are implemented simultaneously with benefits expansions or reductions in cost-sharing, which makes it difficult to isolate the effects of the carve-out. Furthermore, cost, utilization, and quality are all interrelated, and studies that exclude some measures may fail to capture the full impact of carve-outs on enrollees' health care. For example, reports that exclude analysis of prescription drug utilization may create an incomplete view of the total cost of mental health services.[25] This is especially important given that prescription drug spending has been growing during a period when inpatient and outpatient mental health care has not been growing. Last, some evidence indicates that the impact of a carve-out may change over time as it is implemented and matures,[16] so results at a given point in time may not hold true over the long term.

Despite these issues, studies have consistently shown that carve-outs have led to cost savings for behavioral health services (see Table 1). Studies of private payers carving out behavioral health from fee-for-service or preferred provider organization (PPO) plans report aggregate behavioral health cost decreases in the 30%-40% range.[c] Cost savings are demonstrated across contracts with different payers (private firms and state employers), different MBHOs, and different models of general health insurance (fee-for-service and PPO). Studies that examine a subset of expenditures, such as costs for individuals with a particular diagnosis (e.g., depression care in Merrick[49]) or for a particular type of service (e.g., substance abuse in Stein et al.[58]) also conclude that the carve-out led to significant spending reductions. Whereas many evaluations examine one-time spending decreases, Sturm[60] notes that several studies also show continued savings over time.

Analysis of public payers (primarily state Medicaid programs) that carve out behavioral health care also reveals significant cost savings on those services, although there is wider variation in study results (owing to a wider range of carve-out arrangements).[d] Frank & Lave's 2003 review of studies[25]

---

[c] Cuffel et al.[18] shows even larger aggregate savings per covered life on the basis of the authors' calculations. Studies of carve-outs from health maintenance organizations (HMOs) show mixed results with respect to costs. See Frank & Lave.[25]

[d] For example, the evaluation of Colorado's carve-out.

Table 1	Summary of findings from selected carve-out evaluations costs	
Finding	**Studies**	**Study setting (sample)**
Aggregate costs decline	Bloom et al. 2002 (6) (MBHO only)	CO Medicaid (enrollees with SMI)
	Bouchery & Harwood 2003 (7)	NE Medicaid
	Burns et al. 1999 (9)	NC Medicaid (youths)
	Callahan et al. 1995 (13)	MA Medicaid
	Christianson et al. 1995 (14)	UT Medicaid
	Cuffel et al. 1999 (18)	Private firm
	Frank & McGuire 1997 (26)	MA Medicaid
	Goldman et al. 1998 (33)	Private firm
	Grazier et al. 1999 (34)	Private firm (outpatient services)
	Hodgkin et al. 2004 (36)	MI Medicaid (substance abuse)
	Ma & McGuire 1998 (42)	MA state employees
	McCarty & Argeriou 2003 (47)	IA Medicaid (substance abuse)
	Shepard et al. 2001 (56)	MA Medicaid (substance abuse)
	Stein et al.1999 (58)	Private firm (substance abuse)
	Sturm et al.1998 (61)	OH state employees
Cost per service/user episode decline	Bloom et al. 2002 (6) (MBHO only)	CO Medicaid (enrollees with SMI)
	Callahan et al. 1995 (13)	MA Medicaid
	Cuffel et al. 1999 (18)	Private firm
	Grazier et al. 1999 (34)	Private firm (outpatient services)
	Goldman et al. 1998 (33)	Private firm
	Huskamp 1998 (37)	MA state employees
	Libby et al.2002 (41)	CO Medicaid (youth)
	Ma & McGuire 1998 (42)	MA state employees
	McCarty & Argeriou 2003 (47)	IA Medicaid (substance abuse)
	Merrick 1998 (49)	MA state employees (depression)
	Rothbard et al.2004 (54)	PA Medicaid (schizophrenia)
	Shepard et al. 2002 (57)	MA Medicaid (substance abuse)
	Shepard et al. 2001 (56)	MA Medicaid (substance abuse)
	Stein et al.1999 (58)	Private firm (substance abuse)

shows cost savings in Colorado, Massachusetts, North Carolina, and Utah ranging from 17% to 33%. Some more recent reviews note that some states with immediate cost decreases have found that the declines may have represented one-time savings because these levels were difficult to sustain over time.[6,16,59] As with private payers, studies that focus on subpopulations (e.g., youth in Burns et al.[9] and seriously mentally ill in Bloom et al.[6]) or specific services (e.g., substance abuse in Shepard et al.[56]) also find cost decreases per enrollee under Medicaid carve-outs.

One key component to understanding cost savings under carve-outs is assessing how savings were achieved. If savings under the carve-out are due to costs being shifted to other services, such as prescription drugs or physical health services, then estimates of cost savings may be overstating actual results. Frank & Lave[25] note that the similarity of cost savings in studies that examine only services included in the carve-out and those that examine all be-

havioral health services (regardless of contractual responsibility) indicates minimal cost shifting to primary care providers. Similarly, Cuffel et al.[18] explicitly compare costs for general medical care before and after a carve-out and find lower overall health care spending after the carve-out. Studies do note, however, that there is evidence of cost shifting to some behavioral health services not included in carve-out contracts, such as prescription drugs[e,4,10,12] or child welfare services.[41]

Another possible source of cost savings under carve-outs stems from managed care techniques used by MBHOs, such as negotiation for lower payment rates and coordination of care to reduce duplication or inefficiencies. Many of the studies showing cost savings also find lower costs per service or per user (see Table 1), and several analyses note that lower

[e]Zuvekas et al. (68) state that, though prescription drug costs increased after implementation of a carve-out, the increase may have been smaller than it would have without the carve-out.

payment rates for services were a factor in reducing these costs.[f,13,33,42,49,54,61] Others note lower costs per episode or service category,[34,37] which may be linked to lower payment rates or, alternatively, could be due to less intense service mix within that spending category. Utilization management techniques such as precertification and case management are widely used among MBHOs[40] and frequently cited as a key component of savings,[33,42] although the exact impact they have on costs under behavioral health carve-outs is not usually estimated in evaluations.[g] The fact that denials of authorizations are

rare[40] and that few enrollees ever come near limits on care[51] implies that payment policies and contract incentives[25,42] along with more nuanced approaches to care management are responsible for cost control.

Most studies of carve-outs point to dramatic changes in utilization patterns after implementation, particularly declines in inpatient hospitalization, as the main source of savings (see Table 2). Both utilization rates and length of stay for inpatient care decline following implementation of carve-outs in both the private and public sector. In many cases, reductions in inpatient use are accompanied by increases in intensive outpatient care (e.g., partial hospitalization), although not all studies measure such outcomes. Whether carve-outs lead to decreased outpatient utilization or whether services shift to increase outpatient care is not clear because findings are mixed. Some variation is due to different ways that utilization is measured (e.g., utilization rates or

---

[f]In Montana, low payment rates under the carve-out were cited as a primary reason for providers' unwillingness to participate in the program and the eventual termination of the carve-out.[16]
[g]An exception is Wickizer and Lessler,[67] who concluded that concurrent review had an impact on hospital length of stay under a MBHO.

Table 2	Summary of findings from selected carve-out evaluations: utilization	
Finding	**Studies**	**Study setting**
Inpatient use declines	Bloom et al. 2002 (6) Bouchery & Harwood 2003 (7) Burns et al. 1999 (9) Callahan et al. 1995 (13) Christianson et al. 1995 (14) Goldman et al. 1998 (33) Libby et al. 2002 (41) McCarty & Argeriou 2003 (47) Merrick 1998 (49) Rothbard et al. 2004 (54) Stein et al. 1999 (58) Stoner et al. 1997 (59) Sturm et al. 1998 (61)	CO Medicaid (enrollees with SMI) NE Medicaid NC Medicaid (youths) MA Medicaid UT Medicaid Private firm CO Medicaid (youth) IA Medicaid (substance abuse) MA state employees (depression) PA Medicaid (schizophrenia) Private firm (substance abuse) UT Medicaid OH state employees
Intermediate care increases	Burns et al. 1999 (9) Callahan et al. 1995 (13) Libby et al. 2002 (41) Shepard et al. 2001 (56) Stein et al. 1999 (58) Sturm et al. 1998 (61)	NC Medicaid (youths) MA Medicaid CO Medicaid (youth) MA Medicaid (substance abuse) Private firm (substance abuse) OH state employees
Outpatient use declines	Bloom et al. 2002 (6) Callahan et al. 1995 (13) Goldman et al. 1998 (33) Ma & McGuire 1998 (42) Stein et al. 1999 (58) Sturm et al. 1998 (61)	CO Medicaid (enrollees with SMI) MA Medicaid Private firm MA state employees Private firm (substance abuse) OH state employees
Outpatient use does not change	Grazier et al.1999 (34) Rothbard et al. 2004 (54)	Private firm (outpatient services) PA Medicaid (schizophrenia)
Outpatient use increases	Bouchery & Harwood 2003 (7) Burns et al. 1999 (9) McCarty & Argeriou 2003 (47) Shepard et al. 2001 (56)	NE Medicaid NC Medicaid (youths) IA Medicaid (substance abuse) MA Medicaid (substance abuse)

days of care per enrollee) or to different utilization rates prior to the carve-out, but other variations stem from a real difference in findings of across-the-board utilization decreases versus shifts in service site under carve-outs.

Additional information on utilization patterns under carve-outs can be gleaned from studies that examine the impact these arrangements have on overall access to behavioral health care (see Table 3). Even though some studies find that overall probability of using services declines, most studies find that access remains unchanged or even increases under the carve-out. Studies that report both a decrease in utilization and an increase in access typically show a decline in the days per user but an increase in the likelihood of using that service. The combination of utilization and access outcomes leads to the conclusion that the expanded benefits, decreased cost sharing, and broader provider panels offered by MBHOs may expand access to services, whereas the carve-out structure lessens the intensity of service use.

An overriding concern about carve-outs is whether such arrangements impact the quality of services and mental health outcomes for enrollees. The potential for carve-outs to fragment care delivery for individuals, as well as general concerns about the appropriateness of managed care techniques for behavioral health care, has been a long-standing issue in debates over carve-outs. Given findings that costs decline while access is generally maintained and that patterns of care change so quickly following implementation, some worry that the quality of services delivered under carve-outs may in fact be below acceptable levels (see reference 39). Unlike issues of cost and utilization, which have been widely studied using well-established measures, quality under carve-

outs has been more difficult to evaluate. By nature, quality is more difficult to measure, and accepted guidelines for what care "should" look like for a given population or service are not always available. Furthermore, a wide range of outcomes could be measured to assess quality, which makes comparisons across studies difficult.

A limited number of studies that focus on depression care find an improvement in quality under carve-outs (see Table 4), such as increased follow-up rates[49] or adherence to treatment guidelines.[12,66] A consumer satisfaction survey of Massachusetts Medicaid's carve-out enrollees also finds that, although satisfaction is generally high, enrollees with depression are more likely to be satisfied with their care than are patients with other diagnoses.[19] However, a larger number of studies of general behavioral health services, depression care, or serious mental illness or schizophrenia find no change in quality following carve-out implementation. These studies use measures ranging from readmission rates[7,49] to satisfaction[5,13] to symptoms and functioning levels.[5,17] Other assessments report problems with quality under carve-outs. Most of these evaluations focus on individuals with severe mental health disorders (e.g., schizophrenia) and thus (given the role of Medicaid in caring for individuals with severe mental disorders) evaluate Medicaid carve-outs.

The inclusion of quality measures in studies of carve-outs is a relatively recent addition to the literature on MBHOs. As such, little work has been done to reconcile disparate findings. Sturm[60] posits that poor experiences with Medicaid carve-outs may be a consequence of higher levels of need in the public sector and fewer years of experience with MBHOs than in the private sector. Frank & Lave[25] question

Table 3	Summary of findings from selected carve-out evaluations: access	
Finding	**Studies**	**Study setting**
No change in likelihood of use	Callahan et al. 1995 (13) Cuffel et al. 1999 (18) Zuvekas et al. 2005 (69)	MA Medicaid Private firm Single insurer
Decrease in likelihood of use	Bloom et al. 2002 (6) Hodgkin et al. 2004 (36) Ma & McGuire 1998 (42)	CO Medicaid (enrollees with SMI) MI Medicaid (substance abuse) MA state employees
Increase in likelihood of use	Bouchery & Harwood 2003 (7) Burns et al. 1999 (9) Goldman et al.1998 (33) Grazier et al.1999 (34) McCarty & Argeriou 2003 (47) Merrick 1998 (49) Shepard et al. 2001 (56)	NE Medicaid NC Medicaid (youths) Private firm Private firm (outpatient services) IA Medicaid (substance abuse) MA state employees (depression) MA Medicaid (substance abuse)

Table 4	Summary of findings from selected carve-out evaluations: quality and outcomes	
Finding	**Studies**	**Study setting**
No change in quality compared with no carve-out	Bianconi et al. 2006 (5)	OR Medicaid (enrollees with SMI)
	Bouchery & Harwood 2003 (7)	NE Medicaid
	Bush et al. 2004 (Rx) (10)	Medicaid (schizophrenia)
	Callahan et al. 1995 (adults) (13)	MA Medicaid
	Cuffel et al. 2002 (17)	CO Medicaid (enrollees with SMI)
	Merrick 1998 (readmissions) (49)	MA state employees (depression)
	Wallace et al. 2005 (Rx, symptoms) (65)	Medicaid (schizophrenia)
Improvement in quality compared with no carve-out	Busch 2002 (12)	Single insurer (depression)
	Merrick 1998 (follow up) (49)	MA state employees (depression)
	Shepard et al. 2002 (continuity) (57)	MA Medicaid (substance abuse)
	West et al. 2000 (66)	National (psychiatry patients)
Deterioration of quality compared with no carve-out	Busch et al. 2004 (therapy) (10)	Medicaid (schizophrenia)
	Callahan et al. 1995 (children) (13)	MA Medicaid
	Manning et al. 1999 (46)	UT Medicaid (schizophrenia)
	Ray et al. 2003 (52)	TN Medicaid (enrollees with SMI)
	Shepard et al. 2002 (readmission) (57)	MA Medicaid (substance abuse)
	Wallace et al. 2005 (therapy) (65)	Medicaid (schizophrenia)

whether there have been enough studies of quality to build a representative body of literature. Other explanations include wide variation in the inclusion of quality measures in contracts, requirements that state programs accept lowest bids for contracts, and low payment rates under Medicaid programs.[39]

A final note about the performance of MBHO carve-outs is that the general review above may mask variations within the findings. The potential for carve-outs to affect certain groups disproportionately—namely high-need groups or other vulnerable populations—is a frequently mentioned concern. Some evidence does point to this possibility. For example, Huskamp[37] finds unequal effects of the carve-out for enrollees with unipolar depression or substance dependence. Similarly, analysis of outcomes and quality by Manning and colleagues[46] and Ray et al.[52] both show the largest deterioration for groups with the poorest health or highest risk. Others express concern about the differential impact of carve-outs on children or low-income families[38]; findings of higher readmission rates for children than for other Medicaid populations in Callahan et al.[13] and greater declines in utilization for Aid to Families with Dependent Children-related groups than for other beneficiaries in Christianson et al.[14] indicate that experiences in Medicaid carve-outs for children

and families may differ from those of disabled adult beneficiaries. Performance may also differ for individuals who experience substance abuse problems and mental health care problems,[11,56] although few studies allow for comparisons of these two types of services within the same evaluation.[h] Finally, the variation in findings may be due to ownership of carve-outs, as evidenced by Colorado's experience where larger impacts were observed under the for-profit relative to community-based Medicaid carve-outs. Donohue & Frank's[20] review of several states' Medicaid carve-outs concludes, "ownership status is not a reliable predictor of program success."

THE EVOLVING CARVE-OUT

Like managed care generally, the behavioral health care carve-out is not a static institution. Over time, it has evolved to address some of its own shortcomings that have become apparent to purchasers. The carve-out structure is also being put to new uses to address longstanding policy and management challenges in the mental health and substance abuse delivery system.

---

[h]Exceptions are Ma & McGuire[42] and Huskamp.[37]

The first challenge is coordination of care. One common criticism of MBHC carve-outs has been that they contribute to fragmentation of the delivery system, especially in clinical areas where primary care providers play an important therapeutic role.[24] Primary care treatment of depression is perhaps the most widely studied example of such difficulties. Primary care providers treat ~50% of all patients treated for depression. Carve-out arrangements can interfere with the effective management of treatment for depression in primary care settings by *(a)* making cumbersome the process of referring patients to mental health and substance abuse specialists, *(b)* not reimbursing primary care physicians (who are not in the MBHO's network and thus cannot bill for behavioral health services) for the extra time required to attend to people with depression, and *(c)* impeding communication between primary care physicians and mental health specialists when they are used. Recent demonstrations of new models of interaction between carve-outs and primary care providers are being used across the nation to address these problems.[21]

For example, one large national managed behavioral health care firm, United Behavioral Health, has developed a demonstration partnership with Blue Cross of Northern California and the University of California San Francisco's (UCSF) department of internal medicine. In the partnership, the behavioral health carve-out and the health plan have agreed to credential internists interested and trained in the provision of evidence-based treatment for depression. This agreement means that the carve-out company treats these internists as members of its provider network. It also means that payments to the primary care provider recognize the extra effort and time required to attend to patients with depression. Moreover, the care managers employed by the carve-out play an expanded role in assisting the primary care physicians to track and follow up with patients being treated for depression.

In this demonstration, the fragmentation problem is overcome by altering the standard carve-out arrangement to bring the primary care provider into the managed behavioral health care network and using the carve-out's information technology capacity to promote evidence-based medicine. Integration is accomplished while taking advantage of economies of scale and specialization offered by the MBHC carve-out. Similar models are being adopted by other payers as well. For example, Massachusetts has assigned to its Medicaid MBHC carve-out a role that resembles the use of the carve-out in the UCSF demonstration. In this role, the MBHO oversees the management of mental health care in the primary care setting within the state's primary care case management program.

New Mexico has also developed a new carve-out model to address integration concerns, in this case within its public financing system for behavioral health care. As in other states, over the past 50 years, New Mexico's public mental health system has changed from a relatively centralized system with a single point of decision making (the state mental health authority) to a relatively decentralized one that includes numerous governmental agencies.[23] Low-income individuals with mental health and substance abuse disorders commonly receive mental health care through the state mental health authority, the state Medicaid program, the criminal justice system, public schools, and the foster care system. This decentralization leads to a constellation of public programs that define elements of mental health care differently, pay providers different prices for the same services, and have unique definitions of appropriate care and approaches to quality in behavioral health. These circumstances result in inefficient delivery, poor use of federal and state funds, and inconsistent treatment of the same clinical situations.

To address this public policy challenge, New Mexico established a purchasing cooperative among all the state agencies that purchase behavioral health services. This purchasing cooperative contracted with a single MBHC carve-out to manage all public behavioral health services in the state. The contract requires that a common set of service definitions be applied, that common prices be paid for the same services, and that uniform clinical criteria for appropriate care and quality be put into practice.[i] The aim is to reduce fragmentation within public mental health and substance abuse delivery, to create incentives to use federal matching dollars and state general funds efficiently, and to improve the quality of care. This initiative relies on the carve-out's specialized information technology organization and specialized expertise in managing mental health and substance abuse care. This adaptation of the carve-out form could address some persistent shortcomings of public mental health delivery.

The carve-out model could address a second challenge in mental health delivery, that of concerns about cost shifting. As noted earlier, MBHOs are not typically responsible for coverage of prescription drugs; rather, management of psychotropic drugs has been the nearly exclusive domain of PBMs. Because

---

[i]The State of New Mexico completed its "hold harmless" start up year in July 2006, and the vendor will be permitted to change service delivery arrangements in the coming fiscal year.

prescription drugs are essentially free goods to the carve-out, the carve-out faces incentives (upon which the empirical evidence shows they act) to orient treatment toward the use of pharmacotherapies. Thus, there exists a fundamental misalignment of incentives between PBMs and MBHC carve-outs. To address this issue, several MBHOs are exploring new products and joint ventures.[43] These new arrangements include organizational and contractual arrangements that bring the specialized expertise of the MBHC carve-out to the task of managing psychotropic drug use. This disease-management approach addresses concerns about carve-outs and extends the model beyond its traditional management of specialty inpatient, outpatient, residential, and day-treatment services to prescription drugs and related medical care.

A third area in which carve-out models may be used as solutions to policy issues is market fragmentation, which undermines quality-improvement initiatives. Most major health care markets have multiple health plans that compete for business, and a single health plan rarely accounts for more than 25% of the market share. It is common to see ten health plans competing in a market, with any single health plan enrolling 5%-20% of potential enrollees. Therefore, a typical provider could face dozens of different clinical criteria, formularies, and compensation arrangements. Economic research shows that medical practices tend to manage their affairs in a fashion that is responsive to the overall composition of their payer arrangements.[31] The implication is that a given health plan will usually have very limited ability to affect provider behavior, a challenge to quality-improvement efforts based on payment incentives or guidelines implemented at the health plan level. Recent assessment of pay-for-performance initiatives shows that this issue likely constrained the impact of the effort.[53]

The economies of scale in a carve-out, along with the concentration in the industry, create unique opportunities for carve-outs to improve quality by altering provider behavior. One of the salient features of MBHC carve-outs is that they use a single provider network, telephone intake process, care manager system, and clinical guidelines to serve a variety of individual customers (employers, state government, health plans). This means that an MBHC carve-out firm will serve as purchaser of mental health and substance abuse services for multiple health plans within a market. This purchaser function means carve-outs concentrate the purchasing power of multiple health plans operating in the same market. Through its aggregation of data and its concentrated

purchasing power in markets, a carve-out may have greater potential to affect provider behavior. This potential is predicated on carve-out contracts being structured such that quality improvement is a priority.

ASSESSING THE CARVE-OUT INSTITUTION

The MBHC carve-out is a relatively new institution in the mental health and substance abuse care delivery system. Most people with private health insurance that receive specialty mental health or substance abuse treatment do so in the context of an MBHC carve-out. A large number of Medicaid recipients treated for mental or addictive disorders receive that care via MBHC carve-out arrangements. Many revile the MBHC carve-out because it is the institutional face of managed care in the mental health sector. It is blamed for many of the problems in mental health and substance abuse care delivery, including unmet need for care, increased fragmentation in care delivery, compromised professional autonomy, constraints on care giving, and greater bureaucracy and administrative costs.[39] Some of these criticisms are supported by the facts and merit attention from health care purchasers, policy makers, and consumers. Frequently overlooked, however, are the important contributions that carve-outs have made to solving some longstanding problems in mental health and substance abuse care delivery.

Three basic challenges have confounded mental health policy makers for the 30 years spanning 1963 to 1993. Challenges included (*a*) the high proportion of mental health and substance abuse treatment devoted to inpatient care; (*b*) the relatively low level of access to care, given relatively high measured levels of clinical need; and (*c*) the unequal coverage of mental health and substance abuse care in private insurance. The rise of the MBRC carve-out has accelerated progress on all three of these policy fronts.

The empirical research on carve-outs summarized earlier shows that MBHC carve-outs' first priority has been reducing inpatient psychiatric care as well as reliance on 30-day inpatient substance abuse treatment programs. A large number of studies, summarized in Table 2, shows that utilization and spending on inpatient psychiatric care declined with the advent of the MBHC carve-out. The use of 30-day inpatient substance abuse treatment programs was also dramatically curtailed. This outcome was true for both privately insured populations and those served by the Medicaid program. For 30 years, a central policy goal for mental health and substance abuse care was to reorient care from inpatient to community-based ambulatory care, and only with the wide use of MBHC carve-out was significant progress made in this area.

Most experiences with implementation of MBHC carve-outs have shown that rates of treatment in enrolled populations have increased. That is, a larger portion of a given population receives some treatment for a mental health or substance-abuse problem. This change occurred in part because out-of-pocket costs for outpatient care nearly always declined when a carve-out arrangement was put into place.[23] Again, mental health care had long been viewed as an area where there was substantial underuse of care, in part owing to financial barriers to care.[39] A by-product of this barrier was that high-income people disproportionately used mental health care, implying that private insurance expansions of mental health benefits were regressive financing mechanisms. In the era of the MBHC carve-out, a phenomenon has occurred that Mechanic & McAlpine[48] refer to as "democratization" of care: More people are getting some care, and the variation in what people received has declined. The result is that expanding mental health coverage today is much less regressive than it would have been in the 1970s and 1980s.

MBHC carve-out arrangements have fundamentally altered the political economy of the parity debate, the movement to have mental health and substance abuse services covered by private insurance on the same terms as other medical conditions.[3] The expectations of the high cost of increasing coverage for mental health and substance abuse care stood in the way of parity since the debate ensued over the benefit design for Medicare.[23] Since the mid-1990s, a growing body of evidence has emerged showing that expansion of mental health and substance abuse coverage under MBHC carve-out arrangements did not lead to notable increases in total spending on these services.[3,32,33,37] The Congressional Budget Office has recognized this evidence and has repeatedly adjusted its estimates of the costs of parity. The result is that numerous states and the Federal Employees Health Benefit Program have implemented policies directing private insurers to cover mental health services on terms equal to those of other medical care.

Although the MBHC carve-out has contributed to the gains described, there are instances of less salutary effects. Although, overall, carve-out arrangements do not appear to reduce the average quality of care, especially in privately insured populations, persuasive evidence indicates that disadvantaged populations with complex clinical problems are more likely to experience declines in quality of care under carve-out arrangements than those with less complex problems (summarized in Table 4). This appears to be the case for people with schizophrenia enrolled in Medicaid. Addressing mental health problems in the context of either primary care or serious medical illnesses (e.g., breast cancer) is typically complicated by carve-out arrangements because the carve-out form inhibits coordination, communication, and hand-offs between specialty mental health care and medical care. Although some evidence shows that carve-outs are moving toward solutions to these problems, solutions have not been widely put into practice yet.

Carve-out arrangements carry administrative costs that can be substantial (8%-15% of behavioral health care spending). They also insert themselves into clinical decision-making, a practice that care providers resent. The aggressive price bargaining by carve-outs has resulted in reduced incomes and fees for mental health professionals and significant financial stresses for providers of inpatient psychiatric and substance abuse care. There also exist potential incentives for MBHC carve-outs to emphasize pharmacotherapy over psychosocial treatments. This action may distort clinical decision-making away from the best care for a particular patient.[22]

CONCLUSION

In assessing the overall performance of carve-out arrangements in the context of the recent history of mental health and substance abuse delivery, the evidence suggests that these organizations are not the source of many or most difficulties in mental health and substance abuse care. It is easy to forget that the good old days of fee-for-service delivery routinely failed to meet policy goals and use of evidence-based care for people with mental and addictive disorders. Progress has been made, and the carve-out form has contributed to those gains. Carve-outs have also created some new problems, compromised clinical autonomy, and made many providers financially worse off. It is appropriate to recognize the gains that have been made and also to note the importance of addressing the weaknesses of the MBHC carve-out form in order to develop systems of care for individuals with behavioral health needs.

ACKNOWLEDGMENT
We are grateful for financial support of NIDA Grant P60DA010233.

● ● ● References

1. Am. Manag. Behav. Health Assoc. 2006. *Welcome.* http://www.ambha.org/index.htm.

2. Am. Psychiatr. Assoc. 1988. *The Coverage Catalogue.* Washington, DC: APA.

3. Barry CL, Frank RG, McGuire TG. 2006. The costs of mental health parity: still an impediment. *Health Aff.* 25(3):623-34.

4. Berndt ER, Frank RG, McGuire TG. 1997. Alternate insurance arrangements and the treatment of depression: What are the facts? *Am. J.Manag. Care* 3(2):243-52.

5. Bianconi JM, Mahler JM, McFarland BH. 2006. Outcomes for rural Medicaid clients with severe mental illness in fee for service versus managed care. *Adm. PolicyMent. Health Ment. Health Serv. Res.* 33(4):411-22.

6. Bloom JR, Hu T, Wallace N, Cuffel B, Hausman JW, et al. 2002. Mental health costs and access under alternative capitation systems in Colorado. *Health Servo Res.* 37(2): 31540.

7. Bouchery E, Harwood H. 2003. The Nebraska Medicaid managed behavioral health care initiative: impacts on utilization, expenditures, and quality of care for mental health. *J. Behav. Health Serv. Res.* 30(1):93-108.

8. Brubaker B. 2002. One stressed out industry: managed care meets mental health with mixed results. *Wash. Post* Oct. 29:E1.

9. Burns BJ, Teagle SE, Schwartz M, Angold A, Holtzman A. 1999. Managed behavioral health care: a Medicaid carve-out for youth. *Health Aff.* 18(5):214-25.

10. Busch AB, Frank RG, Lehman A. 2004. The effect of a managed behavioral health care carve-out on quality of care for Medicaid patients diagnosed as having schizophrenia. *Arch. Gen. Psychiatry* 61:442-48.

11. Busch AB, Frank RG, Lehman A. 2006. Schizophrenia, co-occurring substance abuse disorders and quality of care: the differential effect of a managed behavioral health care carve-out. *Adm. Policy Ment. Health Ment. Health Serv. Res.* 33:388-97.

12. Busch SH. 2002. Specialty health care, treatment patterns, and quality: the impact of a mental health carve-out on care for depression. *Health Serv. Res.* 37(6): 1583-1601.

13. Callahan JJ, Shepard DS, Beinecke RH, Larson MH, Cavanaugh D. 1995. Mental health/substance abuse treatment in managed care: the Massachusetts Medicaid experience. *Health Aff.* 14(3):173-84.

14. Christianson JB, Manning W, Lurie N, Stoner TJ, Gray DZ, et al. 1995. Utah's prepaid mental health plan: the first year. *Health Aff.* 14(3):160-72.

15. Coffey RM, Mark T, King E, Harwood H, McKusick D, et al. 2000. *National estimates of expenditures for mental health and substance abuse treatment,* 1997. SAMHSA Pub No. SMA-00-3499. Rockville, MD: CSAT and CMHS, SAMHSA.

16. Coleman M, Schnapp W, Hurwitz D, Hedberg S, Cabral L, et al. 2005. Overview of publicly funded managed behavioral health care. *Adm. PolicyMent. Health* 32(4):321-40.

17. Cuffel BJ, Bloom JR, Wallace N, Hausman JW, Hu T. 2002 Two-year outcomes in fee-for-service and capitated Medicaid programs for people with severe mental illness. *Health Serv. Res.* 37(2):341-59.

18. Cuffel BJ, Goldman W, Schlesinger H. 1999. Does managing behavioral health care services increase the cost of providing medical care? *J.Behav. Health Serv. Res.* 26(4):372-80.

19. Delman J, Beinecke RH. 2005. Assessing consumer satisfaction in the Massachusetts behavioral health partnership. *Adm. Policy Ment. Health.* 32(4): 373-86.

20. Donohue JM, Frank RG. 2000. Medicaid behavioral health carve-outs: a new generation of privatization decisions. *Harvard Rev. Psychiatry J.* 8(5):231-41.

21. Feldman MD, Ong MK, Lee DL, Perez-Stable EJ. 2006. Realigning economic incentives for depression care at UCSF. *Adm. Policy Ment. Health.* 33(1): 34-38.

22. Frank RG, Conti RM, Goldman HH. 2005. Mental health policy and psychotropic drugs. *Milbank Q.* 83(2):271-98.

23. Frank RG, Glied S. 2006. *Better but Not Well.* New York: Johns Hopkins Press.

24. Frank RG, Huskamp HA, Pincus HA. 2003. Aligning incentives in the treatment of depression in primary care with evidence-based practice. *Psychiatr. Serv.* 54(5):682-87.

25. Frank RG, Lave J. 2003. Economics. In *Managed Behavioral Health Services,* ed. S Feldman, 6:146-65. Springfield, IL: Thomas

26. Frank RG, McGuire TG. 1997. Savings from a Medicaid carve-out for mental health and substance abuse services in Massachusetts. *Psychiatr. Serv.* 48(9):1147-52.

27. Frank RG, McGuire TG. 1998. The economic functions of carve outs in managed care. *Am. J. Manag. Care* 4:SP31-39.

28. Frank RG, McGuire TG. 2000. Economics and mental health. In *Handbook of Health Economics,* ed. JP Newhouse, A Culyer, 16:893-54. Amsterdam: North Holland.

29. Frank RG, Salkever DS, Sharfstein SS. 1991. A look at rising mental health insurance costs. *Health Aff.* 10(2):116-24.

30. Gibson R. 1989. Private hospitals share of mental services rises. *Mod. Healthc.* 8:14.

31. Glied S, Zivin JG. 2002. How do doctors behave when some (but not all) of their patients are in managed care. *J. Health Econ.* 21(2):337-53.

32. Goldman HH, Frank RG, Burnam MA, Huskamp HA, Ridgely MS, et al. 2006. Behavioral health insurance parity for federal employees. *N. Engl. J. Med.* 354(13): 1378-86.

33. Goldman W, McCulloch J, Sturm R. 1998. Costs and use of mental health services before and after managed care. *Health Aff.* 17(2):40-52.

34. Grazier KL, Eselius LL, Hut Shore KK, G'sell WA. 1999. Effects of a mental health carve-out on use, costs and payers: a four year study. *J. Behav. Health Serv. Res.* 26(4):381-89.

35. Hodgkin D, Horgan CM, Garnick DW, Merrick EL, Goldin D. 2000. Why carve out? Determinants of behavioral health contracting choice among large U.S. employers. *J.Behav. Health Serv. Res.* 27(2): 178-93.

36. Hodgkin D, Shepard DS, Anthony YE, Strickler GK 2004. A publicly managed Medicaid substance abuse carve-out: effects on spending and utilization. *Adm. Policy Ment. Health.* 31(3):197-17.

37. Huskamp HA. 1998. Howa managed behavioral health care carve-out plans affected spending for episodes of treatment. *Psychiatr. Serv.* 49(12): 1559-62.

38. Hutchinson AB, Foster EM. 2003. The effect of Medicaid managed care on mental health care for children: a review of the literature. *Ment. Health Serv. Res.* 5(1):39-54.

39. Inst. Med. 2006. *Improving the Quality of Health Care for Mental and Substance-Use Conditions.* Washington, DC: Natl. Acad.

40. Koike A, Klap R, Unutzer J. 2000. Utilization management in a large managed behavioral health organization. *Psychiatr. Serv.* 51(5):621-26.

41. Libby AM, Cuellar A, Snowden LR, Orton HD. 2002. Substitution in a Medicaid mental health carve-out: services and costs. *J. Health Care Financ.* 28(4):11-23.

42. Ma CA, McGuire TG. 1998. Costs and incentives in a behavioral health carve-out. *Health Aff.* 17(2): 53-69.

43. Manag. Care Week. 2005. Behavioral firms build disease management capacity to address med/psych interaction. *Manag. Care Week.* Jan. 31.

44. Manag. Care Week. 2005. More MCOs may bring behavioral health services in-house, following Aetna's lead. *Manag. Care Week.* Jan. 3.

45. Manderscheid RW, Atay JE, Hernandez-Cartagena MR, Edmond PY, Male A, et al. 2001. Highlights of organized mental health services in 1998 in major national and state trends. *Mental Health, United States, 2000,* U.S. Dep. Health Hum. Serv., Rockville, MD.

46. Manning WG, Lui CF, Stoner TJ, Gray DZ, Lurie N, et al. 1999. Outcomes for Medicaid beneficiaries with schizophrenia under a prepaid mental health carve-out. *J. Behav. Health Serv. Res.* 26(4):442-50.

47. McCarty D, Argeriou M. 2003. The Iowa managed substance abuse care plan: access, utilization, and expenditures for Medicaid recipients. *J. Behav. Health Serv. Res.* 30(1):18-25.

48. Mechanic D, McAlpine DD. 1999. Mission unfulfilled: potholes on the road to mental health parity. *Health Aff.* 18(5):7-21.

49. Merrick EL. 1998. Treatment of major depression before and after implementation of a behavioral health carve-out plan. *Psychiatr. Serv.* 49(12): 1563-67.

50. Oss ME. 1994. Managed behavioral health market share in the United States, 1994. Gettysburg, PA: Open Minds.

51. Peele PB, Lave JR, Xu Y. 1999. Benefit limits in managed behavioral health care: Do they matter? *J. Behav. Health Serv. Res.* 26(4):430-41.

52. Ray WA, Daugherty JR, Meador KG. 2003. Effect of a mental health "carve-out" program on the continuity of antipsychotic therapy. *N. Engl. J.Med.* 348(19):1885-94.

53. Rosenthal MB, Frank RG, Li Z, Epstein AM. 2005. Early experience with pay-for-performance: from concept to practice. *JAMA* 294(14):1788-93.

54. Rothbard AB, Juno E, Hadley TR, DoginJ. 2004. Psychiatric service utilization and cost for persons with schizophrenia in a Medicaid managed care program. *J.Behav. Health Serv. Res.* 31(1):1-12.

55. Salkever DS, Shinogle JA. 2000. Empirical evidence on the demand for carve-outs in employment group mental health coverage. *J. Ment. Health Pol. Fcon.* 3:83-95.

56. Shepard DS, Daley M, Ritter GA, Hodgkin D, Beinecke RH. 2001. Effects of a statewide carve out on spending and access to substance abuse treatment in Massachusetts, 1992 to 1996. *Health Serv. Res.* 36(6):32-44.

57. Shepard DS, Daley M, Ritter GA, Hodgkin D, Beinecke RH. 2002. Managed care and the quality of substance abuse treatment. *J. Ment. Health Policy Econ.* 5(4):163-74.

58. Stein B, Reardon E, Sturm R. 1999. Substance abuse service utilization under managed care: HMOs versus carve-out plans. *J. Behav. Health Serv. Res.* 26(4):451-56.

59. Stoner T, Manning W, Christianson J, Gray DZ, Marriott S. 1997. Expenditures for mental health

services in the Utah prepaid mental health plan. *Health Care Financ. Rev.* 18(3):73-93.

60. Sturm R. 1999. Tracking changes in behavioral health services: How have carve-outs changed care? *J. Behav. Health Serv. Res.* 26(4):360-71.

61. Sturm R, Goldman W, McCulloch J. 1998. Mental health and substance abuse parity: a case study of Ohio's state employee program. *J. Mental Health Policy Econ.* 1:129-34.

62. TeichJL, Melek SP. 2000. Characteristics of managed behavioral health care organizations in 1996. *Psychiatr. Serv.* 51(11):1422-27.

63. Tigner R. 1989. Charter hospital's aggressiveness sparks criticism. *Bus J.* July 31.

64. U.S. Dep. Health Hum. Serv. 1999. *Mental Health: A Report of the Surgeon General.* Rockeville, MD: U.S. Dep. Health Hum. Serv., Substance Abuse Ment. Health Serv. Adm., Cent. Ment. Health Serv., Natl. Inst. Health, Natl. Inst. Ment. Health.

65. Wallace NT, Bloom JR, Hu TW, Libbt AM. 2005. Medication treatment patterns for adults with schizophrenia in Medicaid managed care in Colorado. *Psychiatr. Serv.* 56(11):1402-8.

66. West JC, Leaf PJ, Zarin DA. 2000. Health plan characteristics and conformance with key psychopharmacologic treatment recommendations for major depression. *Ment. Health Serv. Res.* 2(4):223-37.

67. WIckizer TM, Lessler D. 1998. Effects of utilization management on patterns of hospital care among privately insured adult patients. *Med Care* 36:1545-54.

68. Zuvekas SH, Rupp AE, Norquist GS. 2005. Spillover effects of benefit expansions and carve-outs on psychotropic medical use and costs. *Inquiry* 42(1):86-97.

69. Zuvekas SH, Rupp AE, Norquist GS. 2005. The impacts of mental health parity and managed care in one large employer group: a reexamination. *Health Aff.* 24(6):1668-71.

Achieving the Promise: Transforming Mental Health Care in America

Source: New Freedom Commission on Mental Health. 2003. *Achieving the Promise: Transforming Mental Health Care in America. Executive Summary.* DHHS Pub. No. SMA-03-3831. Rockville, MD: Department of Health and Human Services, pp. 1-8.

We envision a future when everyone with a mental illness will recover, a future when mental illnesses can be prevented or cured, a future when mental illnesses are detected early, and a future when everyone with a mental illness at any stage of life has access to effective treatment and supports—essentials for living, working, learning, and participating fully in the community.

In February 2001, President George W. Bush announced his New Freedom Initiative to promote increased access to educational and employment opportunities for people with disabilities. The Initiative also promotes increased access to assistive and universally designed technologies and full access to community life. Not since the Americans with Disabilities Act (ADA)—the landmark legislation providing protections against discrimination—and the Supreme Court's *Olmstead v. L.C.* decision, which affirmed the right to live in community settings, has there been cause for such promise and opportunity for full community participation for all people with disabilities, including those with psychiatric disabilities.

On April 29, 2002, the President identified three obstacles preventing Americans with mental illnesses from getting the excellent care they deserve:

- Stigma that surrounds mental illnesses,
- Unfair treatment limitations and financial requirements placed on mental health benefits in private health insurance, and
- The fragmented mental health service delivery system.

The President's New Freedom Commission on Mental Health (called *the Commission* in this report) is a key component of the New Freedom Initiative. The President launched the Commission to address the problems in the current mental health service delivery system that allow Americans to fall through the system's cracks.

In his charge to the Commission, the President directed its members to study the problems and gaps in the mental health system and make concrete recommendations for immediate improvements that the Federal government, State governments, local agencies, as well as public and private health care providers, can implement. Executive Order 13263 detailed the instructions to the Commission.

The Commission's findings confirm that there are unmet needs and that many barriers impede care for people with mental illnesses. Mental illnesses are shockingly common; they affect almost every American family. It can happen to a child,[a] a brother, a grandparent, or a co-worker. It can happen to someone from any background—African American, Alaska Native, Asian American, Hispanic American, Native American, Pacific Islander, or White American. It can occur at any stage of life, from childhood to old age. No community is unaffected by mental illnesses; no school or workplace is untouched.

In any given year, about 5% to 7% of adults have a serious mental illness, according to several nationally representative studies.[1-3] A similar percentage of children—about 5% to 9%—have a serious emotional disturbance. These figures mean that millions of adults and children are disabled by mental illnesses every year.[1,4]

President Bush said,

Americans must understand and send this message: mental disability is not a scandal—it is an illness. And like physical illness, it is treatable, especially when the treatment comes early.

Over the years, science has broadened our knowledge about mental health and illnesses, showing the potential to improve the way in which mental health care is provided. The U.S. Department of Health and Human Services (HHS) released *Mental Health: A Report of the Surgeon General*,[5] which reviewed scientific advances in our understanding of mental health and mental illnesses. However, despite substantial investments that have enormously increased the scientific knowledge base and have led to developing many effective treatments, many Americans are not benefiting from these investments.[6,7]

Far too often, treatments and services that are based on rigorous clinical research languish for years rather than being used effectively at the earliest opportunity. For instance, according to the Institute of Medicine (IOM) report, *Crossing the Quality Chasm: A New Health System for the 21st Century,* the lag between discovering effective forms of treatment and incorporating them into routine patient care is unnecessarily long, lasting about 15 to 20 years.[8]

In its report, the Institute of Medicine described a strategy to improve the quality of health care dur-

ing the coming decade, including priority areas for refinement.[9] These documents, along with other recent publications and research findings, provide insight into the importance of mental heath, particularly as it relates to overall health.

> **In this *Final Report* . . .**
>
> ***Adults with a serious mental illness*** are persons age 18 and over, who currently or at any time during the past year, have had a diagnosable mental, behavioral, or emotional disorder of sufficient duration to meet diagnostic criteria specified within DSM-III-R *(Diagnostic and Statistical Manual for Mental Disorders)*[10], that has resulted in functional impairment[b] which substantially interferes with or limits one or more major life activities.
>
> **A serious emotional disturbance** is defined as a mental, behavioral, or emotional disorder of sufficient duration to meet diagnostic criteria specified in the DSM-III-R that results in functional impairment that substantially interferes with or limits one or more major life activities in an individual up to 18 years of age. Examples of functional impairment that adversely affect educational performance include an inability to learn that cannot be explained by intellectual, sensory, or health factors; an inability to build or maintain satisfactory interpersonal relationships with peers and teachers; inappropriate types of behavior or feelings under normal circumstances; a general pervasive mood of unhappiness or depression; or a tendency to develop physical symptoms or fears associated with personal or school problems.[11]

MENTAL ILLNESSES PRESENTS SERIOUS HEALTH CHALLENGES

Mental illnesses rank first among illnesses that cause disability in the United States, Canada, and Western Europe.[12] This serious public health challenge is under-recognized as a public health burden. In addition, one of the most distressing and preventable consequences of undiagnosed, untreated, or under-treated mental illnesses is suicide. The World Health Organization (WHO) recently reported that suicide

---

[a]In this *Final Report,* whenever *child* or *children* is used, it is understood that parents or guardians should be included in the process of making choices and decisions for minor children. This allows the family to provide support and guidance when developing relationships with mental health professionals, community resource representatives, teachers, and anyone else the individual or family invites. This same support and guidance can also include family members for individuals older than 18 years of age.

[b]*Functional impairment* is defined as difficulties that substantially interfere with or limit role functioning in one or more major life activities, including basic daily living skills (e.g., eating, bathing, dressing); instrumental living skills (e.g., maintaining a household, managing money, getting around the community, taking prescribed medication); and functioning in social, family, and vocational/educational contexts (Section 1912 (c) of the Public Health Services Act, as amended by Public Law 102-321).

worldwide causes more deaths every year than homicide or war.[13]

In addition to the tragedy of lost lives, mental illnesses come with a devastatingly high financial cost. In the U.S., the annual economic, indirect cost of mental illnesses is estimated to be $79 billion. Most of that amount—approximately $63 billion—reflects the loss of productivity as a result of illnesses. But indirect costs also include almost $12 billion in mortality costs (lost productivity resulting from premature death) and almost $4 billion in productivity losses for incarcerated individuals and for the time of those who provide family care.[14]

In 1997, the latest year comparable data are available, the United States spent more than $1 trillion on health care, including almost $71 billion on treating mental illnesses. Mental health expenditures are predominantly publicly funded at 57%, compared to 46% of overall health care expenditures. Between 1987 and 1997, mental health spending did not keep pace with general health care because of declines in private health spending under managed care and cutbacks in hospital expenditures.[15]

THE CURRENT MENTAL HEALTH SYSTEM IS COMPLEX

In its *Interim Report to the President,* the Commission declared, ". . . the mental health delivery system is fragmented and in disarray. . . lead[ing] to unnecessary and costly disability, homelessness, school failure and incarceration." The report described the extent of unmet needs and barriers to care, including:

- Fragmentation and gaps in care for children,
- Fragmentation and gaps in care for adults with serious mental illnesses,
- High unemployment and disability for people with serious mental illnesses,
- Lack of care for older adults with mental illnesses, and
- Lack of national priority for mental health and suicide prevention.

The *Interim Report* concluded that the system is not oriented to the single most important goal of the people it serves—the hope of recovery. State-of-the-art treatments, based on decades of research, are not being transferred from research to community settings. In many communities, access to quality care is poor, resulting in wasted resources and lost opportunities for recovery. More individuals could recover from even the most serious mental illnesses if they had access in their communities to treatment and supports that are tailored to their needs.

The Commission recognizes that thousands of dedicated, caring, skilled providers staff and manage the service delivery system. The Commission does not attribute the shortcomings and failings of the contemporary system to a lack of professionalism or compassion of mental health care workers. Rather, problems derive principally from the manner in which the Nation's community-based mental health system has evolved over the past four to five decades. In short, the Nation must replace unnecessary institutional care with efficient, effective community services that people can count on. It needs to integrate programs that are fragmented across levels of government and among many agencies.

Building on the research literature and comments from more than 2,300 consumers,[c] family members, providers, administrators, researchers, government officials, and others who provided valuable insight into the way mental health care is delivered, after its yearlong study, the Commission concludes that traditional reform measures are not enough to meet the expectations of consumers and families.

To improve access to quality care and services, the Commission recommends fundamentally transforming how mental health care is delivered in America. The goals of this fundamental change are clear and align with the direction that the President established.

THE GOAL OF A TRANSFORMED SYSTEM: RECOVERY

To achieve the promise of community living for everyone, new service delivery patterns and incentives must ensure that every American has easy and continuous access to the most current treatments and best support services. Advances in research, technology, and our understanding of how to treat mental illnesses provide powerful means to transform the system. In a transformed system, consumers and family members will have access to timely and accurate information that promotes learning, self-monitoring, and accountability. Health care providers will rely on up-to-date knowledge to provide optimum care for the best outcomes.

---

[c]In this *Final Report, consumer* identifies people who use or have used mental health services (also known as mental health consumers, survivors, patients, or clients).

When a serious mental illness or a serious emotional disturbance is first diagnosed, the health care provider—in full partnership with consumers and families—will develop an individualized plan of care for managing the illness. This partnership of personalized care means basically choosing *who, what,* and *how* appropriate health care will be provided:

- Choosing which mental health care professionals are on the team,
- Sharing in decision making, and
- Having the option to agree or disagree with the treatment plan.

The highest quality of care and information will be available to consumers and families, regardless of their race, gender, ethnicity, language, age, or place of residence. Because recovery will be the common, recognized outcome of mental health services, the stigma surrounding mental illnesses will be reduced, reinforcing the hope of recovery for every individual with a mental illness.

> **In this *Final Report* . . .**
>
> **Stigma** refers to a cluster of negative attitudes and beliefs that motivate the general public to fear, reject, avoid, and discriminate against people with mental illnesses. Stigma is widespread in the United States and other Western nations.[1] Stigma leads others to avoid living, socializing, or working with, renting to, or employing people with mental disorders—especially severe disorders, such as schizophrenia. It leads to low self-esteem, isolation, and hopelessness. It deters the public from seeking and wanting to pay for care.[5] Responding to stigma, people with mental health problems internalize public attitudes and become so embarrassed or ashamed that they often conceal symptoms and fail to seek treatment.

As more individuals seek help and share their stories with friends and relatives, compassion will be the response, not ridicule.

Successfully transforming the mental health service delivery system rests on two principles:

- **First, services and treatments must be consumer- and family-centered,** geared to give consumers real and meaningful choices about treatment options and providers—not oriented to the requirements of bureaucracies.
- **Second, care must focus on increasing consumers' ability to successfully cope with life's** **challenges, on facilitating recovery, and on building resilience,** not just on managing symptoms.

Built around consumers' needs, the system must be seamless and convenient.

> **In this *Final Report* . . .**
>
> **Recovery** refers to the process in which people are able to live, work, learn, and participate fully in their communities. For some individuals, recovery is the ability to live a fulfilling and productive life despite a disability. For others, recovery implies the reduction or complete remission of symptoms. Science has shown that having hope plays an integral role in an individual's recovery.
>
> **Resilience** means the personal and community qualities that enable us to rebound from adversity, trauma, tragedy, threats, or other stresses—and to go on with life with a sense of mastery, competence, and hope. We now understand from research that resilience is fostered by a positive childhood and includes positive individual traits, such as optimism, good problem-solving skills, and treatments. Closely knit communities and neighborhoods are also resilient, providing supports for their members.

Transforming the system so that it will be both consumer- and family-centered and recovery-oriented in its care and services presents invigorating challenges. Incentives must change to encourage continuous improvement in agencies that provide care. New, relevant research findings must be systematically conveyed to front-line providers so that they can be applied to practice quickly. Innovative strategies must inform researchers of the unanswered questions of consumers, families, and providers. Research and treatment must recognize both the commonalities and the differences among Americans and must offer approaches that are sensitive to our diversity. Treatment and services that are based on proven effectiveness and consumer preference—not just on tradition or outmoded regulations—must be the basis for reimbursements.

The Nation must invest in the infrastructure to support emerging technologies and integrate them into the system of care. This new technology will enable consumers to collaborate with service providers, assume an active role in managing their illnesses, and move more quickly toward recovery.

The Commission identified the following six goals as the foundation for transforming mental health care in America. The goals are intertwined. No single step can achieve the fundamental restructuring that is needed to transform the mental health care delivery system.

● ● ● References

1. United States Public Health Service Office of the Surgeon General (2001). *Mental Health: Culture, Race, and Ethnicity: A Supplement to Mental Health: A Report of the Surgeon General*. Rockville, MD: Department of Health and Human Services, U.S. Public Health Service.

2. Department of Health and Human Services: Substance Abuse and Mental Health Services Administration (2002). *National Household Survey on Drug Abuse: Volume I. Summary of National Findings; Prevalence and Treatment of Mental Health Problems*.

3. Kessler, R. C., Berglund, P. A., Bruce, M. L., Koch, J. R., Laska, E. M., Leaf, P. J. et al. (2001). The prevalence and correlates of untreated serious mental illness. *Health Services Research, 36,* 987-1007.

4. Farmer, E. M. Z., Mustillo, S., Burns, B. J., & Costello, E. J. (2003). The epidemiology of mental health programs and service use in youth: Results from the Great Smoky Mountains Study. In M. H. Epstein, K. Kutash, & A. Duchnowsk (Eds.), *Outcomes for Children and Youth with Behavioral and Emotional Disorders and Their Families: Programs and Evaluation Best Practices*, 2nd ed., [in press].

5. United States Public Health Service Office of the Surgeon General (1999). *Mental Health: A Report of the Surgeon General*. Rockville, MD: Department of Health and Human Services, U. S. Public Health Service.

6. Lehman, A. F. & Steinwachs, D. M. (1998). Patterns of usual care for schizophrenia: Initial results from the Schizophrenia Patient Outcomes Research Team (PORT) Client Survey. *Schizophrenia Bulletin, 24,* 11-20.

7. Wang, P. S., Demler, O., & Kessler, R. C. (2002). Adequacy of treatment for serious mental illness in the United States. *American Journal of Public Health, 92,* 92-98.

8. Balas, E. A. & Boren, S. A. (2000). Managing clinical knowledge for health care improvement. In *Yearbook of Medical Informatics* (pp. 65-70). Bethesda, MD: National Library of Medicine.

9. Institute of Medicine Committee on Quality of Health Care in America (2001). *Crossing the Quality Chasm: A New Health System for the 21st Century*. Washington, DC: National Academies Press.

10. American Psychiatric Association (1987). *Diagnostic and Statistical Manual of Mental Disorders*. (3rd Revision Edition.) Washington, DC: American Psychiatric Association.

11. Individuals with Disabilities Education Act (IDEA), Pub. L. No. 105-117. (1997).

12. World Health Organization. (2001). *The World Health Report 200-Mental Health: New Understanding, New Hope*. Geneva: World Health Organization.

13. World Health Organization. (2002). *World Report on Violence and Health*. Geneva: World Health Organization.

14. Rice, D. P. & Miller, L. S. (1996). The economic burden of schizophrenia: Conceptual and methodological issues and cost estimates. In M. Moscarelli, A. Rupp, & N. Sartorius (Eds.), *Schizophrenia* (pp. 321-334). Chichester, UK: Wiley.

15. Coffey, R. M., Mark, T., King, E., Harwood, H., McKusick, D., Genuardi, J. et al. (2000). *National Estimates of Expenditures for Mental Health and Substance Abuse Treatment, 1997* (Rep. No. SAMHSA Publication SMA-00-3499). Rockville, MD: Substance Abuse and Mental Health Services Administration.

INTERVENTIONS TO IMPROVE HEALTH

Part V provides the critical action elements that are needed to fundamentally improve our health care system and health outcomes. This part consists of three chapters that address both non-medical (Chapter 15) and medical interventions (Chapter 16), and lessons that can be learned from abroad (Chapter 17). Chapter 15 focuses on non-medical interventions. Since many health determinants are non-medical, focusing on non-medical interventions is essential to improving population health. Chapter 16 focuses on medical interventions. The appropriate balance in medical care delivery should include not only secondary and tertiary care—emphasised in the United States—but also primary and preventive care, and public health which are critical for both population and individual health. Chapter 17 introduces lessons from abroad. Many countries have developed health care systems that promote better access, quality, and efficiency than the U.S. Their experience and lessons could be helpful to the U.S. as we grapple with health care reform.

15

Non-Medical Interventions

Since health status is determined by environmental, behavioral, and social factors, as well as medical care, medical intervention alone is not sufficient for improving the health status of a population. A clean, toxin-free environment and sanitation reduce exposure to microorganisms that cause various air-, water-, and food-borne diseases. Most of the causes of the current leading chronic diseases such as heart disease, cancer, and injury can be associated with a host of behavior risk factors: cigarette smoking, alcohol abuse, lack of exercise, unsafe driving, poor dietary habits and uncontrolled hypertension. In addition, nutritious foods help increase resistance to disease elements and maintain the initial changes brought on by environmental and nutritional improvement. Social factors are external to the individual and examples of social risk factors include low income, poor education, long-term unemployment, unstable family environment, and lack of community structure and cohesion. All these are linked to poor social outcomes which are associated with poor health outcomes.

Recently, there has been a shift in focus from the biological determinants of health to the social and environmental determinants as dramatic differences in health within countries have been observed. The differences have been attributed to social stratification that occurs in a nation as a result of socio-economic status, politics, ethnicity, and culture. Stratification is a worldwide occurrence, and the World Health Organization's (WHO) Commission on Social Determinants of Health has examined the ties between social factors and health outcomes in a global scale.[1]

In the United States, the focus on social factors came to the forefront with President Clinton's Racial and Ethnic Health Disparities Initiative in 1998. Diminishing racial and ethnic disparities then became one of the two major goals of Health People 2010 as studies showed that social and environmental factors, including discrimination and inequality for housing, employment, and education, placed minorities at a distinct disadvantage and affected health outcomes negatively.[2]

The earlier chapters have looked at determinants of health. Specifically, social determinants of health reflect personal and community-level influences, including demographics, SES factors, and aspects of social interactions. These factors include race/ethnicity, SES (such as income, education, and occupation), behavioral factors, and social interactions (such as social networks at the individual level and social cohesion at the community level) that influence health care access and health. Behavior, it should be noted, should not be isolated from the social and environmental contexts that influence what choices are available and made.

While social determinants influence the health and resources that patients bring to the health care system, the medical care system focuses primarily on treating poor health. While public health, preventive care, and primary care contribute to general health status, other services, such as specialty and long-term care, are more influential in end-of-life care services and mortality. Without access to medical care, individuals will have difficulty treating health problems. Patients who gain access and move across the spectrum of care have to contend with continuity and coordination of care.

In considering solutions for health disparities, policymakers should examine the balance of social and medical influences on health. While social factors are likely to have stronger influences on health than medical care (since medical care typically intervenes only when a problem is identified), there are important roles for medical care in improving health, promoting well-being, enhancing quality of life, and ultimately lengthening life expectancy. In trying to improve population health and reduce health disparities, one should consider the respective contributions and likely effectiveness of social and medical interventions.

Since medical care absorbs such a large proportion of national spending, special consideration should be given to where resources are directed. Should equal investments be made in all health services, or are some investments better than others? Increasing resources for primary care, for example, may make basic health services available to more individuals but would reduce the availability of specialty care. Directing resources toward specialty care (such as higher-technology services) may enhance care and extend life for people with more severe health conditions but would draw away resources from basic primary care services for all. Other considerations, such as the quality of care and access to alternative therapies, may also have an impact on health care experiences and health outcomes.

Considering that both social and medical determinants are responsive to numerous outside forces, improvement in population health and reduced health disparities is obtainable through interventions at four levels: (1) policy interventions, (2) community-based

interventions, (3) health care interventions, and (4) individual interventions.

Policy Interventions: Social or public policy influences the health and health care of the population in many ways. Product safety regulations, screening food and water sources, and enforcing safe work environments are a few of the ways in which public policy directly guards the welfare of the nation. With fewer resources at their disposal, however, vulnerable populations are uniquely dependent on programs created through social and public policy to address basic nutritional, safety, social, and health care needs. Many of the mechanisms relating vulnerable status to poor health are amenable to policy intervention, and policy initiatives can be primary prevention strategies to alter the fundamental dynamics linking social factors to poor health.

Community-Based Interventions: Disparities in health vary substantially at the community level, suggesting that some sources of health disparities may be addressed at the community level. Neighborhood poverty, the presence of local social resources, and societal cohesion and support are all likely to contribute to the level of health and health inequalities in a community. Intervention strategies have to be tailored to address these community health risks. Because community partnerships reflect the priorities of a local population and are managed by members of the community, they minimize cultural barriers and improve community buy-in to the program.

Community-based strategies have the particular benefit of mobilizing resources at the local level to address these problems. Community resources can be applied directly to community members, providing businesses and other local organizations with greater incentives to contribute to local health causes. Community approaches also benefit from community participatory decision making, where local researchers, practitioners, social services, businesses, and community members are invited to contribute to the process of designing, implementing, evaluating, and sustaining interventions. Many community programs are operated by nonprofit organizations and, in exchange for providing services, receive subsidies through federal, state, or local funds and receive tax exemptions. Thus, they are able to offer health services at lower cost than private organizations which must earn a profit for their stockholders.

Health Care Interventions: Billions of dollars are spent annually to monitor and improve facets of health care in the United States. Interventions have been designed for systems of care (such as designing integrated electronic medical record systems to better coordinate care for populations with multiple chronic and acute conditions), health care providers (such as continuing education for pediatricians to better target developmental services to children most in need), and consumers of health services (such as educating pregnant women to attend regular prenatal care visits). Health care monitoring initiatives in national, state, and local surveys have been designed to monitor the quality of care provided in health plans and can be used to examine and reduce disparities across demographic groups.

Individual-Level Interventions: While less comprehensive in scale and scope, individual-level initiatives intervene and minimize the effects of negative health-related behaviors. Altering individual behaviors that influence health, such as reducing smoking and encouraging exercise, is the focus of these individual-targeted interventions, and there are numerous theories that identify the complex pathways and barriers to elicit improvements in behavior. The integration of behavioral science into the public health field has been a valuable contribution, providing a toolbox of health-related behavior change strategies.

One of the most prominent models integrating behavioral science and public health is social action theory. Behavior in this model is described as the interaction of biology, environment, and social context, which is critical in determining the success of any health-related behavior intervention (Institute of Medicine Committee on Health and Behavior: Research Practice and Policy, 2001). Behavioral change programs can be implemented at the community level, such as in neighborhoods or in community groups, but the focus of behavior change is nonetheless on each individual.

Integrated Interventions: Like behavioral risk factors, social risk factors tend to come in clusters and therefore should be dealt with as a whole. Medical intervention should be incorporated into a coherent, intertwined strategy that also includes social and behavioral interventions. Such a comprehensive program should focus on the community (e.g., a county), rather than individuals, with broad-based participation from local health department, interdisciplinary teamwork among health care providers (i.e., practicing physicians, hospitals, HMOs, health centers), social services agencies, community organizations, and citizen groups. A community-wide information system could be developed based on data available from the health department, providers, and insurance companies. Epidemiologic analysis of the frequency of clinical

problems and an assessment of social and environmental factors would need to be done. Consensus could then be reached on the priority conditions that should be addressed in a comprehensive manner.

This chapter includes a collection of readings focusing on non-medical strategies to improve health and reduce health disparities. In **Approaching Health Disparities from a Population Perspective: The National Institutes of Health Centers for Population Health and Health Disparities,** Warnecke and colleagues looked at determinants of population health disparities. With the publication of Healthy People 2010 in 1999, focus was shifted toward the modification and elimination of health disparities. It became more widely known that many health outcomes that resulted within different population sub-groups were preventable. In September 2003, eight Centers for Population Health and Health Disparities (CPHHD) were launched to "create new paradigms to explore the determinants of health disparities and to develop and conduct multilevel, trans-disciplinary research" combining a mix of population, social and behavioral, and clinical methods.

Disparities, studies showed, were a result of an imbalance in the distribution of and access to resources that promote better health outcomes. Determinants for the disparities were split into population-level and individual-level. Population level determinants looked at the group as a whole, including educational level, gender, race/ethnicity, and aggregate poverty while individual level determinants were based solely on the achievements of the individual such as individual or household outcome, behaviors, and heredity and genes. The influences on health by these determinants were examined through a multitude of studies.

Animal models were tested to see the effects of stress on tumor development. In rat models, it was seen that the stress of social isolation led to tumor developments by the activation of a stress hormone receptor. The animal studies were used to explore downward causation of the social environment in relation to the development of breast tumors in African American women. The study found that the stress of social factors (i.e., crime, poor housing, etc.) can create a biological environment that can contribute to cancer growth. Studies also examined the interaction between genes and the environment, and found that genetic predisposition for cancer can be exacerbated by the social environment in a prostate cancer study that examined the relationship between the census block characteristics of where the patients resided and their genetic predisposition to prostate cancer.

Current research on health disparities are only cross-sectional studies and still require more longitudinal studies that examine longer periods of time before making stronger associations between population and individual factors and health outcomes.

In **Closing the Gap in a Generation: Health Equity through Action on the Social Determinants of Health,** Marmot et al., representing the Commission on Social Determinants of Health, have studied the effects of social determinants on health both globally and locally. They determined that negative health outcomes among low-income groups were a result of unequal distribution of resources, such as power, money, and services, along with poor social policies and programs. Premature loss of life can be attributed to the conditions, both social and physical, of daily living. The commission aspires to close the disparities that occur as a result of unequal distribution of resources and poor daily living conditions.

Improvements in daily conditions involve creating a safer and better built environment. Infants and children need good nutrition, even before birth, which means teaching expectant mothers how to eat properly and how to feed their children properly. Governments and social agencies need to commit to better education programs that promote not only cognitive abilities but foster emotional and social development. In cities, the design of the urban landscape needs to promote healthier living in addition to providing housing and sanitation.

In addition to daily living conditions, politics is another factor that can influence health. The commission has deemed that more aid is needed in poor countries to improve their health systems and close the disparities gap. They also called for debt relief for poor nations from more powerful nations to alleviate some of the burdens on these developing countries. While the Commission understands that social gradients will most likely remain intact, a well-executed plan to eliminate social structures that cause disparities can close the gap significantly.

In **The Inequality Paradox: The Population Approach and Vulnerable Populations,** Frohlich and Potvin focus on the more vulnerable subpopulation. Despite gains in health that have been achieved in the recent past, the improvement of the general population's health has been unevenly distributed, creating widening health disparities. Health interventions take different approaches to improving health, either dealing with the population as a whole or placing a focus on vulnerable populations. While interventions aimed at the general population have proven to be effective, they do have drawbacks and may have also exacerbated the gap in health outcomes.

Geoffrey Rose's population approach to intervention does not address differences in the distribution. The basis of his approach stems from two ideas: risk exposure is shaped on a population-level rather than by individual factors and the majority of the population is at an average level of risk exposure. The aggregate risk exposure of an entire population, then, is much larger than the risk exposure of a subgroup, and thus the Rose population approach concludes that the most effective health interventions are ones directed at a population, such as environment control methods and smoking bans. Interventions aimed at general populations do not always work because of the uneven distribution of risk exposure that must be acknowledged in order to prevent disparities in health outcomes. Using general population approaches can leave those at a higher risk for disease with poorer health than the majority of the population.

Another approach focuses on specific population groups to improve health outcomes. This approach either targets populations at risk, as described in the Lalonade Report published in 1974 in Canada, or vulnerable populations. Populations at risk are individuals with elevated risk for a disease or a condition while vulnerable populations are a subgroup or subpopulation with similar social characteristics that place them at higher risk for risk exposure. Creating health interventions with these specific subpopulations in mind is important for narrowing the gap in health disparities. These populations need more focused programs in order to reach similar gains as the rest of the population.

In **Beyond Health Care: New Directions to a Healthier America,** The Robert Wood Johnson Foundation Commission to Build a Healthier America has the charge to identify interventions beyond the health care system that can produce substantial health effects, are likely to achieve a significant positive impact on Americans' health, address the needs of those who are most at risk or most vulnerable, are feasible and achievable in the current economic environment, and are supported by a strong knowledge base. The Commission found the strongest evidence for interventions that can have a lasting effect on the quality of health and life in programs that promote early childhood development and that support children and families. Their recommendations that aim to ensure that children have the best start in life and health are as follows: (1) Ensure that all children have high-quality early developmental support (child care, education, and other services). (2) Fund and design WIC and SNAP (Food Stamps) programs to meet the needs of hungry families for nutritious food. (3) Create public-private partnerships to open and sustain full-service grocery stores in communities without access to healthful foods. (4) Feed children only healthy foods in schools. (5) Require all schools (K-12) to include time for all children to be physically active every day. (6) Become a smoke-free nation. (7) Create "healthy community" demonstrations to evaluate the effects of a full complement of health-promoting policies and programs. (8) Develop a "health impact" rating for housing and infrastructure projects that reflects the projected effects on community health and provides incentives for projects that earn the rating. (9) Integrate safety and wellness into every aspect of community life. (10) Ensure that decision-makers in all sectors have the evidence they need to build health into public and private policies and practices.

• • • References

1. Marmot, M. "Achieving health equity: from root causes to fair outcomes." *Lancet*. 2007; 370:1153–1163.

2. Gehlert, S; Sohmer, D; Sacks, T; Miniger, C; McClintock, M; and Olopade, O. "Targeting health disparities: a model linking upstream determinants to downstream interventions." *Health Affairs*, 2008; 27:339-349.

Institute of Medicine Committee on Quality of Health Care in America. (2001.) *Crossing the Quality Chasm: A New Health System for the 21st Century*. Washington, D.C.: National Academy Press.

Approaching Health Disparities from a Population Perspective: The National Institutes of Health Centers for Population Health and Health Disparities

Source: Warnecke RB, Oh A, Breen N, et al. Approaching health disparities from a population perspective: the National Institutes of Health Centers for Population Health and Health Disparities. *Am J Public Health* 2008;98:1608-15. Reprinted with permission of the American Public Health Association.

ADDRESSING HEALTH DISPARITIES AS A PUBLIC HEALTH GOAL

Although the *Report of the Secretary's Task Force on Black and Minority Health* was published in 1985 by the U.S. Department of Health and Human Services,[1] racial and ethnic disparities in health care were seriously addressed only with the 1999 publication of *Healthy People 2010*.[2,3] At that time, the Centers for Disease Control and Prevention introduced the Racial and Ethnic Approaches to Community Health program, which features community-based participatory research as a tool to achieve social justice in health care.[2,3]

When the National Center on Minority Health and Health Disparities was established as part of the Minority Health and Health Disparities Research and Education Act of 2000, all National Institutes of Health (NIH) institutes and centers were required to develop strategic plans for modifying and eliminating health disparities. This initiative incorporated into the federal public health discourse the idea that disparities in health outcomes are not inevitable. Federally funded researchers were challenged to adopt research models combining social, behavioral, clinical, and basic science.[4] Reports published by the Institute of Medicine, the National Academy of Sciences, also described new multilevel, transdisciplinary research paradigms that integrated theories from the social and behavioral sciences with new research on genetics and molecular biology, thus expanding the scientific understanding of determinants of health. Together, all these developments created a strong stimulus for a new approach to research by the federal government.[2,3,5-14]

The National Institute of Environmental Health Sciences and the National Cancer Institute, National Institute on Aging, and Office of Behavioral and Social Sciences initiated a broad NIH effort to study the determinants of population health disparities. In April 2002, the National Institute of Environmental Health Sciences invited applications to establish Centers for Population Health and Health Disparities (CPHHDs).[15] Eight CPHHDs were launched in September 2003. Their primary goals were to create new paradigms to explore the determinants of health disparities and to develop and conduct multilevel, trans-disciplinary research combining population, social and behavioral, clinical, and biological theory and methods. At the same time, the Agency for Healthcare Research and Quality initiated several programs that addressed disparities in health services, so this focus was excluded from the CPHHD initiative.[16]

Reflecting the design of the Racial and Ethnic Approaches to Community Health program, each CPHHD was required to include at least one community-based participatory research project to ensure that resulting new interventions would have external validity and relevance to public health concerns and policy. Participating community-based organizations included groups from inside and external to the universities and at many levels from community to government (Table 1). All had either successfully organized to address community priorities or shaped and defined policies influencing disparate health outcomes. Participation by community-based organizations in each center's research and outreach programs fosters local ownership and institutionalization of proven strategies. Partnerships forged through local public health programs, advisory boards, and the direct participation of community members in the research process have expanded the research and service delivery infrastructure at the state and local level.

A POPULATION HEALTH APPROACH TO HEALTH DISPARITIES

To elucidate health disparities, research must focus on the determinants of disparate health outcomes across populations.[17-22] The recent Institute of Medicine review of the national plan for addressing disparities differentiated between disparities as inequities and differences in population health.[4,23] Inequitable health outcomes result from inequities in the distribution of or access to resources that promote good health outcomes; differences refer to outcomes that are the result of biological risk or other factors that are not a matter of policy or discrimination in access. A difference may become a disparity when some subgroups and not others are given access to resources to manage their differential risk from biology or other factors and the groups without access have poorer outcomes. Thus, differences and disparities may have different determinants requiring different forms of intervention.[4,23]

Population-level determinants of health outcomes are distinct from the determinants of individual health outcomes. Determinants of population health are expressed as rates, averages, and distributions of population characteristics, such as aggregate poverty, education levels, gender and racial/ethnic distributions, and patterns of segregation.[17-22] Individuals have risk factors, such as household or individual income, educational attainment, behavior, heredity, and genes. It has been shown that population characteristics affect health outcomes independently of the characteristics of individuals. For example, in studies by Marmot et al., the social status gradient was a population-level determinant of the distribution of health outcomes in a population of British civil servants. In several analyses, the researchers showed that social status defined by the gradient had an effect on individual risk of heart disease onset that was independent of an individual's biological risk factors.[20,21]

An underlying question addressed by CPHHD centers was phrased by Taylor et al. as, "How does the unhealthy environment get under the skin?"[24(p411)] In other words, how does population risk relate to individual risk? We drew on the works of Berkman et al.,[25] Glass and McAtee,[26] and Taylor et al.[24] to design our model for approaching this question from a multilevel perspective (Figure 1).[27] Three primary types of determinants are shown on the left side of the figure. Distal determinants include the population social conditions, policies that affect social conditions, and the policymaking bodies that influence or determine them. They are considered fundamental causes because their influence is solely reflected at the population level in the variation in rates of disease or poor health, such as the epidemic of HIV in Africa or rates of obesity in the United States. Their roots are embedded in policy, shared social norms about health and social practices, socioeconomic disadvantage, and policies that affect public availability of health services, including who receives them and the level and quality of service. They are the determinants of inequities rather than differences.[28]

Intermediate determinants, the second level of our model, include the immediate social and physical contexts and social relationships in which the distal effects are experienced, such as the community or neighborhood.[29,30] The social context includes neighborhood or community poverty level, extent of residential segregation, median income and education, and opportunities for social interaction to redress the effect of the distal factors.[31-36] Social relationships include social networks, social engagement, and social influence and are forms of social capital that suppress the negative effects of impoverished social environments. These negative effects can, in the absence of such networks, be increased by social isolation.[37-44] The physical environment includes availability and accessibility of local health

Table 1 Partnerships Developed by the Centers for Population Health and Health Disparities: 2003–2008

Centers and Their Partners at Other Universities	Partners in Other University Departments	Government and Quasi-Government Partners	Community-Based Organization Partners
Ohio State University and University of Michigan			
University of Kentucky	Ohio State Agricultural Extension Service	Ohio Department of Breast Health and Cervical Cancer	Ohio Division, American Cancer Society
Ohio University	College of Public Health College of Medicine Economics Department Psychology Department Comprehensive Cancer Center	National Cancer Institute Cancer Information Service Centers for Disease Control and Prevention	Appalachia Community Cancer Network and four community coalitions
RAND Corp University of Michigan University of California, Berkeley University of California, Los Angeles Rutgers University		Los Angeles Department of Park and Recreation District of Columbia City Council	Multicultural Area Health Education Center District of Columbia Primary Care Association
Tufts University and Northeastern University	Jean Mayer, USDA, Human Nutrition Research Center on Aging at Tufts University Tufts Friedman School of Nutrition Science and Policy Tufts School of Medicine Northeastern University Department of Sociology Northeastern Center for Urban Health Research	USDA Agricultural Research Service Massachusetts Department of Public Health	La Alianza Hispana Tufts–New England Medical Center
University of Chicago University of Ibadan, Nigeria Ohio State University, RAND Corp, Tufts/Northeastern University, University of Illinois at Chicago, University of Texas Medical Branch, Wayne State University, University of Pennsylvania	School of Social Service Administration Center of Excellence in Health Promotion Economics (CDC) Biological Sciences Division Social Sciences Division Institute for Mind and Biology Robert Wood Johnson National Program Office for Health Disparities Solutions	John H. Stroger Jr Hospital of Cook County, IL Mt Sinai Hospital of Chicago Methodist Hospitals of Gary, IN	Faith-Based Wellness Network
University of Illinois at Chicago University of Chicago, Wayne State University, University of Pennsylvania, Rand Corp, Tufts/Northeastern	Institute for Research on Race and Public Policy Midwest Latino Health Research Training and Policy Center International Center for Health Leadership Development University of Illinois at Chicago Cancer Center School of Public Health College of Nursing Department of Sociology Vice Chancellor for Research Institute for Health Research and Policy Survey Research Laboratory	Illinois Department of Public Health–Illinois State Cancer Registry Chicago Department of Public Health John H. Stroger Jr Hospital of Cook County Illinois State Cancer Plan Institute for Health Care Quality (Medicare)	Healthcare Consortium of Illinois (Greater Roseland Health District and Healthy South Chicago) Cook County Breast Health Consortium Illinois Division-American Cancer Society

(continued)

Table 1	Partnerships Developed by the Centers for Population Health and Health Disparities: 2003–2008 (continued)		
University of Pennsylvania			
	Cheikh Anta Diop University, Dakar, Senegal	U.S. Veterans Administration Hospitals	National Physician and Family Referral Project
	Robert Wood Johnson Health and Society Scholars Program		Philadelphia Chapter, National Black Leadership Initiative on Cancer
	Leonard Davis Institute for Health Economics		
	Abramson Cancer Center		
	Institute on Aging		
	Wharton School of Business		
	Annenberg School of Communication		
	School of Social Work Law School		
University of Texas Medical Branch			
	University of Maryland Population Center	Area Health Education Center	Liberty County Cancer Awareness Network
	University of Texas, Austin Population Research Center	Social Security Administration	Parent-Teacher Association of Los Angeles
	Baylor College of Medicine Department of Medicine, Health Services Research	Galveston County Health District	Morgan School
	School of Nursing	National Center for Health Statistics–Mortality Division	Galveston County Cancer Coalition
	Department of Preventive Medicine and Community Health		Jesse Tree
	Infectious Disease		
	Obstetrics and Gynecology Division		
Wayne State University			
	University of Michigan Inter-University Consortium for Political and Social Research	Detroit Department of Public Health	Movement for Life Initiative
	Case Western Reserve University	Detroit Medical Center	American Heart Association/Detroit
	African American Initiative for Male Health Improvement (Henry Ford Hospital)		Healthy Black Elders Project Health Living
	Minority Center or Urban African American Aging Research		Metropolitan Christian Council
	College of Nursing		
	College of Liberal Arts		
	Center for Urban Studies		
	Karmanos Cancer Institute		
	Wayne State University Community Relations		

Note: USDA = US Department of Agriculture; CDC = Centers for Disease Control and Prevention.

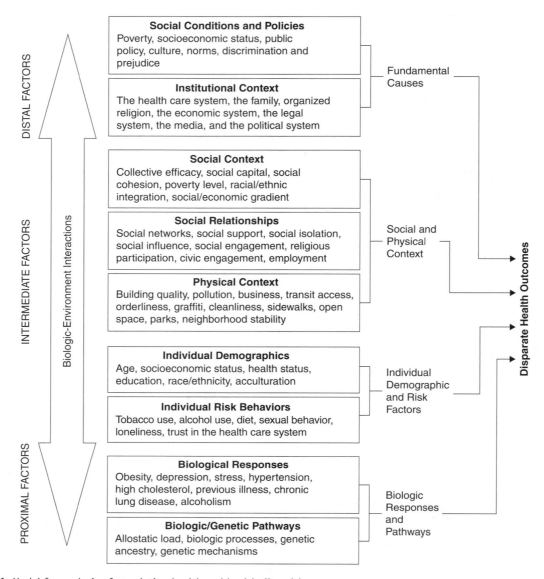

Figure 1 Model for analysis of population health and health disparities.

care resources to the public; availability of transportation, quality air and water, and healthy food; presence of crime; degree of neighborhood disorder; and quality of the built environment.[34,35,45-47] We hypothesize that these intermediate determinants are the links through which the environment affects individual demographic factors and risks as well as biological responses and pathways, which compose the proximal determinants. Proximal determinants refer to individuals. Demographic factors characterize both contexts and individuals and in the model can have independent effects. Risk factors and biological responses and pathways refer only to individuals.

Individual determinants include socioeconomic status (SES), race/ethnicity, gender, and level of acculturation. These determinants affect individuals' capacity to respond to environmental challenges and include where they live, their capacity to address health care needs, the degree to which they have social support, and their level of social integration or isolation. Behaviors such as dietary and sexual practices, exercise, and tobacco use are also individual-level determinants, as are cultural beliefs, which mediate behavior and the capacity to respond to health needs.[48,49]

In addition to risk behaviors and individual demographics, proximal determinants include biological markers or processes that result from behavior or intermediate determinants and may include risk from heredity or spontaneous mutation or environmental stress. Markers include elevated cholesterol or other indicators of prolonged or intense stress, such as body mass index, high blood pressure, abnormal cells in the cervix, or a lump in the breast.[50-57]

CPHHD research employs a well-recognized model of how environmental context affects individual health outcomes. The model assumes that the capacity to respond to differences and disparities in the distribution of health outcomes—and the ultimate effectiveness of that response—requires interventions capable of addressing both contextual and individual factors.

APPLYING TRANSDISCIPLINARY STRATEGIES TO UNDERSTANDING HEALTH DISPARITIES

CPHHD investigators at the Center for Interdisciplinary Health Disparities Research (CIHDR) at the University of Chicago have studied both nonhuman animal and human models to elucidate the interactions between the social environment and biology. They established that socially isolated rats developed an acquired vigilant state and died with mammary tumors at younger ages than did their group-housed peers,[58] a process that was confirmed in a second project that used SV-40 T-antigen mice. The preliminary conclusion is that the stress of social isolation in nonhuman animals promotes tumor development by activating stress hormone receptors and ultimately preventing the death of malignant cells.[59] The nonhuman animal studies enabled CIHDR investigators to isolate a multifaceted suite, made up of depression, loneliness, and vigilance, that is linked to the physiological stress system that is secondary to social isolation. These results suggest directions in which the research can move to better understand these pathways and explore strategies for tumor prevention and therapy.[28-30]

From Animal to Human Models

The CPHHDs are using our model and findings from the CIHDR to assess the pathways by which the environment may affect health and health status. Although there is an extensive literature on how the environment and social isolation relate to poor health outcomes, this research has not focused on pathways of differences or disparities in health outcomes.[41,44,50,51,54,60,61]

The results of work with animal models informed the CIHDR investigators' model of downward causation from social environmental conditions to psychosocial factors, biological responses, and breast tumor development in newly diagnosed African American women living in Chicago. The investigators used in-home interviews, investigations of the built environment, and publicly available community health data geocoded to the study participants' addresses to uncover a pathway with significant associations between community-level factors and individual characteristics as minute as the genetic information in the nucleus of a cell.

At the community level, dilapidated housing, crime, and general social disorganization lead to isolation, physical assault, and depression. This environment alters the stress hormone response (measured as nighttime rise of cortisol levels, including awakening response). Investigators have identified glucocorticoid receptors in tumors, as well as serum- and glucocorticoid-inducible kinase 1, which is involved in cell survival. Expression of this enzyme occurs when stress hormone travels across the cell membrane and binds with the glucocorticoid receptor complex, creating an environment conducive to cancer growth. This is a possible route by which external, community-level conditions may play a role in the occurrence of cancer.[24]

Environmental Stressors and Biological Response

These preliminary results have stimulated investigators at other CPHHDs to examine the relationship between physiological stress and health outcomes. For example, investigators at Ohio State University are conducting a case-control study to examine how social, behavioral, and biological factors contribute to the elevated risk of developing cervical abnormalities among Appalachian women. One research aim is to use surrogate markers of chronic Epstein-Barr virus infection to identify molecular markers associated with environmental stressors leading to cervical abnormalities. Preliminary data indicate that Epstein-Barr antigen titers are significantly higher among women with cervical abnormalities. In a stratified analysis adjusted for age, region, and presence of human papilloma virus, the investigators found a significant inverse relationship between SES and levels of Epstein-Barr antigen titers. Borderline statistically significant differences were observed between women at high risk for developing cervical cancer and those with human papilloma virus infection.

At the University of Texas Medical Branch in Galveston, investigators are linking social, geographical, behavioral, and biological data that will contribute to better understanding of the interplay between stress and health among Hispanics. The

Hispanic population exhibits the paradox of high morbidity and disability but unexpectedly low mortality, even though Hispanics are clearly disadvantaged in income, education, and access to health care. The investigators analyzed Texas and California vital statistics registries from 1999 to 2001 linked to the 2000 Census and contributed to mounting evidence that mortality rates are substantially lower among Hispanic immigrants, particularly at older ages, than among non-Hispanic Whites but are similar among U.S.-born Hispanics and non-Hispanic Whites.[62,63]

To better understand the social and biological stress processes that contribute to these differences, the Texas researchers studied a cohort of Hispanics, non-Hispanic African Americans, and non-Hispanic Whites living close to a large petrochemical complex. Preliminary analyses suggested that lower-SES groups, non-Hispanic African Americans, and foreign-born Hispanics exhibited greater concern about refinery danger and greater change in mental health scores after a refinery explosion. The respondents had similar patterns of disparities in biological stress markers. For example, in a case-control study that followed the protocol used by the Ohio State University center, the Texas CPHHD researchers also found evidence that reactivation of latent Epstein-Barr viruses (a marker for immune dysregulation) was associated with lower SES and minority ethnic status. Elevated levels of interleukin-6 and interleukin-10, which signal inflammatory stress response, were associated with distance from a petrochemical complex in multivariate models accounting for age, gender, ethnicity, and education. These early findings suggest that SES and ethnic disparities in stress and health are consistent across psychosocial and biological analyses.[64,65]

Contextual Stressors and Health Outcomes

Cumulative biological stress, or allostatic load, describes the human body's physiological response to its environment over time.[61] This stress is manifested in dysregulation in multiple physiological systems, including metabolic, cardiac, and inflammatory. Investigators at the RAND Corporation are using National Health and Nutrition Examination Survey III data merged with census tract data to study associations between environmental and biological characteristics. They are analyzing neighborhood or census tract characteristics to elucidate the effects of social, economic, and racial segregation on allostatic load. Preliminary results indicate that low neighborhood SES is associated with increased individual-level allostatic load, even after individual characteristics are controlled.

Neighborhood influences tend to operate differently for men and women. Women living in neighborhoods with low household incomes, a high percentage of male unemployment, and a high percentage of households on public assistance were found to experience increased allostatic load. Men living in neighborhoods with a high percentage of African American households had high allostatic loads. High allostatic loads also were found in neighborhoods with a high proportion of adults younger than 25 years and with less than a high school education. Further, although these effects differed for men and women, they appeared to be similar among Whites, African Americans, and Mexican Americans, suggesting that poverty and segregation experienced in the immediate environment (neighborhood) affect allostatic load independently of race or ethnicity.

Investigators at the University of Illinois at Chicago examined the effects of upward neighborhood SES change on the probability of distant metastasis at diagnosis of breast cancer.[66] The researchers analyzed data from 1137 Cook County census tracts from the 1990 and 2000 censuses and data from the Illinois State Cancer Registry for 21,516 female breast cancer cases diagnosed in these census tracts from 1994 to 2000. They constructed a multilevel model of 1990 baseline SES of neighborhoods and degree of neighborhood change from 1990 to 2000 (compositional characteristics) and patient's age and race or Hispanic status (individual characteristics) to predict distant metastasis (vs. local and regional stage) at cancer diagnosis. Residence in a census tract experiencing SES improvement was associated with increased odds of distant metastasis at diagnosis, as were being African American and residence in a census tract with lower baseline SES in 1990. Paradoxically, both measures of initial neighborhood disadvantage and upward neighborhood SES change were independently associated with greater odds of the metastasis outcome, suggesting that even in socioeconomically distressed areas, disruption of the social and physical environment may worsen health outcomes, at least in the variable measured.

The investigators conducted a second analysis, with the same data, of breast cancer stage at diagnosis. They used an ordered logistic regression model rather than an arbitrary dichotomization (e.g., late-stage vs. others) and a random-effects model that accounted for the nesting of cases within census tracts. This analysis disentangled the effects of race/ethnicity and poverty and found that the effects of race/ethnicity diminished with age and completely disappeared after age 60 years, although poverty remained a predictor of late-stage diagnosis. Investigators at 5 other CPHHDs are collaborating with the Chicago researchers to compare the results of both studies with similar analyses from their own locations.

Biological Stress Responses

Investigators at Tufts and Northeastern universities are examining the effect of life experiences and psychosocial stress on allostatic load as a marker of biological risk among Puerto Ricans 65 years and older in the greater Boston area. This population was shown to suffer from an excess burden of chronic conditions, including type 2 diabetes, depression, and physical disability, compared with non-Hispanic Whites of similar age and living in similar neighborhoods.[53,57,67] In a study with a prospective cohort design, the researchers are exploring how the relationship of psychosocial stress and its effect on allostatic load affects previously identified health disparities in depression, cognitive impairment, and functional limitation in the same population. They hypothesize that the association between life stress, physiological response, and chronic conditions is modified by biological effects. The investigators are measuring markers of inflammation, hypothesized to be key mediators of the associations of dietary intake and nutritional status with environmental social support. They are also investigating how these associations are modified by genetic variability.

Researchers at Wayne State University's Center for Urban and African American Health (Detroit, MI) are investigating the effects of vitamin D on obesity and breast cancer recurrence among African American women. They are studying obesity-linked influences on oxidative stress and how such stress affects nitric oxide metabolism, leading to salt-induced rises in blood pressure that may contribute to heightened risk for cancer recurrence in breast cancer survivors.

The investigators in Detroit are also exploring how vitamin D and elevated parathyroid hormone contribute to weight gain. Preliminary analyses found that participants with low vitamin D levels, with or without elevated parathyroid hormone levels, had more body fat than did those with normal vitamin D and parathyroid hormone levels. Vitamin D has antiproliferative and antiinflammatory properties and may affect body composition, cellular proliferation, and vascular function. The investigators hypothesize that vitamin D may have an important role in causing or mediating high levels of oxidative stress in ductal fluid in breast cancer survivors. Alone or with parathyroid hormone, vitamin D may be involved in mediating the known link between weight gain and breast cancer recurrence.

Gene-Environment Interactions

Variations in neighborhood SES were included in a study of the interaction of genes and environment in prostate cancer at the CPHHD at the University of Pennsylvania. Investigators there have begun to expand the definition of environment in genotype and environment studies to include both individual- and neighborhood-level risk factors. They evaluated the joint relationship of income and education level in residential census tracts with genetic effects on prostate cancer in 1002 White men with prostate cancer and a control group of 387 men.[68] Participants' addresses were geocoded to 2000 Census tracts. The researchers used the tract data to group participants by per capita income, poverty, and educational attainment. The interaction of these neighborhood factors with genotypes of the androgen receptor CAG repeats and SRD5A2-V89L or SRD5A2-A49T variants were evaluated to determine their joint effect on prostate cancer risk and severity. Statistically significant interactions between SRD5A2-V89L genotypes and census tract per capita income were associated with later-stage prostate tumors.

In addition, a significant genotype-neighborhood interaction was observed for androgen receptor CAG genotypes among men living in areas with a high percentage of high school graduates compared with men residing in tracts with a low percentage of high school graduates. These findings suggest that genetic effects on prostate tumor severity are affected by neighborhood characteristics, including poverty and educational attainment. Further, the results indicate that research on genotypes should include neighborhood context.

CONCLUSIONS

Collaborations among 8 CPHHDs across the United States reflect a new approach to elucidating the determinants of health disparities. This research explores the question of "how environment gets under the skin."[24(p411)] A preliminary finding is that the neighborhood context has a significant effect on individual risk that is independent of individual characteristics.[64,66] If confirmed, this information could inform policies on the availability of screening and treatment facilities.

The NIH Roadmap for Medical Research is designed to encourage studies that fill the gaps in biomedical research and to promote collaboration across NIH agencies. The roadmap aims to significantly affect the progress of biomedical research, disseminate new scientific findings, and transform them into tangible benefits for American populations.[69] The principal elements include (1) interdisciplinary teams that cover the complete spectrum of research (basic, clinical, and social and behavioral science), (2) expanded efforts to include minority and medically underserved communities, (3) new partnerships with private and public health care organizations, and (4) enriched educational environments for training the next generation of researchers in the complexities of translating research from bench to bedside and from behavior to policy. All of these elements are key components of the CPHHDs, positioning the centers' work at the cutting edge of research sponsored by NIH.

CPHHD research to date is almost exclusively cross-sectional, but elucidating health disparities ultimately will require longitudinal studies that examine the entire life span. University of Chicago investigators are employing a lifespan approach in rat models; a next step is to move from preliminary nonhuman animal models to the population level. The animal models are transdisciplinary and multilevel and have the potential to elucidate poorly understood population-level determinants of disparities.

Ultimately, public health policies and resources dedicated to service delivery must be the focus of attempts to eliminate disparities. CPHHDs have adopted the recommendations of the NIH Roadmap for Medical Research, which calls for combining clinical, basic, and social science research to examine the relationships between policy, the social and physical environment, and disparities in health outcomes. The preliminary results described here illustrate the need for multilevel interventions that address context as a key pathway to improving health outcomes. These outcomes are most likely to be seen in clinical and public health practice.

Thus, the next step is to develop interventions that can address population factors as well as individual behavior and risk. Community-based participatory research provides a platform for introducing context into intervention strategies as a component to be evaluated and not simply controlled. The community partnerships developed by the CPHHDs and shown in Table 1 are critical to the effective translation of research findings into applications in community settings. Partners provide important local knowledge, as well as access to political leaders, and these partnerships are the likely channels for dissemination of research findings about health disparities and for implementation of effective interventions.

About the Authors

Richard B. Warnecke and April Oh are with the Center for Population Health and Health Disparities (CPHHD), University of Illinois, Chicago. Nancy Breen, Shobha Srinivasan, and Jon Kerner are with the National Cancer Institute, National Institutes of Health, Bethesda, MD. Ronald Abeles is with the Office of Behavioral and Social Science Research, National Institutes of Health, Bethesda. Frederick L. Tyson is with the National Institute of Environmental Health Sciences, National Institutes of Health, Bethesda, and Georgeanne Patmios is with the National Institute on Aging, National Institutes of Health, Bethesda. Sarah Gehlert is with the Center for Interdisciplinary Health Disparities, University of Chicago, Chicago. Electra Paskett is with the CPHHD, Ohio State University, Columbus, and University of Michigan, Ann Arbor. Katherine L. Tucker is with the CPHHD, Tufts University and Northeastern University, Boston, MA. Nicole Lurie is with the CPHHD, RAND Corporation, Santa Monica, CA, Washington, DC, and Pittsburgh, PA. Timothy Rebbeck is with the CPHHD, University of Pennsylvania, Philadelphia. James Goodwin is with the CPHHD, University of Texas Medical Branch, Galveston. John Flack is with the Center for Urban and African American Health, Wayne State University, Detroit, MI. At the time of the study, Suzanne Heurtin-Roberts was with the Behavioral Research Program, National Cancer Institute, National Institutes of Health, Bethesda. Robert A. Hiatt is with the University of California, San Francisco.

Requests for reprints should be sent to Richard B. Warnecke, Program in Cancer Control and Population Science, University of Illinois Cancer Center, 1747 W Roosevelt Rd, Ste 558, MC 275, Chicago, IL 60608-1264 (e-mail: warnecke@uic.edu).

This article was accepted October 15, 2007.

Contributors

R. B. Warnecke was the lead author. A. Oh did the bibliographic work for the article and contributed to its content. N. Breen contributed to the conceptualization of the article and participated in writing the final draft. S. Gehlert contributed to the content of the article and assisted with writing. E. Paskett contributed to content of the article and its preparation. K. L. Tucker, N. Lurie, T. Rebbeck, J. Goodwin, J. Flack,

S. Srinivasan, and J. Kerner contributed to the content of the article. S. Heurtin-Roberts, R. Abeles, F. L. Tyson, and G. Patmios critically read drafts of the article. R. A. Hiatt critically read the article and provided important insights that guided its development.

ACKNOWLEDGMENTS
This research was funded by the National Institute of Environmental Health Sciences (grants P50 ES012395, P50 ES012382, and P50 ES012383), the National Institute of Aging (grant P01 AG02323394), and the National Cancer Institute (grants P50 CA1065631, P50 CA015632, P50 CA106743, and P50 CA105641).

This article was originated by the leadership of the CPHHD program.

The authors acknowledge the editorial assistance of Lisa Kelly-Wilson at the Survey Research Laboratory, University of Illinois at Chicago.

● ● ● References

1. *Report of the Secretary's Task Force on Black and Minority Health*. Washington, DC: US Dept of Health and Human Services; 1985.

2. Stoto, MA, Green, LW, Bailey LA, eds. *Linking Research and Public Health Practice: A Review of CDC's Program of Centers for Research and Demonstration of Health Promotion and Disease Prevention*. Washington, DC: National Academy Press; 1997.

3. *Healthy People 2010: Understanding and Improving Health*. Washington, DC: US Dept of Health and Human Services; 2000.

4. Committee on the Review and Assessment of the NIH's Strategic Research Plan and Budget to Reduce and Ultimately Eliminate Health Disparities. *Examining the Health Disparities Research Plan of the National Institutes of Health: Unfinished Business*. Washington, DC: National Academy Press; 2006.

5. Haynes MA, Smedley B, eds. *The Unequal Burden of Cancer: An Assessment of NIH Research and Programs for Ethnic Minorities and the Medically Underserved*. Washington, DC: Institute of Medicine, National Academy Press; 1999.

6. Martin LG, Soldo BJ, eds. *Racial and Ethnic Differences in the Health of Older Americans*. Washington, DC: National Academy Press; 1997.

7. Anderson NB. Levels of analysis in health science: a framework for integrating sociobehavioral and biomedical research. *Ann N Y Acad Sci*. 1999:563–576.

8. Office of Behavioral and Social Sciences Research. Toward Higher Levels of Analysis: Progress and Promise in Research on Social and Cultural Dimensions of Health. Bethesda, MD: National Institutes of Health; 2001. NIH publication 01-5020.

9. Singer BH, Ryff CD, eds.; Committee on Future Directions for Behavior and Social Sciences Research at the National Institutes of Health. *New Horizons in Health: An Integrative Approach*. Washington, DC: National Academies Press; 2001.

10. Smedley BD, Syme SL, eds. *Promoting Health: Intervention Strategies From Social and Behavioral Research*. Washington, DC: National Academy Press; 2000.

11. Hanna K, Coussens C. *Rebuilding the Unity of Health and the Environment: A New Vision of Environmental Health for the 21st Century*. Washington, DC: National Academies Press; 2001.

12. Institute of Medicine, Committee on Health and Behavior. *Health and Behavior: The Interplay of Biological, Behavioral, and Societal Influences*. Washington, DC: National Academies Press; 2001.

13. Stern PC, Carstensen LL, eds. *The Aging Mind: Opportunities in Cognitive Research*. Washington, DC: National Academy Press; 2000.

14. Finch CE, Vaupel JW, Kinsella K, eds. *Cells and Surveys: Should Biological Measures Be Included in Social Science Research?* Washington, DC: National Academies Press; 2001.

15. National Institutes of Health. *Centers for Population Health and Health Disparities*. Available at: http://grants2.nih.gov/grants/guide/rfa-files/RFA-ES-02-009.html. Accessed August 10, 2006.

16. *AHRQ Focus on Research: Disparities in Health Care*. Rockville, MD: Agency for Healthcare Research and Quality; 2002. AHRQ publication 02-M027. Available at: http://www.ahrq.gov/news/focus/disparhc. htm. Accessed August 28, 2007.

17. Rose G. Sick individuals and sick populations. *Int J Epidemiol*. 1985;14:32–38.

18. Rose G. *The Strategy of Prevention*. New York, NY: Oxford Press; 1992.

19. Kindig DA. Understanding population health terminology. *Milbank Q*. 2007;85:139–161.

20. Marmot M, Wilkinson RG. *Social Determinants of Health*. 2nd ed. New York, NY: Oxford University Press; 2006.

21. Marmot M. *The Status Syndrome: How Social Standing Affects Our Health and Longevity*. New York, NY: Henry Holt; 2004.

22. Evans R, Barer M, Marmour T. *Why Are Some People Healthy and Others Not? The Determinants of Health in Populations*. New York, NY: Aldine de Gruyter; 1994.

23. Harper S, Lynch J. *Methods for Measuring Cancer Disparities: Using Data Relevant to Healthy People 2010 Cancer-Related Objectives*. Cancer Control Monograph Series, No. 6. Bethesda, MD: National Cancer Institute; 2005. NIH publication 05-5777.

24. Taylor SE, Repetti RL, Seeman T. Health psychology: what is an unhealthy environment and how does it get under the skin? *Annu Rev Psychol*. 1997; 48:411–417.

25. Berkman LF, Glass T, Brissette I, Seeman TE. From social integration to health: Durkheim in the new millennium. *Social Sci Med*. 2000;51:843–857.

26. Glass TA, McAtee MJ. Behavioral science at the crossroads in public health: extending horizons, envisioning the future. *Soc Sci Med*. 2006;62:1650–1671.

27. Subramanian SV, Jones K, Duncan C. Multilevel methods for public health research. In: Kawachi I, Berkman LF, eds. *Neighborhood and Health*. New York, NY: Oxford University Press; 2003:65–111.

28. Link BG, Phelan J. Social conditions as fundamental causes of disease. *J Health Soc Behav*. 1995;Spec No:80–94.

29. Diez-Roux AV, Nieto GJ, Muntaner C, Tyroler HA, Comstock GW. Neighborhood environments and coronary heart disease: a multilevel analysis. *Am J Epidemiol.* 1997;146:48–63.

30. Jones K, Duncan C. Individuals and their ecologies: analyzing the geography of chronic disease within a multilevel modeling framework. *Health Place.* 1995; 1:27–30.

31. Boardman JD, Saint Onge JM, Rogers RG, Denny JT. Race differentials in obesity: the impact of place. *J Health Soc Behav.* 2005;26:229–243.

32. Hill TD, Ross CE, Angell RJ. Neighborhood disorder, psychophysiological distress, and health. *J Health Soc Behav.* 2005;46:140–186.

33. Jenks C, Meyer SE. The social consequences of growing up in a poor neighborhood. In: Lynn LE, McGeary MGH, eds. *Inner City Poverty in the United States.* Washington DC: National Academy Press; 1990:111–186.

34. Raudenbush SW, Sampson RJ. Econometrics toward a science of assessing ecological settings with application to systematic social observation of neighborhoods. *Sociol Methodol.* 1999;29:1–41.

35. Ross CE, Mirowsky J. Neighborhood disadvantage, disorder and health. *J Health Soc Behav.* 2001;42: 258–276.

36. Sampson RJ. How do communities undergird or undermine human development? Relevant contexts and social mechanisms. In: Booth A, Crouter N, eds. *Does It Take a Village? Community Effects on Children, Adolescents, and Families.* Mahwah, NJ: Lawrence Erlbaum; 2001:3–30.

37. Sampson RJ. Neighborhood level context and health: lessons from sociology. In: Kawachi I, Berkman LF, eds. *Neighborhood and Health.* New York, NY: Oxford University Press; 2003:132–146.

38. Heaney CA, Israel BA. Social networks and social support. In: Glanz K, Rimer BK, Lewis FM, eds. *Health Behavior and Health Education: Theory, Research and Practice.* San Francisco, CA: Jossey-Bass. 2002:185–209.

39. Kawachi I, Berkman LF. Social cohesion, social capital, and health. In: Berkman LF, Kawachi I, eds. *Social Epidemiology.* New York, NY: Oxford University Press; 2000:174–189.

40. Lochner KA, Kawchi I, Brennan RT, Buka SL. Social capital and neighborhood mortality rates in Chicago. *Soc Sci Med.* 2003;56:1797–1805.

41. Seeman TE. Social ties and health: the benefits of social integration. *Ann Epidemiol.* 1996;5:442–451.

42. Subramanian SV, Lochner KA, Kawachi I. Neighborhood differences in social capital: a compositional artifact or a contextual construct? *Health Place.* 2003;9:33–44.

43. Szreter S, Woolcock M. Health by association? Social capital, social theory, and the political economy of public health. *Int J Epidemiol.* 2004;33: 650–667.

44. Thoits PA. Stress coping, and social support processes: where are we? What next? *J Health Soc Behav.* 1995;Spec No:53–79.

45. Fitzpatrick K, LaGory M. *Unhealthy Places: The Ecology of Risk in the Urban Landscape.* New York, NY: Routledge; 2000.

46. Sloggett A, Joshi H. Higher mortality in deprived areas: community or personal disadvantage? *BMJ.* 1994;309:1470–1474.

47. Waitzman NJ, Smith KR. Phantom of the area: poverty-area residence and mortality in the United States. *Am J Pub Health.* 1998;88:973–976.

48. Emmons KM. Health behaviors in a social context. In: Berkman L, Kawachi I, eds. *Social Epidemiology.* New York, NY: Oxford University Press; 2000:242–266.

49. Glanz K, Rimer BK, Lewis FM, eds. *Health Behavior and Health Education: Theory, Research and Practice.* San Francisco, CA: Jossey-Bass; 2002.

50. Baum A, Garafalo JP, Yali AM. Socioeconomic status and chronic stress. *Ann N Y Acad Sci.* 1999; 896:131–144.

51. Cacioppo JT, Hawkley LC, Crawford LE, et al. Loneliness and health: potential mechanisms. *Psychosom Med.* 2002;64:407–414.

52. Elliott M. The stress process in neighborhood context. *Health Place.* 2000;6:287–299.

53. Falcon LM, Tucker KL. Prevalence and correlates of depressive symptomatology among Hispanic elders in Massachusetts. *J Gerontol B Psychol Sci Soc Sci.* 2000;55(2):S108–S116.

54. Gallo LC, Matthews KA. Do negative emotions mediate the association between socioeconomic status and health? *Ann N Y Acad Sci.* 1999;896:226–245.

55. McClintock MK, Conzen SD, Gehlert S, Masi C, Olopade F. Mammary cancer and social interactions: identifying multiple environments that regulate gene expression throughout the life span. *J Gerontol B Psychol Sci Soc Sci.* 2005;60(Spec No 1):32–41.

56. Ryff CD, Singer B. From social structure to biology: integrative science in pursuit of human health and well-being. In: Snyder, CR, Lopez SJ, eds. *Handbook of Positive Psychology.* New York, NY: Oxford University Press; 2002.

57. Tucker KL, Bermudez O, Castanada C. Type 2 diabetes is prevalent and poorly controlled among Hispanic elders. *Am J Pub Health.* 2000;90: 1288–1293.

58. Hermes GL, Rosenthal L, Montag A, et al. Social isolation and the inflammatory response: sex differences in the enduring effects of a prior stressor. *Am J Physiol Regul Integr Comp Physiol.* 2006;290: 273–282.

59. Wu W, Chaudhuri S, Brickley DR, Pang D, Karrison T, Conzen SD. Microarray analysis reveals glucocorticoid-regulated survival genes that are associated with inhibition of apoptosis in breast epithelial cells. *Cancer Res.* 2004;64:1757–1764.

60. House JA, Landis KR, Umberson D. Social relationships and health. *Science.* 1988;241:540–545.

61. McEwen BS, Seeman T. Protective and damaging effects of mediators of stress: elaborating and testing the concepts of allostasis and allostatic load. *Ann N Y Acad Sci.* 1999;896:30–45.

62. Eschbach K, Kuo YF, Goodwin JS. Ascertainment of Hispanic ethnicity on California death certificates: implications for the explanation of the Hispanic mortality advantage. *Am J Pub Health.* 2006;96:2209–2215.

63. Eschbach K, Stimpson JP, Kuo YF, et al. Mortality of Hispanic immigrants and US-born Hispanics at younger ages: a re-examination of recent patterns. *Am J Pub Health.* 2007;97(7):1297–1304.

64. Peek MK, Cutchin MP, Freeman DH, et al. Perceived health change in the aftermath of a petro-chemical accident: an examination of pre-disaster, within-disaster, and post-disaster variables. *J Epidemiol Community Health.* 2008;62(2): 106–112.

65. Cutchin MP, Martin KR, Owen SV, et al. Concerns about petrochemical health risk before and after a refinery explosion. *Risk Anal.* In press.

66. Barrett RE, Cho YI, Weaver KE, et al. Neighborhood change and distant metastasis at diagnosis of breast cancer. *Ann Epidemiol.* 2008;18:43–47.

67. Tucker KL, Falcon LM, Bianchi LI, Cacho E, Bermudez OI. Self reported prevalence and health correlates of functional limitation among Massachusetts elderly Puerto Ricans, Dominicans, and a non-Hispanic white neighborhood comparison group. *J Gerontol A Biol Sci Med Sci.* 2000;55(2):M90–M97.

68. Zeigler-Johnson CM, Friebel T, Walker AH, et al. CYP3A4, CYP3A5, and CYP3A43 genotypes and haplotypes in the etiology and severity of prostate cancer. *Cancer Res.* 2004;64:8461–8467.

69. Division of Strategic Coordination, Office of Portfolio Analysis and Strategic Initiatives, National Institutes of Health. *NIH Roadmap for Medical Research.* Available at: http://nihroadmap.nih.gov. Accessed September 11, 2006.

Closing the Gap in a Generation: Health Equity Through Action on the Social Determinants of Health

Source: Reprinted from *The Lancet*; 372:1661-9. Marmot M, Friel S, Bell R, Houweling TA, Taylor S, Commission on Social Determinants of Health. Closing the gap in a generation: health equity through action on the social determinants of health, Copyright 2008, with permission from Elsevier.

The Commission on Social Determinants of Health, created to marshal the evidence on what can be done to promote health equity and to foster a global movement to achieve it, is a global collaboration of policy makers, researchers, and civil society, led by commissioners with a unique blend of political, academic, and advocacy experience. The focus of attention is on countries at all levels of income and development. The commission launched its final report on August 28, 2008. This paper summarises the key findings and recommendations; the full list is in the final report.

INTRODUCTION

Life chances differ greatly depending on where people are born and raised. A person who has been born and lives in Japan or Sweden can expect to live more than 80 years; in Brazil, 72 years; India, 63 years; and in several African countries, less than 50 years. Within countries, the differences in life chances are also great. The poorest people have high levels of illness and premature mortality—but poor health is not confined to those who are worst off. At all lev-

els of income, health and illness follow a social gradient: the lower the socioeconomic position, the worse the health.

If systematic differences in health for different groups of people are avoidable by reasonable action, their existence is, quite simply, unfair. We call this imbalance health inequity. Social injustice is killing people on a grand scale, and the reduction of health inequities, between and within countries, is an ethical imperative.

SOCIAL DETERMINANTS OF HEALTH AND HEALTH EQUITY

The commission took a holistic view of social determinants of health.[1] The poor health of poor people, the social gradient in health within countries, and the substantial health inequities between countries are caused by the unequal distribution of power, income, goods, and services, globally and nationally, the consequent unfairness in the immediate, visible circumstances of people's lives—their access to health care and education, their conditions of work and leisure, their homes, communities, towns, or cities—and their chances of leading a flourishing life. This unequal distribution of health-damaging experiences is not in any sense a natural phenomenon but is the result of a combination of poor social policies and programmes, unfair economic arrangements, and bad politics. Together, the structural determinants and conditions of daily life constitute the social determinants of health and cause much of the health inequity between and within countries.

A NEW APPROACH TO DEVELOPMENT

Health and health equity might not be the aim of all social and economic policies, but they will be a fundamental result. For example, economic growth is, without question, important, particularly for poor countries, because it gives the opportunity to provide resources to invest in improvement of the lives of their populations. But growth by itself, without appropriate social policies to ensure reasonable fairness in the way its benefits are distributed, brings little benefit to health equity.

Society has traditionally looked to the health sector to deal with its concerns about health and disease. Certainly, maldistribution of health care—i.e., not delivering care to those who most need it—is one social determinant of health. But much of the high burden of illness leading to appalling premature loss of life arises because of the immediate and structural conditions in which people are born, grow, live, work, and age.

Action on the social determinants of health must involve the whole of government, civil society, local communities, business, and international agencies. Policies and programmes must embrace all sectors of society, not just the health sector. However, ministries of health and their ministers are crucial to the realisation of change. Health ministries that champion approaches based on social determinants of health can demonstrate effectiveness through good practice and support other ministries in creating policies that promote health equity. WHO must do the same, but on an international scale.

CLOSING THE HEALTH GAP IN A GENERATION

The Commission on Social Determinants of Health calls for the closing of the health gap in a generation: this is an aspiration not a prediction. Great improvements in health, worldwide and within countries, have been made in the past 30 years. We are optimistic that the knowledge exists to continue to make a huge difference to people's life chances and hence to provide improved health equity. We are also realistic and know that action must start now.

The commission's analysis leads to three principles of action: improve the conditions of daily life (i.e., the circumstances in which people are born, grow, live, work, and age); tackle the inequitable distribution of power, money, and resources (the structural drivers of those conditions of daily life) globally, nationally, and locally; and measure the problem, evaluate action, expand the knowledge base, develop a workforce that is trained in the social determinants of health, and raise public awareness about these determinants. These three principles of action are embodied in the three overarching recommendations (panel). The recommendations have to be seen in light of the commission's global reach. Recognition of inequities in health is recognition of the plight of people living on U.S. $1 a day in rural Africa, urban dwellers in shanty towns in low-income and middle-income countries, and the social gradient in health in high-income countries. Although one set of specific recommendations will not apply to all of these particular settings, the general principles will. The recommendations that follow should be seen as principles of action that need to be developed for, and applied in, specific national and local contexts. The full list of recommendations can be found in the final report of the Commission on Social Determinants of Health.[1]

IMPROVE DAILY LIVING CONDITIONS

Equity from the Start

Investment during the early years of life has some of the greatest potential to reduce health inequities within a generation. Child survival, rightly, has been a focus of worldwide interest. The Commission on Social Determinants of Health has gone further and emphasised the importance of early child development, including not only physical and cognitive or linguistic development but also, crucially, social and emotional development. Early child development affects subsequent life chances through skills development, education, and occupational opportunities;[2] it also affects the risks of obesity, malnutrition, mental-health problems, heart disease, and criminality in later life. At least 200 million children worldwide are not achieving their full development potential.[3]

Brain development is highly sensitive to external influences in early childhood that can have life-long effects. Good nutrition is crucial and begins before birth with adequate nourishment of mothers. Mothers and children need a continuum of care from before pregnancy, through pregnancy and childbirth, to the early days and years of life.[4] Children need safe, healthy, supporting, nurturing, caring, and responsive living environments. Preschool educational

Panel: The Commission on Social Determinants of Health's overarching recommendations

Improve Daily Living Conditions

Improve the well-being of girls and women and the circumstances in which their children are born, put major emphasis on early child development and education for girls and boys, improve living and working conditions and create social protection policy supportive of all, and create conditions for a flourishing older life. Policies to achieve these goals will involve civil society, governments, and global institutions.

Tackle the Inequitable Distribution of Power, Money, and Resources

To address health inequities and inequitable conditions of daily living it is necessary to address inequities—such as those between men and women—in the way society is organised. A strong, committed, capable, and adequately financed public sector is needed. To achieve that requires more than strengthened government—it requires strengthened governance: legitimacy, space, and support for civil society, for an accountable private sector, and for people across society to agree on public interests and reinvest in the value of collective action. In a globalised world, the need for governance dedicated to equity applies equally from the community level to global institutions.

Measure and Understand the Problem and Assess the Results of Action

Acknowledging that there is a problem and ensuring that health inequity is measured—within countries and globally—are essential for action. National governments and international organisations, supported by WHO, should set up national and global health-equity surveillance systems for routine monitoring of health inequity and the social determinants of health and should asses the health-equity impact of policy and action. Creating the organisational space and capacity to act effectively on health inequity requires investment in training of policy makers and health practitioners, public understanding of social determinants of health, and a stronger focus on social determinants in public health research.

programmes and schools, as part of the wider environment that contributes to development, can play a vital part in building children's capabilities. The combined effects of good nutrition and psychosocial stimulation completely reversed the effects of stunting on intellectual development in a randomised controlled trial in stunted children.[5]

To build equity from the start of life, governments and international agencies need to commit to and implement a comprehensive approach to early life, building on existing child-survival programmes and extending interventions in early life to include social-emotional and language-cognitive development. This approach will require interagency mechanisms to provide a comprehensive package that extends to all children, mothers, and other carers regardless of ability to pay. These principles of early child development should extend to the education system. Key principles for the education system include provision of high-quality compulsory primary and secondary education for all children regardless of ability to pay, abolishing fees for primary school, and identifying barriers to enrolment in school.

Healthy Places Healthy People

In 2007, for the first time, more people worldwide were living in urban than in rural settings.[6] Almost 1 billion people live in slums. The proportion of urban residents varies enormously among countries: from less than 10% in Uganda to 100%, or close to it, in Singapore and Belgium. Policies and investment patterns driven by urban needs[7] lead to underinvestment in infrastructure and amenities for rural communities worldwide, including indigenous people,[8] creating disproportionate poverty and poor living conditions for these populations.[9,10]

Infectious diseases and undernutrition will continue to dominate in particular regions and groups around the world. However, urbanisation is reshaping population health problems, particularly among poor people in urban areas, towards non-communicable diseases, accidental and violent injuries, and effects of ecological disaster.[11,12]

Access to good-quality housing and shelter, clean water, and sanitation are human rights and basic needs for healthy living.[13,14] Growing dependence on cars, land-use change to facilitate car use, and increased inconvenience of non-motorised modes of travel have knock-on effects on local air quality, greenhouse-gas emission, and physical inactivity.[15] The planning and design of urban environments has a major effect on health equity through its influence on behaviour and safety.

The current model of urbanisation poses substantial environmental challenges, particularly climate change—the effect of which is greater in low-income countries and among vulnerable subpopulations.[16,17] At present, greenhouse-gas emissions are determined mainly by consumption patterns in cities in developed countries.

Communities and neighbourhoods that ensure access to basic goods, that are socially cohesive, that are designed to promote good physical and psychological well-being, and that are protective of the natural environment are essential for health equity. Therefore, health and health equity need to be at the heart of urban governance and planning. Upgrading of urban slums should be a priority, including provision of water and sanitation, electricity, and paved streets for all households regardless of ability to pay. Affordable housing must be high on any agenda to improve health equity.

Urban planning should promote healthy and safe behaviours equitably, through investment in active transport, through retail planning to manage access to unhealthy foods, and through good environmental design and regulatory controls, including control of the number of alcohol outlets.

The Commission on Social Determinants of Health focused particularly on urban areas, but relief of pressure of migration to urban areas and equity between urban and rural areas requires sustained investment in rural development, addressing the exclusionary policies and processes that lead to rural poverty, landlessness, and displacement of people from their homes.

Fair Employment and Decent Work

Work is the origin of many important determinants of health.[18] Work can provide financial security, social status, personal development, social relations, and self-esteem and protection from physical and psychosocial hazards. Employment conditions and the nature of work are both important to health. A flexible workforce is seen as good for economic competitiveness but brings with it effects on health.[19] Mortality seems to be significantly higher in temporary workers than in permanent workers.[20] Poor mental health outcomes are associated with precarious employment (figure 1).[21,22]

Adverse working conditions can expose individuals to a range of physical health hazards and cluster in low-status occupations. Improved working conditions in high income countries, which have been hard won over many years of organised action and regulation, are sorely lacking in many middle-income and low-income countries. Stress at work, defined as a combination of high psychological demands and low control or as an imbalance between effort and reward,[23] is associated with a 50% excess risk of coronary heart disease[24] and other indicators of mental and physical ill health.[25]

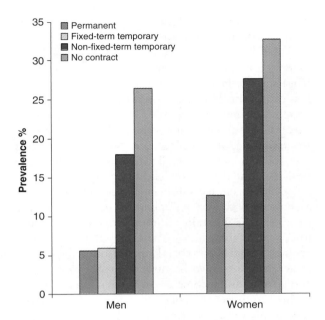

Figure 1 Poor mental health among manual workers in Spain by type of contract[21]

Although work is seen as a route out of poverty in high-income countries, this is not the case worldwide (Figure 2, not included).[26] Through fair employment and decent working conditions, government, employers, and workers can help eradicate poverty, alleviate social inequities, reduce exposure to physical and psychosocial hazards, and improve opportunities for health and well-being. To this end, full and fair employment and decent work must be a central goal of national and international social and economic policy making, and should involve strengthened representation of workers in the creation of policy, legislation, and programmes relating to employment and work.

Employment policy should aim to provide a living wage (that takes into account the real cost of healthy living) and to protect all workers. International agencies should support countries to implement standards of labour for formal and informal workers, to develop policies to ensure balance between work-life and home-life, and to reduce the negative effects of insecurity among workers in precarious work arrangements. Policies that reduce all workers' exposure to material hazards, work-related stress, and health-damaging behaviours are also needed.

Social Protection Throughout Life

Low living standards are a powerful determinant of health inequity. The fundamental principle of social protection is that all people need support at some point in their lives. A feature of all high-income countries is that society provides, to a greater or lesser extent, for vulnerable periods and for protection from specific factors, such as illness, disability, and loss of income or work. However, four in every five people worldwide lack basic social-security coverage.[27] Government policies can make a difference—for example, in Sweden and Norway generous transfer payments to socially vulnerable families have been associated with low child poverty.[28]

Generous universal social protection systems are associated with better population health, including lower excess mortality among elderly people and lower mortality among socially disadvantaged groups. Budgets for social protection are typically larger in countries with universal protection systems and poverty and income inequality tend to be smaller in these countries than in countries with systems that specifically target poor people.

Reduction of the health gap in a generation requires that governments build systems allowing a healthy standard of living below which nobody should fall because of circumstances beyond his or her control. Social protection should be extended to all people, including those in precarious work, informal work, and household or care work.

Although limited institutional infrastructure and financial capacity remains an important barrier in many countries, social protection systems can be initiated, even in low-income countries. Such systems can be instrumental in realising developmental goals rather than being dependent on these goals having been reached. Social protection systems can reduce poverty, and local economies can benefit from them. Therefore, the Commission on Social Determinants of Health recommends that governments establish and strengthen universal comprehensive social protection policies that support a level of income sufficient for healthy living for all.

Universal Health Care

The health-care system is itself a social determinant of health, influenced by and influencing the effect of other social determinants. Gender, education, occupation, income, ethnicity, and place of residence are all closely linked to access to, experiences of, and benefits from health care (Figure 3, not included).[29] Leaders in health care have an important stewardship role across all branches of society to ensure that policies and actions in other sectors improve health equity.

Health care is a common good, not a market commodity. Nearly all high-income countries or-ganise their healthcare systems around the principle of universal coverage; this approach requires that everyone within a country can access the same range of services according to needs and preferences, regardless of income, social status, or residency, and that people are empowered to use these services.

The commission advocates the financing of health-care systems through general taxation or mandatory universal insurance. The evidence is compellingly in favour of publicly funded health-care systems. In particular, out-of-pocket spending on health care must be kept to a minimum. The policy imposition of user fees for health care in low-income and middle-income countries has led to an overall reduction in use and worsening of health outcomes. Upwards of 100 million people are pushed into poverty each year through catastrophic household health costs.

Health-care systems have the best health outcomes when based in primary health care. The emphasis in the best systems is both on locally appropriate action across the range of social determinants, where prevention and promotion are in balance with investment in curative interventions, and on primary care with adequate referral to higher levels of care.

In all countries, but most pressingly in the poorest and those experiencing brain-drain losses, adequate numbers of appropriately skilled health workers at the local level are fundamental to extending coverage and improving the quality of care. Investment in training and retaining health workers is vital to the strengthening of health-care systems. This strengthening involves global attention to the flows of health personnel as much as national and local attention to investment and skills development. Medical and health practitioners—from those at WHO to those in local clinics—have powerful voices, affecting society's ideas and decisions about health, and bear witness to the ethical imperative and benefit to effciency of working more coherently through the health-care system to target social causes of poor health.

TACKLE INEQUITY OF POWER, MONEY, AND RESOURCES

Health Equity in All Policies, Systems, and Programmes

Every feature of government and the economy has the potential to affect health and health equity. Coherent action across government-including finance, education, housing, employment, transport, and health—at all levels, is essential for improving health equity.[30] Traffic injury, a major public-health issue, is an example of where action must come from outside the health sector. Legislation for the mandatory wearing of helmets by cyclists reduced bicyle-related head and other injuries in Canada in the 1990s.[31]

Policy coherence is crucial. For example, trade policy that actively encourages the unfettered production, trade, and consumption of foods high in fats and sugars to the detriment of fruit and vegetable production is contradictory to health policy, which recommends low consumption of high-fat, high-sugar foods and increased consumption of fruit and vegetables.[32] Intersectoral action for health-co-ordinated policy and action among health and non-health sectors can be a key strategy to achieve policy coherence.[33] Reaching beyond government to involve civil society and the voluntary and private sectors is vital for health equity and can help to ensure fair decision making.

Health, and health equity, should become corporate issues for the whole of government, placing responsibility for action at the highest level and ensuring its coherent consideration across all policies. The results of all policies and programmes on health equity also need to be assessed. Although action across government is required, ministries of health have central roles in stewardship and information. This function requires strong leadership from government ministers of health, with support from WHO.

Fair Financing

For countries at all levels of economic development, public financing of action on the social determinants of health is fundamental to welfare and health equity. The socioeconomic development of rich countries was strongly supported by publicly financed infrastructure and progressively universal public services. The emphasis on public finance, given the substantial failure of markets to supply vital goods and services equitably, implies strong public-sector leadership and adequate public expenditure.

Many low-income countries have weak direct tax institutions and mechanisms and most of their workforce are employed informally. These countries commonly rely on indirect taxes, such as trade tariffs, for government income. Economic agreements that require tariff reduction can reduce domestic revenue in low-income countries. Strengthened progressive tax capacity is a necessary prerequisite of any further tariff-cutting agreements. At the same time, measures to combat the use of offshore financial centres to reduce unethical avoidance of national tax regimes could provide resources for development at least comparable to those made available through new taxes. As globalisation increases the interdependence among countries, the argument for global approaches to taxation becomes stronger.

Aid is important for social development. But the volume of aid is appallingly low-absolutely, relative to wealth in donor countries (Figure 4, not included),[34] and relative to the level of aid commitment of about 0.7% of gross domestic product in such countries. Independent of increased aid, the Commission on Social Determinants of Health urges greater debt relief for more countries than currently provided.

The strengthening of public finance to improve social determinants of health will entail the building of national capacity for progressive taxation and the assessment of potential for new national and global public finance mechanisms; fair allocation between geographical regions and ethnic groups is also necessary.

Increased international finance for health equity and increased finance through a social determinants of health action framework means that existing commitments to increase global aid to the 0.7% of gross domestic product must be honoured and the Multilateral Debt Relief Initiative expanded. The quality of aid must be improved, too, focusing on better coordination among donors and stronger alignment with recipient development plans. Poverty reduction planning at the national and local levels in recipient countries should adopt a framework addressing social determinants of health to create coherent, cross-sectoral financing. This framework must be transparent and accountable.

Market Responsibility

Markets can bring health benefits in the form of new technologies, goods, and services and improved standard of living. But the marketplace can also generate negative conditions for health, including economic inequalities, resource depletion, environmental pollution, unhealthy working conditions, and the circulation of dangerous and unhealthy goods.

Health is not a tradeable commodity. It is a matter of rights and a public-sector duty. As such, resources for health must be equitable and universal. Experience shows that commercialisation of vital social goods, such as education and health care, produces health inequity. The Commission on Social Determinants of Health views certain goods and services as basic human and societal needs—access to clean water, for example, and health care. Such goods and services must be made available universally, regardless of ability to pay, with the public sector, rather than the market sector, underwriting adequate supply and access. The unit price of a commodity commonly gets cheaper as consumption goes up, making the first units difficult for people on low incomes to puchase and encouraging overconsumption by people who can afford the first units, as was the case with water prices in Johannesburg.[35] A fairer tarrif structure would subsidise the price for poorer consumers and have price disincentives for overconsumption.

Also, public-sector leadership is needed for effective national and international regulation of products, activities, and conditions that damage health or lead to health inequities. Global governance mechanisms—such as the Framework Convention on Tobacco Control—are required with increasing urgency as market integration expands and accelerates circulation of and access to health-damaging commodities. Processed foods and alcohol are two prime candidates for stronger global, regional, and national regulatory controls.

Finally, regular health equity impact assessment of all policy making and market regulation should be institutionalised nationally and internationally. In recent decades, under globalisation, market integration has increased. Some of the effects on employment and distribution of goods and services will be beneficial for health, some of them disastrous. The commission urges that caution be applied in the consideration of new global, regional, and bilateral economic policy commitments. Before such commitments are made, the effect of the existing framework of agreements on health, the social determinants of health, and health equity must be fully understood.

Public-sector leadership does not displace the responsibilities and capacities of the private sector. Stakeholders in the private sector are influential, and have the power to do much for global health equity. Although, to date, initiatives such as those under corporate social responsibility have shown limited evidence of real effect. Corporate social responsibility may be a valuable way forward, but evidence is needed to demonstrate this. Corporate accountability may be a stronger basis on which to build responsible collaborations between private and public interests.

The effect of economic agreements on people's lives should be made obvious. Outcomes of health and health equity must be considered in national and international economic agreements and policy mak-

ing. The roles of the state as the primary provider of basic services essential to health (e.g., water and sanitation) and regulator of goods and services with a major effect on health (e.g., tobacco, alcohol, and food) need to be reinforced.

Gender Equity

Gender inequities are pervasive in all societies. Biases in power, resources, entitlements, norms and values, and the way in which organisations are structured and programmes are run damage the health of millions of girls and women. The position of women in society is also associated with child health and survival. Gender inequities influence health through, for example, discriminatory feeding patterns, violence against women, lack of decision-making power, and unfair divisions of work, leisure, and possibilities of improving one's life.

Although the position of women has improved substantially over the past century in many countries, progress has been uneven and many challenges remain. Women earn less than men, even for equivalent work (Figure 5, not included);[36] girls and women lag behind in education and employment opportunities. Maternal mortality and morbidity remain high in many countries, and reproductive health services remain inequitably distributed within and between countries. The intergenerational effects of inequity between the sexes make the imperative to act even stronger.

There are several ways in which governments, donors, international organisations, and civil society can promote gender equity. First, legislation can promote equity and make discrimination on the basis of sex illegal. Second, gender equity units within central administration of governments and international institutions can strengthen assessments of gender implications of planned actions to ensure that men and women benefit equitably. Third, national accounts can include the economic contribution of housework, care work, and voluntary work. Fourth, finance policies and programmes can close gaps in education and skills and support economic participation by women. Finally, investment in sexual and reproductive health services and programmes leading to universal coverage and rights should be increased.

Political Empowerment-Inclusion and Voice

Empowerment is central to the social determinants of health. Material, psychosocial, and political empowerment comes from inclusion in society and fulfilment of rights to the conditions necessary to achieve the highest attainable standard of health. The risk of these rights being violated is the result of entrenched structural inequities.[37] The freedom to participate in economic, social, political, and cultural relationships has intrinsic value.[38] Inclusion, agency, and control are each important for social development, health, and well-being.

A particularly egregious form of social exclusion is seen among indigenous peoples in many countries. But social inequity is also manifest across various intersecting social categories, such as class, education, gender, age, ethnicity, disability, and geography. Exclusion is a sign of not simple difference but hierarchy and reffects deep inequities in the wealth, power, and prestige of different people and communities.

Serious effort to reduce health inequities will involve changing of the distribution of power within society and global regions and empowerment of individuals and groups to represent effectively their needs and interests. Such changes will challenge the unfair and graded distribution of social resources to which all citizens have claims and rights.

Changes in power relationships can take place at various levels, from the level of individuals, households, or communities to the sphere of structural relations among economic, social, and political stakeholders and institutions. Community or civil society action on health inequities cannot be separated from the responsibility of the state to guarantee a comprehensive set of rights and ensure the fair distribution of essential material and social goods among population groups. Top-down and bottom-up approaches are equally vital.

All groups in society can be empowered through fair representation in decisions about how society operates, particularly in relation to health equity by a socially inclusive framework for policy making. Such inclusion can enable civil society to organise and act in a manner that promotes and realises the political and social rights affecting health equity.

Good Global Governance

Great differences in the health and life chances of peoples around the world reffect imbalance in the power and prosperity of nations. The benefits of globalisation remain profoundly unequally distributed. Progress in global economic growth and health equity made between 1960 and 1980 has been significantly dampened since (Figure 6, not included),[39] as global economic policy hit social-sector spending and social development hard. Also associated with the second (post-1980) phase of globalisation, the world has seen significant increase in, and regularity

of, financial crises, proliferating conflicts, and forced and voluntary migration.

Through the recognition of common interests and interdependent futures, the international community must commit to a multilateral system in which all countries, rich and poor, engage with an equitable voice. Only through such a system of global governance—that places fairness in health at the heart of the development agenda and genuine equality of influence at the heart of its decision making—will coherent attention to global health equity be possible. Therefore health equity should become a global development goal, and a framework of social determinants of health should be adopted to strengthen multilateral action on development. The UN, through WHO and the Economic and Social Council, should lead and use indicators of social determinants of health to monitor progress by establishing multilateral working groups on thematic social determinants of health. WHO should lead in global action by enshrining social determinants of health as guiding principles across its departments and country programmes.

UNDERSTAND THE PROBLEM AND EVALUATE ACTION

Action on the social determinants of health will be more effective if basic data systems are in place and there are mechanisms to ensure that the data can be understood and applied to develop more effective policies, systems, and programmes. Education and training in social determinants of health are essential.

Lack of data often means that problems are unrecognised. Good evidence on levels of health and its distribution, and on the social determinants of health, is essential for the scale of the problem to be understood, the effects of actions assessed, and progress monitored. Experience shows that countries without basic data on mortality and morbidity stratified by socioeconomic indicators have difficulties in moving forward on health equity.[40] Countries with the worst health problems have the poorest data. Many countries do not even have basic systems to register all births and deaths (Table).[41]

The evidence base on health inequity, the social determinants of health, and what works to improve them needs further strengthening. Unfortunately, most health research funding remains overwhelmingly biomedically focused. Also, much research remains gender biased. Traditional hierarchies of evidence (which put randomised controlled trials and laboratory experiments at the top) generally do not

Unregistered births (1000s) in 2003 by region and level of development

	Births	Unregistered children
World	133,028	48,276 (36%)
Sub-Saharan Africa	26,879	14,751 (55%)
Middle East and north Africa	9790	1543 (16%)
South Asia	37,099	23,395 (63%)
East Asia and Pacific	31,616	5901 (19%)
Latin America and Caribbean	11,567	1787 (15%)
CEE, CIS, and Baltic states	5250	1218 (23%)
Industrialised countries	10,827	218 (2%)
Developing countries	119,973	48,147 (40%)
Least developed countries	27,819	16,682 (71%)

Data are number (%). CEE = Central and eastern Europe. CIS = Commonwealth of Independent States. Data from UNICEF.[41]

work for research on the social determinants of health. Rather, evidence needs to be judged on fitness for purpose—that is, does it convincingly answer the question asked?

Evidence is only one part of what swings policy decisions—political will and institutional capacity are important too. Policy makers need to understand what affects population health and how the gradient operates. Action on the social determinants of health also requires capacity building among practitioners, including the incorporation of teaching on social determinants of health into the curricula of health and medical personnel. In addition, training of policy makers and other stakeholders on social determinants of health and investment in public awareness are needed.

Routine monitoring systems for health equity and the social determinants of health are needed, locally, nationally, and internationally. Combined with investment, such systems will enable generation and sharing of new evidence on the ways in which social determinants influence population health and health equity and on the effectiveness of measures to reduce health inequities through action on social determinants.

CONCLUSION

Is closing the gap in a generation possible? This question has two clear answers. If we continue as we are, there is no chance at all. If there is a genuine desire to

change, if there is a vision to create a better and fairer world where people's life chances and their health will no longer be blighted by the accident of where they happen to be born, the colour of their skin, or the lack of opportunities afforded to their parents, then the answer is: we could go a long way towards it.

Action can be, and is being, taken. But coherent action must be fashioned across the determinants, rooting out structural inequity as much as ensuring more immediate well-being. In calling to close the gap in a generation, we do not imagine that the social gradient in health within countries, or the great differences between countries, will be abolished in 30 years. But the evidence, produced in the final report[1] of the Commission on Social Determinants of Health, encourages us that significant closing of the gap is indeed achievable.

This is a long-term agenda, requiring investment starting now, with major changes in social policies, economic arrangements, and political action. At the centre of this action is empowerment of the people, communities, and countries that currently do not have their fair share. The knowledge and the means to change are at hand. What is needed now is the political will to implement these eminently difficult but feasible changes. Not to act will be seen, in decades to come, as failure on a grand scale to accept the responsibility that rests on all our shoulders.

Conflict of Interest Statement

We declare that we have no conflict of interest.

ACKNOWLEDGMENTS

This publication contains the collective views of the Commission on Social Determinants of Health and does not necessarily represent the decisions or the stated policy of WHO. This paper is based on the executive summary of the final report of the commission. Permission for reproducing text from this report has been granted by WHO. We wrote this paper on behalf of the Commission on Social Determinants of Health. The commissioners are Michael Marmot (Chair), Frances Baum, Monique Bégin, Giovanni Berlinguer, Mirai Chatterjee, William H Foege, Yan Guo, Kiyoshi Kurokawa, Ricardo Lagos Escobar, Alireza Marandi, Pascoal Mocumbi, Ndioro Ndiaye, Charity Kaluki Ngilu, Hoda Rashad, Amartya Sen, David Satcher, Anna Tibaijuka, Denny Vågerö, Gail Wilensky. We are indebted to all those who contributed to the work of the commission, including commissioners, Hernan Sandoval (special adviser), Knowledge Networks, country partners, civil society facilitators, and colleagues in WHO. The WHO arm of the commission secretariat was led by Jeanette Vega and Nico Drager, and was housed in the cluster headed by Assistant Director-General Tim Evans. Team members in Geneva included Daniel Ernesto Albrecht Alba, Erik Blas, Lucy Mshana, Susanne Nakalembe, Anand Sivasankara Kurup, Amit Prasad, Kumanan Rasanathan, Lina Reinders, Ritu Sadana, Michel Thieren, Nicole Valentine, and Eugenio Raul Villar Montesinos. We also thank all former members of the Geneva arm of the secretariat, in particular Lexi Bambas-Nolen, Chris Brown, Alex Irwin, Bongiwe Peguillan, Richard Poe, Gabrielle Ross, Sarah Simpson, Orielle Solar, and Rene Loewenson (consultant).

● ● ● References

1. Commission on Social Determinants of Health. CSDH final report: closing the gap in a generation: health equity through action on the social determinants of health. Geneva: World Health Organization, 2008.

2. Early Child Development Knowledge Network of the Commission on Social Determinants of Health. Early child development: a powerful equalizer. Geneva: World Health Organization, 2007.

3. Grantham-McGregor SM, Cheung YB, Cueto S, Glewwe P, Richter L, Strupp B. Development potential in the first 5 years for children in developing countries. *Lancet.* 2007;369:60–70.

4. WHO. World Health Report 2005: make every mother and child count. Geneva: World Health Organization, 2005.

5. Grantham-McGregor SM, Powell CA, Walker SP, Himes JH. Nutritional supplementation, psychosocial stimulation, and mental development of stunted children: the Jamaican Study. *Lancet.* 1991;338:1–5.

6. WorldWatch Institute. State of the world 2007: our urban future. Washington, DC: The WorldWatch Institute, 2007.

7. Vlahov D, Freudenberg N, Proietti F, et al. Urban as a determinant of health. *J Urban Health* 2007;84(3 suppl):i16–26.

8. Indigenous Health Group. Social determinants and indigenous health: the international experience and its policy implications. http://www.who.int/social_ determinants/resources/indigenous_health_ adelaide_report_07.pdf. Accessed Oct 2, 2008.

9. Ooi GL, Phua KH. Urbanization and slum formation. *J Urban Health.* 2007;84(3 suppl):i27–34.

10. Eastwood R, Lipton M. Rural-urban dimensions of inequality change. Helsinki: World Institute for Development, 2000.

11. Campbell T, Campbell A. Emerging disease burdens and the poor in cities of the developing world. *J Urban Health.* 2007;84(3 suppl):i54–64.

12. Yusuf S, Reddy S, Ounpuu S, Anand S. Global burden of cardiovascular diseases, part I: general considerations, the epidemiologic transition, risk factors, and impact of urbanization. *Circulation.* 2001;104:2746–53.

13. UNESCO. Water: a shared responsibility—United Nations world water development report 2. Paris: UN Educational, Scientific and Cultural Organization, 2006.

14. Shaw M. Housing and public health. *Annu Rev Public Health.* 2004;25:397–418.

15. National Heart Forum. Building health—creating and enhancing places for healthy living, active lives: blueprint for action. London: UK National Heart Forum, 2007.

16. McMichael AJ, Friel S, Nyong A, Corvalan C. Global environmental change and health: impacts, inequalities, and the health sector. *BMJ.* 2008;336: 191–94.

17. Stern, N. The Stern review: the economics of climate change. London: HM Treasury, 2006.

18. Marmot M, Wilkinson R, eds. Social determinants of health. Oxford: Oxford University Press, 2006.

19. Benach J, Muntaner C. Precarious employment and health: developing a research agenda. *J Epidemiol Community Health.* 2007;61:276–77.

20. Kivimaki M, Vahtera J, Virtanen M, Elovainio M, Pentti J, Ferrie JE. Temporary employment and risk of overall and cause specific mortality. *Am J Epidemiol.* 2003;158:663–68.

21. Artazcoz L, Benach J, Borrell C, Cortes I. Social inequalities in the impact of flexible employment on different domains of psychosocial health. *J Epidemiol Community Health.* 2005;59:761–67.

22. Kim IH, Muntaner C, Khang YH, Paek D, Cho SI. The relationship between nonstandard working and mental health in a representative sample of the South Korean population. *Soc Sci Med.* 2006;63: 566–74.

23. Marmot M. Status syndrome. London: Bloomsbury, 2004.

24. Kivimaki M, Virtanen M, Elovainio M, Kouvonen A, Vaananen A, Vahtera J. Work stress in the etiology of coronary heart disease—a meta-analysis. *Scand J Work Environ Health*. 2006;32:431–442.

25. Stansfeld S, Candy B. Psychosocial work environment and mental health—a meta-analytic review. *Scand J Work Environ Health*. 2006;32:443–462.

26. International Labour Organization. Global employment trends. Geneva: International Labour Organization, 2008.

27. International Labour Organization. ILO launches global campaign on social security for all. http://www.ilo.org/global/About_the_ILO/Media_and_public_information/Press_releases/lang--en/WCMS_005285/index.htm. Accessed May 8, 2008.

28. Lundberg O, Åberg Yngwe M, Kölegård Stjärne M, Björk L, Fritzell J. The nordic experience: welfare states and public health (NEWS): health equity studies no 12-report for the Commission on Social Determinants of Health. Stockholm: Centre for Health Equity Studies (CHESS), Stockholm University/Karolinska Institutet, 2008.

29. Gwatkin DR, Wagstaff A, Yazbeck AS, eds. Reaching the poor with health, nutrition, and population services. Washington, DC: World Bank, 2005.

30. Kickbusch I. Health promotion: not a tree but a rhizome. In: O'Neill M, Pederson A, Dupere S, Rootman I, eds. Health promotion in Canada, 2nd edn. Toronto: Canadian Scholars Press, 2007.

31. Macpherson AK, To TM, Macarthur C, Chipman ML, Wright JG, Parkin PC. Impact of mandatory helmet legislation on bicycle-related head injuries in children: a population-based study. *Pediatrics*. 2002;110:e60.

32. Elinder LS. Obesity, hunger, and agriculture: the damaging role of subsidies. *BMJ*. 2005;331:1333–336.

33. Public Health Agency of Canada. Crossing sectors-experiences in intersectoral action, public policy and health. Ottawa: Public Health Agency of Canada, 2007.

34. Randel J, German A, Ewing D, eds. The reality of aid 2004: an independent review of poverty reduction and development assistance. London: IBON Books Manila/Zed Books, 2004.

35. Globalisation Knowledge Network of the Commission on Social Determinants of Health. Towards health-equitable globalisation: rights, regulation and redistribution. Geneva: World Health Organization, 2007.

36. UNICEF. State of the World's Children 2007: Women and children: the double dividend of gender equality. http://www.unicef.org/sowc07/report/full_report.php. Accessed Nov 30, 2007.

37. Farmer P. Pathologies of power: rethinking health and human rights. *Am J Public Health*. 1999;89:1486–1496.

38. Sen A. Development as freedom. New York: Alfred A Knopf, Inc, 1999.

39. Moser K, Shkolnikov V, Leon DA. World mortality 1950–2000: divergence replaces convergence from the late 1980s. *Bull World Health Organ*. 2005:83:202–209.

40. Mackenbach JP, Bakker MJ. Tackling socioeconomic inequalities in health: analysis of European experiences. *Lancet*. 2003;362:1409–1414.

41. UNICEF. The 'rights' start to life. New York: United Nations Children's Fund, 2005.

The Inequality Paradox:
The Population Approach and
Vulnerable Populations

Source: Frohlich, Katherine L; and Potvin, Louise. The Inequality Pradox: The Population Approach and Vulnerable Populations. *American Journal of Public Health* 2008; 98:216-221. Reprinted with permission of the American Public Health Association.

Using the concept of vulnerable populations, we examine how disparities in health may be exacerbated by population approach interventions. We show, from an etiologic perspective, how life-course epidemiology, the concentration of risk factors, and the concept of fundamental causes of diseases may explain the differential capacity, throughout the risk-exposure distribution, to transform resources provided through population-approach interventions into health. From an intervention perspective, we argue that population-approach interventions may be compromised by inconsistencies between the social and cultural assumptions of public health practitioners and targeted groups. We propose some intervention principles to mitigate the health disparities associated with population-approach interventions. (*Am J Public Health.* 2008;98:216-221.doi:10.2105/AJPH.2007.114777)

In western societies, significant efforts during the last half century to improve health systems have resulted in spectacular gains for a wide range of health indicators.[1] A growing number of studies, however, show that these gains have not benefited everyone equally; inequalities in health seem to have increased, at least for some health outcomes.[2–4] This unexpected consequence is particularly troublesome in the case of population-level interventions, which seek to improve the health of the entire population.

We distinguish between 3 intervention approaches: the populations-at-risk approach, based on Lalonde's notion of the health field[5]; Rose's population approach,[6] which addresses the conditions shaping the distribution of individual risk in a population; and a vulnerable population approach that addresses the conditions that put social groups "at risk of risks"—that is, risks that generate exposure to other risks. By shifting the focus to whole populations, population level interventions, which are based on Geoffrey Rose's population approach, represented an advancement over a population at-risk approach.

We propose, however, that interventions based on population approaches are not free from criticism and may have led to unintended exacerbations of health disparities. Using the concept of vulnerable populations, we attempt to explain how this can be so. We begin by reviewing the notion of "populations at risk" and its relationship to Rose's population approach and then proceed with a critique of Rose's approach based on the notion of vulnerable populations. We conclude by suggesting that interventions addressing the needs of vulnerable populations should be used as a complement to population approaches.

LALONDE'S NOTION OF "POPULATIONS AT RISK"

The Lalonde Report,[5] published in Canada in 1974, constitutes a landmark in public health policy. The report was innovative in two key respects. First, it organized the understanding of the determinants of health in a new way by proposing the following 4 health fields: human biology, the social and physical environment, lifestyle, and health care organization. Second, it proposed that public health interventions should focus attention on that segment of the population with the highest level of risk exposure as indicated by health risk behaviors (e.g., smoking, alcohol consumption) or biological markers (e.g., body mass index, blood pressure). This second proposal was based on an analysis of the major causes of mortality and morbidity and the underlying reasons for their occurrence, which had been identified by large-scale longitudinal studies such as the Framingham study.[7] It is important to note that according to Lalonde, populations at risk are composed of individuals who all showed an elevated risk for some specific disease. This segment of the population is now often referred to as the upper end of the risk distribution.

Since the 1970s, however, several critiques have been launched at Lalonde's "populations-at-risk" approach. First, his profile of populations at risk was based on risk factors rooted in behaviors that he considered selfimposed, individual-level lifestyle choices. It was argued by others that the creation of targeted populations based on these criteria lead to victim blaming, thereby potentially stigmatizing these populations.[8]

In a second critique of the populations-at-risk approach, Syme noted that although interventions based on this approach might well diminish the risk profiles of those targeted by the intervention, the distribution of newly emerging risk in society remains unaffected by the intervention because it does not target change at the level of the societal forces that induce people to engage in high-risk behaviors in the first place.[9] The persistence of these forces allows the conditions for new people to enter the at-risk population to replace those who have modified their high-risk behaviors.[10] Also, in his rebuttal to high-risk approaches, Rose argued that a focus on populations at risk addresses neither the conditions influencing incidence nor the shape of each population's distribution. Rose proposed a different strategy based on the conditions that lead to the distribution of individual risk in a given population, which is now known as the population approach.

ROSE'S POPULATION APPROACH

Rose's population approach was based on two important premises: the distribution of risk exposure in a population is shaped by contextual conditions[11] and most cases in a population are represented by individuals with an average level of risk exposure.[6] To illustrate the validity of his first premise, he famously demonstrated, using multiple empirical studies, that the causes of cases (of individual-level disease) are not the same as the causes of incidence (of population-level disease). An insightful example, provided by Cronin,[12] shows that although the shape of the age distribution graph of homicides per million per annum across the lifespan of males is the same for England and Wales and for Chicago, the incidence of homicide in Chicago is 30 times higher. Thus, although the biological factors (such as age) underlying the individual cases might be the same for the two areas (the causes of cases of disease), what shapes the distributions (the causes of incidence) is different. With regard to the second premise, Rose demonstrated, again empirically, that although the excess risk for each individual at low or average risk exposure is small, so many are exposed to it that in absolute terms the effect is large. He therefore argued that focusing efforts on the entire population and not just on high-risk individuals would be most effective in diminishing negative outcomes.

Population approaches to intervention based on Rose's ideas involve mass environmental control methods and interventions that attempt to alter some of society's behavioral norms.[11] A current example includes the denormalization of smoking through public bans. An underlying assumption of Rose's approach is that, as shown in Figure 1, everyone's risk exposure in the distribution is shifted to the left (i.e., reduced) by the same amount, regardless of one's initial position in the risk exposure distribution.

Some empirical examples demonstrate that the effects of population-approach interventions have not always fulfilled Rose's expectations (Table 1). For example, among many populations exposed to population approach interventions, there is an increase in the variation in the distribution of risk, where those who were formerly at lower exposure to risk derive more benefits from the interventions than those who were formerly at greater exposure to risk. This has been signaled of late in a growing literature on the social inequalities in smoking.[16,17] As can be seen in Figure 2, the main overall effect of risk reduction in such a situation may mask a differential intervention effect on risk modified by the initial level of risk exposure. Assuming that the underlying relationship between

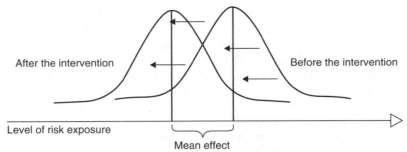

Note: Arrows indicate where the lines of the distribution would be after a population-level approach.

Figure 1 Hypothetical homogeneous effect of a population-approach intervention on the distribution of risk in a population.

Table 3	Effective Population Approach Interventions That Increased Health Disparities	
Intervention	Study	Resulting Disparity
Cervical cancer screening	Katz and Hofer 1994[13]	Women with higher incomes were more likely to be screened for cervical cancer in Ontario and the United States than those with lower incomes.
Neonatal intensive care and surfactant therapy to reduce rates of infant low birthweight	Victora et al. 2001[14]	New population-level interventions in Brazil increased inequity because they initially reached those who were already better off socioeconomically.
Health information campaigns regarding smoking	Federico et al. 2007[15]	Gaps in initiation rates among educational groups may be because of comprehensive information campaigns that were most effective among individuals with higher levels of education.

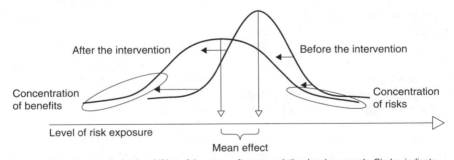

Note: Arrows depict the shifting of the curve after a population-level approach. Circles indicate where the variation in risk is most flagrant.

Figure 2 Illustration of a potential increase in the variation of risk following a population-approach intervention. Adapted from Rose.[6(p74)]

risk exposure and the probability of developing an adverse outcome is not affected by the intervention, such a situation is potentially a powerful generator of health inequalities. Although we are well aware that Rose did not target inequalities in health in his strategy, we offer what we feel is a necessary complementary position to alleviate some of the unintended consequences of this approach on inequalities in health.

THE NOTION OF VULNERABLE POPULATIONS

One of the major shortcomings of Rose's approach is that it does not address the underlying mechanisms that lead to different distributions of risk exposure between socially defined groups within populations. Rose rejected Lalonde's notion of the at-risk group as the primary target for public health interventions. We contend, however, that a focus on vulnerable populations is complementary to a population approach and necessary for addressing social inequalities in health.

The notion of vulnerable populations differs from that of populations at risk. A population at risk is defined by a higher measured exposure to a specific risk factor. All individuals in a population at risk show a higher risk exposure. A vulnerable population is a subgroup or subpopulation who, because of shared social characteristics, is at higher risk of risks. The notion of vulnerable populations refers to groups who, because of their position in the social strata, are commonly exposed to contextual conditions that distinguish them from the rest of the population. As a consequence, a vulnerable population's distribution of risk exposure has a higher mean than that of the rest of the population.

Although they partly overlap, vulnerable populations are different from populations at risk (Table 2). The former are defined by shared social characteristics, whereas the latter are characterized by a homogeneously high level of exposure to a single risk factor. The distinction between exposure to single biologically based risk factors and sharing social characteristics is key. Virtually all of the examples used by Rose to illustrate his population approach were based on risk factors for chronic disease that he explained as being largely caused by biological, genetic, or environmental factors.

What we refer to as vulnerable populations, on the other hand, are populations that share social characteristics that put them at higher risk of risks. In Canada, for example, those vulnerable populations whose mean distributions of risk exposure are significantly higher than those of the general population are people of aboriginal descent, those with an income lower than the poverty threshold, and those who have not completed secondary education.[18] Although on average people of aboriginal descent show a higher exposure to many risk factors, not everyone in this vulnerable group belongs to the high-risk population for any one risk factor.

The unintended adverse consequence for vulnerable populations of applying Rose's approach is because of, we believe, a lack of attention to what has been referred to as the "fundamental cause." According to Link and Phelan,[19,20] risk factors and their accumulation are the expression of fundamental causes linked to one's position in the social structure. These "causes" are the risks that generate exposure to other risks (e.g., low socioeconomic position, being of aboriginal descent, having a low level of education, etc.).

We argue that the fundamental cause mechanism works through two correlated pathways, the first of which relates to the life course. Kuh et al.[21] showed that a person's position in a health indicator distribution is the result of all previous experiences, including those that may not be directly related to health. Thus, for instance, not only are children who live in poor families at higher risk of conditions such as uncontrolled asthma (because of differential levels of medical care received as well as differentials in compliance), but the cumulative effect of poor health from childhood into adulthood seems to be higher for people from lower-income families.[22,23] By not considering the life trajectory of risk exposure, Rose's approach is blind to the crucial effect of the life course. The life course tells us that an individual's position in a distribution is the end product of a life trajectory. Therefore, shifting a distribution implies curbing as many life trajectories as there are individuals in the distribution. There is no reason to assume that curbing individual adverse life trajectories is the same as shifting individual positions in a risk exposure distribution.

The second pathway relates to the concentration of risk. Moderate correlations between several risk factor exposures in the general population may mask highly differentiated experiences in specific subpopulations. Indeed, exposure to multiple risk factors and a greater number of comorbidities are more frequent in some vulnerable populations (e.g., populations with low socioeconomic positions, aboriginal peoples, etc.). By focusing on single risk factors, Rose's approach cannot account for multiple risk exposure. Vulnerable populations, we argue, are those who concentrate numerous risk factors throughout their life course because of shared fundamental causes associated with their position in the social structure.

Population-approach interventions themselves seem to have abetted the augmentation of social inequalities in health through their unintended effect of concentrating risk in vulnerable populations. It appears from empirical observations that individuals from vulnerable populations are the least able to positively respond to population-approach interventions. This "inverse care law" states that those with the most resources at hand to adapt to new situations will be the first to derive maximum benefits from population-approach interventions.[14,20] Population-approach interventions may also have unfortunate effects on vulnerable populations because of incongruities in social and cultural assumptions between public health practitioners and targeted groups.[24-26] There is a growing disconnect, for example, between

Table 2	Three Different Public Health Approaches to Improving Health		
Intervention Approach	Objective	Target for Intervention	Critiques[a]
Populations at risk (Lalonde[5])	Prevent disease in those individuals at higher risk	Reduce the specific risk exposure for individuals at higher risk through behavioral (or biochemical) changes	Blames the victim; does not prevent other individuals from becoming at risk
Population approach (Rose[5])	Increase overall population health	Shift distribution of population risk exposure toward a lower mean through changes in environmental conditions that lead to increased risk	May increase health inequalities
Vulnerable populations (this essay)	Decrease health inequalities between socially defined groups	Shift to a lower level the risk exposure distribution of socially defined groups through changes in social and environmental conditions that make groups at higher risk of risks	May lead to positive discrimination; may lead to stigmatization; may be less efficient in terms of population health

[a]The critiques directed at the populations-at-risk approach are empirically documented. The critique listed for the population approach is currently being researched, and those associated with vulnerable populations are speculative.

the assumptions that tobacco control practitioners take as self-evident (e.g., the preeminent importance of health, the value of knowledge as a determinant of health)[27] and how smokers view their smoking and their health. A recent article by Bottoroff et al.,[28] for instance, explores the important role that smoking plays in reinforcing dominant ideals of masculinity for men, particularly those becoming first-time fathers.

CONCLUSION

We have explored the pathways through which the laudable public health objectives of improving the health of the overall population may lead to increasing health disparities between various social groups. That the objective of improving population health may not necessarily be compatible with the objective of reducing health disparities is becoming acknowledged in an increasing number of health policies.[29] One way to ensure that vulnerable populations are not left behind in the improvement of population health is to distinguish these objectives and design public health strategies that use both population and vulnerable population approaches to interventions. Many national jurisdictions have adopted policy recommendations that couple the reduction in health disparities with the improvement of overall population health. Such policies can be found in various reports, such as "Integrated Pan-Canadian Healthy Living Strategy,"[30] the Swedish "Health on Equal Terms Public Health Policy,"[31] and "Tackling Heath Inequalities: A Program for Action" in the United Kingdom.[32]

There remains the question of what a vulnerable population approach to intervention should look like. Although an authoritative answer is clearly outside the scope of this essay, a tentative answer would identify two characteristics for vulnerable population interventions. The first is that such interventions must be based on intersectoral approaches. Fundamental causes that create vulnerability are rooted in everyday life, and their alleviation lies mostly outside of the health sector (the prevention of illiteracy is one case in point). In such cases, the role of the health sector is not so much to invest directly in the transformation of social determinants as to take a leadership role and "engage with other sectors in health disparities' reduction."[29] The second characteristic is that such interventions should be participatory. Given that one of our critiques of population approaches is that the targeted populations often

have different concerns than those of public health promoters, an essential attribute of a vulnerable population approach would be its inclusion of members of vulnerable populations in the articulation of the problem and the development of the program and its evaluation. This is not to say that the vulnerable population approach should be the only one to involve the participation of populations, but it emphasizes that participation is a key intervention feature of this approach.[33]

Finally, no intervention approach can singly fulfill all public health goals. The more we intervene in the name of the public's health, the more we learn about the positive and adverse effects of our strategies. A vulnerable population approach to public health is no exception, and it is likely to produce unintended effects. We can only speculate about such adverse effects, as shown in Table 2. We believe, however, that the notion of vulnerability, as distinct from that of being at risk, offers a useful framework to address the question of health inequalities.

About the Authors
The authors are with the Lea Roback Centre for Research on Health Inequalities, Department of Social and Preventive Medicine, University of Montreal, and le Groupe de Recherche Interdisciplinaire en Santé, Montreal, Quebec.

Requests for reprints should be sent to Katherine L. Frohlich, PhD, CP 6128 succursale Centre-Ville, Montreal, QC, H3C 3J7, Canada (e-mail: katherine.frohlich@umontreal.ca).

This essay was accepted June 8, 2007.

Contributors
The authors were equally responsible for the conceptualization and writing of this essay.

ACKNOWLEDGMENTS
L. Potvin holds the Chair on Community Approaches and Health Inequalities funded by the Canadian Health Services Research Foundation and the Canadian Institute of Health Research (CHSRFCIHR-022605).

The authors are most grateful for insightful comments from Norman Frohlich and S. Leonard Syme.

● ● ● References
1. Detels R, Breslow L. Current scope and concerns in public health. In: Detels R, McEwen J, Beaglehole R, Tanaka H, eds. *The Scope of Public Health.* 4th ed. Oxford, England: Oxford University Press; 2002: 3–20. *Oxford Textbook of Public Health;* vol 1.
2. Goel V. Socioeconomic status and cancer incidence and survival. *Cancer Prev Control.* 1998;2:211-212.

3. Choinière R, Lafontaine P, Edwards AC. Distribution of cardiovascular disease risk factors by socioeconomic status among Canadian adults. *CMAJ.* 2001; 162:S13-S24.

4. Heymann D. Infectious agents. In: Detels R, McEwen J, Beaglehole R, Tanaka H, eds. *The Scope of Public Health.* 4th ed. Oxford, England: Oxford University Press; 2002:171-194. *Oxford Textbook of Public Health;* vol 1.

5. Lalonde M. A new perspective on the health of Canadians. 1974. Available at: http://www.hc-sc.gc.ca/hcs-sss/alt_formats/hpb-dgps/pdf/pubs/1974-lalonde/lalonde_e.pdf. Accessed October 22, 2007.

6. Rose G. *The Strategy of Preventive Medicine.* Oxford, England: Oxford University Press; 1992.

7. Dawber TR. *The Framingham Study: The Epidemiology of Atherosclerotic Disease.* Cambridge, Mass: Harvard University Press; 1980.

8. Labonté R. Death of program, birth of metaphor: the development of health promotion in Canada. In: Pederson A, O'Neill M, Rootman I, eds. *Health Promotion in Canada. Provincial, National & International Perspectives.* Toronto, Ontario: W.B. Saunders; 1994:72-90.

9. Syme SL. The social environment and health. *Daedalus.* Fall 1994:79-86.

10. McKinlay JB. The promotion of health through planned sociopolitical change: challenges for research and policy. *Soc Sci Med.* 1993;36:109-117.

11. Rose G. Sick individuals and sick populations. *Int J Epidemiol.* 1985;14:32-38.

12 Cronin H. *The Ant and the Peacock.* Cambridge, England: Cambridge University Press; 1991.

13. Katz SJ, Hofer TP. Socioeconomic disparities in preventive care persist despite universal coverage: breast and cervical cancer screening in Ontario and the United Kingdom. *JAMA.* 1994; 272:530-534.

14. Victora CG, Barros FC, Vaughan JP. The impact of health interventions on inequalities: infant and child health in Brazil. In: Leon D, Walt G, eds. Poverty, Inequality and Health. Oxford, England: Oxford University Press; 2001:125-136.

15. Federico B, Costa G, Kunst AE. Educational inequalities in initiation, cessation, and prevalence of smoking among 3 Italian birth cohorts. Am J Public Health. 2007;97:838-845.

16. Barbeau EM, Krieger N, Soobader MJ. Working class matters: socioeconomic disadvantage, race/ethnicity, gender, and smoking in NHIS 2000. *Am J Public Health.* 2004;94:269-278.

17. The National Strategy: Moving Forward. The 2005 Progress Report on Tobacco Control. Prepared by the Tobacco Control Liaison Committee of the Federal-Provincial Territorial Advisory Committee on Population Health and Health Security in collaboration with non-governmental organizations, 2005. Available at: http://www.hc-sc.gc.ca/hl-vs/alt_formats/hecs-sesc/pdf/pubs/tobac-tabac/foward-avant/foward-avant_e.pdf. Accessed October 22, 2007.

18. Frohlich KL, Ross N, Richmond C. Health disparities in Canada today: evidence and pathways. *Health Policy.* 2006;79:132-143.

19. Link BG, Phelan J. Social conditions as fundamental causes of diseases. *J Health Soc Behav.* 1995;(spec no.):80-94.

20. Phelan J, Link B. Controlling disease and creating disparities: a fundamental cause perspective. *J Gerontol B Psychol Sci Soc Sci.* 2005;60(spec no.): 27-33.

21. Kuh D, Power C, Blane D, Bartley M. Social pathways between childhood and adult health. In: Kuh D, Ben-Shlomo Y, eds. *A Life Course Approach to Chronic Disease Epidemiology.* Oxford, England: Oxford University Press; 1997:169-198.

22. Kuh D, Ben-Shlomo Y, eds. *A Life Course Approach to Chronic Disease Epidemiology.* Oxford, England: Oxford University Press; 1997.

23. Power C, Matthews S. Origins of health inequalities in a national population sample. *Lancet.* 1997;350: 1584-1589.

24. Laurier E, McKie L, Goodwin N. Daily and life-course contexts of smoking. *Sociol Health Illn.* 2000;22:289-309.

25. Krumeich A, Weijts W, Reddy P, Meijer-Weitz A. The benefits of anthropological approaches for health promotion research and practice. *Health Educ Res.* 2001;16:121-130.

26. Garcia A. Is health promotion relevant across cultures and the socioeconomic spectrum? *Fam Community Health.* 2005;29:20S-27S.

27. Caplan R. The importance of social theory for health promotion: from description to reflexivity. *Health Promot Int.* 1993;8:147-157.

28. Bottoroff JL, Oliffe J, Kalaw C, Carey C, Mroz L. Men's constructions of smoking in the context of women's tobacco reduction during pregnancy and postpartum. *Soc Sci Med.* 2006;62:3096-3108.

29. Health Disparities Task Group of the Federal/Provincial/Territorial Advisory Committee on Population Health and Health Security. *Reducing Health Disparities-Roles of the Health Sector.* Discussion paper, 2005. Available at: http://www.phac-aspc.gc.ca/ph-sp/disparities/pdf06/disparities_recommended_policy.pdf. Accessed January 4, 2008.

30. Secretariat for the Healthy Living Network. The integrated pan-Canadian healthy living strategy, 2005. Available at: http://www.phac-aspc.gc.ca/hl-vsstrat/pdf/hls_e.pdf. Accessed October 18, 2007.

31. Hogstedt C, Lundgren B, Moberg H, Pettersson B, Ágren G. Forward. *Scand J Public Health.* 2004;32:3.

32. *Tackling Health Inequalities: A Program for Action.* London, England: UK Department of Health; 2003.

33. Potvin L. Managing uncertainty through participation. In: McQueen DM, Kickbusch I, Potvin L, Pelikan JM, Balbo L, Abel T, eds. *Health & Modernity: The Role of Theory in Health Promotion.* New York, NY: Springer; 2007:103-128.

Beyond Health Care: New Directions to a Healthier America

Source: Robert Wood Johnson Foundation Commission to Build a Healthier America. Beyond health care: New directions to a healthier America. New York: Author. Copyright 2009 Robert Wood Johnson Foundation Commission to Build a Healthier America, pp.1-14. Courtesy of Robert Wood Johnson Foundation.

Shortfalls in health take years off the lives of Americans and subject us to often-avoidable suffering. As co-chairs of the *Robert Wood Johnson Foundation Commission to Build a Healthier America*, we have been charged to identify knowledge-based actions—both short- and long-term that are outside the medical care system—for reducing and, ultimately, eliminating those shortfalls.

That is an urgent charge, one that each of us on this Commission has taken with utmost seriousness.

The Commission is a national, independent and nonpartisan body comprising innovators and leaders who, together, represent a rich diversity of experience and tremendous depth of knowledge. As a group, we have sought to go beyond traditional definitions of health to identify promising and important policies and programs that can help each person and each family live a healthier life. Supporting us in this endeavor have been our research partners at the Center on Social Disparities in Health at the University of California, San Francisco, the Commission staff at The George Washington University

School of Public Health and Health Services and Commission Staff Director David R. Williams, Harvard School of Public Health.

This past year, we have explored and shed misconceptions about the state of our nation's health and taken a broader look at how health is shaped by how and where we live our lives. Our journey has led us to many places and discoveries across America—from North Carolina to Philadelphia to Denver to Tennessee, from school playgrounds to farmers' markets to workplaces.

Despite the economic challenges we face as a nation, across America, we have found good news: solutions are in plain sight and stakeholders are coming together to improve health and remove the obstacles that prevent people in particularly stressed circumstances and communities from making healthy choices. These pockets of success provide evidence that improving health and reducing disparities are within our reach. They energize us and give us hope, but they also show us how far we have to go. The scattered examples tell us we are far from incorporating health into all aspects of our society and our communities. This is something we must do, and do together, because the stakes for our nation and especially for our children are too high not to act. It will take all of us working together to create and nurture a culture of health, where we each take responsibility for improving our own health and building the kind of society that supports and enables all of us to live healthy lives.

Because Americans can't afford to wait, we hope that the findings and recommendations offered here spark a national conversation about committing to health and wellness for everyone—and then move us to collaborative action. The health of our nation depends on improving the health of *every* American.

Mark McClellan, M.D., Ph.D.

Alice M. Rivlin, Ph.D.

Co-Chair Co-Chair

RECOMMENDATIONS FROM THE ROBERT WOOD JOHNSON FOUNDATION COMMISSION TO BUILD A HEALTHIER AMERICA

Given the seriousness of our nation's economic condition, we chose our recommendations with particular care, focusing on those with the strongest potential to leverage limited resources and optimize the impact of federal investments. Commissioners studied and debated several options and crafted recommendations that:

- address the Commission's charge to identify interventions beyond the health care system that can produce substantial health effects;
- are likely to achieve a significant positive impact on Americans' health;
- address the needs of those who are most at risk or most vulnerable;
- are feasible and achievable in the current economic environment; and
- are supported by a strong knowledge base.

We found the strongest evidence for interventions that can have a lasting effect on the quality of health and life in programs that promote early childhood development and that support children and families. Therefore, many of our recommendations aim to ensure that our children have the best start in life and health. Along with social advantage and disadvantage, health is often passed across generations. Strategies for giving children a healthy start will help ensure future generations of healthy adults. This is indeed a wise long-term investment of scarce resources.

EXECUTIVE SUMMARY

For the first time in our history, the United States is raising a generation of children who may live sicker, shorter lives than their parents. We must act now to reverse this trend.

Why aren't Americans among the healthiest people in the world? Why are some Americans so much healthier than others? What can be done to create opportunities for all Americans to live long and healthy lives?

These questions prompted the Robert Wood Johnson Foundation in 2008 to establish the Commission to Build a Healthier America, enlisting national leaders in business, labor, education, community development, health care services, philanthropy, media and research and public policy to find solutions *outside* of the medical care system for advancing the nation's health. This Executive Summary describes the context for the Commission's work and recommendations for moving forward to improve America's health, for harnessing forces across many sectors and for prompting action.

AMERICANS ARE NOT AS HEALTHY AS WE COULD AND SHOULD BE

Despite Spending More on Medical Care Than Any Other Nation

A nation's health is its most precious asset. Yet there are tremendous gaps between how healthy Americans are and how healthy we could be. At every income and education level, Americans should be healthier. Many people with middle-class incomes and education die prematurely from preventable health problems. And for those with more limited incomes and education, health outcomes are far worse. Diabetes is twice as common and heart disease rates are 50 percent higher among poor adults when compared with those in the highest income group. An obesity epidemic threatens our children's future health and the number of uninsured and underinsured Americans continues to climb.

Despite breakthroughs in medical science and a $1 trillion increase in annual health care spending over the past decade, America is losing ground relative to other countries when it comes to health. Astronomical medical bills strain family and government budgets and threaten America's global competitiveness. Health care spending consumes about 16 percent of the U.S. gross domestic product (GDP), much more than in any other industrialized nation, and is expected to climb to over 20 percent of GDP by 2018. The costs of medical care and insurance are now out of reach for many American households, pushing some families into bankruptcy, draining businesses, reducing employment and severely straining public budgets.

More health care spending will not solve our health problems. Even with technologically advanced care for conditions such as preterm births, diabetic complications and heart disease, we cannot expect this care to close the global health gap. Infant mortality and life expectancy rates in the United States lag behind most of Europe, Japan, Canada and Australia and in the last two decades, U.S. rankings have fallen lower on the scale relative to other nations, despite our rapid increases in spending. In 1980, the United States ranked 18th in infant mortality rates among industrialized nations. By 2002, 24 industrialized nations—including Korea, Hungary, the Czech Republic and Greece—had lower infant mortality rates than the United States. Meanwhile, the United States slipped from 14th among industrialized countries in life expectancy at birth in 1980 to 23rd by 2004. We need to look beyond medical care to other factors that can improve America's health.

HEALTH IS MORE THAN HEALTH CARE

And Some Americans Face Much Poorer Prospects for Good Health and Long Life Than Others

Although medical care is essential for relieving suffering and curing illness, only an estimated 10 to 15 percent of preventable mortality has been attributed to medical care. A person's health and likelihood of becoming sick and dying prematurely are greatly influenced by powerful social factors such as education and income and the quality of neighborhood environments. These *social determinants* of health can have profound effects. For example:

- American college graduates can expect to live at least five years longer than Americans who have not completed high school.

- Poor Americans are more than three times as likely as Americans with upper middle-class incomes to suffer physical limitations from a chronic illness.

- Upper middle-class Americans can expect to live more than six years longer than poor Americans.

- People with middle incomes are less healthy and can expect to live shorter lives than those with higher incomes—even when they are insured.

This shouldn't be the case in a nation whose highest ideals and values are based on fairness and equality of opportunity.

Where people live, learn, work and play affects how long and how well they live—to a greater extent than most of us realize. What constitutes health includes the effects of our daily lives—how our children grow up, the food we eat, how physically active we are, the extent to which we engage in risky behaviors like smoking and our exposure to physical risks and harmful substances—as well as the neighborhoods and environments in which we live. We must identify where people can make improvements in their own health and where society needs to lend a helping hand.

WE MUST OVERCOME OBSTACLES AND IMPROVE OPPORTUNITIES FOR ALL AMERICANS TO MAKE HEALTHY CHOICES

Assuming responsibility for one's health may appear straightforward. But our society's institutions, from government to business to not-for-profits, must provide support to bring healthy choices within everyone's reach. Our society's leaders and major institutions can create incentives and lower barriers so that individuals and families can take steps to achieve better health. These are not necessarily easy steps for everyone to take. For many Americans, they may be quite difficult.

Many people live and work in circumstances and places that make healthy living nearly impossible. Many children do not get the quality of care and support they need and grow up to be less healthy as a result; many Americans do not have access to grocery stores that sell nutritious food; still others live in communities that are unsafe or in disrepair, making

---

Good Health Requires Personal Responsibility

Good health depends on personal choice and responsibility. No government or private program can take the place of people making healthy choices for themselves or their families. To build a healthier nation each of us must make a commitment to:

- eat a healthy diet;
- include physical activity as a part of daily life;
- avoid risky behaviors including smoking, excessive drinking, misusing medications and abusing illegal substances;
- avoid health and safety hazards at home and at work; and
- provide safe, nurturing and stimulating environments for infants and children.

it difficult or risky to exercise. While individuals must make a commitment to their own health, our society must improve the opportunities to choose healthful behaviors, especially for those who face the greatest obstacles.

For example, members of disadvantaged racial and ethnic groups are more likely to live in poor neighborhoods. The characteristics of such neighborhoods—factors like limited access to nutritious food; living near toxic wastes, abandoned or deteriorating factories, freeway noise and fumes; and exposure to crime and violence and other hazards—increase the chances of serious health problems. All of these factors that increase illness or risk of injury are more common in the daily lives of our nation's poor and minority families.

Living in health-damaging situations often means that individuals and families don't have healthy choices they can afford to make. Protecting and preserving good health will mean focusing on communities and people, how and where they work, where their children learn; fixing what impairs our health and strengthening what improves it. The road to a healthier nation requires us all to understand that this is about everyone, rich and poor, minority and majority, rural and urban. We cannot improve our health as a nation if we continue to leave so many far behind.

THE CHARGE TO THE COMMISSION

The Robert Wood Johnson Foundation asked the Commission to Build a Healthier America to identify practical, feasible ways to reduce barriers to good health and promote and facilitate healthy choices by individuals, for themselves and their families. The Foundation charged the Commission with three tasks:

- Raise awareness among policy-makers and the public about the substantial shortfalls in health experienced by many Americans.

- Identify interventions beyond clinical services that demonstrate promise for improving overall health and reducing disparities.

- Recommend to the Foundation and the nation's leaders key actions outside medical care that communities, businesses, unions, philanthropies, faith-based organizations, civic groups, local governments, the states and the federal government can take to create greater opportunities for long and healthy lives for all Americans.

Commissioners solicited advice and information from experts, innovators, stakeholders and the public through activities including field hearings, public testimony, roundtable discussions, experts' meetings and fact-finding site visits. Commissioners and staff met and consulted with elected and executive agency officials, representatives of business, advocacy, professional and policy organizations and the public. Through a portal on its Web site at *commissionon health.org*, the Commission solicited information about successful interventions.

The Commission reached consensus on findings and recommendations through a series of meetings, monthly teleconferences and one-on-one discussions among Commissioners and with senior Commission and Foundation staff.

WHAT WE LEARNED

Although accessible, high-quality medical care is crucial, a healthy America cannot be achieved solely through the health care system. The solutions to our health problems lie not principally in hospitals and doctors' offices but in our homes, our schools, our workplaces, our playgrounds and parks, our grocery stores, sidewalks and streets, in the air we breathe and the water we drink.

Ultimately, the responsibility for healthy behaviors rests with each of us. Too many Americans, however, face daunting obstacles to healthy choices. Achieving a healthy America for everyone, therefore, will require *both* personal responsibility and policies and programs that break down barriers to good health, particularly for those who face the greatest obstacles.

The Commission identified a range of successful ways to improve health at the local, state and federal levels—practical, feasible and effective solutions often hiding in plain sight. But too often, they exist in isolation—too scattered to have a broad effect on the health of a community at large. To be fully effective, these programs need greater scale and geographic spread.

Still, these promising programs, policies and initiatives—and their successes—provide both hope and direction. Across populations and geographic regions, the Commission saw more similarities than differences. Commonalities among programs that work include collaboration, flexibility, leadership and continuity in funding. Repeatedly, we heard testimony that continuity of funding is a chronic problem. Too often, while start-up funds are provided to establish programs, funders move on to other issues once programs are underway. The value of collaboration to create a broader base of support is a key theme of this report and a necessity if successful programs are to expand across sectors and across the nation.

We recognize that a one-size-fits-all approach will not work to improve the health of all Americans. Rather, removing barriers to health and creating opportunities to promote more healthful behaviors must involve pursuing multiple strategies and adopting promising approaches across diverse settings. Federal intervention is not sufficient to produce and sustain the changes that need to be made in our society; national leadership and public/private collaboration are needed at the local, state and national levels. We must also develop standards of accountability for programs aimed at improving health and measure progress toward our goals. As a nation we simply cannot afford to invest in programs that do not perform well and do not meet standards that should be demanded by taxpayers, funders and beneficiaries.

We were particularly impressed by the strong evidence and testimony across cities and regions about the need—and many opportunities—for intervening on behalf of our children in the first stages of life, when the foundation for health is being established. We found promising ways to build that foundation that cut across multiple sectors. Many of our recommendations address how to improve children's health-and thus their future health as adults.

Finally, we recognize that *income* and *education* are two of the most critical factors for enabling improvements in health and reducing health disparities. Given the short tenure of the Commission and our charge to issue recommendations that can have a direct, positive effect on health in years, not decades, we do not make specific recommendations to address persistent poverty and lack of education in our nation. But until we reduce poverty, particularly child poverty, and improve overall educational attainment and quality, America cannot and will not be as healthy as it should be.

CREATING A NATIONAL CULTURE OF HEALTH

Achieving better health requires action both by individuals and by society. If society supports and enables healthier choices—and individuals make them—we can achieve large improvements in our nation's health. Too often, we focus on how medical care can make us healthier, but health care alone isn't sufficient. We need to cultivate a national culture infused with health and wellness—among individuals and families and in communities, schools and workplaces. Just as America has "greened" in response to global warming, we can and must integrate healthier decisions in all we do.

A CALL FOR COLLABORATION

Building a healthier nation will require substantial collaboration among leaders across all sectors, including some—for example, leaders in child care, education, housing, urban planning and transportation—who may not fully comprehend the importance of their roles in improving health. This Commission challenges individuals, communities, employers and unions, the business community, media, faith leaders and congregants, philanthropy and government officials at all levels to work together on promising strategies and solutions:

Community-based groups can adopt a "health lens" to view their communities by:

- establishing farmers' markets and advocating for local supermarkets where none exist;
- ensuring streets are pedestrian- and bike-safe, and advocating for cross walks, bike paths, sidewalks and security lighting; and
- assessing and remediating hazardous conditions in housing.

Schools can provide a quality education to give students the best opportunity to achieve good health throughout life; promote healthy personal choices by students; and provide a safe and healthy physical and social environment by:

- ensuring all school lunch and breakfast offerings meet the most current U.S. dietary guidelines; removing all junk food from cafeterias, vending machines and canteens; and
- making daily physical activity one of the highest priorities.

Businesses and employers can exercise local leadership and promote employee health by:

- making a visible commitment to increase physical activity at work;
- selecting health plans that include wellness benefits; and
- implementing a comprehensive smoke-free workplace policy and offering proven tobacco-use treatment to smokers.

Health care providers, particularly those whose patients have lower incomes or live in disadvantaged communities, can help connect patients with community services and resources.

Governments at all levels can provide incentives; seed assessments and plans; fund research and evaluations to identify effective approaches to improving health; and provide the foundation for collaborative efforts.

Local and state governments can lead by:

- making early child development services a highest priority;
- offering financial incentives for grocery stores to locate in underserved neighborhoods;
- incorporating health-conscious designs into building codes and zoning;
- adopting state-wide smoke-free workplace and public spaces laws.

The federal government can lead by:

- ensuring that the early developmental needs of children in low-income families are met;
- fully funding WIC and SNAP and ensuring that these programs are designed to support the needs of hungry families with nutritious food; and
- funding research and evaluation of effective non-medical and community-based interventions in all sectors that influence health; holding programs that receive federal support accountable for achieving results.

Philanthropies can lead by:

- supporting initiatives in disadvantaged communities that create opportunities for healthy living and healthy choices; and
- identifying, supporting and championing innovative models of community building and design; joining with federal and state agencies and businesses as partners in supporting and rigorously evaluating place-based, multisector demonstrations.

We strongly support a realignment of existing and new private and public resources to support improved health for all Americans. This will require a concerted focus on achieving the most rapid progress among those who are farthest behind on the road to optimal health. Together, we can and must achieve a healthy America for all.

16

Medical Interventions

Performance improvement of health care delivery has gained much importance in recent years. It is a critical issue for every country. It is also a challenging area because performance improvement requires grappling with difficult questions. The OECD initiated the Health Project in 2001 to address some of the key challenges faced by the health systems of various countries. Some of the key issues are: What can be done to ensure that spending on health is affordable today and sustainable tomorrow? What is needed to improve the quality and safety of health care, and to ensure that health systems are responsive to the needs of patients and other stakeholders? How should equitable and timely access to necessary care be supported? And, perhaps the most challenging question of all: what can be done to increase value for money? (OECD 2004). In the United States, the Institute of Medicine (IOM) has taken the lead by identifying key areas of deficiency in the U.S. health care delivery system. The IOM published several reports, two of which—the 1999 report, *To Err is Human: Building a Safer Health System* and the 2001 report, *Crossing the Quality Chasm: A New Health System for the 21st Century*—gained wide attention.

Recommendations in the first report are directed mainly at health care organizations, health care professionals, professional licensure boards, regulators, accrediting agencies, and professional societies. The report's recommendations include establishing a mandatory system for reporting errors and adverse events, organizing a national quality forum, requiring states to establish reporting systems, encouraging regulatory and accreditation organizations to require patient safety programs, requiring licensing bodies to implement re-examination and re-licensure of professionals, and incorporating patient safety into clinical practice guidelines. The National Quality Forum (NQF)—a private, nonprofit organization founded in 1999—aims to improve the quality of health care for all Americans. Its three-part mission includes setting national priorities and goals for performance improvement, endorsing national consensus standards for measuring and publicly reporting on performance, and promoting the attainment of national goals through education and outreach programs. NQF's membership includes a wide variety of health care stakeholders, including consumer organizations, public and private purchasers, physicians, nurses, hospitals, accrediting and certifying bodies, supporting industries, and health care research and quality improvement organizations (NQF 2010). The second IOM report identifies gaps in the delivery of health care. It calls for leadership in health care organizations that would facilitate change and foster and reward improvement. Its recommendations include preparing the workforce for a world of expanding knowledge and rapid change. The report recommends the creation of an information infrastructure to support evidenced-based decision-making by members of the health care delivery team. The report articulates six aims for improvement that include making the system safe, avoiding injury, delivering services that are based on scientific knowledge and are patient centered, delivering services in a timely manner, delivering services efficiently, and delivering services in an equitable manner. In December 2002, the Hospital Quality Alliance (HQA) was created. The HQA is a national public-private collaboration whose mission is to develop and implement measures that would improve the quality of care in hospitals and to make information about hospital performance available to the public.

In 2005, the Centers for Medicare and Medicaid Services (CMS) began requiring hospitals to report certain quality measures for public disclosure. In collaboration with other stakeholders, the CMS developed a tool called Hospital Compare which contains information on how well hospitals care for patients with certain medical conditions or surgical procedures, and the results from a survey of patients about the quality of care they received during a recent hospital stay. This information is intended to help consumers make better choices by comparing the quality of care hospitals provide. In 2008, this initiative was expanded to link payments for health care services to quality of care. Under the Hospital-Acquired Conditions initiative, Medicare no longer pays hospitals at a higher rate when a patient acquires a preventable condition while in the hospital and increased costs are incurred as a result of the preventable condition.

Interventions needed to improve health care delivery include a focus on improving health outcomes for people over the course of their lives through better organization and coordination. Programs designed to manage patient conditions over time are more effective than short-term interventions. There is a need to link patients, care teams, and information together; and at the same time, to redesign processes that deliver safer and more reliable care (Commonwealth Fund 2006). The provision of evidence-based care is still remarkably uneven

(McGlynn et al. 2003). Furthermore, there are dramatic differences in spending across both regions and hospitals which have highlighted the need to improve efficiency by providing better care at lower cost (Fisher et al. 2009). A variety of approaches will be needed to realize these seemingly conflicting goals. One such intervention is through innovations that use less costly personnel, materials, and facilities, and that permit patients to do for themselves some of what has been done to them. Recent examples of this approach include generic drugs, self-administered tests for pregnancy and urinary tract infection, diagnostic kits that measure blood glucose levels, and remote monitoring technology that transmits information from the home to the clinic (Robinson & Smith 2008). Evidence also suggests that disease management (DM) can improve quality of care, and at least some DM programs have the potential to decrease costs as well. DM programs are typically designed to ensure that (1) preventive measures are taken when appropriate (e.g., screening tests) and (2) complications that could result in costly hospitalizations or emergency room visits are avoided. Providing better communications, management, and follow-up for certain patients has the potential to improve patient health and reduce overall costs by reducing hospital stays and emergency room visits, and by changing other aspects of utilization (McKethan et al. 2009).

The success of various interventions to improve health will be realized only if the patient becomes one of the central players in health care. Partnerships between patients, physicians and other providers are essential.

The first reading for this chapter, **10 Years, 5 Voices, 1 Challenge**, expresses the views of five prominent health care leaders to assess the impact of IOM's report, *To Err is Human: Building a Safer Health System*, up to now and what should be done next. Above all else, the report created enhanced awareness of how unsafe the care environment really was. It then triggered a sense of momentum that did not exist before. This has led to tangible changes in the culture of organizations. Some organizations have made extraordinary progress in embracing patient safety, but others are just starting the journey. Successful organizations have used strategies that employ the use of data, accountability to data, and transparency. Transparency must include public reports on individual institutions that show adverse events, why they happened, and what has been done to keep them from happening again. The Hospital Compare data show that an increasing number of hospitals are demonstrating 90% plus compliance with national standards of care; but there is a need to validate standardized data reporting. We are moving in the right direction, but not fast enough. Additional progress can be made with more pressure from payers and regulators. Financial incentives are necessary to curtail wasteful care.

Physician performance measurement should be regarded as a public good because its implications extend to the population as a whole. In **Physician Performance Measurement: A Key to Higher Quality and Lower Cost Growth or a Lost Opportunity?** Draper concludes that physician performance measurement offers tremendous promise to improve the quality and efficiency of care. To accomplish this goal, however, certain challenges need to be overcome. (1) Medical record review provides data that are more reliable than claims or administrative data that are commonly used by health plans, but they are also more expensive to collect. (2) More often than not performance assessment is not based on standardized measures and other methodological issues persist. (3) Proprietary rather than uniform approaches to assess quality and cost make the results uncomparable between plans. (4) Measurement alone is not likely to improve performance unless it is accompanied by support to improve performance and rewards to encourage and reinforce desired behaviors.

In **Hospital Strategies to Engage Physicians in Quality Improvement,** Liebhaber and colleagues report on several strategies that hospitals are using to engage physicians in their quality improvement (QI) programs. For various reasons, hospital employment is becoming a better fit for both physicians and hospitals than the traditional voluntary medical staff model. Economic incentives built around a shared quality agenda can improve physicians' participation in QI. Physicians are likely to respond to reliable data that are useful in making decisions. Another approach is to assign hospital staff to serve as project managers for physician-led QI projects. Involvement of the governing board and the CEO in the hospital's QI agenda sends a positive message to motivate physicians. Hospitals need to nurture and support physician leaders who are also highly respected clinicians. These physician champions can make some difference in seeking participation from a larger number of physicians in QI activities; only a small fraction of the medical staff is generally engaged in QI.

Finally, through education and communication, physicians need to understand that QI is not a regulatory or administrative exercise, and that it results in better patient outcomes.

The final reading, **Navigating Health Care: Why It's So Hard and What Can Be Done to Make It Easier for the Average Consumer,** is based on the premise that a broader understanding of patients' experiences, as they move through the multiple parts of the health care system to gain access and use services, will help inform potential solutions. Vulnerable populations can particularly fall victim to poorly navigated health care. Both consumers and payers pay the price when care is not well coordinated. Some models of care coordination have been proposed but not adequately evaluated. Other issues of navigation are associated with how best to use the benefits that are available in an individual's health plan, and how to choose the best health care providers that are covered under the plan. Learning about one's illness, treatment options, and managing one's health present challenges for many people. Research needs to demonstrate the effectiveness of various types of coordination mechanisms currently in use.

● ● ● **References**

Commonwealth Fund. 2006. *Why Not the Best? Results From a National Scorecard on U.S. Health System Performance.* New York: The Commonwealth Fund.

Fisher, E.S. et al. 2009. Fostering accountable health care: Moving forward in Medicare. *Health Affairs— Web Exclusive* 28 (supplement 1): w219–w231.

McGlynn, E.A. et al. 2003. The quality of health care delivered to adults in the United States. *New England Journal of Medicine* 348 (26): 2635–2645.

McKethan, A. et al. 2009. *Improving Quality and Value in the U.S. Health Care System.* Washington, DC: Bipartisan Policy Center.

National Quality Forum (NFQ). 2010. *About NFQ.* Retrieved February 2010 from http://www.quality forum.org/About_NQF/About_NQF.aspx

OECD. 2004. *Towards High-Performing Health Systems: Summary Report.* Paris: Organisation for Economic Cooperation and Development.

Robinson, J.C. and M.D. Smith. 2008. Cost-reducing innovation in health care. *Health Affairs* 27 (5): 1353–1356.

1

---

10 years, 5 Voices, 1 Challenge

Source: Reprinted from *Hospitals & Health Network,* by permission, October 2009, Copyright 2009, by Health Forum, Inc.

To Err Is Human jump-started a movement to improve patient safety. How far have we come? Where do we go from here?

A decade ago, the prestigious Institute of Medicine shocked the nation by highlighting studies suggesting that medical errors kill up to 98,000 patients in American hospitals every year. To address the problem, the 1999 report *To Err Is Human: Building a Safer Health System* made recommendations in four areas: create leadership, research, tools and protocols to enhance knowledge of safety issues; identify and learn from errors by creating nationwide mandatory and voluntary error reporting systems; raise safety standards through actions by oversight organizations, professional groups and health care purchasers; and implement safety systems in health care organizations to enhance safe practice at the delivery level. *Hospitals & Health Networks* asked five prominent health care leaders representing a variety of stakeholders, from providers to payers to patients, to assess the report's impact up to now and where patient safety efforts should focus next.

CONSISTENTLY ADVANCING QUALITY REQUIRES TRANSPARENCY, CLARITY OF PURPOSE

James B. Conway, *senior vice president, Institute for Healthcare Improvement. Shortly after Boston Globe reporter Betsy Lehman died from a medical error at Boston's Dana-Farber Cancer Institute in 1994, Conway took over as chief operating officer and led an institution-wide effort to improve care quality and patient safety. He also took part in the first national meeting on patient safety that led to the formation of the National Patient Safety Foundation in 1996.*

A lot of work was done leading up to the IOM report. By 1999, Dana-Farber and other organizations began to learn what the unique properties of organizations were that enabled them to achieve dramatically higher levels of quality and safety. No one from Dana-Farber was on the IOM report committee, but what we learned was a fundamental part of the report.

I think most people did not anticipate the extraordinary press coverage the report received. President Clinton embraced it and kicked off an effort to address the problem with the Quality Interagency Coordination Task Force. The effort to evaluate and respond to the IOM report findings across all federal agencies was led by Health & Human Services Secretary Donna Shalala. We were pleasantly surprised.

But the question remains: Are we safer? The answer is, "Yes in many places more of the time." It is very hard to say if we are safer nationally. Some organizations have made extraordinary progress while others are just starting the journey.

One thing we have learned is it is hard to have safety where you don't have transparency. As IHI looks at hospitals and communities where there is the greatest improvement, one thing we consistently find is data, accountability to data and transparency.

We have really struggled with transparency. Data inputs and outputs vary dramatically by state. Most of what is collected is reported in aggregate, if at all. It is not possible to assess the performance of individual institutions. The emphasis is more on protecting organizations than protecting patients.

In Massachusetts, we had two systems: a confidential report to the state used for informing and learning and a public report of aggregate data. This year we started public reports by institution showing what their events were, why they happened and what the organization has done to keep them from happening again.

We were able to close the information circle in Massachusetts because of health system reform. We now have business and consumer representatives on the state quality and cost council that sets health policy. When you ask them if you need to report incidents by organization they say sure, why not? When you change who is sitting at the table you get different outcomes.

The question for national reform is: Are we going to reshape the health care system or just tinker with payment mechanisms?

I frankly believe we have had too much "democracy" and not enough clarity of purpose. We have to decide to create a system that safely and reliably provides high quality care 100 percent of the time, set a date to achieve it and hold ourselves to it. It's complicated but it is absolutely doable. But we have to decide to do it.

HOSPITALS HAVE ADOPTED AND CONTINUE TO BUILD A CULTURE OF QUALITY

Rich Umbdenstock, *president and CEO, American Hospital Association. In 1999 Umbdenstock was CEO of Providence Health & Services, then a nine-hospital system serving eastern Washington state and Montana. He joined the AHA board in November 1999, about the time the IOM report was released.*

Everyone wants to see care improved locally and nationally. There is a lot of difference of opinion on how to do it and the obstacles. But there is no opposition to the consensus that improvement is needed. The IOM report created a sense of momentum that we didn't have before.

Significant progress has been made. Fundamentally what changed is the willingness to recognize the challenge and not argue about the numbers, but appreciate that care must be safe for each patient. This has led to palpable changes in the culture of organizations. Mistakes are no longer seen as inevitable, but as something that can be actively worked on and prevented.

Not every organization is as far along as others. But in our own work with the Quest for Quality Prize we have found an incredible amount of positive change. The Hospital Compare data show that more hospitals follow nationally agreed upon care steps. An ever-increasing number are demonstrating 90 percent-plus compliance with 90 percent-plus patients. But we can improve on that and there are some areas where we need to start from the beginning. We are constantly seeing new challenges, such as drug-resistant bacteria and more immune-compromised patients, which require new approaches. Quality is a moving target.

Hospitals have been strong advocates of public reporting. At the national level, the AHA is one of the founding entities of the Hospital Quality Alliance. Acute care hospitals are leaders in reporting quality and patient satisfaction at the state level. About 40 states report not just quality measures, but also financial measures. We have been strong supporters of reporting sentinel events and have learned a lot from the reports and related root cause analyses. We are seeing hospitals learn from unfortunate events elsewhere and prevent them from happening locally.

One challenge is the huge number of reporting measures requested not only by Medicare and other federal agencies, but by state agencies and private-sector payers and business coalitions. The volume of requests and different measures sometimes work against improvement because they consume financial and clinical resources that could be used to improve care. We are not seeing much progress on standardizing clinical measures, though everyone agrees these measures should be individually vetted and the National Quality Forum is the group to do it.

We want reform to build on the momentum that exists. We have substantial partnerships in the NQF and HQA that we should build on rather than replace with something that excludes the work and commitment of the private sector. We want changes that enable greater integration and coordination among providers. We need to remove some legal barriers, such as the Stark law, that were set up to deal with abuses but have had the unintended consequence of keeping the system fragmented. We want to see payment reforms that reward quality and care coordination. We are very much in favor of demonstration projects and private initiatives to understand how to do this while preventing unintended adverse consequences.

EXPERIENCE HAS DEEPENED UNDERSTANDING OF QUALITY ISSUES, BUT OVERALL PROGRESS IS SLOW

Janet Corrigan, *president and CEO, National Quality Forum. As a senior board director at the Institute of Medicine, Corrigan directed the Quality of Care in America initiative that produced* To Err Is Human *and* Crossing the Quality Chasm.

In many ways, the greatest significance of this report is the enhanced awareness of how unsafe the care environment really is. That is a necessary prerequisite for improvement. A good deal of the public today is aware that there are safety issues. It also unleashed a lot of improvement initiatives among health care professionals, hospitals and nursing homes.

Over the last decade, we have gained a deeper understanding of how complex the issues are. It is hard to change the culture of an institution. Many forces work against transparency and continuous quality improvement. It takes time and leadership and you have to stick with it.

Making significant improvements requires an overhaul of the delivery system. We can't get there without sizable investments in information technology to create a complete electronic health record and access to it. You need strong organizational support, a team with good communication, a common treatment plan, a variety of decision support tools, and a way to engage family members and caregivers as part of the team.

It will require changing the payment system. Current systems don't reward investments in safety as they should. We are just now starting to see efforts to reward safety and penalize unsafe environments by withholding payments for preventable events.

We have not made enough progress on transparency. I applaud states that have established reporting systems, but we need a nationwide system. The IOM recommended two types of reports; mandatory reports for the small fraction of events resulting in death or serious harm to patients, and voluntary reports focusing on errors that result in minor or temporary harm or near-misses. The voluntary reporting system should provide protection from legal discovery to create a learning environment in which providers would not have reservations about coming forward.

In both cases we have fallen short. Mandatory reporting is required in some states but not all. Health care is the only part of our society in which someone can die and there is no investigation. I continue to think it is critical that we have public reporting on a variety of safety measures including health care-acquired infections.

However, progress has been made, and many examples go beyond individual hospitals. In Michigan, more than 100 hospitals reduced catheter-related bloodstream infections that saved an estimated 1,500 lives and $100 million over 18 months. Everything from small rural hospitals to major academic medical centers participated. The question is why haven't we been able to take those accomplishments to scale across all 50 states?

We haven't accomplished everything and improvement has been slower than we expected. But overall, the glass is more than half full.

WITHOUT PUBLIC REPORTING, THERE'S NO WAY TO TELL WHAT PROGRESS HAS BEEN MADE

Lisa McGiffert, *director, Safe Patient Project, Consumers Union. She is co-author of the Consumers Union report* To Err is Human—To Delay is Deadly: Ten Years Later a Million Lives Lost, Billions of Dollars Wasted.

The IOM report initially produced a flurry of activity, but things died down. Legislation was introduced and some money was given to the Agency for Healthcare Research & Quality, but the impact was less significant than many of us hoped.

One problem was there was no organization to oversee implementation. The intent of the IOM report was to create such an entity, but we as a country fell short. The IOM committee did the report and dispersed. When we did our 10-year follow-up, we found it difficult to get anything new on the subject from the IOM. They referred us to people on the committee.

There have been a lot of individual improvements in care processes. People take risks and try things and significantly reduce infections or medication errors or bed sores and report their results at conferences. As a nation we could be safer because of this. But nobody knows because we are not measuring it. There is no validated standardized data reporting.

To show how little progress has been made, the latest AHRQ report used the IOM's 1999 work as the best estimate of the magnitude of medical errors. The best information we have now comes from AHRQ's 2008 National Healthcare Quality Report. Based on paper chart reviews and billing records, it estimates that patient safety declined by 1 percent in each of the six years following the IOM report. According to this data, we are less safe than in 1999.

Even when projects involving hundreds of hospitals are undertaken, the results often are not shared with the public. The Michigan keystone project looked at measures to reduce bloodstream infections for two years and found that half of hospitals reduced their rate to zero and sustained it and half did not. But they would not publish which did and which didn't. If you only have aggregate data you can't make an informed decision.

Our belief is public reporting is a key element to bring about systemic change. As long as this harm is kept secret, we are not going to be able to end it. We have decades of experience with secret voluntary reporting and it has been ineffective in bringing about real change.

That does not mean there are not places where care is safer. There are. Individual institutions are stepping up. But progress is spotty and it depends on who is in charge. We are moving in the right direction, but not fast enough.

GREATER SAFETY FOCUS IS NEEDED TO KEEP EMPLOYER-SPONSORED COVERAGE VIABLE

Helen Darling, *president, National Business Group on Health, which provides a forum for employers to discuss and develop policy positions on health care.*

Shockingly modest progress has been made given the impact of the problem, how many people were made aware of it, and how many efforts have been made to address it. From the employer community's perspective, we think more should have occurred.

We are finally starting to see some action. CMS is making "never events" unreimbursable. There are longer lists of events at the National Quality Forum. We have gone from saying "patient safety is an important thing that you should do" to tying money to it. I anticipate more progress as we see more pressure from payers and regulators. There has to be less tolerance for waste if we are going to cover 46 million people who have nothing now.

The potential savings are huge. A study in the *American Journal of Medical Quality* found that just improving discharge planning could reduce hospital readmissions enough to save about $400 per admission. We are talking about billions of dollars not to mention a reduction in human suffering.

A lot can be done with financial incentives. Almost everything we have in health care was developed in response to market demand. The roughly $22 billion investment in health care IT will make it possible to provide and track services in ways that were not possible before. With the new technology we will know sooner when people are being readmitted and there will be a financial consequence.

There are a lot of good examples. We recognized two this year with our first patient safety leadership awards: Henry Ford in Detroit and Memorial Hermann in Houston. They have ambitious goals on safety. They achieve them and sustain them with support from the board level on down.

But we are not going to accomplish delivery and finance reform unless we harmonize the activities of the public and private sectors. They don't have to be identical and we can still have multiple payers, but we have to harmonize how we pay hospitals and doctors to get them to collaborate. The AHA has put forward principles that we all agree on.

Our for-profit employers are in the worst economy in 70 years. Companies are eliminating or reducing 401(k) matches rather than cut health care. They can't afford to go much further. If nothing happens to slow health cost increases, companies will cease to fund it.

Physician Performance Measurement: A Key to Higher Quality and Lower Cost Growth or a Lost Opportunity?

Source: Draper, D.A. 2009. *Physician Performance Measurement: A Key to Higher Quality and Lower Cost Growth or a Lost Opportunity?* Commentary: Insights into the Health Care Marketplace. Used with the permission of The Center for Studying Health System Change.

Although the United States spends more than $2 trillion annually on health care, patient outcomes lag other developed countries that spend far less per capita. Physicians wield significant influence—directly and indirectly—over the quality and cost of health care, and efforts to measure and improve physician performance have gained momentum. Much of the impetus has come from purchasers seeking to engage consumers to be more active participants in their health and health care decisions. In response, health plans have developed physician performance measurement programs to provide information to consumers. However, methodological limitations, including the use of claims data, small sample sizes, and non-standardized measures and assessments, have fueled skepticism about plan programs. While measuring performance is an important step, health plans often fail to take the next step—supporting and rewarding physician performance improvement to encourage and reinforce desired behaviors. Arguably, physician performance measurement has such profound implications for all Americans' health and health care that it should be a public good, transcending competitive dynamics. Standardizing measures, combining payers' data, providing effective support for improvement,

and creating robust rewards for good results offer some ways to improve the current state of physician performance measurement.

PHYSICIANS KEY TO HIGHER QUALITY AND LOWER COST GROWTH

U.S. health care costs continue to spiral upward. In 2007, the United States spent $2.2 trillion on health care, or 16 percent of the nation's gross domestic product (GDP), and spending grew more than 6 percent from the previous year.[1] Yet, despite the highest per-capita health expenditures in the world, U.S. patient outcomes are comparatively worse than those of many other developed countries with much lower spending.[2] The disconnect between money spent on health care and the often less-than-stellar results has sparked national awareness of the critical importance of measuring and improving health care quality and slowing spending growth through increased efficiency. As a result, nascent efforts are underway to measure and improve physician performance on both quality and cost dimensions.

Physicians are the linchpin of care delivery, and, directly and indirectly, they have significant influence on health care quality and costs.[3] Measuring physician performance to identify weaknesses that warrant change and working to make those changes, therefore, creates tremendous opportunity to improve health care quality and efficiency. Although physician performance measurement and improvement offers a potentially powerful tool, it may prove a lost opportunity for improving the nation's health care system if methodological and other shortcomings of existing efforts are not appropriately addressed.

EFFORTS TO MEASURE AND REWARD PHYSICIAN PERFORMANCE

To date, most performance measurement programs have been developed by health plans seeking to differentiate physicians on the basis of quality and costs. Much of the impetus has come from purchasers, notably large national employers, hoping to address quality and cost concerns by engaging consumers to be more active participants in decisions about their health and health care.[4] As the responsibility for health care decision making and costs increasingly shifts to consumers, there is a recognized need to provide more and better information about health care providers, including the quality and cost-effectiveness of the services these providers deliver.[5] Plans have embraced these measurement efforts as a way of creating value for their employer clients and to help distinguish themselves in a competitive marketplace.

Plan efforts often are manifest and marketed in the form of physician ranking programs or some type of narrow, tiered or high-performance provider network.[6] These programs operate under a variety of names such as the Aexcel Specialist Network (Aetna), Blue Precision (Blue Cross Blue Shield), Care Network (CIGNA), Preferred Network (Humana), and Premium Designation Program (United Healthcare). The underlying premise of these initiatives is to provide a systematic and objective method of measuring physician performance based on quality and cost metrics that can be assessed using plans' claims or other administrative data and making the results publicly available to enrollees. Most often, the results are used only to inform consumers; in some cases, consumers have incentives, such as reduced copayments, to use the higher-performing physicians. Plans rarely pay bonuses to physicians they deem high performing. In these programs, quality and efficiency improvements are achieved to the extent that patient volume shifts to higher-performing physicians as a result of changes in physician referrals and consumer choices and lower-performing physicians improving the care they provide.

Although plans' physician performance measurement programs are broadly similar, they vary in the methodologies employed. Methodologies often differ on dimensions such as the specific measures used, sample-size requirements, and the comparative emphasis placed on quality vs. cost measures. Consequently, gauging the comparability of individual plan results is difficult because the decision algorithm each plan uses to conduct the assessments is proprietary with little, if any, transparency. This variability can result in physicians deemed high performing by one plan but not another, as was the case, for example, for a large integrated delivery system in Seattle, Virginia Mason Medical Center, as plans rolled out their respective programs in that market.[7]

Limited physician input and lack of transparency, which the American Medical Association describes as "black-box methodologies," has resulted in considerable physician skepticism and outright dismissal by some. It also has resulted in legal action. In 2006, for example, the Washington State Medical Association filed suit against Regence Blue Shield, alleging Regence used flawed methods and outdated information to exclude physicians from the plan's high-performance network. The pushback resulted in Regence discontinuing the program, at least until it could be revamped.[8] In 2007, New York Attorney General Andrew Cuomo launched an investigation into the physician ranking programs of health plans operating in New York, raising concerns that plans' profit motives affected the accuracy of the rankings and encouraged consumers to choose physicians solely on the basis of cost.[9] As a result of the investigation, health plans agreed to make a number of changes, including basing their assessments not solely on costs, using national quality and efficiency measures, and using measures that help facilitate consumers' comparisons of physicians. The agreement also required plans to score 100 percent compliance on external reviews of their ranking programs.[10]

As these reactions to health plans' programs suggest, performance measurement can evoke anxiety generally and be especially threatening to physicians who are unlikely to show good performance. The stakes are high for physicians deemed poor performing, because their professional reputations are at risk and, potentially, their financial interests. Ensuring that a valid methodological approach is used to measure performance is therefore crucial because egregious, albeit unintended, consequences could include incorrectly labeling a physician as a poor performer or having a consumer choose a physician based on an inaccurate assessment whose care resulted in an adverse outcome. As recent history suggests, methodologies to assess physician performance are subject to intense scrutiny, and weaknesses in objectivity, credibility and transparency can undermine, if not derail, the intended objectives of improving health care quality and efficiency. Engaging physicians as active participants in plans' performance improvement efforts has proved difficult because of these weaknesses. And when there are problems with one plan's performance measurement effort, physicians often construe problems more broadly to all plan efforts.

METHODOLOGICAL SHORTCOMINGS TARNISH CREDIBILITY

Although strong methodological approaches to physician performance measurement are vital to its success, shortcomings have tarnished—at least initially—the credibility of many health plans' efforts. Much of the controversy has focused on data credibility, sample sizes and methods used to analyze the data.

Lack of Data Credibility.

Plans typically use their own claims and other administrative data to measure physician performance. However, these data can be considerably less reliable and accurate than data extracted through medical record review, which is more expensive to collect. Claims and administrative data have inherent weaknesses in documenting all services provided to a patient by a physician and in capturing legitimate reasons why certain services were or were not provided—information that is critical for an accurate assessment of physician performance. Typically, health plans do not collaborate with other entities, for example, a large physician group with robust electronic medical record data, to compare and validate claims data and factor in any needed data adjustments.

Inadequate Sample Size

Although plans typically require a minimum sample size to assess a physician's performance, these thresholds tend to be set relatively low (e.g., fewer than a dozen patients) in part because of limitations associated with an individual plan's use of only their own claims data to conduct the assessment. But because any single plan's patients may represent only a small fraction of a physician's entire patient panel, there is a greater likelihood that the assessment may yield incomplete, if not erroneous, results. For example, if a plan's patients are disproportionately sicker with higher costs of care than the physician's overall patient panel, the plan's assessment might tag the physician as a poor performer, when the opposite may be true.

Non-Standardized Measures

There is no standardized set of measures used by plans to assess physician performance, and even if the measures are the same or similar, plans may define and operationalize them differently. The same is true of methods to adjust for differences in risk among patients—whether and how these methods are applied to the measures. Adjustment for patient differences is important because many physicians believe their patients are more challenging than average. Plans typically use evidence-based medical guidelines and consensus-based quality standards to assess physician quality. Efficiency is generally measured using episodes of care and attributing all related costs, including those of other providers, to the physician deemed primarily responsible for the patient's care, regardless of whether that physician has control over the other providers rendering the care. Physician organizations have been critical of the tools—called groupers—used to sort claims into episodes of care in part because this methodology is still evolving, but also because of the way in which physicians are assigned and held accountable for all of the costs of a patient's care.

Non-Standardized Assessment

There is little, if any, consensus among plans about how physicians' performance should be assessed, including, for example, the relative emphasis of quality vs. cost measures. This is at least partially rooted in plans' desire to use their physician performance measurement efforts as a way of gaining a competitive advantage in the marketplace—to have something different and seemingly better than their competitors to offer employer clients. The difficulty with such a proprietary approach, however, is that it creates distrust because of the limited transparency of the process and how the results were derived. It also diminishes the overall credibility and effectiveness of the assessments because there is no comparability between plans, leading to physicians deemed high performing by one plan but not another and creating confusion for those that may rely on the information.

MEASUREMENT NECESSARY BUT NOT SUFFICIENT

Measuring performance is an important and necessary initial step to improving the quality and efficiency of care provided, but measurement alone is likely insufficient to prompt physicians to improve performance. Support to improve performance and rewards to encourage and reinforce desired behaviors also are needed. However, these elements are largely absent from many health plan efforts, and when they do exist, they are inadequate to bring about meaningful or sustained performance improvement.[11]

Support for Improving Performance

It is of little use to measure performance and not also support physicians willing to improve. Health plan assessment efforts generate considerable data, but many fail to provide physicians the information in a clear and actionable manner. A case study of Virginia Mason Medical Center is illustrative in understanding the value of providing meaningful data to foster performance improvement.[12] In this particular case, Aetna provided detailed claims data by individual physicians, practice sites, patients and cost centers, such as pharmaceuticals and emergency services, which then allowed the system to conduct further analyses to identify cost-reduction opportunities. Through this process, for example, Virginia Mason identified that its costs per migraine episode were high, in part because patients went to the emergency department for severe headaches when they lacked "rescue" medication. The analysis provided the system with important information to help guide physicians in changing their care of patients with migraines.

Benchmarking an individual physician's performance to a relevant peer group can also support improvement. This performance comparison appeals to the competitiveness of physicians to improve and, to the extent the comparisons are public, provides even greater impetus to improve. Additionally, the timeliness of the performance assessment is important. Plans typically conduct their physician performance assessments at most annually, using data that is often at least a year old. Consequently, the assessments may preclude the timely detection of performance changes and yield results that are no longer valid. This can be particularly frustrating for physicians who are engaged in the process and making improvements.

There are a number of other ways plans can support physicians to improve their performance. For example, it would be useful to provide physicians guidance on the quality and costs of other providers to whom they refer. Although this is not a common practice among plans, without this information, physicians are likely to continue existing referral patterns even though the recipient providers may be poor performers. Finally, providing peer-learning and support opportunities to physicians, including disseminating best practices and encouraging broader

adoption would also be beneficial to help physicians improve performance.

Rewards for Good Performance

Key to any successful performance improvement effort is the inclusion of meaningful incentives that motivate and reward good results. However, the incentives currently associated with most health plans' physician performance measurement programs are minimal at best and do little to gain physicians' attention, engage them in the process or motivate them to improve. When incentives are offered, they are generally too inconsequential to be effective. Often, the incentive is limited to a physician designated as high performing in a plan's provider directory. Plans have been largely unwilling to offer rewards for better performance, in part because they do not want to increase aggregate payments, but also because they do not have a strong basis for penalizing low-performing physicians.

SIGNIFICANT POTENTIAL OR A POTENTIAL LOST OPPORTUNITY?

Physician performance measurement, if credible and with relevant and robust improvement opportunities and rewards, offers tremendous promise to improve the quality and efficiency of care. Yet, most existing health plan programs have yielded information of limited value and usefulness, particularly for physicians and consumers. Many of these efforts also have been mired in underlying skepticism and distrust about plan motivations and methodological concerns, aggravated by sometimes conflicting results when plans pursue their own individual measurement efforts.

The measurement of physician performance has implications far beyond any single plan and its enrollees, extending to the population as a whole. Consequently, it is ill-advised to think of physician performance measurement as something other than a public good. Transcending competitive dynamics and encompassing a broader scope can position physician performance measurement as a legitimate and valuable activity that yields demonstrable improvements in quality and costs. But, there are several critical challenges to moving physician performance measurement forward.

One challenge is that there is little consensus on what standards should guide these programs although the recent efforts in New York that require compliance to a prescribed set of standards may offer a good starting point toward national standardization.

Additionally, the Consumer-Purchaser Disclosure Project, a consortium of purchasers, is working collaboratively with plans and providers to create a national set of principles to guide how health plans measure physicians' performance and report the information to consumers.[13]

Another important challenge is measuring physicians' performance across their entire patient panel, not piecemeal as is the case now with individual plans focusing only on their respective subset of patients. However, this requires combining data from all payers, including Medicare and Medicaid, to conduct an accurate assessment and likely will require some legal authority, such as the federal government, to mandate that it happen. The Centers for Medicare and Medicaid Services' (CMS) Generating Medicare Physician Quality Performance Measurement Results (GEM) project, which provides physician group practice performance data on a limited set of quality measures derived from Medicare Part B claims data offers a potential model and framework. The intended purpose of the project is to make this information available to Chartered Value Exchanges— regional collaboratives focused on health care quality and efficiency—to combine with commercial payer data to obtain a more complete profile of physician group practices.[14]

The absence of a convening entity with the necessary capacity, wherewithal and clout to neutralize existing competitive dynamics and champion physician performance measurement is another key challenge. In the current context, CMS may be the only candidate that fits this bill. A convener would be instrumental, if not essential, in helping to standardize the process and could serve as a central data repository into which payers reported, improving efficiencies and eliminating conflicting results that ensue from individual plan efforts.

Finally, effective support for physicians willing to improve and robust rewards for physicians demonstrating good results are important. Otherwise, as the experience to date suggests, it is difficult, if not impossible, to engage physicians in the process. The support and rewards have to be of value to physicians to avoid distraction by competing demands. Although the challenges outlined here are formidable, failure to take the appropriate steps to improve the current state of physician performance measurement may result in a lost opportunity to improve the quality and efficiency of the underperforming U.S. healthcare system.

● ● ● **References**

1. Centers for Medicare and Medicaid Services (CMS), *National Health Expenditures: 2007 Highlights*, Washington, D.C.

2. Kaiser Family Foundation, *Health Care Spending in the United States and OECD Countries (Snapshots: Health Care Costs)*, Washington, D.C. (January 2007).

3. CMS, *National Health Expenditures: 2007 Highlights*. At a minimum, physicians influence spending for hospital care (32 percent of total national health expenditures), physician/clinical services (22 percent), and prescription drugs (10 percent).

4. Tynan, Ann, Allison Liebhaber and Paul B. Ginsburg, *A Health Plan Work in Progress: Hospital-Physician Price and Quality Transparency*, Research Brief No. 7, Center for Studying Health System Change, Washington, D.C. (August 2008).

5. Christianson, Jon, Paul B. Ginsburg and Debra A. Draper, "The Transition from Managed Care to Consumerism: A Community-Level Status Report," *Health Affairs*, Vol. 27, No. 5 (September/October 2008).

6. Draper, Debra A., Allison Liebhaber and Paul B. Ginsburg, *High-Performance Health Plan Networks: Early Experiences*, Issue Brief No. 111, Center for Studying Health System Change, Washington, D.C. (May 2007).

7. Pham, Hoangmai H., et al., "Redesigning Care Delivery in Response to a High-Performance Network: The Virginia Mason Medical Center," *Health Affairs*, Vol. 26, No. 4 (July/August 2007).

8. "Regence BlueShield Sued Over 'Select' Network," *Seattle Post-Intelligencer* (Sept. 21, 2006).

9. Langston, Edward L., "Pay for Performance Programs," Report of the Board of Trustees, American Medical Association (December 2007).

10. "NCQA posts reviews of health plans under 2007 physician ranking settlement," *Health Plan & Provider Report* (Jan. 7, 2009).

11. Rosenthal, Meredith B., et al., "Paying for Quality: Providers' Incentives for Quality Improvement," *Health Affairs*, Vol. 23, No. 2 (March/April 2004); Rosenthal, Meredith B., and Richard G. Frank, "What is the Empirical Basis for Paying for Quality in Health Care?" *Medical Care Research and Review*, Vol. 64, No. 2 (April 2006).

12. Pham, et al. (July/August 2007).

13. Consumer-Purchaser Disclosure Project, *http://www.healthcaredisclosure.org/* (accessed March 3, 2009).

14. CMS, Generating Medicare Physician Quality Performance Measurement Results (GEM), *http://www.cms.hhs.gov/GEM/* (accessed March 3, 2009).

Hospital Strategies to Engage Physicians in Quality Improvement

Source: Liebhaber, A., D.A. Draper, and G.R. Cohen. 2009. *Hospital Strategies to Engage Physicians in Quality Improvement*. Issue Brief No. 127. Washington, DC: Center for Studying Health System Change. Used with the permission of The Center for Studying Health System Change.

In the last decade, growing evidence that the quality of U.S. health care is uneven at best has prompted greater attention to quality improvement, especially in the nation's hospitals. While physicians are integral to hospital quality improvement efforts, focusing physicians on these activities is challenging because of competing time and reimbursement pressures. To overcome these challenges, hospitals need to employ a variety of strategies, according to a Center for Studying Health System Change (HSC) study of four communities—Detroit, Memphis, Minneapolis-St. Paul and Seattle. Hospital strategies include employing physicians; using credible data to identify areas that need improvement; providing visible support through hospital leadership; identifying and nurturing physician champions to help engage physician peers; and communicating the importance of physicians' contributions. While hospitals are making gains in patient care quality, considerably more progress likely could be made through greater alignment of hospitals and physicians working together on quality improvement.

PHYSICIAN INVOLVEMENT KEY TO HOSPITAL QUALITY IMPROVEMENT

In recent years, such reports as the Institute of Medicine's *Crossing the Quality Chasm* have brought quality of care issues to the forefront. The dissonance between costs and outcomes has also heightened awareness about the need to improve health care quality, including the quality of care provided in the nation's hospitals. The United States spends about $2.4 trillion on health care annually—nearly a third of which is for hospital care.[1] Yet, health outcomes in the United States are comparatively worse than those of many other developed countries that have lower spending.[2]

Although hospitals have long engaged in quality improvement (QI) activities, they continue to face escalating demands to participate in a wide range of quality improvement and reporting programs. Moreover, hospitals' financial and reputational interests are increasingly at stake to demonstrate high quality and to improve when weaknesses are identified. The Joint Commission, for example, requires hospitals seeking accreditation, which is often required by payers for reimbursement, to demonstrate compliance with the National Patient Safety Goals—a set of standards focusing on the reduction of hospital-acquired infections and other patient safety issues. Additionally, the Centers for Medicare and Medicaid Services (CMS) collects data on a core set of quality measures from hospitals as part of its

Reporting Hospital Quality Data for Annual Payment Update program. Hospitals that do not participate in the program or fail to meet CMS reporting requirements receive a 2-percentage-point reduction in their annual payment update. More recently, CMS also began disallowing payment to hospitals for so-called never events—medical errors such as foreign bodies left in surgical patients and preventable postoperative deaths.[3]

Given the increasing pressures on hospitals to improve the quality of patient care, the need to engage physicians in hospital quality improvement initiatives is critical. Physicians are the key decision makers related to the care a hospitalized patient receives and are integral to hospitals' QI projects, ranging from improving hand-washing hygiene to reducing ventilator-associated pneumonia. Yet, hospitals' attempts to engage physicians in improving patient care come at a time when physicians face growing reimbursement and time pressures. Hospitals are using a variety of strategies to address these challenges and ensure physician involvement in QI, according to an HSC study examining physician involvement in hospital QI activities in four communities: Detroit, Memphis, Minneapolis–St. Paul and Seattle. These strategies include: employing physicians; using credible data to encourage physician involvement; demonstrating visible commitment to quality improvement through hospital leadership; identifying and nurturing physician champions; and communicating the importance of physicians' contributions.

EMPLOYMENT ENGAGES PHYSICIANS

While there is wide acknowledgment that physician involvement is critical for hospital QI initiatives, hospitals face a major challenge in securing physicians' time to participate. Even some of the more straightforward activities associated with hospital quality improvement, such as attending meetings or reviewing proposed changes in hospital processes, are difficult for a physician with a large patient load. As one physician respondent lamented, "These things are terribly time consuming . . . and your patient responsibilities never go away." Nearly all respondents commented that the trade-offs for physicians—sacrificing either personal or billable time—are difficult to resolve.

Many hospitals have historically relied on the voluntary medical staff model to solicit physician participation—a model that is generally premised on a loose affiliation between hospitals and community-based physicians. However, as more services shift to outpatient settings and physicians confront quality-of-life issues and financial stresses, physicians increasingly feel less obligated to perform such functions as participating on hospital committees in exchange for hospital privileges. As a result, engaging loosely affiliated physicians in hospital QI projects can be particularly challenging because of competing priorities. Moreover, while respondents often described medical staff bylaws as encouraging physicians to "be good citizens" and participate in QI activities, bylaws often lack the specificity or accountability that clearly outline physicians' responsibilities.

Hospital employment of physicians is becoming more prevalent, often as part of a larger set of alignment strategies, such as securing emergency call coverage and initiating new service lines to attract more patients. For physicians, employment may be attractive because it eliminates the administrative burden of a private practice, secures a predictable income, offers relief from high malpractice premiums and allows for a better work-life balance. Typically, quality improvement is not the main reason driving tighter alignment of physicians and hospitals, but employment can create incentives for physician involvement in QI activities as one chief medical officer (CMO) described by "achieving economic alignment around the shared quality agenda." To ensure alignment, hospital executives reported increasing use of formal job descriptions and contractual arrangements that detail physician responsibilities to the hospital related to QI participation and increased accountability for results.

Employment of physicians can lessen competing pressures on physicians' time to participate in QI activities. Other benefits include increased physician accessibility and visibility, as well as a pool of potential champions to help garner support and engagement of physician peers. However, respondents frequently cautioned that employment alone is insufficient to gain and sustain physician involvement in the absence of other factors, including credible data to motivate engagement, personal interest, and other support and encouragement from the hospital.

CREDIBLE DATA MOTIVATES IMPROVEMENT

Credible data to identify areas that need improvement and systematically assess progress are essential to securing physician participation in hospital quality improvement. As one hospital chief executive officer (CEO) said, "People rally toward data, toward measurement and toward evidence-based practice." Many respondents recounted how physicians assume they are providing good quality of care until they are shown data proving otherwise. For example, at one hospital, physicians had lower hand-washing rates than other caregivers. Only when the data were broken down by caregiver type were physicians able to see they were less compliant and begin to focus on improving.

Although hospitals' participation in CMS, Joint Commission and other programs has prompted increased data collection, many hospitals still report they are "starving" for good data. Many data sources are retrospective and administrative in nature (e.g., billing data), which makes physicians skeptical. Hospitals are trying to use other data sources, such as chart reviews, which are expensive. As a national hospital association representative stated, "I would first give a caveat that we are not lacking for data, we're lacking for useful information to make decisions. You can fall on your sword by giving physicians data that are not reliable, not representative, or not useful."

Using external, risk-adjusted data is a way to improve data credibility. Several respondents noted the American College of Surgeons' National Surgical Quality Improvement Program[4] (NSQIP) as a particularly useful data source for surgical specialties. Benchmarking data against other institutions is important as well. Academic medical centers placed high value on benchmarking against other University HealthSystem Consortium[5] hospitals, and children's hospitals reported great value in benchmarking against other Child Health Corporation of America[6] hospitals.

Although still a work in progress, some hospitals are moving toward using benchmarked data, when available, to provide feedback to physicians about their performance relative to their peers, either within the hospital or with physicians in similar care settings. Some hospitals give individual-level data to physicians, while others distribute aggregated quality scorecards. Hospital executives reported that this feedback appeals to the competitive nature of physicians. As one hospital director of quality improvement noted, "Helping them [physicians] understand goals and then providing them with information about how they're doing on those goals on an individual basis against one another is another tried and true strategy for gaining involvement."

Providing physicians with data support for QI—staff to collect and analyze the data—also is important. This is typically done by assigning hospital staff to serve as project managers for physician-led QI projects. Hospital executives emphasized the positive impact of quality departments taking more ownership of the data, collecting it, and making it accessible to physicians so physicians do not have to spend their limited time pulling information together.

The impact of information technology (IT) on quality improvement is "a mixed bag." Respondents acknowledged that it has provided access to more information in a timelier, more organized manner, allowing hospitals to improve reporting of individual physician and department performance. IT also has enhanced hospitals' ability to communicate with physicians by posting messages related to QI or performance results on a Web site or through physician portals. In some ways, however, IT also reportedly makes it more difficult and complex to get information. Common complaints about IT were the lack of interoperability or uniformity across inpatient and outpatient settings and across different hospitals campuses, which means collecting comprehensive data is still cumbersome. Many hospital executives reported they were in the early stages of implementing an electronic medical record (EMR) system and were not yet at the point where they could use it to its full potential for QI.

COMMITTED HOSPITAL LEADERSHIP ENGENDERS PHYSICIAN SUPPORT

Visible commitment by hospital leadership can foster physician involvement in quality improvement activities. For example, several respondents noted how helpful it was when hospital boards became involved in the hospital QI agenda. As one respondent observed, "We're seeing a growing interest at the board level in hospitals around quality . . . that connection between the board and medical staff seems to be one where there's also a good potential for support. If the board is supportive of quality endeavors and they're more engaged, that sets the tone."

An important role of hospital leadership is creating a strong quality culture by publicly demonstrating that QI is important, supported and encouraged. Respondents from several hospitals noted that leadership turnover often created changes in QI priorities and methods, but hospitals with a well-established QI culture were better able to keep physicians involved despite the changes. As one hospital chief nursing officer (CNO) said, it's an environment where "you get on the boat or the boat's going without you." This is reportedly achieved by providing clarity about what's expected in terms of QI, establishing the appropriate infrastructure and institutionalizing that direction from an organizational perspective.

Respondents praised senior leaders who go out on patient floors to talk with patients and staff to see for themselves the quality challenges and issues the hospital faces. Some noted how useful it was to have senior leadership accompany physicians on patient care rounds, which enables some of the quality discussion to occur in real time.

QI also needs adequate resources, which is challenging for hospitals as QI demands continue to increase. As one CMO noted, "If they're [physicians] going to get engaged in quality projects, they want to be sure the hospital is going to back them up. Once they've done a project they need to be sure the hospital has the will to maintain the gains." However, several respondents noted that after implementing initiatives mandated by external organizations, they often were left with limited, if any, resources to pursue other activities of interest to hospital staff.

PHYSICIAN CHAMPIONS FOSTER BROADER PARTICIPATION

Physician involvement in hospital QI is reportedly often limited to a fraction of the active medical staff. While respondents were generally favorable when describing the efforts of these physicians, they were frustrated that it was "always the same people." Finding ways to engage more physicians is critical to QI, which ultimately requires all members of the medical staff to adopt process and practice changes. Respondents cautioned that continued reliance on the same set of individuals can lead to burnout and also limit the number of QI activities that can reasonably be pursued.

Hospitals often look to physician champions to help promote their quality agendas and elicit broader physician participation. Respondents emphasized the importance of physician champions being highly respected in their area of clinical expertise. Most respondents also noted that physicians who have emerged as champions appear to possess certain personality traits, such as a willingness to challenge the status quo, a capacity to command the attention of others and an ability to ignite passion in others. As one CEO described a physician champion in his hospital, "Every thought process he has always has a filter of 'what is this going to do to quality?'"

To nurture physician champions, hospitals often provide support for leadership training or attendance at national quality meetings, which helps to broaden perspectives and heighten awareness in areas such as systems and change management. Physician respondents spoke of the importance of hospitals investing in training physicians through courses and seminars to create "true believers" in quality improvement. The more forward-thinking hospitals have a succession plan in place for their quality leaders to identify young physicians who need to be exposed and educated on QI to ultimately assume the quality mantle.

Several respondents had experience with successfully converting naysayers—physicians who initially criticized the purpose and methodology of QI initiatives—into champions. Strategies included bringing naysayers into the process early and asking for their input. For example, one CNO recounted an experience where hospital staff worked with a physician who was critical of the Joint Commission's National Safety Patient Goals and the hospital's EMR to make sure he was fully trained and could see the benefit. Now that physician, who was initially a naysayer, reportedly "beats the drum for the thing." However, at some point, as one CMO stated, "You have to keep marching on and not fret a lot about them [naysayers]."

EFFECTIVE COMMUNICATION SPURS INVOLVEMENT

In soliciting physician involvement in hospital quality improvement, it is important to have clear communications and effective messaging. Many hospital executives found they were often dealing with an "educational deficit"—that many physicians did not understand QI and its importance, contributing to their reluctance to participate. Strategies that hospitals have used to communicate to physicians about QI include one-on-one meetings, newsletters, posters and e-mails.

A particularly effective message frames quality improvement as advantageous for patients. If hospitals can demonstrate to physicians that QI activities result in better patient outcomes, respondents believed that participation was appealing to physicians. As one respondent noted, "If physicians understand that it's not for a regulatory or administrative requirement, but . . . it's about the care they're providing patients, they're all over it, they're very enthusiastic." Other effective messages include how QI will ultimately protect physicians' time by improving efficiency and how poor quality costs money and impacts the reputation of the hospital, which could also affect physicians' reputations and bottom lines.

Hospital staff can also maximize physician involvement by recognizing that physicians have a limited amount of time to devote to QI and being strategic about using that time. Strategies to achieve this include inviting physicians to meetings that result in concrete decision making and scheduling meetings far in advance and for times early in the morning or in the evenings to accommodate physicians' clinical responsibilities.

Once physicians do agree to participate, respondents reported the importance of hospital leadership providing recognition and positive feedback, an area where several respondents believed their hospitals were lacking. For physicians to participate in QI, it often means voluntarily contributing their time and forgoing compensation; they want to be recognized by hospital leadership for that sacrifice. To achieve this goal, some hospitals have employed strategies such as publicly posting performance data, holding poster sessions to provide visibility and encouraging physicians to present their work to the broader staff.

IMPLICATIONS

While hospitals are working to improve their quality of care and are making incremental gains, considerably more progress can be made. Recognizing that physicians are essential to hospitals' quality improvement efforts, it is unlikely that significant progress can be achieved unless physicians are more effectively integrated into the process. Because many physicians are spending less time in the hospital and are increasingly reticent about voluntarily giving their time to hospitals, finding effective strategies to engage physicians in QI activities will become even more important.

To identify and promote policies and practices that encourage hospitals and physicians to work together to achieve results, it is important for policy makers driving the nation's health care quality improvement agenda to focus on:

- Rationalizing the demands placed on hospitals and physicians, focusing on a limited number of QI initiatives that demonstrate the most

promise for significant improvement and striving for consistency across programs;

- Creating mechanisms to facilitate hospitals' efforts to use data to improve patient care quality, such as centralized data repositories; and

- Establishing financial and other incentives that best support hospital quality improvement while also examining state and federal regulations, such as gainsharing prohibitions, that may impede hospitals' engagement of physicians in quality improvement.

● ● ● **Notes**

1. Centers for Medicare and Medicaid Services (CMS), *National Health Expenditure Projections, 2008-2018*, Washington, D.C.

2. Kaiser Family Foundation, *Health Care Spending in the United States and OECD Countries (Snapshots: Health Care Costs)*, Menlo Park, Calif. (January 2007).

3. CMS, *Eliminating Serious, Preventable, and Costly Medical Errors—Never Events*, News Release, Washington, D.C. (July 31, 2008).

4. NSQIP is a nationally validated, risk-adjusted, outcomes-based program to measure and improve the quality of surgical care. The program employs a prospective, peer-controlled, validated database to quantify 30-day risk-adjusted surgical outcomes, which allows comparison of outcomes among all hospitals in the program.

5. The University HealthSystem Consortium is an alliance of 103 academic medical centers and 210 affiliated hospitals. The consortium offers databases that provide comparative data in clinical, operational, faculty practice management, financial, patient safety and supply chain areas.

6. Child Health Corporation of America is a business alliance of 38 children's hospitals. The alliance provides a range of programs and services, including group purchasing and supply chain management; pediatric data management; performance improvement and patient safety initiatives; and Web-based training programs and strategic planning.

4

Navigating Health Care: Why It's So Hard and What Can Be Done to Make It Easier for the Average Consumer

Source: Rein, A. 2007. *Navigating Health Care: Why It's So Hard and What Can Be Done to Make It Easier for the Average Consumer.* Issue Brief. Washington, DC/Princeton, NJ: AcademyHealth/Robert Wood Johnson Foundation.

In February 2007, AcademyHealth conducted a meeting on behalf of the Robert Wood Johnson Foundation to examine the role of consumer engagement in improving the quality of health care. In preparation for this meeting, five papers were commissioned on the following subjects: consumer activation, consumer choice of health plan and provider, consumer choice of treatment, patient navigation and the appropriate role for consumers. This issue brief is based on the paper exploring the challenges faced by consumers as they attempt to navigate the health care system, which was authored by Shoshanna Sofaer, Dr.P.H.

CARVING OUT A ROLE FOR THE HEALTH CARE CONSUMER

In the last several decades, efforts have been made to reduce rapidly escalating health care costs by applying pressure to various players in the sector. These efforts have been largely inadequate. In 2005, total national health expenditures rose 6.9 percent—two times the rate of inflation—and represented 16 per-

cent of the gross domestic product. Furthermore, the overall financing and affordability picture for health care in the United States looks bleak.

More recently, policy-makers and researchers have begun to examine the relationship between health care cost and the quality of care received. In the discussion of possible approaches to reducing the former while improving the latter, the direct role of health care consumers has assumed a more prominent place. Previously, the patient—the central player in the health care space—was not seen as part of the solution. Now certain health care stakeholders have come to believe that patients need to take a more active role in all parts of their care. Some efforts in this area are intended to make consumers more aware of the costs associated with their use of health care services and selection of providers (e.g., "consumer-directed" health plans), while others focus on improving patient experiences and clinical outcomes (e.g., patient self management, shared decision making between patients and providers and greater patient "activation").

Taken together these efforts may foster some improvements, but none constitute a big-picture "fix" for the cost/quality problems that currently exist, nor do they introduce the elements of ease and continuity that are so lacking for consumers trying to get care in today's highly fractured health care sector. Perhaps this challenge—as seen from the health care consumer's perspective—is best expressed by Jessie Gruman, Ph.D., who laments that "being a patient in the United States is like being drop-kicked into a foreign country. You don't know the language, you don't have a map, you can't tell who's in charge, and all you want to do is go home." Fixing discrete segments of the sector may do little to improve this experience, but there is hope that a broader understanding of patients' experiences, as they move through entire episodes of care and beyond, will help inform potential policy solutions.

PATIENT NAVIGATION: WHAT IS IT AND WHY IS IT IMPORTANT?

The concept of patient navigation has emerged as a way of characterizing the experiences of consumers in health care. For the purposes of this issue brief and the paper on which it is based, patient navigation is defined as "the process(es) by which patients and/or their health caregivers move into and through the multiple parts of the health care enterprise in order to gain access to and use its services in a manner that maximizes the likelihood of gaining the positive health outcomes available through those services." Given the highly fractured and—to many—inscrutable nature of the U.S. health care sector, this process is fraught with challenges for most consumers, especially those who are sick, stressed, busy with their everyday lives or otherwise disadvantaged in taking on the tasks involved.

For patients to get timely, appropriate, affordable and quality care, they must be able to navigate the health care system. When it is too burdensome, patients and their caregivers respond by delaying or failing to get needed care or by seeking care in inappropriate but more easily accessible settings, such as emergency departments. Navigation challenges may also inhibit the capacity of certain individuals more than others, which can exacerbate health disparities. This leaves many vulnerable to the clinical consequences of poorly navigated health care. For example, those with limited English proficiency face the additional challenge of literally understanding what they need to do to gain access to appropriate care. It is no wonder that, on average, Americans receive appropriate health care only about half the time.

In addition to poor clinical consequences, health care efficiency is also seriously compromised by poor navigation. An enormous amount of time and energy is expended in trying to explain the workings of the health care system to patients and their caregivers. Just think of all the forms that people need to read, understand and sign. They often end up signing whether they understand a form or not. Despite the system's effort to make things clear up front, the complexity of most situations leads to problems or miscommunications that need to be untangled later. These problems often result in overuse, under-use or inappropriate use of services (e.g., duplication of diagnostic tests, missed physician visits and visits that are useless because necessary information has not arrived on time). All this, in turn, undermines the goal of getting value out of every health care dollar.

WHY IS NAVIGATION OF HEALTH CARE SO HARD?

To understand why navigating health care is so hard, it is instructive to think about providers—both individuals and organizations—in the context of organizational theory. We know that all organizations need to both specialize and coordinate. We expect health care providers to specialize in order to perform tasks with a high degree of technical expertise and effectiveness, but we also need them to coordinate within and across their own settings in the health care space to maximize outcomes, including the patient's experience of care. Up to this point, U.S. providers have generally done well in specializing and rather poorly in coordinating. Our payment mechanisms have likely fostered this environment. The dominant fee-for-service paradigm has engendered support for numerous specialized medical technologies and complex procedures but has failed to encourage care coordination across providers, settings and time.

Historically, the bottom line for health care organizations has not been affected by poor coordination. It is consumers (and payers) who have paid the price—both directly in terms of cost and indirectly in terms of hassle, wasted time and diminished outcomes. Given the extremely challenging prospect of redesigning organizational structures in health care to be more accommodating to patients, it is not surprising that most of the efforts thus far have simply tried to help patients deal with obstacles in the existing system. In other words, trying to make the best of what you've got. For example, "care managers," "patient navigators" and other specialists have been brought in to help individual patients make their way through one or several episodes of care.

WHAT CAN BE DONE TO MAKE IT EASIER FOR PATIENTS?

To fully address patient navigation problems and their consequences, system-level interventions are needed. For example, at the medical appointment level, some have suggested having group appointments, which could expand and perhaps improve the time available to patients and providers for discussing conditions and treatments. Another model might be for medical teams to be constructed around patient needs, so that complex diagnoses or treatment issues could be fully discussed and decisions made with the benefit of having all relevant parties at the table.

Though not yet a reality, there are some examples of structural innovations that may facilitate patient navigation. Integrated delivery systems, which allow multiple health services to be managed by the same organizing entity, may improve coordination and ease patient navigation. This could be especially true in systems where health care coverage is integrated with delivery, such as Kaiser Permanente and Group Health of Puget Sound. Another idea being promoted to enhance patient navigation is the "focused factory," which involves the reorganization of health care reimbursement and competition around care for particular health conditions, such as cancer and diabetes. This "one-stop shopping" model enables patients to get all the care they need in one place, so long as it is related to the particular condition. However, the most serious navigation, quality and cost problems frequently arise for patients with multiple conditions, not just one. Presumably, communication and information sharing between the various actors in these systems would be better, but we do not yet know whether this would translate into easier patient navigation. And while the creation of interdisciplinary teams has been cited as a possible solution and can lead to improved coordination and quality, there is no evidence to suggest that this would necessarily improve patient navigation, particularly given that teams do not follow patients though transitions of care from one setting to another.

WHAT DOES NAVIGATION MEAN TO THE AVERAGE PATIENT?

Thus far, the health care system has assumed that with some guidance consumers will "figure it out" for themselves. Even to the savviest of consumers, however, this can be a daunting and often unpleasant task.

Coverage Decisions

At the outset, and assuming that they have a choice of coverage (and assuming they can afford one or more of the options), consumers need to select and figure out how to use a health plan. People getting coverage through employers or public payers can, to some extent, rely on those parties to provide some guidance, but people in the individual market are basically on their own. Even assuming that the volumes of forms and paperwork are written to be comprehended by a lay audience, there is considerable variation in people's abilities to understand the information and apply it to their own situation. Once a plan has been selected, patients still need to learn to use it to their advantage. This involves knowing what is covered at what level, following ground rules for using services (e.g., referral processes) and learning what to do in the case of a reimbursement dispute. For those in need of public assistance, another set of hurdles must be cleared just to prove eligibility for coverage.

Health Care Service Decisions

Choosing the best health care services—and then using those services effectively—adds yet another set of potentially challenging tasks for consumers. Even a simple doctor's visit can pose a navigational challenge. Much emphasis is placed on the selection of a health care provider, and there is an ever-expanding body of information being disseminated to consumers in the hopes that they will select high-quality, low-cost providers. Yet the extent to which this choice is meaningful depends on whether providers are covered under the plans consumers choose, and are willing to accept new patients.

Once patients have successfully chosen providers, their navigational tasks are highly dependent on the level of health care services required to prevent or manage their illnesses. In addition to the emotional burden of illness, people challenged with major clinical events may have to assume an even greater responsibility for managing their own care. That may include learning about a variety of highly technical treatment options, working with providers to make appropriate treatment decisions, and ensuring that their care is being coordinated, since the system is not inherently coordinated. For those managing multiple conditions over a long period of time, this workload is compounded, and the job of navigation becomes even more challenging.

FACILITATING PATIENT NAVIGATION: WHERE WE ARE NOW AND WHERE WE NEED TO GO

Thus far, efforts to improve patient navigation have not challenged the existing care delivery structure;

they have only introduced professional or lay "navigators" to assist patients within specific domains of care. In many of these instances, the role of the navigator is to (1) help patients access and use services, and (2) provide psychosocial support. This support function has been demonstrated to be a life-saving element of cancer care.

Health plans have used nurse navigators to manage complex conditions. Care managers and coordinators represent another version of this approach. Humana, for example, employs a set of trained nurses who initiate contact with beneficiaries whose diagnoses or service utilization patterns suggest a higher risk and or cost. Though this practice is common, there is little evidence to suggest that it improves patient outcomes or facilitates patient navigation. Researchers looking at the use of navigators in cancer care suggest that these team members "differ from other cancer support personnel in their orientation toward flexible problem solving to overcome perceived barriers to care rather than the provision of a predefined set of services." This suggests the need for further research to better understand the value proposition of such navigators.

Moving forward, it will be important to consider three primary questions in order to develop a research agenda that will help to better understand patient navigation:

1. Where should attention be focused?
2. Which patients should attention be focused on?
3. Which points in the health care sector should be areas of focus?

With respect to the first question, given the role of the primary care provider as the de facto coordinator of care (whether it actually happens or not), it may be instructive to focus research in this area. Given the limited time and capacity of solo and small practice providers coupled with reimbursement pressures, it may be best to start with larger, multispecialty groups. This would also afford the opportunity to explore navigation both within and between complex institutions.

Whatever settings are determined most appropriate for initial exploration, patient navigation researchers may wish to look for opportunities to piggyback on work that is going on in related areas, such as care coordination, transitions management and disease management. They may also wish to explore opportunities for introducing more patient-centered tools that can facilitate coordination and integration of care, such as personal health records.

These specifics aside, several priority issues for initial research have been suggested, including:

1. Using population surveys to develop a baseline "epidemiology" of patient navigation in order to better appreciate and enumerate all of the elements involved and to identify who is most affected by navigation issues, under what circumstances they are affected and how patients currently deal with system complexity

2. Conducting observational studies that look at different patient navigation interventions currently being used, as well as treatment settings with different levels of intended structural "integration" models to measure their effect on patient outcomes and experiences

3. Developing interventions at the systems level to re-engineer the health care sector so that it becomes more inherently navigable by consumers

4. Documenting the health and financial consequences associated with problems in patient navigation

While research in all of these issue areas would require significant work, we will not fully appreciate the societal cost associated with the status quo—nor the potential savings associated with evidence-based solutions—until we better understand navigation problems in U.S. health care.

About the Author
Alison Rein is a Senior Associate with AcademyHealth.

17

Lessons from Abroad

The United States spends more than any other country on healthcare. In 2005, the U.S. spent $6,041 per capita on healthcare, which was more than double the median per capita expenditures of the other 30 industrialized countries in the Organization for Economic Cooperation and Development (OECD) at $2,922. Spending in the U.S. was 16% of GDP in 2008 and is estimated to be around 20% by 2017.[2] In comparison, other OECD countries spent about 9.1% of their GDP on healthcare. Despite all the money spent on the healthcare system, the U.S. still scores average or below average on health outcomes and quality measures. The data indicate that the U.S. is not getting value for the money it puts into healthcare, as numerous other countries spend less to produce better health outcomes.[1] The structure and organization of other nations' health systems could provide lessons for the U.S. as it embarks on healthcare reform.

A recent example of a country's successful attempt at healthcare reform is the Netherland's market-oriented reforms throughout the past couple of decades, eventually culminating in the Health Insurance Act (HIA) of 2006. In 1987, the Dekker Committee, appointed by the Dutch government to evaluate the healthcare system, recommended a market-oriented healthcare reform alongside the creation of a national health insurance system.[3,4] Between 1987 and 2006, a series of small reforms took place that laid the foundation for the HIA. A system of risk equalization, product classification, and medical pricing was established. Coupled with outcome and quality measures, the system was designed to emphasize competition based on better patient care rather than prices. With the passage of HIA, every individual living or working in the Netherlands were required to purchase, at the very least, a basic insurance plan from private companies. Unlike the United Kingdom, Australia, or New Zealand with universal healthcare through a single-payer system, the Netherlands utilizes private insurance companies to foster competition in a managed market. The basic plan that is required for purchase includes care by primary care physicians and specialists, pharmaceuticals, and hospital visits for up to one year. Competition is driven more on the quality of each coverage and its providers, rather than the prices. If individuals want additional coverage, supplemental plans are also available for purchase at the discretion of the enrollee. Under the law, insurance companies are not allowed to reject any applicants or charge different premiums. In order to balance out enrollees who may cost more or less than average, risk equalization became an important feature of Dutch healthcare. Enrollees of each insurance company are evaluated and companies with enrollees that cost more than average are paid by the government from the Risk Equalization Fund, while companies with enrollees that cost less than average pay into the fund. Since the full implementation of HIA, 98% of the population has been under an insurance plan, a percentage much higher than the proportion of insured Americans.[3,4,5] The reform of the Dutch system provides a suitable example for U.S. to emulate. It is more compatible with the American culture of "individual choice, multiple competing approaches, local control, and pluralism" than single-payer systems controlled entirely by the government.[4]

Other countries also see universal coverage as an important aspect of society. Germany, the United Kingdom, Israel, Australia, and New Zealand are just some of the countries that provide universal coverage to their citizens. In Germany, 90% of the population pays into a statutory health insurance fund, which is supplemented by employers and taxes, while the remaining 10% with above average income purchase private insurance schemes. The statutory health insurance fund covers any service for the patient deemed necessary and cost-effective. The Institute for Quality and Efficiency in Health Care provides the government with comparative-effectiveness research and scientific recommendations of any new, innovative medical products and treatments. In order to be covered by the state's insurance system, the new product or service must be more advantageous than those already available and in the market, thus limiting access to expensive procedures that may not be cost-effective. Patients may still receive these services, but have to pay out-of-pocket to do so. Admittedly, the German system is being pressured into reform as many are dissatisfied with the service they are receiving.[6]

In Israel, the National Health Insurance Law (NHIL) passed in 1995 provided every citizen in the country with a basic package of healthcare. healthcare is funded by general-revenue taxation and income-tax. Much like other systems, Israel also allows its citizens to purchase supplemental coverage if they so desire. Four sickness plans compete to manage and provide care for its members, and the government distributes funds to these plans according to need and efficiency. The plans are mandated by law to accept all applicants despite pre-existing conditions. To fund this healthcare system, Israel only spends 8% of its GDP, only $2,000 per capita, which is significantly less than the United States. Their health outcomes are also better than the US. For example, life expectancy at birth in Israel is 80.3 years compared with 77.8 years in the US.[7]

Not only are other countries' health outcomes much better than the US, there is a significant difference between the actual life expectancy in the U.S. compared to the predicted average life expectancy based on GDP per capita. Based on a bivariate regression that looked at life expectancy and GDP per capita, the predicted U.S. life expectancy was found at 80.9 years, a 3.1 year difference. On this same regression, Italy, Japan, Spain, and Australia showed better actual life expectancies than the predicted number from the model, indicating that it is possible to get more with less.[1]

Americans are also generally more dissatisfied with the performance of the healthcare system than people from most other countries, with the majority of the concerns stemming from affordability. A survey of adults across the United States, Australia, New Zealand, Germany, the Netherlands, Canada, and the United Kingdom indicates that the organization and structure of these other countries allows for more patient-centered care which is viewed more positively than the fragmented healthcare system of the US. Adults in Australia, the Netherlands, Germany, and New Zealand reported easy accessibility to their primary care providers outside of the normal nine-to-five work week. The Netherlands have an after-hours cooperative that handles patient concerns after 6 pm, and the majority of Dutch and German practices also have early morning hours. The after-hour co-ops seemed the most effective at providing after-hours care since Dutch patients were the least likely to voice concerns about difficulty in access. Primary care that is both easily accessible and coordinates further care received the most positive survey results. Limiting financial barriers to healthcare through universal coverage was also an important aspect of patient satisfaction. Fragmented coverage seemed to only act as a barrier to higher-quality and more efficient care.[8]

The most important lesson that the U.S. can learn from these countries is perhaps not on universal coverage, but on how to cut costs while enhancing value through comparative-effectiveness research, implementation of information technology (IT), and financial incentives to meet quality performance measures. Both Britain and Australia have organizations that evaluate the value of any new medical technology and treatments. Britain's National Institute for Health and Clinical Excellence evaluates new drugs, devices, and diagnostic tools and evaluates the cost against the quality-adjusted life years (QALY) it produces. It only recommends new technologies to the National Health Service, which is the entity that provides healthcare in Britain, if the cost per unit of health benefit falls below a threshold such as $50,000 per QALY. There is no comparable organization in the U.S. that examines cost-effectiveness of new technology, which results in the proliferation of expensive new techniques that may or may not be as effective or cost-beneficial as current methods. The implementation of IT has also been slow with only a quarter of U.S. primary care physicians utilizing electronic medical records, whereas 90% or more use IT in Britain, the Netherlands, and New Zealand. Implementing IT is expensive, but over time, it would be able to save the U.S. healthcare system more than $80 billion. In addition, primary care physicians in Britain are given financial incentives to reach certain quality performance measures. If targets are met in preventive care, the management of chronic conditions, and patient feedback, general practitioners could receive a 25% bonus. Financial incentives to reach quality targets are different from the U.S. system that pays not for quality, but for the quantity of services rendered. Pay-for-performance has the potential to improve the value of the care received by patients.[2,9]

Admittedly, the U.S. is not the only healthcare system struggling to provide care for its population while keeping costs contained. China is currently struggling with the same problems of a large uninsured population and rapidly rising costs. When China re-oriented its economy, it also put an end to its universal coverage system and placed healthcare on the same market-oriented economy as the rest of its businesses. Now, healthcare coverage is received through employment and does not cover dependents and migrant workers so that most healthcare expenses are paid out-of-pocket. In China, healthcare has turned into a profitable business in which the focus is not always on patients. Physicians over-prescribe drugs and tests while hospitals provide expensive, innovative procedures to turn profits. Services are also fragmented, with little coordination between primary and secondary/tertiary services, similar to the system in the US. China and the United States are both in need of healthcare reform for similar problems. Both countries need to determine how to extend coverage to the uninsured, cut costs, and provide better service.[10]

In this chapter, we included readings and excerpts of reports that showcase both successful and less successful international experiences. In **Slowing the Growth of Health Care Costs—Learning from International Experience,** Davis provided the rationale for learning from other countries when it comes to healthcare delivery and financing. The U.S. spends more money on healthcare than any other country in the world, and yet, it is still the only industrialized nation without universal health coverage, and the differences do not end there. The structure of the U.S. healthcare system is widely different from that of other countries with its focus on specialties rather than primary care. It has been slow to adopt the policies of its counterparts in the developed world in reducing healthcare spending. The U.S. has also been slow in the use of information technology, such as electronic medical records.

In Britain, the National Institute of Health and Clinical Excellence judge the effectiveness of new drugs, devices, and diagnostic tools before determining whether to recommend the item to the medical community. The organization evaluates the cost of the new technology and determines how many quality-adjusted life years (QALY) it can impact based on the cost. New technology is recommended only if it is below a certain threshold, which is currently at $50,000 per QALY. There is no similar process in the United States.

Information technology is another area in which the U.S. has fallen behind other nations where its use is widespread. Only 25% of primary care providers have electronic medical records in the U.S., while 90% of physicians use them in countries such as Great Britain, New Zealand, and the Netherlands.

The organization of the U.S. healthcare system presents another major difference between U.S. and other nations. Patients outside of the U.S. are required to have a primary care provider. They cannot immediately see specialists, but must be referred by their primary care physician. There is also a larger focus on preventive care in other nations than in the U.S. Primary care physicians in Britain receive bonuses if they hit quality targets, such as managing chronic diseases and providing preventive care. Primary care is also more widely accessible in some European nations, including the Netherlands, providing an excellent system for receiving after-hour care. Specialists in these nations are often salaried, hospital employees, rather than physicians in private practice.

Partisan division within the U.S. federal government is at least partially responsible for the lack of progress in reforming healthcare compared to what other industrialized countries have been able to achieve. New policies pushed by a strong presidential leadership is necessary to move beyond the status quo. The U.S. cannot afford to keep the healthcare system as is. By 2017, the percentage of GDP spent on healthcare is estimated to reach 20% while those without adequate insurance will continue to suffer from preventable diseases if nothing significant is done.

In **Comparative Effectiveness in Health Care Reform: Lessons from Abroad,** Helen Evans of the Heritage Foundation sheds insights on learning from other countries in the context of comparative effectiveness research currently advocated in the US. The American Recovery and Reinvestment Act, also known as the economic stimulus bill, establishes a Federal Coordinating Council for Comparative Effectiveness Research. The organization would act similar to Britain's National Institute for Health and Clinical Excellence (NICE), investigating the cost-effectiveness of new drugs and medical devices before they enter the market. Comparative effectiveness research (CER) was fueled by the variations in medical decisions and outcomes in the 20th century. Variations in healthcare services indicated that some places were providing too much or too little care. CER attempts to impose a strict algorithm on medical decisions in the context of economic rationality, though it mostly succeeds, instead, in reflecting the political climate of the times. Rationing healthcare technology, however, limits personal freedom and choice. International examples show that these organizations severely limit the access of patients to innovative treatments that, while expensive, may actually help their conditions. Without a body to regulate the cost-effectiveness of treatments, the United States is currently able to rapidly diffuse new medical technology, providing patients with better levels of availability than in European nations. Imposing an Institute for Comparative Effectiveness Research, as suggested by President Barack Obama would only be counterproductive in improving the health status of the country and the health system towards the "European-style medical interventionism." CER is only useful if the assessment is done in the private sector with a basis on competition and non-coercion, and still provides health professionals with the freedom to choose the treatments they see fit, rather than adhering to uniform treatments mandated by the government.

President Obama has proposed the creation of an Institute for Comparative Effectiveness as a key component of an ambitious healthcare reform. The institute would have the authority to make official determinations of the clinical effectiveness and cost-effectiveness of medical treatments, procedures,

drugs, and medical devices. Today, in virtually every country, healthcare is heavily influenced by government policy that fosters a professional monopoly of supply and strict top-down regulation. The creation of an Institute for Comparative Effectiveness would mean more government control of private medical decisions. The idea that government is intrinsically superior to a spontaneous and free market is groundless. American policymakers who believe the healthcare systems in many European countries to be ideal should learn about citizens of the United Kingdom being denied the medicines they need. It is clear from the British experience and other international examples that a comparative effectiveness strategy that relies on central planning and coercion would be counterproductive and also would lead to cost constraints that could worsen patients' medical conditions and damage the quality of their lives.

In **Evaluating the WHO Assessment Instrument for Mental Health Systems by Comparing Mental Health Policies in Four Countries,** Dr. Hamid and colleagues examined mental health policies in four countries. Mental health is often an overlooked aspect of healthcare and labeled as a low priority despite its importance in the general well-being of an individual. In order to gather information on the mental health systems and infrastructure of each country, the World Health Organization (WHO) developed the Assessment Instrument for Mental Health System (AIMS). It evaluates each mental health system through six sectors: policy and legislative framework, mental health services, mental health in primary care, human resources, education of the public, and surveillance and research.

Using AIMS, the mental health services of four countries—the Philippines, Iraq, the former Yugoslav Republic of Macedonia, and Japan—were evaluated. These four countries were chosen because of their recent attempts at building better systems in place to deal with mental health.

Among the four countries, only Japan has a string of mental health policies and laws, though the budget focusing on this sector is meager. The Yugoslav Republic of Macedonia has the highest ratio of mental health professionals per 100,000 patients, with Japan coming in second. Overall, there are not enough professionals performing the service in a community health setting where it is needed. There is a limited amount of mental health services in the primary care sector, despite WHO's push for the shift of psychiatry into primary care. In Iraq, only 7% of primary care providers and 1% of nurses receive post-graduate training in mental health. Additionally, the monitoring and surveillance of mental health in all four countries is limited, thus providing an incomplete picture of the problem.

While AIMS assessment can provide information on mental health systems across the globe, it also has its limitations. It does not evaluate the data based on the cultural context of the region. For example, extended family networks in both Iraq and the Philippines are an important aspect of the culture, which often results in better prognosis for mentally ill patients by providing a smoother transition back into society through a support network of close family members and friends. It also does not account for spiritual leaders and their efforts in treating the mentally ill. In some countries, individuals seek help from spiritual leaders rather than doctors for their health concerns. Furthermore, data does not account for the political climate that shapes the healthcare systems and influences the quality and accessibility of the services. Despite these shortcomings, AIMS assessment is an informative tool that can provide a general picture of the mental health system and infrastructure of a country.

Finally, in **China's Health System Performance**, Yuanli Liu, and others reviewed health systems performance achieved by China in recent years. Despite tremendous growth in the Chinese economy, recent trends suggest that dissatisfaction with healthcare services is growing within the population. In 1998, 12% of Chinese in urban areas and 7% of the population in rural areas were dissatisfied with hospital services. By 2003, the percentage increased sharply to 61% and 54%, respectively. To evaluate the performance of the health system, healthcare delivery and healthcare financing were reviewed.

The study showed that China did not have many health interventions in place. While it has safe drinking water, prenatal care, hospital delivery, and childhood vaccination programs, it is lacking in other significant areas. Only 21% of people in rural areas have access to sanitary toilets. There are very few smoking cessation programs and policies despite its large population of smokers. Programs that monitor infectious disease are also insufficient with a low rate of examinations from suspected tuberculosis cases. There is a struggle to provide access to health interventions that are cost-efficient but unprofitable.

In addition to the shortcomings of its interventions, there is also a significant gap between the poor and rich. Low-income populations face particular hardships in accessing healthcare services. This population group often has no money to pay for services, or is at risk of incurring catastrophic medical spending. Inability to pay for services was cited by 75% of people in urban areas and 83% in rural villages.

The evaluation of China's health system, however, is limited by the availability of data. Only four sets of national surveys were used, and despite the large sample size for each survey it may not be nationally and regionally representative. There is also limited information on public health interventions, such as seatbelt use and mental health services. More comprehensive datasets are needed to develop a better picture of the country's current health system and more accurately monitor its progress.

• • • References

1. Anderson, Gerard; Frogner, Bianca K. "Health Spending in OECD Countries: Obtaining Value Per Dollar." *Health Affairs*, 2008; 1718–1727.

2. Davies, Karen. "Slowing the Growth of Health Care Costs—Learning from International Experience." *New England Journal of Medicine*, 2008; 359: 1751–1755.

3. van Den Ven, Wynand P.M.M.; Schut, Frederik. "Universal Mandatory Health Insurance in the Netherlands: A Model for the United States?" *Health Affairs*, 2008; 27: 771–781.

4. Enthoven, Alain C.; Van de Ven, Wynand P.M.M. "Going Dutch—Managed Competition Health Insurance in the Netherlands." *New England Journal of Medicine*, 2007; 357: 2421–2423

5. Enthoven, Alain. "A Living Model of Managed Competition: A Conversation with Dutch Health Minister Ab Kink." *Health Affairs*, 2008; 27:w196–w203.

6. Sawicki, Peter T. "Communal Responsibility for Health Care—The Example of Benefit Assessment in Germany." *New England Journal of Medicine*, 2009; 361: e42

7. Chernichovsky, Dov. "Not 'Socialized Medicine'— An Israeli View of Health Care Reform." *New England Journal of Medicine*, 2009; 361: e46

8. Schoen, Cathy; Osborn, Robin; Doty, Michelle M.; Bishop, Meghan; Peugh, Jordan; Murukutla. "Toward Higher-Performance Health Systems: Adults' Health Care Experiences in Seven Countries, 2007." *Health Affairs*, 2007; 26: w717–w734.

9. Campbell, Stephen; Reeves, David; Kontopantellis, Evangelos; Middleton, Elizabeth; Sibbald, Bonnie; Roland, Martin. "Quality of Primary Care in England with Pay For Performance." *New England Journal of Medicine*, 357: 181–190.

10. Yip, Winnie; Hsiao, William C. "The Chinese Health System at a Crossroads." *Health Affairs*, 2008; 27:460–468

Slowing the Growth of Health Care Costs—Learning from International Experience

Source: Davis K. Slowing the growth of health care costs—learning from international experience. N Engl J Med 2008;359:1751-5. Copyright © 2008 Massachusetts Medical Society. All rights reserved.

High health care expenditures and the growing number of people without health insurance set the United States apart from all other industrialized countries. The United States spends twice per capita what other major industrialized countries spend on health care[1,2] but is the only one that fails to provide near-universal health insurance coverage. We also fail to achieve health outcomes as good, or value for health spending as high, as what is achieved in other countries(see figures).

The United States has been slow to learn from countries that have systematically adopted policies that curtail spending and enhance value. Chief among these are mechanisms for assessing the comparative cost-effectiveness of drugs, devices, diagnostic tests, and treatment procedures; implementation of information technology, including electronic repositories of patient medical information, across sites of care; easy access to primary care, including organized systems of off-hours care; a strong role for government in negotiating payment for care; and payment systems that reward preventive care, management of chronic conditions, care coordination, and health outcomes rather than volume of services.

No single silver bullet will transform the U.S. health care system, but a series of coordinated policy changes has the potential to substantially bend the curve of projected health care spending.[4] Recent estimates prepared for the Commonwealth Fund Commission on a High Performance Health System indicate that $1.5 trillion could be saved over a 10-year period if a combination of options, including universal health insurance, was adopted. These options were specifically designed for the U.S. health care system and would preserve its mixed private-public system of financing rather than being contingent on the adoption of a single-payer system.

The option currently receiving the most attention is a system for generating more information about the effectiveness of medical treatments, weighing it against that of other diagnostic or treatment options, and assessing cost relative to benefits to determine whether more expensive therapies warrant their additional cost.[5] In this effort, the United States can learn from the cost-effectiveness review systems in Britain and Australia.[1] Britain's National Institute for Health and Clinical Excellence makes a judgment about the effectiveness of new drugs, devices, and diagnostic tools relative to existing technology and provides advice on clinical guidelines and management of individual medical conditions that is grounded in a systematic review of available evidence. It evaluates the incremental cost of a new technology per quality-adjusted life year and recommends that the National Health Service cover new technologies whose cost per unit of health benefit is below a certain threshold, such as $50,000 per quality-adjusted life-year.

We have no comparable process.[5] Even a recent legislative proposal calling for a private organization funded by public and private sources to undertake effectiveness research stops short of recommending assessment of the cost-effectiveness of technologies or systematically basing insurance coverage decisions on such evidence. We need to ensure that new technology yields value over and above existing technologies, commensurate with its incremental cost. Investing in the knowledge needed to improve decision making and incorporating information about relative clinical value and cost-effectiveness into the design of insurance benefits would yield an estimated 10-year savings of $368 billion for our health care system (see table).[3]

We also lag behind other industrialized countries in the adoption of information technology.[1,2] Only about one fourth of U.S. primary care physicians have electronic medical records, as compared with 90% in countries such as Britain, the Netherlands, and New Zealand.[1] Denmark has a national health information exchange that contains all of a patient's relevant clinical information in a repository that is accessible to patients and all the providers caring for them. In the United States, accelerating providers' adoption of health information technology with the capacity to support decision making and share patient health information across sites of care could be financed through an assessment of 1% on insurance premiums and Medicare outlays. Estimates are that the initial investment could be recouped after 7 years, and the estimated net savings to the health care system could reach $88 billion over 10 years (see table).

The third area in which the United States differs markedly from other industrialized countries is the financing and organization of primary care.[2] Patients in many other countries are required to enroll with a primary care physician. In Britain, general practitioners receive bonuses accounting for up to 25% of their compensation in exchange for meeting quality targets in preventive care, managing chronic conditions, organizing care, and collecting patient feedback. In addition, primary care in Britain is easily accessible. The Netherlands and Denmark have excellent organized systems of off-hours care. The Netherlands funds the salaries of nurses placed in private physicians' practices to work with patients with selected chronic conditions. Analysis of the cost-savings potential of developing a system of "patient-centered medical homes" for primary care in the United States indicates that Medicare alone could save $194 billion over 10 years (see table).

Other countries control high-cost services through payment practices and patient incentives. France, among other countries, negotiates prices for pharmaceuticals and eliminates cost sharing for highly effective medications. Germany uses a reference-pricing approach, whereby the insurance system pays the lowest price for comparably effective drugs, with patients paying any difference between the reference price and the actual price. Negotiating pharmaceutical prices would generate savings of $43 billion over 10 years in the United States. Japan, though it uses a fee-for-service system of payment, tightly controls rates of payments and, as a matter of deliberate policy, reduces the price of new technologies over time to encourage improved efficiency and productivity.

In some countries, specialist physicians are typically salaried hospital employees. Germany has also set aside a portion of its payments for contracts with providers delivering integrated care, such as cancer care. Moving to a bundled episode-of-care payment system that combines hospital and physician services for episodes of acute care in the United States would generate 10-year savings of $229 billion (see table).

The issue, therefore, is not so much whether we know how to slow down the escalation of health care costs. Abundant international evidence, and even examples in the United States, demonstrate that higher quality, better access, and lower costs can achieved simultaneously. Rather, the United States has been paralyzed by partisan divisions at the level of the federal government and by organized opposition from those who benefit from the status quo. The key to progress may lie in both a presidential administration committed to transformation of the health care system and a new policy process that is better insulated from special-interest political pressures. At a recent summit sponsored by the Senate Finance Committee, both Chairman Max Baucus and Federal Reserve Board Chairman Ben Bernanke raised the possibility of a "Health Fed" or a "MedPAC (Medicare Payment Advisory Commission) with teeth," which would be delegated by Congress to make specific payment and policy decisions under a broad policy framework established by Congress. This approach, applied first to Medicare, could accelerate the diffusion of policy innovations throughout the country and provide a testing ground for broader application to Medicaid and commercial insurers.

The status quo is unacceptable. Without serious commitment to change, health spending as a percentage of the gross domestic product will rise from 16% currently to 20% by 2017; and Americans

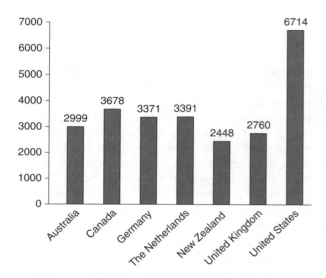

Panel A Health Expenditures per Capita (U.S. dollars)

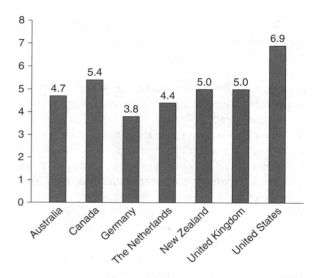

Panel C Infant Deaths per 1000 Births Health Expenditures per Capita (U.S. dollars)

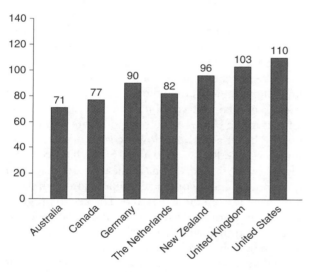

Panel B Deaths before the Age of 75 That Could Be Averted through Medical Care (per 100,000)

Dr. Davis is the president of the Commonwealth Fund, New York.

About the Author
Alison Rein is a Senior Associate with AcademyHealth.

• • •   References

1. American College of Physicians. Achieving a high-performance health care system with universal access: what the United States can learn from other countries. Ann Intern Med 2008;148:55-75. [Erratum, Ann Intern Med 2008;148:635.] .

2. Schoen C, Osborn R, Doty MM, Bishop M, Peugh J, Murukutla N. Toward higher-performance health systems: adults' health care experiences in seven countries, 2007. Health Aff (Millwood) 2007;26: w717-w734.

3. Nolte E, McKee CM. Measuring the health of nations: updating an earlier analysis. Health Aff (Millwood) 2008;27:58-71.

4. Schoen C, Guterman S, Shih A, et al. Bending the curve: options for achieving savings and improving value in U.S. health spending. New York: The Commonwealth Fund, 2007.

5. Orszag PR, Ellis P. Addressing rising health care costs—a view from the Congressional Budget Office. N Engl J Med 2007; 357:1885-7.

without adequate insurance and access to essential services will continue to suffer avoidable health consequences. American resources and ingenuity are adequate for the challenge. What is required is national leadership and commitment to moving toward a high-performance health care system.

No potential conflict of interest relevant to this article was reported.

Policy Options and Their Projected 10-Year Impact on Spending.*					
Policy Option	**Spending**				
	Total National	Federal Government	State and Local Government	Private Payer	Household
			billions of $		
Producing and using better information					
Promoting health information technology	−88	−41	−19	0	−27
Establishing a Center for Medical Effectiveness and Health Care Decision Making	−368	−114	−49	−98	−107
Instituting patient-shared decision making	−9	−8	0	0	−1
Promoting health and disease prevention					
Promoting public health: reducing tobacco use (through new taxes invested in prevention programs)	−191	−68	−35	−39	−49
Promoting public health: reducing obesity (through new taxes invested in prevention programs)	−283	−101	−52	−57	−73
Instituting positive incentives for healthy behavior (through federally funded wellness programs)	−19	2	−12	−4	−5
Aligning incentives with quality and efficiency					
Instituting Medicare hospital pay-for-performance	−34	−27	−1	−2	−4
Instituting Medicare episode-of-care payment	−229	−377	18	90	40
Strengthening primary care and care coordination in Medicare	−194	−157	−4	−9	−23
Limiting federal tax exemptions for premium contributions	−131	−186	−19	−55	130
Correcting price signals in the health care market					
Resetting benchmark rates for Medicare Advantage plans	−50	−124	0	0	74
Instituting competitive bidding between traditional Medicare and private plans	−104	−283	0	0	178
Instituting negotiated prescription-drug prices	−43	−72	4	17	8
Applying Medicare provider-payment methods and rates to all payers	−122	0	0	−105	−18
Limiting payment updates in high-cost areas	−158	−260	13	62	27

* A negative number indicates a decrease in spending as compared with projected expenditures (i.e., savings); a positive number indicates an increase in spending. In some cases, because of rounding, the sum of the effects on spending by the various payers does not add up to the total effect on national health expenditures. Data are from Schoen et al.[2] and are based on modeling by the Lewin Group.

2

Comparative Effectiveness in Health Care Reform: Lessons from Abroad

Source: Evans, Helen. Comparative Effectiveness in Health Care Reform: Lessons from Abroad. The Heritage Foundation. *Backgrounder* #2239, February 4, 2009. Courtesy of the Heritage Foundation.

President Barack Obama has proposed the creation of an Institute for Comparative Effectiveness as a key component of an ambitious health care reform.[1] The institute would have the authority to make official determinations of the clinical effectiveness and cost-effectiveness of medical treatments, procedures, drugs, and medical devices.

President Obama's initial nominee as Secretary of Health and Human Services (HHS), former Senator Tom Daschle (D-SD), has likewise proposed the creation of a supremely powerful Federal Health Board, which would have similar authority to make decisions that would be binding on health plans and providers financed by federal taxpayers, and potentially on private health insurance coverage.[2] While Senator Daschle has withdrawn his name from Senate consideration, the concept of such a board or institute is strongly indicative of the Obama Administration's policy orientation toward centralized health policy decision-making.

The U.S. House of Representatives has just passed the $850 billion American Recovery and Reinvestment Act (H.R. 1), the so-called economic stimulus bill, which would establish a Federal Coordinating Council for Comparative Effectiveness Research. The bill would provide $1.1 billion for the new council and delegate spending authority to the HHS Secretary to investigate the effectiveness of different drugs and medical devices.[3] The Senate version of the economic stimulus package contains a similar provision.

Of course, there is no reason why private-sector or government officials should not have access to the best information on what works and what doesn't.

---

[1] For a brief discussion of the Obama proposal, see Robert E. Moffit and Nina Owcharenko, "The Obama Health Plan: More Power to Washington," Heritage Foundation *Backgrounder* No. 2197, October 15, 2008, at *http://www.heritage.org/research/healthcare/bg2197.cfm*.

[2] For a brief discussion of Daschle's proposed Federal Health Board, see Senator Tom Daschle, with Scott S. Greenberger and Jeanne M. Lambrew, *Critical: What We Can Do About the Health Care Crisis* (New York: Thomas Dunne Books, 2008). See also Robert E. Moffit, "How a Federal Health Board Will Cancel Private Coverage and Care," Heritage Foundation *WebMemo* No. 2155, December 4, 2008, at *http://www.heritage.org/research/healthcare/wm2155.cfm*.

[3] The provision is included in Title IX of Subtitle B of the American Recovery and Reinvestment Act of 2009. According to the report language accompanying the House bill, "By knowing what works best and presenting this information more broadly to patients and health care professionals, those items, procedures, and interventions that are most effective to prevent, control and treat health conditions will be utilized, while those that are found to be less effective and in some cases, more expensive, will no longer be prescribed."

Talking Points

- Today, in virtually every country, health care is heavily influenced by government policy that fosters a professional monopoly of supply and strict top-down regulation.
- President Barack Obama has proposed the creation of an Institute for Comparative Effectiveness would mean more government control of private medical decisions.
- The idea that government is intrinsically superior to a spontaneous and free market is groundless. American policymakers who believe the health care systems in many European countries to be ideal should learn about citizens of the United Kingdom being denied the medicines they need.
- It is clear from the British experience and other international examples that a comparative effectiveness strategy that relies on central planning and coercion would be counterproductive and also would lead to cost constraints that could worsen patients' medical conditions and damage the quality of their lives.

Nor is there any reason why such scientific evaluations should not be widely available to doctors and patients alike. But studies of the comparative effectiveness of medical devices, drugs, and technology should be conducted primarily within the private sector, and there should be no government monopoly over either the research or the distribution of information. The key issue is the personal freedom of patients to be able to choose the health care that, in the professional judgment of their doctors, best serves their personal needs.

Focus on Medical Technology

Technology, in particular, can be expensive. Over the past 20 years, health technology assessment (HTA)—the synthetic coordination of information assessing medicines and treatments—has become increasingly popular with policymakers and legislators around the world. Advocates of HTA invariably believe that such an approach has the capacity to provide decision-makers in the public and private sectors with objective information on the value of medical technologies, devices, and medicines. Driven by concerned perceptions of "unproven technology," "spiraling costs" and "increasing consumer expectations," its proponents aim to produce synthesized research information that they believe sheds light on the effects and costs of various forms of health technology.

Such an approach, however, would guarantee the incremental advance of government control of private medical decisions. While formally touted as an instrument of efficiency and effectiveness, it would distort scientific research in the service of political or budgetary objectives while denying individual freedom of choice. In that sense, this approach would serve as a propaganda tool designed to legitimize anti-consumerist rationing.

COMPARATIVE EFFECTIVENESS IN HEALTH CARE: HOW IT STARTED

The intellectual roots of effectiveness research can be traced back to mid-18th century Scotland and the "arithmetical medicine" practiced by the graduates of the Edinburgh medical school. It was there that James Lind famously undertook a controlled trial of six separate treatments for scurvy.[4] During the 1830s, Pierre Louis developed the *méthode numérique* in Paris, whereby he demonstrated that phlebotomy did not actually improve the survival rates of patients suffering from pneumonia.

At the beginning of the 20th century, Ernest Codman, an American physician, founded what is today known as "outcomes management" in patient care. Shunned by established institutions, he set up his own unit, the End Result Hospital. In line with his teachings and the findings from this unit, end results were made public in a privately published book, *A Study in Hospital Efficiency*.[5] Of 337 patients discharged from the hospital between 1911 and 1916, Codman recorded and publicized 123 errors.

In England, the 1930s saw the development of health services research. In a world increasingly obsessed with egalitarian uniformity, J. A. Glover found a tenfold variation in tonsillectomy.[6] Subsequently, following several decades of socialized health care in the United Kingdom, the 1970s and 1980s witnessed the release of a range of studies that highlighted wide geographical variations in general medical admissions including operations such as appendectomy, caesarean section, cholecystectomy, hys-

---

[4]Stephen R. Brown, *Scurvy: How a Surgeon, a Mariner, and a Gentleman Solved the Greatest Medical Mystery of the Age of Sail* (New York: St. Martin's Press, 2003).
[5]Ernest A. Codman, *A Study in Hospital Efficiency* (Boston, Mass.: Privately printed, 1916).
[6]J. A. Glover, "The Incidence of Tonsillectomy in School Children," *Proceedings of the Royal Society of Medicine*, Vol. XXXI (1938), pp. 1219-1236.

terectomy, tonsillectomy, and prostatectomy.[7] Such variations not only demonstrated the inequities of the National Health Service (NHS), but also raised questions about the probity and cost-effectiveness of many of its treatments.

Following the publication of Archie Cochrane's *Effectiveness and Efficiency: Random Reflections on Health Services*[8] in the United States, researchers demonstrated large variations in the rates of prostatectomy for patients with benign prostatic hyperplasia.[9] This work and others suggested that such variations "meant either under-provision in some places and/or over-provision (and possibly ineffective treatment) in others."[10] While "comparative effectiveness" builds on skepticism, the investigation of variations, randomized control trials, and cost-benefit analysis, its reviews purport to be systematic. As such, they attempt to go beyond the more narrative-based reviews that used to dominate the typical review article in medical literature.

COMPARATIVE EFFECTIVENESS: THE RATIONALE

In recent decades, health care has advanced in significant ways. Across the developed world, not only has medical knowledge progressed, but investment in equipment and drugs has delivered unprecedented gains. Treatments are safer and more effective than ever before. Quality of life and life expectancy have been enhanced. Alongside aging populations has come the world of ever-increasing consumer expectations.

The rapid growth of medical knowledge and technology means it is much harder for doctors and other health care providers to keep up to date. Indeed, the problem of information and practice transference is rendered almost impossible by the fact that health care is now a highly statist and corporatist venture. Today, there is no such thing as a free market in health care, and many of the problems popularly associated with it are in fact the result of state failure.

Today, in virtually every country in the world, health care is heavily influenced by government policy and fosters professional monopoly of supply and strict top-down regulation.[11] While there is nothing inherent in health care that guarantees such an outcome, governments, either actively or passively, grant special legislative favor to interest groups when it comes to people's medical treatments and insurance.

The idea that government is intrinsically a superior agent, over and above a spontaneous and free market, is groundless. As David Friedman, a professor of law at Santa Clara University in California, has argued, both the notion of market failure in health economics and its popularity with most opinion leaders have arisen because many health policy analysts "interpret the problem in terms of fairness rather than efficiency."[12] This almost unconscious adherence to the notion of market failure in health care is rooted in:

the error of judging a system by the comparison between its outcome and the best outcome that can be described, rather than judging it by a comparison between its outcome and the outcome that would actually be produced by the best alternative system available. If, as seems likely, all possible sets of institutions fall short of producing perfect outcomes, then a policy of comparing observed outcomes to ideal ones will reject any existing system. . . . The question we should ask, and try to answer, is not what outcome would be ideal but what outcome we can expect from each of various alternative sets of institutions, and which, from that limited set of alternatives, we prefer. . . . My conclusion is that there is no good reason to expect government involvement in the medical market, either the extensive involvement that now exists or the still more extensive involvement that many advocated, to produce desirable results.[13]

---

[7]D. Sanders, A. Coulter, K. McPherson, *Variations in Hospital Admission Rates: A Review of the Literature* (London: King Edward's Hospital Fund for London, 1989), p. 31.

[8]Archie Cochrane, *Effectiveness and Efficiency: Random Reflections on Health Services* (Leeds: Nuffield Provincial Hospitals Trust, 1972).

[9]J. E. Wennberg, A. G. Mulley, D. Hanley, *et al.*, "An Assessment of Prostatectomy for Benign Urinary Tract Obstruction: Geographic Variations and the Evaluation of Medical Care Outcomes," JAMA, Vol. 259, No. 20 (1988), pp. 3027-3030.

[10]Andrew Stevens, Ruairidh Milne, and Amanda Burls, "Health Technology Assessment: History and Demand," *Journal of Public Health Medicine*, Vol. 25, No. 2 (1998), p. 99.

[11]Brian Micklethwait, "How and How Not to Demonopolise Medicine," *Political Notes* No. 56, Libertarian Alliance, London, 1991.

[12]David Friedman, "Should Medicine Be a Commodity? An Economist's Perspective," *Philosophy and Medicine: Rights to Health Care*, Vol. 38 (1991), at *http://www.daviddfriedman.com/Academic/Medicine_Commodity/Medicine_Commodity.html* (January 29, 2009).

[13]*Ibid.*

Curiously, it is within the context of government control and anti-competitive corporatism that new and innovative medical treatments are met with initiatives for even more rationing by government officials, as well as other highly regulated players including private medical insurers. In recent years, many countries have introduced comparative effectiveness or HTA programs, ostensibly to improve their decision-making and their allocation of relatively scarce medical resources. In reality, many politicians and officials have done so not least because they are trying to get themselves off the hook of past promises they made concerning the provision of comprehensive, unlimited, or, as in the case of the United Kingdom, seemingly "free" health care at the point of service.

Since extensive government intervention has distorted health care markets and has made it impossible for individuals to determine a clear and transparent value of the costs and benefits of health care technology through a normally functioning price system, the proponents of comparative effectiveness, or health technology assessment, have instead resorted to a predictably pseudoscientific methodology to give their bureaucratic determinations a sheen of objectivity. As with other forms of centralized government planning, the practitioners of these bureaucratic arts attempt to capture and mathematically profile and model their assessments; in assessing health technology, they seek "to compare and prioritize new technologies based on different units that aggregate . . . benefits."[14]

In a study of HTA for the Stockholm Network, a prominent European think tank, research has focused on these assessments in terms of the value of human life:

> In HTA, the dominant aggregate natural unit is called quality-adjusted life years (QALYs). Generally, QALYs factor in both the quantity and the quality of life generated by new health care interventions. It is the arithmetic calculation of life expectancy and a measure of the quality of the remaining life years. . . . To date QALYs are the preferred indicator of HTAs calculations, although one may find additional tools in use by HTA bodies such as HRQol ("health related quality of life," which considers physical function, social function, cognitive function, distress, pain: in brief, anything to do

with quality of life), DALYs ("disability life adjusted years"—of life lost due to premature mortality in the population and the years lost due to disability for incidents of the studied health condition), and healthy-year equivalents (HYEs).[15]

Despite the pretense of scientific objectivity, this type of health technology assessment is nothing of the sort. It is designed primarily to provide policymakers with a legitimizing rubric by which they can mimic a few elements of the market and therefore deploy a degree of fake economic rationality in justifying their decisions. In this way, practitioners of HTA attempt to balance the requirement to provide innovative health care technologies with ham-fisted efforts at controlling the costs of those technologies.

Consider the quality of human life and lifespan. The use of QALYs is pseudoscience. It is nothing more than a tool for central planning that attempts to objectify what is inherently subjective. The limited attempts to capture accurately the various "units of healthcare benefit" mean that there is an inevitable gulf between the theoretical underpinnings of QALYs and the actual behavior of ordinary people. Moreover, the artificial prioritization of so-called cost-based considerations by practitioners of health technology assessment is invariably made at the expense of other considerations. As Dr. Meir Pugatch and Francesca Ficai of the Stockholm Network note, "Thus, a decision to prioritize a less therapeutically effective medicine because of cost-based considerations over an effective, but more expensive, medicine could lead to some serious political, social and moral dilemmas."[16]

Not only is this type of health technology assessment methodologically flawed: It is incompatible with personal freedom and contradicts the subjective choices of genuine economic agents. When deployed at the national level through the power of a government agency, it is inevitably subject to additional political pressures. Indeed, in 2009, it is clear that national organizations that conduct these assessments—such as the National Institute for Health and Clinical Excellence in the United Kingdom or the Institute for Quality and Efficiency in Health Care in Germany—are in the business of rationing health care technologies so that they mesh with the politically fixed budgetary allocations of the national government.

---

[14]Meir P. Pugatch and Francesca Ficai, "A Healthy Market? An Introduction to Health Technology Assessment," Stockholm Network, London, 2007, p. 5.

[15]*Ibid.*
[16]*Ibid.*, p. 6.

Today, it is clear that the political economy of these government bodies means that their structures, processes, and pseudoscientific constructs have a significant and detrimental impact on the practice of, and even the public discourse on, health care. Far from reflecting scientific rationality and economics, health technology assessments often reflect either politically driven social judgments of the decision-makers in these agencies or, worse, a thinly veiled attempt to accommodate whatever political pressures happen to be momentarily dominant.

HOW COMPARATIVE EFFECTIVENESS WORKS IN EUROPE

According to the International Network of Agencies for Health Technology Assessments (INAHTA),[17] many industrialized countries have bodies that are charged with health technology assessments or comparative effectiveness studies. Despite this, the evolution of these bodies and their responsibilities at the national decision-making level has been far from uniform.

For example, some of these bodies have an advisory role. They make reimbursements or pricing recommendations to a national or regional governing body, as is the case in Denmark. Others have a more explicit regulatory role. They are accountable to government ministers and are responsible for listing and pricing medicines and devices. This is the case in France, Germany, and the United Kingdom.

The United Kingdom

The experience of the United Kingdom in making the difficult decisions about what kind of health care technologies, devices, drugs, and medical treatments and procedures should be favored in Britain's National Health Service has been cited favorably by Senator Daschle.

The NHS was established in 1948. It is a single-payer health care system, directly administered by the British government, funded through taxation, and provided mainly by public-sector institutions. Because the NHS is a fully nationalized entity, the central government specifies the capital and current budgets of its regional health authorities and determines the expenditure on drugs by controlling the budgets given to each general practitioner. Overall, NHS health care is rationed through long waiting lists and, in some cases, omission of various treatments.[18]

For the British government, the practice of HTA facilitates rationing by delay. It is a tool that aims to ensure that expensive new technologies are initially provided only in hospitals that have the technical capacity to evaluate them. While the NHS Research and Development Health Technology Assessment Programme is funded by the Department of Health and, according to its criteria, researches the costs, effectiveness, and impact of health technologies, the Medicines and Healthcare Products Regulatory Agency (MHRA) ensures that drugs and devices are safe.[19]

In 1999, the government went a step further and set up the National Institute of Health and Clinical Excellence (NICE).[20] At its heart is the Centre for Health Technology Evaluation that issues formal guidance on the use of new and existing medicines based on rigid and proscriptive "economic" and clinical formulas. With the NHS obliged to adhere to NICE's pronouncements, criticism of NICE has been ceaseless, particularly from various patient organizations.

NICE is a controversial body. It has tried repeatedly to stop breast cancer patients from receiving the powerful breakthrough drug Herceptin and patients with Alzheimer's disease from receiving the drug Aricept. The criteria by which this agency makes its decisions have been kept largely secret from the public. As is inevitable with any nationalized health care system, life-extending medicines such as those to treat renal cancers are refused on the grounds of limited resources and the need to make decisions based not on genuine market economics but on an artificial assessment of the benefit that may be gained by the patient and society "as a whole."

In 2001, NICE deliberately restricted state-insured sufferers of multiple sclerosis from receiving the innovative medicine Beta Interferon. Claiming that its relatively high price jeopardized the efficacy of the NHS, patients with the more severe forms of the disease were told that they would have to go on suffering in the name of politically defined equity.[21]

---

[17]See INAHTA home page at *http://www.inahta.org* (January 30, 2009).

[18]Helen Evans, *Sixty Years On—Who Cares for the NHS?* (London: Institute of Economic Affairs, 2008), pp. 26-54.

[19]See MHRA home page at *http://www.mhra.gov.uk* (January 30, 2009).

[20]Pugatch and Ficai, "A Healthy Market? An Introduction to Health Technology Assessment," p. 8.

[21]"MS Research Urges End of NHS Bar on Drug," *The Daily Telegraph*, June 19, 2001.

In more recent years, patients with painful and debilitating forms of rheumatoid arthritis have been informed by NICE that in many instances they will not be allowed to receive a sequential range of medicines that have often been proved to be of significant benefit. Instead, the institute decreed that "people will be prevented from trying a second anti-TNF treatment if the first does not work for their condition."[22]

Similarly, in August 2008, patients with kidney cancer continued to be denied effective treatments designed to prolong their lives, often by months or even a few years. The calculations used by NICE have been systematically disputed by clinical experts who are more concerned with patient welfare than with vote-seeking, but the institute has also come under fire for not involving doctors who are active on the front line of medicine: "With Sutent for instance, there was just one oncologist on the panel."[23]

In January 2009, patients with osteoporosis also fell foul of NICE. The institute declared that only a small minority of patients with this debilitating disease would receive the medicine Protelos, and even they would receive it only as an extreme last resort. While clinicians and osteoporosis support groups have pointed out that more than 70,000 hip fractures result in 13,000 premature deaths in the U.K. each year and that these otherwise avoidable episodes needlessly cost the NHS billions of pounds, not only are patients being denied necessary treatments, but taxpayers' money is wasted.[24]

Indeed, according to its annual reports and accounts, NICE is now spending more money on communicating its decisions than would be spent if it allowed patients access to many of the medicines it is so busy denying them. The money that the institute now spends on public relations campaigns "could have paid for 5,000 Alzheimer's sufferers to get £2.50-a-day drugs for a year," according to *The Daily Mail.*[25]

Devoid of a market and the language of price, this top-down system ironically ignores many of the

societal costs associated with failure to treat severe illness, such as illness-related unemployment. Moreover, the fact that preventing access to more costly medicines may save money in the short term overlooks the costs for the future. If older medicines lead to more rapid deterioration of a condition, the effect could be a more expensive hospital or nursing home episode later.

Denmark

The Danish health care system is completely state-funded, with public provision of hospital beds representing more than 90 percent of the hospital sector. Under the Healthcare Act, citizens are covered for all or part of expenditures for treatment, including reimbursement for all pharmaceutical products listed with the Danish Medicines Agency. Therefore, there is no need for price regulation of drugs. With central and municipal government having significant control of the funding and provision of health care, the acquisition of new technology is left initially to the five regions that run the hospitals.

Denmark's national HTA system was explicitly established on the basis of its making prioritized resource-allocation decisions. Carried out by the unit known as the Danish Centre for Evaluation and Health Technology Assessment (DACEHTA), it operates within the framework of the National Board of Health (NBH), itself a part of the Danish Ministry of Health.[26] In reality, this means that "[t]he Ministry keeps a close watch on it in order to neutralize 'expensive' healthcare technologies, as their adoption results in requests for extra funding from the regions."[27]

France

In France, health care is a statutory right enshrined in the Constitution of the Fifth Republic. Unlike in Denmark or the United Kingdom, however, French health care is financed mainly by social insurance and delivered by a mixture of public and private providers. While two-thirds of French hospitals are state-owned, one-third are private, with half of the latter group being not-for-profit.

There have been various attempts in recent years to extend government control of health care costs. In 1991, the French government extended its Health

[22]See press release, "NICE Limits Options for People with Rheumatoid Arthritis," Arthritis Cares, London, July 21, 2008.

[23]"Nasty Truth About NICE: It's the Body that Rations NHS Drugs. But This Leading Cancer Specialist Says Its Decisions Are Deeply Flawed," *The Daily Mail,* August 8, 2008.

[24]"NICE Decision to Block Osteoporosis Drug Access Was 'Irrational,'" *The Daily Telegraph,* January 20, 2009.

[25]"Drug Watchdog NICE 'Spends More on "Spin" than Tests on New Treatments,'" *The Daily Mail,* September 10, 2008, at *http://www.dailymail.co.uk/health/article-1054049/Drug-watchdog-NICE-spends-spin-tests-new-treatments.html* (January 30, 2009).

[26]See National Board of Health home page at *http://www.sst.dk* (January 30, 2009).

[27]Meir P. Pugatch and Helen Davison, "A Healthy Market? Health Assessment Technology in Context," Stockholm Network, London, 2007, p. 9.

Map system by which it controls the capital construction of all hospitals as well as their budgets, the purchase of medical equipment, the rates charged by private hospitals, the number of pharmacies per head, and even the price of drugs.[28]

In 2005, the government went a stage further with the establishment of a centralized High Health Authority. While this body has had only a limited impact—and France continues to enjoy a comparatively higher diffusion rate for new technologies than is found in many other countries in Europe—it is nevertheless designed to stipulate the benefits of medicines and determine their price-reimbursement levels. As such, it is set to raise the focus on cost-containment and bring its decision-making under closer state control.

Germany

As in France, health care in Germany is financed primarily by social insurance and provided by a mixture of public and private providers. While all services are contracted instead of being provided directly by the government, more than 10 percent of Germans opt for full private medical insurance.[29] Providing a potent source of exit from the state, the regulated private sector puts pressure on the government to ensure that the sectoral differences in service do not become so wide that ever-larger numbers of young, high-income consumers defect by going private and delegitimizing a central pillar of the Bismarckian philosophy.

While the pressure to maintain some semblance of parity with the private sector meant that state spending rose dramatically for many years after the introduction of a formal reference pricing system in 1989, the strategic objective of the German Ministry of Health has been to reduce supply, particularly through the use of published positive and negative lists concerning medicines and treatments. Through these lists, pressure is applied to the statutory sick funds to control costs.[30]

It is in this context that health technology assessment has played an ever-greater role in German health policy since the 1990s. In 1990, the Office of Technology Assessment at the German Parliament

(TAB) was established, and in 2004, the government set up the Institute for Quality and Economic Efficiency in the Healthcare Sector (IQWiG).

Tasked with the central goal of efficiency, IQWiG investigates and stipulates which therapeutic and diagnostic services are appropriate.[31] Disseminating its pronouncements to various self-governing bodies, its information is used concerning the coverage of technologies in the benefits catalogue. With such ventures being funded primarily by the German Ministry for Health and Social Affairs, assessment bodies can refuse a hospital's claim for reimbursement for the unauthorized use of new technology.

LESSONS FOR AMERICAN POLICYMAKERS

There is a pervasive European mythology: a widespread belief that American health care is rooted in the free market. In reality, much of American health care is a highly planned, regulated, and government-funded system. Through major entitlement and welfare programs such as Medicare and Medicaid, which contribute to rapidly growing American health care costs, government takes a historically higher proportion of gross domestic product than does even the British NHS. Moreover, by virtue of the structure and financing of private-sector health insurance, there is little consumer control over health care dollars.

Nonetheless, the United States is not only a major consumer of health care services, but also the world's largest producer of medical technology. Investment in new medical technology is comparatively high, as is its rate of diffusion: "This is demonstrated by cross-national examinations of the comparative availability of selected medical technologies such as radiation therapy and open-heart surgery. Measured in units per million, the United States experiences levels of availability up to three times greater than in Canada and Germany."[32]

During the presidential campaign, Barack Obama proposed an Institute for Comparative Effectiveness that would make formal recommendations on medical technologies, devices, and drugs. In

[28]Brian Abel-Smith and Elias Mossialos, "Cost Containment and Health Care Reform: A Study of the European Union," London School of Economics and Political Science *Occasional Paper in Health Policy* No. 2, 1994, pp. 33-35.

[29]Pugatch and Davison, "A Healthy Market? Health Assessment Technology in Context," p. 10.

[30]*Ibid.*, p. 11.

[31]*Ibid.*

[32]"American Democracy and Health Care," *British Journal of Political Science*, Vol. 27, No. 4 (October 1997), p. 573.

Congress, champions of comprehensive overhaul of U.S. health care favor policies that would explicitly accelerate America's trajectory downward toward a European-style medical interventionism.

Fearing the impact of the rising costs of Medicare, Medicaid, and the highly regulated arrangements of the private insurance sector, many American legislators and other top policymakers are becoming attracted to the idea of a body that would make top-down pronouncements on the cost-effectiveness of new medical technologies. The idea of a statutorily created agency charged with system-wide cost containment and rationing of medical services and technologies is becoming surprisingly fashionable in Washington policy circles.

The implications of this trend are alarming for U.S. citizens, particularly when one considers that the technology a society uses reflects the wider and underlying incentive structures it adopts for using it: "An incentive structure that encourages providers to trade off the costs and benefits of health care gives providers little incentive to use expensive technologies and thus researchers will have little incentive to create it."[33]

In the long term, a statist, centralized control of medical technology offers little if any regulatory benefit. Through its own logic, it not only stifles innovation, but also, in doing so, ends up precluding those very inventions that could turn out to be of immeasurable benefit to individuals and to society in general.

If comparative effectiveness and health technology assessment especially are to be useful, they must be generated primarily by the private sector on a competitive and non-coercive basis. In avoiding the imposition of a uniformity of rules that comes with government intervention, physicians and other medical professionals would and should remain free to pick and choose from the best practices and professional insights into the treatment of medical conditions as they see fit (with, of course, the informed consent of their patients).

It is only by returning health care to a genuinely patient-centered and consumer-driven health care marketplace that information, innovation, and best practice will permeate the complex array of health care arrangements in both the public and the private sectors. It is only through open competition and the economic discipline of the free market that real progress and productivity can be secured.

Therefore, in framing a policy on comparative effectiveness, America's policymakers should be governed by four principles:

- **They should reject the statutory creation of a board, council, or institute that would centralize government control of patient access to drugs, devices, medical technologies, treatments, or procedures.** This is especially the case if such an agency were to have the power to override the considered judgment of competing professional expertise, especially the professional judgment of a patient's attending physician.

- **Comparative effectiveness research and health technology assessments should be undertaken primarily by the private sector.** While government can contribute to research efforts and promote the widespread availability of the best information, it must not exercise monopoly power over the conduct of research itself or the distribution of information.

- **Comparative effectiveness research should be patient-centered and supportive of quality and value, not focused simply on cost-containment.** In this respect, it should foster scientific advances, health information technology, and the emerging science of personalized medicine.

- **Comparative effectiveness research must move beyond randomized clinical trials and embrace practical clinical trials.** It should include observational data, and its methodologies should fully address issues such as the validity and applicability of findings.

CONCLUSION

As is clear from the British experience and other international examples, a comparative effectiveness strategy that relies on central planning and coercion would not only be counterproductive in the long run—because it would undermine the incentives for medical innovation—but would also lead to the imposition of cost constraints that would worsen patients' medical conditions and damage the quality of their lives.

Helen Evans, Ph.D., is a citizen of the United Kingdom. A registered general nurse, she is the Director of Nurses for Reform and a Health Fellow with the Adam Smith Institute of London, England.

---

[33]Pugatch and Davison, "A Healthy Market? Health Assessment Technology in Context," p. 16.

3

Evaluating the WHO Assessment Instrument for Mental Health Systems by Comparing Mental Health Policies in Four Countries

Source: Hamid, Hamada; Abanilla, Karen; and Huang, Keng-Yen. Evaluating the WHO Assessment Instrument for Mental Health Systems by comparing mental health policies in four countries. *Bulletin of the World Health Organization* 2008; 86: 467-473. Courtesy of the World Health Organization.

ABSTRACT

Mental health is a low priority in most countries around the world. Minimal research and resources have been invested in mental health at the national level. As a result, WHO has developed the Assessment Instrument for Mental Health Systems (WHO-AIMS) to encourage countries to gather data and to re-evaluate their national mental health policy. This paper demonstrates the utility and limitations of WHO-AIMS by applying the model to four countries with different cultures, political histories and public health policies: Iraq, Japan, the Philippines and the former Yugoslav Republic of Macedonia.

WHO-AIMS provides a useful model for analysing six domains: policy and legislative framework; mental health services; mental health in primary care; human resources; education of the public at large; and monitoring and research. This is especially important since most countries do not have experts in mental health policy or resources to design their own evaluation tools for mental health systems.

Furthermore, WHO-AIMS provides a standardized database for cross-country comparisons. However, limitations of the instrument include the neglect of the politics of mental health policy development, underestimation of the role of culture in mental health care utilization, and questionable measurement validity.

INTRODUCTION

Countries across the globe have long overlooked the issue of mental health and mental illness. Countries spend little on mental health, especially developing countries that allocate less than 1% of their gross domestic product (GDP), while developed countries only spend about 5% of their GDP.[1] These figures are remarkable given that one single mental illness, unipolar major depression, is today one of the top five leading causes of disability worldwide and is expected to be the second leading cause of disability worldwide by 2020.[2]

In 2003, almost half (40-50%) of low- to middle-income countries did not have mental health policies.[3] In response, WHO developed the Assessment Instrument for Mental Health Systems (WHO-AIMS), designed to gather information on specific components of a country's mental health system and its infrastructure, in order to promote the development of mental health policies.[4]

WHO-AIMS may have a significant influence on how developing countries view the "model" mental health system. The WHO-AIMS tool provides a template for regional mental health care experts to enter essential data regarding six domains of mental health care systems: policy and legislative framework; mental health services; mental health in primary care; human resources; education of the public at large; and monitoring and research.

The initial instrument was piloted in several countries. While the overall conclusion of the pilot test was that WHO-AIMS was useful, the initial length of the instrument precluded several countries from completing it. Currently, 50 countries have agreed to use WHO-AIMS as an instrument to assess their mental health care systems. However, although WHO-AIMS has been used in many countries, its utility has never been evaluated. This paper examines the utility of the WHO-AIMS instrument in developing and developed countries by applying it to the mental health systems of Iraq, Japan, the Philippines and the former Yugoslav Republic of Macedonia. These four countries have distinct cultural and historical circumstances, which make it especially interesting to use the WHO-AIMS model to compare their mental health systems and policies. These comparisons allow us to demonstrate how WHO-AIMS may be used in countries with different political and cultural situations, and to assess its possible limitations given these differences.

Mental Health Systems in Four Countries

Iraq, the Philippines and the former Yugoslav Republic of Macedonia, are three low- to middle-income countries that are currently in the process of evaluating their mental health systems through the application of the WHO-AIMS instrument (Table 1).

Policy and Legislative Framework

WHO-AIMS provides a useful model for evaluating the mental health policy of each country. As reported in Table 1, The former Yugoslav Republic of Macedonia is the only country without any policy on mental health; however, it does have provision for coverage of mental health under primary care.[5] In the last two years, with the establishment of policy institutes such as the Center for Research and Policy Making, its health-care services are being utilized in mental health care.[6]

The Philippines has a mental health policy that is hampered by a miniscule budget and limited legislative authority.[7,8] No mental health law has been established.[9] Its mental health budget is only 0.02% of its total health budget, the latter being 3% of its GDP.[7]

Like the Philippines and the former Yugoslav Republic of Macedonia, Iraq is also in the early stage of developing a mental health system. With the help of the Substance Abuse and Mental Health Services Administration (SAMHSA) in the United States of America, the United Kingdom's National Health Service and WHO, Iraqi mental health policymakers have started to develop a detailed plan for implementing a policy on mental health. In 2005, Iraq passed mental health legislation focusing on the rights of consumers, patients' families, and caregivers (e.g., access of care, determination of capacity, guardianship, voluntary and involuntary hospitalizations, law enforcement, and mechanisms for implementing legislation).

Japan, on the other hand, has passed several mental health laws since 1900. In 1995, it passed a mental health act that for the first time legally defined mental illness as a disability, and established strict criteria for involuntary hospitalization. This law promotes the concept of "normalization", viewing mental illness as a disability and encouraging the integration of psychiatric inpatients into the community.[10,11] Relative to the three developing countries, Japan has a higher expenditure on mental health, spending 0.5% of its GDP on mental health (and a total of 8.6% of its GDP on health).[12] Although spending on mental health is higher in Japan than in the other three countries, it is still a small percentage of total health spending, considering the large impact of this disability. This demonstrates a global trend of mental health continuing to have a low priority, regardless of the country's culture, economic strength and resources.

Mental Health Services

Compared to Japan, the other three countries' mental health services are meagre. The number of psychiatric beds in Japan is the highest in the world.[13] In 2000, the ratio of psychiatric beds per 10,000 individuals in Japan was 28.4, three times higher than in the United Kingdom, and there was also a 95% occupancy of these beds.[5] The former Yugoslav Republic of Macedonia has the next highest ratio of inpatient psychiatric beds, at 8.2 per 10,000 individuals, with Iraq and the Philippines having 0.6 and 0.9 per 10,000 individuals, respectively.[5] The distribution of inpatient psychiatric beds in all four countries is similar, with the majority of beds located in cities. In the Philippines, 77% are located in the national capital[8] and in Iraq, 97% are located around its three largest cities (Baghdad, Basra and Mosul). Although Iraq, the Philippines and the former Yugoslav Republic of Macedonia are shifting

Table 1	Mental health system comparisons across four countries[a]			
WHO-AIMS	**Iraq**	**Japan**	**Philippines**	**The former Yugoslav Republic of Macedonia**
1. Policy and legislative framework				
Mental health policy	Yes	Yes	Yes	No
Mental health policy (1st, latest) year	1982, 2005	1950, 1995	1990, 2001	n/a (draft 2005)
Mental health programme	Yes	Yes	Yes	No
Law in mental health	Yes (1982)	Yes (2000)	No	No
Insurance policy	No	Universal coverage	Poor policy	Yes—not comprehensive
Financing mental health—main method	Tax-based	Tax-based	Tax-based	Social insurance
Mental health budget/health budget	n/a	5%	0.02%	n/a
Substance abuse policy	Yes (1966)	Yes (1953)	Yes (1972)	Yes (1999)
Therapeutic drug policy—essential list of drugs	Yes	No	Yes	Yes
Inspecting human rights	No	Yes	No	No
2. Mental health services				
Disability benefits for mental health	Yes	Yes	Yes	Yes
Community care in mental health	Yes	Yes	No	Yes
Psychiatric beds/10,000 individuals	0.63	28.4	0.9	8.2
Psychiatric beds in general hospitals/ 10,000 individuals	0.06	7.8	0.3	2
Psychiatric beds in mental hospitals/ 10,000 individuals	0.55	20.6	0.56	6.2
Disproportion services (city)	Yes	Yes	Yes	Yes
Medication	Limited access	Adequate	Short/limited	Short/limited
3. Mental health in primary care				
Treatment for severe mental disorders in primary care	Yes	No	No	No
Mental health care facilities in primary care	Yes	Yes	Yes	Yes
Training for primary care personnel in mental health	Yes	Yes	Yes	Yes
Trained physician interaction of primary doctor with mental health services	No information	No information	No information	No information
Links between mental health facilities and alternative practitioners	No information	No information	No information	No information
4. Human resources				
Psychiatric training	Yes	Yes	Yes	Yes
Psychiatrist/100,000 individuals	0.7	9.4	0.4	7.5
Psychologist in mental health/100,000 individuals	0.05	7	0.9	2
Social workers in mental health/100,000	0.2	15.7	16	1.5
Psychiatric nurses/100,000 individuals	0.1	59	0.4	24
Family/consumer association involvement in policies and plans	No information	No information	No information	No information
5. Public education and links with other sectors				
Mental health policy promotion	Few	Yes	Few	No information
Mental health policy advocacy	Yes	Yes	Yes	No information
NGO in mental health	Yes	Yes	Yes	Yes
Mental health care for prisoners	Minimal	Yes	None	No information
6. Monitoring and research				
Mental health monitor/inspection system	Yes/poor monitor	Yes	No monitor	Yes/inspection
Research	Few	Yes/larger scale	Few	Few
Data collection system in mental health	Yes	Yes (periodically)	No	No
Reporting system for mental health	Yes	Yes	No	Yes

n/a, not applicable; NGO, nongovernmental organization; WHO-AIMS, WHO Assessment Instrument for Mental Health Systems.

[a]Statistical data were gathered from WHO website (2005) and from the Ministries of Health of Iraq, Japan, the Philippines and the former Yugoslav Republic of Macedonia.

towards de-institutionalization, very few community mental health programmes and social services exist.

In all three of the developing countries, psychotropic medication is very limited. In Iraq, the current state of violence prevents distribution of goods and limits access to medication. As a result of the low appropriations designated for mental health services in Iraq, the Philippines and the former Yugoslav Republic of Macedonia, psychopharmacologic agents, although listed in the country's essential drug list, are often in short supply.[8]

Mental Health in Primary Care

Given the stigma and lack of resources allocated to mental health care, WHO has encouraged mental health policymakers to shift the responsibility to the primary care sector. All four countries need to improve in this particular domain. Although professional training in mental health for primary care workers exists in Japan, it is not rigorously evaluated.[14] In the Philippines, there was a push in the 1990s for psychiatric care to be integrated within the general health services and, as a first step, the country's National Mental Health Programme proposed opening acute psychiatric units and outpatients in 72 general hospitals under its Department of Health. However, as of 2004, only 10 of those hospitals opened outpatient clinics due to a lack of funds.[8] In Iraq, only 7% of primary care physicians and 1% of nurses receive postgraduate training in mental health. Only 1-20% of the physician-based primary care clinics, and no non-physician-based primary care clinics, have protocols for management of mental illness or dispense psychotropic medication.

All four countries lack data on how primary care or mental health facilities are currently linked with alternative care practitioners, yet these latter groups are the ones who, in certain instances, have initial contact with the mentally ill.

Human Resources

Among the four countries, Japan has the highest per capita ratio of individuals providing mental health services.[14] Despite the fact that Japan has 13-23 times more psychiatrists than Iraq and the Philippines, it still has an inadequate number of mental health staff providing community care; this has slowed its progress in carrying out its de-institutionalization policy. Of the three developing countries, the former Yugoslav Republic of Macedonia has the highest ratio of psychiatrists per 100,000 individuals.[5,15]

All four countries lack data on refresher training for mental health staff, as well as data on the number of organizations, associations or nongovernmental organizations (NGOs) involved in mental health policies, legislation or advocacy. Having data in these areas would help service planning and resource allocation.

Public Education and Links with Other Sectors

Iraq, Japan, the Philippines and the former Yugoslav Republic of Macedonia have education and awareness programmes on specific mental health issues. The Iraqi mental health council has published brochures and participated in media campaigns to promote mental health. In the Philippines, the National Mental Health Programme launched an advocacy programme, *Lusog Isip* (Mental Health), which conducts annual mental health celebrations including seminars for government (nationwide and local) and nongovernmental offices, symposia and radio programmes.[16] There are no published data regarding the efficacy of these efforts.

Monitoring and Research

In all three developing countries, limited monitoring and research exists. Iraq, the Philippines and the former Yugoslav Republic of Macedonia lack both epidemiological and area catchment studies of the mentally ill, and thus have no empirical basis for determining where their resources should be allocated. In the Philippines, in addition to funding difficulties, there are sociocultural reasons why little attention has been paid to either the documentation of mental illness or the evaluation of its treatment. Filipinos have traditionally viewed mental illness as a form of evil possession, sorcery or punishment for wrongdoing, and relatives with mental illness are often sent to traditional healers or priests for exorcism.[17]

The Philippines' Department of Health is beginning to make some progress, albeit at a very slow pace. The crafting of the national mental health policy is a potentially important first step, as is the national registration of persons with disabilities. Established in the 1990s, its goal is to identify individuals with disabilities, including those with mental illness, and to develop rehabilitation programmes and raise awareness. Unfortunately, only 12% of the estimated numbers of individuals with disabilities have registered.[18]

In contrast to the three developing countries, the Japanese Ministry of Health provides more resources for research and monitoring its mental health system, including patients' rights and quality of mental health care. Japan's updated national database has been useful in guiding the existing mental health policy and evaluating new policies.

COMMENTS

Utility and Application of WHO-AIMS

WHO-AIMS allows for multidimensional evaluation and provides much needed evidenced-based data, which can be used to inform public mental health policy. WHO-AIMS provides information about financing, provision of services, management, and other key components of the mental health system of each country. Since the WHO-AIMS criteria are standardized, we were able to effectively compare our four countries as well as evaluate their mental health systems' strengths and weaknesses. The synchronization of mental health data between countries in a systematic uniform method allows for cross-regional comparisons that facilitate a useful exchange of information and experience.[19] For instance, the WHO-AIMS data revealed that the integration and improvement in primary care, provision of care for special populations (e.g., children, the elderly), community mental health services, and training in mental health are sorely lacking in Iraq, the Philippines and the former Yugoslav Republic of Macedonia. In politically unstable countries, such as Iraq and the former Yugoslav Republic of Macedonia, where there is a high turnover of administration, including in the Ministry of Health, WHO-AIMS creates a centralized information resource that provides experts with critical mental health data that they can analyse. Furthermore, collaboration with mental health experts from other countries has played a large role in informing policy and service development in all four countries.

Another advantage of WHO-AIMS is that it is comprehensive and easy for non-specialists to use. This is especially useful in countries such as Iraq, the Philippines and The former Yugoslav Republic of Macedonia, where public health institutions lack resources and experts. The domains covered by WHO-AIMS were determined by hundreds of global health policy experts over many years. Developing countries presumably do not have the resources to develop, as well as pilot, such a comprehensive model for assessing mental health systems. In spite of its comprehensiveness, WHO-AIMS provides a template for local professionals to collect information relatively quickly, with minimal training and at little cost.

Limitations of WHO-AIMS

While the parameters used in the WHO-AIMS model are useful in assessing mental health systems, they do not include critical dimensions such as cultural values and political processes within the country under study. Furthermore, the WHO-AIMS parameters have limited ability to describe the scope or degree of problems in a country or region's mental health services and policies.

Cultural Dimension

WHO-AIMS lacks a section detailing the cultural context of the region of interest. Societies have their own distinct idioms of distress as well as indigenous methods for coping, some of which are quite effective. For instance, several WHO-sponsored, international multi-centre studies have suggested that in developing countries cultural factors may influence the course of schizophrenia. In some cultures, such as Filipino and Iraqi, extended family systems and support networks are thought to improve integration and resilience among the mentally ill. Evidence of the impact of culture is illustrated by the work of Kulhara et al.,[20] who found that the presence of extended family systems increased social integration, and higher expectations contributed to better prognosis in patients from some Asian and Middle Eastern countries compared to those from Europe and North America.

In many cultures, changes in mood are attributed to social or spiritual stressors, which can often be addressed by the social support systems, alternative caregivers and traditional healers as opposed to, or in conjunction with, psychotropic medications. Traditional healers, for instance, are commonly used in Iraq, the Philippines and the former Yugoslav Republic of Macedonia with minimal or no integration with the mental health system.[15,21] Indigenous and religious healers are often the first people contacted by patients or their families, especially in the rural areas. Their role in referring the patient to mental health services needs to be further explored. Lieban[21] looked at the role traditional healers played in the treatment of people living in Cebu, the second largest city in the Philippines. Despite a relatively high concentration of modern medical resources in this city, Lieban found the practice of folk medicine by shamanistic healers and other practitioners quite robust, with practitioners treating 25-100 patients a day.

WHO-AIMS does not take into account these valuable social and cultural mechanisms, which may impact on the utilization of services and the course of illness.

Political Process

Kingdon described "three streams" that form or change policies: problem defining, proposal generating, and political shifts; clearly, these are unique in each region.[22] Iraq, the Philippines and the former Yugoslav Republic of Macedonia all have distinct colonial histories that have shaped their political and, consequently, health-care systems. Recent wars and multinational interventions in Iraq and in the former Yugoslav Republic of Macedonia[23] continue to force the restructuring of the overall health-care system, not to mention its mental health-care component. In the Philippines, the end of the Marcos government brought about significant improvements in the country's mental health system. The Philippines' Department of Health organized a task force to implement the National Programme for Mental Health. As this programme was a "favourite" of the then secretary of health, it was allocated resources, despite not having a specific budget from the Department of Health. Owing to a shift in political power, the programme increasingly lost support to the point of termination. However, with the introduction of another administration in 2002, the programme was revived and renamed the National Mental Health Programme.[8] These simplified examples demonstrate how a country's mental health system cannot be adequately analysed without taking into account its political climate.

Questionable Measurement Validity

Another concern of the WHO-AIMS instrument is the accuracy and validity of its measurements. Many of the WHO-AIMS items are written in broad terms that do not provide adequate information about the quality of the item measured (Table 2). For example, items 1.4.4 and 1.4.5 are designed to explore the level of training of mental health professionals and primary care providers, yet there is no attempt at measuring the quality of training or the impact of the level of training on quality of care. In items 1.5.4, 1.5.5 and 2.10, WHO-AIMS assesses the availability and accessibility of psychotropic medications, but an assessment of a country's regulations regarding medications is not included. In Iraq, the Philippines and the former Yugoslav Republic of Macedonia, dispensing of psychotropic medication (including tranquillizers, antipsychotics, sedatives and anxiolytics) is poorly controlled and these

medications may be purchased freely at local pharmacies. Inadequate regulations may lead to substance misuse or abuse, thereby increasing morbidity and mortality. Under the WHO-AIMS criteria, a country could misleadingly score well on psychotropic medication availability, yet that very "availability" could contribute to an increase in mental health problems.

WHO provided an exceptional service to mental health policy-makers by developing WHO-AIMS, theoretically a sophisticated, data-driven framework, but its neglect of assessing social histories, cultural strengths and political processes limits its usefulness. Its overemphasis on the biomedical model and pharmacological therapies tends to undervalue cultural models and coping mechanisms for mental distress. Many studies in developing countries have demonstrated that there are other variables that can contribute to a better prognosis in patients with mental illnesses such as schizophrenia.[24-28] Without taking social history, cultural strengths and political processes into account when assessing a country's mental health system, we can only have a restricted picture of mental health systems.

WHO-AIMS, while limited in scope, is useful as an initial tool for assessing mental health systems. Following complaints by participants in initial pilot studies, the authors of WHOAIMS decreased the number of questions, yet key, especially qualitatively, questions need to be included. Mental health policy-makers in the developing world need to recognize the limitations of WHO-AIMS and acquire more qualitative data tailored to their own region.

ACKNOWLEDGMENTS

The authors would like to thank Dr Victor Rodwin for his feedback on the manuscript. Dr Hamid would like to thank the Institute of Social Policy and Understanding for its support.

Competing Interests:
None declared.

● ● ● References

1. *World health report 2001*—Mental health: new understanding, new hope. Geneva: WHO; 2001.

2. Murray CJL, Lopez AD. Evidence-based health policy: lessons from the global burden of disease study. *Science* 1996;274:740-3. PMID:8966556 doi:10.1126/science.274.5288.740.

3. Saxena S, Maulik PK. Mental health services in low- and middle-income countries: an overview. *Curr Opin Psychiatry* 2003;16:437-42. doi:10.1097/00001504-200307000-00010.

Table 2	Sample items WHO-AIMS

Item	Detail
Item 1.4.4	**Training staff in mental hospitals on human rights protection of patients**
Definition	Proportion of mental hospitals with at least one-day training, meeting or other type of working session on human rights protection of patients in the last two years
Measure	Proportion; UN = unknown; NA = non applicable
Numerator	Number of mental hospitals with at least one-day training, meeting or other type of working session on human rights protection of patients in the last two years
Denominator	Total number of mental hospitals (#)
Item 1.4.5	**Training staff in community-based inpatient psychiatric units and community residential facilities on human rights protection of patients**
Definition	Proportion of community-based inpatient psychiatric units and community residential facilities with at least one-day training, meeting or other type of working session on human rights protection of patients in the last two years
Measure	Proportion; UN = unknown; NA = non applicable
Numerator	Number of community-based inpatient psychiatric units and community residential facilities with at least one-day training, meeting or other type of working session on human rights protection of patients in the last two years
Denominator	Total number of community-based inpatient psychiatric units and community residential facilities (#)
Item 1.5.4	**Free access to essential psychotropic medications**
Definition	Proportion of population with free access (at least 80% covered) to essential psychotropic medicines
Measure	Proportion; UN = unknown; NA = non applicable
Numerator	Number of people with free access (at least 80% covered) to essential psychotropic medicines
Denominator	Number of people in general population
Notes	This item is specific for psychotropic drugs (in many countries psychotropic drugs are not covered by government or insurance schemes) Free access to essential psychotropic medicines means that essential psychotropics—once prescribed—are provided to people with mental disorders free of cost or with reimbursement equal or more than 80% of the retail price. The funding sources for free access/reimbursement may be the government or insurance schemes (employment, social or private)
Item 2.10.3	**Availability of medicines in mental health outpatient facilities**
Definition	Proportion of mental health outpatient facilities in which at least one psychotropic medicine of each therapeutic category (antipsychotic, antidepressant, mood stabilizer, anxiolytic and antiepileptic medicines) is available in the facility or in a nearby pharmacy all year long
Measure	Proportion; UN = unknown; NA = non applicable
Numerator	Number of mental health outpatient facilities in which at least one psychotropic medicine of each therapeutic category is available in the facility or in a nearby pharmacy
Denominator	Total number of mental health outpatient facilities (#)

WHO-AIMS, WHO Assessment Instrument for Mental Health Systems.

4. *World Health Organization Assessment Instrument for Mental Health Systems (WHO-AIMS)*, version 2.2. Geneva: WHO; 2005.

5. *Project atlas: resources for mental health and neurological disorders*. Geneva: WHO; 2005. Available from: http://www.who.int/globalatlas/default.asp [accessed on 28 February 2008].

6. *Rationalization of hospital services in Macedonia*. The former Yugoslav Republic of Macedonia: Center for Research and Policy Making; 2006. Available from: http://www.crpm.org.mk/Home.htm [accessed on 28 February 2008].

7. Tolentino, UJl. The state of mental health in the Philippines. *Bulletin of the Board of International Affairs of the Royal College of Psychiatrists* 2004;6:8-11.

8. Conde B. Philippine mental health country profile. *Int Rev Psychiatry* 2004;16:159-66. PMID:15276948 doi:10.1080/095402603100016.

9. *National Mental Health Policy, 2 April 2001*. Republic of the Philippines, Department of Health Administrative Order No. 8, series 2001.

10. Ito H, Sederer LI. Mental health services reform in Japan. *Harv Rev Psychiatry* 1999;7:208-15. PMID:10579100 doi:10.1093/hrp/7.4.208.

11. Nakatani Y. Psychiatry and the law in Japan: history and current topics. *Int J Law Psychiatry* 2000;23:589-604. PMID:11143956 doi:10.1016/S0160-2527(00)00061-3.

12. *Ministry of Health, labour and welfare data on mental health and welfare* [in Japanese]. Ichikawa: National Institute of Mental Health in Japan; 2002.

13. Oshima I, Mino Y, Inomata Y. Institutionalisation and schizophrenia in Japan: social environments and negative symptoms. *Br J Psychiatry* 2003;183:50-6. PMID:12835244 doi:10.1192/bjp.183.1.50.

14. Tsuchiya KJ, Takei N. Focus on psychiatry in Japan. *Br J Psychiatry* 2004; 184:88-92. PMID:14719534 doi:10.1192/bjp.184.1.88.

15. Gater R, Jordanova V, Maric N, Alikaj V, Bajs M, Cavic T, et al. Pathways to psychiatric care in Eastern Europe. *Br J Psychiatry* 2005;186:529-35. PMID:15928365 doi:10.1192/bjp.186.6.529.

16. *The national healthy lifestyle campaign*. Manila: Philippine Department of Health; 2003.

17. Querubin L, Rodriguez S. *Beyond the physical. The state of a nation's mental health. The Philippine Report*. Melbourne: CIMH; 2002.

18. *Philippine registry for persons with disabilities*. Manila: National Center for Disease Prevention and Control, Degenerative Diseases Office, Department of Health; 2005. Available from: *http://www.doh.gov.ph/programs/person_disabilities* [accessed on 4 March 2008].

19. Jenkins R, Gulbinat W, Manderscheid R, Baingana F, Whiteford H, Khandelwal S, et al. The mental health country profile: background, design, and use of a systematic method appraisal. *Int Rev Psychiatry* 2004;16:31-47. PMID:15276936 doi:10.1080/09540260310001635087.

20. Kulhara P, Chakrabarti S. Culture and schizophrenia and other psychotic disorders. *Psychiatr Clin North Am* 2001;24:449-64. PMID:11593856 doi:10.1016/S0193-953X(05)70240-9.

21. Lieban RW. Fatalism and medicine in Cebuano areas of the Philippines. *Anthropol Q* 1966;39:171-9. doi:10.2307/3316802.

22. Kingdon J. The reality of public policy making. In: Danis, M, Clancy C, Churchill L, eds. *Ethical dimensions of health policy*. New York: Oxford University Press; 2002:97-116.

23. Rechel B, Schwalbe N, McKee M. Health in southeastern Europe: a troubled past, an uncertain future. *Bull World Health Organ* 2004;82:539-46. PMID:15500286.

24. Craig TJ, Siegel C, Hopper K, Lin S, Sartorius N. Outcome in schizophrenia and related disorders compared between developing and developed countries. A recursive partitioning re-analysis of the WHO DOSMD data. *Br J Psychiatry* 1997;170:229-33. PMID:9229028.

25. Leff J, Sartorius N, Jablensky Karten A, Ernberg G. The international pilot study of schizophrenia: five-year follow-up findings. *Psychol Med* 1992;22:131-45. PMID:1574549.

26. Mathews M, Basil B, Mathews M. Better outcomes for schizophrenia in non-Western countries. *Psychiatr Serv* 2006;57:143-4. PMID:16399986 doi:10.1176/appi.ps.57.1.143-a.

27. Miller G. Mental health in developing countries. A spoonful of medicine— and a steady diet of normality. *Science* 2006;311:464-5. PMID:16439640 doi:10.1126/science.311.5760.464.

28. Kulhara P, Chakrabarti S. Culture and schizophrenia and other psychotic disorders. *Psychiatr Clin North Am* 2001;24:449-64. PMID:11593856 doi:10.1016/S0193-953X(05)70240-9.

4

China's Health System Performance

Source: Reprinted from *The Lancet;* 372: 1914-1923. Liu, Yuanli; Rao, Keqin; and Gakidou, Emmanuela. China's health system performance. Copyright 2008, with permission from Elsevier.

We created a comprehensive set of health-system performance measurements for China nationally and regionally, with health-system coverage and catastrophic medical spending as major indicators. With respect to performance of health-care delivery, China has done well in provision of maternal and child health services, but poorly in addressing non-communicable diseases. For example, coverage of hospital delivery increased from 20% in 1993 to 62% in 2003 for women living in rural areas. However, effective coverage of hypertension treatment was only 12% for patients living in urban areas and 7% for those in rural areas in 2004. With respect to performance of health-care financing, 14% of urban and 16% of rural households incurred catastrophic medical expenditure in 2003. Furthermore, 15% of urban and 22% of rural residents had affordability difficulties when accessing health care. Although health-system coverage improved for both urban and rural areas from 1993 to 2003, affordability difficulties had worsened in rural areas. Additionally, substantial inter-regional and intra-regional inequalities in health-system coverage and healthcare affordability measures exist. People with low income not only receive lower health-system coverage than those with high income, but also have an increased probability of either not seeking health care when ill or undergoing catastrophic medical spending. China's current health-system reform efforts need to be assessed for their effect on performance indicators, for which substantial data gaps exist.

INTRODUCTION

Is China's health system doing well? Existing published work has been mixed so far. On the one hand, with China's economy growing at an annual rate of 9.7% from 1978 to 2006 and lifting more than 210 million people from poverty, Chinese people now have improved nutrition, drinking water, housing conditions, and health care.[1] Not surprisingly, the health status of China's people, measured by broad population health indicators, has continuously improved. Life expectancy at birth increased from 67.9 years in 1981 to 71.4 years in 2000. From 1991 to 2005, the infant mortality rate fell from 50.2 to 19.0 per 1000 livebirths, and the maternal mortality rate declined from 88.9 to 47.7 per 100,000.[2]

On the other hand, self-reported morbidity rate and bedridden days increased remarkably from 1993 to 2003, according to China's three national household health surveys done in 1993, 1998, and 2003.[3] Furthermore, the mismatch between increasing demand for and inadequate supply of safe and effective health care, escalating medical costs, and absence of insurance coverage made the general public identify the problem of "too difficult to see a doctor" and "too expensive to see a doctor" as one of the key public policy issues in China's opinion polls.[4,5] In 1998, for example, only 12% of patients living in urban areas and 7% of those living in rural areas were dissatisfied with the inpatient services they received. By 2003, hospital dissatisfaction rate in patients living in urban and rural areas increased to 61% and 54%, respectively.[3] To answer people's mounting demand for policy actions to reform China's health system, the State Council Health-Care Reform Leading Group, involving 14 ministries, was formed in September, 2006, to develop new policies aiming to establish a more effective and equitable health-care system. The package of new health-system reform policies is likely to be announced late 2008.[6-8]

However, because health-care reform is a means to an end and not an end in itself, several crucial questions can be raised: how has China's overall health-system performance been? In what particular areas has China done well or not well? Will China's reform efforts improve health-system performance nationally and sub-nationally? How can we assess health-system performance? Despite vigorous discussions among China's major stakeholders about different reform strategies and approaches, little attention has been paid to the issue of how to monitor health-system reform initiatives and to measure their success and failures in China.[9] Comprehensive analysis of health-system performance sub-nationally (e.g., in provinces) is absent. This is a crucially important unit of analysis, if not more important than the country-wide analysis, because of China's decentralised fiscal system.[10] Furthermore, because substantial disparities exist in China's many socioeconomic dimensions, the issue of how China's health system performs differently for different groups of people needs to be addressed. Therefore, as indicated by experiences in Mexico and other countries, the measurement of a country's (or region's) performance of health-care system is crucially important for monitoring progress, providing evidence-based assessment of reform policies, identifying determinants of success and failure, and fostering a culture of accountability.[11,12]

MEASUREMENT ISSUES

Initiatives by WHO, Organisation of Economic Cooperation and Development, World Bank, and other organisations in the past 15 years have generated worldwide interests in performance measurement of health systems between countries and within countries.[13-16] Even though health systems can be defined in many ways, a consensus that has emerged is on the two fundamental approaches to measurement of how a health system performs.

First is the measurement of health-system coverage. The defining goal of any health system is generally accepted to be to improve health. However, because health is determined by many factors, including non-health-care factors such as environmental pollution, we cannot merely attribute changes in health status to the performance of a health system. Therefore, a measure of health-system performance should focus on the delivery of health interventions to individuals in need, because it is a key process through which health systems can contribute to improvement of population health and reduction of health inequalities. Shengelia and colleagues[17] argued that provision of health services can be assessed more comprehensively through the measure of coverage, which they defined as the probability of people in need to receive services. Furthermore, effective coverage takes into account the quality of interventions delivered and aims to measure the estimated health gain associated with every health intervention.

Second is the measurement of health-care affordability. Besides improvement of health, another intrinsic goal of a health system is to reduce financial barriers to health care, especially protection of households from incurring catastrophic medical expenditures. Financial hardship caused by out-of-pocket payments has been measured in different ways in published studies. Measurement of the impoverishing effect: if the income of a household has fallen below the poverty line after out-of-pocket payments for health care, then this household would be defined as being medically impoverished.[18,19] Measurement of so-called catastrophic spending: if a household's out-of-pocket payments for health care are equal or greater than 30-40% of the household's capacity to pay (disposable income minus food expenditure),[20-22] or 10% of the household's income,[23] then that household would be defined as having undergone catastrophic spending. Here, we mainly adopt WHO's framework of effective coverage and catastrophic spending (30% of household capacity to pay) to measure China's health-system performance. We also measure people's foregone health care due to cost concerns.

INDICATORS OF HEALTH-SYSTEM COVERAGE

We identified four major types of health interventions: (1) curative interventions to treat different diseases (e.g., tuberculosis treatment and hypertension control); (2) preventive interventions (e.g., immunisations); (3) behavioural interventions (e.g., smoking cessation); and (4) intersector public-health interventions (e.g., safe drinking water). To measure the effective coverage of health interventions in China, we selected those that represent these four major types of interventions and that are relevant for China's major health problems. Ideally, we should have a comprehensive list of indicators for all the major interventions that target the most common diseases and their risk factors in China. On the basis of a review of all available data, only 11 interventions could be measured for all provinces for at least one period during the 10 years of investigation (from 1993 to 2003) (Table 1).

A composite measure of coverage was constructed with simple averages from the 11 interventions to help to summarise the overall pattern of service delivery at national and provincial levels. This set of interventions, even though not exhaustive or ideal, is the basis of the first generation of measurements of health-system coverage in China. The panel shows in detail China's most important data sources. Although data collectors (i.e., the Chinese Ministry of Health) assessed data validity and reliability, no independent evaluation exists.

On the basis of these data, Table 2 shows the latest national and provincial benchmarks for measurement of health-system coverage. We have taken advantage of the recently completed 2004 China Adult Chronic Diseases Risk Factors Surveillance Survey (panel) to measure effective coverage of treatment of hypertension—the only intervention for which information about quality is available. For other interventions, we used crude coverage—i.e., the proportion of those in need of the intervention who reported having obtained the intervention. Table 2 also shows catastrophic medical spending by region.

| Table 1 | Indicators and associated measurement strategies |

	Intervention	Population in need	Definition of indicator	Year of survey
Water	Access to safe drinking water	All households	Percentage of households with access to safe drinking water	1993, 1998, 2003
Toilet	Access to sanitary toilets	All households	Percentage of households with access to a sanitary toilet	1993, 1998, 2003
Cessation	Smoking cessation	Smokers	Percentage of smokers who either quit smoking or tried to quit in the year before the survey	1993, 1998, 2003
Antenatal	Antenatal care	Expectant mothers	Percentage of expectant mothers who received any antenatal visit in the year before the survey	1993, 1998, 2003
Delivery	Hospital delivery	Women who gave birth in a specific period	Percentage of women who gave birth, delivering their baby in a hospital in the year before the survey	1993, 1998, 2003
Postnatal	Postnatal care	Women who gave birth in a specific period	Percentage of women who gave birth in the year before the survey, who received any postnatal visit by medical staff	1993, 1998, 2003
Vaccine	Immunisation	Children aged 0–1 years	Percentage of children younger than 1 year who were immunised for all of the following: BCG, DTP3, Hep B, measles, and OPV	1993, 1998, 2003
TB examination	Examination of suspected TB cases	Population with self-reported symptoms of TB (coughing or coughing up blood for 3 weeks)	Ratio of people who reported having gone through formal clinical examination to people who reported having TB-like symptoms	2003
TB DOTS	Treatment of confirmed TB cases	TB patients	Percentage of confirmed TB patients who self-reported having completed the whole treatment protocol	2003
Hypertension treatment	Treatment of hypertension	Hypertension patients	Percentage of hypertensive people who reported having taken control measures in the past year	2004
Hypertension effectiveness	Effective treatment of hypertension	Hypertension patients	Percentage of hypertensive people who reported having taken control measures and whose blood pressure was normal during the survey period	2004

BCG = Bacille Calmette Guérin. DOTS = directly observed treatment, short-course. DTP3 = diphtheria–tetanus–pertussis vaccine. Hep B = Hepatitis B. OPV = oral polio vaccine. TB = tuberculosis.

| Table 2 | Performance indicators of health-system coverage in 2003 and 2004 by region |

	Water	Toilet	Cessation	Antenatal	Delivery	Postnatal	Vaccine	TB examination	TB DOTS	Hypertension treatment	Hypertension effectiveness	Catastrophic medical expenditures
National	85.8 (0.2)	40.1 (0.2)	6.1 (0.2)	87.7 (0.3)	68.2 (0.5)	53.2 (0.5)	86.3 (0.8)	30.6 (0.8)	57.0 (3.3)	26.7 (0.5)	8.9 (0.3)	15.3 (0.2)
Urban	99.2 (0.1)	86.5 (0.3)	6.9 (0.5)	96.5 (0.4)	92.7 (0.6)	59.63 (1.1)	94.5 (1.3)	36.3 (1.5)	48.9 (7.3)	33.6 (0.8)	11.7 (0.6)	13.8 (0.3)
Rural	80.2 (0.2)	20.7 (0.2)	5.8 (0.3)	85.5 (0.4)	61.9 (0.6)	51.5 (0.6)	84.7 (0.9)	28.2 (0.9)	59.1 (3.7)	21.8 (0.6)	7.0 (0.4)	15.8 (0.2)
Urban vs rural p value	<0.0001	<0.0001	<0.05	<0.0001	<0.0001	<0.0001	<0.0001	<0.0001	>0.10	<0.0001	<0.0001	<0.0001
Beijing	98.6 (0.3)	46.1 (1.4)	8.4 (1.9)	96.9 (1.8)	97.9 (1.5)	80.2 (4.1)	100.0 (0.0)	38.6 (6.5)	..	40.0 (3.6)	11.6 (2.3)	27.5 (1.4)
Tianjin	85.7 (1.0)	54.8 (1.4)	3.1 (1.1)	95.5 (2.0)	95.2 (2.1)	69.1 (4.4)	100.0 (0.0)	36.8 (7.8)	66.7 (27.2)	37.6 (4.2)	17.3 (3.3)	14.7 (1.1)
Hebei	68.5 (0.9)	28.5 (0.9)	3.90 (0.9)	94.1 (1.1)	75.0 (2.1)	43.43 (2.4)	85.5 (4.0)	22.9 (3.4)	83.3 (15.2)	33.5 (2.5)	9.6 (1.6)	17.7 (0.8)
Shanxi	98.3 (0.3)	12.3 (0.8)	6.2 (1.3)	92.8 (1.5)	60.1 (2.8)	40.9 (2.8)	83.3 (5.1)	19.7 (4.6)	71.4 (17.1)	26.1 (2.2)	8.2 (1.4)	16.7 (1.2)
Neimeng	87.3 (0.8)	1.7 (0.3)	2.3 (0.9)	91.4 (1.5)	53.0 (2.6)	55.4 (2.6)	86.8 (4.1)	29.5 (3.5)	80.0 (17.9)	21.7 (2.7)	4.8 (1.4)	23.8 (1.0)
Liaoning	98.8 (0.3)	48.2 (1.4)	3.8 (1.2)	98.7 (0.9)	80.1 (3.3)	68.9 (3.8)	100.0 (0.0)	34.0 (6.7)	100.0 (0.0)	24.6 (2.2)	6.0 (1.2)	15.0 (1.1)
Jilin	96.2 (0.4)	54.8 (1.2)	4.5 (1.3)	98.1 (0.9)	97.7 (1.0)	43.3 (3.4)	100.0 (0.0)	17.2 (3.9)	100.0 (0.0)	27.3 (2.5)	6.8 (1.4)	19.9 (1.0)
Heilongjiang	99.4 (0.2)	14.1 (0.8)	6.3 (1.4)	98.2 (0.7)	82.1 (2.1)	50.0 (2.8)	100.0 (0.0)	24.8 (4.0)	66.7 (19.2)	20.9 (1.8)	5.7 (1.0)	17.2 (0.9)
Shanghai	100.0 (0.0)	86.7 (1.0)	6.2 (1.5)	98.9 (1.1)	98.9 (1.1)	68.9 (4.9)	85.7 (9.4)	38.0 (4.9)	..	54.4 (4.1)	18.8 (3.2)	18.4±0.8
Jiangsu	90.8 (0.6)	50.7 (1.0)	7.4 (1.2)	93.0 (1.6)	98.8 (0.7)	58.2 (3.2)	95.7 (2.4)	34.5 (4.0)	55.6 (16.6)	46.7 (3.1)	22.2 (2.6)	14.2±0.8
Zhejiang	98.4 (0.3)	68.5 (1.1)	9.9 (1.5)	100.0 (0.4)	99.5 (0.4)	69.7 (3.0)	95.0 (3.5)	39.0 (4.5)	100.0 (0.0)	22.9 (2.4)	6.0 (1.3)	15.0±0.9
Anhui	96.8 (0.4)	29.2 (0.9)	8.5 (1.5)	90.4 (1.7)	72.4 (2.5)	39.0 (2.8)	88.0 (3.8)	27.2 (4.0)	28.6 (12.1)	33.6 (2.8)	11.2 (.9)	15.4 (0.8)
Fujian	76.4 (1.0)	46.4 (1.2)	10.1 (1.7)	96.9 (1.0)	90.8 (1.7)	78.1 (2.4)	94.1 (2.6)	30.9 (4.8)	75.0 (21.7)	15.9 (2.4)	3.1 (1.2)	11.2 (0.8)
Jiangxi	88.5 (0.7)	26.6 (1.0)	10.4 (1.6)	72.5 (3.2)	48.3 (3.4)	60.7 (3.4)	61.8 (6.5)	31.9 (4.0)	58.3 (14.2)	33.3 (3.8)	15.0 (2.9)	12.0 (0.8)
Shandong	98.7 (0.2)	39.1 (1.0)	4.5 (1.0)	96.6 (1.0)	95.2 (1.1)	62.8 (2.6)	91.7 (4.0)	27.9 (5.0)	50.0 (35.4)	25.3 (2.4)	8.1 (1.5)	14.9 (0.9)
Henan	91.3 (0.6)	32.0 (1.0)	5.1 (1.0)	88.8 (1.4)	70.0 (2.1)	21.0 (1.8)	75.8 (4.5)	32.1 (4.5)	50.0 (17.7)	24.1 (2.6)	5.0 (1.3)	18.4 (0.8)
Hubei	91.3 (0.6)	53.7 (1.0)	5.2 (1.1)	91.2 (1.7)	70.5 (2.8)	63.4 (2.9)	83.3 (4.8)	22.4 (3.7)	55.6 (16.6)	34.6 (2.6)	11.5 (1.8)	9.3 (0.6)
Hunan	80.9 (0.8)	75.1 (0.9)	5.2 (1.1)	88.5 (1.9)	60.7 (2.9)	59.9 (2.9)	89.4 (3.8)	25.6 (3.7)	33.3 (19.2)	21.7 (2.5)	8.3 (1.7)	14.4 (0.7)
Guangdong	97.2 (0.3)	72.9 (0.9)	8.6 (1.3)	92.1 (1.4)	89.6 (1.6)	54.6 (2.6)	98.7 (1.3)	30.4 (4.0)	12.5 (11.7)	39.0 (3.8)	14.0 (2.7)	11.1 (0.8)
Guangxi	73.7 (1.0)	25.5 (1.0)	6.7 (1.4)	81.8 (2.3)	68.6 (2.7)	43.3 (2.9)	79.0 (4.7)	32.1 (4.5)	71.4 (17.1)	25.6 (2.8)	10.9 (2.0)	8.4 (0.7)
Hainan	98.9 (0.3)	65.9 (1.4)	6.6 (1.9)	95.0 (1.5)	98.6 (0.8)	63.4 (3.2)	100.0 (0.0)	45.1 (7.0)	57.1 (18.7)	31.2 (4.8)	9.7 (3.1)	16.3 (1.1)
Chongqing	84.5 (0.8)	54.5 (1.2)	5.4 (1.2)	9.8 (2.1)	67.6 (3.4)	54.6 (3.7)	89.2 (5.1)	37.9 (3.)	64.7 (11.6)	19.2 (3.5)	4.8 (1.9)	18.5 (0.9)
Sichuan	81.3 (0.9)	41.3 (1.2)	8.5 (1.6)	91.4 (2.8)	73.8 (4.3)	59.6 (4.8)	86.4 (7.3)	35.7 (4.5)	100.0 (0.0)	18.0 (2.4)	6.3 (1.5)	15.9 (0.9)
Guizhou	63.8 (1.1)	7.6 (0.6)	1.4 (0.6)	66.8 (2.3)	29.8 (2.2)	56.1 (2.4)	68.2 (5.1)	30.9 (4.2)	66.7 (12.2)	12.4 (2.1)	4.9 (1.4)	17.0 (0.8)
Yunan	82.2 (0.9)	34.0 (1.1)	7.1 (1.4)	72.4 (2.2)	38.2 (2.4)	47.8 (2.5)	72.5 (5.4)	28.6 (3.6)	63.6 (14.5)	17.8 (2.7)	6.1 (1.7)	17.8 (0.9)
Tibet	65.4 (1.4)	48.3 (1.4)	7.1 (2.3)	75.6 (2.3)	38.2 (2.7)	33.0 (2.6)	97.7 (1.6)	43.5 (5.4)	52.2 (10.4)	29.2 (3.1)	16.7 (2.5)	10.2 (0.9)
Shanxi	78.3 (1.0)	48.9 (1.2)	7.7 (1.4)	88.3 (2.1)	77.4 (2.8)	68.0 (3.1)	78.4 (6.8)	24.5 (4.2)	50.0 (25.0)	25.1 (2.9)	12.1 (2.2)	13.0 (0.8)
Gansu	46.9 (1.2)	5.7 (0.5)	5.7 (1.4)	86.5 (1.8)	47.5 (2.6)	58.8 (2.6)	93.7 (3.1)	36.4 (6.5)	69.2 (12.8)	15.8 (2.03)	2.8 (0.9)	12.7 (0.8)
Qinghai	53.0 (1.4)	2.9 (0.5)	2.5 (1.1)	84.8 (1.8)	34.4 (2.4)	54.9 (2.5)	80.3 (4.7)	13.6 (3.7)	80.0 (17.9)	29.6 (5.4)	8.5 (3.3)	22.9 (1.2)
Ningxia	90.0 (0.6)	33.4 (1.0)	4.1 (1.1)	97.1 (0.7)	92.8 (1.1)	85.02 (1.6)	98.0 (1.4)	39.0 (4.2)	28.6 (17.1)	18.0 (4.4)	1.3 (1.3)	16.8 (0.8)
Xinjiang	88.1 (0.8)	40.9 (1.2)	2.5 (1.2)	60.7 (2.4)	36.0 (2.4)	16.0 (1.8)	61.9 (5.3)	28.0 (4.7)	22.2 (13.9)	25.5 (2.1)	10.8 (1.5)	16.2 (0.9)
Inter-province p value	<0.0001	<0.0001	<0.005	<0.0001	<0.0001	<0.0001	>0.0001	<0.005	>0.10	<0.005	<0.005	<0.005

Data are percentages (SD). DOTS= directly observed treatment, short-course. TB = tuberculosis. Data sources: reference 3 and 2004 China Adult Chronic Risk Diseases Factors Surveillance Survey (unpublished).

In 2003, China's health system seemed to do well in terms of access to safe drinking water, antenatal care, hospital delivery, and childhood vaccinations, as indicated by the high coverage of these interventions. Coverages of these interventions were 99%, 96%, 93%, and 95% for urban areas, and 80%, 86%, 62%, and 85% for rural areas, respectively. However, concerns may arise about access to sanitary toilets for rural households (only 21%), the low rate of examination of suspected tuberculosis (36% for urban and 28% for rural areas), and low effective coverage of hypertension in 2004 (only 12% and 7% for urban and rural areas, respectively). Because China's high rate of cigarette smoking (45% of urban and 50% of rural male adults were regular smokers in 2003) and the associated disease burden, we find it particularly troublesome to see such a low smoking cessation rate (only about 6% of the smokers have tried to quit).

Data Sources

China National Health Services Survey[3]

Since 1993, the Chinese Ministry of Health has done a national household interview survey every 5 years. A four-stage stratified random sampling procedure was used to select the households for interview to represent China's urban and rural populations. In the first stage, urban cities and rural provinces were selected after they were grouped into three urban types (big, middle-sized, and small cities) and four rural types (ranging from the richest to the poorest counties). In the second stage, five streets in every city and five towns in every county were randomly chosen. In the third stage, two residential committees and villages in every selected street and town were chosen. Finally, 60 households were randomly identified in every residential committee and village. The total number of households sampled in 1993, 1998, and 2003 were 50,700, 50,690, and 57,023, respectively. In addition to demographic and socioeconomic data (including self-reported income and expenditure), the interviewers, who are trained medical professionals, also obtained comprehensive information about self-reported health status, health-care utilisation, and behavioural factors, such as smoking and drinking. Informed consent was obtained from every person before being interviewed. The response rate has been on average more than 90%.

2004 China Adult Chronic Diseases Risk Factors Surveillance Survey

Because of the increasing prevalence of chronic diseases, China did the first Adult Chronic Diseases Risk Factors Surveillance Survey in 2004, and is planning to do one every 3 years. The survey is done by the China Centre for Disease Control, which is in the process of completing the second survey. The sample was selected on the basis of the adjusted National Disease Surveillance Points (DSPs), which included 154 counties, representing China in terms of, for example, geographical and demographic distribution, and socioeconomic development status. The survey adopted a multistage stratified random sampling framework, with a final sample size of 32,760 households. From every household, an adult (18-69 years of age) was randomly selected. The contents of the survey included two parts: a structured questionnaire and a physical examination. The structured questionnaire asked questions about the person's demographic characteristics, self-reported health status, chronic diseases, and relative risk factors (such as smoking, drinking, diet, and exercise), and health-service utilisation. The physical examination included measurement of height, weight, waist and sternum, and blood pressure.

China Statistics Digest

The State Statistics Bureau publishes a China Statistics Digest every year, which gives a comprehensive set of information about China's demographic, economic, and social characteristics nationally and provincially. We drew from this dataset information about province variables that might explain variations in effective coverage and occurrence of household catastrophic health-care spending.

Furthermore, we noticed remarkable inter-regional inequalities in health-system coverage. Except for the effective coverage of tuberculosis treatment, differences between urban and rural coverage rates and inter-provincial differences were all significant. On average, coverage in urban areas (61%) was 15% higher than in rural areas (46%) (Table 2). Figure 1 maps composite coverage of different provinces. The geographical distribution of health-system coverage is remarkable, with the southeast regions having the best performance indicator, followed by the northern, central, and western regions. This pattern corresponds almost perfectly with China's different economic development in these regions (China's eastern provinces tend to have higher economic development level than the central provinces, which in turn are better than their western counterparts).[10]

With respect to the income-related inequality in coverage, the rate difference in composite coverage between the highest and lowest income quintile groups ranged from 12% to 27%. For urban populations, the greatest income-related inequality was in access to sanitary toilets, with the rate difference between rich and poor groups being as high as 40% in 1998. For rural populations, income-related inequality was most pronounced in hospital delivery rate, with the rate difference between the highest and the poorest income quintile being as high as 43% in 1998. The hospital delivery rate for the poorest women living in urban areas was 88%, which was even higher than that for the richest women living in rural areas (78%). China's urban healthcare system has done better than the rural system on almost all the coverage indicators, except for coverage of tuberculosis treatment. A small percentage (36% for the urban and 28% for the rural samples) of interviewed people, who reported tuberculosis-like symptoms, underwent formal testing for tuberculosis (including radiographic and smear examination). Therefore, China's ability to detect tuberculosis cases remains questionable despite recent progress in tuberculosis control.[24] Once diagnosed, however, a high percentage of patients received treatment, which was provided free of charge at government-run facilities. The overall percentage of confirmed patients with tuberculosis who received treatment was 90% for urban and 97% for rural patients in 2003. A higher percentage of tuberculosis patients living in rural areas (59% vs 49% of patients living in urban areas) completed the whole treatment episode. The higher effective coverage of tuberculosis treatment in rural China might be explained, in part, by the fact that rural populations are less mobile than their urban counterparts, and thus patient compliance issues in rural areas may be easier to manage. Other

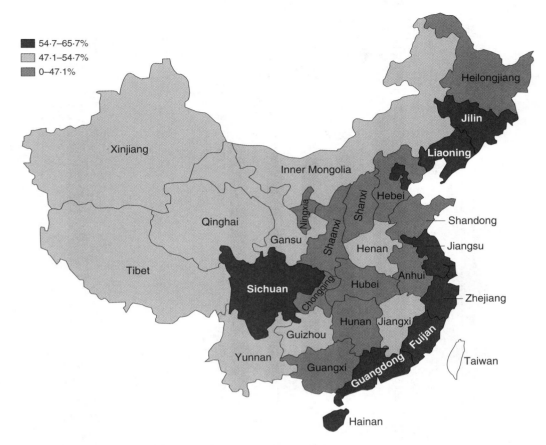

■	54·7–65·7%
▨	47·1–54·7%
▨	0–47·1%

Figure 1 Health-system coverage in Chinese provinces in 2003

studies showed that, although tuberculosis drugs are free in China, patients still had to pay for other related medicines and diagnostic tests during the course of their treatment, a reason that may also explain why many patients failed to complete the appropriate treatment.[25,26]

How did coverage and its distribution change between 1993 and 2003? Both urban and rural sectors have overall improved coverage of all major interventions (Table 3). However, changes seemed to have been non-linear and unstable during the 10 years.

Although inter-provincial inequalities in coverage seemed reduced between 1993 and 2003, as indicated by the decreased coefficient of variation, income-related inequality in composite coverage in terms of rate difference between the lowest and highest income quintile increased only slightly in the rural and urban areas between 1993 and 2003 (Table 3). Even though coverage of hospital delivery for women living in rural areas increased from 1993 to 2003, income-related inequality also increased (Table 3), showing that serious inequity problems persisted in China, especially in rural China.

Moreover, our findings strongly suggest that attention should be paid to China's inadequate disease prevention programmes. Rates of coverage of immunisation in children aged 0-1 years living in urban and rural areas fell between 1998 and 2003 (Table 3), mainly because of rate reduction in the poorest populations. This finding shows a widespread challenge to China's public-health system in terms of how to provide equitable access to those health interventions that are cost effective, yet non-profitable, to the fee-for-service health-care providers.[27,28] Furthermore, the rate of smoking cessation is low and the rate of smoking in men living in rural areas remains high, especially in the poor population. As previously shown,[29] smoking control is not only an important public-health issue for China, but also a poverty-reduction issue. The fact that, in 2004, only 42% and 27% of individuals living in urban and rural areas, respectively, with high blood pressure were aware of their condition draws attention to the absence of health literacy.

We did a multivariate regression analysis to understand which provincial characteristics could explain the differences across provinces in terms of

Table 3	Health-system coverage in 1993, 1998, and 2003						
	Water	Toilet	Prenatal	Hospital delivery	Postnatal	Vaccines	Composite
Urban*							
1993	97.15 (96.89–97.41)	69.39 (68.67–70.11)	82.85 (81.98–83.72)	85.85 (85.05–86.66)	41.88 (40.74–43.02)	84.86 (81.54–88.17)	77%
1998	96.98 (96.72–97.24)	68.63 (67.93–69.33)	96.59 (95.24–97.93)	92.32 (92.30–92.34)	61.59 (58.00–65.19)	95.26 (92.39–98.13)	85%
2003	99.19 (99.06–99.33)	86.55 (86.03–87.06)	96.46 (95.62–97.30)	92.65 (91.46–93.84)	59.63 (59.61–59.66)	94.50 (94.49–94.55)	88%
Rural*							
1993	52.49 (52.00–2.99)	5.20 (4.98–5.42)	31.34 (30.77–31.90)	19.97 (19.49–20.46)	48.99 (48.38–49.59)	48.05 (45.93–50.17)	34%
1998	58.78 (58.30–59.26)	8.23 (7.96–8.50)	81.04 (79.69–82.38)	41.43 (41.41–41.45)	50.41 (48.70–52.12)	89.34 (87.54–91.13)	55%
2003	80.24 (79.85–80.62)	20.71 (20.31–21.10)	85.48 (84.66–86.29)	61.92 (60.8–63.05)	51.52 (51.51–51.53)	84.70 (84.72–84.76)	64%
Urban inequity¹							
1993	1.40 (1.39–1.41)†	34.36 (34.33–34.39)†	15.28 (15.23–15.33)†	14.05 (14.00–14.10)†	2.05 (2.03–2.07)†	5.68 (5.13–6.23)†	12%
1998	7.48 (7.46–7.49)†	39.61 (39.58–39.64)†	8.13 (7.75–8.50)†	17.34 (16.82–17.86)†	22.74 (22.16–23.32)†	7.75 (6.59–8.91)†	17%
2003	1.31 (1.31–1.32)†	24.95 (24.93–24.98)†	10.50 (10.33–10.68)†	13.12 (12.93–13.31)†	24.17 (23.93–24.41)†	11.54 (10.47–12.61)†	13%
Rural inequity¹							
1993	17.35 (17.34–17.36)†	5.16 (5.15–5.16)†	19.36 (19.34–19.37)†	20.04 (20.03–20.06)†	19.27 (19.25–19.28)†	17.66 (17.48–17.85)†	16%
1998	32.49 (32.47–32.50)†	18.61 (18.60–18.62)†	30.30 (30.16–30.45)†	43.22 (43.06–43.37)†	29.22 (29.08–29.36)†	8.08 (7.84–8.32)†	27%
2003	18.69 (18.68–18.70)†	19.73 (19.72–19.74)†	20.82 (20.76–20.88)†	36.27 (36.20–36.34)†	21.65 (21.59–21.70)†	9.33 (9.12–9.53)†	20%
Inequity²‡							
1993	0.34†	0.70†	0.40†	0.59†	0.36†	0.43†	0.47
1998	0.09†	0.52†	0.16†	0.48†	0.36†	0.07†	0.28
2003	0.17†	0.55†	0.11†	0.31†	0.28†	0.13†	0.26

Data are percentages (95% CI), unless otherwise stated. Inequity¹ = rate difference between the income quintile 1 and 5. *Urban-rural difference in the same year is significant at p < 0.0001, except for vaccines in 1998 where p value < 0.01. †Intertemporal difference of the same indicator is significant at p < 0.0001. ‡Inequity² = coefficient of variation for provincial indicators.

coverage. Explanatory variables included population size, gross domestic product (GDP) per head, dependency ratio (i.e., the ratio of the number of dependants [aged 0-14 years and >65 years] to the total working-age poputation [aged 15-64 years]), urbanisation index, illiteracy rate, healthcare supply, and insurance coverage. We showed that only GDP per head was a significant predictor of both hospital delivery and composite coverage. Another significant predictor (of composite coverage only) was insurance coverage. Figure 2 illustrates the relation between a province's GDP per head and its hospital delivery. These results support the claim that a strong relation between economic development of a province and its health system coverage exists, which clearly suggests China's absence of transfer payments to provinces by central government. An article in this *Lancet* series by Hu and colleagues[30] provides a detailed discussion about the inadequate and inequitable government financing in China.

INDICATORS OF HEALTH-CARE AFFORDABILITY IN CHINA

On the basis of Xu and colleagues' publications,[20,21] we defined a household as having incurred catastrophic medical spending if the family's total reported out-of-pocket medical expenditure in the past year exceeded 30% of the family's yearly non-subsistence spending, which equals total household spending minus subsistence food expenditure. Unfortunately, the national health-service survey in 1993 did not obtain information on total household expenditures. Therefore, we were not able to include the data from 1993 in our time analysis on financial risks.

Financial effect of out-of-pocket payments for households cannot be fully captured by measuring catastrophic spending. Because of inability to pay, some people may choose not to seek health care when ill. To identify those individuals who cannot afford health care, we used questions from the China Health Services Survey in 1998 and 2003 on the reasons for: (1) not seeking health care when ill; (2) forgoing admission to hospital recommended by doctors; and (3) self-discharging from the hospital against medical advice. Here, we classify individuals as having affordability problems if they cited inability to pay as the major reason for not seeking health care.

We showed variation of the rate of catastrophic medical spending between rural and urban settings (Table 2) Besides the difference in income, the urban-rural rate difference is also related to the differential insurance coverage of the two populations, with the urban populations having a substantially higher

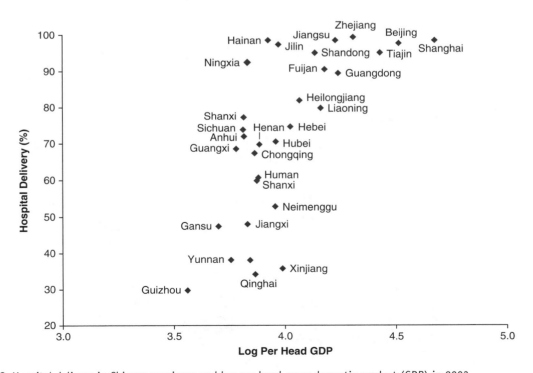

Figure 2 Hospital delivery in Chinese provinces and log per head gross domestic product (GDP) in 2003

insurance coverage than their rural counterparts.[3] We also showed a wide variation of the rate of catastrophic medical spending in different provinces (Table 2). Notably, poor provinces do not always have higher rates of catastrophic medical spending, as one might expect. For example, in Beijing, despite being a high-income city, the rate of catastrophic medical spending is high, whereas in Guizhou, despite being a low-income province, the rate is low. This result is not wholly unexpected, because the extent of catastrophic medical spending is dependent on utilisation rate and price, in addition to income. Low-income regions may have low health-care utilisation rates and low average medical prices, both of which might cause a low probability of catastrophic medical spending.

How did catastrophic medical spending change between 1998 and 2003 in China? The average rate of catastrophic medical spending increased but this rise is entirely attributable to the increased rural rate, because the rate in urban households declined (Table 4). Although all income groups in rural China had an increasing rate of catastrophic medical spending, the poorest rural group was the hardest hit. The fraction of rural households in the lowest income quintile that incurred catastrophic medical spending increased from 21.5% in 1998 to 25.7% in 2003.

Although the inter-province inequality in catastrophic spending seemed to have narrowed from 1998 to 2003 (the coefficient of variation decreased), the income-related inequality for rural households increased. Therefore, all indicators point to a worsening financial risk protection for the rural population.

Table 5 shows rates of foregone medical care (outpatient and inpatient) and early hospital discharge due to cost concerns. In 1998, less than 1% of urban and rural residents reported feeling ill during the 2 weeks before interview but did not seek health care because of cost concerns. This trend leads to an estimated yearly rate of 14% for urban and 19% for rural populations. Furthermore, around 1% of the interviewed urban and rural residents reported having refused to be admitted to hospital against medical advice in the year before the interview be-

Table 4	Rate of catastrophic medical spending in 1998 and 2003
	Households with medical expenditure high than 30% of the capacity to pay
Urban*	
1998	16.42 (15.74−17.10)
2003	13.77 (13.21−14.33)
Rural*	
1998	12.78 (12.42−13.14)
2003	15.83 (15.47−16.19)
Urban inequity[1]	
1998	17.29 (16.73−17.85)†
2003	11.25 (10.86−11.64)
Rural inequity[1]	
1998	13.93 (13.60−14.26)†
2003	14.81 (14.53−15.09)†
Inequity[2] ‡	
1998	0.35†
2003	0.28†

Data are percentages (95% CI), unless stated otherwise. Inequity[1] = rate difference between the income quintile 1 and 5. *Urban–rural difference in the same year is significant at $p < 0.0001$. †Intertemporal difference of the same indicator is significant at $p < 0.0001$. ‡Inequity[2] = coefficient of variation for provincial indicators.

| Table 5 | Rate of foregone medical care due to cost concerns in 1998 and 2003 |

		Foregone outpatient care due to cost	Foregone inpatient care due to cost	Early discharge due to cost
Urban*				
	1998	14.36 (14.03−14.69)	1.01 (0.92−1.11)	0.74 (0.66−0.82)
	2003	13.61 (13.31−13.91)	0.78 (0.70−0.86)	0.69 (0.62−0.77)
Rural*				
	1998	18.69 (18.48−18.89)	0.97 (0.93−1.02)	0.74 (0.70−0.79)
	2003	19.73 (19.52−19.93)	0.9 (0.85−0.95)	0.93 (0.88−0.98)
Urban inequity[1]				
	1998	28.86 (28.23−29.49)†	1.36 (1.21−1.51)†	0.91 (0.78−1.04)†
	2003	33.80 (33.08−34.52)†	1.39 (1.24−1.54)†	1.03 (0.90−1.16)†
Rural inequity[1]				
	1998	28.86 (28.58−29.14)†	1.10 (1.03−1.17)†	0.58 (0.54−0.62)†
	2003	29.12 (28.86−29.38)†	0.96 (0.90−1.20)†	0.36 (0.34−0.38)†
Inequity[2]‡				
	1998	0.53†	0.49†	0.52†
	2003	0.57†	0.61†	0.41†

Data are percentages (95% CI), unless stated otherwise. Inequity[1] = rate difference between the income quintile 1 and 5. *Urban−rural difference in the same year is significant at $p < 0.0001$. †Intertemporal difference of the same indicator is significant at $p < 0.0001$. ‡Inequity[2] = coefficient of variation for provincial indicators.

cause of cost concerns. Inability to pay was cited by less than 1% of urban and rural residents for their decision to discharge themselves ahead of schedule in 1998. Overall, 16% of urban and 20% of rural residents reportedly had financial difficulties in accessing health care in 1998. Although urban rate of foregone medical care decreased to 15% in 2003, the rural rate rose to 22% in the same year, explained by 5% increase in foregone outpatient care and 25% rise in early hospital discharge from the rural rate in 1998.

We also showed that the poorest income groups had not only a higher rate of foregone medical care than their better-off counterparts, but also a higher probability of attributing their decision to inability to pay. For example, in 2003, 75% and 83% of poor urban and rural patients who refused to be admitted cited inability to pay as the major reason for foregone inpatient care. The income-related inequality in foregone health care and early hospital discharge due to inability to pay had increased for urban residents from 1998 to 2003, whereas it increased only for foregone outpatient care for rural residents dur-

ing the same period. During 1998 and 2003, however, the rural rate was consistently higher than the urban one.

DISCUSSION

We have done a comprehensive measurement of China's health-system performance, considering two major variables: health-care delivery (addressing the basic question of whether people in need of certain health interventions receive them), and health-care financing (addressing the basic issue of whether households can afford to pay for the health care they need).

We showed that China's health system did well for some indicators (e.g., delivering maternal and child health services), but not so well for others. For example, the increases in antenatal visit and hospital delivery rates for women living in urban areas between 1993 and 2003 approached the performance of Mexico for skilled birth attendance.[31] These rates also increased for women living in rural areas; however, indicators that capture specific quality measures showed that big gaps exist between crude and effective coverage. For example, even though most urban and rural confirmed tuberculosis cases underwent some treatment, only about half of urban and almost 60% of rural patients completed the treatment protocol. Effective control rate of patients with hypertension is even lower: only 12% and 7% of patients with hypertension living in urban and rural areas had their blood pressure lowered to normal values as a result of treatment. China's future health-system reform programmes should not only aim to expand access to more health-care services, but also ensure and enhance quality of these services.

Indicators of both China's health status and health-system coverage are not international outliers because of their income (Table 6). However, according to a recent study of 23 selected countries that account for around 80% of the total burden of chronic-disease mortality in developing countries, death rates for chronic respiratory disease are highest in China.[32] Increasing evidence exists about the cost-effectiveness of tobacco control measures, salt reduction, and use of multidrug regimens for patients at high risk of cardiovascular diseases.[33] In this respect, China's health system seems to be far less advanced than that of other developing countries. For example, in the examination survey only 42% and 27% of people living in urban and rural areas, respectively, with high blood pressure knew about their condition. Moreover, although 45% and 50% of men living in urban and rural areas were regular smokers in 2003, only 5-6% of them tried to quit. Therefore, the biggest challenge for the future is to scale up cost-effective interventions for chronic disease prevention and to use measurement of effective coverage to monitor progress in China.

Irrespective of specific indicators, remarkable inequalities in health-system coverage exist in China. According to our analysis, these inequalities are mainly related to income differentials. Indeed, our multiple regression analysis showed that the only significant predictor of provincial health-system coverage is GDP per head. This finding not only emphasises the fundamental role of wealth in health development, but also indicates a serious absence of effective transfer payment mechanisms between provinces in the health sector on the part of the central government

With respect to affordability, we measured the rate of both catastrophic medical spending and foregone health care due to inability to pay. According to WHO's definition (i.e., 30% of a household's capacity to pay), 14% of urban and 16% of rural households incurred catastrophic medical spending in 2003. In other words, catastrophic medical spending affected about 184 million Chinese people—a record that puts China's health-system performance for financial risk protection among the poorest in the world. A recent study of 89 countries showed that the rate of catastrophic medical spending ranged from zero in the Czech Republic, Slovakia, and the UK to more than 10% in Brazil and Vietnam.[20]

Furthermore, on the basis of the proportion of residents reported having either foregone medical care (outpatient or inpatient) or early hospital discharge due to cost concerns in 2003, we can extrapolate that about 438 million Chinese people had affordability difficulties in 2003. The fact that many people were affected by financial access difficulties might explain both people's high dissatisfaction rate with the services they received and erosion of trust in the system, as Tang and colleagues[34] discussed in a report about health equity in China. Moreover, the low-income groups were the hardest hit because they had a higher probability not only of not seeking health care when ill, but also of incurring catastrophic medical spending when seeking medical care.

Our analysis has several limitations, which need to be taken into consideration in the interpretation of the findings. First, analysis of the provincial health-system performance is based on four sets of nationally representative survey data, which, although large in terms of sample size, are not always representative of every province. Therefore, our results on benchmarking provinces should be interpreted with caution, and considered as an illustrative example of what can and should be done if more data were available. Second, in most cases we are able to provide only crude rather than effective coverage indicators. For many indicators in this analysis, either no information or only proxies were available to capture the quality of the intervention being delivered. Third, our analysis is based on cross-sectional surveys that are done only every 5 years. Finally, the selection of indicators used in the coverage estimation is opportunistic and does not mirror the changing epidemiological profile of the Chinese population. No information exists on the coverage of interventions for most chronic diseases. Therefore, our measure of coverage is only the first step towards benchmarking performance and needs to be re-estimated once information about coverage of other important interventions becomes available.

We have shown the urgent need for China to construct a more comprehensive nationally and regionally representative dataset (whether a cohort or repeated cross-sections) to be able to monitor and

Table 6   Indicators of health and coverage in selected countries and areas in WHO member states

	Population (×10³) in 2005	Gross national income per head (PPP in $) in 2005	Male life expectancy at birth (years) in 2005	Infant mortality rate (per 1000 livebirths) in 2005	Maternal mortality ratio (per 100 000 livebirths) in 2005	Immunisation coverage among children aged 1 year (DTP3) in 2005*	TB detection rate under DOTS in 2005	TB treatment success under DOTS in 2004	Access to improved drinking water sources (urban) in 2004*	Access to improved drinking water sources (rural) in 2004*	Access to improved sanitation (urban) in 2004*	Access to improved sanitation (rural) in 2004*
Vietnam	84 238	3010 (111)	69 (72)	16 (117)	130 (77)	95% (70)	84% (34)	93% (12)	99% (56)	80% (83)	92% (75)	50% (91)
India	1103 371	3460 (107)	62 (126)	56 (55)	540 (42)	59% (180)	61% (87)	86% (43)	95% (100)	83% (75)	59% (129)	22% (141)
Indonesia	222 781	3720 (105)	66 (103)	28 (83)	230 (61)	70% (170)	66% (71)	90% (21)	87% (133)	69% (109)	73% (109)	40% (111)
Egypt	74 033	4440 (98)	66 (103)	28 (83)	84 (96)	98% (26)	63% (84)	70% (123)	99% (56)	97% (41)	86% (91)	58% (79)
Philippines	83 054	5300 (90)	64 (118)	25 (92)	200 (66)	79% (152)	75% (50)	87% (38)	87% (133)	82% (77)	80% (99)	59% (78)
China	1323 345	6600 (78)	71 (50)	23 (96)	56 (108)	87% (121)	80% (43)	94% (9)	93% (114)	67% (114)	69% (116)	28% (132)
Brazil	186 405	8230 (61)	68 (83)	28 (83)	260 (58)	96% (55)	53% (105)	81% (78)	96% (96)	57% (129)	83% (96)	37% (115)
Thailand	64 233	8440 (59)	67 (95)	18 (107)	44 (113)	98% (26)	73% (52)	74% (103)	98% (72)	100% (1)	98% (46)	99% (27)
USA	298 213	41 950 (2)	75 (33)	7 (152)	14 (140)	96% (55)	85% (30)	61% (148)	100% (1)	100% (1)	100% (1)	100% (1)
Southeast Asia	1656 529	3557	62	51	460	66%	64%	87%	92%	81%	64%	31%

Data are numbers (indicator ranking in all WHO member states), unless otherwise stated. PPP = purchasing power parity. Int $ = the international dollar is a hypothetical unit of currency that has the same purchasing power that the US dollar has in the USA at a specific time. DTP3 = diphtheria–tetanus–pertussis vaccine. DOTS = directlyobserved therapy. TB = tuberculosis.
*Data are percentages (indicator ranking among all WHO member states). Data source: 2007 World Health Statistics.

assess health-policy changes properly. In particular, China needs to obtain information on non-personal, public-health interventions, such as seatbelt use and mental-health services. Future studies should also establish a more comprehensive understanding of the major underlying determinants of the health-system performance.

——————

ACKNOWLEDGMENTS
We thank the editors and reviewers for their comprehensive comments that helped revision of our manuscript. Comments from participants of *The Lancet*-CMB Authors Workshop in October, 2007, in Beijing were also appreciated.

● ● ● **References**

1. Wen J. Keynote speech presented at Summer Davos, Dalian, China. http://www.gov.cn/english/2007-09/07/content_741508.htm (accessed April 18, 2008).

2. The Chinese Ministry of Health. China Health Statistics Digest. Beijing: the Peking Union Medical College Press, 2007.

3. Centre for Health Statistics and Information, MOH. An Analysis Report of National Health Services Survey in 2003. Beijing: the Peking Union Medical College Press, 2004.

4. Ma K. Implementation of the central government's economic work conference for the benefit of 2007 development and reform. *Macroeconomic Management* 2007; 1: 8-13.

5. The Chinese Social Sciences Academy. 2007 Social Development Report. Beijing: the Chinese Social Sciences Academy Press, 2006.

6. Gao Q. Using creative system mechanisms to stimulate health reform and development. *China Development Observation* 2007; 4: 44-47.

7. Wen J. Keynote speech presented at the National Urban Residents Basic Medical Insurance Pilot Study Conference in Beijing, P. R. China, July, 23, 2007.

8. Chen Z, Gao Q. Health reform and development with Chinese characteristics: ensuring medical and health care services for each and every citizen. *Qiu Shi* 2008; 1: 35-38.

9. Yip W, Hsiao WC. The Chinese health system at a crossroads. *Health Affairs* 2008; 27: 460-68.

10. Dollar D. Poverty, inequality and social disparities during China's economic reform. World Bank Policy research Working Paper 4253, 2007. http://econ.worldbank.org/external/default/main?pagePK=64165259&piPK=64165421&theSitePK=469372&menuPK=64166093&e ntityID=000016406_20070613095018 (accessed Aug 26, 2008).

11. Gakidou E, Lozano R, Gonzalez-Pier E, et al. Assessing the effect of the 2001-06 Mexican health reform: an interim report card. *Lancet* 2006; 368: 1920-35.

12. Frenk J. Bridging the divide: global lessons from evidence-based health policy in Mexico. *Lancet* 2006; 368: 954-61.

13. WHO. The World Health Report 2000: Health Systems: Improving Performance. Geneva: World Health Organization, 2000.

14. World Bank. Technical Note No 5: Assessing health sector performance. Washington, DC: World Bank, 2001. http://www.healthsystemsrc.org/Pdfs/HNP_tecnnote5a.pdf (accessed May 1, 2008).

15. Roberts MJ, Hsiao, WC, Berman P, Reich MR. Getting health reform right—a guide to improving performance and equity. Oxford: Oxford University Press, 2004.

16. Liu Y. What is wrong with China's health system? *Harvard China Review* 2006; 3: 14-18.

17. Shengelia B, Murray CJL, Adams OB. Beyond access and utilization: defining and measuring health system coverage. In: Murray CJL, Evans DB eds. Health systems performance assessment: debates, methods and empiricism. Geneva: World Health Organization, 2003: 221-34.

18. Liu Y, Rao K, Hsiao WC. Medical spending and rural impoverishment in rural China. *JHPN* 2003; 21: 216-22.

19. Wagstaff A, Yu S. Do health sector reforms have their intended impacts? The World Bank's Health VIII project in Gansu province, China. *J Health Econ* 2007; 26: 505-35.

20. Xu K, Evans D, Carrin G, et al. Protecting households from catastrophic health spending. *Health Aff* 2007; 26: 972-83.

21. Xu K, Evans B, Kawabata K, Zeramdini R, Klavus J, Murray CJL. Household catastrophic health expenditure: a multi-country analysis. *Lancet* 2003; 362: 111-17.

22. Murray CJL. Assessing the Distribution of Household Financial Contributions to the Health System: Concepts and Empirical Application. In: Murray CJL, Evans DB eds. Health systems performance assessment: debates, methods and empiricism. Geneva: World Health Organization, 2003: 513-31.

23. Wagstaff A, van Doorslaer E. Catastrophe and impoverishment in paying for health care with applications to Vietnam, 1993-98. *Health Econ* 2003; 12: 921-34.

24. Wang L, Liu J, Chin DP. Progress in tuberculosis control and the evolving public-health system in China. *Lancet* 2007; 369: 691-96.

25. Zhang T, Tang S, Jun G, Whitehead, M. Persistent problems of access to appropriate, affordable TB services in rural China: experiences of different socio-economic groups. *BMC Public Health* 2007; 7: 19.

26. Meng Q, Li R, Cheng G, Blas E. Provision and financial burden of TB services in a financially decentralized system: a case study from Shandong, China. *Int J Health Planning Management* 2004; 19 (suppl 1): S45-S62.

27. Blumenthal D, Hsiao W. Privatization and its discontents—the evolving Chinese health care system. *N Engl J Med* 2005; 353: 1165-70.

28. Liu Y. China's public health-care system: facing the challenges. *World Health Organ Bull* 2004; 82: 532-37.

29. Liu Y, Rao K, Hu T, Sun Q, Mao Z. Cigarette smoking and poverty in China. *Soc Sci Med* 2006; 63: 2784-90.

30. Hu S, Tang S, Liu Y, Zhao Y, Escobar ML, de Ferranti D. Reform of how health care is paid for in China: challenges and opportunities. *Lancet* 2008; published online October 20, 2008. DOI:10.1016/S0140-6736(08)61368-9.

31. Lozano R, Soliz P, Gakidou E, et al. Benchmarking of performance of Mexican states with effective coverage. *Lancet* 2006; 368: 1729-41.

32. Abegunde DO, Mathers CD, Adam T, Ortegon M, Strong K. The burden and costs of chronic diseases in low-income and middleincome countries. *Lancet* 2008; 370: 1929-38.

33. Gaziano TA, Galea G, Reddy KS. Scaling up interventions for chronic disease prevention: the evidence. *Lancet* 2008; 370: 1939-46.

34. Tang S, Meng Q, Chen L, Bekedam H, Whitehead M. Health equity in China: tackling the "perfect storm". *Lancet* 2008; published online October 20, 2008. DOI:10.1016/S0140-6736(08)61364-1.

VI

Directions for the Future

The future of the nation's health rests primarily in the hands of the American people. This does not discount the role of sound government policies and partnerships with healthcare professionals. The three entities all have significant roles to play in determining the future directions that can produce the most returns in improving health at an affordable cost. Dominance by either the government or the healthcare industry without significant participation by others is unlikely to succeed. The individual must first and foremost be responsible for his or her own health. The government should support the individual through sound public health initiatives and by ensuring access for the most vulnerable in our society. The healthcare industry, with support from the government and in partnership with healthcare professionals and consumers, can start laying the foundation of a system that values the roles of individual responsibility, self-management support to live productively with chronic conditions, patient activation, disease prevention, health education, and access to routine primary care. All three entities also need to engage in building an understanding that high-tech care is not necessarily the best care and that technological progress and utilization should be based firmly on demonstrated cost-effectiveness. The readings provided in this book furnish ample evidence for the direction just outlined. The four readings in the chapter that follows provide guidelines for the future that are based on these principles.

The Future of Health Care Delivery

Just as it was with managed care bashing during the 1990s—and with some it still is—bashing of the U.S. healthcare system has become a popular pastime with some critics. The use of invectives such as "a broken system" and "a failed system" that we sometimes encounter in literature perhaps do a good job of providing political fodder, but do little to offer pragmatic solutions that would expand basic services in a manner that balances personal responsibility, cost-effectiveness, and quality without jeopardizing the level of satisfaction that the majority of insured Americans express with the healthcare services they receive. Many of these same critics are also proponents of a government-controlled system similar to the ones in Canada and Great Britain with little acknowledgment that these systems also face serious problems in the areas of cost, access, and quality. Having health insurance but not the ability to access services when needed is something that no American would want to see. Yet, this is what we are likely to get if we only focus on giving everyone a "health insurance card" without adequate attention to the capacity of the system's ability to meet people's basic preventive health and primary care needs.

Discussion of organizational capacity should take into account the fact that many uninsured currently do receive healthcare. The safety net infrastructure (such as American's health centers and public hospitals) and charity care obligations of nonprofits have to be taken into account.

Expanding health insurance without organizational reform in healthcare delivery is like the old adage of putting the horse before the cart. As a society, Americans also need to reach some consensus on the innovation, dissemination, and use of technology that accounts for roughly half of healthcare cost inflation. The government has and will always have a role to play in the nation's health, but what should that role be and how should accountability be established regarding the value created in return for the tax dollars spent?

Few people disagree that the U.S. healthcare system is in need of reform, and so is the case with other delivery systems around the world. The question is not whether but how the U.S. healthcare system should be reformed. What should be the priorities? What incremental steps are likely to steer us in the right direction without dislocating what is good about U.S. healthcare, and there is much that is good, critics notwithstanding. "Clearly a $2.4 trillion healthcare system has plenty of room for pluralism, and it's silly to expect one-size-fits-all solutions" (Dentzer, 2008). In other words, an acknowledgment that individual situations differ and call for a plurality of approaches to meet varied needs must be at the foundation of any health reform.

Incremental reform must be driven by an overarching philosophy that currently does not exist. Education, information, and transparency on goals to be achieved and how they would be achieved are necessary for Americans to "buy-into" a philosophical framework for reform. New mindsets need to be adopted. As Paulus, Davis, and Steele (2008) have proposed, the underpinnings for such a philosophy should be healthcare value. Seeking value necessitates asking the question, "What do we propose to get in return for what we pay and how much should we pay for what we should reasonably expect to get?" Most Americans are uncomfortable with a simplistic "tax and spend" approach. The mindset that needs to change is what we see portrayed in some TV commercials in which consumers are prompted to get a mobility gadget because Medicare pays for it. A value-added philosophy will seek to promote mobility without the use of the gadget unless it is absolutely necessary. The pillars of a value-driven reform will emphasize individual responsibility for one's own health, self-management support, patient activation, preventive services, health education, and an infrastructure based on primary care. These areas must be the focus of reform because they have the potential to return the biggest dividends in improving the nation's health. On the other hand, waste that does not add value must be squeezed out of the system. Examples include malpractice reform and the practice of defensive medicine, utilization of technology that does not meet the standards of cost-efficiency, and overutilization of specialty services.

In the first reading, **The Present and Future Organization of Medicine**, Falk draws lessons from history to inform the future direction of the organization of medical care. Throughout history, in many parts of the world, the form of medical practice has been determined by the structure and customs of society. Some of the details furnished by Falk on the current trends and future direction of medical care are open to debate; however, Americans would agree with most of the principles and goals to be achieved. The controversial area is how it should be done. Falk proposes that any national plan for the organization of medicine should be designed through joint action of lay and professional groups. He further warns that

unless such cooperative action is accomplished, solutions to healthcare problems are likely to be imposed upon the public and the professionals by ambitious politicians and bureaucrats.

In his testimony before Congress titled, **Options for Controlling the Cost and Increasing the Efficiency of Health Care,** Elmendorf points to lack of incentives in the healthcare system for physicians, hospitals, and other providers of healthcare to control costs. Uncertainty exists regarding the effects of various proposals such as changes in how providers are paid, taxation of employer-sponsored health insurance, more health benefit research, adoption of information technology (IT), and changes in the Medicare program. There is a general lack of evidence about the likely impact of such proposals in making a significant impact in achieving cost effectiveness. Elmendorf provides an overview of the inefficiencies in the U.S. healthcare system and discusses the payment options and provider incentives currently in place. Referring to a 2008 report by the Congressional Budget Office (CBO), Elmendorf points to some novel options to pay providers such as cutting payment rates in high-spending geographic areas, paying physicians a blend of capitation and fee-for-service rates that include bonuses and penalties based on the total spending for Medicare services, and bundling together payments for hospital and post-acute services. Adoption of IT is not likely to produce substantial savings. For instance, according to the CBO, only modest reductions in spending are expected from the American Recovery and Reinvestment Act of 2009 which includes payment incentives for adopting IT. As for research, the American Recovery and Reinvestment Act provides $1.1 billion in federal funding, but without cost-effectiveness assessment the effect on cost savings will be smaller if the focus is only on clinical effectiveness. Various options are likely to reduce spending only if they bring about a change in the behavior of physicians and patients to utilize fewer and less intensive services.

In developed countries in particular, the primary burden of disease has been shifting from communicable and acute illnesses to chronic and multifaceted illnesses. Both public health and medical care have played major roles in conquering communicable disease. Chronic illnesses, on the other hand, are mainly attributed to environmental, behavioral, genetic, and lifestyle factors. Personal responsibility for one's own health and access to preventive and therapeutic services are keys to addressing the rising problem of chronic conditions. In the article, **Rising Rates of Chronic Health Conditions: What Can Be Done?**

Cassil points to the growing problem of chronic disease and areas in which the current healthcare system is not adequately prepared to address the challenges posed by obesity and chronic conditions. A redesigned chronic care model will incorporate a system design to facilitate interaction between healthcare teams and patients, decision support for best care, clinical information systems to make all critical information available to caregivers, and self-management support to help manage the conditions and make behavioral changes to improve health. Perceptual gaps that exist between consumers and those who are pushing consumers to be more involved in their health need to be narrowed for future progress in health improvement.

The concept of a *medical home* is currently being explored in the United States with the aim of providing accessible, continuous, coordinated, and patient-centered care to populations with chronic illnesses. Based on their expertise in medical home initiatives, the authors of **Making Medical Homes Work: Moving from Concept to Practice** discuss four critical areas that can make or break a successful program. The areas identified are (1) how to qualify physician practices as medical homes, (2) how to match patients to their medical homes, (3) how to engage patients and other providers to work with medical homes in care coordination, and (4) how to pay practices that serve as medical homes.

● ● ● **References**

Dentzer, S. 2008. Innovations: Medical home or medical Motel 6? *Health Affairs* 27 (5): 1216–1217.

Paulus, R.A., K. Davis, and G.D. Steele. 2008. Continuous innovation in health care: Implications of the Geisinger experience. *Health Affairs* 27 (5): 1235–1245.

The Present and Future Organization of Medicine

Source: Falk, I.S. 2005. The present and future organization of medicine. *The Milbank Quarterly* 83 (4): 1-9.

I

Today medicine stands at a crossroad. No one can fully grasp the content of medical science and medical art or foresee the path which the newer knowledge will follow more than a decade hence. No one can fully comprehend the present position of medical practice in society or anticipate the form it is destined to take. This much is clear: Every serious effort to contemplate the course of future developments must draw a clear distinction between the *content* of medicine and the *form* of medical practice. This distinction may be brought into sharp relief by a few simple illustrations.

A patient appears in a physician's office. How the doctor shall proceed to take the medical history, upon what signs and symptoms he shall make his diagnosis and what course of therapeusis he shall prescribe—these are part of the content of medicine and are wholly within the domain of the physician. A patient comes to a dentist. The examination, the diagnosis, the program of care and treatment, decisions as to the need for cleansing, extraction, prosthesis, or orthodontia, and the performance of the services—these are part of the content of dentistry and are within the province of the dentist.

For its own protection, society has for many centuries regulated the privilege of the individual to hold himself out as a physician. Both in olden times and in modern, society has established standards which must be met by those who would qualify as practitioners. The individuals who receive approval are then entrusted to choose the procedures which will best serve each patient in his time of medical need. Physicians and dentists have had, have, and undoubtedly will continue to have, the sole right and duty to decide *what* shall be practised. This, the content of medicine, belongs to the practitioner.

We find another picture when we inquire into the circumstances under which the physician practises and the nature of his economic relations to society or to the individual patient. Everywhere and always, the physician has been a product of his times and the conditions under which he has practised have invariably reflected the customs of the period. In primitive times, he was physician, priest, and magician; in classical times he was variously slave, craftsman, honored citizen, and body-physician at the court of prince, king, or emperor. In early Christian times, in the Middle Ages, during the Renaissance, in the imperial, and in the liberal periods, his roles have been many and varied.

Between 1850 and 1930, the industrial revolution changed the world at a pace which has almost defied understanding or analysis. Simultaneously, medicine made more progress and became more efficient than ever before in history. Medical art and medical practice grew beyond the competence of any individual; and medical specialization—though not new in the world—attained such a state of development as to constitute substantially a new phenomenon in the history of science.

The profound economic changes which came with industrialization (and urbanization) brought colossal forces to play upon medical practice. The number and variety of practitioners grew in a manner hitherto unknown. Tremendous competition developed. Through circumstances which no one planned and no one foresaw, a profession fell into a business world. In order to survive, medicine began to adapt itself to the world about it. The older order of so-called "private practice" was transformed into a system of competitive practice which no one consciously willed and which in an insidious way has interfered with the great social task which medicine is destined to perform. The practitioners of the healing arts were compelled to become businessmen and entrepreneurs.

Fifty years ago, the world began to seek an answer to the paradox which the industrial revolution presented to the practice of medicine. In 1883, in an effort to weaken the growing influence of the Social Democrats, the Iron Chancellor gave Germany sickness insurance. Fundamental changes came into the conditions of medical practice—first in Germany and later in the forty countries of the world which followed her lead in establishing compulsory or voluntary systems of furnishing medical care through insurance. Health and sickness insurance evolved in the same period which saw the gestation of modern medicine. In the same year in which sickness insurance was being instituted in Germany (1882), Louis Pasteur published his first communication on rabies and Robert Koch read his classic paper on the etiology of tuberculosis. This coincidence is not cited to prove that insurance against medical costs was responsible for medical advance, but to challenge the converse: The history of medicine since 1882 does not lend itself readily to the argument that the international spread of sickness insurance *impeded* medical progress.

The conditions under which medicine is practised, the nature of the physician's relation to the society of his times, the manner in which he is remunerated—these and other characteristics of the *organization of medicine* have known many patterns. In all countries of the world and for many centuries, the form of medical practice has been determined by the structure and the customs of society. And this is true in the United States today. In the light of this unquestionable lesson from history, it is absurd for the editor of a leading American medical journal to express the view: ". . . the right to say how medicine shall be practised must remain with the medical profession." The medical profession has not now that "right" any more than they had it in centuries past when physicians were permitted to practise as licensed wanderers, or as the salaried "bodyphysicians" of kings or princes, or as university faculties. Society has never delegated such a "right" to the medical profession; and today it might be difficult to discover evidences that society contemplates an innovation in this regard.

If the expression quoted above were merely the casual blurb of a journalist, it would be deserving of no specific attention. But it warrants comment because it represents the opinion of a number of self-styled leaders of the medical profession. There are signs everywhere in the United States that profound change impends in the organization of medicine. If physicians, dentists, and other members of the medical professions, are to exert useful and constructive influence, if they are to serve wisely in guiding the practice of medicine to a form of organization more esteemed by society than is the present one, they must take cognizance of the forces which are at work. The medical practitioner must range himself with—and not against—these forces if he would influence the course of events. It is not difficult to imagine the grave consequences which might befall if society should seek a new organization of medicine and did not have the counsel of the medical professions. As surely as the professions determine *what* they shall practice, society determines *how* they shall practice. The interest of lay people is centered not on what the physician shall practice, but upon how he shall be paid for his services.

II

There is a ferment at work in American medicine. There is a vast unrest; physicians, dentists, nurses, hospital administrators, pharmacists, and others are conscious of a national uncertainty in the future of medical organization. The order of the nineteen-twenties has been under critical fire. This was already clearly evident in 1927 when the Committee on the Costs of Medical Care first came into being. It was concern over the future which brought the Committee into existence as a voluntary organization dedicated to dispassionate investigation of the needs of the times. The economic depression has only intensified the need for action.

To visualize the issues at stake, it is necessary to study the research reports prepared by the staff of the Committee on the Costs of Medical Care. Though there were differences of opinion within the Committee concerning *recommendations,* the *facts* disclosed by the Committee's investigations were accepted by all factions. The data are now a year or two old. But in this, they err only in understating the need for certain obvious changes in the organization of medicine.[1]

Among some groups it has become almost a pastime to lay the blame for the burden of medical costs on the drugstore and the cultist. Others frequently imply that most of our troubles would be over if these expenditures were eliminated and other recognized wastes were curtailed. We should not fall into the habit of taking these delusions too seriously. The obvious savings which are possible would amount to three-quarters of a billion dollars a year, or 20 per cent of the total costs of medical care in a normal year. But to effect savings of these kinds would, in the best of circumstances, be a slow and difficult task. Spending habits are deeply rooted and ignorance is not easily overcome. Even granting that these savings were effected, the facts in the case point conclusively that the major problems of medical costs would still demand other solutions. For the major problems are:

a. The uncertain, uneven, and unbudgetable size of medical costs for the individual or the family.

b. The difficulty of knowing how, when, and where to secure good medical care.

c. The uncertain and inadequate remuneration of practitioners and institutions.

Neither professional nor lay groups will make real progress on issues in medical economics until they recognize that these are the real issues which face the public and the professions and that the three are interlocked, one with another. The professions and the public will be toiling at cross purposes until they realize that each has an equal and fundamental interest in medicine and that the interests of both must be safeguarded in any solution which may be proposed. In principle, it is obviously desirable that any plan designed to equalize costs should also discourage waste. Experience in many places has shown that it is possible to combine these two desirable objectives. Indeed, the success of an organization which equalizes costs depends, in greater or lesser measure, upon the fact that it simultaneously reduces wastes, familiarizes the beneficiaries with the path to authorized medical agencies, and stabilizes the incomes of practitioners. By comparison with what has been and is easily accomplished in the reduction of wastes through organized medical agencies operating under non-profit insurance plans, reduction in wastes by educational measures alone is costly and ineffective. Proposals to reduce costs and to eliminate wastes must inevitably be linked with proposals to equalize costs among groups of people and over periods of time. In any final sense, the economic and professional needs of modern medicine call for group payment by the public, group practice by the professions, and a conjunction of the two.

III

The public and the professions are convinced that on the whole "all's well" with the science and the art of medicine. No one knows its destination; but it is on its way and its way seems to be a highroad. But the serenity with which the *content* of medicine is viewed has no counterpart in the attitude toward the *form* of medical organization. On the contrary, it is a common belief that, in respect to organization and social relations, medicine is at a crossroad and has not yet found the signpost. The view is extremely prevalent in the public mind; it is almost general among hospital and public health authorities, and it is—to put the matter conservatively—common among the members of the medical professions.

There are two distinct but interrelated questions before society and the professions: Toward what form of organization is medicine heading? How shall it be most wisely guided to a desirable form? Let us consider these in turn.

A vast experimentation is in progress in the United States and in foreign countries. Disregarding details, we can discern at least six major movements:

1. An increasing prevalence of group payment of medical costs. This is notably evident for hospital service and has become quite common for care furnished by physicians.

2. An expanding activity of government agencies in furnishing diagnostic and curative as well as preventive care.

3. An expanding interest of private practitioners in preventive medicine.

4. A growing tendency toward group—as distinguished from individual—practice.

5. An increasing demand for the effective control of excessive specialization in the professions.

6. A widening interest in the possibilities of improving the education of general practitioners and restoring them to a central place among their professional colleagues.

These and other important movements must somehow be fused into a single current. All must be encompassed in any sound program of medical organization for the future. In this country and abroad, many experiments have been (and are being) tried to attain these six objectives. A study of experience suggests that, whatever the near future holds, sound planning must rest upon the following basic principles:

1. The provision of good medical care to all of the population is essential to the nation's well-being.

2. The costs of medical care should be distributed over groups of people and over periods of time, whether through taxation, insurance, or combinations of the two.

3. Those who render medical care should be adequately remunerated.

4. Quality in medical care should not be sacrificed to economy in cost.

5. The medical care of the dependent and indigent sick is an obligation of society.

6. Group payment of medical costs should be restricted to this purpose and should not be combined with insurance against the loss of wages during a period of illness.

7. Group payment of medical costs should embrace all economic groups in the population to whom the private purchase of medical care brings variable costs which are burdensome and which are incapable of being budgeted on an individual or family basis.

8. The costs of medical care must be distributed according to ability to pay.

9. Group payment of medical costs should be grounded on a compulsory basis.

10. A system of group payment for medical care should not include or permit the operation of proprietary or profit-making agencies or of any independent intermediary between the potential patient and the medical agencies.

Whether we like them or not, an evaluation of European and American experiences reveals that these principles are sound. The form of organization to which medicine is moving should be conceived in these principles. In addition, experience shows that effective operation of a system of compulsory insurance against medical costs requires:

a. Flexibility in the scope of medical benefits so as to permit adaptation to local variations in available personnel and facilities.

b. Professional control of professional personnel and procedures.

c. Freedom of all competent practitioners who subscribe to necessary rules of procedure to engage in insurance practice.

d. Freedom of all persons to choose their physician or dentist from among all practitioners in the community who engage in insurance practice.

e. Freedom of insurance practitioners to accept or reject patients.

f. Minimum interference of the insurance system with the private practice of medicine.

On these premises, the immediate task is to design a form of organization which is in accord with these basic concepts and which will operate effectively.

IV

How shall we proceed to formulate a program for the place which medicine shall occupy in society? Can it be done by the medical professions alone? There are no evidences in medical writings that medical practitioners have either the training or experience in the social or economic problems which would qualify them to act *alone*. In addition, medical practitioners would be subject to popular suspicion in such an undertaking because they have a large stake in the outcome. Furthermore, the lay world has so profound an interest in the subject that one can anticipate a general revolt against anything which would seem to be dictation to society from the professions. There is an old adage which is pertinent: "He that reckons without his host must reckon again."

Can an adequate program be formulated by the public or by their leaders in government? The answer is written indelibly in history. Bismarck, single-handed, gave Germany sickness insurance; Lloyd-George and his small coterie gave Great Britain national health insurance. The place which medicine shall occupy in the social order has for centuries been determined by the lay world and this can be done again. Unfortunately, there is a very clear lesson in modern history that such action is not in the best interests of society. Success in the operation of any national plan for the organization of medicine has been almost directly proportional to the extent to which there has been professional, conjointly with lay, participation in designing the program. The history of health insurance in European countries is replete with illuminating examples on this point. The role which the British medical professions played in compelling a revision of Lloyd-George's program, before the National Health Bill was enacted and during the first years of its operation, is a case in point. Today, satisfaction with national health insurance is so general in Great Britain that no responsible group would propose its abolition. Both the public and the organized medical and dental professions are clamoring for extension of the system. The demand is for more, not for less, national health insurance. And this is especially evident in the official proposals of the British Medical Association.

If we learn anything from history, we must be resolved that the economic problems which confront American medicine should be solved by the joint action of lay and professional groups. Yet we must recognize that if such cooperative action does not become a reality, solutions may be imposed upon both the public and the professions by ambitious politicians or by designing bureaucrats. And these solutions may not be the best which can be designed in the public interest.

Many persons, lay and professional, are convinced of the need and the opportunity for public service in a sound reordering of the functional relations of medicine. No good purpose is served by denying existence of the problem or by acrimony between lay and professional groups which have fundamentally common interests. Neither denials nor hard names will create a current or stem a tide. The times call for action and the problems for wise and judicious solutions.

● ● ● Reference

1. The factual information and its analysis are available in a single volume: Falk, I.S.; Rorem, C. Rufus; and Ring, M.D.: *The Costs of Medical Care: A Summary of Investigations on the Economic Aspects of the Prevention and Care of Illness.* Chicago, University of Chicago Press, 1933. A brief resumé (Fundamental Facts on the Costs of Medical Care, by I.S. Falk) appeared in the Milbank Memorial Fund *Quarterly Bulletin*, April 1933, xi, No. 2, pp. 130-153.

Options for Controlling the Cost and Increasing the Efficiency of Health Care

Source: Congressional Budget Office. 2009. *Options for Controlling the Cost and Increasing the Efficiency of Health Care*. Statement of Douglas W. Elmendorf before the Subcommittee on Health Committee on Energy and Commerce, U.S. House of Representatives on March 10. 2009. Washington, DC: Congressional Budget Office.

Chairman Pallone, Ranking Member Deal, and Members of the Subcommittee, thank you for inviting me to testify this morning about the opportunities and challenges that the Congress faces in trying to make the health care system more efficient—so that it can continue to improve Americans' health but at a lower cost. Policymakers could seek to improve efficiency by changing the ways that public programs pay for health care services or by encouraging such changes in private health plans; in both sectors, those changes could in turn exert a strong influence on the delivery of care.

In designing proposals to control costs and improve the efficiency of health care, policymakers must take into account a number of important factors:

- Spending on health care has generally grown much faster than the economy as a whole, and that trend has continued for decades. Studies attribute the bulk of that cost growth to the development and diffusion of new treatments and other forms of medical technology. That

expansion in the capabilities of medical care has conferred tremendous benefits by extending and improving lives, but it has also absorbed a rising share of the nation's resources.

- The cost of health care is imposing an increasing burden on the federal government, as well as on state governments and the private sector. According to the Congressional Budget Office's (CBO's) projections, under current policies federal spending on Medicare and Medicaid will increase from about 5 percent of gross domestic product (GDP) in 2009 to more than 6 percent in 2019 and about 12 percent by 2050. Most of that increase will result from growth in per capita costs rather than from the aging of the population. In the private sector, the escalation of health care costs has contributed to slow growth in wages because workers must give up other forms of compensation to offset the rising costs of employment-based insurance.

- Rapidly rising costs for health care have generated rapid increases in the price of health insurance—an important factor behind the ongoing increase in the number of uninsured people. As health insurance premiums rise faster than workers' productivity and total compensation, people need to give up more of other goods and services to obtain insurance, and the rates at which people obtain insurance fall.

- The available evidence suggests that a substantial share of spending on health care contributes little if anything to the overall health of the nation, but finding ways to reduce such spending without also affecting services that improve health will be difficult. In many cases, the current system does not create incentives for doctors, hospitals, and other providers of health care—or their patients—to control costs. Significantly reducing the level or slowing the growth of health care spending below current projections will require substantial changes in those incentives.

- Given the central role of medical technology in the growth of health care spending, reducing or slowing that spending over the long term will probably require decreasing the pace of adopting new treatments and procedures or limiting the breadth of their application. Such changes need not involve explicit rationing but could occur as a result of market mechanisms or policy changes that affect the incentives to develop and adopt more costly treatments.

Controlling costs and improving efficiency present many challenges, but there are a number of approaches about which many analysts would probably concur:

- Many analysts would agree that payment systems should move away from a fee-for-service design—which tends to encourage the delivery of more services—and should instead provide stronger incentives to control costs, reward value, or both. A number of alternative approaches could be considered—including fixed payments per patient, bonuses based on performance, or penalties for substandard care—but their precise effects on spending and health are uncertain. Policymakers may thus want to test various options (for example, using demonstration programs in Medicare) to see whether they work as intended or to determine which design features work best. Almost inevitably, though, reducing the amount that is spent on health care will involve some cutbacks or constraints on the number and types of services provided relative to the currently projected levels.

- Many analysts would agree that the current tax exclusion for employment-based health insurance—which exempts most payments for such insurance from both income and payroll taxes—dampens incentives for cost control be-

cause it is open-ended. Those incentives could be changed by replacing the tax exclusion or restructuring it to encourage workers to join health plans with lower premiums (reflecting some combination of higher cost-sharing requirements and tighter management of benefits).

- Many analysts would agree that more information is needed about which treatments work best for which patients and about what quality of care different doctors, hospitals, and other providers deliver. The broad benefits that such information provides suggest a role for the government in funding research on the comparative effectiveness of treatments, in generating measures of quality, and in disseminating the results to doctors and patients. Wider adoption of health information technology (IT) would facilitate all of those efforts. But absent stronger incentives to control costs and improve efficiency, the effect of information alone on spending will generally be limited.

- Many analysts would agree that controlling federal costs over the long term will be very difficult without addressing the underlying forces that are also causing private costs for health care to rise. Private insurers generally have more flexibility than Medicare's administrators to adapt to changing circumstances, but changes made in the Medicare program can also stimulate broader improvements in the health sector.

Many of the steps that analysts would recommend might not yield substantial budgetary savings or reductions in national spending on health care within a 10-year window—and others might increase federal costs or total spending—for several reasons:

- In some cases, savings may materialize slowly because an initiative is phased in. For example, Medicare could save money by reducing payments to hospitals that have a high rate of avoidable readmissions (for complications following a discharge) but would have to gather information about readmission rates and notify hospitals before such reductions could be implemented. More generally, the process of converting innovative ideas into successful programmatic changes could take several years. Of course, for proposals that would increase the budget deficit, phasing them in would reduce the amount of the increase that is within a 10-year budget window.

- Even if they generate some offsetting savings, initiatives are not costless to implement. For example, expanding the use of disease management services can improve health and may well be cost-effective—that is, the value of the benefits could exceed the costs. But those efforts may still fail to generate net reductions in spending on health care because the number of people receiving the services is generally much larger than the number who would avoid expensive treatments as a result. In other cases, most of the initial costs would be incurred in the first 10 years, but little of the savings would accrue in that period.

- Moreover, the effect on the federal budget of a policy proposal to encourage certain activities often differs from the impact of those activities on total spending for health care. For example, a preventive service could be cost-reducing overall, but if the government began providing that service for free, federal costs would probably increase—largely because many of the payments would cover costs for care that would have been received anyway.

- In some cases, additional steps beyond a proposal are needed for the federal government to capture savings generated by an initiative. For example, getting hospitals to adopt electronic health records would lower their costs for treating Medicare patients, but the program's payment rates would have to be reduced in order for much of those savings to accrue to the federal government.

- Savings from some initiatives may not materialize because incentives to reduce costs are lacking. For example, proposals to establish a "medical home" might have little impact on spending if the primary care physicians who would coordinate care were not given financial incentives to economize on their patients' use of services. Those proposals could increase costs if they simply raised payments to those primary care physicians.

- In some cases, estimating the budgetary effects of a proposal is hampered by limited evidence. Studies generally examine the effects of discrete policy changes but typically do not address what would happen if several changes were made at the same time. Those interactions could mean that the savings from combining two or more initiatives will be greater than or less than the sum of their individual effects.

On a broad level, many analysts agree about the direction in which policies would have to go in order to make the health care system more cost-effective: Patients and providers both need stronger incentives to control costs as well as more information about the quality and value of the care that is provided. But much less of a consensus exists about crucial details regarding how those changes are made (and similar disagreements arise about how to expand insurance coverage). In part, those disagreements reflect different values or different assessments of the existing evidence, but often they reflect a lack of evidence about the likely impact of making significant changes to the complex system of health insurance and health care.

Those difficulties notwithstanding, CBO recently analyzed the budgetary and other effects of numerous proposals designed to increase the efficiency of public health insurance programs or of the health sector more broadly—and identified a number of options that would probably reduce federal spending and would seem likely to enhance the quality of care. To provide a context for those options, my testimony first discusses some evidence about the inefficiency of the current health care system and then briefly reviews the incentives created by different payment methods and their implications for health care delivery and costs. Finally, I consider in more detail two commonly cited approaches for improving the system's performance: expanding the use of health IT and investing in research that compares the effectiveness of medical treatments. Those examples illustrate the important role of incentives in determining the effects of enhanced information on health care spending.

BACKGROUND ON HEALTH CARE SPENDING AND INEFFICIENCY

Spending on health care and related activities will account for nearly 18 percent of GDP in 2009—an expected total of $2.5 trillion—and under current policies, that share is projected to exceed 20 percent in 2018.[1] Annual health expenditures per capita are projected to rise from about $8,000 to about $13,000 over that period. Federal spending accounts for roughly one-third of those totals, and federal

---

[1]See Andrea Sisko and others, "Health Spending Projections Through 2018: Recession Effects Add Uncertainty to the Outlook," *Health Affairs*, Web Exclusive (February 24, 2009), pp. w346-w357. Spending on related activities includes the administrative costs of public and private insurance plans, funding for medical research, and the costs of constructing medical facilities.

outlays for the Medicare and Medicaid programs are projected to grow from about $720 billion in 2009 to about $1.4 trillion in 2019. Over the longer term, rising costs for health care represent the single greatest challenge to balancing the federal budget.[2]

Concerns about the level and growth of health care spending in this country might be less prominent if it was clear that the spending was producing commensurately good and improving health, but substantial evidence suggests that more spending does not always mean better care. Although many treatments undoubtedly save lives and improve patients' health, much spending is not cost-effective and in many cases does not even improve health. Indeed, despite spending more per capita than other nations, the United States lags behind lower-spending nations on several metrics, including life expectancy and infant mortality.[3] Statistics on health can be affected by a number of factors outside the scope of the health care system, but one recent study found that, compared with other industrialized countries, the United States also had higher mortality rates for conditions that are considered amenable to medical care.[4]

Recent studies have highlighted three types of shortcomings in the quality of care that people receive, each of which may constitute a form of inefficiency:

- **Overuse.** Overuse occurs when a service is provided even though its risk of harm exceeds its likely benefit—that is, when it is not warranted on medical grounds. A more expansive definition would include cases in which the added costs of a more expensive service did not exceed the added benefits it was expected to provide. A number of studies have found, on the basis of after-the-fact reviews by independent panels of doctors, that a sizable share of certain surgeries were performed despite their being clinically inappropriate or of equivocal value; those findings held true under various types of insurance plans.[5]

- **Underuse.** At the same time that some services are overused, others do not get provided even though they would have been medically beneficial. One recent study found that Medicare enrollees frequently did not receive care that was recommended or deemed appropriate; another study, which examined a broader population, found that patients typically received about half of recommended services, whether for preventive care, treatment of acute conditions, or treatment of chronic conditions.[6]

- **Misuse.** That term includes incorrect diagnoses as well as medical errors and other sources of avoidable complications (such as infections that patients acquire during a hospital stay). Over the past decade, the Institute of Medicine has issued several reports documenting the extent of medical errors and their consequences. Recently, Medicare has stopped paying for what are termed "never events"—mistakes such as operating on the wrong body part. The range of avoidable errors is undoubtedly much larger, but other types may be more difficult for an insurer to identify.

GEOGRAPHIC VARIATION IN SPENDING FOR HEALTH CARE

Perhaps the most compelling evidence suggesting inefficiency in the health sector is that per capita health care spending varies widely within the Medicare program, and yet that variation is not correlated with available measures of the quality of care or of health outcomes overall. In 2004, for example, Medicare spending per beneficiary ranged from about $5,600 in South Dakota to about $8,700 in Louisiana. Yet a comparison of composite quality scores for medical centers and average Medicare spending per beneficiary shows that facilities in states with high average costs are no more likely to provide recommended care for some common health problems than are facilities in states with lower costs (see Figure 1). For the country generally, health care spending per capita

[2]For additional discussion, see Congressional Budget Office, *The Long-Term Outlook for Health Care Spending* (November 2007).
[3]See, for example, Gerard F. Anderson and Bianca K. Frogner, "Health Spending in OECD Countries: Obtaining Value per Dollar," *Health Affairs,* vol. 27, no. 6 (November/December 2008), pp. 1718-1727.
[4]Cathy Schoen and others, "U.S. Health System Performance: A National Scorecard," *Health Affairs,* Web Exclusive (September 20, 2006), pp. w457-w475.
[5]See Elizabeth A. McGlynn, "Assessing the Appropriateness of Care: How Much Is Too Much?" RAND Research Brief (Santa Monica, Calif.: RAND, 1998).

[6]See Stephen F. Jencks, Edwin D. Huff, and Timothy Cuerdon, "Change in the Quality of Care Delivered to Medicare Beneficiaries, 1998-1999 to 2000-2001," *Journal of the American Medical Association,* vol. 289, no. 3 (January 15, 2003), pp. 305-312; and Elizabeth A. McGlynn and others, "The Quality of Health Care Delivered to Adults in the United States," *New England Journal of Medicine,* vol. 348, no. 26 (June 26, 2003), pp. 2635-2645.

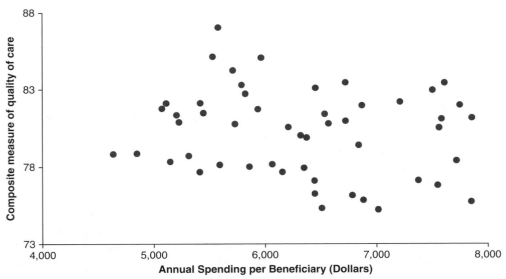

Notes: The composite measure of the quality of care, based on Medicare beneficiaries in the fee-for-service program
who were hospitalized in 2004, conveys the percentage who received recommended care for myocardial infarction,
heart failure, or pneumonia.
Spending figures convey average amounts by state.

Figure 1 The Relationship Between Medicare Spending and Quality of Care, by State, 2004 *Source:* Congressional Budget Office based on data from Department of Health and Human Services, Agency for Healthcare Research and Quality, National Healthcare Quality Report, 2005 (December 2005), Data Tables Appendix, available at www.ahrq.gov/qual/nhqr05/index.html, and data from the Centers for Medicare and Medicaid Services' Continuous Medicare History Sample.

also varies widely, ranging from roughly $4,000 in Utah to $6,700 in Massachusetts in 2004, but the connection between that variation and health outcomes has not been examined as closely. In addition, Medicaid spending per enrollee varies considerably among states for many reasons.

The observed variations in Medicare spending per enrollee are even greater when examined using smaller geographic areas that reflect where enrollees get their hospital care—but a link between higher spending and better health is still hard to discern. In 2005, average costs ranged from about $5,200 in the areas with the lowest spending to nearly $14,000 in the areas with the highest spending (those averages were adjusted to account for differences in the age, sex, and race of Medicare beneficiaries in the various areas). According to one study, higher-spending regions did not have lower mortality rates than lower-spending regions, even after adjustments were made to control for different rates of illness among patients and in various regions.[7] That

study also found that higher spending did not slow the rate at which the elderly developed functional limitations (reflecting their difficulties in taking care of themselves).

Other studies of spending variation reach somewhat different conclusions, but they also suggest opportunities to improve the efficiency of the health sector. For example, some research suggests that health overall might not suffer in the process of changing medical practice to match that of lower-cost regions but that patients who would benefit most from more expensive treatments might be made worse off as a result, while patients who would do better with less expensive treatments would gain.[8] Other, older, studies of geographic variation indicate that there may be room to reduce spending without harming health in both high-use and low-use areas of the country, because—in both types of regions—a large share of certain surgeries were found to be clinically inappropriate or of equivocal value.

[7]Elliott S. Fisher and others, "The Implications of Regional Variations in Medicare Spending, Part 2: Health Outcomes and Satisfaction with Care," *Annals of Internal Medicine,* vol. 138, no. 4 (February 18, 2003), pp. 288-298. The study divided the country into about 300 "hospital referral regions" by determining where Medicare enrollees were most likely to get their hospital care.

[8]See Amitabh Chandra and Douglas Staiger, "Productivity Spillovers in Health Care: Evidence from the Treatment of Heart Attacks," *Journal of Political Economy,* vol. 115, no. 1 (2007), pp. 103-140; and Mary Beth Landrum and others, "Is Spending More Always Wasteful: The Appropriateness of Care and Outcomes Among Colorectal Cancer Patients," *Health Affairs,* vol. 27, no. 1 (January/February 2008), pp. 159-168.

What factors contribute to geographic variation? Some of the differences in spending reflect varying rates of illness as well as differences in the prices that Medicare pays for the same service (which are adjusted on the basis of local costs for labor and equipment in the health sector). But according to researchers at Dartmouth, differences in illness rates account for less than 30 percent of the variation in spending among areas, and differences in prices can explain another 10 percent—indicating that more than 60 percent of the variation is due to other factors.[9] Differences in income or the stated preferences of individuals for specific types of care also appear to explain little of the variation in spending, although unmeasured differences in the demand for care could be important.

Some evidence suggests that the degree of geographic variation in treatment patterns is greater when less of a consensus exists within the medical community about the best treatment to use. For example, patients who have fractured their hip clearly need to be hospitalized, and there is relatively little variation in admission rates for Medicare beneficiaries with that diagnosis. For hip replacements and for knee replacements, however, more discretion is involved, and the surgery rates vary more widely. There appears to be even more variation in the rates of back surgery—a treatment whose benefits have been the subject of substantial questions.[10]

A significant part of the variation in medical practice appears to be attributable to regional differences in the supply of medical resources and the use of those resources. For example, lower-cost areas tend to have a lower ratio of specialists to primary care physicians. Analysis by the Dartmouth researchers that focused on spending in the last 6 months of Medicare patients' lives and on patients with similar medical conditions also found substantial differences between high-cost and low-cost areas in the number of visits to the doctor, the number of tests conducted, and number of days spent in the hospital.[11] Overall, patterns of treatment in high-spending areas tend to be more intensive than those in low-spending areas. That is, in high-spending areas, a broader array of patients will receive costly treatments.[12]

PAYMENT METHODS AND PROVIDERS' INCENTIVES

Before turning to specific options for encouraging efficiency, it is useful to consider the broad range of payment methods that are currently in use and the incentives that they create for doctors and hospitals. Most care provided by physicians in the United States is paid for on a fee-for-service basis, meaning that a separate payment is made for each procedure, each office visit, and each ancillary service (such as a laboratory test). Hospitals are often paid a fixed amount per admission (a bundled payment to cover all of the services that the hospital provides during a stay) or an amount per day. Such payments may encourage doctors and hospitals to limit their own costs when delivering a given service or bundle, but they can also create an incentive to provide more services or bundles that are more expensive if the additional payments exceed the added costs.

Other arrangements, such as salaries for doctors or periodic capitation payments (fixed amounts per patient), do not provide financial incentives to deliver additional services. One study randomly assigned enrollees to different health plans and found that those in an integrated plan (which owns the hospitals used by enrollees and pays providers a salary) used 30 percent fewer services than enrollees in a fee-for-service plan, but whether those results could be replicated more broadly is unclear. Moreover, those approaches raise concerns about providers' incentives to stint on care or avoid treating sicker patients. A number of intermediate options exist that would provide fewer incentives to limit services, including episode-based payments (fixed amounts for all services related to treating a given health problem) or partial capitation (a blend

---

[9]See John E. Wennberg, Elliott S. Fisher, and Jonathan S. Skinner, "Geography and the Debate Over Medicare Reform," *Health Affairs,* Web Exclusive (February 13, 2002), pp. w96-w97.

[10]See Dartmouth Atlas Project, *The Dartmouth Atlas of Health Care.* Determining what share of any geographic variation in the use of specific procedures is attributable to differences in the treatments that doctors recommend and what share is attributable to differences in the prevalence or intensity of the underlying illness is challenging, so the comparison of procedures may be sensitive to the manner in which differences in illness rates are estimated.

[11]Elliott S. Fisher and others, "The Implications of Regional Variations in Medicare Spending, Part 1: The Content, Quality, and Accessibility of Care," *Annals of Internal Medicine,* vol. 138, no. 4 (February 18, 2003), pp. 273-287. The study did not find substantial differences among areas in the number of hospital admissions or the types of surgeries performed.

[12]For further discussion, see Congressional Budget Office, *Geographic Variation in Health Care Spending* (February 2008).

of a smaller fixed payment per patient and reduced fees per service).

Proposals could seek to change payment methods either indirectly or directly. They could change the payment methods used by private health plans indirectly by encouraging shifts in enrollment toward plans that have lower-cost payment systems. In particular, modifying the current tax preference for employer-sponsored health care—so that it did not encourage workers to purchase more expensive plans than they would otherwise choose—could make lower-cost, integrated health plans more attractive. For public programs, such as Medicare and Medicaid, policymakers could directly change payment methods. Depending on the extent of the changes that were made, implementing them could prove to be very challenging, both because the government would have to determine the appropriate level and structure of the new payments and because providers might have to alter decades-long practices about how they organize and deliver health care.

The financial incentives created by different payment systems—and the spending amounts they yield—also depend on the level at which payment rates, or prices, are set. Those rates depend partly on the methods that are used to set them. Private-sector payment rates are set by negotiation, reflecting the underlying costs of the services and the relative bargaining power of providers and health plans; in turn, bargaining power depends on factors such as the number of competing providers or provider groups within a local market area. Fee-for-service payment rates in Medicare and Medicaid are generally set administratively (with any bargaining generally taking place through the legislative process of determining or modifying statutory rate-setting formulas). Administered pricing poses a number of challenges, particularly in deciding how to determine providers' costs for services that require substantial training or that become cheaper to provide when they are performed more frequently. Additional issues include how to account for the quality of those services and their value to patients, and what impact rate setting might have on the development of new medical technology.[13]

CBO'S ANALYSIS OF BUDGET OPTIONS

Addressing the strong interest of policymakers in health care financing and health care issues, CBO recently released *Budget Options, Volume 1: Health Care*.[14] That December 2008 report comprises 115 discrete options to alter federal programs, affect the private health insurance market, or both. It includes many options that would reduce the federal budget deficit and some that would increase it. Although similar to CBO's previous reports on budget options, that volume reflects an extensive and concerted effort to substantially expand the range of topics and types of proposals considered and includes estimates of many approaches that the agency had not previously analyzed.

The options stem from a variety of sources, including discussions with Congressional staff; reviews of legislative proposals, past versions of the President's budget, and academic literature; and analyses conducted by CBO staff, other government agencies such as the Medicare Payment Advisory Commission, and private groups. Although the number of health-related policy options is significantly greater than in previous volumes, it is not an exhaustive list. CBO's estimates are sensitive to the precise specifications of each option and could change in the future for a variety of reasons, including changes in economic conditions or other factors that affect projections of baseline spending or the availability of new evidence about an option's likely effects. It should also be noted that the options' effects may not be additive; that is, there could be important interactive effects among options that make their cumulative impact larger or smaller than the sum of the estimates. Some of the options that are particularly complex may be candidates for demonstration projects or pilot programs, which could reduce the uncertainty about their effects.

Chapter 5 of CBO's *Budget Options* volume examines a number of policies that could change the way that providers are paid—and thus the incentives they have—in ways that are designed to enhance the quality and efficiency of health care. Most of those options focus on Medicare, but others address Medicaid or the larger health care system. Some options would involve relatively modest changes in payment methods, but others would make more dramatic changes to those methods and thus to

---

[13]For additional discussion of payment methods and rate-setting techniques, see Congressional Budget Office, *Key Issues in Analyzing Major Health Insurance Proposals* (December 2008), pp. 102-108.

[14]Another volume, containing budget options that are not related to health care, is forthcoming.

incentives for providers. (Chapter 6 describes several options for reducing the geographic variation in spending for Medicare, primarily by cutting payment rates in high-spending areas, but the effects of those options on care quality are less clear.)

Option 38 provides one example of how Medicare could move away from fee-for-service payments to physicians toward a blend of capitated and per-service payments. That option would require the Centers for Medicare and Medicaid Services to assign each beneficiary who participates in the traditional Medicare program to a primary care physician. Those physicians would receive approximately three-fourths of their Medicare payments on a per-service basis and approximately one-fourth under a capitated arrangement; they would also receive bonuses or face penalties, depending on the total spending for all Medicare services incurred by their panel of beneficiaries. In response to the incentives created by that payment approach, physicians would probably try to reduce spending among their panel of patients in several ways—for example, by limiting referrals to specialists, increasing their prescribing of generic medications, and reducing hospitalizations for discretionary procedures. According to CBO's estimates, this option would increase payments to physicians and decrease payments to all other Medicare providers, with a net federal savings of about $5 billion between 2010 and 2019.

Option 30 focuses instead on Medicare's payments for hospital and post-acute care, which would be bundled together. Under the specifications of that option, federal spending would be reduced by about $19 billion over the 2010-2019 period, CBO estimates. That approach would constitute a significant change in the way Medicare pays for post-acute care (which includes services provided by skilled nursing facilities and home health agencies). Medicare would no longer make separate payments for post-acute care services following an acute care inpatient hospital stay. Instead, the unit of payment for acute care provided in hospitals would be redefined and expanded to include post-acute care provided both there and in nonhospital settings. Hospitals would have incentives to reduce the cost of post-acute care for Medicare beneficiaries by lessening its volume and intensity or by contracting with lower-cost providers.

Chapters 7 and 8 examine a much wider range of ways in which payment rates for medical services and supplies could be changed under both the Medicare and Medicaid programs. For example,

Option 55 would reduce (by 1 percentage point) the annual update factor under Medicare for inpatient hospital services; by CBO's estimates, that change would yield $93 billion in savings over 10 years. Option 59 includes several alternatives for increasing payment rates for physicians under Medicare, which (under current law) are scheduled to fall by about 21 percent in 2010 and by about 5 percent annually for several years thereafter. The 10-year cost of those alternatives ranges from $318 billion to $556 billion.

Chapters 3 and 9 examine several options that could improve the efficiency of the health sector by changing incentives about how much insurance to purchase and how much care to demand. For example, Option 11 would replace the current tax exclusion for employment-based health insurance with a refundable but more limited tax credit. In addition to encouraging workers to choose less expensive health insurance plans, that option would increase federal revenues by $606 billion through 2018 (as estimated by the staff of the Joint Committee on Taxation). Option 83 would change the Medicare program's cost-sharing requirements and restrict supplemental insurance coverage of those requirements (known as medigap plans) in ways that would reduce federal costs by $73 billion over the 2010-2019 period. That approach would encourage enrollees to be more prudent in their use of Medicare services.

THE POTENTIAL AND LIMITS OF HEALTH INFORMATION TECHNOLOGY

Health information technology has the potential to significantly increase the efficiency of the health sector by helping providers manage information. In particular, electronic health records—comprising electronic documentation of providers' medical notes, electronic viewing of laboratory and radiological results, electronic prescribing of medications, and an interoperable connection among providers of health care—could have a significant impact on medical practice.[15] When used effectively, electronic health records could reduce the duplication of diagnostic tests; remind physicians about appropriate preventive care; identify harmful drug interactions

---

[15]Definitions of what constitutes a health IT system vary, which can affect the measured adoption rates. Capabilities that are sometimes considered separate from an electronic health record include computerized physician order entry (for ordering tests and medications within a hospital) and computer-based decision support systems.

or possible allergic reactions to prescribed medicines; and help physicians manage the care of patients with complex chronic conditions. Such steps could yield significant health benefits for patients, but research indicates that the extent to which health IT also generates reductions in health care spending depends largely on the incentives facing providers who have adopted it. By itself, the adoption of more health IT is generally not sufficient to produce substantial savings because the incentives for many providers to use that technology in ways that control costs are not strong.

Factors Affecting Adoption of Health IT

The most auspicious examples of health IT have tended to involve relatively integrated health care systems. Such systems typically involve a hospital network or a health plan that owns the hospitals that provide most care to enrollees, with doctors and other providers who work exclusively for the organization (either for a salary or under contract). In such systems, most savings generated by health IT care are captured by the hospital or the health plan—thus providing incentives to adopt health IT and use it effectively. A number of integrated delivery systems, including Kaiser Permanente, Intermountain Healthcare, Geisinger Health System, and Partners HealthCare—as well as the Department of Veterans Affairs—have implemented electronic health records either across their organizations or in some regions, and officials of those systems believe that both the efficiency and quality of the care they provide have improved as a result.

For providers and hospitals that are not part of integrated systems, however, the financial benefits of health IT are not as easy to capture. Correspondingly, those physicians and facilities have adopted electronic health records at a much slower rate. Office-based physicians in particular may see no benefit if they purchase and install such a product—and may even suffer financial harm. Even though the use of health IT could reduce costs for the health system as a whole so as to offset the start-up and operating costs involved, many physicians might not be able to reduce their own office expenses or increase their own revenue sufficiently to pay for it. The health benefits deriving from health IT are probably lower in unintegrated settings, but whether that tendency reflects the lack of financial incentives for effective use of health IT in such settings or stems from other limitations of a more fragmented system of care is not clear.

All in all, despite the potential gains from health IT, relatively few providers have adopted it—about 12 percent of physicians and 11 percent of hospitals as of 2006.[16]

Effects of Recent Legislation Regarding Health IT

The recently enacted American Recovery and Reinvestment Act establishes payment incentives in the Medicare and Medicaid programs to encourage providers to adopt health IT. Although the direct effect of those provisions involves participation in those programs, providers would use the newly purchased IT systems for all of their patients. Thus, both public and private health care delivery will benefit from the increased use of health IT. Consequently, CBO expects, the adoption of health IT brought about by the law will modestly reduce total spending on health care services by diminishing the number of inappropriate tests and procedures, reducing paperwork and administrative overhead, and decreasing the number of adverse events resulting from medical errors. Before the new law, CBO had assumed that nearly all doctors and hospitals would adopt health IT eventually, but that process would probably take about 25 years. As a result of the law's provisions, about 90 percent of doctors and 70 percent of hospitals will adopt health IT by 2019, CBO estimates.

Although the use of health care services in Medicare and Medicaid is projected to decline as a result of the increased adoption of health IT, the net effect of the Reinvestment and Recovery Act's provisions for health IT is to increase federal spending in the near term, because those programs bear the full cost of the incentive payments. Specifically, CBO estimates that the law's payment incentives will increase spending for the Medicare and Medicaid programs by about $33 billion over the 2009-2019 period. The expanded use of health IT will reduce direct federal spending for benefits by Medicare and Medicaid (and by the Federal Employees Health Benefits program) by about $13 billion over the same period. Taking into account about $1 billion in funding for administering the payment-incentive provisions, CBO estimates that those provisions will increase direct spending on net by about $21 billion over the 2009-2019 period. Because accelerating the

---

[16]For further discussion, see Congressional Budget Office, *Evidence on the Costs and Benefits of Health Information Technology* (May 2008).

adoption and use of health IT will lower health care costs for private payers, the law will also yield lower health insurance premiums in the private sector. Consequently, private employers will pay less of their employees' compensation in the form of tax-advantaged health insurance premiums and more in the form of taxable wages and salaries—so federal tax revenues will, by CBO's estimates, increase by about $3 billion between 2009 and 2019.

COMPARING THE EFFECTIVENESS OF MEDICAL TREATMENTS

Patients with a given disease or medical condition often have several treatment options available to them, but rigorous evaluation of the relative effectiveness of those options is rarely available to them or their doctors. Drugs and medical devices must be certified as safe and effective before they can be marketed, but with limited exceptions the regulatory process for approving those products does not evaluate them relative to alternatives. Meanwhile, medical procedures—which account for a much larger share of total health care spending—can be in widespread use without a systematic review of their impact. Appraisals of the current situation vary widely, but some experts believe that less than half of all medical care is based on adequate evidence about its effectiveness—a gap that may never close entirely but that remains troubling.

Consequently, many analysts recommend conducting additional research that compares the effectiveness of different treatments—and reflecting that view, the Recovery and Reinvestment Act provided $1.1 billion in federal funding for such research. Studies of comparative effectiveness may examine similar treatments, such as competing drugs, or they may analyze very different approaches, such as surgery and drug therapy. The analysis may focus only on the relative clinical benefits and risks of each option, or it may go on to weigh both the costs and the benefits of those options. In some cases, a given treatment may be found more effective for all types of patients, but more commonly a key issue is determining which specific types would benefit most from it. Assessing cost-effectiveness as well as clinical effectiveness would probably yield a somewhat larger effect on health care spending than would research focused only on clinical effectiveness, because it would help highlight cases in which the additional benefits of a more costly treatment are relatively small.

By itself, however, generating additional information is likely to have a very limited effect on spending for health care.[17] To affect medical treatment and reduce health care spending, the results of comparative effectiveness analyses would ultimately have to change the behavior of doctors and patients—that is, to get them to use fewer services or less intensive and less expensive services than are currently projected. Bringing about those changes would probably require action by public and private insurers to incorporate the results into their coverage and payment policies in order to affect the incentives for doctors and patients. Making such changes to the Medicare program would require legislative action; private insurers would not face the same constraint but might be reluctant to take such steps if Medicare did not do so.[18]

---

[17]For further discussion, see Option 45 in CBO's *Budget Options* volume.

[18]For further discussion, see Congressional Budget Office, *Research on the Comparative Effectiveness of Medical Treatments: Issues and Options for an Expanded Federal Role* (December 2007).

3

Rising Rates of Chronic Health Conditions: What Can Be Done?

Source: Cassil, A. 2008. *Rising Rates of Chronic Health Conditions: What Can Be Done?* Issue Brief No. 125. Washington, DC: Center for Studying Health System Change. Used with the permission of The Center for Studying Health System Change.

The growing prevalence of chronic health conditions—about 60 percent of the adult U.S. population had at least one chronic condition in 2005—has added costs to the U.S. health care system. Prevention and better management of chronic conditions are often cited as ways to improve health outcomes and slow U.S. health care spending growth—or at least generate better value for the $2.1 trillion spent annually on health care in the United States. Yet, the health care system remains largely focused on acute, episodic care, according to experts at a Center for Studying Health System Change (HSC) conference titled, Rising Rates of Chronic Health Conditions: What Can Be Done? Panelists explored the role of obesity in rising rates of chronic conditions, the need for better information on how to treat patients with multiple chronic conditions, how to help patients improve self-management skills and how difficult changing unhealthy behaviors can be.

U.S. HEALTH CARE SYSTEM FOCUSED ON ACUTE CARE NOT CHRONIC CONDITIONS

In some respects, America's rising rates of chronic conditions reflect the huge advances in public health, industrial safety and medical care over the last century. A hundred years ago, most people didn't live long enough to develop a chronic condition. In 1900, an average American's life expectancy was 47 years; today it's 78 years. A hundred years ago, the top causes of death were infections—such as pneumonia, influenza and tuberculosis—accidents and child birth.

Today, the leading causes of death are heart disease, cancer and stroke. While advances in public health and medical care have been spectacular, the U.S. health care system is behind the times when it comes to providing early intervention and high-quality care for people with chronic conditions.

"We have a system that remains focused on providing acute episodes of care. We're pretty good at treating a heart attack, but not so good at preventing and managing the underlying heart disease that leads to that heart attack," said HSC President Paul B. Ginsburg, who moderated the conference.

Tremendous attention has been focused on identifying effective clinical care for individual chronic illnesses, such as heart disease or diabetes, but more than one in four Americans has two or more chronic conditions, according to panelist Carolyn Clancy, M.D., director of the Agency for Healthcare Research and Quality.

"Where our evidence base is pretty thin is how to manage effectively people who have several chronic illnesses, particularly people for whom one of those illnesses is a mental health disorder," she said.

"When you're looking at people with multiple conditions, you've not only got interactions between illnesses and between treatments, you've got people on multiple medications, multiple providers . . . so many [providers] that it's really hard to imagine that there's a common script across this array of clinicians," Clancy continued.

THE ECONOMICS OF OBESITY

Two-thirds of Americans are overweight or obese, and the prevalence of obesity—a clear risk factor for many chronic diseases—has more than doubled in the United States in the last three decades, according to panelist Eric Finkelstein, an economist at RTI and author of *The Fattening of America: How the Economy Makes Us Fat, If It Matters, and What to Do About It.*

As cheap and fattening food abounds, Americans have steadily increased their caloric intake, Finkelstein noted, saying, "The argument that I'm selling is—the increase in food consumption is a direct result of a decrease in food prices, both the monetary price of food, as well as the opportunity or acquisition cost of getting that food into your mouths."

Flipping to the caloric expenditure side of things, Finkelstein pointed out that leisure-time physical activity is losing out to new technologies, such as DVDs, the Internet, cable TV and computer games. The same is true for "accidental exercise," or the exercise people typically used to get through the work day, he said, adding, "You'd have to think pretty hard to find an occupation that hasn't been mechanized to the extent that you get almost no physical activity at all—so accidental exercise is almost nonexistent."

New technologies, such as statins to control high cholesterol, have helped reduce some of the adverse health consequences of obesity over time, Finkelstein said, citing a recent study that found today's obese population has a better cardiovascular disease profile than normal-weight individuals did several decades ago.

"The changing economy has lowered the cost of food consumption, price and non-price, raised the cost of physical activity in terms of the opportunity cost, as well as being physically active on the job, and that's essentially lowered the health cost of being obese," Finkelstein said. "These three factors have really combined to create an environment where we would expect to see rising rates of obesity, which is exactly what we've seen."

While obesity is clearly costly on many levels, Finkelstein urged caution against citing the high cost of obesity as justification for public obesity interventions because public-funded, cost-saving interventions for obesity "just don't exist."

Instead, Finkelstein suggested that the government's role in stemming obesity should be to examine "past policies that probably helped promote obesity rates . . . agricultural subsidy policies, for example, even zoning policies that essentially encourage people to use automobile transportation as opposed to other forms of transportation."

MEDICAID: TRAIN WRECK OR LAND OF OPPORTUNITY?

Nowhere does the cost of chronic conditions hit harder than for the approximately 7 million people who are dually eligible for Medicaid and Medicare, according to panelist Melanie Bella, senior vice president at the Center for Health Care Strategies, a nonprofit that works with state Medicaid programs to improve care for enrollees with costly and complex health needs.

The so-called dual eligibles account for about 42 percent of Medicaid costs and 25 percent of Medicare costs, Bella said. Among the most expensive 1 percent of Medicaid enrollees, 83 percent have three or more chronic conditions and 60 percent have five or more chronic conditions.

"So you might look at this and think, this is a train wreck, what in the world are we going to do about this," Bella said. "We look at this and say Medicaid is the land of opportunity. There is no better place to tackle chronic illness than in Medicaid."

Echoing Clancy's point about the need to identify effective interventions for patients with multiple chronic conditions, Bella said, "Medicaid and Medicare have realized you cannot do single-disease, silo disease management programs, yet trying to figure out how to go from that all the way to a program that's going to be responsive and nimble to every single beneficiary's needs regardless of the set of chronic conditions was fairly overwhelming."

Many states are moving to identify "high-opportunity" beneficiaries and develop tailored care management interventions, she said, but states face formidable challenges, including:

- Most high-need, high-cost beneficiaries get their care in a fragmented fee-for-service environment.
- Reimbursement rates are generally insufficient to support complex care management.
- Medicaid's financing structure makes it difficult to invest in long-term solutions because of pressure to show immediate cost savings.

- Misaligned payment incentives between Medicare and Medicaid result in cost shifting and poor quality. For example, Medicare pays for hospital care, while Medicaid covers nursing home care, so if better care coordination prevents a Medicaid nursing home patient from hospitalization, the savings accrue to Medicare rather than Medicaid.

"The majority of folks in Medicare and Medicaid who are the highest cost and have the highest needs . . . are still in a very fragmented, uncoordinated fee-for-service system. The very folks who need it the most are stuck, arguably, in the worst place," Bella said.

EMPLOYER INITIATIVES

While more and more employers are adopting health promotion and wellness programs, panelist Ron Goetzel, Ph.D., director of the Institute for Health and Productivity at Emory University, questioned whether most employer programs are effective.

"We're seeing a sea change in terms of the number of employers that are beginning to think about and implement these kinds of programs in the workplace," Goetzel said. "The main problem out there is that they don't know how to do it well."

Noting the strong link between modifiable health risk factors—such as smoking, diet and uncontrolled high blood pressure—and chronic conditions, Goetzel said the evidence is growing that workplace health promotion and disease prevention programs can be effective.

"There's a growing body of literature that suggests that if you do things that are evidence-based, well-designed, well-implemented and well-evaluated, that these kinds of programs can improve workers' health, lower their risk for disease, save businesses money by reducing health-related loss and limiting absence and disability, heighten work morale and work relations, and improve worker productivity," he said.

Efforts to improve workplace wellness initiatives could include identifying and disseminating best practices, establishing public-private technical assistance services, and funding large-scale studies to evaluate the effectiveness of different interventions, he said.

"There's a lot of ignorance out there in terms of what works and what does not, and a lot of things that don't work are being put in place in these companies," Goetzel said. "So there is a lot of knowledge that can be distributed, disseminated, communicated to organizations that want to put these programs in place."

REDESIGNING CARE

Existing research consistently finds that the U.S. health care delivery system generally does a "poor" job of helping patients with chronic conditions get their diseases under control, according to panelist Michele Heisler, M.D., an associate professor of medicine at the University of Michigan and research scientist at the Veterans Affairs Health Services Research and Development Center for Excellence.

Numerous studies show that patients with chronic conditions are not on the right medications at the right doses, Heisler said. And, and even when providers prescribe the correct medications, research also shows that only about 50 percent of patients with chronic conditions take their prescribed medications, and the numbers are even worse for diet and exercise.

"The costs of this are huge," Heisler said. "Just counting unnecessary emergency room admissions and preventable hospitalizations, the costs of poor medication adherence alone is greater than $100 billion a year . . . drugs don't work in patients who don't take them."

Patient self-management is an essential component of good chronic care, Heisler said, adding that "chronic disease outcomes depend critically—once patients are on the right medications, once they get appropriate advice and support for self-management—on what they have to do between office visits."

Citing an Institute of Medicine report on the quality of U.S. health care, Heisler said physicians and patients are working as hard as they can "but current care systems cannot do the job, we have to change systems."

At the physician-practice level, Heisler suggested efforts to redesign care should focus on four key components of the Wagner Chronic Care Model:

- Delivery system design (who's on the health care team and how do we interact with patients).
- Decision support (what is the best care and how do we make it happen every time).
- Clinical information systems (how do we capture and use critical information for clinical care).
- Self-management support (how we help patients live with their conditions and make behavioral changes to improve health).

"Ideally what we're looking for is well-organized, efficient practices, satisfied patients on the right medication with excellent self-management and healthy behaviors, and satisfied providers able to provide outstanding patient care without feeling overwhelmed," Heisler concluded.

INVOLVING PATIENTS

A key element of improving care for people with chronic conditions is improved self-management, several panelists noted. "We need self-management support—how we help patients live with their conditions and make behavioral changes to improve health," Heisler said.

The learning curve for patients is likely to be high since many are unfamiliar with such concepts as evidence-based care and clinical guidelines, said panelist Kristin Carman, co-director of the Health Policy & Research Program at the American Institutes for Research.

"If you think about it, and this is not just true for people for chronic disease, we want people to be using and applying information about staying healthy, preventing disease and managing disease," Carman said, adding that "consumers are not always on the same page" as employers, insurers and others who are pushing consumers to be more involved in their care.

"So when you say guidelines suggest you do this, guidelines suggest you do that, this is what many of them have in their head: 'These are about restrictions on my choice. They're designed to protect everyone but the patient. They represent an inflexible, one-size-fits-all approach. I'm an individual,'" Carman said.

As part of a recent project to design an employer toolkit to communicate with employees about evidence-based care, Carman and her colleagues surveyed people about how active they were in managing their health. About three-quarters of the respondents said they were attempting to make a lifestyle change to improve their health, with about half of those saying the change was moderate and about 40 percent reporting the change was small or very small.

"The bad news is, no matter how they viewed it, they all thought it was hard or very hard. . . ." Carman said. "If people's self-conception is virtually everything they're trying to do is hard, it's not very likely they're going to do it or be able to sustain it."

Making Medical Homes Work: Moving from Concept to Practice

Source: Ginsburg, P.B. et al. 2008. *Making Medical Homes Work: Moving from Concept to Practice*. Policy Perspective No. 1. Washington, DC: Center for Studying Health System Change. Used with the permission of The Center for Studying Health System Change.

Widespread concern about high and rising costs, coupled with increasing evidence that the quality of U.S. health care varies greatly, has put health care reform near the top of the domestic policy agenda. Policy makers face mounting pressure to reform provider payment systems to spur changes in how providers are organized and deliver care.

In many communities, physician practices, hospitals and other providers are poorly integrated in terms of culture, organization and financing. While these independent arrangements may offer some benefit, such as broadened patient choice, the flip side of independence is fragmentation—across care sites, providers and in clinical decision making for patients. Current payment systems, particularly fee-for-service arrangements, reinforce delivery systems that offer care in silos and reward greater volume but not quality of care. Fee-for-service payment also provides few incentives for providers to invest in improving care for chronic illnesses, which account for a far greater proportion of health care spending than do acute illnesses.

Among the many proposals for payment and delivery system reform under discussion, the medical home model has gained significant momentum in both the public and private sectors. The concept has been promoted by primary care physician societies. And a broad range of insurers and payers—for example, United HealthCare, Aetna, the Blue Cross Blue Shield Association, and Medicaid programs—are developing medical home initiatives. Likewise, Congress has mandated a medical home demonstration in fee-for-service Medicare.

Although medical home definitions vary and continue to evolve, at the heart of a medical home is a physician practice committed to organizing and coordinating care based on patients' needs and priorities, communicating directly with patients and their families, and integrating care across settings and practitioners. If enough physician practices become medical homes, a critical mass might be attained to transform the care delivery system to provide accessible, continuous, coordinated, patient-centered care to high-need populations—usually considered to be patients with chronic illnesses.

Some advocates ascribe a broader goal to the medical home model—to improve the quality of care, reduce the need for expensive medical services and generate savings for payers. Medical homes are expected to accomplish this goal by changing how physicians practice medicine.

Yet despite the enormous energy and resources invested in the medical home model to date, relatively little has been written about moving from theoretical concept to practical application, particularly on a large scale. What would an effective medical home program look like? And how should it be implemented? Forging ahead with medical home initiatives without such analyses to ground their design and identify potential pitfalls and solutions may result in ineffective programs that alienate patients and/or physicians. That would put at risk not only the resources invested by clinicians and payers/insurers in early initiatives, but also the political viability of the model itself in the long-term as a vehicle for wider health care reform.

The Center for Studying Health System Change (HSC) and Mathematica Policy Research (MPR) are uniquely positioned to address operational issues related to medical homes. Along with conducting independent and collaborative research relevant to medical homes, care coordination, payment policy and the organization of care delivery, HSC and MPR researchers have direct experience with both public- and private-sector medical home initiatives, including leading the design of the Medicare medical home demonstration.

Based on these experiences, we've identified four critical operational issues in the implementation of most medical home models that we believe have potential to make or break a successful program: (1) how to qualify physician practices as medical homes; (2) how to match patients to their medical homes; (3) how to engage patients and other providers to work with medical homes in care coordination; and (4) how to pay practices that serve as medical homes. Drawing on published data and our on-the-ground expertise, we hope that these analyses will guide clinicians, payers and policy makers as they attempt to build a solid foundation for successful medical home initiatives. Doing so will improve the chances that the medical home concept can serve as a stepping stone to broader reforms in health care payment and delivery systems.

QUALIFYING A PHYSICIAN PRACTICE AS A MEDICAL HOME

BY ANN S. O'MALLEY, DEBORAH PEIKES AND PAUL B. GINSBURG

Identifying an effective and efficient way to determine if a physician practice has the capabilities to serve as a medical home is a pressing challenge as public and private payers develop pilots to determine whether additional payment to medical homes can improve the quality and efficiency of care. Ensuring that a qualification tool validly captures the capa-

bilities a practice needs to be a medical home can help practices focus on the most important activities to improve care. Most medical home initiatives rely on the joint principles of the patient-centered medical home developed by the primary care physician specialty societies, which lay out the general attributes of a patient-centered medical home. They emphasize four key primary care elements—accessibility, continuity, coordination and comprehensiveness—that research shows positively affect health outcomes, satisfaction and costs. An ideal qualification tool would ensure that medical homes are built on a firm foundation of these critical primary care pillars. A qualification tool that either gives insufficient emphasis to these bedrock primary care elements or gives too much emphasis to factors that may not be related to better performance risks excluding physician practices that truly function as medical homes and including those that don't. Moreover, overly burdensome documentation requirements for practice structures that ultimately may not improve patient outcomes run the risk of posing a barrier to practices seeking to participate as medical homes and distracting physicians from improving care for patients.

Building Medical Homes on a Solid Primary Care Foundation

Public and private payers are launching patient-centered medical home (PCMH) experiments as one strategy to improve the quality and coordination of care, potentially lower costs, and increase financial support to primary care physicians. These experiments seek to test a medical home concept that emphasizes the central importance of primary care to an organized and patient-centered health care system.[1-3] The medical home concept posits that primary care physicians' direct and trusted relationship with patients, coupled with a depth and breadth of clinical training across body systems, position them to assess an individual's health needs and to tailor a comprehensive approach to care across conditions, care settings and providers.

Not all primary care practices are set up to function as a PCMH. In part, this shortcoming results from inadequate financial support for such activities as care coordination, along with inadequate training of providers on how to work together as a team. In an attempt to remedy this, payers are experimenting with providing additional payment to participating practices that can demonstrate the capabilities of a patient-centered medical home. Most current pilots and demonstrations require practices to "qualify" as a medical home via an objective measurement tool. The tool's measures, in effect, are a blueprint for practices' efforts to build medical-home capabilities.

Primary Care and Chronic Care Models

While there are different views about what makes a physician practice a medical home, the specialty societies' joint principles are the widely accepted starting point for most current demonstrations and pilots.[4] The joint principles originate from two distinct conceptual frameworks, the primary care model[1,2,5] and the chronic care model,[6] each of which was developed for different purposes.

The primary care model[1,2,5] focuses on all patients in a practice and emphasizes whole-person care over time, rather than single-disease-oriented care. The primary care model identifies four elements as essential to the delivery of high-quality primary care: accessible first contact care, or serving as the entry point to the health care system for the majority of a person's problems; a continuous relationship with patients over time; comprehensive care that meets or arranges for most of a patient's health care needs; and coordination of care across a patient's conditions, providers and settings in consultation with the patient and family.[1,2,5]

The chronic care model focuses on "system changes intended to guide quality improvement and disease management activities" for chronic illness.[6] The chronic care model includes six interrelated elements—patient self-management support, clinical information systems, delivery system redesign, decision support, health care organization and community resources. Three aspects of the model in particular—self-management support, delivery system design and decision support—used in combination have improved single chronic condition care, in particular for diabetes.[6-8] The designers of the chronic care model assumed that before implementation "every chronically ill person has a primary care team that organizes and coordinates their care."[6] In other words, the chronic care model is meant to be developed on a "solid platform of primary care."[6,9,10] Consequently, both the primary care and chronic care models suggest that a medical home qualification tool must first capture and measure the four defining primary care elements before emphasizing capabilities to treat individual chronic diseases.

Recognizing the benefits and evidence behind each of the key primary care elements—accessibility, continuity, coordination and comprehensiveness—on patient and population health outcomes, patient and provider satisfaction, and costs, the joint principles require the medical home to provide each.[2,5,11-18] To the four primary care elements, the physician societies added aspects of the chronic care model-team functioning in a physician-directed practice, quality and safety tools for evidence-based medicine, decision support, performance measurement, quality improvement, enlisting patient feedback and "appropriate" use of information technology.[4]

Common attributes across the primary care and chronic care models can inform selection of the most relevant measures for a patient-centered medical home qualification tool (see Table 1 for a summary of elements of the two care models as they align with the physician societies' joint principles). In sum, these conceptual frameworks and the evidence supporting them suggest that a tool to determine whether a practice is a medical home would ideally measure that a practice has in place processes to ensure that care is accessible, continuous, coordinated and comprehensive. Capabilities that could help support these elements include a searchable patient registry, a mutual agreement between the patient and the medical home team on their respective roles and expectations, tools for comprehensive care such as planned visits that include pre- and post-visit planning, the use of care plans when appropriate, and enhanced access via phone and same-day appointment availability. Lastly, because of the time and resource constraints under which primary care practices already operate, it is particularly important that the qualification tool not create an onerous documentation burden for participating practices.

Current Qualification Tool

Most medical home demonstrations and pilots are measuring whether a practice is a medical home via the National Committee for Quality Assurance (NCQA) Physician Practice Connections-Patient Centered Medical Home tool (PPC-PCMH version 2008).[29] The PPC-PCMH is a modification of an earlier NCQA tool, the PPC (Physician Practice Connections) that focused on recognizing practices that use systematic processes and information technology to enhance the quality of care.[29] The PPC and the PPC-PCMH are based on the chronic care model[6] and have less emphasis on the primary care model's four elements. While it is difficult to succinctly describe the PPC-PCMH or its scoring algorithm, the tool has nine standards:

- Access and Communication;
- Patient Tracking and Registry Functions;
- Care Management;

Table 1	Commonalities Between the Physician Societies' Joint Principles, the Primary Care Model and the Chronic Care Model that Can Guide Measurement of the Patient-Centered Medical Home (PCMH)

PCMH Elements as Outlined by the Physician Societies' Joint Principles[4]	Capabilities related to this PCMH Element from the Joint Principles, the Primary Care Model & Chronic Care Model
Accessibility of the practice PCMH is an accessible point of entry into the health care system each time new care is needed (i.e., first contact care).	• Open scheduling.[4, 19–21] • Ease of making appointments and wait times.[2] • Expanded hours.[2, 4] • Options for patients to communicate with personal physician and office staff.[4] • 24–7 phone coverage.[2, 4.]
Continuity of care "Each patient has an ongoing relationship with a personal physician in the PCMH." Person-focused (not just disease specific) care over time.	• Each patient has an identifiable primary care clinician for ongoing care.[2, 4, 5, 13] • Patient is able to make appointments with that particular clinician.[2, 5, 13] • Discussion about PCMH role and expectations with the patient—Discussion between personal physician and patient on the roles and expectations for the medical home, including making visible to the patient who the team members are.[2, 21, 22] • Registry of patients.[2, 4, 6] PCMH has a list of patients for which it is responsible. • Complete medical records are retrievable and accessible.[2]
Coordination of care "across all domains of the health care system."	• PCMH coordinates care that patients receive from other providers (e.g., specialists, hospitals, home health agencies to assure that patients get the indicated care when and where they need and want it, including medication review and management.[2, 5, 14, 23]) • Referral tracking and follow up.[2] • Evidence-based decision making around referrals.[5, 24]
Comprehensiveness PCMH recognizes and provides, or arranges for "care for all stages of life, including: acute care, chronic care, preventive services and end-of-life care."	• Planned visits.[6, 25, 26] • Registry of patients[2, 4, 6] facilitates comprehensive care and population health management by enabling searches of patients with particular conditions and characteristics.[2, 6] • Range of services offered by PCMH.[2, 5]
Physician directed medical practice with a team that "takes collective responsibility for ongoing care of patients."	• A team approach can, in theory, leverage the relative clinical and organizational training skills of each member (e.g., physician, nurse, medical assistant) to ensure that the increasingly complex and inter-related needs of patients with multiple chronic conditions are met. Teamwork can facilitate comprehensiveness and coordination of care.[2, 6, 27]
Quality & Safety	• Decision making guided by evidence-based medicine and decision-support tools.[6] • Quality improvement efforts.[4, 6] • Patients participate in decision making.[4, 6] • Patient feedback is sought to ensure expectations are met.[4, 6]
Information Technology "Uses IT appropriately to support optimal patient care, performance measurement, patient education and enhanced communication."	• Registry of patients.[2, 4, 6] Consensus statement focused on aspects of information systems most relevant to the immediate progress of the PCMH emphasizes the use of a registry to identify the PCMH's patients, facilitate disease management, population health and evidence-based care.[28]

- Patient Self-Management Support;
- Electronic Prescribing;
- Test Tracking;
- Referral Tracking;
- Performance Reporting and Improvement; and
- Advanced Electronic Communication.

Embedded within the tool's nine standards are 30 elements containing a total of 166 items, or measures (see Table 2 for a summary of the measures and the capabilities captured). Depending on the score achieved, the PPC-PCMH can qualify a practice at one of three levels of medical-home capabilities (basic, intermediate, advanced). So, for example, at Level 1, a practice must pass 5 of 10 "must-pass"

Table 2	**Frequency of Items from the PPC-PCMH Organized by Concept Captured**	

Percentage*	Number of Items	Capability**
46	77	Information Technology • 19 items on e-prescribing • 18 items on electronic data system for patient demographic data • 14 items on the use of e-mail, e-communication, or interactive Web site • 11 items on electronic system for basic clinical data • 8 items on electronic system for managing tests • 7 items on electronic system for population management
14	24	Care for three specific conditions that the practice identifies as important to their patient panel, e.g., including identifying those patients, use of condition-specific guidelines, care management and self-management support.
13	21	Coordination of care • 1 item on scheduling visits to different providers into one trip for the patient • 4 items on referral-tracking • 6 items on test tracking and follow up • 10 items assess information continuity across settings, e.g., care transitions
9	15	Accessibility
5	8	Performance reporting
4	7	Organizing clinical data via tools such as problem lists and medication lists
2	4	Use of non-physician staff (an important element of team work)
2	4	Does the practice collect data on patient experience with care • 1 item on access to care • 1 item on physician communication • 1 item on patient confidence in self-care • 1 item on satisfaction with care
1	2	Preventive services
1	2	Continuity of care with a personal clinician
1	2	Patient communication preferences

* Percentage of the total of 166 items.
** These item counts have been organized by content area rather than by their labels in the PPC-PCMH.

elements. Practices seeking PPC-PCMH recognition complete the Web-based tool and provide documentation to validate responses.[29]

How the Tool Performs in Measuring Medical-Home Capabilities

The PPC-PCMH tool has notable strengths, first of which is its support from payers, specialty societies and the National Quality Forum. The tool allows for flexibility in how practices meet some of the requirements. This is important because procedures for achieving particular capabilities will likely vary with practice culture, resources and patient-panel characteristics. In addition, the NCQA tool requires supporting documentation from practices for those capabilities where validation appears to be necessary to ensure their presence.[2,30] NCQA's experience and infrastructure for fielding and scoring quality measures also are strengths. Thus, the tool is a good start for de-

veloping consistent measurement across medical home initiatives.

However, the current PPC-PCMH may not be ideal for ascertaining medical-home capabilities because it underemphasizes some of the defining primary care elements and overemphasizes issues not specific to a medical home. The tool has a fairly strong emphasis on access and some aspects of coordination, such as referral tracking, but other important aspects of coordination (e.g., between the primary care physician and specialists) are not part of the 2008 version that most pilots plan to use. The tool has only two items on continuity of care and few items on comprehensiveness.

Many of the measures in the PPC-PCMH focus not on primary care, but on such issues as information technology or condition-specific performance reporting. So a practice could potentially score well on the PPC-PCMH without providing patient-centered primary care.

First, the tool places great weight on information technology (IT) capabilities—77 of the 166 measures relate to IT. Information technology clearly has potential to make clinical data available to providers in real time, when it is needed for shared decision making with patients. When an affordable, interoperable electronic medical record (EMR) eventually becomes a reality, it will likely be an enormous advance in information continuity across care settings and, thus, potentially foster care coordination.

In the meantime, however, it may be premature to require practices to have more than a searchable patient registry. Many primary care physicians, particularly those in small practices that make up the bulk of the U.S. primary care infrastructure,[31] lack the economies of scale that facilitate purchasing and maintaining an EMR and do not want to do so until an affordable and interoperable option is widely available. Moreover, the evidence of commercial EMRs' effectiveness in primary care practices is mixed. To date, the vast majority of effectiveness studies come from four large institutions with internally developed EMRs.[32,33] Most of the positive outcomes from outpatient studies involve the use of computer-generated, paper-based reminders or registries.[32-34] The presence of an EMR correlates only weakly with clinical quality of care measures. Nevertheless, practices with fully functional EMRs scored the highest on the PPC.[35]

Two other IT capabilities that are heavily emphasized in the PPC-PCMH, but for which the evidence is mixed, include e-mail communication with patients[36,37] and e-prescribing.[32,33,38,39] Research on e-mail's effectiveness in patient care is still in its infancy. As of 2006, only 3 percent of physicians used e-mail frequently to communicate with patients.[37] While there is momentum in federal policy behind e-prescribing, improved outcomes from e-prescribing have predominantly been demonstrated with computerized physician order entry (CPOE) in the hospital setting. In the primary care setting, results have been more mixed.[32,33,38-40] The PPC-PCMH's heavy IT emphasis raises the concern that practices with IT structures may score well without necessarily providing better clinical outcomes or continuous and coordinated care. The large number of IT measures in the NCQA tool could also create barriers to qualification among practices that provide good primary care but don't necessarily emphasize IT.

Second, the tool requires extensive documentation around single-condition care. The goal of this requirement was to provide practices with the motivation to consider how a systematic approach to work flow and documentation could promote broader changes within a practice. This incremental approach could help practices to systematically address particular chronic conditions and important population-based health issues. The tool allows practices the flexibility to identify what those important conditions are for its patient panel. A caution, however, is that among Americans 65 and older, almost two-thirds have multiple chronic conditions.[41,42] Given this, there is a risk that a measurement approach that overemphasizes adherence to condition-specific guidelines could create incentives to simply treat a patient's individual condition to achieve benchmarks rather than to provide comprehensive and coordinated care across a patient's complex health needs.[43]

Illustrating these risks, a high score on the current PPC-PCMH tool does not guarantee that a practice actually functions as a medical home. One study in predominantly large groups in Minnesota found that particular components (e.g., decision support, clinical information system) of the PPC, a forerunner to the PPC-PCMH were correlated with performance in diabetes care (HgA1c <= 8%, LDL <130 mg/dL).[44] At the same time, performance on the tool does not appear to correlate with patient experiences with care.[35] Thus, while the tool has promise in terms of capturing important elements of diabetes care, a medical home qualification tool should better identify whether patients are experiencing care that is truly patient-centered.

The time required to qualify via the PPC-PCMH tool, both in terms of developing processes to meet the tool's measures and completion of the application itself, may be a barrier to participation among smaller practices that have fewer resources. After completing a shorter online screening tool that provides practices with an opportunity to estimate where they might fall in relation to the tool's criteria, the practice can decide whether to move forward with the actual PPC-PCMH. Only anecdotal information is available to date on the 2008 version of the PPC-PCMH. Based on information from the older version, NCQA estimates that the newer PPC-PCMH tool and its documentation take a practice on average between 40 and 80 hours to complete. This does not include time a practice spends developing new processes to address certain capabilities measured by the tool. Several practices report that the older PPC (2004-05) application was time-consuming, taking 80 to 100 hours to complete.[45] Given that practices with five or fewer physicians constitute 95 percent of office-based medical practices,[31] such time and resource considerations could pose significant barriers to participation among the very practices medical home initiatives are targeting.

Next Steps

One approach to modifying the PPC-PCMH tool would be to focus initially on measures that capture the key primary care elements, are supported by evidence, and that experience suggests are feasible or have the strongest face validity with practitioners and patients. If certain measures require a good deal of time and documentation from a practice, then there should be strong evidence that they lead to improved patient outcomes.

The burden on practices to complete the PPC-PCMH documentation could be reduced by decreasing the number of IT items, particularly those with inconclusive data on effectiveness. Practices that have an EMR should get credit for their efforts, but this can be ascertained with fewer IT measures. Existing data do support keeping a measure of whether a practice has an electronic patient registry, including a list of patients for whom a practice serves as a medical home and that can be used to identify patients needing preventive services and chronic condition management.[2,6,28]

At this point, the PPC-PCMH might be viewed as a starting point for developing a future tool that more comprehensively captures the four primary care elements. Validated measures for these primary care elements exist,[46,47] and selected domains from validated provider surveys could be incorporated into the PPC-PCMH.[46] For example, in addition to the tool's two current measures of continuity of care-scheduling each patient with a personal clinician and visits with the assigned personal clinician-validated items on continuity could be added, such as how long on average patients stay with the practice and what percentage of patients use the practice for most of their non-emergency sick and well care needs.

The tool could include measures on processes to improve communication between the medical home and specialists related to referrals and consultations. With respect to comprehensiveness, a practice could check off services provided, ranging from preventive, acute and chronic care to basic procedures that can be done in the office setting with a focus on those known to be cost-effective and of sufficient need in the population, such as immunizations, family planning and pulmonary function tests.[2]

Validation that the medical home is indeed patient-centered could be enhanced by the inclusion of patient feedback in a qualification tool. While most demonstrations and pilots will delay enlisting patient feedback until the evaluation phase (rather than doing so in the qualification phase), confirmation of the presence of particular PCMH elements during the qualification phase could be assisted by incorporating patient input using validated measures.[46,47]

Recognizing many of these concerns, the physician specialty societies endorsed the PPC-PCMH for testing purposes only. NCQA is working to incorporate stakeholder input into future versions of the tool, including measures of coordination between the primary care physician and specialists and an important measure on mutual acknowledgment of the partnership between the patient and the medical home. Unfortunately, these revisions are not likely to be incorporated in time for the tool that will be used in the qualification phase of most pilots. The reality of current medical home initiatives is that payers want to see documentation of improved capabilities from providers if they are going to increase reimbursement for medical home services. In an effort to be responsive to that request, the medical home qualification tool train has, perhaps, prematurely left the station.

Past experience with performance measurement linked to payment suggests that "we will get what we measure." Both the primary care and chronic care models suggest that the qualification of practices as medical homes should be based on the conceptual underpinnings of primary care. Measures in a medical home qualification tool, therefore, should capture the structures and processes that ensure accessibility, continuity, coordination and comprehensiveness. Additional capabilities that could help deliver these elements and enhance chronic care provision include a patient registry, mutual acknowledgment between the patient and the medical home physician on their respective roles and expectations, 24-7 phone access, some same-day appointments, team-based care, and the use of planned care visits.

At this critical turning point for the nation's fragile and underfunded primary care infrastructure, a medical home qualification tool that insufficiently emphasizes key primary care elements risks excluding physician practices that actually deliver patient-centered primary care as medical homes and including those that don't. Moreover, an overly burdensome tool with large documentation requirements for structures that ultimately may not be associated with improved clinical outcomes runs the risk of distracting physicians from developing the practice capabilities that can truly improve patient care.

MATCHING PATIENTS TO MEDICAL HOMES: ENSURING PATIENT AND PHYSICIAN CHOICE

By Deborah Peikes, Hoangmai H. Pham, Ann S. O'Malley and Myles Maxfield

For medical homes to achieve their potential to improve care, payers must link each eligible patient to a medical home practice in a way that ensures transparency, clinical face validity and fairness for physicians. Equally important are adequate choice and awareness of the medical home model for patients and operational feasibility for payers that must determine which physician practices are eligible for enhanced payments. The approach the payer uses to assign, or attribute, patients to medical homes will ultimately influence how successfully medical home initiatives can engage patients and physicians.

Why Patient Assignment Matters, Or It Takes Three to Tango

Physician practices acting as medical homes need to know which patients they are responsible for so the practices can coordinate those patients' care. If physicians can clearly identify the patients they are responsible for, they can more accurately predict the additional revenue they can expect for acting as a medical home. More accurate revenue prediction in turn allows practices to make informed decisions about whether they want to become a medical home and what additional staff or infrastructure, such as information technology, they can afford to purchase. Finally, giving physicians some choice about which patients they will form medical home relationships with rather than having this dictated by a payer will enhance physician buy in.

Patients need to know which practice serves as their medical home so they know who to count on to coordinate and manage their overall care. In addition, patients need to be aware of what the medical home will provide if they are to work closely with the medical home and change the way they use care. To be sure, a patient can garner some benefit from practice transformations resulting from their physician's practice becoming a medical home—such as ensuring that abnormal lab results are tracked—without knowing about the medical home model. Ideally, however, the medical home will help patients decide when to see a specialist, select a specialist that will both serve the patient's clinical needs and coordinate with the medical home physician, and achieve smooth transitions after a hospital discharge.

The current fee-for-service payment system lacks incentives for primary care physicians to consistently play an active role in integrating and coordinating care. Without a conversation explaining the new medical home model of care, many patients will continue to use care outside of the medical home without telling their medical home physician. If physicians are unaware of patients' self-referrals to specialists, or emergency room and hospital use, they cannot help patients coordinate their care. Similarly, if medical homes provide expanded access, this should also be explained to patients so they do not simply use the emergency room or seek out another primary care physician for problems that can be addressed in the medical home practice.

Evidence suggests that educating patients about the roles and responsibilities of both the medical home physician and the patient can help patients transform the way they use care. Indeed, the British Columbia Primary Care Demonstration found that patients' use of specialty, emergency room and primary care delivered by other physicians declined only after the program changed the registration process to require that physicians educate patients about the benefits of continuity of care with the primary care physician, as well as providing extended hours.

The final reason patients should be informed of the medical home is to address potential privacy concerns. If patients are not informed, they may be alarmed to find out that payers are sharing confidential information with the medical home physician about their use of emergency room, hospital and specialist care.

Payers, typically insurers, need to link patients to specific physicians for three reasons. First, since most insurers in part use capitated payments, or per-patient, per-month fees, to compensate physicians for providing medical home services, insurers need to know which patients belong to which physicians so that payment goes to the correct physicians. Second, some insurers provide feedback data on quality and utilization for individual patients or the entire patient panel to physicians as part of their medical home initiatives. Finally, insurers need to know which patients belong with which physicians when they evaluate the effectiveness of the medical home.

Payers can link patients to physicians using four general approaches:

- apply claims-based algorithms;
- ask physicians to identify patients;
- ask patients to identify physicians; or
- employ hybrids of these three approaches.

Each of the approaches has different strengths and weaknesses on six important dimensions: patient choice, physician choice, ease for physician, ease for insurer, correct assignments and encouraging patient understanding of medical home rights and responsibilities (see Table 3).

Claims-Only Approach Common but Prone to Errors

The most commonly used approach to linking patients to physicians in commercial insurers' medical home pilots relies on claims-based algorithms. Such algorithms typically search historical claims for the physician billing for the most recent claims with an evaluation and management (E&M) code or pharmacy claim, or the largest share of E&M visits for the patient.[48] Claims-based approaches are expeditious because the insurer avoids the costs of collecting information from patients and physicians.

An approach that relies exclusively on claims is operationally easy for both insurers, who simply review historical claims data, and physicians, who do not participate in any way. However, by excluding physician and patient input, this approach does not allow either to select the person with whom they perceive they have a medical home relationship. Moreover, automatic assignment may interfere with existing patient-physician relationships and risk alienating both parties. Even if claims could get the assignment correct, the success of the medical home intervention depends on educating patients about the new services medical homes are providing and how to use care in a way that facilitates efficiency and coordination. Without involving patients, this opportunity is lost.

Perhaps most importantly, while the efficiency of using historical claims data is tempting from an operational perspective, claims can be inaccurate and may not reflect clinical realities. Because many patients see multiple physicians, claims algorithms cannot always indentify the correct provider. For example, in a given year, Medicare beneficiaries see a median of two primary care providers and five specialists working in four different practices.[49] The Medicare Health Support (MHS) study examined how often a group of physicians identified via a claims algorithm actually included the patient's self-reported primary physician for heart disease. While the algorithm identified on average five doctors per beneficiary that might be the personal physician, it failed to include the primary physician as identified by 17 percent of patients.[50]

Another illustration of the inaccuracy of claims-based algorithms comes from the seeming instability of care relationships suggested by claims data, which may not be consistent with patient self-reports. The Medicare Current Beneficiary Survey indicates that patients' care relationships are more stable than the claims-based algorithm would suggest, as 70 percent of beneficiaries reported having the same physician as their usual provider for at least three years; the analogous figure would be less than 40 percent based on claims assignment.[49]

Anecdotal evidence suggests patients with other types of insurance also see multiple primary care practices. For example, one state Medicaid program found that half of all patients whose claims suggested they saw a large primary care practice as their medical home—they had one or more well-child visits or two or more sick visits with the practice in the prior year—also had visits with other nearby practices. United Healthcare's analysis of claims data convinced the company to supplement claims information with patient and physician input. The analysis used the prior 18 months of claims to identify the likely medical home practice of commercially insured patients aged 18 to 64. A year later, claims data suggested that 72 percent of the patients with a medical home

Table 3	Trade-Offs of Different Medical Home Assignment Procedures			
	Claims-Based Algorithms	**Physician Reports**	**Patient Reports**	**Hybrid (Claims, Physicians, Patients)**
Ensures Patient Choice	No	No	Yes	Yes
Ensures Physician Choice	No	Yes	No	Yes
Operationally Easy for Physician	Yes	No	Yes	No
Operationally Easy for Payer	Yes	No	No	No
Correct Assignments	Not Always	Not Always	Not Always	Yes
Encourages Patient Understanding of Medical Home Rights and Responsibilities	No	No	Yes	Yes

the year before who still had coverage with United had the same medical home practice, 16 percent had moved to another practice, and 12 percent did not use a primary care practice.[51] Claims data alone cannot answer whether these patients truly changed the practice they consider to be their medical home.

Another problem with most current claims-based approaches is that they do not address patients who lack a primary care physician, or the "medically homeless." One study found that in a one-year period, 15 percent of all Medicare beneficiaries saw only specialists without seeing any primary care doctors, and 6 percent had no E&M visits with any type of doctor.[49] Another study reported that more than one-third of working-age adults did not have an accessible primary care provider, and half of children did not have a medical home.[52] Approaches based purely on claims would not be able to assign these patients.

Physicians May Be Unaware of Other Providers

An approach that asks physicians to identify which patients to assign to their practice still requires insurers to reconcile each physician's patient list to ensure the patients are eligible for coverage and have not been identified by another physician. While physicians would have input into which patients they would like to serve, in many cases, they may not be aware of other physicians that their patients see.

Thus, an approach that relies on physician input without patient input may not always generate correct assignments. And like claims-only approaches, physician-driven approaches would not assist patients in receiving adequate information about the new medical home services.

Patient Reports Operationally Challenging

Turning to a patient-focused approach, where patients would be asked to submit the name of their medical home, the burden on insurers to collect this information from patients would be high. People don't always turn in their forms. For example, often only one-third to one-half of people respond to social science surveys without substantial effort to collect their responses. Even when money is at stake, not all people file the necessary forms. Only 80 percent to 86 percent of tax filers eligible for the earned income tax credit actually claim the credit.[53]

The patient-based approach has three strengths. First, there is no operational burden on physicians. Second, the assignments will be correct from the patient perspective. Third, because insurers will need to

inform patients about the medical home concept when their input is solicited, insurers likely would inform patients of their medical home rights and responsibilities. However, the physician's perception of who their core patients are may vary from the patient's perspective.

A Hybrid Approach Can Help Build Medical Home Relationships

A hybrid approach that combines features of the claims-based, physician-driven and patient-driven approaches would best help build medical home relationships while honoring existing patient-physician relationships. For example, insurers could send practices a list of their potential patients (e.g., those who claims indicate they saw the physician one or more times in the prior two years). The physicians would then be expected to obtain the patient's consent to be matched to their practice, and the physician could explain medical home features to the patients. This approach also ensures that patients can decline if they prefer another medical home.

Insurers could send patients who had not seen a physician in the prior two years a list of medical homes in their area that are accepting new patients and ask patients to select one, or opt in. While insurers might not wish to simply assign patients to a practice and give them the opportunity to change that assignment—an opt-out approach—there may be a role for such an approach for patients who do not voluntarily select a medical home. The insurer could assign those patients to a practice and notify both the practice and patient of the assignment and the patient's ability to change to another medical home if desired. Seeking patient input, and only assigning patients if they do not provide it, decreases the burden for the insurer, while still maximizing patient and physician choice.

The insurer could also require a formal, bilateral acknowledgment between the medical home physician and the patient that explains the respective roles of the medical home and the patient. Patients would retain the right to change their medical home if they are not satisfied with their care.

Accurate Assignment Matters

Accurate and meaningful linkages between the patient and the medical home physician are critical and require the input of physicians and patients. Having a process in place that requires patients to participate actively is pivotal to the potential of medical homes to transform patterns of care.

An approach that balances the needs and preferences of patients, physician practices and payers carries four benefits. First, such an approach helps obtain patient buy in to understand and use new medical home services effectively. Second, physicians will have clear responsibility for individual patients and be better able to coordinate care for those patients. Third, insurers can direct payment and provide information on service use and prevention or treatment needs to each physician for the appropriate patients. Finally, the most accurate approaches to assignment will facilitate rigorous evaluations of the medical home model.

MEDICAL HOMES: THE INFORMATION EXCHANGE CHALLENGE

By MYLES MAXFIELD, HOANGMAI H. PHAM AND DEBORAH PEIKES

The potential of medical homes to improve quality and reduce costs by improving coordination of care across providers, care settings and clinical conditions will be limited without effective mechanisms for exchanging clinical information with patients and providers outside of the medical home. An explicit agreement between the medical home and the patient detailing the roles and responsibilities of both could assist with the exchange of information. Exchanging information with specialists may not be feasible without some form of electronic exchange or incentives for specialists to participate.

Closing the Circuit Among Medical Homes, Patients and Other Providers

Medical home initiatives typically have two overarching goals—to reduce costs and improve the quality of care. Medical homes are expected to reduce costs directly by avoiding redundant or unneeded tests, imaging, procedures and medications, hereafter generically called unnecessary services. These reductions are expected to be large enough to offset any increased spending on medical home services. By maintaining comprehensive clinical information on patients, medical homes can avoid unnecessary services in three ways: (1) using the results of tests, imaging and services ordered by other providers; (2) advising patients who seek care from another provider whether that care is needed; and (3) increasing the delivery of primary and secondary preventive care.

The second overarching goal of medical home programs is improving the quality of care by maintaining comprehensive clinical information on the care patients receive from other providers, providing a sounder basis for the medical home physician's diagnoses and treatment decisions. In addition, use of evidence-based guidelines and registries can help medical homes ensure patients receive recommended care. Improved quality of care also may reduce health care costs by avoiding preventable hospitalizations, complications, medical errors and unnecessarily long episodes of care.

Coordinating care across providers is one critical way to reduce overuse of services. The medical home ideally will help patients use appropriate specialists and coordinate the testing and treatment that all providers deliver. But whether medical homes can achieve this goal depends on the behavior of patients and other providers—behavior that medical homes cannot completely control. Medical home physicians rely on patients to report plans to see other providers, including specialists. Without such knowledge, medical home physicians cannot make appropriate decisions to instead provide the care themselves, steer the patient to a high-quality specialist or determine if another type of specialist would be more appropriate.

Unfortunately, there is a risk that patients may not share this information with the medical home. Fee-for-service payment systems provide few incentives, penalties or restrictions on patients' use of other providers, and some patients may view efforts to coordinate with the medical home physician as restrictive and time-consuming.

Specialists must in turn share information about their clinical findings, prescribed medications and care plan with the medical home, either directly or through the patient, so the medical home can ensure that the patient's overall care is consistent and integrated. But under neither fee-for-service nor current medical home models do specialists receive additional compensation or other incentives for communicating with the medical home or patients. While some might argue that existing standards of care and payment rates already include expectations for such communication, the reality is that it often does not occur.

Medical Home Information Exchange

Effective information exchange between the medical home and the patient relies on an agreement between the medical home and the patient. Under such an agreement, patients agree to tell the medical home when they wish to see another primary care physician or specialist and why. In return, the medical home agrees to oversee the entirety of patients' care, including advising patients whether or not to seek care from another practitioner. If patients are unwilling to share complete information on the care they receive, or wish to receive, from other providers, the medical home will not be able to comprehensively manage patient care. Such a breakdown in the exchange of information between the medical home and patient would leave the patient's care as fragmented and inefficient as under current fee-for-service arrangements.

The exchange of clinical information between the medical home and patients' other providers—specialists, other primary care physicians, hospitals, post-acute care facilities, nursing homes—is equally essential to the medical home model.

Patient Challenges

There are two major challenges to exchanging clinical information between the medical home and patients. The first is that many patients in fee-for-service systems may not want to put all their information eggs in one medical home basket. Specifically, many patients, and especially many Medicare beneficiaries with chronic conditions, see many practitioners, including multiple primary care physicians. Some patients believe that doing so offers the advantages of multiple perspectives on the best treatment approach. These patients may not want to place all their trust in the hands of a single medical home provider in the belief that "two physician heads are better than one."

The second major challenge is that some patients may fear their medical homes will function as a gatekeeper to control access to other providers. While the medical home model tries to avoid the mandatory gatekeeper model used by some managed care organizations, medical homes are likely to have a "soft gatekeeper" function. One of the most important mechanisms for medical homes to achieve cost savings is for the medical home to identify potentially redundant tests and services before they occur and counsel patients to avoid redundant services. While some patients may dislike this oversight, others may simply not take the time to circle back and inform their medical home about care they plan to receive, or have received, elsewhere.

Specialist Challenges

As challenging as the medical home-patient exchange of information is, the medical home-specialist exchange may be more so. The primary challenge in exchanging information with other providers is that the number of other providers can be large. One study found that the typical primary care physician shares his or her Medicare patients with 229 other physicians working in 117 other practices.[54]

In most communities, different physician practices operate autonomously of one another, with little integration in terms of common culture, administrative procedures, financing or information systems. Many medical homes may find it practically infeasible to negotiate "service agreements" with all providers seeing their patients to lay out common expectations about how each party will share clinical information. Even if service agreements were negotiated with all other providers, many medical homes would find it infeasible to exchange information with all providers seeing all of the medical home's patients. Without some form of electronic information exchange among providers beyond fax machines, implementing information flows among networks of this magnitude may not be practical for many practices.

Second, medical homes cannot establish service agreements with every other provider because some of those encounters, such as those in emergency departments or during hospital admissions, cannot be easily anticipated. Thus, a related issue for coordinating care with outside providers is how to improve information flow so that medical homes know when their patients use emergency departments or are hospitalized. With more complete information on incidental care encounters, medical homes would be better able to educate patients about potential alternatives for care, provide relevant clinical history to emergency and inpatient providers, assist in communicating with patients' families, and help patients understand hospital discharge instructions and coordinate transitional care.

Third, many specialists may not see the value of entering into service agreements with medical homes. Specifically, payers typically pay a fee to the medical home that includes the time and equipment devoted to the information exchange, but specialists are not paid directly. If the specialist is practicing in a geographic area containing many medical homes, the costs of exchanging information on many patients with many medical homes may be substantial. In theory, the medical home could compensate specialists for the time and equipment used in the information exchange by sharing medical home fees with specialists. Such an arrangement may require modification to law and regulation pertaining to provider fee-splitting. In practice, many sponsors of medical home initiatives do not include the full cost of exchanging information with other providers in medical home fees. In such instances, the medical home is unlikely to share fees with specialists.

Overcoming the Challenges

Several approaches can mitigate the challenges of the medical home-patient information exchange. The first is to make the agreement between the medical home and the patient as explicit and formal as possible. This means the agreement should be written, and the medical home should discuss the agreement with the patient, ideally in person. The agreement should describe the responsibilities of, and benefits to, the patient and the medical home. Patients agree to share information on all aspects of their care with the medical home provider and to consider the medical home physician's advice seriously, even when it pertains to care provided by a different physician. In return, the medical home offers the patient better coordinated care and a more satisfactory patient experience. Both parties should sign the agreement.

A second approach is for the medical home program to exclude patients who are unwilling to enter into such an agreement. The medical home should attempt to persuade the patient to join the medical home program, but failing that, the medical home and program sponsors should recognize that the medical home model may not be well suited to all patients.

Turning to the medical home-specialist information exchange, the less expensive it is to exchange a particular type of information, the more feasible it will be for medical homes to exchange information with large numbers of specialists. One way to minimize the cost of information exchange is for medical home programs to focus on practices that already participate in a network of providers, such as an integrated service delivery network (ISDN), health information exchange (HIE) or regional health information organization (RHIO). For example, such networks can include information exchanges with local hospitals through electronic physician portals[55] that can push information to the medical home practice when a patient is evaluated at a hospital. Such an approach was used successfully with several disease management providers in recent Medicare demonstrations. Such networks minimize the cost of setting information exchange agreements with specialists, as well as minimize the transaction cost of exchanging clinical information.

A second approach specific to ambulatory care physicians is for payers to require specialists to enter into service agreements with medical homes as a condition of inclusion in their plan network. Third, payers could leverage other financial incentives they may already be offering providers to use electronic information systems. For example, Medicare could combine the financial incentives in its electronic health record (EHR) demonstration with the Medicare medical home demonstration. The combined incentive may encourage more practices to invest in EHR technology, which would in turn reduce the transaction cost of the information exchange. For this strategy to be effective, payers would have to require interoperable EHR systems.

Fourth, payers could use claims data to provide feedback to the medical home on the patient's health care from other providers. Information on hospital admissions, emergency room use and the need for preventive services would be particularly useful. Clearly this strategy raises privacy concerns, but the agreement between the medical home and the patient could include the patient's informed consent for the release of such information to the medical home.

Fostering Care Delivery Changes

The medical home model can serve as an impetus for increasing primary care physicians' responsibility and authority to coordinate the care of their patients, as well as foster greater patient self-management of medical conditions. Ultimately, piecemeal incentives will likely have limited ability to ensure effective coordination of care across multiple providers that remain unaffiliated and poorly integrated in their management, culture and financing.

Policy makers might consider an improved medical home model as a bridge to broader reforms of the organization of delivery systems, in which they encourage the "virtual" networks defined by service agreements to gradually become actual networks of affiliated providers. Favorable payment systems that focus on provider organizations that *are* integrated can create incentives for medical practices—and health care markets—to evolve toward greater cohesion through enlarging existing practices, mergers among practices or practices and hospital systems, or other creative arrangements. The medical home model is unlikely to result in sustainable, meaningful improvements in care coordination and outcomes without confronting and addressing these underlying issues in the organization of care delivery.

PAYING FOR MEDICAL HOMES: A CALCULATED RISK

By Hoangmai H. Pham, Deborah Peikes and Paul B. Ginsburg

The resurgence in interest among policy makers in the medical home concept stems from goals of improving quality and reducing health care costs. Another driver of recent advocacy for the model is the search for vehicles to increase financial support for primary care physicians, whose services are widely acknowledged to be undercompensated in current fee-for-service payment systems. Moreover, existing fee-for-service payment systems typically do not pay for important activities that primary care physicians perform, such as care coordination and patient education.

Partial Capitation Payment Dominates Medical Home Pilots and Demonstrations

Payment approaches for medical homes under current fee-for-service payment systems essentially focus on additional payment for currently uncovered services. But the signal challenge is that payers have limited data both on what these uncovered services are in current practice and what the ideal array of services should be—that is, services that dependably result in high-quality, efficient patient care.

Payers recognize that medical home services, such as care coordination, are difficult to itemize, may occur outside face-to-face patient visits, and can legitimately vary in type and intensity across different patients or over time for a given patient. Paying for medical home services effectively requires some sort of capitation, or fixed per-patient fees. Most payers sponsoring medical home demonstrations or pilots offer additional payment in the form of partial capitation—a single per-patient, per-month or per-practice, per-year fee that is prospectively calculated.

Across public- and private-sector medical home initiatives, it is also clear that payers are more focused on paying for the *processes* that medical homes engage in than on the *outcomes* of those processes. Generally, if medical home initiatives incorporate any variation in payment levels, they tend to link payments to levels of medical-home capability. Frequently they do not consider patients' disease burden or physicians' performance on standardized quality measures. Although a few medical home initiatives—for example, those sponsored by the state of Vermont and the Blue Cross Blue Shield Association—recommend incorporating bonuses tied to physicians' performance on clinical quality or pa-

tient satisfaction measures, most payers are taking a wait-and-see approach on bonuses. Even fewer payers are considering payment adjustments based on patients' illness burden, a posture that makes it difficult to adapt payment levels from one program to another if the programs serve markedly different patient populations—for example, working-age, healthy commercially insured patients vs. sicker Medicare patients. One major exception is the Medicare medical home demonstration (MMHD), which will adjust payment rates based on illness severity.

The Constraint of Budget Neutrality

The most straightforward approach to setting capitated payments would be to first identify the services to be covered—those payers deem effective and currently not reimbursed—and then estimate their unit costs and frequency of delivery to the typical patient. Summing the product of unit costs and service frequency for a given time period would yield a per-capita amount, such as a monthly care management fee. However, calibrating even limited capitated payments proves a thorny endeavor, because payers currently place a high priority on budget neutrality. The hope is that potential savings from delivery of medical home services, such as reduced hospitalizations from improved care coordination, will offset any additional payments to physician practices for serving as medical homes.

But there is so little experience with medical homes that, as yet, there is no certainty that additional services will actually increase efficiency through lower costs and/or improved quality. This uncertainty makes it difficult to set payment levels that will achieve spending neutrality and to determine whether such levels will be sufficient to underwrite the costs of the activities that payers expect medical homes to perform.

Setting payments is particularly challenging in the context of demonstrations and pilots. Physicians naturally are concerned about how they will fare financially in a program of limited duration. They have reason to worry about payers' long-term commitment to pay for medical-home capabilities and the amount of time practices would have to amortize costs incurred to become medical homes. And physicians' perception of the adequacy of payments arguably carries more weight for medical home services than other services, because physicians have to be willing to participate if payers are to establish and sustain this new model.

Lastly, not all patients need the same amount of care coordination and not all medical homes offer the same services-the "typical" unit of medical home care is more difficult to define than that of more discrete services, such as a colonoscopy. For example, one medical home practice might attempt to improve coordination by implementing electronic data exchange with other providers—a resource-intensive strategy—while another practice might opt instead to implement team meetings for particular patients—a far less expensive strategy. Because most medical home initiatives allow physicians to choose different qualifying capabilities, fixed payment levels may not match the actual costs of a particular medical-home capability.

So physicians may expect payments to reflect differences both in disease burden and medical-home capabilities, adding layers of administrative complexity. Unfortunately, the lack of sound cost data to provide different medical home services to different types of patients leaves payers and physicians dependent on educated guesswork for setting cost-based prices.

Given the complexity of setting medical home payment levels, it is no wonder that payment levels range as broadly as they do across different programs—from an expected $20,000 to $30,000 per practice, per year in Vermont to $35,000 to $85,000 per full-time physician per year in Philadelphia. Fees in the Medicare demonstration could total $104,232 or $133,386 per year for the typical primary care physician.[56]

Calibrating Payments

Payers can employ three general methods to set the capitation payment. First, payment can reflect the costs of providing the extra services expected of a medical home, which requires estimating the costs of acquiring and maintaining medical-home capabilities, such as disease management and "open-access" scheduling. Second, payers can set payments to be budget neutral. Payers would estimate the total they expect to spend for eligible patients, make assumptions regarding the savings that medical home services might generate through more efficient delivery of care and set fees to equal those theoretical savings. Finally, payers can set payments to represent a target share of physician income to ensure adequate participation, which in turn requires estimating a physician's current revenues and determining the percentage upon which to base the new fees. Payers can improvise hybrid approaches that try to balance all three objectives of accurately reflecting costs, budget neutrality and adequate physician participation.

In most currently planned public- and private-sector initiatives, the overriding priority is achieving budget neutrality for payers. For example, this is an explicit consideration in the multi-payer medical home pilot in Rhode Island. Payers base payment levels on estimates of the savings they might achieve-for example, from reduced use of emergency department services and redundant testing. Payers would expect these savings to be offset by increases in other spending categories, such as preventive care. At the extreme, one private initiative has cautiously adopted a "pay-as-you-go" approach, by promising to share actual savings with physicians.

Payers are not yet at the point where they are willing to *add* payment for currently nonreimbursed services without a reasonable chance that it will be offset by savings elsewhere. Yet, in the setting of pilots and demonstrations, payers are much better positioned than physicians to take risks and absorb potential losses from the experiment. They could do so by reducing their focus on budget neutrality and relying more heavily on cost estimates of services and/or the level of incentive that will entice physicians to participate.

The Medicare medical home demonstration will actually attempt to price medical home services and reimburse physicians based on costs, as estimated by the Relative Value Update Committee (RUC). In contrast, few private-sector initiatives are taking this bottom-up approach, which physicians may perceive as more scientifically sound and fair but which requires much more painstaking data collection than private payers have been willing to wait or pay for. One notable exception is the Vermont medical home pilot, which reviewed related public and private programs and consulted with physician organizations, other stakeholders and payment experts to assess costs of typical "transformation of care processes," such as hiring part-time nurses.

To anticipate how physicians might react to different payment levels, payers have to consider not only the costs of required medical-home capabilities, but also the average proportion of practice revenues that eligible patients represent for a typical physician. Most medical home initiatives involve a single payer, with payments that would, therefore, represent a minority, although possibly a substantial one, of a physician's revenues. This is true even for the MMHD (Medicare accounts for roughly 30% of a primary care physician's revenues) and initiatives in communities with highly concentrated private payer markets. The revenue sources for a given practice are important to consider because physicians will judge proposed payment levels based on whether they are high enough to amortize investment costs and cover operating costs of new medical-home capabilities. Most initiatives do not explicitly cover investment costs, and the size of a physician's patient panel is largely fixed. Therefore, physicians' interest in participating may depend on whether they believe that payments exceed their likely operating costs by a large enough margin to offset their investment costs. Multi-payer initiatives would cover a larger percentage of a physician's patient panel, dangling the promise of greater revenue gains to entice physicians to invest in practice improvements.

With the many uncertainties in the cost and value of medical home services, there is a golden opportunity for payers and physician organizations to collect detailed information on how physician practices transform themselves to achieve medical-home capabilities and the associated costs of those changes. Such data could not only help inject scientific rigor into the correction of payment levels as programs evolve, but also could clarify the level of effort that patients with different disease burdens require of medical homes, help identify the medical-home capabilities that are most cost effective, and inform judgments about the long-term sustainability of the model.

Taking Reasonable Risks Ahead of Data

From a broader policy perspective, it is worth questioning whether the earnest efforts to accurately price medical home services are a useful first step to achieving lasting payment reform. If the risk to the primary care infrastructure of doing nothing is as grave as consensus suggests, then payers may need to take a comparable risk to address the problem. At the moment, payers have much greater capacity to assume risk than do physicians—both in terms of resources and their potential to influence the behavior of other providers. Moreover, physicians are far less likely to invest in transforming their practices for pilots of limited duration than for an ongoing program with sustained political support.

Broad and lasting reform involves many technical and political steps pursued over many years. Demonstrations and pilots may merely be the first step in reform. Physicians are trained to order diagnostic tests only when they expect the results to affect future decision making, and not just to gather information for its own sake, because of the inconvenience and potential risk of complications to patients and the expense involved. Similarly, payers might consider whether their commitment to paying for medical home services or increasing their financial support for primary care in other ways will wane if they discover that medical home initiatives do not save money.

If payers are committed to increasing support for primary care regardless of the outcomes of medical home pilots, then they could design payments that at best achieve budget neutrality or even result in spending increases. That is, budget neutrality may be an admirable long-term goal, but an unrealistic expectation at every step of reform. Payers could implement such payments broadly—for all primary care physicians who achieve medical-home capabilities—rather than just in isolated initiatives. Then they could track physician performance and patient outcomes and adjust the program as needed over time. Precedents for this more aggressive approach include some of the most dramatic changes to Medicare payment policy—establishment of the Medicare inpatient prospective payment system and the resource-based relative value scale for physician services.

Medical Homes as a Stepping Stone to Broader Payment Reform

In the long term, medical home payment approaches could serve as a model for transitioning payment for care of chronic conditions from fee for service to capitation as much as possible. Coupling capitation with bonuses based on system cost savings and quality outcomes would better align incentives for preventive care, coordination and quality improvement.[57,58]

The daunting constraints of already soaring health care spending imply that long-term improvements in primary care payment might need to occur in a zero-sum fashion involving shifts of resources from non-primary care services. Payers can influence the degree to which this shift is gradual and acceptable to specialists. Paying for medical home services without immediate expectations of budget neutrality might begin to correct the imperfections of the fee-for-service system in a way that would minimize opposition from non-primary care providers, bettering the chances of broad reform stepping ahead.

• • • References

1. World Health Organization, *Alma-Ata 1978: Primary Health Care, Report of the International Conference on Primary Health Care*, Web exclusive (September 1978).

2. Starfield, Barbara, *Primary Care: Balancing Health Needs, Services and Technology,* Oxford University Press, New York, N.Y. (Oct. 15, 1998).

3. American Academy of Pediatrics, "Medical Home Initiatives for Children with Special Needs Project Advisory Committee," *Pediatrics*, Vol. 110, No. 1 (July 2002).

4. Joint Principles of the Patient-Centered Medical Home, *http://www.acponline.org/hpp/approve_jp.pdf?hp*. Accessed on June 2, 2008.

5. Institute of Medicine, *Primary Care: America's Health in a New Era*, Washington, D.C. (1996).

6. Wagner, Edward H., et al., "Improving Chronic Illness Care: Translating Evidence into Action," *Health Affairs*, Vol. 2, No. 6 (November/December 2001).

7. Tsai, Alexander C., et al., "A Meta-analysis of Interventions to Improve Care for Chronic Illnesses," *American Journal of Managed Care*, Vol. 11, No. 8 (August 2005).

8. Bodenheimer, Thomas, Edward H. Wagner and Kevin Grumbach, "Improving Care for Patients with Chronic Illness, The Chronic Care Model, Part 2," *Journal of the American Medical Association*, Vol. 288, No. 15 (Oct. 16, 2002).

9. Rothman, Arlyss A., and Edward H. Wagner, "Chronic Illness Management: What is the Role of Primary Care?" *Annals of Internal Medicine*, Vol. 138, No. 3 (Feb. 4, 2003).

10. Berenson, Robert A., et al., "A House is Not a Home: Keeping Patients at the Center of Practice Redesign," *Health Affairs*, Vol. 27, No. 5 (September/October 2008).

11. Schoen, Cathy, et al., "Toward Higher-Performance Health Systems: Adults' Health Care Experiences in Seven Countries," *Health Affairs*, Web exclusive (Oct. 31, 2007).

12. Anderson, Roger, Angela Barbara and Steven Feldman, "What Patients Want: A Content Analysis of Key Qualities that Influence Patient Satisfaction," *Medical Practice Management*, Vol. 22, No. 5 (March/April 2007).

13. Cabana, Michael D., and Sandra H. Jee, "Does Continuity of Care Improve Patient Outcomes?" *Journal of Family Practice*, Vol. 53, No. 12 (December 2004).

14. Stille, Christopher, et al., "Coordinating Care across Diseases, Settings and Clinicians: A Key Role for Generalist in Practice," *Annals of Internal Medicine*, Vol. 142, No. 8 (April 19, 2005).

15. Alpert, Joel. J., et al., "Delivery of Health Care for Children: Report of an Experiment," *Pediatrics*, Vol. 57, No. 6 (June 1976).

16. Grumbach, Kevin, et al., "Resolving the Gatekeeper Conundrum: What Patients Value in Primary Care and Referrals to Specialists," *Journal of the American Medical Association*, Vol. 282, No. 3 (July 21, 1999).

17. Fisher, Elliot S., et al., "The Implications of Regional Variations in Medicare Spending, Part 1: The Content, Quality and Accessibility of Care," *Annals of Internal Medicine*, Vol. 138, No. 4 (February 2003).

18. Flocke, Susan A., Kurt C. Stange and Stephen J. Zyzanski, "The Association of Attributes of Primary Care with the Delivery of Clinical Preventive Services," *Medical Care*, Vol. 36, No. 8 (August 1998).

19. Murray, Mark, et al., "Improving Timely Access to Primary Care: Case Studies of the Advanced Access Model," *Journal of the American Medical Association*, Vol. 289, No. 8 (Feb. 26, 2003).

20. Bundy, David G., et al., "Open Access in Primary Care: Results of a North Carolina Pilot Project," *Pediatrics*, Vol. 116, No. 1 (July 2005).

21. Health Transition Fund, Health Canada, *Primary Care Demonstration Project, Final Report to the Health Transition Fund*, Vancouver, Canada (April 10, 2001).

22. Safran, Dana G., "Defining the Future of Primary Care: What Can We Learn from Patients?" *Annals of Internal Medicine*, Vol. 138, No. 3 (Feb. 4 2003).

23. McDonald, Kathryn M., et al., *Closing the Quality Gap: A Critical Analysis of Quality Improvement Strategies: Volume 7—Care Coordination*," Publication No. 04(07)-0051-7, Agency for Healthcare Research and Quality, Rockville, Md. (June 2007).

24. Grimshaw, Jeremy M., et al., "Interventions to Improve Outpatient Referrals from Primary Care to Secondary Care (Review)," *Cochrane Database of Systematic Reviews*, Issue 3 (July 20, 2005).

25. Sinsky, Christine A., "Improving Office Practice: Working Smarter, Not Harder," *Family Practice Management*, Vol. 13, No. 10 (November/December 2006).

26. Bodenheimer, Thomas, "Helping Patients Improve Their Health-Related Behaviors: What System Changes Do We Need?" *Disease Management*, Vol. 8, No. 5 (Oct. 8, 2005).

27. Grumbach, Kevin, and Thomas Bodenheimer, "Can Health Care Teams Improve Primary Care Practice?" *Journal of the American Medical Association*, Vol. 291, No. 10 (Mar. 10, 2004).

28. Phillips, Robert L., Michael Klinkman and Larry A. Green, "Conference Report: Harmonizing Primary Care Clinical Classification and Data Standards," Washington, D.C. (Oct. 10-11, 2007).

29. National Committee for Quality Assurance (NCQA), Physician Practice Connections (PPC) and the Physician Practice Connections—Patient Centered Medical Home (PPC-PCMH), Version 2008 can both be found at *http://www.ncqa.org/tabid/141/ Default.aspx* and at *http://www.ncqa.org/tabid/ 631/Default.aspx*, respectively. Accessed Nov. 11, 2008.

30. Scholle, Sarah H, et al., "Measuring Practice Systems for Chronic Illness Care: Accuracy of Self-Reports from Clinical Personnel," *Joint*

Commission Journal on Quality and Safety, Vol. 34, No. 7 (July 2008).

31. Hing, Esther, and Catharine W. Burt, "Office-Based Medical Practices: Methods and Estimates from the National Ambulatory Medical Care Survey," *Advance Data,* Vol. 12, No. 383 (March 2007).

32. Chaudhry, Basit, et al., "Systematic Review: Impact of Health Information Technology on Quality, Efficiency and Costs of Medical Care," *Annals of Internal Medicine,* Vol. 144, No.10 (May 16, 2006).

33. Shekelle, Paul, Sally Morton and Emmett Keeler, *Costs and Benefits of Health Information Technology,* Agency for Healthcare Research and Quality, Rockville, Md. (April 2006).

34. Dexheimer, Judith W., et al., "Prompting Clinicians About Preventive Care Measures: A Systematic Review of Randomized Controlled Trials," *Journal of the American Informatics Association,* Vol. 15, No. 3 (May/June 2008*).*

35. Torda, Phyllis, *Qualifying Patient Centered Medical Homes,* National Committee for Quality Assurance, Washington, D.C. (June 11, 2007). *http://www.eric. org/forms/uploadFiles/BA7F00000017.filename.tor da_-_PPC_and_PCMH_June_11_PCPCC_ TORDA.ppt.* Accessed Nov. 11, 2008.

36. Car, Josip, and Aziz Sheikh, "E-mail Consultations in Health Care, Part 2: Acceptability and Safe Application," *British Medical Journal,* Vol. 329 (Aug. 21, 2004).

37. Brooks, Robert G., and Nir Menachemi, "Physicians' Use of E-mail with Patients: Factors Influencing Electronic Communication and Adherence to Best Practices," *Journal of Medical Internet Research,* Vol. 8, No. 1 (March 24, 2006).

38. Palen, Ted E., et al., "Evaluation of Laboratory Monitoring Alerts Within a Computerized Physician Order Entry System for Medication Orders," *American Journal of Managed Care,* Vol. 12, No. 7 (July 2006).

39. Gandhi, Tejal K., et al., "Outpatient Prescribing Errors and the Impact of Computerized Prescribing," *American Journal of Managed Care,* Vol. 20, No. 9 (September 2006).

40. McMullin, S. Troy, Thomas P. Lonergan and Charles S. Rynearson, "Twelve-Month Drug Cost Savings Related to Use of an Electronic Prescribing System with Integrated Decision Support in Primary Care," *Journal of Managed Care Pharmacy,* Vol. 11, No. 4 (May 2005).

41. Richardson, William C., et al., *Crossing the Quality Chasm: A New Health System for the 21st Century,* Institute of Medicine, National Academy Press (2001).

42. Anderson, Gerard F., et al., "Chronic Conditions: Making the Case for Ongoing Care," Partnership for Solutions, Johns Hopkins University

(December 2002). Can be found at *http://www .partnershipforsolutions.org/DMS/files/chronicbook 2002.pdf.*

43. Boyd, Cynthia M., et al., "Clinical Practice Guidelines and Quality of Care for Older Patients with Multiple Comorbid Diseases: Implications for Pay for Performance," *Journal of the American Medical Association,* Vol. 294, No. 6 (August 2005).

44. Solberg, Leif I., et al., "Practice Systems are Associated with High-Quality Care for Diabetes," *American Journal of Managed Care,* Vol. 14, No. 2 (February 2008).

45. Bridges to Excellence Program Evaluation, Thomson Medstat for Bridges to Excellence, Inc., *http://www.bridgestoexcellence.org/Documents/ BTE-Program-Evaluation-7-26-06.pdf.* Accessed Nov. 11, 2008.

46. Starfield, Barbara, "Adult Primary Care Assessment Tool," Johns Hopkins University, *http://www.jhsph. edu/hao/pcpc/tools.htm.* Accessed June 11, 2008.

47. Safran, Dana G., et al., "The Primary Care Assessment Survey: Tests of Data Quality and Measurement Performance," *Medical Care,* Vol. 36, No. 5 (May 1998).

48. Rosenblatt, Roger A., et al., "The Generalist Role of Specialty Physicians: Is There a Hidden System of Primary Care?" *Journal of the American Medical Association,* Vol. 279, No. 17 (May 6, 1998).

49. Pham, Hoangmai H., et al., "Care Patterns in Medicare and Their Implications for Pay for Performance," *New England Journal of Medicine,* Vol. 356, No. 11 (March 2007).

50. Simon, Samuel, et al., "Identification of Usual Source of Care Providers for Frail Medicare Beneficiaries: Development and Use of a Claims-Based Approach." Paper presented at the Academy Health Annual Research Meeting, Orlando, Fla. (June 2007).

51. Sullivan, Eric, et al., "Patient-Centered Medical Home Program," United Healthcare Health Services (2008).

52. Schoen, Cathy, et al., "U.S. Health System Performance: A National Scorecard," *Health Affairs,* Web exclusive (Sept. 20, 2006).

53. Scholz, John C., *The Earned Income Tax Credit: Participation, Compliance, and Antipoverty Effectiveness,* Discussion Paper No. 1020-93, Institute for Research on Poverty, Madison, Wis. (September 1993). Available at: *http://www.irp.wisc. edu/publications/dps/pdfs/dp102093.pdf.*

54. Pham, Hoangmai H., et al., "Primary Care Physicians' Links to Other Physicians through Medicare Patients: The Scope of Care Coordination," *Annals of Internal Medicine,* forthcoming.

55. Grossman, Joy M., Thomas S. Bodenheimer and Kelly McKenzie, "Hospital-Physician Portals: The Role of Competition in Driving Clinical Data Exchange," *Health Affairs*, Vol. 25, No. 6 (November/December 2006).

56. Estimates of payments in the Medicare demonstration are based on assumptions that each medical home physician treats 250 beneficiaries per year, with 86 percent eligible for the demonstration and participating for the entire year. Average payments for the lower and higher tier of medical-home capabilities are equal to $40.40 and $51.70 per benefici-ary per month, respectively. Based on these assumptions, each medical home physician could earn $104,232 or $133,386 per year for meeting the lower or higher tier of medical-home capabilities, respectively.

57. Berenson, Robert A., and Jane Horvath, "Confronting the Barriers to Chronic Care Management in Medicare," *Health Affairs*, Web exclusive (Jan. 22, 2003).

58. Anderson, Gerard F., "Medicare and Chronic Conditions," *New England Journal of Medicine*, Vol. 353, No. 3 (July 21, 2005).

Index